to Estate Planning

JEFFREY A. SCHOENBLUM

Editorial Staff

Editors . . . . Barbara L. Post, Esq.
Production . . . . Jennifer Schencker, Gokiladevi Sashikumar
Prabhu Meenakshisundaram

This publication is designed to provide accurate and authoritative information in regard to the subject matter covered. It is sold with the understanding that the publisher is not engaged in rendering legal, accounting, or other professional services. If legal advice or other professional assistance is required, the services of a competent professional person should be sought.

—From a *Declaration of Principles* jointly adopted by a Committee of the American Bar Association and a Committee of Publishers and Associations

ISBN: 978-0-8080-5033-9

2700 Lake Cook Road
Riverwoods, IL 60015
800 344 3734
CCHCPELink.com

Portions of this work were published in a previous edition.

Printed in the United States of America

FSC
www.fsc.org
MIX
Paper from
responsible sources
FSC® C103525

Introduction

The *2019 Multistate Guide to Estate Planning* is designed as a comprehensive practical reference for estate planning professionals. It enables the practitioner to keep abreast of the increasingly complex state rules that govern important estate planning issues. Each table provides citations with which to access current state statutes and case law governing important estate planning issues.

This book explores a number of the vital differences distinguishing the laws of the states pertaining to the transfer of family wealth. At one time, the local practitioner could be proud of his or her provincialism. Today, too many factors make ignorance of other states' laws a dangerous proposition. In our mobile society, with its geographically scattered families, out-of-state vacation homes, retirees moving to sunnier climes, and individuals with far-flung investments, proper estate planning means planning that addresses the cosmopolitan nature of most clients' lives. In both the transfer tax and income tax contexts, different states impose often markedly different tax burdens. Some states are also willing to assert taxing jurisdiction in a far more aggressive manner than other states. Only by being alert to the differences among the states can the estate planning professional and probate lawyer successfully serve his or her client and safely fulfill professional obligations. This book provides a detailed, readily accessible tool for researching the differences in both the non-tax and tax areas, thereby facilitating inquiry into appropriate estate planning and probate administration. In addition, a comparison of the present and prior editions of this book affords insight into the evolution of estate and trust law and the many changes that have been occurring.

The easy-to-use format of the *2019 Multistate Guide to Estate Planning* enables the reader to readily locate information concerning one state's treatment of a particular issue—or compare the treatment required by several states—all on the same table. There are 14 tables, each addressing a different topic. Each table is broken into detailed, separate analyses. The analyses consist of a series of detailed questions. The tables are designed for state-by-state comparison.

The answers to the questions posed are to the point, whenever possible. In almost every case, the answer is followed by a relevant statutory, and occasional case, cite. The reader is thus provided with both a brief, reliable response to the query and a reference if he or she wishes to research the matter further. This approach is intended to save valuable time and reduce the cost of online research.

What are the typical scenarios in which this book would prove of considerable benefit to the user? A number of these situations can be readily anticipated:

1. *When a client's property is located in a number of states.* An initial analysis has to be made of such matters as:

   - Who can serve as personal representative?

   - What are the likely state death taxes?

   - What claims will a spouse and/or descendants have with regard to estate assets in each of the various states?

   - Will ancillary probate be necessary, and what are some of the requirements in the particular states?

   - If assets of relatively limited value are involved, will a small-estate procedure be available?

   - Who can serve as a guardian of the property of a minor situated in the state?

   - Will the will be deemed valid even though not executed with the formalities required by the law of the other state?

   - Is there a Rule Against Perpetuities and, if so, what is it?

   - What will substitutes work without adhering to the formalities of will execution?

   - Can personal property be disposed of by a separate signed writing?

2. *When a client has moved to your state, perhaps to retire or due to a change in employment.* Suppose he or she has left property, beneficiaries, or relatives behind. How do the former state's rules impact on the property and rights of relatives? What are the likely state income and death tax consequences?

3. *When a client has been named personal representative or fiduciary for an out-of-state relative.* Can he, she, or it serve? What formal steps must be taken?

4. *When a client or other member of the family is in need of a guardianship due to minority or incompetency.* If property is owned in another jurisdiction, who can serve as a guardian or conservator?

5. *When there is a desire to use a testamentary substitute in place of a will.* Which states will give effect to alternatives like P.O.D. and T.O.D. designations? How are joint tenancies, tenancies by the entirety and joint bank accounts treated? Can a writing dispose of tangible personal property? Are the doctrines of incorporation by reference and acts of independent significance recognized?

6. *When a client dies with property in other jurisdictions.* What steps need to be taken in particular states to pay off creditors and retrieve the property? Can all this be accomplished without an ancillary probate?

7. *When a client is concerned about creditor claims.* As the exposure to creditors and the amount of judgments increase, many clients are seeking whatever asset protection is available to them. Various states offer substantial protection for particular types of assets. Through location of the property in the state, potential creditors' claims that may be made in the future can be avoided. What are the positions of various states as to life insurance, annuities, pension plans and jointly owned property? Which claims will succeed?

8. *When a client is concerned about "dying with dignity."* The recent highly visible public controversies and evolving law have made this a focus of primary concern for clients. There are tremendous differences from one state to another. What is a state's position with regard to living wills, durable powers of attorney, and health care directives? Just how much can be authorized and what exposure do doctors and hospitals have? Will an out-of-state document be given effect?

These are just some of the questions addressed in this book on a topic-by-topic, state-by-state basis. Considerable emphasis has been placed on formal validity of wills, probate, state taxation, family protections, ancillary administration, nonresident fiduciary qualification, small and informal estate administration, testamentary substitutes, living wills, asset protection, and the rule against perpetuities. These are topics that raise day-to-day, commonly encountered problems in estate practice. Nevertheless, these topics often involve analysis of some of the most convoluted and incomprehensible statutes.

And the 2019 edition links to a URL containing the 2018 recommended Advance Directives for all fifty states.

There is a great deal of material contained in the tables found in this publication. Over the years, a number of former and present students have been of substantial assistance in helping me compile the raw material, confirm the answers to the questions, and proofread. I am very grateful to them. Thank you.

Jeffrey A. Schoenblum

October 2018

Dedication

To Renee Hawkins, an extraordinary professional

About the Author

JEFFREY A. SCHOENBLUM, Centennial Professor of Law at Vanderbilt University, is a graduate of the Johns Hopkins University and Harvard Law School, where he was a Note Editor of the Harvard Law Review. After law school, he served as a clerk for Judge J. Edward Lumbard of the U.S. Court of Appeals for the Second Circuit and then was an associate with the New York law firm of Willkie Farr & Gallagher. Professor Schoenblum is the author of a number of books and articles and has spoken at numerous seminars, including the University of Miami Annual Institute on Estate Planning, the Notre Dame Tax and Estate Planning Institute and the Southern Federal Tax Institute. He has been elected to the Estate Planning Hall of Fame. In addition, Professor Schoenblum is a member of the American Law Institute. He is an academician of the International Academy of Estate and Trust Law and a fellow of the American College of Estate and Trust Counsel. He has served as Chairman of the ABA Real Property, Probate, and Trust Law Section's Committee on International Property, Estate and Trust Law, and was an advisor to the Restatement (Third) of Property Donative Transfers.

Multistate Guide to Estate Planning
Table of Contents

SUPPLEMENTAL MATERIAL

The supplemental material for Wolters Kluwer's 2019 *Multistate Guide to Estate Planning* is provided at *download.cchcpelink.com/MGEP2019.zip*

NONTAX

Table 1: Formal Will Requirements 1001
Table 2: Proving Foreign Wills 2001
    Table 2.01, Part 1: Proof of a Foreign Will 2002
    Table 2.01, Part 2: Proof of a Foreign Will 2032
    Table 2.02, Part 1: Ancillary Probate 2036
    Table 2.02, Part 2: Ancillary Probate 2045
    Table 2.02, Part 3: Ancillary Probate 2062
Table 3: Nonresident Qualification as a Fiduciary 3001
    Table 3.01: Nonresident Individual as Executor or Administrator 3002
    Table 3.02: Nonresident Individual as Guardian of Minor's or Incompetent's Property 3011
    Table 3.03: Nonresident Bank as Executor or Administrator 3018
    Table 3.04: Nonresident Bank as Guardian of Minor's or Incompetent's Property 3028
Table 4: Small Estates Procedure 4001
Table 5: Will Substitutes 5001
    Table 5.01, Part 1: Principal Will Substitutes 5003
    Table 5.01, Part 2: Principal Will Substitutes 5018
    Table 5.02: Incorporation by Reference and Facts of Independent Significance 5036
Table 6: The Rights of a Spouse 6001
    Table 6.01: Rights Available in Addition to the Elective Share 6002
    Table 6.02: How Is the Elective Share Obtained? 6013
    Table 6.03, Part 1: Calculation of Elective Share 6035
    Table 6.03, Part 2: Calculation of Elective Share 6064
    Table 6.03, Part 3: Calculation of Elective Share 6080
    Table 6.04: Waiver of Spousal Rights, Including Antenuptial Agreements 6090
Table 7: Intestate Succession 7001
Table 8: Asset Protection 8001
    Table 8.01: Life Insurance 8003
    Table 8.02: Annuities 8024
    Table 8.03: Pension Plans 8031
    Table 8.04: Jointly-Owned Property 8040
Table 9: Rule Against Perpetuities 9001
Table 10: Living Will 10,001
    Table 10.01, Part 1: Coverage of Living Will Statute 10,002
    Table 10.01, Part 2: Coverage of Living Will Statute 10,030
    Table 10.02, Part 1: Formal Requirements 10,054
    Table 10.02, Part 2: Formal Requirements 10,064
    Table 10.02, Part 3: Formal Requirements 10,072
    Table 10.02, Part 4: Formal Requirements 10,102
    Table 10.03, Part 1: Revocation 10,116
    Table 10.03, Part 2: Revocation 10,130
    Table 10.04: Civil or Criminal Liability for Failure to Act 10,147
    Table 10.05: Effect Regarding Insurance 10,168
    Table 10.06: Governing Law 10,171
Table 11: Status of Children Conceived by Assisted Reproduction Techniques 11,001

TAX

Table 12: Contacts Resulting in State Taxation of an Estate's Income 12,001

Table 13: Income Tax Rates for Trusts and Estates 13,001

Table 14: State Inheritance, Estate, Generation-Skipping Transfer, and Gift Taxes 14,001

Table 14.01: Freestanding Inheritance, Estate and Succession Tax 14,005

Table 14.02: Estate Tax 14,020

Table 14.03: Generation-Skipping Transfer Tax 14,059

Table 14.04: Gift Tax 14,078

Table 14.05: Waivers 14,079

Table 14.06: Conflicts Between States 14,086

Table 14.07: Inheritance, Estate, Succession, Transfer, and Gift Tax Rates 14,093

Table 14.08: State-by-State Summary of Current State Inheritance and Estate Tax
Situation 14,109

Table 14.09: Internal Revenue Code Section 2011(b): State Death Tax Credit Before
Repeal 14,113

Table 1
Formal Will Requirements
(current through 5/1/18)

A very large percentage of clients will have property located in another state. Most typically, this will be in the nature of a summer or winter home, or, perhaps, a farm or apartment inherited from a parent or grandparent. In other cases, the client may have moved due to employment considerations to another state. Property may have been left behind, possibly with the expectation of an eventual return to the prior state of residence. Still other cases may involve an elderly client, who has moved in with relatives or to a nursing home in a different state than the one in which she has previously resided.

In all of these cases, as well as numerous others, one question that the lawyer must address is the formal validity of the will. In other words, to be given effect, a will must comply with the formal execution requirements found in the state's statute of wills. Some attorneys assume that formalities are a collection of antiquated technicalities that have no practical effect and will certainly not be cited in invalidating a will. This is a grave misconception. A review of recent case law demonstrates that well-drafted wills can founder on the shoals of formal requirements. All the effort put into the estate plan may be wasted by this neglect. Additionally, lawyers may well be creating an exposure to malpractice liability.

Certain attorneys are careful to observe their own state's technical formalities. However, they fail to take account of other states' formalities. In the present-day world, this is a dangerous oversight. As noted, many clients have some assets linked to another state. There should be no blithe assumption that the local formalities with which the lawyer is familiar govern the disposition of these assets as well.

The common law rule is that the law of the domicile of the decedent at the time of his death governs a will disposing of personal property. The law of the state in which the real property is situated governs wills disposing of real property. Several jurisdictions, such as North Carolina and the District of Columbia, still follow this approach.

Clearly, separate wills are not typically drafted for personal property and each parcel of real property located in a different state. Thus, careful attention must be paid to the identification and situation of assets of the client. Once this has been accomplished, care must be taken to assure that the formalities of the *single* will of the testator and its execution be in accordance with the law of *all* relevant jurisdictions. The formalities of each of the 50 states and the District of Columbia are set out in Table 1 on a state-by-state basis for easy reference.

There is wide diversity among the states. Not all states adhere to the common law rule. Many have adopted statutes that provide for the formal validity of a will if it is valid under the law of any of a number of states. For example, the Uniform Probate Code approach validates a will if it is valid under the law of the state in which the will was executed, or the state in which the testator was domiciled or has his place of abode at *either* the time of his death or of will execution. In addition, if the will is valid under the local law where it is being probated, it will be given effect. This means that if there is local property, a locally valid will should work, even though the will is invalid, for example, at the testator's domicile, place of abode, or the place of execution. Note also that this approach abandons the separate common law rules for personal and real property. Uniform Probate Code §2-506. The Uniform Probate Code also validates a will that is valid under the law of the country of which the person is a national.

Not all states have gone as far as the Uniform Probate Code. Thus, again, no assumptions can be made as to whether a will validly executed elsewhere will be given effect locally or whether a will valid locally will be valid where certain estate assets are located.

Obviously, the concerns addressed by this table would not be of importance if all states had the same formal requirements for a valid will. They simply do not! Accordingly, careful review of the relevant state's formal requirements for execution of a will is unavoidable.

Alabama
Formal Will Requirements

Minimum age for executing will	Real Property—18 years. (§ 43-8-130) Personal Property—18 years. (§ 43-8-130)
Number of witnesses required	Two. (§ 43-8-131)
Holographic wills	No. (§ 43-8-131 (commentary); Black v. Seals, 474 So. 2d 696 (1985))
Wills admitted to probate if valid under the law of:	Alabama presently (§ 43-8-131) or if its execution complies with the law at the time of execution of the place where the will is executed, or the place where, at the time of execution or death, the testator is domiciled, has a place of abode, or is a national. (§ 43-8-135)
Does the signing by the testator and/or witnesses just of the self-proving affidavit constitute the execution of the will?	Yes. (§ 43-8-132(c))
Can self-proving affidavit be signed later by testator and/or witnesses?	Yes. At any time after execution, the will may be self-proved by the testator's acknowledgment of the will and the witnesses' affidavits attached or annexed to the will in substantially the form provided for in the statute. (§ 43-8-132(b))
If a witness is a devisee, does this result in the disqualification to serve as a witness or the invalidation of the devise?	No. (§ 43-8-134(b)) (commentary)
Can any other person sign the will?	Yes, if in testator's presence and at his direction. (§ 43-8-131)
When must witnesses sign?	At signing of will by testator or his later acknowledgment of his signature or of the will. (§ 43-8-131 & commentary)
Must they sign in the presence of the testator?	No, if later acknowledgment of signature or will by the testator in presence of the witness. (§ 43-8-131 commentary)
Must they sign in the presence of each other?	No. (Fulks v. Green, 20 So. 2d 787, 789 (1945)) See also § 43-8-131 commentary.
Must the testator publish the will?	No. (§ 43-8-131 commentary)
Must the will be signed in a particular place?	No. (§ 43-8-131 commentary)
Must the required number of witnesses be present at the same time for the signing or acknowledgment by the testator?	No. (§ 43-8-131 & commentary)
May the testator acknowledge either his will or his signature?	Yes. (§ 43-8-131)
Requirements to be witness	Any person generally competent to be a witness. (§ 43-8-134(a)) This means at the time of execution a person competent to testify in court as to the facts of execution. (*Id.* commentary)

Alaska
Formal Will Requirements

Minimum age for executing will	Real Property—18 years. (§ 13.12.501) Personal Property—18 years. (§ 13.12.501)
Number of witnesses required	Two. (§ 13.12.502(a)(3))
Holographic wills	Yes. (§ 13.12.502(b))
Wills admitted to probate if valid under the law of:	Alaska; place of execution at time of execution; place where, at time of execution or death, the testator is domiciled, has a place of abode, or is a national. (§ 13.12.506) But see § 13.06.068(c), which omits place of abode and where the testator is a national. § 13.12.506 applies "except as provided" in § 13.06.068. Quaere whether this means that these two bases for will validity are no longer applicable. Why are both of these choice of law sections, that is, §§ 13.12.506 and 13.06.068(c), in effect with regard to formal validity? An "international will" is also valid. (§ 13.12.912)
Does the signing by the testator and/or witnesses just of the self-proving affidavit constitute the execution of the will?	Yes. (§ 13.12.504(c))
Can self-proving affidavit be signed later by testator and/or witnesses?	Yes. At any time after execution, the will may be self-proved by the testator's acknowledgment of the will and the witnesses' affidavits attached or annexed to the will in substantially the form provided for in the statute. (§ 13.12.504(b))
If a witness is a devisee, does this result in the disqualification to serve as a witness or the invalidation of the devise?	No. (§ 13.12.505(b))
Can any other person sign the will?	Yes, if in testator's "conscious presence" and by the testator's direction. (§ 13.12.502(a)(2))
When must witnesses sign?	Within a "reasonable time" after witnessing the signing of the will or testator's acknowledgment of the signature or of the will. (§ 13.12.502(a)(3))
Must they sign in the presence of the testator?	No. (§ 13.12.502(a)(3))
Must they sign in the presence of each other?	No. (§ 13.12.502(a)(3))
Must the testator publish the will?[1]	No. (U.P.C. § 2-502 cmt.)
Must the will be signed in a particular place?	No. (U.P.C. § 2-502 cmt.[2])
Must the required number of witnesses be present at the same time for the signing or acknowledgment by the testator?	No. (§ 13.12.502(a)(3))
May the testator acknowledge either his will or his signature?	Yes. (§ 13.12.502(a)(3))

Alaska
Formal Will Requirements

Requirements to be witness	An individual generally competent to be a witness (§ 13.12.505(a)). There is no age requirement to be a witness. (Sevier v. State, 614 P.2d 791 (1980); Alaska Rules of Evidence, Rule 601)

---

[1] Although adopting the Uniform Probate Code, the editorial board comments of the U.P.C. have not been included in Alaska Statutes. Nonetheless, the assumption is that they would be relied upon in construing the statutory provisions.

[2] *Id.*

Arizona
Formal Will Requirements

Minimum age for executing will	Real Property—18 years. (§ 14-2501) Personal Property—18 years. (§ 14-2501)
Number of witnesses required	Two. (§ 14-2502(A)(3))
Holographic wills	Yes. (§ 14-2503)
Wills admitted to probate if valid under the law of:	Arizona; place of execution at time of execution; place where, at the time of execution or death, the testator is domiciled, has a place of abode, or is a national. (§ 14-2506)
Does the signing by the testator and/or witnesses just of the self-proving affidavit constitute the execution of the will?	Yes. (§ 14-2504(C); In re Estate of McKay, 802 P.2d 443, 445 (Ct. App. 1990))
Can self-proving affidavit be signed later by testator and/or witnesses?	Yes. At any time after execution, the will may be self-proved by the testator's acknowledgment of the will and the witnesses' affidavits made before an officer authorized to administer oaths in the state where the acknowledgement occurs and evidenced by the officer's certificate, under the official seal, and attached or annexed to the will in substantially the form provided for in the statute. (§ 14-2504(B))
If a witness is a devisee, does this result in the disqualification to serve as a witness or the invalidation of the devise?	No. (§ 14-2505(B))
Can any other person sign the will?	Yes, if in testator's "conscious presence" and by the testator's direction. (§ 14-2502(A)(2))
When must witnesses sign?	Within a "reasonable time" after witnessing the signing of the will or testator's acknowledgment of the signature or of the will. (§ 14-2502(A)(3))
Must they sign in the presence of the testator?	No. (§ 14-2502(A)(3))
Must they sign in the presence of each other?	No. (§ 14-2502(A)(3))
Must the testator publish the will?	No. (§ 14-2502; see also cmt. to UPC 2-502, the source of § 14-2502; cf In re Harber's Estate, 428 P. 2d 662,670 (1967) ("There is no obligation on the part of the testatrix to publish her will to all the world."))
Must the will be signed in a particular place?	No. (In re Harris' Estate, 296 P. 267, 269 (1931))
Must the required number of witnesses be present at the same time for the signing or acknowledgment by the testator?	No. (§ 14-2502(A)(3))
May the testator acknowledge either his will or his signature?	Yes. (§ 14-2502(A)(3))
Requirements to be witness	A person who is generally competent to be a witness. (§ 14-2505(A)) Under § 12-2202, persons of unsound mind and children under age 10, who appear incapable of receiving just impressions of the facts respecting which they testify, or of relating them truly, may not be witnesses in a civil action.

Arkansas
Formal Will Requirements

Minimum age for executing will	Real Property—18 years. (§ 28-25-101) Personal Property—18 years. (§ 28-25-101)
Number of witnesses required	Two. (§ 28-25-103(a)); three "credible disinterested witnesses to the handwriting and signature" of the testator in the case of a holographic will without attesting witnesses. (§ 28-25-104)
Holographic wills	Yes. (§ 28-25-104)
Wills admitted to probate if valid under the law of:	Arkansas; place of execution at the time of execution; place of testator's domicile at the time of execution. (§ 28-25-105)
Does the signing by the testator and/or witnesses just of the self-proving affidavit constitute the execution of the will?	Probably not. The affidavit must be written on the "will." "[I]f that is impracticable," then it must be "securely affixed to the will or to a true copy of the will by the officer administering the oath." (§ 28-25-106(c); Shamoon v. Tombridge, 723 S.W.2d 827 (1987))
Can self-proving affidavit be signed later by testator and/or witnesses?	Yes, "at any time," even after the testator's death, and even if not requested by an interested person. There is no provision for a testator signing. (§ 28-25-106(b))
If a witness is a devisee, does this result in the disqualification to serve as a witness or the invalidation of the devise?	There is no disqualification of the witness. The devise is invalid, at least in part, if there are not two disinterested witnesses. The portion in excess of the witness's intestate share is forfeited. (§ 28-25-102(b))
Can any other person sign the will?	Yes, at testator's "discretion and in his or her presence." (§ 28-25-103(b)(1)(D)(i)) The person must write his own name and state that he signed the testator's name at the request of the testator. (§ 28-25-103(b)(1)(D)(ii))
When must witnesses sign?	Apparently, can sign it at any time if other requirements are fulfilled. (Upton v. Upton, 759 S.W.2d 811 (1988)) For example, the testator may declare his will and acknowledge his signature already made. (§ 28-25-103(b)(1)(B))
Must they sign in the presence of the testator?	Yes. Furthermore, it must be at his request. (§ 28-25-103(c))
Must they sign in the presence of each other?	Apparently not, as long as at testator's request and in his presence. See § 28-25-103(c) (Upton v. Upton, 759 S.W.2d 811, 812 (1988))
Must the testator publish the will?	Yes. He must declare to the attesting witnesses that the instrument is his will. (§ 28-25-103(b)(1))
Must the will be signed in a particular place?	At the end. (§ 28-25-103(b)(2)(A)) However, superfluous or administrative language can follow. (Clark v. National Bank, 802 S.W.2d 452, 454 (1991)) A will signed in the attestation clause with requisite intent is valid compliance. (Scritchfield v. Loyd, 589 S.W.2d 557, 559 (1979))
Must the required number of witnesses be present at the same time for the signing or acknowledgment by the testator?	Yes. (§ 28-25-103(b)(2)(B))

Arkansas
Formal Will Requirements

May the testator acknowledge either his will or his signature?	No. Provision is made only for the acknowledgment of the testator's signature. (§ 28-25-103(b)(1)(B))
Requirements to be witness	18 years or older and generally competent to be a witness in the state. (§ 28-25-102(a))

California
Formal Will Requirements

Minimum age for executing will	Real Property—18 years. (Prob. § 6100) Personal Property—18 years. (Prob. § 6100) An emancipated minor can make a will. See Family Code § § 7002 and 7050(e)(6).
Number of witnesses required	Two. (Prob. § 6110(c)(1)) However, clear and convincing evidence that, at the time the testator signed the will, the testator intended the will to constitute the testator's will shall result in the will being treated as compliant with Prob. § 6110(c)(1), though not in compliance with Prob. § 6110(c)(1). (Prob. § 6110(c)(2)
Holographic wills	Yes. (Prob. § 6111)
Wills admitted to probate if valid under the law of:	California; place where executed at time of execution; place at time of execution or, if at death the testator is domiciled, has a place of abode, or is a national. (Prob. § 6113) An "international will" is also valid. (Prob. § 6381)
Does the signing by the testator and/or witnesses just of the self-proving affidavit constitute the execution of the will?	Possibly so, since one form of evidence of execution is "an affidavit in the original will that includes or incorporates the attestation clause." (Prob. § 8220(b)) The result might be different with the alternative form of permitted affidavit, "to which there is attached a photographic copy of the will." (*Id.*)
Can self-proving affidavit be signed later by testator and/or witnesses?	No. (Prob. § § 8220(b), 8221(b)(1)) However, provision is made for a separate affidavit by a person with personal knowledge of the circumstances of the execution. (Prob. § 8221(b)(2)) See also Prob. § 8220, which provides for an affidavit, with a photographic copy of the will attached.
If a witness is a devisee, does this result in the disqualification to serve as a witness or the invalidation of the devise?	There is no disqualification of the witness. (Prob. § 6112(b)) The devise is invalid, at least in part, if there are not two disinterested witnesses. The interested witness is entitled to "take such proportion of the devise made to the witness in the will as does not exceed the share of the estate which would be distributed to the witness if the will were not established." (Prob. § 6112(d)) Nevertheless, there is only a presumption of duress, menace, or fraud, or undue influence, which can be rebutted by the witness. Presumption does not apply if the devise is made to a witness solely in a fiduciary capacity. (Prob. § 6112(c))
Can any other person sign the will?	Yes, in the testator's name by a person in testator's presence and by testator's direction. (Prob. § 6110(b)(2)) Alternatively, by a conservator pursuant to a court order to make a will. (Prob. § 6110(b)(3))
When must witnesses sign?	During the testator's lifetime. The witnesses must be present at the same time. (Prob. § 6110(c)(1))
Must they sign in the presence of the testator?	No. The 1983 law repealed the former requirement to this effect. (Prob. § 6110 comment) However, clear and convincing evidence that, at the time the testator signed the will, the testator intended the will to constitute the testator's will shall result in the will being treatment as compliant with Prob. § 6110(c)(1), though not in compliance with Prob. § 6110(c)(1). (Prob. § 6110(c)(2))

California
Formal Will Requirements

Must they sign in the presence of each other?	No. (Prob. § 6110, cmt; In re Armstrong, 64 P.2d 1093, 1096 (1937))
Must the testator publish the will?	No, but witnesses must understand that the instrument they sign is testator's will. (Prob. § 6110(c)(1)(B))
Must the will be signed in a particular place?	No. The new law repealed the former requirement to this effect. (Prob. § 6110 comment)
Must the required number of witnesses be present at the same time for the signing or acknowledgment by the testator?	Yes. (Prob. § 6110(c)(1)(A))
May the testator acknowledge either his will or his signature?	Yes. (Prob. § 6110(c)(1)(A))
Requirements to be witness	Any person generally competent to be a witness. (Prob. § 6112(a)) Under § 700 of the Evidence Code, age, per se, does not bar a person from being a competent witness.

Colorado
Formal Will Requirements

Minimum age for executing will	Real Property—18 years. (§ 15-11-501) Personal Property—18 years. (§ 15-11-501)
Number of witnesses required	Two witnesses are required or the will must be acknowledged by the testator before a notary public or other individual authorized to take acknowledgments. (§ 15-11-502(1)(c))(I) and (II))
Holographic wills	Yes. (§ 15-11-502(2))
Wills admitted to probate if valid under the law of:	Colorado; place of execution at time of execution; place where, at the time of execution or death, the testator is domiciled, has a place of abode, or is a national. (§ 15-11-506) An "international will" is also valid. (§ 15-11-1003)
Does the signing by the testator and/or witnesses just of the self-proving affidavit constitute the execution of the will?	Yes. (§ 15-11-504(3))
Can self-proving affidavit be signed later by testator and/or witnesses?	At any time after execution, the will may be self-proved by the testator's acknowledgment of the will and the witnesses' affidavits attached or annexed to the will in substantially the form provided for in the statute. (§ 15-11-504(2))
If a witness is a devisee, does this result in the disqualification to serve as a witness or the invalidation of the devise?	No. (§ 15-11-505(2))
Can any other person sign the will?	Yes, if in testator's "conscious presence" and by the testator's direction. (§ 15-11-502(1)(b)) "Conscious presence" means physical proximity, but not necessarily within testator's line of sight. (§ 15-11-502(4))
When must witnesses sign?	Prior to or after the testator's death. Each witness must sign within a reasonable time after witnessing the signing of the will or testator's acknowledgment of that signature or acknowledgment of the will. (§ 15-11-502(c)(1)) With regard to witnessing, the witnesses need not be in the line of sight of the testator if in the testator's conscious presence, which requires physical proximity to the testator but not necessarily within testator's line of sight. (§ 15-11-502(c)(4))
Must they sign in the presence of the testator?	No. (§ 15-11-502(1)(c)(I)
Must they sign in the presence of each other?	No. (U.P.C. § 2-502 cmt;[1] In re Estate of Wiltfong, 148 P.3d 465, 467 (Ct. App. 2006))
Must the testator publish the will?	No. (U.P.C. § 2-502 cmt.; In re Estate of Wiltfong, 148 P.3d 465, 467 (Ct. App. 2006)[2])
Must the will be signed in a particular place?	No. (U.P.C. § 2-502 cmt.[3])
Must the required number of witnesses be present at the same time for the signing or acknowledgment by the testator?	No. (§ 15-11-502(1)(c)(I)
May the testator acknowledge either his will or his signature?	Yes. (§ 15-11-502(1)(c)(I)

Colorado
Formal Will Requirements

Requirements to be witness	A person who is generally competent to be a witness. (§ 15-11-505(1)) Under § 13-90-106, persons of unsound mind and certain children under age 10 may not be witnesses.

---

[1] Although adopting the Uniform Probate Code, the editorial board of the U.P.C. has not been included in Colorado Revised Statutes. Nonetheless, the assumption is that they would be relied upon in construing the statutory provisions.

[2] *Id.*

[3] *Id.*

Connecticut
Formal Will Requirements

Minimum age for executing will	Real Property—18 years. (§ 45a-250) Personal Property—18 years. (§ 45a-250)
Number of witnesses required	Two. (§ 45a-251)
Holographic wills	No. (§ 45a-251)
Wills admitted to probate if valid under the law of:	Connecticut; place of execution. (§ 45a-251) An "international will" is also valid. (§ 50a-2)
Does the signing by the testator and/or witnesses just of the self-proving affidavit constitute the execution of the will?	The issue would probably not arise regarding the testator, since only the witnesses, and not the testator, sign the affidavits. Moreover, the witnesses must state in the affidavits "such facts as they would be required to testify to in court to prove [the] will," which would presumably include that the testator signed the will or acknowledged his signature in their presence. (§ 45a-285)
Can self-proving affidavit be signed later by testator and/or witnesses?	Yes, at any time, including after the testator's death, any or both of the witnesses may sign an affidavit. However, it must be at the testator's request or, if the testator is deceased, at the request of the executor or any person "interested" in the will. (§ 45a-285)
If a witness is a devisee, does this result in the disqualification to serve as a witness or the invalidation of the devise?	There is no disqualification of the witness. Unless there are sufficient other witnesses, or unless the witness devisee is an heir, a devise to the witness or the spouse of the witness is void. A person may be a witness without voiding the devise to a community, church, society, association, or corporation in which the witness has an interest. (§ 45a-258)
Can any other person sign the will?	No provision or reported case specifically authorizes this.
When must witnesses sign?	No provision, other than that they must subscribe in testator's presence (§ 45a-251) and after testator signs, which is a requirement not in the statute but represents a "judicial gloss on the word 'subscribed'" in the statute. (Gardner v. Balboni, 588 A.2d 634, 639 n.8 (1991))
Must they sign in the presence of the testator?	Yes. (§ 45a-251)
Must they sign in the presence of each other?	No. (Wheat v. Wheat, 244 A.2d 359, 363 n.4 (1968))
Must the testator publish the will?	No. (In re Simmons' Will, 132 N.Y.S.2d 795, 796 (Sur. Ct. 1954), construing the predecessor of § 45a-251)
Must the will be signed in a particular place?	It must be subscribed, that is, to "write underneath." However, this does not bar it from following certain nondispositive clauses. (Gardner v. Balboni, 588 A.2d 634, 638 (1991))
Must the required number of witnesses be present at the same time for the signing or acknowledgment by the testator?	Apparently, there is no requirement that the witnesses be present at all at the signing or that there be an acknowledgment. (Wheat v. Wheat, 244 A.2d 359, 364 (1968))
May the testator acknowledge either his will or his signature?	No acknowledgment at all is required. (Wheat v. Wheat, 244 A.2d 359 (1968))
Requirements to be witness	No provision or reported case specifically addresses this.

Delaware
Formal Will Requirements

Minimum age for executing will	Real Property—18 years. (12 § 201) Personal Property—18 years. (12 § 201)
Number of witnesses required	Two. (12 § 202(a)(2))
Holographic wills	No. (12 § 202(a),(b))
Wills admitted to probate if valid under the law of:	Delaware; place of execution at time of execution; place where, at the time of execution or death, the testator is domiciled, has a place of abode, or is a national. (12 § 1306) An "international will" is also valid. (12 § 252)
Does the signing by the testator and/or witnesses just of the self-proving affidavit constitute the execution of the will?	Yes. The will can be made self-proved by acknowledgment of testator and affidavits of witnesses if "attached or annexed to the will in form and content substantially as [provided herein.]" (12 § 1305) the signature on the affidavit alone suffices under the doctrine of integration. (In re Will of Carter, 565 A.2d 933, 936 (Del. 1989))
Can self-proving affidavit be signed later by testator and/or witnesses?	Yes. Acknowledgment "at any subsequent date" of testator and affidavits of witnesses attached or annexed to the will in substantially the form provided for in the statute. (12 § 1305)
If a witness is a devisee, does this result in the disqualification to serve as a witness or the invalidation of the devise?	There is no disqualification of the witness or the devise. (12 § 203(b))
Can any other person sign the will?	Yes, in the testator's presence and by the testator's express direction. (12 § 202(a)(1))
When must witnesses sign?	At any time. The witnesses need not even have seen testator sign, nor need they know the instrument is testator's will. (In re Kemp's Will, 186 A. 890, 894 (Super. Ct. 1936))
Must they sign in the presence of the testator?	Yes. (12 § 202(a)(2))
Must they sign in the presence of each other?	No. (In re Estate of Hallett, 295 A.2d 755, 756 (Ch. 1972))
Must the testator publish the will?	No. (In re Kemp's Will, 186 A. 890, 894 (Super. Ct. 1936))
Must the will be signed in a particular place?	Yes. Despite no requirement in the statute, the case law requires that the witnesses subscribe their names below the dispositive provisions, even though this may not be required of the testator. Owens v. Bennett, 5 Del. 367 (Super. Ct. 1852); In re Will of Panousseris, 52 Del. 21, 31, 151 A.2d 518, 523-24 (Orph. Ct. 1959).
Must the required number of witnesses be present at the same time for the signing or acknowledgment by the testator?	Apparently not. (In re Kemp's Will, 186 A. 890, 894 (Super. Ct. 1936); In re Estate of Hallett, 295 A.2d 755, 756 (Ch. 1972))
May the testator acknowledge either his will or his signature?	Probably yes. It suffices for the testator to request that the witnesses subscribe their names as witnesses to his signature in his presence. (In re Kemp's Will, 186 A. 890, 894 (Super. Ct. 1936))

Delaware
Formal Will Requirements

Requirements to be witness	Any person generally competent to be a witness. (12 § 203(a)) The requirement, however, of 12 § 202(a)(2) is that "credible" witnesses sign. Credible is construed to mean "competent," as provided in 12 § 203. (Hudson v. Flood, 94 A. 760, 761 (Super. Ct. 1915)) To be credible and competent, the person must be capable of testifying in court. (*Id.*)

District of Columbia
Formal Will Requirements

Minimum age for executing will	Real Property—18 years. (§ 18-102) Personal Property—18 years. (§ 18-102)
Number of witnesses required	Two. (§ 18-103(2))
Holographic wills	No. (§ 18-103)
Wills admitted to probate if valid under the law of:	There is no statutory provision. The common law rule is in effect. Thus, the law of the situs governs real property. (Greenwood v. Page, 138 F.2d 921, 923 (D.C. Cir. 1943); Farrar v. Bingham, 93 F.2d 252, 254 (D.C. Cir. 1937)) The law of the domicile at death of the testator governs personal property. (In re Kerr's Estate, 433 F.2d 479, 481 n.10 (D.C. Cir. 1970)) However, "international wills" under the Washington Convention are valid. (§ 18-702)
Does the signing by the testator and/or witnesses just of the self-proving affidavit constitute the execution of the will?	There is no provision for a self-proving affidavit. A will can be admitted to abbreviated probate pursuant to which "due execution of the will shall be presumed." The will should have a recital by the attesting witnesses of facts constituting due execution. Alternatively, a verified statement of any person with personal knowledge of the circumstances of the execution may be used. (§ 20-312(b))
Can self-proving affidavit be signed later by testator and/or witnesses?	There is no provision for a self-proving affidavit.
If a witness is a devisee, does this result in the disqualification to serve as a witness or the invalidation of the devise?	There is no disqualification of the witness. (§ 18-104(d)) The devise is void to the extent it exceeds the amount that would be taken as an intestate share if there was no will. (§ 18-104(b)) A creditor for whom there is a charge in the will can serve as a witness without diminishing the charge for the creditor's benefit with respect to real estate; no mention of personalty. (§§ 18-106; 18-104(c)) Interestingly, the statute does not provide for the interested witness taking if there are two other disinterested witnesses. This, however, is suggested by In re Estate of Pye, 325 F. Supp. 321, 323 (D.D.C. 1971).
Can any other person sign the will?	Yes, if in his presence and by his express direction. (§ 18-103(1))
When must witnesses sign?	No statute or case authority directly on point. However, witnesses should not sign before testator. If they do, the will may, nevertheless, still be valid if testator and witnesses signed "at substantially the same time and in each other's presence." (Billings v. Woody, 167 F.2d 756 (D.C. Cir. 1948))
Must they sign in the presence of the testator?	Yes. (§ 18-103(2))
Must they sign in the presence of each other?	No. (Notes v. Doyle, 32 App. D.C. 413, 416 (D.C. Cir. 1909))
Must the testator publish the will?	Maybe. (Homovich v. Chapman, 191 F.2d 761 (D.C. Cir. 1951) (considering publication of the will as a factor in determining validity.))
Must the will be signed in a particular place?	No. (In re Estate of Hall, 328 F. Supp. 1305 (D.D.C. 1971), aff'd, 466 F.2d 340 (D.C. Cir. 1972))

District of Columbia
Formal Will Requirements

Must the required number of witnesses be present at the same time for the signing or acknowledgment by the testator?	No. (Davis v. Davis, 471 A.2d 1008 (D.C. 1984))
May the testator acknowledge either his will or his signature?	Document must be acknowledged by the testator to be his or her will. (Davis v. Davis, 471 A.2d 1008 (Ct. App. 1984))
Requirements to be witness	The witnesses must be "credible." (§ 18-103(2))

Florida
Formal Will Requirements

Minimum age for executing will	Real Property—18 years. (§ 732.501) Personal Property—18 years. (§ 732.501). An emancipated minor can execute a will as well. (§ 732.501)
Number of witnesses required	Two. (§ 732.502(1)(b))
Holographic wills	No. (§ 732.502(2)); In re Estate of Salathe, 703 So. 2d 1167, 1168 (Fl. App. 1997))
Wills admitted to probate if valid under the law of:	In the case of a resident, the Florida law as to execution requirements must be observed. There is no choice of law statute for the benefit of residents. In the case of a will "executed by a nonresident of Florida," the will shall be valid if valid "under the laws of the state or country where the will was executed." (§ 732.502(2)) This rule does not, however, allow for a holographic or nuncupative will even though allowed at the place of execution. See also In re Estate of Swanson, 397 So. 2d 465, 466 (Fl. App. 1981).
Does the signing by the testator and/or witnesses just of the self-proving affidavit constitute the execution of the will?	One court agrees for witnesses (In re Estate of Charry, 359 So. 2d 544 (Dist. Ct. App. 1978)), since there is no requirement as to where witnesses sign. The decision distinguishes the witnesses from the testator in this regard. As for the testator, it may also be acceptable, since a testator's signature in the attestation clause has been approved. (In re Schiele's Estate, 51 So. 2d 287 (1951)) However, each case would, with regard to the testator, turn on the particular facts. As for the statute, the implication is that it would not treat this as a proper execution of the will, since the self-proving form must be attached *to* or *follow* the will; it requires the testator's signature in addition to the signature in the will, and the affidavit must be attached to or follow *the* will in substantially the prescribed form. (§ 732.503)
Can self-proving affidavit be signed later by testator and/or witnesses?	Yes, by later acknowledgment of will by testator, affidavits of the witnesses, and officer's certificate "attached to or following the will, in substantially the [statutory] form. . . . " (§ 732.503)
If a witness is a devisee, does this result in the disqualification to serve as a witness or the invalidation of the devise?	There is no disqualification of the witness. (§ 732.504(2)) There is no reference to voiding the devise to an interested witness. The provision is intended to parallel U.P.C. § 2-504 and, thus, the devise to the witness probably is not invalid.
Can any other person sign the will?	Yes, in the testator's presence and at his direction. (§ 732.502(1)(a)(2))
When must witnesses sign?	No time specified. (§ 732.502(1)(c))
Must they sign in the presence of the testator?	Yes. (§ 732.502(1)(c))
Must they sign in the presence of each other?	Yes. (§ 732.502(1)(c))
Must the testator publish the will?	No. (York v. Smith, 385 So. 2d 1110, 1111 (Dist. Ct. App. 1980); In re Beakes' Estate, 306 So. 2d 99, 101 (Fl. 1974))

Florida
Formal Will Requirements

Must the will be signed in a particular place?	Yes, the testator, but not the witnesses, must sign at the end. (§ 732.502(1)(a)(1)) However, if the testator signs, for example, in the attestation clause, this may be permissible if testamentary intent is established. (In re Schiele's Estate, 51 So. 2d 287, 289 (Fl. 1951))
Must the required number of witnesses be present at the same time for the signing or acknowledgment by the testator?	Yes. (§ 732.502(1)(b)(2)) (See also Jordan v. Fehr, 902 So. 2d 198, 201 (Fl. Dist. Ct. App. 2005))
May the testator acknowledge either his will or his signature?	The acknowledgment may be either of the fact that he has previously signed the will or that another person subscribed his name to it. (§ 732.502(1)(b)(2)(a)-(b))
Requirements to be witness	Any person competent to be a witness. (§ 732.504(1))

Georgia Note that the references herein are to the Probate Code for estates of decedents dying on or after January 1, 1998.
Formal Will Requirements

Minimum age for executing will	Real Property—14 years. (§ 53-4-10) Personal Property—14 years. (§ 53-4-10)
Number of witnesses required	Two. (§ 53-4-20(b))
Holographic wills	No. (§ 53-4-20)
Wills admitted to probate if valid under the law of:	In the case of a domiciliary of Georgia at death, Georgia law determines the validity of the will. (Carr v. Kupfer, 296 S.E.2d 560, 562 (1982)) In the case of any other testator, the law of his domicile. (Arrington v. Hosemann, 163 S.E.2d 722, 723 (1968)) In the case of real property, the law of the situs controls. (Veach v. Veach, 53 S.E.2d 98, 102 (1949)) A statute now restates, at least in part, the common law. If a will is a "foreign will" or an "out-of-state will," and is "valid under the laws of this state," it can be offered for original probate under certain conditions. (§ 53-5-31) A "foreign will" is a will of a nondomiciliary who dies while domiciled in a jurisdiction that is not a state or territory governed by the Constitution of the United States and who at death owns property located in this state or a cause of action the venue of which lies in this state. (§ 53-5-30(2)) An "out-of-state will" is the will of a nondomiciliary who dies while domiciled in a state or territory that is governed by the Constitution of the United States and who at death owns property located in this state or a cause of action the venue of which lies in this state. (§ 53-5-30(4)) *Quaere* whether it is a foreign will if the person later becomes a resident (*i.e.*, domiciliary) of Georgia and is one at the time of death.
Does the signing by the testator and/or witnesses just of the self-proving affidavit constitute the execution of the will?	Probably yes. (Westmoreland v. Tallent, 549 S.E.2d 113, 116 (2001))
Can self-proving affidavit be signed later by testator and/or witnesses?	Yes, at any time during "the lifetime of the testator and the witnesses." The testator and witnesses can sign an affidavit that is to be attached or annexed to the will in the form and contents substantially as provided in the statute. (§ 53-4-24(a) & (b))
If a witness is a devisee, does this result in the disqualification to serve as a witness or the invalidation of the devise?	There is no disqualification of the witness. However, unless there are two other subscribing witnesses who are not devisees, the devise to witness is void. (§ 53-4-23(a)) The fact that a spouse of a witness receives a devise under the will simply is a "fact going only to the credibility of the witness." (§ 53-4-23(b))
Can any other person sign the will?	Yes, if in the testator's presence and by his express direction. (§ 53-4-20(a))
When must witnesses sign?	Either at the testator's execution of the will or at a later acknowledgment of his signature. See In re Estate of Brannon, 441 S.E.2d 248, 248-49 (1994); Thornton v. Hulme, 128 S.E.2d 744, 745 (1962). § 53-4-20, which addresses witnessing in general, "carries forward" its predecessor, § 53-2-40. See Comment to § 53-4-20. The cited cases were decided under § 53-2-40.

Georgia Note that the references herein are to the Probate Code for estates of decedents dying on or after January 1, 1998.
Formal Will Requirements

Must they sign in the presence of the testator?	Yes. (§ 53-4-20(b)) A "line-of-vision" test under the current law: "'it is not necessary for the testator to have watched the witnesses sign, as long as the testator could have watched them sign.'" (McCormick v. Jeffers, 637 S.E.2d 666, 669 (Ga. 2006), citing to Restatement (Third) of Property § 3.1 at 177)) In addition, no special request of the witnesses to attest the will is required, since this is implied from the act itself of witnessing. (Whitfield v. Pitts, 53 S.E.2d 549 (1949)) Note also that one witness must not sign for the other. (§ 53-4-20(b))
Must they sign in the presence of each other?	No. (In re Estate of Brannon, 441 S.E.2d 248, 249 (Ga. 1994); Whitfield v. Pitts, 53 S.E.2d 549 (1949))
Must the testator publish the will?	No, as long as the witnesses are "requested by the testator to subscribe the memorandum of attestation" or are otherwise requested to attest his signature. (Slade v. Slade, 118 S.E. 645, 648 (1923))
Must the will be signed in a particular place?	Apparently not. (In re Estate of Brannon, 441 S.E.2d 248, 249 (1994) ("Where all of the signature pages are physically connected as part of the will, the fact that a testator's signature and the signatures of witnesses do not appear on the same page does not in itself invalidate the execution of the will"; the court points out that nothing in the statute requires signing on the same page; the implication is that there is no rule as to placement of signatures, although the decision's language leaves open the possibility of a different result under certain circumstances))
Must the required number of witnesses be present at the same time for the signing or acknowledgment by the testator?	No. (Miles v. Bryant, 589 S.E.2d 86, 87 (2003); Thornton v. Hulme, 128 S.E.2d 744, 745 (1962))
May the testator acknowledge either his will or his signature?	The testator must acknowledge his signature. (Norton v. Georgia R.R. Bank & Tr., 285 S.E.2d 910, 912 (1982), *aff'd*, 322 S.E.2d 870 (1984)) The acknowledgment may be implied. (Thornton v. Hulme, 128 S.E.2d 744, 745 (1962); Glenn v. Mann, 214 S.E.2d 911, 914 (1975))
Requirements to be witness	The witnesses must be competent to be a witness and at least be 14 years old. (§ 53-4-22)

Hawaii
Formal Will Requirements

Minimum age for executing will	Real Property—18 years. (§ 560:2-501) Personal Property—18 years. (§ 560:2-501)
Number of witnesses required	Two. (§ 560:2-502(a)(3))
Holographic wills	Yes. (§ 560:2-502(b))
Wills admitted to probate if valid under the law of:	Hawaii; place of execution at time of execution; place where, at the time of execution or death, the testator is domiciled, has a place of abode, or is a national. (§ 560:2-506)
Does the signing by the testator and/or witnesses just of the self-proving affidavit constitute the execution of the will?	Yes. (§ 560:2-504(a) & (c))
Can self-proving affidavit be signed later by testator and/or witnesses?	At any time after execution, the will may be self-proved by the testator's acknowledgment of the will and the witnesses' affidavits attached or annexed to the will in substantially the form provided for in the statute. (§ 560:2-504(b))
If a witness is a devisee, does this result in the disqualification to serve as a witness or the invalidation of the devise?	No. (§ 560:2-505(b))
Can any other person sign the will?	Yes, if in testator's "conscious presence" and by the testator's direction. (§ 560:2-502(a)(2))
When must witnesses sign?	Within a "reasonable time" after witnessing the signing of the will or testator's acknowledgment of the signature or of the will. (§ 560:2-502(a)(3))
Must they sign in the presence of the testator?	No. (§ 560:2-502(a)(3))
Must they sign in the presence of each other?	No. (§ 560:2-502(a)(3))
Must the testator publish the will?	No. (U.P.C. § 2-502 cmt.[1])
Must the will be signed in a particular place?	No. (U.P.C. § 2-502 cmt.[2])
Must the required number of witnesses be present at the same time for the signing or acknowledgment by the testator?	No. (§ 560:2-502(a)(3) & U.P.C. § 2-502 cmt.[3])
May the testator acknowledge either his will or his signature?	Yes, as long as each witness signs within a "reasonable time" after the testator's acknowledgment. (§ 560:2-502(a)(3) & U.P.C. § 2-502 cmt.[4])
Requirements to be witness	An individual generally competent to be a witness. (§ 560:2-505(a))

[1] Although adopting the Uniform Probate Code, the editorial comments of the U.P.C. have not been included in Hawaii Code Annotated. Nonetheless, the assumption is that they would be relied upon in construing the statutory provisions.

[2] *Id.*

[3] *Id.*

[4] *Id.*

Idaho
Formal Will Requirements

Minimum age for executing will	Any person 18 years old or an emancipated minor under age 18 who is of sound mind may also execute a will. (§ 15-2-501)
Number of witnesses required	Two. (§ 15-2-502)
Holographic wills	Yes. (§ 15-2-503)
Wills admitted to probate if valid under the law of:	Idaho; place of execution at time of execution; place where, at the time of execution or death, the testator is domiciled, has a place of abode, or is a national. (§ 15-2-506)
Does the signing by the testator and/or witnesses just of the self-proving affidavit constitute the execution of the will?	Yes. (§ 15-2-504(1),(3))
Can self-proving affidavit be signed later by testator and/or witnesses?	Yes, at any time after execution, the will may be self-proved by the testator's acknowledgment of the will and the witnesses' affidavits attached or annexed to the will in substantially the form provided for in the statute. (§ 15-2-504(2))
If a witness is a devisee, does this result in the disqualification to serve as a witness or the invalidation of the devise?	No. (§ 15-2-505(b))
Can any other person sign the will?	Yes, if in the testator's presence and by his direction. (§ 15-2-502)
When must witnesses sign?	No time limit specified. (§ 15-2-502) (In re Estate of Miller, 149 P.3d 840, 842 (2006) (witness may sign after testator's death))
Must they sign in the presence of the testator?	No. (§ 15-2-502 cmt.)
Must they sign in the presence of each other?	No. (§ 15-2-502 cmt.)
Must the testator publish the will?	No. (§ 15-2-502 cmt.)
Must the will be signed in a particular place?	No. (§ 15-2-502 cmt.)
Must the required number of witnesses be present at the same time for the signing or acknowledgment by the testator?	No. (§ 15-2-502 cmt.)
May the testator acknowledge either his will or his signature?	Yes. (§ 15-2-502 cmt.)
Requirements to be witness	Any person 18 or older who is generally competent to be a witness. (§ 15-2-505(a))

Illinois
Formal Will Requirements

Minimum age for executing will	Real Property—18 years. (755 ILCS § 5/4-1) Personal Property—18 years. (755 ILCS § 5/4-1)
Number of witnesses required	Two. (755 ILCS § 5/4-3(a))
Holographic wills	No. (755 ILCS § 5/4-3)
Wills admitted to probate if valid under the law of:	Illinois; place where executed at time of execution; place where testator domiciled at the time of execution. (755 ILCS § 5/7-1) An "international will" is also valid. (755 ILCS § 10/2)
Does the signing by the testator and/or witnesses just of the self-proving affidavit constitute the execution of the will?	Unlikely that testator would even sign, since the testator's signature is not required on affidavit. (755 ILCS § 5/6-4) However, since will can be signed anywhere and affidavit forms a part of or is attached to will, signing of affidavit by testator might well suffice. (755 ILCS § 5/6-4(b))
Can self-proving affidavit be signed later by testator and/or witnesses?	Yes, by an affidavit signed after attestation and forming part of the will or attached to will or accurate facsimile. (755 ILCS 5/6-4(b))
If a witness is a devisee, does this result in the disqualification to serve as a witness or the invalidation of the devise?	There is no disqualification of the witness. Unless the will can be proved without the witness, the witness cannot take the excess over what the witness would have taken by intestate succession. (755 ILCS § § 5/4-6(a) & 4-6(b))
Can any other person sign the will?	Yes, in the testator's presence and by his direction. (755 ILCS 5/4-3(a))
When must witnesses sign?	No time limit. Each can sign at a later date than testator, as long as signed in presence of testator by each witness and following acknowledgment of testator that the instrument was his act or deed, even if not revealing it is his will. (Martin v. Martin, 165 N.E. 644, 649-50 (1929))
Must they sign in the presence of the testator?	Yes. (755 ILCS 5/4-3(a))
Must they sign in the presence of each other?	No. (Heavner v. Heavner, 174 N.E. 413, 414 (1930)), construing the same language, "attested in the presence of the testator by two or more credible witnesses." (735 ILCS § 5/4-3(a)), that appears in the current statute.
Must the testator publish the will?	No. (In re Estate of Carroll, 548 N.E.2d 650, 653 (1989))
Must the will be signed in a particular place?	No. (In re Estate of Carroll, 548 N.E.2d 650, 653 (1989))
Must the required number of witnesses be present at the same time for the signing or acknowledgment by the testator?	No. (755 ILCS § 5/4-3) Construing the same language, "attested in the presence of the testator by two or more credible witnesses," that appears in the current statute.
May the testator acknowledge either his will or his signature?	The testator would have to acknowledge before the witness signs that the instrument is his act or deed. (In re Estate of Carroll, 548 N.E.2d 650, 653 (1989))
Requirements to be witness	The witness must be "credible" (755 ILCS 5/4-3(a)), which means legally competent to testify to the facts attested at the time the will is subscribed. (Smith v. Goodell, 101 N.E. 255, 256 (1913))

Indiana
Formal Will Requirements

Minimum age for executing will	Real Property—18 years. (§ 29-1-5-1) Personal Property—18 years. (§ 29-1-5-1) In both instances, if a member of the armed forces or merchant marines of the United States or its allies, a person younger than 18 may make a will.
Number of witnesses required	Two. (§ 29-1-5-3(a))
Holographic wills	No. (§ 29-1-5-3)
Wills admitted to probate if valid under the law of:	Under law in force at time of execution or death in Indiana, place of execution; or domicile of testator at the time of execution or death. (§ 29-1-5-5)
Does the signing by the testator and/or witnesses just of the self-proving affidavit constitute the execution of the will?	Yes. (§ 29-1-5-3.1; Wynick v. Gentry, 796 N.E.2d 342, 348-49 (Ct. App. 2003) (holding also that statute has retroactive effect))
Can self-proving affidavit be signed later by testator and/or witnesses?	Yes. (§ 29-1-5-3.1(b))
If a witness is a devisee, does this result in the disqualification to serve as a witness or the invalidation of the devise?	There is no disqualification of the witness. Unless the will can be proved without the witness, the witness cannot take the excess over what the witness would have taken by intestate succession. (§ 29-1-5-2(c))
Can any other person sign the will?	Yes, at the testator's direction and in the testator's presence. (§ 29-1-5-3(b)(1)(C))
When must witnesses sign?	No time specified, as long as other requirements in *Can self-proving affidavit be signed later by testator and/or witnesses?* and *May the testator acknowledge either his will or his signature?* are met. (§ 29-1-5-3(b))
Must they sign in the presence of the testator?	Yes. (§ 29-1-5-3(b)(2))
Must they sign in the presence of each other?	Yes. (§ 29-1-5-3(b)(2))
Must the testator publish the will?	Yes. (§ 29-1-5-3(b)(1))
Must the will be signed in a particular place?	No. There is no statutory provision. Earlier case law did not require a signature in a particular place. (Thrift Realty Co. v. White, 168 N.E. 250, 251 (1929))
Must the required number of witnesses be present at the same time for the signing or acknowledgment by the testator?	Yes. (§ 29-1-5-3(b))
May the testator acknowledge either his will or his signature?	Yes. (§ 29-1-5-3(b)(1)(A)-(B)(Signature))
Requirements to be witness	Any person competent to be a witness generally in Indiana. (§ 29-1-5-2(b))

Iowa
Formal Will Requirements

Minimum age for executing will	"Any person of full age and sound mind may dispose by will of all the person's property . . . ." (§ 633.264) Generally, full age would be 18, except if married at an earlier age. (§ 599.1)
Number of witnesses required	Two. (§ 633.279(1))
Holographic wills	No. (§ 633.279) See also Olsen v. Olsen, 2001 WL 246570 (Ct. App. Mar. 14, 2001)
Wills admitted to probate if valid under the law of:	Iowa; place where executed; place where testator domiciled. (§ 633.283)
Does the signing by the testator and/or witnesses just of the self-proving affidavit constitute the execution of the will?	No. The acknowledgment of the will by the testator and verifications of the witnesses must be evidenced by their signatures "attached or annexed to the will, in form and content substantially as [provided in the statute]." (§ 633.279(2)) But see Delaware, *Does the signing by the testator and/or witnesses just of the self-proving affidavit constitute the execution of the will?*
Can self-proving affidavit be signed later by testator and/or witnesses?	Yes. (§ 633.279(2))
If a witness is a devisee, does this result in the disqualification to serve as a witness or the invalidation of the devise?	There is no disqualification of the witness. (§ 633.281) Unless there are two other disinterested witnesses, the witness cannot take the excess over what the witness would have taken by intestate succession. (§ 633.281)
Can any other person sign the will?	Yes, in the testator's presence and by the testator's express direction. (§ 633.279(1))
When must witnesses sign?	No time limit specified.
Must they sign in the presence of the testator?	Yes. (§ 633.279(1))
Must they sign in the presence of each other?	Yes. (§ 633.279(1))
Must the testator publish the will?	Yes. (§ 633.279(1))
Must the will be signed in a particular place?	No. (In re Johnson's Estate, 229 N.W. 261, 263 (1930))
Must the required number of witnesses be present at the same time for the signing or acknowledgment by the testator?	No. (In re Hull's Will, 89 N.W. 979, 981 (1902)) (decided under the former law)
May the testator acknowledge either his will or his signature?	The later acknowledgment of the signature is an alternative, but must, apparently, be done in the presence of the two witnesses. (In re McElderry's Estate, 251 N.W. 610, 612 (1933)
Requirements to be witness	Any person who is at least 16 and who is competent to be a witness generally in the state. (§ 633.280)

Kansas
Formal Will Requirements

Minimum age for executing will	"[R]ights of majority." (§ 59-601) This is generally 18 years (§ 38-101). However, it is age 16, if married or has been married. (Id.)
Number of witnesses required	Two. (§ 59-606)
Holographic wills	No. (§ 59-606; Matter of Reed's Estate, 229 Kan. 431 (1981))
Wills admitted to probate if valid under the law of:	Kansas; place where executed; place of testator's residence at the time of execution or death. (§ 59-609)
Does the signing by the testator and/or witnesses just of the self-proving affidavit constitute the execution of the will?	Yes, with respect to witnesses signing the affidavit and not the will itself. (§ 59-606) There is no similar reference to the testator, who also must sign the affidavit. However, In re Estate of Petty, 608 P.2d 987, 992 (1980), though involving witnesses, would appear to support the result that a will is duly executed even if the testator signs the self-proving affidavit.
Can self-proving affidavit be signed later by testator and/or witnesses?	Yes, "at any subsequent date during the lifetimes of the testator and the witnesses," by affidavits of testator and witnesses "in form and contents substantially as [provided by statute]." (§ 59-606)
If a witness is a devisee, does this result in the disqualification to serve as a witness or the invalidation of the devise?	Devise is void, unless there are two other disinterested witnesses or to the extent the witness would take by intestate succession. (§ 59-604)
Can any other person sign the will?	Yes, in the presence of the testator and by the testator's express direction. (§ 59-606)
When must witnesses sign?	No time specified.
Must they sign in the presence of the testator?	Yes. (§ 59-606) This may occur after the witness "saw" testator's signing or "heard" later acknowledgment of the will. (§ 59-606)
Must they sign in the presence of each other?	No. (In re Perkins' Estate, 504 P.2d 564, 568-69 (Kan. 1972)) However, the self-proving affidavit form has an express provision stating that the witnesses stated that "they did sign the will as witnesses in the presence of each other and in the presence of the testator and at the testator's request." To be valid, the self-proving affidavit must be in "form and contents substantially" as specified in the statute. (§ 59-606)
Must the testator publish the will?	No. (In re Estate of Koellen, 176 P.2d 544, 549 (1947))
Must the will be signed in a particular place?	At the end. (§ 59-606)
Must the required number of witnesses be present at the same time for the signing or acknowledgment by the testator?	No. (§ 59-606) The statute states that the will "shall be attested and subscribed in the presence of such party by two or more competent witnesses . . . ." In Humphrey v. Wallace, 216 P.2d 781, 783 (1950), presence at the same time was not required.

Kansas
Formal Will Requirements

May the testator acknowledge either his will or his signature?	The acknowledgment must be of the will, since the law describes two or more witnesses who "saw the testator subscribe or heard the testator acknowledge the will." (§ 59-606)
Requirements to be witness	Competency. (§ 59-607)

Kentucky
Formal Will Requirements

Minimum age for executing will	Real Property—18 years. (§ 394.020) Personal Property—18 years. (§ 394.020) However, "except in pursuance of a power given to the effect, and except also, that a parent, though under eighteen (18) years of age, may by will appoint a guardian of his child." (§ 394.030)
Number of witnesses required	Two. (§ 394.040)
Holographic wills	Yes. (§ 394.040)
Wills admitted to probate if valid under the law of:	Place where testator is domiciled, if he is not domiciled in Kentucky at the time of his death. (§ 394.120)
Does the signing by the testator and/or witnesses just of the self-proving affidavit constitute the execution of the will?	Yes. (§ 394.225(1))
Can self-proving affidavit be signed later by testator and/or witnesses?	Yes, by the acknowledgment by testator of will and the affidavits of witnesses before "an officer authorized to administer oaths." (§ 394.225(2))
If a witness is a devisee, does this result in the disqualification to serve as a witness or the invalidation of the devise?	No. However, if the will cannot otherwise be proved without the witness, and the witness *or the witness' spouse* is a devisee, then the witness or witness' spouse cannot take more than the witness would take by intestate succession. (§ 394.210(2))
Can any other person sign the will?	Yes, in testator's presence and by his direction. (§ 394.040)
When must witnesses sign?	At either testator's execution or later acknowledgment. (§ 394.040)
Must they sign in the presence of the testator?	Yes. (§ 394.040)
Must they sign in the presence of each other?	Yes. (§ 394.040)
Must the testator publish the will?	No. (Wroblewski v. Yeager, 361 S.W.2d 108, 110 (Ct. App. 1962))
Must the will be signed in a particular place?	At the end or close of the writing. (§ 446.060(1)) This requirement is met in the case of a holographic will even if signature precedes date. (Fairweather v. Nord, 388 S.W.2d 122, 125 (Ky. 1965))
Must the required number of witnesses be present at the same time for the signing or acknowledgment by the testator?	Yes. (§ 394.040)
May the testator acknowledge either his will or his signature?	The *will* must be acknowledged. (§ 394.040)
Requirements to be witness	Must be credible. (§ 394.040), which means not disqualified by mental imbecility, interest or crime from giving testimony in a court of justice. (Savage v. Bulger, 77 S.W. 717 (1903)) Also, subsequent incompetency does not invalidate attestation though witness is incompetent to prove its execution. (§ 394.210(1))

Louisiana
Formal Will Requirements

Minimum age for executing will	Real Property—16 years. (Civ. Code art. 1476) Personal Property—16 years. (Civ. Code art. 1476) If a minor is under 16, he may not make a will unless the donation is in favor of his spouse or children. (Id.)
Number of witnesses required	Two, plus a notary for a notarial or sealed testament. (Civ. Code art. 1577(1))
Holographic wills	Yes. (Civ. Code art. 1575)
Wills admitted to probate if valid under the law of:	Louisiana; place of execution; place where testator domiciled at the time of execution. (Rev. Stat. § 9:2401)

Note: Great caution should be exercised with regard to execution of a will because, while Louisiana allows for two types of wills, neither is precisely identical to those recognized in the other states or under the common law. These are holographic and notarial testaments. (Civ. Code art. 1574)

Maine
Formal Will Requirements

Minimum age for executing will	Real Property—18 years. (18–A § 2-501) Personal Property—18 years. (18–A § 2-501)
Number of witnesses required	Two. (18–A § 2-502)
Holographic wills	Yes. (18–A § 2-503)
Wills admitted to probate if valid under the law of:	Maine; place of execution at the time of execution; place where, at time of execution or death, testator is domiciled, has a place of abode, or is a national. (18–A § 2-506)
Does the signing by the testator and/or witnesses just of the self-proving affidavit constitute the execution of the will?	Yes. (18–A § 2-504(a) & cmt.)
Can self-proving affidavit be signed later by testator and/or witnesses?	Yes, if acknowledgment of will by testator and affidavits of witnesses before notary attached or annexed to will in substantially the [prescribed statutory] form. (18–A § 2-504(b))
If a witness is a devisee, does this result in the disqualification to serve as a witness or the invalidation of the devise?	There is no disqualification of the witness. (18–A § 2-505(b) cmt.) The devise is not invalidated. (18–A § 2-505(b) cmt.)
Can any other person sign the will?	Yes, if in the testator's presence and by his direction. (18–A § 2-502)
When must witnesses sign?	While they must witness (1) at the time the will is signed; (2) the acknowledgment that the document is the testator's will; or (3) the acknowledgment by the testator that the signature is the testator's, no particular time for signing the will is prescribed. (18–A § 2-502 & cmt.)
Must they sign in the presence of the testator?	No. (18–A § 2-502 cmt.)
Must they sign in the presence of each other?	No. (18–A § 2-502 cmt.)
Must the testator publish the will?	No. (18–A § 2-502 cmt.)
Must the will be signed in a particular place?	No. (18–A § 2-502 cmt.)
Must the required number of witnesses be present at the same time for the signing or acknowledgment by the testator?	No. (18–A § 2-502 cmt.)
May the testator acknowledge either his will or his signature?	Yes. (18–A § 2-502)
Requirements to be witness	Any person generally competent to be a witness. (18–A § 2-505(a))

Maryland
Formal Will Requirements

Minimum age for executing will	Real Property—18 years. (Est. & Trusts § 4-101) Personal Property—18 years. (Est. & Trusts § 4-101)
Number of witnesses required	Two. (Est. & Trusts § 4-102)
Holographic wills	Yes, if entirely in the handwriting of a testator serving in the U.S. armed forces, who signs it outside the United States and its territories. The will is void one year after discharge of testator from the armed services. (Est. & Trusts § 4-103)
Wills admitted to probate if valid under the law of:	Maryland; place where executed; place where testator domiciled. (Est. & Trusts § 4-104)
Does the signing by the testator and/or witnesses just of the self-proving affidavit constitute the execution of the will?	There is no provision for self-proving a will.
Can self-proving affidavit be signed later by testator and/or witnesses?	There is no provision for self-proving a will.
If a witness is a devisee, does this result in the disqualification to serve as a witness or the invalidation of the devise?	No. (Leitch v. Leitch, 79 A. 600, 602-03 (1911))
Can any other person sign the will?	Yes, in his presence and by his express direction. (Est. & Trusts § 4-102)
When must witnesses sign?	No provision. (Casson v. Swogell, 500 A.2d 1031 (1985))
Must they sign in the presence of the testator?	Yes. (Est. & Trusts § 4-102)
Must they sign in the presence of each other?	No. (O'Neal v. Jennings, 455 A.2d 66, 67 (Md. App. 1983))
Must the testator publish the will?	No. (Casson v. Swogell, 500 A.2d 1031, 1032 (1985))
Must the will be signed in a particular place?	Uncertain. There is some language in Greenhawk v. Quimby, 184 A. 485, 487 (1936), about the signature being affixed "in the appropriate place for his signature."
Must the required number of witnesses be present at the same time for the signing or acknowledgment by the testator?	Apparently no. (Van Meter v. Van Meter, 183 Md. 614, 39 A.2d 752, 754 (1944))
May the testator acknowledge either his will or his signature?	Apparently either. (Slack v. Truitt, 791 A.2d 129, 135-36 (2002))
Requirements to be witness	Must be "credible," (Est. & Trusts, § 4-102) which means competent. This in turn is determined under the common law which bars the insane, those so young as to want discretion, and those guilty of an infamous crime. (McGarvey v. McGarvey, 405 A.2d 250, 253 (1979) (holding, however, that "'the dead hand of the common-law rule . . . should no longer be applied' to disqualify As [sic] an attesting witness to a will one who has been convicted of an 'infamous' crime."))

Massachusetts
Formal Will Requirements

Minimum age for executing will	Real Property—18 years. (190B § 2-501) Personal Property—18 years. (190B § 2-501)
Number of witnesses required	Two. (190B § 2-502(a)(3))
Holographic wills	No. (190B § 2-502) Note that the subsequent U.P.C. Comment subsection (b) "authorizes holographic wills." The actual statute does not do so. The U.P.C. Comment was not properly edited to comport with the Massachusetts version enacted.
Wills admitted to probate if valid under the law of:	Massachusetts; place where executed at time of execution, place where at time of execution or death where testator is domiciled, has place of abode or is a national. (190-B § 2-506)
Does the signing by the testator and/or witnesses just of the self-proving affidavit constitute the execution of the will?	Yes, if the form and content is substantially as provided by the statute. (190B § 2-504(a))
Can self-proving affidavit be signed later by testator and/or witnesses?	Yes. (190B § 2-504(b))
If a witness is a devisee, does this result in the disqualification to serve as a witness or the invalidation of the devise?	There is no disqualification of the witness. However, the devise to the witness, or to the witness' spouse, is void, in the absence of two other disinterested witnesses. (190B § 2-505(b))
Can any other person sign the will?	Yes, in testator's conscious presence and by his express direction. (190B § 2-502(a)(2))
When must witnesses sign?	No specific time requirement, but definitely after testator signs. Note that 190B § 2-502(a)(3) omits "within a reasonable time" language of the U.P.C.
Must they sign in the presence of the testator?	No. (190B § 2-502(a)(3))
Must they sign in the presence of each other?	No. (190B § 2-502)
Must the testator publish the will?	No. (190B § 2-502 comment)
Must the will be signed in a particular place?	No. (190B § 2-502 comment)
Must the required number of witnesses be present at the same time for the signing or acknowledgment by the testator?	No. (190B § 2-502 comment)
May the testator acknowledge either his will or his signature?	If an acknowledgment of a signature is involved, the witnesses must actually see the signature, unless concealment was unintentional. (In re Dunham, 134 N.E.2d 915, 916 (1956)) (Prior to July 1, 2011) Yes. (190B § 2-502(a)(3))
Requirements to be witness	An individual competent to be a witness. (190B § 2-505(a))

Michigan
Formal Will Requirements

Minimum age for executing will	Real Property—18 years. (§ 700.2501) Personal Property—18 years. (§ 700.2501)
Number of witnesses required	Two. (§ 700.2502(1)(c))
Holographic wills	Yes. (§ 700.2502(2))
Wills admitted to probate if valid under the law of:	Michigan; place of execution at time of execution; or place where at the time of execution or death, the testator is domiciled, has a place of abode, or is a national. (§ 700.2506)
Does the signing by the testator and/or witnesses just of the self-proving affidavit constitute the execution of the will?	Yes. (§ 700.2504(1))
Can self-proving affidavit be signed later by testator and/or witnesses?	Yes. (§ 700.2504(2))
If a witness is a devisee, does this result in the disqualification to serve as a witness or the invalidation of the devise?	The signing of a will by an interested witness does not invalidate the will or any provision of it. (§ 700.2505(2))
Can any other person sign the will?	Yes, in the testator's "conscious" presence and by the testator's direction. (§ 700.2502(1)(b))
When must witnesses sign?	A reasonable time after witnessing the signing or the acknowledgment by the testator. (§ 700.2502(1)(c)) However, the signatures must be before the testator's death. (In re Estate of Mikeska, 362 N.W.2d 906, 910-11 (Ct. App. 1985))
Must they sign in the presence of the testator?	No specific requirement. (§ 700.2502)
Must they sign in the presence of each other?	No specific requirement. (§ 700.2502)
Must the testator publish the will?	No. (In re Estate of Clark, 603 N.W.2d 290, 293 (Ct. App. 1999); In re Balk's Estate, 298 N.W. 779, 780 (1941))
Must the will be signed in a particular place?	No, under prior law. (In re Thomas' Estate, 220 N.W. 764, 765 (1928) (former statute); In re Norris' Estate, 191 N.W. 238, 241 (1922) (former statute)) (See also In re Dodson's Estate, 326 N.W.2d 532, 533 (Ct. App. 1982) ("Even when Michigan's statutes required that a will be 'subscribed' by the testator, a will signed at the top was held valid...")
Must the required number of witnesses be present at the same time for the signing or acknowledgment by the testator?	No specific requirement. (§ 700.2502; In re Estate of Allen, 2002 WL 31951319 at *1-2 (Ct. App. Dec. 6, 2002))
May the testator acknowledge either his will or his signature?	Yes. (§ 700.2502(1)(c))
Requirements to be witness	Any individual "generally competent to be a witness." (§ 700.2505(1))

Minnesota
Formal Will Requirements

Minimum age for executing will	Real Property—18 years. (§ 524.2-501) Personal Property—18 years. (§ 524.2-501)
Number of witnesses required	Two. (§ 524.2-502(3))
Holographic wills	No. (§ 524.2-502)
Wills admitted to probate if valid under the law of:	Minnesota; place of execution at time of execution; place where, at the time of execution or death, the testator is domiciled, has a place of abode, or is a national. (§ 524.2-506) An "international will" is also valid. (§ 524.2-1002)
Does the signing by the testator and/or witnesses just of the self-proving affidavit constitute the execution of the will?	Yes. (§ 524.2-504(a))
Can self-proving affidavit be signed later by testator and/or witnesses?	Yes, if acknowledgment of will by testator and affidavits of witnesses before notary attached or annexed to will in substantially the [prescribed statutory] form. (§ 524.2-504(b))
If a witness is a devisee, does this result in the disqualification to serve as a witness or the invalidation of the devise?	No. (§ 524.2-505(b))
Can any other person sign the will?	Yes, if in the testator's conscious presence and by his direction. (§ 524.2-502(2)) Or by a conservator authorized to do so by court order. (§§ 524.2-502(2) & 524.5-411)
When must witnesses sign?	Either within a reasonable time after the will is signed, the acknowledgment that the document is the testator's will, or the acknowledgment by the testator that the signature is his. (524.2-502 & U.P.C. § 2-502 cmt.[1])
Must they sign in the presence of the testator?	No. (U.P.C. § 2-502 cmt.[2])
Must they sign in the presence of each other?	No. (U.P.C. § 2-502 cmt.[3])
Must the testator publish the will?	No. (U.P.C. § 2-502 cmt.[4])
Must the will be signed in a particular place?	No. (U.P.C. § 2-502 cmt.[5])
Must the required number of witnesses be present at the same time for the signing or acknowledgment by the testator?	No. (U.P.C. § 2-502 cmt.[6])

Minnesota
Formal Will Requirements

May the testator acknowledge either his will or his signature?	Yes. (§ 524.2-502(3); U.P.C. § 2-502 cmt.[7])
Requirements to be witness	Any person generally competent to be a witness. (§ 524.2-505(a))

---

[1] Although adopting the Uniform Probate Code, the editorial board comments of the U.P.C. have not been included in Minnesota Statutes. Nonetheless, the assumption is that they would be relied upon in construing the statutory provisions.

[2] *Id.*

[3] *Id.*

[4] *Id.*

[5] *Id.*

[6] *Id.*

[7] *Id.*

Mississippi
Formal Will Requirements

Minimum age for executing will	Real Property—18 years. (§ 91-5-1) Personal Property—18 years. (§ 91-5-1)
Number of witnesses required	Two. (§ 91-5-1)
Holographic wills	Yes. (§ 91-7-10)
Wills admitted to probate if valid under the law of:	There is no statutory prohibition.
Does the signing by the testator and/or witnesses just of the self-proving affidavit constitute the execution of the will?	No support for this. However, there is no decision stating that it does not constitute due execution (e.g., through use of doctrine of integration). See Delaware, *Does the signing by the testator and/or witnesses just of the self-proving affidavit constitute the execution of the will?*
Can self-proving affidavit be signed later by testator and/or witnesses?	The statute provides for only witness affidavits. Although it only states that the witness affidavits "may" be signed at the will execution, this is not required. (§§ 91-7-7, 91-7-9)
If a witness is a devisee, does this result in the disqualification to serve as a witness or the invalidation of the devise?	There is no disqualification of the witness. The devise is void to the extent it exceeds what the witness would have received by intestate succession if there are not two other credible witnesses. (§ 91-5-9) A creditor is a competent witness, but any special provision for payment or preference in the will is void. (§ 91-5-13)
Can any other person sign the will?	Yes, if in testator's presence and by testator's express direction. (§ 91-5-1)
When must witnesses sign?	There is no specific time requirement. But see *Can self-proving affidavit be signed later by testator and/or witnesses?*
Must they sign in the presence of the testator?	Yes. (§ 91-5-1)
Must they sign in the presence of each other?	No. (Phifer v. McCarter, 76 So. 2d 258, 259 (1954))
Must the testator publish the will?	Yes, but may be construed by testator's actions, rather than words. (Green v. Pearson, 110 So. 862, 864 (1927))
Must the will be signed in a particular place?	No. (Wilson v. Polite, 218 So.2d 843, 850 (1969)) (name of testator may be written any place on the instrument, so long as it is declared to be his signature))
Must the required number of witnesses be present at the same time for the signing or acknowledgment by the testator?	No. (Phifer v. McCarter (above) noted that the statute did not require the testator to sign in the presence of witnesses.)
May the testator acknowledge either his will or his signature?	Uncertain. One case holds that the testator needs to acknowledge both his signature and his will. (Austin v. Patrick, 176 So. 714, 716 (1937)) A later case refers to the need to "acknowledge signing the document." (In re Estate of McKellar, 380 So. 2d 1273, 1274 (1980))
Requirements to be witness	They must be "credible," (§ 91-5-1) which means competent. (Wallace v. Harrison, 65 So. 2d 456, 459 (1953))

Missouri
Formal Will Requirements

Minimum age for executing will	Real Property—18 years. (§ 474.310) Personal Property—18 years. (§ 474.310) Any minor emancipated by adjudication, marriage or entry into active military duty is also able to execute a valid will.
Number of witnesses required	Two. (§ 474.320)
Holographic wills	No. (§ 474.320)
Wills admitted to probate if valid under the law of:	Missouri; place of execution at time of execution; place where, at time of execution or death, the testator is domiciled, has a place of abode, or is a national. (§ 474.360)
Does the signing by the testator and/or witnesses just of the self-proving affidavit constitute the execution of the will?	No support for this. However, there is no decision stating that it does not constitute due execution (e.g., through use of doctrine of integration). See Delaware, *Does the signing by the testator and/or witnesses just of the self-proving affidavit constitute the execution of the will?*
Can self-proving affidavit be signed later by testator and/or witnesses?	Yes, "at any subsequent date," by "acknowledgment" of the testator and witnesses attached or annexed to the will in form and content substantially as provided in the statute. (§ 474.337(1))
If a witness is a devisee, does this result in the disqualification to serve as a witness or the invalidation of the devise?	There is no disqualification of the witness. In the event there are not sufficient disinterested witnesses, the devise is void to the extent it exceeds the share the witness would take by intestate succession. (§ 474.330(2))
Can any other person sign the will?	Yes, if by the direction of the testator and in his presence. (§ 474.320)
When must witnesses sign?	No time constraint, but must do so in the presence of the testator. See also *Can self-proving affidavit be signed later by testator and/or witnesses?* (§ 474.320)
Must they sign in the presence of the testator?	Yes. (§ 474.320) However, the testator does not actually have to see them sign. (Callaway v. Blankenbaker, 141 S.W.2d 810, 816 (1940))
Must they sign in the presence of each other?	No. (Grimm v. Tittmann, 20 S.W. 664, 665 (1892))
Must the testator publish the will?	Yes, but need not be done by express words, as opposed to acts. (Maurath v. Sickles, 586 S.W.2d 723, 726 (Ct. App. 1979), *citing* Hughes v. Dwyer, 546 S.W.2d 733, 736 (Ct. App. 1977))
Must the will be signed in a particular place?	No. (Potter v. Richardson, 230 S.W.2d 672, 676 (1950))
Must the required number of witnesses be present at the same time for the signing or acknowledgment by the testator?	No. The prospect of acknowledgment, as an alternative to witnessing the signing by the testator, has been confirmed. (Lopiccolo v. Semar, 890 S.W.2d 754, 759 (Ct. App. 1995))
May the testator acknowledge either his will or his signature?	No. The testator must make known to witnesses that he has signed the instrument as his will. (Grimm v. Tittman, 20 S.W. 664, 665 (1892))
Requirements to be witness	Any person who is competent to be a witness generally. (§ 474.330(1))

Montana
Formal Will Requirements

Minimum age for executing will	Real Property—18 years. (§ 72-2-521) Personal Property—18 years. (§ 72-2-521)
Number of witnesses required	Two. (§ 72-2-522(1)(c))
Holographic wills	Yes. (§ 72-2-522(2))
Wills admitted to probate if valid under the law of:	Montana; place of execution at time of execution; place where, at the time of execution or death, the testator is domiciled, has a place of abode, or is a national. (§ 72-2-526) An "international will" is also valid. (§ 72-2-902)
Does the signing by the testator and/or witnesses just of the self-proving affidavit constitute the execution of the will?	Yes. (§ 72-2-524(1) & (3))
Can self-proving affidavit be signed later by testator and/or witnesses?	At any time after execution, the will may be self-proved by the testator's acknowledgment of the will and the witnesses' affidavits attached or annexed to the will in substantially the form provided for in the statute. (§ 72-2-524(2))
If a witness is a devisee, does this result in the disqualification to serve as a witness or the invalidation of the devise?	No. (§ 72-2-525(2))
Can any other person sign the will?	Yes, if in the testator's conscious presence and by the testator's direction. (§ 72-2-522(1)(b))
When must witnesses sign?	Within a reasonable time after having witnessed either the signing of the will or the testator's acknowledgment of the signature or of the will. (§ 72-2-522(1)(c))
Must they sign in the presence of the testator?	No. (U.P.C. § 2-502 cmt.[1])
Must they sign in the presence of each other?	No. (U.P.C. § 2-502 cmt.[2])
Must the testator publish the will?	No. (U.P.C. § 2-502 cmt.[3])
Must the will be signed in a particular place?	No. (U.P.C. § 2-502 cmt.[4])
Must the required number of witnesses be present at the same time for the signing or acknowledgment by the testator?	No. (U.P.C. § 2-502 cmt.[5])
May the testator acknowledge either his will or his signature?	Yes. (§ 72-2-522(1)(c); U.P.C. § 2-502 cmt.[6])
Requirements to be witness	An individual must be generally competent to be a witness. (§ 72-2-525(1))

[1] Although adopting the Uniform Probate Code, the editorial board comments of the U.P.C. have not been included in Montana Code Annotated. Nonetheless, the assumption is that they would be relied upon in construing the statutory provisions.
[2] *Id.*
[3] *Id.*
[4] *Id.*
[5] *Id.*
[6] *Id.*

Nebraska
Formal Will Requirements

Minimum age for executing will	Real Property—18 years or is not a minor. (§ 30-2326) Personal Property—18 years or is not a minor. (§ 30-2326)
Number of witnesses required	Two. (§ 30-2327)
Holographic wills	Yes. (§ 30-2328)
Wills admitted to probate if valid under the law of:	Nebraska, place of execution at the time of execution; place where, at the time of execution or death, the testator is domiciled, has a place of abode, or is a national. (§ 30-2331)
Does the signing by the testator and/or witnesses just of the self-proving affidavit constitute the execution of the will?	The following language would appear to allow this: "Any will may be simultaneously executed, attested, and made self-proved by the acknowledgment thereof by the testator and the affidavits of the witnesses . . . ." (§ 30-2329(1))
Can self-proving affidavit be signed later by testator and/or witnesses?	Yes. "An attested will may at any time subsequent to its execution be made self-proved, by the acknowledgment thereof by the testator and the affidavits of the witnesses . . . in form and content substantially as [provided in the statute]." (§ 30-2329(2))
If a witness is a devisee, does this result in the disqualification to serve as a witness or the invalidation of the devise?	There is no disqualification of the witness. However, unless there is at least one disinterested witness, the devise is void to the extent it exceeds the share the interested witness would take by intestate succession. (§ 30-2330(b))
Can any other person sign the will?	Yes, if in the testator's presence and by his direction. (§ 30-2327)
When must witnesses sign?	No time constraint, although it must be after either the signing of the will or the testator's acknowledgment of the signature or of the will. (§ 30-2327) The law has been interpreted as requiring that witnesses must sign prior to the testator's death. (In re Estate of Flicker, 339 N.W.2d 914, 915 (1983))
Must they sign in the presence of the testator?	No. (U.P.C. § 2-502 cmt.[1])
Must they sign in the presence of each other?	No. (U.P.C. § 2-502 cmt.[2])
Must the testator publish the will?	No. (U.P.C. § 2-502 cmt.[3])
Must the will be signed in a particular place?	No. (U.P.C. § 2-502 cmt.[4])
Must the required number of witnesses be present at the same time for the signing or acknowledgment by the testator?	No. (U.P.C. § 2-502 cmt.[5])

Nebraska
Formal Will Requirements

May the testator acknowledge either his will or his signature?	Yes. (§ 30-2327; U.P.C. § 2-502 cmt.[6])
Requirements to be witness	Any individual generally competent to be a witness. (§ 30-2330(a))

---

[1] Although adopting the Uniform Probate Code, the editorial comments of the U.P.C. have not been included in Revised Statutes of Nebraska Annotated. Nonetheless, the assumption is that they would be relied upon in construing the statutory provisions.

[2] *Id.*

[3] *Id.*

[4] *Id.*

[5] *Id.*

[6] *Id.*

Nevada
Formal Will Requirements

Minimum age for executing will	Real Property—18 years. (§ 133.020) Personal Property—18 years. (§ 133.020)
Number of witnesses required	Two. (§ 133.040)
Holographic wills	Yes. (§ 133.090) See also approval of electronic wills. (§ § 133.040 & 133.085)
Wills admitted to probate if valid under the law of:	Nevada; place of execution; testator's domicile. (§ 133.080) See also approval of electronic wills. (§ 133.040)
Does the signing by the testator and/or witnesses just of the self-proving affidavit constitute the execution of the will?	Yes. (§ 133.055: A signature affixed to a self-proving affidavit or a self-proving declaration. attached to a will and executed at the same time as the will is a signature affixed to the will if necessary to prove the execution of the will.)
Can self-proving affidavit be signed later by testator and/or witnesses?	Yes. (§ 133.050(2) & (3))
If a witness is a devisee, does this result in the disqualification to serve as a witness or the invalidation of the devise?	There is no disqualification of the witness. However, the devise to an interest witness is void unless there are two other competent witnesses. (§ 133.060) A mere charge on the estate does not make a creditor incompetent to serve as a witness. (§ 133.070)
Can any other person sign the will?	Yes, "if by an attending person at the testator's express direction." (§ 133.040)
When must witnesses sign?	No statute or case authority directly on point. Since it must be in testator's presence, the signing must be before testator's death. (§ 133.040)
Must they sign in the presence of the testator?	Yes. (§ 133.040)
Must they sign in the presence of each other?	No statute or case authority directly on point. However, the self-proving declaration or self-proving affidavit must be in "substantially" the form set forth in the statute, which states that the witnesses signed "in the presence of each other." (§ 133.050(2))
Must the testator publish the will?	No statute or case authority directly on point. However, the self-proving declaration or self-proving affidavit must be in substantially the form set forth in the statute which states that the testator declared it to be his or her last will and testament in their presence. (§ 133.050(2)-(3))
Must the will be signed in a particular place?	No statute or case authority directly on point.
Must the required number of witnesses be present at the same time for the signing or acknowledgment by the testator?	No statute or case authority directly on point.
May the testator acknowledge either his will or his signature?	No statute or case authority directly on point.
Requirements to be witness	An individual competent to be a witness. (§ 133.040)

New Hampshire
Formal Will Requirements

Minimum age for executing will	Real Property—18 years. (§ 551:1) Personal Property—18 years. (§ 551:1) Married persons under 18 may make a will. (§ 551:1)
Number of witnesses required	Two. (§ 551:2 (IV)) Two witnesses are required (for wills executed on or after January 1, 1993).
Holographic wills	No. (§ 551:2)
Wills admitted to probate if valid under the law of:	New Hampshire; place of execution. (§ 551:5(I) & (II))
Does the signing by the testator and/or witnesses just of the self-proving affidavit constitute the execution of the will?	Probably not. (§ 551:2-a(I) & (II))
Can self-proving affidavit be signed later by testator and/or witnesses?	No restriction if signatures of testator and witnesses are followed by a sworn acknowledgment by the testator and witnesses as provided in the statute. (§ 551:2-a) The language conspicuously omits a statement that the form can be in "substantially" the form and content set forth in the statute. Rather, the self-proving document must be "as follows." Furthermore, it must be notarized by an officer authorized "in the place of execution" of the will.
If a witness is a devisee, does this result in the disqualification to serve as a witness or the invalidation of the devise?	There is no disqualification of the witness. However, the devise to the witness or the witness' spouse is void unless there are two other disinterested witnesses. A provision for payment of a debt does not disqualify a creditor. (§ 551:3)
Can any other person sign the will?	Yes, if at the testator's express direction in the testator's presence. (§ 551:2(III))
When must witnesses sign?	There is no time constraint. But see *Must they sign in the presence of the testator?*
Must they sign in the presence of the testator?	Yes. (§ 551:2(IV))
Must they sign in the presence of each other?	Apparently not. Each witness must see the signature on the will and subscribe his name. (Welch v. Adams 1 A. 1 (1885)) However, they must sign in each other's presence if a self-proving affidavit is to be used. (§ 551:2-a(I))
Must the testator publish the will?	No. (Welch v. Adams, 1 A. 1 (1885))
Must the will be signed in a particular place?	No statute or case authority directly on point.
Must the required number of witnesses be present at the same time for the signing or acknowledgment by the testator?	No. (Welch v. Adams, 1 A. 1 (1885))
May the testator acknowledge either his will or his signature?	Yes. (Welch v. Adams, 1 A. 1 (1885))
Requirements to be witness	The witness must be "credible." (§ 551:2(IV)) This term is intended to mean "competent." (Ross v. Carlino, 417 A.2d 13, 13 (1980)) A person under age 14 is presumed incompetent, but this presumption can be rebutted. (Carlton v. Carlton, 40 N.H. 14, 19 (1859))

New Jersey
Formal Will Requirements

Minimum age for executing will	Real Property—18 years. (§ 3B:3-1) Personal Property—18 years. (§ 3B:3-1)
Number of witnesses required	Two. (§ 3B:3-2(a)(3))
Holographic wills	Yes. (§ § 3B:3-2(b); 3B:3-3)
Wills admitted to probate if valid under the law of:	New Jersey; place where executed; place where, at time of execution or death, testator was domiciled, had a place of abode, or was a national. (§ 3B:3-9)
Does the signing by the testator and/or witnesses just of the self-proving affidavit constitute the execution of the will?	Yes. (§ 3B:3-4)
Can self-proving affidavit be signed later by testator and/or witnesses?	No restriction if acknowledgment of will by testator and affidavits of witnesses attached or annexed to the will in substantially the statutory form. (§ 3B:3-5)
If a witness is a devisee, does this result in the disqualification to serve as a witness or the invalidation of the devise?	No. (§ 3B:3-8)
Can any other person sign the will?	Yes, if in the testator's conscious presence and at his direction. (§ 3B:3-2)
When must witnesses sign?	Within a reasonable time after witnessing either the signing of the will or the acknowledgement of the will or signature. (§ 3B:3-2 (a)(3))
Must they sign in the presence of the testator?	No. (§ 3B:3-2(a)(3); U.P.C. § 2-502 cmt.[1])
Must they sign in the presence of each other?	No. (§ 3B-2(a)(3); U.P.C. § 2-502 cmt.[2])
Must the testator publish the will?	No. (U.P.C. § 2-502 cmt.[3]) Yes, apparently, if using self-proving affidavit. (§ 3B:3-4)
Must the will be signed in a particular place?	No. (U.P.C. § 2-502 cmt.) *Cf.* In re Will of Ranney, 573 A.2d 467, 471 (Ct. App. 1990), *aff'd*, 589 A.2d 1339 (1991). Under former law, see In re Potts' Estate, 61 A.2d 649, 649 (Co. Ct. 1948); In re Phelan's Estate, 87 A. 625, 626 (1913), *aff'd*, 91 A. 1070 (1914).
Must the required number of witnesses be present at the same time for the signing or acknowledgment by the testator?	No. (U.P.C. § 2-502 cmt.[4])
May the testator acknowledge either his will or his signature?	Yes. (3B:3-2(a)(3)). See also U.P.C. § 2-502 cmt.[5]
Requirements to be witness	Any person who is generally competent to be a witness. (§ 3B:3-7)

[1] Although adopting the Uniform Probate Code, the editorial comments of the U.P.C. have not been included in New Jersey Statutes. Nonetheless, the assumption is that they would be relied upon in construing the statutory provisions.

[2] *Id.*

[3] *Id.*

[4] *Id.*

[5] *Id.*

New Mexico
Formal Will Requirements

Minimum age for executing will	Real Property—18 years or an emancipated minor. (§ 45-2-501) Personal Property—18 years or an emancipated minor. (§ 45-2-501)
Number of witnesses required	Two. (§ 45-2-502(C))
Holographic wills	No. (§ 45-2-502)
Wills admitted to probate if valid under the law of:	A will is valid if executed in compliance with New Mexico law (§ 45-2-502) or if the will complies with the laws of the place of execution at the time of execution or the place where, at the time of execution or death, the testator is domiciled, has a place of abode, or is a national (§ 45-2-506). An "international will" is also valid. (§ 45-2-1002)
Does the signing by the testator and/or witnesses just of the self-proving affidavit constitute the execution of the will?	Yes, based on language that "will may be simultaneously executed, attested and made self-proved by acknowledgment thereof by the testator and affidavits of the witnesses." (§ 45-2-504(A)) See also § 45-2-504(C) which provides "A signature affixed to a self-proving affidavit attached to a will is considered a signature affixed to the will if necessary to prove the will's due execution."
Can self-proving affidavit be signed later by testator and/or witnesses?	No restriction if acknowledgment of will by testator and affidavits of witnesses attached or annexed to the will in substantially the statutory form. (§ 45-2-504(B))
If a witness is a devisee, does this result in the disqualification to serve as a witness or the invalidation of the devise?	No. (§ 45-2-505(B))
Can any other person sign the will?	Yes, if in the testator's conscious presence and by the testator's direction. (§ 45-2-502(B))
When must witnesses sign?	Uncertain. Provision states: "after each [witness] witnessed the signing of the will . . . ." (§ 45-2-502(C))
Must they sign in the presence of the testator?	Yes. (§ 45-2-502(C))
Must they sign in the presence of each other?	Yes. (§ 45-2-502(C))
Must the testator publish the will?	Yes. Even though § 45-2-502 is derived from the U.P.C., which does not require publication, publication is still required under New Mexico law. Publication may be by words or conduct. (In re Kelly's Estate, 660 P.2d 124, 129-30 (Ct. App. 1983))
Must the will be signed in a particular place?	No. (U.P.C. § 2-502 cmt.[1])
Must the required number of witnesses be present at the same time for the signing or acknowledgment by the testator?	Yes. Implied from requirement that witnesses must sign will "after each witnessed the signing of the will . . . ." (§ 45-2-502(C))
May the testator acknowledge either his will or his signature?	No. (§ 45-2-502(c))
Requirements to be witness	An individual who is generally competent to be a witness. (§ 45-2-505(A))

---

[1] *Id.*

New York
Formal Will Requirements

Minimum age for executing will	Real Property—18 years. (Est., Powers & Tr. Law § 3-1.1) Personal Property—18 years. (Est., Powers & Tr. Law § 3-1.1)
Number of witnesses required	Two. (Est., Powers & Tr. Law § 3-2.1(a)(4))
Holographic wills	Yes, but only for members of the military while serving in armed conflict or for a person serving with or accompanying the armed services under these circumstances, or a mariner while at sea. (Est., Powers & Tr. Law §§ 3-2.2(a)(2), (b)) A holographic will made by a member of the armed services becomes invalid one year after his discharge from the armed services. It becomes invalid for a person serving with or accompanying the armed services one year after ceasing to do so. It becomes invalid for a mariner three years after the making of the will. (Est., Powers & Tr. Law § 3-2.2(c)(1)(3))
Wills admitted to probate if valid under the law of:	New York; place of execution at time of execution; place where testator is domiciled at the time of execution or death; applies to will of personal property located anywhere or real property in the state. (Est., Powers & Tr. Law § 3-5.1(c))
Does the signing by the testator and/or witnesses just of the self-proving affidavit constitute the execution of the will?	Probably not, since only the witnesses, and not the testator, sign the affidavits. Moreover, the witnesses must state in the affidavits "such facts as would if uncontradicted establish the . . . validity of its execution," which would presumably include that the testator signed the will or acknowledged his signature in their presence. (Sur. Ct. Proc. Act § 1406(1)) Notwithstanding the foregoing, one lower court has held witnesses validly executed the will when they signed the self-proving affidavit. (In re Will of Zuracino, 561 N.Y.S.2d 397, 398 (Sur. Ct. 1990)) Unlike witnesses, the testator must sign in a particular place, at the end (Est., Powers & Tr. Law § 3-2.10), so a different rule may apply to the testator. See also Florida.
Can self-proving affidavit be signed later by testator and/or witnesses?	Yes, at any time, including after the testator's death, any or both of the witnesses may sign an affidavit. However, it must be at the testator's request or, if the testator is deceased, at the request of the executor, the proponent, the attorney of the proponent, or any person "interested" in the will. (Sur. Ct. Proc. Act § 1406(1))
If a witness is a devisee, does this result in the disqualification to serve as a witness or the invalidation of the devise?	There is no disqualification of the witness. (Est., Powers & Tr. Law § 3-3.2(a)) However, the devise is void if there are not sufficient other disinterested witnesses, in which case the witness is denied the excess over the share he would take by intestate succession. (Est., Powers & Tr. Law § 3-3.2(a)(1) & (a)(3))
Can any other person sign the will?	Yes, if in the presence of the testator and by his direction. (Est., Powers & Tr. Law § 3-2.1(a)(1)) The person must also sign his own name and "affix his residence address," although failure to comply with this latter requirement will not invalidate the will. (Est., Powers & Tr. Law § 3-2.1(a)(1)(C))

New York
Formal Will Requirements

When must witnesses sign?	Both must sign within a 30-day period. (Est., Powers & Tr. Law § 3-2.1(a)(4)) There is a rebuttable presumption that the 30-day requirement has been met. (Id.) The signatures must follow a request to do this by the testator. (Id.) When signing, the witnesses must also affix their residence addresses, although failure to do so "shall not affect the validity of the will." (Id.)
Must they sign in the presence of the testator?	No, as long as *When must witnesses sign?* above is satisfied.
Must they sign in the presence of each other?	No. (Est., Powers & Tr. Law § 3-2.1(a)(2))
Must the testator publish the will?	Yes. (Est., Powers & Tr. Law § 3-2.1(a)(3))
Must the will be signed in a particular place?	Yes, at the end. (Est., Powers & Tr. Law § 3-2.1(a)(1)(A)) However, if it comes before the end, preceding material may be given effect. (*Id.*) Material that follows the signature, other than the attestation clause, will not be given effect. (Est., Powers & Tr. Law § 3-2.1(a)(1)(B))
Must the required number of witnesses be present at the same time for the signing or acknowledgment by the testator?	No. (Est., Powers & Tr. Law § 3-2.1(a)(2),(4))
May the testator acknowledge either his will or his signature?	No. The signature must be acknowledged in the presence of the witnesses. (Est., Powers & Tr. Law § 3-2.1(a)(4))
Requirements to be witness	The general rule of evidence applies. If the statute, as with respect to probate, does not specify a minimum age, there is none. As was stated in connection with a sworn deposition of a child below age 12 in a matter governed by the Family Court Act: "Although age is a relevant factor in determining the capacity of a person to make a statement under oath, the Family Court Act does not contain any age limitations . . . ." (In re Nelson R., 683 N.E.2d 329, 331, 660 N.Y.S.2d 707, 708-09 (Ct. App. 1997))

North Carolina
Formal Will Requirements

Minimum age for executing will	Real Property—18 years. (§ 31-1) Personal Property—18 years. (§ 31-1)
Number of witnesses required	Two. (§ 31-3.3(a))
Holographic wills	Yes. (§ 31-3.4)
Wills admitted to probate if valid under the law of:	There is no general statutory provision. Even if the law of North Carolina has not been complied with, the clerk of the court may take proof and the will may be adjudged duly proved. (§ 28A-2A-6) A will is valid if valid under North Carolina law at the time of its execution or at the time of the death of the testator. A will is also valid if it complies with the law of the place it was executed at execution, or with the law of the place where the testator is domiciled at execution or at testator's death, or if it is a military testamentary instrument complying with 10 U.S.C. § 1044d.
Does the signing by the testator and/or witnesses just of the self-proving affidavit constitute the execution of the will?	Yes, based on language that "will may be simultaneously executed, attested and made self-proved by acknowledgment thereof by the testator and affidavits of the witnesses." (§ 31-11.6(a)) However, if the witnesses sign the self-proving affidavit after the execution, there may be a problem, since in this case the affidavit can be made only if the will has been properly attested already. One court has recognized this problem but decided to adhere to a substantial compliance approach. See New Jersey and In re Will of Ranney, 573 A.2d 467 (Ct. App. 1990). North Carolina courts might not do so.
Can self-proving affidavit be signed later by testator and/or witnesses?	Yes "at any time subsequent to its execution." (§ 31-11.6(b))
If a witness is a devisee, does this result in the disqualification to serve as a witness or the invalidation of the devise?	There is no disqualification of the witness. A devise to the witness, the witness' spouse, or "anyone claiming under him" is void, unless there are at least two other disinterested witnesses. (§ 31-10(a))
Can any other person sign the will?	Yes, if in the testator's presence and at his direction. (§ 31-3.3(b))
When must witnesses sign?	After the testator's signature or acknowledgment, but no specific time period is prescribed. Since witnesses must sign in testator's presence (§ 31-3.3(d)), this must occur before his death. The witness cannot sign before the testator, at least not on a prior day. (In re McDonald's Will, 13 S.E.2d 239, 239 (1941) although there may be an exception if they signed at "practically" the same time.)
Must they sign in the presence of the testator?	Yes. (§ 31-3.3(d))
Must they sign in the presence of each other?	No. (§ 31-3.3(d))
Must the testator publish the will?	No requirement that testator inform witnesses that the instrument is his will. The statute provides that he must signify that the "instrument is his instrument by signing it in their presence or by acknowledging to them his signature previously affixed thereto." (§ 31-3.3(c))

North Carolina
Formal Will Requirements

Must the will be signed in a particular place?	No. (In re Roberts' Will, 112 S.E.2d 505, 510 (1960))
Must the required number of witnesses be present at the same time for the signing or acknowledgment by the testator?	No. (§ 31-3.3(c))
May the testator acknowledge either his will or his signature?	The testator must acknowledge the signature. (§ 31-3.3(c))
Requirements to be witness	The witness must be competent. (§ 31-8.1) The question of competency is one of law to be decided by the judge. (McLean v. Elliott, 72 N.C. 70 (1875))

North Dakota
Formal Will Requirements

Minimum age for executing will	Real Property—18 years. (§ 30.1-08-01) Personal Property—18 years. (§ 30.1-08-01 & U.P.C. cmt. 2-501)
Number of witnesses required	Two. (§ 30.1-08-02(1)(c)) Alternatively, the testator may sign or acknowledge the will before a notary public. (Id.)
Holographic wills	Yes. (§ 30.1-08-02(2) & U.P.C. cmt. 2-501)
Wills admitted to probate if valid under the law of:	North Dakota; place of execution at time of execution; place where, at time of execution or death, testator is domiciled, has a place of abode, or is a national. (§ 30.1-08-06) An "international will" is also valid. (§ 30.1-08.2-02)
Does the signing by the testator and/or witnesses just of the self-proving affidavit constitute the execution of the will?	Yes. (§ 30.1-08-04(3))
Can self-proving affidavit be signed later by testator and/or witnesses?	Yes, at any time after execution of will. (§ 30.1-08-04(2))
If a witness is a devisee, does this result in the disqualification to serve as a witness or the invalidation of the devise?	No. (§ 30.1-08-05(2))
Can any other person sign the will?	Yes, if in the testator's conscious presence and by the testator's direction. (§ 30.1-08-02(1)(b))
When must witnesses sign?	Within a reasonable time after witnessing either the signing of the will or the testator's acknowledgment of the signature or of the will. (§ 30.1-08-02(1)(c)) This can be after the testator's death. (§ 30.1-08-02 cmt.)
Must they sign in the presence of the testator?	No. (§ 30.1-08-02 cmt.)
Must they sign in the presence of each other?	No. (§ 30.1-08-02 cmt.)
Must the testator publish the will?	No. (§ 30.1-08-02 cmt.; In re Estate of Polda, 349 N.W.2d 11, 16 (1984))
Must the will be signed in a particular place?	No. (§ 30.1-08-02 cmt.)
Must the required number of witnesses be present at the same time for the signing or acknowledgment by the testator?	No. (§ 30.1-08-02 cmt.)
May the testator acknowledge either his will or his signature?	Yes. (§ 30.1-08-02(1)(c)(1); cmt.)
Requirements to be witness	Any person who is generally competent to be a witness. (§ 30.1-08-05(1))

Ohio
Formal Will Requirements

Minimum age for executing will	Real Property—18 years. (§ 2107.02) Personal Property—18 years. (§ 2107.02)
Number of witnesses required	Two. (§ 2107.03)
Holographic wills	No. (§ 2107.03)
Wills admitted to probate if valid under the law of:	Ohio; place of execution at the time of execution; or domicile at the time of death. (§ 2107.18)
Does the signing by the testator and/or witnesses just of the self-proving affidavit constitute the execution of the will?	There is no provision for a self-proved will. A probate court is required to admit a will to probate "if it appears from the face of the will . . . that the execution of the will complies with the law . . . ." (§ 2107.18)
Can self-proving affidavit be signed later by testator and/or witnesses?	There is no provision for a self-proved will. A probate court is required to admit a will to probate "if it appears from the face of the will . . . that the execution of the will complies with the law . . . ." (§ 2107.18)
If a witness is a devisee, does this result in the disqualification to serve as a witness or the invalidation of the devise?	There is no disqualification of the witness. However, the devise is void if there are not two other disinterested witnesses, to the extent the devise exceeds the share that the witness would take by intestate succession. The share is contributed to by devisees as if the witness was an absent or afterborn child. (§ 2107.15)
Can any other person sign the will?	Yes, if in the testator's conscious presence and at his express direction. (§ 2107.03)
When must witnesses sign?	No time restriction, but must be after the witnesses saw the testator sign or "heard him acknowledge his signature." (§ 2107.03) Since the will must be attested and subscribed in the presence of the testator, the signing cannot occur after the testator's death.
Must they sign in the presence of the testator?	Yes, in the testator's "conscious presence." (§ 2107.03) This means "within the range of any of the testator's senses, excluding the sense of light or sound that is sensed by telephone, electronic or other distant communication." (Id.)
Must they sign in the presence of each other?	No. (McFadden v. Thomas, 96 N.E.2d 254, 257 (Sup. Ct. 1951))
Must the testator publish the will?	The answer is uncertain. Probably no. Underwood v. Rutan, 101 Oh. St. 306, 128 N.E. 78 (1920) (no declaration required). See also In re Maurer, 31 Ohio N.P. (N.S.) 247 (Prob. Ct. 1933) (unlike in *Underwood*, the witnesses did not know the document was a will). But see Shinn v. Phillips, 220 N.E.2d 674, 677 (Ct. App. 1964), citing Collins v. Collins, 110 Ohio St. 105, 112-28, 143 N.E. 561, 565-67 (1924) (publication required for revival of will on the basis that it was required when the will was originally executed).
Must the will be signed in a particular place?	At the end. (§ 2107.03)
Must the required number of witnesses be present at the same time for the signing or acknowledgment by the testator?	No. (§ 2107.03)

Ohio
Formal Will Requirements

May the testator acknowledge either his will or his signature?	No. The testator must acknowledge the signature. (§ 2107.03)
Requirements to be witness	The witnesses must be competent. (§ 2107.03) They must also not be under 18 years of age. (§ 2107.06)

Oklahoma
Formal Will Requirements

Minimum age for executing will	Real Property—18 years. (84 § 41) Personal Property—18 years. (84 § 41)
Number of witnesses required	Two. (84 § 55(4))
Holographic wills	Yes. (84 § 54)
Wills admitted to probate if valid under the law of:	Oklahoma; place of execution; place where testator is domiciled at execution. (84 § 71)
Does the signing by the testator and/or witnesses just of the self-proving affidavit constitute the execution of the will?	From the statutory language, it would appear not, since the affidavit must be attached or annexed to the "testamentary instrument." (84 § 55(5)(a)) Even the alternative declaration that is allowed, see 84 § 55(5)(b), refers to a "will." But see In re Estate of Cutsinger, 445 P.2d 778, 782 (1968), holding to contrary and validating a witness' signatures appearing only on the affidavit. The court deemed the sworn attestation statement to be part of the will and in "substantial compliance" with the statute. But see also Delaware.
Can self-proving affidavit be signed later by testator and/or witnesses?	No restriction if acknowledgment of will by testator and affidavits of witnesses "during the lifetimes of the testator and witnesses" attached or annexed to the will in substantially the statutory form. (84 § 55(5)(a)) The notary must be authorized to act in Oklahoma. (*Id.*) A written declaration in place of the notarized acknowledgment and affidavits is also allowed, but it must be in substantially the form provided for by statute. (84 § 55(5)(b))
If a witness is a devisee, does this result in the disqualification to serve as a witness or the invalidation of the devise?	There is no disqualification of the witness. However, the devise is void if there are not two other competent witnesses. (84 § 143) If void, the witness is still entitled to the devise to the extent it does not exceed the witness' share under intestate succession. (84 § 144) The other devisees contribute based on the proportion of the amount and parts devised to them. (84 § 144) A creditor is a competent witness despite a charge on the estate for the payment of debts. (84 § 143)
Can any other person sign the will?	Yes, if in the testator's presence and by his direction. (84 § 55(1))
When must witnesses sign?	At the testator's request and in his presence. (84 § 55(4)) Thus, they must sign before the testator's death.
Must they sign in the presence of the testator?	Yes, and sign at the testator's request and at the end of the will. (84 § 55(4)) They should also write their places of residence, although failure to do does not invalidate the will. (84 § 56)
Must they sign in the presence of each other?	No. (Moore v. Glover, 163 P.2d 1003, 1007 (1945) (decided under substantially identical former law)
Must the testator publish the will?	Yes. (84 § 55(3))
Must the will be signed in a particular place?	Yes, at the end. (84 § 55(1))
Must the required number of witnesses be present at the same time for the signing or acknowledgment by the testator?	No. (84 § 55(2))

Oklahoma
Formal Will Requirements

May the testator acknowledge either his will or his signature?	No. The testator must acknowledge his subscription in the presence of the witnesses. (84 § 55(2)) He must also declare to them that the instrument is his will. (84 § 55(3))
Requirements to be witness	84 § 55, which sets forth the "formal requisites in execution" of a will, refers only to the "attesting witnesses." However, 84 § 145 states that if the witnesses "are competent at the time of attesting its execution, their subsequent incompetency, from whatever cause it may arise, does not prevent the probate and allowance of the will, if it is otherwise satisfactorily proved." On the other hand, 58 § 82 requires the proof of two "credible" witnesses in the case of a lost or destroyed will.

Oregon
Formal Will Requirements

Minimum age for executing will	Real Property—18 years. (§ 112.225) Personal Property—18 years. (§ 112.225) A married person under 18 may make a will, as may a minor who is emancipated in accordance with §§ 419B.550–419B.558. (§ 112.225)
Number of witnesses required	Two. (§ 112.235(1)(b))
Holographic wills	No. (§ 112.235) But see § 112.238, admitting writing as a will, though not in compliance with § 112.235, if proven by clear and convincing evidence that it was intended as a will by decedent.
Wills admitted to probate if valid under the law of:	The will must be in writing and signed by the testator or at his direction. Then, it is valid if it is valid under the law of Oregon, at time of execution or death; domicile of testator at execution or death; place of execution at time of execution. (§ 112.255) An "international will" is also valid. (§ 112.255)
Does the signing by the testator and/or witnesses just of the self-proving affidavit constitute the execution of the will?	No, since the affidavit is submitted by each witness and not by the testator. As to the witnesses, no specific form of affidavit is provided. However, the language of the statute strongly suggests that there would have to be a will already signed by the testator and witnesses, since the affidavit is intended to give evidence of the execution of the will. (§ 113.055(1))
Can self-proving affidavit be signed later by testator and/or witnesses?	At the time of will execution or any time thereafter, presumably including after the testator's death, since the witness submits the affidavit. (§ 113.055(1))
If a witness is a devisee, does this result in the disqualification to serve as a witness or the invalidation of the devise?	There is no disqualification of the witness. (§ 112.245) The provision does not specifically address whether the devise is void, and there is no direct case authority on point. Curiously, the statute proceeds to define an "interested witness" after stating that the will is not "invalidated" though attested by an interested witness.
Can any other person sign the will?	Yes, if at the direction of the testator. (§ 112.235(1)(b)) A witness can sign for the testator. Id.(1)(a)(B)
When must witnesses sign?	After witnessing the testator's signature or after each "[h]ear[s] the testator acknowledge the signature on the will," or "[h]ear[s]or observe[s] the testator direct some other person to sign the name of the testator." The witnesses must attest by signing the will "within a reasonable time before the testator's death." (§ 112.235(1)(b)(A)-(B))
Must they sign in the presence of the testator?	No. The statute simply states that the two witnesses shall each "attest the will by signing the witness' name to it within a reasonable time before the testator's death." (§ 112.235(1)(b)(B); Rogers v. Rogers, 691 P.2d 114 (Ct. App. 1984))
Must they sign in the presence of each other?	No. The statute simply states that the two witnesses shall each "attest the will by signing the witness' name to it." (§ 112.235(3)(c); Wishard v. Turner, 478 P.2d 438, 440 (1970) (former statute))

Oregon
Formal Will Requirements

Must the testator publish the will?	Probably not. Although there is no specific requirement, the witnesses must "[s]ee the testator sign the will" or "[h]ear the testator acknowledge the signature on the will." (§ 112.235(1)(b)(A)) Under a prior statute requring that the will be "attested by two or more competent witnesses, subscribing their name to the will, in the presence of the testator," the Oregon Supreme Court held that "nor is it necessary that the testator should declare the instrument to be his last will and testament." In re Neil's Estate, 111 Or. 282, 293, 226 P. 439, 442 (1924). See also In re Christofferson's Estate, 190 P.2d 928, 931 (1948).
Must the will be signed in a particular place?	There is no statutory provision or definite case authority on point.
Must the required number of witnesses be present at the same time for the signing or acknowledgment by the testator?	No. (§ 112.235(1)(a))
May the testator acknowledge either his will or his signature?	No. The testator must acknowledge to each witness that the "signature on the will" is the testator's. (§ 112.235(1)(a)(C))
Requirements to be witness	There is no statutory provision relating to the requirements for serving as a witness. Presumably, general competency requirements apply. The statute states that "any person who, having organs of sense can perceive, and perceiving can make known the perception to others, may be a witness." (§ 40.310, Rule 601)

Pennsylvania
Formal Will Requirements

Minimum age for executing will	Real Property—18 years. (20 § 2501) Personal Property—18 years. (20 § 2501)
Number of witnesses required	Two. (20 § 3132 (1)) However, the witnesses need not subscribe a will signed by the testator at the end. Rather, the will must be proved by the oaths or affirmations of two competent witnesses. Proof of subscribing witnesses, however, shall be preferred to the extent that they are available and proof of the signature of the testator is preferred to proof of the signature of a subscribing witness. (Id.)
Holographic wills	There is no statutory provision but holographs are recognized by case law. (In re Estate of Sidlow, 543 A.2d 1143, 1144 (Super. Ct. 1988); In re Young's Estate, 58 Pa. D.&C.2d 659 (1972))
Wills admitted to probate if valid under the law of:	Pennsylvania; place where testator domiciled at time of execution or death. (20 § 2504.1)
Does the signing by the testator and/or witnesses just of the self-proving affidavit constitute the execution of the will?	The acknowledgment of the testator and affidavits of the witnesses can be "substantially as set forth in the Uniform Probate Code" or as set forth in the statute. The provision is not precise on which version of the Uniform Probate Code is determinative. Certain forms in the Code would support the conclusion that the will had been validly executed. If the Pennsylvania form were followed, there might be a problem since the testator acknowledges that his "name is signed to the attached or foregoing instrument." (20 § 3132.1)
Can self-proving affidavit be signed later by testator and/or witnesses?	Yes, by testator and witnesses, although the witnesses can submit separate affidavits if not done at same time as the required acknowledgment by the testator. The self-proving documents can be executed before an officer authorized in Pennsylvania or where executed, or before "an attorney at law," who must be "a member of the bar of the Supreme Court of Pennsylvania or of the highest court of the state in which execution of the will occurs . . . " and who then must certify to the officer authorized to take oaths that the acknowledgment and affidavit was made before him. (20 § 3132.1(c))
If a witness is a devisee, does this result in the disqualification to serve as a witness or the invalidation of the devise?	The witness's interest does not automatically render him incompetent, but it may. (In re Elias' Estate, 239 A.2d 393 (1968); In re Pochron's Estate, 80 A.2d 794, 796 (1951); In re Umble's Estate, 186 A. 75, 76 (1936)) The witness is not barred from taking a devise. (In re Janney's Estate, 446 A.2d 1265, 1266 (1982))
Can any other person sign the will?	Yes, if in the testator's presence and by his express direction. (20 § 2502(3))
When must witnesses sign?	Witnesses are not required to subscribe if the testator has signed at the end of the will. (20 § 2502; Ligo v. Dodson, 151 A. 694 (1930)) Thus, there is no specific time constraint.

Pennsylvania
Formal Will Requirements

Must they sign in the presence of the testator?	Yes (20 § 2502(3)), at the execution, but only if someone else is signing for the testator or if the testator signs by mark instead of by signature. If the testator signs by his own signature, the witnesses are not required to sign.
Must they sign in the presence of each other?	Apparently not, if based on *acknowledgment* of the signature. (McClure v. Redman, 107 A. 25 (1919); In re Hoffmann's Estate, 15 Pa. D.&C. 2d 331 (1959), *aff'd,* 160 A.2d 237 (1960); In re Norton's Estate, 16 Erie 329 (1934); In re Kovel's Will, 24 Fid. 304 (1974))
Must the testator publish the will?	Yes, if subscribed by another for the testator. (20 § 2502(3)) Otherwise, publication of the will is not required. (In re Brantlinger's Estate, 210 A.2d 246, 251 (1965); In re Lillibridge's Estate, 69 A. 1121 (1908); (20 § 2502(3))
Must the will be signed in a particular place?	At the end. (20 § 2502) Although the presence of subsequent writing will not, in and of itself, invalidate the will (20 § 2502(1)), the entire will is invalidated if any dispositive provisions follow the signature (Evans' Appeal, 58 Pa. 238 (1868)).
Must the required number of witnesses be present at the same time for the signing or acknowledgment by the testator?	No. The testator may acknowledge his signature to the witnesses. There is no requirement that they both be present at the same time. (Leckey v. Cunningham, 56 Pa. 370 (1867)) Indeed, the statute itself does not mention the possibility of acknowledgment. However, if the testator simply makes his mark, or if another signs at his direction, the statute requires that it be made in the presence of the two witnesses. (20 § 2502(2)(3))
May the testator acknowledge either his will or his signature?	Apparently, the signature must be acknowledged. (Leckey v. Cunningham, 56 Pa. 370 (1867))
Requirements to be witness	Competency. 20 § 3132 requires that "[a]ll wills shall be proved by the oaths or affirmations of two competent witnesses." See also In re Goodwin's Estate, 12 Pa. D.&C. 77 (1928).

Rhode Island
Formal Will Requirements

Minimum age for executing will	Real Property—18 years. (§ 33-5-2) Personal Property—18 years. (§ 33-5-2)
Number of witnesses required	Two. (§ 33-5-5)
Holographic wills	No. (§ 33-5-5) "Any soldier or airman in actual military service, or any mariner or soldier at sea, may dispose of his or her personal estate by will as he or she might heretofore have done." (§ 33-5-6)
Wills admitted to probate if valid under the law of:	Rhode Island; place of execution or domicile. (§ 33-5-7)
Does the signing by the testator and/or witnesses just of the self-proving affidavit constitute the execution of the will?	No, since the affidavit does not provide for the testator's signature, but only that of the witnesses. (§ 33-7-26) It might still be integrated into will if the testator signed there. See Delaware, *Does the signing by the testator and/or witnesses just of the self-proving affidavit constitute the execution of the will?*
Can self-proving affidavit be signed later by testator and/or witnesses?	Yes. The witnesses alone are required to sign affidavits, and they can do this even after the testator's death. (§ 33-7-26(2)) An affidavit "at anytime" "substantially in the form" set forth in the statute meets the requirements. (§ 33-7-26(2)-(3))
If a witness is a devisee, does this result in the disqualification to serve as a witness or the invalidation of the devise?	There is no disqualification of the witness. The will is still valid, but the devise is void to the witness "or any person claiming under that person." (§ 33-6-1) There is no mention of whether the presence of two other disinterested witnesses alters this result. The rule does not apply to a creditor where the will provides for a charge or a direction to pay any debts. (§ 33-6-2)
Can any other person sign the will?	Yes, if in the testator's presence and by the testator's express direction. (§ 33-5-5)
When must witnesses sign?	No specific time, but testator must be present then. (§ 33-5-5)
Must they sign in the presence of the testator?	Yes. (§ 33-5-5)
Must they sign in the presence of each other?	Yes. (§ 33-5-5)
Must the testator publish the will?	"No other publication shall be necessary" other than signature or acknowledgment of signature by the testator. (§ 33-5-5)
Must the will be signed in a particular place?	There is no statutory provision or definite case authority on point.
Must the required number of witnesses be present at the same time for the signing or acknowledgment by the testator?	Yes. (§ 33-5-5)
May the testator acknowledge either his will or his signature?	No. The *signature* must be acknowledged. (§ 33-5-5)

Rhode Island
Formal Will Requirements

Requirements to be witness	There are no specific requirements. The statute simply refers to "witnesses." Presumably, they would have to be competent to testify. See also § 33-7-10, which requires that the witnesses to the signature of the testator be "credible" when at least one of the original witnesses is not available.

South Carolina
Formal Will Requirements

Minimum age for executing will	Real Property—18 years. (§§ 62-2-501, 62-1-201(27)) Personal Property—18 years. (§§ 62-2-501, 62-1-201(27)) A married person under 18 may also make a will, as may an emancipated minor. (§ 62-1-201(27))
Number of witnesses required	Two. (§ 62-2-502)
Holographic wills	No. (§ 62-2-502 cmt.)
Wills admitted to probate if valid under the law of:	South Carolina; place of execution; place where the testator is domiciled at the time of execution or at the time of death. (§ 62-2-505)
Does the signing by the testator and/or witnesses just of the self-proving affidavit constitute the execution of the will?	Yes. (§ 62-2-503(a)) ("Any will may be simultaneously executed, attested, and made self-proved . . . acknowledgment by the testator and the affidavits of at least one witness . . . .") (Id.)
Can self-proving affidavit be signed later by testator and/or witnesses?	Yes. "An attested will may at any time subsequent to its execution be made self-proved, by the acknowledgment thereof of the testator and the affidavit of at least one witness . . . in the following form or in a similar form showing the same intent." (§ 62-2-503(b))
If a witness is a devisee, does this result in the disqualification to serve as a witness or the invalidation of the devise?	There is no disqualification of the witness. However, unless there are two other disinterested witnesses, the devise to the witness or the witness' spouse is void to the extent it exceeds the share that the witness or the spouse would be entitled under intestate succession. (§ 62-2-504) A creditor is a competent witness despite a charge of any debts to the estate. (Id.)
Can any other person sign the will?	Yes, if in the testator's presence and by the testator's direction. (§ 62-2-502)
When must witnesses sign?	There is no specific time constraint.
Must they sign in the presence of the testator?	Probably not. See § 62-2-502 cmt., stating that the prior law was like the current law but it "further required that three witnesses sign and that they do so in the presence of the testator and of each other."
Must they sign in the presence of each other?	Probably not. See § 62-2-502 cmt., stating that the prior law was like the current law but it "further required that three witnesses sign and that they do so in the presence of the testator and of each other."
Must the testator publish the will?	No. (§ 62-2-502 cmt.)
Must the will be signed in a particular place?	No. (§ 62-2-502 cmt.)
Must the required number of witnesses be present at the same time for the signing or acknowledgment by the testator?	No. (§ 62-2-502)

South Carolina
Formal Will Requirements

May the testator acknowledge either his will or his signature?	Yes. (§ 62-2-502)
Requirements to be witness	The witness must be "competent and able to testify." (§ § 62-3-406)

South Dakota
Formal Will Requirements

Minimum age for executing will	Real Property—18 years. (§ 29A-2-501) Personal Property—18 years. (§ 29A-2-501)
Number of witnesses required	Two. (§ 29A-2-502(b)(3))
Holographic wills	Yes. (§ 29A-2-502)
Wills admitted to probate if valid under the law of:	South Dakota; place of execution at time of execution; place where, at time of execution or death, testator is domiciled, has a place of abode, or is a national. (§ 29A-2-506)
Does the signing by the testator and/or witnesses just of the self-proving affidavit constitute the execution of the will?	Yes. (§ 29A-2-504(c))
Can self-proving affidavit be signed later by testator and/or witnesses?	Yes, "at any time after its execution." (§ 29A-2-504(b))
If a witness is a devisee, does this result in the disqualification to serve as a witness or the invalidation of the devise?	No. (§ 29A-2-505(b))
Can any other person sign the will?	Yes, if in the testator's conscious presence and by the testator's direction. (§ 29A-2-502(b)(2))
When must witnesses sign?	There is no time constraint. However, it must occur after the testator signs or acknowledges his signature. (U.P.C. § 2-502 cmt.[1])
Must they sign in the presence of the testator?	Yes, but sufficient if in the "conscious presence" of the testator. (§ 29A-2-502(b)(3))
Must they sign in the presence of each other?	No. (U.P.C. § 2-502 cmt.[2])
Must the testator publish the will?	No. (U.P.C. § 2-502 cmt.[3])
Must the will be signed in a particular place?	No. (U.P.C. § 2-502 cmt.[4])
Must the required number of witnesses be present at the same time for the signing or acknowledgment by the testator?	No. (§ 29A-2-502(b)(3))
May the testator acknowledge either his will or his signature?	There is provision for acknowledgment of the signature. (§ 29A-2-502(b)(3)) No provision is made for the acknowledgment of the will itself, even though the U.P.C., from which this provision is derived, so provides. Compare U.P.C. § 2-502.
Requirements to be witness	An individual generally competent to be a witness. (§ 29A-2-505(a))

---

[1] Although adopting the Uniform Probate Code, the editorial comments of the U.P.C. have not been included in South Dakota Codified Laws. Nonetheless, the assumption is that they would be relied upon in construing the statutory provisions.

[2] *Id.*

[3] *Id.*

[4] *Id.*

Tennessee
Formal Will Requirements

Minimum age for executing will	Real Property—18 years. (§ 32-1-102) Personal Property—18 years. (§ 32-1-102)
Number of witnesses required	Two. (§ 32-1-104)
Holographic wills	Yes. (§ 32-1-105)
Wills admitted to probate if valid under the law of:	Tennessee; place of execution; place of testator's domicile at the time of execution. (§ 32-1-107)
Does the signing by the testator and/or witnesses just of the self-proving affidavit constitute the execution of the will?	Probably not, since only the witnesses, and not the testator, sign the affidavits. Moreover, the witnesses must state in the affidavits "facts to which they would be required to testify in court to prove the will," which would presumably include that the testator signed the will or acknowledged his signature in their presence. (§ 32-2-110) But see Delaware.
Can self-proving affidavit be signed later by testator and/or witnesses?	Yes, at any time, including after the testator's death, any or both of the witnesses may sign an affidavit. However, it must be at the testator's request or, if the testator is deceased, at the request of the executor or any person "interested" in the will. (§ 32-2-110)
If a witness is a devisee, does this result in the disqualification to serve as a witness or the invalidation of the devise?	There is no disqualification of the witness. However, if there are not two other disinterested witnesses, the devise is void to the extent that the aggregate value exceeds the share the witnesses would take by intestate succession. (§ 32-1-103(b)) A creditor would not be an interested witness, since a witness is interested only if the witness is given "some personal and beneficial interest." (§ 32-1-103(c))
Can any other person sign the will?	Yes, if at the testator's direction and in the testator's presence. (§ 32-1-104(1)(C))
When must witnesses sign?	No precise time is specified. However, the witnesses must "sign: (A) In the presence of the testator; and (B) In the presence of each other." (§ 32-1-104(2))
Must they sign in the presence of the testator?	Yes. (§ 32-1-104(2)(A))
Must they sign in the presence of each other?	Yes. (§ 32-1-104(2)(B))
Must the testator publish the will?	Yes (§ 32-1-104(a)(1)), but need not be express signification that the document is testator's will if it can be implied from the facts and circumstances. (Hale v. Bradley, 817 S.W.2d 320, 322 (Ct. App. 1991))
Must the will be signed in a particular place?	No. There is no statutory requirement. See In re Estate of Chastain, 401 S.W. 3d 612, 621 (Tenn. 2012) ("Nor does our holding require a testator to sign in a particular location on the will because Tennessee Code Annotated section 32-1-104 is silent on the issue.")
Must the required number of witnesses be present at the same time for the signing or acknowledgment by the testator?	Yes. (§ 32-1-104(1)(D))

Tennessee
Formal Will Requirements

May the testator acknowledge either his will or his signature?	The testator must acknowledge his signature. (§ 32-1-104(1)(B))
Requirements to be witness	Any person competent to be a witness. (§ 32-1-103(a))

Texas
Formal Will Requirements

Minimum age for executing will	Real Property—18 years. (Estates Code § 251.001) Personal Property—18 years. (Estates Code § 251.001) Estates Code § 251.001 also provides that persons who are married or have been married or are members of armed forces or the auxiliaries thereof or the U.S. Maritime Service may execute wills, even though under age 18.
Number of witnesses required	Two. (Estates Code § 251.051(3))
Holographic wills	Yes. (Estates Code § 251.052)
Wills admitted to probate if valid under the law of:	Texas; where testator domiciled at death. (Estates Code § 502.001)
Does the signing by the testator and/or witnesses just of the self-proving affidavit constitute the execution of the will?	Yes. (Estates Code §§ 251.101 & 251.1045) However, the will is not considered self-proved, since the signature is deemed on the will and missing instead from the self-proving affidavit. (Id.)
Can self-proving affidavit be signed later by testator and/or witnesses?	Yes, by affidavits of the testator and witnesses "at a later date during the lifetime of the testator and the witnesses . . . ." (Estates Code § 251.103)
If a witness is a devisee, does this result in the disqualification to serve as a witness or the invalidation of the devise?	There is no disqualification of the witness. However, if there are not two other competent witnesses, the devise is void to the extent it exceeds the share that the witness would take by intestate succession. (Estates Code § 254.002)
Can any other person sign the will?	Yes, by the testator's direction and in his presence. (Estates Code § 251.051(2)(B))
When must witnesses sign?	There is no time constraint in the statute. Generally, they must sign before the testator's death, since they must sign in his presence. But see James v. Haupt, 573 S.W.2d 285, 289 (Ct. Civ. App. 1978); Estates Code § 251.051.(3) ("where the execution and attestation of a will occurs at the same time and place and from parts of the same transaction, it is immaterial that the witnesses subscribe before the testator signs.")
Must they sign in the presence of the testator?	Yes (Estates Code § 251.051(3)), but it may be "conscious" presence (i.e., even if testator did not actually see), the testator could have with slight physical exertion. (Nichols v. Rowan, 422 S.W.2d 21, 24 (Ct. Civ. App. 1967))
Must they sign in the presence of each other?	No. (Venner v. Layton, 244 S.W.2d 852, 856 (Ct. Civ. App. 1951))
Must the testator publish the will?	Uncertain, although attestation clause constitutes evidence where witnesses are uncertain. (Reese v. Franzheim, 381 S.W.2d 329, 330 (Ct. Civ. App. 1964); but see Brown v. Traylor, 210 S.W.3d 648 (2006))
Must the will be signed in a particular place?	Although there is no statutory requirement, the older case law does not require the testator to sign at the end. (Lawson v. Dawson's Estate, 53 S.W. 64 (1899); In re Brown's Estate, 507 S.W.2d 801 (Ct. Civ. App. 1974))

Texas
Formal Will Requirements

Must the required number of witnesses be present at the same time for the signing or acknowledgment by the testator?	While the testator is not required to sign in the witnesses' presence, there is no provision relating to acknowledgment, and there are few cases. Moreover, the self-proving affidavit recommended form indicates that the testator *signed* in the presence of the witnesses. Since the affidavit used must have "contents substantially" as set forth in the statute, this would seem to support the conclusion that the witnesses must be present when the testator "executed" the will.
May the testator acknowledge either his will or his signature?	See *Must the required number of witnesses be present at the same time for the signing or acknowledgment by the testator?*
Requirements to be witness	They must be "credible" and "above the age of 14." (Estates Code § 251.051(3)) A "credible" witness is a competent witness, that is, one competent to testify to the fact of will execution. (Moos v. First State Bank, 60 S.W.2d 888, 889 (Ct. Civ. App. 1933))

Utah
Formal Will Requirements

Minimum age for executing will	Real Property—18 years. (§ 75-2-501) Personal Property—18 years. (§ 75-2-501)
Number of witnesses required	Two. (§ 75-2-502(1)(c))
Holographic wills	Yes. (§ 75-2-502(2))
Wills admitted to probate if valid under the law of:	Utah; place of execution at time of execution; place where domiciled, abode, or national at time of execution or death. (§ 75-2-506)
Does the signing by the testator and/or witnesses just of the self-proving affidavit constitute the execution of the will?	The following language would appear to allow this: "A will may be simultaneously executed, attested, and made self-proved by acknowledgment thereof by the testator and affidavits of the witnesses . . . ." (§ 75-2-504(1),(3))
Can self-proving affidavit be signed later by testator and/or witnesses?	Yes. "An attested will may be made self-proved at any time after its execution by the acknowledgment thereof by the testator and the affidavits of the witnesses . . . [in form and content] substantially [as provided in the statute]." (§ 75-2-504(2))
If a witness is a devisee, does this result in the disqualification to serve as a witness or the invalidation of the devise?	No. (§ 75-2-505(2))
Can any other person sign the will?	Yes, if in the testator's conscious presence and by his direction. (§ 75-2-502(1)(b))
When must witnesses sign?	Within a reasonable time either after the testator executes the will or he acknowledges his signature or the will. (§ 75-2-502(1)(c))
Must they sign in the presence of the testator?	No. (§ 75-2-502 cmt.)
Must they sign in the presence of each other?	No. (§ 75-2-502 cmt.)
Must the testator publish the will?	No. (§ 75-2-502 cmt.)
Must the will be signed in a particular place?	No. (§ 75-2-502 cmt.)
Must the required number of witnesses be present at the same time for the signing or acknowledgment by the testator?	No. (§ 75-2-502 & cmt.)
May the testator acknowledge either his will or his signature?	Yes. (§ 75-2-502(1)(c) & cmt.)
Requirements to be witness	A person who is generally competent. (§ 75-2-505(1)) Utah imposes a very low bar for competency. (§ 78B-1-128; Ut. R. Evid. 601; State v. Calliham, 57 P.3d 220, 226 (Sup. Ct. 2002))

Vermont
Formal Will Requirements

Minimum age for executing will	"A person of age and sound mind may devise, bequeath and dispose of his estate, real and personal . . . ." (14 § 1) A person of 18 years of age is considered of age. See 1 § 173.
Number of witnesses required	Two. (14 § 5)
Holographic wills	No. (14 § 5) (See also In re Estate of Cote, 848 A.2d 264, 269 (2004))
Wills admitted to probate if valid under the law of:	Vermont; place of execution or domicile. (14 § 112)
Does the signing by the testator and/or witnesses just of the self-proving affidavit constitute the execution of the will?	There is no provision.
Can self-proving affidavit be signed later by testator and/or witnesses?	There is no provision.
If a witness is a devisee, does this result in the disqualification to serve as a witness or the invalidation of the devise?	There is no disqualification of the witness. However, if there are not three other competent witnesses, a devise to the witness, the witness' spouse, or "one claiming under such person" (i.e., the witness) is void in full. On the other hand, regardless of its amount, the devise is valid, if the witness is an heir at law. (14 § 10) A charge for the payment of debts does not prevent creditors from bringing competent witnesses to the testator's will. (*Id.*)
Can any other person sign the will?	Yes, if in the testator's presence and by the testator's express direction. (14 § 5)
When must witnesses sign?	Although they do not have to sign when the testator executes the will, they do have to sign in his presence and the other two witnesses' presence. (14 § 5)
Must they sign in the presence of the testator?	Yes. (14 § 5)
Must they sign in the presence of each other?	Yes. (14 § 5) They need not actually look at each other signing. (In re Claflin's Will, 52 A. 1053, 1057 (1902))
Must the testator publish the will?	No. (In re Claflin's Will, 50 A. 815 (1901), *aff'd*, 52 A. 1053, 1054-56 (1902))
Must the will be signed in a particular place?	There is no statutory provision or definite case authority on point. Nevertheless, the key is the testator's intent in signing and not the actual location of the signature. (Adams v. Field, 21 Vt. 256 (1849))
Must the required number of witnesses be present at the same time for the signing or acknowledgment by the testator?	No. (In re Claflin's Will, 50 A. 815 (1901))

Vermont
Formal Will Requirements

May the testator acknowledge either his will or his signature?	The testator may acknowledge his signature, and this need not be in terms of express words. (In re Claflin's Will, 50 A. 815, 816 (1901)) He may also possibly acknowledge the will. (Roberts v. Welch, 46 Vt. 164, 168 (1873) ("it would be enough that [the testator] declared the instrument, which the witnesses were called to attest, to be his will, or his instrument, which he wished them to attest ... [On the other hand, when] the attesting witness does not know that he is thereby attesting the execution of the instrument by the testator, nor any other fact, and has no knowledge that the paper that he signed was signed or executed by the testator for any purpose, it could not be said that there was attestation of the execution of the instrument.")
Requirements to be witness	The witnesses must be "credible." (14 § 5) Credible means competent. (In re Potter's Will, 95 A. 646, 647 (1915))

Virginia
Formal Will Requirements

Minimum age for executing will	Real Property—18 years. (§ 64.2-401) Personal Property—18 years. (§ 64.2-401) An emancipated minor may also execute a legally valid will. (Id) An emancipated minor must be at least 16 years old. (§ 16.1-331)
Number of witnesses required	Two. (§ 64.2-403(C))
Holographic wills	Yes. (§ 64.2-403(B))
Wills admitted to probate if valid under the law of:	Place where domiciled if not domiciled in Virginia at time of death (limited to personal property). (§ 64.2-407) An "international will" is also valid. (§ 64.2-434)
Does the signing by the testator and/or witnesses just of the self-proving affidavit constitute the execution of the will?	Maybe. Technically, the self-proving forms state that the will has already been signed. There are two types of forms, one which the testator and witnesses sign (§ 64.2-452) and another which the notary alone signs (§ 64.2-452). There is no authority on whether a signature on the first type would substitute for signing the will. The theory of integration arguably could be used. See Delaware.
Can self-proving affidavit be signed later by testator and/or witnesses?	The will may be made self-proved at any subsequent date by the acknowledgment of the testator and affidavits of the witnesses (§ 64.2-452) or "by the acknowledgment thereof by the testator and the attesting witnesses." It must be attached or annexed to the will, and is required to be substantially in form and content as provided in the statute. (§ 64.2-453) However, the certifying officer need not be a notary in Virginia if authorized to administer oaths under the law of the state where the acknowledgment occurred or an appropriate person authorized by the U.S. State Department. (Id.)
If a witness is a devisee, does this result in the disqualification to serve as a witness or the invalidation of the devise?	There is no disqualification of the witness. (§ 64.2-405) The provision does not address whether a devise is void. Presumably, the devise is allowed.
Can any other person sign the will?	Yes, if in the testator's presence and by his direction. (§ 64.2-403(A)) It must be done in manner to make it manifest that the name is intended as a signature. (Id.)
When must witnesses sign?	At the time of the execution or later acknowledgment of will when the testator and witnesses are present. (§ 64.2-403)
Must they sign in the presence of the testator?	Yes. (§ 64.2-403(C))
Must they sign in the presence of each other?	No. (§ 64.2-403)
Must the testator publish the will?	There is nothing in the statute as to the original execution, although the testator must acknowledge his "will." (§ 64.2-403(C)) Still, there is an old case that states that the will must be published, but that the testator has published the will even if he acknowledges it by referring to it as a deed. (Beane v. Yerby, 53 Va. (12 Gratt.) 239 (1855))

**Virginia
Formal Will Requirements**

Must the will be signed in a particular place?	No, but it must be done in a manner to make it manifest that the name is intended as a signature. (§ 64.2-403(A); Slate v. Titmus, 385 S.E.2d 590, 591 (1989); Hamlet v. Hamlet, 32 S.E.2d 729, 731 (1945); McElroy v. Rolston, 34 S.E.2d 241, 243 (1945)) Whereas the testator must "sign," the witnesses must "subscribe," which has been interpreted to mean signing "underneath." (French v. Beville, 62 S.E.2d 883, 886 (1951))
Must the required number of witnesses be present at the same time for the signing or acknowledgment by the testator?	Yes. (§ 64.2-403(C))
May the testator acknowledge either his will or his signature?	No. "[T]he will" must be acknowledged. (§ 64.2-403(C))
Requirements to be witness	The witnesses must be competent. (§ 64.2-403(C)) A competent witness is one competent to testify in court. (Ferguson v. Ferguson, 47 S.E.2d 346, 351 (1948))

Washington
Formal Will Requirements

Minimum age for executing will	Real Property—18 years. (§ 11.12.010) Personal Property—18 years. (§ 11.12.010)
Number of witnesses required	Two. (§ 11.12.020)
Holographic wills	No. (§ 11.12.020)
Wills admitted to probate if valid under the law of:	Washington; place where executed; place where testator is domiciled either at the time of the will's execution or at the time of the testator's death. (§ 11.12.020)
Does the signing by the testator and/or witnesses just of the self-proving affidavit constitute the execution of the will?	In the case of the witnesses, this is recognized as an alternative to signing the will. (§ 11.12.020(1)) Since the testator does not sign the affidavit, and the affidavit states all facts necessary to prove the will in court, including the signature of the testator on the will, the testator's signature on the affidavit instead of the will itself probably would not be valid. Indeed, this was the position taken in invalidating witness signatures on the affidavit before § 11.12.020(1) was revised in 1990 to allow this with regard to witnesses. (Wa. S.B. No. 6392, approv. Mar. 15, 1990, 1990 Wash. Legis. Serv. 79) No similar language authorizes a testator to sign only the self-proving affidavit and the rationale of *Ricketts*, though at times it only involved witnesses, would probably result in finding the instrument invalid. Even though the statute cited above appears to allow this, the statute only mentions the possibility of the witness signature on the affidavit qualifying as a *due attestation* of the will. (In re Estate of Ricketts, 773 P.2d 93, 95 (Ct. App. 1989)). See also In re Estate of Starkel, 134 P.3d 1197 (Ct. App. 2006).
Can self-proving affidavit be signed later by testator and/or witnesses?	Yes. At any time, including after the testator's death, any or both of the witnesses may sign an affidavit. However, it must be at the testator's request or, if the testator is deceased, at the request of the executor or any person "interested" in the will. (§ 11.20.020(2)) However, § 11.12.020 deems to require the affidavit be signed "while in the presence of the testator and at the testator's direction or request . . . ."
If a witness is a devisee, does this result in the disqualification to serve as a witness or the invalidation of the devise?	There is no disqualification of the witness. (§ 11.12.160(2)) If there are not two other competent witnesses, a rebuttable presumption is created that the devise was obtained by duress, menace, fraud, or undue influence. (§ 11.12.160(2)) If the presumption is not rebutted, the witness can take only to the extent of the share the witness would have taken by intestate succession. (§ 11.12.160(3))
Can any other person sign the will?	Yes, if under the testator's direction and in the testator's presence. (§ 11.12.020) Such person must also subscribe his own name and state that he subscribed the testator's name at the testator's request. However, the signing and statement are not required if the testator evidences approval of the signature made at his request by making his mark on the will. (§ 11.12.030)

Washington
Formal Will Requirements

When must witnesses sign?	Unclear. See *Must the required number of witnesses be present at the same time for the signing or acknowledgment by the testator?*, indicating the uncertain status of the law as to a later acknowledgment. (In re Gardner's Estate, 417 P.2d 948, 952 (1966))
Must they sign in the presence of the testator?	Yes, and "at the testator's direction or request." (§ 11.12.020)
Must they sign in the presence of each other?	No. (In re Gardner's Estate, 417 P.2d 948, 952 (1966))
Must the testator publish the will?	No. (In re Chambers' Estate, 60 P.2d 41, 42 (1936))
Must the will be signed in a particular place?	Probably not. (In re Estate of Price, 871 P.2d 1079, 1083 (1994) (formalities reduced to a minimum))
Must the required number of witnesses be present at the same time for the signing or acknowledgment by the testator?	There is conflicting authority on this point. The most recent decision does not require that the testator sign in the presence of the witnesses. (In re Gardner's Estate, 417 P.2d 948 (1966)) However, there is no statutory authority for post-execution acknowledgment and no definite case authority. Earlier cases indicate that the witnesses actually have to see the testator sign. (In re Cronquist's Estate, 274 P.2d 585 (1954))
May the testator acknowledge either his will or his signature?	Unclear. See *Must the required number of witnesses be present at the same time for the signing or acknowledgment by the testator?*
Requirements to be witness	The witnesses must be competent. (§ 11.12.020) "Competent" means persons who could "legally testify in court to the facts which they attest" by signing the will. (In re Mitchell's Estate, 249 P.2d 385, 394 (1952))

West Virginia
Formal Will Requirements

Minimum age for executing will	Real Property—18 years. (§ 41-1-2) Personal Property—18 years. (§ 41-1-2)
Number of witnesses required	Two. (§ 41-1-3)
Holographic wills	Yes. (§ 41-1-3)
Wills admitted to probate if valid under the law of:	West Virginia; domiciliary state at death (limited to personal property located in Virginia). (§ 41-1-5)
Does the signing by the testator and/or witnesses just of the self-proving affidavit constitute the execution of the will?	The production of the will itself appears to suffice for ex parte probate. (§ 41-5-10) Very unlikely; must represent final manifestation of testamentary intent. In Black v. Maxwell, 46 S.E.2d 804 (Sup. Ct. 1948), the court made clear that if there was any uncertainty as to testator's intent regarding placement of signature, the instrument would not be given effect as a will. Statement of testator's writing on envelope containing instrument that it was his will could not be used to clarify testator's intent. (Id. at 812)
Can self-proving affidavit be signed later by testator and/or witnesses?	Yes, by witnesses at testator's request. (§ 41-5-15) This conclusion is based on heading of section which states: "Proof of will while testator living," suggesting that the affidavit does not necessarily have to be signed at the time of execution of the will.
If a witness is a devisee, does this result in the disqualification to serve as a witness or the invalidation of the devise?	There is no disqualification of the witness. The devise to the witness or the witness' spouse is void if there are not other competent witnesses, except an intestate share is given to the witness, to the extent he would be entitled to one if the will were not established, but not in excess of the devise. (§ 41-2-1) A creditor can be a competent witness, as can a spouse of a creditor, despite the will being charged with the debt owed the creditor. (§ 41-2-2)
Can any other person sign the will?	Yes, in the testator's presence and by the testator's direction. (§ 41-1-3)
When must witnesses sign?	The statute does not provide when they must sign, though they are required to sign in the presence of the testator and of each other. Stevens v. Casdorph, 203 W. Va. 450, 508 S.E.2d 610 (1998) (also rejecting the argument of "substantial compliance" with the formalities of will execution). (§ 41-1-3)
Must they sign in the presence of the testator?	Yes. (§ 41-1-3) Technically, the testator must request that they act as witnesses, although the testator's agent can do this, if the testator hears and understands and does not dissent. (Cheatham v. Hatcher, 30 Grat. (71 Va.) 56 (1878))
Must they sign in the presence of each other?	Yes. (§ 41-1-3)
Must the testator publish the will?	Yes. (Freeman v. Freeman, 76 S.E. 657 (1912), overruled on other grounds) However, the testator need not declare it is his will if, for example, the witnesses read the attestation clause, which states that it is the will of the person whose signature they have been asked to witness. (Id.)
Must the will be signed in a particular place?	No. (Black v. Maxwell, 46 S.E.2d 804, 809 (1948))

West Virginia
Formal Will Requirements

Must the required number of witnesses be present at the same time for the signing or acknowledgment by the testator?	Yes. The testator must sign or acknowledge the will "in the presence of at least two competent witnesses, present at the same time." (§41-1-3)
May the testator acknowledge either his will or his signature?	No. The will must be acknowledged. (§41-1-3)
Requirements to be witness	They must be competent. (§41-1-3)

Wisconsin
Formal Will Requirements

Minimum age for executing will	Real Property—18 years. (§ 853.01) Personal Property—18 years. (§ 853.01)
Number of witnesses required	Two. (§ 853.03(2))
Holographic wills	No. (§ 853.03)
Wills admitted to probate if valid under the law of:	Wisconsin; place of execution at the time of execution or death; place where testator resided, was domiciled or was a national at time of execution or death. (§ 853.05)
Does the signing by the testator and/or witnesses just of the self-proving affidavit constitute the execution of the will?	Yes, by both. (§ 853.04(1) & (3))
Can self-proving affidavit be signed later by testator and/or witnesses?	Yes, by both, "at any time." (§ 853.04(2))
If a witness is a devisee, does this result in the disqualification to serve as a witness or the invalidation of the devise?	There is no disqualification of the witness. If there are not two other disinterested witnesses (§ 853.07(2)(c)(1)) or if there is not sufficient evidence that the testator intended the full transfer to take effect (§ 853.07(2)(c)(2)), the devise to the witness or to the witness' spouse is void to the extent it exceeds the share the witness would take by intestate succession. (§ 853.07(2)) A person is not an "interested" witness if the witness or witness' spouse is not devised an interest which is personal and beneficial. Thus, a provision for employment at the usual rate is not a problem (§ 853.07(3)(a)); nor is a "provision which would have conferred no benefit if the testator had died immediately following execution of the will." (§ 853.07(3)(b)) Thus, executors, trustees, and contingent remaindermen or discretionary trust beneficiaries would appear to be among those who are not "interested" witnesses.
Can any other person sign the will?	Yes, if by the testator's direction and in the testator's presence. (§ 853.03(1)) A witness can sign for the testator. (§ 853.03 cmt.) This proxy signing must be in the presence of the witnesses or later acknowledged by the testator in the presence of the witnesses. (Id.)
When must witnesses sign?	Within a reasonable time after witnessing testator's signing or acknowledgment of the will. (§ 853.03(2))
Must they sign in the presence of the testator?	No. (§ 853.03(2)(am))
Must they sign in the presence of each other?	No. (§ 853.03(2)(am) & cmt.)
Must the testator publish the will?	No. (§ 853.03 cmt.)
Must the will be signed in a particular place?	No. (§ 853.03 cmt.)
Must the required number of witnesses be present at the same time for the signing or acknowledgment by the testator?	No. (§ 853.03(2)(am))

Wisconsin
Formal Will Requirements

May the testator acknowledge either his will or his signature?	Yes. (§ 853.03(2)(am)) the acknowledgement may be "implicit or explicit."
Requirements to be witness	Any person competent to testify as a witness in court to the facts relating to execution. (§ 853.07(1))

Wyoming
Formal Will Requirements

Minimum age for executing will	Real Property—18 years. (§ 2-6-101) Personal Property—18 years. (§ 2-6-101) Section 2-6-101 actually refers to "legal age" and does not specify any numerical age. Moreover, there is no definition of the term, "legal age" in Wyoming Statutes Annotated or in Wyoming case law. Section 2-1-301(a)(xvii) defines "full age" as the state of "legal majority having attained the age of eighteen (18) years." Perhaps "legal age" is intended to mean the same as "full age," but there is no specific authority confirming this.
Number of witnesses required	Two. (§ 2-6-112)
Holographic wills	Yes. (§ 2-6-113)
Wills admitted to probate if valid under the law of:	Wyoming; place of execution at time of execution; place where, at time of execution or death, testator is domiciled, has a place of abode, or is a national. (§ 2-6-116)
Does the signing by the testator and/or witnesses just of the self-proving affidavit constitute the execution of the will?	Yes. (§ 2-6-114(b))
Can self-proving affidavit be signed later by testator and/or witnesses?	Yes. "An attested will may . . . at any subsequent date [to its execution] be made self-proven by the acknowledgment thereof by the testator and the affidavits of the witnesses . . . in form and contents substantially as [provided in the statute]." (§ 2-6-114(c))
If a witness is a devisee, does this result in the disqualification to serve as a witness or the invalidation of the devise?	There is no disqualification of the witness. If there are not two other disinterested and competent witnesses, the witness can only take a portion of the estate to the extent it does not exceed the amount the witness would take by intestate succession. (§ 2-6-112)
Can any other person sign the will?	Yes, in the testator's presence and by his express direction. (§ 2-6-112)
When must witnesses sign?	There is no time constraint. The statute simply requires that the "will" be "witnessed." (§ 2-6-112)
Must they sign in the presence of the testator?	Apparently so. Estate of Zelikovitz, 923 P.2d 740, 744 (Sup. Ct. 1996), seems to interpret the language in § 2-6-112, "witnessed by two (2) competent witnesses," as meaning that they saw the testator sign. There is no statutory provision or direct case authority on point.
Must they sign in the presence of each other?	No, except when proof of signing is offered by affidavit. (§ 2-6-205(a)); In re Estate of Meyer, 367 P.3d 629 (Sup. Ct. 2016)); In re Estate of Zelikovitz, 923 P.2d 740, 744 (Sup. Ct. 1996)) There are, however, other means of proving a will under Wyoming law other than by affidavit. (§ 2-6-205)
Must the testator publish the will?	No. (In re Estate of Carey, 504 P.2d 793, 801 (1972))
Must the will be signed in a particular place?	There is no statutory provision or direct case authority on point.

Wyoming
Formal Will Requirements

Must the required number of witnesses be present at the same time for the signing or acknowledgment by the testator?	Since the witnesses must "attest" the "will" (§ 2-6-112), they, presumably, must see its execution or have it acknowledged. However, there is no specific statutory provision or direct case authority on point.
May the testator acknowledge either his will or his signature?	Since the witnesses must "attest" the "will" (§ 2-6-112), they, presumably, must see its execution or have it acknowledged. However, there is no specific statutory provision or direct case authority on point.
Requirements to be witness	They must be competent. (§ § 2-6-112, 2-6-115)

Table 2
Proving Foreign Wills
(current through 5/1/18)

Whenever assets of the estate of an individual are situated outside the state of domicile at death, the personal representative will face the quandary of how to proceed in the other state or states to prove that the will should be given effect with regard to those nondomicile assets and to establish the personal representative's own authority to act on behalf of the estate. Since each state has plenary power over the property within its physical or regulatory control, careful attention must be paid to this matter in order to unify the estate and avoid splintering probate and administration into a number of mini-estates scattered around the country.

Although a very commonplace problem, there has been very little attention paid to this matter. The statutes that do exist are incomplete and often border on, if not cross over into, the incomprehensible. There is little case law, and what there is, tends to consist of very old, highly particularized decisions.

Table 2.01 and Table 2.02 detail the governing principles embodied in each state's law. Where appropriate, inferences have been drawn from the statutory language. Some questions, however, simply have no clear-cut answer. Undoubtedly, these questions are handled based on local county custom and practice.

The emphasis of this table is not on the requirements for original probate of the will in the domiciliary state. The assumption is that the attorney knows or can readily inquire as to how to accomplish this. Rather, the chapter addresses exclusively the situation of what each nondomicile state requires with regard to probate of the out-of-state decedent's will. It explores important aspects of the subject, such as proper venue for local probate, the possibilities of original probate locally of a nondomiciliary's will, the prerequisites to ancillary probate following probate at the domicile, special notice requirements in the state of ancillary probate, and the qualification locally to act on behalf of the estate of the domiciliary personal representative or the person designated in the will, if other than the domiciliary representative. As to which persons from out-of-state can qualify to serve as a personal representative, see Table 3.01.

Ultimately, the question of ancillary probate is crucial because it bears on the transfer of assets of the estate to the primary personal representative in the domiciliary state. The chapter, thus, considers, among other questions, whether and when assets may be transferred to the domiciliary personal representative from the local jurisdiction.

One additional difficulty inherent in this subject matter is the terminology used by various states in dealing with situations involving "original probate" and "ancillary probate." Traditionally, original probate references (i) probate at the domicile, or (ii) probate in a non-domiciliary jurisdiction *before* probate at the domicile. Ancillary probate references probate in a non-domiciliary state *after* probate at the domicile. Especially in the case of UPC states, while the situations described routinely arise and are analyzed in the Table, the traditional terminology is not expressly used in the relevant UPC-based state statutes.

Finally, with respect to the following UPC states, the editorial board comments of the UPC have not been adopted in whole along with the statutory enactment: Alaska, Arizona, Colorado, Hawaii, Idaho, Maine, Massachusetts, Michigan, Minnesota, Montana, Nebraska, New Mexico, North Dakota, South Carolina, South Dakota, and Utah Nonetheless, in providing answers for these states to the questions posed in the Table, the assumption is that the comments would be relied upon in construing the statutory provisions. However, one should proceed with caution in this case, as a state may have deliberately not adopted certain comments.

Table 2.01, Part 1
Proof of a Foreign Will

	What Proof is Required to Establish a Will Already Proved in Another State?	Are There Special Rules For a Will Proved Outside the U.S.?	Is There a Special Rule For Local Property?	Is Original Probate of a Foreign Will Permitted if Not Already Established at the Domicile?	If So, What Are the Circumstances?	What About Original Probate After Probate in Another Jurisdiction?
Alabama	An authenticated and certified copy of the will and its probate. (§ 43-8-175) This assumes that the testator, at the time of his death, was not an inhabitant of Alabama. (*Id.*) Inhabitant means domiciliary. (*Ambrose v. Vandeford*, 167 So. 2d 149 (Ala. 1964))	Yes. It must be probated as an original proceeding with respect to local land and real property, including giving notice to next of kin. (§ 43-8-175)	No, except for a will probated outside the U.S. (See § 43-8-175)	Implied Yes. (See § 43-8-162(2)-(4); see also *Kelley v. Sutliff*, 80, So. 2d 636 (1955))	None specified. See § 43-8-162 for proper venue (discussed in Table 2.02, Part 3 below); see also § 43-8-167 (discussing mode of proving a will generally).	No. When a will, which has already been probated in another U.S. state where testator is an inhabitant at time of death, is presented for probate in Alabama, the only inquiries the court can make are whether the granting court had jurisdiction and whether the will properly authenticated. Duty of the court is then ministerial. (*Carter v. Davis*, 154 So. 2d 9 (1963)
Alaska	For informal probate, an authenticated copy of the will and the statement probating it (§ 13.16.090(d)); for formal probate, a final order of a court in a proceeding determining testacy, validity, or construction, where there was notice to and an opportunity to contest by all interested persons, and there was a finding, or it was based upon a finding, that the decedent was domiciled at death in the state where the order was made. (§ 13.16.175)	Yes. If the will comes from a place that does not provide for probate, it may be proved by a duly authenticated certificate of its legal custodian stating that the copy introduced is true and that the will has become effective under the law of the other place. (Informal probate (§ 13.16.090(e)); formal probate (§ 13.16.180)	Yes. If the will disposes of personal property, wherever situated, or real property situated in Alaska, it must be in writing and be signed by the testator, and otherwise executed and attested to under the local law of: 1) Alaska, 2) the jurisdiction where the will was executed at the time of execution, or 3) the jurisdiction where the testator was domiciled, either at the time of execution or death. (§ 13.06.068(c))	Yes.	Proceedings must be "concluded" in this state before they are concluded at the domicile. (U.P.C. cmt. to § 3-408, which parallels § 13.16.175) The requirements are otherwise the same as those for probate of a domestic will, except for proper venue. (See § 13.16.090 for informal probate and § § 13.16.140-180 for formal)	Generally no. (See § 13.16.090(d) for informal probate and § 13.16.175 for formal probate) However, if probate in the other jurisdiction is informal (§ 13.16.140(b)), or if it was formal probate in a non-domiciliary jurisdiction (§ 13.16.175), formal probate may be sought as an original proceeding.

Table 2.01, Part 1
Proof of a Foreign Will

	What Proof is Required to Establish a Will Already Proved in Another State?	Are There Special Rules For a Will Proved Outside the U.S.?	Is There a Special Rule For Local Property?	Is Original Probate of a Foreign Will Permitted if Not Already Established at the Domicile?	If So, What Are the Circumstances?	What About Original Probate After Probate in Another Jurisdiction?
Arizona	For informal probate, a written application by any interested person together with an authenticated copy of the will and the statement probating it (§ 14-3303(D)); for formal probate, a final order of a court in a proceeding determining testacy, validity, or construction, where there was notice to and an opportunity to contest by all interested persons, and there was a finding, or it was based upon a finding, that the decedent was domiciled at death in the state where the order was made. (§ 14-3408)	Yes. If the will comes from a place that does not provide for probate, it may be proved by a duly authenticated certificate of its legal custodian stating that the copy introduced is true and that the will has become effective under the law of the other place. (Informal probate § 14-3303(E); formal probate § 14-3409)	No.	Yes.	Proceedings must be "concluded" in this state before they are concluded at the domicile. (U.P.C. cmt. to § 3-408, which parallels § 14-3408. The requirements are otherwise the same as those for probate of a domestic will, except for proper venue. (See § 14-3303 for informal probate and §§ 14-3401-14-3409 for formal)	Generally no. (See § 14-3303(D) for informal probate and § 14-3408 for formal probate) However, if probate in the other jurisdiction is informal (§ 14-3401(B)), or if it was formal probate in a non-domiciliary jurisdiction (§ 14-3408), formal probate may be sought as an original proceeding.

Table 2.01, Part 1
Proof of a Foreign Will

	What Proof is Required to Establish a Will Already Proved in Another State?	Are There Special Rules For a Will Proved Outside the U.S.?	Is There a Special Rule For Local Property?	Is Original Probate of a Foreign Will Permitted if Not Already Established at the Domicile?	If So, What Are the Circumstances?	What About Original Probate After Probate in Another Jurisdiction?
Arkansas	When a will of a nonresident has been admitted to probate in another appropriate jurisdiction, an authenticated copy thereof, and an authenticated copy of the order admitting the will to probate must be filed. When so filed, together with a petition for admission of the will to probate in the state, the court shall presume, in the absence of evidence to the contrary, that the will was duly executed and proved and admitted to probate in the foreign jurisdiction, and the court will then admit the will if it appears the will was executed and proved in the manner prescribed by the law of its place of execution, laws of the testator's domicile at the time of execution, or by the laws of Arkansas. (§ 28-40-120(a) & (b) If not executed in accordance with Arkansas law, the petition must state the time and place of execution and the testator's domicile at the time of its execution and at the time of his or her death. (§ 28-40-120(c))	No.	No.	Yes. (McPherson v. McKay, 172 S.W.2d 911 (1943))	If the testator owned property in Arkansas that might be the subject of administration in Arkansas, or where there was a debt or demand due the testator that requires administration to collect. (McPherson v. McKay, 172 S.W.2d 911 (1943))	No provision.

Table 2.01, Part 1
Proof of a Foreign Will

	What Proof is Required to Establish a Will Already Proved in Another State?	Are There Special Rules For a Will Proved Outside the U.S.?	Is There a Special Rule For Local Property?	Is Original Probate of a Foreign Will Permitted if Not Already Established at the Domicile?	If So, What Are the Circumstances?	What About Original Probate After Probate in Another Jurisdiction?
California	The will or an authenticated copy of the will, an authenticated copy of the order admitting the will to probate, or other evidence of the establishment or proof of the will. (Prob. § 12521(a)) However, see the grounds to contest ancillary probate in Table 2.02, Part 2 below.	Yes. The court shall admit the will to probate, and may not permit a contest or revocation of probate, if it appears that the following conditions are satisfied: (1) foreign nation's determination is based on a finding that at the time of death the decedent was domiciled in the foreign nation; (2) all interested parties were given notice and an opportunity for contest in the proceedings in the foreign nation; (3) the determination in the foreign nation is final. The court may refuse to admit the will, even though it is shown to satisfy the conditions provided in subdivision (a), where the order admitting the will was made under a judicial system that does not provide impartial tribunals or procedures compatible with the requirements of due process of law. (See Prob. §§ 12522 for other states and §§ 12523 for foreign jurisdictions)	No.	Yes. (Prob. §§ 12520, 8000, et seq.)	If it has not been probated elsewhere or it fails to qualify for ancillary administration under Prob. § 12520. (cmt. to Prob. § 12520)	No, unless the original probate is not based on a finding that decedent was domiciled in that jurisdiction at death, there was inadequate notice, or the order of probate is not final. (See Prob. §§ 12522 for other states and §§ 12523 for foreign jurisdictions)

Table 2.01, Part 1
Proof of a Foreign Will

	What Proof is Required to Establish a Will Already Proved in Another State?	Are There Special Rules For a Will Proved Outside the U.S.?	Is There a Special Rule For Local Property?	Is Original Probate of a Foreign Will Permitted if Not Already Established at the Domicile?	If So, What Are the Circumstances?	What About Original Probate After Probate in Another Jurisdiction?
Colorado	For informal probate, an authenticated copy of the will and the statement probating it (§ 15-12-303(4)); for formal probate, a final order of a court in a proceeding determining testacy, validity, or construction, where there was notice to and an opportunity to contest by all interested persons, and there was a finding, or it was based upon a finding, that the decedent was domiciled at death in the state where the order was made. (§ 15-12-408)	Yes. If the will comes from a place that does not provide for probate, it may be proved by a duly authenticated certificate of its legal custodian stating that the copy introduced is true and that the will has become effective under the law of the other place. (Informal probate § 15-12-303(5); formal probate § 15-12-409)	No. However, Wimbush v. Wimbush, 587 P.2d 796 (1978), may allow for separate determination of validity of will for purposes of local real property.	Yes.	Proceedings must be "concluded" in this state before they are concluded at the domicile. (U.P.C. cmt. to § 3-408, which parallels § 15-12-408) The requirements are otherwise the same as those for probate of a domestic will, except for proper venue. (See § 15-12-303 for informal probate and §§ 15-12-401-15-12-409 for formal)	Generally no. (See § 15-12-303(4) for informal probate and § 15-12-408 for formal probate) However, if probate in the other jurisdiction is informal (§ 15-12-401(2)), or if it was formal probate in a non-domiciliary jurisdiction (§ 15-12-408), formal probate may be sought as an original proceeding.
Connecticut	An authenticated and exemplified copy of will and record of proceedings proving and establishing will. (§ 45a-288) A complete statement in writing of the property and estate of the decedent in Connecticut shall be included. (Id.)	No.	No.	Yes. (§ 45a-287(b))	There must not have been a denial of probate or establishment by a judge or court in the domicile jurisdiction, or if probate was denied, it was for a cause that is not grounds for rejection in this state. (§ 45a-287(b))	There is no authority on point in the statutes or case law.

Table 2.01, Part 1
Proof of a Foreign Will

	What Proof is Required to Establish a Will Already Proved in Another State?	Are There Special Rules For a Will Proved Outside the U.S.?	Is There a Special Rule For Local Property?	Is Original Probate of a Foreign Will Permitted if Not Already Established at the Domicile?	If So, What Are the Circumstances?	What About Original Probate After Probate in Another Jurisdiction?
Delaware	A verified copy of will and a verified copy of record admitting the same to probate. (12 Del. C. §1307(a)) To be verified, it must be certified by the proper officer under the officer's hand and seal of office with a certificate from the state or presiding judge stating the copy is certified in due form. A will admitted to probate in Delaware by submitting the proof described in this answer will have the same force and effect as an originally probated will. (12 Del. C. §1307(a))	Yes. A verification certificate may come from presiding judge or attested by resident U.S.-Consul General or Consul-General deputy under seal of U.S. Consulate General. (12 Del. C. §1307(b))	No.	Yes.	The will must not have been probated at the domicile, must not have been rejected from probate at the domicile for a reason that is also a valid reason for rejection in Delaware, and it must be a valid will under the laws of Delaware. (12 Del. C. §1307(a))	The statute implies original probate in Delaware is allowed after original probate in another non-domiciliary jurisdiction so long as it has not yet been probated at the domicile. (12 Del. C. §1307(a))
District of Columbia	A duly certified copy or transcript of record of proceedings admitting will. (§14-504)	No.	No.	There is no statute or case authority.	There is no statute or case authority.	There is no statute or case authority.

Table 2.01, Part 1
Proof of a Foreign Will

	What Proof is Required to Establish a Will Already Proved in Another State?	Are There Special Rules For a Will Proved Outside the U.S.?	Is There a Special Rule For Local Property?	Is Original Probate of a Foreign Will Permitted if Not Already Established at the Domicile?	If So, What Are the Circumstances?	What About Original Probate After Probate in Another Jurisdiction?
Florida	Authenticated copy of probated will that is determined to comply with the Florida execution formalities or those of some other permissible jurisdiction under §732.502(1) or §732.502(2). (§734.104(3)) A special procedure is provided for estates with less than $50,000 in value in Florida. (§734.1025) Otherwise, a full-blown ancillary probate is required.	A will in a foreign language must be accompanied by a true and complete English translation. (§733.204)	Yes as to real property. (§734.104) It requires authenticated copies of the will, the petition for probate, and the order admitting the will to probate in the proper foreign court and executed as provided in col. 1. If a petition is not required, then there must be proof by affidavit or certificate that a petition is not required. The order admitting the will to probate must state that no petition was required in the foreign jurisdiction. Note that §734.104(2) could be read as applying to other property as well. An ancillary proceeding challenging a will re local situs real property can even override a determination of the validity of the will at the domicile. (In re Roberg's Estate, 396 So. 2d 235 (Dist. Ct. App. 1981))	Yes. (§§ §731.106, 733.103) (Cuevas v. Kelly, 873 So. 2d 367 (Dist. Court App. 2004); Biederman v. Cheatham, 161 So. 2d 538 (Dist. Court App. 1964).) In particular, if will of a nonresident provides that it is to be "construed and regulated" by Florida law, then the validity and effect is determined by Florida law with respect to all property having a situs in Florida. (§731.106(2)) This would require an original determination by a Florida court. Certain intangibles will have a Florida situs, even if the decedent was not domiciled in Florida. (§731.106(1))	See Col. 4.	Unclear, but may be allowed. (§733.103(2)) Only bars collateral attack with respect to "the probate of a will in Florida." On the other hand, §733.103 provides that until a will is admitted "in this state or in the state where the decedent was domiciled," the will is ineffective. The implication is that, if proved at the domicile, it is effective. Furthermore, a contest re a will disposing of Florida situs realty is permitted despite a foreign probate. (Trotter v. Van Pelt, 198 So. 215 (Fla. 1940); In re Roberg's Estate, 396 So. 2d 235 (Dist. Ct. App. 1981); In re Estate of Barteau, 736 So. 2d 57 (Dist. Ct. App. 1999) In re Estate of Swanson, 397 So. 2d 465 (Dist. Ct. App. 1981); In re Hatcher, 439 So. 2d 977, 979-80 (Dist. Ct. App. 1983)) *But see* Loewenthal v. Mandell, 170 So. 169, 174 (Fla. 1936) and Cuevas v. Kelly, 873 So. 2d 367 (Dist. Ct. App. 2004) (personal property), which seem to hold to the contrary.

Table 2.01, Part 1
Proof of a Foreign Will

	What Proof is Required to Establish a Will Already Proved in Another State?	Are There Special Rules For a Will Proved Outside the U.S.?	Is There a Special Rule For Local Property?	Is Original Probate of a Foreign Will Permitted if Not Already Established at the Domicile?	If So, What Are the Circumstances?	What About Original Probate After Probate in Another Jurisdiction?
Georgia	A properly certified copy of the will and a properly authenticated copy of the final probate proceedings at the domicile, certified in accordance with §24-9-922, which may be attacked or resisted on the same grounds as other judicial proceedings from a state of the United States. (§53-5-33(b))	Yes. The same proof is required as in the prior question, but serves merely as prima facie evidence of due execution, and may be objected to by caveat or rebutted by proof, as in the case of a will offered for original probate. (§53-5-33(c))	No. See §53-5-33 cmt., which notes extension of provision to real property.	Yes. (§53-5-36)	Upon proof that the will is valid under the laws of this state and has not been offered for probate in the domiciliary jurisdiction or that it has been offered for probate but no timely objection was filed or the grounds of a pending objection would not, if proved, cause the denial of probate. (§§53-5-31, 53-5-32).	No.
Hawaii	For informal probate, an authenticated copy of the will and the statement probating it (§560:3-303(d)); for formal probate, a final order of a court in a proceeding determining testacy, validity, or construction, where there was notice to and an opportunity to contest by all interested persons, and there was a finding, or it was based upon a finding, that the decedent was domiciled at death in the state where the order was made. (§560:3-408)	Yes. If the will comes from a place that does not provide for probate, it may be proved by a duly authenticated certificate of its legal custodian stating that the copy introduced is true and that the will has become effective under the law of the other place. (Informal probate §560:3-303(e); formal probate §560:3-409)	No.	Yes.	Proceedings must be "concluded" in this state before they are concluded at the domicile. (U.P.C. cmt. to §3-408, which parallels §560:3-408) The requirements are otherwise the same as those for probate of a domestic will, except for proper venue. (See §560:3-303 for informal probate and §§560:3-401–560:3-409 for formal)	Generally no. (See §560:3-303(d) for informal probate and §560:3-408 for formal probate) However, if probate in the other jurisdiction is informal(§560:3-401(b)), or if it was formal probate in a non-domiciliary jurisdiction (§560:3-408), formal probate may be sought as an original proceeding.

Table 2.01, Part 1
Proof of a Foreign Will

	What Proof is Required to Establish a Will Already Proved in Another State?	Are There Special Rules For a Will Proved Outside the U.S.?	Is There a Special Rule For Local Property?	Is Original Probate of a Foreign Will Permitted if Not Already Established at the Domicile?	If So, What Are the Circumstances?	What About Original Probate After Probate in Another Jurisdiction?
Idaho	For informal probate, an authenticated copy of the will and the statement probating it (§ 15-3-303(d)); for formal probate, a final order of a court in a proceeding determining testacy, validity, or construction, where there was notice to and an opportunity to contest by all interested persons, and there was a finding, or it was based upon a finding, that the decedent was domiciled at death in the state where the order was made. (§ 15-3-408)	Yes. If the will comes from a place that does not provide for probate, it may be proved by a duly authenticated certificate of its legal custodian stating that the copy introduced is true and that the will has become effective under the law of the other place. (Informal probate § 15-3-303(e); formal probate § 15-3-409)	No.	Yes.	Proceedings must be "concluded" in this state before they are concluded at the domicile. (U.P.C. cmt. to § 3-408, which parallels § 15-3-408) The requirements are otherwise the same as those for probate of a domestic will, except for proper venue. (See § 15-3-303 for informal probate and §§ 15-3-401-15-3-409 for formal)	Generally no. (See § 15-3-303(d) for informal probate and § 15-3-408 for formal probate) However, if probate in the other jurisdiction is informal (§ 15-3-401(b)), or if it was formal probate in a non-domiciliary jurisdiction (§ 15-3-408), formal probate may be sought as an original proceeding.
Illinois	An authenticated copy of the written will and the probate thereof. (755 ILCS § 5/7-3(a))	No. But if the laws of the other jurisdiction do not require the will to be probated, an authenticated certificate of the legal custodian that the will is a true copy and has become operative by the laws of that jurisdiction will be required. (755 ILCS § 5/7-3(b)) A will admitted to probate by submitting copies of the will and domiciliary probate order has the same effect as the probate of a domestic will. (755 ILCS § 5/7-5)	No.	Yes. (755 ILCS § 5/7-4(a), (b), (c))	If the will can be proved under the laws of Illinois, place of execution, or place of domicile at the time of execution. (755 ILCS § 5/7-4(a), (b), (c))	Implied yes. (755 ILCS § 5/7-4) But see 755 ILCS § 5/7-3(a), allowing for probate of foreign will already admitted to probate in another jurisdiction by submitting copies of the will and probate order.)

Table 2.01, Part 1
Proof of a Foreign Will

	What Proof is Required to Establish a Will Already Proved in Another State?	Are There Special Rules For a Will Proved Outside the U.S.?	Is There a Special Rule For Local Property?	Is Original Probate of a Foreign Will Permitted if Not Already Established at the Domicile?	If So, What Are the Circumstances?	What About Original Probate After Probate in Another Jurisdiction?
Indiana	Certified will or a certified copy of the will and probate of the will. In all cases, the documents must be attested as to authenticity. (§ 29-1-7-26) The court probating the will must be satisfied the will ought to be allowed as the last will of the decedent. (§ 29-1-7-27) Generally, the will must be received and recorded before the deadlines set out in § 29-1-7-15.1(d). (§ 29-1-7-25) Finally, if the will was executed in Indiana and then proved or allowed in another state or country it cannot be admitted to probate in Indiana unless executed in accordance with Indiana law. (§ 29-1-7-28)	No.	No.	Not specifically addressed. (§§ 29-1-7-25 – 29-1-7-29)	Not specifically addressed. (§§ 29-1-7-25 – 29-1-7-29)	Not specifically addressed. (§§ 29-1-7-25 – 29-1-7-29)
Iowa	Copy of the will and of the original probate record, both of which must be properly authenticated and certified. (§ 633.496)	No. (§ 633.496)	No. (§ 633.495)	Yes. (§ 633.495)	Only if not probated in another state; only in a county where either real or personal property of the deceased non-resident is located. (§ 633.495)	No provision.

Table 2.01, Part 1
Proof of a Foreign Will

	What Proof is Required to Establish a Will Already Proved in Another State?	Are There Special Rules For a Will Proved Outside the U.S.?	Is There a Special Rule For Local Property?	Is Original Probate of a Foreign Will Permitted if Not Already Established at the Domicile?	If So, What Are the Circumstances?	What About Original Probate After Probate in Another Jurisdiction?
Kansas	Copy of will and the probate of it, both authenticated. (§59-2229) Court will then have a hearing to determine if the will was probated and that the will was executed in accordance with the laws of the testator's residence, the laws of the state in which it was executed, or the laws of Kansas. (§59-2230) A will admitted to probate by submitting evidence of probate elsewhere and proof of compliance with the applicable law shall have the same force and effect as the original probate of the will. (§59-2230)	No. (§59-2229)	No.	Not specified.	N/A	Yes, since probate of wills probated elsewhere is allowed (§§ 29-2229 – 59-2230), and all probate proceedings are original, not ancillary. (§59-804)
Kentucky	An authenticated copy of the will and certificate of probate create a presumption of proper execution. (§ 394.150)	No. (§ 394.150)	No.	No, except under peculiar circumstances. (Payne v. Payne, 39 S.W.2d 205 (Ct. App. 1931))	N/A	No.

Table 2.01, Part 1
Proof of a Foreign Will

	What Proof is Required to Establish a Will Already Proved in Another State?	Are There Special Rules For a Will Proved Outside the U.S.?	Is There a Special Rule For Local Property?	Is Original Probate of a Foreign Will Permitted if Not Already Established at the Domicile?	If So, What Are the Circumstances?	What About Original Probate After Probate in Another Jurisdiction?
Louisiana	An authenticated copy of the will and probate thereof, with a petition for the probate, must be filed and proper proceedings had as required by law on a petition for the original probate of a domestic will. The court must determine the will has been duly proved, allowed, and admitted to probate outside Louisiana, and that it was executed according to the law of the place where it was made, or in which the testator at the time of death was domiciled, or in conformity with Louisiana law. (La. Rev. Stat. §§ 9:2421, 9:2422, 9:2423) Foreign wills admitted to probate shall have the same force and effect as the original probate of a domestic will. (La. Rev. Stat. § 9:2423)	No. But if probate was not required in the foreign jurisdiction, an authenticated copy of the will and a certificate from the legal custodian verifying the will is a true copy and has become operative by the laws of the foreign jurisdiction will be required. (La. Rev. Stat. § 9:2424)	No.	Yes.	It must be in a form that is valid in either the decedent's domicile or place of execution. Evidence must be provided proving the will's validity. (Code Civ. Pro. §§ 2888, 3401)	Implied no. (Code Civ. Pro. § 3405)

Table 2.01, Part 1
Proof of a Foreign Will

	What Proof is Required to Establish a Will Already Proved in Another State?	Are There Special Rules For a Will Proved Outside the U.S.?	Is There a Special Rule For Local Property?	Is Original Probate of a Foreign Will Permitted if Not Already Established at the Domicile?	If So, What Are the Circumstances?	What About Original Probate After Probate in Another Jurisdiction?
Maine	For informal probate, an authenticated copy of the will and the statement probating it (18-A §3-303(d)); for formal probate, a final order of a court in a proceeding determining testacy, validity, or construction, where there was notice to and an opportunity to contest by all interested persons, and there was a finding, or it was based upon a finding, that the decedent was domiciled at death in the state where the order was made. (18-A §3-408)	Yes. If the will comes from a place that does not provide for probate, it may be proved by a duly authenticated certificate of its legal custodian stating that the copy introduced is true and that the will has become effective under the law of the other place. (Informal probate 18-A §3-409)	No.	Yes.	Proceedings must be "concluded" in this state before they are concluded at the domicile. (U.P.C. cmt. to §3-408, which parallels 18-A §3-408) The requirements are otherwise the same as those for probate of a domestic will, except for proper venue. (See 18-A §3-303 for informal probate and 18-A §3-401 - 18-A §3-409 for formal)	Generally no. (See 18-A §3-303(d) for informal probate and 18-A §3-408 for formal probate) However, if probate in the other jurisdiction is informal (18-A §3-401), or if it was formal probate in a non-domiciliary jurisdiction (18-A §3-408), formal probate may be sought as an original proceeding.
Maryland	A certified copy of the will and the order admitting it to probate. (Roach v. Jurchak, 35 A.2d 817 (1944); however, note that the executor of a foreign domiciliary's estate does not have to take out letters to act in Maryland, eliminating the usual ancillary procedure. (Est. & Trust, §5-501)	Not specified.	See Col. 1.	Yes. Probate proceedings must be brought in the proper venue under the statute, (Est. & Trust §5-103), and the will must be properly executed. (Est. & Trust § 4-104) See Table 2.02, Part 3 for a discussion of proper venue.	A will executed out side this state is properly executed if it is (1) in writing; (2) signed by the testator; and (3) executed in conformity with the provisions of Est. & Trusts §4-102, the law of the domicile of the testator, or the place where the will is executed. (Est. & Trusts §4-104)	Not specified.

Table 2.01, Part 1
Proof of a Foreign Will

	What Proof is Required to Establish a Will Already Proved in Another State?	Are There Special Rules For a Will Proved Outside the U.S.?	Is There a Special Rule For Local Property?	Is Original Probate of a Foreign Will Permitted if Not Already Established at the Domicile?	If So, What Are the Circumstances?	What About Original Probate After Probate in Another Jurisdiction?
Massachusetts	For informal probate, an authenticated copy of the will and the statement probating it (190B §3-303(d)); for formal probate, a final order of a court in a proceeding determining testacy, validity, or construction, where there was notice to and an opportunity to contest by all interested persons, and there was a finding, or it was based upon a finding, that the decedent was domiciled at death in the state where the order was made. (190B §3-408)	Yes. If the will comes from a place that does not provide for probate, it may be proved by a duly authenticated certificate of its legal custodian stating that the copy introduced is true and that the will has become effective under the law of the other place. (Informal probate 190B §3-303(e); formal probate 190B §3-409)	No.	Yes.	Proceedings must be "concluded" in this state before they are concluded at the domicile. (U.P.C. cmt. to §3-408, which parallels 190B §3-408) The requirements are otherwise the same as those for probate of a domestic will, except for proper venue. (See 190B §3-303 for informal probate and 190B §3-401 - 190B §3-409 for formal)	Generally no. (See 190B §3-303(d) for informal probate and 190B §3-408 for formal probate) However, if probate in the other jurisdiction is informal (190B §3-401(b)), or if it was formal probate in a non-domiciliary jurisdiction (190B §3-408), formal probate may be sought as an original proceeding.
Michigan	For informal probate, an authenticated copy of the will and the statement probating it (§700.3303(4); for formal probate, a final order of a court in a proceeding determining testacy, validity, or construction, where there was notice to and an opportunity to contest by all interested persons, and there was a finding, or it was based upon a finding, that the decedent was domiciled at death in the state where the order was made. (§700.3408)	Yes. If the will comes from a place that does not provide for probate, it may be proved by a duly authenticated certificate of its legal custodian stating that the copy introduced is true and that the will has become effective under the law of the other place. (Informal probate §700.3303(5); formal probate §700.3409)	No.	Yes.	Proceedings must be "concluded" in this state before they are concluded at the domicile. (U.P.C. cmt. to §3-408, which parallels §700.3408) The requirements are otherwise the same as those for probate of a domestic will, except for proper venue. (See §700.3303 for informal probate and §700.3401 - 700.3409 for formal)	Generally no. (See §700.3303(4) for informal probate and §700.3408 for formal probate) However, if probate in the other jurisdiction is informal (§700.3401(2)), or if it was formal probate in a non-domiciliary jurisdiction (§700.3408), formal probate may be sought as an original proceeding.

Table 2.01, Part 1
Proof of a Foreign Will

	What Proof is Required to Establish a Will Already Proved in Another State?	Are There Special Rules For a Will Proved Outside the U.S.?	Is There a Special Rule For Local Property?	Is Original Probate of a Foreign Will Permitted if Not Already Established at the Domicile?	If So, What Are the Circumstances?	What About Original Probate After Probate in Another Jurisdiction?
Minnesota	For informal probate, an authenticated copy of the will and the statement probating it (§524.3-303(d)); for formal probate, a final order of a court in a proceeding determining testacy, validity, or construction, where there was notice to and an opportunity to contest by all interested persons, and there was a finding, or it was based upon a finding, that the decedent was domiciled at death in the state where the order was made. (§524.3-408)	Yes. If the will comes from a place that does not provide for probate, it may be proved by a duly authenticated certificate of its legal custodian stating that the copy introduced is true and that the will has become effective under the law of the other place. (Informal probate §524.3-303(e); formal probate §524.3-409)	No.	Yes.	Proceedings must be "concluded" in this state before they are concluded at the domicile. (U.P.C. cmt. to §3-408, which parallels §524.3-408) The requirements are otherwise the same as those for probate of a domestic will, except for proper venue. (See §524.3-303 for informal probate and §§524.3-401 - 524.3-409 for formal)	Generally no. (See §524.3-303(d) for informal probate and §524.3-408 for formal probate) However, if probate in the other jurisdiction is informal (§524.3-401(b)), or if it was formal probate in a non-domiciliary jurisdiction (§524.3-408), formal probate may be sought as an original proceeding.
Mississippi	An authenticated copy of a will proven according to the laws of another jurisdiction. (§91-7-33) Such will may be contested as the original might have been if it had been executed in this state. (Id.)	No.	Yes. All personal property in this state shall descend and be distributed according to the laws of this state, regardless of rights accruing in other states, and notwithstanding the domicile of the deceased may have been in another state. (§ 91-1-1)	Yes.	The same as probate for a domestic will. (§91-7-33)	Yes. (§91-7-33)
Missouri	An authenticated copy of the will, probated in another state, and the probate thereof. (§§ 474.370, 474.380)	Yes. Such wills are not covered by §§ 474.370 and 474.380, and thus must be proven as an original will would be in this state.	In counties where real estate is affected, a will admitted to probate together with an authenticated order admitting the same to probate are required. (§474.380)	Yes.	It must be proved in the manner of a domestic will. (White v. Greenway, 263 S.W. 104 (1924))	Yes, foreign wills admitted to probate shall have the same force and effect as the original probate of a domestic will. (§474.380)

Table 2.01, Part 1
Proof of a Foreign Will

	What Proof is Required to Establish a Will Already Proved in Another State?	Are There Special Rules For a Will Proved Outside the U.S.?	Is There a Special Rule For Local Property?	Is Original Probate of a Foreign Will Permitted if Not Already Established at the Domicile?	If So, What Are the Circumstances?	What About Original Probate After Probate in Another Jurisdiction?
Montana	For informal probate, an authenticated copy of the will and the statement probating it (§72-3-213(3)); for formal probate, a final order of a court in a proceeding determining testacy, validity, or construction, where there was notice to and an opportunity to contest by all interested persons, and there was a finding, or it was based upon a finding, that the decedent was domiciled at death in the state where the order was made. (§72-3-312)	Yes. If the will comes from a place that does not provide for probate, it may be proved by a duly authenticated certificate of its legal custodian stating that the copy introduced is true and that the will has become effective under the law of the other place. (Informal probate §72-3-213(4); formal probate §72-3-316)	No.	Yes.	Proceedings must be "concluded" in this state before they are concluded at the domicile. (U.P.C. cmt. to §3-408, which parallels §72-3-312) The requirements are otherwise the same as those for probate of a domestic will, except for proper venue. (See §§72-3-201 - 72-3-203 for informal probate and §72-3-301 - §72-3-316 for formal)	Generally no. (See §72-3-213(3) or informal probate and §72-3-312 for formal probate) However, if probate in the other jurisdiction is informal (§72-3-302(3)), or if it was formal probate in a non-domiciliary jurisdiction (§72-3-312), formal probate may be sought as an original proceeding.
Nebraska	For informal probate, an authenticated copy of the will and the statement probating it (§30-2416(d)); for formal probate, a final order of a court in a proceeding determining testacy, validity, or construction, where there was notice to and an opportunity to contest by all interested persons, and there was a finding, or it was based upon a finding, that the decedent was domiciled at death in the state where the order was made, so long as such state has similar reciprocal provisions in place. (§30-2432)	Yes. If the will comes from a place that does not provide for probate, it may be proved by a duly authenticated certificate of its legal custodian stating that the copy introduced is true and that the will has become effective under the law of the other place. (Informal probate §30-2416(e); formal probate §30-2433)	No.	Yes.	Proceedings must be "concluded" in this state before they are concluded at the domicile. (U.P.C. cmt. to §3-408, which parallels §30-2432) The requirements are otherwise the same as those for probate of a domestic will, except for proper venue. (See §30-2416 for informal probate and §§30-2425 - 30-2433 for formal)	Generally no. (See §30-2416(d) for informal probate and §30-2432 for formal probate) However, if probate in the other jurisdiction is informal (§30-2425), or if it was formal probate in a non-domiciliary jurisdiction (§30-2432), formal probate may be sought as an original proceeding. This answer assumes there is a similar reciprocal provision in the domicile state.

Table 2.01, Part 1
Proof of a Foreign Will

	What Proof is Required to Establish a Will Already Proved in Another State?	Are There Special Rules For a Will Proved Outside the U.S.?	Is There a Special Rule For Local Property?	Is Original Probate of a Foreign Will Permitted if Not Already Established at the Domicile?	If So, What Are the Circumstances?	What About Original Probate After Probate in Another Jurisdiction?
Nevada	A certified copy of a will and the order admitting its probate must be presented with a petition for probate to schedule a hearing to determine if (a) the will has been "duly proved and admitted to probate" outside of Nevada and (b) it was executed in accordance with the laws of the state of execution, decedent's domicile, or Nevada. (§ 136.260(2) & (3))	No. But if the laws of the foreign jurisdiction do not require the will to be probated, a certified copy of the will, and the legal custodian's certification as to the authenticity of the will and that it has become operative by the laws of such jurisdiction, must be presented to schedule a hearing on the matter, and proper notice must be given as would be required for the original probate of a domestic will. (§ 136.260(4)) Foreign wills admitted to probate shall have the same force and effect as the original probate of a domestic will. (§ 136.260(1)-(3))	No.	Yes. (§ 136.010)	Not specified.	Not specified.
New Hampshire	Authenticated copy of will and its probate. (§ 552:13) Foreign wills admitted to probate shall have the same effect as domestic wills proved in the state. (§ 552:13)	No. (§ 552:13)	No.	Yes.	Not specified.	Not specified.

Table 2.01, Part 1
Proof of a Foreign Will

	What Proof is Required to Establish a Will Already Proved in Another State?	Are There Special Rules For a Will Proved Outside the U.S.?	Is There a Special Rule For Local Property?	Is Original Probate of a Foreign Will Permitted if Not Already Established at the Domicile?	If So, What Are the Circumstances?	What About Original Probate After Probate in Another Jurisdiction?
New Jersey	A copy of the will or record of the will and the certificate/judgment for probate and, if real estate being transferred, the record of the grant of testamentary letters. The will shall be admitted to probate if valid under New Jersey laws. (§ 3B:3-27) A will probated in New Jersey by filing a copy of the foreign probate records shall have the same force and effect in respect to real estate as an originally probated domestic will. (§ 3B:3-27)	No. (§ 3B:3-27)	No.	Yes. (§ 3B:3-28)	No proceeding is pending at the domicile and the proceeding takes place in a county where the decedent owned property. (§ 3B:3-28)	Not specified.
New Mexico	For informal probate, an authenticated copy of the will and the statement probating it (§ 45-3-303(D)); for formal probate, a final order of a court in a proceeding determining testacy, validity, or construction, where there was notice to and an opportunity to contest by all interested persons, and there was a finding, or it was based upon a finding, that the decedent was domiciled at death in the state where the order was made. (§ 45-3-408)	Yes. If the will comes from a place that does not provide for probate, it may be proved by a duly authenticated certificate of its legal custodian stating that the copy introduced is true and that the will has become effective under the law of the other place. (Informal probate § 45-3-303(E); formal probate § 45-3-409)	No.	Yes.	Proceedings must be "concluded" in this state before they are concluded at the domicile. (U.P.C. cmt. to § 3-408, which parallels § 45-3-408) The requirements are otherwise the same as those for probate of a domestic will, except for proper venue. (See § 45-3-303 for informal probate and §§ § 45-3-401 - 45-3-409 for formal)	Generally no. (See § 45-3-303(D) for informal probate and § 45-3-408 for formal probate) However, if probate in the other jurisdiction is informal (§ 45-3-401(B)), or if it was formal probate in a non-domiciliary jurisdiction (§ 45-3-408), formal probate may be sought as an original proceeding.

Table 2.01, Part 1
Proof of a Foreign Will

	What Proof is Required to Establish a Will Already Proved in Another State?	Are There Special Rules For a Will Proved Outside the U.S.?	Is There a Special Rule For Local Property?	Is Original Probate of a Foreign Will Permitted if Not Already Established at the Domicile?	If So, What Are the Circumstances?	What About Original Probate After Probate in Another Jurisdiction?
New York	Proof that the written will has been admitted to probate at the testator's domicile or has been established by the laws of the jurisdiction and, if it remains subject to contest at domicile, proof that it is not being contested. (Surr. Ct. Proc. Act § 1602(1))	No. (Surr. Ct. Proc. Act § 1602)	No.	Yes. (Surr. Ct. Proc. Act § 1605)	It must have been validly executed for probate in New York. (Surr. Ct. Proc. Act § 1605(1)) Otherwise, if it has been denied probate or establishment at the testator's domicile, it may only be probated in New York if the denial of probate is not grounds for denial in New York. (Surr. Ct. Proc. Act § 1605(3))	Only if (1) the New York court is satisfied that ancillary probate would be unduly expensive, inconvenient, or impossible; (2) the testator has directed that the will be offered for probate in New York; or (3) laws of testator's domicile discriminate against domiciliaries of New York either as a beneficiary or a fiduciary. (Surr. Ct. Proc. Act § 1605(2))
North Carolina	A certified copy of the will and the probate proceedings. (§ 28A-2A-17) However, to pass title to real estate in North Carolina, the proper execution in accordance with North Carolina law at the time of execution or death or as otherwise specified in § 31-46 and this must be established to the satisfaction of the clerk of the superior court by testimony of a witness to the will, or from findings of fact or recitals in the order of probate, or otherwise in such certified copy of the will and the and the probate proceedings. (§ 28A-2A-17(b))	Yes, the copy of the will and probate proceedings shall be certified by any ambassador, minister, consul or commercial agent of the United States under his official seal. (§ 28A-2A-17(a))	A will originally probated outside the state must appear to have been executed according to: (a) the laws of this state at the time of execution or at the testator's death, (b) the laws where it was executed at the time of the execution, (c) the laws where testator is domiciled at the will's execution or time of death, (d) 10 U.S.C. § 1044d if it is a military testamentary instrument, in order to pass title to or dispose of real estate in this state. (§ 28A-2A-17, § 31-46)	Probably not, on reciprocity grounds, since North Carolina requires the original probate of the will of a North Carolina domiciliary to be in North Carolina and any other probate is deemed ancillary. (§ 28A-26-1)	No provision.	No provision.

Table 2.01, Part 1
Proof of a Foreign Will

	What Proof is Required to Establish a Will Already Proved in Another State?	Are There Special Rules For a Will Proved Outside the U.S.?	Is There a Special Rule For Local Property?	Is Original Probate of a Foreign Will Permitted if Not Already Established at the Domicile?	If So, What Are the Circumstances?	What About Original Probate After Probate in Another Jurisdiction?
North Dakota	For informal probate, an authenticated copy of the will and the statement probating it (§30.1-14-03(4)); for formal probate, a final order of a court in a proceeding determining testacy, validity, or construction, where there was notice to and an opportunity to contest by all interested persons, and there was a finding, or it was based upon a finding, that the decedent was domiciled at death in the state where the order was made. (§30.1-15-08)	Yes. If the will comes from a place that does not provide for probate, it may be proved by a duly authenticated certificate of its legal custodian stating that the copy introduced is true and that the will has become effective under the law of the other place. (Informal probate §30.1-14-03(5); formal probate §30.1-15-09)	No.	Yes.	Proceedings must be "concluded" in this state before they are concluded at the domicile. (U.P.C. cmt. to §3-408, which parallels §30.1-15-08) The requirements are otherwise the same as those for probate of a domestic will, except for proper venue. (See §30.1-14-03 for informal probate and §§30.1-15-01 - 30.1-15-09 for formal)	Generally no. (See §30.1-14-03(4) for informal probate and §30.1-15-08 for formal probate) However, if probate in the other jurisdiction is informal (§30.1-15-01(2)), or if it was formal probate in a non-domiciliary jurisdiction (§30.1-15-08), formal probate may be sought as an original proceeding.
Ohio	An authenticated copy of the will, executed and proved under the laws of any other state or territory. (§2129.05) Wills from other states admitted to probate shall be as valid as domestic wills. (§2129.05)	Yes. An authenticated copy of a will executed, proved, and allowed in a foreign country, and the probate thereof must be given to appropriate probate court. (§2129.07) There will be a 2 month application for probate, and notice must be given to all interested persons. (*Id.*) The court will then determine if the instrument ought to be allowed in this state. (*Id.*)	No.	Yes.	If no domiciliary administration has been commenced, the ancillary administrator shall proceed with administration in Ohio as though the decedent had been a resident of Ohio. (§2129.11)	Implied no (§2129.11), except for wills proved in foreign countries. (§2129.07)

Table 2.01, Part 1
Proof of a Foreign Will

	What Proof is Required to Establish a Will Already Proved in Another State?	Are There Special Rules For a Will Proved Outside the U.S.?	Is There a Special Rule For Local Property?	Is Original Probate of a Foreign Will Permitted if Not Already Established at the Domicile?	If So, What Are the Circumstances?	What About Original Probate After Probate in Another Jurisdiction?
Oklahoma	Authenticated copy of the will and the order or decree admitting it to probate must be filed with a petition for letters to schedule a hearing. (58 §52) At the hearing the record must show the will has been proved in another jurisdiction, and that it was executed according to the laws: (a) of this state, (b) of the place where it was made, or (c) of the place where the testator was at the time domiciled. (58 §53) After a foreign will is admitted to probate, it has the same force and effect as a domestically probated will. (Id.)	No. (58 §51)	No.	Yes.	None, must simply petition the court (58 §§22-23)	Not specified.
Oregon	Certified copy of the will and a certified copy of the order admitting the will to probate or establishment of the domicile. (§ 113.065(1))	No. (§ 113.065(1))	No.	Not specified.	N/A	Not specified.
Pennsylvania	An authenticated copy of the will and its probate. It is then entitled to be probated in Pennsylvania. (20 §3136)	Yes. If it is proved an essential requirement for a valid will under Pennsylvania law has not been met, the probate proceedings may be augmented to require submission of additional evidence to the register. (20 §3136)	No.	Not specified.	Not specified.	Not specified.

Table 2.01, Part 1
Proof of a Foreign Will

	What Proof is Required to Establish a Will Already Proved in Another State?	Are There Special Rules For a Will Proved Outside the U.S.?	Is There a Special Rule For Local Property?	Is Original Probate of a Foreign Will Permitted if Not Already Established at the Domicile?	If So, What Are the Circumstances?	What About Original Probate After Probate in Another Jurisdiction?
Rhode Island	Authenticated copy of the will and its probate must be filed to assign a hearing. (§33-7-18) Notice shall then be given as if the will were presented for domestic probate. (§33-7-19) Unless cause to the contrary is given, the will may be placed on file at the hearing. (§33-7-20)	No. (§33-7-18)	Yes. Title in real estate shall not pass until a certified copy of the will is recorded in the records of land evidence where the real estate is situated. (§33-7-20)	Yes. (§33-7-25)	If it complies with the laws of execution in Rhode Island. (§33-7-25(a)) Otherwise, if it has been denied probate or establishment of the testator's domicile it may not be admitted to Original probate in Rhode Island unless the denial was for a cause that is not grounds for rejection in Rhode Island. (§33-7-25(c))	Only if (1) the ancillary probate would be unduly expensive, inconvenient, or impossible; (2) testator directed in the will that probate be offered in Rhode Island; or (3) laws of testator's domicile discriminate against domiciliaries of Rhode Island either as a beneficiary or as a fiduciary. (§33-7-25(b))
South Carolina	For informal probate, an authenticated copy of the will and the statement probating it (§62-3-303(d)); for formal probate, a final order of a court in a proceeding determining testacy, validity, or construction, where there was notice to and an opportunity to contest by all interested persons, and there was a finding, or it was based upon a finding, that the decedent was domiciled at death in the state where the order was made. (§62-3-408)	Yes. If the will comes from a place that does not provide for probate, it may be proved by a duly authenticated certificate of its legal custodian stating that the copy introduced is true and that the will has become effective under the law of the other place. (Informal probate §62-3-303(e); formal probate §62-3-409)	No.	Yes.	Proceedings must be "concluded" in this state before they are concluded at the domicile. (U.P.C. cmt. to §3-408, which parallels §62-3-408) The requirements are otherwise the same as those for probate of a domestic will, except for proper venue. (See §62-3-303; for informal probate and §§62-3-401 - 62-3-409 for formal)	Generally no. (See §62-3-303(d) for informal probate and §62-3-408 for formal probate) However, if probate in the other jurisdiction is informal (§62-3-401), or if it was formal probate in a non-domiciliary jurisdiction (§62-3-408), formal probate may be sought as an original proceeding.

Table 2.01, Part 1
Proof of a Foreign Will

	What Proof is Required to Establish a Will Already Proved in Another State?	Are There Special Rules For a Will Proved Outside the U.S.?	Is There a Special Rule For Local Property?	Is Original Probate of a Foreign Will Permitted if Not Already Established at the Domicile?	If So, What Are the Circumstances?	What About Original Probate After Probate in Another Jurisdiction?
South Dakota	For informal probate, an authenticated copy of the will and the statement probating it (§ 29A-3-303(d)); for formal probate, a final order of a court in a proceeding determining testacy, validity, or construction, where there was notice to and an opportunity to contest by all interested persons, and there was a finding, or it was based upon a finding, that the decedent was domiciled at death in the state where the order was made. (§ 29A-3-408)	Yes. If the will comes from a place that does not provide for probate, it may be proved by a duly authenticated certificate of its legal custodian stating that the copy introduced is true and that the will has become effective under the law of the other place. (Informal probate § 29A-3-303(e); formal probate § 29A-3-409)	No.	Yes.	Proceedings must be "concluded" in this state before they are concluded at the domicile. (U.P.C. cmt. to § 3-408, which parallels § 29A-3-408) The requirements are otherwise the same as those for probate of a domestic will, except for proper venue. (See § 29A-3-303 for informal probate and §§ 29A-3-401 - 29A-3-409 for formal)	Generally no. (See § 29A-3-303(d) for informal probate and § 75-3-408 for formal probate) However, if probate in the other jurisdiction is informal (§ 29A-3-401(b)), or if it was formal probate in a non-domiciliary jurisdiction (§ 29A-3-408), formal probate may be sought as an original proceeding.

Table 2.01, Part 1
Proof of a Foreign Will

	What Proof is Required to Establish a Will Already Proved in Another State?	Are There Special Rules For a Will Proved Outside the U.S.?	Is There a Special Rule For Local Property?	Is Original Probate of a Foreign Will Permitted if Not Already Established at the Domicile?	If So, What Are the Circumstances?	What About Original Probate After Probate in Another Jurisdiction?
Tennessee	An authenticated copy of the will, its probate, and a petition for probate must be presented to file the will in either common or solemn form; if it is filed in solemn form, there must be a hearing on the matter and notice given as for the original probate of a domestic will. At the hearing, it must be shown the will has been duly proved and admitted to probate outside the state, and that it was executed according to the laws of: (1) the place where the will was made, (2) the place where the testator was domiciled at the time, or (3) this state. (§32-5-103) When a court admits a will to probate based on another jurisdiction's probate, it shall have the same force and effect as the original probate of a domestic will. (§32-5-104).	Yes. (§§32-5-104, 32-5-105) A hearing is required. If it is established that the will was duly proved, allowed, and admitted to probate, as well as executed according to the law of the place in which made, or in which the testator was domiciled, or in conformity with the laws of Tennessee, then it must be admitted to probate as if an original probate. (§32-5-104) However, if probate "is not required" in the other jurisdiction, then two steps are involved. First, a duly authenticated copy of the will and a duly authenticated certificate of the legal custodian of the original will that the same is a true copy and that the will has become operable must be presented by an executor or interested person. If the will is a notarial will in the possession of a notary and must remain in the custody of a notary, then the will must be duly authenticated by the notary. The second step is a hearing and notice as in the case of an original will presented for probate. (§32-5-105)	Yes. A contest of a will of another jurisdiction on the issue devisavit vel non shall be allowed as to a devise of realty in this state, but as to devises of personalty, the foreign will shall be conclusive. (§32-5-103)	Yes.	The petition must state the death of the testator, the testator's ownership in lands in the county, the facts of testacy, and be submitted in a county in which the decedent owned property. Then the court shall authorize the taking of proof necessary to prove the will in accordance with the laws of Tennessee. (§32-5-110)	Not specified.

Table 2.01, Part 1
Proof of a Foreign Will

	What Proof is Required to Establish a Will Already Proved in Another State?	Are There Special Rules For a Will Proved Outside the U.S.?	Is There a Special Rule For Local Property?	Is Original Probate of a Foreign Will Permitted if Not Already Established at the Domicile?	If So, What Are the Circumstances?	What About Original Probate After Probate in Another Jurisdiction?
Texas	A copy of the foreign will and the probate order/decree/judgment. (§ 501.002) The copy must be attested by the original signature of the court clerk, include a certificate with the original signature of the judge/presiding magistrate stating the attestation is in proper form, and have the court seal affixed, if one exists. (*Id.*) For wills admitted to probate in the jurisdiction where testator was domiciled at time of death, an indication that probate in Texas is requested on the basis of the authenticated copy of the foreign probate proceedings is also requested. (*Id.*) For wills admitted to probate in jurisdiction other than the one where testator was domiciled at time of death, all the information required for probate of a domestic will, the name and address of each devisee and each person entitled to a portion of the estate in the absence of the will is also required. (*Id.*)	No.	No.	Yes.	Original probate is permitted as long as the will is valid under Texas laws. However, if probate was rejected elsewhere, it must be for a cause that is not grounds for rejection in Texas. Otherwise, it cannot be originally probated in Texas. (§ 502.001)	Implied yes, so long as the will is valid under Texas law, and was not rejected elsewhere for a cause that is valid under Texas law. (§ 502:001)

Table 2.01, Part 1
Proof of a Foreign Will

	What Proof is Required to Establish a Will Already Proved in Another State?	Are There Special Rules For a Will Proved Outside the U.S.?	Is There a Special Rule For Local Property?	Is Original Probate of a Foreign Will Permitted if Not Already Established at the Domicile?	If So, What Are the Circumstances?	What About Original Probate After Probate in Another Jurisdiction?
Utah	For informal probate, an authenticated copy of the will and the statement probating it (§75-3-303(4)); for formal probate, a final order of a court in a proceeding determining testacy, validity, or construction, where there was notice to and an opportunity to contest by all interested persons, and there was a finding, that the decedent was domiciled at death in the state where the order was made. (§75-3-408)	Yes. If the will comes from a place that does not provide for probate, it may be proved by a duly authenticated certificate of its legal custodian stating that the copy introduced is true and that the will has become effective under the law of the other place. (Informal probate §75-3-303(e); formal probate §75-3-409)	No.	Yes.	Proceedings must be ''concluded'' in this state before they are concluded at the domicile. (U.P.C. cmt. to §3-408, which parallels §75-3-408) The requirements are otherwise the same as those for probate of a domestic will, except for proper venue. (See §75-3-303 for informal probate and §§75-3-401 - 75-3-409 for formal)	Generally no. (See §75-3-303(4) for informal probate and §75-3-408 for formal probate) However, if probate in the other jurisdiction is informal (§75-3-401(2)), or if it was formal probate in a non-domiciliary jurisdiction (§75-3-408), formal probate may be sought as an original proceeding.
Vermont	A duly authenticated copy of the will and its allowance, or a certificate of the legal custodian of the will that it is a true copy and has become operative by the laws of the state, or a copy of a notarial will which has been duly authenticated by such notary if the laws require that the notary retain custody of the will. Such documents must be filed to schedule a hearing, and notice must be given per the probate rules. (14 §114)	No. (14 §114)	No.	Yes.	In writing and signed by the testator and in compliance with the law, either of the place where executed or of the testator's domicile. (14 §112)	Not specified.

Table 2.01, Part 1
Proof of a Foreign Will

	What Proof is Required to Establish a Will Already Proved in Another State?	Are There Special Rules For a Will Proved Outside the U.S.?	Is There a Special Rule For Local Property?	Is Original Probate of a Foreign Will Permitted if Not Already Established at the Domicile?	If So, What Are the Circumstances?	What About Original Probate After Probate in Another Jurisdiction?
Virginia	An authenticated copy of the will and certificate of probate create a rebuttable presumption that the will was duly executed and admitted to probate as a will of personal estate where testator was domiciled, and shall be admitted as a will of personal estate. If such copy indicates that the will was admitted to probate in a court of another jurisdiction and was so executed as to be a valid will of real estate in the Commonwealth by the law of the Commonwealth, such copy may be admitted to probate as a will of real estate. An authenticated copy of any will which has been self-proved under the laws of another state shall, when offered with its authenticated certificate of probate, be admitted to probate as a will of personal estate and real estate. (§ 64.2-450)	No. (§ 64.2-450)	If real estate is in Virginia, then the will must be valid under Virginia laws. (§ 64.2-450)	Implied yes.	Must be done in the county where decedent owned property. (§ 64.2-443)	Not specified.
Washington	Copy of the will and the original probate record certified by the clerk, or if there is no clerk, certified by the judge and by the seal of the officers if they have a seal. (§ 11.20.090) Foreign wills admitted to probate appear to have the same force and effect as domestic wills. (§ 11.20.100)	No. (§ 11.20.090)	No.	Yes. (§ 11.12.020(2))	Will complies with laws of the state where it is executed or decedent's domicile. (§ 11.12.020(1))	Not specified.

Table 2.01, Part 1
Proof of a Foreign Will

	What Proof is Required to Establish a Will Already Proved in Another State?	Are There Special Rules For a Will Proved Outside the U.S.?	Is There a Special Rule For Local Property?	Is Original Probate of a Foreign Will Permitted if Not Already Established at the Domicile?	If So, What Are the Circumstances?	What About Original Probate After Probate in Another Jurisdiction?
West Virginia	An authenticated copy and the certificate of probate create a rebuttable presumption as a will of personalty. (§41-5-13)	No. (§41-5-13)	Yes. Wills of real estate must have been proved as valid wills of land in this state by the laws thereof. (§41-5-13)	Yes. (§§ 41-5-4(c) & (d), 41-5-5)	Not specified.	Implied no. (§41-5-13)
Wisconsin	Will with proof that it has been probated or established in testator's domicile and not being contested there. (§868.01(1))	No. (§868.01(1))	No.	Yes. (§ 868.01(5))	If the will has not been rejected from probate or establishment at the testator's domicile, and if so, it was for a reason which is not grounds for rejection of a will in Wisconsin. (§868.01(5))	(§868.01(1))

Table 2.01, Part 1
Proof of a Foreign Will

	What Proof is Required to Establish a Will Already Proved in Another State?	Are There Special Rules For a Will Proved Outside the U.S.?	Is There a Special Rule For Local Property?	Is Original Probate of a Foreign Will Permitted if Not Already Established at the Domicile?	If So, What Are the Circumstances?	What About Original Probate After Probate in Another Jurisdiction?
Wyoming	Satisfaction of the court that the will has been duly proved, allowed, and admitted to probate outside of this state and executed according to the place where made or where the testator was domiciled at the time, or in conformity with the law of Wyoming. (§§ 2-11-102, 2-11-104) Also note that there are special rules for estates not exceeding $200,000. The rules allow for the dispensing of probate proceedings. (§§ 2-11-103, 2-11-201) A petition under oath must be filed with the district judge in the proper county, showing the facts in the case together with certified copies of the petition, order of appointment of personal representative, inventory, and final decree of distribution as well as a full showing that debts have been paid. (§§ 2-11-201, 2-11-202) Provision also made for the sale or other disposition of local property relating to estate being probated and settled elsewhere. (§ 2-11-202) Foreign wills admitted to probate outside of Wyoming, executed according to laws of Wyoming, of the domicile at time of decedent's death, or of the place the will was executed, that are admitted to probate in Wyoming,	Yes. If probate was not required in the foreign jurisdiction, it may be proved by an authenticated copy with a certificate of the legal custodian that the copy is true and the will has become operative by the laws of the foreign jurisdiction. (§ 2-11-105)	No.	Not specified.	N/A	Not specified.

Table 2.01, Part 1
Proof of a Foreign Will

What Proof is Required to Establish a Will Already Proved in Another State?	Are There Special Rules For a Will Proved Outside the U.S.?	Is There a Special Rule For Local Property?	Is Original Probate of a Foreign Will Permitted if Not Already Established at the Domicile?	If So, What Are the Circumstances?	What About Original Probate After Probate in Another Jurisdiction?
shall have the same force and effect as the original probate of a domestic will. (§ 2-11-104)					

Table 2.01, Part 2
Proof of a Foreign Will

	Are There Special Notice Requirements?			
	What If Decedent Was a U.S. Citizen?	What If a Beneficiary Is Not a U.S. Citizen?	What If Decedent Was a Domiciliary of Another State?	What If a Beneficiary Is a Domiciliary of Another State?
Alabama	No distinction is made based on decedent's citizenship, but notice must be given if testator was not an "inhabitant" of Alabama and the will "was admitted to probate" elsewhere outside the jurisdiction of the United States. (§ 43-8-175)	No.	No, no notice requirement. (§ 43-8-175)	Yes. If either surviving spouse or next of kin reside out of state, notice must be given by publication once a week for three successive weeks in a newspaper published in the county where the will is being proved, or as provided by the Alabama Rules of Civil Procedure. (§ 43-8-166)
Alaska	A provision requires notice to be given to spouse, children, heirs, devisees, and executors "named in any will that is … known by the petitioner to have been probated or offered for informal or formal probate elsewhere; and … any personal representative of the decedent whose appointment has not been terminated." This requirement is based on knowledge of petitioner, whereas there is a mandatory notice requirement, regardless of knowledge, in the case of wills that have been or are being probated in the local county. (§ 13.16.150(a)) It is unclear whether persons named in known, but *unprobated*, wills need to be notified. (U.P.C. § 3-403(a) cmt.)			
Arizona	A provision requires notice to be given to spouse, children, heirs, devisees, and executors "named in any will that is … known by the petitioner to have been probated, or offered for informal or formal probate in another jurisdiction, and any personal representative of the decedent whose appointment has not been terminated." This requirement is based on knowledge of petitioner, whereas there is a mandatory notice requirement, regardless of knowledge, in the case of wills that have been or are being probated in the local county. (§ 14-3403(A)) It is unclear whether persons named in known but unprobated wills need to be notified. (§ 14-4301 & U.P.C. § 3-403(a) cmt.; § 14-4203)			
Arkansas			No.	
California			No. (Prob. § 12512)	
Colorado	A provision requires notice to be given to spouse, children, heirs, devisees, and executors "named in any will that is … known by the petitioner to have been probated, or offered for informal or formal probate elsewhere, and any personal representative of the decedent whose appointment has not been terminated." This requirement is based on knowledge of petitioner, whereas there is a mandatory notice requirement, regardless of knowledge, in the case of wills that have been or are being probated in the local county. (§ 15-12-403(1)(b)) It is unclear whether persons named in known but unprobated wills need to be notified. (U.P.C. § 3-403 cmt.)			
Connecticut			No.	
Delaware			No, but the court may order notice as it deems proper in respect to persons not within the state. (12 § 1303)	
District of Columbia	No.	No.	Yes. Notice shall be published once a week for three consecutive weeks in a newspaper of general circulation in the District of Columbia and any other publication as the Court may provide. (§ 20-343)	No.
Florida	The rules for commencing ancillary probate are those set forth in Florida Probate Rules (§ 734.102(2)). Specific notice rules are set forth in Fla. Probate R. 5.470(b). See also In re Estate of Hatcher, 439 So. 2d 977 (Dist. Ct. App. 1983) (need to provide notice to rule on will) If letters are applied for by other than the domiciliary representative, notice must be given to the domiciliary representative. (§ 734.102(1)).			

Table 2.01, Part 2
Proof of a Foreign Will

	Are There Special Notice Requirements?			
	What If Decedent Was Not a U.S. Citizen?	*What If a Beneficiary Is Not a U.S. Citizen?*	*What If Decedent Was a Domiciliary of Another State?*	*What If a Beneficiary Is a Domiciliary of Another State?*
Georgia	No provision.	No provision.	Yes. Notice is to be given by an ancillary personal representative in Georgia to all Georgia-domiciled creditors in the manner required for decedents who die domiciled in Georgia. (§ 53-5-40)	No provision.
Hawaii	A provision requires notice to be given to spouse, children, heirs, devisees, and executors "named in any will . . . that is known by the petitioner to have been probated, or offered for informal or formal probate elsewhere, and any personal representative of the decedent whose appointment has not been terminated." This requirement is based on knowledge of petitioner, whereas there is a mandatory notice requirement, regardless of knowledge, in the case of wills that have been or are being probated in the local county. (§ 560:3-403(a) & (b)) It is unclear whether persons named in known but unprobated wills need to be notified. (U.P.C. § 3-403 cmt.)			
Idaho	A provision requires notice to be given to spouse, children, heirs, devisees, and executors "named in any will . . . that is known by the petitioner to have been probated, or offered for informal or formal probate elsewhere, and any personal representative of the decedent whose appointment has not been terminated." This requirement is based on knowledge of petitioner, whereas there is a mandatory notice requirement, regardless of knowledge, in the case of wills that have been or are being probated in the local county. (§ 15-3-403(1)) It is unclear whether persons named in known but unprobated wills need to be notified. (*Id.* cmt.)			
Illinois	No.			
Indiana	No.			
Iowa	No. (§ 633.498)			
Kansas	The manner of notification is at the court's discretion. (§ 59-2229)	No.	The manner of notification is at the court's discretion. (§ 59-2229)	No.
Kentucky	No.			
Louisiana	No. (Code Civ. Pro. § 3401)			
Maine	A provision requires notice to be given to spouse, children, heirs, devisees, and executors "named in any will . . . that is known by the petitioner to have been probated or offered for informal or formal probate elsewhere, and any personal representative of the decedent whose appointment has not been terminated." This requirement is based on knowledge of petitioner, whereas there is a mandatory notice requirement, regardless of knowledge, in the case of wills that have been or are being probated in the local county. (18A § 3-403(a)) It is unclear whether persons named in known but unprobated wills need to be notified. (*Id.* cmt.)			
Maryland	Yes, but only for real and lease hold property. (Est. & Trusts § 5-503(b)(1))	No.	Yes, but only for real and lease hold property. (Est. & Trusts § 5-503(b)(1))	No.
Massachusetts	A provision requires notice to be given to spouse, children, heirs, devisees, and executors "named in any will . . . that is known by the petitioner to have been probated, or offered for informal or formal probate elsewhere, and any personal representative of the decedent whose appointment has not been terminated." This requirement is based on knowledge of petitioner, whereas there is a mandatory notice requirement, regardless of knowledge in the case of wills that have been or are being probated in the local county. (190B § 3-403(b)) It is unclear whether persons named in known but unprobated wills need to be notified. (U.P.C. cmt. to § 3-403(a), which section parallels 190B § 3-403)			
Michigan	A provision requires notice to be given to the decedent's heirs, devisees, and personal representatives named in the will that is known by petitioner to have been probated or offered for informal or formal probate "elsewhere," and any personal representative of the decedent whose appointment has not been terminated, the trustee of a trust, and notice by publication to known and unknown persons with an interest. (§ 700.3403)			

Table 2.01, Part 2
Proof of a Foreign Will

State	Are There Special Notice Requirements?			
	What If Decedent Was Not a U.S. Citizen?	*What If a Beneficiary Is Not a U.S. Citizen?*	*What If Decedent Was a Domiciliary of Another State?*	*What If a Beneficiary Is a Domiciliary of Another State?*
Minnesota				A provision requires notice to be given to spouse, children, heirs, devisees, and executors "named in any will … that is known by the petitioner to have been probated, or offered for informal or formal probate elsewhere, and any personal representative of the decedent whose appointment has not been terminated." This requirement is based on knowledge of petitioner, whereas there is a mandatory notice requirement, regardless of knowledge, in the case of wills that have been or are being probated in the local county. (§ 524.3-403(a)) It is unclear whether persons named in known but *unprobated* wills need to be notified. (U.P.C. cmt. to § 3-403(a), which section parallels § 524.3-403(a))
Mississippi				
Missouri		No, but court may require notice as it deems fit. (§ 472.100)	No.	
Montana				A provision requires notice to be given to spouse, children, heirs, devisees, and executors "named in any will … that is known by the petitioner to have been probated or offered for informal or formal probate elsewhere; and any personal representative of the decedent whose appointment has not been terminated." This requirement is based on knowledge of petitioner, whereas there is a mandatory notice requirement, regardless of knowledge, in the case of wills that have been or are being probated in the local county. (§ 72-3-305(2)) It is unclear whether persons named in known, but *unprobated*, wills need to be notified. (U.P.C. cmt. to § 3-403(a), which section parallels § 72-3-305(3))
Nebraska				A provision requires notice to be given to spouse, children, heirs, devisees, and executors "named in any will … that is known by the petitioner to have been probated, or offered for informal or formal probate elsewhere, and any personal representative of the decedent whose appointment has not been terminated." This requirement is based on knowledge of petitioner, whereas there is a mandatory notice requirement, regardless of knowledge, in the case of wills that have been or are being probated in the local county. (§ 30-2427(a)) It is unclear whether persons named in known but *unprobated* wills need to be notified. (U.P.C. § 3-403 cmt.)
Nevada		No. (§ 136.100(2))		
New Hampshire		No. (§ 552:15)		
New Jersey		No.		
New Mexico				A provision requires notice to be given to spouse, children, heirs, devisees, and executors "named in any will … that is known by the petitioner to have been probated, or offered for informal or formal probate elsewhere; and any personal representative of the decedent whose appointment has not been terminated." This requirement is based on knowledge of petitioner, whereas there is a mandatory notice requirement, regardless of knowledge, in the case of wills that have been or are being probated in the local county. (§ 45-3-403(B)) It is unclear whether persons named in known but unprobated wills need to be notified. (U.P.C. § 3-403 cmt.)
New York		No.		
North Carolina		No.		
North Dakota				A provision requires notice to be given to spouse, children, heirs, devisees, and executors "named in any will … that is known by the petitioner to have been probated, or offered for informal or formal probate elsewhere; and any personal representative of the decedent whose appointment has not been terminated." This requirement is based on knowledge of petitioner, whereas there is a mandatory notice requirement, regardless of knowledge, in the case of wills that have been or are being probated in the local county. (§ 30.1-15-03(1)) It is unclear whether persons named in known but unprobated wills need to be notified. (*Id.* cmt.)
Ohio	No, but there are special notice requirements if the will was probated in a foreign country or U.S. territory. (§ 2129.07(A))	No.		
Oklahoma		No. (58 § 25)		
Oregon	No, but the court may change the notice requirements for good cause. (§ 111.215)			
Pennsylvania		No.		

Table 2.01, Part 2
Proof of a Foreign Will

	Are There Special Notice Requirements?			
	What If Decedent Was a U.S. Citizen?	What If a Beneficiary Is Not a U.S. Citizen?	What If Decedent Was a Domiciliary of Another State?	What If a Beneficiary Is a Domiciliary of Another State?
Rhode Island	No. (§ 33-7-19)			
South Carolina	A provision requires notice to be given to spouse, children, heirs, devisees, and executors "named in any will … that is known by the petitioner to have been probated, or offered for informal or formal probate elsewhere, and any personal representative of the decedent whose appointment has not been terminated." This requirement is based on knowledge of petitioner, whereas there is a mandatory notice requirement, regardless of knowledge, in the case of wills that have been or are being probated in the local county. (§62-3-403(a)) It is unclear whether persons named in known but *unprobated* wills will need to be notified. (*Id.* cmt.)			A provision requires notice to be given to spouse, children, heirs, devisees, and executors "named in any will … that is known by the petitioner to have been probated, or offered for informal or formal probate elsewhere, and any personal representative of the decedent whose appointment has not been terminated." This requirement is based on knowledge of petitioner, whereas there is a mandatory notice requirement, regardless of knowledge, in the case of wills that have been or are being probated in the local county. (§62-3-403(a)) It is unclear whether persons named in known but *unprobated* wills will need to be notified. (*Id.* cmt.)
South Dakota	A provision requires notice to be given to spouse, children, heirs, devisees, and executors "named in any will … that is known by the petitioner to have been probated, or offered for informal or formal probate elsewhere, and any personal representative of the decedent whose appointment has not been terminated." This requirement is based on knowledge of petitioner, whereas there is a mandatory notice requirement, regardless of knowledge, in the case of wills that have been or are being probated in the local county. (U.P.C. §3-403 cmt.)			A provision requires notice to be given to spouse, children, heirs, devisees, and executors "named in any will … that is known by the petitioner to have been probated, or offered for informal or formal probate elsewhere, and any personal representative of the decedent whose appointment has not been terminated." This requirement is based on knowledge of petitioner, whereas there is a mandatory notice requirement, regardless of knowledge, in the case of wills that have been or are being probated in the local county. (§29A-3-403(b)) It is unclear whether persons named in known but *unprobated* wills need to be notified.
Tennessee	No. (§32-5-103)			
Texas	Only that notice to devisees and heirs should be made through registered or certified mail if no original probate in the domicile has been established. (§501.003)	No.	Only that notice to devisees and heirs should be made through registered or certified mail if no original probate in the domicile has been established. (§501.003)	No.
Utah	A provision requires notice to be given to spouse, children, heirs, devisees, and executors "named in any will … that is known by the petitioner to have been probated, or offered for informal or formal probate elsewhere, and any personal representative of the decedent whose appointment has not been terminated." This requirement is based on knowledge of petitioner, whereas there is a mandatory notice requirement, regardless of knowledge, in the case of wills that have been or are being probated in the local county. (§75-3-403(1)) It is unclear whether persons named in known but *unprobated* wills need to be notified. (*Id.* cmt.)			A provision requires notice to be given to spouse, children, heirs, devisees, and executors "named in any will … that is known by the petitioner to have been probated, or offered for informal or formal probate elsewhere, and any personal representative of the decedent whose appointment has not been terminated." This requirement is based on knowledge of petitioner, whereas there is a mandatory notice requirement, regardless of knowledge, in the case of wills that have been or are being probated in the local county. (§75-3-403(1)) It is unclear whether persons named in known but *unprobated* wills need to be notified. (*Id.* cmt.)
Vermont	No. (14 §114(b))			
Virginia	No.			
Washington	No.			
West Virginia	No. (§41-5-13)			
Wisconsin	No.	Yes. (§879.03(3))		
Wyoming	No.			

Table 2.02, Part 1
Ancillary Probate

	For Ancillary Probate, Must:				
	There Be Proof of No Pending Contest at Domicile?	There Be Proof That Period for Contesting Will at the Domicile Has Expired?	There Be Proof That Decedent Was Domiciled in Other Jurisdiction?	All Interested Parties Be Notified?	Other Considerations?
Alabama	No.	No.	No.	No. (§ 43-8-175)	No.
Alaska	No. But see Table 2.02, Part 2 regarding contesting the will during ancillary proceedings. (§ 13.16.090(d) - informal probate; § 13.16.175 - formal probate)	No. But see Table 2.02, Part 2 regarding contesting the will during ancillary proceedings. (§ 13.16.090(d) - informal probate; § 13.16.175 - formal probate)	Proof of Domicile is necessary to establish there has been a formal probate (U.P.C. jurisdictions) or solemn form probate (common law jurisdictions) elsewhere. If there has been such probate then there can be only ancillary, and not original probate, if the other probate was at the domicile. That is why proof of domicile is necessary. (§§ 13.16.175, 13.16.180)	See Table 2.01, Part 2	No.
Arizona	No. But see Table 2.02, Part 2 regarding contesting the will during ancillary proceedings. (§ 14-3303(D) - informal probate; § 14-3408 -formal probate)	No. But see Table 2.02, Part 2 regarding contesting the will during ancillary proceedings. (§ 14-3303(D - informal probate; § 14-3408 -formal probate)	Proof of Domicile is necessary to establish there has been a formal probate (U.P.C. jurisdictions) or solemn form probate (common law jurisdictions) elsewhere. If there has been such probate then there can be only ancillary, and not original probate, if the other probate was at the domicile. That is why proof of domicile is necessary. (§§ 14-3408, 14-3409)	See Table 2.01, Part 2	No.
Arkansas	It is presumed in the absence of evidence to the contrary. (§ 28-40-120)	It is presumed in the absence of evidence to the contrary. (§ 28-40-120)	Petition for probate shall state the time and place of execution, testator's domicile at execution, and testator's domicile at the time of death. (§ 28-40-120(c))	Yes. (§ 28-40-111(a)(4))	No. Except where special provision is made otherwise, the law and procedure relating to the administration of estates of resident decedents shall apply to the ancillary administration of estates of nonresident decedents. (§ 28-42-101)
California	No.	No.	No.	Yes. (Prob. § 12512)	Yes. These answers assume: (1) original probate was based on domicile, (2) proper notice was given, and (3) original probate is final. If these assumptions do not hold true in a particular case, the answers given do not apply. (Prob. §§ 12522, 12523)

Table 2.02, Part 1
Ancillary Probate

	There Be Proof of No Pending Contest at Domicile?	There Be Proof That Period for Contesting Will at the Domicile Has Expired?	For Ancillary Probate, Must:		
			There Be Proof That Decedent Was Domiciled in Other Jurisdiction?	All Interested Parties Be Notified?	Other Considerations?
Colorado	No. But see Table 2.02 Part 2 regarding contesting the will during ancillary proceedings. (§ 15-12-303(4) - informal probate; § 15-12-408 - formal probate)	No. But see Table 2.02, Part 2 regarding contesting the will during ancillary proceedings. (§ 15-12-303(4) - informal probate; § 15-12-408 - formal probate)	Proof of Domicile is necessary to establish there has been a formal probate (U.P.C. jurisdictions) or solemn form probate (common law jurisdictions) elsewhere. If there has been such probate then there can be only ancillary, and not original probate, if the other probate was at the domicile. That is why proof of domicile is necessary. (§§ 15-12-408, 15-12-409)	See Table 2.01, Part 2	No.
Connecticut	No. Only "proved and established" will required. (§ 45a-288)	No.	At least a claim of domicile out of state. (§ 45a-288)	Yes. (§ 45a-288)	Yes. A filing for ancillary probate is open to objection. (§ 45a-288)
Delaware	(12§ 1307)	(12§ 1307)	(12§ 1307)	(12§ 1307)	No.
District of Columbia[1]	No. (§ 14-504)	No. (§ 14-504)	No. (§ 14-504)	A foreign personal representative must afford notice through publication in D.C. as provided in § 20-343(a).	No.
Florida	See Table 2.01, Part 1.	No provision. See also Staum v. Rubano, 120 So. 3d 109, 111 (Dist. Ct. App. 2013) ("We are aware of no authority providing a Florida court with jurisdiction to determine that a creditor's pending claim against a foreign domiciliary estate is untimely.")	No, but foreign probate can be challenged on this ground. See Table 2.02, Part 2.	Yes. See Table 2.02, Part 2.	If a foreign notarial will is in the possession of the notary pursuant to foreign law, a copy will suffice only if duly authenticated by the notary, whose position, signature, and seal of office are authenticated by a U.S. consular officer in jurisdiction of notary's residence (i.e., domicile). (§733.205)

Table 2.02, Part 1
Ancillary Probate

	There Be Proof of No Pending Contest at Domicile?	There Be Proof That Period for Contesting Will at the Domicile Has Expired?	For Ancillary Probate, Must: There Be Proof That Decedent Was Domiciled in Other Jurisdiction?	All Interested Parties Be Notified?	Other Considerations?
Georgia	Yes, based on requirement of a copy of "final proceedings" of domicile for jurisdiction, but this does not bar will contest in ancillary proceeding. (§ 53-5-33(c))	Yes, based on requirement of a copy of "final proceedings" of domicile for jurisdiction, but this does not bar will contest in ancillary proceeding. (§ 53-5-33(c))	Yes, based on requirement of copy of "final proceedings" of domiciliary jurisdiction. (§ 53-5-33(c))	Yes. Statute provides particularly for notice to be given to all creditors of the nondomiciliary decedent who are domiciled in Georgia as is required for Georgia-domiciled decedents. (§ 53-5-40)	Ancillary probate can only be accomplished in solemn form. Also, it is not available until the proof is presented that the "will has not been offered for probate in this state in proceedings in which a caveat to such probate has been finally sustained or is pending." (§ 53-5-33(a)) This provision is necessary due to the possibility of original probate of a foreign will in Georgia. See Table 2.01, Part 1.
Hawaii	No. But see Table 2.02, Part 2 regarding contesting the will during ancillary proceedings. (§ 560:3-303(d) - informal probate; § 560:3-408 - formal probate)	No. But see Table 2.02, Part 2 regarding contesting the will during ancillary proceedings. (§ 560:3-303(d) - informal probate; § 560:3-408 - formal probate)	Proof of Domicile is necessary to establish there has been a formal probate (U.P.C. jurisdictions) or solemn form probate (common law jurisdictions) elsewhere. If there has been such probate then there can be only ancillary, and not original probate, if the other probate was at the domicile. That is why proof of domicile is necessary. (§§ 560:3-408, 560:3-409)	See Table 2.01, Part 2	No.
Idaho	No. But see Table 2.02, Part 2 regarding contesting the will during ancillary proceedings. (§ 15-3-303(d) - informal probate; § 15-3-408 - formal probate)	No. But see Table 2.02, Part 2 regarding contesting the will during ancillary proceedings. (§ 15-3-303(d) - informal probate; § 15-3-408 - formal probate)	Proof of Domicile is necessary to establish there has been a formal probate (U.P.C. jurisdictions) or solemn form probate (common law jurisdictions) elsewhere. If there has been such probate then there can be only ancillary, and not original probate, if the other probate was at the domicile. That is why proof of domicile is necessary. (§§ 15-3-408, 15-3-409)	See Table 2.01, Part 2	No.
Illinois	No. (755 ILCS § 5/7-3)	No. (755 ILCS § 5/7-3)	No. (755 ILCS § 5/7-3)	Yes. (755 ILCS §§ 5/7-2, 5/6-10)	No.
Indiana	No. (§§ 29-1-7-26, 27)	No.	No.	No.	No.
Iowa	No. (§ 633.496)	No. (§ 633.496)	No. (§ 633.496)	No. (§ 633.496)	No.

Table 2.02, Part 1
Ancillary Probate

	For Ancillary Probate, Must:				
	There Be Proof of No Pending Contest at Domicile?	There Be Proof That Period for Contesting Will at the Domicile Has Expired?	There Be Proof That Decedent Was Domiciled in Other Jurisdiction?	All Interested Parties Be Notified?	Other Considerations?
Kansas	No. (§§ 59-2229, 59-2230)	No. (§§ 59-2229, 59-2230)	No. (§§ 59-2229, 59-2230)	Yes, as the court directs, in the case of a will executed and originally probated outside of the state. (§ 59-2229)	No.
Kentucky	No. § 394.150	No. § 394.150	Implied yes. Says any will offered for probate must contain a statement of the residence of the testator in the probate application. (§ 394.145; see also § 394.150)	Not specified for ancillary probate, but normally notice to all interested parties is not essential to give court jurisdiction of application to probate or set aside probate of a will. (Miller v. Hill, 168 S.W.2d 769 (1943))	Yes, filing for ancillary probate creates a presumption of proper execution that can be rebutted; rebuttal may create a need for proof of these matters. (§ 394.150)
Louisiana	No. (§§ 9:2422-9:2423)	No. (§§ 9:2422-9:2423)	No. (§§ 9:2422-9:2423)	Procedure for notice shall be the same as for a Louisiana domiciliary. (Code Civ. Pro. § 3401)	No.
Maine	No. But see Table 2.02, Part 2 regarding contesting the will during ancillary proceedings. (18-A § 3-303(d) - informal probate; 18-A § 3-408 - formal probate)	No. But see Table 2.02, Part 2 regarding contesting the will during ancillary proceedings. (18-A § 3-303(d) - informal probate; 18-A § 3-408 - formal probate)	Proof of Domicile is necessary to establish there has been a formal probate (U.P.C. jurisdictions) or solemn form probate (common law jurisdictions) elsewhere. If there has been such probate then there can be only ancillary, and not original probate, if the other probate was at the domicile. That is why proof of domicile is necessary. (18-A §§ 3-408, 3-409)	See Table 2.01, Part 2	No.
Maryland	No.	No.	No.	Yes, but only for real and leasehold property. (Est. & Trusts § 5-503(b)(1))	Because a foreign personal representative is not required to take out letters, it eliminates the usual ancillary procedure. (Est. & Trust § 5-501)

Table 2.02, Part 1
Ancillary Probate

	There Be Proof of No Pending Contest at Domicile?	*There Be Proof That Period for Contesting Will at the Domicile Has Expired?*	*There Be Proof That Decedent Was Domiciled in Other Jurisdiction?*	*All Interested Parties Be Notified?*	*Other Considerations?*
			For Ancillary Probate, Must:		
Massachusetts	No. But see Table 2.02, Part 2 regarding contesting the will during ancillary proceedings. (190B §3-303(d) - informal probate; 190B §3-408 - formal probate)	No. But see Table 2.02, Part 2 regarding contesting the will during ancillary proceedings. (190B §3-303(d) - informal probate; 190B §3-408 - formal probate)	Proof of Domicile is necessary to establish there has been a formal probate (U.P.C. jurisdictions) or solemn form probate (common law jurisdictions) elsewhere. If there has been such probate then there can be only ancillary, and not original probate, if the other probate was at the domicile. That is why proof of domicile is necessary. (190B §§3-408, 3-409)	See Table 2.01, Part 2	No.
Michigan	No. But see Table 2.02, Part 2 regarding contesting the will during ancillary proceedings. (§700.3303(4) - informal probate; §700.3408 - formal probate)	No. But see Table 2.02, Part 2 regarding contesting the will during ancillary proceedings. (§700.3303(4) - informal probate; §700.3408-formal probate)	Proof of Domicile is necessary to establish there has been a formal probate (U.P.C. jurisdictions) or solemn form probate (common law jurisdictions) elsewhere. If there has been such probate then there can be only ancillary, and not original probate, if the other probate was at the domicile. That is why proof of domicile is necessary. (§§700.3408, 700.3409)	See Table 2.01, Part 2	No.
Minnesota	No. But see Table 2.02, Part 2 regarding contesting the will during ancillary proceedings. (§524.3-303(d) - informal probate; §524.3-408-formal probate)	No. But see Table 2.02, Part 2 regarding contesting the will during ancillary proceedings. (§524.3-303(d) - informal probate; §524.3-408 - formal probate)	Proof of Domicile is necessary to establish there has been a formal probate (U.P.C. jurisdictions) or solemn form probate (common law jurisdictions) elsewhere. If there has been such probate then there can be only ancillary, and not original probate, if the other probate was at the domicile. That is why proof of domicile is necessary. (§§524.3-408, 524.3-409)	See Table 2.01, Part 2	No.
Mississippi	Not necessarily, but such may be required if the will is contested, since ancillary probate may be contested as the original might have been. (§91-7-33)	Not necessarily, but such may be required if the will is contested, since ancillary probate may be contested as the original might have been. (§91-7-33)	Not necessarily, but such may be required if the will is contested, since ancillary probate may be contested as the original might have been. (§91-7-33)	No.	Mississippi law will govern, regardless of the decedent's domicile in another state. (§91-1-1)

Table 2.02, Part 1
Ancillary Probate

	For Ancillary Probate, Must:				
	There Be Proof of No Pending Contest at Domicile?	There Be Proof That Period for Contesting Will at the Domicile Has Expired?	There Be Proof That Decedent Was Domiciled in Other Jurisdiction?	All Interested Parties Be Notified?	Other Considerations?
Missouri	No (§ 474.380), but such may be required if the will is contested, since ancillary probate may be contested as wills proved in Missouri. (§ 474.390)	No (§ 474.380), but such may be required if the will is contested, since ancillary probate may be contested as wills proved in Missouri. (§ 474.390)	No (§ 474.380), but such may be required if the will is contested, since ancillary probate may be contested as wills proved in Missouri. (§ 474.390)	Yes. (§ 474.380)	No.
Montana	No. But see Table 2.02, Part 2 regarding contesting the will during ancillary proceedings. (§ 72-3-213(3) - informal probate; § 72-3-312 - formal probate)	No. But see Table 2.02, Part 2 regarding contesting the will during ancillary proceedings. (§ 72-3-213(3) - informal probate; § 72-3-312 - formal probate)	Proof of Domicile is necessary to establish there has been a formal probate (U.P.C. jurisdictions) or solemn form probate (common law jurisdictions) elsewhere. If there has been such probate then there can be only ancillary, and not original probate, if the other probate was at the domicile. That is why proof of domicile is necessary. (§§ 72-3-312, 72-3-316)	See Table 2.01, Part 2	No.
Nebraska	No. But see Table 2.02, Part 2 regarding contesting the will during ancillary proceedings. (§ 30-2416(d) - informal probate; § 30-2432 -formal probate)	No. But see Table 2.02, Part 2 regarding contesting the will during ancillary proceedings. (§ 30-2416(d) - informal probate; § 30-2432 -formal probate)	Proof of Domicile is necessary to establish there has been a formal probate (U.P.C. jurisdictions) or solemn form probate (common law jurisdictions) elsewhere. If there has been such probate then there can be only ancillary, and not original probate, if the other probate was at the domicile. That is why proof of domicile is necessary. (§§ 30-2432, 30-2433)	See Table 2.01, Part 2	Yes. Although largely based on the UPC, Nebraska has a unique reciprocity requirement for formal ancillary probate proceedings. (§ 30-2432) These answers assume this requirement is satisfied.
Nevada	No. (§ 136.260)	No. (§ 136.260)	Implied yes because the court examines the will to ensure that it was executed in accordance with the laws of the state of execution, decedent's domicile, or Nevada. (§ 136.260(3))	Yes. (§ 136.260(2))	No.
New Hampshire	No. (§ 552:13)	No. (§ 552:13)	No. (§ 552:13)	Only as the court shall order. (§ 552:13)	No.
New Jersey	No. (3B:3-27)	No. (3B:3-27)	No. (3B:3-27)	No. (3B:3-27)	No.

Table 2.02, Part 1
Ancillary Probate

For Ancillary Probate, Must:

	There Be Proof of No Pending Contest at Domicile?	There Be Proof That Period for Contesting Will at the Domicile Has Expired?	There Be Proof That Decedent Was Domiciled in Other Jurisdiction?	All Interested Parties Be Notified?	Other Considerations?
New Mexico	No. But see Table 2.02, Part 2 regarding contesting the will during ancillary proceedings. (§45-3-303(D)) - informal probate; §45-3-408 - formal probate)	No. But see Table 2.02, Part 2 regarding contesting the will during ancillary proceedings. (45-3-303(D) - informal probate; §45-3-408 - formal probate)	Proof of Domicile is necessary to establish there has been a formal probate (U.P.C. jurisdictions) or solemn form probate (common law jurisdictions) elsewhere. If there has been such probate then there can be only ancillary, and not original probate, if the other probate was at the domicile. That is why proof of domicile is necessary. (§§45-3-408, 45-3-409)	See Table 2.01, Part 2	No.
New York	Yes. (Surr. Ct. Proc. Act §1602)	Not necessarily, but if the time has not expired, you need proof there is no pending contest at domicile. (Surr. Ct. Proc. Act §§1602)	Yes. (Surr. Ct. Proc. Act §1602(1))	No. (Surr. Ct. Proc. Act §1602)	No.
North Carolina	No, but see the requirements mentioned in Table 2.01, Part I, column 3. (§28A-2A-17)	No, but see the requirements mentioned in Table 2.01, Part I, column 3. (§28A-2A-17)	If challenged, may have to prove, since there is a requirement that for a North Carolina domiciliary, North Carolina has exclusive domiciliary probate. (§28A-26-1)	No special provision.	No.
North Dakota	No. But see Table 2.02, Part 2 regarding contesting the will during ancillary proceedings. (§30.1-14-03(4) - informal probate; §30.1-15-08 - formal probate)	No. But see Table 2.02, Part 2 regarding contesting the will during ancillary proceedings. §30.1-14-03(4) - informal probate; §30.1-15-08 - formal probate)	Proof of Domicile is necessary to establish there has been a formal probate (U.P.C. jurisdictions) or solemn form probate (common law jurisdictions) elsewhere. If there has been such probate then there can be only ancillary, and not original probate, if the other probate was at the domicile. That is why proof of domicile is necessary. (§§30.1-15-08, 30.1-15-09)	See Table 2.01, Part 2	No.
Ohio	No. (§2129.05)	No. (§2129.05)	No. (§2129.05)	No. (§2129.05)	Provision for notification is made only if the will was probated in a U.S. territory or foreign country. (§2129.07)
Oklahoma	No. (58 §52)	No. (58 §52)	No. (58 §52)	Yes. (58 §52)	No.

Table 2.02, Part 1
Ancillary Probate

	For Ancillary Probate, Must:				
	There Be Proof of No Pending Contest at Domicile?	There Be Proof That Period for Contesting Will at the Domicile Has Expired?	There Be Proof That Decedent Was Domiciled in Other Jurisdiction?	All Interested Parties Be Notified?	Other Considerations?
Oregon	No. Wills proved outside the U.S. may require the evidence discussed here to be proved. (§ 113.065)	No. Wills proved outside the U.S. may require the evidence discussed here to be proved. (§ 113.065)	No. (§ 113.065)	No. (§ 113.065)	No.
Pennsylvania	No. (20 § 3136)	No. (20 § 3136)	No.	No.	Wills proved outside the U.S. may require the evidence discussed here to be proved. (20 § 3136)
Rhode Island	No. (§§ 33-7-18, 33-7-20)	No. (§§ 33-7-18, 33-7-20)	No. (§§ 33-7-18, 33-7-20)	Yes. (§ 33-7-19)	The proof discussed here may be required if cause is shown at the probate hearing. (§ 33-7-20)
South Carolina	No. But see Table 2.02, Part 2 regarding contesting the will during ancillary proceedings. (§ 62-3-303(d) - informal probate; § 62-3-408 - formal probate)	No. But see Table 2.02, Part 2 regarding contesting the will during ancillary proceedings. § 62-3-303(d) - informal probate; § 62-3-408-formal probate)	Proof of Domicile is necessary to establish there has been a formal probate (U.P.C. jurisdictions) or solemn form probate (common law jurisdictions) elsewhere. If there has been such probate then there can be only ancillary, and not original probate, if the other probate was at the domicile. That is why proof of domicile is necessary. (§§ 62-3-408, 62-3-409)	See Table 2.01, Part 2	No
South Dakota	No. But see Table 2.02, Part 2 regarding contesting the will during ancillary proceedings. (§ 29A-3-303(d) - informal probate; § 29A-3-408 - formal probate)	No. But see Table 2.02, Part 2 regarding contesting the will during ancillary proceedings. § 29A-3-303(d) - informal probate; § 29A-3-408 - formal probate)	Proof of Domicile is necessary to establish there has been a formal probate (U.P.C. jurisdictions) or solemn form probate (common law jurisdictions) elsewhere. If there has been such probate then there can be only ancillary, and not original probate, if the other probate was at the domicile. That is why proof of domicile is necessary. (§§ 29A-3-408, 29A-3-409)	See Table 2.01, Part 2	No.
Tennessee	No. (§§ 32-5-103, 32-5-104)	No. (§§ 32-5-103, 32-5-104)	No. (§§ 32-5-103, 32-5-104)	Yes, if probate is in solemn form. (§ 32-5-103)	The will may be contested at a hearing for solemn form probate. If it is, the proof discussed here may be required. (§ 32-5-104)
Texas	No. (§ 501.002)	No. (§ 501.002)	No. (§ 501.002)	No, unless first probate was not at domicile. (§ 501.003)	No.

Table 2.02, Part 1
Ancillary Probate

	For Ancillary Probate, Must:				
	There Be Proof of No Pending Contest at Domicile?	*There Be Proof That Period for Contesting Will at the Domicile Has Expired?*	*There Be Proof That Decedent Was Domiciled in Other Jurisdiction?*	*All Interested Parties Be Notified?*	*Other Considerations?*
Utah	No. But see Table 2.02, Part 2 regarding contesting the will during ancillary proceedings. (§75-3-303(4) - informal probate; §75-3-408 - formal probate)	No. But see Table 2.02, Part 2 regarding contesting the will during ancillary proceedings. §75-3-303(4) - informal probate; §75-3-408 - formal probate)	Proof of Domicile is necessary to establish there has been a formal probate (U.P.C. jurisdictions) or solemn form probate (common law jurisdictions) elsewhere. If there has been such probate then there can be only ancillary, and not original probate, if the other probate was at the domicile. That is why proof of domicile is necessary. (§§75-3-408, 75-3-409)	See Table 2.01, Part 2	No.
Vermont	No. (14 §114)	No. (14 §114)	No. (14 §114)	Yes. (14 §114(b))	If the will is contested, or its probate at the hearing for probate in Vermont, the proof discussed may be required. (14 §114(b))
Virginia	No. (§64.2-450)	No.	There is a rebuttable presumption that domicile was in the original probate jurisdiction. (§64.2-450)	No. (§64.2-450)	No.
Washington	No. (§11.20.090)	No. (§11.20.090)	No. (§11.20.090)	No. (§11.20.090)	No.
West Virginia	No. (§41-5-13)	No. (§41-5-13)	No. (§41-5-13)	No. (§41-5-13)	There is a presumption that domicile was in the original probate jurisdiction for a will of personalty. (§41-5-13)
Wisconsin	Yes. (§868.01(1))	No. (§868.01)	Yes. (§868.01(1) & (6))	No. (§868.01)	No.
Wyoming	No. (§2-11-104)	No. (§2-11-104)	No. (§2-11-104)	No. (§2-11-104)	No. (§2-11-104)

[1] Note: No ancillary probate is necessary. No letters are required to be obtained. If Table 2.01, *What proof is required to establish a will already proved in another estate?*, is complied with, foreign personal representative can act just like a local personal representative who has been duly appointed. (§20-341)

Table 2.02, Part 2
Ancillary Probate

	Can a Will Be Contested in the Ancillary Proceeding?	At What Point in Ancillary Proceedings Can Property Be Transmitted to the Domiciliary Personal Representative?	Will Letters Be Issued to Person Named in Will, Although That person Is Not the Domiciliary Personal Representative?	If No Other Person is Named in the Will, is the Domiciliary Personal Representative Entitled to Letters in the Ancillary Probate Jurisdiction?
Alabama	Yes, except if already probated elsewhere. (§43-8-175; Carter v. Davis, 154 So. 2d 9 (1963))	No provision.	Only if they are Alabama residents (§43-2-22), and the named executor renounces appointment or fails to file within 30 days after probate. (§43-2-26)	Yes. (§43-2-192)
Alaska	No (§13.16.090(d) - informal; §13.16.175 - formal), unless original probate was informal and ancillary probate will be formal. (§13.16.140(b))	After payment of claims locally. (§13.16.520(c)) With regard to debts, personal property, or instrument evidencing debt, obligation, stock, or chose in action, payment or transfer can be made directly to domiciliary personal representative after 60 days following death, if proof of appointment of domiciliary personal representative and affidavit stating: date of death, that no local administration is pending or has been applied for, and that domiciliary personal representative is entitled to payment or delivery. Transfer of securities is covered by §3 of Uniform Act for Simplification of Fiduciary Security Transfers. (§13.21.015 & U.P.C. §4201 cmt.¹) However, cannot make any of these transfers if notified not to do so by local creditors of decedent. (§13.21.025)	Yes, if the will so specifies. (§13.16.065(g))	Yes. (§13.16.065(g))

Table 2.02, Part 2
Ancillary Probate

	Can a Will Be Contested in the Ancillary Proceeding?	At What Point in Ancillary Proceedings Can Property Be Transmitted to the Domiciliary Personal Representative?	Will Letters Be Issued to Person Named in Will, Although That person Is Not the Domiciliary Personal Representative?	If No Other Person is Named in the Will, is the Domiciliary Personal Representative Entitled to Letters in the Ancillary Probate Jurisdiction?
Arizona	No (§ 14-3303(D) - informal; § 14-3408-formal), unless original probate was informal and ancillary probate will be formal. (§ 14-3401(B))	After payment of claims locally. (§ 14-3815(C)) With regard to debts, personal property, or instrument evidencing debt, obligation, stock, or chose in action, payment or transfer can be made directly to domiciliary personal representative after 60 days following death, if proof of appointment of domiciliary personal representative and affidavit stating: date of death, that no local administration is pending or has been applied for, and that domiciliary personal representative is entitled to payment or delivery. Transfer of securities is covered by § 3 of Uniform Act for Simplification of Fiduciary Security Transfers. (§ 14-4201 & U.P.C. § 4201 cmt.²) However, cannot make any of these transfers if notified not to do so by local creditors of decedent. (§ 14-4203)	Yes. (§ 14-3203(G))	Yes. (§ 14-3203(G))
Arkansas	Yes, but only when the grounds of objection are filed within the specified time periods. (§ 28-40-113(b); Schweitzer v. Bean, 242 S.W. 63 (1922))	Prior to the final disposition of the ancillary estate, the domiciliary personal representative may apply to remove assets from Arkansas. An issuance of a bond may be required. The application may or may not be granted at the court's discretion. (§§ 28-42-106, 28-42-109)	Yes, but preference will be given to the domiciliary personal representative, who will be notified and can object. However, the court retains discretion to act in the best interests of the estate. (§§ 28-42-102(b) & (c), 28-42-105(a) & (b))	Any interested person may apply. Domiciliary personal representative will be notified and can object. Preference is given to the domiciliary personal representative. (§§ 28-42-102(b) & (c), 28-42-105(a))

Table 2.02, Part 2
Ancillary Probate

	Can a Will Be Contested in the Ancillary Proceeding?	At What Point in Ancillary Proceedings Can Property Be Transmitted to the Domiciliary Personal Representative?	Will Letters Be Issued to Person Named in Will, Although That person Is Not the Domiciliary Personal Representative?	If No Other Person is Named in the Will, is the Domiciliary Personal Representative Entitled to Letters in the Ancillary Probate Jurisdiction?
California	Only if the sister state did not find the decedent domiciled in the sister state, one or more interested parties were not given notice and an opportunity to contest in the sister state, or the determination of the sister state is not final. (Prob. § 12522)	Representative may petition court for preliminary or final distribution of all or a part of decedent's personal property. (Prob. §§ 11600, 12540(a)) Preliminary distribution may not be made unless two months have elapsed, there is no injury to interested parties, and bond required by the court is filed. (Prob. §§ 11620, 11621) Final distribution may not be ordered unless the estate is in a condition to be closed. (Prob. § 11640) In all cases, the judge must determine the distribution is in the best interest of the estate or interested persons. (Prob. § 12540(a))	Yes. (Prob. § 12513)	Yes, the domiciliary personal representative has priority over all other persons, except where the decedent's will nominates a different person to be the personal representative for California. (Prob. § 12513)
Colorado	No (§ 15-12-303(4) - informal; § 15-12-408 - formal), unless original probate was informal and ancillary probate will be formal. (§ 15-12-401(2))	After payment of claims locally. (§ 15-12-815(3)) With regard to debts, personal property, or instrument evidencing debt, obligation, stock, or chose in action, payment or transfer can be made directly to domiciliary personal representative after 60 days following death, if proof of appointment of domiciliary personal representative and affidavit stating: date of death; that no local administration is pending or has been applied for; and that domiciliary personal representative is entitled to payment or delivery. Transfer of securities is covered by § 3 of Uniform Act for Simplification of Fiduciary Security Transfers. (§ 15-13-201 & U.P.C. § 4-201 cmt.[3]) However, cannot make any of these transfers if notified not to do so by local creditors of decedent. (§ 15-13-203)	Yes. (§ 15-12-203(7))	Yes. (§ 15-12-203(7))
Connecticut	Yes. (§ 45a-288(a) & (c))	No provision.	No provision.	No provision.
Delaware	Only where will is not already probated in another state. (12 § 1307)	60 days after decedent's death, if presented with proof of appointment and an appropriate affidavit. (12 § 1562)	Implied yes. (12 § 1502(a))	Implied yes. (12 § 1502(a))

Table 2.02, Part 2
Ancillary Probate

	Can a Will Be Contested in the Ancillary Proceeding?	At What Point in Ancillary Proceedings Can Property Be Transmitted to the Domiciliary Personal Representative?	Will Letters Be Issued to Person Named in Will, Although That person Is Not the Domiciliary Personal Representative?	If No Other Person is Named in the Will, is the Domiciliary Personal Representative Entitled to Letters in the Ancillary Probate Jurisdiction?
District of Columbia	Yes, after a foreign personal representative publishes the required materials regarding his appointment (§ 20-343), any person may file a complaint. (§ 20-305)	Personal or leasehold property may be removed, leased, or transferred if: (a) after the first publication of notice such representative holds letters from (1) a jurisdiction within the metropolitan area, (2) a jurisdiction outside the metropolitan area and such representative posts a bond; or (b) six months after the first publication of notice (1) no claims are filed or (2) all claims have been released or finally determined in favor of the personal representative. (§ 20-343(b)) Real property may be leased or transferred if the personal representative: (a) posts bond or, (b) allows six months to pass after the first publication and either no claims are filed or all claims have been released or finally determined in favor of the personal representative. (§ 20-343(c)) In the event of a failure of the personal representative to transfer the real or leasehold property in a reasonable time, the Court may order this if (a) the will or an authenticated copy is filed in the Register's Office, (b) notice has been published as specified indicating the property the decedent owned, and (c) all claims of creditors have been satisfied. (§ 20-344)	Yes. (§ 20-303)	No letters are needed. (§ 20-341(a)) The information set forth in Table 2.01, Part 1 must be filed.

Table 2.02, Part 2
Ancillary Probate

	Can a Will Be Contested in the Ancillary Proceeding?	At What Point in Ancillary Proceedings Can Property Be Transmitted to the Domiciliary Personal Representative?	Will Letters Be Issued to Person Named in Will, Although That person Is Not the Domiciliary Personal Representative?	If No Other Person is Named in the Will, is the Domiciliary Personal Representative Entitled to Letters in the Ancillary Probate Jurisdiction?
Florida	Not by an interested person who was notified or appeared in proceeding in another state and did not challenge its domiciliary status. If a person was not bound by earlier proceeding, however, he could claim the decedent had a Florida domicile. See Lowenthal v. Mandell, 170 So. 169 (1936). If the person is shown to be a Florida domiciliary, the will can be challenged locally as if it were admitted for original probate in Florida. (§733.206(3)) See also Table 2.01, Part 1.	After the payment of expenses of administration and claims against the estate. (§734.102(6)) If the claimant is from the domiciliary state, it cannot seek to reach assets under ancillary administration in Florida if the time for making claims in Florida, generally two years after the decedent's death, has expired. (§733.710 (1)) (Staum v. Russo, 120 So. 3d 109 (Dist. Ct. App. 2013)) However, the claimant is still an interested person and, thus, could seek an accounting and a transfer of the remaining ancillary assets to the New York domiciliary representative to satisfy claims against the still pending New York estate. Alternatively, the statute allows distribution to the beneficiaries. (§734.102(6)) This would bypass the domiciliary estate and make the assets more difficult to reach by creditors.	Yes. (§734.102(1)) But see §733.304 as to which nonresidents qualify.	Yes. (§734.102(1)) However, if not qualified to act, then an alternate or successor named in will and qualified to act is entitled to letters. If there are no such persons, then "those entitled to a majority interest of the Florida property may have letters issued to a personal representative selected by them and who is qualified to act in Florida." A special rule applies to cases of intestacy. See also §733.304 as to which nonresidents qualify.
Georgia	Yes. (§53-5-33(b) & (c))	The general rules for a domiciliary personal representative apply, although a court may order after notice to heirs, beneficiaries, and creditors that distribution may only be made after payment to heirs, beneficiaries, and creditors "residing or situated" in Georgia. (§53-5-41)	Yes. (§53-5-37)	Yes, "in the absence of an objection," or failure to qualify within a "reasonable time." If "good cause" to the objection is found, then an administrator c.t.a. who qualifies under Georgia law will be appointed. (§53-5-37)

Table 2.02, Part 2
Ancillary Probate

	Can a Will Be Contested in the Ancillary Proceeding?	At What Point in Ancillary Proceedings Can Property Be Transmitted to the Domiciliary Personal Representative?	Will Letters Be Issued to Person Named in Will, Although That person Is Not the Domiciliary Personal Representative?	If No Other Person is Named in the Will, is the Domiciliary Personal Representative Entitled to Letters in the Ancillary Probate Jurisdiction?
Hawaii	No (§560:3-303(d) - informal; §560:3-408; C- formal), unless original probate was informal and ancillary probate will be formal. (§560:3-401(b))	After payment of claims locally. (§560:3-815(c)) With regard to debts, personal property, or instrument evidencing debt, obligation, stock, or chose in action, payment or transfer can be made directly to domiciliary personal representative after 60 days following death, if proof of appointment of domiciliary personal representative and affidavit stating; date of death, that no local administration is pending or has been applied for, and that domiciliary personal representative is entitled to payment or delivery. Transfer of securities is covered by §3 of Uniform Act for Simplification of Fiduciary Security Transfers. (§560:4-201 & U.P.C. §4-201 cmt.[4]) However, cannot make any of these transfers if notified not to do so by local creditors of decedent. (§560:4-203)	Yes. (§560:3-203(g))	Yes. (§560:3-203(g))
Idaho	No (§15-3-303(d) - informal; §15-3-408 - formal), unless original probate was informal and ancillary probate will be formal. (§15-3-401(b))	After payment of claims locally. (§15-3-815(c)) With regard to debts, personal property, or instrument evidencing debt, obligation, stock, or chose in action, payment or transfer can be made directly to domiciliary personal representative after 60 days following death, if proof of appointment of domiciliary personal representative and affidavit stating; date of death, that no local administration is pending or has been applied for, and that domiciliary personal representative is entitled to payment or delivery. Transfer of securities is covered by §3 of Uniform Act for Simplification of Fiduciary Security Transfers. (§15-4-201 & cmt.) However, cannot make any of these transfers if notified not to do so by local creditors of decedent. (§15-4-203)	Yes. (§15-3-203(g))	Yes. (§15-3-203(g))

Table 2.02, Part 2
Ancillary Probate

	Can a Will Be Contested in the Ancillary Proceeding?	At What Point in Ancillary Proceedings Can Property Be Transmitted to the Domiciliary Personal Representative?	Will Letters Be Issued to Person Named in Will, Although That person Is Not the Domiciliary Personal Representative?	If No Other Person is Named in the Will, is the Domiciliary Personal Representative Entitled to Letters in the Ancillary Probate Jurisdiction?
Illinois	Yes. (755 ILCS §5/8-1(a))	When the representative delivers: (a) an affidavit from the representative stating he or she has no knowledge of outstanding letters in the state of a petition for letter, and there are no creditors of the estate in the state; and (b) a copy of his or her letters certified within the past 60 days. (755 ILCS §5/22-1)	Yes. (755 ILCS §§5/6-8, 5/7-5)	Yes. (755 ILCS §§5/6-8, 5/7-5)
Indiana	Yes. (§29-1-7-29)	No provision.	Yes. (§29-1-10-1)	Yes. (§29-1-10-1)
Iowa	Yes. (§633.310) However, this may not be the case if the will has already been probated elsewhere. (§633.496)	The court may require payment of all claims filed and allowed belonging to residents of Iowa, and all legacies and distributive shares payable to residents of Iowa, before allowing the property to be removed. (§633.504)	Implied yes. (§633.63)	Yes, and a resident personal representative will also be appointed to serve with the domiciliary personal representative unless good cause is shown that the domiciliary personal representative should act alone. (§§633.502, 633.64)
Kansas	Yes, because proceeding is considered original, not ancillary. (§§59-804, 59-2224)	All probate proceedings are original, not ancillary. (§59-804)	Yes. (§59-701)	Yes. (§§59-701, 59-1707)
Kentucky	Implied yes. The court presumes validity of will in the absence of evidence to the contrary. Therefore, it appears evidence may be brought in to contest the will. (§394.150)	After the payment of debts to Kentucky citizens. (§395.260)	Yes; however, any nonresident must be related by consanguinity, marriage, or adoption or be the spouse of such person so related to the decedent, ward, or incompetent. (§§395.020, 395.005(3))	Yes; however, any nonresident must be related by consanguinity, marriage, or adoption or be the spouse of such person so related to the decedent, ward, or incompetent. (§§395.020, 395.005(3)) See also §395.170, allowing nonresident executors to prosecute actions by giving bond.
Louisiana	Yes, except form and mode of execution. These persons may not have been parties to the foreign probate. (Shimshak v. Cox, 116 So. 714 (1928))	Not specified.	Yes, unless they are disqualified. (Code Civ. Pro. §3082; see §3097 for disqualifications.)	Yes, after qualifying with the court (Code Civ. Pro. §3402), if they appoint a resident agent (Code Civ. Pro. §3097(a)(4)).

Table 2.02, Part 2
Ancillary Probate

	Can a Will Be Contested in the Ancillary Proceeding?	At What Point in Ancillary Proceedings Can Property Be Transmitted to the Domiciliary Personal Representative?	Will Letters Be Issued to Person Named in Will, Although That person Is Not the Domiciliary Personal Representative?	If No Other Person is Named in the Will, is the Domiciliary Personal Representative Entitled to Letters in the Ancillary Probate Jurisdiction?
Maine	Yes, except if there is a final order of a court of another state determining testacy, due process requirements were met, and the decedent was domiciled there. (18-A § 3-408)	After payment of claims locally. (18-A § 3-815(c)) With regard to debts, personal property, or instrument evidencing debt, obligation, stock, or chose in action, payment or transfer can be made directly to domiciliary personal representative after 60 days following death, if proof of appointment of domiciliary personal representative and affidavit stating: date of death, that no local administration is pending or has been applied for, and that domiciliary personal representative is entitled to payment or delivery. Transfer of securities is covered by § 3 of Uniform Act for Simplification of Fiduciary Security Transfers. (18-A § 4-201 & cmt.) However, cannot make any of these transfers if notified not to do so by local creditors of decedent. (18-A § 4-203)	Yes. (18-A § 3-203(g))	Yes. (18-A § 3-203(g))
Maryland	No, because Maryland has effectively dispensed with ancillary proceedings since the personal representative may act without prior court authorization. (Est. & Trusts §§ 5-501, 5-502)	At any point presumably, since there are no ancillary proceedings and the foreign representative may act without prior court authorization. (Est. & Trusts §§ 5-501, 5-502)	Yes. (Est. & Trusts § 5-105)	A foreign representative is not required to take out letters in Maryland. (Est. & Trusts § 5-501)

Table 2.02, Part 2
Ancillary Probate

	Can a Will Be Contested in the Ancillary Proceeding?	At What Point in Ancillary Proceedings Can Property Be Transmitted to the Domiciliary Personal Representative?	Will Letters Be Issued to Person Named in Will, Although That person Is Not the Domiciliary Personal Representative?	If No Other Person is Named in the Will, is the Domiciliary Personal Representative Entitled to Letters in the Ancillary Probate Jurisdiction?
Massachusetts	No (190B § 3-303(d) - informal; 190B §§ 3-408- formal), unless original probate was informal and ancillary probate will be formal. (190B § 3-401(b))	After payment of claims locally. (190B § 3-815) With regard to debts, personal property, or instrument evidencing debt, obligation, stock, or chose in action, payment, or transfer can be made directly to domiciliary personal representative after 60 days following death, if proof of appointment of domiciliary personal representative and affidavit stating; date of death, that no local administration is pending or has been applied for, and that domiciliary personal representative is entitled to payment or delivery. Transfer of securities is covered by § 3 of Uniform Act for Simplification of Fiduciary Security Transfers. (190B § 4-201) However, cannot make any of these transfers if notified not to do so by local creditors of decedent. (190B § 4-203)	Yes. (190B § 3-203(g))	Yes. (190B § 3-203(g))
Michigan	No (§700.3303(4) - informal; §700.3408 - formal), unless original probate was informal and ancillary probate will be formal. (§700.3401(2))	After payment of claims locally. (§700.3815(3)) With regard to debts, personal property, or instrument evidencing debt, obligation, stock, or chose in action, payment or transfer can be made directly to domiciliary personal representative after 63 days following death, if proof of appointment of domiciliary personal representative and affidavit stating; date of death, that no local administration is pending or has been applied for, and that domiciliary personal representative is entitled to payment or delivery. (§700.4201 & U.P.C. §4-201 cmt.[5])	Yes. (§700.3203(1)(a))	Yes. (§700.3203(1)(a))

Table 2.02, Part 2
Ancillary Probate

	Can a Will Be Contested in the Ancillary Proceeding?	At What Point in Ancillary Proceedings Can Property Be Transmitted to the Domiciliary Personal Representative?	Will Letters Be Issued to Person Named in Will, Although That person Is Not the Domiciliary Personal Representative?	If No Other Person is Named in the Will, is the Domiciliary Personal Representative Entitled to Letters in the Ancillary Probate Jurisdiction?
Minnesota	No (§ 524.3-303(d) - informal; § 524.3-408 - formal), unless original probate was informal and ancillary probate will be formal. (§ 524.3-401(b))	After payment of claims locally. (§ 524.3-815(c)) With regard to debts, personal property, or instrument evidencing debt, obligation, stock, or chose in action, payment or transfer can be made directly to domiciliary personal representative after 60 days following death, if proof of appointment of domiciliary personal representative and affidavit stating; date of death, that no local administration is pending or has been applied for, and that domiciliary personal representative is entitled to payment or delivery. Transfer of securities is covered by § 3 of Uniform Act for Simplification of Fiduciary Security Transfers. (§ 524.4-201 & U.P.C. § 4-201 cmt.⁶) However, cannot make any of these transfers if notified not to do so by local creditors of decedent. (§ 524.4-203)	Yes. (§ 524.3-203(g))	Yes. (§ 524.3-203(g))
Mississippi	Yes. (§ 91-7-33)	Not specified, but there are penalties for removing property from the state. (§ 91-7-257)	Yes. (§ 91-7-35)	Yes. (§ 91-7-35)
Missouri	Yes. (§ 474.390)	60 days after death, if no demand has been made by someone authorized in this state. (§ 473.691)	Yes. (§ 473.678)	Yes, assuming there is no local administration pending. (§ 473.676)

Table 2.02, Part 2
Ancillary Probate

	Can a Will Be Contested in the Ancillary Proceeding?	At What Point in Ancillary Proceedings Can Property Be Transmitted to the Domiciliary Personal Representative?	Will Letters Be Issued to Person Named in Will, Although That person Is Not the Domiciliary Personal Representative?	If No Other Person is Named in the Will, is the Domiciliary Personal Representative Entitled to Letters in the Ancillary Probate Jurisdiction?
Montana	No (§72-3-213(3) - informal; §72-3-312 - formal), unless original probate was informal and ancillary probate will be formal. (§72-3-302(3))	After payment of claims locally. (§72-3-821(3)) With regard to debts, personal property, or instrument evidencing debt, obligation, stock, or chose in action, payment or transfer can be made directly to domiciliary personal representative after 60 days following death, if proof of appointment of domiciliary personal representative and affidavit stating: date of death; that no local administration is pending or has been applied for; and that domiciliary personal representative is entitled to payment or delivery. Transfer of securities is covered by § 3 of Uniform Act for Simplification of Fiduciary Security Transfers. (§72-4-306 & U.P.C. § 4-201 cmt.) However, cannot make any of these transfers if notified not to do so by local creditors of decedent. (§72-4-308)	Yes. (§72-3-506)	Yes. (§72-3-506)
Nebraska	No (§30-2416(d) - informal; § 30-2432-formal), unless original probate was informal and ancillary probate will be formal. (§30-2425) The foregoing applies if there is a reciprocal provision in the domicile state.	After payment of claims locally. (§30-2497(c)) With regard to debts, personal property, or instrument evidencing debt, obligation, stock, or chose in action, payment or transfer can be made directly to domiciliary personal representative after 60 days following death, if proof of appointment of domiciliary personal representative and affidavit stating: date of death; that no local administration is pending or has been applied for; and that domiciliary personal representative is entitled to payment or delivery. (§ 30-2502) Transfer of securities is covered elsewhere. (U.P.C. § 4-201 & cmt.) However, cannot make any of these transfers if notified not to do so by local creditors of decedent. (§ 30-2504)	Yes. (§ 30-2412(g))	Yes. (§ 30-2412(g))

Table 2.02, Part 2
Ancillary Probate

	Can a Will Be Contested in the Ancillary Proceeding?	At What Point in Ancillary Proceedings Can Property Be Transmitted to the Domiciliary Personal Representative?	Will Letters Be Issued to Person Named in Will, Although That person Is Not the Domiciliary Personal Representative?	If No Other Person is Named in the Will, is the Domiciliary Personal Representative Entitled to Letters in the Ancillary Probate Jurisdiction?
Nevada	Implied yes, since there is a hearing. (§ 136.260)	Not specified, but the personal representative generally has a right to possession of decedent's property (§143.020), and a duty to take possession. (§ 143.030)	Yes. (§§ 138.010(1), 138.020)	Yes. (§§ 138.010(1), 138.020)
New Hampshire	Yes, implied. (§ 552:14)	Not specified.	Yes. (§ 553:2)	Yes, if the domiciliary personal representative was named in the will (§553:2), and appoints a resident agent. (§ 553:25)
New Jersey	Implied yes. (§ 3B:3-28)	Not specified. (§ 3B:23-42)	Implied yes. (§ 3B:23-42)	Yes, provided letters have not been issued in New Jersey or an action for letters is not pending in New Jersey. (§§ 3B:14-28, 3B:14-29)
New Mexico	No. (§ 45-3-303(D) - informal; § 45-3-408 - formal), unless original probate was informal and ancillary probate will be formal. (§ 45-3-401(B))	After payment of claims locally. (§ 45-3-815(C)) With regard to debts, personal property, or instrument evidencing debt, obligation, stock, or chose in action, payment or transfer can be made directly to domiciliary personal representative after 60 days following death, if proof of appointment of domiciliary personal representative and affidavit stating: date of death, that no local administration is pending or has been applied for, and that domiciliary personal representative is entitled to payment or delivery. Transfer of securities is covered by § 3 of Uniform Act for Simplification of Fiduciary Security Transfers. (§ 45-4-201 & U.P.C. § 4-201 cmt.) However, cannot make any of these transfers if notified not to do so by local creditors of decedent. (§ 45-4-203)	Yes. (§ 45-3-203(G))	Yes. (§ 45-3-203(G))
New York	Yes, but only on the grounds that the foreign proof requirements have not been satisfied or that the will has been denied probate in New York. (Surr. Ct. Proc. Act § 1602(2))	As per Surr. Ct. Proc. Act § 1603. See Table 2.02, Part 1. However, the court may have ordered direct distribution after payment of local and other creditors. (Surr. Ct. Proc. Act § 1610)	Yes. (Surr. Ct. Proc. Act § 1604(1)(a))	Yes. (Surr. Ct. Proc. Act § 1604(1)(b) & (c)

Table 2.02, Part 2
Ancillary Probate

	Can a Will Be Contested in the Ancillary Proceeding?	At What Point in Ancillary Proceedings Can Property Be Transmitted to the Domiciliary Personal Representative?	Will Letters Be Issued to Person Named in Will, Although That person Is Not the Domiciliary Personal Representative?	If No Other Person is Named in the Will, is the Domiciliary Personal Representative Entitled to Letters in the Ancillary Probate Jurisdiction?
North Carolina	Yes. § 28A-3-1(2) affords the jurisdiction. A decision under the prior law anticipates availability of caveat procedure. (See In re Mark's Will, 259 N.C. 326, 331-32, 130 S.E.2d 673, 677 (1963))	With regard to debts, personal property, or instrument evidencing debt, obligation, stock, or chose in action, payment or transfer can be made directly to domiciliary personal representative after 60 days following death, if proof of appointment of domiciliary personal representative and affidavit stating: date of death, that no local administration is pending or has been applied for, and that domiciliary personal representative is entitled to payment or delivery. (§ 28A-26-2(a)) However, cannot make any of these transfers if notified not to do so by local creditors of decedent. (§ 28A-26-2(c)) Payment of claims must be made before the property can be transferred to the domiciliary personal representative. (§ 28A-26-9)	Implied yes. (§§ 28A-26-1, 28A-26-3)	Yes. (§ 28A-26-3(a)) Note that domiciliary personal representative may be substituted once appointed, even though local representative was previously serving. (§ 28A-26-3(b)) A local representative can be appointed if application for local appointment is not made by the domiciliary personal representative within 60 days of issuance of domiciliary letters or, if shorter, 90 days after the death of the decedent. (Id.) To be appointed, the domiciliary personal representative must present a certified or exemplified copy of letters to the county clerk of the superior court. (§ 28A-26-3(a))
North Dakota	No. (§ 30.1-14-03(4) - informal; § 30.1-15-08 - formal), unless original probate was informal and ancillary probate will be formal. (§ 30.1-15-01(2))	After payment of claims locally. (§ 30.1-19-15(3)) With regard to debts, personal property, or instrument evidencing debt, obligation, stock, or chose in action, payment or transfer can be made directly to domiciliary personal representative after 60 days following death, if proof of appointment of domiciliary personal representative and affidavit stating: date of death; that no local administration is pending or has been applied for; and that domiciliary personal representative is entitled to payment or delivery. Transfer of securities is covered by § 3 of Uniform Act for Simplification of Fiduciary Security Transfers. (§ 30.1-24-02 & cmt.) However, cannot make any of these transfers if notified not to do so by local creditors of decedent. (§ 30.1-24-04)	Yes. (§ 30.1-13-03(7))	Yes. (§ 30.1-13-03(7))

Table 2.02, Part 2
Ancillary Probate

	Can a Will Be Contested in the Ancillary Proceeding?	At What Point in Ancillary Proceedings Can Property Be Transmitted to the Domiciliary Personal Representative?	Will Letters Be Issued to Person Named in Will, Although That person Is Not the Domiciliary Personal Representative?	If No Other Person is Named in the Will, is the Domiciliary Personal Representative Entitled to Letters in the Ancillary Probate Jurisdiction?
Ohio	No, if probated in another state. (§ 2129.05; Jones v. Robinson, 17 Ohio St. 171 (1867)); yes, if not proved elsewhere and involving Ohio real property (Thomas v. Taylor, 2001 WL 992086 (Ct. App. Aug. 31, 2001)).	Not specified, but prior to filing a final account, the ancillary administrator shall file an application for a certificate of transfer for real estate. (§ 2129.19)	Yes, provided that person meets the Ohio qualifications in § 2109.21(B)(2).	Yes, provided that person meets the Ohio qualifications in § 2109.21(B)(2).
Oklahoma	Implied yes because admitting a foreign will to probate has the same force and effect as a will first admitted to probate in Oklahoma, and Oklahoma allows for contest of wills of the probate. (58 §§ 53, 61)	After final settlement of the administrative accounts, an application must be filed and the court determines whether it is in the best interest of the estate. (58 § 633)	Yes. (58 § 101)	Yes. (58 § 101)
Oregon	Yes, if it would be grounds for rejection in Oregon. (§ 113.065(2))	When administration has been completed and the estate is in a condition to be distributed. (§ 116.163)	Yes. (§ 113.085(1)(a))	Yes. (§ 113.085(1)(a))
Pennsylvania	Yes, with respect to wills already probated outside the U.S. (20 § 3136) As for domestic wills, the contestant can challenge the will authenticated in another state if the decedent's domicile is shown to have been in Pennsylvania. See, e.g., In re Salwaroski's Estate, 37 Northam. 18 (1963)	Not specified. See 20 § 3311.	Yes. (20 § 3155)	Yes. (20 § 3155)
Rhode Island	Yes, by showing cause why the will should not be filed and recorded. (§ 33-7-19)	Not specified.	May issue letters to the named executor. (§ 33-7-21)	May issue letters to the named executor. (§ 33-7-21)

Table 2.02, Part 2
Ancillary Probate

	Can a Will Be Contested in the Ancillary Proceeding?	At What Point in Ancillary Proceedings Can Property Be Transmitted to the Domiciliary Personal Representative?	Will Letters Be Issued to Person Named in Will, Although That person Is Not the Domiciliary Personal Representative?	If No Other Person is Named in the Will, is the Domiciliary Personal Representative Entitled to Letters in the Ancillary Probate Jurisdiction?
South Carolina	No. (§ 62-3-303(d) - informal; § 62-3-403 formal), unless original probate was informal and ancillary probate will be formal. (§ 62-3-401)	After payment of claims locally. (§ 62-3-815(c)) With regard to debts, personal property, or instrument evidencing debt, obligation, stock, or chose in action, payment or transfer can be made directly to domiciliary personal representative after 60 days following death, if proof of appointment of domiciliary personal representative and affidavit stating: date of death, that no local administration is pending or has been applied for, and that domiciliary personal representative is entitled to payment or delivery. Transfer of securities is covered by § 3 of Uniform Act for Simplification of Fiduciary Security Transfers. (§ 62-4-201 & cmt.) However, cannot make any of these transfers if notified not to do so by local creditors of decedent. (§ 62-4-203)	Yes. (§ 62-3-203(f)	Yes. (§ 62-3-203(f)
South Dakota	No. § 29A-3-303(d) - informal; § 29A-3-408 - formal), unless original probate was informal and ancillary probate will be formal. § 29A-3-401(b)	After payment of claims locally. (§ 29A-3-815(c)) With regard to debts, personal property, or instrument evidencing debt, obligation, stock, or chose in action, payment or transfer can be made directly to domiciliary personal representative after 60 days following death, if proof of appointment of domiciliary personal representative and affidavit stating: date of death; that no local administration is pending or has been applied for; and that domiciliary personal representative is entitled to payment or delivery. Transfer of securities is covered by § 3 of Uniform Act for Simplification of Fiduciary Security Transfers. (§ 29A-4-201 & U.P.C. § 4-201 cmt.) However, cannot make any of these transfers if notified not to do so by local creditors of decedent. (§ 29A-4-203)	Yes. (§ 29A-3-203(g))	Yes. (§ 29A-3-203(g))

Table 2.02, Part 2
Ancillary Probate

	Can a Will Be Contested in the Ancillary Proceeding?	At What Point in Ancillary Proceedings Can Property Be Transmitted to the Domiciliary Personal Representative?	Will Letters Be Issued to Person Named in Will, Although That person Is Not the Domiciliary Personal Representative?	If No Other Person is Named in the Will, is the Domiciliary Personal Representative Entitled to Letters in the Ancillary Probate Jurisdiction?
Tennessee	Yes, but not as to devises of personality. (§§ 32-5-103, 32-5-106)	Not specified.	Not specified.	Yes. (§ 32-5-102)
Texas	Yes. (§ 503.003) However, if it has been probated in decedent's domicile, the only grounds for contest are: (a) that the foreign proceedings were not duly authenticated or recorded in the deed records; (b) will has been finally rejected for probate in Texas; or (c) probate has been set aside in decedent's domicile. (§ 504.001)	There is no specific provision relating to ancillary probate; it appears the original probate laws of Texas govern distribution.	The executor named in the will is entitled to letters. (§ 501.006)	The executor named in the will is entitled to letters. (§ 501.006)
Utah	No. (§75-3-303(4) - informal; §75-3-408- formal), unless original probate was informal and ancillary probate will be formal. (§75-3-401(2))	After payment of claims locally. (§75-3-815(3)) With regard to debts, personal property, or instrument evidencing debt, obligation, stock, or chose in action, payment or transfer can be made directly to domiciliary personal representative after 60 days following death, if proof of appointment of domicilliary personal representative and affidavit stating: date of death; that no local administration is pending or has been applied for; and that domiciliary personal representative is entitled to payment or delivery. Transfer of securities is covered by §3 of Uniform Act for Simplification of Fiduciary Security Transfers. (§75-4-201 & cmt.) However, cannot make any of these transfers if notified not to do so by local creditors of decedent. (§75-4-203)	Yes. (§75-3-203(7))	Yes. (§75-3-203(7))

Table 2.02, Part 2
Ancillary Probate

	Can a Will Be Contested in the Ancillary Proceeding?	At What Point in Ancillary Proceedings Can Property Be Transmitted to the Domiciliary Personal Representative?	Will Letters Be Issued to Person Named in Will, Although That person Is Not the Domiciliary Personal Representative?	If No Other Person is Named in the Will, is the Domiciliary Personal Representative Entitled to Letters in the Ancillary Probate Jurisdiction?
Vermont	Not specified. Only states that there is a hearing and notice as to whether the will shall be allowed as the will of the decedent. Objections to allowance of the will in Vermont shall be filed in writing no less than 14 business days prior to the hearing. In the event that no objections are filed, the will shall be allowed without hearing. Whether will can be contested is not addressed. (14 §§ 114(b), 115)	Not specified. Only states that after the payment of debts and administration the estate will be disposed of according to the will and the residue will be disposed of as provided in case of estates in Vermont belonging to persons who are not inhabitants of Vermont. (14 § 116)	Yes. (14 §§ 902, 904)	Yes, if they appoint a resident agent who accepts appointment as the resident agent of the nonresident estate fiduciary and agrees to accept service of legal process; may be made as agent of the nonresident executor, administrator or trustee and other communications on behalf of the executor or administrator. (14 §§ 902, 904)
Virginia	Yes. See Table 2.01, Part 1. (§ 64.2-450)	Not specified.	Implied yes. (§ 64.2-511)	Yes. (§ 64.2-1426)
Washington	Yes. (§§ 11.20.100, 11.24.010)	Not specified.	Yes. (§ 11.36.010)	Yes, if they appoint a resident agent. (§ 11.36.010)
West Virginia	Yes, but only if contesting whether it is a true copy of the will, that the probate of the will was set aside by the original probate court, or that such probate was improperly made. (§ 41-5-13)	After the inventory or appraisement has been filed with the required bond. (§ 44-5-3(d))	Implied yes. (§ 44-1-1)	Yes. (§ 44-5-3)
Wisconsin	Yes, but only that the proof required for ancillary probate has not been met or that the will has been finally rejected from probate in Wisconsin. (§ 868.01(2))	Prior to the final disposition of the ancillary estate but after notice, acceptance of service of process, and the posting of a bond. (§ 868.03(7))	Yes. (§§ 868.03(2)(a), 868.03(6))	Yes, domiciliary personal representative is given preference unless the court determines it is not in the best interest of the estate. (§ 868.03(2)(a))
Wyoming	Yes. (§§ 2-2-103, 2-6-301)	Not specified.	Yes. (§ 2-11-301)	Yes, if they designate a resident agent. (§ 2-11-301)

[1] Although adopting the Uniform Probate Code, the editorial board comments of the U.P.C. have not been included in Alaska Statutes. Nonetheless, the assumption is that they would be relied upon in construing the statutory provisions.

[2] Although adopting the Uniform Probate Code, the editorial board comments of the U.P.C. have not been included in Arizona Revised Statutes. Nonetheless, the assumption is that they would be relied upon in construing the statutory provisions.

[3] Although adopting the Uniform Probate Code, the editorial board comments of the U.P.C. have not been included in Colorado Revised Statutes. Nonetheless, the assumption is that they would be relied upon in construing the statutory provisions.

[4] Although adopting the Uniform Probate Code, the editorial comments of the U.P.C. have not been included in Hawaii Code Annotated. Nonetheless, the assumption is that they would be relied upon in construing the statutory provisions.

[5] Although adopting the provision from the Uniform Probate Code, the editorial board comments of the U.P.C. have not been included in the Michigan Statutes. Nonetheless, the assumption is that they would be relied upon in construing the statutory provision.

[6] Although adopting the Uniform Probate Code, the editorial board comments of the U.P.C. have not been included in Minnesota Statutes. Nonetheless, the assumption is that they would be relied upon in construing the statutory provision.

[7] Although adopting the Uniform Probate Code, the editorial comments of the U.P.C. have not been included in Revised Statutes of Nebraska Annotated. Nonetheless, the assumption is that they would be relied upon in construing the statutory provision.

Table 2.02, Part 3
Ancillary Probate

	Is Provision Made for Cases Where the Foreign Domiciliary Jurisdiction Does Not Issue Letters?	May Creditors File a Local Probate Petition?	The Proper Venue in the State for Ancillary Probate Is …
Alabama	No.	Yes, because they are interested persons. (§§ 43-8-160, 43-8-1(14))	When the testator, not an inhabitant of the state, dies in a county in Alabama in which the testator owns assets, that county's probate court. If the testator dies outside the county, then the county where such assets are located. If the testator dies not leaving assets in Alabama, and assets thereafter come into any county, then that county into which such assets are brought. If the testator designates a county in which he/she owns property, then that county's probate court. (§ 43-8-162)
Alaska	Yes, in terms of probating the will (§ 13.16.090(5) - informal probate; § 13.16.180 - formal probate; see also Table 2.01, Part 1, column 2); not specifically in terms of issuing letters.	Yes. (§§ 13.16.090(a)(3) (informal proceeding), 13.16.145(a)(2) (formal proceeding), 13.16.080(a)(1)(A) (application must list interest of person), 13.06.050(26) (interested person includes creditor))	If not domiciled in state, (A) in any county or state where property at decedent's death (§ 13.16.055(a)(2)(A)) (B) a fiduciary who is subject to the laws of this state and who comes into the control of property owned by the decedent at the time of death resides or has principle office. (§ 13.16.055(a)(2)(B)) Note that a debt is located where the debtor resides or has its principal office, if not an individual. Commercial paper, investment paper, and other instruments are located where the instrument is. An interest in trust is located where the trustee may be sued. Note, as well, that if there is a challenge to venue, it must be brought in same court having exclusive jurisdiction. As for conflicting determination of domicile, the first determination of domicile is controlling. (§ 13.16.055(d))
Arizona	Yes, in terms of probating the will (§ 14-3303(E) - informal probate; § 14-3409 - formal probate; see also Table 2.01, Part 1, column 2); not specifically in terms of issuing letters.	Yes, 45 days after decedent's death (§ 14-3301), or through a formal hearing. (§§ 14-3402(A)(2), 14-1201(28))	If not domiciled in state, in any county in state where property at decedent's death. Note that a debt is located where the debtor resides or has its principal office, if not an individual. Commercial paper, investment paper, and other instruments are located where the instrument is. An interest in trust is located where the trustee may be sued. Note, as well, that if there is a challenge to venue, it must be brought in same court having exclusive jurisdiction. As for conflicting determination of domicile, the first determination of domicile is controlling. (§ 14-3201)
Arkansas	No.	Any interested person may petition the court. (§§ 28-40-107(a)(1), 28-1-102(11))	The county where property with the greatest value is located; if there is no property, the county of death if the testator died in Arkansas; if the testator died out of state with no property in Arkansas, then in any county where a cause of action may be maintained by the personal representative. (§ 28-40-102(a)(2)–(4))

Table 2.02, Part 3
Ancillary Probate

	Is Provision Made for Cases Where the Foreign Domiciliary Jurisdiction Does Not Issue Letters?	May Creditors File a Local Probate Petition?	The Proper Venue in the State for Ancillary Probate Is . . .
California	Only states that if the will is admitted to probate or established or proved in accordance with the laws of the foreign jurisdiction, then the will is to be admitted into probate in California. (Prob. §12521(a))	Yes, any interested person may file. (Prob. §12510) A creditor is an interested person. (Prob. §48)	In the county where the nonresident decedent died if the decedent had property there; if no property of the nonresident decedent is located in the country where the decedent died, or if the decedent did not die in the state, then any county where the decedent's property is located; if property of the nonresident decedent is located in more than one county, then proper venue is the county in which a petition for ancillary administration is first filed, and the court in that county has jurisdiction of the administration of the estate. (Prob. §12511, §7052(a), (b))
Colorado	Yes, in terms of probating the will (§15-12-303(5) - informal probate; §15-12-409- formal probate; see also Table 2.01, Part 1, column 2); not specifically in terms of issuing letters.	Yes. (§§15-12-303(1)(c), 15-12-401, 15-10-201(27))	If not domiciled in state, in any county in state where property at decedent's death. Note that a debt is located where the debtor resides or has its principal office, if not an individual. Commercial paper, investment paper, and other instruments are located where the instrument is. An interest in trust is located where the trustee may be sued. Note, as well, that if there is a challenge to venue, it must be brought in same court having exclusive jurisdiction. As for conflicting determination of domicile, the first determination of domicile is controlling. (§15-12-201)
Connecticut	No.	Any person interested in such property may file. (§§45a-287(b), 45a-288(a))	Any of the following districts in which: (1) the testator last resided; (2) any of the testator's real or tangible property is situated; (3) any of the testator's intangible property is situated; (4) the executor or trustee named in the will resides; or (5) any cause of action in favor of the testator arose or any debtor of the testator resides or has an office. If more than one applies, the court which first assumes jurisdiction is to retain jurisdiction. (§45a-287(a))
Delaware	No.	Implied yes. (12 §1307(a))	Any county in Delaware where there are any goods or chattels, rights or credits, or lands or tenements of the deceased. (12 §1302(a))
District of Columbia	No.	Yes. (§§ 20-301, 20-101(d)) Also, a creditor may file a claim in a book known as "Claims Against Nonresident Decedents." Until the claim is resolved, it constitutes a lien on decedent's D.C. real property and proceeds of an authorized sale. (§20-343(d))	No provision presumably since there are not several counties in D.C.
Florida	Yes, at least in part, when a notary is involved. See 2.02, Part 2, col. 4.	Creditors as a category are not among those who are named as possible appointees as personal representative. (§733.301) However, they can petition the court for the appointment of a personal representative. See, e.g., In re Bush's Estate, 80 So. 2d 673 (1955).	If not domiciled in state, in any county in state where property at decedent's death; if no property in the state, then where any debtor of decedent is domiciled. (§733.101) Also, a statute recognizes that a married woman may have a Florida domicile even if her husband is a nonresident of Florida. (§733.101(2))

2064

Table 2.02, Part 3
Ancillary Probate

	Is Provision Made for Cases Where the Foreign Domiciliary Jurisdiction Does Not Issue Letters?	May Creditors File a Local Probate Petition?	The Proper Venue in the State for Ancillary Probate Is . . .
Georgia	Yes. Ancillary probate may be granted, even though a will has not been probated at the domicile, if it has been "established" there, provided it has not been offered for probate and successfully caveated in Georgia. (§ 53-5-33) See above for proof of establishment of will at the domicile.	Yes. (§ 53-5-44)	Probate court of any county in which property owned by decedent or "any cause of action of which the decedent was possessed at death the venue of which lies in this state." (§ 53-5-36)
Hawaii	Yes, in terms of probating the will (§ 560.3-303(e) - informal probate; § 560:3-409 - formal probate; see also Table 2.01, Part 1, column 2); not specifically in terms of issuing letters.	Yes. (§§ 560:3-302(b), 560:3-401, 560:1-201)	If not domiciled in state, in any judicial circuit in state where property at decedent's death. Note that a debt is located where the debtor resides or has its principal office, if not an individual. Commercial paper, investment paper, and other instruments are located where the instrument is. An interest in trust is located where the trustee may be sued. Note, as well, that if there is a challenge to venue, it must be brought in same court having exclusive jurisdiction. As for conflicting determination of domicile, the first determination of domicile is controlling. (§ 560:3-201)
Idaho	Yes, in terms of probating the will (§ 15-3-303(e) - informal probate; § 15-3-409 - formal probate; see also Table 2.01, Part 1, column 2); not specifically in terms of issuing letters.	Yes. (§§ 15-3-303, (application for informal probate), 15-3-401 (an interested person may file a formal testacy petition), 15-3-402, 15-1-201(25) (a creditor is an interested person))	If not domiciled in state, in any county in state where property at decedent's death. Note that a debt is located where the debtor resides or has its principal office, if not an individual. Commercial paper, investment paper, and other instruments are located where the instrument is. An interest in trust is located where the trustee may be sued. Note, as well, that if there is a challenge to venue, it must be brought in same court having exclusive jurisdiction. As for conflicting determination of domicile, the first determination of domicile is controlling. (§ 15-3-201)
Illinois	Yes, in terms of probating the will (755 ILCS § 5/7-3(b)); not specifically in terms of serving as the personal representative.	Yes. (755 ILCS §§ 5/7-2, 5/6-2), 5/1-2.11 (creditor included within meaning of interested person entitled to file)	The county in which the greater part of real estate is located or, if no real estate, where the greater part of his personal estate is located. (755 ILCS § 5/5-1(a), (b), & (c))
Indiana	No.	Any interested person may petition. (§§ 29-1-7-4(a), 29-1-7-27) and creditors are interested (§ 29-1-3(14)).	Any county in Indiana where decedent's property resides. If more than one county commences a proceeding, the county that first commences probate proceedings shall determine venue. (§ 29-1-7-1(a) & (b))
Iowa	No.	Only if they are an interested person. (§ 633.290)	In a county where real or personal property of testator is located. (Brown v. Monticello State Bank of Monticello, 360 N.W.2d 81 (1984); §§ 633.12, 633.495)
Kansas	No.	Yes, may be made by any person interested in the will. (§ 59-2229)	Any county where the decedent left any estate to be administered. (§ 59-2203)
Kentucky	No.	Yes, it is implied that any person may file. (§ 394.150)	If he had no known place of residence in this state, and land is devised, then in the county where the land or part thereof lies; if no land is devised, then in the county where any part of the estate is located, or where there is a debt or demand owing to the decedent. (§ 394.140)

Table 2.02, Part 3
Ancillary Probate

	Is Provision Made for Cases Where the Foreign Domiciliary Jurisdiction Does Not Issue Letters?	May Creditors File a Local Probate Petition?	The Proper Venue in the State for Ancillary Probate Is . . .
Louisiana	Yes, in terms of probating the will. (§9:2424) Not specifically in terms of issuing letters.	Yes, any person interested in the will may file. (§9:2422)	Any parish where immovable property of the deceased is located or movable property of the deceased is located if the deceased owned no immovable property in Louisiana at death. (Code Civ. Pro. §§2811, 3401)
Maine	Yes, in terms of probating the will (18-A §3-303(e) - informal probate; 18-A §3-409- formal probate; see also Table 2.01, Part 1, column 2); not specifically in terms of issuing letters.	Yes. (18-A §§3-303(a), 3-401, 1-201(20))	If not domiciled in state, in any county in state where property at decedent's death. Note that a debt is located where the debtor resides or has its principal office, if not an individual. Commercial paper, investment paper, and other instruments are located where the instrument is. An interest in trust is located where the trustee may be sued. Note, as well, that if there is a challenge to venue, it must be brought in same court having exclusive jurisdiction. (18-A §3-201)
Maryland	Not specifically, but a foreign representative is not required to take out letters in Maryland. (Est. & Trusts §5-501)	No, since they are NOT interested persons. (Est. & Trusts §§5-301, 5-401, 1-101)	The situs of tangible personal property. (Est. & Trusts §5-103(b))
Massachusetts	Yes, in terms of probating the will (190B §3-303(e) - informal probate; 190B §3-409 - formal probate; see also Table 2.01, Part 1, column 2); not specifically in terms of issuing letters.	Yes. (§§190B §§3-303, 3-401, 1-201(24))	If not domiciled in state, in any county in state where property at decedent's death. Note that a debt is located where the debtor resides or has its principal office, if not an individual. Commercial paper, investment paper, and other instruments are located where the instrument is. An interest in trust is located where the trustee may be sued. Note, as well, that if there is a challenge to venue, it must be brought in same court having exclusive jurisdiction. (190B §3-201)
Michigan	Yes, in terms of probating the will (§700.3303(5) - informal probate; §700.3409 - formal probate; see also Table 2.01, Part 1, column 2); not specifically in terms of issuing letters.	Yes. (§§700.3105, 700.1105(c))	If not domiciled in state, in any county in state where property at decedent's death. Note that a debt is located where the debtor resides or where the debtor has its principal office, if not an individual. Commercial paper, investment paper, and other instruments are located where the instrument is. An interest in trust is located where the trustee may be sued. Note, as well, that if there is a challenge to venue, it must be brought in same court having exclusive jurisdiction. As for conflicting determination of domicile, the first determination of domicile is controlling. (§700.3201)

Table 2.02, Part 3
Ancillary Probate

State	Is Provision Made for Cases Where the Foreign Domiciliary Jurisdiction Does Not Issue Letters?	May Creditors File a Local Probate Petition?	The Proper Venue in the State for Ancillary Probate Is …
Minnesota	Yes, in terms of probating the will (§524.3-303(e) - informal probate; §524.3-409 - formal probate; see also Table 2.01, Part 1, column 2); not specifically in terms of issuing letters.	Yes. (§§524.3-303, 524.3-401, 524.1-201(33))	If not domiciled in state, in any county in state where property at decedent's death. Note that a debt is located where the debtor resides or has its principal office, if not an individual. Commercial paper, investment paper, and other instruments are located where the instrument is. An interest in trust is located where the trustee may be sued. Note, as well, that if there is a challenge to venue, it must be brought in same court having exclusive jurisdiction. (§524.3-201)
Mississippi	Not specifically.	Yes. (§91-7-3, Greenville Lumber Co., Inc. v. Hammett, 889 So. 2d 502 (Miss. 2004))	In the county of residence, or where land to be devised is located; if no residence or land is in state, in the county where testator died, or where some property may be. (§91-7-1)
Missouri	Not specifically.	Not specified.	In any county wherein decedent left property, unless decedent owned real estate in Missouri, in the county where a major part of the real estate is located. (§473.010)
Montana	Yes, in terms of probating the will (§72-3-213(4) - informal probate; §72-3-316- formal probate; see also Table 2.01, Part 1, column 2); not specifically in terms of issuing letters.	Yes. (§§72-3-105, 72-1-103)(25)	If not domiciled in state, in any county in state where property at decedent's death. (§72-3-112) Note that a debt is located where the debtor resides or has its principal office, if not an individual. Commercial paper, investment paper, and other instruments are located where the instrument is. An interest in trust is located where the trustee may be sued. Note, as well, that if there is a challenge to venue, it must be brought in same court having exclusive jurisdiction. As for conflicting determination of domicile, the first determination of domicile is controlling. (§72-3-113)
Nebraska	Yes, in terms of probating the will (§30-2416(e) - informal probate; §30-2433 - formal probate; see also Table 2.01, Part 1, column 2); not specifically in terms of issuing letters.	Yes. (§§30-2416(a)(3), 30-2425, 30-2209(21))	If not domiciled in state, in any county in state where property at decedent's death. Note that a debt is located where the debtor resides or has its principal office, if not an individual. Commercial paper, investment paper, and other instruments are located where the instrument is. An interest in trust is located where the trustee may be sued. Note, as well, that if there is a challenge to venue, it must be brought in same court having exclusive jurisdiction. As for conflicting determination of domicile, the first determination of domicile is controlling. (§30-2410)
Nevada	Yes, in terms of probating the will (§136.260(4)); not specifically in terms of issuing letters.	Any person interested in the will may file. (§136.260(2)) An interested person is a person whose right or interest under an estate may be materially affected by a decision of a fiduciary or a decision of the court. The fiduciary or court shall determine who is an interested person according to the particular purposes of, and matter involved in, a proceeding. (§132.185)	Any county in which the testator left any estate. (§136.260(1))

Table 2.02, Part 3
Ancillary Probate

State	Is Provision Made for Cases Where the Foreign Domiciliary Jurisdiction Does Not Issue Letters?	May Creditors File a Local Probate Petition?	The Proper Venue in the State for Ancillary Probate Is . . .
New Hampshire	•	Yes, any party in interest may file. (§ 552:13)	Any county where there is an estate on which the will operates. (§ 552:14)
New Jersey	No provision.	Implied yes. (§§ 3B:3-26, 3B:3-27)	The surrogate's court of any county. (§ 3B:3-26)
New Mexico	Yes, in terms of probating the will (§ 45-3-303(E) - informal probate; § 45-3-409 - formal probate; see also Table 2.01, Part 1, column 2); not specifically in terms of issuing letters.	Yes. (§§ 45-3-303(A)(3), 45-3-402, 45-1-201(A)(26))	If not domiciled in state, in any county in state where property at decedent's death. Note that a debt is located where the debtor resides or has its principal office, if not an individual. Commercial paper, investment paper, and other instruments are located where the instrument is. An interest in trust is located where the trustee may be sued. Note, as well, that if there is a challenge to venue, it must be brought in same court having exclusive jurisdiction. As for conflicting determination of domicile, the first determination of domicile is controlling. (§ 45-3-201)
New York	Yes. (Surr. Ct. Proc. Act § 1607(1))	Yes. (Surr. Ct. Proc. Act § 1609(1))	The court having jurisdiction over the property. (Surr. Ct. Proc. Act § 1602(1))
North Carolina	No.	If executor has not applied for probate within 60 days after the testator's death, a creditor, as a "person interested in the estate, may make such application, upon 10 days' notice thereof to the executor." (§ 28A-2A-2)	If not domiciled in North Carolina, then any county where left property or assets or into which they may have come (§ 28A-3-1(2)); if more than one county in which property or assets, then county where proceedings first commenced (§ 28A-3-1(2)); if nondomiciliary motorist who died in North Carolina, then any county in North Carolina. (§ 28A-3-1(3))
North Dakota	Yes, in terms of probating the will (§ 30.1-14-03(5) - informal probate; § 30.1-15-09 - formal probate; see also Table 2.01, Part 1, column 2); not specifically in terms of issuing letters.	Yes. (§§ 30.1-14-03(1)(c), 30.1-15-01(1), 30.1-01-06(25))	If not domiciled in state, in any county in state where property at decedent's death. Note that a debt is located where the debtor resides or has its principal office, if not an individual. Commercial paper, investment paper, and other instruments are located where the instrument is. An interest in trust is located where the trustee may be sued. Note, as well, that if there is a challenge to venue, it must be brought in same court having exclusive jurisdiction. (§ 30.1-13-01)
Ohio	No.	Yes. (§ 2129.04)	Where property of the decedent is located or where a debtor of the decedent resides. (§ 2129.04)
Oklahoma	No.	Yes, any person interested in the will may file. (58 § 52(A))	Where any portion of the estate is left, or any portion of the estate for which claim is made. (58 § 51)
Oregon	No.	Yes, any interested person may file. (§ 113.035)	Where property is located. (§ 113.015)
Pennsylvania	No.	Not specified. (20 § 3136)	Any county where any of the property is located. (20 § 3131)
Rhode Island	No.	Yes, any person interested in the will may file. (§ 33-7-18)	Any town or city where the testator had property upon which the will may operate. (§ 33-7-18)

Table 2.02, Part 3
Ancillary Probate

	Is Provision Made for Cases Where the Foreign Domiciliary Jurisdiction Does Not Issue Letters?	May Creditors File a Local Probate Petition?	The Proper Venue in the State for Ancillary Probate Is …
South Carolina	Yes, in terms of probating the will (§ 62-3-303(e)) - informal probate; § 62-3-409 - formal probate; see also Table 2.01, Part 1, column 2); not specifically in terms of issuing letters.	Yes. (§§ 62-3-303(a)(3), 62-3-401, 62-1-201(23))	If not domiciled in state, in any county in state where property at decedent's death. Note that a debt is located where the debtor resides or has its principal office, if not an individual. Commercial paper, investment paper, and other instruments are located where the instrument is. An interest in trust is located where the trustee may be sued. Note, as well, that if there is a challenge to venue, it must be brought in same court having exclusive jurisdiction. (§ 62-3-201)
South Dakota	Yes, in terms of probating the will (§ 29A-3-303(e) - informal probate; § 29A-3-409- formal probate; see also Table 2.01, Part 1, column 2); not specifically in terms of issuing letters.	Yes. (§§ 29A-3-303(a)(3), 29A-3-401, 29A-1-201(23))	if not domiciled in state, in any county in state where property at decedent's death. Note that a debt is located where the debtor resides or has its principal office, if not an individual. Commercial paper, investment paper, and other instruments are located where the instrument is. An interest in trust is located where the trustee may be sued. Note, as well, that if there is a challenge to venue, it must be brought in same court having exclusive jurisdiction. (§ 29A-3-201)
Tennessee	Yes, in terms of probating the will (§ 32-5-105(a)): not specifically in terms of issuing letters. (§ 32-5-102)	Yes, any interested person may file. (§ 32-5-103)	Where any part of the estate is left. (§ 32-5-101)
Texas	No.	Yes, any person interested may file (§§ 256.051, 22.018)	If testator died in state, either county where testator died or where the principal part of the estate was located at death. If testator did not die in the state, in the county where the nearest of kin resides. If there is no kindred, in the county where the principal part of the estate was located at death. (§ 33.001)
Utah	Yes, in terms of probating the will (§ 75-3-303(5) - informal probate; § 75-3-409 - formal probate; see also Table 2.01, Part 1, column 2); not specifically in terms of issuing letters.	Yes. (§§ 75-3-303(1)(c), 75-3-401(1), 75-1-201(24))	If not domiciled in state, in any county in state where property at decedent's death. Note that a debt is located where the debtor resides or has its principal office, if not an individual. Commercial paper, investment paper, and other instruments are located where the instrument is. An interest in trust is located where the trustee may be sued. Note, as well, that if there is a challenge to venue, it must be brought in same court having exclusive jurisdiction. (§ 75-3-201)
Vermont	No.	Yes, any person interested may file. (14 § 114(a))	In the probate division of the Superior Court. (14 § 113))
Virginia	No.	Not specified as to whom may file. (§ 64.2-450)	In the county or city where any real estate lies that is devised or was owned by the decedent. If there be no such real estate, then in the county or city of death or where there is estate. (§ 64.2-443)

Table 2.02, Part 3
Ancillary Probate

	Is Provision Made for Cases Where the Foreign Domiciliary Jurisdiction Does Not Issue Letters?	May Creditors File a Local Probate Petition?	The Proper Venue in the State for Ancillary Probate Is …
Washington	No.	Implied yes. (§ 11.24.010)	In any county in which any part of probate estate is situated. (§ 11.96A.050(4)(b)(i)) If there are no assets in the state, any county where a nonprobate asset might be. (§ 11.96A.050(4)(b)(i)) Alternatively, proper venue for probate is the county in which the decedent died. (§ 11.96A.050(4)(b)(i)): see also § 11.96A.040(1)(b) & (1)(c))
West Virginia	No.	Yes. (§§ 41-5-5, 41-5-13)	Where any real estate devised is located, or if there be none, the county where the testator died, or where any property is located. (§ 41-5-4)
Wisconsin	No.	Yes, any interested person may file. (§ 856.07(1))	In any county where property of the decedent is located. The court that first exercises jurisdiction shall retain jurisdiction. (§ 856.01(2))
Wyoming	Yes, in terms of probating the will (§ 2-11-105); not specifically in terms of issuing letters.	Yes, any interested person may file. (§ 2-11-103)	Where any estate is left. (§ 2-11-102)

Table 3
Nonresident Qualification as a Fiduciary
(current through 5/1/18)

Often a relative or bank from another state has the relationship and has engendered trust to manage affairs of an individual or administer an estate. Quite commonly, the individual being represented has retired to a state other than the one in which the most trusted individuals or bank are resident. In other cases, the individual has remained, but other members of the family or close friends have moved out of state. When naming fiduciaries in a will, or seeking qualification of a personal representative or guardian,[1] careful consideration must be given to whether such person can qualify. In many instances, states draw distinctions between residents (usually meaning more precisely domiciliaries) and nonresidents (usually meaning more precisely nondomiciliaries). In some situations, nonresidents may serve, but only with the joint appointment of a resident or the designation of a resident agent.

The rules regarding fiduciaries vary widely, even within a state, based on the particular category of fiduciary involved. The rules also tend to vary, depending whether a domiciliary or ancillary estate or guardianship administration is involved. There are even distinct rules often for executors, as opposed to administrators. Finally, sharp differences exist in the treatment of nonresident individuals on the one hand and nonresident corporate entities on the other hand. With regard to the former, there may be a further differentiation between certain nonresident relatives, who are permitted to serve as fiduciaries locally, and other relatives and unrelated individuals, who do not qualify to serve under local law.

The ensuing tables address these issues. Table 3.01 is specifically concerned with the appointment of nonresident executors and administrators. The table considers both nonresidents appointed in cases of domiciliary administration as well as in cases of ancillary administration. Thus, if a nonresident is seeking approval to serve in a state where some of the decedent's property is located, but the decedent was not domiciled (ancillary administration), the rules as to qualification may differ from the case where the nonresident is seeking to serve at the decedent's domicile. If the same person is seeking to serve in both places, he may be a resident in one state and a nonresident in the other state, thus requiring a review of the law of more than one state.

Table 3.02 follows the same analysis, but with respect to individuals serving as domiciliary and ancillary guardians of minor and incompetent persons. Table 3.03 shifts the focus to nonindividual banks[2] serving as executors and administrators. Table 3.04 considers the same issues from the standpoint of institutions serving as guardians of the property of minors and incompetents.

Because fiduciaries may, in fact, be required to qualify in a number of foreign states, careful consideration must be given to the requirements imposed by any number of several states in which qualification will be sought. The failure to satisfy the relevant state requirements can have dire consequences. The local court may appoint a local attorney or institution completely unknown to the family. Alternatively, a local member of the family may be appointed, even though not one preferred by the testator or ward, as the case may be. Nevertheless, this person may exercise considerable control over family wealth and have tremendous impact on the futures of members of the family. Especially if appointed by the court, this person may be entitled to substantial fees that otherwise would not have been paid. Routine supervision by the court may also complicate and delay matters.

---

[1] The table uses the term "guardian" generally, although in a particular state a different term, such as conservator or curator, may be used when referring, for example, to the party charged with responsibility for an incompetent adult or his assets.

[2] Similar rules would typically apply to trust companies and other institutions authorized to serve in a fiduciary capacity.

Table 3.01
Nonresident Individual as Executor or Administrator

	Nonresident Individual as Executor	Nonresident Individual as Administrator	Nonresident Individual as Ancillary Executor	Nonresident Individual as Ancillary Administrator
Alabama	Yes. (§43-2-191)	Yes. (§43-2-42)	Yes. (§43-2-191)	§43-2-193 indicates that it is permissible to have a nonresident administrator for a nonresident decedent leaving property in Alabama if a relative, or otherwise if that administrator is also the administrator of the decedent's estate at his domicile.
Alaska	Yes. (§13.16.245)	See col. 1.	Yes. (§13.16.245) If no local administration is pending, a foreign domiciliary personal representative can act locally after filing proof of appointment and of any bond given. (§§13.21.035, 13.21.045)	Yes, same requirements as in the prior column.
Arizona	Yes. (§14-3203(f))	Yes. (§14-3203(f))	Yes. (§14-3203(f)) If no local administration is pending, a foreign domiciliary personal representative can act locally after filing proof of appointment and of any bond given. (§§14-4204 –14-4207)	Yes, same requirements as in the prior column.
Arkansas	Yes, if resident agent is appointed. (§28-48-101(b)(6)(A))	Yes, if resident agent is appointed. (§28-48-101(b)(6)(A))	Yes, if the person is a personal representative in the domiciliary state and a resident agent is appointed. (§§28-42-102, 28-42-104) However, this is not the case if not in the best interests of the estate. (§28-42-102(b)) Appointment of a nonresident might not be in best interests of estate when most of the assets are situated in Arkansas. (Phillips v. Sherrod Estate, 453 S.W.2d 60 (1970))	See prior col.
California	Yes. (Prob. §§8570, 8572) The person must be a resident of the U.S. (Prob. §8402(a)(4))	Same as prior col.	Note that a sister state personal representative has priority of appointment but a foreign nation personal representative does not. ((Prob. §12513 & Law Revision Comm'n Comments)	Yes. (Prob. §12513)
Colorado	(§15-12-601)	Yes. §15-12-601	Yes. (§15-12-601)	Yes, same requirements as in the prior column.
Connecticut	Yes, after filing in the court of probate making the appointment a certificate appointing the probate judge as agent for service of process. (§52-60(a))	See col. 1.	See col. 1.	See col. 1.
Delaware	Yes, after filing in the office of the Register of Wills an irrevocable power of attorney designating the Register as agent. (12 §1506)	See col. 1.	Yes. (12 §§1506, 1566, 1568)	Yes. (12 §§1505, 1506, 1566, 1568)

Table 3.01

Nonresident Individual as Executor or Administrator

	Nonresident Individual as Executor	Nonresident Individual as Administrator	Nonresident Individual as Ancillary Executor	Nonresident Individual as Ancillary Administrator
District of Columbia	Yes, after filing in the office of the Register of Wills an irrevocable power of attorney designating the Register as agent. (§ 20-303(b)(7)) Aliens who are not admitted as U.S. permanent residents may not serve. (§ § 20-303(b)(5))	Yes, after filing in the office of the Register of Wills an irrevocable power of attorney designating the Register as agent. (§ 20-303(b)(7)) Aliens not lawful permanent residents of U.S. may not serve. (§ 20-303(b)(5))	Yes, after filing in the office of the Register of Wills an irrevocable power of attorney designating the Register as agent. (§ § 20-303, 20-341, 20-342) A foreign personal representative of a nondomiciliary is not required to obtain letters in the District of Columbia. If a foreign personal representative is administering an estate that has property located in the District of Columbia, he must file with the Register a copy of the appointment as personal representative and a copy of the decedent's will, if any, authenticated pursuant to 28 U.S.C. § 1738.	Yes, after filing in the office of the Register of Wills an irrevocable power of attorney designating the Register as agent. (§ § 20-303, 20-341, 20-342) A foreign personal representative of a nondomiciliary is not required to obtain letters in the District of Columbia. If a foreign personal representative is administering an estate that has property located in the District of Columbia, he must file with the Register a copy of the appointment as personal representative and a copy of the decedent's will, if any, authenticated pursuant to 28 U.S.C. § 1738.
Florida	No, unless he is a legally adoptive parent or adopted child, lineal relative, spouse, brother, sister, uncle, aunt, nephew, niece of decedent or lineal relative of such person, or spouse of a person otherwise qualified. (§ 733.304)	No, unless he is a legally adoptive parent or adopted child, lineal relative, spouse, brother, sister, uncle, aunt, nephew, niece of decedent or lineal relative of such person, or spouse of person otherwise qualified. (§ 733.304)	Yes, if qualified to act in Florida. (§ 734.102) A nondomiciliary of Florida can only act if a legally adopted child or adoptive parent of the decedent; related by lineal consanguinity; a spouse or a brother, sister, uncle, aunt, nephew or niece of decedent, or someone related by lineal consanguinity to such person; or the spouse of a person otherwise qualified. (§ 733.304) Persons not qualified to serve are felons, those mentally or physically unable to perform duties, and those persons under the age of 18. (§ 733.303)	Yes. See prior column.
Georgia	Yes. (§ § 53-6-1)	Yes. (§ § 53-6-1) A nonresident administrator must post bond, unless waived by the unanimous consent of the heirs of the estate. (§ 53-6-50(c)) There is also a surety requirement in connection with the bond. (§ § 53-6-51)	Yes. (§ 53-5-37) However, ancillary proceedings may not be necessary. (§ 53-5-42)	Yes. (§ § 53-5-37) However, ancillary proceedings may not be necessary. (§ 53-5-42)
Hawaii	Yes. (§ 560:3-601)	Yes. (§ 560:3-601)	Yes, same requirements as in the first column. If no local administration is pending, a foreign domiciliary personal representative can act locally after filing proof of appointment and of any bond given. (§ § 560:3-203(g))	Yes, same requirements as in the prior column.
Idaho	(§ 15-3-601)	Yes. (§ 15-3-601)	Yes, same requirements as in the first column. If no local administration is pending, a foreign domiciliary personal representative can act locally after filing proof of appointment and of any bond given. (§ § 15-3-203(g))	Yes, same requirements as in the prior column.

Table 3.01
Nonresident Individual as Executor or Administrator

	Nonresident Individual as Executor	Nonresident Individual as Administrator	Nonresident Individual as Ancillary Executor	Nonresident Individual as Ancillary Administrator
Illinois	Yes, if a resident of the U.S., over 18 years old, of sound mind, and not a convicted felon. The court has the discretion to require a nonresident executor to post a bond notwithstanding any contrary provision of the will. (755 ILCS §5/6-13)	Yes, if a resident of the U.S., over 18 years old, of sound mind, and not a convicted felon. (755 ILCS §5/9-1)	Yes, if a resident of the U.S., over 18 years old, of sound mind, not disabled, and not a convicted felon. (755 ILCS §5/6-13)	Yes, if a resident of the U.S., over 18 years old, of sound mind, not disabled, and not a convicted felon. (755 ILCS §5/9-1)
Indiana	Yes, if serving jointly with a resident (§ 29-1-10-1(c)); or by appointing a resident agent and posting a bond. (§ 29-1-10-1(d))	Yes, if serving jointly with a resident (§ 29-1-10-1(c)); or by appointing a resident agent and posting a bond. (§ 29-1-10-1(d))	There is no statutory prohibition. However, § 29-2-1-1 states that a "local personal representative includes any personal representative appointed in this state pursuant to appointment proceedings described in article 1 of this title." That could include § 29-1-10-1(c), requiring joint appointment of a resident. Note that if a domiciliary foreign personal representative has established his appointment the domiciliary personal representative can act like a local personal representative in Indiana. (§§ 29-2-1-5, 29-2-1-6)	There is no statutory prohibition. However, § 29-2-1-1 states that a "local personal representative includes any personal representative appointed in this state pursuant to appointment proceedings described in article 1 of this title." That could include § 29-1-10-1(c), requiring joint appointment of a resident. Note that if a domiciliary foreign personal representative has established his appointment the domiciliary personal representative can act like a local personal representative in Indiana. (§§ 29-2-1-5, 29-2-1-6)
Iowa	Yes, if a resident fiduciary is also appointed to serve with the nonresident or alone if good cause is shown. (§ 633.64(1))	Yes, if a resident fiduciary is also appointed to serve with the nonresident or alone if good cause is shown. (§ 633.64(1))	Yes. There is a provision specifically addressing qualification of a fiduciary appointed in another state under a will admitted to probate in the other state. It permits appointment if a resident is also appointed to serve with the nonresident or alone if good cause is shown. (§ 633.502)	Yes, although provision implies that a resident co-administrator may also be appointed. (§ 633.501)

Table 3.01
Nonresident Individual as Executor or Administrator

	Nonresident Individual as Executor	Nonresident Individual as Administrator	Nonresident Individual as Ancillary Executor	Nonresident Individual as Ancillary Administrator
Kansas	Yes, if a resident agent is appointed. (§59-807(b)) See also §59-706(b)) providing that if the decedent was a nonresident and the person designated in the will does not seek appointment in Kansas, and no other interested person seeking appointment has qualified, then letters of administration can be granted to the spouse, nominee of the spouse, or devisee who court believes will be best able to manage and preserve the estate, or to a nominee of a devisee. Quaere how provision in last sentence relates to provision in prior sentence. If court is not satisfied with any of the foregoing choices, it can grant letters to some other person. (§59-807(c))	Yes, if a resident agent is appointed. (§59-706(a))	Yes, if a resident agent is appointed. (§§59-807, 59-1706) See also §59-804.	Same as prior col.
Kentucky	Only if over 18 and related by consanguinity, marriage, adoption, or the spouse of such person so related. (§395.005(3))	Only if over 18 and related by consanguinity, marriage, adoption, or the spouse of such person so related. (§395.005(3))	Yes. (§395.005(3))	Yes. (§395.005(3))
Louisiana	Yes, if resident agent is appointed. (Code Civ. Pro. art. 3097(A)(4)) The rules of the next column apply if the appointment is of a dative testamentary executor. (Id.; §3097(B))	Yes, if resident agent is appointed and if nonresident is the surviving spouse, heir, legatee, legal representative of an heir or legatee, the nominee of any of the above, a creditor of the deceased, property with the deceased or a co-owner of immovable property with the deceased. (Code Civ. Pro. art. 3097(B))	Yes, if resident agent is appointed. Also, a bond will have to be furnished on the application of an interested person for good cause shown. (Code Civ. Pro. arts. 3402, 3404, 3097) The rules of the next column apply if the appointment is of a dative testamentary executor. (Id.; §3097(B))	Yes, if resident agent is appointed and if nonresident is the surviving spouse, heir, legatee, legal representative of an heir or legatee, the nominee of any of the above, or a creditor of the deceased, or a co-owner of immovable property with the deceased. (Code Civ. Pro. arts. 3402, 3404, 3097(B))
Maine	Yes, if appointed at the domicile, if named in the will, or if nominated by the domiciliary personal representative. (18-A §3-203(g))	Yes. See prior col.	Yes, same requirements as in the first column. If no local administration is pending, a foreign domiciliary personal representative can act locally after filing proof of appointment and of any bond given. (18-A §§4-204–4-207, 3-203(g))	Yes, same requirements as in the prior col. (18-A §§4-205, 4-207, 3-203)
Maryland	Yes, if resident agent is appointed. (Est. & Trusts §5-105(c)(6))	Yes, if resident agent is appointed. (Est. & Trusts §5-105(c)(6))	Yes, if resident agent is appointed. (Est. & Trusts §5-105(c)(6))	Yes, although a foreign personal representative is not required to take out letters in Maryland. (Est. & Trusts §5-501)

Table 3.01
Nonresident Individual as Executor or Administrator

	Nonresident Individual as Executor	Nonresident Individual as Administrator	Nonresident Individual as Ancillary Executor	Nonresident Individual as Ancillary Administrator
Massachusetts	Yes, if appointed at the domicile, if named in the will, or if nominated by the domiciliary personal representative. (190B §3-203(g))	Yes. See prior col.	Yes. (190B §§4-204-4-207)	Yes; same requirements as in the prior col. (190B §§4-204—4-207)
Michigan	There is no statutory prohibition. (§700.3203)	There is no statutory prohibition. (§700.3203)	Yes. An out-of-state domiciliary personal representative can be appointed in Michigan if there is no local administration. (§700.4203) Without court approval, and after 63 days from a nonresident decedent's death, the afore said person can receive payment or delivery regarding personal property, a debt, obligation, stock, or chose in action. (§700.4201)	Yes. See prior column.
Minnesota	Yes, if appointed at the domicile, if named in the will, or if nominated by the domiciliary personal representative. (§524.3-203(g))	Yes. See prior col.	Yes, same requirements as in the first column. If no local administration is pending, a foreign domiciliary personal representative can act locally after filing proof of appointment and of any bond given. (§§524.4-204– 524.4-207, 524.3-203(g))	Yes, same requirements as in the prior col. (§§524.4-204 et seq., 524.3-203(g))
Mississippi	There is no statutory prohibition. (§91-7-35)	There is no statutory prohibition. (§91-7-65)	Yes, after appropriate filing in county where property located. (§91-7-259)	Yes, after appropriate filing in county where property located. (§91-7-259)
Missouri	Yes, after designation of resident agent. (§473.117(3))	Yes, after designation of resident agent. (§473.117(3))	Yes, after appropriate filing in county where property located if no local administration is pending. (§§473.676, 473.677, 473.678)	Yes, after appropriate filing in county where property located if no local administration is pending. (§§473.676, 473.677, 473.678)
Montana	Yes, in that there is no specific prohibition. (§72-3-501) A domiciliary personal representative or a person nominated by such person has priority. (§72-3-506)	Same as prior col.	Yes. (§§72-4-201 et seq., 72-3-506)	Yes. (§§72-4-201 et seq., 72-3-506)
Nebraska	Yes, if appointed at the domicile, if named in the will, or if nominated by the domiciliary personal representative. (§30-2412(g))	See prior col.	Yes, same requirements as in the first col. If no local administration is pending, a foreign domiciliary personal representative can act locally after filing proof of appointment and of any bond given. (§§30-2506–2508)	Yes, same requirements as in the prior col. (§§30-2506, 30-2508, 30-2412(g))

Table 3.01

Nonresident Individual as Executor or Administrator

	Nonresident Individual as Executor	Nonresident Individual as Administrator	Nonresident Individual as Ancillary Executor	Nonresident Individual as Ancillary Administrator
Nevada	Yes, in that there is no specific prohibition. (§ 138.020)	The individual must either (i) associate as co-administrator or a resident of Nevada or a banking corporation authorized to do business in the state, or (ii) be named as a personal representative in a will subject to a pending petition for probate, if the court, in its discretion, believes it would be appropriate to make such an appointment. (§ 139.010(4)(a)-(b))	Yes, since there is no statutory prohibition. (§ 138.020)	The individual must either (i) associate as co-administrator or a resident of Nevada or a banking corporation authorized to do business in the state, or (ii) be named as a personal representative in a will subject to a pending petition for probate, if the court, in its discretion, believes it would be appropriate to make such an appointment. (§ 139.010(4))
New Hampshire	No, unless judge deems proper. (§ 553:5)	No, unless judge deems proper. (§ 553:5)	No, but in the court's discretion. (§ 553:5; see also § 554:28)	No, but in the court's discretion. (§ 553:5; see also § 554:28)
New Jersey	Yes, after filing power of attorney with the surrogate of the county or clerk of the court. (§ 3B:14-47)	Yes, after filing power of attorney with the surrogate of the county or clerk of the court. (§§ 3B:14-47, 3B:10-2)	Yes, after filing power of attorney with the surrogate of the county or clerk of the court. (§ 3B:14-25 et seq.)	Yes, after filing power of attorney with the surrogate of the county or clerk of the court. (§§ 3B:14-25 et seq., 3B:10-7)
New Mexico	Yes, if appointed at the domicile, if named in the will, or if nominated by the domiciliary personal representative. (§ 45-3-203(G))	Yes. § 45-3-203 does not condition appointment on domicile or residence in-state. Furthermore, § 45-3-203(G) recognizes a personal representative appointed at the domicile or if nominated by the domiciliary personal representative.	Yes, same requirements as in the first col. If no local administration is pending, a foreign domiciliary personal representative can act locally after filing proof of appointment and of any bond given. (§§ 45-4-205, 45-4-207)	Yes, same requirements as in the prior col. (§§ 45-3-203(g), 45-4-205, 45-4-207)
New York	Yes. (Surr. Ct. Proc. Act §§ 707, 708) A nonresident alien can be an executor if he serves with one or more co-fiduciaries, at least one of whom must be a resident of New York. Any appointment of a resident or nonresident alien fiduciary is made in the court's discretion. No mention is made of a nonresident from another state. Also, the court may declare ineligible any fiduciary "unable to read and write the English language." (Surr. Ct. Proc. Act § 707(2)	Yes. (Surr. Ct. Proc. Act §§ 707, 708) A nonresident alien can be an executor if he serves with one or more co-fiduciaries, at least one of whom must be a resident of New York. Any appointment of a resident or nonresident alien fiduciary is made in the court's discretion. No mention is made of a nonresident from another state. Also, the court may declare ineligible any fiduciary "unable to read and write the English language." (Surr. Ct. Proc. Act § 707(2))	Yes, subject to the requirements of § 707. (Surr. Ct. Proc. Act § 1608) See first column.	Yes, subject to the requirements of § 707. (Surr. Ct. Proc. Act § 1608) See first column.
North Carolina	Yes, if a resident agent is appointed. (§ 28A-4-2(4))	Yes, if a resident agent is appointed. (§ 28A-4-2(4))	Yes. (§ 28A-26-3)	Yes. (§ 28A-26-3)

Table 3.01

Nonresident Individual as Executor or Administrator

	Nonresident Individual as Executor	Nonresident Individual as Administrator	Nonresident Individual as Ancillary Executor	Nonresident Individual as Ancillary Administrator
North Dakota	Yes, if appointed at the domicile, if named in the will, or if nominated by the domiciliary personal representative. (§ 30.1-13-03(7))	Same as prior col.	Yes, same requirements as in the first col. If no local administration is pending, a foreign domiciliary personal representative can act locally after filing proof of appointment and of any bond given. (§§ 30.1-24-06, 30.1-24-08, 30.1-13-03(7))	Yes, same requirements as in the prior col. (§§ 30.1-24-06, 30.1-24-08, 30.1-13-03(7))
Ohio	Yes. (§ 2109.21(B)(1)) To qualify for appointment, a nonresident shall be either an individual who is related to the maker of the will by consanguinity or affinity or a person who resides in a state that allows appointment of a nonresident not related to the maker. The court may order the assets to remain in the state until distribution. (Id.)	No. (§ 2109.21(A))	Yes, to qualify for appointment, a nonresident must be either an individual who is related to the maker of the will by consanguinity or affinity or a person who resides in a state that allows appointment of a nonresident not related to the maker. (§§ 2129.08, 2109.21(B)(2); see also § 2129.25)	Yes. To qualify for appointment, a person who is not a resident of this state shall be an individual who is related to the maker of the will by consanguinity or affinity, or a person who resides in a state that allows the appointment of a nonresident who is not related to the maker of the will. (§§ 2109.21(B)(2), 2129.08, 2129.25)
Oklahoma	Yes, after appointing resident agent. (58 § 162)	Yes, after appointing resident agent. (58 § 162)	Yes. (58 § 262)	Yes. (58 § 262)
Oregon	Yes, but pursuant to the discretion of the court. (§§ 113.085, 113.087)	Yes, but pursuant to the discretion of the court. (§§ 113.085, 113.087)	Yes, but ancillary appointment may not be necessary. (§§ 113.085, 113.087, 116.263)	Yes, but ancillary appointment may not be necessary. (§§ 113.085, 113.087, 116.263)
Pennsylvania	Yes, in that there is no specific prohibition. (20 § 3155)	Yes, at the discretion of the register. (20 §§ 3155, 3157)	Yes. (20 §§ 3151, 3155, 4101 et seq.)	Yes, at the discretion of the register. (20 §§ 3151, 3155, 3157, 4101 et seq.)
Rhode Island	Yes, if resident agent is appointed. (§ 33-18-9)	No, person who is not an "inhabitant," unless other circumstances, in the opinion of the court, render such appointment proper. (§ 33-8-7) To the extent a person appointed is "residing out of state" then a resident agent in the state must be appointed). (§ 33-18-9)	Yes, if resident agent is appointed. (§§ 33-18-9, § 33-8-1)	No, person who is not an "inhabitant," unless other circumstances, in the opinion of the court, render such appointment proper. (§ 33-8-7) To the extent a person appointed is "residing out of state" then a resident agent in the state must be appointed). (§ 33-18-9)
South Carolina	Yes, § 62-3-203 does not condition appointment on domicile or residence in state. Furthermore, § 62-3-203(f) recognizes a personal representative appointed at the domicile or if nominated by the decedent's will or by the domiciliary personal representative.	Yes, § 62-3-203 does not condition appointment on domicile or residence in state. Furthermore, § 62-3-203(f) recognizes a personal representative appointed at the domicile or if nominated by the decedent's will or by the domiciliary personal representative.	Yes, § 62-3-203 does not condition appointment on domicile or residence in state. Furthermore, § 62-3-203(f) recognizes a personal representative appointed at the domicile or if nominated by the decedent's will or by the domiciliary personal representative.	Yes, same requirements as in the prior column. (§§ 62-3-203, 62-4-201, 62-4-203)

Table 3.01

Nonresident Individual as Executor or Administrator

	Nonresident Individual as Executor	Nonresident Individual as Administrator	Nonresident Individual as Ancillary Executor	Nonresident Individual as Ancillary Administrator
South Dakota	Yes, if appointed at the domicile, if named in the will, or if nominated by the domiciliary personal representative. (§29A-3-203(g))	Yes. §29A-3-203 does not condition appointment on domicile or residence in-state. Furthermore, §29A-3-203(g) recognizes a personal representative appointed at the domicile or if nominated by the domiciliary personal representative.	Yes, same requirements as in the first column. If no local administration is pending, a foreign domiciliary personal representative can act locally after filing proof of appointment and of any bond given. (§§29A-4-204, 29A-4-207)	Yes, same requirements as in the prior column. (§29A-3-203)
Tennessee	Yes, any resident or nonresident person may serve.(§35-50-107(a)(2)(B))	Same as prior col.	Same as 1st col.	Same as 1st col.
Texas	Yes, if resident agent is appointed. (Estates §304.003(3))	Yes, if resident agent is appointed. (Estates §304.003(3))	Provision is made for receipt of ancillary letters by an executor named in a foreign will admitted to ancillary probate in Texas. (Estates §501.006)	Yes, if resident agent is appointed. (Estates §304.003(3))
Utah	Yes, if appointed at the domicile, if named in the will, or if nominated by the domiciliary personal representative. (§75-3-203(7))	Yes. §75-3-203 does not condition appointment on domicile or residence in-state. Furthermore, §75-3-203 recognizes a personal representative appointed at the domicile or if nominated by the domiciliary personal representative.	Yes, same requirements as in the first column. If no local administration is pending, a foreign domiciliary personal representative can act locally after filing proof of appointment and of any bond given. (§§75-4-204, 75-4-207)	Yes, same requirements as in the prior column. (§§75-4-205, 75-4-207, 75-3-203)
Vermont	Yes, in the court's discretion. (14 §904(a)) Title 14 §904(b) provides that where a nonresident executor is appointed, the executor must designate a resident agent. See also R. of Prob. P. 68.	Yes, in the court's discretion. (14 §904(a)) Title 14 §904(b) provides that where a nonresident administrator is appointed, the administrator must designate a resident agent. See also R. of Prob. P. 68.	Probably; there is no specific provision. Tit. 14 §904 applies only when the principal administration is in Vermont; but see 14 §§1215, 1216.	Probably; there is no specific provision. Tit. 14 §904 applies only when the principal administration is in Vermont; but see 14 §§1215, 1216.
Virginia	Yes, after appointing a resident agent or accepting service upon clerk of court in which he is qualified/appointed. (§64.2-1426)	Same as col. 1.	Same as col. 1.	Same as col. 1.
Washington	Yes, after appointing an agent who is a resident of the county or who is the attorney of record of the estate, upon whom service of all papers may be made. (§11.36.010)	Same as col. 1.	Same as col. 1.	Same as col. 1.

Table 3.01

Nonresident Individual as Executor or Administrator

	Nonresident Individual as Executor	Nonresident Individual as Administrator	Nonresident Individual as Ancillary Executor	Nonresident Individual as Ancillary Administrator
West Virginia	Yes, if resident decedent names the individual executor. (§44-5-3(a)(4)) Appointment as executor constitutes the clerk of the county commission where appointment is made as attorney-in-fact for service of notice and process. (§44-5-3(c))	Yes, if distributees apply in the county court that would have jurisdiction as to the probate of his will, if there were one. Preference is given to husband or wife and persons applying within 30 days of death of the intestate. (§§44-5-3(a)(5), 44-1-4)) Appointment as administrator constitutes that the clerk of the county commission wherein appointment was made is attorney-in-fact for service of notice and process. (§44-5-3(c))	Yes, but only if serving as such in decedent's state of domicile. (§44-5-3(a)(1))	Yes, but only if serving as such in decedent's state of domicile. (§44-5-3(a)(1), (a)(2))
Wisconsin	Yes, after appointment of a resident agent. (§856.23) However, nonresidency may be a sufficient cause for non-appointment or removal, in the court's discretion. (§856.23(2))	Same as col. 1.	Yes, unless the court finds that it will not be for the best interests of the estate or the decedent has otherwise directed. (§868.03(2)(a); see also §877.16)	Yes, unless the court finds that it will not be for the best interests of the estate or the decedent has otherwise directed. (§868.03(2)(a); see also §877.16)
Wyoming	Yes, after appointment of a resident agent. (§2-11-301)	No, unless a resident of Wyoming is appointed co-administrator. (§2-4-203)	Yes, after appointment of a resident agent. No probate is necessary if property in state has a value of less than $200,000. (§§2-11-301, 2-11-201)	No, unless a resident of Wyoming is appointed co-administrator. (§§2-4-203, 2-11-201) However, no probate is necessary if property in state is less than $200,000. (§§2-4-203, 2-11-201)

Table 3.02

Nonresident Individual as Guardian of Minor's or Incompetent's Property

	Nonresident Individual as Guardian of Minor's Property	*Nonresident Individual as Guardian of Incompetent's Property*	*Nonresident Individual as Ancillary Guardian of Minor's Property*	*Nonresident Individual as Ancillary Guardian of Incompetent's Property*
Alabama	Yes. (§§ 26-2A-76, 26-2A-138)	Yes. (§§ 26-2A-104, 26-2A-138)	Yes. (§§ 26-2A-138, 26-2A-160)	Yes. (§§ 26-2A-138, 26-2A-160)
Alaska	Yes. (§§ 13.26.121, 13.26.143, 13.26.465, 13.26.580)	Yes. (§§ 13.26.121, 13.26.143, 13.26.465, 13.26.580)	Yes. (§§ 13.26.211, 13.26.311, 13.26.465, 13.26.580)	Yes. (§§ 13.26.211, 13.26.311, 13.26.465, 13.26.580)
Arizona	Yes. (§§ 14-5202, 14-5206, 14-5410, 14-5432)	Yes. (§§ 14-5301, 14-5311, 14-5410, 14-5432)	Yes. (§§ 14-5202, 14-5206, 14-5410, 14-5432)	Yes. (§§ 14-5301, 14-5311, 14-5410, 14-5432)
Arkansas	Yes; resident agent must be appointed. (§ 28-65-203(f))	Yes; resident agent must be appointed. (§ 28-65-203(f))	Yes; resident agent must be appointed. (§ 28-65-203(f)) However, a guardian appointed in the state of the minor's residence may serve upon petition. (§ 28-65-601)	Yes; resident agent must be appointed. (§ 28-65-203(f)) However, a guardian appointed in the state of the incompetent's residence may serve upon petition. (§ 28-65-601)
California	Yes. (Prob. §§ 1514 & note 22, 1812)	Yes. (Prob. §§ 1514 & note 22, 1812)	Yes. (Prob. §§ 2801, 3800)	Yes. (Prob. §§ 2801, 3800)
Colorado	Yes.[1] (§§ 15-14-202, 15-14-206, 15-14-413, 15-14-433)	Yes.[2] (§§ 15-14-301, 15-14-310, 15-14-413, 15-14-433)	Yes. (§§ 15-14-202, 15-14-206, 15-14-413, 15-14-433)	Yes. (§§ 15-14-301, 15-14-310, 15-14-413, 15-14-433)
Connecticut	Yes, so long as judge is appointed as local agent. (§§ 45a-629, 52-60)	Yes. (§§ 45a-645, 45a-650, 52-60)	Yes. (§§ 45a-629, 45a-632, 52-60)	Yes. (§§ 45a-659, 52-60)
Delaware	Yes. (12 §§ 3901, 3902)	Yes. (12 § 3901)	Yes. (12 §§ 3901, 3902, 3904)	Yes. (12 §§ 3901, 3904)
District of Columbia	Yes, after filing in the office of the Register of Wills an irrevocable power of attorney designating the Register as agent. (§ 21-110) See also § 21-106.	There is no direct authority.	Yes, after filing in the office of the Register of Wills an irrevocable power of attorney designating the Register as agent. (§ 21-110) See also §§ 21-106, 21-111, 21-112.	There is no direct authority. However, see also § 21-2077, allowing person appointed in the domicile to serve if no conservator has been appointed locally, if authenticated copies of the appointment and bond, if any, are filed with the court.
Florida	Yes, if lineal relative, legally adopted child or adoptive parent, spouse, brother, sister, uncle, aunt, niece or nephew of ward, or lineal relative of such person, or spouse of a person otherwise qualified. (§744.309)	Yes, if lineal relative, legally adopted child or adoptive parent, spouse, brother, sister, uncle, aunt, niece or nephew of ward, or lineal relative of such person, or spouse of a person otherwise qualified. (§744.309)	Yes, if a resident agent is designated. (§§744.306, 744.307)	Yes, if a resident agent is designated. (§§744.306, 744.307)

Table 3.02

Nonresident Individual as Guardian of Minor's or Incompetent's Property

	Nonresident Individual as Guardian of Minor's Property	Nonresident Individual as Guardian of Incompetent's Property	Nonresident Individual as Ancillary Guardian of Minor's Property	Nonresident Individual as Ancillary Guardian of Incompetent's Property
Georgia	In Georgia, the relevant person regarding property in excess of $15,000 is the conservator. There does not appear to be a restriction on a nonresident serving as conservator or guardian ($15,000 or less). (§§ 29-3-5, 29-3-6, 29-2-2, 29-2-4, 29-3-1(b))	Implied. (§§ 29-4-2; 29-4-3)	See first column.	Probably yes. (§§ 29-4-2; 29-4-3).
Hawaii	Yes. The court is required to make an appointment "in the best interest of the minor." There is no residency requirement. (§§ 560:5-206(a) 560:5-204)	Probably yes. (§§ 560:5-306; 560:5-304)	Yes. (§ 560:5-433)	Yes. (§ 560:5-433)
Idaho	Yes. (§§ 15-5-202, 15-5-206, 15-5-410(1))	Yes. (§§ 15-5-301, 15-5-311, 15-5-410(1))	Yes. (§§ 15-5-202, 15-5-206, 15-5-410(1))	Yes. (§§ 15-5-301(c), 15-5-311, 15-5-410(1))
Illinois	Yes, if a resident of the U.S. and who court finds capable of providing an active and suitable program of guardianship for the minor. (755 ILCS §5/11-3)	Yes, if a resident of the U.S. and who court finds capable of providing an active and suitable program of guardianship for the minor. (755 ILCS §5/11a-5)	Yes, if a resident of the U.S. (755 ILCS §5/11-3) There does not seem to be a specific provision as to ancillary guardians.	Yes, if a resident of the U.S. (755 ILCS §5/11a-5) There does not seem to be a specific provision as to ancillary guardians.
Indiana	Yes. (§29-3-5-5) There is no prohibition. Furthermore, if no one is appointed locally, a guardian appointed at the protected person's domicile may prove his foreign appointment and then act as a guardian appointed in Indiana. (§29-3-13-2)	Yes. (§ 29-3-5-5) There is no prohibition. Furthermore, if no one is appointed locally, a guardian appointed at the protected person's domicile may prove his foreign appointment and then act as a guardian appointed in Indiana. (§29-3-13-2)	Yes, after the guardian proves his foreign appointment. (§29-3-13-2)	Yes, after the guardian proves his foreign appointment. (§29-3-13-2)
Iowa	Yes, if a resident is also appointed to serve with the nonresident or alone if good cause is shown. (§633.64)	Yes, if a resident is also appointed to serve with the nonresident or alone if good cause is shown. (§633.64)	Yes, if no conservatorship, nor application therefor, pending in this state. (§633.603)	Yes, if no conservatorship, nor application therefor, pending in this state and a resident is also appointed to serve with the nonresident, although the foreign conservator may serve alone if good cause is shown. (§633.603)
Kansas	Yes, if a resident agent is appointed. (§§ 59-3054, 59-3069(h))	Yes, if a resident agent is appointed. (§§ 59-3054, 59-3069(h))	Yes, if a resident agent is appointed. (§§ 59-3051(n), 59-3054; 59-3062, 59-3069(h))	Yes, if a resident agent is appointed. (§§ 59-3051(n), 59-3062, 59-3069(h))

Table 3.02
Nonresident Individual as Guardian of Minor's or Incompetent's Property

	Nonresident Individual as Guardian of Minor's Property	Nonresident Individual as Guardian of Incompetent's Property	Nonresident Individual as Ancillary Guardian of Minor's Property	Nonresident Individual as Ancillary Guardian of Incompetent's Property
Kentucky	Only if over 18 and related by consanguinity, marriage, adoption, or the spouse of such person so related. (§395.005)	Only if over 18 and related by consanguinity, marriage, adoption, or the spouse of such person so related. (§§387.185, 395.005)	Yes, if appointed and qualified according to the laws of the ward's domicile. (§§387.185, 395.005)	Yes, if appointed and qualified according to the laws of the ward's domicile. (§§387.185, 395.005; notes on the applicability of §387.185 to incompetents)
Louisiana	Yes, if resident agent is appointed. (Code Civ. Pro. art. 4273; Rev. Stat. §9:751)	Yes, if resident agent is appointed for service of process. (Code Civ. Pro. arts. 4273, 4556, 4561)	Yes, assuming the minor is residing outside Louisiana. (Code Civ. Pro. art. 4431)	Yes, assuming the ward is residing outside Louisiana. (Code Civ. Pro. arts. 4556, 4561(B)(1)(c))
Maine	Yes. (18-A §§5-202, 5-206, 5-410, 5-432)	Yes. (18-A §§5-301, 5-311, 5-410, 5-432)	Yes. (18-A §§5-202, 5-206, 5-410, 5-432)	Yes. (18-A §§5-311, 5-410, 5-432)
Maryland	Yes, if resident agent is appointed. (Est. & Trusts §13-207(d))	Yes, if resident agent is appointed. (Est. & Trusts §13-207(d))	Yes, although a foreign guardian or other fiduciary is not required to qualify as an ancillary. (Est. & Trusts §§13-222, 13-207(d))	Yes, although a foreign guardian or other fiduciary is not required to qualify as an ancillary. (Est. & Trusts §§13-222, 13-207(d))
Massachusetts	Yes. (190B §§5-409, 5-431)	Yes. (190B §§5-409, 5-431)	Yes. (202 §33) This statute authorizes the foreign guardian to act with respect to local property, if there is no local guardian, upon petition to the county court where the property is situated.	Yes. (202 §33) This statute authorizes the foreign guardian or other fiduciary to act with respect to local property, if there is no local guardian, upon petition to the county court where the property is situated.
Michigan	There seems to be no statutory prohibition. (§§700.5212, 700.5201, 700.5409)	There seems to be no prohibition. (§§700.5313, 700.5301, 700.5409)	There seems to be no prohibition. (§§700.5409, 700.5432, 700.5433)	There seems to be no prohibition. (§§700.5409, 700.5432, 700.5433)
Minnesota	Yes. (§§524.5-202, 524.5-206, 524.5-413, 524.5-433).	Yes, by implication, since there is no statutory prohibition. (§§524.5-301, 524.5-309), 524.5-413, 524.5-433).	Yes. (§§524.5-202, 524.5-206, 524.5-413, 524.5-433).	Yes, by implication, since there is no statutory prohibition. (§§524.5-301, 524.5-309), 524.5-413, 524.5-433).
Mississippi	The parties may appoint a nonresident as a testamentary guardian. (§§93-13-7, 93-13-13)	There is no statutory prohibition. (§93-13-121 et seq.)	Yes. (§§93-13-181 et seq.)	Yes. (§93-13-181 et seq.)
Missouri	Yes. (§§475.055(1)(1), 475.055(3), 475.055(4), after designation of resident agent (§473.117(3)).	Yes. (§§475.055(1)(1), 475.055(3), 475.055(4) after designation of resident agent (§473.117(3)).	Yes. (§§475.055(.3), 475.339)	Yes. (§§475.055(.3), 475.339)
Montana	Yes. (§§72-5-211, 72-5-223, 72-5-410)	Yes. (§§72-5-312, 72-5-410)	Yes. (§§72-5-211, 72-5-223)	Yes. (§72-5-312)
Nebraska	Yes. (§§30-2606, 30-2610, 30-2639(b)(2), 30-2661)	Yes. (§§30-2617, 30-2627, 30-2639, 30-2661)	Yes. (§§30-2606, 30-2610, 30-2639(b)(2), 30-2661)	Yes. (§§30-2617, 30-2627, 30-2639(b)(2), 30-2661)

Table 3.02

Nonresident Individual as Guardian of Minor's or Incompetent's Property

	Nonresident Individual as Guardian of Minor's Property	*Nonresident Individual as Guardian of Incompetent's Property*	*Nonresident Individual as Ancillary Guardian of Minor's Property*	*Nonresident Individual as Ancillary Guardian of Incompetent's Property*
Nevada	Yes. The court will appoint a qualified person most suitable to be a guardian to a minor. (AB 319 (2017)/§ 46(6)(a)) Nevada will recognize guardians registered in a different state. (§ 159.2027) See also § 159.0487 specifying for whom a guardian may be appointed, including persons not resident, but physically present in the state and nonresidents with property in the state.	Yes. The court shall not give preference to a resident over a nonresident if the court determines that the nonresident is more qualified and suitable to serve as guardian; and the distance from the proposed guardian's place of residence and the adult's place of residence will not affect the quality of the guardianship or the ability of the proposed guardian to make decisions and respond quickly to the needs of the adult because (1) A person or care provider in this State is providing continuing care and supervision for the adult; or (2) The adult is in a secured residential long-term care facility in this State; or (3) Within 30 days after the appointment of the proposed guardian, the proposed guardian will move to this State or the adult will move to the proposed guardian's state of residence. (§ 159.0613) See also § 159.0487 specifying for whom a guardian may be appointed, including persons not resident, but physically present in the state and nonresidents with property in the state.	Yes. The court will appoint a qualified person most suitable to be a guardian to a minor. (AB 319 (2017)/§ 46(6)(a)) Nevada will recognize guardians registered in a different state. (§ 159.2027) See also § 159.0487 specifying for whom a guardian may be appointed, including persons not resident, but physically present in the state and nonresidents with property in the state.	Yes. The court shall not give preference to a resident over a nonresident if the court determines that the nonresident is more qualified and suitable to serve as guardian; and the distance from the proposed guardian's place of residence and the adult's place of residence will not affect the quality of the guardianship or the ability of the proposed guardian to make decisions and respond quickly to the needs of the adult because (1) A person or care provider in this State is providing continuing care and supervision for the adult; or (2) The adult is in a secured residential long-term care facility in this State; or (3) Within 30 days after the appointment of the proposed guardian, the proposed guardian will move to this State or the adult will move to the proposed guardian's state of residence. (§ 159.0613) See also § 159.0487 specifying for whom a guardian may be appointed, including persons not resident, but physically present in the state and nonresidents with property in the state.
New Hampshire	Yes. (§ 464-A:10)	Yes. (§ 464-A:10)	Yes. (§§ 463:10, 463:30, 554:28)	Yes. (§§ 464-A:10, 464-C:18, 554:28)
New Jersey	Yes, after filing power of attorney with the surrogate of the county or clerk of the court. (§§ 3B:14-47, 3B:12-21; 3B:1-1)	Yes, after filing power of attorney with the surrogate of the county or clerk of the court. (§ 3B:14-47; 3B:1-1)	Yes, after filing power of attorney with the surrogate of the county or clerk of the court. (§§ 3B:14-47, 3B:12-21; 3B:1-1) See also § 3B:12-19 requiring supervision of surrogate.	Yes, after filing power of attorney with the surrogate of the county or clerk of the court. (§§ 3B:14-47, 3B:1-1)
New Mexico	Yes. (§§ 45-5-202, 45-5-206, 45-5-410)	Yes. (§§ 45-5-301, 45-5-311, 45-5-410)	Yes. (§§ 45-5-202(C), 45-5-311, 45-5-410(A)(1))	Yes. (§§ 45-5-301(C), 45-5-311, 45-5-410(A)(1))
New York	There seems to be no prohibition. (Surr. Ct. Proc. Act § 1707)	There does not seem to be a prohibition. (Men. Hyg. §§ 81.01, 81.19)	Yes. (Surr. Ct. Proc. Act § 1716(4)) However, ancillary proceedings may not be necessary. (Surr. Ct. Proc. Act § 1716(1))	There does not seem to be a prohibition. (Men. Hyg. §§ 81.01, 81.09) However, there is a special provision if the incapacitated person is not present in the state and a guardian has been appointed elsewhere. The foreign guardian can be appointed with regard to New York property management in the discretion of the court. (Men. Hyg. § 81.18)
North Carolina	Possibly under § 35A-1224(b), but nonresidency appears to be grounds for removal. (§ 35A-1290(b)(4))	Yes, if a resident agent is appointed and the nonresident agrees in a writing to the jurisdiction of North Carolina. If a resident has "likely" to become a nonresident, the clerk has the duty to remove the resident or take other action sufficient to protect the ward's interests. (§§ 35A-1213(b), 35A-1290(b)(4))	Possibly. § 35A-1280 states that the clerk *may* appoint an ancillary guardian if it is established that:	Possibly. § 35A-1280 states that the clerk *may* appoint an ancillary guardian if it is established that:

Table 3.02

Nonresident Individual as Guardian of Minor's or Incompetent's Property

	Nonresident Individual as Guardian of Minor's Property	Nonresident Individual as Guardian of Incompetent's Property	Nonresident Individual as Ancillary Guardian of Minor's Property	Nonresident Individual as Ancillary Guardian of Incompetent's Property
North Dakota	Yes. (§§ 30.1-27-06, 30.1-29-10)	Yes. (§§ 30.1-28-01, 30.1-28-11, 30.1-29-10)	Yes. (§§ 30.1-27-06, 30.1-29-10(3)(a))	Yes. (§§ 30.1-28-01, 30.1-28-11, 30.1-29-10(3)(a))
Ohio	Yes, if named in a will by a parent of the minor, or selected by a minor over 14 years old (§ 2111.12) or appointed, after being nominated in or pursuant to a durable power of attorney as described in § 1337.24 or § 2111.121. See § 2109.21(C).	No. (§§ 2109.21(D), 2111.02(A))	No. (§ 2111.37)	No. (§ 2111.37)
Oklahoma	Yes, if citizen or resident of the U.S. and at the court's discretion for the best interest of the minor. (30 § 4-104(a)) Generally, the person appointed must be a resident of the state for one year in good faith, but that requirement does not apply if the person appointed will be guardian for a spouse, child, children, grandchildren, parent, grandparent, brother, sister, aunt, uncle, niece or nephew, (30 § 4-104(b)) after appointing resident agent (58 § 162).	Yes, if citizen or resident of the U.S. and at the court's discretion for the best interest of the minor. (30 § 4-104(a)) Generally, the person appointed must be a resident of the state for one year in good faith, but that requirement does not apply if the person appointed will be guardian for a spouse, child, children, grandchild, grandchildren, parent, grandparent, brother, sister, aunt, uncle, niece or nephew, (30 § 4-104(b)) after appointing resident agent (58 § 162).	Yes, if citizen or resident of the U.S. and at the court's discretion for the best interest of the minor. (30 § 4-104(a)) Generally, the person appointed must be a resident of the state for one year in good faith, but that requirement does not apply if the person appointed will be guardian for a spouse, child, children, grandchild, grandchildren, parent, grandparent, brother, sister, aunt, uncle, niece or nephew, (30 § 4-104(b)) However, if the incompetent ward and domiciliary guardian are both nonresidents, then no appointment of the guardian may even be required, since, pursuant to court approval, the ward's estate can be removed from the state. (30 §§ 4-601, 4-605, 4-607)	Yes, if citizen or resident of the U.S. and at the court's discretion for the best interest of the minor. (30 § 4-104(a)) Generally, the person appointed must be a resident of the state for one year in good faith, but that requirement does not apply if the person appointed will be guardian for a spouse, child, children, grandchild, grandchildren, parent, grandparent, brother, sister, aunt, uncle, niece or nephew, (30 § 4-104(b)) However, if the incompetent ward and domiciliary guardian are both nonresidents, then no appointment of the guardian may even be required, since, pursuant to court approval, the ward's estate can be removed from the state. (30 §§ 4-601, 4-605, 4-607)
Oregon	Yes. (§ 125.200)	Yes. (§ 125.200)	Yes. (§ 125.200)	Yes. (§ 125.200)
Pennsylvania	Yes. (20 §§ 5112, 5147)	Yes. (20 §§ 5515, 5512)	Yes. (20 §§ 5111, 4101 et seq.)	Yes. (20 §§ 4101 et seq., 5512, 5511(b))
Rhode Island	Yes, if it is a testamentary appointment. (§§ 33-15.1-8) and if a resident agent is appointed (§ 33-18-9).	Yes, there is no statutory prohibition, as long as a resident agent is appointed. (§ 33-18-9)	Yes. (§§ 33-15.1-9) Moreover, the guardian may be able to remove property without local appointment. (§ 33-15-42)	Yes. There is no statutory prohibition. Moreover, the guardian may be able to remove property without local appointment. (§ 33-15-42)
South Carolina	Yes. (§§ 62-5-301, 62-5-408, 62-5-308, 62-5-430)	Yes. (§§ 62-5-301, 62-5-408, 62-5-308, 62-5-430)	Yes. (§§ 62-4-204, 62-5-429, 62-5-430, 62-5-301(c), 62-5-408(a)(1))	Yes. (§§ 62-5-301 et seq., 62-5-308, 62-5-430)

Table 3.02
Nonresident Individual as Guardian of Minor's or Incompetent's Property

	Nonresident Individual as Guardian of Minor's Property	Nonresident Individual as Guardian of Incompetent's Property	Nonresident Individual as Ancillary Guardian of Minor's Property	Nonresident Individual as Ancillary Guardian of Incompetent's Property
South Dakota	Yes, if capable of providing an active and suitable program of guardianship. (§29A-5-110) A resident agent must be designated. (§29A-5-113)	Yes, if capable of providing an active and suitable program of guardianship. (§29A-5-110) A resident agent must be designated. (§29A-5-113)	Yes. (§29A-5-114) However, ancillary proceedings may not be necessary. (§29A-5-115)	Yes. (§29A-5-114) However, ancillary proceedings may not be necessary. (§29A-5-115)
Tennessee	Yes, any person may serve as the guardian. (§35-50-107(a)(2)(E)) There is no statutory provision for guardian of the property. This would require resident cofiduciary. (§35-50-107(a)(1)) But see Brimhall v. Simmons, 338 F.2d 702, 707 (6th Cir. 1964), which construes Tennessee law as permitting nonresident guardian of incompetent appointed in another state to serve in Tennessee with respect to a nonresident ward in absence of statute and without requiring resident cofiduciary.	Yes, any person may serve as guardian, referred to in statute as "conservator." (§35-50-107(a)(2)(F)) See also §30-1-116. There is no statutory provision for guardian of the property. This would require resident cofiduciary. (§35-50-107(a)(1)) But see Brimhall v. Simmons, 338 F.2d 702, 707 (6th Cir. 1964), which construes Tennessee law as permitting nonresident guardian of incompetent appointed in another state to serve in Tennessee with respect to a nonresident ward in absence of statute and without requiring resident cofiduciary.	See first column.	Same as 2d column.
Texas	Yes, if resident agent is appointed. (Estates §§1104.351, 1104.352, 1104.357)	Yes, if resident agent is appointed. (Estates §§1104.351, 1104.352, 1104.357)	Yes, but the guardian must have been appointed where the ward resides, the guardian is qualified as a fiduciary in that jurisdiction, and a complete transcript is filed of the proceedings in which the appointment took place. (Estates §1252.051)	Yes, but the guardian must have been appointed where the ward resides, the guardian is qualified as a fiduciary in that jurisdiction, and a complete transcript is filed of the proceedings in which the appointment took place. (Estates §1252.051) However, ancillary proceedings may not be necessary. (Estates §1252.055) (removal of personal property of the ward from the state under certain circumstances)
Utah	Yes. (§§75-5-202, 75-5-206, 75-5-410, 75-5-432)	Yes. (§§75-5-301, 75-5-311, 75-5-410, 75-5-432)	Yes. (§§75-5-202, 75-5-206, 75-5-410(1)(a), 75-5-432)	Yes. (§§75-5-301, 75-5-311, 75-5-410(1)(a), 75-5-432)
Vermont	Yes, in the court's discretion if the guardian is named in a will or is a relative of the ward. (14 §2603) A nonresident guardian of a minor's property must appoint a resident agent. See R. Prob. P. Rule 68(b).	Yes, in the court's discretion if the guardian is named in a will or is a relative of the ward. (14 §2603) A nonresident guardian of an incompetent's property must appoint a resident agent. (R. Prob. P. Rule 68(b)).	Yes, in the court's discretion if the guardian is named in a will or is a relative of the ward. (14 §2603) A nonresident guardian of a minor's property must appoint a resident agent. See also 14 §2649; R. Prob. P. Rule 68(b).	Yes, in the court's discretion if the guardian is named in a will or is a relative of the ward. (14 §2603) A nonresident guardian of an incompetent's property must appoint a resident agent. See also 14 §2649; R. Prob. P. Rule 68(b).

Table 3.02
Nonresident Individual as Guardian of Minor's or Incompetent's Property

	Nonresident Individual as Guardian of Minor's Property	Nonresident Individual as Guardian of Incompetent's Property	Nonresident Individual as Ancillary Guardian of Minor's Property	Nonresident Individual as Ancillary Guardian of Incompetent's Property
Virginia	Yes, after appointing a resident agent. (§64.2-1426(A))	Yes, after appointing a resident agent. (§64.2-1426(A))	Yes, after appointing a resident agent. (§64.2-1426) However, ancillary proceedings may not be necessary. (§64.2-1427)	Yes, after appointing a resident agent. (§64.2-1426) However, ancillary proceedings may not be necessary. (§64.2-1427)
Washington	Yes, after appointing a resident agent. (§§11.36.010, 11.88.020(1)(d))	Yes, after appointing a resident agent. (§§11.36.010, 11.88.020(1)(d))	Yes, after appointing a resident agent. (§§11.36.010, 11.88.020(1)(d))	Yes, after appointing a resident agent. (§§11.36.010, 11.88.020(1)(d))
West Virginia	Yes, for resident infants if appointed by infant's father or mother by last will and testament. (§§44-5-3(a)(6), 44-10-1) Appointment as testamentary guardian constitutes the clerk of the county commission where appointment is made as attorney-in-fact for service of notice and process. (§44-5-3(c))	Yes. (§§44-5-3(a)(7), 44-10-1)	Yes, as testamentary guardian if serving as such in minor's state of domicile. (§44-5-3(a)(3)) Appointment as testamentary guardian constitutes the clerk of the county commission where appointment is made as attorney-in-fact for service of notice and process. (§44-5-3(c))	Yes. (§§44-5-3(a)(7), 44-10-1)
Wisconsin	There is no statutory prohibition. (§54.15)	Yes. There is no statutory prohibition. (§54.15)	Yes. There is no statutory prohibition. (§54.15)	Yes. There is no statutory prohibition. (§54.15)
Wyoming	Yes. There is no statutory prohibition. (§§3-2-101, 3-2-107)	Yes. There is no statutory prohibition. (§§3-2-101, 3-2-107, 3-3-401)	Yes. There is no statutory prohibition. (§§3-2-101, 3-2-107, 3-3-401)	Yes. There is no statutory prohibition. (§§3-2-101, 3-3-401)

[1] §15-14-413(1)(a) gives highest priority to the appointment of a person recognized by the appropriate court of the foreign jurisdiction in which the protected person "resides." The provision, however, does not specifically address the appointment of a foreign person when the protected person resides in Colorado. Presumably, no limitation is placed on such person serving, if the person otherwise complies with the statute.

[2] Id.

Table 3.03
Nonresident Bank as Executor or Administrator

	Nonresident Bank as Executor	Nonresident Bank as Administrator	Nonresident Bank as Ancillary Administrator	Nonresident Bank as Ancillary Executor	Nonresident Bank as Ancillary Administrator
Alabama	Yes, if reciprocal treatment is accorded Alabama banks. (§10A-2-15.41(a)(2)) Nonresident bank must file a verified statement with the Commissioner of Revenue. (§10A-2-15.42)	Yes, if reciprocal treatment is accorded Alabama banks. (§10A-2-15.41(a)(2)) Nonresident bank must file a verified statement with the Commissioner of Revenue. (§10A-2-15.42)	Yes, if reciprocal treatment is accorded Alabama banks. (§10A-2-15.41(a)(2)) Nonresident bank must file a verified statement with the Commissioner of Revenue. (§10A-2-15.42)	Yes, if reciprocal treatment is accorded Alabama banks. (§10A-2-15.41(a)(2)) Nonresident bank must file a verified statement with the Commissioner of Revenue. (§10A-2-15.42)	Yes, if reciprocal treatment is accorded Alabama banks. (§10A-2-15.41(a)(2)) Nonresident bank must file a verified statement with the Commissioner of Revenue. (§10A-2-15.42)
Alaska	Yes, if qualified doing business in Alaska under §06.26.010(a)(8) or otherwise as indicated in §43.31.300 that a nonresident may serve as executor for a nonresident decedent if that executor is also the executor of the decedent's estate in the state of decedent's domicile. The provision, however, does not specifically address the appointment of a foreign executor when the decedent is an Alaska resident.	No specific authorization. But see §13.16.110 for informal appointment. See also §§13.21.030 and 13.21.035 allowing the duly authorized personal representative to serve in Alaska if there is no local administration or application for one.	Yes. (§§06.26.010(a)(8), 43.31.300) See also §§13.21.030 and 13.21.035 allowing the duly authorized personal representative to serve in Alaska if there is no local administration or application for one.	Yes. (§§06.26.010(a)(8), 43.31.300) See also §§13.21.030 and 13.21.035 allowing the duly authorized personal representative to serve in Alaska if there is no local administration or application for one.	No specific authorization. But see §13.16.110 for informal appointment. See also §§13.21.030 and 13.21.035 allowing the duly authorized personal representative to serve in Alaska if there is no local administration or application for one.
Arizona	No. (§14-3203(F)(3))	No. (§14-3203(F)(3))	No. (§14-3203(F)(3))	No. (§14-3203(F)(3))	No. (§14-3203(F)(3))
Arkansas	Yes, if authorized to act as a fiduciary in the state. (§28-48-101(b)(4))	Yes, if authorized to act as a fiduciary in the state. (§28-48-101(b)(4))	Yes, if the person is a personal representative in the domiciliary state and a resident agent is appointed. (§§28-42-102, 28-42-104) Alternatively, the same as Executor, as long as the domiciliary representative is given notice and is not appointed instead. (§28-42-102(c)) In any event, all ancillary appointments of nonresidents appear to be discretionary with the courts. See Phillips v. Sherrod Estate, 453 S.W.2d 60 (Ark. 1970). The bank, if a corporation, does not have to be authorized to do business in the state. (§28-42-102(a)(2))	Yes, if the person is a personal representative in the domiciliary state and a resident agent is appointed. (§§28-42-102, 28-42-104) Alternatively, the same as Executor, as long as the domiciliary representative is given notice and is not appointed instead. (§28-42-102(c)) In any event, all ancillary appointments of nonresidents appear to be discretionary with the courts. See Phillips v. Sherrod Estate, 453 S.W.2d 60 (Ark. 1970). The bank, if a corporation, does not have to be authorized to do business in the state. (§28-42-102(a)(2))	Yes, if the person is a personal representative in the domiciliary state and a resident agent is appointed. (§§28-42-102, 28-42-104) Alternatively, the same as Executor, as long as the domiciliary representative is given notice and is not appointed instead. (§28-42-102(c)) In any event, all ancillary appointments of nonresidents appear to be discretionary with the courts. See Phillips v. Sherrod Estate, 453 S.W.2d 60 (Ark. 1970). The bank, if a corporation, does not have to be authorized to do business in the state. (§28-42-102(a)(2))
California	Yes, if authorized to conduct business of a trust company in the state. (Prob. §§83 and notes, 300, 8572)	Yes, if authorized to conduct business of a trust company in the state. (Prob. §§83 and notes, 300, 8461(r), 8402)	Yes, if authorized to conduct business of a trust company in the state. (Prob. §§83 and notes, 300, 12540, 12541)	Yes, if authorized to conduct business of a trust company in the state. (Prob. §§83 and notes, 300, 12540, 12541)	Yes, if authorized to conduct business of a trust company in the state. (Prob. §§83 and notes, 300, 12540, 12541)

Table 3.03

Nonresident Bank as Executor or Administrator

	Nonresident Bank as Executor	*Nonresident Bank as Administrator*	*Nonresident Bank as Ancillary Executor*	*Nonresident Bank as Ancillary Administrator*
Colorado	Yes, but may first be required to obtain a certificate of authority to transact business. (§§ 15-10-201(35), 15-12-203) The relevant provision is found at § 7-115-101.	Yes, but may first be required to obtain a certificate of authority to transact business. (§§ 15-12-203, 15-10-201(35)) The relevant provision is found at § 7-115-101.	Yes, but may first be required to obtain a certificate of authority to transact business. (§§ 15-12-203, 15-13-205) The relevant provision is found at § 7-115-101.	Yes, but may first be required to obtain a certificate of authority to transact business. (§§ 15-12-203, 15-13-205) The relevant provision is found at § 7-115-101.
Connecticut	Yes, if reciprocal treatment is accorded Connecticut banks. (§ 45a-206)	Uncertain.	Yes, if reciprocal treatment is accorded Connecticut banks. (§ 45a-206)	Uncertain.
Delaware	Yes, if reciprocal treatment accorded Delaware corporations, (8 § 380) and after filing in the office of the Register of Wills an irrevocable power of attorney designating the Register an agent. (12 § 1506)	Yes, if reciprocal treatment accorded Delaware corporations, (8 § 380) and after filing in the office of the Register of Wills an irrevocable power of attorney designating the Register an agent. (12 § 1506)	Yes, if reciprocal treatment accorded Delaware corporations. (8 § 380)	Yes, if reciprocal treatment accorded Delaware corporations. (8 § 380)
District of Columbia	Yes. (§§ 26-1301, 26-1309, 26-1310, 26-1335)	Yes. (§§ 26-1301, 26-1309, 26-1310, 26-1335)	Yes. (§§ 26-1301, 26-1309, 26-1310, 26-1335, 20-341, 20-342)	Yes. (§§ 26-1301, 26-1309, 26-1310, 26-1335, 20-341, 20-342)
Florida	No. (§ 660.41(1))	No. (§ 660.41(1))	Yes. (§ 660.41(1))	Yes. (§ 660.41(1))
Georgia	Yes, if it is a bank authorized to act in a fiduciary capacity in the state in which it is incorporated or organized or, if the foreign entity is a national banking association, in the state which has its principal place of business. (§ 53-12-321)	Yes, if it is a bank authorized to act in a fiduciary capacity in the state in which it is incorporated or organized or, if the foreign entity is a national banking association, in the state which has its principal place of business. (§ 53-12-321)	Yes, if it is a bank authorized to act in a fiduciary capacity in the state in which it is incorporated or organized or, if the foreign entity is a national banking association, in the state which has its principal place of business. (§ 53-12-321)	Yes, if it is a bank authorized to act in a fiduciary capacity in the state in which it is incorporated or organized or, if the foreign entity is a national banking association, in the state which has its principal place of business. (§ 53-12-321)
Hawaii	Yes, if named in will. (§ 560:3-203(a)(1)) Any bank, after having obtained approval (§ 412:5-205), can serve as a trust company. A trust company can serve as a personal representative or trustee. (§ 412:8-201)	Identical to prior column, except a court appointment of an administrator would only occur if persons with priority under the statute could not serve or were objected to by persons with a right to object. (§ 560:3-203)	Same as first column. If appointed at domicile, a foreign personal representative may exercise all powers of a local representative.	Same as second column. If appointed at domicile, a foreign personal representative may exercise all powers of a local representative.
Idaho	Yes. (§§ 15-3-203)	Yes. (§§ 15-3-203)	Yes. (§§ 15-3-203)	Yes. (§§ 15-3-203)

Table 3.03
Nonresident Bank as Executor or Administrator

	Nonresident Bank as Executor	Nonresident Bank as Administrator	Nonresident Bank as Ancillary Executor	Nonresident Bank as Ancillary Administrator
Illinois	Yes, if the corporation is authorized by the laws of the state of its organization or domicile to act as a fiduciary in that state and reciprocal treatment is accorded Illinois banks. (205 ILCS §620/4-2) Prior to the time any corporation can act, it must obtain from the Commissioner of Banks and Real Estate a certificate of authority. (205 ILCS §620/4-5)	Yes, if the corporation is authorized by the laws of the state of its organization or domicile to act as a fiduciary in that state and reciprocal treatment is accorded Illinois banks. (205 ILCS §620/4-2) Prior to the time any corporation can act, it must obtain from the Commissioner of Banks and Real Estate a certificate of authority. (205 ILCS §620/4-5)	Yes, if the corporation is authorized by the laws of the state of its organization or domicile to act as a fiduciary in that state and reciprocal treatment is accorded Illinois banks. (205 ILCS §620/4-2) Prior to the time any corporation can act, it must obtain from the Commissioner of Banks and Real Estate a certificate of authority. (205 ILCS §620/4-5)	Yes, if the corporation is authorized by the laws of the state of its organization or domicile to act as a fiduciary in that state and reciprocal treatment is accorded Illinois banks. (205 ILCS §620/4-2) Prior to the time any corporation can act, it must obtain from the Commissioner of Banks and Real Estate a cer tificate of authority. (205 ILCS §620/4-5)
Indiana	Yes, if serving jointly with a resident. (§29-1-10-1(c))	Yes, if serving jointly with a resident. (§29-1-10-1(c))	There is no statutory prohibition. However, §29-2-1-1 states that a "local personal representative includes any personal representative appointed in this state pursuant to appointment proceedings described in article 1 of this title." That could include §29-1-10-1(c), requiring joint appointment of a resident. Note that if a domiciliary foreign personal representative has established his appointment the domiciliary personal repre sentative can act like a local personal representative in Indiana. (§§29-2-1-5, 29-2-1-6)	There is no statutory prohibition. However, §29-2-1-1 states that a "local personal representative includes any personal representative appointed in this state pursuant to appointment proceedings described in article 1 of this title." That could include §29-1-10-1(c), requiring joint appointment of a resident. Note that if a domiciliary foreign personal representative has established his appointment the domiciliary personal repre sentative can act like a local personal representative in Indiana. (§§29-2-1-5, 29-2-1-6)
Iowa	Yes, if reciprocal treatment is accorded Iowa banks. (§633.64(2))	Yes, if reciprocal treatment is accorded Iowa banks. (§633.64(2))	Yes, if reciprocal treatment is accorded Iowa banks. (§§633.64(2), 633.502)	Yes, if reciprocal treatment is accorded Iowa banks. (§§633.64(2), 633.502)

Table 3.03

Nonresident Bank as Executor or Administrator

	Nonresident Bank as Executor	Nonresident Bank as Administrator	Nonresident Bank as Ancillary Executor	Nonresident Bank as Ancillary Administrator
Kansas	Yes, if it is organized under the laws of, and has a principal place of business in, another state that permits a bank or other corporation that is similarly organized in Kansas to act in a like fiduciary capacity in the other state under similar conditions (§59-1701(a)(3)) and a resident agent is appointed (§59-1706). An officer, employee, or agent of a bank or corporation which is not authorized to act as a fiduciary in Kansas may himself or herself not act as a fiduciary in Kansas, whether a resident or nonresident of Kansas, if such person is acting as a fiduciary on behalf of such bank or corporation. (§59-1701(b))	Yes, if it is organized under the laws of, and has a principal place of business in, another state that permits a bank or other corporation that is similarly organized in Kansas to act in a like fiduciary capacity in the other state under similar conditions (§59-1701(a)(3)) and a resident agent is appointed (§59-1706). An officer, employee, or agent of a bank or corporation which is not authorized to act as a fiduciary in Kansas may himself or herself not act as a fiduciary in Kansas, whether a resident or nonresident of Kansas, if such person is acting as a fiduciary on behalf of such bank or corporation. (§59-1701(b))	Yes, if it is organized under the laws of, and has a principal place of business in, another state that permits a bank or other corporation that is similarly organized in Kansas to act in a like fiduciary capacity in the other state under similar conditions (§59-1701(a)(3)) and a resident agent is appointed (§59-1706). An officer, employee, or agent of a bank or corporation which is not authorized to act as a fiduciary in Kansas may himself or herself not act as a fiduciary in Kansas, whether a resident or nonresident of Kansas, if such person is acting as a fiduciary on behalf of such bank or corporation. (§59-1701(b))	Yes, if it is organized under the laws of, and has a principal place of business in, another state that permits a bank or other corporation that is similarly organized in Kansas to act in a like fiduciary capacity in the other state under similar conditions (§59-1701(a)(3)) and a resident agent is appointed (§59-1706). An officer, employee, or agent of a bank or corporation which is not authorized to act as a fiduciary in Kansas may himself or herself not act as a fiduciary in Kansas, whether a resident or nonresident of Kansas, if such person is acting as a fiduciary on behalf of such bank or corporation. (§59-1701(b))
Kentucky	No. (§395.005)	No. (§395.005)	No. (§395.005)	No. (§395.005)
Louisiana	Yes; resident agent must be appointed. (Civ. Code Pro. arts. 3097(A)(4), 5251(11); Rev. Stat. §12:308)	Yes; resident agent must be appointed. (Civ. Code Pro. arts. 3097(A)(4), 5251(11); Rev. Stat. §12:308)	Yes; resident agent must be appointed. (Civ. Code Pro. arts. 3097(A)(4), 3402, 3404, 5251(11); Rev. Stat. §12:308)	Yes; resident agent must be appointed. (Civ. Code Pro. arts. 3097(A)(4), 3402, 3404, 5251(11); Rev. Stat. §12:308)
Maine	Yes, if reciprocal treatment is accorded Maine banks. (18 §4161)	Yes, if reciprocal treatment is accorded Maine banks. (18 §4161)	Yes, if reciprocal treatment is accorded Maine banks. (18 §4161)	Yes, if reciprocal treatment is accorded Maine banks. (18 §4161)
Maryland	Yes. (Est. & Trusts §5-105)	Yes. (Est. & Trusts §5-105)	Yes, although a foreign personal representative is not required to take out letters in Maryland. (Est. & Trusts §5-501)	Yes, although a foreign personal representative is not required to take out letters in Maryland. (Est. & Trusts §5-501)
Massachusetts	Yes, if reciprocal treatment is accorded Massachusetts banks. (167C §17)	Yes, if reciprocal treatment is accorded Massachusetts banks. (167C §17)	Yes, if reciprocal treatment is accorded Massachusetts banks. (167C §17)	Yes, if reciprocal treatment is accorded Massachusetts banks. (167C §17)
Michigan	There is no specific prohibition (§700.3601, §700.4201)	See previous column.	There is no specific mention of banks or corporations. See §700.4201 indicating that ancillary proceedings may not even be necessary.	See previous column.

Table 3.03
Nonresident Bank as Executor or Administrator

	Nonresident Bank as Executor	Nonresident Bank as Administrator	Nonresident Bank as Ancillary Executor	Nonresident Bank as Ancillary Administrator
Minnesota	The bank must have its principal office in a state that accords reciprocal treatment to Minnesota banks and must designate Secretary of State as attorney for service of process. (§ 303.25)	The bank must have its principal office in a state that accords reciprocal treatment to Minnesota banks and must designate Secretary of State as attorney for service of process. (§ 303.25)	The bank must have its principal office in a state that accords reciprocal treatment to Minnesota banks and must designate Secretary of State as attorney for service of process. (§ 303.25)	The bank must have its principal office in a state that accords reciprocal treatment to Minnesota banks and must designate Secretary of State as attorney for service of process. (§ 303.25)
Mississippi	Yes, if reciprocal treatment is accorded Mississippi banks and must appoint Secretary of State as service agent. (§ 81-5-43(1))	Yes, if reciprocal treatment is accorded Mississippi banks and must appoint Secretary of State as service agent. (§ 81-5-43(1))	Yes, if reciprocal treatment is accorded Mississippi banks and must appoint Secretary of State as service agent. (§ 81-5-43(1))	Yes, if reciprocal treatment is accorded Mississippi banks and must appoint Secretary of State as service agent. (§ 81-5-43(1))
Missouri	Yes, if reciprocal treatment is accorded Missouri banks and (a) if the bank is organized under another state's laws, or (b) if the bank is a national bank. (§§ 362.600, 473.117)	Yes, if reciprocal treatment is accorded Missouri banks and (a) if the bank is organized under another state's laws, or (b) if the bank is a national bank. (§§ 362.600, 473.117)	Yes, if reciprocal treatment is accorded Missouri banks and (a) if the bank is organized under another state's laws, or (b) if the bank is a national bank. (§§ 362.600, 473.117)	Yes, if reciprocal treatment is accorded Missouri banks and (a) if the bank is organized under another state's laws, or (b) if the bank is a national bank. (§§ 362.600, 473.117)
Montana	Yes, (§ 72-3-501) though may have to qualify to do business (§ 35-1-1026).	Yes, (§ 72-3-501) though may have to qualify to do business (§ 35-1-1026).	Yes, (§§ 72-3-506, 72-4-201) though may have to qualify to do business (§ 35-1-1026).	Yes (§§ 72-4-201 et seq., 72-3-506) though may have to qualify to do business (§ 35-1-1026).
Nebraska	Yes. (§§ 30-2412, 8-158)	Yes. (§§ 30-2412, 8-158))	Yes. (§§ 30-2412(g), 30-2505, 30-2506, 30-2508, 8-158))	Yes. (§§ 30-2412(g), 30-2505, 30-2506, 30-2508, 8-158)
Nevada	§ 138.020(1)(d) provides that a banking corporation, the principal place of business of which is not Nevada, may serve as an executor, but only if it associates as co-executor a banking corporation the principal place of business of which is Nevada.	§ 139.010 provides that a banking corporation the principal place of business of which is not Nevada, may serve as an administrator, but only if it associates as co-administrator a banking corporation the principal place of business of which is Nevada, and the court in its discretion believes it would be appropriate to make such appointment.	§ 138.020(1)(d) provides that a banking corporation, the principal place of business of which is not Nevada, may serve as an executor, but only if it associates as co-executor a banking corporation the principal place of business of which is Nevada.	§ 139.010 provides that a banking corporation, the principal place of business of which is not Nevada, may serve as an administrator, but only if it associates as co-administrator a banking corporation the principal place of business of which is Nevada or named as personal representative in a will pending probate at the court's discretion.

Table 3.03
Nonresident Bank as Executor or Administrator

	Nonresident Bank as Executor	Nonresident Bank as Administrator	Nonresident Bank as Ancillary Executor	Nonresident Bank as Ancillary Administrator
New Hampshire	Yes, if bank is licensed to establish and maintain a state branch or state agency and has obtained a certificate of authority from the commissioner to engage in fiduciary activities at such office (§384-F:15) or if bank files as Foreign Trust Company with the commissioner. (§383-C-:1104)	Yes, if bank is licensed to establish and maintain a state branch or state agency and has obtained a certificate of authority from the commissioner to engage in fiduciary activities at such office (§284-F:15) or if bank files as Foreign Trust Company with the commissioner. (§383-C:1104)	Yes, if bank is licensed to establish and maintain a state branch or state agency and has obtained a certificate of authority from the commissioner to engage in fiduciary activities at such office (§284-F:15) or if bank files as Foreign Trust Company with the commissioner. (§383-C:1104)	Yes, if bank is licensed to establish and maintain a state branch or state agency and has obtained a certificate of authority from the commissioner to engage in fiduciary activities at such office (§284-F:15) or if bank files as Foreign Trust Company with the commissioner. (§383-C:1104)
New Jersey	Yes, if named in a decedent's will or codicil, and if the state in which such bank has its principal office accords reciprocal treatment to New Jersey banks. (§17:9A-316(B) See also definition of "trust business" in §17:9A-316(D)) There may also be a basis if the bank is operating an office in New Jersey. (Id.; §17:9A-418 et seq.)	Yes, if named in a decedent's will or codicil, and if the state in which such bank has its principal office accords reciprocal treatment to New Jersey banks. (§17:9A-316(B) See also definition of "trust business" in §17:9A-316(D)) There may also be a basis if the bank is operating an office in New Jersey. (Id.; §17:9A-418 et seq.)	Yes, if named in a decedent's will or codicil, and if the state in which such bank has its principal office accords reciprocal treatment to New Jersey banks. (§17:9A-316(B) See also definition of "trust business" in §17:9A-316(D)) There may also be a basis if the bank is operating an office in New Jersey. (Id.; §17:9A-418 et seq.)	Yes, if named in a decedent's will or codicil, and if the state in which such bank has its principal office accords reciprocal treatment to New Jersey banks. (§17:9A-316(B) See also definition of "trust business" in §17:9A-316(D)) There may also be a basis if the bank is operating an office in New Jersey. (Id.; §17:9A-418 et seq.)
New Mexico	Yes, if qualified to do business in New Mexico. (§§45-3-203, 53-17-1)	Yes, if qualified to do business in New Mexico. (§§45-3-203, 53-17-1)	Yes. (§§45-4-204, 45-4-207, 45-3-203, 53-17-1)	Yes. (§§45-4-204, 45-4-207, 53-17-1, 45-3-203)
New York	Yes, if reciprocal treatment is accorded New York banks. (Banking Law §131(3))	Yes, if reciprocal treatment is accorded New York banks. (Banking Law §131(3))	Yes, if reciprocal treatment is accorded New York banks, (Banking Law §131(3)) or according to the court's discretion (Surr. Ct. Proc. Act §1608(6)).	Yes, if reciprocal treatment is accorded New York banks, (Banking Law §131(3)) or according to the court's discretion (Surr. Ct. Proc. Act §1608(6)).
North Carolina	Yes, if under will and a resident agent is appointed. (§§55-15-05, 28A-4-2(4))	Yes, if under will. (§55-15-05)	Yes. (§28A-26-3(a))	Yes. (§28A-26-3(a))

Table 3.03

Nonresident Bank as Executor or Administrator

	Nonresident Bank as Executor	Nonresident Bank as Administrator	Nonresident Bank as Ancillary Executor	Nonresident Bank as Ancillary Administrator
North Dakota	Yes, after filing copy of charter and power of attorney with Secretary of State if reciprocal treatment is accorded North Dakota banks. (§§ 6-08-25, 6-08-26) There is a $50 filing fee and a $25 fee for the for warding of notice or service of process by the Secretary of State to the foreign bank.	Yes, after filing copy of charter and power of attorney with Secretary of State if reciprocal treatment is accorded North Dakota banks. (§§ 6-08-25, 6-08-26) There is a $50 filing fee and a $25 fee for the for warding of notice or service of process by the Secretary of State to the foreign bank.	Yes, after filing copy of charter and power of attorney with Secretary of State if reciprocal treatment is accorded North Dakota banks. (§§ 6-08-25, 6-08-26) There is a $50 filing fee and a $25 fee for the for warding of notice or service of process by the Secretary of State to the foreign bank.	Yes, after filing copy of charter and power of attorney with Secretary of State if reciprocal treatment is accorded North Dakota banks. (§§ 6-08-25, 6-08-26) There is a $50 filing fee and a $25 fee for the for warding of notice or service of process by the Secretary of State to the foreign bank.
Ohio	A foreign corporation may be licensed to do business in Ohio as a trust company for one year after meeting extensive filing and fee requirements. (§§ 1119.08, 1119.17, 2109.21 note 3)	A foreign corporation may be licensed to do business in Ohio as a trust company for one year after meeting extensive filing and fee requirements. (§§ 1119.08, 1119.17)	Yes, if reciprocal treatment is accorded Ohio banks. (§ 1109.02)	Yes, if reciprocal treatment is accorded Ohio banks. (§1109.02)
Oklahoma	Yes, if reciprocal treatment is accorded Oklahoma banks. (6 § 1002)	Yes, if reciprocal treatment is accorded Oklahoma banks. (6 § 1002)	Yes, if reciprocal treatment is accorded Oklahoma banks. (6 § 1002)	Yes, if reciprocal treatment is accorded Oklahoma banks. (6 § 1002)
Oregon	Yes. (§§ 113.085, 113.087)	Yes. (§§ 113.085, 113.087)	Yes. (§§ 113.085, 113.087)	Yes. (§§ 113.085, 113.087)
Pennsylvania	Yes, if reciprocal treatment is accorded Pennsylvania banks. (7 § 106) In addition, there must be compliance with minimal capital requirements. (7 § 106(b)(ii))	Yes, if reciprocal treatment is accorded Pennsylvania banks. (7 § 106) In addition, there must be compliance with minimal capital requirements. (7 § 106(b)(ii))	Yes, if reciprocal treatment is accorded Pennsylvania banks. (7 § 106) In addition, there must be compliance with minimal capital requirements. (7 § 106(b)(ii))	Yes, if reciprocal treatment is accorded Pennsylvania banks. (7 § 106) In addition, there must be compliance with minimal capital requirements. (7 § 106(b)(ii))
Rhode Island	Yes, if appointment of state official as true and lawful attorney for receipt of process and reciprocal treatment is accorded Rhode Island banks. (§ 19-3.1-6)	Yes, if appointment of state official as true and lawful attorney for receipt of process and reciprocal treatment is accorded Rhode Island banks. (§ 19-3.1-6)	Yes, if appointment of state official as true and lawful attorney for receipt of process and reciprocal treatment is accorded Rhode Island banks. (§ 19-3.1-6)	Yes, if appointment of state official as true and lawful attorney for receipt of process and reciprocal treatment is accorded Rhode Island banks. (§ 19-3.1-6)
South Carolina	No and neither may officers, employees, or agents of such corporations if acting on behalf of the corporation. (§ 62-3-203(e)(3))	No and neither may officers, employees, or agents of such corporations if acting on behalf of the corporation. (§ 62-3-203(e)(3))	Yes. (§ 62-3-203) Applies only to estates of nonresident decedents. (§ 62-3-203(f))	Yes. (§ 62-3-203) Applies only to estates of nonresident decedents. (§ 62-3-203(f))

Table 3.03
Nonresident Bank as Executor or Administrator

	Nonresident Bank as Executor	Nonresident Bank as Administrator	Nonresident Bank as Ancillary Executor	Nonresident Bank as Ancillary Administrator
South Dakota	Yes, if reciprocal treatment is accorded South Dakota banks and if filing provisions are met, especially naming the office of the Secretary of State for the receipt of process. (§§51A-5-7-51A-5-10)	Yes, if reciprocal treatment is accorded South Dakota banks and if filing provisions are met, especially naming the office of the Secretary of State as agent for the receipt of process. (§§51A-5-7-51A-5-10)	Yes, if reciprocal treatment is accorded South Dakota banks and if filing provisions are met, especially naming the office of the Secretary of State as agent for the receipt of process. (§§51A-5-7-51A-5-10)	Yes, if reciprocal treatment is accorded South Dakota banks and if filing provisions are met, especially naming the office of the Secretary of State as agent for the receipt of process. (§§51A-5-7-51A-5-10)
Tennessee	Yes, if reciprocal treatment is accorded Tennessee banks. (§35-50-107(a)(2)(A)) The secretary of state must be appointed as agent for service of process. (§35-50-107(b)(2)) See also §30-1-116.	Yes, if reciprocal treatment is accorded Tennessee banks. (§35-50-107(a)(2)(A)) The secretary of state must be appointed as agent for service of process. (§35-50-107(b)(2)) See also §30-1-116.	Yes, if reciprocal treatment is accorded Tennessee banks. (§35-50-107(a)(2)(A)) The secretary of state must be appointed as agent for service of process. (§35-50-107(b)(2)) See also §30-1-116.	Yes, if reciprocal treatment is accorded Tennessee banks. (§35-50-107(a)(2)(A)) The secretary of state must be appointed as agent for service of process. (§35-50-107(b)(2)) See also §30-1-116.
Texas	Yes, if reciprocal treatment is accorded Texas banks and if filing provisions are met. (Estates §505.003)	Yes, if reciprocal treatment is accorded Texas banks and if filing provisions are met. (Estates §505.003)	Yes, if reciprocal treatment is accorded Texas banks and if filing provisions are met. (Estates §505.003)	Yes, if reciprocal treatment is accorded Texas banks and if filing provisions are met. (Estates §505.003)
Utah	A foreign depository institution may not engage in the trust business. (§7-18a-302) However, "trust business" does not include that of a court-appointed trustee accountable to the court. (§7-5-1(c)(viii)) Generally, an institution will qualify to do business as a trust company in the state if it is an out-of-state depository institution authorized to engage in business as a depository institution in Utah or its wholly-owned subsidiary. (§7-5-1(d)) Also, "trust business" includes serving as a personal representative, an administrator, or an executor. (§7-5-1(1)(b))	A foreign depository institution may not engage in the trust business. (§7-18a-302) However, "trust business" does not include that of a court-appointed trustee accountable to the court. (§7-5-1(c)(viii)) Generally, an institution will qualify to do business as a trust company in the state if it is an out-of-state depository institution authorized to engage in business as a depository institution in Utah or its wholly-owned subsidiary. (§7-5-1(d)) Also, "trust business" includes serving as a personal representative, an administrator, or an executor. (§7-5-1(1)(b))	A foreign depository institution may not engage in the trust business. (§7-18a-302) However, "trust business" does not include that of a court-appointed trustee accountable to the court. (§7-5-1(c)(viii)) Generally, an institution will qualify to do business as a trust company in the state if it is an out-of-state depository institution authorized to engage in business as a depository institution in Utah or its wholly-owned subsidiary. (§7-5-1(d)) Also, "trust business" includes serving as a personal representative, an administrator, or an executor. (§7-5-1(1)(b))	A foreign depository institution may not engage in the trust business. (§7-18a-302) However, "trust business" does not include that of a court-appointed trustee accountable to the court. (§7-5-1(c)(viii)) Generally, an institution will qualify to do business as a trust company in the state if it is an out-of-state depository institution authorized to engage in business as a depository institution in Utah or its wholly-owned subsidiary. (§7-5-1(d)) Also, "trust business" includes serving as a personal representative, an administrator, or an executor. (§7-5-1(1)(b))

Table 3.03

Nonresident Bank as Executor or Administrator

	Nonresident Bank as Executor	Nonresident Bank as Administrator	Nonresident Bank as Ancillary Executor	Nonresident Bank as Ancillary Administrator
Vermont	Yes. To qualify, the nonresident's domiciliary state must permit Vermont banks and trust companies to act as executors and trustees within its borders, and the nonresident bank must obtain a certificate of authority from the Vermont Secretary of State. (11A §15.01(d)) See also R. of Prob. P. 68.	Tit. 11A §15.01 can be interpreted two ways. Since it only mentions executors and trustees, it can be read as not imposing the requirements set forth in *Nonresident Bank as Executor* for other types of nonresident fiduciaries. However, it could also be read as not allowing certification of nonresident banks acting in their other fiduciary roles.	Yes. To qualify, the nonresident's domiciliary state must permit Vermont banks and trust companies to act as executors and trustees within its borders, and the nonresident bank must obtain a certificate of authority from the Vermont Secretary of State. (11A §15.01(d)) See also R. of Prob. P. 68.	Tit. 11A §15.01 can be interpreted two ways. Since it only mentions executors and trustees, it can be read as not imposing the requirements set forth in *Nonresident Bank as Executor* for other types of nonresident fiduciaries. However, it could also be read as not allowing certification of nonresident banks acting in their other fiduciary roles.
Virginia	No, unless authorized to do business in the state. (§64.2-1426(B))	No, unless authorized to do business in the state. (§64.2-1426(B))	No, unless authorized to do business in the state. (§64.2-1426(B))	No, unless authorized to do business in the state. (§64.2-1426(B))
Washington	Yes, if appoints an agent who is a resident of the county where the estate is being probated or is an attorney of record of the estate. Otherwise, no, except if a national bank authorized to so act, if upon petition of a person having a right to such appoint. The bank must not have drawn a will appointing it to the position. (§11.36.010)	Yes, if appoints an agent who is a resident of the county where the estate is being probated or is an attorney of record of the estate. Otherwise, no, except if a national bank authorized to so act, if upon petition of a person having a right to such appoint. The bank must not have drawn a will appointing it to the position. (§11.36.010)	Yes, if appoints an agent who is a resident of the county where the estate is being probated or is an attorney of record of the estate. Otherwise, no, except if a national bank authorized to so act, if upon petition of a person having a right to such appoint. The bank must not have drawn a will appointing it to the position. (§11.36.010)	Yes, if appoints an agent who is a resident of the county where the estate is being probated or is an attorney of record of the estate. Otherwise, no, except if a national bank authorized to so act, if upon petition of a person having a right to such appoint. The bank must not have drawn a will appointing it to the position. (§11.36.010)
West Virginia	No, unless a main or branch office in the state. However, the provision then states that a nonresident corporation cannot have its principal office or place of business outside the state. (§44-5-3)	No, unless a main or branch office in the state. However, the provision then states that a nonresident corporation cannot have its principal office or place of business outside the state. (§44-5-3)	No, unless a main or branch office in the state. However, the provision then states that a nonresident corporation cannot have its principal office or place of business outside the state. (§44-5-3)	No, unless a main or branch office in the state. However, the provision then states that a nonresident corporation cannot have its principal office or place of business outside the state. (§44-5-3)

Table 3.03

Nonresident Bank as Executor or Administrator

	Nonresident Bank as Executor	Nonresident Bank as Administrator	Nonresident Bank as Ancillary Executor	Nonresident Bank as Ancillary Administrator
Wisconsin	Yes, if (a) authorized to act as a fiduciary in its state of organization, and (b) the law of that state allows the following to act as a fiduciary "not unduly restrictive when compared with the laws of this state:" a corporation organized in Wisconsin, a national banking association having its principal place of business in Wisconsin, and a federal savings association or a federal savings bank having its principal place of business in Wisconsin, and authorized to act as a fiduciary in Wisconsin. (§ 223.12)	Yes, if (a) authorized to act as a fiduciary in its state of organization, and (b) the law of that state allows the following to act as a fiduciary "not unduly restrictive when compared with the laws of this state:" a corporation organized in Wisconsin, a national banking association having its principal place of business in Wisconsin, and a federal savings association or a federal savings bank having its principal place of business in Wisconsin and authorized to act as a fiduciary in Wisconsin. (§ 223.12)	Yes, if (a) authorized to act as a fiduciary in its state of organization, and (b) the law of that state allows the following to act as a fiduciary "not unduly restrictive when compared with the laws of this state:" a corporation organized in Wisconsin, a national banking association having its principal place of business in Wisconsin, and a federal savings association or a federal savings bank having its principal place of business in Wisconsin and authorized to act as a fiduciary in Wisconsin. (§ 223.12) If the bank has been appointed at the domicile, it qualifies without satisfying § 223.12. See also § 877.16.	Yes, if (a) authorized to act as a fiduciary in its state of organization, and (b) the law of that state allows the following to act as a fiduciary "not unduly restrictive when compared with the laws of this state:" a corporation organized in Wisconsin, a national banking association having its principal place of business in Wisconsin, and a federal savings association or a federal savings bank having its principal place of business in Wisconsin and authorized to act as a fiduciary in Wisconsin. (§ 223.12) If the bank has been appointed at the domicile, it qualifies without satisfying § 223.12. See also § 877.16.
Wyoming	Yes, after appointment of a resident agent if not doing business in the state. (§ 2-11-301)	No, unless a resident of Wyoming is appointed co-administrator. (§ 2-4-203)	Yes, after appointment of a resident agent if not doing business in the state. (§§ 2-11-301, 2-11-201)	Yes, likely requires a Wyoming resident to be appointed as co-administrator. (§ 2-4-203) See also § 2-11-201.

Table 3.04
Nonresident Bank as Guardian of Minor's or Incompetent's Property

	Nonresident Bank as Guardian of Minor's Property	Nonresident Bank as Guardian of Incompetent's Property	Nonresident Bank as Ancillary Guardian of Minor's Property	Nonresident Bank as Ancillary Guardian of Incompetent's Property
Alabama	Yes, if reciprocal treatment is accorded Alabama banks. (§10A-2-15.41(a)(2)) Nonresident banks must file a verified statement with the Commissioner of Revenue. (§10A-2-15.42)	Yes, if reciprocal treatment is accorded Alabama banks. (§10A-2-15.41(a)(2)) Nonresident banks must file a verified statement with the Commissioner of Revenue. (§10A-2-15.42)	Yes, if reciprocal treatment is accorded Alabama banks. (§10A-2-15.41(a)(2)) Nonresident banks must file a verified statement with the Commissioner of Revenue. (§10A-2-15.42)	Yes, if reciprocal treatment is accorded Alabama banks. (§10A-2-15.41(a)(2)) Nonresident banks must file a verified statement with the Commissioner of Revenue. (§10A-2-15.42)
Alaska	Yes. (§§06.26.010, 43.31.300, 13.26.121, 13.26.143, 13.26.465, 13.26.580)	Yes. (§§06.26.010, 43.31.300, 13.26.211, 13.26.311, 13.26.465, 13.26.580)	Yes. (§§06.26.010, 43.31.300, 13.26.121, 13.26.143, 13.26.465, 13.26.580)	Yes. (§§06.26.010, 43.31.300, 13.26.211, 13.26.311, 13.26.465, 13.26.580)
Arizona	Yes. (§§14-5206, 14-5410, 14-5432)	Yes. (§§14-5301, 14-5311, 14-5410, 14-5432)	Yes. (§§14-5206, 14-5410, 14-5432)	Yes. (§§14-5301, 14-5311, 14-5410, 14-5432)
Arkansas	Yes, if authorized to do business in the state and properly empowered by its charter to serve as guardian. (§28-65-203(e)(1)) A separate provision states that a bank may serve if it has trust powers. (§28-65-203(e)(2)) The provision is unclear as to whether the requirements of §28-48-101(b)(6) must also be satisfied.	Yes, if authorized to do business in the state and properly empowered by its charter to serve as guardian. (§28-65-203(e)(1)) A separate provision states that a bank may serve if it has trust powers. (§28-65-203(e)(2)) The provision is unclear as to whether the requirements of §28-48-101(b)(6) must also be satisfied.	Generally, the same standards apply as for personal representatives. (§28-65-103) Moreover, a guardian appointed in the state of the incompetent's residence may serve upon petition. (§28-65-601) The bank, if a corporation, does not have to be authorized to do business in the state. (§28-65-603)	Generally, the same rules apply for conservators of a disabled person as for guardians of minors. (§28-67-106)
California	Yes, if authorized to conduct business of a trust company in the state and in the best interest of the ward. (Prob. §§83, 300, 1514 & note 22)	Yes, if authorized to conduct business of a trust company in the state. The court has sole discretion in the selection. (Prob. §§83, 300, 1514 & note 22)	Yes, if authorized to conduct business of a trust company in the state. (Prob. §§83, 300, 2801) Domiciliary proceedings in California may not be necessary. (Prob. 3800)	Yes, if authorized to conduct business of a trust company in the state. (Prob. §§83, 300, 1812, 2801) Domiciliary proceedings in California may not be necessary. (Prob. 3800)
Colorado	Yes, but first may be required to obtain a certificate of authority to transact business.[1] (§§15-14-202, 15-14-206, 15-14-413) See also §7-115-101.	Yes, but first may be required to obtain a certificate of authority to transact business.[2] (§§15-14-301, 15-14-311, 15-14-413) See also §7-115-101.	Yes, but first may be required to obtain a certificate of authority to transact business.[3] (§§15-14-202, 15-14-206, 15-14-413, 15-14-433) See also §7-115-101.	Yes, but first may be required to obtain a certificate of authority to transact business.[4] (§§15-14-301, 15-14-311, 15-14-413, 15-14-433) See also §7-115-101.
Connecticut	There is no statutory prohibition. (§45a-629)	No general statutory prohibition against foreign corporation as conservator. (§45a-659) Only Connecticut corporations can be guardians of mentally disabled wards. (§45a-669)	No statutory prohibitions. See §45a-635 for right of foreign guardian to removal personal property. See also §45a-632 providing that a guardian may be appointed in ancillary proceeding.	No statutory prohibition against foreign corporation as conservator. (§45a-659) Only Connecticut corporations can be guardians of mentally retarded wards. (§45a-669)

Table 3.04
Nonresident Bank as Guardian of Minor's or Incompetent's Property

	Nonresident Bank as Guardian of Minor's Property	Nonresident Bank as Guardian of Incompetent's Property	Nonresident Bank as Ancillary Guardian of Minor's Property	Nonresident Bank as Ancillary Guardian of Incompetent's Property
Delaware	Yes, if reciprocal treatment accorded Delaware corporations. (8 §§ 380; 12 § 3901, 3902)	Yes, if reciprocal treatment accorded Delaware corporations. (8 §§ 380; 12 § 3901)	Yes, if reciprocal treatment accorded Delaware corporations. (8 §§ 380; 12 § 3901, 3902, 3904) If the minor is resident out of state, then it is the court's discretion. (12 § 3902(d))	Yes, if reciprocal treatment accorded Delaware corporations. (8 §§ 380; 12 § 3901, 3904)
District of Columbia	Yes. (§§ 26-1309, 26-1310, 26-1335)	Yes, there is no statutory prohibition. (§§ 26-1309(5), 26-1310, 26-1335)	Yes. (§§ 26-1309, 26-1310, 26-1335, 21-111, 21-112)	Yes. (§ 21-2057(a)(1)) See also §§ 26-1309, 26-1310, 26-1335. §§ 21-2076-21-2077 indicate that ancillary proceedings may not be necessary. The cited section relates to foreign conservators. See definition in § 21-2011(3).
Florida	There is no specific prohibition. (§ 744.309(4)) If the ward moves to Florida, the foreign guardian can act after filing its appointment papers. (§ 744.306) A foreign guardian can maintain or defend lawsuits locally. (§ 744.306(2))	There is no specific prohibition. (§ 744.309(4)) If the ward moves to Florida, the foreign guardian can act after filing its appointment papers. (§ 744.306) A foreign guardian can maintain or defend lawsuits locally. (§ 744.306(2))	A guardian of nonresident ward, if duly appointed in court of another state, may manage property in Florida. (§ 744.307) A foreign guardian may also maintain or defend an action. (§ 744.306(2)) If the ward moves to Florida, the foreign guardian can act locally after filing its appointment papers. (§ 744.306(1))	A guardian of nonresident ward, if duly appointed in court of another state, may manage property in Florida. (§ 744.307) A foreign guardian may also maintain or defend an action. (§ 744.306(2)) If the ward moves to Florida, the foreign guardian can act locally after filing its appointment papers. (§ 744.306(1))
Georgia	Yes, if it is a bank eligible to act in a fiduciary capacity in the state where it is incorporated or organized, or where it has its principal place of business. (§ 53-12-321)	Yes, if it is a bank eligible to act in a fiduciary capacity in the state where it is incorporated or organized, or where it has its principal place of business. (§ 53-12-321)	Yes, if it is a bank eligible to act in a fiduciary capacity in the state where it is incorporated or organized, or where it has its principal place of business. (§ 53-12-321)	Yes, if it is a bank eligible to act in a fiduciary capacity in the state where it is incorporated or organized, or where it has its principal place of business. (§ 53-12-321)
Hawaii	No, unless recognized by the appropriate court of some other jurisdiction where the protected person resides as a guardian of the protected person's property. (§ 560:5-410(a)(1))	No, unless recognized by the appropriate court of some other jurisdiction where the protected person resides as a guardian of the protected person's property. (§ 560:5-410(a)(1))	No, unless recognized by the appropriate court of some other jurisdiction where the protected person resides as a guardian of the protected person's property. (§ 560:5-410(a)(1))	No, unless recognized by the appropriate court of some other jurisdiction where the protected person resides as a guardian of the protected person's property. (§ 560:5-410(a)(1))
Idaho	Yes. (§§ 15-5-202, 15-5-206, 15-5-410)	Yes. (§§ 15-5-301, 15-5-311, 15-5-410)	Yes. (§§ 15-5-202, 15-5-206, 15-5-410)	Yes. Provision is specifically made for recognition of appointment under will probated at testator's domicile in another state. (§§ 15-5-301, 15-5-311, 15-5-410)

Table 3.04

Nonresident Bank as Guardian of Minor's or Incompetent's Property

	Nonresident Bank as Guardian of Minor's Property	Nonresident Bank as Guardian of Incompetent's Property	Nonresident Bank as Ancillary Guardian of Minor's Property	Nonresident Bank as Ancillary Guardian of Incompetent's Property
Illinois	Yes, if the corporation is authorized by the laws of the state of its organization or domicile to act as a fiduciary in that state and reciprocal treatment is accorded Illinois banks. (205 ILCS § 620/4-2) Prior to the time any corporation can act, it must obtain from the Commissioner of Banks and Real Estate a certificate of authority. (205 ILCS § 620/4-5)	Yes, (755 ILCS § 5/11a-5(c)) if the corporation is authorized by the laws of the state of its organization or domicile to act as a fiduciary in that state and reciprocal treatment is accorded Illinois banks. (205 ILCS § 620/4-2) Prior to the time any corporation can act, it must obtain from the Commissioner of Banks and Real Estate a certificate of authority. (205 ILCS § 620/4-5)	Yes, if the corporation is authorized by the laws of the state of its organization or domicile to act as a fiduciary in that state and reciprocal treatment is accorded Illinois banks. (205 ILCS § 620/ 4-2) Prior to the time any corporation can act, it must obtain from the Commissioner of Banks and Real Estate a certificate of authority. (205 ILCS § 620/4-5)	Yes, (755 ILCS § 5/11a-5(c)) if the corporation is authorized by the laws of the state of its organization or domicile to act as a fiduciary in that state and reciprocal treatment is accorded Illinois banks. (205 ILCS § 620/4-2) Prior to the time any corporation can act, it must obtain from the Commissioner of Banks and Real Estate a certificate of authority. (205 ILCS § 620/4-5)
Indiana	Yes. There is no prohibition. Furthermore, if no one is appointed locally, a guardian appointed at the protected person's domicile may prove his foreign appointment and then act as a guardian appointed in Indiana. (§ 29-3-13-2) A bank or trust company can also act if the state in which it has its principal place of business gives reciprocal treatment. (§ 28-1-12-1(b)(2)(B) & (3))	Yes. There is no prohibition. Furthermore, if no one is appointed locally, a guardian appointed at the protected person's domicile may prove his foreign appointment and then act as a guardian appointed in Indiana. (§ 29-3-13-2) A bank or trust company can also act if the state in which it has its principal place of business gives reciprocal treatment. (§ 28-1-12-1(b)(2)(B) & (3))	Yes. There is no prohibition. Furthermore, if no one is appointed locally, a guardian appointed at the protected person's domicile may prove his foreign appointment and then act as a guardian appointed in Indiana. (§ 29-3-13-2) A bank or trust company can also act if the state in which it has its principal place of business gives reciprocal treatment. (§ 28-1-12-1(b)(2)(B) & (3))	Yes. There is no prohibition. Furthermore, if no one is appointed locally, a guardian appointed at the protected person's domicile may prove his foreign appointment and then act as a guardian appointed in Indiana. (§ 29-3-13-2) A bank or trust company can also act if the state in which it has its principal place of business gives reciprocal treatment. (§ 28-1-12-1(b)(2)(B) & (3))
Iowa	Yes, if reciprocal treatment is accorded Iowa banks. (§ 633.64)	Yes, if reciprocal treatment is accorded Iowa banks. (§ 633.64)	Yes, if reciprocal treatment is accorded Iowa banks. (§§ 633.64, 633.502)	Yes, if reciprocal treatment is accorded Iowa banks. (§§ 633.64, 633.502)

Table 3.04
Nonresident Bank as Guardian of Minor's or Incompetent's Property

	Nonresident Bank as Guardian of Minor's Property	Nonresident Bank as Guardian of Incompetent's Property	Nonresident Bank as Ancillary Guardian of Minor's Property	Nonresident Bank as Ancillary Guardian of Incompetent's Property
Kansas	Yes, if it is organized under the laws of, and has a principal place of business in, another state that permits a bank or other corporation that is similarly organized in Kansas to act in a like fiduciary capacity in the other state under similar conditions (§59-1701(a)(3)) and a resident agent is appointed (§59-1706). An officer, employee, or agent of a bank or corporation which is not authorized to act as a fiduciary in Kansas may himself or herself not act as a fiduciary in Kansas, whether a resident or nonresident of Kansas, if such person is acting as a fiduciary on behalf of such bank or corporation. (§59-1701(b))	Yes, if it is organized under the laws of, and has a principal place of business in, another state that permits a bank or other corporation that is similarly organized in Kansas to act in a like fiduciary capacity in the other state under similar conditions (§59-1701(a)(3)) and a resident agent is appointed (§59-1706). An officer, employee, or agent of a bank or corporation which is not authorized to act as a fiduciary in Kansas may himself or herself not act as a fiduciary in Kansas, whether a resident or nonresident of Kansas, if such person is acting as a fiduciary on behalf of such bank or corporation. (§59-1701(b))	Yes, if it is organized under the laws of, and has a principal place of business in, another state that permits a bank or other corporation that is similarly organized in Kansas to act in a like fiduciary capacity in the other state under similar conditions (§59-1701(a)(3)) and a resident agent is appointed (§59-1706). An officer, employee, or agent of a bank or corporation which is not authorized to act as a fiduciary in Kansas may himself or herself not act as a fiduciary in Kansas, whether a resident or nonresident of Kansas, if such person is acting as a fiduciary on behalf of such bank or corporation. (§59-1701(b))	Yes, if it is organized under the laws of, and has a principal place of business in, another state that permits a bank or other corporation that is similarly organized in Kansas to act in a like fiduciary capacity in the other state under similar conditions (§59-1701(a)(3)) and a resident agent is appointed (§59-1706). An officer, employee, or agent of a bank or corporation which is not authorized to act as a fiduciary in Kansas may himself or herself not act as a fiduciary in Kansas, whether a resident or nonresident of Kansas, if such person is acting as a fiduciary on behalf of such bank or corporation. (§59-1701(b))
Kentucky	No. (§395.005)	No. (§395.005)	Yes. (§§387.010(3), 387.185)	Yes. (§§387.010(3), 387.185)
Louisiana	Yes, if resident agent is appointed. (Code Civ. Pro. arts. 4273, 5251(11))	Yes, if resident agent is appointed for service of process. (Code Civ. Pro. arts. 4273, 4556, 5251(11))	Yes. (Code Civ. Pro. art. 4431)	Yes, if resident agent is appointed for service of process. (Code Civ. Pro. arts. 4431, 4556, 5251(11))
Maine	Yes, if reciprocal treatment is accorded Maine banks. (18 §4161)	Yes, if reciprocal treatment is accorded Maine banks. (18 §4161)	Yes, if reciprocal treatment is accorded Maine banks. (18 §4161)	Yes, if reciprocal treatment is accorded Maine banks. (18 §4161)
Maryland	Yes, if resident agent is appointed. (Est. & Trusts §13-207(d))	Yes, if resident agent is appointed. (Est. & Trusts §13-207(d))	Yes, although a foreign guardian or other fiduciary is not required to qualify as an ancillary. (Est. & Trusts §§13-222, 13-207(d))	Yes, although a foreign guardian or other fiduciary is not required to qualify as an ancillary. (Est. & Trusts §§13-222, 13-207(d))
Massachusetts	Yes, if reciprocal treatment is accorded Massachusetts banks. (167C §17)	Yes, if reciprocal treatment is accorded Massachusetts banks. (167C §17)	Yes, if reciprocal treatment is accorded Massachusetts banks. (167C §17)	Yes, if reciprocal treatment is accorded Massachusetts banks. (167C §17)
Michigan	Yes, no specific prohibition. (§700.5409)	Yes, no specific prohibition. (§700.5409)	Yes. (§700.5409(1)(a))	Yes. (§700.5409(1)(a))
Minnesota	The bank must have its principal office in a state that accords reciprocal treatment to Minnesota banks. (§303.25)	The bank must have its principal office in a state that accords reciprocal treatment to Minnesota banks. (§303.25)	The bank must have its principal office in a state that accords reciprocal treatment to Minnesota banks. (§303.25)	The bank must have its principal office in a state that accords reciprocal treatment to Minnesota banks. (§303.25)

Table 3.04

Nonresident Bank as Guardian of Minor's or Incompetent's Property

	Nonresident Bank as Guardian of Minor's Property	Nonresident Bank as Guardian of Incompetent's Property	Nonresident Bank as Ancillary Guardian of Minor's Property	Nonresident Bank as Ancillary Guardian of Incompetent's Property
Mississippi	Yes, if reciprocal treatment is accorded Mississippi banks. (§ 81-5-43)	Yes, if reciprocal treatment is accorded Mississippi banks. (§ 81-5-43)	Yes, if reciprocal treatment is accorded Mississippi banks. (§ 81-5-43)	Yes, if reciprocal treatment is accorded Mississippi banks. (§ 81-5-43)
Missouri	Yes, if reciprocal treatment is accorded Missouri banks and (a) if the bank is organized under another state's laws, or (b) if the bank is a national bank, after designation of a resident agent. (§§ 362.600, 473.117, 475.055(4))	Yes, if reciprocal treatment is accorded Missouri banks and (a) if the bank is organized under another state's laws, or (b) if the bank is a national bank, after designation of a resident agent. (§§ 362.600, 473.117, 475.055(4))	Yes, if reciprocal treatment is accorded Missouri banks and (a) if the bank is organized under another state's laws, or (b) if the bank is a national bank. (§§ 362.600, 473.117, 475.055(4), 475.095, 475.339)	Yes, if reciprocal treatment is accorded Missouri banks and (a) if the bank is organized under another state's laws, or (b) if the bank is a national bank. (§§ 362.600, 473.117, 475.055(4), 475.095, 475.339)
Montana	Yes, (§§ 72-5-211, 72-5-223, 72-5-410) though may have to qualify to do business (§ 35-1-1026).	Yes, (§ 72-5-312) though may have to qualify to do business (§ 35-1-1026).	Yes, (§ 72-5-312) though may have to qualify to do business (§ 35-1-1026).	Yes, (§§ 72-5-312, 72-5-410(1)(a)) though may have to qualify to do business (§ 35-1-1026).
Nebraska	Yes. (§ § 30-2639, 30-2606, 30-2610, 30-2661)	Yes. (§§ 30-2639, 30-2661, 30-2620)	Yes. (§§ 30-2639, 30-2606, 30-2610, 30-2661)	Yes. (§§ 30-2639, 30-2661, 30-2620)
Nevada	Yes. The court will appoint a qualified person most suitable to be a guardian to a minor and will consider a person nominated in a will of a parent. (AB 319(2017),§ 46(6)(a)) See also § 159.0487 specifically for whom a guardian may be appointed, including persons not resident, but physically present in the state and nonresidents with property in the state.	Yes, the court may appoint a nonresident guardian when it has jurisdiction, the guardian designates a resident agent in this State, and if necessary completes applicable training. (§ 159.0613(6)(a)-(c)) Nevada will recognize guardians registered in a different state. (§ 159.2027) See also § 159.0487 specifically for whom a guardian may be appointed, including persons not resident, but physically present in the state and nonresidents with property in the state.	Yes. The court will appoint a qualified person most suitable to be a guardian to a minor and will consider a person nominated in a will of a parent. (AB319(2017),§ 46(6)(a)) See also § 159.0487 specifically for whom a guardian may be appointed, including persons not resident, but physically present in the state and nonresidents with property in the state.	Yes, the court may appoint a nonresident guardian when it has jurisdiction, the guardian designates a registered agent in this State, and if necessary completes applicable training. (§ 159.0613(6)(a)-(c)) Upon registration, Nevada will recognize guardians authorized in a different state, but subject to limitation on powers under Nevada law, and subject to conditions impressed on nonresident parties in litigation.
New Hampshire	Yes. The court may appoint "any person or entity whose appointment is appropriate." (§ 463:10(II)) (emphasis added)	Yes. The court may appoint "any person or entity whose appointment is appropriate." (§ 463:10(II)) (emphasis added)	Yes. (§ 464-A:10(II))	Yes. (§ 464-A:10(II))

Table 3.04
Nonresident Bank as Guardian of Minor's or Incompetent's Property

	Nonresident Bank as Guardian of Minor's Property	Nonresident Bank as Guardian of Incompetent's Property	Nonresident Bank as Ancillary Guardian of Minor's Property	Nonresident Bank as Ancillary Guardian of Incompetent's Property
New Jersey	Yes, if named in a decedent's will or codicil, if the state in which such bank has its principal office accords reciprocal treatment to New Jersey banks, and if the nonresident bank has secured from the commissioner a certificate to transact trust business. (§17:9A-316) There may also be a basis if the bank is operating an office in New Jersey. (*Id.*; §17:9A-418 et seq.)	Yes, if named in a decedent's will or codicil, if the state in which such bank has its principal office accords reciprocal treatment to New Jersey banks, and if the nonresident bank has secured from the commissioner a certificate to transact trust business. (§17:9A-316) There may also be a basis if the bank is operating an office in New Jersey. (*Id.*; §17:9A-418 et seq.)	Yes, if named in a decedent's will or codicil, if the state in which such bank has its principal office accords reciprocal treatment to New Jersey banks, and if the nonresident bank has secured from the commissioner a certificate to transact trust business. (§17:9A-316) There may also be a basis if the bank is operating an office in New Jersey. (*Id.*; §17:9A-418 et seq.)	Yes, if named in a decedent's will or codicil, if the state in which such bank has its principal office accords reciprocal treatment to New Jersey banks, and if the nonresident bank has secured from the commissioner a certificate to transact trust business. (§17:9A-316) There may also be a basis if the bank is operating an office in New Jersey. (*Id.*; §17:9A-418 et seq.)
New Mexico	Yes, if authorized to transact business in New Mexico. (§§45-5-201, 45-5-202, 45-5-206, 53-17-1)	Yes, if authorized to transact business in New Mexico. (§§45-5-301, 45-5-311, 45-5-410, 53-17-1)	Yes, if authorized to transact business in New Mexico. (§§45-5-201, 45-5-202, 45-5-206, 53-17-1)	Yes, if authorized to transact business in New Mexico. (§§45-5-301, 45-5-311, 45-5-410, 53-17-1)
New York	Yes, if reciprocal treatment is accorded New York banks. (Banking Law §131(3))	Yes, if reciprocal treatment is accorded New York banks. (Banking Law §131(3))	Yes, if reciprocal treatment is accorded New York banks, (Banking Law §131(3)) or according to the court's discretion. (Surr. Ct. Proc. Act §1716(3) & (4))	There does not seem to be a prohibition. (Men. Hyg. §§ 81.01, 81.09) However, there is a special provision if the incapacitated person is not present in the state and a guardian has been appointed elsewhere. The foreign guardian can be appointed with regard to New York property management in the discretion of the court. (Men. Hyg. §81.18)
North Carolina	Yes, if authorized to exercise fiduciary power in North Carolina. (§§55-15-05, 35A-1224(c))	Yes, if authorized to exercise fiduciary power in North Carolina. (§§55-15-05, 35A-1213(c))	§35A-1280 states that clerk *may* appoint an ancillary guardian if it is established that: 1. Nonresident has property in North Carolina; 2. Nonresident is a minor or incompetent; and 3. Nonresident has no guardian in North Carolina. However, ancillary proceedings may not be necessary. (§35A-1281(c))	§35A-1280 states that clerk *may* appoint an ancillary guardian if it is established that: 1. Nonresident has property in North Carolina; 2. Nonresident is a minor or incompetent; and 3. Nonresident has no guardian in North Carolina. However, ancillary proceedings may not be necessary. (§35A-1281(c))

3034

Table 3.04
Nonresident Bank as Guardian of Minor's or Incompetent's Property

	Nonresident Bank as Guardian of Minor's Property	Nonresident Bank as Guardian of Incompetent's Property	Nonresident Bank as Ancillary Guardian of Minor's Property	Nonresident Bank as Ancillary Guardian of Incompetent's Property
North Dakota	Yes, after filing copy of charter and power of attorney with Secretary of State if reciprocal treatment is accorded North Dakota banks. (§§ 6-08-25, 6-08-26) There is a $50 filing fee and a $25 fee for the forwarding of notice or service of process by the Secretary of State to the foreign bank.	Yes, after filing copy of charter and power of attorney with Secretary of State if reciprocal treatment is accorded North Dakota banks. (§§ 6-08-25, 6-08-26) There is a $50 filing fee and a $25 fee for the forwarding of notice or service of process by the Secretary of State to the foreign bank.	Yes, after filing copy of charter and power of attorney with Secretary of State if reciprocal treatment is accorded North Dakota banks. (§§ 6-08-25, 6-08-26) There is a $50 filing fee and a $25 fee for the forwarding of notice or service of process by the Secretary of State to the foreign bank.	Yes, after filing copy of charter and power of attorney with Secretary of State if reciprocal treatment is accorded North Dakota banks. (§§ 6-08-25, 6-08-26) There is a $50 filing fee and a $25 fee for the forwarding of notice or service of process by the Secretary of State to the foreign bank.
Ohio	A foreign corporation may be licensed to do business in Ohio as a trust company for one year after meeting extensive filing and fee requirements. (§§ 1111.01(I) (defining "trust business" as including serving as a guardian or conservator), 1111.02(A)(2), 1109.02)	A foreign corporation may be licensed to do business in Ohio as a trust company for one year after meeting extensive filing and fee requirements. (§§ 1111.01(I) (defining "trust business" as including serving as a guardian or conservator), 1111.02, 1109.02)	A foreign corporation may be licensed to do business in Ohio as a trust company for one year after meeting extensive filing and fee requirements. (§§ 1111.01(I) (defining "trust business" as including serving as a guardian or conservator), 1111.02, 1109.02)	A foreign corporation may be licensed to do business in Ohio as a trust company for one year after meeting extensive filing and fee requirements. (§§ 1111.01(I) (defining "trust business" as including serving as a guardian or conservator), 1111.02, 1109.02)
Oklahoma	No, although a nonresident may be appointed guardian of his or her own relatives and may also be appointed upon the written request of the father, mother, or next of kin. (30 § 4-104)	No, although a nonresident may be appointed guardian of his or her own relatives and may also be appointed upon the written request of the father, mother, or next of kin. (30 § 4-104)	No, although a nonresident may be appointed guardian of his or her own relatives and may also be appointed upon the written request of the father, mother, or next of kin. (30 § 4-104) However, if the incompetent ward and domiciliary guardian are both nonresidents, then no appointment of the guardian may be required, since pursuant to court approval, the ward's estate can be removed from the state. (30 §§ 4-605, 4-607)	No, although a nonresident may be appointed guardian of his or her own relatives and may also be appointed upon the written request of the father, mother, or next of kin. (30 § 4-104) However, if the incompetent ward and domiciliary guardian are both nonresidents, then no appointment of the guardian may be required, since pursuant to court approval, the ward's estate can be removed from the state. (30 §§ 4-605, 4-607)
Oregon	Yes. (§ 125.200)	Yes. (§ 125.200)	Yes. (§ 125.200)	Yes. (§ 125.200)
Pennsylvania	Yes, if reciprocal treatment is accorded Pennsylvania banks. (7 § 106) Any bank must meet minimum capital requirements. (7 § 106(b)(ii))	Yes, if reciprocal treatment is accorded Pennsylvania banks. (7 § 106) Any bank must meet minimum capital requirements. (7 § 106(b)(ii))	Yes, if reciprocal treatment is accorded Pennsylvania banks. (7 § 106) Any bank must meet minimum capital requirements. (7 § 106(b)(ii))	Yes, if reciprocal treatment is accorded Pennsylvania banks. (7 § 106) Any bank must meet minimum capital requirements. (7 § 106(b)(ii))
Rhode Island	Yes, if appointment of state official as true and lawful attorney for receipt of process. (§ 19-3.1-6)	Yes, if appointment of state official as true and lawful attorney for receipt of process. (§ 19-3.1-6)	Yes, if appointment of state official as true and lawful attorney for receipt of process. (§ 19-3.1-6) Moreover, the guardian may be able to remove property without local appointment. (§ 33-15-42)	Yes, if appointment of state official as true and lawful attorney for receipt of process. (§ 19-3.1-6) Moreover, the guardian may be able to remove property without local appointment. (§ 33-15-42)
South Carolina	Yes. (§§ 62-5-311, 62-5-410)	Yes. (§§ 62-5-311, 62-5-410)	Yes. (§§ 62-4-204, 62-5-431, 62-5-432, 62-5-410)	Yes. (§§ 62-4-204, 62-5-431, 62-5-432, 62-5-410)

Table 3.04

Nonresident Bank as Guardian of Minor's or Incompetent's Property

	Nonresident Bank as Guardian of Minor's Property	Nonresident Bank as Guardian of Incompetent's Property	Nonresident Bank as Ancillary Guardian of Minor's Property	Nonresident Bank as Ancillary Guardian of Incompetent's Property
South Dakota	Yes, if capable of providing a suitable program of conservatorship, and if reciprocal treatment is accorded South Dakota banks and if filing provisions are met, especially naming the office of the Secretary of State as agent for the receipt of process. (§§ 51A-5-7-51A-5-10, 29A-5-110)	Yes, if capable of providing a suitable program of conservatorship, and if reciprocal treatment is accorded South Dakota banks and if filing provisions are met, especially naming the office of the Secretary of State as agent for the receipt of process. (§§ 51A-5-7-51A-5-10, 29A-5-110)	Yes, if reciprocal treatment is accorded South Dakota banks and if filing provisions are met, especially naming the office of the Secretary of State as agent for the receipt of process. (§§ 51A-5-7-51A-5-10, 29A-5-110)	Yes, if reciprocal treatment is accorded South Dakota banks and if filing provisions are met, especially naming the office of the Secretary of State as agent for the receipt of process. (§§ 51A-5-7-51A-5-10, 29A-5-110)
Tennessee	Yes, if reciprocal treatment is accorded Tennessee banks. (§ 35-50-107(a)(2)(A)) The secretary of state must be appointed as agent for service of process. (§ 35-50-107(b)(2)) See also § 30-1-116.	Yes, if reciprocal treatment is accorded Tennessee banks. (§ 35-50-107(a)(2)(A)) The secretary of state must be appointed as agent for service of process. (§ 35-50-107(b)(2)) See also § 30-1-116.	Yes, if reciprocal treatment is accorded Tennessee banks. (§ 35-50-107(a)(2)(A)) The secretary of state must be appointed as agent for service of process. (§ 35-50-107(b)(2)) See also § 30-1-116.	Yes, if reciprocal treatment is accorded Tennessee banks. (§ 35-50-107(a)(2)(A)) The secretary of state must be appointed as agent for service of process. (§ 35-50-107(b)(2)) See also § 30-1-116.
Texas	Yes, if reciprocal treatment is accorded Texas banks and if filing provisions are met. (Estates § 505.003)	Yes, if reciprocal treatment is accorded Texas banks and if filing provisions are met. (Estates § 505.003)	Yes, if reciprocal treatment is accorded Texas banks and if filing provisions are met. (Estates § 505.003)	Yes, if reciprocal treatment is accorded Texas banks and if filing provisions are met. (Estates § 505.003)
Utah	No, unless all requirements are met. (§§ 7-18a-302, 7-5-1)	No, unless all requirements are met. (§§ 7-18a-302, 7-5-1)	No, unless all requirements are met. (§§ 7-18a-302, 7-5-1)	No, unless all requirements are met. (§§ 7-18a-302, 7-5-1)
Vermont	Tit. 11A § 15.01 can be interpreted two ways. Since it only mentions executors and trustees, it can be read as not imposing the requirements set forth in *Nonresident Bank as Executor* for other types of nonresident fiduciaries. However, it could also be read as not allowing certification of nonresident banks acting in their other fiduciary roles.	Tit. 11A § 15.01 can be interpreted two ways. Since it only mentions executors and trustees, it can be read as not imposing the requirements set forth in *Nonresident Bank as Executor* for other types of nonresident fiduciaries. However, it could also be read as not allowing certification of nonresident banks acting in their other fiduciary roles.	Tit. 11A § 15.01 can be interpreted two ways. Since it only mentions executors and trustees, it can be read as not imposing the requirements set forth in *Nonresident Bank as Executor* for other types of nonresident fiduciaries. However, it could also be read as not allowing certification of nonresident banks acting in their other fiduciary roles.	Tit. 11A § 15.01 can be interpreted two ways. Since it only mentions executors and trustees, it can be read as not imposing the requirements set forth in *Nonresident Bank as Executor* for other types of nonresident fiduciaries. However, it could also be read as not allowing certification of nonresident banks acting in their other fiduciary roles.
Virginia	No, unless authorized to do business in the state. (§ 64.2-1426(B))	No, unless authorized to do business in the state. (§ 64.2-1426(B))	No, unless authorized to do business in the state. (§ 64.2-1426) Ancillary proceedings may not be necessary. (§ 64.2-1427)	No, unless authorized to do business in the state. (§ 64.2-1426) Ancillary proceedings may not be necessary. (§ 64.2-1427)

Table 3.04

Nonresident Bank as Guardian of Minor's or Incompetent's Property

	Nonresident Bank as Guardian of Minor's Property	Nonresident Bank as Guardian of Incompetent's Property	Nonresident Bank as Ancillary Guardian of Minor's Property	Nonresident Bank as Ancillary Guardian of Incompetent's Property
Washington	Yes, if appoints an agent who is a resident of the county where the estate is being probated or is an attorney of record of the estate. Otherwise, no, except if a national bank authorized to so act, if upon petition of a person having a right to such appoint. The bank must not have drawn a will appointing it to the position. (§11.36.010)	Yes, if appoints an agent who is a resident of the county where the estate is being probated or is an attorney of record of the estate. Otherwise, no, except if a national bank authorized to so act, if upon petition of a person having a right to such appoint. The bank must not have drawn a will appointing it to the position. (§ 11.36.010)	Yes, if appoints an agent who is a resident of the county where the estate is being probated or is an attorney of record of the estate. Otherwise, no, except if a national bank authorized to so act, if upon petition of a person having a right to such appoint. The bank must not have drawn a will appointing it to the position. (§ 11.36.010)	Yes, if appoints an agent who is a resident of the county where the estate is being probated or is an attorney of record of the estate. Otherwise, no, except if a national bank authorized to so act, if upon petition of a person having a right to such appoint. The bank must not have drawn a will appointing it to the position. (§ 11.36.010)
West Virginia	No, unless a main or branch office in the state. However, the provision then states that a nonresident corporation cannot have its principal office or place of business outside the state. (§ 44-5-3)	No, unless a main or branch office in the state. However, the provision then states that a nonresident corporation cannot have its principal office or place of business outside the state. (§ 44-5-3)	No, unless a main or branch office in the state. However, the provision then states that a nonresident corporation cannot have its principal office or place of business outside the state. (§44-5-3)	No, unless a main or branch office in the state. However, the provision then states that a nonresident corporation cannot have its principal office or place of business outside the state. (§44-5-3)
Wisconsin	Yes, if (a) authorized to act as a fiduciary in its state of organization, and (b) the law of that state allows the following to act as a fiduciary "not unduly restrictive when compared with the laws of this state:" a corporation organized in Wisconsin, a national banking association having its principal place of business in Wisconsin, and a federal savings association or a federal savings bank having its principal place of business in Wisconsin and authorized to act as a fiduciary in Wisconsin. (§ 223.12)	Yes, if (a) authorized to act as a fiduciary in its state of organization, and (b) the law of that state allows the following to act as a fiduciary "not unduly restrictive when compared with the laws of this state:" a corporation organized in Wisconsin, a national banking association having its principal place of business in Wisconsin, and a federal savings association or a federal savings bank having its principal place of business in Wisconsin and authorized to act as a fiduciary in Wisconsin. (§ 223.12)	Yes, if (a) authorized to act as a fiduciary in its state of organization, and (b) the law of that state allows the following to act as a fiduciary "not unduly restrictive when compared with the laws of this state:" a corporation organized in Wisconsin, a national banking association having its principal place of business in Wisconsin, and a federal savings association or a federal savings bank having its principal place of business in Wisconsin. (§ 223.12) If the bank has been appointed at the domicile, it qualifies without satisfying § 223.12. See also § 54.64(6).	Yes, if (a) authorized to act as a fiduciary in its state of organization, and (b) the law of that state allows the following to act as a fiduciary "not unduly restrictive when compared with the laws of this state:" a corporation organized in Wisconsin, a national banking association having its principal place of business in Wisconsin, and a federal savings association or a federal savings bank having its principal place of business in Wisconsin. (§ 223.12) If the bank has been appointed at the domicile, it qualifies without satisfying § 54.64(6).

Table 3.04
Nonresident Bank as Guardian of Minor's or Incompetent's Property

	Nonresident Bank as Guardian of Minor's Property	Nonresident Bank as Guardian of Incompetent's Property	Nonresident Bank as Ancillary Guardian of Minor's Property	Nonresident Bank as Ancillary Guardian of Incompetent's Property
Wyoming	Section 13-5-101(b)(i) provides that a trust company may "act or be appointed by any court to act in like manner as an individual, as executor, administrator, guardian or conservator."	Section 13-5-101(b)(i) provides that a trust company may "act or be appointed by any court to act in like manner as an individual, as executor, administrator, guardian or conservator."	Section 13-5-101(b)(i) provides that a trust company may "act or be appointed by any court to act in like manner as an individual, as executor, administrator, guardian or conservator."	Section 13-5-101(b)(i) provides that a trust company may "act or be appointed by any court to act in like manner as an individual, as executor, administrator, guardian or conservator."

[1] § 15-14-413(1)(a) gives highest priority to the appointment of a person recognized by the appropriate court of the foreign jurisdiction in which the protected person "resides." The provision, however, does not specifically address the appointment of a foreign person when the protected person resides in Colorado. Presumably, no limitation is placed on such person serving, if the person otherwise complies with the statute.

[2] *Id.*

[3] *Id.*

[4] *Id.*

Table 4
Small Estates Procedure
(current through 5/1/18)

Almost every state has a simplified procedure for small estates. This table considers the option, which may be of particular relevance in the case of a decedent who dies domiciled in one state, but leaves a small amount of property in another state or states. By use of the small estates procedure, considerable expense, delay, conflicting decisions, and multiple will contests can be avoided. This table should be considered in conjunction with Table 2, which deals with ancillary or original probate in a state other than the domiciliary state, when the local assets are too substantial to qualify for the use of the small estate procedure.

There are several crucial issues that must be confronted before the small estates procedure can be utilized. First, the procedure may not necessarily be available to nonresidents at all. Second, if it is, there may be precise requirements for obtaining the benefit. For example, in some states, a hearing may be required. In others, a simple affidavit may be prepared and submitted to those in possession of the decedent's property. This table provides details as to the required contents of the petition and/or affidavit. It also indicates what notice requirements must be observed.

The small estates procedure is not available for all assets. Moreover, certain assets, such as automobiles, may have to be handled specially. Regardless of the nature of the assets allowed, each state also imposes a maximum dollar amount. If the "estate" exceeds this amount, the small estates procedure cannot be employed.

Difficult questions often arise as to authority to deal with the property. At what point can the assets be disposed of and by whom? In other words, there may be creditors, whose rights have to be addressed first. There is also the question whether an executor or administrator appointed in another state might seek to act and have priority. Alternatively, a nonresident fiduciary may be barred from acting in that capacity locally. Finally, a transferor of assets, who delivers the property upon presentation of an affidavit or petition, may want to be assured that there will be no liability if later someone else claims a right to the property. All of these matters are dissected and addressed, along with statutory references for further inquiry, if deemed necessary by the reader.

Lastly, each state table is headed with the title or type of small estate procedure. In some states, only a procedure for collection of assets by presentation of an affidavit to the holder is in effect. In other states, the statute only addresses the procedure for prompt probate of a will through summary administration. In a large number of states, the statute provides for both procedures.

Alabama
Summary Distribution of Small Estates

Who can initiate process?	The surviving spouse, if there is one; otherwise distributees of an estate of personal property only. (§§ 43-2-692(a), 43-2-691(2)(defines distributees))
Can it be used if claims outstanding?	No, payments or arrangements for payment of all claims against the estate must be made. (§ 43-2-692(b)(9))
Different rules if die testate or intestate?	If the decedent dies intestate, the awards due under Alabama law to the surviving spouse and children must be determined by a probate judge. If the decedent died testate, the will must be filed in the probate judge's office. (§ 43-2-692(b)(6) & (7))
Notice?	Notice of filing must be published once in a newspaper of general circulation in the county of decedent's domicile. If no such newspaper exists, notice must be posted at county courthouse for one week. (§ 43-2-692(b)(8))
heirs	No provision.
creditors	No provision.
others	No provision.
Which of the following must be observed?	
hearing	No provision.
affidavit, petition, other	Petition. (§ 43-2-692(a)) Can use an affidavit/order to claim decedent's property from another party in possession. (§ 43-2-694)
bond	No bond is required. (§ 43-2-692(a)).
What are basic contents of petition or affidavit?	Petition shall describe the estate of decedent. (§ 43-2-692(a))
Is procedure available in the case of nonresident decedents?	No. (§ 43-2-692(b)(2))
Maximum allowable value of estate	$25,000 (adjusted for inflation). (§ 43-2-692(b)(1)), $28,417 for the period March 1, 2017 – February 28, 2018).
What property can be transferred by this means?	Personal property. (§ 43-2-692(b))
Special rules for certain assets (e.g., automobile)	No provision.
Can the spouse or other person take summarily if under certain amount?	Yes. The surviving spouse or distributee has a defeasible right to personal property of the decedent if the entire estate is less than $25,000 and certain other criteria are satisfied. (§ 43-2-692(b))
Minimum period before filing allowed	Can file any time. (§§ 43-2-692(b)(4), 43-2-692(a))
Rights/obligations of party with affidavit	May have property transferred. (§ 43-2-694) Liable to personal representative of estate, surviving spouse, or minor children, or anyone with a superior right to the property. (§ 43-2-696)

Are some creditors given special privileges/ preference (e.g., medical expenses, funeral expenses)?	Yes, there is a priority imposed. In rank order: funeral expenses, probate fees, last illness expenses, state and municipality taxes, secured creditors, unsecured lienholders, unsecured creditors, and distributees or devisees. (§ 43-2-692(b)(9))
Creditors' rights, if insufficient assets	If there are insufficient assets to pay debts, and other arrangements are not made, summary distribution is not available. (§ 43-2-692(b)(9))
May the distribution of the estate proceed without appointment of personal representative?	Yes, as long as no petition for the appointment of a personal representative is pending or has been granted. (§ 43-2-692(b)(3)) Note that there is no indication whether this applies to a petition filed in Alabama or anywhere.
Must court approve affidavit?	No. Must be executed by a person with knowledge of compliance with the requirements of summary distribution. (§ 43-2-694)
Waiting period before authority to act	30 days after notice of filing of petition was first published. (§ 43-2-692(b)(4))
With whom do you file petition or affidavit?	Probate judge's office in county of decedent's domicile at death. (§ 43-2-692(a))
Is there an informal procedure for appointment of executor or administrator?	No provision.
Can a nonresident serve?	The power to utilize summary distribution is subject to any pre-existing right to administer. (§ 43-2-695)
Can the nonresident act locally based on appointment in another state?	Yes. (§§ 43-2-192 (executor), 43-2-193 (administrator), 43-2-191 (generally))
What does a transferor need so as to be relieved of liability if challenged by another person later on who claims the particular property (e.g., copy of affidavit)?	Payor is relieved upon payment to same extent as if payment made to a personal representative. The payor need not investigate the truthfulness of the affidavit. (§ 43-2-696)

Alaska
Collection of Personal Property by Affidavit; Summary Administration

Who can initiate process?	There are two different procedures, depending on whether or not there is a personal representative. If there is no personal representative, the procedure is collection of personal property by affidavit and can be initiated by a person claiming to be the successor of the decedent. (§ 13.16.680(a)) If there is a personal representative, then the personal representative may initiate the procedure called summary administration. (§ § 13.16.690, 13.16.695(a))
Can it be used if claims outstanding?	*Affidavit.* No provision. *Summary Administration.* Yes. (§ 13.16.690)
Different rules if die testate or intestate?	No provision.
Notice?	
heirs	*Affidavit.* No provision. *Summary Administration.* No notice is required to distribute the estate, but must send closing statement to distributees. (§ 13.16.695(a)(3))
creditors	*Affidavit.* No provision. *Summary Administration.* No notice is required to distribute the estate, but a closing statement must be sent to creditors. (§ § 13.16.690, 13.16.695(a)(3))
others	*Affidavit.* No provision. *Summary Administration.* All distributees, creditors and other claimants of whom personal representative is aware and whose claims are neither paid nor barred must be sent a copy of the closing statement. (§ 13.16.695(a)(3))
Which of the following must be observed?	
hearing	No provision.
affidavit, petition, other	*Affidavit.* Affidavit. (§ 13.16.680(a)) *Summary Administration.* A verified statement. (§ 13.16.695(a))
bond	No provision.
What are basic contents of petition or affidavit?	*Affidavit:* Must show that the estate, less liens and encumbrances, consists only of not more than: vehicles with a maximum total value of $100,000 and other personal property with a maximum value of $50,000; 30 days have elapsed since death; no application or petition for appointment of personal representative is pending or has been granted in *any* jurisdiction; party claiming to be successor is entitled to property. (§ 13.16.680) (emphasis added) *Summary Administration.* Closing statement must show that value of estate did not exceed certain allowances and expenses; that estate is fully administered; and that a closing statement was sent to all distributees, creditors and other claimants. (§ 13.16.695(a))

Is procedure available in the case of nonresident decedents?	No provision.
Maximum allowable value of estate	*Affidavit.* Value of entire estate, wherever located, less liens and encumbrances, must consist only of not more than vehicles valued at $100,000 or less and other personal property that does not exceed $50,000. (§ 13.16.680(a)(1)) *Summary Administration.* Value of entire estate, less liens and encumbrances, cannot exceed homestead, exempt property, family allowance, administration costs, funeral expenses, and medical expenses for last illness. (§ 13.16.690)
What property can be transferred by this means?	*Affidavit.* Personal property. (§ 13.16.680) *Summary Administration.* The estate. (§ 13.16.690)
Special rules for certain assets (e.g., automobile)	Stock in corporations organized under the Alaska Natives Claims Settlement Act is not to be considered under this section for distribution or estate valuation purposes. (§ 13.16.705(a))
Can the spouse or other person take summarily if under certain amount?	*Affidavit.* Yes, "a person claiming to be successor" can take if the value of the entire estate, less liens and encumbrances, consists only of not more than vehicles with a total value not exceeding $100,000 and other personal property that does not exceed $50,000. (§ 13.16.680(a)(1)) *Summary Administration.* Yes, "persons entitled" can take if the value of the entire estate does not exceed certain allowances and expenses. (§ 13.16.690)
Minimum period before filing allowed	*Affidavit.* 30 days after death. (§ 13.16.680(a)(2)) *Summary Administration.* Any time after disbursement and distribution of estate. (§ 13.16.695(a))
Rights/obligations of party with affidavit	*Affidavit.* Accountable to anyone with a superior right or a personal representative. (§ 13.16.685) *Summary Administration.* No provision.
Are some creditors given special privileges/ preference (e.g., medical expenses, funeral expenses)?	*Affidavit.* No provision. *Summary Administration.* Yes, administration expenses, funeral expenses, and last illness medical expenses. (§ 13.16.690)
Creditors' rights, if insufficient assets	*Affidavit.* See *Rights/obligations of party with affidavit* above. *Summary Administration.* No right beyond a right to a closing statement. (§ 13.16.695(a)(3))
May the distribution of the estate proceed without appointment of personal representative?	*Affidavit.* Yes. (§ 13.16.680) *Summary Administration.* No specific provision. All the relevant provisions reference the personal representative, but there is no specific requirement. See, e.g. §§ 13.16.690, 3.16.695.
Must court approve affidavit?	No provision.

Waiting period before authority to act	*Affidavit.* 30 days after death. (§ 13.16.680(a)(2)) *Summary Administration.* Immediately after the entire estate is deemed to not exceed certain allowances and expenses. (§ 13.16.690)
With whom do you file petition or affidavit?	*Affidavit.* With those in possession of property or transfer agent of any security. (§ 13.16.680(a), (b)) *Summary Administration.* File with the court. (§ 13.16.695(a)(3))
Is there an informal procedure for appointment of executor or administrator?	Yes, the judge may appoint if no qualified person has come forward to take charge of the assets and estate consists only of not more than vehicles with a total value not exceeding $100,000 and other personal property that does not exceed $50,000. (§ 13.16.700)
Can a nonresident serve?	Yes. (§ § 13.21.015 through 13.21.040)
Can the nonresident act locally based on appointment in another state?	Yes, if no local administration is pending, a foreign personal representative may exercise in this state all powers of a local personal representative. (§ § 13.21.035, 13.21.030)
What does a transferor need so as to be relieved of liability if challenged by another person later on who claims the particular property (e.g., copy of affidavit)?	Payor is released from liability upon payment. No need to inquire into the truth of the affidavit. (§ 13.16.685)

Arizona
Transfer of Title to Small Estates by Affidavit and Summary Administration

Who can initiate process?	There are two procedures: (1) collection of personal/real property by affidavit, and (2) summary administration. *Personal and Real Property by Affidavit* (§ 14-3971). This procedure has three components—one for compensation owing to the decedent by the employer (§ 14-3971(A)), one for the collection of personal property (§ 14-3971(B)), and one for real property (§ 14-3971(E)). Under § 14-3971(A), the surviving spouse or someone acting on behalf of the surviving spouse may initiate. Under § 14-3971(B) & (E), a person claiming to be a successor may initiate. *Summary Administration.* (§ 14-3973) The personal representative. (§ 14-3973)
Can it be used if claims outstanding?	*Affidavit.* The affidavit procedure for real property requires unsecured debt, funeral expenses, expenses of last illness, and federal estate taxes to be paid. (§ 14-3971(E)(3) & (6)) *Summary Administration.* No provision.
Different rules if die testate or intestate?	No provision.
Notice?	*Affidavit.* Once the affidavit is filed and the registrar determines that it is complete, the registrar shall cause the affidavit to be recorded in the county where real property is located. (§ 14-3971(F)) *Summary Administration.* No general provision, but see below.
heirs	*Affidavit.* No provision. *Summary Administration.* A copy of the closing statement must be sent to all known distributees whose claims are neither paid nor barred. (§ 14-3974(A)(3))
creditors	*Affidavit.* No provision. *Summary Administration.* A copy of the closing statement must be sent to all known creditors whose claims are neither paid nor barred. (§ 14-3974(A)(3))
others	*Affidavit.* No provision. *Summary Administration.* A copy of the closing statement must be sent to other claimants of whom the personal representative is aware and whose claims are neither paid nor barred. (§ 14-3974(A)(3)).
Which of the following must be observed?	
hearing	No provision.
affidavit, petition, other	*Affidavit.* All types of collection by affidavit require the collector to present an affidavit that states the necessary information for that type of collection. (§ 14-3971) *Summary Administration.* Must have a closing statement. (§ 14-3974)
bond	No provision.

What are basic contents of petition or affidavit?	*Affidavit:*
	A. With regard to an employer owing compensation of no more than $5,000, the affidavit must state that: (1) affiant is surviving spouse or is authorized to act on the spouse's behalf; and (2) no application for the appointment of a personal representative pending or granted in Arizona or, if granted, the personal representative has been discharged or more than one year has elapsed since a closing statement has been filed. (§ 14-3971(A))
	B. With regard to personal property, the affidavit must state that: (1) the value of all personal property in the estate, less liens and encumbrances, does not exceed $25,000; (2) 30 days have lapsed since decedent's death; (3) no application or petition for a personal representative is pending and a personal representative has not been appointed in any jurisdiction, or the personal representative has been discharged or more than one year has lapsed since a closing statement has been filed; and (4) successor is entitled to the property. (§ 14-3971(B))
	C. With respect to real property, the affidavit may be filed in the county court of the decedent's domicile, or if not a domiciliary, the county in which the property is situated: (1) describing the real property and decedent's interest; (2) value of real property in Arizona, less liens and encumberances, does not exceed $100,000; (3) six months have lapsed since death; (4) no application or petition for personal representative is pending in any jurisdiction and no personal representative has been appointed in any jurisdiction, or the personal representative has been discharged or more than one year has elapsed since a closing statement has been filed; (5) funeral, last illness, and unsecured debts have been paid; (6) why the affiant is entitled to the property; (7) no other person has a right to the property; (8) no federal estate tax due on decedent's estate; and (9) an affirmation that the information is true. (§ 14-3971(E))
	Summary Administration. Closing statement must state that to the best of personal representative's knowledge the estate value does not exceed the homestead, exempt property, and family allowances, plus reasonable administrative, funeral, and medical expenses. It must state that the personal representative has fully administered the estate by disbursing and distributing it to the persons entitled thereto. The closing statement must also state that the personal representative has distributed the assets and that copies of the closing statement have been sent to the required parties. (§ 14-3974(A))
Is procedure available in the case of nonresident decedents?	Yes. (§§ 14-4201, 14-4207)

Maximum allowable value of estate	*Affidavit.* $5,000 in compensation. (§ 14-3971(A)) $75,000 for personal property, less liens and encumbrances. (§ 14-3971(B)) $100,000 real property, less liens and encumbrances. (§ 14-3971(E)) *Summary Administration.* Entire estate, less liens and encumbrances, does not exceed homestead, exempt property, family allowance, administration costs, and funeral/last illness expenses. (§ 14-3973)
What property can be transferred by this means?	*Affidavit.* Wages, personal property, and real property. (§ 14-3971) *Summary Administration.* The estate. (§ 14-3973)
Special rules for certain assets (e.g., automobile)	Registered ownership of any securities shall be changed by a tranfer agent. (§ 14-3971(C)) Automobile must be transferred through the motor vehicle division. (§ 14-3971(D))
Can the spouse or other person take summarily if under certain amount?	Yes, if the entire estate, less liens and encumbrances, does not exceed allowance in lieu of homestead, exempt property, family allowance, costs and expenses of administration, reasonable funeral expenses, and reasonable and necessary medical and hospital expenses of the last illness of the decedent, the personal representative may do so. (§ 14-3973)
Minimum period before filing allowed	*Affidavit.* For personal property, must wait 30 days after the death of decedent. (§ 14-3971(B)). For real property, must wait 6 months after the death of decedent. (§ 14-3971(E)(2)) No minimum period for compensation owed to the decedent by the employer. (§ 14-3971(A)) *Summary Administration.* No minimum period. (§ 14-3973)
Rights/obligations of party with affidavit	Accountable to personal representative or anyone with a superior right. (§ 14-3972(A))
Are some creditors given special privileges/preference (e.g., medical expenses, funeral expenses)?	*Affidavit.* For real property, funeral expenses, last illness expenses, unsecured debts, and federal estate tax must be paid first. (§ 14-3971(E)(3), (6)) *Summary Administration.* Administration expenses, funeral expenses, and last illness expenses have priority. (§ 14-3973)
Creditors' rights, if insufficient assets	No provision beyond the right to receive closing statement in summary administration. (§ 14-3974)
May the distribution of the estate proceed without appointment of personal representative?	*Affidavit.* Must proceed without personal representative. (§ 14-3971) *Summary Administration.* Personal representative appears to be required, as relevant section references personal representative. (§ 14-3973)
Must court approve affidavit?	Only for real property. (§ 14-3971(E), (F))
Waiting period before authority to act	See *minimum period before filing allowed* above.

With whom do you file petition or affidavit?	For real property, an affidavit must be filed in the court in the county of decedent's domicile at time of death or, if decedent was not domiciled in Arizona, then in any county in which real property of the decedent is located. (§ 14-3971(E))
Is there an informal procedure for appointment of executor or administrator?	Yes. (§ § 14-3301, 14-3307 to -3311)
Can a nonresident serve?	Yes. (§ 14-3203(G))
Can the nonresident act locally based on appointment in another state?	Yes, if there is no local administration and the appropriate documentation is filed with local courts. (§ § 14-4204, 4205).
What does a transferor need so as to be relieved of liability if challenged by another person later on who claims the particular property (e.g., copy of affidavit)?	The transferor is discharged upon payment without need to investigate truth of affidavit. (§ 14-3972(A))

Arkansas
Distribution Without Administration

Who can initiate process?	In Arkansas, distributees can collect small estates by engaging in an affidavit procedure. (§ 28-41-101) If the court determines that the value of the estate does not exceed certain statutory allowances to which the widow or minor children are entitled free of debt, the affidavit procedure is not necessary and the court will vest the estate in the widow or minor children. (§ 28-41-103) *Affidavit.* Distributees of an estate. (§ 28-41-101) *No Administration.* Interested person. (§ 28-41-103)
Can it be used if claims outstanding?	*Affidavit.* No. (§ 28-41-101(a)(4)(A)) *No Administration.* Yes. (§ 28-41-103)
Different rules if die testate or intestate?	No provision.
Notice?	*Affidavit.* If real property is involved, notice shall contain (1) the name of the decedent and last known address, (2) the date of death, (3) a statement that an affidavit was filed, date of filing, a legal description of all real property, (4) a statement requiring all persons having claims against the estate to exhibit them, properly verified, within 3 months from the date of the first publication of the notice, (5) the name, mailing address and telephone number of the distributee or attorney, and (6) the date the notice was first published. (§§ 28-41-101(b)(2)(B)) *No Administration.* Court discretion. (§ 28-41-103(c))
heirs	*Affidavit.* If the estate contains real property, notice shall be published in accordance with § 28-1-112(b) (listing several methods). In addition, within one month of first notice by publication, notice must be served upon all heirs whose names and addresses are known. (§§ 28-41-101(b)(2)(C), 28-40-111(a)(4)) *No Administration.* Court discretion. (§ 28-41-103(c))
creditors	*Affidavit.* If the estate contains real property, notice shall be published in accordance with § 28-1-112(b) (listing several methods). In addition, within one month of first notice by publication, notice must be served upon all unpaid creditors whose names, status as creditors, and addresses are known or reasonably ascertainable. (§§ 28-41-101(b)(2)(C), 28-40-111(a)(4)) *No Administration.* Court discretion. (§ 28-41-103(c))
others	*Affidavit.* If the estate contains real property. notice shall be published in accordance with §§ 28-1-112(b)(4) and 28-40-111(a)(4) (§§ 28-41-101(b)(2)(C)) *No Administration.* Court discretion. (§ 28-41-103(c))
Which of the following must be observed?	
hearing	No provision.
affidavit, petition, other	*Affidavit.* Affidavit. (§ 28-41-101) *No Administration.* Petition. (§ 28-41-103(c))

bond	No provision.
What are basic contents of petition or affidavit?	*Affidavit.* Affidavit must set forth (1) that there are no unpaid claims, and the Department of Human Services has provided no state or federal benefits or has been reimbursed; (2) an itemized description and valuation of real and personal property; (3) the names and addresses of those in possession of real or personal property; and (4) the names, addresses, and relationship to decedent of persons entitled to property. (§ 28-41-101(a)(4)(A)–(D)) *No Administration.* Petition must establish that value of estate (personal property) does not exceed amounts that the widow or minor children are entitled to under the surviving spouse marital share or statutory allowance. (§ 28-41-103(a))
Is procedure available in the case of nonresident decedents?	Except where special provisions apply, same for nonresident decedents as resident decedents. (§ 28-42-101)
Maximum allowable value of estate	*Affidavit.* All property, less encumberances, excluding homestead and statutory allowances, must not exceed $100,000. (§ 28-41-101(a)(3)(A), (B)) *No Administration.* See *contents of petition* in § 28-41-103(a).
What property can be transferred by this means?	*Affidavit.* Entire estate. (§ 28-41-101(a)) *No Administration.* Personal property. (§ 28-41-103(a))
Special rules for certain assets (e.g., automobile)	No provision.
Can the spouse or other person take summarily if under certain amount?	No provision.
Minimum period before filing allowed	*Affidavit.* 45 days after death. (§ 28-41-101(a)(2)) *No Administration.* No provision.
Rights/obligations of party with affidavit	Distributee will be treated like a trustee who is answerable to anyone with a prior right or any personal representative. (§ 28-41-102(b))
Are some creditors given special privileges/ preference (e.g., medical expenses, funeral expenses)?	*Affidavit.* Department of Human Services ("DHS") is given specific attention—Affidavit must indicate whether DHS furnished benefits to the decedent and, if so, whether those funds were reimbursed. (§ 28-41-101(a)(4)(A)) *No Administration.* No provision.
Creditors' rights, if insufficient assets	*Affidavit.* Cannot use affidavit procedure if there are unpaid claims. (§ 28-41-101(a)(4)(A)) *No Administration.* No provision.
May the distribution of the estate proceed without appointment of personal representative?	Yes. (§§ 28-41-101(a), 28-41-103)
Must court approve affidavit?	No. Affidavit must simply be filed by probate clerk. (§ 28-41-101(b)(1))
Waiting period before authority to act	*Affidavit.* 45 days have elapsed since the death of the decedent. (§ 28-41-101(a)(2)) *No Administration.* None. (§ 28-41-103)

With whom do you file petition or affidavit?	Clerk of the Probate Court. (§ 28-41-101(a)(4) & (b)(1))
Is there an informal procedure for appointment of executor or administrator?	No provision.
Can a nonresident serve?	Yes, if appointed as agent to accept service of process and notice. (§ 28-48-101(b)(6))
Can the nonresident act locally based on appointment in another state?	Yes, after filing an authenticated copy of domiciliary letters in the proper venue. (§ 28-42-102(a)(1))
What does a transferor need so as to be relieved of liability if challenged by another person later on who claims the particular property (e.g., copy of affidavit)?	The person making payment is discharged to the same extent as if payment made to a personal representative. Such person is not required to examine truthfulness of the affidavit. (§ 28-41-102(a))

California
Small Estate Set Aside/Disposition of Estate Without Administration

Who can initiate process?	There are two procedures: small estate set aside ("Set Aside") (Prob. § 6600 et seq.) and disposition of estate without administration ("No Administration") (Prob. § 13000 et seq.). *Set Aside.* The following may initiate the process: (1) person named as executor in will; (2) surviving spouse; (3) guardian of minor child; (4) child who was a minor at time of death; or (5) personal representative. (Prob. § 6606(a)) *No Administration.* The successor of decedent may initiate the process. (Prob. § 13107.5) A successor is a person who is entitled to succeed to a particular item of property under a will or under the laws of intestate succession. (Prob. § 13006) The "No Administration" procedure is divided into a personal property procedure (Prob. §§ 13100-13116) and real property procedure. (Prob. §§ 13200-13210)
Can it be used if claims outstanding?	*Set Aside.* Discretionary. (Prob. § 6609(b)) *No Administration.* Under personal property procedure, yes, but the successor remains liable for unsecured debt of decedent. (Prob. §§ 13101, 13109) Under real property procedure, affiant must swear that funeral expenses, last illness expenses, and unsecured debts are paid. (Prob. § 13200(a)(8)) Successor remains liable for unsecured debt. (Prob. § 13204) Liability limited to fair market value of decedent's property, "net income the person received from the property," and "if the property has been disposed of, interest on the fair market value of the property from the date of disposition." (Prob. § 13207)
Different rules if die testate or intestate?	*Set Aside.* No provision. *No Administration.* Only to the extent that testacy/intestacy determines the successor. (Prob. §§ 13100, 13006)
Notice?	*Set Aside.* If administration proceedings are not pending, notice shall be delivered at least 15 days in advance of hearing to (1) each person named as executor in a will; (2) each heir and devisee known to petitioner; and (3) copy of petition to the surviving spouse, each child, and each devisee who is not petitioning. (Prob. §§ 6607(a), 1220) If proceedings are pending, notice must be delivered to each known heir and each devisee, executor, and alternate executor in the will at least 15 days in advance of hearing. (Prob. §§ 6607(c), 8110) *No Administration.* No notice required for personal property unless there is a hearing for a court order to determine succession. If there is such a hearing, notice of the hearing is to be delivered to each known heir, devisee, and conservator or guardian of the decedent. (Prob. §§ 13153, 13152, 1220) For real property, the succession hearing rules are the same, and a copy of the affidavit must be delivered to each known guardian/conservator. (Prob. § 13200(f))

heirs	See *Notice?* above.
creditors	See *Notice?* above.
others	See *Notice?* above.
Which of the following must be observed?	
hearing	*Set Aside.* Yes. (Prob. § 6607) *No Administration.* No provision.
affidavit, petition, other	*Set Aside.* Petition. (Prob. § 6602) *No Administration.* Affidavit or "declaration." (Prob. § § 13101, 13200) For the real property procedure there is a $30 fee. (Prob. § § 13201, Government § 70626(b)(9))
bond	No provision.

What are basic contents of petition or affidavit?

Set Aside. Petition shall allege that chapter of code applies and request for an order for set aside and shall include: (1) if administration not pending, facts necessary to determine the county in which the estate of the decedent may be administered; (2) name, age, address, relation of each known heir/devisee; (3) description and estimated value of decedent's estate and a list of all liens and encumbrances; (4) description and estimated value of real property outside of California that passed to surviving spouse/minor child; (5) description and estimated value of any joint property or multiple party accounts that passed to the surviving spouse/minor child; (6) any property outside of estate by virtue of homestead; (7) unpaid funeral, last illness, administration expenses; (8) requested disposition of estate and the considerations that support such a disposition. (Prob. § 6604) An inventory and appraisal must accompany the petition. (Prob. § 6608)

No Administration. For personal property: (1) decedent's name; (2) date and place of decedent's death; (3) statement that 40 days have passed since death; (4) statement that either no administration proceeding is pending in California or that the personal representative has consented to this procedure; (5) gross fair market value of decedent's real and personal property in California (less exclusions of Prob. § 13050) does not exceed $150,000; (6) description of the property to be given to affiant; (7) name of the successor to the property; (8) statement that affiant is the successor or authorized to act on successor's behalf; (9) statement that no person has a superior right in the described property; (10) request for delivery; (11) affirmation as to truth; (12) attachment of death certificate; and (13) attachment of personal representative's consent if appropriate. (Prob. § 13101) Also required: in some cases, evidence of any ownership (Prob. § 13102); inventory and appraisal of California real property (Prob. § 13103); proof of affiant's identity (Prob. § 13104).

For real property: (1) decedent's name; (2) date and place of death; (3) legal description of property and the interest of the decedent therein; (4) name/address of known guardians/conservators of estate; (5) statement that gross value of California real property (less exclusions of Prob. § 13050) does not exceed $50,000; (6) statement that six months have passed since death; (7) no administration proceeding has been conducted, or the decedent's personal representative has consented to this procedure; (8) statement that funeral expenses, last illness expenses, and unsecured debt have been paid; (9) statement that affiant is successor and no person has a superior right; (10) affirmation of truth of affidavit; (11) notarized; (12) attachment of inventory/appraisal of non-excluded California real property; (13) if affiant is claiming under a will and there is no estate proceeding, a copy of the will must also be attached; and (14) attached certified copy of death certificate or personal representative's consent to use of affidavit procedure. (Prob. § 13200)

Is procedure available in the case of nonresident decedents?	No provision.
Maximum allowable value of estate	*Set Aside.* Net value less liens, encumbrances, and homestead interest must not exceed $20,000. (Prob. § 6602) *No Administration.* Personal property—current gross fair market value of real and personal property must not exceed $150,000 less certain exclusions. (Prob. §§ 13101(a)(5), 13050) Real property—gross value of California real property less exclusions must not exceed $50,000. (Prob. §§ 13200(a)(5), 13050)
What property can be transferred by this means?	*Set Aside.* Entire estate. (Prob. § 6602) *No Administration.* Personal property—personal only. (Prob. § 13101(a)) Real property—real only. (Prob. § 13200(a))
Special rules for certain assets (e.g., automobile)	Under all procedures, certain property does not count for valuation purposes. (Prob. §§ 6600, 13050)
Can the spouse or other person take summarily if under certain amount?	Yes, the surviving spouse can take property that passes by will or intestate succession without administration. (Prob. § 13500 et seq.)
Minimum period before filing allowed	*Set Aside.* Any time before order for final distribution. (Prob. § 6605(c)) *No Administration.* Personal property—40 days after death. (Prob. § 13101(a)(3)) Real property—six months after death. (Prob. § 13200(a)(6))
Rights/obligations of party with affidavit	*Set Aside.* Not applicable. *No Administration.* Personal property—liable for (1) unsecured debt (Prob. § 13109); (2) liable to those with superior claims (Prob. § 13110(a)); (3) liable for treble damages if fraudulently secures the payment, delivery, or transfer of the decedents' property (Prob. § 13110(b)); (4) liable to personal representative if administration proceedings later commenced or if personal representative revokes consent to use of this procedure. (Prob. § 13111) Real property—liable for (1) unsecured debt (Prob. § 13204); (2) liable to those with superior claims (Prob. § 13205(a)); (3) liable for treble damages if fraudulent execution or filing of affidavit (Prob. § 13205(b)); (4) liable to personal representative if administration proceedings later commenced or if personal representative revokes consent to use this procedure (Prob. § 13206).
Are some creditors given special privileges/ preference (e.g., medical expenses, funeral expenses)?	*Set Aside.* If an order is made to set aside the small estate, the court will make an additional order requiring that unpaid last illness expenses, funeral charges, and administration expenses be paid. (§ 6609(d)) *No Administration.* Real property—the affiant must swear that funeral expenses, last illness expenses, and unsecured debts have been paid. (Prob. § 13200(a)(8))

Creditors' rights, if insufficient assets	*Set Aside.* No provision. *No Administration.* For personal property, affiants are liable for unsecured debt to the extent provided in § 13112. (Prob. § 13109) For real property, affiants are liable for unsecured debt to the extent provided in § 13207. (Prob. § 13204)
May the distribution of the estate proceed without appointment of personal representative?	*Set Aside.* Yes. (Prob. § 6606) *No Administration.* Yes. (Prob. § § 13108, 13210)
Must court approve affidavit?	*Set Aside.* While there is no affidavit, the court must approve a petition to assign the whole of the decedent's estate to the surviving spouse and the minor children. (Prob. § 6609) *No Administration.* For personal property, no court involvement is necessary. (Prob. § 13101) For real property, the affidavit must be filed in the Superior Court in the county of decedent's domicile at time of death, or if decedent was not domiciled in California, then in the any county in which real property of the decedent is located. (Prob. § 13200(a))
Waiting period before authority to act	*Set Aside.* None. (Prob. § 6605) *No Administration.* Personal property—40 days. (Prob. § 13101(a)(3)) Real property—six months. (Prob. § 13200(a))
With whom do you file petition or affidavit?	*Set Aside.* "Petition shall be filed in the superior court of a county in which the estate may be administered." (Prob. § 6603) *No Administration.* Real property—Superior court in county of decedent's domicile at death or if the decedent was not domiciled in California then in any county in which real property of the decedent is located. (Prob. § 13200(a)); Personal property—with holder of decedent's property (Prob. § 13101)
Is there an informal procedure for appointment of executor or administrator?	No provision.
Can a nonresident serve?	No provision.
Can the nonresident act locally based on appointment in another state?	No provision.
What does a transferor need so as to be relieved of liability if challenged by another person later on who claims the particular property (e.g., copy of affidavit)?	*Set Aside.* No provision. *No Administration.* Transferor is released from liability under personal property procedures. If the requirements of Section 13100-13104 are satisfied, receipt of an affidavit by the holder of decedent's property discharging the holder from any further liability. (Prob. § 13106(a)) No provision for real property procedures.

Colorado
Collection of Personal Property by Affidavit/Summary Administration Procedure for Small Estates

Who can initiate process?	*Affidavit.* Successor. (§ 15-12-1201(1)) *Summary Administration.* Personal representative. (§ 15-12-1203)
Can it be used if claims outstanding?	*Affidavit.* Yes. (§ 15-12-1201) *Summary Administration.* Yes. (§ 15-12-1203)
Different rules if die testate or intestate?	*Affidavit.* Same rules by implication. (§ 15-12-1201) *Summary Administration.* Same rules. (§ 15-12-1203)
Notice?	*Affidavit.* No provision. *Summary Administration.* Closing statement must be sent to all distributees of the estate and to known creditors and other claimants of whom the personal representative is aware and whose claims are neither paid nor barred. (§ 15-12-1204(1)(c))
heirs	*Summary Administration.* Closing statement must be sent to all distributees of the estate whose interests are affected. (§ 15-12-1204(1)(c))
creditors	*Summary Administration.* If the net value of the estate, less liens and encumbrances, does not exceed the value of the personal property held by the decedent as fiduciary or trustee, exempt property allowance, family allowance, cost of administration, reasonable funeral and medical/ hospital expenses of the last illness of the decedent, the representative may distribute the property without giving notice to creditors. (§ 15-12-1203) But a closing statement must be sent to known creditors whose claims are neither paid nor barred. (§ 15-12-1204(1)(c))
others	*Summary Administration.* Closing statement must be sent to all other claimants of whom the personal representative is aware and whose claims are neither paid nor barred. (§ 15-12-1204(1)(c))
Which of the following must be observed?	
Hearing	No provision.
affidavit, petition, other	Affidavit. (§ 15-12-1201) *Summary Administration.* Closing statement. (§§ 15-12-1203, 15-12-1204)
Bond	No provision.

What are basic contents of petition or affidavit?	*Affidavit.* The affidavit must assert that (1) the fair market value of property at time of death, wherever located, less liens and encumbrances, does not exceed $66,000 for 2017 (amount adjusted for inflation); (2) at least 10 days have lapsed since death; (3) no application/petition for a personal representative is pending or has been granted in any jurisdiction; and (4) the claimant is entitled to the property in the proportion set forth. (§ 15-12-1201(1)(a)–(d)) *Summary Administration.* Closing statement must assert that (1) to the best of personal representative's knowledge, the value of the entire estate, less liens and encumbrances, did not exceed the value of personal property held by the decedent or in the decedent's possession as fiduciary or trustee, exempt property, family allowance, costs of administration, funeral/last illness expenses; (2) the personal representative has fully administered the estate by disbursing and distributing it to the persons entitled; and (3) copies of the closing statement were sent to all distributees and creditors whose claims are neither paid nor barred, along with an accounting to those whose interests are affected. (§ 15-12-1204(1)(a)-(c))
Is procedure available in the case of nonresident decedents?	Yes. (§§ 15-13-201, 15-13-207)
Maximum allowable value of estate	*Affidavit.* Fair market value of all property at the time of death, less liens and encumbrances, must not exceed $66,000 for 2017 (amount adjusted for inflation). (§ 15-12-1201(1)(a)) *Summary Administration.* Value of entire estate less liens and encumbrances must not exceed the value of personal property held by the decedent or in possession of decedent as fiduciary/trustee, exempt property, family allowance, costs and expenses of administration, funeral/last illness expenses. (§ 15-12-1203)
What property can be transferred by this means?	*Affidavit.* Personal. (§ 15-12-1201) *Summary Administration.* All. (§ 15-12-1203)
Special rules for certain assets (e.g., automobile)	Registered ownership of any securities shall be changed by a tranfer agent upon presentation of the affidavit. (§ 15-12-1201(2)) A public official that is aware of any registered title of the decedent shall change the registered ownership from the decedent to the successor(s) upon presentation of the affidavit. (§ 15-12-1201(3))
Can the spouse or other person take summarily if under certain amount?	No provision.
Minimum period before filing allowed	*Affidavit.* 10 days after death. (§ 15-12-1201(1)(b)) *Summary Administration.* Any time after disbursement and distribution of estate. (§ 15-12-1204(1))
Rights/obligations of party with affidavit	Answerable and accountable to any personal representative or person with superior right. (§ 15-12-1202)

Are some creditors given special privileges/ preference (e.g., medical expenses, funeral expenses)?	*Affidavit.* No provision. *Summary Administration.* Funeral/last illness expenses. (§ 15-12-1203)
Creditors' rights, if insufficient assets	No provisions. Must be sent a closing statement. (§ 15-12-1204(1)(c))
May the distribution of the estate proceed without appointment of personal representative?	*Affidavit.* Not if an application or petition for the appointment of a personal representative is pending or has been granted in *any* jurisdiction. (§ 15-12-1201(1)(c)) (emphasis added) *Summary Administration.* Must proceed with personal representative. (§ 15-12-1203)
Must court approve affidavit?	No. (§ 15-12-1201)
Waiting period before authority to act	*Affidavit.* 10 days after death. (§ 15-12-1201) *Summary Administration.* No waiting period. (§ 15-12-1203)
With whom do you file petition or affidavit?	*Affidavit.* Need not file. (§ 15-12-1201) *Summary Administration.* Closing statement filed with the court. (§ 15-12-1204(1))
Is there an informal procedure for appointment of executor or administrator?	Yes. (§ § 15-12-301, 15-12-307–311)
Can a nonresident serve?	Yes. (§ 15-13-205)
Can the nonresident act locally based on appointment in another state?	Yes, if there is no local administration and the appropriate documentation is filed with local courts. (§ 15-13-206)
What does a transferor need so as to be relieved of liability if challenged by another person later on who claims the particular property (e.g., copy of affidavit)?	Transferror is released to the same extent as if payor dealt with a personal representative, without any need to inquire into the truth of the affidavit. (§ 15-12-1202)

Connecticut
Settlement of Certain Small Estates Without Letters of Administration or Probate of Will

Who can initiate process?	(1) Surviving spouse; (2) if no surviving spouse, next of kin; or (3) if no next of kin or if surviving spouse and next of kin refuse, any person the court deems to have a sufficient interest. (§ 45a-273(a))
Can it be used if claims outstanding?	No, at least to the value of the decedent's estate. (§ 45a-273(a))
Different rules if die testate or intestate?	Yes. If a party seeks to use, and qualifies, for this procedure and the fair market value of estate exceeds claims and family allowances of § 45a-320, the court will proceed as follows: (1) if no will, court will order distribution per law of intestate succession; (2) if will provides for distribution which is the same as intestate succession, court will order distribution per law of intestate succession; (3) if will provides for method other than intestate succession and heirs sign a waiver, court will order excess to be paid in accordance with will; (4) if will provides for method other than intestate succession and the persons entitled to distribution under the will consent to distribution under intestate succession, the excess will be distributed in accordance with the laws of intestate succession; (5) if the will directs a distribution different from the laws of intestate succession, the heirs at law do not waive their right to contest the admission of such will, and the persons entitled to bequests under the will do not consent to the distribution of the estate in accordance with the laws of intestate succession, the court shall dismiss the affidavit and permit any party to petition for admission of the will to probate in accordance with section 45a-286. (§ 45a-273(f))
Notice?	No provision, except the court may act on the affidavit without notice and hearing. (§ 45a-273(c))
heirs	No provision.
creditors	No provision.
others	No provision.
Which of the following must be observed?	
hearing	No provision, except the court may act on the affidavit without notice and hearing. (§ 45a-273(c))
affidavit, petition, other	Affidavit. (§ 45a-273(a))
bond	As a condition to a transfer under § 45a-273(e), the holder may require the execution of a bond of indemnity. (§ 45a-273(h))

What are basic contents of petition or affidavit?	Affidavit stating: (1) A statement whether the decedent received aid or care from the state; (2) a list of the decedent's solely owned assets, excluding assets that pass outside of probate by operation of law; and (3) a list of all claims, expenses and taxes due from the decedent's estate including: funeral expenses, expenses of settling the estate, claims due for the last sickness of the decedent, all lawful taxes and all claims due, all claims due any laborer or mechanic for personal wages for labor performed for the decedent within three months immediately before the decease of such person, other preferred claims, and all other claims allowed in proportion to their respective amounts. The list shall indicate if any of the claims, expenses and taxes have been paid and, if so, by whom. (§45a-273(b), §45a-365)
Is procedure available in the case of nonresident decedents?	Yes, may use another state's procedures as a matter of comity if that state grants same privilege to Connecticut. (§45a-276(a))
Maximum allowable value of estate	The aggregate value of any solely owned tangible and intangible personal property cannot exceed $40,000. (§45a-273(a))
What property can be transferred by this means?	After claims have been satisfied, all excess tangible and intangible solely owned personal property excluding property that passes outside of probate by operation of law. (§45a-273(a) & (f))
Special rules for certain assets (e.g., automobile)	No provision.
Can the spouse or other person take summarily if under certain amount?	No provision.
Minimum period before filing allowed	This procedure is available only if no will is presented for probate within 30 days of death. (§45a-275)
Rights/obligations of party with affidavit	Liable to commissioner of revenue for any succession or transfer tax and to the executor or administrator of the estate of the decedent thereafter appointed. (§45a-273(j))
Are some creditors given special privileges/ preference (e.g., medical expenses, funeral expenses)?	Yes: state aid or state humane institution, and incarceration costs. (§45a-273(e))
Creditors' rights, if insufficient assets	No provision.
May the distribution of the estate proceed without appointment of personal representative?	Yes. (§45a-273(a))
Must court approve affidavit?	Yes. (§45a-273(c) & (f))
Waiting period before authority to act	30 days after death. (§45a-275)
With whom do you file petition or affidavit?	Court of probate in district where decedent resided. (§45a-273(a))
Is there an informal procedure forappointment of executor or administrator?	No provision.
Can a nonresident serve?	No provision.

Can the nonresident act locally based on appointment in another state?	No provision.
What does a transferor need so as to be relieved of liability if challenged by another person later on who claims the particular property (e.g., copy of affidavit)?	Payor may require the filing of waivers, the execution of a bond of indemnity, and a receipt for such transfer or payment. (§ 45a-273(h))

Delaware
Distribution of Decedent's Property Without Grant of Letters

Who can initiate process?	Spouse, grandparent, lineal descendant of a grandparent, the personal representative of any of the foregoing who may be deceased, or the guardian or trustee of any of the foregoing who may be incapacitated, or a trustee of a trust created by the decedent, or a funeral director licensed in the state or the named executor in the decedent's will. (12 § 2306(a)) Preference is given in the following order: (1) spouse; (2) child; (3) parent; (4) sibling; (5) grandchild or grandparent; (6) funeral director licensed in the state. (12 § 2306(b))
Can it be used if claims outstanding?	Only if "all known debts of the decedent are paid or provided for." (12 § 2306(a)(4))
Different rules if die testate or intestate?	Yes. If testate, the person receiving the estate must distribute per the will. If intestate, per intestate succession. (12 § 2306(a))
Notice?	"Every account filed by an executor or administrator shall be accompanied by a statement of the names and mailing addresses of each beneficiary entitled to share in the distribution of the estate." (12 § 2302(a))
heirs	No provision.
creditors	No provision.
others	No provision.
Which of the following must be observed?	
hearing	No provision.
affidavit, petition, other	Affidavit. (12 § 2306(a))
bond	No provision.
What are basic contents of petition or affidavit?	Affidavit must state the following: (1) no petition for appointment of a personal representative pending or granted; (2) 30 days have elapsed since death; (3) value of personal estate (less jointly owned property, family Bible, clothes of decedent, family stores laid in before the death, insurance policy, pensions, bonds, stock options or other employee benefits payable to someone other than the decedent) does not exceed $30,000; (4) all known debts are paid or provided for; (5) surviving spouse allowance has been paid, waived, or lapsed; (6) decedent did not own solely owned real estate located in Delaware; (7) the right of affiant to receive the money or property. (12 § 2306(a)(1)-(7))
Is procedure available in the case of nonresident decedents?	No provision.
Maximum allowable value of estate	Other than either property described in § 1901(b) & (c) or jointly owned property, $30,000. (12 § 2306(a)(3))
What property can be transferred by this means?	Personal estate. (12 § 2306(a))

Special rules for certain assets (e.g., automobile)	Property described in § 1901(b) & (c), such as family Bible, decedent's clothes, family stores laid in before death, property or death benefit, employee or incentive plan, and jointly owned property excluded from maximum allowed value. (12 § 2306(a)(3)) Next of kin has a right to take possession of the decedent's motor vehicle(s) and can enter any premises to remove clothing for the burial and can take possession of property in residential rental units of decedent. (12 § 2306(c))
Can the spouse or other person take summarily if under certain amount?	No provision.
Minimum period before filing allowed	No filing required, but must wait until 30 days after death to distribute the personal estate. (12 § 2306(a)(2))
Rights/obligations of party with affidavit	Answerable to anyone with a prior right, "accountable to any intestate distributee or any personal representative thereafter appointed." (12 § 2307(a))
Are some creditors given special privileges/ preference (e.g., medical expenses, funeral expenses)?	No provision. All known debts must be paid or provided for. (12 § 2306(a)(4))
Creditors' rights, if insufficient assets	No provision. All known debts must be paid or provided for. (12 § 2306(a)(4))
May the distribution of the estate proceed without appointment of personal representative?	Must proceed without personal representative. (12 § 2306(a)(1))
Must court approve affidavit?	No. (12 § 2306)
Waiting period before authority to act	30 days after death. (12 § 2306(a)(2))
With whom do you file petition or affidavit?	No filing required. (12 § 2306)
Is there an informal procedure for appointment of executor or administrator?	No provision.
Can a nonresident serve?	No provision.
Can the nonresident act locally based on appointment in another state?	No provision.
What does a transferor need so as to be relieved of liability if challenged by another person later on who claims the particular property (e.g., copy of affidavit)?	Transferor is released as if payment made to a personal representative. No need to inquire into the truthfulness of the affidavit. (12 § 2307(a))

District of Columbia
Small Estates

Who can initiate process?	Any person eligible for appointment as personal representative to an estate. (§§ 20-352, 20-303)
Can it be used if claims outstanding?	Yes. (§§ 20-352, 20-353)
Different rules if die testate or intestate?	No provision.
Notice?	All notice is at the discretion of the court. If the court directs notice, claims or objections must be made within 30 days of its publication. (§ 20-353(b))
heirs	No provision.
creditors	No provision.
others	No provision.
Which of the following must be observed?	
hearing	No provision.
affidavit, petition, other	Verified petition. (§ 20-352)
bond	No. (§ 20-354(a))
What are basic contents of petition or affidavit?	In addition to information required for standard probate petition under § 20-304, petition must include [a] statement that petitioner has made a diligent search to discover all property and debts of the decedent; [a] list of the known creditors of the decedent, with the amount of each claim, including contingent and disputed claims; and [a] statement of any legal proceedings pending in which the decedent was a party. (§ 20-352(a)-(c))
Is procedure available in the case of nonresident decedents?	No provision.
Maximum allowable value of estate	$40,000. (§ 20-351)
What property can be transferred by this means?	Property subject to administration. (§ 20-351)
Special rules for certain assets (e.g., automobile)	If the only property of decedent is two or fewer automobiles, the Mayor may transfer title to the motor vehicles in accordance with § 50-1501.02(d).
Can the spouse or other person take summarily if under certain amount?	No provision.
Minimum period before filing allowed	No provision.
Rights/obligations of party with affidavit	There is no affidavit for the small estate procedure.
Are some creditors given special privileges/preference (e.g., medical expenses, funeral expenses)?	Funeral expenses and family allowance. (§ 20-353(a)(3))
Creditors' rights, if insufficient assets	Right to file objection to small estates proceeding pursuant to notice. (§ 20-354(b))
May the distribution of the estate proceed without appointment of personal representative?	No. (§ 20-353(a)(1))

Must court approve affidavit?	Court must approve petition. (§ 20-353(a))
Waiting period before authority to act	No provision.
With whom do you file petition or affidavit?	Court. (§§ 20-352, 20-353)
Is there an informal procedure for appointment of executor or administrator?	No provision.
Can a nonresident serve?	Yes. Court appoints personal representatives after filing of a petition (§ 20-353), and any person eligible for appointment as a personal representative under § 20-303 may file a petition. Under § 20-303(b)(7), to qualify for appointment as a personal representative, a nonresident must file "an irrevocable power of attorney with the Register designating the Register and the Register's successors in office as the person upon whom all notices and process issued by a competent court in the District of Columbia may be served with the same effect as personal service, in relation to all suits or matters pertaining to the estate in which the letters are to be issued."
Can the nonresident act locally based on appointment in another state?	No provision.
What does a transferor need so as to be relieved of liability if challenged by another person later on who claims the particular property (e.g., copy of affidavit)?	No provision.

Florida
Summary Administration, Disposition of Personal Property Without Administration

Who can initiate process?	*Summary Administration.* Any beneficiary or personal representative. (§ 735.203(1)) *Disposition Without Administration.* Any interested party. (§ 735.301(2))
Can it be used if claims outstanding?	*Summary Administration.* Yes, if provision for payment of known or reasonably ascertainable creditors has been made. (§ 735.206(2)) *Disposition Without Administration.* Disposition without administration can proceed where decedent leaves only personal property exempt under § 732.402, personal property exempt under the Constitution of Florida, and nonexempt personal property which does not exceed funeral expenses and medical/ hospital expenses of the last 60 days of last illness. (§ 735.301(1))
Different rules if die testate or intestate?	*Summary Administration.* If testate, decedent's will must not direct administration as required by Chapter 733. (§ 735.201(1)) *Disposition Without Administration.* No provision.
Notice?	*Summary Administration.* Any person who has received an order of summary administration may publish notice. If notice to creditors is published once per week for two consecutive weeks in the county in which the Order of Summary Administration was entered, creditors must file claims with court within three months from first publication, or be forever barred. (§§ 735.2063, 733.2121(2), 733.702) *Disposition Without Administration.* No provision.
heirs	No provision.
creditors	*Summary Administration.* Prior to entry of the order of summary administration, petitioner shall make a diligent search and reasonable inquiry for known or reasonably ascertained creditors, serve a copy of the petition on them, and make provision for payment to the extent that assets are available. (§ 735.206(2))
others	*Summary Administration.* Any beneficiary who does not join the order for summary administration must receive notice. (§ 735.203(1), (3))
Which of the following must be observed?	
hearing	*Summary Administration.* No provision *Disposition Without Administration.* No provision.
affidavit, petition, other	*Summary Administration.* Petition. (§ 735.203) *Disposition Without Administration.* Informal application required. May take the form of letter, affidavit, or other form. (§ 735.301(2))
bond	No provision.

What are basic contents of petition or affidavit?	*Summary Administration.* [M]ust be signed and verified by the surviving spouse, if any, and any beneficiaries. (§ 735.203(1)) Any beneficiary who does not join must receive formal notice. (*Id.*) *Disposition Without Administration.* No provision.
Is procedure available in the case of nonresident decedents?	*Summary Administration.* Yes. (§ 735.201) *Disposition Without Administration.* No provision.
Maximum allowable value of estate	*Summary Administration.* Value of estate less value of exempt property must not exceed $75,000 or decedent must have been dead for more than two years. (§ 735.201(2)) *Disposition Without Administration.* Nonexempt personal property value must not exceed sum of preferred funeral expenses and reasonable and necessary medical and hospital expenses of the last 60 days of the illness. (§ 735.301(1))
What property can be transferred by this means?	*Summary Administration.* Entire estate (§ 735.201) *Disposition Without Administration.* Personal property. (§ 735.301)
Special rules for certain assets (e.g., automobile)	No provision.
Can the spouse or other person take summarily if under certain amount?	No provision.
Minimum period before filing allowed	*Summary Administration.* May be filed at any stage of administration of the estate if it currently appears to qualify. (§ 735.2055) *Disposition Without Administration.* No provision.
Rights/obligations of party with affidavit	No provision.
Are some creditors given special privileges/ preference (e.g., medical expenses, funeral expenses)?	*Summary Administration.* No provision. *Disposition Without Administration.* Funeral and medical expenses of the last 60 days of the last illness. (§ 735.301(1))
Creditors' rights, if insufficient assets	*Summary Administration.* Beneficiaries or heirs remain liable on creditors' claims for up to two years after decedent's death. (§ 735.206(4)(d), (f)) "Any known or reasonably ascertainable creditor who did not receive notice and for whom provision for payment was not made may enforce the claim and, if successful, shall be awarded reasonable attorney's fees." (§ 735.206(4)(d)) *Disposition Without Administration.* No provision.
May the distribution of the estate proceed without appointment of personal representative?	*Summary Administration.* Yes. (§ 735.206) *Disposition Without Administration.* Yes. (§ 735.301(2))
Must court approve affidavit?	*Summary Administration.* No provision. *Disposition Without Administration.* Yes. (§ 735.301(2))
Waiting period before authority to act	*Summary Administration:* No waiting period. (§ 735.2055) *Disposition Without Administration.* No provision.
With whom do you file petition or affidavit?	*Summary Administration.* Court. (§ 735.206) *Disposition Without Administration.* Court. (§ 735.301)

Is there an informal procedure for appointment of executor or administrator?	*Summary Administration.* No provision. *Disposition Without Administration.* Yes. (§ 735.301(2))
Can a nonresident serve?	*Summary Administration.* No provision, but an opinion from the Florida Attorney General states: "A personal representative of a nonresident decedent must proceed through ancillary administration . . . in the absence of an order of family administration . . . or an order of summary administration . . . or a letter or other writing under the seal of the court." (Op. Atty. Gen., 84-59, June 21, 1984) *Disposition Without Administration.* No provision.
Can the nonresident act locally based on appointment in another state?	No provision.
What does a transferor need so as to be relieved of liability if challenged by another person later on who claims the particular property (e.g., copy of affidavit)?	*Summary Administration.* Entered Order of Summary Administration. (§ 735.206(4)(b)) *Disposition Without Administration.* Court authorization. (§ 735.301)

Georgia
Order Dispensing with Administration

Who can initiate process?	Any heir of the deceased. (§ 53-2-40(a))
Can it be used if claims outstanding?	Only if all of the known creditors have consented or will be served. (§ 53-2-40(b))
Different rules if die testate or intestate?	Only applicable to the estate of a person dying intestate. (§ 53-2-40(a))
Notice?	If a petition is filed that states there are known creditors, a citation is issued, and the known creditors are served (§ 53-2-41(a)), typically by the sheriff. (§ 53-11-3(b))
heirs	The court is required to "ascertain the heirs." (§ 53-2-41(c)) Heirs must agree upon a division of the estate among themselves. (§ 53-2-40(b))
creditors	See above.
others	When the court approves a petition for an order that "no administration is necessary, where there is an interest in real property, the court shall file, within 30 days of granting such petition, a certified copy of the order granting the petition" in each Georgia county in which the deceased owned property. (§ 53-2-40(d))
Which of the following must be observed?	
hearing	No provision.
affidavit, petition, other	Need to file a petition to obtain an order dispensing with administration. (§ 53-2-40)
bond	No provision.
What are basic contents of petition or affidavit?	The petition must show the name and domicile of the decedent, the names, ages, majority status, and domicile of the heirs of the decedent; the description of the property in this state owned by the deceased owner; and a statement that the decedent owes no debts or that there are known debts and all creditors have consented or will be served; and that the heirs have agreed upon a division of the estate among themselves. (§ 53-2-40(b))
Is procedure available in the case of nonresident decedents?	The petition is available to nonresident decedents, if there is real property located in this state. (§ 53-2-40(a))
Maximum allowable value of estate	No provision.
What property can be transferred by this means?	Real and personal property. (§ 53-2-40(a))
Special rules for certain assets (e.g., automobile)	No provision.
Can the spouse or other person take summarily if under certain amount?	No provision.
Minimum period before filing allowed	No provision.
Rights/obligations of party with affidavit	No provision.

Are some creditors given special privileges/ preference (e.g., medical expenses, funeral expenses)?	No provision.
Creditors' rights, if insufficient assets	After the granting of an order that no administration was necessary, any creditor has a right of action on the unsatisfied debts against the heirs to the extent of value of property received by the heirs. (§ 53-2-42) In addition, a creditor may object to the order prior to the grant and the order will not be issued as long as the objection is not withdrawn. (§ 53-2-41(b))
May the distribution of the estate proceed without appointment of personal representative?	Yes. (§ 53-2-40(a))
Must court approve affidavit?	Yes. If no objections to the order are filed and the court finds that the estate owes no debts or that all creditors have consented or withdrawn any objections and that the heirs are of age and under no disabilities or are represented by a guardian or a personal representative, the court must enter an order finding that no administration is necessary. (§ 53-2-41(c))
Waiting period before authority to act	No provision.
With whom do you file petition or affidavit?	The petition must be filed with the Probate Court of the county of domicile of the decedent, if the decedent was a resident of Georgia; if the decedent was not a Georgia resident, the petition must be filed in the county in which the real property is located. (§ 53-2-40(a))
Is there an informal procedure for appointment of executor or administrator?	No provision.
Can a nonresident serve?	No provision.
Can the nonresident act locally based on appointment in another state?	No provision.
What does a transferor need so as to be relieved of liability if challenged by another person later on who claims the particular property (e.g., copy of affidavit)?	No provision.

Hawaii
Collection of Personal Property by Affidavit and Summary Administration Procedure for Small Estates

Who can initiate process?	*By Affidavit.* A person claiming to be the successor of the decedent, or the Department of Human Services if it has a claim against the estate pursuant to § 346-15 or 346-37. (§ 560:3-1201(a)) *Summary Administration.* Personal representative. (§ 560:3-1203) *Clerk Administration.* Clerk of court of residence or domicile, or any interested person. (§ 560:3-1205)
Can it be used if claims outstanding?	*By Affidavit.* No provision. *Summary Administration.* Yes. (§ 560:3-1203) *Clerk Administration.* Yes. (§ 560:3-1206(a))
Different rules if die testate or intestate?	No provision.
Notice?	*By Affidavit.* No provision. *Summary Administration.* A copy of the closing statement must be sent to all distributees of the estate. (§ 560:3-1204(a)(3)) *Clerk Administration.* If the estate has a total value of $10,000 or less, the clerk is to publish the fact by posting a notice thereof at the front entrance of the court house of the judicial circuit and by advertising the notice in the English language at least once in a newspaper of general circulation in the judicial circuit. Notice must state that all creditors of the deceased must file with the clerk duly verified claims within 60 days from the date of publication, and that all persons claiming to be heirs of the estate must also file their claims with the clerk in that 60-day period. (§ 560:3-1206(a)) If the estate has a total value in excess of $10,000, the content and method of giving notice shall be as provided for informal probates in § 560:3-306. (§ 560:3-1206(b))
heirs	No provision.
creditors	*Summary Administration.* The distribution of the estate may be accomplished without notice being given to creditors. (§ 560:3-1203)
others	No provision.
Which of the following must be observed?	
hearing	No provision.
affidavit, petition, other	*By Affidavit.* Affidavit. (§ 560:3-1201) *Summary Administration.* Closing statement. (§ 560:3-1204) *Clerk Administration.* Petition. (§ 560:3-1205)
bond	No provision.

What are basic contents of petition or affidavit?	*By Affidavit.* Statements affirming the following: the gross value of the decedent's estate does not exceed $100,000, except that any motor vehicles registered in the decedent's name may be transferred regardless of value; no application or petition for the appointment of a personal representative is pending or has been granted in Hawaii; and the claimed successor or successors are entitled to the property and explain the relationship of the claimed successor to the decedent, or the Department of Human Services has a claim against the estate pursuant to section 346-15 or 346-37, dealing with recovery of payments and of medical assistance and expenses of burial. (§ 560:3-1201(a)) *Summary Administration.* After distribution, a verified statement must be filed that states that the value of entire estate, less liens and encumbrances, did not exceed homestead and family allowances, exempt property, administration expenses, and funeral and last illness expenses; the estate has been fully administered and distributed; and the closing statement sent to all known distributees and claimants. (§ 560:3-1204(a)) *Clerk Administration.* No provision.
Is procedure available in the case of nonresident decedents?	No provision.
Maximum allowable value of estate	*By Affidavit.* $100,000, apart from the value of any motor vehicle registered in decedent's name. (§ 560:3-1201(a)(1)) *Summary Administration.* "[V]alue of the entire estate, less liens and encumbrances does not exceed homestead allowance, exempt property, family allowance, costs and expenses of administration, reasonable funeral expenses, and reasonable and necessary medical and hospital expenses of the last illness of the decedent. (§ 560:3-1203) *Clerk Administration.* $100,000. (§ 560:3-1205)
What property can be transferred by this means?	*By Affidavit.* Personal property. (§ 560:3-1201) *Summary Administration.* Entire estate. (§ 560:3-1203) *Clerk Administration.* Entire estate. (§ 560:3-1205)
Special rules for certain assets (e.g., automobile)	*By Affidavit.* Any motor vehicles registered in the decedent's name may be transferred by affidavit regardless of value. (§ 560:3-1201(a)(1)) *Summary Administration.* No provision. *Clerk Administration.* No provision.
Can the spouse or other person take summarily if under certain amount?	No provision.
Minimum period before filing allowed	No provision.

Rights/obligations of party with affidavit	*By Affidavit.* Rights: to compel transfer of property in a proceeding. Obligations: is answerable and accountable to any personal representative of the estate or to any other person having a superior right. (§ 560:3-1202) *Summary Administration.* No provision. *Clerk Administration.* The Clerk shall make diligent effort to ascertain the names and whereabouts of the devisees of the decedent and present evidence relating thereto to the court having jurisdiction of the proceedings. (§ 560:3-1209)
Are some creditors given special privileges/ preference (e.g., medical expenses, funeral expenses)?	*By Affidavit.* The Department of Human Services, if it has paid for the decedent's burial, crematory, mortuary, or cemetery services, or if it has paid out various other types of state funds, will have priority over those of other successors. (§ § 560:3-1201(a)(3)(b) 346-15, 346-37) *Summary Administration.* Funeral and last illness medical expenses. (§ 560:3-1204(a)(1)) *Clerk Administration.* No provision.
Creditors' rights, if insufficient assets	*By Affidavit.* Payee is accountable to the personal representative, or any person having a superior right in the property. (§ 560:3-1202) *Summary Administration.* No provision. *Clerk Administration.* No provision.
May the distribution of the estate proceed without appointment of personal representative?	*By Affidavit.* Yes. (§ 560:3-1201(a)(2)) *Summary Administration.* No. (§ 560:3-1203) *Clerk Administration.* Yes. (§ 560:3-1205)
Must court approve affidavit?	*By Affidavit.* No, but a death certificate must be presented with the affidavit. (§ 560:3-1201(a)) *Summary Administration.* No provision. *Clerk Administration.* No provision.
Waiting period before authority to act	*By Affidavit.* No provision. *Summary Administration.* No provision. *Clerk Administration.* The clerk is to, after the expiration of four months after the first publication, in the case of an estate valued in excess of $10,000, or after 60 days in the case of an estate valued at $10,000 or less, pay or distribute the money, funds, or property of the estate. (§ 560:3-1209)
With whom do you file petition or affidavit?	*By Affidavit.* No provision. *Summary Administration.* Closing statement must be filed with court. (§ 560:3-1204(a)) *Clerk Administration.* Petition must be filed with court. (§ 560:3-1205)
Is there an informal procedure for appointment of executor or administrator?	Yes. (§ § 560:3-301, 560:3-307 to 311)
Can a nonresident serve?	Yes. (§ § 560:3-301, 560:3-203)
Can the nonresident act locally based on appointment in another state?	Yes. If there is no local administration, and the domiciliary foreign personal representative has filed in a local court, the foreign personal representative may exercise with regard to assets in Hawaii all powers of a local personal representative. (§ 560:4-204)

What does a transferor need so as to be relieved of liability if challenged by another person later on who claims the particular property (e.g., copy of affidavit)?

By Affidavit. Payor is discharged and released to the same extent as if that person dealt with a personal representative of the decedent. (§ 560:3-1202)
Summary Administration. No provision.
Clerk Administration. No provision.

Idaho
Collection of Personal Property by Affidavit and Summary Administration Procedure for Small Estates

Who can initiate process?	*By Affidavit.* The person claiming to be the successor. (§ 15-3-1201(a)) *Summary Administration.* Personal representative or surviving spouse (i.e., sole beneficiary). (§ § 15-3-1203, 15-3-1205(a))
Can it be used if claims outstanding?	*By Affidavit.* No provision. *Summary Administration.* Yes. (§ 15-3-1204(a)(1))
Different rules if die testate or intestate?	*By Affidavit.* No provision. *Summary Administration.* If surviving spouse is sole beneficiary and decedent died testate, original will must accompany petition. (§ 15-3-1205(a))
Notice?	
heirs	*By Affidavit.* No provision. *Summary Administration.* A copy of the closing statement must be sent to all distributees of the estate. (§ 15-3-1204(a)(3))
creditors	*By Affidavit.* No provision. *Summary Administration.* The distribution of the estate may be accomplished without giving notice to creditors. (§ 15-3-1203 and Comment) A copy of the closing statement must be sent. (§ 15-3-1204(a)(3))
others	No provision.
Which of the following must be observed?	
hearing	*By Affidavit.* No provision. *Summary Administration.* If the spouse is the sole beneficiary/devisee, there is a hearing to determine that the person was married to the decedent and was the sole beneficiary. (§ 15-3-1205(a))
affidavit, petition, other	*By Affidavit.* Affidavit. (§ 15-3-1201) *Summary Administration.* Closing statement. (§ 15-3-1203) If spouse is sole beneficiary/devisee, must file a petition. (§ 15-3-1205)
bond	No provision.

What are basic contents of petition or affidavit?	*By Affidavit.* Statements affirming the following: the fair market value of the estate which is subject to probate, less liens and encumbrances, does not exceed $100,000; 30 days have elapsed since death of decedent; "[n] o application or petition for the appointment of a personal representative or for summary administration is pending or has been granted in any jurisdiction;" and "[t]he claiming successor is entitled to payment or delivery of the property." (§ 15-8-1201(a)(1)-(4)) *Summary Administration.* Closing statement must state that the estate value, less liens and encumbrances, did not exceed homestead and family allowances, exempt property, and funeral and medical expenses; of last illness; that estate has been administered and distributed by the personal representative; and that closing statement has been sent to all distributees and claimants whom the personal representative is aware whose claims are neither paid nor barred and has furnished a full account in writing of his administration to the distributees whose interests are affected. (§ 15-3-1204(a)(1)-(3)) If decedent leaves surviving spouse as sole devisee or beneficiary, the petition must set out marriage and the death of a person leaving a surviving spouse. If decedent died testate, the original of the last will and testament must accompany the petition. (§ 15-3-1205(a))
Is procedure available in the case of nonresident decedents?	No provision.
Maximum allowable value of estate	*By Affidavit.* For the use of an affidavit the fair market value of the entire estate, less liens, and encumbrances, cannot exceed $100,000. (§ 15-3-1201(a)(1)) *Summary Administration.* The value of the entire estate, less liens and encumbrances, cannot exceed homestead allowance, exempt property, family allowance, costs and expenses of administration, reasonable funeral expenses, and reasonable and necessary medical and hospital expenses of the last illness of the decedent. (§ 15-3-1203)
What property can be transferred by this means?	*By Affidavit.* Personal property. (§ 15-3-1201) *Summary Administration.* Entire estate. (§ 15-3-1203)
Special rules for certain assets (e.g., automobile)	*By Affidavit.* "[T]ransfer agent of any security shall change the registered ownership on the books of a corporation... upon the presentation of an affidavit." (§ 15-3-1201(b)) *Summary Administration.* No provision.
Can the spouse or other person take summarily if under certain amount?	Yes. Surviving spouse who is sole beneficiary may take summarily. (§ 15-3-1205)
Minimum period before filing allowed	*By Affidavit.* 30 days after death of decedent must pass before offering affidavit. (§ 15-3-1201(a)) *Summary Administration.* Estate must be fully administered and distributed before closing statement may be filed. (§ 15-3-1204(a)(2))

Rights/obligations of party with affidavit	*By Affidavit.* Rights: to bring a proceeding to compel adherence to affidavit. Obligations: is answerable and accountable to any personal representative of the estate or to any other person having a superior right. (§ 15-3-1202) *Summary Administration.* No provision.
Are some creditors given special privileges/ preference (e.g., medical expenses, funeral expenses)?	*By Affidavit.* No provision. *Summary Administration.* Funeral and last illness medical expenses. (§ 15-3-1204(a)(1))
Creditors' rights, if insufficient assets	*By Affidavit.* Payee is answerable to any person with a superior right in the property. (§ 15-3-1202) *Summary Administration.* No provision.
May the distribution of the estate proceed without appointment of personal representative?	*By Affidavit.* Yes. (§ 15-3-1201(a)(3)) *Summary Administration.* Generally there must be a personal representative, but if surviving spouse is the sole beneficiary, she/he may petition. (§§ 15-3-1203, 15-3-1205)
Must court approve affidavit?	*By Affidavit.* No provision. *Summary Administration.* If spouse proceeds as sole beneficiary, court must approve. (§ 15-3-1205)
Waiting period before authority to act	*By Affidavit.* 30 days must pass before the presentation of an affidavit. (§ 15-3-1201(a)) *Summary Administration.* May act immediately. (§ 15-3-1203)
With whom do you file petition or affidavit?	*By Affidavit.* No provision. *Summary Administration.* Closing statement and any petition by surviving spouse are filed with court. (§§ 15-3-1204(a), 15-3-1205(a))
Is there an informal procedure for appointment of executor or administrator?	Yes. (§§ 15-3-301, 15-3-307–311)
Can a nonresident serve?	Yes. (§§ 15-3-203, 15-3-301)
Can the nonresident act locally based on appointment in another state?	Yes. If there is no local administration, and the domiciliary foreign personal representative has filed in a local court, the foreign personal representative may exercise with respect to assets in Idaho all powers of a local personal representative, subject to conditions imposed upon nonresidents generally. (§§ 15-4-204, 15-4-205)
What does a transferor need so as to be relieved of liability if challenged by another person later on who claims the particular property (e.g., copy of affidavit)?	*By Affidavit.* Payor is discharged and released to the same extent as if he dealt with a personal representative of the decedent. (§ 15-3-1202) *Summary Administration.* No provision.

Illinois
Small Estates

Who can initiate process?	"[a]ny person or corporation or financial institution (1) indebted or holding personal estate of a decedent, (2) controlling the right of access to decedent's safe deposit box or (3) acting as registrar or transfer agent of particular interests of decedent." (755 ILCS § 5/25-1(a))
Can it be used if claims outstanding?	Yes, if claims are paid before distributions (755 ICLS § 5/25-1(b)(7.5))
Different rules if die testate or intestate?	If decedent dies intestate, the names, addresses, and relationships of decedent's heirs, and the portion of the estate to which each heir is entitled must be listed in the affidavit. (755 § ILCS 5/25-1(b)(10)(a)) If decedent dies testate, affiant must attach certified copy of will to affidavit and state that to the best belief the will on file is the "decedent's last will and was signed by the decedent and the attesting witnesses." (755 ILCS § 5/25-1(b)(10)(b))
Notice?	No provision.
heirs	No provision.
creditors	No provision.
others	No provision.
Which of the following must be observed?	
hearing	No provision.
affidavit, petition, other	Affidavit. (755 ILCS § 5/25-1)
bond	No provision.
What are basic contents of petition or affidavit?	Name and address of the affiant; information about the decedent including: name, date of death, place of residency before death, and a copy of the death certificate; statements affirming the following: no letters of office are now outstanding on the decedent's estate and no petition for letters is contemplated or pending in Illinois or in any other jurisdiction; "gross value of the personal estate does not exceed $100,000; all decedent's funeral expenses have been paid or list the amounts and the person entitled thereto;" there is no known unpaid claim or contested claim against the decedent; "the names and places of residence of any surviving spouse, minor children, and adult dependent children;" the award allowable to the surviving spouse or child of a decedent who was an Illinois resident; the affiant is unaware of any dispute or potential conflict as to the heirship or will of the decedent; a description of how the property should be distributed. (755 ILCS § 5/25-1(b))
Is procedure available in the case of nonresident decedents?	No provision.
Maximum allowable value of estate	$100,000. (755 ILCS § 5/25-1(b)(6))

What property can be transferred by this means?	Personal property. (755 ILCS § 5/25-1(a)) ("personal estate")
Special rules for certain assets (e.g., automobile)	If a vehicle is part of the estate, the transferee is to "mail or deliver to the Secretary of State, within 120 days, the last certificate of title, if available, the documentation required under the provisions of the Probate Act of 1975, and an application for certificate of title. The small estate affidavit [is to] be furnished by the Secretary of State." (625 ILCS § 5/3-114(b))
Can the spouse or other person take summarily if under certain amount?	No provision.
Minimum period before filing allowed	No provision.
Rights/obligations of party with affidavit	Rights: to recover the personal estate in a civil action, if someone refuses to transfer the property. (755 ILCS § 5/25-3) Obligations: indemnify and hold harmless all creditors and heirs of the decedent and other persons relying upon the affidavit who incur loss because of such reliance. (755 ILCS § 5/25-1(e))
Are some creditors given special privileges/ preference (e.g., medical expenses, funeral expenses)?	All claims but funeral expenses must be paid. If funeral expenses have not been paid, they must be listed on the affidavit. (755 ILCS § 5/25-1(b)(7)(a))
Creditors' rights, if insufficient assets	Payee is answerable to any representative of the estate, or person having a prior right. (755 ILCS § 5/25-1(d))
May the distribution of the estate proceed without appointment of personal representative?	No provision.
Must court approve affidavit?	No provision.
Waiting period before authority to act	No provision.
With whom do you file petition or affidavit?	No provision.
Is there an informal procedure for appointment of executor or administrator?	No provision.
Can a nonresident serve?	A nonresident may be an affiant. The nonresident affiant shall provide contact information for agent as service of process within jurisdiction; if no agent is named, then court clerk in decedent's residence of death serves as agent. (755 ILCS § 5/25-1(f))
Can the nonresident act locally based on appointment in another state?	Yes, since there will be a designated agent for service of process. (755 ILCS § 5/25-1(f))
What does a transferor need so as to be relieved of liability if challenged by another person later on who claims the particular property (e.g., copy of affidavit)?	Payor is released to the same extent as if payment had been made to the representative of the estate. (755 ILCS § 5/25-1(d))

Indiana
Dispensing with Administration

Who can initiate process?	*By Affidavit.* The affidavit is submitted by the distributee, being a person entitled to a share of the property of the decedent or it is submitted by a person acting on the distributee's behalf. (§ 29-1-8-1(b)) *Summary Distribution.* Personal representative or person acting on behalf of distributees. (§ 29-1-8-3(a))
Can it be used if claims outstanding?	*By Affidavit.* No provision. *Summary Distribution.* Yes. (§ 29-1-8-4(a)(3))
Different rules if die testate or intestate?	No provision.
Notice?	
heirs	*By Affidavit.* No provision. *Summary Distribution.* A copy of the closing statement [must be sent] to all distributees of the estate. (§ 29-1-8-4(a)(3))
creditors	*By Affidavit.* No provision. *Summary Distribution.* The distribution of the estate may be accomplished without notice being given to creditors. (§ 29-1-8-3(a) and Comment) But see § 29-1-8-4(a)(3).
others	No provision.
Which of the following must be observed?	
hearing	No provision.
affidavit, petition, other	*By Affidavit.* Affidavit. (§ 29-1-8-1) *Summary Distribution.* Closing statement. (§ 29-1-8-4)
bond	No provision.
What are basic contents of petition or affidavit?	*By Affidavit.* Must state the following: value of the gross probate estate, less liens and encumbrances "and reasonable funeral expenses," does not exceed $50,000; 45 days have elapsed since the death of the decedent; "no application or petition . . . of a personal representative is pending or has been granted in any jurisdiction;" "name and address of each other person . . . entitled to a share of the property and the part of the property to which each person is entitled;" "claimant has notified each person identified in the affidavit of the claimant's intention to present an affidavit;" and the "claimant is entitled to payment or delivery of the property." (§ 29-1-8-1(b)(1)-(6)) *Summary Distribution.* Closing statement must state that the value of the gross estate, less liens and encumbrances, does not exceed sum of $50,000 (so long as after 2007), the costs and expenses of administration, and reasonable funeral expenses; that estate is fully distributed; and that the closing statement was sent to all claimants, creditors the representative is aware of, and distributees. (§ 29-1-8-4(a))

Is procedure available in the case of nonresident decedents?	No provision.
Maximum allowable value of estate	*By Affidavit.* $50,000. (§ 29-1-8-1(b)(1)) *Summary Distribution.* The gross value of the estate cannot exceed the sum of: $50,000, the costs and expenses of administration, and reasonable funeral expenses. (§ 29-1-8-3(a))
What property can be transferred by this means?	*By Affidavit.* Personal property. (§ 29-1-8-1) *Summary Distribution.* Entire estate. (§ 29-1-8-3)
Special rules for certain assets (e.g., automobile)	*By Affidavit.* If a motor vehicle or a watercraft is part of the estate, transfer of the certificate of title can take place five days after the death of the decedent, if the appointment of a personal representative is not contemplated. The transfer will be made by the bureau of motor vehicles upon receipt of an affidavit duly executed by the distributees of the estate. (§ 29-1-8-1(c)) A transfer agent of a security shall change the registered ownership on the books of a corporation upon presentation of an affidavit. (§ 29-1-8-1(d)) *Summary Distribution.* For real property, affiant must record affidavit in the office of the recorder in the county in which the real property is located. (§ 29-1-8-3(b))
Can the spouse or other person take summarily if under certain amount?	No provision.
Minimum period before filing allowed	*By Affidavit.* An affidavit can only be presented 45 days after the death of the decedent. (§ 29-1-8-1(b)(2)) *Summary Distribution.* Estate must be fully administered and distributed before filing closing statement. (§ 29-1-8-4(a))
Rights/obligations of party with affidavit	*By Affidavit.* Rights: to bring a proceeding to compel adherence to affidavit, after proving their right to the property. Obligations: are answerable and accountable to any personal representative of the estate or to any other person having a superior right. (§ 29-1-8-2) *Summary Distribution.* No provision.
Are some creditors given special privileges/ preference (e.g., medical expenses, funeral expenses)?	Last illness medical and funeral expenses must be paid in full. (§ 29-1-8-9)
Creditors' rights, if insufficient assets	*By Affidavit.* Payee is accountable to any person having a superior right. (§ 29-1-8-2) *Summary Distribution.* No provision.
May the distribution of the estate proceed without appointment of personal representative?	*By Affidavit.* Yes. (§ 29-1-8-1(b)(3)) *Summary Distribution.* Yes. (§ 29-1-8-3(a))
Must court approve affidavit?	No provision.
Waiting period before authority to act	*By Affidavit.* An affidavit can only be presented 45 days after the death of the decedent. (§ § 29-1-8-1(a), (b)(2), 29-1-8-1(a)) *Summary Distribution.* May act immediately. (§ 29-1-8-3(a))

With whom do you file petition or affidavit?	*By Affidavit.* No provision. *Summary Distribution.* Must file closing statement with court. (§ 29-1-8-4) If estate includes real property, must record affidavit with recorder in county where real property is located. (§ 29-1-8-3(b))
Is there an informal procedure for appointment of executor or administrator?	No provision.
Can a nonresident serve?	No provision.
Can the nonresident act locally based on appointment in another state?	No provision.
What does a transferor need so as to be relieved of liability if challenged by another person later on who claims the particular property (e.g., copy of affidavit)?	*By Affidavit.* Payor is discharged and released to the same extent as if he dealt with a personal representative. (§ 29-1-8-2) *Summary Distribution.* No provision.

Iowa
Administration of Small Estates

Who can initiate process?	If "there is no will, administration shall be granted to any qualified person on the petition of (1) the surviving spouse; (2) the heirs of the decedent; (3) creditors of the decedent; or (4) other persons showing good grounds therefor." (§ 633.227) If there is a will at the time the will of a decedent is filed with the clerk, or thereafter, any interested person may file a verified petition in the district court of the proper county to have the will admitted to probate; for the appointment of the executor. A petition for probate may be combined with a petition for appointment of the executor, and any person interested in either the probate of a will or in the appointment of the executor, may petition for both. (§ 633.290)
Can it be used if claims outstanding?	Yes. (§ 635.13)
Different rules if die testate or intestate?	Yes. (§ 635.2) (See *Who can initiate process?* and *What are the basic contents of petition or affidavit?*)
Notice?	Administrator or executor must publish notice once a week for two consecutive weeks in a daily or weekly newspaper of general circulation published in the county in which the estate is pending and must mail notice to all claimants which may not be paid during administration. (§§ 635.13, 633.230, 633.304)
heirs	A copy of the closing statement must be sent to "all interested parties." "Interested parties" is a term that is not defined by statute. (§ 635.8(1)(d))
creditors	A copy of the closing statement must be sent to "all known interested parties." (§ 635.8(1)(d)) Claimants of the estate are "interested parties." (§ 635.13) There are special notice requirements. (§ 635.13)
others	Notice is to be given (§ 635.13) to the following parties: Spouse (§ 633.237); publication notice (§§ 633.230 (intestacy) & 633.304 (testacy)); department of human services (§ 633.231 (intestacy)).
Which of the following must be observed?	
hearing	A copy of the closing statement and an opportunity to object and request a hearing must be sent by proper notice to all interested parties (§ 635.8(1)(d))
affidavit, petition, other	Petition. (§ 635.1)
bond	Petition must include statement that probate property does not "exceed an aggregate gross value of more than [$100,000]... and the approximate amount of personal property and income, for the purposes of setting bond." (§§ 635.2, 635.1)

What are basic contents of petition or affidavit?	Petition requirements: (1) name, domicile, and date of death of decedent; (2) name and address of the surviving spouse and name and relationship of each beneficiary in a testate estate or known heirs in an intestate estate; (3) whether decedent died intestate or testate and, if testate, the date of will execution; (4) statement that the probate property does not exceed a gross value of $100,000 and the approximate amount of personal property and income for the purposes of setting a bond; (5) the name and address of the proposed personal representative. (§ 635.2)
Is procedure available in the case of nonresident decedents?	No provision.
Maximum allowable value of estate	Gross value of the probate assets cannot exceed $100,000. (§ 635.1)
What property can be transferred by this means?	Any property of the estate. (§§ 635.7, 633.361)
Special rules for certain assets (e.g., automobile)	Personal property that is of a perishable nature and for which there is a regularly established market can be sold by the personal representative without order of the court. (§ 633.387)
Can the spouse or other person take summarily if under certain amount?	No provision.
Minimum period before filing allowed	For surviving spouse, 20 days after the death of decedent. For each other class in succession, 10 days after the death of decedent. (§ 633.228)
Rights/obligations of party with affidavit	"The personal representative is required to file the report and inventory for which provision is made in § 633.361 including all probate and nonprobate assets." (§ 635.7(1)) The personal representative must also file a closing statement "within a reasonable time from the date of issuance of the letters of appointment." (§ 635.8(1))
Are some creditors given special privileges/ preference (e.g., medical expenses, funeral expenses)?	No provision.
Creditors' rights, if insufficient assets	Creditors may file claims against the estate "within the applicable time periods provided in such notices." (§ 635.13)
May the distribution of the estate proceed without appointment of personal representative?	No. (§ 635.1)
Must court approve affidavit?	No provision.
Waiting period before authority to act	Upon issuance of letters of appointment for administration. (§ 635.1)
With whom do you file petition or affidavit?	Clerk of Probate Court. (§ 635.1)
Is there an informal procedure for appointment of executor or administrator?	No provision.

Can a nonresident serve?	A natural person who is a nonresident of Iowa and who is otherwise qualified may serve, provided a resident fiduciary is appointed to serve with such nonresident fiduciary or, if good cause is shown, the nonresident may serve alone. (§ 633.64(1))
Can the nonresident act locally based on appointment in another state?	No. (§ 633.64)
What does a transferor need so as to be relieved of liability if challenged by another person later on who claims the particular property (e.g., copy of affidavit)?	No Provision.

Kansas
Summary Proceedings and Payment of Certain Benefits to Certain Relatives

Who can initiate process?	*By Affidavit.* "[S]urviving spouse or other relative by whom or on whose behalf request for payment is made." (§ 59-1507a(b)) *Summary Proceedings.* Executor or administrator. (§ 59-1507)
Can it be used if claims outstanding?	*By Affidavit.* Yes, with respect to personal property. The affidavit required is "sufficient if in substantial compliance with the form set forth by the judicial council." (§ 59-1507b) *Summary Proceedings.* Yes. (§ 59-1507)
Different rules if die testate or intestate?	*By Affidavit.* No. (§ 59-1507b) *Summary Proceedings.* No provision.
Notice?	*By Affidavit.* No provision. *Summary Proceedings.* The court with or without notice may adjust, correct, settle, allow or disallow account of the executor and administrator, and if the account is allowed, summarily determine the heirs, legatees, and devisees, and close the administration. (§ 59-1507)
heirs	No provision.
creditors	No provision.
others	No provision.
Which of the following must be observed?	
hearing	No provision.
affidavit, petition, other	*By Affidavit.* Affidavit. (§ § 59-1507a, 59-1507b) *Summary Proceedings.* Executor or administrator can present his or her account with an application for the settlement and allowance thereof. (§ 59-1507)
bond	No provision.
What are basic contents of petition or affidavit?	*By Affidavit.* Affidavit for certain benefits must list: "(1) the date of death of the deceased, (2) the relationship of the affiant to the deceased, (3) that no executor or administrator for the deceased has qualified or been appointed, and (4) that, to the affiant's knowledge, there exists at the time of the filing of such affidavit, no relative of a closer degree of kindred to the deceased than the affiant." (§ 59-1507a(b)) In addition, the affidavit must comply "with the form set forth by the judicial counsel." (§ 59-1507b) *Summary Proceedings.* No provision.
Is procedure available in the case of nonresident decedents?	No. (§ 59-1507) *Summary Proceedings.* No provision.

Maximum allowable value of estate	*By Affidavit.* For the use of the affidavit for certain personal property, $40,000. (§ 59-1507b), for certain monthly benefits, $5,000 (§ 59-1507a) *Summary Proceedings.* "[T]he estate, exclusive of the homestead and allowances to the spouse and minor children," cannot exceed the "amounts required for funeral expenses, expenses of last sickness, wages of servants during the last sickness, costs of administration, debts having preference under the laws of the United States or [Kansas], and taxes." (§ 59-1507)
What property can be transferred by this means?	*By Affidavit.* "[M]onthly benefits" (e.g., under title II of Social Security Act) or under any veterans administration program or public or private retirement or annuity plan. (§ 59-1507a(a)) Any personal property of whatever nature. (§ 59-1507b) *Summary Proceedings.* Entire estate. (§ 59-1507) ("estate of a decedent")
Special rules for certain assets (e.g., automobile)	No provision beyond §§ 59-1507a and 59-1507b. See *What property can be transferred by this means?*
Can the spouse or other person take summarily if under certain amount?	*By Affidavit.* If certain benefits, as specified in § 59-1507a, do not exceed totally $5,000, spouse and certain other recipient relatives can take summarily based on prescribed affidavit. (§ 59-1507a) *Summary Proceedings.* No provision.
Minimum period before filing allowed	No provision.
Rights/obligations of party with affidavit	*By Affidavit.* No provision. *Summary Proceedings.* No provision.
Are some creditors given special privileges/ preference (e.g., medical expenses, funeral expenses)?	*By Affidavit.* No provision. *Summary Proceedings.* Funeral expenses, expenses of last sickness, costs of administration, debts having preference under laws of U.S. or Kansas, and taxes. (§ 59-1507)
Creditors' rights, if insufficient assets	No provision.
May the distribution of the estate proceed without appointment of personal representative?	*By Affidavit.* No. (§§ 59-1507a, 59-1507b) *Summary Proceedings.* Yes. (§ 59-1507)
Must court approve affidavit?	No provision.
Waiting period before authority to act	*By Affidavit.* Certain benefits to decedent must be paid to relatives at least 180 days after decedent's death. (§ 59-1507a(a)) *Summary Proceedings.* No provision.
With whom do you file petition or affidavit?	*By Affidavit.* "[W]ith the appropriate governmental office or private company or person." (§§ 59-1507a(b), 59-1507(b) *Summary Proceedings.* Court. (§ 59-1507)
Is there an informal procedure for appointment of executor or administrator?	No provision.
Can a nonresident serve?	Yes. (§§ 59-1706 through -1708)

Can the nonresident act locally based on appointment in another state?	A nonresident fiduciary may assign, extend, release, satisfy or foreclose any mortgage, judgment or lien, or collect any debts secured thereby. (§ 59-1707) A nonresident fiduciary may also sue or be sued in any court in Kansas. (§ 59-1708)
What does a transferor need so as to be relieved of liability if challenged by another person later on who claims the particular property (e.g., copy of affidavit)?	*By Affidavit.* Receipt of affidavit shall constitute a full discharge and release from any further claim for such transfer to the same extent as if transfer had been made to an executor or administrator of the decedent's estate. (§ 59-1507b) See also § 59-1507a (regarding payments). *Summary Proceedings.* No provision.

Kentucky
Dispensing with Administration by Agreement

Who can initiate process?	A representative, legatee, distributee or creditor. (§ 395.510(1))
Can it be used if claims outstanding?	Yes, but only if the written agreement to dispense with administration designates a trustee with power to collect claims and demands. (§ 395.470(1))
Different rules if die testate or intestate?	Only available to the estate of a person dying intestate. (§ 395.470(1))
Notice?	
heirs	See *Who can initiate process?*
creditors	The persons applying for an order dispensing with administration shall advertise for creditors of the intestate to appear and present their claims. . . . The person and place shall be designated in the advertisement. The advertisement shall also give notice when, where, and by whom the order dispensing with administration will be applied for. The advertisement shall be posted at the courthouse door for six . . . weeks, and published pursuant to § 424. (§ 395.470(4))
others	No provision.
Which of the following must be observed?	
hearing	No provision.
affidavit, petition, other	Need to file a written agreement (affidavit) to obtain an order dispensing with administration. (§ 395.470(2)) Must also file an affidavit showing that advertisement for creditors has been made. (§ 395.470(4))
bond	Person applying for order shall give bond before the order is granted with surety in the amount of the personal estate. (§ 395.470(5))
What are basic contents of petition or affidavit?	All persons beneficially entitled to the personal estate have agreed in writing that there shall be no administration; and either there are no claims or demands due the estate, or the written agreement to dispense with the administration designates a trustee with power to collect claims and demands. (§ 395.470(1))
Is procedure available in the case of nonresident decedents?	No provision.
Maximum allowable value of estate	No provision.
What property can be transferred by this means?	All property contained in the personal estate. (§ 395.470(1))
Special rules for certain assets (e.g., automobile)	No provision.

Can the spouse or other person take summarily if under certain amount?	Yes, "[w]here the exemption of the surviving spouse alone, or together with preferred claims paid by a widow or by the widower where the wife's estate is legally liable for payment, equals or exceeds the amount of probatable assets." This provision does not distinguish between testate and intestate decedents' estates. (§ 395.455(1))
Minimum period before filing allowed	If brought by someone other than the personal representative then 6 months, otherwise no provision. (§ 395.510)
Rights/obligations of party with affidavit	No provision.
Are some creditors given special privileges/ preference (e.g., medical expenses, funeral expenses)?	No provision.
Creditors' rights, if insufficient assets	Bond provided by the persons applying for the order dispensing with administration for the benefit of creditors who, within six months from the order dispensing with administration, file their claims with the court. (§ 395.470(5))
May the distribution of the estate proceed without appointment of personal representative?	Yes. (§§ 395.455, 395.470)
Must court approve affidavit?	The court must approve the written agreement. (§ 395.470(2))
Waiting period before authority to act	No provision.
With whom do you file petition or affidavit?	The written agreement with a motion for an order dispensing with administration must be filed in district court. (§ 395.470(2))
Is there an informal procedure for appointment of executor or administrator?	No provision.
Can a nonresident serve?	Yes. (§ 395.170)
Can the nonresident act locally based on appointment in another state?	Yes, if there is no local administration. (§ 395.170(2))
What does a transferor need so as to be relieved of liability if challenged by another person later on who claims the particular property (e.g., copy of affidavit)?	No provision.

Louisiana
Small Successions

Who can initiate process?	"[T]he surviving spouse, if any, and one or more competent major heirs." (Code Civ. Pro. Art. 3432(A))
Can it be used if claims outstanding?	Yes. (Code Civ. Pro. Art. 3431(C))
Different rules if die testate or intestate?	Testate decedents do not qualify for small successions administration. Intestate decedents may qualify for small successions administration, depending on the survival of certain heirs and the value of the estate. (Code Civ. Pro. Arts. 3421, 3431(a), 3441)
Notice?	No notice required, unless decedent dies single and without an heir in Louisiana and a public administrator takes possession of the estate. In that case, the public administrator must advertise one time in the official journal of the parish. (Code Civ. Pro. Art. 3431(B))
heirs	Notice given pursuant to Art. 3431(B) shall read: "Notice is hereby given to any heirs or creditors . . . " (Code Civ. Pro. Art. 3431(C))
creditors	Notice given pursuant to Art. 3431(B) shall read: "Notice is hereby given to any heirs or creditors . . . " (Code Civ. Pro. Art. 3431(C))
others	No provision.
Which of the following must be observed?	
hearing	No provision.
affidavit, petition, other	Affidavit. (Code Civ. Pro. Art. 3432)
bond	No provision.
What are basic contents of petition or affidavit?	Decedent's date of death and domicile at death; statement that decedent died intestate; marital status of deceased; the location of the last residence of the deceased; name, address, domicile, and location of last residence of surviving spouse, if any; and names and last known addresses of heirs and relationship to decedent; the statement that an heir not signing the affidavit either could not be located after the exercise of reasonable diligence or was given 10 days notice by U.S. mail of affiant's intent to execute an affidavit for small succession and did not object; a description of whether the property left by the decedent is separate or community; sufficient identification of nonmovable property; a showing of the value of each item of property, and the aggregate value of all such property, at the time of death; the respective interests of heirs and whether the surviving spouse has a usufruct; and an affirmation that the affidavit is true, correct; complete; an affirmation that the affiant has accepted the succession. (Code Civ. Pro. Art. 3432(A))

Is procedure available in the case of nonresident decedents?	No. Code Civ. Pro. Art. 3421, Official Revision Comments states that the procedure is only available to domiciliaries of Louisiana. Nevertheless, Code Civ. Pro. Art. 3432.1 provides for affidavit procedure in case of person domiciled outside of Louisiana who died testate. In addition to providing much of the same information as when a Louisiana domiciliary died intestate (Code Civ. Pro. Art. 3432(A)), Code Civ. Pro. Art. 3432.1 requires attachment of certified copies of the testament and the probate order of another state if the affidavit is being used in lieu of an ancillary probate proceeding.
Maximum allowable value of estate	$75,000 gross value of interests in property in Louisiana of decedent. (Code Civ. Pro. Art. 3421)
What property can be transferred by this means?	No provision.
Special rules for certain assets (e.g., automobile)	No provision.
Can the spouse or other person take summarily if under certain amount?	Yes, if decedent died intestate with less than $75,000 of property, provided decedent's sole heirs are his descendants, his ascendants, his brothers or sisters or descendants thereof, and a surviving spouse. (Code Civ. Pro. Arts. 3421, 3431)
Minimum period before filing allowed	No provision.
Rights/obligations of party with affidavit	A copy of an affidavit endorsed by the inheritance tax collector is full authority for the delivery of property. (Code Civ. Pro. Art. 3434 Comments)
Are some creditors given special privileges/ preference (e.g., medical expenses, funeral expenses)?	No provision.
Creditors' rights, if insufficient assets	If a public administrator takes possession of the estate, creditors are entitled to notice and have the right to object. (Code Civ. Pro. Art. 3431(C))
May the distribution of the estate proceed without appointment of personal representative?	Yes. (Code Civ. Pro. Art. 3432)
Must court approve affidavit?	No. (Code Civ. Pro. Art. 3432)
Waiting period before authority to act	No provision.
With whom do you file petition or affidavit?	"[A]ny officer or person authorized to administer oaths in the place where the affidavit is executed." (Code Civ. Pro. Art. 3432)
Is there an informal procedure for appointment of executor or administrator?	No provision.
Can a nonresident serve?	No provision.
Can the nonresident act locally based on appointment in another state?	No provision.

What does a transferor need so as to be relieved of liability if challenged by another person later on who claims the particular property (e.g., copy of affidavit)?	"The receipt of the persons named in the affidavit as heirs of the deceased, or surviving spouse in [the] community thereof, constitutes a full release and discharge for the payment of money or delivery of property made under the provisions of this Article." (Code Civ. Pro. Art. 3434(B))

Maine
Collection of Personal Property by Affidavit; Summary Administration for Small Estates

Who can initiate process?	*Affidavit.* Persons claiming to be successors. (18-A § 3-1201(a)) *Summary Administration.* Personal representative. (18-A § 3-1204(a))
Can it be used if claims outstanding?	*Affidavit.* Yes. (18-A § 3-1201(a)(1)) *Summary Administration.* Yes. (18-A § 3-1204(a)(3))
Different rules if die testate or intestate?	No provision.
Notice?	*Affidavit.* No provision. *Summary Administration.* All distributees and claimants must receive a copy of the closing statement. (18-A § 3-1204(a)(3))
heirs	No provision.
creditors	*Summary Administration.* If the net value of the estate does not exceed homestead allowance, exempt property, family allowance, administration expenses, funeral expenses, and medical/hospital expenses of last illness, then no notice to creditors is necessary. (18A § 3-1203)
others	No provision.
Which of the following must be observed?	
hearing	No provision.
affidavit, petition, other	*Affidavit.* Affidavit. (18-A § 3-1201(a)) *Summary Administration.* Closing statement. (18-A § 3-1204(a))
bond	No provision.

What are basic contents of petition or affidavit?	*Affidavit.* Statement that: value of entire estate, wherever located, less liens and encumbrances, does not exceed $20,000; 30 days elapsed since death of decedent; no application or petition for the appointment of a personal representative is pending or has been granted in any jurisdiction; claiming successor is entitled to payment or delivery of the property. (18-A § 3-1201(a))
	Summary Administration. Closing statement must state: "(1) to the best of the personal representative's knowledge, the value of the entire estate, less liens and encumbrances, did not exceed homestead allowance, exempt property, family allowance, costs and expenses of administration, reasonable funeral expenses, and reasonable and necessary medical and hospital expenses of the last illness of the decedent; (2) the personal representative has fully administered the estate by disbursing and distributing it to the persons entitled thereto; and (3) the personal representative has sent a copy of the closing statement to all distributees of the estate and to all creditors or other claimants of whom he is aware whose claims are neither paid nor barred and has furnished a full account in writing of his administration to the distributees whose interests are affected." (18-A § 3-1204(a))
Is procedure available in the case of nonresident decedents?	No provision.
Maximum allowable value of estate	*Affidavit.* Value of entire estate, wherever located, less liens and encumbrances, may not exceed $20,000. (18-A § 3-1201(a)(1))
	Summary Administration. The value of the entire estate, less liens and encumbrances, must not exceed homestead allowance, exempt property, family allowance, costs and expenses of administration, reasonable funeral expenses, and reasonable and necessary hospital expenses of the last illness of the decedent. (18-A § 3-1204(a)(1))
What property can be transferred by this means?	*Affidavit.* "[T]angible personal property or an instrument evidencing a debt, obligation, stock, or chose in action." (18-A § 3-1201(a))
	Summary Administration. Entire estate. (18-A § 3-1204(a)) ("The estate")
Special rules for certain assets (e.g., automobile)	*Affidavit.* Within 30 days of death of Maine resident, the surviving spouse, deceased's child/child's descendants, father/mother, or brother/sister may request deceased's Social Security owed if less than $1,000. (18A § 3-1205) "A transfer agent of any security shall change the registered ownership on the books of a corporation from the decedent to the successor . . . upon the presentation of an affidavit." (18-A § 3-1201(b))
Can the spouse or other person take summarily if under certain amount?	*Affidavit.* Social security benefits if less than $1,000. (18A § 3-1205)

Minimum period before filing allowed	*Affidavit.* There is no filing for this procedure. See *Waiting period before authority to act.* *Summary Administration.* Estate must be fully administered and distributed before a closing statement can be filed. (18-A §3-1204(a)(2))
Rights/obligations of party with affidavit	*Affidavit.* Successor with affidavit is entitled to payment of indebtedness or delivery of property, but is accountable to those with superior rights. (18-A §§3-1201(a), 3-1202) *Summary Administration.* No provision.
Are some creditors given special privileges/ preference (e.g., medical expenses, funeral expenses)?	*Affidavit.* No provision. *Summary Administration.* Funeral and last illness medical expenses. (18-A §3-1204(a)(1))
Creditors' rights, if insufficient assets	*Affidavit.* Payees are accountable to persons with superior rights. (18-A §3-1202) *Summary Administration.* No provision.
May the distribution of the estate proceed without appointment of personal representative?	*Affidavit.* Yes; absence of personal representative is required. (18-A §3-1201(a)(3)) *Summary Administration.* No. (18-A §3-1204(a))
Must court approve affidavit?	No provision.
Waiting period before authority to act	*Affidavit.* 30 days after death of decedent. (18-A §3-1201(a)(2)) *Summary Administration.* No minimum period after appointment of personal representative. (18-A §3-1204(a))
With whom do you file petition or affidavit?	*Affidavit.* No provision. *Summary Administration.* Court. (18-A §3-1204(a))
Is there an informal procedure for appointment of executor or administrator?	Yes. (18-A §§3-301, 3-307 to -311)
Can a nonresident serve?	Yes. (18-A §§4-201 to -207)
Can the nonresident act locally based on appointment in another state?	If the foreign personal representative has complied with §4-204, the foreign personal representative may exercise as to assets in [Maine] all powers of a local personal representative and may maintain actions and proceedings in [Maine] subject to any conditions imposed upon nonresident parties generally. (18-A §4-205)
What does a transferor need so as to be relieved of liability if challenged by another person later on who claims the particular property (e.g., copy of affidavit)?	*Affidavit.* Payor is "discharged and released to the same extent as if he dealt with a personal representative." (18-A §3-1202) *Summary Administration.* No provision.

Maryland
Small Estates and Modified Administration

Who can initiate process?	*Small Estates.* Any person entitled to administration pursuant to § 5-104. (Est. & Trusts § 5-602) Under Est. & Trusts § 5-104, any person with a pecuniary interest in the estate's proper administration qualifies. *Modified Administration.* Personal representative. (Est. & Trusts § 5-702)
Can it be used if claims outstanding?	*Small Estates.* Yes. (Est. & Trusts § 5-602(c)) *Modified Administration.* No provision.
Different rules if die testate or intestate?	No provision.
Notice?	*Small Estates.* If it appears there will be property remaining after payments, allowances, and expenses, unless prior notice of appointment of personal representative has been published, the register shall publish notice of the appointment in a newspaper of general circulation in the county of appointment once a week in three successive weeks pursuant to § 7-103. (Est. & Trusts § 5-603(b)) *Modified Administration.* Unless an interested person waives notice of the verified final report under modified administration, the personal representative shall provide a copy to each interested person within 10 months from the date of the appointment. (Est. & Trust § 5-706(5))
heirs	No provision.
creditors	Notice made under § 7-103 is meant to notify creditors of the estate to present their claims. (Est. & Trusts § 5-603(a)-(b))
others	No provision.
Which of the following must be observed?	
hearing	No provision.
affidavit, petition, other	*Small Estates.* Petition. (Est. & Trusts § 5-602) *Modified Administration.* Election, final report. (Est. & Trusts § 5-702)
bond	*Small Estates.* Unless bond is expressly excused by the will or by written consent of all interested persons, personal representative must post bond if value of estate after payment of expenses and allowances is greater than $10,000. (Est. & Trusts § 5-604(a)(1)) If the estate is established to have a gross value of less than $10,000 after the payment of expenses and allowances, a person appointed as a personal representative may not be required to give bond. (Est. & Trusts § 5-604(a)(2)) *Modified Administration.* No provision.

What are basic contents of petition or affidavit?	*Small Estates.* In addition to information required by Est. & Trusts §§ 5-201 and 5-202, petition shall contain a statement that petitioner has made a diligent search to discover all property and debts of the decedent; a list of known property and its value; a list of known creditors, and the amount of each claim; and a statement of any legal proceedings pending in which decedent was a party. (Est. & Trusts § 5-602) *Modified Administration.* There is no specific provision. Presumably, the petition would have to show all statutory prerequisites have been satisfied: (1) all residuary legatees of a testate decedent and heirs at law of an intestate decedent are limited to: the personal representative and individuals or entities exempt from an inheritance tax; (2) all trustees of each trust that is a residuary legatee are limited to the decedent's personal representative, surviving spouse, and children; (3) the estate is solvent and sufficient assets exist to satisfy all testamentary gifts; (4) a final report is filed within 10 months from date of appointment, (5) distribution can occur no later than 12 months from the date of appointment; and (6) all residuary legatees or heirs at law must consent to modified administration under the detailed procedures of Est. & Trusts § 5-706. (Est. & Trusts § 5-702) Final report "shall include (1) [a] statement representing the continued qualification for modified administration; (2) [a]n itemized schedule of property and the basis of its valuation; (3) [a]n itemized schedule of liens, debts, taxes, and funeral expenses of the decedent and administration expenses of the estate; and (4) [s]chedules setting forth distributive shares of the estate and the applicable inheritance tax." (Est. & Trusts § 5-707)
Is procedure available in the case of nonresident decedents?	No provision.
Maximum allowable value of estate	*Small Estates.* Fair market value of property less debts secured by the property is $50,000 or less. (Est. & Trusts § 5-601(a), (d)) If the surviving spouse is the sole legatee or heir and before filing of an initial account in administration under Subtitle 3 or 4, fair market value of property less debts secured by the property must be $100,000 or less. (Est. & Trusts § 5-601(c)) *Modified Administration.* No provision.
What property can be transferred by this means?	*Small Estates.* Entire estate. (Est. & Trusts § 5-601(a) ("the estate")) *Modified Administration.* Entire estate. (Est. & Trusts § 5-702(2) ("the estate"))
Special rules for certain assets (e.g., automobile)	No provision.
Can the spouse or other person take summarily if under certain amount?	Yes, if the surviving spouse is the sole legatee or heir of the decedent and the property is valued at $100,000 or less. (Est. & Trusts § 5-601(c))

Minimum period before filing allowed	*Small Estates.* No provision. *Modified Administration.* Election for modified administration must be filed within 3 months of the date of appointment of a personal representative. (§ 5-702) Final report must be filed within 10 months from date of appointment. (§ 5-702(3))
Rights/obligations of party with affidavit	No provision.
Are some creditors given special privileges/ preference (e.g., medical expenses, funeral expenses)?	*Small Estates.* Immediate payment of allowable funeral expenses and family allowances. (Est. & Trusts § 5-603(a)(2)) *Modified Administration.* A final report under modified administration shall include an itemized schedule of funeral expenses, liens, debts, taxes and administration expenses of the estate. (Est. & Trusts § 5-707(3))
Creditors' rights, if insufficient assets	*Small Estates.* Right to object within 30 days of publication of notice. (Est. & Trusts § 5-603(b)(1)) *Modified Administration.* Filing of written objection by an interested person revokes procedure. (Est. & Trusts § 5-708(a)(2))
May the distribution of the estate proceed without appointment of personal representative?	*Small Estates.* No. (Est. & Trusts § 5-603(a)(1)) *Modified Administration.* No. (Est. & Trusts § 5-702)
Must court approve affidavit?	*Small Estates.* Register must find that petition is accurate. (Est. & Trusts § 5-603(a)) *Modified Administration.* No provision.
Waiting period before authority to act	No provision.
With whom do you file petition or affidavit?	*Small Estates.* Register of wills. (Est. & Trusts § 5-603(a)) *Modified Administration.* Register of wills. (Est. & Trusts § 5-703(b))
Is there an informal procedure for appointment of executor or administrator?	*Small Estates.* If the register finds the petition is accurate, the petitioner shall serve as personal representative. (Est. & Trusts § 5-603(a)(1)) *Modified Administration.* No provision.
Can a nonresident serve?	Yes. (Est. & Trusts §§ 5-501 to -506)
Can the nonresident act locally based on appointment in another state?	Yes. (Est. & Trusts § 5-502)
What does a transferor need so as to be relieved of liability if challenged by another person later on who claims the particular property (e.g., copy of affidavit)?	No provision.

Massachusetts
Collection of Personal Property by Voluntary Administration Proceedings for Small Estates (Post Jan 1, 2012)

Who can initiate process?	*Affidavit.* Interested person, any person designated to act as a voluntary personal representative of the estate of the person by the department of mental health, the department of developmental services or the division of medical assistance, in the case of a person who at the person's death, was receiving services from those departments. (190B § 3-1201). *Summary Administrative Proceedings.* Personal representative. (190B § 3-1203)
Can it be used if claims outstanding?	*Affidavit.* Yes. (190B § 3-1201) *Summary Administrative Proceedings.* Yes, if the value of the entire estate, less liens and encumbrances, does not exceed family allowances, exempt property, costs and expenses of administration, reasonable funeral expenses, and reasonable and necessary medical and hospital expenses of the last illness of the decedent. (190B § 3-1203)
Different rules if die testate or intestate?	*Affidavit.* No provision. *Summary Administrative Proceedings.* No provision.
Notice?	*Affidavit.* No provision. *Summary Administrative Proceedings.* A copy of the closing statement must be sent to all distributees, creditors, and other claimants. (190B § 3-1204(a)(3))
heirs	No provision.
creditors	*Summary Administrative Proceedings.* Personal representative may disburse and distribute the estate without giving notice to creditors. (190B § 3-1203)
others	No provision.
Which of the following must be observed?	
hearing	*Affidavit.* No. (190B § 3-1201) *Summary Administrative Proceedings.* No. (190B § 3-1203)
affidavit, petition, other	*Affidavit.* Sworn Statement, coupled with death certificate. (190B § 3-1201) *Summary Administrative Proceedings.* Closing statement. (190B § 3-1204)
bond	*Affidavit.* Upon payment of the proper fee, the register may issue a certificate of appointment to such voluntary personal representative. (190B § 3-1201) *Summary Administrative Proceedings.* No provision.

What are basic contents of petition or affidavit?	*Affidavit.* Sworn statement providing (a) the name and residential address of petitioner; (b) name, residence, and date of death of decedent; (c) the relationship of the petitioner to the deceased; (d) a schedule showing every asset of the estate known to the petitioner and the estimated value of each such asset; (e) a statement that the petitioner has undertaken to act as voluntary personal representative of the estate of the deceased and will administer the same according to law and apply the proceeds in accord with this section; (f) the names and addresses of surviving joint owners of property with the deceased known to the petitioner; (g) the names and addresses known to the petitioner of the persons taking by intestacy; and (h) the names and addresses known to the petitioner of the persons who would take under the provisions of the will, if any. (190B § 3-1201) *Summary Administrative Proceedings.* The closing statement must indicate (1) that the value of the net estate, less liens and encumbrances, did not exceed family allowances, exempt property, and reasonable administration, funeral, and last illness expenses; (2) all disbursements have been made to those entitled; and (3) a copy of the closing statement has been sent to all distributees, creditors, and other claimants. (190B § 3-1204(a))
Is procedure available in the case of nonresident decedents?	No provision.
Maximum allowable value of estate	*Affidavit.* Personal property not including a motor vehicle owned by the decedent, cannot exceed $25,000. (190B § 3-1201) *Summary Administrative Proceedings.* To the extent the entire estate, less encumbrances and liens, does not exceed administrative costs and expenses, reasonable funeral and burial expenses, homestead, family allowance, exempt property, and reasonable and necessary last illness medical and hospital expenses. (190B § 3-1203)
What property can be transferred by this means?	*Affidavit.* Personal property. (190B § 3-1201) *Summary Administrative Proceedings.* Entire estate. (190B § 3-1203)
Special rules for certain assets (e.g., automobile)	No provision.
Can the spouse or other person take summarily if under certain amount?	*Affidavit.* After first paying funeral expenses, expenses of last sickness, administration expenses and debts, distributions are made consistent with intestacy provisions. (190B § 3-1201)
Minimum period before filing allowed	*Affidavit.* 30 days from death of decedent. (190B § 3-1201) *Summary Administrative Proceedings.* None

Rights/obligations of party with affidavit	*Affidavit.* The person holding the sworn statement is essentially a personal representative and has a right to collect from those holding property or owing the estate. (190B § 3-1201)
Are some creditors given special privileges/preference (e.g., medical expenses, funeral expenses)?	*Affidavit.* The priority is: (1) funeral and last illness expenses; (2) administration expenses; (3) debts. (190B § 3-1201) *Summary Administrative Proceedings.* Liens, encumbrances, family allowances, exempt property, administrative expenses, reasonable funeral expenses, and reasonable and necessary medical and hospital expenses of the last illness. (190B § 3-1203)
Creditors' rights, if insufficient assets	*Affidavit.* If any person to whom a statement is delivered refuses to pay, deliver, transfer, or issue any personal property or evidence thereof, it may be recovered or its payment, delivery, transfer, or issuance compelled upon proof of their right in a proceeding brought for the purpose by or on behalf of the persons entitled thereto. (190B § 3-1202) *Summary Administrative Proceedings.* No provision.
May the distribution of the estate proceed without appointment of personal representative?	*Affidavitt.* Yes. (190B § 3-1201) *Summary Administrative Proceedings.* No. (190B § 3-1203)
Must court approve affidavit?	*Affidavit.* No. (190B § 3-1201) *Summary Administrative Proceedings.* No approval necessary. (190B § 3-1203)
Waiting period before authority to act	*Affidavit.* Must be more than 30 days after decedent's death. (190B § 3-1201) *Summary Administrative Proceedings.* No provision.
With whom do you file petition or affidavit?	*Affidavit.* File with court. (190B § 3-1201) *Summary Administrative Proceedings.* Closing statement must be filed with court. (190B § 3-1204(a))
Is there an informal procedure for appointment of executor or administrator?	Yes. (190B § 3-1201)
Can a nonresident serve?	Yes. (190B §§ 3-1201, 4-201, 4-205, 207)
Can the nonresident act locally based on appointment in another state?	Yes. (190B § 4-205)
What does a transferor need so as to be relieved of liability if challenged by another person later on who claims the particular property (e.g., copy of affidavit)?	*Affidavit.* Payor is released and discharged simply by making the transfer upon presentation of a copy of a statement attested by the register of the court and a receipt for surrender of evidentiary instrument, such as a policy, passbook, or certificate. (190B § 3-1201) *Summary Administrative Proceedings.* No provision

Michigan
Summary Administrative Proceedings*

Who can initiate process?	*Sworn Statement.* Decedent's successor. (§ 700.3983(1)) *Summary Administrative Proceedings.* Personal representative. (§ § 700.3987, 700.3988(1))
Can it be used if claims outstanding?	*Sworn Statement.* Yes. (§ 700.3983(1)) *Summary Administrative Proceedings.* Yes. (§ 700.3988(1)(c))
Different rules if die testate or intestate?	*Sworn Statement.* No provision. *Summary Administrative Proceedings.* No provision.
Notice?	*Sworn Statement.* No provision. *Summary Administrative Proceedings.* A copy of the closing statement must be sent to all distributees, creditors, and other claimants. (§ 700.3988(1)(c))
heirs	No provision.
creditors	*Summary Administrative Proceedings.* Personal representative may disburse and distribute the estate without giving notice to creditors. (§ 700.3987)
others	No provision.
Which of the following must be observed?	
hearing	*Sworn Statement.* No provision. *Summary Administrative Proceedings.* No provision.
affidavit, petition, other	*Sworn Statement.* Sworn Statement, coupled with death certificate. (§ 700.3983(1)) *Summary Administrative Proceedings.* Closing statement. (§ § 700.3987, 700.3988)
bond	*Sworn Statement.* No provision. *Summary Administrative Proceedings.* No provision.
What are basic contents of petition or affidavit?	*Sworn Statement.* Sworn statement that (1) estate does not include real property and the value of the entire estate, net of encumbrances and liens, does not exceed $22,000 for 2016; (2) 28 days have elapsed since decedent's death; (3) no application for appointment as personal representative is pending; (4) the claimant is entitled to property; and (5) the names and addresses of others entitled to property and their shares. (§ 700.3983(1)) *Summary Administrative Proceedings.* The closing statement must indicate (1) that the value of the net estate, less liens and encumbrances, did not exceed homestead allowance, family allowance, exempt property, and reasonable administration, funeral, and last illness expenses; (2) all disbursements have been made to those entitled; and (3) a copy of the closing statement has been sent to all distributees, creditors, and other claimants. (§ 700.3988(1)) In addition to the foregoing, identification and a simple sworn statement can be provided by a decedent's spouse, child, or parent so as to collect $500 or less and wearing apparel from a hospital, convalescent or nursing home, morgue, or law enforcement agency. (§ 700.3981)

Is procedure available in the case of nonresident decedents?	No provision.
Maximum allowable value of estate	*Sworn Statement.* Personal property, net liens and encumbrances, cannot exceed $22,000 for 2016. (§ 700.3983(1)(a)) *Summary Administrative Proceedings.* To the extent the entire estate, less encumbrances and liens, does not exceed administrative costs and expenses, reasonable funeral and burial expenses, homestead, and family allowance, exempt property, and reasonable and necessary last illness medical and hospital expenses. (§ 700.3987)
What property can be transferred by this means?	*Sworn Statement.* Personal property. (§ 700.3983(1)) *Summary Administrative Proceedings.* Entire estate. (§ 700.3987)
Special rules for certain assets (e.g., automobile)	Hospital, convalescent or nursing home, morgue, or law enforcement agency holding cash less than $500 and wearing apparel of decedent may deliver such property to a person furnishing identification and a sworn statement that the person is the decedent's spouse, child, or parent, and that no application is pending for administration of the estate. (§ 700.3981) Also, a transfer agent of a security shall change the registered ownership on the books of a corporation upon presentation of a sworn statement. (§ 700.3983(2))
Can the spouse or other person take summarily if under certain amount?	*Sworn Statement.* If funeral expenses have been paid and value of estate is less than $22,000 for 2016, property is turned over to surviving spouse. If funeral expenses have not been paid and estate is less than $22,000 for 2016, funeral expenses are paid first, and surviving spouse receives the balance. (§ 700.3982)
Minimum period before filing allowed	*Sworn Statement.* Filing not required. (§ 700.3983(1)) *Summary Administrative Proceedings.* None, other than after review of inventory and appraisal. (§ 700.3987)
Rights/obligations of party with affidavit	Affiant who claims wearing apparel and petty cash is answerable to fiduciaries of the estate and to persons having a prior right to wearing apparel or cash. (§ 700.3981) *Sworn Statement.* The person holding the sworn statement has a right to collect from those holding property or owing the estate. The transferee is answerable and accountable for the property to a person having superior right. (§ 700.3984(2))
Are some creditors given special privileges/ preference (e.g., medical expenses, funeral expenses)?	*Sworn Statement.* Not applicable since assumes a net estate after payment of debts and expenses. (§ 700.3983(1)(a)) *Summary Administrative Proceedings.* Funeral and burial expenses, and last illness medical expenses, and administration costs and expenses. (§ 700.3987)

Creditors' rights, if insufficient assets	*Sworn Statement.* The transferee is answerable and accountable for the property to a person having superior right and can compel payment or delivery upon proof of right to the property. (§ 700.3984(2)) *Summary Administrative Proceedings.* No provision.
May the distribution of the estate proceed without appointment of personal representative?	*Sworn Statement.* Yes. There must not be an application or petition for appointment of a personal representative pending or granted in any jurisdiction. (§ 700.3983(1)(c)) *Summary Administrative Proceedings.* No. (§§ 700.3987, 700.3988)
Must court approve affidavit?	*Sworn Statement.* No. However, a standard form will be available for use. (§ 700.3983(3)) *Summary Administrative Proceedings.* No approval necessary. (§ 700.3987)
Waiting period before authority to act	*Sworn Statement.* Must be more than 28 days after decedent's death. (§ 700.3983(1)) *Summary Administrative Proceedings.* May act immediately. (§ 700.3987)
With whom do you file petition or affidavit?	*Sworn Statement.* Not required. (§ 700.3983) *Summary Administrative Proceedings.* Closing statement must be filed with court. (§ 700.3988(1))
Is there an informal procedure for appointment of executor or administrator?	Yes. (§§ 700.3301, 700.3307–.3311)
Can a nonresident serve?	Yes. (§§ 700.4101–.4205)
Can the nonresident act locally based on appointment in another state?	If domiciliary foreign personal representative files authenticated copies of appointment and official bond with the court, such person may exercise the power of a local representative subject to conditions imposed upon nonresidents generally. (§ 700.4203(1))
What does a transferor need so as to be relieved of liability if challenged by another person later on who claims the particular property (e.g., copy of affidavit)?	*Sworn Statement.* Payor is released and discharged simply by making the transfer under a sworn statement to the same extent as if the person dealt with the personal representative. (§ 700.3984(1)) *Summary Administrative Proceedings.* No provision.

*

---

* For cost-of-living adjustments for §§ 700.3982 and 700.3983, see Letter of Andy Dillon, State Treasurer, Estates and Protected Individuals Code Cost-Of-Living Adjustments To Specific Dollar Amounts (Jan. 24, 2013). See also § 700.1210.

Minnesota
Collection of Personal Property by Affidavit; Summary Administration Procedure for Small Estates

Who can initiate process?	*Affidavit.* Person claiming to be the successor of the decedent or a state or county agency with a claim authorized by § 256B.15. (§ 524.3-1201(a)) *Summary Administration.* Any interested person. (§ 524.3-1203(1))
Can it be used if claims outstanding?	*Affidavit.* No provision. *Summary Administration.* No summary closing to distributees other than by family allowance is to be made without a showing that all claims have been paid. If the estate does not exceed $150,000 and is not exhausted by priority payments and exclusive of homestead, summary administration may proceed. (§ 524.3-1203(3), (5))
Different rules if die testate or intestate?	No provision.
Notice?	*Affidavit.* No provision. *Summary Administration.* All distributees and known claimants whose claims are neither paid nor barred must be sent a copy of the closing statement. (§ 524.3-1204(a)(3))
heirs	*Summary Administration.* All distributees must be sent a copy of the closing statement. (§ 524.3-1204(a)(3))
creditors	*Summary Administration.* All known claimants whose claims are neither paid nor barred must be sent a copy of the closing statement. (§ 524.3-1204(a)(3)).
others	No provision.
Which of the following must be observed?	
hearing	If the closing and distribution of assets is made pursuant to the terms of a will, no decree shall issue until a hearing has been held for formal probate of the will as provided in §§ 524.3-401 to 524.3-413. (§ 524.3-1203(5))
affidavit, petition, other	*Affidavit.* Affidavit. (§ 524.3-1201(a)) *Summary Administration.* Petition & closing statement. (§§ 524.3-1203(1), 524.3-1204(a)(3))
bond	*Affidavit.* No provision. *Summary Administration.* If personal representative not appointed, court may require petitioner to file a corporate surety bond. If a personal representative is appointed, a representative's bond must be filed conditioned upon the fact that all exempt property, allowances, and claims listed in M.S.A. § 524.3-805(a)(1)-(6) have been paid. (§ 524.3-1203(4), (5))

What are basic contents of petition or affidavit?	*Affidavit.* (1) Value of estate, less liens and encumbrances, does not exceed $75,000; (2) 30 days have elapsed since death of decedent; (3) no application for appointment of personal representative is pending or granted; (4) amount of claim in multi-party financial accounts, if applicable; and (5) claiming successor is entitled to payment or delivery of the property. (§ 524.3-1201(a)(1)-(5)) Certified death certificate must be presented with affidavit. (§ 524.3-1201(a)) *Summary Administration.* Closing statement must state that (1) the value of the estate, less liens and encumbrances, did not exceed homestead and family allowances, administration expenses, and funeral and last illness expenses; (2) that the estate has been fully administered and distributed; and (3) that the closing statement has been sent to all distributees and claimants whose claims are neither paid nor barred. (§ 524.3-1204(a))
Is procedure available in the case of nonresident decedents?	No provision.
Maximum allowable value of estate	*Affidavit.* Value of estate, less liens and encumbrances, does not exceed $75,000. (§ 524.3-1201(a)(1)) *Summary Administration.* If the estate will not be exhausted in payment of the priority items enumerated in subdivisions 1 to 4, the estate may nevertheless be summarily closed if the gross value of the estate exclusive of exempt homestead and any exempt property does not exceed $150,000. (§ 524.3-1203(5))
What property can be transferred by this means?	*Affidavit.* Payment of indebtedness; tangible personal property; instrument evidencing a debt, obligation, stock, or chose in action; and contents of safe deposit box. (§ 524.3-1201(a)) *Summary Administration.* "[A]ny real, personal, or other property in kind." (§ 524.3-1203(3))
Special rules for certain assets (e.g., automobile)	*Affidavit.* If presented with a proper affidavit, a motor vehicle registrar shall issue a new certificate of title. (§ 524.3-1201(d)) Also, in the case of a safe deposit box, payor need not deliver it if he has received an objection or if the key is not available. (§ 524.3-1201(e)) A transfer agent of any security shall change the registered ownership on the books of a corporation . . . upon presentation of an affidavit. (§ 524.3-1201(b)) *Summary Administration.* No provision.
Can the spouse or other person take summarily if under certain amount?	*Affidavit.* No provision. *Summary Administration.* Court may summarily determine and assign shares. (§ 524.3-1203(1), (3))
Minimum period before filing allowed	*Affidavit.* 30 days after death of decedent. (§ 524.3-1201(a)) *Summary Administration.* No provision.

Rights/obligations of party with affidavit	*Affidavit.* (1) Party can compel recovery of property upon proof of their right in a proceeding; (2) party with affidavit is answerable to any personal representative of the estate or to any other person having a superior right. (§ 524.3-1202) *Summary Administration.* No provision.
Are some creditors given special privileges/ preference (e.g., medical expenses, funeral expenses)?	*Affidavit.* No provision. *Summary Administration.* Yes, funeral, last illness medical expenses, and the classification of claims in M.S.A. § 524.3-805. (§ § 524.3-1203(1), (3), 524.3-1204(a)(1))
Creditors' rights, if insufficient assets	*Affidavit.* Payees are answerable to those with superior rights. (§ 524.3-1202) *Summary Administration.* See *Can it be used if claims outstanding?*
May the distribution of the estate proceed without appointment of personal representative?	*Affidavit.* Must proceed without personal representative. (§ 524.3-1201(a)(3)) *Summary Administration.* May proceed without personal representative. (§ 524.3-1203(4))
Must court approve affidavit?	*Affidavit.* No provision. *Summary Administration.* Yes (petition). (§ 524.3-1203(1))
Waiting period before authority to act	*Affidavit.* 30 days. (§ 524.3-1201(a)(2)) *Summary Administration.* No provision.
With whom do you file petition or affidavit?	*Affidavit.* No provision. *Summary Administration.* Probate Court. (§ 524.3-1203(1))
Is there an informal procedure for appointment of executor or administrator?	Yes. (§ § 524.3-301, 524.3-307–311)
Can a nonresident serve?	Yes. (§ § 524.4-201–207)
Can the nonresident act locally based on appointment in another state?	60 days after filing authentication of appointment and notice of intent, a domiciliary foreign personal representative may exercise as to assets in Minnesota all powers of a local personal representative subject to any conditions imposed upon nonresident parties generally. (§ 524.4-205)
What does a transferor need so as to be relieved of liability if challenged by another person later on who claims the particular property (e.g., copy of affidavit)?	*Affidavit.* Payor is discharged and released after transferring property pursuant to the affidavit to the same extent as if he dealt with a personal representative. (§ 524.3-1202) *Summary Administration.* No provision.

Mississippi
Payment of Indebtedness or Delivery of Personal Property of Decedent to Decedent's Successor; Affidavit of Successor

Who can initiate process?	Persons claiming to be "successors" of decedent, defined as: (1) decedent's spouse; (2) if no spouse, then adult with whom minor children of decedent are residing; (3) if no minor children, any adult child of decedent; or (4) if no adult child, either parent of the decedent. (§ 91-7-322(1)–(2))
Can it be used if claims outstanding?	No provision.
Different rules if die testate or intestate?	No provision.
Notice?	No provision.
heirs	No provision.
creditors	No provision.
others	No provision.
Which of the following must be observed?	
hearing	No provision.
affidavit, petition, other	Affidavit. (§ 91-7-322(1))
bond	No provision.
What are basic contents of petition or affidavit?	(1) Value of estate, excluding liens and encumbrances, does not exceed $50,000; (2) 30 days elapsed since death of decedent; (3) no application or petition for appointment of personal representative can be pending or granted; and (4) facts of relationship establishing affiant as a successor of the decedent. (§ 91-7-322(1)(a)-(d))
Is procedure available in the case of nonresident decedents?	No provision.
Maximum allowable value of estate	Value of entire estate, less liens and encumbrances, cannot exceed $50,000. (§ 91-7-322(1)(a))
What property can be transferred by this means?	Payment of indebtedness, tangible personal property; or instrument evidencing a debt, obligation, stock or chose in action. (§ 91-7-322(1))
Special rules for certain assets (e.g., automobile)	No provision.
Can the spouse or other person take summarily if under certain amount?	No provision.
Minimum period before filing allowed	No filing required. See *Waiting period before authority to act.*

Rights/obligations of party with affidavit	(1) Affiant can compel recovery of property upon proof of right in a proceeding brought in Chancery Court; (2) affiant is answerable to any personal representative of the estate or to any other person having a superior right. (§ 91-7-322(5)) Affiant is also empowered to negotiate, transfer ownership and exercise all other incidents of ownership with respect to the personal property and other instruments described in § 91-7-322(1). (§ 91-7-322(4))
Are some creditors given special privileges/ preference (e.g., medical expenses, funeral expenses)?	No provision.
Creditors' rights, if insufficient assets	Payees are answerable to persons with superior rights. (§ 91-7-322(5))
May the distribution of the estate proceed without appointment of personal representative?	Must proceed without appointment of personal representative. (§ 91-7-322(1)(c))
Must court approve affidavit?	No provision.
Waiting period before authority to act	30 days after death of decedent. (§ 91-7-322(1)(b))
With whom do you file petition or affidavit?	No provision.
Is there an informal procedure for appointment of executor or administrator?	No provision.
Can a nonresident serve?	No provision.
Can the nonresident act locally based on appointment in another state?	No provision.
What does a transferor need so as to be relieved of liability if challenged by another person later on who claims the particular property (e.g., copy of affidavit)?	Payor is discharged and released to the same extent as if such person had dealt with a personal representative. (§ 91-7-322(5))

Missouri
Small Estates—Distribution of Assets Without Letters, When Affidavit; Procedure; Fee

Who can initiate process?	Personal representative under the will if a will has been presented for probate; otherwise, any distributee entitled to receive property of the decedent. (§ 473.097(2))
Can it be used if claims outstanding?	Yes, if claims will be paid. (§ 473.097(2)(2))
Different rules if die testate or intestate?	No provision beyond *Who can initiate process?*
Notice?	
heirs	No provision.
creditors	If value of property in affidavit is greater than $15,000, clerk must publish notice to creditors in the newspaper for two consecutive weeks. (§ 473.097(5))
others	No provision.
Which of the following must be observed?	
hearing	No provision.
affidavit, petition, other	Affidavit and certificate. (§ 473.097(3))
bond	Yes. (§ 473.097(1)(3))
What are basic contents of petition or affidavit?	Affidavit must set forth: (1) decedent left no will or will has been presented for probate; (2) all unpaid debts or demands against decedent's estate will be paid, up to value of the property received; (3) itemized description and valuation of the property of the decedent; (4) names and addresses of persons having possession of the property; (5) names, addresses, and relationship to decedent of persons who will receive items included in the affidavit; and (6) facts establishing the right to such specific items of property. (§ 473.097(2)(1)-(6))
Is procedure available in the case of nonresident decedents?	No provision.
Maximum allowable value of estate	Value of entire estate, less liens and encumbrances, cannot exceed $40,000. (§ 473.097(1)(1))
What property can be transferred by this means?	Real property and personal property. (§ 473.097(1))
Special rules for certain assets (e.g., automobile)	No provision.
Can the spouse or other person take summarily if under certain amount?	No provision.
Minimum period before filing allowed	30 days after death of decedent. (§ 473.097(1)(2))

Rights/obligations of party with affidavit	Affiant is liable for debts of the decedent's estate up to the value of the property received. Secured creditors retain their right to decedent's property. Affiant is entitled to collect property of decedent described in the affidavit and may liquidate property as necessary to pay debts. (§ 473.097(2)(2), (6) & (7)) Affiant is also answerable and accountable to anyone having a superior right. (§ 473.100)
Are some creditors given special privileges/ preference (e.g., medical expenses, funeral expenses)?	Must file bond ensuring payment of all the debts of the decedent, including any debts to the state and any debts related to funeral and burial. (§ 473.097(1)(3))
Creditors' rights, if insufficient assets	Right to payment up to the value of the property received by the affiant. (§ 473.097(2)(2))
May the distribution of the estate proceed without appointment of personal representative?	Yes. (§ 473.097(2), 473.097(2))
Must court approve affidavit?	Certificate of clerk showing names and addresses of the persons entitled to the described property must be annexed to or endorsed on the affidavit. (§ 473.097(2))
Waiting period before authority to act	30 days after death of decedent. (§ 473.097(1)(2))
With whom do you file petition or affidavit?	Office of the clerk of the probate division. If receiving real property, must file affidavit and certificate of the clerk in the office of the recorder of deeds of each county where the real property is situated. (§ 473.097(3)–(4))
Is there an informal procedure for appointment of executor or administrator?	No provision.
Can a nonresident serve?	No provision.
Can the nonresident act locally based on appointment in another state?	No provision.
What does a transferor need so as to be relieved of liability if challenged by another person later on who claims the particular property (e.g., copy of affidavit)?	Transferor is discharged and released to the same extent as if made to an executor or administrator of the decedent. Transferor need not inquire into the truth of the affidavit. (§ 473.100)

Montana
Collection of Personal Property by Affidavit; Summary Administration Procedure for Small Estates

Who can initiate process?	*Affidavit.* "[P]erson claiming to be the successor of the decedent." (§ 72-3-1101(1)) *Summary Administration.* Personal representative. (§ 72-3-1103)
Can it be used if claims outstanding?	*Affidavit.* Yes. (§ 72-3-1101(1)(a)) *Summary Administration.* Yes. (§ 72-3-1103)
Different rules if die testate or intestate?	No provision.
Notice?	
heirs	*Affidavit.* No provision. *Summary Administration.* All distributees of estate must get a copy of the closing statement. (§ 72-3-1104(1)(c))
creditors	*Affidavit.* No provision. *Summary Administration.* Must send copy of the closing statement to all creditors whose claims are neither paid nor barred. (§ 72-3-1104(1)(c)) Summary administration may proceed without notice to creditors. (§ 72-3-1103)
others	No provision.
Which of the following must be observed?	
hearing	No provision.
affidavit, petition, other	*Affidavit.* Affidavit. (§ 72-3-1101) *Summary Administration.* Closing statement. (§ 72-3-1104)
bond	No provision.
What are basic contents of petition or affidavit?	*Affidavit.* (1) Value of estate, less liens and encumbrances, does not exceed $50,000; (2) 30 days elapsed since death of decedent; (3) no application for appointment of personal representative is pending or granted; and (4) claiming successor is entitled to payment or delivery of property. (§ 72-3-1101(1)(a)-(d)) *Summary Administration.* Verified closing statement filed with the court must state (1) value of the estate, less liens and encumbrances, does not exceed family and homestead allowances, exempt property, and funeral, last medical, and administrative expenses; (2) estate has been fully administered and all inheritance taxes have been paid; and (3) copy of the closing statement has been distributed to distributees and creditors. (§ 72-3-1104(1)(a)-(c))
Is procedure available in the case of nonresident decedents?	No provision.

Maximum allowable value of estate	*Affidavit.* Value of estate, less liens and encumbrances, cannot exceed $50,000. (§72-3-1101(1)(a)) *Summary Administration.* Value of the entire estate, less liens and encumbrances, does not exceed homestead allowance, exempt property, family allowance, costs and expenses of administration, reasonable funeral expenses, and necessary medical and hospital expenses of the last illness of the decedent. (§72-3-1103)
What property can be transferred by this means?	*Affidavit.* (1) Payment of indebtedness; (2) tangible personal property; or (3) instrument evidencing a debt, obligation, stock, or chose in action. (§72-3-1101(1)) *Summary Administration.* Entire estate. (§72-3-1103)
Special rules for certain assets (e.g., automobile)	A transfer agent must change the registered ownership of a security upon presentation of an affidavit. (§72-3-1101(3))
Can the spouse or other person take summarily if under certain amount?	No provision.
Minimum period before filing allowed	*Affidavit.* No filing required for affidavit procedure. See *Waiting period before authority to act.* *Summary Administration.* File any time after disbursement and distribution of estate. (§72-3-1103)
Rights/obligations of party with affidavit	*Affidavit.* (1) Party can compel recovery of property upon proof of right in a proceeding; (2) party with affidavit is answerable to any personal representative of the estate or to any other person having a superior right. (§72-3-1102(2)–(3)) *Summary Administration.* No provision.
Are some creditors given special privileges/ preference (e.g., medical expenses, funeral expenses)?	*Affidavit.* No provision. *Summary Administration.* Funeral and last illness medical expenses. (§72-3-1103)
Creditors' rights, if insufficient assets	*Affidavit.* Payee is answerable to any person with a superior right. (§72-3-1102(3)) *Summary Administration.* No provision.
May the distribution of the estate proceed without appointment of personal representative?	*Affidavit.* Administration must proceed without application or appointment in any jurisdiction. (§72-3-1101(1)(c)) *Summary Administration.* No. (Must have personal representative.) (§72-3-1103)
Must court approve affidavit?	No provision.
Waiting period before authority to act	*Affidavit.* 30 days after death of decedent. (§72-3-1101(1)(b)) *Summary Administration.* May act immediately. (§72-3-1103)
With whom do you file petition or affidavit?	*Affidavit.* No provision. *Summary Administration.* Must file verified closing statement with the court. (§72-3-1104(1))
Is there an informal procedure for appointment of executor or administrator?	Yes. (§§72-3-201–202, 221–225)

Can a nonresident serve?	Yes. (§§72-4-303, 72-4-305)
Can the nonresident act locally based on appointment in another state?	If domiciliary foreign personal representative files authenticated copies of appointment and official bond with the court, such person may exercise as to assets in Montana all of the powers of a local representative subject to conditions imposed upon nonresidents generally. (§§72-4-310, 72-4-309)
What does a transferor need so as to be relieved of liability if challenged by another person later on who claims the particular property (e.g., copy of affidavit)?	*Affidavit.* Payor is discharged to the same extent as if he dealt with a personal representative of decedent after transferring property pursuant to the affidavit. (§72-3-1102(1)) *Summary Administration.* No provision.

Nebraska
Collection of Personal Property by Affidavit; Summary Administration Procedure for Small Estates

Who can initiate process?	*Affidavit.* Any person claiming to be the successor of the decedent. (§ 30-24,125(a)) *Summary Administration.* Personal representative. (§ 30-24, 127)
Can it be used if claims outstanding?	*Affidavit.* Yes. (§ 30-24,125(a)) *Summary Administration.* Yes. (§ 30-24,127)
Different rules if die testate or intestate?	No provision.
Notice?	
heirs	*Affidavit.* No provision. *Summary Administration.* Must send copy of the closing statement to all distributees of estate. (§ 30-24,128(a)(3))
creditors	*Affidavit.* No provision. *Summary Administration.* Must send copy of the closing statement to all creditors whose claims are neither paid nor barred. (§ 30-24,128(a)(3)) Summary administration may proceed without notice to creditors. (§ 30-24,127)
others	No provision.
Which of the following must be observed?	
hearing	No provision.
affidavit, petition, other	*Affidavit.* Affidavit. (§ 30-24,125(a)) *Summary Administration.* Closing statement. (§ 30-24,128(a))
bond	No provision.
What are basic contents of petition or affidavit?	*Affidavit.* (1) Value of personal property, less liens and encumbrances, does not exceed $50,000; (2) 30 days elapsed since death of decedent; (3) claiming successor's relationship to decedent or basis of claim; (4) claiming successor affirms that all statements are true; (5) no application for appointment of personal representative is outstanding or granted; and (6) claiming successor is entitled to delivery of the property. (§ 30-24,125(a)(1)-(6)) A copy of decedent's death certificate must be attached to the affidavit. (§ 30-24,125(a)(2)) *Summary Administration.* Verified closing statement filed with the court must state: (1) value of the estate, less liens and encumbrances, did not exceed family and homestead allowances, exempt property, and funeral, last illness medical, and administrative expenses; (2) estate has been fully administered; and (3) copy of the closing statement has been distributed to distributees and claimants. (§ 30-24,128(a)(1)-(3))
Is procedure available in the case of nonresident decedents?	No provision.

Maximum allowable value of estate	*Affidavit.* Value of estate, less liens and encumbrances, did not exceed $50,000. (§ 30-24,125(a)(1)) *Summary Administration.* "[V]alue of the entire estate, less liens and encumbrances, does not exceed homestead allowance, exempt property, family allowance, costs and expenses of administration, reasonable funeral expenses, and reasonable and necessary medical and hospital expenses of the last illness of the decedent." (§ 30-24,127)
What property can be transferred by this means?	*Affidavit.* Tangible personal property, instruments evidencing a debt, obligation, stock or chose in action and payment of indebtedness. (§ 30-24,125(a)) *Summary Administration.* Entire estate. (§ 30-24,127)
Special rules for certain assets (e.g., automobile)	*Affidavit.* If seeking to transfer certificate of title to a motor vehicle, motor boat, all-terrain vehicle, utility-type vehicle, or minibike, affiant must furnish to the department of motor vehicles an affidavit showing applicability of, and compliance with, Section 30-24.125. (§ 30-24,125(c)) Transfers of securities must change the registered ownership on the corporate books upon presentation of affidavit. (§ 30-24,125(b)) *Summary Administration.* No provision.
Can the spouse or other person take summarily if under certain amount?	No provision.
Minimum period before filing allowed	*Affidavit.* No filing required. See *Waiting period before authority to act.* *Summary Administration.* May file any time after disbursement and distribution of estate. (§ 30-24,127)
Rights/obligations of party with affidavit	*Affidavit.* (1) Party can compel recovery of property upon proof of right in a proceeding; (2) party is answerable to any personal representative of the estate or to any other person having a superior right. (§ 30-24,126) *Summary Administration.* No provision.
Are some creditors given special privileges/ preference (e.g., medical expenses, funeral expenses)?	*Affidavit.* No provision. *Summary Administration.* Funeral and last illness medical expenses. (§ 30-24,127)
Creditors' rights, if insufficient assets	*Affidavit.* Payee is answerable to persons having a superior right. (§ 30-24,126) *Summary Administration.* No provision.
May the distribution of the estate proceed without appointment of personal representative?	*Affidavit.* Yes. It *must* proceed without application for or appointment of a personal representative. (§ 30-24,125(a)(5)) *Summary Administration.* No. (§ 30-24,127)
Must court approve affidavit?	No provision.
Waiting period before authority to act	*Affidavit.* 30 days after death of decedent. (§ 30-24,125(a)(2)) *Summary Administration.* No provision.
With whom do you file petition or affidavit?	*Affidavit.* No provision. *Summary Administration.* Must file verified closing statement with the court. (§ 30-24,128(a))

Is there an informal procedure for appointment of executor or administrator?	Yes. (§ § 30-2414, 30-2420–2424)
Can a nonresident serve?	Yes. (§ § 30-2501–2508)
Can the nonresident act locally based on appointment in another state?	If domiciliary foreign personal representative files authenticated copies of appointment and official bond with the court, such person may exercise as to assets in Nebraska all of the powers of a local representative subject to conditions imposed upon nonresidents generally. (§ § 30-2506, 30-2505)
What does a transferor need so as to be relieved of liability if challenged by another person later on who claims the particular property (e.g., copy of affidavit)?	*Affidavit.* Payor is released and discharged to the same extent as if he had dealt with a personal representative after transferring property pursuant to affidavit. (§ 30-24,126) *Summary Administration.* No provision.

Nevada
Distribution of Small Estates

Who can initiate process?	*Estates Not Exceeding $100,000*: No provision, but if deceased leaves a surviving spouse or minor child, procedure is automatic; (§ 146.070(3)-(5)) *Affidavit*: With respect to an affidavit process not involving a court, an affidavit which can show the right to receive the money or property, or to have evidence of an interest transferred. (§ 146.080(1)). *Court Petition*: An alternative is an affidavit procedure to set aside the estate by court order, without subsequent administration, which is also available, by petition. (§ 146.070) The petition may be filed by a person who has a right to succeed to the property of the decedent pursuant to the laws of succession, or under the direction of the Department of Health and Human Services or Public Administration. (§ 146.070(1))
Can it be used if claims outstanding?	Yes. (§ 146.070(8)(d)) *Affidavit Procedure*: Yes, but there must be a statement that all debts, if not paid already, have been "Provided for." (§ 146.080(2)(f)) There must also be a statement that the affiant has no knowledge of any existing claims for personal injury or damages against the decedent. (§ 146.080(2)(j)) *Court Petition*: The petition itself may seek to set aside the estate to pay debts. (§ 146.070(2))
Different rules if die testate or intestate?	*Affidavit*: No. (§ 146.080(1)) *Court Petition*: No. (§ 146.070(i),(2)(d))
Notice?	
heirs	*Estates Not Exceeding $100,000*: Petitioner shall give notice to all heirs and devisees. (§ 146.070(11)) *Affidavit*: Notice to every person whose right to succeed to decedent's property is equal to or superior to the affiant's right (§ 146.080(2)(h)) *Court Petition*: Notice in accord with § 155.010 to heirs, devisees, and Department of Health and Human Services (§ 146.070(11))
creditors	No provision.
others	*Estates Not Exceeding $100,000*: Petitioner shall give notice to the Director of the Department of Human Resources. (§ 146.070(11)) *Affidavit*: No provision. *Court Petition*: No provision.
Which of the following must be observed?	
hearing	*Estates Not Exceeding $100,000*: Yes. (§ 146.070(11)) *Affidavit*: No. *Court Petition*: Yes. (§ 146.070(1))
affidavit, petition, other	*Estates Not Exceeding $100,000*: Yes. (§ 146.070(8)) *Affidavit*: Need an affidavit. (§ 146.080(1)) *Court Petition*: Need a petition. (§ 146.070(1))

bond	No provision.
What are basic contents of petition or affidavit?	*Estates Not Exceeding $100,000*: (1) A specific description of all property in the decedent's estate; (2) a list of all liens and encumbrances against estate property at death; (3) an estimate of value of the property together with an explanation of how the estimated value was determined; (4) a statement of decedent's debts; (5) names, ages, and residences or decedent's heirs and devisees and the relationship of the heirs and devisees to decedent; and (6) If the decedent left a will, a statement concerning all evidence known to the petitioner that tends to prove that the will is valid (§ 146.070(8)(a)-(f)) *For Estates Not Exceeding $100,000 Only for the Benefit of the Decedent's Surviving Spouse and/or Minor Children Without Payment to Creditors*: The petition must also contain: (1) A specific description and estimated value of property passing by nonprobate transfers by decedent to surviving spouse and/or minor children; and (2) nonprobate transfers and estimated value of property sought to be set aside that is less than $100,000. (§ 146.070(9)) *Local Estates Not Exceeding $100,000 if Surviving Spouse Is a Claimant, or $25,000 if Any Other Claimant, and Estate Not Involving an Interest in or Lien on Real Property*: The affidavit must contain: (1) affiant's name and address and statement that affiant is entitled by law to succeed to the property; (2) the date and place of death of decedent; (3) gross value of estate property in Nevada does not exceed $100,000 if surviving spouse is the claimant or $25,000 if any other claimant, and that there is no real property or interest therein; (4) at least 40 days have elapsed since death of decedent; (5) no petition for appointment of personal representative is pending or granted; (6) all debts of decedent including funeral and burial expenses and money owed to the Department of Human Resources as result of Medicaid payments have been paid or provided for; (7) description of personal property and portion claimed; (8) 14 days' notice given to every person whose right to succeed to decedent's property is equal or superior to that of the affiant; (9) statement that affiant is personally entitled or the Director of the Department of Human Resources is entitled to delivery of the property; (10) That the affiant has no knowledge of any existing claims for personal injury or tort damages against the decedent; and (11) affiant acknowledges understanding that filing a false affidavit is a felony in Nevada. (§ 146.080(2)(a)-(k)). *Court Petition*: (1) Description of all decedent's property; (2) list of all liens and mortgages at death; (3) estimate of value of the property; (4) statement of decedent's debts; (5) names, ages, and residences of decedent's heirs and devisees and the relationship of the heirs and devisees to the decedent; (6) if decedent left a will, a statement concerning evidence known to petitioner that tends to prove the will is valid. (§ 146.070(3)(a)-(e))

Is procedure available in the case of nonresident decedents?	*Affidavit*: This procedure applies with respect to "the decedent's property in this state . . . " (§ 146.080(1)) *Court Petition*: The statute references "decedent's estate," although court would presumably not have jurisdiction if decedent did not die domiciled there or did not have property with a situs in the state. (§ 146.070(1))
Maximum allowable value of estate	*Affidavit*: $100,000 if the claimant is a surviving spouse, otherwise, $25,000. (§ 146.080(7)(a)) The gross value of the decedent's property in the estate, except amounts due to the decedent's services in the Armed Forces of the U.S. or the value of any motor vehicles registered to the decedent, must not exceed the forgoing "applicable amount." (§ 146.080(2)(c)) *Court Petition*: $100,000, including nonprobate transfers to surviving spouse and minor children. (§ 146.070(9)(b)) Presumably, the "estate" value referred to is simply property with a Nevada situs when the decedent was not domiciled in Nevada at death. *Local Estates Not Exceeding $100,000 if Surviving Spouse is a Claimant, or $25,000 if Any Other Claimant, and Not Involving an Interest in or Lien on Real Property*: Must leave no real property, nor interest therein, nor lien thereon in the state and gross value of decedent's property in the state over and above amounts due to decedent for services in the U.S. armed forces, and the value of any motor vehicles registered to the decedent does not exceed $100,000 if surviving spouse is the claimant or $25,000 if any other claimant. (§ 146.080(1))
What property can be transferred by this means?	*Estates Not Exceeding $100,000*: Entire estate. (§ 146.070(2)) ("the whole estate") *Affidavit*: A procedure not available if there is an interest in real property in the state, or a mortgage or lien thereon. (§ 146.080(1)) *Court Petition*: No provision.
Special rules for certain assets (e.g., automobile)	*Affidavit*: Upon receiving proof of death of decedent and affidavit, transfer agent of securities shall change the registered ownership; government agencies shall issue a new certificate of title, ownership or registration. (§ 146.080(5)(a), (b)) *Court Petition*: No provision. *Local Estates Not Exceeding $100,000 if Surviving Spouse is a Claimant, or $25,000 if Any Other Claimant, and Not Involving an Interest in or Lien on Real Property*: Upon receiving proof of death of decedent and affidavit, transfer agent of securities shall change the registered ownership; government agencies shall issue a new certificate of title, ownership or registration. The government agency cannot refuse to accept an affidavit containing the information required, regardless of the form of the affidavit.
Can the spouse or other person take summarily if under certain amount?	Yes, spouse and/or minor children (146.070(3)–(5)) Court has great discretion and considers the needs and resources of the surviving spouse and/or minor children, and non-probate transfers. (§ 146.070(6)).

Minimum period before filing allowed	Estates Not Exceeding $100,000: 30 days after death of decedent. (§ 146.070(8)) No filing required. See *Waiting period before authority to act*. (§ 146.080(1)) *Court Petition:* $100,000. 30 days after death of decedent. (§ 146.070(8))
Rights/obligations of party with affidavit	*Affidavit:* Collect money due to decedent, receive property of the decedent, and have evidence of interest, indebtedness, or right transferred to the claimant (§ 146.080(1)) Right to have property transferred. (§ 146.080(1)) *Court Petition:* No provision.
Are some creditors given special privileges/ preference (e.g., medical expenses, funeral expenses)?	*Estates Not Exceeding $100,000:* If no surviving spouse or minor child, estate is first used for payment of the petitioner's attorney's fees and costs incurred relative to the proceeding under this section, payment of funeral expenses, expenses of last illness, and money owed to Medicaid and creditors. The remaining balance goes to claimants pursuant to the will, or intestate succession. (§ 146.070(2)(a)-(d)) *Affidavit:* All debts of decedent, including funeral burial and Medicaid expenses, must be provided for. (§ 146.080(2)(f)) *Court Petition:* If no surviving spouse or minor child, estate is paid in the following order: payment of funeral expenses, expenses of last illness, and money owed to Medicaid and creditors. The remaining balance goes to claimants pursuant to the will, or intestate succession. (§ 146.070(2)) If there is a surviving spouse or minor child, the court "must" set aside the estate for them. (§ 146.070(3)); However, the court may alter this if it would result in a "manifest injustice" with respect to creditors. (§ 146.070(4)) An adjustment is specifically provided for the benefit of creditors of the spouse or minor child is receiving nonprobate transfers already benefiting them. (§ 146.070(5)).
Creditors' rights, if insufficient assets	*Affidavit:* No provision. *Court Petition:* No provision.
May the distribution of the estate proceed without appointment of personal representative?	*Affidavit:* Yes. (§ 146.080(1)) *Court Petition:* Yes. (§ 146.070(1))
Must court approve affidavit?	No. The affiant must acknowledge an understanding that a false affidavit constitutes a felony. (§ 146.080(2)(k))
Waiting period before authority to act	*Local Estates Not Exceeding $100,000 if Surviving Spouse is a Claimant, or $25,000 if any Other Claimant, and Not Involving an Interest In or Lien on Real Property:* No, however a false affidavit constitutes a felony (§ 146.080(2)(k)). *Estates Not Exceeding $100,000:* 30 days after death of decedent. (§ 146.070(8)) *Affidavit:* 40 days after death of decedent. (§ 146.080(1)) *Court Petition:* 30 days after death of decedent. (§ 146.070(8))

With whom do you file petition or affidavit?	Estates Not Exceeding $100,000: Court (§ 146.070(12)) *Affidavit:* No filing. Simply furnish decedent's debtor, custodian, registrar or transfer agent with an affidavit. (§ 146.080(1)) *Court Petition:* Court. (§ 146.070(13))
Is there an informal procedure for appointment of executor or administrator?	No provision.
Can a nonresident serve?	No provision.
Can the nonresident act locally based on appointment in another state?	No provision.
What does a transferor need so as to be relieved of liability if challenged by another person later on who claims the particular property (e.g., copy of affidavit)?	*Estates Not Exceeding $100,000*: No provision, since the distribution occurs under the aegis of the court, but the court might require additional evidence at the hearing. (§ 146.070(13)) *Affidavit*: If a person who receives an affidavit relies in good faith on that affidavit, such person is immune from civil liability resulting from that reliance. (§ 146.080(4)) *Court Petition*: No provision, since the distribution occurs under the aegis of the court.

New Hampshire
Waiver of Administration

Who can initiate process?	The administrator of the estate. Statute specifies who will be the administrator. (§ 553:32(I))
Can it be used if claims outstanding?	No. (§ 553:32(I)(b))
Different rules if die testate or intestate?	No. (§ 553:32)
Notice?	No provision.
heirs	No provision.
creditors	No provision.
others	No provision.
Which of the following must be observed?	
hearing	No provision.
affidavit, petition, other	Affidavit of administration. (§ 553:32(I))
bond	Bond not required. (§ 553:32(I)(a))
What are basic contents of petition or affidavit?	"[A]ffidavit of administration shall [(1)] state that to the best of the knowledge and belief of the administrator, there are no outstanding debts or obligations attributable to the estate, and [(2)] list all real estate owned by decedent at the time of death, including location, book and page." (§ 553:32(I)) The administrator, if nonresident, must also appoint some person residing in New Hampshire as an agent. (§ 553:25)
Is procedure available in the case of nonresident decedents?	No provision.
Maximum allowable value of estate	No provision.
What property can be transferred by this means?	Entire estate. (§ 553:32(I)) ("the estate")
Special rules for certain assets (e.g., automobile)	No provision.
Can the spouse or other person take summarily if under certain amount?	No provision.
Minimum period before filing allowed	Affidavit of administration must be filed no earlier than 6 months and no later than one year after the date of appointment of the administrator. (§ 553:32(I)(b))
Rights/obligations of party with affidavit	Affiant does not need to do an inventory of the estate or account for assets. Administration of the estate is complete once the probate court approves of the affidavit. (§ 553:32(I)(a)–(b))
Are some creditors given special privileges/ preference (e.g., medical expenses, funeral expenses)?	No provision.

Creditors' rights, if insufficient assets	Not applicable; there are no outstanding debts allowed for this procedure. (§ 553:32(I)) "Any interested person may petition for a full administration of the estate at any time from the original grant of administration to the filing of the affidavit of administration." (§ 533:32(II))
May the distribution of the estate proceed without appointment of personal representative?	No. (§ 553:32(I)) (requires administrator)
Must court approve petition?	Yes. (§ 553:32(I))
Waiting period before authority to act	6 months from date of death. (§ 553:32(I))
With whom do you file petition or affidavit?	Probate court. (§ 553:32(I))
Is there an informal procedure for appointment of executor or administrator?	No provision.
Can a nonresident serve?	Yes, provided a New Hampshire resident is appointed as agent. (§ 553:25)
Can the nonresident act locally based on appointment in another state?	No, unless the judge deems proper based on circumstances. (§ 553:5)
What does a transferor need so as to be relieved of liability if challenged by another person later on who claims the particular property (e.g., copy of affidavit)?	No provision.

New Jersey
Small Estate Administration

Who can initiate process?	Surviving spouse partner in a civil union, or domestic partner (§ 3B:10-3), or any heir if there is no surviving spouse or domestic partner (§ 3B:10-4).
Can it be used if claims outstanding?	Yes. (§ § 3B:10-3, 3B:10-4)
Different rules if die testate or intestate?	Both § § 3B:10-3 and 3B:10-4 expressly apply only to estates of an intestate decedent.
Notice?	Spouse/Partner in a Civil Union/Domestic Partner—No provision. Heirs—see below.
heirs	Heirs—Must obtain the other remaining heirs' consent in writing, and file the written consent with the affidavit. (§ 3B:10-4)
creditors	No provision.
others	No provision.
Which of the following must be observed?	
hearing	No provision.
affidavit, petition, other	Affidavit. (§ § 3B:10-3, 3B:10-4)
bond	No bond required. (§ 3B:10-4)
What are basic contents of petition or affidavit?	Spouse/Partner in a Civil Union/Domestic Partner: (1) the affiant is the surviving spouse or partner in a civil union or domestic partner of the intestate; (2) the value of the intestate's real and personal assets will not exceed $50,000; (3) the residence of the intestate at his or her death; and (4) the nature, location, and value of the intestate's real and personal assets. (§ 3B:10-3) Heirs: (1) Residence of the intestate at his or her death; (2) names, residences, and relationships of all of the heirs; (3) the nature, location, and value of the intestate's real and personal assets; and (4) statement that the value of the intestate's real and personal assets will not exceed $20,000 (§ 3B:10-4)
Is procedure available in the case of nonresident decedents?	Yes. Sections 3B:10-3 and 3B:10-4 specifically provide for nonresident decedents.
Maximum allowable value of estate	Spouse/Domestic Partner—$50,000. (§ 3B:10-3) Heirs—$20,000. (§ 3B:10-4)
What property can be transferred by this means?	Real and personal. (§ § 3B:10-3, 3B:10-4)
Special rules for certain assets (e.g., automobile)	No provision.
Can the spouse or other person take summarily if under certain amount?	No provision.
Minimum period before filing allowed	No provision.

Rights/obligations of party with affidavit	Spouse/Domestic Partner: Affiant (1) has the rights, powers, and duties of an administrator duly appointed for the estate, (2) is entitled absolutely to all the real and personal assets without administration, (3) is entitled to assets of the estate up to $10,000 free from all debts of the intestate, and (4) may be sued and required to account as if he had been appointed administrator. (3B:10-3) Heirs: Affiant (1) has the rights, powers, and duties of an administrator duly appointed for the estate; (2) is entitled to receive the assets of the benefit of all the heirs and creditors without administration or entering into a bond, and (3) may be sued and required to account as if he had been appointed administrator. (3B:10-4)
Are some creditors given special privileges/ preference (e.g., medical expenses, funeral expenses)?	No provision.
Creditors' rights, if insufficient assets	May sue the surviving spouse or domestic partner and require an accounting as if the spouse had been appointed administrator. (§§ 3B:10-3, 3B:10-4)
May the distribution of the estate proceed without appointment of personal representative?	Yes. (§§ 3B:10-3, 3B:10-4)
Must court approve affidavit?	No provision.
Waiting period before authority to act	No provision.
With whom do you file petition or affidavit?	The office of the surrogate, or if proceeding before the superior court, then in the office of the clerk of that court. If affiant is a not a resident of New Jersey, the surrogate may authorize in writing the affidavit to be executed in the affiant's domicile. (§§ 3B:10-3, 3B:10-4)
Is there an informal procedure for appointment of executor or administrator?	No provision.
Can a nonresident serve?	An affiant may be a nonresident. (§§ 3B:10-3, 3B:10-4)
Can the nonresident act locally based on appointment in another state?	Yes. Both §§ 3B:10-3 and 3B:10-4 provide that a nonresident affiant, with written authorization of the surrogate, may execute the affidavit in the affiant's domicile before certain officers authorized by §§ 46:14-7 and 46:14-8. However, §§ 46:14-7 and 46:14-8 have both been repealed, and §§ 3B:10-3 and 3B:10-4 have not been amended to reflect the repeals. Note, however, that the Law Revision Commission Comment accompanying § 46:14-6.1 states that § 46:14-6.1 includes the same officers as repealed under §§ 46:14-7 and 46:14-8.
What does a transferor need so as to be relieved of liability if challenged by another person later on who claims the particular property (e.g., copy of affidavit)?	Payors are permanently discharged if they are presented a copy of the affidavit marked a true copy by the surrogate or the clerk of the Superior Court. (§ 3B:10-5)

New Mexico
Summary Administration Procedure for Small Estates

Who can initiate process?	*By Affidavit.* Person claiming to be successor of the decedent, defined in §45-1-201(A)(50) as "persons, other than creditors, who are entitled to property of a decedent under his will or the Uniform Probate Code." (§45-3-1201(A)) *Summary Administration.* Personal representative. (§45-3-1203)
Can it be used if claims outstanding?	*By Affidavit.* Yes. (§45-3-1201(A)) *Summary Administration.* Yes. (§45-3-1203)
Different rules if die testate or intestate?	*By Affidavit.* No provision. *Summary Administration.* No provision. Although these statutes do not expressly limit themselves to testate estates, the statutes are located in Article 3 of Chapter 45, which is entitled "Probate of Wills and Administration." No such procedures are discussed in Part 1 of Article 2, which deals with intestate succession.
Notice?	*By Affidavit.* No provision. *Summary Administration.* Personal representative must send a copy of the closing statement to several parties (see below) and must also provide a full accout in writing of the administration to the distributees whose interests are affected. (§45-3-1204(A)(3))
heirs	*Summary Administration.* Must send a copy of the closing statement to all distributees of the estate. (§45-3-1204(A)(3))
creditors	*Summary Administration.* Must send a copy of the closing statement to all creditors of whom he is aware whose claims are neither paid or barred. (§45-3-1204(A)(3)) Summary administration allows for disbursement without notice to creditors. (§45-3-1203)
others	*Summary Administration.* Must send a copy of the closing statement to all "other claimants" of whom he is aware whose claims are neither paid or barred. (§45-3-1204(A)(3))
Which of the following must be observed?	
hearing	No provision.
affidavit, petition, other	*By Affidavit.* Affidavit. (§45-3-1201) *Summary Administration.* Closing statement. (§45-3-1203)
bond	No provision.

What are basic contents of petition or affidavit?	*By Affidavit.* Affidavit must state that (1) the value of entire estate, wherever located, less liens and encumbrances, does not exceed $50,000; (2) 30 days have elapsed since death of decedent; (3) no application or petition for appointment of a personal representative is pending or has been granted in any jurisdiction; and (4) the claiming successor is entitled to payment or delivery of the property. (§ 45-3-1201(A)(1)-(4)) *Summary Administration.* Closing statement must state that "(1) to the best knowledge of the personal representative, the value of the entire estate, less liens and encumbrances, did not exceed the family allowance, personal property allowance, costs and expenses of administration, reasonably necessary medical and hospital expenses of the last illness of the decedent, and reasonable funeral expenses; (2) the personal representative has fully disbursed the estate to persons entitled thereto; and (3) the personal representative has sent a copy of the closing statement to all distributees of the estate and to all creditors or other claimants of whom he is aware whose claims are neither paid nor barred and has furnished a full account in writing of his administration to the distributees whose interests are affected." (§ 45-3-1204(A)(1)-(3))
Is procedure available in the case of nonresident decedents?	*By Affidavit.* No provision. *Summary Administration.* No provision.
Maximum allowable value of estate	*By Affidavit.* $50,000. (§ 45-3-1201(A)(1)) *Summary Administration.* Value of the entire estate, less liens and encumbrances, cannot exceed the family allowance, personal property allowance, costs and expenses of administration, reasonable and necessary medical and hospital expenses of the last illness of the decedent, and reasonable funeral expenses. (§ 45-3-1204(A)(1))
What property can be transferred by this means?	*By Affidavit.* Payment of debts, tangible personal property or instruments evidencing a debt, obligation, stock or chose in action belonging to the decedent. (§ 45-3-1201(A)) The affidavit may not be used to perfect title to real estate. (§ 45-3-1201(C)) *Summary Administration.* Entire estate. (§ 45-3-1203)
Special rules for certain assets (e.g., automobile)	*By Affidavit.* A transfer agent of any security shall change the registered ownership on the books of a corporation from the decedent to the successors upon the presentation of an affidavit. (§ 45-3-1201(B)) Affidavit may not be used to perfect title to real estate. (§ 45-3-1201(C)) *Summary Administration:* Homestead. (§ 45-3-1205)
Can the spouse or other person take summarily if under certain amount?	No provision.
Minimum period before filing allowed	*By Affidavit.* No filing required. See *Waiting period before authority to act.* *Summary Administration.* May file any time after disbursing and distributing estate. (§ 45-2-1203)

Rights/obligations of party with affidavit	*By Affidavit.* The affiant is (1) entitled to payment of debts and delivery of certain assets upon presentation of affidavit (§ 45-3-1201(A)); (2) can bring a proceeding to recover property if the other party refuses to recognize the affidavit (§ 45-3-1202); and (3) after payment is made, is answerable to any personal representative of the estate or any other person having a superior right (§ 45-3-1202). *Summary Administration.* No provision.
Are some creditors given special privileges/ preference (e.g., medical expenses, funeral expenses)?	*By Affidavit.* No provision. *Summary Administration.* Reasonable and necessary medical and hospital expenses of the last illness of the decedent and reasonable funeral expenses. (§ 45-3-1203)
Creditors' rights, if insufficient assets	*By Affidavit.* Payee is liable to any person with superior rights. (§ 45-3-1202) *Summary Administration.* No provision.
May the distribution of the estate proceed without appointment of personal representative?	*By Affidavit.* Yes. Affiant can only use procedure if no personal representative has been appointed and no appointment is pending. (§ 45-3-1201(A)(3)) *Summary Administration.* No. (§ 45-3-1203)
Must court approve affidavit?	*By Affidavit.* No provision. *Summary Administration.* No provision.
Waiting period before authority to act	*By Affidavit.* 30 days after date of death. (§ 45-3-1201(A)(2)) *Summary Administration.* May act immediately. (§ 45-3-1203)
With whom do you file petition or affidavit?	*By Affidavit.* No provision. *Summary Administration.* Verified closing statement is filed with the court. (§ 45-3-1204(A))
Is there an informal procedure for appointment of executor or administrator?	Yes. (§ § 45-3-301, 45-3-307–311)
Can a nonresident serve?	Yes. "If no local administration or application or petition therefor is pending in New Mexico, a domiciliary foreign personal representative may file with the court of a county in which property belonging to the decedent is located authenticated copies of his appointment and of any official bond he has given and a statement of the domiciliary foreign personal representative's address." (§ 45-4-204)
Can the nonresident act locally based on appointment in another state?	If there is no local administration and the domiciliary foreign personal representative files authenticated copies of appointment and official bond with the court, such person "may exercise as to assets in New Mexico all [of the] powers of a local representative . . . subject to conditions imposed upon nonresidents generally." (§ § 45-4-204, 45-4-205)
What does a transferor need so as to be relieved of liability if challenged by another person later on who claims the particular property (e.g., copy of affidavit)?	*By Affidavit.* Payor is discharged and released to the same extent as if he or she dealt with a personal representative of the decedent when he or she pays after being presented the affidavit. (§ 45-3-1202) *Summary Administration.* No provision.

New York
Settlement of Small Estates

Who can initiate process?	A voluntary administrator as defined in Surr. Ct. Proc. Act § 1301(2). See also Surr. Ct. Proc. Act § 1303.
Can it be used if claims outstanding?	Yes. The voluntary administrator can settle claims against the estate up to $100,000. (Surr. Ct. Proc. Act § 1306). See also Surr. Ct. Proc. Act. § 1301.
Different rules if die testate or intestate?	If the deceased dies intestate, the right to act as a voluntary administrator follows a line of succession based on the closeness of relation to the decedent, starting with a surviving adult spouse. (Surr. Ct. Proc. Act § 1303(a)) If the decedent dies testate, the named executor or alternate executor has the first right to act as voluntary administrator, and if this person renounces or fails to qualify, any adult person who would be entitled to petition for letters of administration may act as voluntary administrator. (Surr. Ct. Proc. Act § 1303(b))
Notice?	The clerk of the Surrogate's Court must mail to each distributee, other than those who have renounced the right to act, and to beneficiaries listed in the affidavit, notice of the proceeding by postcard or letter. (Surr. Ct. Proc. Act § 1304(4))
heirs	No provision.
creditors	No provision.
others	No provision.
Which of the following must be observed?	
hearing	No provision.
affidavit, petition, other	Affidavit and certified copy of death certificate. (Surr. Ct. Proc. Act § 1304(3))
bond	No. (Surr. Ct. Proc. Act § 1304(2))
What are basic contents of petition or affidavit?	Affidavit is to be in the form of Official Form No. 5, which is appended to Article 13 of the Surrogate Court Procedure Act, and is filed with a certified copy of the death certificate. (Surr. Ct. Proc. Act § 1304(3))
Is procedure available in the case of nonresident decedents?	Yes. (Surr. Ct. Proc. Act § 1301(1))
Maximum allowable value of estate	Personal property with a gross value of $100,000. (Surr. Ct. Proc. Act § 1301(1))
What property can be transferred by this means?	Personal property only. (Surr. Ct. Proc. Act § 1302)
Special rules for certain assets (e.g., automobile)	No provision.
Can the spouse or other person take summarily if under certain amount?	No provision.
Minimum period before filing allowed	None. (Surr. Ct. Proc. Act § 1304(1))

Rights/obligations of party with affidavit	Rights: (1) may maintain an action to recover property if payor refuses to pay after presentation of a certificate and receipt (Surr. Ct. Proc. Act § 1306(1)); (2) may sell any personal property coming into his or her possession for reasonable value (Surr. Ct. Proc. Act § 1306(2)); (3) rights, powers, and duties with respect to personal property of an administrator duly appointed for the estate (Surr. Ct. Proc. Act § 1306(3)). Obligations: (1) deposit all money received in an estate bank account and pay expenses of the decedent before distributing balance to persons entitled (Surr. Ct. Proc. Act § 1307(1)); (2) account to the court for all personal property of the decedent received and disbursed (Surr. Ct. Proc. Act § 1307(2)).
Are some creditors given special privileges/ preference (e.g., medical expenses, funeral expenses)?	Funeral expenses. (Surr. Ct. Proc. Act § 1307(1))
Creditors' rights, if insufficient assets	If an issue arises about sufficiency of the assets to satisfy all of the decedent's debts and administration expenses, claimants' priorities are determined under Surr. Ct. Proc. Act § 1811. (Surr. Ct. Proc. Act § 1307, Practice Commentaries)
May the distribution of the estate proceed without appointment of personal representative?	Yes. (Surr. Ct. Proc. Act § § 1301(2), 1303, 1304)
Must court approve affidavit?	No provision.
Waiting period before authority to act	None. (Surr. Ct. Proc. Act § 1304(1))
With whom do you file petition or affidavit?	Clerk of the decedent's domicile or, if decedent is a nondomiciliary, of the county in which his personal property is located. (Surr. Ct. Proc. Act § 1304(3))
Is there an informal procedure for appointment of executor or administrator?	Yes, voluntary administrator. (Surr. Ct. Proc. Act § § 1301(2), 1304(3))
Can a nonresident serve?	Yes. If a nominated executor requests preliminary letters and qualifies under Surr. Ct. Proc. Act § 708, the court must appoint him. (Surr. Ct. Proc. Act § 1412, Practice Commentaries) There is no residency requirement in Surr. Ct. Proc. Act § 708. With intestate decedents, Surr. Ct. Proc. Act § 1001 does not expressly disqualify nonresidents, but an example in the Practice Commentaries to Surr. Ct. Proc. Act § 1001 suggests nondomiciliary alien distributees are not eligible.
Can the nonresident act locally based on appointment in another state?	Yes, provided non-domiciliary debtors, transfer agents, safe deposit companies, banks, trust companies or persons holding personal property in the domiciliary state recognize and pay or transfer the personal property of a New York domiciliary, pursuant to a short certificate of court as made under the Surr. Ct. Proc. Act. (Surr. Ct. Proc. Act § 1309(2))

What does a transferor need so as to be relieved of liability if challenged by another person later on who claims the particular property (e.g., copy of affidavit)?

Delivery by a voluntary administrator to the debtor of the short form certificate of the court, the receipt of the administrator, and the surrender of any evidentiary document shall constitute a complete release and discharge. (Surr. Ct. Proc. Act § 1305)

North Carolina
Small Estates

Who can initiate process?	If decedent died intestate, the public administrator appointed pursuant to § 28A-12-1, or an heir or creditor of the decedent, not disqualified under § 28A-4-2. (§ 28A-25-1(a)) If decedent died testate, proceedings can be initiated by a public administrator, person named or designated as executor in the will, a devisee, heir, or creditor of the decedent not disqualified under § 28-A-4-2 (§ 28A-25-1.1(a)) Whether decedent died testate or intestate, there is a special provision if the affiant is a surviving spouse and the sole heir of the decedent. (§ 28A-25-1.1(a))
Can it be used if claims outstanding?	Yes. (§ 28A-25-3(a)(1)(b))
Different rules if die testate or intestate?	Yes. The differences relate only to who may initiate the process (see *Who can initiate process?*) and particular details required to be in the affidavit (see *What are basic contents of petition or affidavit?*).
Notice?	Prior to recovery of any assets of the decedent, the clerk of the superior court of the county where decedent had his domicile at the time of his death mails a copy of the affidavit to persons shown in the affidavit as entitled to the property. (§§ 28A-25-1(b), 28A-25-1.1(b))
heirs	No provision.
creditors	No provision.
others	No provision.
Which of the following must be observed?	
hearing	No provision.
affidavit, petition, other	Affidavit. (§§ 28A-25-1(a), 28A-25-1.1(a))
bond	No provision.

What are basic contents of petition or affidavit?

If decedent dies intestate: (1) name and address of the affiant and that he or she is a public administrator or an heir or creditor of the decedent; (2) the name of the decedent and his residence at time of death; (3) the date and place of death of the decedent; (4) that 30 days have elapsed since the death of the decedent; (5) that the value of all the personal property owned by the estate of the decedent, less liens and encumbrances thereon, does not exceed $20,000; (6) that no application or petition for appointment of a personal representative is pending or has been granted in any jurisdiction; (7) names and addresses of those persons who are entitled, under the provisions of the Intestate Succession Act, to the personal property of the decedent and their relationship, if any, to the decedent; and (8) a description sufficient to identify each tract of real property owned by the decedent at the time of his death. (§ 28A-25-1(a))

If decedent dies testate: (1) the name and address of the affiant and the fact that he or she is the public administrator, or a person named or designated as executor in the will, or devisee or an heir or creditor of the decedent; (2) the name of the decedent and his residence at time of death; (3) the date and place of death of the decedent; (4) that 30 days have elapsed since the death of the decedent; (5) that the decedent died testate leaving personal property, less liens and encumbrances thereon, not exceeding $20,000 in value; (6) that the decedent's will has been admitted to probate in the court of proper county and a duly certified copy of the will has been recorded in each county in which is located any real property owned by the decedent at the time of his death; (7) that a certified copy of the decedent's will is attached to the affidavit; (8) that no application or petition for appointment of a personal representative is pending or has been granted in any jurisdiction; (9) the names and addresses of those persons who are entitled, under the provisions of the will, or if applicable, of the Intestate Succession Act, to the property of the decedent and their relationship, if any, to the decedent; and (10) a description sufficient to identify each tract of real property owned by the decedent at the time of his death. (§ 28A-25-1.1(a))

If the affiant is a surviving spouse and sole heir of the decedent: (1) name and address of the affiant and the fact that he or she is the surviving spouse and is entitled, under the provisions of the Intestate Succession Act or under the provisons of the decedent's will, to all of the property of the decedent; (2) that the value of all of the personal property owned by the estate of the decedent, less liens and encumbrances thereon, does not exceed $30,000; and (3) the information required in subdivisions (2), (3), (4), (6), and (8) of N.C. Gen. Stat. § 28A-25-1(a), if the decedent died intestate, or the information required in subdivisions (2), (3), (4), (6), (7), (8), and (10) of N.C. Gen. Stat. Ann. § 28A-25-1.1(a), if the decedent died testate. (§§ 28A-25-1(a), 28A-25-1.1(a))

Is procedure available in the case of nonresident decedents?	No. (§ § 28A-25-1(b), 28A-25-1.1(b))
Maximum allowable value of estate	Personal property, less liens and encumbrances, valued at $20,000. (§ § 28A-25-1(a), 28A-25-1.1(a)) The maximum is $30,000 if the affiant is the surviving spouse and sole heir of the decedent. (§ § 28A-25-1(a), 28A-25-1.1(a))
What property can be transferred by this means?	Payment of indebtedness, tangible personal property or an instrument evidencing a debt, obligation, stock or chose in action. (§ § 28A-25-1(a), 28A-25-1.1(a))
Special rules for certain assets (e.g., automobile)	For motor vehicles, checking and savings accounts, and stocks or securities, presentation of an affidavit shall be sufficient to require transfer. (§ § 28A-25-1(c), 28A-25-1.1(c))
Can the spouse or other person take summarily if under certain amount?	Yes. (§ § 28A-25-1(a), 28A-25-1.1(a))
Minimum period before filing allowed	30 days from date of death. (§ § 28A-25-1(a)(4), 28A-25-1.1(a)(4))
Rights/obligations of party with affidavit	Affiant is entitled, upon presentation of the affidavit, to any property or contract right owned by decedent at the time of his death. (§ § 28A-25-1(c), 28A-25-1.1(c)) The affiant may bring an action to compel payment if a person to whom an affidavit is delivered refuses to pay. (§ 28A-25-2) The affiant must disburse and distribute collected personal property in the proper order (§ 28A-25-3(a)(1)), and file an affidavit with the clerk of superior court that he has collected the personal property of the decedent and describe the manner in which he has disbursed and distributed the personal property. (§ 28A-25-3(a)(2)) If it appears to be in the best interest of the estate to sell, lease, mortgage any real property, the affiant must petition the clerk of superior court for the appointment of a personal representative to conclude the administration of the decedent's estate pursuant to § 28A-25-5. (§ 28A-25-3(b))
Are some creditors given special privileges/ preference (e.g., medical expenses, funeral expenses)?	Creditors must be paid in the order prescribed in § 28A-19-6. (§ 28A-25-3(a)(1)(b))
Creditors' rights, if insufficient assets	Payee is answerable to any person having an interest in the estate. (§ 28A-25-2)
May the distribution of the estate proceed without appointment of personal representative?	Yes. There must not be an application or petition for appointment of a personal representative pending or granted in any jurisdiction. (§ § 28A-25-1(a)(6), 28A-25-1.1(a)(8))
Must court approve affidavit?	No provision.
Waiting period before authority to act	30 days after date of death. (§ § 28A-25-1(a)(4), 28A-25-1.1(a)(4))
With whom do you file petition or affidavit?	The office of the clerk of superior court of the county where the decedent had his domicile at the time of his death. (§ § 28A-25-1(b), 28A-25-1.1(b))

Is there an informal procedure for appointment of executor or administrator?	Yes. Any interested person, including the affiant, can petition the clerk of superior court for the appointment of a personal representative or collector to conclude administration of the estate. (§ 28A-25-5)
Can a nonresident serve?	Yes. The nonresident must appoint a resident agent to accept service of process in all actions or proceedings with respect to the estate and file such appointment with the court. (§ 28A-4-2(4))
Can the nonresident act locally based on appointment in another state?	No provision.
What does a transferor need so as to be relieved of liability if challenged by another person later on who claims the particular property (e.g., copy of affidavit)?	Payor is discharged and released to the same extent as if he dealt with a duly qualified personal representative of the decedent if presented with a proper affidavit. Payor need not inquire into the truth of the affidavit. (§ 28A-25-2)

North Dakota
Summary Administration Procedure for Small Estates

Who can initiate process?	*By Affidavit.* Any person claiming to be the successor of the decedent or a person claiming to have incurred reasonable expense by providing funeral services for the decedent. (§ 29A-3-1201(a)). *Summary Administration.* Personal representative. (§ § 30.1-23-03, 30.1-23-04)
Can it be used if claims outstanding?	*By Affidavit.* Yes. (§ 30.1-23-01(1)) *Summary Administration.* Yes. (§ 30.1-23-03)
Different rules if die testate or intestate?	*By Affidavit.* Although these statutes do not expressly limit themselves to testate estates, the statutes are located in Article 3, which is entitled "Probate of Wills and Administration." No such procedures are discussed in Article 2, which deals with intestate succession. *Summary Administration.* Although these statutes do not expressly limit themselves to testate estates, the statutes are located in Article 3, which is entitled "Probate of Wills and Administration." No such procedures are discussed in Article 2, which deals with intestate succession.
Notice?	*By Affidavit:* No provision.
heirs	*Summary Administration.* Must send copy of closing statement to all distributees of the estate. (§ 30.1-23-04(1)(c))
creditors	*Summary Administration.* Must send copy of closing statement to all creditors of whom the personal representative is aware whose claims are neither barred nor paid. (§ 30.1-23-04(1)(c)) Under summary administration, the personal representative may disburse without giving notice to creditors. (§ 30.1-23-03)
others	*Summary Administration.* Must send copy of closing statement to all "other claimants of whom the personal representative is aware whose claims are neither paid nor barred . . . " (§ 30.1-23-04(1)(c))
Which of the following must be observed?	
hearing	No provision.
affidavit, petition, other	*By Affidavit.* Affidavit. (§ 30.1-23-01(1)) *Summary Administration.* Closing statement. (§ 30.1-23-04(1))
bond	No provision.

What are basic contents of petition or affidavit?	*By Affidavit.* (1) That the value of the entire estate, wherever located, less liens and encumbrances, does not exceed $50,000; (2) that 30 days have elapsed since death of decedent; (3) that no application or petition for the appointment of a personal representative is pending or has been granted in any jurisdiction; and (4) that the claiming successor is entitled to payment or delivery of the property; and (5) a description sufficient to identify each tract of real property owned by the decedent at the time of the decedent's death. (§ 30.1-23-01(1)(a)-(e)) *Summary Administration.* Closing statement must state that (1) to the best knowledge of personal representative, the value of the entire estate, less liens and encumbrances, did not exceed the homestead, plus exempt property, family allowance, costs and expenses of administration, reasonable funeral expenses, and reasonable and necessary medical and hospital expenses of the last illness of the decedent; (2) personal representative has fully administered the estate by disbursing and distributing it to the persons entitled thereto; and (3) personal representative has sent a copy of the closing statement to all distributees and to all creditors of whom the personal representative is aware whose claims are neither barred nor paid and has furnished a full account in writing of the administration to distributees whose interests are affected. (§ 30.1-23-04(1)(a)-(c))
Is procedure available in the case of nonresident decedents?	*By Affidavit.* Yes. (§ 30.1-23-02, Editorial Board Comment) *Summary Administration.* No provision.
Maximum allowable value of estate	*By Affidavit.* $50,000. (§ 30.1-23-01(1)(a)) *Summary Administration.* The value of entire estate, less liens and encumbrances, must not exceed the homestead, plus exempt property, family allowance, costs and expenses of administration, reasonable funeral expenses, and reasonable and necessary medical and hospital expenses of the last illness of the decedent. (§ 30.1-23-03)
What property can be transferred by this means?	*By Affidavit.* Payment of indebtedness, tangible personal property, real property, or an instrument evidencing a debt, obligation, stock, or chose in action. (§ 30.1-23-01(1)) *Summary Administration.* Entire estate. (§ 30.1-23-04(1)(a))
Special rules for certain assets (e.g., automobile)	*Affidavit.* "[T]ransfer agent of any security shall change the registered ownership on the books of a corporation . . . upon presentation of an affidavit." (§ 30.1-23-01(2)) *Summary Administration.* No provision.
Can the spouse or other person take summarily if under certain amount?	No provision.
Minimum period before filing allowed	*By Affidavit.* No filing required under affidavit procedure. See *Waiting period before authority to act.* *Summary Administration.* Entire estate must have been inventoried and appraised. (§ 30.1-23-03) May file any time after disbursement and distribution of the estate. (§ 30.1-23-04(1))

Rights/obligations of party with affidavit	*By Affidavit.* Affiant is entitled to payment from person possessing property belonging to the decedent. (§ 30.1-23-01) The affiant can bring an action if a party refuses to pay upon presentation of the affidavit. Affiant is accountable to any person having a superior right. (§ 30.1-23-02) *Summary Administration.* No provision.
Are some creditors given special privileges/ preference (e.g., medical expenses, funeral expenses)?	*By Affidavit.* No provision. *Summary Administration.* Reasonable funeral expenses and reasonable and necessary medical and hospital expenses of the last illness of the decedent. (§ 30.1-23-03)
Creditors' rights, if insufficient assets	*By Affidavit.* Payees are answerable to any person having a superior right. (§ 30.1-23-02) *Summary Administration.* No provision.
May the distribution of the estate proceed without appointment of personal representative?	*By Affidavit.* Yes. There must not be an application or petition for appointment of a personal representative pending or granted in any jurisdiction. (§ 30.1-23-01(1)(c)) *Summary Administration.* No. (§ 30.1-23-03)
Must court approve affidavit?	*By Affidavit.* No provision. *Summary Administration.* No provision.
Waiting period before authority to act	*By Affidavit.* 30 days after date of death. (§ 30.1-23-01(1)(b)) *Summary Administration.* May act immediately. (§ 30.1-23-03)
With whom do you file petition or affidavit?	*By Affidavit.* No provision. *Summary Administration.* Verified closing statement is filed with the court. (§ 30.1-23-04(1))
Is there an informal procedure for appointment of executor or administrator?	Yes. (§ § 30.1-14-01, 30.1-14-07–11)
Can a nonresident serve?	Yes. (§ 30.1-24-01–08)
Can the nonresident act locally based on appointment in another state?	Yes. If there is no local administration and the domiciliary foreign personal representative has filed in a local court, such person may exercise as to assets in North Dakota all powers of a local personal representative, subject to conditions imposed upon nonresidents generally. (§ § 30.1-24-06, 30.1-24-05)
What does a transferor need so as to be relieved of liability if challenged by another person later on who claims the particular property (e.g., copy of affidavit)?	*By Affidavit.* Payor is discharged to the same extent as if the person dealt with a personal representative. (§ 30.1-23-02) *Summary Administration.* No provision.

Ohio
Release from Administration

Who can initiate process?	Any interested party. (§ 2113.03(B))
Can it be used if claims outstanding?	No provision.
Different rules if die testate or intestate?	"If the decedent died testate, the will shall be presented for probate, and, if admitted to probate, the court may relieve the estate from administration and order distribution of the estate under the will." (§ 2113.03(F))
Notice?	All interested parties must be given notice by publication in a newspaper of general circulation in the county, unless notices are waived or found unnecessary (§ 2113.03(B))
heirs	Surviving spouse and heirs at law must be given notice in advance of filing application for release from administration. The length of time prior is set by the probate court. (§ 2113.03(B))
creditors	No provision.
Which of the following must be observed?	
hearing	No provision.
affidavit, petition, other	Application. (§ 2113.03(B))
bond	No provision.
What are basic contents of petition or affidavit?	Application must satisfy court that § 2113.03(A) requirement is met. (§ 2113.03(B)) See *Maximum allowable value of estate.*
Is procedure available in the case of nonresident decedents?	No provision.
Maximum allowable value of estate	(1) $35,000; or (2) $100,000 if: (a) decedent devised and bequeathed all assets to a person named in the will as a spouse and is survived by that person; or (b) decedent is survived by a spouse who married decedent in accordance with Chapter 3101 of the Ohio Code or a similar foreign law, decedent died without a valid will, and the spouse gets all assets under § 2105.06 or under a combination of §§ 2105.06 and 2106.13. (§ 2113.03(A))
What property can be transferred by this means?	Real and personal. (§ 2113.03(B))
Special rules for certain assets (e.g., automobile)	No provision.
Can the spouse or other person take summarily if under certain amount?	Yes. (§ 2113.031(B)(1)-(2))
Minimum period before filing allowed	An interested party can only apply after proper notice has been given. (§ 2113.03(B))
Rights/obligations of party with affidavit	No provision.
Are some creditors given special privileges/ preference (e.g., medical expenses, funeral expenses)?	No provision.

Creditors' rights, if insufficient assets	"Any delivery of personal property or transfer of real property pursuant to an order relieving an estate from administration is made subject to the limitations pertaining to the claims of creditors." (§ 2113.03(H))
May the distribution of the estate proceed without appointment of personal representative?	Yes. (§ 2113.03(B))
Must court approve affidavit?	Court may approve after being satisfied that § 2113.03(A) is satisfied. (§ 2113.03(B))
Waiting period before authority to act	No provision. See *Minimum period before filing allowed*. (§ 2113.03(B))
With whom do you file petition or affidavit?	The Probate Court. (§ 2113.03(B))
Is there an informal procedure for appointment of executor or administrator?	If there is a "delay in granting letters testamentary or of administration, the probate court may appoint a special administrator" who functions until an executor or administrator is appointed. (§ 2113.15)
Can a nonresident serve?	A nonresident cannot administer an intestate estate. (§ 2113.06) If the decedent died testate, the probate court shall issue letters testamentary to the executor named in the will, nominated by holders of a power as described in § 2107.65, or to the executor named in the will and to a coexecutor nominated by holders of such a power. (§ 2113.05)
Can the nonresident act locally based on appointment in another state?	No provision.
What does a transferor need so as to be relieved of liability if challenged by another person later on who claims the particular property (e.g., copy of affidavit)?	No provision.

Oklahoma
Dispensing with Regular Proceedings; Petition for Summary Administration

Who can initiate process?	*Dispensing with Regular Proceedings.* Personal representative. (58 § 241(A)) *Petition for Summary Administration.* Any interested person. (58 § 245(A))
Can it be used if claims outstanding?	*Dispensing with Regular Proceedings.* Yes. (58 § 241(C)) *Petition for Summary Administration.* Yes. (58 § 245(B)(7))
Different rules if die testate or intestate?	*Dispensing with Regular Proceedings.* No provision. Although these statutes do not expressly limit themselves to testate estates, the statutes are located in Title 58, which is entitled "Probate Procedure." *Petition for Summary Administration.* Yes. See *What are basic contents of petition or affidavit?*
Notice?	*Dispensing with Regular Proceedings.* Notice to creditors and all persons interested in the estate. (58 § 241(C)) *Petition for Summary Administration.* Notice to creditors and notice of hearing upon petition for summary administration and final accounting, determination of heirship, distribution and discharge must be combined in one notice filed with the petition. (58 § 246(B)) Within 10 days of filing of the petition and combined notice, notice of the petition, notice to creditors, and notice of final accounting, determination of heirship, distribution and discharge must be published once a week for two consecutive weeks in a newspaper that is authorized by law to publish legal notices and published in the county where the petition is filed. If no newspaper, then it must be posted in three public places in the county, including the courthouse. (58 § 246(C))
heirs	*Dispensing with Regular Proceedings.* Notice must be mailed to all interested persons at their respective last-known addresses not less than ten days prior to date of hearing. (58 § 241(C)) *Petition for Summary Administration.* No provision.
creditors	*Dispensing with Regular Proceedings.* Notice of hearing must be published once each week for two consecutive weeks in a generally circulated newspaper published in filing county, or if there is no such newspaper, notice shall be published in an adjoining county having a legal newspaper. (58 § 241(C)) *Petition for Summary Administration.* "Combined notice" must be mailed to all creditors of the decedent. (58 § 246(B)-(C)) To preserve a claim not shown in a petition a creditor must present the claim to the personal representative no more than 30 days following the filing of the petition and combined notice. (§ 246(B))

others	*Dispensing with Regular Proceedings.* No provision. *Petition for Summary Administration.* "Combined notice" must be sent to all interested persons at their last known addresses within ten days of filing the petition. (58 § 246(B), (C))
Which of the following must be observed?	
hearing	*Dispensing with Regular Proceedings.* Yes. (58 § 241(D)) *Petition for Summary Administration.* Yes. (58 §§ 246(D), 247)
affidavit, petition, other	*Dispensing with Regular Proceedings.* Petition for probate (58 § 241(A)). *Petition for Summary Administration.* Petition (58 § 245)
bond	*Dispensing with Regular Proceedings.* Yes. Initially the bond is required. (58 § 171) After the personal representative has been appointed, and notice has been given, the court will discharge the personal representative and sureties from the personal representative's bond, unless the court defers such discharge as necessary or desirable. (58 § 241(D)) *Petition for Summary Administration.* Discretion of the court. (58 § 245(D))
What are basic contents of petition or affidavit?	*Dispensing with Regular Proceedings.* No provision. *Petition for Summary Administration.* Petition must state (1) interest of petitioner; (2) name, age, date of death of decedent, county of decedent's domicile at time of death; (3) names, ages, and last-known addresses of the administrators, executors, nonpetitioning conominees, heirs, legatees and devisees of the decedent; (4) names and last-known addresses of all known creditors of the decedent; (5) probable value and character of the property of the estate and the legal description of all real property owned by the decedent in Oklahoma; (6) whether an application or petition for the appointment of a personal representative is pending or has been granted in any jurisdiction; (7) a statement of the relief requested; and (8) if the decedent died intestate, the petitioners diligently searched for and failed to find a will. (58 § 245(B)) In addition, if decedent died testate, (1) a copy of the will must be attached and petition must state (a) the petitioner, to the best of their knowledge, believes the will to have been validly executed and (b) the petitioner is unaware of any instrument revoking the will, and believes that the instrument attached to the application is the decedent's last will; and (2) the petition must state whether the attached will has been admitted to probate in any other jurisdiction. (58 § 245(B))
Is procedure available in the case of nonresident decedents?	*Dispensing with Regular Proceedings.* No provision. *Petition for Summary Administration.* Yes. (§ 245(A)(3))

Maximum allowable value of estate	*Dispensing with Regular Proceedings.* $150,000 of real and personal property. (58 § 241(A)) *Petition for Summary Administration.* $200,000. (58 § 245(A)(1))
What property can be transferred by this means?	*Dispensing with Regular Proceedings.* Real and personal. (58 § 241(B)) *Petition for Summary Administration.* Entire estate. (58 § 245(B)(8)) ("the estate")
Special rules for certain assets (e.g., automobile)	*Dispensing with Regular Proceedings.* No provision. *Petition for Summary Administration.* No provision.
Can the spouse or other person take summarily if under certain amount?	*Dispensing with Regular Proceedings.* No provision. *Petition for Summary Administration.* No provision.
Minimum period before filing allowed	*Dispensing with Regular Proceedings.* Court must be satisfied with estate valuation before personal representative may apply for summary administration. (58 § 241(B)) *Petition for Summary Administration.* No provision.
Rights/obligations of party with affidavit	*Dispensing with Regular Proceedings.* No provision. *Petition for Summary Administration.* No provision.
Are some creditors given special privileges/ preference (e.g., medical expenses, funeral expenses)?	*Dispensing with Regular Proceedings.* Funeral expenses, last illness medical expenses, administration expenses, and allowed claims. (58 § 241(D)) *Petition for Summary Administration.* Funeral expenses, last illness medical expenses, and administration expenses and allowed claims. (58 § 247(A))
Creditors' rights, if insufficient assets	*Dispensing with Regular Proceedings.* Liens upon property for estate or transfer taxes are fully protected (58 § 241(B)); otherwise, no provision. *Petition for Summary Administration.* Creditors can object at the hearing if they file in time. (58 § 247(A))
May the distribution of the estate proceed without appointment of personal representative?	*Dispensing with Regular Proceedings.* No. (58 § 241(A) & (B)) *Petition for Summary Administration.* Yes. (58 § 245(A))
Must court approve affidavit?	*Dispensing with Regular Proceedings.* No provision. *Petition for Summary Administration.* Court must approve petition. (58 § 247(A))
Waiting period before authority to act	*Dispensing with Regular Proceedings.* No waiting period stated following the hearing. Hearing must be at least 35 days after first publication of notice. (58 § 241(D)) *Petition for Summary Administration.* Hearing must be at least 45 days following the first publication of notice. (58 § 246(D)).
With whom do you file petition or affidavit?	*Dispensing with Regular Proceedings.* Petition and application are filed with court. (58 § 241(A) & (B)) *Petition for Summary Administration.* No provision.
Is there an informal procedure for appointment of executor or administrator?	*Dispensing with Regular Proceedings.* No provision. *Petition for Summary Administration.* No provision.

Can a nonresident serve?	*Dispensing with Regular Proceedings.* Yes, but nonresident must appoint an agent to accept service of legal process that resides in the county where the nonresident is appointed personal representative. (58 § 162) *Petition for Summary Administration.* Yes. (58 § 262)
Can the nonresident act locally based on appointment in another state?	*Dispensing with Regular Proceedings.* No provision. *Petition for Summary Administration.* Yes. (58 § 262)
What does a transferor need so as to be relieved of liability if challenged by another person later on who claims the particular property (e.g., copy of affidavit)?	*Dispensing with Regular Proceedings.* No provision. *Petition for Summary Administration.* No provision.

Oregon
Small Estates

Can initiate process?	One or more of the claiming successors, as defined in Or. Rev. Stat. § 114.505, or, if decedent died testate, any person named as personal representative in the will. (§ 114.515(1)) Also, the Director of Human Services, Director of the Oregon Health Authority or an attorney in certain specified circumstances. (*Id.*) A creditor may file an affidavit if a decedent dies intestate and without heirs and if the creditor has received written authorization from an estate administrator of the Department of State Lands who has been appointed. (§ 114.520(1))
Can it be used if claims outstanding?	Yes, but affiant must pay claims. (§ 114.545(1)(c))
Different rules if die testate or intestate?	Who can initiate the process is differerent depending on whether the decedent died testate or intestate. See *Who can initiate process?* "Claiming Successors" has different definitions if the decedent dies testate or intestate. (§ 114.505(2))
Notice?	The affiant must, within 30 days after filing, "mail, deliver or cause to be recorded each instrument which the affidavit states will be mailed, delivered or recorded." (§ 114.545(1)(b))
heirs	See *Notice?*
creditors	See *Notice?*
others	See *Notice?*
Which of the following must be observed?	
hearing	No provision.
affidavit, petition, other	Affidavit. (§ 114.515)
bond	No provision.

What are basic contents of petition or affidavit?	(1) Name, age, domicile, address, and social security number of the decedent; (2) date and place of decedent's death with a copy of the death certificate attached; (3) fair market value of all property of the estate, with a legal description of real property; (4) statement that no application or petition for the appointment of a personal representative has been granted in Oregon; (5) whether decedent died testate or intestate, and if testate, attached copy of the will (6) list of heirs and their interest in property described in the affidavit and that a copy of the affidavit will be delivered or mailed to each heir; (7) list of devisees if decedent died testate, and their interest in property described in the affidavit and state that a copy of the affidavit has been delivered or mailed to each devisee; (8) the interest in the property described in the affidavit to which each heir or devisee is entitled and the interest, if any, that will escheat; (9) statement that reasonable efforts have been made to ascertain creditors and estimated amounts of the claims; (10) list of creditors known with unpaid expenses and claims against the estate and state that a copy of the affidavit has been delivered or mailed to each creditor who has not been paid in full; (11) list of persons known to assert a against the estate and estimated amount of the claims; (12) statement that a copy of the affidavit will be mailed or delivered to the Department of Human Services or to the Oregon Health Authority; (13) statement that claims not listed or disputed will be barred unless presented to affiant in four months or if a personal representative is appointed; and (14) if affiant lists one or more claims that affiant disputes, statement that such claim(s) are barred unless (a) petition for summary determination is filed within 4 months, or (b) a personal representative is appointed within the time allowed under ORS § 114.555. (§ 114.525(1)-(14))
Is procedure available in the case of nonresident decedents?	No provision.
Maximum allowable value of estate	Maximum fair market value of total estate of $275,000; maximum personal property fair market value of $75,000; and maximum real property fair market value of $200,000. (§ 114.515(2))
What property can be transferred by this means?	Personal and real property. (§ 114.545(1)(f)) See also § 114.515(2).
Special rules for certain assets (e.g., automobile)	No provision.
Can the spouse or other person take summarily if under certain amount?	If, after four months from the first publication of notice to interested parties, it appears that reasonable provision for support of the spouse and/or dependent children of decedent "warrants that the whole estate, after payment of claims, taxes, and expenses of administration, be set apart for such support, the court may so order. There shall be no further proceeding in the administration of the estate, and the estate shall be summarily closed." (§ 114.085)

Minimum period before filing allowed	30 days after date of death. (§ 114.515(3))
Rights/obligations of party with affidavit	*Rights:* (1) entitled to delivery of personal property of the decedent upon presenting a certified copy of the affidavit (§ 114.535(1)); (2) may bring an action to recover if a person to whom an affidavit is delivered refuses to pay (§ 114.535(6)). *Duties:* (1) take control of property of the estate (§ 114.545(1)(a)); (2) "mail, deliver or cause to be recorded each instrument which the affidavit states will be mailed, delivered or recorded." (§ 114.545(1)(b)); (3) pay claims and expenses (§ 114.545(1)(c)); (4) record deeds executed by the affiant or claiming successor (§ 114.545(3)).
Are some creditors given special privileges/ preference (e.g., medical expenses, funeral expenses)?	No provision.
Creditors' rights, if insufficient assets	Affiants are answerable to creditors whose claims must be paid. (§ 114.545(2))
May the distribution of the estate proceed without appointment of personal representative?	Yes. Must proceed without personal representative. (§ 114.525(4))
Must court approve affidavit?	No provision.
Waiting period before authority to act	Affiant may not file affidavit until 30 days after the death of the decedent. (§ 114.515(3)) Affiant cannot collect personal property until 10 days after filing the affidavit. (§ 114.535(1)) Affiant may convey real or personal property with the consent of heir/devisee, any time within four months after affidavit is filed. (§ 114.545(1)(f)) If personal representative not appointed by the end of four months after the affidavit has been filed, it is automatically conveyed to those entitled to it. (§ 114.555)
With whom do you file petition or affidavit?	"[C]lerk of the probate court in any county where there is venue for a proceeding seeking the appointment of a personal representative for the estate." (§ 114.515(1))
Is there an informal procedure for appointment of executor or administrator?	No provision.
Can a nonresident serve?	Generally, a nonresident can be a personal representative. (§ 113.095) There is no exclusion in § 113.085, which lists the preferences in appointing the personal representative. Nonresident personal representatives also are not excluded in § 113.095, which lists qualifications for personal representatives.
Can the nonresident act locally based on appointment in another state?	No provision.
What does a transferor need so as to be relieved of liability if challenged by another person later on who claims the particular property (e.g., copy of affidavit)?	"Any person that pays, transfers, delivers, provides access to or allows possession of property of a decedent in the manner provided in this section is discharged and released from any liability or responsibility for the property in the same manner and with the same effect as if the property had been transferred, delivered, or paid to a personal representative." (§ 114.535(4))

Pennsylvania
Settlement of Small Estates on Petition

Who can initiate process?	Any party in interest. (20 § 3102)
Can it be used if claims outstanding?	No provision.
Different rules if die testate or intestate?	No provision.
Notice?	All notice is at the discretion of the court. (20 § 3102)
heirs	No provision.
creditors	No provision.
others	No provision.
Which of the following must be observed?	
hearing	No provision.
affidavit, petition, other	Petition. (20 § 3102)
bond	No provision.
What are basic contents of petition or affidavit?	No provision.
Is procedure available in the case of nonresident decedents?	Not available for nondomiciliaries. (20 § 3102)
Maximum allowable value of estate	$50,000, excluding real property and payments to family and funeral directors, but including personal property claimed as family exemption. (20 § 3102)
What property can be transferred by this means?	Personal property. (20 § 3102)
Special rules for certain assets (e.g., automobile)	No provision.
Can the spouse or other person take summarily if under certain amount?	No provision.
Minimum period before filing allowed	No provision.
Rights/obligations of party with affidavit	Right to receive the property as though there had been a decree of distribution after an accounting. (20 § 3102)
Are some creditors given special privileges/ preference (e.g., medical expenses, funeral expenses)?	Funeral expenses. (20 § 3101)
Creditors' rights, if insufficient assets	Any party in interest may petition court for improper distribution within one year of decree of distribution. (20 § 3102)
May the distribution of the estate proceed without appointment of personal representative?	Yes. (20 § 3102)
Must court approve affidavit?	After petition, court may direct property distribution at its discretion. (20 § 3102)
Waiting period before authority to act	No provision.
With whom do you file petition or affidavit?	Orphan's court division of county of domicile at death. (20 § 3102)

Is there an informal procedure for appointment of executor or administrator?	No provision.
Can a nonresident serve?	No provision.
Can the nonresident act locally based on appointment in another state?	No provision.
What does a transferor need so as to be relieved of liability if challenged by another person later on who claims the particular property (e.g., copy of affidavit)?	No provision.

Rhode Island
Payments in Small Estates

Who can initiate process?	Decedent's surviving spouse, child, grandchild, parent, sibling, niece, nephew, aunt, uncle or any interested party. (§ 33-24-1) If will exists, then named executor, otherwise an alternate is chosen, or another person in descending priority from the same list as in § 33-24-1. (§ 33-24-2)
Can it be used if claims outstanding?	Yes. (§ 33-24-1 & 33-24-2)
Different rules if die testate or intestate?	The small estate procedure is available even if there is a will. (§ 33-24-2) The only difference is who can initiate the process. See *Who can initiate the process?*
Notice?	The statute does not specify, but payors may receive a written demand for payment from a personal representative. (§ § 33-24-1(c) & 33-24-2(d)))
heirs	No provision.
creditors	No provision.
others	No provision.
Which of the following must be observed?	
hearing	No hearing is required, (§ § 33-24-1(b) & 33-24-2) but the probate judge may require a hearing to take place in order to determine whether to issue a certification of appointment of executor. (§ § 33-24-2(c) & 33-24-2(b))
affidavit, petition, other	Affidavit. (§ § 33-24-1 & 33-24-2)
bond	No provision.
What are basic contents of petition or affidavit?	In case of intestate decedent, the affidavit must also contain:(a) name and address of affiant; (b) name, address, date of death of decedent, with death certificate attached; (c) relationship of affiant to the deceased; (d) schedule of decedent's assets, with estimated values; (e) statement that affiant has undertaken to act as voluntary administrator; and (f) names and addresses, known to affiant, of those who would take under § 33-1-10 in the case of intestacy. (§ 33-24-1(a)(1)–(6)) In case of will naming executor, the affidavit must also contain names and addresses known to the affiant of persons who take under the will. (§ 33-24-2(a)(1)–(7))
Is procedure available in the case of nonresident decedents?	No. (§ § 33-24-1 & 33-24-2)
Maximum allowable value of estate	$15,000, exclusive of "tangible personal property." (§ § 33-24-1 & 33-24-2)
What property can be transferred by this means?	Personal property. (§ § 33-24-1 & 33-24-2)
Special rules for certain assets (e.g., automobile)	No provision.
Can the spouse or other person take summarily if under certain amount?	No provision.

Minimum period before filing allowed	30 days from the death of the decedent. (§§ 33-24-1(a) & 33-24-2(a))
Rights/obligations of party with affidavit	Voluntary administrator/executor is "liable as an executor in his or her own wrong to all persons aggrieved by his or her administration of the estate and if letters testamentary or letters of administration are at any time granted, shall be liable as such an executor to the rightful executor or administrator." (§§ 33-24-1(f) & 33-24-2(g))
Are some creditors given special privileges/ preference (e.g., medical expenses, funeral expenses)?	Payment for funeral, last illness, administration, and then other debts in order specified under R.I. Gen. L. § 33-12-11. (§§ 33-24-1(e) & 33-24-2(f))
Creditors' rights, if insufficient assets	As per R.I. Gen. L. § 33-12-11. (§§ 33-24-1(e) & 33-24-2(f))
May the distribution of the estate proceed without appointment of personal representative?	Yes. (§§ 33-24-1(a) & 33-24-2(a))
Must court approve affidavit?	Yes. (§§ 33-24-1(b) & 33-24-2(c))
Waiting period before authority to act	30 days after death. (§§ 33-24-1(a) & 33-24-2(a))
With whom do you file petition or affidavit?	Probate Court. (§§ 33-24-1(a) & 33-24-2(a))
Is there an informal procedure for appointment of executor or administrator?	Voluntary administrator, who can be a surviving spouse, child, grandchild, parent, sibling, niece, nephew, aunt, uncle or interested party. (§ 33-24-1)
Can a nonresident serve?	No (§ 33-24-1(a)); however, if there is a will naming an executor, there is no specific restriction. (§ 33-24-2)
Can the nonresident act locally based on appointment in another state?	No specific provision.
What does a transferor need so as to be relieved of liability if challenged by another person later on who claims the particular property (e.g., copy of affidavit)?	"Payments and deliveries made under this section shall discharge the liability of the debtor, obligor or deliverer to all persons with respect to such debt." (§§ 33-24-1(c) & 33-24-2(d))

South Carolina
Collection of Personal Property by Affidavit; Summary Administration Procedure for Small Estates

Who can initiate process?	*By Affidavit.* Person claiming to be successor of decedent. (§ 62-3-1201(a)) *Small Estates.* Personal representative. (§ 62-3-1203(a))
Can it be used if claims outstanding?	*By Affidavit.* Yes. (§ 62-3-1201(a)) *Small Estates.* Yes. (§ 62-3-1203(a))
Different rules if die testate or intestate?	No provision.
Notice?	*By Affidavit.* No provision.
heirs	*Small Estates.* Closing statement must be sent to all distributees of the estate. (§ 62-3-1204(a)(3))
creditors	*Small Estates.* Yes, pursuant to § 62-3-801 but no additional notice is needed. (§ 62-3-1203(a)) Closing statement must be sent to all creditors of whom the affiant is aware whose claims are neither paid nor barred. (§ 62-3-1204(a)(3))
others	*Small Estates.* Closing statement must be sent to all "other claimants" of whom the affiant is aware whose claims are neither paid nor barred. (§ 62-3-1204(a)(3))
Which of the following must be observed?	
hearing	No provision.
affidavit, petition, other	*By Affidavit.* Affidavit. (§ 62-3-1201(a)) *Small Estates.* Closing statement. (§ 62-3-1204(a))
bond	No provision.
What are basic contents of petition or affidavit?	*By Affidavit.* Affidavit must state (1) the value of the entire probate estate, less liens and encumbrances, does not exceed $25,000; (2) 30 days have elapsed since death of decedent; (3) no petition has been filed/granted for personal representative; and (4) a statement that the claiming successor is entitled to payment/delivery. (§ 62-3-1201(a)) *Small Estates.* Closing statement must provide (1) that the value of the entire estate, less liens and encumbrances, did not exceed $25,000 and exempt property and administrative, funeral, and medical expenses, or, alternatively, that summary administration was available under § 62-3-1203(b); (2) that the estate is fully administered; and (3) that a copy of the closing statement was sent to distributees, creditors, and other claimants. (§ 62-3-1204(a))
Is procedure available in the case of nonresident decedents?	No provision.
Maximum allowable value of estate	*By Affidavit.* $25,000, less liens and encumbrances. (§ 62-3-1201(a)(1)) *Small Estates.* $25,000, less liens and encumbrances. (§ 62-3-1203(a))

What property can be transferred by this means?	*By Affidavit.* Tangible personal property or instrument evidencing debt, obligation, stock, or chose in action belonging to decedent. (§ 62-3-1201(a)) *Small Estates.* Entire estate. (§ 62-3-1203(a))
Special rules for certain assets (e.g., automobile)	*By Affidavit.* A transfer agent of any security shall change the registered ownership. (§ 62-3-1201(b)) *Small Estates.* No provision.
Can the spouse or other person take summarily if under certain amount?	Yes. If personal representative(s) is/are the sole devisee(s) or heir(s), the personal representative may immediately disburse after giving notice to creditors and must file a closing statement afterward. (§ 62-3-1203(b))
Minimum period before filing allowed	*By Affidavit.* 30 days after decedent's death. (§ 62-3-1201(a)(2)) *Small Estates.* May file at any time after disbursement and distribution of the estate. (§ 62-3-1203)
Rights/obligations of party with affidavit	*By Affidavit.* Right to collect tangible personal property, (§ 62-3-1201(a)(4)) or on an instrument evidencing a debt, obligation, stock, or chose in action. *Small Estates.* No provision.
Are some creditors given special privileges/ preference (e.g., medical expenses, funeral expenses)?	*By Affidavit.* No provision. *Small Estates.* Funeral and last illness medical expenses. (§ 62-3-1204(a)(1)(i))
Creditors' rights, if insufficient assets	*By Affidavit.* Affiants are answerable to any person with a superior right. (§ 62-3-1202) *Small Estates.* No provision.
May the distribution of the estate proceed without appointment of personal representative?	*By Affidavit.* Yes. There must not be an application or petition for appointment of a personal representative pending or granted in any jurisdiction. (§ 62-3-1201(a)(3)) *Small Estates.* No. (§ 62-3-1203(a))
Must court approve affidavit?	*By Affidavit.* Yes. (§ 62-3-1201(a)(5)) *Small Estates.* Not applicable.
Waiting period before authority to act	*By Affidavit.* 30 days after decedent's death. (§ 62-3-1201(a)(2)) *Small Estates.* Under summary administration personal representative may immediately disburse. (§ 62-3-1203)
With whom do you file petition or affidavit?	*By Affidavit.* Probate court. (§ 62-3-1201(a)(6)) *Small Estates.* Closing statement must be filed with court. (§ 62-3-1204(a))
Is there an informal procedure for appointment of executor or administrator?	Yes. (§§ 62-3-301, 307-311)
Can a nonresident serve?	Yes. (§§ 62-4-201 to -207)
Can the nonresident act locally based on appointment in another state?	Yes. If there is no local administration, and the domiciliary foreign personal representative has filed in a local court, such person may exercise with respect to assets in South Carolina all powers of a local personal representative, subject to conditions imposed upon nonresidents generally. (§§ 62-4-205, 62-4-204)

What does a transferor need so as to be relieved of liability if challenged by another person later on who claims the particular property (e.g., copy of affidavit)?

By Affidavit. Payor is "discharged and released to the same extent as if he dealt with a personal representative." (§ 62-3-1202)

South Dakota
Collection of Personal Property by Affidavit; Summary Administration Procedure for Small Estates

Who can initiate process?	Person claiming to be successor of decedent. (§ 29A-3-1201(a))
Can it be used if claims outstanding?	Yes. (§ 29A-3-1202(d))
Different rules if die testate or intestate?	No provision.
Notice?	No provision.
heirs	No provision.
creditors	No provision.
others	No provision.
Which of the following must be observed?	
hearing	No provision.
affidavit, petition, other	Affidavit. (§ 29A-3-1201(a))
bond	No provision.
What are basic contents of petition or affidavit?	Affidavit must state that (1) the value of estate, less liens and encumbrances, does not exceed $50,000; (2) 30 days have elapsed since death of decedent; (3) no application for personal representative is pending/granted; (4) decedent incurred no debt to Department of Social Services for medical care/nursing home; and (5) the claiming successor is entitled to payment/delivery of property. (§ 29A-3-1201(a)(1)-(5))
Is procedure available in the case of nonresident decedents?	No provision.
Maximum allowable value of estate	$50,000 less liens and encumbrances. (§ 29A-3-1201(a)(1))
What property can be transferred by this means?	Tangible personal property or an instrument evidencing a debt, obligation, stock, or chose in action belonging to decedent. (§ 29A-3-1201(a))
Special rules for certain assets (e.g., automobile)	Transfer agent of any security shall change registered ownership upon presentation of the affidavit. (§ 29A-3-1201(b))
Can the spouse or other person take summarily if under certain amount?	No provision.
Minimum period before filing allowed	No filing required. See *Waiting period before authority to act.*
Rights/obligations of affiant	Entitled to collect personal property (§ 29A-3-1201(a)); right to hearing on refusal of estate debtor to transfer asset (§ 29A-3-1202(b)); liable to personal representative or any person with superior right (§ 29A-3-1202(c)); duty to distribute property to creditors and eligible distributees (§ 29A-3-1202(d)); submits to jurisdiction of probate court (§ 29A-3-1202(e)).

Are some creditors given special privileges/ preference (e.g., medical expenses, funeral expenses)?	Any affiant receiving payment or delivery of personal property must ensure that property is applied to funeral and administrative expenses, among other things. (§ 29A-3-1202(d))
Creditors' rights, if insufficient assets	Affiant is liable to persons having a superior right. (§ 29A-3-1202(c))
May the distribution of the estate proceed without appointment of personal representative?	Yes. It *must* proceed without a personal representative. (§ 29A-3-1201(a)(3))
Must court approve affidavit?	No provision.
Waiting period before authority to act	30 days after death of decedent. (§ 29A-3-1201(a)(2))
With whom do you file petition or affidavit?	No provision.
Is there an informal procedure for appointment of executor or administrator?	Yes. (§ § 29A-3-301, 29A-3-307–311)
Can a nonresident serve?	Yes. (§ § 29A-4-201–207)
Can the nonresident act locally based on appointment in another state?	Yes. If there is no local administration, and the domiciliary foreign personal representative has filed in a local court, such person may exercise with respect to assets in South Dakota all powers of a local personal representative, subject to conditions imposed upon nonresidents generally. (§ § 29A-4-205, 29A-4-204)
What does a transferor need so as to be relieved of liability if challenged by another person later on who claims the particular property (e.g., copy of affidavit)?	Transferor is discharged and released as if he had dealt with a personal representative and is not required to inquire into the truth of the affidavit. (§ 29A-3-1202(a))

Tennessee
Small Estates

Who can initiate process?	One or more of decedent's competent, adult legatees/devisees/ personal representative (if testate), or heirs or next of kin (if intestate), or any creditor. (§ 30-4-103(1))
Can it be used if claims outstanding?	Yes. (§ 30-4-104(c))
Different rules if die testate or intestate?	If testate, distribute according to will; if intestate, distribute by intestate succession. (§ 30-4-104(c)) See also *Who Can Institute Process?*
Notice?	
heirs	No provision.
creditors	No provision.
others	No provision.
Which of the following must be observed?	
hearing	No provision.
affidavit, petition, other	Affidavit. (§ 30-4-103)
bond	Bond payable to state, with two or more sureties or one corporate surety, in amount equal to value of decedent's estate. (§ 30-4-103(4))
What are basic contents of petition or affidavit?	Affidavit must (1) state whether decedent left a will; (2) list decedent's unpaid debts, amounts due, creditors; (3) describe decedent's property and known possessors at time of death, and insurance payments to decedent's estate; (4) provide the name, age, address, and relationship of each devisee/legatee/heir entitled to receive property; and (5) whether or not the affiant elects to give notice to creditors. (§ 30-4-103(1))
Is procedure available in the case of nonresident decedents?	No provision.
Maximum allowable value of estate	Value of personal property does not exceed $50,000. (§ 30-4-102(5))
What property can be transferred by this means?	Personal property; life insurance on decedent payable to estate; any stock, bond, note or other evidence of ownership, indebtedness; right belonging to decedent's estate. (§§ 30-4-102(4), 30-4-104(a))
Special rules for certain assets (e.g., automobile)	No provision.
Can the spouse or other person take summarily if under certain amount?	No provision.
Minimum period before filing allowed	45 days from date of decedent's death, subject to court's discretion to shorten period on motion. (§ 30-4-103(1))

Rights/obligations of party with affidavit	Right to collect property. (§ 30-4-104(a)) Obligation to provide no false/misleading statement in affidavit. (§ 30-4-103(1)(B)) Affiant liable to unpaid creditors/other valid claimants or later-appointed personal representative. (§ 30-4-104(c)) Affiant must pay tax on estate property. (§ 30-4-104(d)) Affiant may have hearing for debtor's refusal to honor payment/transfer under affidavit. (§ 30-4-104(e))
Are some creditors given special privileges/ preference (e.g., medical expenses, funeral expenses)?	No provision, other than any creditor's right to file and present an affidavit. (§ 30-4-103(1))
Creditors' rights, if insufficient assets	Bond. (§ 30-4-103(5)) Affiant remains liable to unpaid creditors of estate. (§ 30-4-104(c))
May the distribution of the estate proceed without appointment of personal representative?	Yes. There must not be an application or petition for appointment of a personal representative pending or granted in any jurisdiction. (§ 30-4-103(1))
Must court approve affidavit?	Court must file the affidavit, but no provision explicity requires approval. (§ 30-4-103(2))
Waiting period before authority to act	45 days from date of decedent's death. (§ 30-4-103(1))
With whom do you file petition or affidavit?	Court exercising probate jurisdiction in county of decedent's legal residence on date of death. (§§ 30-4-103(1), 30-4-102(2))
Is there an informal procedure for appointment of executor or administrator?	No provision.
Can a nonresident serve?	No provision.
Can the nonresident act locally based on appointment in another state?	No provision.
What does a transferor need so as to be relieved of liability if challenged by another person later on who claims the particular property (e.g., copy of affidavit)?	Payor is discharged and released as if he had dealt with a personal representative and is not required to inquire into the truth of the affidavit. (§ 30-4-104(b))

Texas
Small Estates

Who can initiate process?	Distributees of decedent's estate if the value of the estate assets exceed known liabilities of the estate and the value of estate assets does not exceed $75,000 on the date of the affidavit not including homestead allowance and exempt property. (Est. Code § 205.001)
Can it be used if claims outstanding?	Yes. (Est. Code § 205.001)
Different rules if die testate or intestate?	Available only to distributees of intestates. (Est. Code § 205.001)
Notice?	A copy of the affidavit must be furnished to the person(s) owing money to the estate, having custody or possession of property of the estate, or acting as a registrar/ fiduciary/transfer agent for an interest belonging to the estate. (Est. Code § 205.004)
heirs	No provision.
creditors	No provision.
others	No provision.
Which of the following must be observed?	
hearing	No provision.
affidavit, petition, other	Affidavit. (Est. Code § § 205.001, 205.002)
bond	No provision.
What are basic contents of petition or affidavit?	Affidavit must state that (1) no petition for personal representative granted/pending; (2) 30 days have elapsed since death of decedent; (3) the value of the estate, excluding homestead and exempt property, does not exceed $75,000; (4) must list all known assets/ liabilities of estate and indicate which assets the applicant claims are exempt; and (5) must list other relevant family history facts and names/addresses of distributees. (Est. Code. § 205.001, 205.002)
Is procedure available in the case of nonresident decedents?	No provision.
Maximum allowable value of estate	$75,000, not including homestead allowance and exempt property. (Est. Code § 205.001)
What property can be transferred by this means?	Decedent's estate. (Est. Code § 205.001)) If a homestead is the only real property in decedent's estate, this procedure is also available for the homestead. (Est. Code § 205.006)
Special rules for certain assets (e.g., automobile)	Homestead is real property subject to affidavit if it is the only real property of the estate. (Est. Code § 205.006)
Can the spouse or other person take summarily if under certain amount?	No provision.
Minimum period before filing allowed	30 days since death of decedent. (Est. Code § 205.001)

Rights/obligations of party with affidavit	Right to collect property. (Est. Code § 205.001) Right to hearing on refusal of estate debtor to transfer asset. Transferee/affiant liable to personal representative or any person with prior right. (Est. Code § 205.007)
Are some creditors given special privileges/ preference (e.g., medical expenses, funeral expenses)?	No provision.
Creditors' rights, if insufficient assets	Affiant is answerable to any person having a prior right. (Est. Code § 205.007)
May the distribution of the estate proceed without appointment of personal representative?	Yes. It *must* proceed without a personal representative. (Est. Code § 205.001)
Must court approve affidavit?	Yes. (Est. Code § 205.001)
Waiting period before authority to act	30 days since death of decedent. (Est. Code § 205.001)
With whom do you file petition or affidavit?	Clerk of court with jurisdiction and venue. (Est. Code § 205.001)
Is there an informal procedure for appointment of executor or administrator?	No provision.
Can a nonresident serve?	No provision.
Can the nonresident act locally based on appointment in another state?	No provision.
What does a transferor need so as to be relieved of liability if challenged by another person later on who claims the particular property (e.g., copy of affidavit)?	Transferor of property needs merely to have been presented with valid affidavit to be discharged and is not required to inquire into the truth of the affidavit. (Est. Code § 205.007)

Utah
Collection of Personal Property by Affidavit; Summary Administration Procedure for Small Estates

Who can initiate process?	*By Affidavit.* Person claiming to be successor of decedent. (§ 75-3-1201) *Summary Administration.* Personal representative. (§ 75-3-1203)
Can it be used if claims outstanding?	*By Affidavit.* Yes. (§ 75-3-1201(1)) *Summary Administration.* Yes. (§ 75-3-1203)
Different rules if die testate or intestate?	No provision.
Notice?	
heirs	*By Affidavit.* No provision. *Summary Administration.* Closing statement must be sent to all distributees of the estate. (§ 75-3-1204(1)(d))
creditors	*By Affidavit.* No provision. *Summary Administration.* Under summary administration, may disburse without giving notice to creditors and file closing statement. (§ 75-3-1203) Closing statement must be sent to all creditors of whom the personal representative is aware and whose claims are neither paid nor barred. (§ 75-3-1204(1)(d))
others	*By Affidavit.* No provision. *Summary Administration.* Closing statement must be sent to all "other claimants" of whom the affiant is aware and whose claims are neither paid nor barred. (§ 75-3-1204(1)(d))
Which of the following must be observed?	
hearing	No provision.
affidavit, petition, other	*By Affidavit.* Affidavit. (§ 75-3-1201) *Summary Administration.* Closing statement. (§ 75-3-1203)
bond	No provision.
What are basic contents of petition or affidavit?	*By Affidavit.* Statement including (1) value of entire estate less liens and encumbrances, does not exceed $100,000; (2) 30 days elapsed since decedent's death; (3) no application/petition for appointment of personal representative is pending/has been granted; and (4) claiming successor entitled to payment/delivery of property. (§ 75-3-1201(1)(a)-(d)) *Summary Administration.* Closing statement must state (1) the nature and value of estate assets; (2) that the value of the estate, less liens and encumbrances, did not exceed the value of exempt property, the homestead and family allowances, and administrative, funeral, and medical expenses; (3) that the estate is fully administered; and (4) that a copy of the closing statement has been sent to all distributees and claimants. (§ 75-3-1204(1)(a)-(d))
Is procedure available in the case of nonresident decedents?	*By Affidavit.* Yes. (Comment to § 75-3-1202) *Summary Administration.* No provision.

Maximum allowable value of estate	*By Affidavit.* $100,000, less liens and encumbrances. (§ 75-3-1201(1)(a)) *Summary Administration.* "[E]ntire estate, less liens and encumbrances, [cannot] exceed homestead allowance, exempt property, family allowance, costs and expenses of administration, reasonable funeral expenses, and reasonable and necessary medical and hospital expenses." (§ 75-3-1203)
What property can be transferred by this means?	*By Affidavit.* "[T]angible personal property or an instrument evidencing a debt, obligation, stock, or chose in action belonging to the decedent." (§ 75-3-1201(1)) *Summary Administration.* Entire estate. (§ 75-3-1203)
Special rules for certain assets (e.g., automobile)	*By Affidavit.* Not more than four boats, motor vehicles, trailers, or semi-trailers are exempt from calculation of estate value. (§ 75-3-1201(3)) Also, transferors of securities shall change registered ownership. (§ 75-3-1201(2)) *Summary Administration.* No provision.
Can the spouse or other person take summarily if under certain amount?	No provision.
Minimum period before filing allowed	*By Affidavit.* No filing required. See *Waiting period before authority to act.* *Summary Administration.* Estate must be fully administered before closing statement can be filed. (§ 75-3-1204(1)(c))
Rights/obligations of party with affidavit	*By Affidavit.* Right to collect property. (§ 75-3-1201) Right to proceeding on refusal of estate debtor to transfer asset. Transferee/affiant liable to personal representative or any person with superior right. (§ 75-3-1202) *Summary Administration.* No provision.
Are some creditors given special privileges/ preference (e.g., medical expenses, funeral expenses)?	*By Affidavit.* No provision. *Summary Administration.* Reasonable funeral expenses, reasonable and necessary medical/hospital expenses of last illness. (§ 75-3-1204(1)(b))
Creditors' rights, if insufficient assets	*By Affidavit.* Affiant is liable to any person having a superior right. (§ 75-3-1202) *Summary Administration.* Right to file action against personal representative is implied. (§ 75-3-1204(2))
May the distribution of the estate proceed without appointment of personal representative?	*By Affidavit.* Yes. There must not be an application or petition for appointment of a personal representative pending or granted in any jurisdiction. (§ 75-3-1201(1)(c)) *Summary Administration.* No. (§ 75-3-1203)
Must court approve affidavit?	No provision.
Waiting period before authority to act	*By Affidavit.* 30 days after decedent's death. (§ 75-3-1201(1)(b)) *Summary Administration.* "[M]ay immediately disburse and distribute the estate to the persons entitled." (§ 75-3-1203)

With whom do you file petition or affidavit?	*By Affidavit.* No provision. *Summary Administration.* Closing statement is to be filed with the court. (§ 75-3-1204(1))
Is there an informal procedure for appointment of executor or administrator?	Yes. (§ § 75-3-301, 75-3-307–311)
Can a nonresident serve?	Yes. (§ § 75-4-201–207)
Can the nonresident act locally based on appointment in another state?	Yes. If there is no local administration, and the domiciliary foreign personal representative has filed in a local court, such person may exercise with respect to assets in Utah all powers of a local personal representative, subject to conditions imposed upon nonresidents generally. (§ § 75-4-205, 75-4-204)
What does a transferor need so as to be relieved of liability if challenged by another person later on who claims the particular property (e.g., copy of affidavit)?	*By Affidavit.* Transferor of property needs merely to have been presented with valid affidavit to be fully discharged and is released to the same extent as if he dealt with a personal representative. The transferor is not required to inquire into the truth of the affidavit. (§ 75-3-1202) *Summary Administration.* No provision.

Vermont
Small Estates

Who can initiate process?	Any "petitioner or some other suitable person." (14 § 1902) No specific persons are listed.
Can it be used if claims outstanding?	Yes (14 § 1901(2)); must show that the funeral expenses have been paid or post a bond.
Different rules if die testate or intestate?	Yes, but only for discharge. If dies intestate, 14 § 1903(a). If dies testate, 14 § 1903(b).
Notice?	The court may grant administration of the estate to the petitioner without notice. (14 § 1902(b))
heirs	No provision.
creditors	No provision.
others	No provision.
Which of the following must be observed?	
hearing	No provision.
affidavit, petition, other	Petition. (14 § 1901)
bond	If funeral expenses have not been paid, a bond in an amount determined by the judge is required conditioned on the payment of funeral expenses. (14 § 1901(2))
What are basic contents of petition or affidavit?	Inventory of estate; verification of bond; will (if any). (14 § 1901)
Is procedure available in the case of nonresident decedents?	No provision.
Maximum allowable value of estate	$10,000 (personal property only). (14 § 1902(b)(3))
What property can be transferred by this means?	Decedent's personal estate. If estate contains real property, small estates procedure cannot be used. (14 § 1902(b)(2))
Special rules for certain assets (e.g., automobile)	No provision.
Can the spouse or other person take summarily if under certain amount?	No provision.
Minimum period before filing allowed	No provision.
Rights/obligations of party with affidavit	No provision.
Are some creditors given special privileges/ preference (e.g., medical expenses, funeral expenses)?	Funeral expenses paid or guaranteed by bond. (14 § 1901(2))
Creditors' rights, if insufficient assets	No provision.
May the distribution of the estate proceed without appointment of personal representative?	No specific provision.
Must court approve affidavit?	Yes. (14 § 1902(b))

Waiting period before authority to act	Petitioner must wait for court approval before being allowed to administer estate. But no waiting period before filing with court. (14 § 1902)
With whom do you file petition or affidavit?	Probate court. (14 § 1902)
Is there an informal procedure for appointment of executor or administrator?	Court may grant administration to "petitioner or some other suitable person." (14 § 1902(b))
Can a nonresident serve?	No provision.
Can the nonresident act locally based on appointment in another state?	No provision.
What does a transferor need so as to be relieved of liability if challenged by another person later on who claims the particular property (e.g., copy of affidavit)?	If it appears to the satisfaction of the judge that the administrator has paid funeral and burial expenses and has paid over all the balance and residue of the estate, the administrator shall be discharged and excused from liability to distributees. (14 § 1903)

Virginia
Payments, Settlements or Administration Without Appointment of Representative

Who can initiate process?	Affidavit must be made by all of the known successors. (§ 64.2-601(A))
Can it be used if claims outstanding?	No provision.
Different rules if die testate or intestate?	No provision.
Notice?	
heirs	No provision.
creditors	No provision.
others	No provision.
Which of the following must be observed?	
hearing	No provision.
affidavit, petition, other	Affidavit. If a person is in possession of a small asset valued at $25,000 or less, then no affidavit required. (§ 64.2-602)
bond	No provision.
What are basic contents of petition or affidavit?	Affidavit must state (1) that the value of the personal estate does not exceed $50,000; (2) 60 days have elapsed since decedent's death; (3) that no application granted/ pending for personal representative; (4) will, if any, was duly probated; and (5) that claiming successor entitled to payment/delivery of property; (6) and the basis upon which such entitlement is claimed; (7) names and addresses of all successors to the extent known; (8) the name of each successor designated to receive payment or delivery of the small asset on behalf of all successors; (9) that the designated successor shall have a fiduciary duty to safeguard and promptly pay or deliver the small asset as required by the laws of the Commonwealth. (§ 64.2-601(A)(1)–(8))
Is procedure available in the case of nonresident decedents?	No provision.
Maximum allowable value of estate	$50,000. If a person is in possession of a small asset valued at $25,000 or less, then no affidavit required. (§ § 64.2-601(A)(1), 64.2-602)
What property can be transferred by this means?	"A small asset." "A small asset" means "any indebtedness . . . to or any asset belonging or presently distributable to the decedent, other than real property, having a value, on the date of the decedent's death, of no more than $50,000." (§ 64.2-601)
Special rules for certain assets (e.g., automobile)	Transferor of security shall change registered ownership from decedent to successor. (§ 64.2-601(D))
Can the spouse or other person take summarily if under certain amount?	No provision.

Minimum period before filing allowed	No filing required. See *Waiting period before authority to act*.
Rights/obligations of party with affidavit	Right to collect property. (§ 64.2-601) Right to hearing on refusal of estate debtor to transfer asset. Transferee/affiant is answerable to personal representative or any person with an equal or superior right. (§ 64.2-603)
Are some creditors given special privileges/ preference (e.g., medical expenses, funeral expenses)?	No provision.
Creditors' rights, if insufficient assets	Affiant is answerable to persons having an equal or a superior right. (§ 64.2-603)
May the distribution of the estate proceed without appointment of personal representative?	Yes. There must not be an application for appointment of a personal representative pending or granted in any jurisdiction. (§ 64.2-601(A)(3))
Must court approve affidavit?	No provision.
Waiting period before authority to act	60 days after death of decedent. (§ 64.2-601(A)(2))
With whom do you file petition or affidavit?	No provision.
Is there an informal procedure for appointment of executor or administrator?	No provision.
Can a nonresident serve?	No provision.
Can the nonresident act locally based on appointment in another state?	No provision.
What does a transferor need so as to be relieved of liability if challenged by another person later on who claims the particular property (e.g., copy of affidavit)?	"Any person paying or delivering a small asset . . . is discharged and released to the same extent as if [he] dealt with a personal representative." No requirement to inquire into the truth of the affidavit. (§ 64.2-603)

Washington
Estates Under $60,000—Disposition of Property

Who can initiate process?	Person claiming to be successor of decedent, excluding creditors but including persons entitled to take under will/by intestate succession, surviving spouse or surviving domestic partner to extent entitled to one-half interest in property, department of social and health services to extent funds were expended, and/or the state in case of escheat property. (§§ 11.62.005(2)(a) & (b), 11.62.010(1))
Can it be used if claims outstanding?	All debts must have been satisfied or provided for. (§ 11.62.010(2)(f))
Different rules if die testate or intestate?	No provision.
Notice?	
heirs	Claiming successor must provide written notice to all other successors. (§ 11.62.010(2)(h))
creditors	No provision.
others	No provision.
Which of the following must be observed?	
hearing	No provision.
affidavit, petition, other	Affidavit. (§ 11.62.010)
bond	No provision.
What are basic contents of petition or affidavit?	Affidavit must state (1) names and addresses of claiming successor; (2) decedent was a state resident; (3) value of estate, less liens and encumbrances, is under $100,000; (4) 40 days have elapsed since decedent's death; (5) no petition filed/granted for appointment of personal representative; (6) all debts, including funeral expenses, paid or provided for; (7) description of personal property; (8) notice has been given to all successors, and that a minimum of ten days have elapsed since the service or mailing of the notice; and (9) that the successor is entitled to property or to the delivery of the property. (§ 11.62.010(2)(a)-(i))
Is procedure available in the case of nonresident decedents?	No. (§ 11.62.010(2)(b))
Maximum allowable value of estate	$100,000, less spouse's or domestic partner's community property interest, liens, and encumbrances. (§ 11.62.010(2)(c))
What property can be transferred by this means?	Tangible and intangible personal property belonging to decedent and decedent's surviving spouse or surviving domestic partner as community property, including any instrument of debt, obligation, stock, chose in action, license or ownership. (§§ 11.62.005(1), 11.62.010(1))

Special rules for certain assets (e.g., automobile)	Up to $1,000 from decedent's credit union account may be summarily transferred to surviving spouse or surviving domestic partner. (§ 11.62.030) A transfer agent of any registered security shall change the registered ownership. (§ 11.62.010 (3))
Can the spouse or other person take summarily if under certain amount?	See *Special rules for certain assets.*
Minimum period before filing allowed	No filing is required. See *Waiting period before authority to act.*
Rights/obligations of party with affidavit	Right to collect property. (§ 11.62.010) Right to hearing on refusal of estate debtor to transfer asset. Transferee/affiant liable to personal representative or any person with superior right. (§ 11.62.020)
Are some creditors given special privileges/preference (e.g., medical expenses, funeral expenses)?	Department of Social and Health Services and state may qualify as "successor." (§ 11.62.005) All debts including funeral and burial expenses must be paid or provided for. (§ 11.62.010(2)(f))
Creditors' rights, if insufficient assets	All debts must be paid or provided for. (§ 11.62.010(2)(f))
May the distribution of the estate proceed without appointment of personal representative?	Yes. There must not be an application or petition for appointment of a personal representative pending or granted in any jurisdiction. (§ 11.62.010(2)(e))
Must court approve affidavit?	No provision.
Waiting period before authority to act	40 days from date of decedent's death. (§ 11.62.010(1)) Also, 10 days must have elapsed since notice given to distributees. (§ 11.62.010(2)(h))
With whom do you file petition or affidavit?	Must mail copy along with decedent's social security number to department of social and health services, office of financial recovery. (§ 11.62.010(5))
Is there an informal procedure for appointment of executor or administrator?	No provision.
Can a nonresident serve?	No provision.
Can the nonresident act locally based on appointment in another state?	No provision.
What does a transferor need so as to be relieved of liability if challenged by another person later on who claims the particular property (e.g., copy of affidavit)?	Transferor of property needs merely to have been presented with valid affidavit for discharge/release. Transferor must not have had actual knowledge of the falsity of any statement required to be in the affidavit. (§ 11.62.020)

West Virginia

There are no provisions.

Wisconsin
Transfer by Affidavit; Summary Assignment of Small Estates; Summary Settlement of Small Estates

Who can initiate process?	*Affidavit.* Any heir of decedent, trustee of a revocable trust created by decedent, a person named in the will to act as personal representative, or guardian of decedent at time of death. (§ 867.03(1g)) *Summary Assignment.* Personal representative or any interested person. If 30 days after decedent's death, nobody has petitioned the court, anyone with an interest in the property of the estate, any creditor of the decedent, or anyone who needs the appointment of a personal representation for the maintenance of a cause of action may petition. (§§ 867.02(2) & 856.07) *Summary Settlement.* Personal representative or any interested person. If 30 days after decedent's death, nobody has petitioned the court, anyone with an interest in the property of the estate may petition. (§§ 867.01(3) & 856.07)
Can it be used if claims outstanding?	*Affidavit.* Yes. (§ 867.03(1g)) *Summary Assignment.* Yes. (§ 867.02) *Summary Settlement.* Yes. (§ 867.01(1))
Different rules if die testate or intestate?	No provision.
Notice?	*Affidavit.* Department of health and family services entitled to notice if decedent or spouse ever received certain state aid. (§ 867.03(1m)) *Summary Assignment.* All notice is at the discretion of the court. (§ 867.02(2)(d)) Petitioner must mail/deliver a copy of the order to all interested persons whose addresses are known by the petitioner. (§ 867.02(2)(i)) *Summary Settlement.* The court may hear the matter without notice. (§ 867.01(3)(d))
heirs	No provision.
creditors	*Summary Assignment*: The petitioner shall publish notice to creditors in a newspaper published in the county. (§ 867.02(2)(d))
others	*Summary Assignment*: The petitioner shall give notice by certified mail to the department of health services. (§ 867.02(2)(d)) *Summary Settlement*: If the decedent received medical assistance, then petitioner shall give notice by certified mail to the department of health services as soon as practicable. (§ 867.01(3)(d))
Which of the following must be observed?	
hearing	No provision.
affidavit, petition, other	*Affidavit.* Affidavit. (§ 867.03(1g)) *Summary Assignment.* Petition (§ 867.02(2)(am)). Order (§ 867.02(2)(g)). *Summary Settlement.* Petition (§ 867.01(3)(am)) Order. (§ 867.01(3)(f))

bond	*Affidavit.* No provision. *Summary Assignment.* Court may require as it sees fit. (§ 867.02(2)(c)) *Summary Settlement.* Court may require as it sees fit. (§ 867.01(3)(c))
What are basic contents of petition or affidavit?	*Affidavit.* (1) Description and value of property to be transferred, (2) total value of decedent's property in the state at date of death, and (3) whether decedent or spouse ever received certain state aid. (§ 867.03(1g)(a)–(c)) *Summary Assignment.* (1) Statement that the estate does not exceed $50,000 in value and cannot be summarily settled under § 867.01; (2) statement as to whether petitioner has been able to locate decedent's will; (3) statement of property in which decedent had an interest; (4) names and addresses of all of decedent's creditors known by petitioner and the amount claimed by each; (5) names and addresses of all persons interested; and (6) whether the decedent or decedent's spouse received family care, medical assistance, long-term community support services, or other aid as listed in the statute. (§ 867.02(2)) *Summary Settlement.* (1) Statement that the value of the estate, less the amount of debts for which any property in the estate is security, does not exceed in value all allowed claims, OR that the estate, less secured debts, does not exceed $50,000 in value, and that decedent is survived by a spouse or at least one minor child or both; (2) detailed statement of property in which decedent had an interest; (3) names and addresses of all persons interested, ascertained by petitioner with reasonable diligence; and (4) whether the decedent or the decedent's spouse received statutory family care benefit, medical assistance, long-term community support services or aid relating to cystic fibrosis, treatment of kidney disease, or hemophilia treatment services. (§ 867.01(3)(am))
Is procedure available in the case of nonresident decedents?	No provision.
Maximum allowable value of estate	*Affidavit.* Any heir of decedent, trustee of a revocable trust created by decedent, any person named in the will to act as a personal representative or guardian of decedent at time of death. (§ 867.03(1g)) *Summary Assignment.* $50,000, exclusive of secured debts. (§ 867.02(1)) *Summary Settlement.* Value of the estate, less the amount of debts for which any property in the estate is security, must not exceed in value all allowed claims, OR estate, less secured debts, must not exceed $50,000 in value, and decedent is survived by a spouse or at least one minor child or both. (§ 867.01(1))

What property can be transferred by this means?	*Affidavit.* Property subject to administration in Wisconsin. (§ 867.03(1g)) *Summary Assignment.* Entire estate. (§ 867.02(1)) ("the estate") *Summary Settlement.* Entire estate. (§ 867.01(1)) ("the estate")
Special rules for certain assets (e.g., automobile)	No provision.
Can the spouse or other person take summarily if under certain amount?	No provision.
Minimum period before filing allowed	No provision.
Rights/obligations of party with affidavit	*Affidavit.* Right to property upon presentation of affidavit to person owing estate. (§ 867.03(1g)) *Summary Assignment.* See *Creditors' rights,* if insufficient assets. *Summary Settlement.* No provision.
Are some creditors given special privileges/ preference (e.g., medical expenses, funeral expenses)?	*Affidavit.* No provision. *Summary Assignment.* Secured creditors. (§ 867.02(1)) *Summary Settlement.* Secured creditors. (§ 867.01(1)(b))
Creditors' rights, if insufficient assets	*Affidavit.* No provision. *Summary Assignment.* Unsatisfied creditors may recover from assignees. (§ 867.02(4)) *Summary Settlement.* Court may order notice to unsatisfied creditors. (§ 867.01(3)(g))
May the distribution of the estate proceed without appointment of personal representative?	*Affidavit.* No provision. *Summary Assignment.* Yes. (§ 867.02(1)) *Summary Settlement.* Yes. (§ 867.01(1))
Must court approve affidavit?	No provision.
Waiting period before authority to act	No provision.
With whom do you file petition or affidavit?	*Affidavit.* No provision. *Summary Assignment.* Court. (§ 867.02) *Summary Settlement.* Court. (§ 867.01)
Is there an informal procedure for appointment of executor or administrator?	*Affidavit.* No provision. *Summary Assignment.* Court may appoint special administrator. (§ 867.02(2)(f)) *Summary Settlement.* Court may appoint special administrator. (§ 867.01(3)(b))
Can a nonresident serve?	No provision.
Can the nonresident act locally based on appointment in another state?	No provision.

What does a transferor need so as to be relieved of liability if challenged by another person later on who claims the particular property (e.g., copy of affidavit)?	*Affidavit.* Upon transfer to affiant, transferor is released to the same extent as if the transfer had been made to a personal representative of the estate. (§ 867.03(2)) *Summary Assignment.* Transferors are released to the same extent as if the same had been made to a personal representative of the estate. (§ 867.02(3)) *Summary Settlement.* Transferors are released to the same extent as if the same had been made to a personal representative of the estate. (§ 867.01(4))

Wyoming
Distribution by Affidavit and Summary Procedure

Who can initiate process?	Person or persons claiming to be distributees. (§§ 2-1-201, 2-1-205) Under certain circumstances, government may initiate process. (§ 2-1-204)
Can it be used if claims outstanding?	*Personal Property.* Yes. (§ 2-1-201(a)) *Real Property.* Yes. (§ 2-1-205(c))
Different rules if die testate or intestate?	No provision.
Notice?	Notice must be published once per week for two consecutive weeks in a newspaper of general circulation in the county in which the application was filed. (§ 2-1-205(d)) Notice to the agent to attorney of any party is considered notice. (§ 2-1-205(j))
heirs	The notice of application shall be served by first class mail to the last known address, with copy of application attached, to the surviving spouse of the decedent, if any, and to all other distributees, so far as known, or to their guardians if any of them are minors, or to their personal representatives if any of them are deceased. (§ 2-1-205(d))
creditors	First class mail to any reasonably ascertainable creditors no later than ten (10) days after the date of first publication. (§ 2-1-205(d))
others	No provision.
Which of the following must be observed?	
hearing	No provision.
affidavit, petition, other	*Personal Property.* Affidavit. (§ 2-1-201(a)) *Real Property.* Application for decree pursuant to summary procedure. (§ 2-1-205(a))
bond	No provision.

What are basic contents of petition or affidavit?	*Personal Property.* (1) Statement that value of entire estate, less liens and encumbrances, does not exceed $200,000; (2) statement that 30 days has elapsed since decedent's death; (3) statement that no application for a personal representative is pending or has been granted in any jurisdiction in this state; (4) statement that claiming distributee is entitled to payment or delivery of property, including facts concerning distributee's relationship to decedent, and facts concerning the legal basis upon which the distributee or distributees claim entitlement to such property, and that there are no other distributees having a right to succeed the property under probate and (5) if an application for appointment of a personal representative has been made in a jurisdiction outside of Wyoming: (a) The name and address of the proposed or appointed personal representative, the date of the application and the date of any appointment; and (b) The title of the proceedings and name of the court and jurisdiction in which the application was made. (§ 2-1-201(a)(i)–(v)) *Real Property.* Same as personal property, but application must also include a description and valuation of the real property. (§ 2-1-205(b))
Is procedure available in the case of nonresident decedents?	No provision.
Maximum allowable value of estate	*Personal Property.* $200,000, less liens and encumbrances. (§ 2-1-201(a)(i)) *Real Property.* $200,000 of personal property. There is no maximum value of real property provided.. (§ 2-1-205(a))
What property can be transferred by this means?	*Personal Property.* Tangible personal property or an instrument evidencing a debt, obligation, stock, or chose in action belonging to the decedent. (§ 2-1-201(a)) *Real Property.* Real and personal property including mineral interest. (§ 2-1-205(a))
Special rules for certain assets (e.g., automobile)	Clerk shall transfer title of vehicle from decedent to distributee upon presentation of affidavit. (§ 2-1-201(d)) Upon presentation of an affidavit, a person with custody of the decedent's property or a holder of the decedent's property shall pay any deposit in the sole name of the decedent, with interest and dividends thereon, to the distributee(s). (§ 2-1-201(e)) The transfer agent for any security shall change the registered ownership on the books of the corporation. (§ 2-1-201(b))
Can the spouse or other person take summarily if under certain amount?	No provision.
Minimum period before filing allowed	30 days after death of decedent. (§ § 2-1-201(a)(ii), 2-1-205(a))

Rights/obligations of party with affidavit	*Personal Property.* Right to payment or delivery from persons indebted to decedent or in possession of property belonging to decedent. Must also file affidavit, and remains liable to those with superior rights. (§§ 2-1-201, 2-1-202) *Real Property.* False statements made are subject to the appropriate penalties for perjury and prevents title to property from passing. (§ 2-1-205(d))
Are some creditors given special privileges/ preference (e.g., medical expenses, funeral expenses)?	Governments. (§ 2-1-204)
Creditors' rights, if insufficient assets	*Personal Property.* Affiant is liable to persons having a superior right. (§ 2-1-202) *Real Property.* No provision.
May the distribution of the estate proceed without appointment of personal representative?	*Personal Property.* Yes. (§ 2-1-201(a)) Must proceed without. *Real Property.* Yes. (§ 2-1-205(c))
Must court approve affidavit?	*Personal Property.* No provision. *Real Property.* Court must approve application. (§ 2-1-205(c))
Waiting period before authority to act	30 days after death of decedent. (§§ 2-1-201(a), 2-1-205(a))
With whom do you file petition or affidavit?	*Personal Property.* County clerk. (§ 2-1-201(c)) *Real Property.* District court of county where property is located (§ 2-1-205(a)).
Is there an informal procedure for appointment of executor or administrator?	No provision.
Can a nonresident serve?	No provision.
Can the nonresident act locally based on appointment in another state?	No provision.
What does a transferor need so as to be relieved of liability if challenged by another person later on who claims the particular property (e.g., copy of affidavit)?	*Personal Property.* Payor is discharged and released to the same extent as if he dealt with a personal representative and he is not required to inquire into the truth of the affidavit. (§ 2-1-202) *Real Property.* No provision.

Table 5
Will Substitutes
(current through 5/1/18)

Increasingly, clients' assets are held in forms that pass outside the probate process. Oftentimes, planners advise their clients to use these ownership vehicles and techniques in order to avoid probate, simplify planning, and defeat or at least frustrate creditor's claims.

Despite the remarkable shift of individual wealth to these will substitutes, states disagree on which ones should be recognized and which ones should remain governed by the formal requirements of the wills law. The major categories reviewed in this table are:

Revocable Trusts: The settlor keeps control during life, but probate is avoided. Property is administered after the settlor's death or incompetency pursuant to the terms of the trust instrument. Note that the Uniform Trust Code does not actually provide that the revocable trust is a valid testamentary substitute. Thus, Table 5.01, Part 1 cites prior case law so holding in states that have enacted the Uniform Trust Code.

Deeds: The grantor ordinarily provides for real property to pass at his death to a designated grantee. The key question seems to be whether the execution of the deed creates a present interest in the grantee, so that no interest passes at the time of the grantor's death. One unsettled question relates to the scope of original U.P.C. § 6-201, which one court has construed as not requiring delivery of a deed, while another has construed as requiring such delivery. The U.P.C. has been revised to clarify that delivery is not required. A number of states have enacted this clarification. Other states have enacted transfer on death deed or beneficiary deed statutes. These, generally, do not require lifetime delivery, but may well require prescribed, explicit language in the deed itself indicating that it becomes effective on death. The statute may also require recording of the deed during life. In these states, however, the statute tends not to be exclusive, so that if it has not been complied with, other pertinent statutes or the common law would be controlling as to whether the deed is nontestamentary in character.

Joint Tenancies: These create a right of survivorship in the other joint tenant(s). The joint tenancy serves as a valid substitute for a will, but is subject to severe deficiencies. It restricts flexibility in terms of tax planning and requires surrender of economic control of a pro rata share during life and complete control of the whole to the surviving joint tenant upon the death of the other joint tenant(s). Some states require specific language to create a joint tenancy or limit its availability to either personal or real property.

Tenancies by the Entirety: Similar to a joint tenancy in almost every respect, except that it can only be created between husband and wife. Unlike a joint tenancy, there is no right of partition available to a single joint tenant. Although it originally developed to protect the wife, it has been supplanted by other spousal protections in many states. In certain states, the status of this testamentary substitute is in limbo.

Totten Trusts: A technique approved of in a famous New York case, this form of ownership of a bank account as "A in trust for B," is essentially an implied revocable trust. Not all states recognize this form of account and, if they do, that is a valid testamentary substitute that need not comply with will formalities.

Joint-Name Bank Accounts: In many situations, a bank account will be in joint name, but there will be no reference to survivorship. An important question is whether the account will be deemed to create a right of survivorship or whether an interest is created that will pass under a will or, if no will, by intestate succession.

Payable on Death (P.O.D.) Bank Accounts: A bank account may indicate that at the death of the depositor, the account is to pass to a designated person. This designation will not typically comply with will formalities. The question is, therefore, whether it is a valid substitute that need not comply with those formalities. There is a considerable amount of ferment in this area and much disagreement among the states. The fact that a bank permits this designation does not mean that the designation is valid under the particular state's law.

Transfer on Death (T.O.D.) Securities Accounts: The T.O.D. designation is essentially the securities analogue to the P.O.D. bank account. However, there has been less acceptance of the T.O.D. as a valid testamentary substitute.

Life Insurance Proceeds: The life insurance designation seems almost wholly uncontroversial as a valid testamentary substitute. The beneficiary receives the life insurance proceeds as a third-party beneficiary of the contract between the owner of the policy and the insurance company.

Gifts: Many of the other testamentary substitutes that are recognized rest on the assumption that a lifetime transfer of an interest has occurred, so that no attempt at death-time transfer is deemed to have occurred. Certainly, this is true of a completed outright gift. However, different states set forth their own requirements for finding that a gift has been completed. While the requirements from state to state are often similar, there are nuances that need to be carefully observed. Otherwise, the property will be deemed still owned by the owner and pass pursuant to his will or by intestacy, as the case may be.

A Writing Disposing of Tangible Personal Property: In order to facilitate the disposition of personal effects and the like, a number of states allow for the disposition of items by a simple writing. In most cases, the writing does not have to be completely in the decedent's hand, as is true of a holographic will; nor need it be attested by witnesses or comply with the other requirements of a formally executed will. Many states have resisted the adoption of this streamlined mechanism. Concerns include potential for fraud, disruptive effect on and conflict with other dispositive instruments, and the lack of any limitation on the value of tangible assets that can be disposed of by this method.

In addition to the foregoing, consideration is given by Table 5.02 to the doctrines of incorporation by reference and facts of independent significance. In many cases, these doctrines obviate the need for repeated codicils or a new will, and allow for simplification of the content of the will. Thus, incorporation by reference allows for the inclusion of a pre-existing independent document, such as a list of assets, as part of the will. Facts of independent significance allow reference in a will to the disposition of assets acquired later on or even consistent with the terms of a subsequently executed instrument, such as a trust. An example might be: "I devise the stock owned at my death to Sally." Another example would be: "I leave the contents of my safe deposit box at my death to Bill." Still another example would be: "I leave my residuary estate in accord with the terms of the revocable trust of my wife, as she may amend it from time to time, both before and after my death." However, not all states recognize both incorporation by reference and facts of independent significance. Moreover, some states have statutory enactments acknowledging these doctrines and setting forth their parameters, while other states' enforcement of these doctrines is based on decisional law that is exemplified by contradictory holdings and/or ambiguities.

Since property is commonly situated in more than one jurisdiction and some of the aforementioned will substitutes may be subject to regulation by several states, careful review of the law of any potentially interested state is warranted. This is particularly true since this area of the law is currently in a state of considerable flux. If a particular will substitute is not, in fact, recognized by a state, the consequence could well be intestacy or the transmission of property by will to persons and in a form of ownership not intended by the decedent.

A vital planning dimension is also implicated as a result of differences among states with result to bank accounts and securities. This area of law is in a state of uncertainty, so that great care must be exercised. Opportunities, however, are available. For example, to the extent that the simple vehicle of a p.o.d. designation is preferred, opening an account in one neighboring state rather than another may be a winning strategy. Thus, in the New York metropolitan area, New York will not recognize such an account as a valid testamentary substitute. However, New Jersey will do so. The situation in Connecticut and Pennsylvania is unsettled, so these jurisdictions would not be as appealing as New Jersey.

Table 5.01, Part 1
Principal Will Substitutes

Which of the Following Are Valid to Pass Property at Death without Complying with Wills Formalities?

	Revocable Trust?	Transfer by Deed Effective at Death, Assuming Intent to Make Present Conveyance of Title?	Joint Tenancy?	Tenancy by the Entirety?	Totten Trust Bank Account?	Joint-Name Bank Account with No Reference to Right of Survivorship?
Alabama	No direct explicit authority, even under the Trust Code, although almost certainly not testamentary. (Tierce v. Macedonia United Methodist Church of Northport, 519 So. 2d 451 (1987) (transfer to inter vivos trust with a retained life income interest; however, court emphasized that the remainder was not revocable or contingent)) See also UTC cmt accompanying §19-3B-603.	Yes. (Stephens v. Stephens, 193 So. 2d 755 (1967) (instrument executed by husband and wife conveying certain land to son and providing that deed should become effective at end of natural life of one of grantors who had life estate was deed with reservation of life estate and not a will))	Yes, if right of survivorship mentioned (§35-4-7) then, upon death, his interest passes to other joint tenants. Otherwise, his interest does not survive but descends and vests as if interest had been severed and ascertained. See Barron v. Scroggins, 910 So. 2d 780 (Ala. Civ. App. 2005) in which this statute was applied to a bank account which was titled "JOF – Joint or First." (§5-5A-41)	There is debate as to whether Alabama recognizes a tenancy by the entirety. (§8-9A-1 cmt.)	Yes. (§5-5A-40)	Yes. Any deposit made in any bank in the names of two or more persons payable to any of such persons, upon death of either person, "may" be paid by the bank to the survivor, or to the survivors jointly, even if no words of survivorship are used and only one person contributed the funds, only one person had a right of withdrawal, there was delivery of the bank book or other writing by the person making a deposit to the other person, and regardless of whether there was any intention at the time of making a deposit to vest the other person with a present interest. Despite the use of "may" the intent of the legislation is to create survivorship rights, although the bank may hold off payment for set-off purposes. (§5-5A-41) But see Barron v. Scroggins, 910 So. 2d 780 (Ala. Civ. App. 2005) in which the court relied on §35-4-7, which presumes a tenancy in common and no right of survivorship. The court failed to even mention §5-5A-41.

Table 5.01, Part 1
Principal Will Substitutes

Which of the Following Are Valid to Pass Property at Death without Complying with Wills Formalities?

	Revocable Trust?	Transfer by Deed Effective at Death, Assuming Intent to Make Present Conveyance of Title?	Joint Tenancy?	Tenancy by the Entirety?	Totten Trust Bank Account?	Joint-Name Bank Account with No Reference to Right of Survivorship?
Alaska	Yes. (§13.33.101(a))	No, with the exception of interests in personalty and tenancy by the entirety. (§34.15.130)	Yes. (§13.33.101) The statute is modeled on the language of former U.P.C. §6-201, which has been interpreted by one court as not imposing a delivery requirement. In re Estate of O'Brien, 749 P.2d 154 (Wash. 1988), and by another court as requiring delivery, First Nat'l Bank v. Bloom, 264 N.W. 2d 208, 212 (N.D. 1978), *See generally* Uniform Nonprobate Transfers on Death Act §101 comment (2001) (stating that the court in *In re Estate of O'Brien* was "mistaken" and that the court in *First Nat'l Bank v. Bloom* decided the matter correctly).	Yes. (§34.15.140) Note that spouses who acquire real property hold the estate as tenants by the entirety unless they specify otherwise. (§34.15.110) Personal property involving joint possession and use by spouses is presumed to be held as tenants by the entirety rather than as joint tenants. See Faulk v. Estate of Haskins, 714 P. 2d 354, 654-55 (Alaska 1986) Title to real property acquired by spouses is deemed held as tenants by the entirety (§34.15.110 (b)), unless it is held in a community property trust. (§34.77.100) or unless it is declared otherwise in the conveyance. (§34.15.110 (b)) The conveyance "shall recite" the marital status of the parties acquiring the real property. If the requirement that marital status be stated is not complied with, the spouses are still presumed to hold title as tenants by the entirety. (Faulk v. Estate of Haskins, 714 P. 2d 354, 655-56 (Alaska 1986))	This account has been incorporated into the P.O.D. type account. (§13.33.203)	Yes, except if terms of account specify otherwise. (§§13.33.212, 13.33.214)
Arizona	Yes. (§14-6101(A))	Yes, (§33-405) if beneficiary deed that states it is effective on death.	Yes. Must expressly state the devise or grant vests the estate in the survivor. (§33-431(B))	No statute or cases, since not recognized in state. However, there is an analogous form of ownership described as community property with right of survivorship. (§33-431(C))	Yes. (§6-236)	Yes, except if terms of account specify otherwise. (§§14-6212, 14-6214)

Table 5.01, Part 1
Principal Will Substitutes

Which of the Following Are Valid to Pass Property at Death without Complying with Wills Formalities?

	Revocable Trust?	Transfer by Deed Effective at Death, Assuming Intent to Make Present Conveyance of Title?	Joint Tenancy?	Tenancy by the Entirety?	Totten Trust Bank Account?	Joint-Name Bank Account with No Reference to Right of Survivorship?
Arkansas	Yes. (Gall v. Union Nat. Bank of Little Rock, 159 S.W.2d 757 (1942))	Yes, if beneficiary deed states that it takes effect on death. (§ 18-12-608)	Yes, regardless of the relationship between the parties. (§ 18-12-106)	Yes. (See Weir v. Brigham, 236 S.W.2d 435 (Ark. 1951); § 23-47-204)	Yes. (§ 23-47-204(b))	Yes. (§ 23-47-204(c))
California	Yes. (Prob. § 5000)	Yes. (Prob. § 5000)	Yes (Civ. § 683, Fam Code § 750. See also Estate of Petersen, 28 Cal. App. 4th 1742, 34 Cal. Rptr. 2d 449 (1994))	Not mentioned as recognized form of ownership. (Civ. §§ 682, 683; Hannon v. Southern Pac. R. Co., 12 Cal. App. 350, 107 P. 335 (1909))	Yes. (Prob. §§ 5203, 5404 (definition))	Yes. (Prob. § 5203) Potentially different result for community property account of spouses. (Prob. § 5203(a)(5))
Colorado	Yes. (§ 15-15-101)	Yes, if it is a beneficiary deed, which must be recorded during life and indicates that transfer takes effect on death. (§ 15-15-404)	Yes. Parties do not have to specify a right of survivorship; they just have to specify a joint tenancy. (§ 38-11-101)	Not recognized in state. Any conveyance that purports to create a tenancy by entirety shall create a joint tenancy. (§ 38-31-201(1))	No. Now it is a P.O.D. account. (§ 15-15-203(1))	Yes. (§§ 15-15-212, 15-15-214)
Connecticut	Yes. (Cramer v. Hartford-Connecticut Trust Co., 147 A. 139 (1929) (instrument transferring property to trustee, in which settlor reserved life use and power of revocation and provided for payment to others upon settlor's death, created valid trust)	Depends. If intent is to defer transfer until death, then must comply with wills law. However, can have transfer as a present one, even though possession and enjoyment deferred until after death. Transferor's intent is key. (Smith v. Trinity United Meth. Church, 821 A.2d 291, 294 (Ct. Super. 2002), aff'd, 819 A.2d 225 (Ct. 2003)	Yes. (§ 47-14a)	No. (§ 47-14a)	Yes. (§ 36a-296)	Yes. (§ 36a-290)
Delaware	Yes. (Hanson v. Wilmington Trust Co., 119 A.2d 901 (1955))	No statute or cases on point.	Yes. (25 § 311)	No. (25 § 309)	Yes. (5 § 924)	Yes. (5 § 923)
District of Columbia	Yes. (§ 19-601.01 (a))	Yes. (§ 19-601.01(a)) This statutory provision is modeled on § 101 of the Uniform Nonprobate Transfers on Death Act, which is a revision of U.P.C. § 6-201 of the original U.P.C., designed to clarify that delivery is not required for the disposition by deed to be nontestamentary.	Yes, but it must be "expressly declared to be a joint tenancy." Otherwise it will be treated as a tenancy in common. (§ 42-516)	Yes. (Settle v. Settle, 8 F.2d 911 (D.C. Cir. 1925); § 42-516)	Yes. (Schilt v. Duvall, 479 F.2d 1228, 1230 (D.C. Cir. 1973) ("Totten trust" is tentative trust, revocable at will and beneficiary has no right or title to deposit until death of trustee and while trustee lives he has full control over the deposit))	Yes. (§ 26-804)

Table 5.01, Part 1
Principal Will Substitutes

Which of the Following Are Valid to Pass Property at Death without Complying with Wills Formalities?

	Revocable Trust?	Transfer by Deed Effective at Death, Assuming Intent to Make Present Conveyance of Title?	Joint Tenancy?	Tenancy by the Entirety?	Totten Trust Bank Account?	Joint-Name Bank Account with No Reference to Right of Survivorship?
Florida	Yes, as to written trusts. (§689.075(1)) See generally Alter v. Zuckerman, 585 So. 2d 303 (1991)	Yes. (Williams v. Williams, 6 So. 2d 275 (1942))	Yes. Instrument must expressly provide for survivorship. (§689.15)	Yes. (§689.15; see also Knapp v. Fredricksen, 4 So. 2d 251 (1941))	Yes. See Litsey v. First Federal Sav. & Loan Ass'n of Tampa, 243 So. 2d 239 (Dist. Ct. App. 1971) (trust deposit accounts established by decedent during his lifetime constituted Totten Trusts; and the Totten Trust doctrine, despite claim that it should be overruled or receded from, remains a firmly established rule of law in Florida) See also §655.82.	Yes. (§655.78)
Georgia	Yes, but involving trust with retained life estate. (Jennings v. Jennings, 160 S.E. 405 (Ga. 1931) See also §53-12-100 et. seq., providing for testamentary additions to pre-existing inter vivos trusts, including revocable trusts. But see Wilder v. Howard, 4 S.E.2d 199, 203 (Ga. 1939). (intent of the depositor is controlling, but trust is presumed revocable)	Yes. (Harris v. Neely, 359 S.E.2d 885 (Ga. 1987))	Yes, but only if the instrument expressly refers to the takers as "joint tenants," "joint tenants and not as tenants in common," "joint tenants with survivorship," or as taking "jointly with survivorship." (§44-6-190(a)) If these words are not used, a tenancy in common is created. (*Id.*) The foregoing does not apply to securities or bank accounts. (§44-6-190(b))	Probably not. (State v. Jackson, 399 S.E.2d 88 (1991); Sams v. McDonald, 160 S.E.2d 594 (1968) (recognized, but with suggestion it might just be treated as joint tenancy)) But see In re Watford, 427 B.R. 552, 556-57 (Bankr. S.D. Fla. 2010) (refusing to extend Sams v. McDonald and finding that Georgia law does not recognize tenancy by the entirety).	Yes. (§7-1-813(c))	Yes, rights of survivorship are recognized, unless there is clear and convincing evidence of a contrary intention at the time the account was created. (§§7-1-813(a), 7-1-815)
Hawaii	Yes. (Love v. Love, 17 Haw. 206 (Haw. Terr. 1905))	Yes, by transfer on death deed. (§527-5) (Love v. Love, 17 Haw. 206 (Haw. Terr. 1905))	Yes, but only if "it manifestly appears from the tenor of the instrument that it was intended. . . ." (§§509-1, 509-2)	Yes, but only if "it manifestly appears from the tenor of the instrument that it was intended. . . ." (§§509-1, 509-2)	Yes. (§§560:6-104(c), 560:6-106)	Yes. (§§560:6-104, 560:6-106)
Idaho	Yes. (§15-6-201)	Yes, if delivery of instrument during grantor's lifetime and intent thereby to divest himself of title. (McLaws v. Casey, 400 P.2d 386, 389 (1965)); see also §15-6-201	Yes, but only if declared in its creation to be a joint interest. (§55-104)	No statute or cases directly on point.	Yes. (§§15-6-104(c), 15-6-106)	Yes, but the surviving parties must show an intent to give to account. (§§15-6-104(a), 15-6-106)

Table 5.01, Part 1
Principal Will Substitutes

Which of the Following Are Valid to Pass Property at Death without Complying with Wills Formalities?

	Revocable Trust?	Transfer by Deed Effective at Death, Assuming Intent to Make Present Conveyance of Title?	Joint Tenancy?	Tenancy by the Entirety?	Totten Trust Bank Account?	Joint-Name Bank Account with No Reference to Right of Survivorship?
Illinois	Yes. (Merchants Nat. Bank of Aurora v. Weinold, 138 N.E.2d 840 (1956))	No, at least where deed not delivered or recorded. (Oliver v. Oliver, 36 N.E. 955 (1894))	Yes, but must be expressly declared. (765 ILCS §1005/1)	Yes. (765 ILCS §1005/1c)	Yes. (205 ILCS §625/3)	No, there must be an agreement permitting payment to the surviving party signed by all persons involved at the time the account is opened. (765 ILCS 1005/2(a))
Indiana	Yes. (§29-1-5-9)	Yes, if transfer on death deed that is recorded. (§32-17-14-11) Yes, as well, if intent of grantor is to confer title presently, but simply postpone enjoyment. (VanOrman v. VanOrman, 41 N.E.2d 693 (1942))	Yes. (§§32-17-2-4 (disclaimer); 32-21-10-2, 32-21-10-3 (real property conveyances); Robison v. Fickle, 340 N.E.2d 824 (Ct. App. 1976)) But see last column for bank accounts.	Yes. (Baker v. Cailor, 186 N.E. 769 (1933)) See also §32-21-10-2(c)(3).	Yes. (First Federal Sav. & Loan Assoc. v. Baugh, 310 N.E.2d 101 (Ct. App. 1974)) See also §§32-17-11-1 et seq.)	Yes. (§§32-17-11-4, 32-17-11-5, 32-17-11-18)
Iowa	Yes, if the instrument passes a present interest, even though possession and enjoyment are postponed. (Trustees of Synod v. Horel, 16 N.W.2d 209, 212 (1944))	Yes, if duly executed and recorded, even if recordation occurs after the grantor's death. In the latter case there is a visible presumption of an intent to pass immediate title. (Avery v. Lillie, 148 N.W.2d 474, 477 (1967))	Yes. (In re Murdoch's Estate, 29 N.W.2d 177 (1947)) Also for securities. (§633D.3)	Yes, with respect to securities. (§633D.3) Otherwise, this form of ownership is likely not recognized. See Fay v. Smiley, 209 N.W. 307 (1926). However, §557.15 indicates that a conveyance to two or more persons creates a tenancy in common "unless a contrary intent is expressed."	Yes. (In re Estate of Podhajsky, 115 N.W. 590, 592 (1908))	Notwithstanding general prescription in favor of tenancy in common, in the case of bank accounts, there is a presumption in favor of a joint tenancy. (In re Estate of Kokjohn, 531 N.W.2d 99 (Iowa 1995))
Kansas	Yes. (Moore v. Hayes, 26 P.2d 254 (1933))	Yes. §59-3501 expressly allows this for real estate by use of transfer on death deed.	Yes. Devise must make clear that joint tenancy was intended to be created, otherwise a tenancy by the entirety is created. (§58-501)	No. (Stewart v. Thomas, 68 P. 70 (1902) & Laws of 1891, Ch. 203) See also Shubert v. Hager, 796 P.2d 564 (Kan. Ct. App. 1990) (a grant to the spouses as tenants by the entirety creates a joint tenancy).	Yes. (In re Estate of Morton, 769 P.2d 616 (1987) (Totten trust valid in Kansas; need not comply with statute of wills))	Yes. (§9-1205)

Table 5.01, Part 1
Principal Will Substitutes

Which of the Following Are Valid to Pass Property at Death without Complying with Wills Formalities?

	Revocable Trust?	Transfer by Deed Effective at Death, Assuming Intent to Make Present Conveyance of Title?	Joint Tenancy?	Tenancy by the Entirety?	Totten Trust Bank Account?	Joint-Name Bank Account with No Reference to Right of Survivorship?
Kentucky	Yes. (§ 391.360)	Yes, even if reserved life estate and power to revoke retained. (Commonwealth v. McCauley's Ex'r, 179 S.W. 411 (1915))	While joint tenancy is recognized as a form of ownership and can certainly be provided for, the Kentucky version does not automatically provide for a right of survivorship. (§ 381.120) An estate that is conveyed or devised will be respected as a joint tenancy with right of survivorship "when it manifestly appears, from the tenor of the instrument, that it was intended that the part of the one dying should belong to the others . . . " (§ 381.130) If the right of survivorship exists, it may prevent the partition of the property, as in the case of the traditional joint tenancy. For example, a sharply divided Kentucky Supreme Court held that where a conveyance created a right of survivorship, a joint tenant could not subsequently deed away his interest, but only his joint life estate and his own right of survivorship. (Sanderson v. Saxon, 834 S.W. 2d 676 (Ky. 1992)) Notwithstanding this decision, the result in Sanderson appears to have been overturned by statute with regard to real property. See § 381.130(2)(a)(1), which recognizes the right of a joint tenant to partition during his or her lifetime by deed or other instrument. (§ 381.120)	Yes. (§ 381.050(1)) However, the conveyance to the spouses results in no right of survivorship, but rather a tenancy in common, "unless a right of survivorship is expressly provided for . . . " The will of a spouse cannot eliminate survivorship. (§ 381.050(2))	Yes. (§§ 391.315(3), 391.325)	Yes. (§§ 391.315(1), 391.325)

Table 5.01, Part 1
Principal Will Substitutes

Which of the Following Are Valid to Pass Property at Death without Complying with Wills Formalities?

	Revocable Trust?	Transfer by Deed Effective at Death, Assuming Intent to Make Present Conveyance of Title?	Joint Tenancy?	Tenancy by the Entirety?	Totten Trust Bank Account?	Joint-Name Bank Account with No Reference to Right of Survivorship?
Louisiana[1]	Yes. (Rev. Stat. §§ 9:2011, 9:2013, 9:2046)	Yes. (Succession of Lanata, 18 So. 2d 500 (1944); McKnight v. Comet, 143 So. 726 (Ct. App. 1932))	Joint tenancy is not recognized. (Gathright v. Smith, 352 So. 2d 282 (1977)) However, this form of ownership is recognized for bank accounts if written agreement with bank provides for survivorship. (Rev. Stat. §6:1255)	Tenancy by the entirety is not recognized. (Civ. Code Art. 3526, revision cmt. (h))	Yes. (Rev. Stat. §6:314(A))	No. Written agreement must provide for survivorship. (Rev. Stat. §6:1255)
Maine	Yes. (18-A §6-201)	Not valid if, for example, kept by grantor's attorney, from whom grantor might demand its return at any time. Therefore, it depends on intent. (Eddy v. Pinder, 159 A. 727 (1932)) See also 18-A §6-201.	Yes. (33 §159)	No. (19-A §801; Palmer v. Flint, 161 A.2d 837 (1960))	Yes. (18-A §§6-104(c), 6-106)	Yes. (18-A §§6-104, 6-106)
Maryland	Yes. (Brown v. Mercantile Tr. & Deposit Co., 40 A. 256 (1898))	Yes. (Register of Wills v. Blackway, 141 A.2d 713 (1958))	Yes. To create a joint tenancy, the deed, will, or other written instrument must expressly provide that the property granted is to be held in joint tenancy. (Real Prop. §2-117)	Yes. (McManus v. Summers, 430 A.2d 80 (1981))	Yes. (Financial Institutions Code §1-204; Estates & Trusts Code §1-401)	Yes. (Financial Institutions Code §1-204; Estates & Trusts Code §1-401)
Massachusetts	Yes. (Ascher v. Cohen, 131 N.E.2d 198 (1956))	Yes. (Kelley v. Snow, 70 N.E. 89 (1904)) See also 190B §6-101, which *actually* uses language similar to former U.P.C. §6-201*, which appears to require a lifetime delivery, but in the accompanying Comment to §6-101 states that the language of a revised version of the U.P.C. has been relied upon, thereby eliminating the lifetime delivery requirement. In fact, §6-101 does not use the alternate language.	Yes, but it must be clearly expressed that a joint tenancy is created. (184 §7)	Yes, but it must be clearly expressed that a tenancy by the entirety is created. (184 §7)	Yes, but only if indicated on signature card or beneficiary has notice. (Wolk v. Herbert, 2000 WL 35443740 (Super. Ct. Jan. 25, 2000), citing Cohen v. Newton Savings Bank 67 N.E. 2d 748 (1946))	Presumption of right of survivorship but can be rebutted (Desrosiers v. Germain, 429 N.E. 2d 385 (1981)).

Table 5.01, Part 1
Principal Will Substitutes

Which of the Following Are Valid to Pass Property at Death without Complying with Wills Formalities?

	Revocable Trust?	Transfer by Deed Effective at Death, Assuming Intent to Make Present Conveyance of Title?	Joint Tenancy?	Tenancy by the Entirety?	Totten Trust Bank Account?	Joint-Name Bank Account with No Reference to Right of Survivorship?
Michigan	Yes. (Soltis v. First American Bank Muskegon, 513 N.W.2d 148, *appeal denied*, 522 N.W.2d 639 (1994))	Yes, problem when grantor retains possession of deed and the grantee lacks knowledge of it, even if it was recorded. (Havens v. Schoen, 310 N.W.2d 870, 871 (1981))	Yes. To be relied on, must be an expressly declared joint tenancy. (§ 554.44)	Yes. (In re Selle's Estate, 292 N.W.2d 147 (1980)) See also § 557.71	Yes. (§ 487.702)	Yes. (§ 490.56)
Minnesota	Yes. (Connecticut General Life Ins. Co. v. First Nat. Bank of Minneapolis, 262 N.W.2d 403 (1977))	Yes. (§ 507.071; see also (Hagen v. Hagen, 161 N.W. 380 (1917))	Yes. (Irvine v. Helvering, 99 F.2d 265 (1938)) See also § 500.19(2) (addressing joint tenancies in land)	No. (Wilson v. Wilson, 45 N.W. 710 (1890))	Yes. (In re Estate of Kroyer, 385 N.W.2d 31 (1986))	Yes. (§§ 524.6-204(a), 524.6-206)
Mississippi	No statute or cases on point.	No. Testamentary in nature, even if in form of deed, if the donor's intention was for it to take effect only after the grantor's death. (Simpson v. McGee, 73 So. 55 (1916))	Yes. Must appear from tenor of instrument that it intended to create an estate in joint tenancy. (§ 89-1-7)	Yes. Must appear from tenor of instrument that it intended to create an estate in entirety with right of survivorship. (§ 89-1-7)	Yes. (§ 81-5-62)	Yes. (§ 81-5-63)
Missouri	Yes. (§§ 461.001, 461.009)	Yes, through use of a deed "to take effect upon death." (§ 461.025)	Yes, if expressly declared. (§ 442.450) See also § 442.025; Neagle v. Johnson, 261 F.Supp. 634, *aff'd*, 381 F.2d 9 (1966)	Yes. (Jones v. Cox, 629 S.W.2d 511 (1981)) See also § 442.025	Yes. (§ 362.475)	Yes. (§ 362.470)
Montana	Yes. (§ 72-6-111)	Yes. (§ 72-6-121)	Yes. (§ 70-20-310)	No. (Clark v. Clark, 387 P.2d 907 (1963))	Yes. (§§ 72-6-212, 72-6-214)	Yes. (§§ 72-6-212, 72-6-214)
Nebraska	Yes. (§ 30-2715(a))	Yes. (§ 30-2715(a))	Yes. In order to create a joint tenancy, that purpose must be clearly expressed. (DeForge v. Patrick, 76 N.W.2d 733 (Neb. 1956)). However, joint tenancies are not favored. (In re Ogier's estate, 125 N.W. 2d 68 (Neb. 1963)).	No. (Kern v. McDonald, 84 N.W. 92 (Neb. 1900))	Possibly given effect under § 30-2719(b). (See also Comment § 30-2209) The P.O.D. alternative is enforced. (§ 30-2729)	Right of survivorship if multiple party account. (§ 30-2723)
Nevada	Yes. (Coleman v. First Nat'l Bank, 506 P.2d 86 (Nev. 1973))	Yes, through use of "deed upon death." (§§ 111.671 et seq., 111.661)	Yes. The grant or devise must expressly declare the joint tenancy. (§ 111.060)	No statute—community property state.	Yes. (See also Byrd v. Lanahan, 783 P.2d 426, 428-29 (1989).)	Yes. Deposit into the account must have been intended to be payable to survivors. (§ 100.085)

Table 5.01, Part 1
Principal Will Substitutes

Which of the Following Are Valid to Pass Property at Death without Complying with Wills Formalities?

	Revocable Trust?	Transfer by Deed Effective at Death, Assuming Intent to Make Present Conveyance of Title?	Joint Tenancy?	Tenancy by the Entirety?	Totten Trust Bank Account?	Joint-Name Bank Account with No Reference to Right of Survivorship?
New Hampshire	Yes. (In re Estate of York, 65 A.2d 282 (1949))	Yes. "In the normal course of events persons will use a deed, mortgage, note or contract as a substitute for accomplishing the same purpose by will. When a will is employed we require compliance with the statute of wills. But when a contractual undertaking is employed we do not declare it invalid because it accomplished in part what could have been accomplished by the use of a will." (McGrath v. McGrath, 220 A.2d 760, 762-63 (1966))	Yes. Must clearly express intention to execute a joint tenancy with rights of survivorship. (§477:18)	Yes. Must clearly express intention to create an estate as tenants by the entirety. (§477:18)	Yes. (§ 383-B:4-401(d))	Unclear after repeal of §384.28; general practice is for banks to provide joint account card that provides for survivorship and this can be altered if the depositor does not wish this.
New Jersey	Yes, in case where settlor intends to create a present beneficial interest in favor of the named beneficiary, while postponing his enjoyment thereof until the settlor's death. (In re Kovalyshyn's Estate, 343 A.2d 852 (1975))	Maybe. The key is that there be an intention to part with the deed, even if not actually delivered and to pass title. (Rommell v. Happe, 115 A. 906, 908 (Ch. 1921)) There must be an intention to make deed presently effective. If there is no present intent to pass the title immediately, then the transaction is testamentary in nature and is controlled by the statute of wills. (Montgomery v. Varley, 144 A. 183, 185 (1929))	Yes. (§§ 46:3-17, 46:3-17.1, 46:3-17.5)	Yes. (§§ 46:3-17, 46:3-17.2, 46:3-17.4, 46:3-17.5)	Yes. (§§ 17:16I-5(c), 17:16I-14)	Yes. (§§ 17:16I-5, 17:16I-14)
New Mexico	Yes (§ 46A-6-60(B); Bell v. State of Bell, 181 P.3d 708 (Ct. App. 2008))	Yes. (§ 45-6-405)	Yes. (§40-3-2); Menger v. Otera County State Bank, 98 P.2d 834 (1940) (title is not important, but rather the intent of the transferor)	No, since community property state. (Swink v. Fingado, 850 P.2d 978, 983 n.9 (1993); McDonald v. Senn, 204 P.2d 990, 995 (1949))	Yes. (§§ 45-6-212, 45-6-214) Modeled after U.P.C., which treats Totten trusts as P.O.D. designation. (See § 45-6-201(H))	Yes. (§§ 45-6-212, 45-6-214)

Table 5.01, Part 1
Principal Will Substitutes

Which of the Following Are Valid to Pass Property at Death without Complying with Wills Formalities?

	Revocable Trust?	Transfer by Deed Effective at Death, Assuming Intent to Make Present Conveyance of Title?	Joint Tenancy?	Tenancy by the Entirety?	Totten Trust Bank Account?	Joint-Name Bank Account with No Reference to Right of Survivorship?
New York	Yes. (In re Plotkin's Estate, 290 N.Y.S.2d 46 (1968))	Yes, if deed is absolute. (Slowey v. Hunt, 177 N.Y.S. 505 (1919))	Yes. (Est. Powers & Trusts §6-2.1)	Yes, with respect to real property. It is permitted as well in the case of shares of stock of a cooperative apartment corporation allocated to an apartment or unit together with the appurtenant proprietary lease. (Est. Powers & Trusts §6-2.1(4))	Yes. (Est. Powers & Trusts §7-5.1 et. seq.)	No. A right of survivorship must be included in the instrument. Although, even if there is no right of survivorship, evidence can be presented to show that the decedent intended to create a right of survivorship. (Banking Law §675; In re Estate of Timoshevich, 521 N.Y.S.2d 311, 313 (App. Div. 1987))
North Carolina	Yes. (Ridge v. Bright, 93 S.E.2d 607 (1956))	Yes, if grantor intends title to pass on its execution, despite the fact that enjoyment will be postponed until after grantor's death. (Phifer v. Mullis, 83 S.E. 582 (1914))	Yes, if "the instrument creating the joint tenancy expressly provides for a right of survivorship." (§41-2)	Yes. (§39-13.6; Bank of Greenville v. Gornto, 77 S.E. 222 (1913)) However, it only exists pursuant to contract. Also, it does not exist for personal property. (Bowling v. Bowling, 91 S.E.2d 176 (1956))	Previous section repealed and Code now directs to the section on POD accounts.	No. There must be a written agreement expressly providing for the right of survivorship. (§41-2.1)
North Dakota	Yes. (§30.1-31-01)	Yes. (§30.1-32.1-02)	Yes. (§47-10-23)	No. (Renz v. Renz, 256 N.W.2d 883 (1977))	No. Replaced by P.O.D. account. (§30.1-31-04(2))	Yes, if a multiple party account. (§§30.1-31-09, 30.1-31-11) See also §30.1-31-02(8)(b)
Ohio	Yes. (Central Trust Co. v. McCarthy, 57 N.E.2d 126 (1943))	Yes. (§5302.22) If the terms of the statute are not observed, the common law provides that a deed is effective if intent is not to pass title only upon death; if it is the deed will be testamentary in character. (Tucker v. Morey, 143 N.E.2d 627, 629 (1956))	Yes. Joint tenancy with right of survivorship does not exist at common law in Ohio but is a matter of contract. See, e.g., Spitz v. Rapport, 604 N.E.2d 801 (Ct. App. 1992); §5302.20	No. Instead, effective Apr. 4, 1985, a tenancy of survivorship, akin to a joint tenancy, is the replacement. (§§5302.17; 5302.21)	Yes. (§1109.06)	Yes. (§1109.07)

5013

Table 5.01, Part 1
Principal Will Substitutes

Which of the Following Are Valid to Pass Property at Death without Complying with Wills Formalities?

	Revocable Trust?	Transfer by Deed Effective at Death, Assuming Intent to Make Present Conveyance of Title?	Joint Tenancy?	Tenancy by the Entirety?	Totten Trust Bank Account?	Joint-Name Bank Account with No Reference to Right of Survivorship?
Oklahoma	Yes. (Limb v. Aldridge, 978 P.2d 365, 367 (Okla. Ct. Civ. App. 1998))	Yes. (16 Okla. St., Ch. 1, App. Standard §17.4) Otherwise, not effective, especially where grantor keeps control of property during his lifetime and acts as if he still owns it. (Thomas v. Bank of Oklahoma, 684 P.2d 553, 555 (1984))	Yes. (60 Okla. St. §74)	Yes, but only between husband and wife. (60 Okla. St. §74)	Yes. (6 Okla. St. §902)	Yes. (6 Okla. St. §901)
Oregon	Yes, but care must be exercised. There is some authority that questions the trust's nontestamentary character when the grantor retains secret control over the trust assets and seeks to dispose of the trust assets by will, and the result might be the defeat of creditors. Each case turns on its facts. (Coston v. Portland Tr. Co., 282 P. 442 (1929))	Yes. (§93.963) If the statute is not observed, there is a risk it will be considered testamentary if the deed is not delivered or if it only takes effect at the grantor's death and conveys all of his property. (Witham v. Witham, 66 P.2d 281 (1937); In re Neil's Estate, 226 P. 439 (1924))	Yes. The right of survivorship must be clearly and expressly declared in the conveyance. (§93.180)	Yes. (Gorger v. Gorger, 555 P.2d 1 (1976)) §93.180 does not alter this result. See Noblitt v. Beebe, 35 P. 248 (1882).	Yes. (§§708A.470(3), 708A.480)	Yes. (§§708A.470, 708A.480)
Pennsylvania	Yes. (In re Huested's Estate, 169 A.2d 57 (1961))	Yes. (Damiani v. Lobasco, 79 A.2d 268 (1951))	Yes, but only if right of survivorship is clearly expressed. (68 §110; Margarite v. Ewald, 381 A.2d 480 (1977)) Although this statute seems to be addressing real property, it applies as well to personal property. (Teacher v. Kijurina, 76 A.2d 197 (1950))	Yes. (In re Michael's Estate, 218 A.2d 338 (1966))	Yes. (20 §§6304(b), 6306)	Yes. (20 §§6304(a), 6306)

Table 5.01, Part 1
Principal Will Substitutes

Which of the Following Are Valid to Pass Property at Death without Complying with Wills Formalities?

	Revocable Trust?	Transfer by Deed Effective at Death, Assuming Intent to Make Present Conveyance of Title?	Joint Tenancy?	Tenancy by the Entirety?	Totten Trust Bank Account?	Joint-Name Bank Account with No Reference to Right of Survivorship?
Rhode Island	Yes. (Green v. Green, 559 A.2d 1047 (1989)) Also implied by pourover provision. (§ 33-6-33)	Yes. However, even if grantee is in possession of deed, it is not valid as a testamentary substitute if the grantor intended that it not take effect until death. (Lambert v. Lambert, 77 A.2d 325 (1950))	Yes, but must declare that tenancy is joint or is to those persons and the survivors or survivor of them. (§ 34-3-1)	Yes. § 34-3-1, which creates a presumption in favor of tenancy in common rather than joint tenancy, does not prohibit an estate by the entirety nor did the legislature intend to circumvent the common law as to such estates. (Bloomfield v. Brown, 25 A.2d 354 (1942))	Yes. (§ 19-9-12)	No. (§ 19-9-14) If a joint bank account does not provide for survivorship rights, that absence will be conclusive evidence of an intent not to transfer any right of ownership to the survivor, absent evidence of mistake or fraud. (Robinson v. Delfino, 710 A.2d 154 (R.I. 1998))
South Carolina	Yes. (§ 62-6-201)	Yes. (§ 62-6-201) See also Hydrick v. Hydrick, 141 S.E. 156 (1927)	Yes, but instrument creating joint tenancy must expressly provide for a right of survivorship. (§ 62-2-804)	This estate no longer exists. (Davis v. Davis, 75 S.E.2d 46 (1953))	Yes. (§§ 62-6-104(c), 62-6-106)	Yes. (§§ 62-6-104, 62-6-106)
South Dakota	Yes. (§ 29A-6-113)	Yes. (§ 29A-6-113)	Yes. (§§ 43-2-14, 25-2-3 (with respect to husband and wife); In re Hanson's Estate, 93 N.W.2d 606 (1958))	No. (Schimke v. Karlstad, 208 N.W.2d 710 (1973))	Yes. (§ 51A-10-4, 29A-6-104(3))	Yes. (§§ 29A-6-104, 29A-6-106)
Tennessee	Yes. (§ 35-15-601)	Yes, if duly acknowledged and legally delivered. (Johnson v. Mitchell, 20 Tenn. 168 (1839); Stamper v. Venable, 97 S.W. 812 (1906))	No. A joint tenancy with survivorship is cut down to a tenancy in common. (§ 66-1-107) However, it can be created if there is an express intention. (McLeroy v. McLeroy, 40 S.W.2d 1027 (1931))	Yes. (§§ 31-1-108, 36-3-505)	Yes. (§ 45-2-704)	Yes. (§ 45-2-703)
Texas	Yes. (Est. § 111.052)	Yes. (Est. § 111.052)	Yes, only if agree in writing that the interest of any joint owner who dies shall survive to the surviving joint owner or owners.(Est. § 111.001) (See also Est. Code §§ 111.002, 112.051, pertaining to creation of survivorship right in community property and in agreement between persons, such as cohabitants)	No statute or cases since community property state.	Yes. (Est. §§ 113.153, 113.158, 113.205)	No. A written agreement creating a right of survivorship is necessary. (Est. §§ 113.153, 113.158)

Table 5.01, Part 1
Principal Will Substitutes

Which of the Following Are Valid to Pass Property at Death without Complying with Wills Formalities?

	Revocable Trust?	Transfer by Deed Effective at Death, Assuming Intent to Make Present Conveyance of Title?	Joint Tenancy?	Tenancy by the Entirety?	Totten Trust Bank Account?	Joint-Name Bank Account with No Reference to Right of Survivorship?
Utah	Yes, unless the account, by its terms, has no right of survivorship. (§75-6-201)	Yes. (Controlled Receivables, Inc. v. Harman, 413 P.2d 807 (1966)) This is an interesting case, because the Utah Supreme Court viewed father's comments that he did not intend to pass title to his children until death as "self-serving" and inconsistent with his actions. He argued that in light of his purpose to avoid testamentary formalities, the deed was invalid. The court also emphasized that purpose does not undermine the validity of the deed. *See also* §75-6-201.	Yes. (§57-1-5)	Implied by fact that survivor can disclaim interest devolving by right of survivorship. (§75-2-801)	Yes. (§§75-6-104(3), 75-6-106)	Yes. (§§75-6-104, 75-6-106)
Vermont	Yes, but burden is on the beneficiary to prove a completed trust for his benefit. (Reynolds v. Shambeau, 437 A.2d 1101, 1103 (1981))	Yes, if intent to transfer present interest, even if not present enjoyment. (Blair v. Blair, 10 A.2d 188 (1940); Straw v. Mower, 130 A. 687 (1925)) See also Scott v. Beland, 45 A.2d 641 (1946).	Yes. Conveyance and devises of land must express therein that the grantees or devisees shall take the lands jointly or in joint tenancy or to them and the survivors of them. (27 §2)	Yes. (Buzzell v. Edward H. Everett Co., 180 F. Supp. 893 (1960))	Yes. (In re Estate of Adams, 587 A.2d 958 (1990))	Yes, but there must be evidence to support an intent to create a right of survivorship. (8 §14204)
Virginia	Yes, as long as an interest or estate was intended to pass under the instrument to the trustee or beneficiaries prior to the grantor's death. (Bickers v. Shenandoah Valley Nat'l Bank of Winchester, 90 S.E.2d 865 (1956)) Also implied from pourover statute. (§64.2-426(B)–(C))	Yes, even when there is wording to effect that postponement of enjoyment until grantor's death "is testamentary in nature." (Short v. A. H. Still Inv. Corp., 147 S.E.2d 99 (1966))	Yes, but right of survivorship can only be conferred by the instrument conveying the property. (§§55-20, 55-21)	Yes. Must be manifest from wording of the conveyance that grantor wants to establish a tenancy by entirety. (§§55-20, 55-21)	Yes. (§§6.2-608(c), 6.2-610)	Yes. (§§6.2-608, 6.2-610)

Table 5.01, Part 1
Principal Will Substitutes

Which of the Following Are Valid to Pass Property at Death without Complying with Wills Formalities?

	Revocable Trust?	Transfer by Deed Effective at Death, Assuming Intent to Make Present Conveyance of Title?	Joint Tenancy?	Tenancy by the Entirety?	Totten Trust Bank Account?	Joint-Name Bank Account with No Reference to Right of Survivorship?
Washington	Yes. (In re Estate of Overmire, 794 P.2d 518 (1990); §11.02.091)	Yes. (In re Estate of Mary O'Brien, 749 P.2d 154 (1988); §11.02.091) This court's construction of the provision, adopted from the U.P.C., has been described by the Uniform Nonprobate Transfer on Death Act §101 Comment, as "mistaken," in not requiring a lifetime delivery of the deed.	Yes. (§64.28.010)	No. This statute abolishes the right of survivorship as an incident of tenancy by the entireties. (§11.04.071)	Yes. (§30A.22.100)	The statute is ambiguous. (§30A.22.100) There is a rebuttable presumption that a joint account with right of survivorship has been created. See In re Haden, 2004 WL 2095641 (Wash. Ct. App. Sept. 20, 2004)
West Virginia	Yes. (Davis v. KB & T Co., 309 S.E.2d 45, 49 (1983))	Yes. (Spangler v. Vermillion, 92 S.E. 449 (1917); Lauck v. Logan, 31 S.E. 986 (1898))	No. (§36-1-19) However, §36-1-20 opens a major exception allowing joint tenancies, based on "the tenor of the instrument" or the use of the disjunctive "or" where it links up multiple owners. (Lieving v. Hadley, 423 S.E.2d 600 (1992)) (abrogated on other grounds)	No. It is treated as a tenancy in common. (§36-1-19)	Yes. (§31A-4-33)	Yes. (§31A-4-33)
Wisconsin	Yes. (§705.10)	Yes. (§705.10)	Yes. (§§700.17, 700.19)	No. (Aaby v. Kaupanger, 221 N.W. 417, 418 (1928))	Yes, incorporated into the P.O.D. statute. (§§705.01(8) & 705.04)	Yes. (§705.04)

Table 5.01, Part 1
Principal Will Substitutes

Which of the Following Are Valid to Pass Property at Death without Complying with Wills Formalities?[1]

	Revocable Trust?	Transfer by Deed Effective at Death, Assuming Intent to Make Present Conveyance of Title?	Joint Tenancy?	Tenancy by the Entirety?	Totten Trust Bank Account?	Joint-Name Bank Account with No Reference to Right of Survivorship?
Wyoming	Apparently so. This is implication of Briggs v. Wyoming Nat'l Bank, 836 P.2d 263 (1992).	Yes, if transfer is one of a present interest. (Forbes v. Volk, 358 P.2d 942 (1961))	Yes, but there must be an intent to create the joint tenancy; it will not be presumed. (In re Welty, 217 B.R. 907 (D. Wyo. 1998)) (§ 34-1-140)	Yes, but there must be an express intent to create a tenancy by the entirety if it is in personal property. (In re Anselmi, 52 B.R. 479 (D.Wyo.1985)) (§ 34-1-140)	Yes. (§ 2-1-203(c))	Yes. (§ 2-1-203)

[1] *Caution*: A civil law system with very different concepts is followed. Even though common-law concepts like the trust have been recognized statutorily, they may be approached very differently.

Table 5.01, Part 2
Principal Will Substitutes

Which of the Following Are Valid to Pass Property at Death without Complying with Wills Formalities?

	Payable on Death (P.O.D.) Bank Account?	Transfer on Death (T.O.D.) Security Registration?	Life Insurance Proceeds?	Gift?	A Writing Disposing of Tangible Personal Property Even If Not Entirely in the Testator's Handwriting?
Alabama	Yes, unless the account, by its terms, has no right of survivorship. (§§ 5-24-12, 5-24-14)	Yes. (§§ 8-6-146, 8-6-148)	Yes. (Williams v. Williams, 438 So. 2d 735 (1983) (designation of the beneficiary of a life insurance policy is governed by the provisions of the policy; such provisions are not testamentary))	Yes. The elements of a valid gift are: (a) an intention to give and surrender title to, and dominion over, the property; (b) delivery of the property to the donee; and (c) acceptance by the donee. (Dial v. Dial, 603 So. 2d 1020, 1022 (1992))	No statute or cases on point. There would appear to be no authority in support of this being given effect.
Alaska	Yes. (§§ 13.33.212, 13.33.214)	Yes. (§§ 13.33.307, 13.33.309)	Yes. (§ 13.33.101)	Yes. The donor cannot intend to retain control and ownership, and there must be delivery. (In re Estate of Evanco, 955 P.2d 525, 527 (Alaska 1998))	Yes. Writing must be signed by testator and describe items "other than money or items specifically disposed of by will," with reasonable certainty. The writing may be referred to as one to be in existence at the time of the testator's death; it may be prepared before or after the execution of the will; it may be altered by the testator after its preparation; and it may be a writing that does not have significance apart from its effect in the dispositions made by the will. (§ 13.12.513)
Arizona	Yes. (§§ 14-6212(A)–(B), 14-6214)	Yes. (§§ 14-6307-6311)	Yes. (§ 14-6101)	Yes. A gift of goods or chattel is not valid unless the gift is in writing, duly acknowledged and recorded or by will, duly proved and recorded, or unless actual possession of the gift is passed to and remains with the donee or someone claiming under him. (§ 33-601)	Yes. Writing must be either in handwriting of or signed by testator and describe the items and devisees with reasonable certainty. The writing cannot dispose of money or property specifically devised by will. The writing may be referred to as one to be in existence at the time of the testator's death, prepared before or after the execution of the will, or altered by the testator after its preparation. The writing may have no significance apart from its effect on the dispositions made by the will. (§ 14-2513)

Table 5.01, Part 2
Principal Will Substitutes

Which of the Following Are Valid to Pass Property at Death without Complying with Wills Formalities?

	Payable on Death (P.O.D.) Bank Account?	Transfer on Death (T.O.D.) Security Registration?	Life Insurance Proceeds?	Gift?	A Writing Disposing of Tangible Personal Property Even If Not Entirely in the Testator's Handwriting?
Arkansas	Yes. (§ 23-47-204)	Yes. (§§ 28-14-107, 28-14-109)	Yes. (Slavik v. Estate of Slavik, 880 S.W.2d 524 (1994))	Yes, if proven by clear and convincing evidence that: (a) the donor was of sound mind; (b) an actual delivery of the property took place; (c) the donor clearly intended to make an immediate, present, and final gift; (d) the donor unconditionally released all future dominion and control over the property; and (e) the donee accepted the gift. (Wright v. Union Nat. Bank of Arkansas, Little Rock, Ark., 819 S.W.2d 698, 700 (1991))	Yes. Writing must either be in the handwriting of, or signed by, testator and describe the items and devisees with reasonable certainty. The writing cannot dispose of money, evidences of indebtedness, documents of title, securities, and property used in a trade or business as well as property specifically devised by will. The writing may be referred to as one to be in existence at the time of the testator's death, prepared before or after the execution of the will, or altered by the testator after its preparation. The writing may have no significance apart from its effect on the dispositions made by the will. (§ 28-25-107(b))
California	Yes. (Prob. § 5203)	Yes. (Prob. §§ 5000, 5500 et seq.)	Yes. (Prob. § 5000)	Yes. However, a verbal gift is not valid unless the means of obtaining possession and control of the thing are given, nor is it valid if it is capable of delivery unless there is actual and symbolic delivery of the thing to the donee. (Civ. § 1147)	Yes. (Prob. § 6132) Writing must be referred to by will. Must be dated and written in handwriting of or signed by testator. It must describe the items and recipients with reasonable certainty. It cannot dispose of money that is common coin or currency and property used primarily in a trade or business. The writing may be written or signed before or after execution of the will and need not have significance apart from its effect upon the dispositions of property made by the will.

Table 5.01, Part 2
Principal Will Substitutes

Which of the Following Are Valid to Pass Property at Death without Complying with Wills Formalities?

	Payable on Death (P.O.D.) Bank Account?	Transfer on Death (T.O.D.) Security Registration?	Life Insurance Proceeds?	Gift?	A Writing Disposing of Tangible Personal Property Even If Not Entirely in the Testator's Handwriting?
Colorado	Yes. (§§ 15-15-212, 15-15-214)	Yes. (§§ 15-15-307, 15-15-309)	Yes. (§ 15-15-101)	Yes, the gift is valid if there is a clear and unmistakable intention to make a gift and a complete parting of possession and surrender by the donor of all control and dominion over the same to the donee. (Goemmer v. Hartman, 791 P.2d 1238 (1990))	Yes. Writing must be either in the handwriting of, or signed by, testator and describe items and devisees with reasonable certainty. The writing cannot dispose of money, evidences of indebtedness, documents of title, securities, and property used in a trade or business as well as property specifically devised by will. The writing may be referred to as one to be in existence at the time of the testator's death; it may be prepared before or after the execution of the will; it may be altered by the testator after its preparation; and it may be a writing that has no significance apart from its effect on the dispositions made by the will. (§ 15-11-513)
Connecticut	Yes. (§§ 45a-468; 45a-468)	Yes. (§ 45a-468e-g)	Yes. (Dubno v. Colby, 458 A.2d 396 (1982))	Yes, if valid delivery accompanied by intent that title "pass immediately." (Bergen v. Bergen, 411 A.2d 22, 24 (1979))	No statute or cases on point. There would appear to be no authority in support of this being given effect.

Table 5.01, Part 2
Principal Will Substitutes

Which of the Following Are Valid to Pass Property at Death without Complying with Wills Formalities?

	Payable on Death (P.O.D.) Bank Account?	Transfer on Death (T.O.D.) Security Registration?	Life Insurance Proceeds?	Gift?	A Writing Disposing of Tangible Personal Property Even If Not Entirely in the Testator's Handwriting?
Delaware	Yes. (12 §§ 804-805, 809)	Yes. (12 §§ 804-805, 809)	No statute or cases on point. Implied by 12 § 1901(c), which provides that if someone other than the decedent or decedent's personal representative is designated as beneficiary, insurance proceeds are not included in decedent's estate and such person is entitled to the proceeds.	Yes, if intent and "actual or constructive delivery of the gift during [the donor's] lifetime." The fact that legal title to shares is not to be transferred until after the donor's death "does not make the gift testamentary," at least if the sole purpose of the arrangement was to enable the donor to retain dividend income during her lifetime. (Inre Estate of Surian, Civ. A. No. 9754, 1990 WL 100794 (Ch. 1990); Bothe v. Dennie, 324 A.2d 784, 786 (Super. 1974))	Yes. Writing must either be in the handwriting of or signed by testator and must identify the items and the legatees with reasonable certainty. The writing cannot dispose of money, evidences of indebtedness, documents of title, securities, and property used in a trade or business, as well as property specifically devised by will. The writing must not be inconsistent with the terms of the will and must not be inconsistent with any other writing permitted by the section unless the writing is dated in which case the writing with the latest date will control. The writing may be one referred to as in existence at the time of the testator's death; it may be prepared before or after the execution of the will; it may be altered by the testator after the preparation; and it may be a writing which has no significance apart from its effect upon the dispositions made by the will. (12 §212)
District of Columbia	Yes. (§ 19-602.12)	Yes. (§ 19-603.07)	Yes. (§ 19-601.01(a))	Yes. If donor has died must prove by clear and convincing evidence that there was delivery, intention on the part of the donor to make the gift, and absolute disposition of the subject of the gift. (Uckele v. Jewett, 642 A.2d 119 (1994))	No statute or cases on point. There would appear to be no authority in support of this being given effect.

5022

Table 5.01, Part 2
Principal Will Substitutes

Which of the Following Are Valid to Pass Property at Death without Complying with Wills Formalities?

	Payable on Death (P.O.D.) Bank Account?	Transfer on Death (T.O.D.) Security Registration?	Life Insurance Proceeds?	Gift?	A Writing Disposing of Tangible Personal Property Even If Not Entirely in the Testator's Handwriting?
Florida	Yes. (§ 655.82(n))	Yes. (§§ 711.507, 711.509)	Yes. (Gartley v. Gartley, 622 So. 2d 77 (1993))	Yes. (Canova v. Florida Nat'l Bank, 60 So. 2d 627 (1952) (in case of oral gift, need delivery, surrender by donor, intent to pass title))	Yes. Writing must be signed by testator and must describe the items with reasonable certainty. However, the writing cannot dispose of property used in a trade or business. The writing may be prepared before or after the execution of the will. Testator may alter it after its preparation, and it may be a writing that has no significance apart from its effect on the dispositions made by the will. (§732.515)
Georgia	Yes. (§§ 7-1-813(b), 7-1-815)	Yes. (§ 53-5-67)	Yes. (§ 33-25-11; National Life & Acc. Ins. Co. v. Thornton, 188 S.E.2d 435 (1972))	Yes, if the following requirements are satisfied: (a) the donor must intend to give the gift; (b) the donee must accept the gift; and (c) the gift must be delivered or some act which under the law is accepted as a substitute for delivery must be done. (§ 44-5-80)	No statute or cases on point. There would appear to be no authority in support of this being given effect.
Hawaii	Yes. (§§ 560:6-104(b), 560:6-106, 412:10-308)	Yes. (§§ 539-7, 539-9(a))	No statute or cases on point. But see § 431:10D-114, pertaining to payment of premiums paid in advance and certain dividends to those the insurer deems "to be equitably entitled to such payment ...."	Yes, if delivery, acceptance, and intention to make a gift. (Welton v. Gallagher, 630 P.2d 1077 (1981))	Yes. Writing must be signed by testator and must describe the items and the devisees with reasonable certainty. However, the writing cannot dispose of money or property specifically devised by will. The writing may be referred to as one to be in existence at the time of the testator's death; it may be prepared before or after the execution of the will; it may be altered by the testator after its preparation; and it may be a writing that has no significance apart from its effect on the dispositions made by the will. (§ 560:2-513)

Table 5.01, Part 2
Principal Will Substitutes

Which of the Following Are Valid to Pass Property at Death without Complying with Wills Formalities?

	Payable on Death (P.O.D.) Bank Account?	Transfer on Death (T.O.D.) Security Registration?	Life Insurance Proceeds?	Gift?	A Writing Disposing of Tangible Personal Property Even If Not Entirely in the Testator's Handwriting?
Idaho	Yes. (§§ 15-6-104(b), 15-6-106)	Yes. (§§ 15-6-307, 15-6-309(1))	Yes. (§ 15-6-201)	Yes, if donor competent to contract, freedom of donor's will, a gift that is complete with nothing left undone, the property is delivered and accepted, and the gift goes into immediate and absolute effect. (Goggins v. Herndon, 249 P.2d 203 (1952))	Yes. Must either be in the handwriting of or signed by testator and must describe the items and the devisees with reasonable certainty. The writing cannot dispose of money, evidences of indebtedness, documents of title, securities, and property used in a trade or business as well as property specifically devised by will. The writing may be referred to as one to be in existence at the time of the testator's death; it may be prepared before or after the execution of the will; it may be altered by the testator after its preparation; and it may be a writing which has no significance apart from its effect upon the dispositions made by the will. (§ 15-2-513)
Illinois	Yes. (205 ILCS § 625/4)	Yes. (815 ILCS §§ 10/7, 10/9(a))	Yes. (§ 755 ILCS § 30/1)	Yes, if show donative intent, delivery and acceptance. (Estate of Poliquin, 617 N.E.2d 40, 42-43 (1993))	No statute or cases on point. There would appear to be no authority in support of this being given effect.
Indiana	Yes. (§ 32-17-11-18)	Yes. (§§ 32-17-14-1 et seq.)	Yes. (§ 32-17-11-28)	Yes, if (a) donor is competent to contract, (b) there is freedom of will, (c) the gift is completed with nothing left undone, (d) delivery, unless already in possession of donee, and acceptance, and (e) the gift goes into immediate and absolute effect. (Dunnewind v. Cook, 697 N.E.2d 485, 489 n.3 (1998)) A gift or transfer of title to tangible as well as intangible personal property may be made by written instrument or deed stating a present intent, and this may be done without physical delivery of property. (Lewis v. Burke, 226 N.E.2d 337 (Ct. App. 1967))	Yes, as long as referred to in a will and signed by the testator or settlor of trust and describes the items and beneficiaries with reasonable certainty. However, it cannot dispose of money, evidences of indebtedness, documents of title, securities, and property used in a trade or business as well as property specifically devised by will. The writing may be referred to as in existence at the time of the testator's death; it may be prepared before or after the execution of the will; and the testator may alter it after its preparation (§ 30-4-2-1-11)

Table 5.01, Part 2
Principal Will Substitutes

Which of the Following Are Valid to Pass Property at Death without Complying with Wills Formalities?

	Payable on Death (P.O.D.) Bank Account?	Transfer on Death (T.O.D.) Security Registration?	Life Insurance Proceeds?	Gift?	A Writing Disposing of Tangible Personal Property Even If Not Entirely in the Testator's Handwriting?
Iowa	Yes. (§§ 633D.6, 633D.11)	Yes. (§§ 633D.5, 633D.6, 633D.11)	Yes, unless the proceeds are payable to the decedent's estate. (§ 633.5)	Yes, if donative intent, delivery, and acceptance (Raim v. Stancel, 339 N.W.2d 621 (1983)); need present intent to make gift and divesting of all control and dominion over the property which is the subject of the gift (In re Estate of Crabtree, 550 N.W.2d 168, 170 (1996)).	Yes. Can be disposed of by written statement, letter, or list. Tangible personal property "includes" household goods, furnishings, furniture, personal effects, clothing, jewelry, books, works of art, ornaments, and automobiles. The writing cannot dispose of tangible personal property used in a trade or business or tangible personal property not otherwise disposed of by will. Must either be in testator's handwriting or signed by testator. Must also be dated and must describe items and distributees with reasonable certainty. (§ 633.276)
Kansas	Yes. (§ 9-1215)	Yes. (§§ 17-49a07, 17-49a09)	Yes. (§ 59-3513(a)(1))	The prerequisites for an inter vivos gift are (a) an intent to make a gift; (b) a delivery by the donor to the donee; and (c) an acceptance by the donee. (In re Estate of Button, 830 P.2d 1216, 1218 (1992))	Yes. Writing must be in handwriting of testator or be signed by testator and must describe the items with reasonable certainty. However, the writing cannot dispose of money, evidences of indebtedness, documents of title, securities, and property used in a trade or business as well as property specifically devised by will. The writing may be referred to as in existence at the time of the testator's death; it may be prepared before or after the execution of the will; and the testator may alter it after its preparation. (§ 59-623)
Kentucky	Yes. (§§ 391.315, 391.325)	Yes. (§§ 292.6507, 292.6509)	Yes. (§ 391.360)	A valid gift must include: (a) a donor competent to make gift; (b) a donee capable of taking it; (c) an intent on the part of the donor to absolutely and irrevocably divest himself of title, dominion, and control of gift in praesentia; (d) irrevocable transfer of legal title and dominion to donee; and (e) delivery by donor to donee, and an acceptance by donee. (Bryant's Adm'r v. Bryant, 269 S.W.2d 219, 221 (1954))	No statute or cases on point. There would appear to be no authority in support of this being given effect.

Table 5.01, Part 2
Principal Will Substitutes

Which of the Following Are Valid to Pass Property at Death without Complying with Wills Formalities?

	Payable on Death (P.O.D.) Bank Account?	Transfer on Death (T.O.D.) Security Registration?	Life Insurance Proceeds?	Gift?	A Writing Disposing of Tangible Personal Property Even If Not Entirely in the Testator's Handwriting?
Louisiana[1]	Yes. (Rev. Stat. §6:766.1)	No, although this is under study.	Yes. For example, the law affords the opportunity to make proceeds payable to a trustee and this trust is deemed inter vivos and not testamentary. (Rev. Stat. Title 9, App. 9:1816)	Yes, if simultaneous occurrence of donor's intent to give and actual possession by delivery. (Adams v. Sec. Ins. Co., 533 So. 2d 140 (Ct. App. 1988, rev'd, in part, on other grounds); Montet v. Lyles, 638 So. 2d 727 (Ct. App. 1994)) No formalities are required. (Civ. Code Art. 1543) With respect to immovables or incorporeal property, a donation must be made by authentic act.	No statute or cases on point. There would appear to be no authority in support of this being given effect.
Maine	Yes. (18-A §§6-104(b), 6-106)	Yes. (18-A §§6-308, 6-310)	Yes. (18-A §6-201)	To constitute a valid gift inter vivos, donor must part with all present and future dominion over the property given. There must be a delivery to the donee or to someone for the donee, and gift must be absolute and irrevocable, without any reference to its taking effect at some future period. (Rose v. Osborne, 180 A. 315, 317 (1935))	Yes. Writing must either be in the handwriting of or signed by testator and must describe items and devisees with reasonable certainty. The writing cannot dispose of money or property specifically devised by will. Writing may be referred to as one to be in existence at time of testator's death; it may be prepared before or after the execution of the will; it may be altered by the testator after its preparation; it may be a writing which has no significance apart from its effect upon the dispositions made by the will. (18-C §2-512)
Maryland	Yes. (Fin. Inst. Code §§1-204, Est. & Tr. Code §1-401)	Yes. (Est. & Tr. Code §§16-107, 16-109)	Yes, as to contracts generally. (Reece v. Reece, 212 A.2d 468 (1965))	For valid gift, five factors are needed: a clear intent on the part of the donor; a gratuitous, unconditional transfer of possession; an immediate transfer of title; a delivery of title to the donee; an acceptance of the gift by the donee. (Dulany v. Taylor, 660 A.2d 1046, 1052-53 (1995))	No statute or cases on point. There would appear to be no authority in support of this being given effect.

Table 5.01, Part 2
Principal Will Substitutes

Which of the Following Are Valid to Pass Property at Death without Complying with Wills Formalities?

	Payable on Death (P.O.D.) Bank Account?	Transfer on Death (T.O.D.) Security Registration?	Life Insurance Proceeds?	Gift?	A Writing Disposing of Tangible Personal Property Even If Not Entirely in the Testator's Handwriting?
Massachusetts	Yes. (Shea v. Noble, 2011 WL 855846 (Mass. App. Ct. 2011)	Yes. (190B §§ 6-307, 6-309)	Yes. (Stiles v. Stiles, 487 N.E.2d 874 (1986))	Can even have parol gift, if donor has intent, delivery that is actual or symbolic, all done in manner to transfer during life complete dominion and control. (Kobrosky v. Crystal, 125 N.E.2d 385 (1955))	Yes. Written statement or list disposing of tangible personal property other than money. Must be signed by testator and describe the items and devisees with reasonable certainty. Writing may be referred to as one in existence at time of testator's death, may be prepared before or after the execution of the will, may be altered by the testator after its preparation, and may be a writing which has no significance apart from dispositions made by will. (190B §2-513)
Michigan	Yes. (§§ 700.6304, 700.6305, 700.6309)	Yes. (§§ 700.6304, 700.6305, 700.6309)	Yes. (§ 700.6101(1))	There must be intent to pass title to donee, there must be actual or constructive delivery, and there must be acceptance by the donee. (In re Mensinger Estate, 506 N.W.2d 238 (1993))	Yes. Testator must sign writing, and it must describe items and devisees with reasonable certainty. The writing cannot dispose of money or property specifically devised by will. Writing may be referred to as one in existence at time of testator's death, may be prepared before or after the execution of the will, may be altered by the testator after its preparation, and may be a writing which has no significance apart from dispositions made by will. (§700.2513)
Minnesota	Yes. (§§ 524.6-204(b), 524.6-206)	Yes. (§§ 524.6-307, 524.6-309)	No statute or cases on point.	Key elements are donative intent, delivery of gift, and absolute disposition of the property. (Cooke v. Belzer, 413 N.W.2d 623 (1987))	Yes. Writing must be in hand writing of the testator or be signed by the testator and must describe the items and devisees with reasonable certainty. The writing cannot dispose of money, coin collections, property used in a trade or business, or items specifically disposed of by will. Writing may be referred to as one in existence at the time of testator's death, prepared before execution of the will, altered by the testator after preparation, and may be a writing which has no significance apart from its effect on dispositions made by will. (§524.2-513)

Table 5.01, Part 2
Principal Will Substitutes

Which of the Following Are Valid to Pass Property at Death without Complying with Wills Formalities?

	Payable on Death (P.O.D.) Bank Account?	Transfer on Death (T.O.D.) Security Registration?	Life Insurance Proceeds?	Gift?	A Writing Disposing of Tangible Personal Property Even If Not Entirely in the Testator's Handwriting?
Mississippi	Yes. (§§ 81-5-63, 81-5-62)	Yes. (§§ 91-21-15, 91-21-19)	Yes. (Jones v. Patty, 18 So. 794 (1896))	Property must have been transferred so that the donor surrendered all dominion over it during lifetime; alternatively, the gift must have been made in contemplation of death in the case of a gift cause mortis. (Gilder v. First Nat'l Bank, 214 So. 2d 681, 683 (1968)	No statute or cases on point. There would appear to be no authority in support of this being given effect.
Missouri	Yes. (§ 362.471)	Yes. (§§ 461.028, 461.031)	Yes. (§§ 461.001, 461.009)	Yes, if present intention to make gift on part of donor to donee, acceptance by donee, and ownership takes effect immediately and absolutely. (Kennedy v. Milligan, 915 S.W.2d 784 (1996)	Yes. Written statement or list disposing of tangible personal property other than money. Must be either in testator's handwriting or signed by testator, it must be dated, and must describe the items and devisees with reasonable certainty. Writing may be referred to as one in existence at time of testator's death, may be prepared before or after the execution of the will, may be altered by the testator after its preparation, and may be a writing which has no significance apart from dispositions made by will. However, the writing cannot dispose of money, evidences of indebtedness, documents of title, securities, and property used in a trade or business as well as property specifically devised by will. (§ 474.333)
Montana	Yes. (§§ 72-6-212, 72-6-214)	Yes. (§§ 72-6-307, 72-6-309)	Yes. (§ 72-6-111)	Yes, if intention to make gift, delivery, and acceptance. (Patterson v. Halterman, 505 P.2d 905 (1973))	Yes. Writing must be signed by testator and must describe the items and the devisees with reasonable certainty. However, the writing cannot dispose of money or items specifically disposed of by will. The writing may be: referred to as one to be in existence at the time of the testator's death; prepared before or after the execution of the will; altered by the testator after its preparation; it may be a writing that has no significance apart from its effect upon the dispositions made by the will. (§ 72-2-533)

5028

Table 5.01, Part 2
Principal Will Substitutes

Which of the Following Are Valid to Pass Property at Death without Complying with Wills Formalities?

	Payable on Death (P.O.D.) Bank Account?	Transfer on Death (T.O.D.) Security Registration?	Life Insurance Proceeds?	Gift?	A Writing Disposing of Tangible Personal Property Even If Not Entirely in the Testator's Handwriting?
Nebraska	Yes. (§§ 30-2723(b), 30-2725)	Yes. (§§ 30-2740, 30-2742)	Yes. (§§ 30-2715, 30-2740)	Yes, if intention to transfer title, delivery, and acceptance. (Ralston v. Marget, 293 N.W. 124 (1940))	Yes. Writing must have an indication of the date of the writing or signing and, in the absence of such indication of date, be the only such writing or contain no inconsistency with any other old writing or permit determination of such date of writing or signing from the content of such writing, from extrinsic circumstances, or from other evidence, must either be in the handwriting of the testator or be signed by him, and must describe the items and the devisees with reasonable certainty. However, the writing cannot dispose of money, evidences of indebtedness, documents of title, securities, and property used in a trade or business, or items specifically disposed of by will. (§ 30-2338)
Nevada	Yes. (§§ 111.751, 111.757, 111.729)	Yes. (§ 111.751)	No statute or cases on point.	Yes, if intent to make gift, actual constructive or symbolic delivery of the property in the donor's lifetime to be given without power of revocation. (Edmonds v. Perry, 140 P.2d 566 (1943))	Yes. Writing must have title indicating purpose, date of execution, reference to will to which it relates, reasonable description of items to be disposed of and the legatees, and must have testator's handwritten or electronic signature. The writing cannot dispose of money, evidences of indebtedness, documents of title, securities, property used in a trade or business, or items specifically disposed of by will. The writing may be referred to as a writing in existence at the time of the testator's death, prepared before or after the execution of the will, altered by testator after its preparation, be a writing which has no significance apart from its effect upon the dispositions made by the will. (§ 133.045)

Table 5.01, Part 2
Principal Will Substitutes

Which of the Following Are Valid to Pass Property at Death without Complying with Wills Formalities?

	Payable on Death (P.O.D.) Bank Account?	Transfer on Death (T.O.D.) Security Registration?	Life Insurance Proceeds?	Gift?	A Writing Disposing of Tangible Personal Property Even If Not Entirely in the Testator's Handwriting?
New Hampshire	Yes. (§§ 563-C:5, 563-C:6, 563-C:10)	Yes. (§§ 563-C:5, 563-C:6, 563-C:10)	Yes. "In the normal course of events persons will use a deed, mortgage, note or contract as a substitute for accomplishing the same purpose by will. When a will is employed we require compliance with the statute of wills. But when a contractual undertaking is employed we do not declare it invalid because it accomplished in part what could have been accomplished by the use of a will." (McGrath v. McGrath, 220 A.2d 760, 762-63 (1966))	Yes. (Abbott v. Watson, 202 A.2d 476 (1964)) The requirements for a valid gift are: a manifestation of the donor to give, and an unconditional deliver and acceptance of the gift. (Nashua Tr. Co. v. Mosgovian, 79 A.2d 636, 637 (1951)) (superseded by statute on other grounds, as stated in Brennan v. Timmins, 187 A. 2d 793 (1963)) Other requirements stated are a voluntary transfer, no consideration, and perfected delivery of either the property or a deed. (Curriden v. Chandler, 108 A. 296 (1919)) Gifts causa mortis not valid unless actual delivery proved by two indifferent witnesses, upon petition of donee to the judge to establish the gift, filed within 60 days of death of donor. (§ 551:17)	No statute or cases on point. There would appear to be no authority in support of this being given effect.
New Jersey	Yes. (§ 17:16I-5(b)) P.O.D. account is defined in § 17:16I-2(j).	Yes. (§§ 3B:30-5, 3B:30-6, 3B:30-8, 3B:30-10)	Yes. (In re Posey's Estate, 214 A.2d 713, 719 (1965))	Yes, if there is donative intention, delivery, and to the extent an intangible is involved, the donor's stripping himself of all dominion over the property. (In re Posey's Estate, 214 A.2d 713, 719 (1965))	Yes. Writing must either be in the handwriting of or signed by testator and must describe the items and the devisees with reasonable certainty. However, it cannot dispose of money, evidences of indebtedness, documents of title, securities, and property used in a trade or business, or items specifically disposed of by will. The writing may be referred to as one in existence at the time of the testator's death; it may be prepared before or after the execution of the will; it may be altered by the testator after its preparation; and it may be a writing which has no significance apart from its effect upon the dispositions made by the will. (§ 3A:2A-10)

Table 5.01, Part 2
Principal Will Substitutes

Which of the Following Are Valid to Pass Property at Death without Complying with Wills Formalities?

	Payable on Death (P.O.D.) Bank Account?	*Transfer on Death (T.O.D.) Security Registration?*	*Life Insurance Proceeds?*	*Gift?*	*A Writing Disposing of Tangible Personal Property Even If Not Entirely in the Testator's Handwriting?*
New Mexico	Yes. (§§ 45-6-212, 45-6-214)	Yes. (§§ 45-6-307, 45-6-309)	Yes. (§ 45-6-101)	Yes. Elements of gift are: property subject to gift; a donor competent to make a gift; donative intent not induced by force or fraud; delivery; acceptance by a competent donee; and a present gift fully executed. (Espinoza v. Petritis, 373 P.2d 820 (1962))	Yes. Writing must be signed by testator and describe items and devises with reasonable certainty. The writing cannot dispose of money or property specifically devised by will. The writing may be referred to as in existence at time of testator's death, it may be prepared either before or after execution of will, the writing can be altered by testator after preparation, or can be a writing that has no significance apart from dispositions made by will. (§ 45-2-513)
New York	No. (In re Peno's Estate, 221 N.Y.S. 205, 217 (Sur. Ct. 1927))	Yes. (In re Estate of Crystal, 348 N.Y.S.2d 717, 719 (Sur. Ct. 1973), aff'd, 363 N.Y.S.2d 311 (1974))	Yes. (In re Alvord's Estate, 416 N.Y.S.2d 196 (1979))	Yes, if intent to make an immediate gift, a delivery of the thing given, and an acceptance of the gift, which involves renunciation by donor and acquisition by donee of interest in and title to subject of gift. (In re Peno's Estate, 221 N.Y.S. 205, 217 (Sur. Ct. 1927))	No. (In re Eldridge's Will, 64 N.Y.S.2d 234 (1946))
North Carolina	Yes. (§ 54C-166.1)	Yes. (§ 41-2.2(b)(2)(i))	Yes. Implied in Ballard v. Lance, 169 S.E.2d 199, 202 (Ct. App. 1969). See also Janet McLamb & Lisa K. Vira, Edwards' N.C. Prob. Handbook, § 18:4 (updated 2013)	Yes, if two key elements are present, donative intent and actual or constructive delivery. (Creekmore v. Creekmore, 485 S.E.2d 68 (1997))	No statute or cases on point. There would appear to be no authority in support of this being given effect.
North Dakota	Yes. (§§ 30.1-31-09, 30.1-31-11)	Yes. (§§ 30.1-31-24, 30.1-31-27)	Yes. (§ 30.1-31-01)	Yes, if the following elements are satisfied: donative intent; delivery, actual or constructive; and acceptance of the gift by donee. (In re Paulson's Estate, 219 N.W.2d 132 (1974))	Yes. Writing must be signed by testator and must describe the items and devisees with reasonable certainty. The writing cannot dispose of money or items specifically disposed of by will. Writing may be referred to as one in existence at the time of the testator's death; it may be prepared before or after the execution of the will; it may be altered by the testator after preparation; and it may be a writing that has no significance apart from its effect on the dispositions made by the will. (§ 30.1-08-13)

Table 5.01, Part 2
Principal Will Substitutes

Which of the Following Are Valid to Pass Property at Death without Complying with Wills Formalities?

	Payable on Death (P.O.D.) Bank Account?	*Transfer on Death (T.O.D.) Security Registration?*	*Life Insurance Proceeds?*	*Gift?*	*A Writing Disposing of Tangible Personal Property Even If Not Entirely in the Testator's Handwriting?*
Ohio	Yes. (§ 1109.07)	Yes. (§§ 1709.07, 1709.09)	Yes. (In re Gilger's Estate, 109 N.E.2d 333 (1952))	Yes, if (a) intention to transfer title and right to possession and (b) delivery of property to donee along with relinquishment of ownership, dominion and control over it. (Lauerman v. Destocki, 622 N.E.2d 1122 (1993))	No statute or cases on point. There would appear to be no authority in support of this being given effect.
Oklahoma	Yes. (6 Okla. St. § 901)	Yes. (71 Okla. St. §§ 905, 906, 908, 910)	No statute or cases directly on point, although implied by Graham v. Farmers New World Life Ins. Co., 841 P.2d 1165, 1167-68 (Ct. App. 1992) (insurance contracts are governed by contract law).	A valid gift is one in which the following elements are satisfied: intention to give, complete delivery of the property given, and acceptance by the donee. (McSpadden v. Mahoney, 431 P.2d 432 (1961)) There is not a gift if the donor retains "right of complete control and dominion, and especially the right to take back the 'gift' at any time." (Thomas v. Bank of Oklahoma, 684 P.2d 553, 554 (1984))	No statute or cases on point. There would appear to be no authority in support of this being given effect.
Oregon	Yes. (§§ 708A.470, 708A.480)	Yes. (§§ 59.565, 59.575)	Yes. (Gordon v. Portland Tr. Co., 271 P.2d 653, 655 (1954))	Yes, a gift is valid if there is (a) donative intent, (b) delivery of the property to the donee, (c) intent that the donee have a present interest in it, and (d) acceptance by the donee. (Kesterson v. Cronan, 806 P.2d 134, 136 (1991))	No statute or cases on point. There would appear to be no authority in support of this being given effect.
Pennsylvania	No. However, court may seek to convert it to inter vivos gift creating joint survivorship account. (Nemcek v. Central City Nat. Bank, 149 A.2d 533 (1959))	Yes. (20 §§ 6407, 6409)	Yes. (20 § 6108)	Yes, if donative intent and delivery. (In re Estate of Petro, 694 A.2d 627 (1997))	No statute or cases on point. There would appear to be no authority in support of this being given effect.
Rhode Island	Yes. No statute or cases on point.	Yes. (§§ 7-11.1-8, 7-11.1-10)	Yes. (§ 27-4-11; Murino v. Reynolds, 550 A.2d 1058 (1988)) Note, however, that the same may not be true for other contracts. (Combined Ins. Co. v. Salisbury, 224 A.2d 383 (1966))	Yes. (People's Savings Bank v. Webb, 42 A. 874 (1899); Barrett v. Barrett, 894 A.2d 891 (2006))	No statute or cases on point. There would appear to be no authority in support of this being given effect.

5032

Table 5.01, Part 2
Principal Will Substitutes

Which of the Following Are Valid to Pass Property at Death without Complying with Wills Formalities?

	Payable on Death (P.O.D.) Bank Account?	Transfer on Death (T.O.D.) Security Registration?	Life Insurance Proceeds?	Gift?	A Writing Disposing of Tangible Personal Property Even If Not Entirely in the Testator's Handwriting?
South Carolina	Yes. (§§ 62-6-104(b), 62-6-106)	Yes. (§§ 35-6-70, 35-6-90(A))	Yes. (§ 62-6-201)	Yes. See Worrell v. Lathan, 478 S.E.2d 287, 288 (1996) ("gifts inter vivos and causa mortis must be fully and completely executed —that is, there must be a donative intent to transfer title to the property, a delivery by the donor, and an acceptance by the donee").	Yes. Must either be in the handwriting of or signed by testator and describe items and devisees with reasonable certainty. However, it cannot dispose of money, property used in a trade or business, or items specifically disposed of by will. The writing may be referred to as one to be in existence at the time of the testator's death; it may be prepared before or after the execution of the will; it may be altered by the testator after its preparation; and it may be a writing which has no significance apart from its effect upon the disposition made by the will. (§ 62-2-512)
South Dakota	Yes. (§§ 29A-6-104(2), 29A-6-106)	Yes. (§§ 29A-6-307, 29A-6-309)	Yes. (§ 29A-6-113)	Yes, if intention, delivery, and acceptance. (Bunt v. Fairbanks, 134 N.W.2d 1 (1965))	Yes. Writing must be signed by the testator and must describe the items and the devisees with reasonable certainty. However, the writing cannot dispose of money or items specifically disposed of by will. The writing may be referred to as in existence at the time of the testator's death; it may be prepared before or after the execution of the will; it may be altered by the testator after its preparation; and it may be a writing that has no significance apart from its effect on the dispositions made by the will. (§ 29A-2-513)
Tennessee	Yes. (§ 45-2-704) However, this refers to deposits in trust, so that §§ 35-12-108, 35-12-110 may be more pertinent in certain circumstances.	Yes. (§§ 35-12-108, 35-12-110)	Yes. (Cook v. Cook, 521 S.W.2d 808 (1975))	Yes, if there is (a) an intention on the part of the donor to make a gift and (b) the intent must be accompanied by delivery of the property. (Estate of Bowlin v. Ables, 766 S.W.2d 193 (1988))	Yes. A will may refer to a written statement or list to dispose of items of tangible personal property not otherwise specifically disposed of by the will, other than money, evidences of indebtedness documents if title securities, and property used in a trade or business. (§ Not yet assigned)

Table 5.01, Part 2
Principal Will Substitutes

Which of the Following Are Valid to Pass Property at Death without Complying with Wills Formalities?

	Payable on Death (P.O.D.) Bank Account?	Transfer on Death (T.O.D.) Security Registration?	Life Insurance Proceeds?	Gift?	A Writing Disposing of Tangible Personal Property Even If Not Entirely in the Testator's Handwriting?
Texas	Yes. (Est. §§ 113.152, 113.158, 113.204)	Yes. (Est. § 111.052) However, this provision has been interpreted as not allowing "testamentary disposition of a person's entire estate, including real property, without the requirements of a will or the formalities of will execution." The section allows nontestamentary transfers of "property," "money," or "other benefits," but does not allow nontestamentary transfers of a person's entire estate. In the case, a document attempted in the form of an antenuptial agreement to give the drafter's estate to his wife if they were not separated or divorced at his death. (Hibbler v. Knight, 735 S.W.2d 924, 927 (Ct. App. 1987)	Yes. (Est. § 111.052)	Yes, if intention of donor to make gift, the delivery of the gift to the donee, and the acceptance by the donee of the property. (Dorman v. Arnold, 932 S.W.2d 225 (1996))	No statute or cases on point. There would appear to be no authority in support of this being given effect.
Utah	Yes. (§§ 75-6-104(2), 75-6-106)	Yes. (§§ 75-6-308, 75-6-310)	Yes. (§75-6-201)	Yes, if it enters into immediate and absolute effect. It involves the donor divesting himself and the donee investing himself, with the right of property in the subject of the gift. It must be absolute, irrevocable, and without any reference to its taking place at some future period. The donor has to deliver the property and part with all present and future dominion over it. (Helper State Bank v. Crus, 81 P.2d 359 (1938))	Yes. Writing must be signed by testator and must describe the items and devisees with reasonable certainty. The writing cannot dispose of money. The writing may be referred to as one to be in existence at the time of the testator's death; it may be prepared before or after the execution of the will; it may be altered by the testator after its preparation; and it may be a writing which has no significance apart from its effect upon the dispositions made by the will. (§75-2-513)

Table 5.01, Part 2
Principal Will Substitutes

Which of the Following Are Valid to Pass Property at Death without Complying with Wills Formalities?

	Payable on Death (P.O.D.) Bank Account?	Transfer on Death (T.O.D.) Security Registration?	Life Insurance Proceeds?	Gift?	A Writing Disposing of Tangible Personal Property Even If Not Entirely in the Testator's Handwriting?
Vermont	Yes. (8 § 14205)	Yes. (9 §§ 4357, 4359)	No statute or cases on point.	The elements of a valid inter vivos gift are: (a) manifest intention to create in the donee a present interest during the joint lives of the donor and donee; (b) an unconditional delivery or divestiture of the thing transferred; and (c)acceptance by the donee. Acceptance is presumed if the first two elements are established. (In re Estate of Adams, 587 A.2d 958, 960 (1990))	No statute or cases on point. There would appear to be no authority in support of this being given effect.
Virginia	Yes. (§§ 6.2-608(B), 6.2-610)	Yes. (§§ 64.2-615, 64.2-618)	Yes. (Abbott v. Willey, 479 S.E.2d 528, 529 (1997) (treating policy as nontestamentary instrument); Short v. A. H. Still Inv. Corp., 147 S.E.2d 99 (1966) (relating generally to contracts))	Yes. However, in order for there to be a valid gift, there must be an intention to make a present gift accompanied by a delivery of the thing given or the means of obtaining it. A gift cannot be made to take effect in possession in the future. That would be only a promise to make a gift, and being without consideration is invalid. (Payne v. Tobacco Trading Corp., 18 S.E.2d 281 (1942))	Yes. Written statement or list must be signed by testator and must describe items and recipients with reasonable certainty. The writing cannot dispose of property specifically disposed of by the will. The writing may be referred to as one to be in existence at the time of the testator's death; it may be prepared before or after the execution of the will; it may be altered by the testator after its preparation; and it may be a writing which has no significance apart from its effect upon the dispositions made by the will.
Washington	Yes. (§ 30.22.100)	Yes. (§§ 21.35.035, 21.35.045)	Yes. (§ 11.02.091)	Yes, but only if: (a) an intention of the donor to presently give; (b) a subject matter capable of passing by delivery; (c) an actual delivery; and (d) an acceptance by the donee. (Brin v. Stutzman, 951 P.2d 291, 300 (Ct. App. 1998))	Yes. Will refers to the writing; writing is in handwriting of or signed by testator; and writing describes the items and recipients of property with reasonable certainty. (§ 11.12.260) It cannot dispose of property under a trade or business or items specifically disposed of by the will.

Table 5.01, Part 2
Principal Will Substitutes

Which of the Following Are Valid to Pass Property at Death without Complying with Wills Formalities?

	Payable on Death (P.O.D.) Bank Account?	*Transfer on Death (T.O.D.) Security Registration?*	*Life Insurance Proceeds?*	*Gift?*	*A Writing Disposing of Tangible Personal Property Even If Not Entirely in the Testator's Handwriting?*
West Virginia	Yes. (§31A-4-33(a))	Yes. (§§36-10-7, 36-10-9)	Yes. (Equitable Trust Co. v. Epling, 167 S.E. 820 (1933); Transamerica Occidental Life Ins. Co. v. Burke, 368 S.E.2d 301, 304 (1988))	Yes, but valid only if made by a writing, signed by donor or his agent, or unless actual possession shall have come to and remained with donee or some person holding for or under him. (§36-1-5) However, apart from the statute, case law provides that three requirements must be satisfied: (a) an intention on the part of the donor to make a gift; (b) a delivery or transfer of the subject matter of the gift; and (c) acceptance. Sleigh v. Sleigh, 445 S.E.2d 509, 513 (1994))	No statute or cases on point. There would appear to be no authority in support of this being given effect.
Wisconsin	Yes. (§705.04(2))	Yes. (§§705.27, 705.29)	Yes. (§705.10)	Yes, if there is: (a) an intention to give on the part of the donor; (b) delivery; actual or constructive, to the donee; (c) termination of the donor's dominion over the subject of the gift; and (d) dominion in the donee. (In re Reist's Estate, 281 N.W.2d 86 (1979))	Yes. It must be signed and dated by the testator and describe the property and distribute with reasonable certainty. It does not apply to items specifically disposed of by will. The statute explicitly deals with a writing disposing of digital property. (§853.32(2))
Wyoming	Yes. (§2-1-203(d))	Yes. (§§2-16-108, 2-16-110)	No statute or cases on point.	Yes, if: (a) there is a present intention of the donor to make an immediate gift; (b) actual or constructive delivery of the gift that divests the donor of dominion and control; and (c) acceptance of the gift. (Rose v. Rose, 849 P.2d 1321 (1993))	Yes. Writing must be dated, be signed by testator or in handwriting of testator, and include a description of the items and devisees with reasonable certainty. It cannot dispose of money, evidences of indebtedness, documents of title, securities, property used in a trade or business, or items specifically devised by will. (§2-6-124)

[1] *Caution:* A civil law system with very different concepts like the trust have been recognized statutorily, they may be approached very differently.

Table 5.02
Incorporation by Reference and Facts of Independent Significance

	Incorporation by Reference?	Facts of Independent Significance?
Alabama	Yes. Writing must be in existence when will is executed. Will must describe writing sufficiently to identify it. Language of will must manifest intent to incorporate existing writing. (§ 43-8-139)	Yes. (§ 43-8-141)
Alaska	Yes. Language of will must manifest intent to incorporate existing writing. Will must contain sufficient description to identify writing. (§ 13.12.510)	Yes. (§ 13.12.512)
Arizona	Yes. Writing must: exist at time testator executes will, will must manifest intent to incorporate document, and will must identify document with sufficient specificity to allow its identification. (§ 14-2510)	Yes. (§ 14-2512)
Arkansas	Yes. Writing must be in existence when will is executed. Language of will must manifest intent to incorporate and writing must be sufficiently described to permit its identification. (§ 28-25-107(a))	No statute or case on point.
California	Yes. Writing must be in existence when will is executed. Will must describe writing sufficiently to identify it. Language of will must manifest intent to incorporate existing writing. (Prob. § 6130)	Yes. (Prob. § 6131)
Colorado	Yes. Writing must exist when will is executed, and language of will must manifest intent to incorporate it and sufficiently describe the writing to allow its identification. (§ 15-11-510)	Yes. (§ 15-11-512)
Connecticut	Possibly. (Appeal of Bryan, 58 A. 748 (1904)) See also Waterbury Nat'l Bank v. Waterbury Nat'l Bank, 291 A.2d 737, 741-42 (Conn. 1972)	No statute or case on point.
Delaware	Yes. (Walsh v. St. Joseph's Home for Aged, 303 A.2d 691, 694 (Ch. 1973))	Yes. (Walsh v. St. Joseph's Home for Aged, 303 A.2d 691, 694 (Ch. 1973))
District of Columbia	Yes. (Vestry of St. John's Parish v. Bostwick, 8 App. D.C. 452 (1896))	No statute or case on point.
Florida	Yes. Writing in existence when will executed, will manifests intent to incorporate writing, writing is sufficiently identified by will. (§732.512(1))	Yes. (§732.512(2))

Table 5.02

Incorporation by Reference and Facts of Independent Significance

	Incorporation by Reference?	Facts of Independent Significance?
Georgia	No. Lee v. Swain, 733 S.E.2d 726, 729 (Ga. 2012) (jury instruction involving incorporation by reference was not warranted in action involving construction of will, where proponent of instruction failed to cite any authority indicating doctrine of incorporation by reference has been embraced in the context of wills under Georgia law).	No statute or case on point.
Hawaii	Yes. A writing in existence when a will is executed may be incorporated by reference if the language of the will manifests this intent and describes the writing sufficiently to permit its identification. (§560:2-510)	Yes. (§ 560:2-512)
Idaho	Yes. Writing in existence at will execution, language of will manifests intent to incorporate document, and will sufficiently describes document. (§ 15-2-510)	Yes. (§ 15-2-512)
Illinois	Yes. (In re Meskimen's Estate, 235 N.E.2d 619 (1968))	Yes. (In re Meskimen's Estate, 235 N.E.2d 619 (1968))
Indiana	Yes, must exist at the time of execution of the will and be clearly identified in the will. (§ 29-1-6-1(h))	Yes. (§ 29-1-6-1(i))
Iowa	Yes, must exist at the time the will is executed. (In re Cameron's Estate, 241 N.W. 458 (1932))	No statute or case on point.
Kansas	Yes. The writing must be in existence at the time the will was executed and be accurately described therein so as to assure its identity. (Shulsky v. Shulsky, 157 P. 407, 408 (1916))	No statute or case on point. Mentioned but not ruled on in In re Trusteeship of Will of Daniels, 247 Kan. 349, 353, 799 P.2d 479, 483 (Kan. 1990).
Kentucky	Yes. It is a "well-recognized principle." (Scott v. Gastright, 204 S.W.2d 367 (1947))	Although mentioned favorably, it has not been explicitly endorsed. (Stouse v. First Nat'l Bank, 245 S.W.2d 914, 920 (1952))
Louisiana	Uncertain. A will can refer to another writing for the purpose of making certain the object referred to is in the will, but not for incorporating the writing into the will. (Hessmer v. Edenborn, 199 So. 647, 650-51 (1940); Hall v. Hill, 6 La. Ann. 745 (1851)) It is allowed for trusts. (Rev. Stat. 9:1755)	No statute or case on point.

Table 5.02
Incorporation by Reference and Facts of Independent Significance

	Incorporation by Reference?	Facts of Independent Significance?
Maine	Yes. Writing must: be in existence when will is executed, have language of intent to incorporate writing, and describe writing sufficiently to permit its identification. (18-A § 2-510)	Yes. (18-A § 2-512)
Maryland	Yes. Writing must be in existence when a will or trust is executed. Writing may be incorporated to extent language of will manifests an intent to do so; describes the writing sufficiently to permit its identification. (Est. & Trust § 4-107)	No statute or case on point.
Massachusetts	Yes. (191B §3)	Yes. (190B § 2-512)
Michigan	Yes. Writing must be in existence when will is executed, language of the will manifests the intent to incorporate writing, and identify it sufficiently. (§700.2510)	Yes. (§700.2512)
Minnesota	Yes. The writing must be in existence when the will is executed and the language of the will manifests the intent to incorporate by reference and sufficiently describes the writing. (§524.2-510)	Yes. (§524.2-512)
Mississippi	Yes. However, note negative consequences if incorporation into an otherwise holographic will. (Hewes v. Hewes, 71 So. 4 (1916))	No statute or case on point.
Missouri	Yes. (Rosenblum v. Gibbons, 685 S.W.2d 924, 929 (Ct. App. 1984))	Yes. (Rosenblum v. Gibbons, 685 S.W.2d 924, 929 (Ct. App. 1984))
Montana	Yes. Writing in existence when will is executed, language of will manifests intent to incorporate, and will describes writing sufficiently. (§72-2-530)	Yes. (§72-2-532)
Nebraska	Yes. Writing must be in existence when will is executed, language in will manifest intent to incorporate writing, and will describes writing sufficiently. (§30-2335)	Yes. (§30-2337)
Nevada	No statute or case on point.	No statute or case on point.

Table 5.02

Incorporation by Reference and Facts of Independent Significance

	Incorporation by Reference?	Facts of Independent Significance?
New Hampshire	Yes. The document must exist at the time of the will's execution, be specifically identified, and be accompanied by words manifesting intent to incorporate the document. (In re Estate of Came, 529 A.2d 962, 964-65 (N.H. 1987))	No statute or case on point.
New Jersey	Yes. Any writing in existence when will is executed may be incorporated by reference if the language of the will manifests this intent and describes the writing sufficiently. (§ 3B:3-10)	Yes. (§ 3B:3-12)
New Mexico	Yes. A will may incorporate by reference the provisions of the Uniform Statutory Will Act. (§ 45-2A-4) Writing in existence, intent to incorporate in language of will, reasonably identified writings. (§ 45-2-510)	Yes. (§ 45-2-512)
New York	Generally, the doctrine is not recognized in New York. (Booth v. Baptist Church, 28 N.E. 238 (Ct. App. 1891); In re Estate of O'Brien, 649 N.Y.S.2d 220 (App. Div. 1996)) There are exceptions, such as for pourovers to certain trusts. (Est. Powers & Trusts § 3-3.7)	No statute or case on point.
North Carolina	Yes. (§ 31-51)	Yes. (§ 31-52)
North Dakota	Yes. Writing must be in existence when will executed. Language of will must manifest intent to incorporate writing and must sufficiently identify it. (§ 30.1-08-10)	Yes. (§ 30.1-08-12)
Ohio	Yes. An existing document, book, record, or memorandum may be incorporated in a will by reference if referred to as being in existence at time the will is executed. (§ 2107.05)	Yes. While the theory is recognized in conjunction with pourover trusts, it is not applied generally even regarding pourover trusts. it would not save a pour over to a trust that is unfunded at the testator's death. (Hageman v. Cleveland Tr. Co., 343 N.E.2d 121, 123-24 (1976))

Table 5.02
Incorporation by Reference and Facts of Independent Significance

	Incorporation by Reference?	Facts of Independent Significance?
Oklahoma	Yes. The writing must be in existence when the will is executed, must be referred to in a way that allows it to be reasonably identified, and the reference shows an intent to incorporate the writing. (Miller v. First Nat'l Bank & Trust Co., 637 P.2d 75 (1981))	No statute or case on point. In In re Estate of Richardson, 50 P.3d 584, 588 n.9 (Ct. App. 2002) the court stated that the facts of independent significance doctrine has not been applied in any Oklahoma case. It declined to apply it to overcome a pretermitted heirship statute where the testator explicitly omitted a son in an amendment to an inter vivos trust previously incorporated by reference into a will.
Oregon	Yes. The intention to incorporate, and not mere mention of preexisting document, must clearly appear from the will. (Witham v. Witham, 66 P.2d 281 (1937))	No statute or case on point.
Pennsylvania	Yes. The writing must be clearly identified and in existence at the time the will was written. (Estate of Pew, 655 A.2d 521, 547 (1994))	No statute or case on point.
Rhode Island	Yes. (Ind. Nat'l Bank v. R.I. Hosp., 207 A.2d 286, 293 (R.I. 1965))	No statute or case on point.
South Carolina	Yes. Writing must be in existence when will is executed and language of will must manifest intent to incorporate; will must describe writing sufficiently to identify it. (§ 62-2-509)	Yes. (§ 62-2-511)
South Dakota	Yes. Writing must be in existence when will is executed, language of will manifests intent to incorporate writing, and will describes the writing sufficiently to permit its identification. (§ 29A-2-510)	Yes. (§ 29A-2-512)
Tennessee	Yes. (Goodwin v. Nave, 912 S.W.2d 719 (Ct. App. 1995))	Yes. (In re Will of Tipler, 10 S.W.3d 244, 245 (Ct. App. 1998))
Texas	Yes. The writing must be identified by will so as to leave intention of testator reasonably free from doubt. (Brooker v. Brooker, 106 S.W.2d 247 (1937))	Yes. (Welch v. Trustees of Robt. A. Welch Foundation, 465 S.W.2d 195, 200–01 (1971))
Utah	Yes. Writing must be in existence at time will is executed and language of will manifests intent and describes writing sufficiently to permit its identification. (§ 75-2-510)	Yes. (§ 75-2-512)
Vermont	Possibly, but the law as to incorporation by reference in a will "remains undeveloped." (In re Will of Norris, 183 A.2d 519, 521 (1962))	No statute or case on point.

Table 5.02
Incorporation by Reference and Facts of Independent Significance

	Incorporation by Reference?	Facts of Independent Significance?
Virginia	Yes. The document must be in existence at the time the will is executed; it must appear from the face of the will that the document is in actual existence, and it must be identified and described with reasonable certainty. (Thrasher v. Thrasher, 118 S.E.2d 820 (1961))	No statute or case on point.
Washington	Yes. Writing in existence when will is executed, will manifests intent to incorporate writing, and describes writing sufficiently. If conflict between writing and will, the will controls. (§ 11.12.255)	No statute or case on point.
West Virginia	Yes. The writing must be sufficiently identified in the will and there must have been an intention to incorporate it. (Wible v. Ashcroft, 178 S.E. 516 (1935))	No statute or case on point.
Wisconsin	Yes. There must be an intention to incorporate; the writing must be in existence when the will is executed; the incorporated paper or document must be sufficiently identified therein; and the incorporating testamentary document must be executed in accordance with statutory requirements. (In re Erbach's Estate, 164 N.W.2d 238, 242-43 (1969))	No statute or case on point.
Wyoming	Generally, no statute or case on point. It is expressly allowed in some circumstances, such as gifts for religious and educational uses. (§ 34-5-115)	No statute or case on point.

Table 6
The Rights of a Spouse
(current through 5/1/18)

A client may choose not to leave his entire estate or even a substantial portion of it to his surviving spouse. He may place the interest in trust or impose other restrictions that the surviving spouse finds unappealing. Under the law of states that do not have community property regimes, the surviving spouse may be entitled to elect to take a statutory share rather than be governed by the terms of the will.

Tables 6.01–6.04 explore various aspects of rights accorded a surviving spouse. Table 6.01 inquires into whether the state continues to give recognition to the common law rights of dower and curtesy. It also inventories other measures protective of the family afforded by the state, including homestead, exempt property, and family allowance. However, as this table makes clear, the elective share and these other benefits cannot be viewed in isolation. The availability of one may reduce another.

With particular regard to the statutory right to elect against the will, technical requirements must, typically, be satisfied in order to obtain a share of the estate. These requirements, addressed in Table 6.02, relate to when, what, and with whom must a filing be made. Also, the spouse may not survive long enough or may be incapable to make the election. The table considers who, if anyone, can make the election for the spouse.

In addition to these and other technical matters, the actual calculation of the elective share is examined in Table 6.03. One aspect of this inquiry is the often-complex computation of the base against which the percentage or fractional share of the surviving spouse is multiplied. The base itself may not be limited to the probate estate, but may include various testamentary substitutes, often described as the augmented estate. It may also hinge on the number of years the spouses have been married. Knowledge of the constitutive elements of the base are critical from a planning standpoint to the client who wishes to limit the surviving spouse's elective share claims against the estate. Moreover, the surviving spouse's obligation in some states to take account of her own estate in calculating her elective share and to satisfy any right first from property left to her in the will is also a critical issue. To the extent the surviving spouse is not so constrained, the exercise of any statutory right may have a dire impact on the decedent's dispositive plan. The table explores who bears the burden of satisfying the elective share claim in this situation.

The table also considers how the elective share is calculated and the degree to which it is even available when there is property in more than one state or one or both of the spouses was domiciled outside of the state in which the claim for an elective share has been made. To date, these highly intricate matters have received little attention, although the issues are present in many estates. Much as with multijurisdictional taxation, the possibility of either minimizing or oversatisfying the elective share claim exists, thus requiring proper planning on the part of the client who wishes to minimize the surviving spouse's claim, and careful strategizing on the part of a surviving spouse, who wishes to maximize the election, by taking a share of the estate in as many states as possible. Regardless of the actual burden, it may well have to be satisfied with assets under the control of a foreign jurisdiction. The table also explores how this issue is handled.

Of course, the client may seek to obtain a waiver of any statutory claims before or after marriage. This often takes place in the context of a prenuptial or postnuptial agreement. The general parameters of what is required for a valid waiver are detailed in Table 6.04.

Table 6.01
Rights Available in Addition to the Elective Share

	Is There Still a Right to Common Law Dower?	Is There Still a Right to Common Law Curtesy?	What Are The Alternative Protective Rights Afforded the Surviving Spouse? Can They Be Asserted in Addition to the Elective Share?
Alabama	No. (§ 43-8-57)	No. (§ 43-8-57)	Homestead, exempt property, and family allowance are in addition to elective share. (§ 43-8-74)
Alaska	No provision.	No provision.	Homestead, exempt property, and family allowance are in addition to elective share and supplemental elective share. (§ 13.12.202(c))
Arizona	*Community property—no quasi-community property*		The decedent's share of community property and the decedent's separate property shares are subject to rights to allowance in lieu of homestead, exempt property, and family allowance. (§ 14-3101(A))
Arkansas	Yes. (§ 28-11-101 et seq.)	Yes. (§ 28-11-101 et seq.)	Statutory allowances and homestead are in addition to dower and curtesy. (§ 28-39-401(b)(1), (2) In addition, the surviving spouse may be entitled to any residue not disposed of by will when there are no descendants of great-grandparents surviving the decedent. (§ 28-39-401(b)(3)
California *[Community property state with quasi-community property]*	No, except to the extent provided in Probate Code § 120. (Prob. § 6412)	No, except to extent provided in Probate Code § 120. (Prob. §6412)	Right to one-half of community and quasi-community property. (Prob. § 6401(a), (b)) In addition, there is a right to a family allowance (Prob. § 6540(a)), exempt property (Prob. § 6510(a)), and a probate homestead (also available to the minor children) (Prob. §§ 6520, 6521(a)–(b)).
Colorado	No. (§ 15-11-112)	No. (§15-11-112)	Family allowance and exempt property are in addition to elective share. (§§ 15-11-202(2)(a), 15-11-201(3))
Connecticut	No. *See* Public Acts of 1877, ch. 114. *See generally* Hartford-Connecticut Trust Co. *v.* Lawrence, 138 A-159, 161 (Conn. 1927).	See prior column.	The statutory share is only available once a support allowance has stopped. (§ 45a-436(c) & (d)) The support allowance is provided for in § 45a-436 and defined in § 45a-320. The court has considerable discretion as to amount, lump sum, whether it vests at death, and period during which available. There is also a homestead right and an exemp tion for household goods and possibly certain other personal property as provided for in § 45a-435 and § 45a-321.

Table 6.01

Rights Available in Addition to the Elective Share

	Is There Still a Right to Common Law Dower?	Is There Still a Right to Common Law Curtesy?	What Are The Alternative Protective Rights Afforded the Surviving Spouse? Can They Be Asserted in Addition to the Elective Share?
Delaware	No. (12 §511)	No. (12 §511)	Surviving spouse allowance is in addition to elective share. (12 §2308(a)) The following articles should not be included in the estate inventory: the family Bible, the clothes of the decedent, as well as certain family stores laid in before decedent's death. (12 §1901(b))
District of Columbia	No. (§19-102)	No. (§19-102)	There are exemptions for certain assets not exceeding certain values (§§20-904, 15-501–15-503) and homestead allowance, exempt property, and family allowance. (§§19-101.02–19-101.04)
Florida	No. (§732.111)	No. (§732.111)	Exempt property (§732.402(7)) homestead (§732.4015) and family allowance (§732.403) are in addition to elective share. The elective share is in addition to homestead, exempt property, and allowances. (§732.2105)
Georgia *Georgia Year's Support—No elective share, however, the year's support is like the elective share because if the decedent makes provision for the spouse in lieu of year's support in the will, then the spouse must make an election to take the year's support rather than the provision under the will. (§53-3-3)*	No. (§53-1-3)	No. (§53-1-3)	There is no elective share right at all, but there is a right in the surviving spouse and minor children to a year's support. (§53-3-1) Certain property is also exempt in the case of an intestate insolvent estate. (§44-13-100)
Hawaii	No. (§560:2-112)	No. (§560:2-112)	Homestead allowance, exempt property, and family allowance are in addition to elective share. (§560:2-202(c))

Table 6.01
Rights Available in Addition to the Elective Share

	Is There Still a Right to Common Law Dower?	Is There Still a Right to Common Law Curtesy?	What Are The Alternative Protective Rights Afforded the Surviving Spouse? Can They Be Asserted in Addition to the Elective Share?
Idaho *Community property state—with quasi-community property*	No. (§ 32-914)	No. (§ 32-914)	Homestead allowance, exempt property, and family allowance whether or not takes an elective share. (§ 15-2-206(b))
Illinois	No. (755 ILCS § 5/2-9)	No. (755 ILCS § 5/2-9)	Spouse's award for support for 9 months. (755 ILCS § 5/15-1(a)) as well as a child's award if a minor or adult dependent child does not reside with the surviving spouse. (755 ILCS § 5/15-2(a)) The elective share is calculated on the basis of the estate after payment of just claims. (755 ILCS § 5/2-8(a))
Indiana	No. (§ 29-1-2-11)	No. (§ 29-1-2-11)	Survivor's allowance of $25,000, whether in the form of personal property or a residence. (§ 29-1-4-1) It can be asserted in addition to the elective share. (*Id.*)
Iowa	No. (§ 633.236) (Common-law dower and curtesy abolished by § 2440, Code of 1873; see In re Finch's Estate, 32 N.W.2d 819, 829 (1948))	No. (§ 633.236) (Common-law dower and curtesy abolished by § 2440, Code of 1873; see In re Finch's Estate, 32 N.W.2d 819, 829 (1948))	12-month support and exempt personal property in addition to elective share. (§ § 633.332, 633.374) There is also a homestead right which is available "in lieu of" the elective share (§ 633.240) in legal and equitable estates in real property possessed by the decedent. (§ 633.238(1))
Kansas	No. (Abolished by Rev. Stat. 22-127; see generally Bates v. State Sav. Bank, 18 P.2d 143, 144 (Kan. 1933))	No. (Abolished by Rev. Stat. 22-127; see generally Bates v. State Sav. Bank, 18 P.2d 143, 144 (Kan. 1933))	Homestead and family allowance are in addition to elective share. (§ 59-6a202(c)) There is also an exempt property provision. (§ 59-403)
Kentucky	No. The term is used to describe a statutory right. (§ 392.020)	No. The term is used to describe a statutory right. (§ 392.020)	There is statutory dower and curtesy, which includes personal property. (§ 392.020) Dower and homestead are alternative rights. (In re Gibson, 33 F. Supp. 838 (E.D. Ky. 1940); § 427.070) There is also a right to exempt property (§ 391.030) in addition to the statutory share (Opin. Att'y Gen. 81-256).

Table 6.01

Rights Available in Addition to the Elective Share

	Is There Still a Right to Common Law Dower?	Is There Still a Right to Common Law Curtesy?	What Are The Alternative Protective Rights Afforded the Surviving Spouse? Can They Be Asserted in Addition to the Elective Share?
Louisiana	*Community property state—no quasi-community property* (Article 2338)		There is a homestead allowance (Rev. Stat. § 20:1) and a family allowance during administration if the court concludes that it is necessary. (Code Civ. Pro. Art. 3321).
Maine	No. (18-A § 2-113)	No. (18-A § 2-113)	Homestead, exempt property, and family allowance are available whether or not an elective share is claimed. (18-A § 2-206)
Maryland	No. (Est. & Trusts § 3-202)	No. (Est. & Trusts § 3-202)	The surviving spouse is entitled to receive $10,000 for personal use. (Est. & Trusts § 3-201(a)) This is in addition to the elective share.
Massachusetts	No, dower is abolished effective Jan. 2, 2012. (190B § 2-112)	No, curtesy is abolished effective Jan. 2, 2012. (190B § 2-112)	The surviving spouse is entitled to a value from the estate not exceeding $10,000 in excess of security interests, in household furniture, automobiles, furnishings, appliances, and personal effects. (190B § 2-403) These are in addition to elective share. (*Id.*) There is also a reasonable allowance for maintenance during administration that may not continue more than one year if the estate is inadequate to discharge allowed claims. (190B § 2-404(a)) It is in addition to the elective share. (190B § 2-404(b))
Michigan	Yes. A widow can still elect her dower rights under § 558.1 to § 558.29. (§ 700.2202(1)(b) & (2)(c))	No. (See, e.g., Rockwell v. Estate of Rockwell, 180 N.W.2d 498, 501 (Mich.Ct. App. 1970). Moreover, § 700.2202(2)(c) suggests only dower for a "widow" is recognized.)	Spouse must choose between statutory share, the terms of the will, or dower. (§ 700.2202(2)(a)–(c)) There is additionally a provision for exempt property (§ 700.2404), a family allowance (§ 700.2403) and a homestead allowance of $15,000, all in addition to the elective share. (§ 700.2402)

Table 6.01
Rights Available in Addition to the Elective Share

	Is There Still a Right to Common Law Dower?	*Is There Still a Right to Common Law Curtesy?*	*What Are The Alternative Protective Rights Afforded the Surviving Spouse? Can They Be Asserted in Addition to the Elective Share?*
Minnesota	Yes, upon a notice of *lis pendens* filed with the county recorder or registrar of titles in the county where the property is located, within 15 years after the conveyance on which the action is based. (§ 519.101)	Yes, upon a notice of *lis pendens* filed with the county recorder or registrar of titles in the county where the property is located, within 15 years after the conveyance on which the action is based. (§ 519.101)	Homestead, (§ 524.2-402) exempt property, (§ 524.2-403) and family allowance (§ 524.2-404) are in addition to elective share. (§§ 524.2-202(c), 524.2-204)
Mississippi	No. (§ 93-3-5)	No. (§ 93-3-5)	Exempt property, homestead (§ 91-1-19) and a year's support set aside (§ 91-7-135) are allowed in addition to the elective share.
Missouri	No, if vested after 1955 revisions. (§ 474.110)	No, if vested after 1955 revisions. (§ 474.110)	Exempt property, one-year support allowance, and the homestead exemption are in addition to the elective share. (§§ 474.250, 474.260, 474.290)
Montana	No. (§ 72-2-122)	No. (§ 72-2-122)	Homestead, exempt property, and family allowance are in addition to the elective share. (§§ 72-2-226, 72-2-221(3))
Nebraska	No. (§ 30-104)	No. (§ 30-104)	Homestead, exempt property, and family allowance whether or not takes an elective share. (§ 30-2318(b))
Nevada	*Community property state (§§ 123.220—123.259)— community property* See also § 123.020 (curtesy and dower not allowed)	*Community property state (§§ 123.220—123.259)—no quasi-community property*	Family allowance (§ 146.030(1)) as well as certain exempt property and homestead are allowed (§ 146.020).
New Hampshire	No. (§ 560:3)	No. (§ 560:3)	Homestead, exempt property, support allowance and elective share. To receive the elective share, the spouse must waive homestead. (§ 560:10) Exempt property (§§ 554:4, 554:5) and a family allowance (§ 560:1) are allowed in addition to the elective share.

Table 6.01

Rights Available in Addition to the Elective Share

	Is There Still a Right to Common Law Dower?	Is There Still a Right to Common Law Curtesy?	What Are The Alternative Protective Rights Afforded the Surviving Spouse? Can They Be Asserted in Addition to the Elective Share?
New Jersey	Yes, if real property of which decedent was seized of an estate of inheritance prior to May 28, 1980. (§ 3B:28-1) Otherwise, no. (§ 3B:28-2)	Yes, if real property of which decedent was seized of an estate of inheritance prior to May 28, 1980. (§ 3B:28-1) Otherwise, no. (§ 3B:28-2)	Family allowance during will contest (§ 3B:3-30) and apparel-personal property exemption up to $5,000 (§ 3B:16-5) are in addition to the elective share. (§ 3B:8-1 et seq.)
New Mexico	Dower and curtesy are expressly abolished. (§ 45-2-112)	No. (§ 45-2-112)	Family allowance of $30,000 (§ 45-2-402) and specified exempt property up to $15,000 (§ 45-2-403). They are all in addition to the elective share. (§ 45-2-403)
New York[1]	Only if parties married before September 1, 1930. (Real Prop. § 190)	Only if wife dies by August 31, 1930. (Real Prop. § 189)	Exempt property (Est. Powers & Trusts § 5-3.1) and homestead (CPLR § 5206(b)) can be taken as well. A personal property exemption from creditors claims may also be available (CPLR § 5205). (Power v. Loonam, 266 N.Y.S.2d 865, 866-68 (Sup. Ct. 1966))
North Carolina	No. (§ 29-4)	No. (§ 29-4)	A spousal allowance of $30,000 for one year (§ 30-15) and a year's allowance of $5,000 for minors and certain other children (§ 30-17). The homestead exemption (§ 1C-1602) and Const. Art. X, § 2(1) are homestead protections only available during life (Johnson v. Cross, 66 N.C. 167, 170 (1872)).
North Dakota	No. (§ 30.1-04-13) See also § 14-07-09.	No. (§ 30.1-04-13) See also § 14-07-09.	Family allowance (§ 30.1-07-02), exempt property not to exceed $15,000 (§ 30.1-07-01), and homestead exemption, not to exceed $100,000 (§ 47-18-01) are additional protections. (§ 30.1-05-01)

Table 6.01
Rights Available in Addition to the Elective Share

	Is There Still a Right to Common Law Dower?	Is There Still a Right to Common Law Curtesy?	What Are The Alternative Protective Rights Afforded the Surviving Spouse? Can They Be Asserted in Addition to the Elective Share?
Ohio	Yes. (§2103.02)	No. (§2103.09)	Surviving spouse cannot take dower and elective share. (§2103.02(B)) There is a right to exempt property in the nature of as many as two automobiles, not to exceed $40,000, in addition to any vehicles otherwise passing to the surviving spouse, such as by joint tenancy or will and one watercraft and one outboard motor (§§2106.18, 2106.19), family allowance, not to exceed $40,000, but reduced if the surviving spouse chose two automobiles under §2106.18, by the value of the less valuable automobile of the two automobiles selected (§2106.13), and a year's stay in the house (§2106.15). The surviving spouse may also purchase the following property not specifically devised: (1) the manor house, land on which situated, and adjacent farm land; (2) any other real or personal property not exceeding 1/3 of the estate's gross approved values after counting in (1) above. (§2106.16)
Oklahoma	No. (84 §214)	No. (84 §214)	Yes—homestead (58 §311) (allowing spouse for her lifetime and then minor children to occupy the homestead), family allowance (58 §§311, 312), and also exempt property (58 §§311, 312).
Oregon	No, unless decedent died before July 1, 1970. (§112.685)	No, unless decedent died before July 1, 1970. (§112.685)	Homestead, allowing spouse and dependents, or any of them, to occupy the principal place of abode of decedent for one year after death of decedent, or if leasehold or estate for lifetime of another, until one year after the death of decedent or earlier termination of estate. (§114.005) In addition, there is a provision for support of a spouse and dependent children. (§114.015)
Pennsylvania	No. (20 §2105(A))	No. (20 §2105(B))	Exemption of real and/or personal property up to $3,500 (20 §3121) are additional rights.

Table 6.01

Rights Available in Addition to the Elective Share

	Is There Still a Right to Common Law Dower?	Is There Still a Right to Common Law Curtesy?	What Are The Alternative Protective Rights Afforded the Surviving Spouse? Can They Be Asserted in Addition to the Elective Share?
Rhode Island	No. (§ 33-25-1)	No. (§ 33-25-1)	Family allowance (§ 33-10-1) are additional protections. If there are no issue surviving, then the probate court "shall" set off real estate in excess of amount needed to cover debts, "as may be suitable for her or his situation and support and in accordance with the circumstances of the estate. The interest will be held for the same period as the life estate granted by 33-25-2 et. seq. (§ 33-10-4)
South Carolina	No. (Boan v. Watson, 316 S.E.2d 401, 402-03 (S.C. 1984), prospectively abolished dower, holding it unconstitutional)	No. (Boan v. Watson, 316 S.E.2d 401, 402-03 (S.C. 1984))	Exempt property up to $25,000 in value (§ 62-2-401) is also available.
South Dakota	No. (§ 29A-2-112)	No. (§ 29A-2-112)	Homestead, exempt property, and family allowance are in addition to elective share. (§ 29A-2-202(c))
Tennessee	No. The right to dower is abolished except to the extent that the right vested before April 1, 1977. (§ 31-2-102)	No. The right to curtesy is abolished except to the extent that the right vested before April 1, 1977. (§ 31-2-102)	Homestead, exempt property, and year's support are in addition to elective share. (§ 31-4-101(b))
Texas	*Community property state; no quasi-community property*		Effective Jan. 1, 2014, homestead exempt property, and the family allowance, are available. (Estates Code §§ 353.051, 353.101) They are excluded from the net estate, and are not to be taken for any of the estate's debts, with certain exceptions (Estates Code §§ 353.104, 353.152–353.153, 353.155), known as "class 1 claims," which are funeral expenses and expenses of decedent's last illness, totaling not in excess of $15,000. (Estates Code § 355.102(b))

Table 6.01
Rights Available in Addition to the Elective Share

	Is There Still a Right to Common Law Dower?	*Is There Still a Right to Common Law Curtesy?*	*What Are The Alternative Protective Rights Afforded the Surviving Spouse? Can They Be Asserted in Addition to the Elective Share?*
Utah	No. (§75-2-112)	No. (§75-2-112)	Homestead allowance up to $22,500 (§75-2-402), exempt property up to $15,000 (§75-2-403), and family allowance (§75-2-404) are permitted, but chargeable against the elective share.
Vermont	No. (14 §302)	No. (14 §302)	All furnishings and furniture in the decedent's household. If any objection is made, the court decides what passes to surviving spouse. (14 §312) When the estate "consists principally of vessel, snowmobile, or all-terrain vehicle" title automatically passes to the surviving spouse. (14 §313) There is also a reasonable allowance for the expenses of maintenance of the surviving spouse and minor children or either. It is paid out of the personal estate or income from the real and personal estate from date of death until estate settlement, but no longer than shares in estate are assigned to them, and in the case of an insolvent estate, no more than 8 months after administration is granted. The court has discretion to decide if the allowance takes priority over debts of the estate. (14 §316) There is also a homestead exemption not exceeding $125,000. (27 §§105, 101) Household goods given to the surviving spouse are in addition to other rights. (14 §312) (There is no similar provision specifically relating to 14 §313 and 14 §316.)

Table 6.01
Rights Available in Addition to the Elective Share

	Is There Still a Right to Common Law Dower?	Is There Still a Right to Common Law Curtesy?	What Are The Alternative Protective Rights Afforded the Surviving Spouse? Can They Be Asserted in Addition to the Elective Share?
Virginia	A spouse's interest in common law dower has been abolished, but shall not change or diminish the nature or right of (i) common law dower vested prior to Jan. 1, 1991 and (ii) a creditor or other interested third party in any real estate subject to a right of dower. (§ 64.2-301)	A spouse's interest in common law curtesy has been abolished, but shall not change or diminish the nature or right of (i) common law curtesy vested prior to Jan. 1, 1991 and (ii) a creditor or other interested third party in any real estate subject to a right of curtesy. (§ 64.2-301)	Homestead allowance (maximum $20,000) and elective share are alternative. (§ 64.2-311) However, family allowance (maximum of $24,000) and exempt property (maximum of $20,000) are in addition to elective share. (§§ 64.2-309, 64.2-310)
Washington	*Community property state; no quasi-community property*		There is provision for homestead (§ 11.54.020), family allowance (§ 11.54.010), and exempt property (§ 11.54.080). The homestead is the lesser of total net value of (a) lands, mobile home, improvements, and certain appurtenant personal property, (b) $125,000 in real property, or (c) $15,000 in personal property. *See* § 11.54.020, cross-reference § 6.13.030. In addition, all of the amounts described above can be adjusted as noted to meet basic maintenance and support. (§ 11.54.050) They can also be reduced. (§ 11.54.040) If the total exempt from creditors under § 6.13.030 is less than the minimum $125,000 specified therein with respect to lands, then other property can be substituted. (§ 11.54.080)
West Virginia	No. (§ 43-1-1)	No. (§ 43-1-1)	A homestead exemption of $5,000 and a personal property exemption of $1,000 is provided. (Const. Art. VI, § 48)

Table 6.01
Rights Available in Addition to the Elective Share

	Is There Still a Right to Common Law Dower?	Is There Still a Right to Common Law Curtesy?	What Are The Alternative Protective Rights Afforded the Surviving Spouse? Can They Be Asserted in Addition to the Elective Share?
Wisconsin	Community property state; quasi-community property known as deferred marital property estate is available to the surviving spouse (§ 861.02)		There is provision for family allowance (§ 861.31), in preference to creditors of as much as $10,000 (§ 861.41), and exempt property (§ 861.33).
Wyoming	No. (§ 2-4-101)	No. (§ 2-4-101)	Homestead allowance, exempt property, and family allowance whether or not takes elective share. (§ 2-5-103)

[1] These answers assume that the decedent died after September 1, 1992.

Table 6.02
How Is the Elective Share Obtained?

	By When Must an Election to Take Against the Will Be Made?	What Must Be Filed?	With Whom?	Who Can Make the Election? E.g., Guardian, Executor of Surviving Spouse after Her Death?
Alabama	Within six months after death or within six months after probate, whichever limitation last expires. (§ 43-8-73(a))	Petition. (§ 43-8-73(a))	With court and mailing or delivering to the personal representative, if any. (§ 43-8-73(a))	Personal to surviving spouse during lifetime. Guardian can only upon petition to court if necessary to provide adequate support. (§ 43-8-71)
Alaska	Nine months after death or six months after probate, whichever is later. (§ 13.12.211(a))	Petition. (§ 13.12.211(a))	Court and mailing or delivering to the personal representative, if any. (§ 13.12.211(a))	Spouse personally or guardian, conservator, or agent with power of attorney. (§ 13.12.212(a))
Arizona	*Community property—no quasi-community property*			
Arkansas	Within one month after the period for making claims. (§ 28-39-403(a)) The period for making claims is six months after the first publication of notice. See § 28-50-101 for specified requirements. If at the end of this period litigation is pending concerning the will, the period is extended further to an additional one month after the final order in this litigation. (§§ 28-39-403(b), 28-50-101)	In writing following the form set out in § 28-39-404(a)(2). (§ 28-39-404)	Office of the probate clerk of the circuit court. (§ 28-39-404(a)(1)(B))	Personal to surviving spouse. Guardian of incompetent surviving spouse on permission of the court. (§ 28-39-405)
California	*Community property and quasi-community property (giving surviving spouse same rights in this property as if community property)*			

Table 6.02
How Is the Elective Share Obtained?

	By When Must an Election to Take Against the Will Be Made?	What Must Be Filed?	With Whom?	Who Can Make the Election? E.g., Guardian, Executor of Surviving Spouse after Her Death?
Colorado	Within nine months of death or six months of admission to probate, whichever is later. (§ 15-11-211(1)) Within nine months after the decedent's death, the surviving spouse may petition the court for an extension of time for making an election. (§ 15-11-211(2))	Petition (§ 15-11-211(1))	Filing in the court and mailing or delivering to the personal representative, if any. (§ 15-11-211(1))	Surviving spouse or his or her conservator, guardian, or agent under the authority of a power of attorney. The surviving spouse must be living at time of election. (§ 15-11-212(1)) Note special rules for incapacitated surviving spouse. (§ 15-11-212(2)
Connecticut	Within 150 days after the mailing of the decree admitting the will to probate. (§ 45a-436(c))	Written notice. (§ 45a-436(c))	Probate court. (§ 45a-436(c))	Surviving spouse, conservator, guardian. (§ 45a-436(c))
Delaware	Six months after grant of letters. (12 § 906(a))	Petition. (12 § 906(a))	Court of Chancery and mailing or delivering to the personal representative. (12 § 906(a))	Surviving spouse, personal representative if spouse elected before death, or court if a protected person. (12 § 904) The election may only be exercised during surviving spouse's lifetime. (Id.)
District of Columbia	Within six months after will is admitted to probate. (§ 19-113(a))	Written renunciation following the form set out in § 19-113(a)	Probate Court at D.C. Superior Court. (§§ 19-113, 19-115)	Surviving spouse, or if approved by the court, a guardian or other fiduciary. (§ 19-113(c))
Florida	Within the earlier of six months from date of first publication of notice of administration or two years after the decedent's death. (§ 732.2135 (1)) Within the specified period, surviving spouse or attorney or guardian may petition the court for an extension. (§ 732.2135)	An election. (§ 732.2135(1))	Court having jurisdiction of probate proceeding. (§ 732.2125(2))	Surviving spouse, or with the approval of the court, by an attorney in fact or guardian of the property. (§ 732.2125)

Table 6.02
How Is the Elective Share Obtained?

	By When Must an Election to Take Against the Will Be Made? (§ 53-3-5(c))	What Must Be Filed?	With Whom?	Who Can Make the Election? E.g., Guardian, Executor of Surviving Spouse after Her Death?
Georgia [*Georgia Year's Support*—No elective share. However, the year's support is like the elective share to the extent that if the decedent makes a provision in lieu of year's support in the will, then the spouse may elect to take the year's support rather than the provision under the will. (§ 53-3-3)]	Within 24 months of the date of death of the decedent. (§ 53-3-5(c))	Petition for year's support. (§ 53-3-5(a))	The probate court having jurisdiction over the decedent's estate. (§ 53-3-5(a))	Surviving spouse, guardian, or other person acting on behalf of the spouse or on behalf of minor child. (§ 53-3-5(a))
Hawaii	Within nine months after the date of the decedent's death, or within six months after the probate of the decedent's will, whichever limitation later expires. (§ 560:2-211(a)) Within nine months after the decedent's death, the spouse or reciprocal beneficiary may petition the court for an extension of time for making an election. (§ 560:2-211(b))	Petition. (§ 560:2-211(a))	The probate court and mailing or delivering to the personal representative, if any. (§ 560:2-211(a))	Surviving spouse or reciprocal beneficiary who is living when the petition is filed. (§ 560:2-212(a)) It may also be exercised by the surviving spouse's or reciprocal's conservator, guardian, or agent under a power of attorney. (§ 560:2.212(a)) If exercised by any such persons the surviving spouse or reciprocal is presumed incapacitated, may be required to be placed in a custodial trust. (§ 560:2-212(b))

Table 6.02
How Is the Elective Share Obtained?

	By When Must an Election to Take Against the Will Be Made?	*What Must Be Filed?*	*With Whom?*	*Who Can Make the Election? E.g., Guardian, Executor of Surviving Spouse after Her Death?*
Idaho [Community property state—with quasi-community property]	Within nine months after death of decedent or within six months after the date of filing of the petition for probate, whichever is later. (§ 15-2-205(a)) The court may extend the time for election as it sees fit for cause shown by the surviving spouse before the time for election has expired. (§ 15-2-205(a))	A petition for the elective share. (§ 15-2-205(a))	The court and mailed or delivered to the personal representative. (§ 15-2-205(a))	Surviving spouse during lifetime or by court if protected person. (§ 15-2-204)
Illinois	Within seven months after the admission of the will to probate or within such further time as may be allowed by the court if, within seven months after the admission of the will to probate or before the expiration of any extended period, the surviving spouse files a petition stating that litigation is pending that affects the share of the surviving spouse in the estate. (755 ILCS §5/2-8(b))	A written instrument signed by the surviving spouse and declaring the renunciation. (755 ILCS §5/2-8(b))	The court in which the will was admitted to probate. (755 ILCS §5/2-8(b))	Surviving spouse. If incompetent, conservator, guardian ad litem, or next friend. (In re Klekunas' Estate, 205 N.E.2d 497, 500 (App. Ct. 1965))

Table 6.02
How Is the Elective Share Obtained?

	By When Must an Election to Take Against the Will Be Made?	*What Must Be Filed?*	*With Whom?*	*Who Can Make the Election? E.g., Guardian, Executor of Surviving Spouse after Her Death?*
Indiana	Claims must be filed within three months after the date admitting to probate the will against which the election is made. If litigation is pending as to the validity, the effect or construction of the will, the existence of issue surviving the decedent, or other matters affecting the share of the spouse, then the period is extended until 30 days after the final determination of the litigation. (§ 29-1-3-2)	An election in writing, signed and acknowledged by the surviving spouse or by the guardian of his estate. It may be in the form of that shown in § 29-1-3-3(a). (§ 29-1-3-3(a))	Clerk of the Probate Court. (§ 29-1-3-3(a))	The surviving spouse or the guardian of the surviving spouse's estate may make the election if the spouse is a protected person; otherwise the right to elect is not transferable and cannot be exercised subsequent to the spouse's death. (§ 29-1-3-4)
Iowa	If spouse is not personal representative of the decedent's estate, within four months after service of notice. Otherwise, the spouse shall be deemed to take under the will or to receive the intestate share. (§ 633.237(1)) If the spouse is a personal representative of the estate and fails to file an election under this section within four months of the decedent's death, it shall be conclusively presumed that the surviving spouse elects to take under the will, receive the intestate share, or take under the revocable trust. (§ 633.237(4))	An election in writing. (§ 633.237)	The clerk of the Probate Court. (§ 633.237)	Only the surviving spouse or her conservator may elect to take against the will because the right to elect is personal and not transferable. It cannot be exercised for the spouse subsequent to the spouse's death. (§§ 633.242, 633.236)

Table 6.02
How Is the Elective Share Obtained?

	By When Must an Election to Take Against the Will Be Made?	What Must Be Filed?	With Whom?	Who Can Make the Election? E.g., Guardian, Executor of Surviving Spouse after Her Death?
Kansas	Six months after the date of the decedent's death, or within six months after the notice of the right to the elective share pursuant to § 59-2233, whichever limitation later expires. (§ 59-6a211(a)) The surviving spouse must give notice of the time and place set for hearing, pursuant to court orders, to persons interested in the estate and to the distributees and recipients of portions of the augmented estate whose interests will be adversely affected by the taking of the elective share. (§ 59-6a211(a))	Petition. (§ 59-6a211(a))	The Probate Court and delivered to the personal representative, if any. (§ 59-6a211(a))	Surviving spouse or personal representative if spouse is disabled or deceased. (§ 59-6a212(a)) Right of election to supplemental elective share, homestead, or statutory allowance may be exercised by the surviving spouse, conservator, agent under power of attorney, guardian ad litem or by court on behalf of disabled spouse. (§ 59-6a212(b))
Kentucky	Within six months after the probate, unless an action contesting the will is brought, then the surviving spouse need not make such relinquishment until six months succeeding the time when the action is disposed of. (§ 392.080(1)(b))	A statement relinquishing the will. (§ 392.080(1))	A certificate shall be filed both with the clerk of the court which admitted the will of the deceased spouse to probate and the county clerk of the county where the will of the deceased spouse was admitted to probate. (§ 392.080(b))	Surviving spouse. (§ 392.080)
Louisiana	*Community property state—no quasi-community property*			

Table 6.02
How Is the Elective Share Obtained?

	By When Must an Election to Take Against the Will Be Made?	What Must Be Filed?	With Whom?	Who Can Make the Election? E.g., Guardian, Executor of Surviving Spouse after Her Death?
Maine	The later of within nine months after the date of death or within six months after probate of decedent's will, whichever expires latest. (18-A §2-205(a))	Petition for elective share. (18-A §2-205(a))	Court and mailing or delivery to the personal representative, if any. (18-A §2-205(a))	Surviving spouse only; and if surviving spouse is a protected person, then by court order after a finding that exercise is necessary to provide adequate support for surviving spouse for his/her life expectancy. (18-A §2-203) The surviving spouse's present or future eligibility for public assistance does not diminish the need for support.(18A §2-203(b))
Maryland	The election by a surviving spouse shall be made not later than the later of nine months, after the deceased spouse's death or six months after the date of the first appointment of a personal representative under a will. (Est. & Trusts §3-206(a)(1)) Within the period for making an election, the surviving spouse may file with the court a petition for extension. The court may extend for a period not to exceed three months at a time, but good cause must be shown. (Est. & Trusts §3-206(a)(2))	Must file a writing that may be in conformity with §3-207(b) and which is signed by the surviving spouse or other person entitled to make the election. (Est. & Trusts §3-207)	The election must be filed in the court in which the personal representative of the decedent was appointed. (Est. & Trusts §3-207(a))	Surviving spouse. The right to make an election is personal to him, not transferable, and cannot be exercised after death. If the surviving spouse is under 18 years of age, or under disability, the election may be exercised by order of the court having jurisdiction of the person or property of the spouse or person under disability. (Est. & Trusts §3-204)

Table 6.02
How Is the Elective Share Obtained?

	By When Must an Election to Take Against the Will Be Made?	*What Must Be Filed?*	*With Whom?*	*Who Can Make the Election? E.g., Guardian, Executor of Surviving Spouse after Her Death?*
Massachusetts	Within six months after the probate of the deceased's will. (191 §15) If, after probate of such will, legal proceedings have been instituted wherein its validity or effect is drawn in question, the probate court may, within said six months, on petition and after such notice as it orders, extend the time for filing the aforesaid claim and waiver until the expiration of six months from the termination of such proceedings. (191 §15)	A writing signed by the surviving spouse, waiving any provisions that may have been made for the spouse in the testator's will, or claiming the spouses elective share. (191 §15)	Registry of probate. (191 §15)	The right to an election is purely a personal right and can only be exercised during the life of the surviving spouse. In addition, any election by a guardian or conservator must be approved by the probate court. Friedman v. Andrews, 200 N.E. 575, 576 (Mass. 1936); Old Colony Trust Co. v. Coffman, 172 N.E.2d 609 (Mass. 1936))
Michigan	The election must be made during the life of the surviving spouse and within 63 days after the date for presentment of claims, or within 63 days after filing proof of service of the inventory upon the spouse, whichever is later. (§700.2202(3))	Election in writing filed with the court that the spouse elects one of the choices specified in §700.2202(1)(a)–(b) (intestate) or §700.2202(2)(a)–(c) (testate). (§700.2202(1))	The court. (§700.2202(1))	The spouse can only exercise election during the lifetime of the spouse. In the case of a legally incapacitated person, the right of election may only be exercised by order of the court in which a proceeding as to that person's property is pending. (§700.2202(3 &5)) Guardians generally do not have the right or duty to elect, at least not without the knowledge, consent, and approval of the probate court. (§700.2202(3) & (5); Huntington College v. Moore, 5 F. Supp. 541, 546–47 (W.D. Mich. 1933))

Table 6.02
How Is the Elective Share Obtained?

	By When Must an Election to Take Against the Will Be Made?	What Must Be Filed?	With Whom?	Who Can Make the Election? E.g., Guardian, Executor of Surviving Spouse after Her Death?
Minnesota	Election must be made within nine months after the date of death or within six months after the probate of the decedent's will, whichever time limitation last expires. (§ 524.2-211(a))	Must file a petition claiming the elective share. In addition, "[t]he surviving spouse must give notice of the time and place set for hearing to persons interested in the estate and to the distributees and recipients of portions of the augmented estate whose interests will be adversely affected by the taking of the elective share." (§ 524.2-211(a))	The court and mailed or delivered to the personal representative, if any. (§ 524.2-211(a))	The right of election of the surviving spouse may be exercised only during the surviving spouse's lifetime. In the case of a protected person, the right of election may be exercised only by order of the court in which protective proceedings as to the protected person's property are pending based on factors outlined in § 524.2-212. (§ 524.2-212)
Mississippi	Within 90 days after the probate of the will. (§ 91-5-25)	A renunciation of the deceased's will and an election to take spouse's legal share. (§ 91-5-25)	The court office where the will was probated. (§ 91-5-25)	The elective share right is personal to the surviving spouse and may not be elected by his or her administrator after death. (Shattuck v. Estate of Tyson, 508 So. 2d 1077, 1080-81 (Miss. 1987)) The right to renounce may be exercised by a guardian in the case of an incompetent surviving spouse. (Estate of Mullins v. Estate of Mullins, 125 So. 2d 93, 95-96 (Miss. 1960))

Table 6.02
How Is the Elective Share Obtained?

	By When Must an Election to Take Against the Will Be Made?	What Must Be Filed?	With Whom?	Who Can Make the Election? E.g., Guardian, Executor of Surviving Spouse after Her Death?
Missouri	The election by a surviving spouse must be made within 10 days after the expiration of the time limited for contesting the will of the decedent. If litigation is pending concerning the will, 90 days after the termination of litigation. (§ 474.180)	Form of election must be in writing, signed and acknowledged by the surviving spouse or by the guardian ad litem or conservator of the spouse's estate. It may be filed in accordance with the form of § 474.190. (§ 474.190)	The office of the clerk of the court. (§ 474.190)	The right of election of the surviving spouse is personal to the spouse is not transferable, and cannot be exercised after the surviving spouse's death. But, if the surviving spouse is disabled or a minor, the spouse's guardian ad litem or conservator may elect for the spouses with the approval of the court. (§ 474.200)
Montana	Within nine months after the date of death or within six months after the probate of the decedent's will, whichever time limitation last expires. (§72-2-225(1)) Within nine months after decedent's death, the surviving spouse may petition the court for an extension. (§72-2-225(2))	Must file a petition claiming the elective share. "In addition, the surviving spouse must give notice of the time and place set for hearing to persons interested in the estate and to the distributees and recipients of portions of the augmented estate whose interests will be adversely affected by the taking of the elective share." (§72-2-225(1))	The court and mailed or delivered to the personal representative, if any. (§72-2-225(1))	A surviving spouse who is living when the petition for the elective share is filed with the court. The surviving spouse's conservator, guardian or agent under the authority of a power of attorney may also exercise the election on the surviving spouse's behalf. (§72-2-223(1))

Table 6.02
How Is the Elective Share Obtained?

	By When Must an Election to Take Against the Will Be Made?	What Must Be Filed?	With Whom?	Who Can Make the Election? E.g., Guardian, Executor of Surviving Spouse after Her Death?
Nebraska	Within nine months after the date of death or within six months after the probate of the decedent's will, whichever time limitation last expires. (§ 30-2317(a)) The court may extend the time for election as it sees fit for cause shown by the surviving spouse before the time for election has expired. (§ 30-2317(a))	A petition for the elective share in any designated fraction not in excess of one-half of the augmented estate or, in the absence of any such designation, of one-half of the augmented estate. (§ 30-2317(a)) In addition, the surviving spouse must give notice of the time and place set for hearing to persons interested in the estate and to the distributees and recipients of portions of the augmented estate whose interests will be adversely affected by the taking of the elective share. (§ 30-2317(b))	Petition must be filed in the court and mailed or delivered to the personal representative, if any. (§ 30-2317(a))	Right of election of the surviving spouse may only be exercised by the spouse during the spouse's lifetime. In the case of a protected person, the court in which the protective proceedings are pending may only exercise the election. (§ 30-2315)
Nevada		*Community property state—no quasi-community property*		
New Hampshire	Within six months after appointment of executor or administrator, unless the judge of the probate court grants an extension for good cause shown. (§ 560:14)	Written waiver of will. (§ 560:14)	Probate office. (§ 560:14)	If a ward is insane, a guardian may waive testate distribution. (Wentworth v. Waldron, 172 A. 247, 251 (N.H. 1934)) Otherwise, the right to the elective share is personal and cannot be exercised by surviving spouse's representatives. (Gowing v. Laing, 77 A.2d 32, 32 (N.H. 1950); § 560:10)

Table 6.02
How Is the Elective Share Obtained?

	By When Must an Election to Take Against the Will Be Made?	What Must Be Filed?	With Whom?	Who Can Make the Election? E.g., Guardian, Executor of Surviving Spouse after Her Death?
New Jersey	"[W]ithin 6 months after the appointment of a personal representative of the decedent's estate. The court may, before the time for election has expired and upon good cause shown by the surviving spouse or domestic partner, extend the time for election upon notice to persons interested in the estate and to distributees and recipients of portions of the augmented estate whose interests will be adversely affected by the taking of the elective share." (§ 3B:8-12)	A complaint. (§ 3B:8-12)	Superior Court. (§ 3B:8-12)	Surviving spouse or domestic partner during his lifetime. "In the case of a surviving spouse or domestic partner for whom the court has appointed a guardian to manage his estate, the right of election may be exercised only by order of the court making the appointment and only if election is necessary to provide adequate support of the surviving spouse or domestic partner during his probable life expectancy." (§ 3B:8-11)
New Mexico	*Community property state with quasi-community property* [Quasi-community property is defined in § 40-3-8(C). It is treated as community property for purposes of division of property incident to a dissolution of marriage or a legal separation "if both parties are New Mexico domiciliaries at the time of the dissolution or legal separation." (§ 40-3-8(D)) It is not mentioned in any provision dealing with distribution of an estate.]			

Table 6.02
How Is the Elective Share Obtained?

	By When Must an Election to Take Against the Will Be Made?	What Must Be Filed?	With Whom?	Who Can Make the Election? E.g., Guardian, Executor of Surviving Spouse after Her Death?
New York[1]	"Within six months from date of issuance of letters testamentary or of administration," but not more than two years after decedent's death. (Est. Powers & Trusts §5-1.1-A(d)(1)) The time may be extended by order of the court for up to six months. (Est. Powers & Trusts §5-1.1-A(d)(2))	Written notice. (Est. Powers & Trusts §5-1.1-A(d)(1))	Surrogate's court in which letters testamentary of administration were issued and upon personal representative or executor. (Est. Powers & Trusts §5-1.1-A(d)(1))	Surviving spouse, or upon order of appointing court, an authorized guardian of the property of an infant spouse, an authorized committee of an incompetent spouse, an authorized conservator of a conservatee spouse, an authorized guardian ad litem for the surviving spouse, or an authorized guardian appointed under Article 81 of the Mental Hygiene Law. (Est. Powers & Trusts §5-1.1-A(c)(3))
North Carolina	"[W]ithin six months after the issuance of letters testamentary or... of administration in connection with the will or intestate proceeding." (§30-3.4(b))	A petition. (§30-3.4(b))	The clerk of the county superior court of primary administration and mailing or delivering a copy to personal representative. (§30-3.4(b)(i) & (ii))	Surviving spouse or his or her agent under a power of attorney, or guardian of surviving spouse's estate. If the surviving spouse dies before the claim is settled, his/her personal representative succeeds to the claim. (§30-3.4(a))

Table 6.02
How Is the Elective Share Obtained?

	By When Must an Election to Take Against the Will Be Made?	*What Must Be Filed?*	*With Whom?*	*Who Can Make the Election? E.g., Guardian, Executor of Surviving Spouse after Her Death?*
North Dakota	Within nine months of decedent's death, or within six months after probate of decedent's will, whichever expires later. (§ 30.1-05-05(1)) "The surviving spouse shall serve a copy of the petition for the elective share on, and shall give written notice of the time and place set for hearing to persons interested in the estate and to the distributees and recipients of portions of the augmented estate whose interests may be adversely affected by the taking of the elective share." (*Id.*) The surviving spouse can petition for an extension within 9 months after decedent's death (§ 30.1-05-05(2))	A petition for the elective share. (§ 30.1-05-05(1))	The probate court and mailing or delivering to the personal representative, if any. (§ 30.1-05-05(1))	Surviving spouse or surviving spouse's conservator, guardian, or agent under the authority of a power of attorney, but only if surviving spouse is alive when the petition is filed. (§ 30.1-05-06(1))

Table 6.02
How Is the Elective Share Obtained?

	By When Must an Election to Take Against the Will Be Made?	What Must Be Filed?	With Whom?	Who Can Make the Election? E.g., Guardian, Executor of Surviving Spouse after Her Death?
Ohio	Any time after death of decedent, but not later than five months from the initial appointment of an administrator or executor of the estate. Court may allow more time for good cause if a motion is filed before the expiration of the five-month period. If proceedings for advice or to contest the validity of the will are begun within the time allowed for election, election may be made within three months after the final disposition of the proceedings, if the will is not set aside. (§ 2106.01(E))	Election must be made in person. (§ 2106.06)	Must be before the probate judge or a deputy clerk who has been appointed to act as a referee. (§ 2106.06)	Surviving spouse or any suitable person to whom the probate court, upon the filing of an application on behalf of the surviving spouse, has issued a commission to take the election. (§ 2106.07) If the surviving spouse is unable to make an election because of a legal disability, the court may elect for the spouse. (§ 2106.08)
Oklahoma	"[O]n or before the final date for hearing of the petition for final distribution of the estate." (84 § 44(B)(3))	A writing. (84 § 44(B)(3))	"[D]istrict court in which the estate of the decedent is being administered." (84 § 44(B)(3))	Surviving spouse; if the surviving spouse is incompetent, a guardian or conservator may make the election with court approval. The surviving spouse must be alive when the election is made. (84 § 44(B)(4))

Table 6.02
How Is the Elective Share Obtained?

	By When Must an Election to Take Against the Will Be Made?	What Must Be Filed?	With Whom?	Who Can Make the Election? E.g., Guardian, Executor of Surviving Spouse after Her Death?
Oregon	Within 9 months after spouse dies. (§ 114.610(1)(a))	Either by filing (i) a petition for appointment of personal representative along with a motion to exercise the election, (ii) a motion to exercise the election with a copy served on the personal representative, all persons entitled to receive information, and "all distributees and recipients of the augmented estate known to the surviving spouse who can be located with reasonable effort," or (iii) filing a petition for the exercise of the elective share. (§ 114.610(1)(a)-(c))	Either the probate court or the circuit court, depending on the county. (§§ 114.610, 111.055)	The surviving spouse or by the surviving spouse's "conservator, guardian, or agent under the authority of a power of attorney." (§ 114.625, eff. 2011)
Pennsylvania	Within six months after decedent's death or before expiration of six months after date of probate, whichever is later. (20 § 2210(b)) "The court may extend the time for election for such period and upon such terms and conditions as the court shall deem proper under the circumstances on application of the surviving spouse filed with the clerk within the foregoing time limit." Id	Written and signed election. (20 § 2210(a))	"[C]lerk of the orphan's court division of the county where decedent died domiciled." Notice of election must be given to the decedent's personal representative, if any. (20 § 2210(a))	Surviving spouse or attorney-in-fact, only during spouse's lifetime. Minor spouse's right of election may be exercised only by spouse's guardian, and incapacitated spouse's right of election may be exercised by spouse's guardians or spouse's attorneys-in-fact. (20 § 2206)

Table 6.02
How Is the Elective Share Obtained?

	By When Must an Election to Take Against the Will Be Made?	What Must Be Filed?	With Whom?	Who Can Make the Election? E.g., Guardian, Executor of Surviving Spouse after Her Death?
Rhode Island	Within six months after date of first publication of the qualifications of the fiduciary of the estate. (§ 33-25-4)	Written statement waiving and renouncing devise and bequest, and claiming his or her share in life estate in decedent's real estate. (§ 33-25-4)	Probate court granting probate. The waiver and claim shall also be filed in the records of deeds in each city and town where any real estate is located, if located in any city other than that in which the will is probated. (§ 33-25-4)	Surviving spouse. (§ 33-25-4)
South Carolina	The surviving spouse must make his or her election within eight months after the date of death of the decedent, within six months after the informal or formal probate of the decedent's will, or thirty days after the surviving spouse is served with a petition to set aside or modify a previous probate, whichever limitation last expires. (§ 62-2-205(a))	"[A] summons and petition for the elective share." (§ 62-2-205(a))	The petition must be filed with the court and also mailed or delivered to the personal representative, if any. (§ 62-2-205(a)) The petitioning spouse must also give notice of the time and place set for hearing "to the personal representative and to distributees and recipients of portions of the probate estate whose interests will be adversely affected by the taking of the elective share." (§ 62-2-205)	The right of election may exercised only during by the surviving spouse his lifetime, or by his duly appointed attorney in fact, or, "[i]n the case of a protected person, the right of election may be exercised only by order of the court in which protective proceedings as to his property are pending." (§ 62-2-203) A "protected person" is defined as a minor or incapacitated person for whom a conservator has been appointed or other protective order has been made. (§ 62-5-101(3))

Table 6.02

How Is the Elective Share Obtained?

	By When Must an Election to Take Against the Will Be Made?	*What Must Be Filed?*	*With Whom?*	*Who Can Make the Election? E.g., Guardian, Executor of Surviving Spouse after Her Death?*
South Dakota	The right of election must be exercised within nine months after the date of death of the decedent or within four months after the admission to either formal or informal probate of the decedent's will, whichever limitation later expires. (§29A-2-211(a)) A court may extend the time allowed for good cause shown. (§29A-2-211 (b)) The decedent's nonprobate transfers to others are not included within the augmented estate if the petition for the elective share is filed more than nine months after the decedent's death or beyond the time extended by the court. (§29A-2-211(a))	A petition for the elective share. (§29A-2-211(a))	The petition must be filed with the court and also mailed or delivered to the personal representative, if any. (§ 29A-2-211(a)) "Notice of hearing must be given to persons interested in the estate and to the distributees and recipients of portions of the augmented estate whose interests will be adversely affected by the taking of the elective share." (*Id.*)	"The right of election may be exercised either by the surviving spouse or by [his or her] conservator or agent under the authority of a power of attorney, or, if the surviving spouse dies prior to the expiration of the time for making an election... by the surviving spouse's personal representative." (§29A-2-212)
Tennessee	Within nine months after the date of death. (§ 31-4-102(a)(1)) However, when the title of the surviving spouse to property devised or bequeathed by the will is involved in litigation so that an election cannot be made, the surviving spouse shall have an additional year from the date of the probate of the will, as well as any additional time deemed necessary by the court, within which to elect. (§31-4-102(a)(2))	A petition for the elective share. (§31-4-102(a)(1))	The court and also mailed or delivered to the personal representative, if any. (§ 31-4-102(a)(1))	The surviving spouse may exercise the right of election, or, in the event the surviving spouse dies after the decedent spouse but before the time of election expires, by the personal representative of the decedent's surviving spouse. (§§ 31-4-102, 31-4-105) If surviving spouse is a minor or mentally incompetent, a guardian, conservator, or next friend can make the election. (§31-4-104)
Texas	*Community property state; no quasi-community property*			

Table 6.02
How Is the Elective Share Obtained?

	By When Must an Election to Take Against the Will Be Made?	What Must Be Filed?	With Whom?	Who Can Make the Election? E.g., Guardian, Executor of Surviving Spouse after Her Death?
Utah	"[W]ithin nine months after the date of the decedent's death, or within six months after the probate of the decedent's will, whichever limitation later expires...nonprobate transfers to others are not included within the augmented estate for the purpose of computing the elective-share, if the petition is filed more than nine months after the decedent's death." (§75-2-211(1)) Within nine months after the decedent's death, the surviving spouse may petition the court for an extension of time for making an election. If, within nine months after the decedent's death, the spouse gives notice of the petition to all persons interested in the decedent's nonprobate transfers to others, the court for cause shown by the surviving spouse may extend the time for election. (§75-2-211(2))	A petition for the elective share. (§75-2-211(1))	The court and also mailed or delivered to the personal representative, if any. (§75-2-211(a)) "The petitioning spouse must also give notice of the time and place set for hearing to persons interested in the estate and to the distributees and recipients of portions of the augmented [net] estate whose interests will be adversely affected by the taking of the elective share." (Id.)	The right of election may be exercised only by the surviving spouse who is living when a petition for the elective share is filed in court, or on the surviving spouse's behalf by his conservator, guardian, or agent under the authority of a power of attorney during the life of the surviving spouse. (§75-2-212(1))
Vermont	Within eight months, unless extended by the probate court, after the decedent's will is proved or letters of administration are granted. (R. of Prob. Proc. 13(b))	The election must be filed on the official form given in the rules. (R. of Prob. Proc. 13(b)) See also 14 §319.	The probate court. (R. of Prob. Proc. 13(b))	The surviving spouse is entitled to make the election or a guardian or attorney in fact under a valid durable power of attorney if the surviving spouse is mentally disabled and cannot make the election personally. (14 §319(b)); (R. of Prob. Proc. 13(b))

Table 6.02
How Is the Elective Share Obtained?

	By When Must an Election to Take Against the Will Be Made?	What Must Be Filed?	With Whom?	Who Can Make the Election? E.g., Guardian, Executor of Surviving Spouse after Her Death?
Virginia	Within six months from the later of (a) the time of admission of will to probate or (b) the qualification of an administrator of decedent's estate. (§ 64.2-302(B))	The surviving spouse must file a claim, in person, or in writing for the elective share. The claim must be recorded in the court or clerk's office and must conform to the requirements listed in § 55-106 et seq. (§ 64.2-302(B))	The court or the clerk's office having jurisdiction over administration of decedent's estates. (§ 64.2-302(B))	Reference in the statute is only made to the surviving spouse. (§ 64.2-302(B)) Under prior, but similar law, it was held that if the surviving spouse is incompetent, a guardian cannot make the election, but that a court to which the matter has been addressed has the power either to renounce the will and take the elective share or decline to do so. However, although the court should be motivated by the "best interests," of the surviving spouse, the decision contains language seemingly elevating present value received as the key determinant as to whether to renounce the will or not. (First Nat'l Exch. Bank v. Hughson, 74 S.E.2d 797 (Va. 1953))
Washington	*Community property state; no quasi-community property*			

Table 6.02
How Is the Elective Share Obtained?

	By When Must an Election to Take Against the Will Be Made?	What Must Be Filed?	With Whom?	Who Can Make the Election? E.g., Guardian, Executor of Surviving Spouse after Her Death?
West Virginia	"[W]ithin nine months after the date of the decedent's death or within six months after the probate of the decedent's will, whichever limitation later expires." (§ 42-3-4(a)) The surviving spouse may petition for an extension within nine months of the decedent's death. (§ 42-3-4(b))	A petition for the elective share. (§ 42-3-4(a))	The court and also mailed or delivered to the personal representative, if any. (§ 42-3-4(a)) The petitioning spouse must also serve a copy of the petition and a written notice of the time and place set for hearing on persons interested in the estate and on the distributees and recipients of portions of the augmented estate whose interests may be adversely affected by the taking of the elective share. (*Id.*)	Surviving spouse, conservator, guardian, or agent under the authority of power of attorney. The surviving spouse must be living. (§ 42-3-3(a))
Wisconsin	Community property state; quasi-community property known as *deferred marital property estate is available to the surviving spouse* (§ 851.055)			

Table 6.02
How Is the Elective Share Obtained?

	By When Must an Election to Take Against the Will Be Made?	*What Must Be Filed?*	*With Whom?*	*Who Can Make the Election? E.g., Guardian, Executor of Surviving Spouse after Her Death?*
Wyoming	Within three months after admission of will to probate or within 30 days after being advised by court of right to election, whichever is later. (§2-5-105(a)) Court must advise surviving spouse of right to election within three months after admission of will to probate. (§2-5-104(a))	Petition for elective share. (§2-5-105(a))	Court and also mailed or delivered to the personal representative, if any. (§2-5-105(a))	"The surviving spouse, or a personal representative or guardian of the estate of a deceased or incompetent surviving spouse . . . . . ." (§2-5-105(a)) If spouse of a domiciliary decedent dies or becomes incompetent within three months after will is admitted to probate or before the court advises spouse of right to election, a personal representative or guardian of the estate of the deceased or incompetent surviving spouse has the same right of election as the surviving spouse would have had if living or competent. (§2-5-101(c))

[1] These answers assume that the decedent died after September 1, 1992.

Table 6.03, Part 1
Calculation of Elective Share

	What Percentage Right?	What Is the Right Based On?	Is the Share Based on the Estate Before Subtraction of All Debts, After Subtraction of All Some Debts, After Subtraction of All Debts?	Is Foreign Real Property Taken Into Account?	Is Foreign Personal Property Taken Into Account?
Alabama	Lesser of all of the estate less the surviving spouse's separate estate, or one-third of the estate. (§43-8-70(a)(1) & (2)) Separate estate of surviving spouse is: (1) all property which immediately after death the surviving spouse owns outright or in fee simple absolute; (2) all legal/equitable interests in property acquired by surviving the decedent; and (3) all income and other beneficial interests (a) under a trust, (b) in proceeds of life insurance on the life of decedent, (c) under any broad-based nondiscriminatory pension, profit-sharing, stock bonus, deferred compensation, disability, death benefit, or other such plan established by an employer. (§43-8-70(b)(1)-(3))	Depends on which election spouse is entitled to—one-third or full estate less separate estate. If one-third election, the right is based on the probate estate. (§43-8-70) If full estate less separate estate, other sources of income to surviving spouse and property held by surviving spouse are considered. (§43-8-70(b)) See prior column.	After reduction for allowable claims against the estate. (See §43-8-70; Brakefield v. Hocutt, 779 So. 2d 1165 (Ala. 2000) (construing §43-8-70)	Simply refers to "estate." (§43-8-70(a)(1) & (2))	Simply refers to "estate." (§43-8-70(a)(1) & (2))
Alaska	One-third of augmented estate. (§13.12.202(a))	Augmented estate. (§§13.12.202(a), 13.12.203) The augmented estate is a complicated calculation, the particulars of which should be checked specifically. (§13.12.204–207) In general terms, the augmented estate consists of: (a) decedent's net probate estate; (b) decedent's nonprobate transfers to others (e.g., joint tenancy, insurance, irrevocable transfers in which decedent retained rights to property, transfers which decedent retained power over the income of property); (c) decedent's nonprobate transfers to surviving spouse; (d) surviving spouse's property; and (e) surviving spouse's nonprobate transfers to others. (§§13.12.203, 13.12.205)	See Table 6.03, Part 2. Subtract funeral and administrative expenses, homestead, family allowance, exempt property, and enforceable claims. (§13.12.204)	Yes. (§13.12.203)	Yes. (§13.12.203)
Arizona	*Community property—no quasi-community property*				

Table 6.03, Part 1
Calculation of Elective Share

	What Is the Right Based On?	Is the Share Based on the Estate Before Subtraction of All Debts, After Subtraction of Some Debts, After Subtraction of All Debts?	Is Foreign Real Property Taken Into Account?	Is Foreign Personal Property Taken Into Account?
	What Percentage Right?			
Arkansas	With children: Land—one-third life estate in property in which the decedent was seized. (§ 28-11-301(a)) Personalty—one-third of property which decedent possessed/seized. (§ 28-11-305) Without children: Land—one-half in fee simple of the land that is newly acquired and not an ancestral estate; one-third as against creditors. (§ 28-11-307(a)) If an ancestral estate, one-half; one-third as against creditors. (§ 28-11-307(b)) Personalty—one-half absolutely; one-third as against creditors. (§ 28-11-307(a))	Real property—that which was seized. (§§ 28-11-301, 28-11-307) Personal—that which was possessed or seized. (§ 28-11-305)	No deduction. (§ 28-11-305; Dolton v. Allen, 167 S.W.2d 893, 894 (Ark. 1943); § 28-11-301; Tate v. Jay, 31 Ark. 576, 579 (Ark. 1876))	No apparent distinction made between domestic and foreign property.	Same as prior column.
California[1]	One-half quasi-community property. (Prob. § 101(a))	Quasi-community property. (Prob. § 101) See second column to the right.	The surviving spouse remains liable for debts chargeable against quasi-community property equal to the percent of quasi-community property of the surviving spouse and the community property of the decedent that the surviving spouse takes. (Prob. §§ 13550, 13551) Other general debts can be allocated between surviving spouse and estate property. (Prob. § 11440 et seq.)	Quasi-community property is all property that is not community property and is: (a) all personal property wherever situated and all real property situated in California acquired by the decedent while domiciled elsewhere that would have been community property if the decedent had been domiciled in California at the time of acquisition; and (b) all personal property wherever situated and all real property in California acquired in exchange for real and personal property that would have been community property if the decedent had been domiciled in California at the time the property so exchanged was acquired. (Prob. § 66)	See prior columns.

Table 6.03, Part 1
Calculation of Elective Share

	What Percentage Right?	What Is the Right Based On?	Is the Share Based on the Estate Before Subtraction of All Debts, After Subtraction of Some Debts, After Subtraction of All Debts?	Is Foreign Real Property Taken Into Account?	Is Foreign Personal Property Taken Into Account?
Colorado	Varies depending on length of marriage, maximum one-half of augmented estate. (§15-11-202(1)) If the amount of the surviving spouse's property and the property that passes to a spouse by intestate and testate succession and the amount payable from the decedent's probate estate and nonprobate transfers is less than $50,000 (adjusted for inflation), the surviving spouse is entitled to a supplemental elective share of $50,000 (adjusted for inflation) less the above described amounts. (§15-11-202(2))	Augmented estate is a complicated calculation, and the statute should be carefully checked before computation. Generally, it includes: (a) decedent's net probate estate; (b) decedent's nonprobate transfers to others (e.g., joint tenancy, multiple party accounts, certain life insurance, irrevocable transfers in which decedent reserved rights, any transfer creating a power in decedent over the income or principal of the property); (c) The decedent's nonprobate transfers to the surviving spouse; and (d) The surviving spouse's property and nonprobate transfers to others. (§15-11-203(1)(a)-(d))	Based on the augmented estate which calls for subtraction from probate estate of funeral and administrative expenses, family allowance, exempt property, and enforceable claims. (§15-11-204; See also previous column)	Yes. (§15-11-203(1))	Yes. (§15-11-203(1))
Connecticut	One-third life estate in value of all property passing under will, real and personal, legally or equitably owned by the decedent at the time of death. (§45a-436(a))	Refers only to property passing under will—estate property. (§45a-436(a))	The statute refers to a statutory share that is determined "after the payment of all debts and charges against the estate." (§45a-436(a))	Refers to all property. (§45a-436(a)) But see Banker's Trust Co. v. Greims, 147 A. 290, 292 (Conn. 1929), indicating that foreign real property will not be counted in determining statutory share.	See prior column.
Delaware	One-third of "elective estate," less all transfers to surviving spouse. (12 §901(a))	The "elective estate," less all transfers to surviving spouse valued at date of distribution. (12 §901(a))	The elective estate is based on the federal gross estate less I.R.C. §§2053 and 2054 deductions and certain joint interests of spouse and decedent. (12 §§901(a), 902(a))	Only mentions "gross estate" and "elective estate." (12 §902(a))	Only mentions "gross estate" and "elective estate." (12 §902(a))
District of Columbia	Surviving spouse or domestic partner is entitled to "legal share." The legal share is the share or interest in the real or personal property of the deceased spouse or domestic parter, as he would have taken if the deceased spouse or domestic partner had died intestate, not to exceed one-half of the net estate bequeathed and devised by the will. (§19-113(e))	The "legal share" includes real estate and surplus of the personal estate. (§19-301)	The "surplus of the personal estate" is not defined, but presumably is what remains after expenses of administration.	There is no specific limitation.	There is no specific limitation.

Table 6.03, Part 1
Calculation of Elective Share

	What Percentage Right?	What Is the Right Based On?	Is the Share Based on the Estate Before Subtraction of All Debts, After Subtraction of Some Debts, After Subtraction of All Debts?	Is Foreign Real Property Taken Into Account?	Is Foreign Personal Property Taken Into Account?
Florida	30% of the elective estate (§732.2065) as defined broadly in §732.2035. For the definition of "values" of property interests that make up the elective estate, see §732.2055.	Elective estate (§732.2035) that consists of the sum of values of the following property interests, among others: decedent's probate estate if it is subject to administration in the U.S. (§732.2025(7)); P.O.D.s, T.O.D.s, "In Trust For"; joint tenancy with right of survivorship or in tenancy by the entirety; revocable transfers; property in which the decedent retained an income interest; or person other than surviving spouse had discretion to distribute or appoint the principal for the benefit of the decedent. (§732.2035(1)-(5))	Probate estate reduced by all valid claims against the elective estate and all mortgages, liens, or security interests on the assets. (§732.2055(5))	Probably not if outside the U.S. (§732.2025(7))	Probably yes, if decedent was domiciled in the U.S. so that there is an administration in the U.S. (§732.2025(7))
Georgia²	The surviving spouse is entitled to a year's support in the form of property. (§53-3-1(c)) Personal and real property can be chosen for the year's support. (§§53-3-10, 53-3-11)	Property from the estate can be chosen. (§§53-3-1, 53-3-5)	The year's support is to be preferred before all other expenses since it is among the necessary expenses of administration. (§53-3-1(b))	There is a description of awarding an interest in real property located in Georgia for the year's support. (§53-3-11)	There is only a description of awarding an interest in property located inside or outside the county where the decedent was domiciled at the time of death for the year's support. (§53-3-10)
Hawaii	The percentage share is determined by the length of time the spouse and the decedent were married to each other, or the reciprocal beneficiary and the decedent were in a reciprocal beneficiary relationship, maximum of 50% of augmented estate. (§560:2-202(a)) See §560:2-201 for definition of "reciprocal beneficiary."	Augmented estate (§§560:2-202, 560:2-203), which is composed of: decedent's net probate estate (§560:2-204), the decedent's nonprobate transfers to others (§560:2-205), the decedent's nonprobate transfers to the surviving spouse or reciprocal beneficiary (§560:2-206), and the surviving spouse's or reciprocal beneficiary's property and nonprobate transfers to others (§560:2-207).	The value of the augmented estate includes the decedent's probate estate, reduced by funeral and administrative expenses, homestead allowance, family allowances, exempt property, and enforceable claims. (§560:2-204)	Yes, all real property wherever situated. (§560:2-203)	Yes, all personal property wherever situated. (§560:2-203)

Table 6.03, Part 1
Calculation of Elective Share

	What Percentage Right?	What Is the Right Based On?	Is the Share Based on the Estate Before Subtraction of All Debts, After Subtraction of All or Some Debts, After Subtraction of All Debts?	Is Foreign Real Property Taken Into Account?	Is Foreign Personal Property Taken Into Account?
Idaho[3]	One-half of quasi community property, plus remaining portion of the other half of the quasi-community property not disposed of by will, if any. (§15-2-201(a))	Augmented quasi-community property estate (§15-2-203(a)) composed of: quasi-community property ("all personal property, wherever situated, and all real property situated in this state which… is acquired by the decedent while domiciled elsewhere and which would have been the community property of the decedent and the surviving spouse had the decedent been domiciled in this state at the time of its acquisition" (§15-2-201(b)) and the augmented estate ("transfers of quasi-community property to a person other than the surviving spouse without adequate consideration and without the consent of the surviving spouse" (§15-2-202))	The elective share is reduced by an allocable portion of: general administration expenses, homestead allowance, family allowance, exempt property and enforceable claims. (§15-2-203(b))	Yes. (§15-2-201(b))	Yes. (§15-2-201(b))
Illinois	"[One-third] of the entire estate if the testator leaves a descendant or [one-half] of the entire estate if the testator leaves no descendant." (755 ILCS §5/2-8(a))	Probate estate. Inter vivos transfers can be made to defeat the elective share. (Estate of Mocny, 630 N.E.2d 87, 93 (App. Ct. 1993)) Assets transferred into joint tenancy, where the transfer was made solely to establish a convenience account. (Id.)	Entire estate after payment of all just claims. (755 ILCS §5/2-8; see also In re Grant's Estate, 415 N.E.2d 416 (Ill. 1980))	Real property in another state is not part of the "entire estate." The law of the states where the real estate is located governs the surviving spouse's rights. (In re Estate of Pericles, 641 N.E.2d 10,13 (App. Ct. 1994))	There is no specific limitation.

Table 6.03, Part 1
Calculation of Elective Share

	What Percentage Right?	What Is the Right Based On?	Is the Share Based on the Estate Before Subtraction of All Debts, After Subtraction of Some Debts, After Subtraction of All Debts?	Is Foreign Real Property Taken Into Account?	Is Foreign Personal Property Taken Into Account?
Indiana	One-half of the net personal and real estate of the decedent, unless "the surviving spouse is a second or other subsequent spouse who did not at any time have children by the decedent and the decedent left surviving a child or children or... descendants of a child or children by a previous spouse," then one-third of the net personal estate of the decedent plus 25% of the fair market value of the lands of the decedent minus the value of any liens or encumbrances on the decedent's real property. (§ 29-1-3-1(a))	Not only probate estate. Also, inter vivos trusts where the deceased settlor retains so much control over disposition and management of property in trust that trustee possesses only a naked or nominal title which does not impair full ownership of cestui que trust or beneficiary. (Leazenby v. Clinton Cty. Bank & Trust Co., 355 N.E.2d 861, 864 (Ind. 1976))	Although the term "net personal and real estate" is used, the closest defined term is "net estate." "Net estate" is real and personal property exclusive of the family allowance provided for by § 29-1-4-1 and enforceable claims against the estate. (§§ 29-1-3-1, 29-1-3)	Only "property as would have passed under the laws of descent and distribution." (§ 29-1-3-1(a))	Only mentions net personal estate of testator. (§ 29-1-3-1)
Iowa	(a) "One-third in value of all the legal or equitable estates in real property possessed by the decedent at the time during the marriage, which have not been sold on execution or other judicial sale, and to which the surviving spouse has made no relinquishment of right; (b) [a]ll personal property that, at the time of death, was in the hands of the decedent as the head of a family, exempt from execution; and (c) [o]ne-third of all other personal property of the decedent that is not necessary for the payment of debts and charges; and (d) one-third of property held in trust, not necessary for the payment of the decedent's debts, which the decedent either retained control to alter, revoke, or amend or which the decedent waived such right within one year of death and the surviving spouse had not yet relinquished." (§ 633.238(d))	See prior column. (§ 633.238)	One-third in value of all other personal property of the decedent after the subtraction of all debts. (§ 633.238; In re Estate of Thompson, 512 N.W.2d 560, 564 (Iowa 1994))	All real property possessed by decedent at any time during marriage. (§ 633.238(1))	All personal property. (§ 633.238(1))

Table 6.03, Part 1
Calculation of Elective Share

	What Is the Percentage Right?	What Is the Right Based On?	Is the Share Based on the Estate Before Subtraction of All Debts, After Subtraction of Some Debts, After Subtraction of All Debts?	Is Foreign Real Property Taken Into Account?	Is Foreign Personal Property Taken Into Account?
Kansas	Varies depending on length of marriage, maximum of one-half of augmented estate. (§59-6a202(a)(1))	Augmented estate (§§59-6a202, 59-6a203), which is composed of: decedent's net probate estate, the decedent's non-probate transfers to others (e.g., joint tenancy, insurance, irrevocable transfers in which decedent retained rights to property, transfers which decedent retained power over the income or property). (§59-6a205) the decedent's nonprobate transfers to the surviving spouse (§596a206), and the surviving spouse's property and nonprobate transfers to others (§59-6a207).	The value of the augmented estate includes "the decedent's probate estate, reduced by funeral and administrative expenses, homestead or homestead allowance, family allowances, and enforceable demands." (§59-6a204)	There is no specific mention. (§59-6a203)	There is no specific mention. (§59-6a203)
Kentucky	One-half of the surplus real estate of which the other spouse or anyone for the use of the other spouse was seized of an estate in fee simple at the time of death, and shall have an estate for his or her life in one-third of any real estate which the other spouse or anyone for the use of the other spouse, was seized of in fee simple during the coverture but not at the time of death.... The surviving spouse shall also have an absolute estate in one-half of the surplus personalty left by the decedent. (§392.020)	Not only probate estate. All property transferred with the intent to defeat the surviving spouse's claims to dower. (Harris v. Rock, 799 S.W.2d 10, 12 (Ky. 1990)	Dower is provided from the absolute one-half interest in the surplus personalty of a deceased spouse and is based on the "personalty remaining after the pay ment of the debts, funeral expenses, charges of administration, and widow's exemptions have been deducted from the gross personally possessed by the decedent at the time of his death." Harris v. Rock, 799 S.W. 2d 10,11 (Ky. 1990). See also Mattingly v. Gentry, 419 S.W. 2d 745.747 (Ky. 1967); Talbott's Ex'r v. Goetz, 151 S.W. 2d 369, 372 (Ky. 1941)	There is no specific limitation.	There is no specific limitation.
Louisiana	*Community property state—no quasi-community property*				
Maine	One-third of augmented estate. (18-A §2-201(a))	Augmented estate: probate estate minus funeral and administration expenses, homestead, family allowance, exemptions, and enforceable claims augmented by surviving spouse's property and nonprobate transfers by surviving spouse and decedent. (18-A §2-202)	Probate estate minus "funeral and administrative expenses, homestead allowance, family allowances and exemptions, and enforceable claims." (18-A §2-202)	There is no specific limitation.	There is no specific limitation.

Table 6.03, Part 1
Calculation of Elective Share

	What Percentage Right?	What Is the Right Based On?	Is the Share Based on the Estate Before Subtraction of All Debts, After Subtraction of Some Debts, After Subtraction of All Debts?	Is Foreign Real Property Taken Into Account?	Is Foreign Personal Property Taken Into Account?
Maryland	The surviving spouse may elect to take a one-third share of the net estate if there is surviving issue of the deceased, or a one-half share of the net estate if there is no surviving issue. (Est. & Trusts §3-203(b))	Net estate, that is, property passing by testate succession. (Est. & Trusts §3-203(a))	The property passing by testate succession is reduced by funeral and administration expenses, family allowance, and enforceable claims and debts against the estate. (Est. & Trusts §3-203(a)(1)-(3) There is no deduction for state or federal taxes. (Id.)	Only mentions net estate. (Est. & Trusts §3-203(a))	Only mentions net estate. (Est. & Trusts §3-203(a))
Massachusetts	If the testator left issue, spouse takes one-third of the personal and one-third of the real property; if the deceased left kindred but no issue, spouse takes $25,000 and one-half of the remaining personal and one-half of remaining real property; except that in either case if the spouse would take real and personal property in an amount exceeding $25,000 in value, the spouse receives, in addition to that amount, only the income during the spouse's life of the excess of the spouse's share of such estate above that amount. If the testator left no issue or kindred, the surviving spouse takes $25,000 and one-half of the remaining real and one-half of the remaining personal property absolutely. (191 §15)	Probate estate. (191 §15) In addition, the value of an inter vivos trust estate created after January 23, 1984 is taken into account if the deceased spouse has the power to direct the disposition of the trust estate for his benefit. (Sullivan v. Burkin, 460 N.E.2d 572, 574 (Mass. 1984); See also Bongaards v. Millen, 793 N.E. 2d 335 (Mass. 2003)) See generally Howard J. Alperin, (discussing the Sullivan Rule and making clear that it is limited to revocable trusts created during marriage, a "loophole" in the statute, and does not extend to a general power of appointment) Summary of Basic Law, 14D Mass. Prac. §19.11.	There appears to be no provision for subtraction.	There is no specific limitation.	There is no specific limitation.

Table 6.03, Part 1
Calculation of Elective Share

	What Is the Right Based On?	*What Percentage Right?*	*Is the Share Based on the Estate Before Subtraction of All Debts, After Subtraction of All Debts, or After Subtraction of Some Debts, After Subtraction of All Debts?*	*Is Foreign Real Property Taken Into Account?*	*Is Foreign Personal Property Taken Into Account?*
Michigan	See prior column.	Spouse has two choices if the decedent dies intestate—her intestate share under §700.2102 or her dower right under §558.1 et seq. (§700.2202(1)) If the decedent dies testate, the spouse has three choices—abiding by the terms of the will, if a "widow" that she will take dower rights, or the spouse can take one-half of the sum or share that would have passed to the spouse had the testator died intestate, reduced by one-half of the value of all property "derived by the spouse from the decedent" by any means other than testate or intestate succession upon the decedent's death. (§700.2202(2)) Such property "derived by the spouse from the decedent" includes all the following transfers: (a) a transfer made within two years of the decedent's death to the extent that the transfer is subject to federal gift or estate taxes; (b) a transfer made before the date of death subject to a power retained by the decedent which would make the property, or a portion of the property, subject to federal estate tax; and (c) a transfer effectuated by the death of the decedent through joint ownership, tenancy by the entireties, insurance beneficiary, or similar means. (§700.2202(1), (2), (7))	The reductions in the share are taken into account in arriving at the intestate estate, which serves as the base for calculating the elective share. See first column. The intestate share of the spouse is determined under §700.2102. Under §700.3101, the intestate estate is reduced by creditors' claims.	There is no specific limitation. The key is that the decedent was domiciled in Michigan. (§700.2202(1) and (2)) If the decedent was not domiciled in Michigan, then the law of the place of domicile determines the surviving spouse's rights. (§700.2202(6))	There is no specific limitation. See prior column.

Table 6.03, Part 1
Calculation of Elective Share

	What Percentage Right?	What Is the Right Based On?	Is the Share Based on the Estate Before Subtraction of All Debts, After Subtraction of Some Debts, After Subtraction of All Debts?	Is Foreign Real Property Taken Into Account?	Is Foreign Personal Property Taken Into Account?
Minnesota	Varies depending on length of marriage, maximum of one-half of augmented estate. (§524.2-202(a))	Augmented estate (§§524.2-202, 524.2-203) consists of the sum of: (a) the value of the decedent's probate estate, reduced by funeral and administrative expenses, homestead allowance, family allowances and exemptions, liens, mortgages and enforceable claims; (§524.2-204) (b) the value of the decedent's non-probate transfers to others, other than the homestead, as listed in §524.2-205(1) to (3); (c) the value of the decedent's nonprobate transfers to the surviving spouse, other than homestead and property passing to the spouse under the federal Social Security System, which is composed of all property that passed outside probate at the decedent's death; (§524.2-206) (d) property, other than the homestead, owned by the surviving spouse at the decedent's death; (§524.2-207(a)(1)): (e) property that would have been included in the surviving spouse's non-probate transfers to others had the spouse been the decedent. (§524.2-207(a)(2)) Property is excluded from the decedent's nonprobate transfers to others if: (a) the decedent received adequate and full consideration for the property; or (b) the surviving spouse consented in writing to the transfer. (§524.2-208)	See prior column.	Yes. (§524.2-203) There is no specific limitation.	Yes. (§524.2-203) There is no specific limitation.

Table 6.03, Part 1
Calculation of Elective Share

	What Percentage Right?	What Is the Right Based On?	Is the Share Based on the Estate Before Subtraction of All Debts, After Subtraction of Some Debts, After Subtraction of All Debts?	Is Foreign Real Property Taken Into Account?	Is Foreign Personal Property Taken Into Account?
Mississippi	Such part of the decedent's estate, real and personal, as the spouse would have been entitled if the decedent had died intestate, except that, even if the decedent left no child or descendant of such, the spouse is entitled to only one-half of the real and personal estate of the deceased. (§91-5-25)	The calculation for the elective share is based on the estate of the decedent had the decedent died intestate. (§91-5-25) Also, the separate estate of the surviving spouse, if any, must be calculated. The surviving spouse is only entitled to an elective share to the extent that the elective share exceeds the value of the surviving spouse's separate estate. (§91-5-29)	The estate of the decedent should be reduced for the debts of the decedent, administrative expenses, and funeral expenses. (Banks v. Junk, 264 So. 2d 387, 392 (Miss. 1972))	There is no specific limitation.	There is no specific limitation.
Missouri	"One-half of the estate, subject to the payment of claims, if there are no lineal descendants of the testator; or, if there are lineal descendants of the testator, the surviving spouse shall receive one-third of the estate subject to the payment of claims." This is in addition to exempt property and allowances under §474.260. (§474.160(1)(1))	The estate consists of all the money and property owned by the decedent at death, reduced by funeral and administration expenses, exempt property, family allowance and enforceable claims, and increased by the aggregate value of all money and property derived by the surviving spouse from the decedent by any means other than testate or intestate succession, exempt property or family allowance without full consideration. (§474.163(1)) See §474.163(2)(1)–(6) for examples of property derived by the surviving spouse from the decedent. (§474.163)	See prior column.	Yes, to the extent of the surviving spouse's interest in community property in any other state. (§474.163(2)(6))	Yes, to the extent of the surviving spouse's interest in community property in any other state. (§474.163(2)(6))

Table 6.03, Part 1
Calculation of Elective Share

	What Percentage Right?	What Is the Right Based On?	Is the Share Based on the Estate Before Subtraction of All Debts, After Subtraction of Some Debts, After Subtraction of All Debts?	Is Foreign Real Property Taken Into Account?	Is Foreign Personal Property Taken Into Account?
Montana	Varies depending on length of marriage; maximum of one-half of augmented estate. (§72-2-221(1))	"Augmented estate consists of the sum of: (a) the value of the decedent's probate estate, reduced by funeral and administrative expenses, homestead allowance, family allowances and exemptions, and enforceable claims; (b) the value of the decedent's nonprobate transfers to others, which are composed of all property, whether real or personal, wherever situated, not included in the decedent's estate," of the types listed in §72-2-222(2)(b)(i) to (iii); "(c) the value of the decedent's nonprobate transfers to the surviving spouse, which are composed of all property that passed outside probate at the decedent's death," including that property listed in §72-2-222(2)(c)(i) to (iv); (d) "except to the extent included in the augmented estate" under (a) or (c), the value of property transferred to the spouse by reason of the decedent's death; and owned by the surviving spouse at the decedent's death, including (e) property that would have been included in the surviving spouse's nonprobate transfers to others had the spouse been included in the decedent. (§72-2-222(2)(a)-(d)) Property is excluded from the decedent's nonprobate transfers to others if: (a) the decedent received adequate and full consideration for the property; (b) the surviving spouse consented in writing to the transfer; or (c) the property is life insurance, accident insurance, pension, profit sharing, retirement	See prior column.	Yes. (§72-2-222(1)(a)(vii))	Yes. (§72-2-222(1)(a)(vii))

Table 6.03, Part 1
Calculation of Elective Share

What Percentage Right?	What Is the Right Based On?	Is the Share Based on the Estate Before Subtraction of All Debts, After Subtraction of Some Debts, After Subtraction of All Debts?	Is Foreign Real Property Taken Into Account?	Is Foreign Personal Property Taken Into Account?
	or other benefit plans payable to persons other than the surviving spouse or the decedent's estate. (§72-2-222(3))			

Table 6.03, Part 1
Calculation of Elective Share

	What Percentage Right?	What Is the Right Based On?	Is the Share Based on the Estate Before Subtraction of All Debts, After Subtraction of Some Debts, After Subtraction of All Debts?	Is Foreign Real Property Taken Into Account?	Is Foreign Personal Property Taken Into Account?
Nebraska	Spouse has the right of election to take an elective share in any fraction not in excess of one-half of the augmented estate. (§ 30-2313(a))	Augmented estate is the estate, (§§ 30-2313, 30-2314) first, reduced by the aggregate amount of funeral and administrative expenses, homestead allowance, family allowances and exemptions, and enforceable claims and second, increased by the... amount of the following items: (1) the value of property transferred by the decedent at any time during marriage to the surviving spouse to or for the benefit of any person other than a bona fide purchaser or the surviving spouse (see § 30-2314(a)(1)(i)–(iv) for examples of such transfers); and "(2) the value of property owned by the surviving spouse at the death of the decedent and the value of property transferred by the surviving spouse at any time during marriage to the decedent to or for the benefit of any person other than the decedent, but exclusive of all income earned thereby before the death of the decedent." (§30-2314(a)) The augmented estate does not include the following, otherwise includable, items: (a) accident or life insurance proceeds, joint annuity or pension, any of which are payable to any person other than the surviving spouse; (b) property transferred by the decedent to any person other than the surviving spouse, where the surviving spouse consents to the transfer; and (c) property transferred by the decedent by any means other than intestate succession or testamentary disposition if an elective share	See prior column.	There is no specific limitation.	There is no specific limitation.

Table 6.03, Part 1
Calculation of Elective Share

	What Percentage Right?	What Is the Right Based On?	Is the Share Based on the Estate Before Subtraction of All Debts, After Subtraction of Some Debts, After Subtraction of All Debts?	Is Foreign Real Property Taken Into Account?	Is Foreign Personal Property Taken Into Account?
Nevada			*Community property state—no quasi-community property*		
		petition is not filed within nine months of the death of the decedent. (§ 30-2314(c))			
New Hampshire	Three alternative percentages under § 560:10, as follows: if any children of decedent survive, or any issue of deceased children survive, one-third of personalty and one-third of real estate. If there are no children of deceased and no issue of any deceased children, but the mother, father, brother, or sister of decedent survive, $10,000 of personalty, $10,000 of realty, and one-half of the remainder above $10,000 in each category. If none of the above relations survive, $10,000 of value, plus $2,000 for each full year from date of marriage to date of death, and one-half of the remainder above the said sum, in personalty, and the same in real estate. (§ 560:10)	Probate estate. (§ 560:10)	The probate estate, after subtracting payment of debts and administrative expenses. (§ 560:10) Decedent's inter vivos transfers are not taken into account, if made in good faith and not for the purpose of defeating the widow's statutory rights. (Hanke v. Hanke, 459 A.2d 246, 248 (N.H. 1983))	There is no specific limitation.	There is no specific limitation.

6050

Table 6.03, Part 1
Calculation of Elective Share

	What Percentage Right?	What Is the Right Based On?	Is the Share Based on the Estate Before Subtraction of All Debts, After Subtraction of Some Debts, After Subtraction of All Debts?	Is Foreign Real Property Taken Into Account?	Is Foreign Personal Property Taken Into Account?
New Jersey	"[O]ne-third of the augmented estate." (§ 3B:8-1)	Based on the augmented estate. (§ 3B:8-3) Augmented estate includes: (a) decedent's net probate estate; (b) decedent's nonprobate transfers to others made after May 28, 1980 (i.e., joint tenancy, irrevocable transfers in which decedent retained possession or enjoyment, transfers in which decedent retained right to income, revocable transfers, and transfers within two years of death if amount to any one donee exceeds $3,000.00 in either of the years) (§ 3B:8-3); (c) decedent's nonprobate transfers to surviving spouse or domestic partner (§ 3B:8-6(a)); and (d) surviving spouse's nonprobate transfer to others (§ 3B:8-6(b)). Augmented estate does not include: (a) transfers of property under § 3B:8-3 if made with the written consent or joinder of surviving spouse or domestic partner (§ 3B:8-5); and (b) "life insurance, accident insurance, joint annuity or pension payable to a person other than the surviving spouse or domestic partner" (§ 3B:8-5).	The "estate" minus funeral and administrative expenses and enforceable claims. (§ 3B:8-3)	There is no specific limitation.	There is no specific limitation.
New Mexico	*Community property state with quasi-community property.*				

[Quasi-community property is defined in § 40-3-8(C). It is treated as community property for purposes of division of property incident to a dissolution of marriage or a legal separation if both parties are New Mexico domiciliaries at the time of the dissolution or legal separation. (§ 40-3-8(D)) It is not mentioned in any provision dealing with distribution of an estate.]

Table 6.03, Part 1

Calculation of Elective Share

	What Percentage Right?	What Is the Right Based On?	Is the Share Based on the Estate Before Subtraction of All Debts, After Subtraction of All Debts, or After Subtraction of Some Debts, After Subtraction of All Debts?	Is Foreign Real Property Taken Into Account?	Is Foreign Personal Property Taken Into Account?
New York[4]	Capital value of net estate up to $50,000 or one-third of net estate, whichever is greater. (Est. Powers & Trusts §5-1.1–A(a)(2))	Net probate estate includes: (a) decedent's net probate estate (Est. Powers & Trusts §5-1.1–A(a)); (b) decedent's nonprobate transfers to other (i.e., gifts causa mortis) (Est. Powers & Trusts §5-1.1–A(b)(1)(A)); joint tenancy (Est. Powers & Trusts §5-1.1–A(b)(1)(E)); transfers to trusts where decedent retained right to income, right to revoke, or right to invade principle (Est. Powers & Trusts §5-1.1–A(b)(1)(F)); transfers of property over which decedent had a presently exercisable general power of appointment or if the power was released in the last year of his life or if he exercised the power in favor of someone other than himself or his estate (Est. Powers & Trusts §5-1.1–A(b)(1)(H)); property given away in last year of life (Est. Powers & Trusts §5-1.1A(b)(1)(B)); money deposited, along with dividends and interest thereon, in the name of the decedent in trust for another person in a bank or savings and loan association and remaining on deposit at the date of decedent's death. (Est. Powers & Trusts §5-1.1–A(b)(1)(C)); money deposited, along with dividends and interest thereon, in the name of the decedent and another person and payable on death to the survivor and remaining on deposit in a bank or savings and loan association at the date of decedent's death (Est. Powers & Trusts §5-1.1–A(b)(1)(D)); any money, securities or other property payable under various plans/accounts, such as savings, retirement, pension, deferred	Net probate estate less debts, administrative expenses and reasonable funeral expenses. (Est. Powers & Trusts §5-1.1–A(a)(2))	Yes. (Est. Powers & Trusts §5-1.1–A(c)(7)	Yes. (Est. Powers & Trusts §5-1.1–A(c)(7)

Table 6.03, Part 1
Calculation of Elective Share

	What Percentage Right?	What Is the Right Based On?	Is the Share Based on the Estate Before Subtraction of All Debts, After Subtraction of Some Debts, After Subtraction of All Debts?	Is Foreign Real Property Taken Into Account?	Is Foreign Personal Property Taken Into Account?
		compensation, death benefit stock bonus or profit sharing plan, subject to certain limitations and exceptions (Est. Powers & Trusts §5-1.1A(b)(1)(G)).			
North Carolina	"[T]he applicable share of the Total Net Assets...less the value of Net Property Passing to Surviving Spouse." (§30-3.1(a)) The particular share of the total net assets varies depending on length of the marriage, with a maximum of 50% if married for 15 years or more. (§30-3.1(a)(1)-(4))	Total net assets, less the value of net property passing to the surviving spouse. "Total net assets" is the total assets (defined by §30-3.2(3f)) reduced by year's allowances to persons other than the surviving spouse and claims. (§30-3.2(4)) Net property passing to the surviving spouse is the property passing to the surviving spouse (defined by §30.3.2(3c)) less death taxes of property passing to surviving spouse and claims payable out of, charged against or property allocated to property passing to surviving spouse. (§30.3.2(2c) Property passing to surviving spouse is defined in §30.3.2(3c).	See prior column.	There is no limitation as to situs in calculating Total Net Assets. (§30-3.1)	See prior column.

Table 6.03, Part 1
Calculation of Elective Share

	What Percentage Right?	What Is the Right Based On?	Is the Share Based on the Estate Before Subtraction of All Debts, After Subtraction of Some Debts, After Subtraction of All Debts?	Is Foreign Real Property Taken Into Account?	Is Foreign Personal Property Taken Into Account?
North Dakota	An amount equal to fifty percent of the augmented estate. (§ 30.1-05-01(1))	The augmented estate (§ 30.1-05-02) is a complex calculation, the particulars of which should be checked specifically. Augmented estate consists of: (a) net probate estate (§ 30.1-05-02(2)(a)); (b) nonprobate transfers to others (i.e., property over which decedent alone held presently exercisable general power of appointment (§ 30.1-05-02(2)(b)(1)(a)); property held in joint tenancy accounts with right of survivorship (§ 30.1-05-02(2)(b) (1)(b) & (c)); transfers in which decedent retained right to possession, enjoyment, or income (§ 30.1-05-02(2)(b)(2)(a)); transfers in which decedent could exercise control over the income or principal of transferred property (§ 30.1-05-02(2)(b)(b)); any transfer of property to a person other than surviving spouse in last two years of decedent's life to the extent the aggregate transfer to any one donee in either of the two years preceding death exceeded $10,000 (§ 30.1-05-02(2)(b)(3)(a) & (b); (c) nonprobate transfers to surviving spouse (§ 30.1-05-02(2)(c); (d) surviving spouse's property (§ 30.1-05-02(2)(d)(1)); and (e) surviving spouse's nonprobate transfers to others (§ 30.1-05-02 (2)(d)(2)).	The net probate estate is arrived at by subtracting from the probate estate funeral and administration expenses, homestead allowance, family allowances, exempt property, and enforceable claims. (§30.1-05-02(2)(a))	Yes. (§ 30.1-05-02(1)(a)(7))	Yes. (§ 30.1-05-02(1)(a)(7))

Table 6.03, Part 1
Calculation of Elective Share

	What Percentage Right?	What Is the Right Based On?	Is the Share Based on the Estate Before Subtraction of All Debts, After Subtraction of Some Debts, After Subtraction of All Debts?	Is Foreign Real Property Taken Into Account?	Is Foreign Personal Property Taken Into Account?
Ohio	What surviving spouse would have received under §2105.06 if decedent died intestate. (§2106.01(A)) This is not to exceed one-half of the net estate, unless two or more of decedent's children or their lineal descendants survive, in which case it is not to exceed one-third of the net estate. (§2106.01(C))	"Net estate." (§2106.01(C)) The net estate is what remains of the probate estate after satisfaction of indebtedness of the decedent and the obligations of the estate. (Weeks v. Vandeveer, 233 N.E. 2d 502,506 (Ohio 1968); Winkelfoos v. Mann, 475 N.E. 2d 509, 514 (Ct. App. 1984))	Net estate before payment of federal estate tax, state estate taxes or any other tax that is subject to apportionment. (§2106.01(C)) See also prior column.	There is no specific limitation.	There is no specific limitation.
Oklahoma	Undivided one-half interest in the property acquired by the joint industry during coverture. (84 §44(B)(1) & (2)	Property acquired by the joint industry of the spouses during coverture. (84 §44(B)(1) & (2)) Thus, property acquired before marriage and gifts or devises from others to one spouse would not be covered. (In re Estate of Hardaway, 872 P.2d 395, 397-398 (Okla. 1994)) The same is true of exchanges of separate property between spouses, the purchase by one spouse of separate property with separate funds, and compensation received by one spouse for personal injury. (Id.) Commingling of property that is separate results in a loss of separate property classification. (Catron v. First Nat'l Bank & Trust Co., 434 P.2d 263, 271 (Okla.1967))	Not liable for the payment of estate taxes. (In re Estate of Hardesty, 708 P.2d 596, 598 (Civ. App. 1985))	Yes, so long as it was acquired by joint industry during coverture. (84 §44(B)(1) & (2))	Yes, so long as it was acquired by joint industry during coverture. (84 §44(B)(1) & (2))

Table 6.03, Part 1
Calculation of Elective Share

	What Percentage Right?	What Is the Right Based On?	Is the Share Based on the Estate Before Subtraction of All Debts, After Subtraction of All Debts, or After Subtraction of Some Debts, After Subtraction of All Debts?	Is Foreign Real Property Taken Into Account?	Is Foreign Personal Property Taken Into Account?
Oregon	The percentage share is determined by the length of time the spouse and decedent were married to each other, maximum of 33% of augmented estate upon 15 years of marriage. (§ 114.605(2))	The right is based on the augmented estate. (§ 114.605(1)) The augmented estate consists of the probate estate (as defined in § 114.650), nonprobate estate (as defined in §§ 114.660, 114.665), and the surviving spouse's estate (as defined in § 114.675). (§ 114.630(1)) These assets are reduced by all enforceable claims against the property and all encumbrances on the property. (§ 114.630(2)) Resident's nonprobate estate consists of property with survivorship rights, power to designate a beneficiary, P.O.D., T.O.D., or property over which there was a power of revocation, solely or in conjunction with another, where the decedent could have acquired the property by the exercise of the power. (§ 114.665) The surviving spouse's estate includes all property on the date of decedent's death, including property disclaimed and 50% of the value of a trust in which the spouse had an interest in all of the income and there is no power to distribute principal during the spouse's lifetime to the spouse or anyone else. (§ 114.675(2)(c)) The value attributed to the spouse is 100% if the trustee or spouse has access to the principal solely for the spouse's health, education, support or maintenance. (§ 114.675(2)(b)) The augmented estate does not include irrevocably transferred property to which the surviving spouse consented or joined in the transfer, enhanced future earning capacity, community property, (§ 114.635)	The probate estate is reduced by payment of claims and expenses of administration. (§ 114.650)	Yes. (§ 114.630(1))	Yes. (§ 114.630(1))

Table 6.03, Part 1
Calculation of Elective Share

	What Percentage Right?	What Is the Right Based On?	Is the Share Based on the Estate Before Subtraction of All Debts, After Subtraction of Some Debts, After Subtraction of All Debts?	Is Foreign Real Property Taken Into Account?	Is Foreign Personal Property Taken Into Account?
Pennsylvania	One-third of the property described in the next column. (20 § 2203)	Property passing by will or intestacy; income or use for the remaining life of spouse of property conveyed by decedent during marriage, to the extent that decedent had use of property or an interest in or power to withdraw its income; property conveyed during life where decedent had at his or her death the power to revoke the conveyance or to consume, invade, or dispose of the principal for his or her own benefit; property conveyed during marriage by decedent to his or her ownself and other(s) with right of survivorship where decedent had power at death to unilaterally convey property absolutely or in fee; survivorship rights conveyed to a beneficiary of an annuity contract to the extent it was purchased by decedent during marriage and decedent was receiving annuity payments therefrom at the time of his death; property conveyed by the decedent during marriage and within one year of death, to the extent that the aggregate amount so conveyed to each donee exceeds $3,000, valued at the time of the conveyance. (20 § 2203(a)(1)–(6))	The calculation in the prior column is limited in that it does not include the following: any conveyance made with express consent or joinder of the spouse; life insurance proceeds; interests in any "broad-based nondiscriminatory" pension, profit-sharing, stock bonus, deferred compensation, disability, death benefit, or other employer-established plan for employees and their beneficiaries; property passing by decedent's exercise or nonexercise of a power given to him by someone else. (20 § 2203(b)(1)–(4)) No transferee of or holder of a lien against property subject to a spouse's election is liable to a surviving spouse if the transferee or lienholder has given a bona fide consideration, unless there is an order or decree of court providing otherwise. (20 § 2211(f))	There is no specific limitation.	There is no specific limitation.

| | | | or the present value of any life insurance policy payable on the decedent's death. (§ 114.665(5)) | | |

Table 6.03, Part 1
Calculation of Elective Share

	What Percentage Right?	What Is the Right Based On?	Is the Share Based on the Estate Before Subtraction of All Debts, After Subtraction of Some Debts, After Subtraction of All Debts?	Is Foreign Real Property Taken Into Account?	Is Foreign Personal Property Taken Into Account?
Rhode Island	Life estate in all real estate owned in fee simple by decedent at death. (§33-25-2(a))	Real estate. (§33-25-2(a))	Life estate is subject to any encumbrances existing at decedent's death. Liability of decedent to discharge encumbrances shall not be impaired. (§33-25-2(a)) Also, life estate takes precedence over any claims of decedent's creditors, except claims secured by a lien or any form of encumbrance on the real estate. (§33-25-3)	Possibly. There is provision for filing the waiver and claim in any other city or town than where the will is being probated. (§33-25-4) On the other hand, Rhode Island courts could not exercise authority over out-of-state realty.	No provision
South Carolina	One-third of the decedent's probate estate computed under §62-2-202. (§62-2-201(a))	The decedent's probate estate includes the decedent's property passing by will and by intestacy, reduced by funeral and administration expenses and by enforceable claims. (§62-2-202(a) A trust declared void as illusory may be included in the decedent's estate for the purpose of calculating a surviving spouse's elective share. The trust is illusory if the settlor retained substantial control as in the case of a revocable trust. (Dreher v. Dreher, 634 S.E.2d 646, 649-50 (S.C. 2006)) But see Smith v. McCall, 477 S.E.2d 475, 475-6 (S.C. Ct. App. 1996), which rejected attempt to extend *Seifert* to a joint tenancy account since the joint accounts are valid and are authorized by statute. (§§6-101-113)	The calculation is based on the decedent's probate estate after the subtraction of funeral and administration expenses and of enforceable claims. (§62-2-202)	No provision.	No provision.

Table 6.03, Part 1
Calculation of Elective Share

	What Percentage Right?	What Is the Right Based On?	Is the Share Based on the Estate Before Subtraction of All Debts, After Subtraction of Some Debts, After Subtraction of All Debts?	Is Foreign Real Property Taken Into Account?	Is Foreign Personal Property Taken Into Account?
South Dakota	Varies depending on length of marriage, maximum of one-half of augmented estate. (§ 29A-2-202(a)) If the total is less than $50,000, the surviving spouse is entitled to take a supplemental elective share amount equal to $50,000 minus the sum of certain other amounts. (§ 29A-2-202 (b))	The augmented estate (§ 29A-2-203) is a complex calculation, the particulars of which should be checked specifically. In general terms, the augmented estate consists of: (1) the decedent's net probate estate (decedent's probate estate reduced by funeral and administration expenses, by homestead, family, and exempt property allowances, and by enforceable claims) (§ 29A-2-204); (2) the decedent's nonprobate transfers to others (property over which the decedent alone held a power of appointment; property held by joint tenancy with right of survivorship; property or accounts held in POD, TOD, or co-ownership with right of survivorship; proceeds of insurance; property over which decedent retained right to possession, enjoyment, or income, and others) (§ 29A-2-205); (3) the decedent's nonprobate transfers to the surviving spouse (property held by joint tenancy with right of survivorship; property or accounts held in co-ownership registration with right of survivorship); property passing to the spouse that would have been included in the augmented estate if it has passed to a person other than the spouse) (§ 29A-2-206); and (4) the surviving spouse's property and nonprobate transfers to others (property held in joint tenancy with right of survivorship; property or accounts held in co-ownership registration with right of survivorship; "[p]roperty that passed to surviving spouse by	See prior column.	Yes. (§ 29A-2-203)	Yes. (§ 29A-2-203)

Table 6.03, Part 1
Calculation of Elective Share

	What Percentage Right?	What Is the Right Based On?	Is the Share Based on the Estate Before Subtraction of All Debts, After Subtraction of Some Debts, After Subtraction of All Debts?	Is Foreign Real Property Taken Into Account?	Is Foreign Personal Property Taken Into Account?
		reason of decedent's death, but not including... homestead allowance, family allowance, exempt property, or Social Security payments; property that would have been included in surviving spouse's nonprobate transfers to others had he or she been the decedent)." (§29A2-207)			
Tennessee	Varies depending on length of marriage, maximum of 40% of net estate. (§31-4-101(a)) The elective share is available in the case of intestate decedents as well. (Id.)	The calculation of the elective share is based on the application of the appropriate percentage right to the decedent's "net estate." (§31-4-101(a)) The result is then reduced by the value of all assets includable in the decedent's gross estate that were transferred, or deemed transferred, to, or for the benefit of, the surviving spouse. The term "gross estate" has the meaning it has for inheritance tax purposes pursuant to §67-8-301 et seq. (Id.) Those sections include items in addition to the probate estate, but are not coextensive with the federal gross estate concept.	The "net estate," which includes the decedent's real and personal property subject to disposition under the provisions of the decedent's will or the laws of intestate succession, reduced by [[1]] secured debts to the extent that secured creditors are entitled to realize on the applicable collateral, (§31-4-101(a)) [(2)] funeral and administration expenses, and [(3)] awards of exempt property, homestead allowance and year's support allowance. (§31-4-101(b))	There is no specific limitation.	There is no specific limitation.
Texas	Community property state; no quasi-community property				

Table 6.03, Part 1
Calculation of Elective Share

	What Percentage Right?	What Is the Right Based On?	Is the Share Based on the Estate Before Subtraction of All Debts, After Subtraction of Some Debts, After Subtraction of All Debts?	Is Foreign Real Property Taken Into Account?	Is Foreign Personal Property Taken Into Account?
Utah	[O]ne-third of the augmented estate. (§75-2-202(1)) If the total is less than $75,000, the surviving spouse is entitled to take a supplemental elective share amount equal to $75,000 minus the sum of certain other amounts. (§75-2-202(2))	The augmented estate (§75-2-203) is a complex calculation, the particulars of which should be checked specifically. In general terms, the augmented estate consists of: (1) the net probate estate (the estate reduced by funeral and administrative expenses, homestead allowance, family allowances and exempt property (§75-2-204) and enforceable claims); (2) the decedent's nonprobate transfers to others (property in which decedent alone held, immediately before death, a general power of appointment, or joint tenancy with right of survivorship; P.O.D. accounts, T.O.D. accounts or co-ownership registration; life insurance owned by the decedent or over which he had a general power of appointment, if payable at his death to a person other than the spouse; (3) property transferred by the decedent during marriage, specifically where an income interest was retained, or a transfer in which decedent created a general power of appointment; property that passed during marriage and during the two-year period prior to the decedent's death if an interest terminated in property that otherwise would have been included in the augmented estate, with special provisions for life insurance; and any other transfers made to or for the benefit of a person other than the surviving spouse, not otherwise included in the augmented estate to the extent of aggregate transfers to a donee in excess of $10,000 in either of the	Yes, in that the net probate estate, a component of the augmented estate, is the probate estate reduced by funeral and administration expenses, homestead allowance, family allowances, exempt property and enforceable claims. (§75-2-204)	Yes. (§75-2-203)	Yes. (§75-2-203)

Table 6.03, Part 1
Calculation of Elective Share

	What Percentage Right?	What Is the Right Based On?	Is the Share Based on the Estate Before Subtraction of All Debts, After Subtraction of Some Debts, After Subtraction of All Debts?	Is Foreign Real Property Taken Into Account?	Is Foreign Personal Property Taken Into Account?
Vermont	One half of the balance of the estate after the payment of claims and expenses. (14 §319) The reference to the "estate" limits the elective share to the probate estate. (See *Stephanie Willbanks, Parting is Such Sweet Sorrow, But Does it Have to Be So Complicated? Transmission of Property at Death in Vermont, 29 Vt. L. Rev. 895, 922 (2005)*)	two years (§75-2-205); (4) various transfers to surviving spouse (§75-2-206); (5) the surviving spouse's property and the surviving spouse's nonprobate transfers to others. (§75-2-207) See Table 6.03, Part 2. Note that inter vivos transfers with intent to defeat wife's dower claim, with control by husband during life, was deemed fraudulent and set aside. Same theory might apply under the elective share. (Thayer v. Thayer, 14 Vt. 107, 118-19 (Vt. 1842)) Vermont courts have not addressed the inclusion of nonprobate assets in the calculation of the elective share under various judicial theories. See also *Willbanks, Parting is Such Sweet Sorrow, But Does It Have to Be So Complicated? Transmission of Property at Death in Vermont, 29 Vt. L. Rev. 875, 922 (2005)*.	The decedent's estate after the payment of claims and expenses. (14 §319)	There is no specific limitation.	There is no specific limitation.

Table 6.03, Part 1
Calculation of Elective Share

	What Percentage Right?	What Is the Right Based On?	Is the Share Based on the Estate Before Subtraction of All Debts, After Subtraction of Some Debts, After Subtraction of All Debts?	Is Foreign Real Property Taken Into Account?	Is Foreign Personal Property Taken Into Account?
Virginia	One-third of the decedent's augmented estate, but if no children of the decedent or their descendants survive, the percentage right is one-half of the decedent's augmented estate. (§ 64.2-304)	The augmented estate (§ 64.2-305) is a complex calculation which should be checked specifically. In general terms, the augmented estate consists of: (1) the decedent's net probate estate (estate passing by testate or intestate succession, real and personal, after payment of elected allowance and exemptions, expenses and debts); (2) the value of property, other than tangible personal property received by gift and the proceeds thereof, owned or acquired by surviving spouse at decedent's death, to the extent that the property is derived from decedent by any means other than testate or intestate succession without full consideration in money or money's worth (§ 64.2-305(A)(1)); (3) the decedent's nonprobate transfers to the surviving spouse transferred by the surviving spouse during the marriage to a person other than the decedent which would have been includable in the surviving spouse's augmented estate had he or she predeceased the decedent (§ 64.2-305(A)(2)); (4) the decedent's transfers to any person during the marriage for which the decedent did not receive adequate and full consideration (§ 64.2-305(A)(3)); (5) transfer in which the decedent retained rights over the whole property, the principal, or its income (Id.); (5) transfer within five years preceding death which, in aggregate, exceeds $10,000 to any one donee. (§ 64.2-305(A)(3)(d))	The net probate estate is reduced by allowances, exemptions, funeral expenses, charges of administration, other than federal or state transfer taxes, and debts. (§ 64.2-305(A))	There is no specific limitation.	There is no specific limitation.

6063

Table 6.03, Part 1
Calculation of Elective Share

	What Percentage Right?	What Is the Right Based On?	Is the Share Based on the Estate Before Subtraction of All Debts, After Subtraction of All Some Debts, After Subtraction of All Debts?	Is Foreign Real Property Taken Into Account?	Is Foreign Personal Property Taken Into Account?
Washington			*Community property state; no quasi-community property*		
West Virginia	Varies depending on length of marriage, maximum of one-half of augmented estate. (§42-3-1(a))	The augmented estate (§42-3-2(b)(1)-(4)) is a complex calculation, the particulars of which should be checked specifically. In general terms, the augmented estate consists of: (1) the decedent's net probate estate (probate estate reduced by funeral and administrative expenses, homestead exemption, exempt property, and enforceable claims); (2) the decedent's nonprobate transfers to others (property in which the decedent held a power of appointment, a right of survivorship, a right to income, possession, or enjoyment; property transferred to a donee within the two years before death that exceeds $10,000); (3) the decedent's nonprobate transfers to the surviving spouse (proceeds from insurance, death benefits, or retirement plan); and (4) the surviving spouse's property. (§42-3-2(b))	See prior column.	Yes. (§42-3-2(b)(2))	Yes. (§42-3-2(b)(2))
Wisconsin	*Community property state; the surviving spouse is allowed to elect an amount up to 50% of quasi-community property known as augmented deferred marital property.*				
Wyoming	One-half of probate estate if there is no surviving issue of decedent, or if surviving spouse is also a parent of any surviving issue of the decedent; or one-quarter of probate estate if surviving spouse is not the parent of any surviving issue of decedent. (§2-5-101(a)(i) and (ii))	Property subject to disposition under the will. (§2-5-101)	Probate estate reduced by funeral and administrative expenses, homestead allowance, family allowances and exemption, and enforceable claims. (§2-5-101(a))	Elective share applies to property subject to disposition under the will. (§2-5-101(a))	Elective share applies to property subject to disposition under the will. (§2-5-101(a))

[1] Community property state with quasi-community property.
[2] Georgia Year's Support—No elective share, however, the year's support is like the elective share because if the decedent makes a provision in lieu of year's support in the will, then the spouse may elect. (§53-3-3)
[3] Community property state with quasi-community property.
[4] These answers assume that the decedent died after September 1, 1992.

Table 6.03, Part 2
Calculation of Elective Share

	Is the Election Allowed If Benefits Are Taken Under the Will?	If the Elective Share Is Taken, Are Other Benefits, Like Family Allowance, Reduced, or Vice Versa?	Is the Elective Share Denied If a Surviving Spouse Was Not Living With the Decedent, Abandoned Him, Was Guilty of Adultery, One of the Spouses Had Filed for Divorce, and Similar Circumstances? If So, Which Ones?	Is a Nondomiciliary Spouse of a Domiciliary Decedent Entitled to an Elective Share If the Decedent Died Domiciled in the State?	Is a Spouse Entitled to an Elective Share If the Decedent Was Not a Domiciliary, e.g., Spouse Moves to State After Decedent's Death to Claim Share in Local Real Property?
Alabama	Yes. (§ 43-8-74 commentary) Under the old law, she could not. See, e.g., Dorsey v. Dorsey, 140 So. 540,543 (Ala. 1932); Adams v. Adams, 39 Ala. 274, 275 (Ala. 1864)	Vice versa. (§ § 43-8-70; 43-8-74). Gross estate is reduced by homestead, exempt property, and similar allowances before the elective share is determined. (Garrard v. Long, 514 So. 2d 933, 934 (Ala. 1987)) It is also first reduced by the claims of creditors of the estate. (Brakefield v. Hocutt, 779 So. 2d 1165, 1166–67 (Ala. 2000))	A surviving spouse does not include: (1) a person who obtains or consents to a final device or judgment of divorce or annulment of marriage which decree or judgment is not recognized as valid in this state unless they subsequently participate in a marriage ceremony or live together; (2) a person who, following a divorce or annulment obtained by the decedent, participates in a marriage ceremony with a third person; (3) a person who is a party to a valid proceeding concluded by an order purporting to terminate all marital property rights. (§ 43-8-252)	The domiciliary status of the decedent controls. (§ 43-8-70(a) & (c))	Governed by law of decedent's domicile at death. (§ 43-8-70(c))
Alaska	Yes, but will be used first to satisfy the elective share. (§ 13.12.209)	Vice versa. Homestead, family allowance, exempt property are paid before calculation of elective share. (§ 13.12.202(c))	A surviving spouse does not include: (1) a person who obtains or consents to a final device or judgment of divorce or annulment or marriage, which decree or judgment is not recognized as valid in this state, unless they subsequently participate in a marriage ceremony or live together; (2) a person who, following a divorce or annulment obtained by the decedent, participates in a marriage ceremony with a third person; (3) a person who is a party to a valid proceeding concluded by an order purporting to terminate all marital property rights. (§ 13.12.802(b))	Decedent's domicile controls. (§ 13.12.202(d))	Law of decedent's domicile controls. (§ 13.12.202(d))
Arizona			*Community property—no quasi-community property*		

Table 6.03, Part 2
Calculation of Elective Share

	Is the Election Allowed If Benefits Are Taken Under the Will?	If the Elective Share Is Taken, Are Other Benefits, Like Family Allowance, Reduced, or Vice Versa?	Is the Elective Share Denied If a Surviving Spouse Was Not Living With the Decedent, Abandoned Him, Was Guilty of Adultery, One of the Spouses Had Filed for Divorce, and Similar Circumstances? If So, Which Ones?	Is a Nondomiciliary Spouse of a Domiciliary Decedent Entitled to an Elective Share If the Decedent Died Domiciled in the State?	Is a Spouse Entitled to an Elective Share If the Decedent Was Not a Domiciliary, e.g., Spouse Moves to State After Decedent's Death to Claim Share in Local Real Property?
Arkansas	No, unless will expressly states that it is not in lieu of dower. (§§ 28-11-404, 28-11-405, 28-39-401; Gathright v. Gathright, 1 S.W.2d 809, 810 (Ark. 1928); Chambless v. Gentry, 11 S.W.2d 460 (Ark. 1928) (property given "in lieu of dower" means offer to widow to accept property under will or take dower))	The right to dower or curtesy is in addition to family allowances and homestead. (§ 28-39-401(b)(1))	Divorce only. (Grober v. Clements, 76 S.W. 555, 557 (1903))	Yes, as there is no specific provision restricting the right. (§§ 28-39-401(a), 28-11-301(a))	Yes. (§ 28-39-401) There is a specific provision to the effect that the surviving spouse "of an alien shall be entitled to dower in the estate of the deceased spouse in the same manner as if the alien had been a native-born citizen of the state." (§ 28-11-202) Presumably, the same benefit would be accorded a domiciliary of another state who is not an alien. (See, e.g. Apperson v. Bolton, 29 Ark. 418 (Ark. 1874) (with respect to land in Arkansas))
California	No elective share due to community (Prob. § 100) and quasi-community property (Prob. § 101).	There is no express provision; however, it would seem that the family allowance, which is payable during administration out of estate assets, should not affect quasi-community property which vests upon death. (Prob. §§ 101, 6540)	No provision.	With respect to quasi-community property, decedent's domicile controls. If a domiciliary of California, one-half of decedent's quasi-community property belongs to the surviving spouse. (Prob. § 101)	If California real property was not community property, surviving spouse has same elective share rights as under the law of decedent's domicile. (Prob. § 120)
Colorado	Yes, but the benefits will be used first to satisfy the elective share. (§ 15-11-209(1))	Vice Versa. "If the right of election is exercised by or on behalf of the surviving spouse, the exempt property and family allowance, if any, are not charged against but are in addition to the elective-share and supplemental elective-share amounts." (§ 15-11-202(3))	Only divorce, annulment, and proceedings that terminate marital property rights. A decree of separation that does not terminate the status of husband and wife is not a divorce for purposes of this section. (§ 15-11-802)	Yes. Surviving spouse of domiciliary decedent entitled to elective share. (§ 15-11-202(1))	Maybe. Governed by law of decedent's domicile at death. (§ 515-11-202(5))
Connecticut	No, unless contrary is expressly stated in will or clearly appears therein. (§ 45a-436(b))	Cannot take statutory share until period of support has expired. (§ 45a-436(d))	Abandonment and continued abandonment until death, without sufficient cause. (§ 45a-436(g))	The statute applies with respect to "the death of a spouse" and does not expressly require the decedent to have been a domiciliary of Connecticut. Moreover, there is no provision requiring the surviving spouse to be a domiciliary of the state. (§ 45a436(a))	The section provides that the surviving spouse is entitled to statutory share for any property passing under will. (§ 45a-436) If local real property passes under a foreign will, it is likely that such document will need to be proven in Connecticut and any rights of the spouse in such property will be governed by Connecticut elective share law. (§ 45a-287)

Table 6.03, Part 2
Calculation of Elective Share

	Is the Election Allowed If Benefits Are Taken Under the Will?	If the Elective Share Is Taken, Are Other Benefits, Like Family Allowance, Reduced, or Vice Versa?	Is the Elective Share Denied If a Surviving Spouse Was Not Living With the Decedent, Abandoned Him, Was Guilty of Adultery, One of the Spouses Had Filed for Divorce, and Similar Circumstances? If So, Which Ones?	Is a Nondomiciliary Spouse of a Domiciliary Decedent Entitled to an Elective Share If the Decedent Died Domiciled in the State?	Is a Spouse Entitled to an Elective Share If the Decedent Was Not a Domiciliary, e.g., Spouse Moves to State After Decedent's Death to Claim Share in Local Real Property?
Delaware	Yes. (12 §907(a))	Not reduced. Allowance is a claim against decedent's estate. (12 §2308(c)) But if allowance is taken, the estate is necessarily reduced, which in turn would reduce the elective share. The elective share is one-third of the elective estate. (12 §901)	"[A] complete property settlement entered into, after or in anticipation of separation or divorce is a waiver of all rights to the elective share by each spouse in the property of the other." (12 §905)	The domiciliary status of the decedent controls. If the decedent is a domiciliary, the surviving spouse is entitled to elective share of estate as per this state's law. (12 §901(a))	Governed by law of decedent's domicile. (12 §901(b))
District of Columbia	No. (§§19-112, 19-113)	Homestead, family allowance exempt property not reduced. (§§ 19-101.02 through 19-101.04)	No provision. Section 19-103, which provided for forfeiture due to desertion or adultery, was repealed.	No provision.	No provision for dower election. Decedent must be a D.C. resident for legal share election. (§ 19-301 et seq.)
Florida	No, but accomplished indirectly by satisfying spouse's share in part out of property that has passed to him. (§732.2075)	Not reduced. (§732.2105)	No provision.	The domiciliary status of the decedent controls. If the decedent is a domiciliary, the surviving spouse is entitled to elective share of estate as per this state's law. (§732.201)	See answer to prior question.
Georgia[1]	Yes, as long as the benefits taken under the will were not provided for the spouse in lieu of the year's support, in which case she would have to elect to take either under the will or to take the year's support. (§53-3-3)	No, because a family allowance in addition to the year's support does not exist.	The surviving spouse's right to the year's support is only barred by the marriage or death of the spouse prior to the filing of the petition for year's support. (§53-3-2(a))	Yes. (Farris v. Battle 7 S.E. 262, 264 (Ga. 1887))	No provision.

Table 6.03, Part 2
Calculation of Elective Share

	Is the Election Allowed If Benefits Are Taken Under the Will?	If the Elective Share Is Taken, Are Other Benefits, Like Family Allowance, Reduced, or Vice Versa?	Is the Elective Share Denied If a Surviving Spouse Was Not Living With the Decedent, Abandoned Him, Was Guilty of Adultery, One of the Spouses Had Filed for Divorce, and Similar Circumstances? If So, Which Ones?	Is a Nondomiciliary Spouse of a Domiciliary Decedent Entitled to an Elective Share If the Decedent Died Domiciled in the State?	Is a Spouse Entitled to an Elective Share If the Decedent Was Not a Domiciliary, e.g., Spouse Moves to State After Decedent's Death to Claim Share in Local Real Property?
Hawaii	No, but accomplished indirectly by satisfying spouse's share in part out of property that has passed to her. (§§ 560:2-209(a)(1), 560:2-202))	No, the homestead allowance, exempt property, and family allowance are not charged against but are in addition to the elective share and supplemental share amounts. (§ 560:2-202(c))	Divorce and annulment seem to deny the elective share to the surviving spouse; a decree of separation that does not terminate the status of husband and wife is not a divorce for purposes of this section (§ 560:2-802); the former spouse is not considered a surviving spouse. (§ 560:2-802); Magoon v. Magoon, 780 P.2d 80, 81 (Haw. 1989) (divorced person is not surviving spouse) The same is true for a person "who has terminated" a reciprocal beneficiary relationship with the decedent. That person is not deemed a surviving reciprocal beneficiary. (§ 560: 2-802)	The domiciliary status of the decedent controls. If the decedent is a domiciliary, the surviving spouse is entitled to elective share of estate as per this state's law. (§ 560:2-202(a))	Governed by the law of the decedent's domicile at death. (§ 560:2-202(d))
Idaho	Yes. (§ 15-2-206(a))	No. If the elective share is taken other benefits are not reduced (§ 15-2-206(b)); however, since these benefits are paid out of the quasi-community estate, the elective share will be reduced. (§ 15-2-203(b))	Only divorce or annulment or valid order terminating marital property rights. A decree of separation which does not terminate the status of husband and wife is not a divorce for purposes of this section. (§ 15-2-802 and Comment to Official Text)	Yes. The sole prerequisite is that the deceased spouse was domiciled in the state at death. (§§ 15-2-201, 15-2-202)	Yes. (§ 15-2-209)
Illinois	No. (755 ILCS § 5/2-8(a))	No specific provision or settled case law.	No specific provision or settled case law.	Yes. Governed by the law of the domicile of the deceased at the time of death. (Johnson v. LaGrange State Bank, 365 N.E. 2d 1056, 1059 (Ill. 1978))	No. Governed by the law of the domicile of the deceased at the time of death. (Johnson v. LaGrange State Bank, 365 N.E.2d 1056, 1059 (Ill. 1978)

Table 6.03, Part 2
Calculation of Elective Share

	Is the Election Allowed If Benefits Are Taken Under the Will?	If the Elective Share Is Taken, Are Other Benefits, Like Family Allowance, Reduced, or Vice Versa?	Is the Elective Share Denied If a Surviving Spouse Was Not Living With the Decedent, Abandoned Him, Was Guilty of Adultery, One of the Spouses Had Filed for Divorce, and Similar Circumstances? If So, Which Ones?	Is a Nondomiciliary Spouse of a Domiciliary Decedent Entitled to an Elective Share If the Decedent Died Domiciled in the State?	Is a Spouse Entitled to an Elective Share If the Decedent Was Not a Domiciliary, e.g., Spouse Moves to State After Decedent's Death to Claim Share in Local Real Property?
Indiana	No, the election is not allowed if benefits are taken under the will, unless the value of the property given the surviving spouse under the will is less than the amount the surviving spouse would receive by electing to take against the will, then the surviving spouse may elect to retain any or all specific bequests or devises in the will... and receive the balance due in cash or property. (§ 29-1-3-1(b))	No, the elective share will not reduce the "family allowance." The survivor's allowance ("family allowance") is not chargeable against the distributive share due a spouse when the spouse elects against a will. (Estate of Calcutt v. Calcutt, 576 N.E.2d 1288, 1293 (Ind. Ct. App. 1991); §§ 29-1-3-1, § 29-1-4-1)	"If a person shall abandon his or her "spouse without just cause," or if the husband or wife shall have left the other and shall be living at the time of his or her death in adultery, he or she shall take no part of the estate of the decedent husband or wife." (§§ 29-1-2-14, 29-1-2-15)	There is no specific provision limiting the elective share to the estate of a domiciliary decedent. Arguably, then, there would be an elective share claim regarding Indiana real property by a nondomiciliary decedent. (§ 29-1-3-1)	There is no specific provision distinguishing a nondomiciliary spouse.
Iowa	No. (§ 633.238(2))	The share of the surviving spouse in real estate is set off to include the homestead, or so much there of as will be equal to the share allotted to the spouse by § 633.238. (§ 633.239) The spouse is eligible for 12 months' support. The court considers the estate in making this determination. (§ 633.374)	No provision.	Yes. If decedent is a domiciliary, the surviving spouse is entitled. (§ 633.236)	No. If decedent is a domiciliary, the surviving spouse is entitled. (§ 633.236)
Kansas	Yes, but the benefits under the will are applied first to satisfy the elective share. (§ 59-6a209)	No, the homestead allowance and family allowance are not charged against but are in addition to the elective-share and supplemental share amounts. (§59-6a202(c))	No provision.	The domiciliary status of the decedent controls. If the decedent is a domiciliary, the surviving spouse is entitled to elective share of estate as per this state's law. (§ 59-6a202) (§ 59-6a202)	Uncertain. § 59-6a202(d) refers the issue to art. 8 of ch. 59 and § 59-806(a) makes clear that the dispositions of Kansas property of a nondomiciliary generally is subject to the same substantive provisions as would be a domiciliary. However, § 59-806(a)(2) states that the provision shall not be deemed to affect " (2) The rights of a surviving spouse electing to accept or take against the will of a nonresident [i.e., nondomiciliary] decedent, or the method of such election . . . ." Quaere whether this language is referring to the domiciliary state's elective share provision or Kansas' own elective share provision.

Table 6.03, Part 2
Calculation of Elective Share

	Is the Election Allowed If Benefits Are Taken Under the Will?	If the Elective Share Is Taken, Are Other Benefits, Like Family Allowance, Reduced, or Vice Versa?	Is the Elective Share Denied If a Surviving Spouse Was Not Living With the Decedent, Abandoned Him, Was Guilty of Adultery, One of the Spouses Had Filed for Divorce, and Similar Circumstances? If So, Which Ones?	Is a Nondomiciliary Spouse of a Domiciliary Decedent Entitled to an Elective Share If the Decedent Died Domiciled in the State?	Is a Spouse Entitled to an Elective Share If the Decedent Was Not a Domiciliary, e.g., the Spouse Moves to State After Decedent's Death to Claim Share in Local Real Property?
Kentucky	No. (Hannah v. Hannah, 824 S.W.2d 866, 868 (Ky. 1992); §392.080) However, if the intention of the testator, plainly expressed or clearly inferred, is to provide benefits in addition to statutory rights, then spouse can take both. (§392.080(2))	Must elect between dower (one-third of real estate) and homestead. (In re Gibson, 33 F. Supp. 838, 841 (E.D. Ky. 1940); § 427.070)	"Absolute divorce bars all claims... (§392.090(1)) However, the spouse is entitled to her share when her separation from the decedent is intended as permanent. (Meyers' Adm'r v. Meyers, 50 S.W.2d 81, 82 (1932)) If either spouse voluntarily leaves the other and lives in adultery, the offending party forfeits all right and interest in and to the property and estate of the other, unless they afterward become reconciled and live together as husband and wife." (§392.090)	Only mentions "survivor," without any requirement as to domicile or residence. (§ 392.020)	Only mentions decedent. (§392.020)
Louisiana			*Community property state—no quasi-community property*		
Maine	No. (U.S. Trust Co. of N.Y. v. Douglass, 56 A.2d 633, 636 (Me. 1948)	Homestead, family allowance and exempt property not reduced. (18-A §2-206)	No provision.	Only mentions "surviving spouse," without any requirement as to domicile or residence. (18-A §2-201)	Governed by the law of decedent's domicile at death. (18A §2-201(b))
Maryland	If spouse takes an elective share, all property that would have passed to the spouse under the decedent's will shall be treated as if the surviving spouse died before the execution of the will. The surviving spouse may not receive property under the will. (Est. & Trusts §3-208(a))	No provision.	No provision.	Only mentions "surviving spouse," without any requirement as to domicile or residence. (Est. & Trusts §3-203)	Yes, but only with respect to Maryland real property. (Bish v. Bish, 181 Md. 621, 628 (Md. 1943))

6070

Table 6.03, Part 2
Calculation of Elective Share

	Is the Election Allowed If Benefits Are Taken Under the Will?	If the Elective Share Is Taken, Are Other Benefits, Like Family Allowance, Reduced, or Vice Versa?	Is the Elective Share Denied If a Surviving Spouse Was Not Living With the Decedent, Abandoned Him, Was Guilty of Adultery, One of the Spouses Had Filed for Divorce, and Similar Circumstances? If So, Which Ones?	Is a Nondomiciliary Spouse of a Domiciliary Decedent Entitled to an Elective Share If the Decedent Died Domiciled in the State?	Is a Spouse Entitled to an Elective Share If the Decedent Was Not a Domiciliary, e.g., Spouse Moves to State After Decedent's Death to Claim Share in Local Real Property?
Massachusetts	No. To elect against the will, the surviving spouse must waive all provisions of the testator's will. The waiver of the will must be absolute. (191 §15; Kramer v. Crosby, 165 N.E. 686, 687 (Mass. 1929))	No provision.	A surviving spouse does not include a person who is divorced from decedent or had their marriage annulled or obtained an invalid judgment/decree for that purpose, unless there had been a subsequent remarriage. It also does not include someone who participates in a subsequent marriage with a third person or who is party to a proceeding to terminate all marital property rights. (190B §2-802)	Only mentions surviving husband or wife, without any requirement as to domicile or residence. (191 §15)	Only mentions deceased person. (191 §15)
Michigan	Spouse must choose to take under the will or by elective share, unless the contrary plainly appears by the will to be intended by the testator. (§700.2202(3))	The surviving spouse's homestead allowance, exempt property and family allowance are not charged against, but are in addition to, the elective share. (§§700.2402-700.2404)	Surviving spouse does not include a person who: is divorced from decedent or had prior marriage annulled; consented to a final decree/judgment of divorce/annulment; was party to a proceeding to terminate the marital property rights; and living in a bigamous relationship with another person at the time of decedent's death, or, within one year of death was "willfully absent," deserted," or "willfully neglected" or refused to provide legally required support. (§700.2801). A surviving spouse may regain rights through a subsequent remarriage to decedent. (Id.)	Only mentions "surviving spouse," without any requirement as to domicile or residence. (§700.2202(1) & (2))	Governed by the law of decedent's domicile at death. (§700.2202(6))
Minnesota	Spouse may make election and also take under the provisions of the decedent's will or intestate succession; but property which is part of the augmented estate which passes to the spouse by testate or intestate succession is applied first to satisfy the elective share. (§524.2-209(a)(1))	The surviving spouse's homestead allowance, exempt property and family allowance are not charged against, but are in addition to, the elective share. But, the augmented estate is reduced by homestead allowance, exempt property and family allowance. (§§524.2-202(c), 524.2-204)	A person whose marriage has been dissolved or annulled is not a surviving spouse, unless he or she had subsequently remarried the decedent. (§524.2-802)	Only mentions "surviving spouse," without any requirement as to domicile or residence. (§524.2-202(a))	Governed by the law of the decedent's domicile at death. (§524.2-202(d))

Table 6.03, Part 2
Calculation of Elective Share

	Is the Election Allowed If Benefits Are Taken Under the Will?	If the Elective Share Is Taken, Are Other Benefits, Like Family Allowance, Reduced, or Vice Versa?	Is the Elective Share Denied If a Surviving Spouse Was Not Living With the Decedent, Abandoned Him, Was Guilty of Adultery, One of the Spouses Had Filed for Divorce, and Similar Circumstances? If So, Which Ones?	Is a Nondomiciliary Spouse of a Domiciliary Decedent Entitled to an Elective Share If the Decedent Died Domiciled in the State?	Is a Spouse Entitled to an Elective Share If the Decedent Was Not a Domiciliary, e.g., Spouse Moves to State After Decedent's Death to Claim Share in Local Real Property?
Mississippi	No. (§91-5-25)	Homestead right is not to be considered part of the surviving spouse's separate estate for purposes of determining and reducing the value of the spouse's elective share. (§91-5-25; Matter of Estate of Holloway, 631 So. 2d 127, 137 (Miss. 1993))	Where wife living separate and apart from her husband through husband's fault (evidence sustained finding that wife was justified in living separate and apart from husband at the time of his death), at his death she was entitled to renounce his will. (Stringer v. Arrington, 32 So. 2d 879, 880 (Miss. 1947))	Presumably. Since a surviving spouse of a nondomiciliary decedent spouse can claim a share of property in Mississippi, the same should be true of the surviving spouse of a domiciliary decedent spouse. (Bolton v. Barnett, 95 So. 721 (Miss. 1923))	Husband may renounce wife's will and take child's share, although domicile of the deceased was a foreign state. The right to take the property was governed by the law of the state and not by the law of the decedent's domicile. (§91-5-25; Bolton v. Barnett, 95 So. 721, 726 (Miss. 1923))
Missouri	No. If surviving spouse elects against the will, the spouse shall take nothing under the will. (§474.160(1) & (2))	An election is received in addition to exempt property and family allowance. However, any homestead allowance made to the surviving spouse shall be offset against the elective share. (§474.160(1) & (2))	Yes, if adultery or abandonment under certain circumstances. (§474.140)	Only mentions married testator. (§474.160) However, case law indicates that if decedent was a domiciliary, the surviving spouse is entitled to the elective share. (Colvin v. Hutchison, 92 S.W.2d 667 (Mo. 1936))	Only mentions married testator. (§474.160) However, case law indicates that the elective share is available with regard to local real estate, at least if there has also not been an acceptance of benefits under the will at the decedent's domicile. (Colvin v. Hutchison, 92 S.W.2d 667 (Mo. 1936))
Montana	Spouse's election does not affect the surviving spouse's share under the provisions of the decedent's will or intestate succession. But, property which is part of the augmented estate that passes to the spouse by testate or intestate succession is applied first to satisfy the elective share. (§§72-2-222(2)(a), 72-2-227(1)(a))	The surviving spouse's homestead allowance, exempt property and family allowance are not charged against, but are in addition to, the elective share. But, the augmented estate is reduced by homestead allowance, exempt property and family allowance. (§§72-2-221(3), 72-2-222(2)(a), 72-2-226)	A surviving spouse does not include a person who is divorced from decedent or had their marriage annulled or obtained an invalid judgment/decree for that purpose, unless there had been a subsequent remarriage. It also does not include someone who participates in a subsequent marriage with a third person or who is party to a proceeding to terminate the marital property rights. (§72-2-812)	The domiciliary status of the decedent controls. If the decedent is a domiciliary, the surviving spouse is entitled to elective share of estate as per this state's law. (§72-2-221)	Governed by the law of the decedent's domicile at death. (§72-2-221(4))

Table 6.03, Part 2
Calculation of Elective Share

	Is the Election Allowed If Benefits Are Taken Under the Will?	If the Elective Share Is Taken, Are Other Benefits, Like Family Allowance, Reduced, or Vice Versa?	Is the Elective Share Denied If a Surviving Spouse Was Not Living With the Decedent, Abandoned Him, Was Guilty of Adultery, One of the Spouses Had Filed for Divorce, and Similar Circumstances? If So, Which Ones?	Is a Nondomiciliary Spouse of a Domiciliary Decedent Entitled to an Elective Share If the Decedent Died Domiciled in the State?	Is a Spouse Entitled to an Elective Share If the Decedent Was Not a Domiciliary, e.g., Spouse Moves to State After Decedent's Death to Claim Share in Local Real Property?
Nebraska	Spouse's election does not affect the share of the surviving spouse under the provisions of the decedent's will or intestate succession. But, property which is part of the augmented estate, which passes to the spouse by testate or intestate succession, is applied first to satisfy the elective share and to reduce the amount due from other recipients of portions of the augmented estate. (§§ 30-2318(a), 30-2319(a))	Spouse is entitled to homestead allowance, exempt property and family allowance whether or not an elective share is taken. But, the augmented estate is reduced by homestead allowance, exempt property and family allowance and enforceable claims. (§§ 30-2318(b), 30-2314(a))	An individual who is divorced from the decedent or whose marriage to the decedent has been dissolved or annulled by a decree that has become final is not a surviving spouse unless, by virtue of a subsequent marriage, he is married to the decedent at the time of death. Note that a decree of separation which does not terminate the status of husband and wife does not bar the surviving spouse from claiming the elective share. (§ 30-2353(a)); See 30-2353(b) for more specifications as to who is a "surviving spouse"	The domiciliary status of the decedent controls. If the decedent is a domiciliary, the surviving spouse is entitled to elective share of estate as per this state's law. (§ 30-2313)	Governed by the law of the decedent's domicile at death. (§ 30-2313(b))
Nevada	*Community property state—no quasi-community property*				
New Hampshire	No, unless it appears by will "that such was not the intention." (§ 560:17)	Elective share is reduced by family allowance. (§ 560:1) On the other hand, the homestead allowance may have to be waived if the election is made, although the statutory language is ambiguous. (§ 560:10)	Elective share is denied if husband has abandoned or willfully neglected wife for three years before wife's death, although in that case the husband may still take under any provisions of wife's will. This provision, however, does not apply where the spouses are separated by agreement. (§ 560:18; Foote v. Nickerson, 48 A. 1088, 1089 (N.H. 1901)) In addition, the elective share is denied if, at the time of decedent's death, decedent was justifiably living apart from surviving spouse because surviving spouse was or had been guilty of conduct which constitutes cause for divorce. (§ 560:19) The surviving spouse is still entitled to such as may be given by the will of the deceased. (Id.)	Only mentions "surviving spouse," without any requirement as to domicile or residence. (§ 560:10)	No provision.

Table 6.03, Part 2
Calculation of Elective Share

	Is the Election Allowed If Benefits Are Taken Under the Will?	If the Elective Share Is Taken, Are Other Benefits, Like Family Allowance, Reduced, or Vice Versa?	Is the Elective Share Denied If a Surviving Spouse Was Not Living With the Decedent, Abandoned Him, Was Guilty of Adultery, One of the Spouses Had Filed for Divorce, and Similar Circumstances? If So, Which Ones?	Is a Nondomiciliary Spouse of a Domiciliary Decedent Entitled to an Elective Share If the Decedent Died Domiciled in the State?	Is a Spouse Entitled to an Elective Share If the Decedent Was Not a Domiciliary, e.g., Spouse Moves to State After Decedent's Death to Claim Share in Local Real Property?
New Jersey	Yes, but the "value of all property, estate or interest therein . . . . succeeded to by the surviving spouse or domestic partner as a result of decedent's death" will be first applied to the amount of the surviving spouse's or domestic partner's elective share. (§ 3B:8-18)	Presumably no (no provision).	Yes, if at time of death, decedent and surviving spouse were living separate and apart in different habitations or had ceased to cohabit as man and wife, either as a result of judgment of divorce or under circumstances which would have given rise to a cause of action for divorce or nullity of marriage to decedent prior to his death. (§ 3B:8-1) With respect to jointure, dower, and curtesy, if a spouse "goes away and continues with his par amour in adultery," these benefits will be denied, unless there is a reconciliation and the deserted spouse lives with the deserting spouse. (§§ 3A:37-2; 3B:28-15)	Since surviving spouse must live with a decedent domiciled in New Jersey to be eligible under § 3B:8-1, if spouse is nondomiciliary and decedent is domiciled in New Jersey, there is no elective share.	Governed by the law of decedent's domicile at death. (§ 3B:8-2)
New Mexico	*Quasi-community property is defined in § 40-3-8(C).* [It is treated as community property for purposes of division of property incident to a dissolution of marriage or a legal separation if both parties are New Mexico domiciliaries at the time of the dissolution or legal separation. (§ 40-3-8(D)) It is not mentioned in any provision dealing with distribution of an estate.]				
New York[2]	Not unless decedent has provided otherwise. (Est. Powers & Trusts § 5-1.1-A(a)(4)(A))	The other benefits are not reduced. (Est. Powers & Trusts §§ 5-1.1-A, Practice Commentaries; 5-3.1) The elective share, though, is based on the "net estate." (Est. Powers & Trusts § 5-1.1-A(a)(2))	Divorce, annulment, separation, abandonment, incest, bigamy, and support provisions all determine whether the husband or wife is a "surviving spouse" within the meaning of the statutes. (Est. Powers & Trusts § 5-1.2(a))	Only mentions "surviving spouse," without any requirement as to domicile or residence. (Est. Powers & Trusts § 5-1.1-A)	Not unless nondomiciliary decedent elected to have the disposition of his or her property in New York be governed by New York law. (Est. Powers & Trusts § 5-1.1-A(c)(6))

Table 6.03, Part 2
Calculation of Elective Share

	Is the Election Allowed If Benefits Are Taken Under the Will?	If the Elective Share Is Taken, Are Other Benefits, Like Family Allowance, Reduced, or Vice Versa?	Is the Elective Share Denied If a Surviving Spouse Was Not Living With the Decedent, Abandoned Him, Was Guilty of Adultery, One of the Spouses Had Filed for Divorce, and Similar Circumstances? If So, Which Ones?	Is a Nondomiciliary Spouse of a Domiciliary Decedent Entitled to an Elective Share If the Decedent Died Domiciled in the State?	Is a Spouse Entitled to an Elective Share If the Decedent Was Not a Domiciliary, e.g., Spouse Moves to State After Decedent's Death to Claim Share in Local Real Property?
North Carolina	Yes, but value of net property passing to surviving spouse is used to satisfy the elective share. (§ 30-3.1(a)(iii))	The other benefits are not reduced. (§ 30-15) However, the year's allowance to other persons and claims reduces the total assets subject to the elective share. (§ 30-3.2(4))	Yes. In the event of a spouse (1) who has obtained an absolute divorce or marriage annulment; (2) voluntarily separates from the other spouse and lives in adultery and such has not been condoned; (3) a spouse who willfully and without just cause abandons and refuses to live with the other spouse and is not living with the other spouse at the time of the other spouse's death; (4) a spouse who obtains a divorce not recognized in the state; and (5) a spouse who knowingly contracts a bigamous relationship.(§ 31A-1)	Only mentions "surviving spouse," without any requirement as to domicile or residence. (§ 30-3.1(a))	No. The decedent must have died domiciled in the state. (§ 30-3.1(a))
North Dakota	Yes, but they are included in the augmented estate. (§ 30.1-05-02(2)(d))	Benefits are not charged against, but are in addition to, the elective-share and supplemental elective-share amounts. (§ 30.1-05-01(3))	A surviving spouse does not include a person who is divorced from decedent or had their marriage annulled or obtained an invalid judgment/decree for that purpose, unless there had been a subsequent remarriage. It also does not include someone who participates in a subsequent marriage with a third person or who is party to a proceeding to terminate the marital property rights. (§ 30.1-10-02) Mere voluntary separation or living apart is not enough. (In re Zimmerman, 579 N.W.2d 591, 597 (N.D. 1998))	Only mentions "surviving spouse," without any requirement as to domicile or residence. (§ 30.1-05-01)	Governed by law of decedent's domicile at death. (§ 30.1-05-01(4))
Ohio	No. (Jones v. Lloyd, 33 Ohio St. 572, 577-578 (Ohio 1878) (where a widow elects not to take under the will, she can take nothing in virtue of the bequests, made to her by the will in lieu of dower); § 2106.01)	No. (In re Green's Estate, 410 N.E.2d 812, 814-15 (Com. Pl. 1980); § 2106.01)	Adultery is a bar to dower in real property, unless the offense is condoned by the injured consort. (§ 2103.05)	Only mentions surviving spouse. (§ 2106.01)	No provision.

Table 6.03, Part 2
Calculation of Elective Share

	Is the Election Allowed If Benefits Are Taken Under the Will?	If the Elective Share Is Taken, Are Other Benefits, Like Family Allowance, Reduced, or Vice Versa?	Is the Elective Share Denied If a Surviving Spouse Was Not Living With the Decedent, Abandoned Him, Was Guilty of Adultery, One of the Spouses Had Filed for Divorce, and Similar Circumstances? If So, Which Ones?	Is a Nondomiciliary Spouse of a Domiciliary Decedent Entitled to an Elective Share If the Decedent Died Domiciled in the State?	Is a Spouse Entitled to an Elective Share If the Decedent Was Not a Domiciliary, e.g., Spouse Moves to State After Decedent's Death to Claim Share in Local Real Property?
Oklahoma	No. (84 § 44(B)(2); Turner v. First Nat'l Bank & Trust Co., 262 P.2d 897, 900 (Okla. 1953) (surviving spouse may elect to take under will or as heir at law))	Homestead (84 § 44(B)(1); 58 § 311), other exempt property (58 § 311), and additional allowance (58 § 314) whether or not elective share is sought, are available. See also Oden v. Russell, 371 P.2d 489, 495 (Okla. 1962). The elective share is a one-half interest "in the property acquired by the joint industry of the husband and wife during coverture." (84 § 44(B)(1)) Thus, the elective share would not seem to be affected by these allowances.	No provision.	Yes. (In re Estate of Miller, 768 P.2d 373, 377 (Okla. Civ. App. 1988))	Yes, with respect to property, such as Oklahoma real property, subject to local ancillary administration. (In re Estate of Miller, 768 P.2d 373, 377-78 (Okla. Civ. App. 1988))
Oregon	Yes. If the court determines that the aggregate value of the surviving spouse's estate, the decedent's probate transfers to the surviving spouse, and the decedent's nonprobate transfers to the surviving spouse do not satisfy the amount of the elective share, any additional amount required to satisfy the elective share shall be paid out of the decedent's probate estate and the decedent's nonprobate estate. (§ 114.615)	Support ordered by the court has priority over claims and expenses of administration and is not charged against the person's distributive share. (§ 114.075)	There is no such limitation, so long as the person is a surviving spouse. (§ 114.625) There are provisions for revocation of will in cases of divorce/annulment or subsequent marriage. (§§ 112.305, 112.315)	Yes. (§ 114.600(1))	Governed by the law of the decedent's domicile at death. (§ 114.600(3))
Pennsylvania	No. (20 § 2204)	No provision.	No provision. There are provisions in the context of an intestate decedent, which may be informative. (See 20 § 2106)	Only mentions "surviving spouse," without any requirement as to domicile or residence. (20 § 2203)	"[G]overned by the laws of decedent's domicile at death,... subject to rights of fiduciaries, custodians, and obligors [in Pennsylvania], as well as transferees for value and holders of liens for value on real estate or tangible personal property located in Pennsylvania." (20 § 2202)

Table 6.03, Part 2
Calculation of Elective Share

	Is the Election Allowed If Benefits Are Taken Under the Will?	If the Elective Share Is Taken, Are Other Benefits, Like Family Allowance, Reduced, or Vice Versa?	Is the Elective Share Denied If a Surviving Spouse Was Not Living With the Decedent, Abandoned Him, Was Guilty of Adultery, One of the Spouses Had Filed for Divorce, and Similar Circumstances? If So, Which Ones?	Is a Nondomiciliary Spouse of a Domiciliary Decedent Entitled to an Elective Share If the Decedent Died Domiciled in the State?	Is a Spouse Entitled to an Elective Share If the Decedent Was Not a Domiciliary, e.g., Spouse Moves to State After Decedent's Death to Claim Share in Local Real Property?
Rhode Island	No. (§ 33-25-4)	At least with respect to real estate set aside for the support of the surviving spouse (§ 33-10-4), this right is in addition to the statutory estate. (Id.) There is no provision as to any other benefits.	No provision.	Probably. The statute simply refers to a surviving spouse of a person who dies, with rights granted in "the real estate owned by the decedent." (§ 33-25-2)	Probably. The statute simply refers to a surviving spouse of a person who dies, with rights granted in "the real estate owned by the decedent." (§ 33-25-2)
South Carolina	Yes. However, the amounts of benefits taken under the will are to be applied first to satisfy the surviving spouse's right to the elective share. (§§ 62-2-206, 62-2-207(a))	No, but other benefits accruing to the surviving spouse, including property passed to him or her by will, by intestacy, by homestead allowance, or by exempt property, will be applied first to satisfy the elective share. (§ 62-2-207(a))	Yes. A person is not considered a "surviving spouse" for the purposes of any right to an elective share if there exists a final, valid decree of divorce, annulment, or valid proceeding terminating marital property rights. (§ 62-2-802) Also not a surviving spouse if had been party to a proceeding to terminate marital property rights or if spouse was a common law spouse that had not been adjudicated. (Id.)	Only mentions "surviving spouse," without any requirement as to domicile or residence. (§ 62-2-201)	Governed by the law of the decedent's domicile at death. (§ 62-2-201(b))
South Dakota	No provision. However, "amounts which pass or have passed to the surviving spouse by testate succession" are first applied to satisfy the elective share. (§ 29A-2-209(a)(1))	If the right of election is exercised by or on behalf of the surviving spouse, the surviving spouse's homestead allowance, exempt property, and family allowance, if any, are not charged against but are in addition to the elective share and supplemental elective share amounts. (§ 29A-2-202(c))	"An individual who is divorced from the decedent or whose marriage has been annulled is not a surviving spouse" unless the spouse was subsequently remarried to the decedent. (§ 29A-2-802)	Only mentions "surviving spouse," without any requirement as to their domicile or residence. (§ 29A-2-202(a))	Governed by the law of the decedent's domicile at death. (§ 29A-2-202(d))

Table 6.03, Part 2
Calculation of Elective Share

	Is the Election Allowed If Benefits Are Taken Under the Will?	If the Elective Share Is Taken, Are Other Benefits, Like Family Allowance, Reduced, or Vice Versa?	Is the Elective Share Denied If a Surviving Spouse Was Not Living With the Decedent, Abandoned Him, Was Guilty of Adultery, One of the Spouses Had Filed for Divorce, and Similar Circumstances? If So, Which Ones?	Is a Nondomiciliary Spouse of a Domiciliary Decedent Entitled to an Elective Share If the Decedent Died Domiciled in the State?	Is a Spouse Entitled to an Elective Share If the Decedent Was Not a Domiciliary, e.g., Spouse Moves to State After Decedent's Death to Claim Share in Local Real Property?
Tennessee	Yes, but the elective share is reduced by the transfers and deemed transfers to the surviving spouse. (§31-4-101(c))	Vice versa. Net estate for elective share purposes is reduced by the following: secured debts to the extent that secured creditors are entitled to realize on the applicable collateral, funeral and administration expenses, and award of exempt property, homestead allowance, and year's support allowance. (§31-4-101(b))	The misconduct of a widow will not bar her from making an election. (Fogo v. Griffin, 551 S.W.2d 677, 679 (Tenn. 1977) ("all that is required is a valid marriage and survival of widow")) A surviving spouse does not include a person who is divorced from decedent or had their marriage annulled or obtained an invalid judgment/decree for that purpose, unless there had been a subsequent remarriage. It also does not include someone who participates in a subsequent marriage with a third person or who is party to a proceeding to terminate the marital property rights. (§31-1-102)	Only mentions "surviving spouse," without any requirement as to domicile or residence. (§31-4-101)	Only mentions decedent. (§31-4-101)
Texas			*Community property state; no quasi-community property*		
Utah	Yes, but benefits received under the will are charged against the elective share. (§75-2-209(1)(a))	The surviving spouse is entitled to homestead allowance, exempt property, and family allowance whether or not he or she elects to take the elective share. However, unless specified in the will or governing instrument, the homestead (§75-2-402), exempt property allowance (§75-2-403), and the family allowance (§75-2-404(2)) are all chargeable against the spouse's elective share. (See also §75-2-202(3))	"An individual who is divorced from the decedent or whose marriage has been annulled is not a surviving spouse unless, by virtue of a subsequent marriage, the individual is married to decedent at the time of death. A decree of separation that does not terminate the status of husband and wife is not a divorce.... A surviving spouse does not include: (a) an individual who obtains or consents to a final decree or judgment of divorce from the decedent; (b) an individual who... participates in a marriage ceremony with a third individual; or (c) an individual who... terminates all marital property rights." (§75-2-802)	Only mentions "surviving spouse," without any requirement as to domicile or residence. (§75-2-202(1))	Governed by the law of the decedent's domicile at death. (§75-2-202(4))

Table 6.03, Part 2
Calculation of Elective Share

	Is the Election Allowed If Benefits Are Taken Under the Will?	If the Elective Share Is Taken, Are Other Benefits, Like Family Allowance, Reduced, or Vice Versa?	Is the Elective Share Denied If a Surviving Spouse Was Not Living With the Decedent, Abandoned Him, Was Guilty of Adultery, One of the Spouses Had Filed for Divorce, and Similar Circumstances? If So, Which Ones?	Is a Nondomiciliary Spouse of a Domiciliary Decedent Entitled to an Elective Share If the Decedent Died Domiciled in the State?	Is a Spouse Entitled to an Elective Share If the Decedent Was Not a Domiciliary, e.g., Spouse Moves to State After Decedent's Death to Claim Share in Local Real Property?
Vermont	The elective share is "in lieu" of provisions under the will. (14 §319(a))	The elective share is one-half of the balance of the probate estate after the payment of allowances, claims, and expenses. (14 §319(a)) The family support allowance may be given priority over debts of the estate in the discretion of the court. (14 §316) However, the elective share would not seem to be a debt. The household goods are in addition to the "distributive share of the estate to which the surviving spouse is entitled under other provisions of law." (14 §312) Is the elective share a "distributive share?" As for a vessel, snowmobile, or all-terrain vehicle, which passes directly to the surviving spouse, there is uncertainty whether its value is taken into account for elective share purposes, and it is not a claim or expense. (14 §313, 319(a))	No. In the case of divorce, there must be a final divorce order. (14 §320) Note that if there is such order, the former spouse may not take an elective share of the will unless the will provides to the contrary. (Id.)	Only mentions "surviving spouse," without any mention of domicile. (14 §319)	Only mentions "decedent," without any mention of domicile. (14 §319)
Virginia	No, because if the election is made, the electing spouse is only entitled to a specified fraction of the "augmented estate." (§64.2-304)	The right to an elective share is in addition to a right to family allowance and exempt property. (§64.2-309, §64.2-310) If the surviving spouse claims and receives an elective share of the decedent's estate, the surviving spouse shall not have the benefit of homestead allowance. (§64.2-311)	A spouse who willfully deserts or abandons the decedent spouse is barred from all interest in the elective share. (§64.2-308)	Only mentions "surviving spouse," without any requirement as to domicile or residence. (§64.2-302)	Governed by the law of the decedent's domicile at death. (§64.2-302)
Washington	Community property state; no quasi-community property. (§26.16.030)				
West Virginia	This section does not expressly require the surviving spouse to elect between rights under the will and under general law, but such is within the plain spirit and intention of the statute. (Beard v. Callison, 54 S.E.2d 568, 572-73 (W. Va. 1949); §42-3-1)	No provision.	No provision.	Only mentions "surviving spouse," without any requirement as to domicile or residence. (§42-3-1)	Governed by the law of the decedent's domicile at death. (§42-3-1(c))

Table 6.03, Part 2
Calculation of Elective Share

	Is the Election Allowed If Benefits Are Taken Under the Will?	If the Elective Share Is Taken, Are Other Benefits, Like Family Allowance, Reduced, or Vice Versa?	Is the Elective Share Denied If a Surviving Spouse Was Not Living With the Decedent, Abandoned Him, Was Guilty of Adultery, One of the Spouses Had Filed for Divorce, and Similar Circumstances? If So, Which Ones?	Is a Nondomiciliary Spouse of a Domiciliary Decedent Entitled to an Elective Share If the Decedent Died Domiciled in the State?	Is a Spouse Entitled to an Elective Share If the Decedent Was Not a Domiciliary, e.g., Spouse Moves to State After Decedent's Death to Claim Share in Local Real Property?
Wisconsin	*Community property state; quasi-community property known as deferred marital property estate is available to the surviving spouse (§851.055)*				
Wyoming	Yes. The surviving spouse has a right of election whenever the will deprives the surviving spouse of more than the elective share. This clearly anticipates situations in which a spouse has devised some amount under the will, but, nevertheless, makes the election. Note that there does not appear to be offset for the amount devised by will. (§2-5-101)	No, unless will expressly provides otherwise. (§2-5-103)	No provision, but there are provisions for revocation of will in situations of divorce or annulment which may be informative. (§2-6-118)	Only mentions "surviving spouse," without any requirement as to domicile or residence. (§2-5-101(a))	Governed by the law of decedent's domicile at death. (§2-5-101(b))

[1] Georgia Year's Support—No elective share, however, the year's support is like the elective share because if the decedent makes a provision in lieu of year's support in the will, then the spouse may elect to take the year's support rather than the provision under the will. (§53-3-3)

[2] These answers assume that the decedent died after September 1, 1992.

Table 6.03, Part 3
Calculation of Elective Share

	Are Amounts That Pass to the Surviving Spouse or Owned by the Surviving Spouse Used to Satisfy the Elective Share?	Are These Interests Valued in a Special Way, e.g., Life Income Interest at One-Half Value of Trust Property in Which the Surviving Spouse has an Interest?	How is the Burden of the Elective Share Apportioned Among Estate and/or Nonprobate Beneficiaries?
Alabama	When satisfying the elective share, values...in the estate which have passed to surviving spouse or would have passed to surviving spouse but were renounced "are applied first to satisfy the elective share and to reduce any contributions due from other recipients of transfers included in the estate." (§ 43-8-75(a))	The special valuation does not pertain to determining the value of the elective share (§ 43-8-70 (b)), but when determining how the share is satisfied, beneficial interests in life estates and trusts are valued at one-half "unless higher or lower values for these interests are established by proof."(§ 43-8-75(a))	Equitably apportioned among recipients of the estate in proportion to the value of their interests therein. (§ 43-8-75(b))
Alaska	Yes. First, amounts included in the augmented estate that pass or have passed to spouse under will, intestate succession or covered nonprobate transfers to the spouse; next, the portion of the augmented estate consisting of the surviving spouse's property, and covered nonprobate transfers, but no more than two-thirds of the augmented estate. If these are insufficient, then the decedent's probate estate transfers and nonprobate transfers to others are reached. (§ 13.12.209)	Commuted value is to be used for present and future interests, life insurance settlement option, annuity contract and amount payable under a trust. Pensions, disability compensation, or similar arrangement. (§ 13.12.208(b)(2)) The calculation method is not specified. If there is an overlap under various provisions, only one of the values is relied upon, but it is the highest one. (§ 13.12.208(c)) The value of community property is not included in the augmented estate. (§ 13.12.208(d))	After taking account of values in the first column, liability is equitably apportioned among recipients of the amounts transferred by decedent's probate estate and by decedent's nonprobate transfers to others. If the elective share is still not fully satisfied, the remaining portion of the decedent's nonprobate transfers to others is applied so that the liability is equitably apportioned among recipients of decedent's nonprobate transfers. (§ 13.12.209(b)&(c))
Arizona		Community Property—no quasi-community property	
Arkansas	No provision.	No provision.	No provision.
California[1]	No provision.	No provision.	No provision.
Colorado	Yes. Amounts included in the decedents net probate estate by testate or intestate succession, along with the decedent's nonprobate transfers to spouse, and the marital property portion adjustable per schedule found at § 15-11-203(2) based on length of marriage, are used to satisfy the elective share. Any amounts disclaimed by the surviving spouse shall not be applied to the extent such property passes to someone else. (§ 15-11-209(1))	The augmented estate is reduced by enforceable claims against the property. Commuted value is used for any present or future interest and for amounts payable under any trust, life insurance settlement option, annuity contract, public or private pension, disability compensation, death benefit or retirement plan, or any similar arrangement, exclusive of the federal social security system. Statute does not specify how to determine commuted value. (§ 15-11-208(2)(a)-(b))	After taking account of value in the first column, the decedent's remaining net probate estate and certain nonprobate transfers to others are applied first to satisfy the balance of the elective-share, proportioned among the recipients in proportion to the value of their interests. If the elective share is then not fully satisfied, the remaining portion of the decedent's nonprobate transfers to others is so applied that liability for the unsatisfied balance of the elective share is apportioned among the recipients in proportion to the value of their interests. (§ 15-11-209(3))
Connecticut	No provision.	No provision.	Shall be set out by the fiduciary, the Probate Court in it discretion, or the distributors appointed by the court and shall be determined according to the judgment of the fiduciary or distributors as to personal or real property or both of them. (§ 45a-436(e))

Table 6.03, Part 3
Calculation of Elective Share

	Are Amounts That Pass to the Surviving Spouse or Owned by the Surviving Spouse Used to Satisfy the Elective Share?	Are These Interests Valued in a Special Way, e.g., Life Income Interest at One-Half Value of Trust Property in Which the Surviving Spouse has an Interest?	How is the Burden of the Elective Share Apportioned Among Estate and/ or Nonprobate Beneficiaries?
Delaware	Yes, transfers to the spouse will reduce the amount of elective share. (12 §901) Transfers to the spouse which are counted in this calculation include property passing to spouse by will or intestate succession; property transferred to spouse by decedent during decedent's lifetime and includible in decedent's gross estate under 26 U.S.C. §2036; joint tenancies; any other beneficial interests in a trust created by the decedent during his lifetime; "property appointed to the spouse by decedent's exercise of a general or special power of appointment," insurance on the life of the decedent including accidental death benefits attributable to premiums paid by the decedent; any lump sums and the commuted value of proceeds of annuity contracts of which the decedent was the primary annuitant attributable to premiums paid by the decedent; and the commuted value of amounts payable of the decedent's death under a public or private pension, disability compensation, death benefit or retirement plan, exclusive of the federal Social Security System, by reason of service performed or disabilities incurred by the decedents, and the value of the share of the surviving spouse resulting from rights in property formerly owned by the decedent; and "the value of the share of the surviving spouse resulting from rights in community property owned by the decedent," wherever situated. (12 §903)	Yes, "[p]roperty owned by the spouse at the decedent's death is valued as of date it is valued for purposes of computing the elective estate. Income earned by included property prior to decedent's death is not treated as property derived from the decedent." (12 §903(2))	After application of the amounts described in the first column, liability is apportioned among recipients of the "contributing estate." The "contributing estate" consists of the portion of the "elective estate" that was solely owned by decedent at death and was not transferred or deemed transferred to the surviving spouse. The contributing estate does not include joint tenancy property of the decedent, insurance proceeds payable to a beneficiary other than an estate, or any property held in trust. (12 §908(b)) The "elective estate" is the federal gross estate less deductions allowable under I.R.C. §§2053 & 2054 and transfers by the decedent during life that were made with the written consent or joinder of the surviving spouse. (12 §902(a)) The apportionment will be made in the proportion that the value of each recipient's property bears to the total value of all recipients' property, although this does not include a temporary interest, which is due from the corpus. (12 §908(a))
District of Columbia	No provision.	No provision.	No provision.
Florida	Yes. Unless otherwise provided in the will or testamentary trust, the following apply first to satisfy the elective share: (a) property interests that pass or have passed to a benefit of the surviving spouse, including interests contingent on making the election; (b) retirement plan benefits paid to or for the benefit of the surviving spouse; (c) to the extent paid is for decedent, the surviving spouse any community property interest of the decedent; (d) if owned by a person other than the surviving spouse at the decedent's death, any life insurance proceeds on the decedent's life to the extent paid to or for the benefit of the surviving spouse; (e) property held for the surviving spouse in a qualifying special needs trust; and (f) property that would have been covered by (a)-(e), but was disclaimed. (§732.2075(1))	Value is determined at decedent's death, except if there has been an earlier irrevocable transfer within one year of death, in which case the date of transfer is utilized. (§732.2055)	Only direct recipients included in the elective estate (essentially the augmented estate) and the beneficiaries of the decedent's probate estate or of any trust that is a direct recipient are liable toward satisfaction of the elective share. (§732.2085(1)) Within a class of recipients, liability is apportioned based on proportional value received. (§732.2085(1)(a)) Trust and probate estate beneficiaries, who receive a distribution of principal after the decedent's death are liable in an amount equal to the value of the principal distributed to them multiplied by the contribution percentage of the distributing trust or estate. (§732.2085(1)(b))

Table 6.03, Part 3
Calculation of Elective Share

	Are Amounts That Pass to the Surviving Spouse or Owned by the Surviving Spouse Used to Satisfy the Elective Share?	Are These Interests Valued in a Special Way, e.g., Life Income Interest at One-Half Value of Trust Property in Which the Surviving Spouse has an Interest?	How is the Burden of the Elective Share Apportioned Among Estate and/ or Nonprobate Beneficiaries?
Georgia[2]	If there is no objection, the court will enter an order setting aside year's support. (§53-3-7(a)) If an objection is made to the amount or nature of the property proposed to be set aside as year's support, then the court shall set apart an amount taking into consideration "[t]he support available to the individual for whom the property is to be set apart from sources other than year's support, including but not limited to the principal of any separate estate and the income and earning capacity of that individual; the solvency of the estate and such other criteria as the court deems equitable." (§53-3-7(c))	No provision.	No provision.
Hawaii	First, amounts which pass or have passed to the surviving spouse or reciprocal beneficiary by testate or intestate succession, as well as amounts otherwise included in the augmented estate and passing to the surviving spouse; then property included in the augmented estate that was owned by the surviving spouse and property that passed to the surviving spouse from the decedent, with certain exceptions; and certain nonprobate transfers to others by the surviving spouse that would have been included in her augmented estate if she had died, but not more than the applicable percentage, which is "twice the elective share percentage." (§560:2-209)	Commuted value is to be used for present and future interests amount payable under any trust, life insurance settlement option, annuity contract, pensions disability compensation, death benefit, retirement plan, or similar arrangement, exclusive of the federal social security system. The calculation method is not specified. If there is an overlap under various provisions, only one of the values is relied upon, but it is the highest one. (§560:2-208(b)&(c)) Any amounts included are reduced by any enforceable claims against the included property. (§560:2-208(a))	After taking account of values in the first column, liability is equitably apportioned among recipients of the amounts transferred by decedent's probate estate and by decedent's nonprobate transfers to others. If the elective share is still not fully satisfied, the remaining portion of the decedent's nonprobate transfers to others is applied so that the liability is equitably apportioned among recipients of the remaining portion decedent's nonprobate transfers. (§560:2-209(b)&(c))
Idaho[3]	The "property which passes or has passed to the surviving spouse by testate or intestate succession and property included in the augmented estate which has not been renounced is applied first to satisfy the elective share." (§15-2-207(a))	No provision.	If amounts described in the first column are not sufficient to satisfy the elective share, "then [t]he remaining amount of the elective share is equitably apportioned among beneficiaries of the will and transferees of the augmented estate in proportion to the value of their interest therein." (§15-2-207(b))
Illinois	No provision.	No provision.	Proportionate reductions. (755 ILCS §5/2-8(d); Kane v. Schofield, 76 N.E.2d 216, 221-22 (Ill. App. Ct. 1947))
Indiana	No explicit provision. The spouse's share will be taken from "only such property as would have passed under the laws of descent and distribution." (§29-1-3-1(a))	No. (§29-1-3-1)	The shares of the distributees abate, for the payment of the share of the surviving spouse who elects to take against the will, without any preference or priority between real and personal property, in the following order: (1) property not disposed of by the will, (2) property devised to the residuary devisee, (3) property disposed of by the will but not specifically devised and not devised to the residuary devisee, and (4) property specifically devised, (§29-1-17-3(a)) unless otherwise necessary "to give effect to the intention of the testator." (§29-1-17-3(b))

Table 6.03, Part 3
Calculation of Elective Share

	Are Amounts That Pass to the Surviving Spouse or Owned by the Surviving Spouse Used to Satisfy the Elective Share?	Are These Interests Valued in a Special Way, e.g., Life Income Interest at One-Half Value of Trust Property in Which the Surviving Spouse has an Interest?	How is the Burden of the Elective Share Apportioned Among Estate and/or Nonprobate Beneficiaries?
Iowa	No. (§633.238)	No. (§633.238)	By mutual consent or by referees appointed by the court after an application in writing submitted to the court. (§633.247)
Kansas	First, amounts which pass or have passed to the surviving spouse by testate or intestate succession, as well as amounts otherwise included in the augmented estate and passing to the surviving spouse; then amounts included in the augmented estate, but which were disclaimed by the surviving spouse; then property included in the augmented estate which was owned by the surviving spouse and property that passed to the surviving spouse from the decedent, with certain exceptions, and certain nonprobate transfers to others by the surviving spouse that would have been included in her augmented estate if she had died, but not more than the "applicable percentage," "which is" twice the elective share percentage." (§59-6a209(a))	Commuted value is to be used for present and future interests, and amounts payable under a trusts, life insurance settlement option, annuity contract, pensions, disability compensation, or similar arrangement exclusive of social security. The calculation method is not specified. If there is an overlap under various provisions, only one of the values is relied upon, but it is the highest one. (§59-6a208(b)(2)&(c))	After taking account of values in the first column, liability equitably apportioned among recipients of the amounts transferred by decedent's probate estate and by decedent's nonprobate transfers to others. If the elective share is still not fully satisfied, the remaining portion of the decedent's nonprobate transfers to others is applied so that the liability is equitably apportioned among recipients of decedent's nonprobate transfers. (§59-6a209(b)&(c))
Kentucky	No. (§392.020)	No. (§392.020)	No provision.
Louisiana	*Community Property state—no quasi-community property*		
Maine	Yes. " . . . [V]alues included in the augmented estate which pass or have passed to the surviving spouse, or which would have passed to the spouse but were renounced, are applied first to satisfy the elective share." (18-A §2-207(a))	Spouse's interest in life estate or trust is to be valued at one-half of total value of the property in which surviving spouse has interest, unless higher or lower values are established by proof. (18-A §2-207(a))	After taking into account values in first column, "[R]emaining property of the augmented estate is so applied that liability for the balance of the elective share is equitably apportioned among the recipients of augmented estate in proportion to the value of their interests." (18-A §2-207(b))
Maryland	No. (Estated & Trusts §3-203(a))	No provision.	Contribution to the payment of the elective share shall be prorated among all legatees. Instead of contributing an interest in specific property, a legatee may pay the surviving spouse in cash or other property acceptable to the surviving spouse. (Est. & Trusts §3-208(b))
Massachusetts	(No. 191 §15)	No provision.	The loss falls first on the residue. (Crocker v. Crocker, 120 N.E. 110, 111 (Mass. 1918))
Michigan	Spouse takes "[one-half] of the sum or share that would have passed to the spouse had the testator died intestate, reduced by [one-half] of the value of all property derived by the spouse from the decedent by any means other than testate or intestate succession." (§700.2202(2)(b))	No provision.	"It is the duty of courts to accomplish as near as may be done equitably the same result between the beneficiaries as would have resulted from distribution of the estate in accordance with the terms of the will." Thus, a residuary devise is reduced before a specific devise. (In re Povey's Estate, 261 N.W. 98, 100 (Mich. 1935))

Table 6.03, Part 3
Calculation of Elective Share

	Are Amounts That Pass to the Surviving Spouse or Owned by the Surviving Spouse Used to Satisfy the Elective Share?	Are These Interests Valued in a Special Way, e.g., Life Income Interest at One-Half Value of Trust Property in Which the Surviving Spouse has an Interest?	How is the Burden of the Elective Share Apportioned Among Estate and/or Nonprobate Beneficiaries?
Minnesota	Yes. Amounts which have passed or pass to the spouse by testate and intestate succession are applied first to satisfy the elective share, along with nonprobate transfers to the spouse that constitute part of the augmented estate. (§524.2-209(a)(1)) Then, amounts included in the augmented estate which are disclaimed by the spouse are taken into account (§524.2-209(a)(2)); then property owned by the surviving spouse or which would have been taken into account if the spouse had died, up to the applicable percentage, which is twice the elective share percentage set forth in §524.2-202. (§524.2-209(a)(3))	Commuted value is to be used for present or future interests and amounts payable under any trust, life insurance settlement option, annuity contract, pension, disability compensation, death benefit, retirement plan, or any similar arrangement, exclusive of the federal social security system. Commuted value of spouse's interest in a life estate or interest "in any trust" is valued at one-half the total property that is subject to the life estate or trust estate, unless there are higher or lower values for these interests are established by proof. (§524.2-208(c)(2)) If there is an overlap under various provisions, only one of the values is relied upon, but it is the highest one. (§524.2-208(d))	After taking account of values in the first column, liability for property of the augmented estate due to the surviving spouse is equitably apportioned among the recipients of the decedent's probate estate and the recipients of the decedent's nonprobate transfers in proportion to the value of their interests therein. (§524.2-209(b)) If the elective share is still not fully satisfied, the liability is equitably apportioned among the recipients of the remaining nonprobate transfers of the decedent. (§524.2-209(c))
Mississippi	Yes. If the surviving spouse's "separate estate" is equal to the elective share she is not entitled to dissent from the will. If it is less, then she is only entitled to the difference. However, the surviving spouse is entitled to the entire elective share if separate property is no greater than one-fifth of the elective share value. As to the "separate estate," it includes such items as beneficiary of life insurance on decedent spouse's life, as well as bank accounts in the names of both spouses. (§ 91-5-29; Matter of Estate of Mason 616 So. 2d 322, 331-32. (Miss. 1993)	In order to value the lawful elective share and the surviving spouse's separate estate, the court "may" appoint three commissioners to make the determinations and report to the court. (§91-5-29)	No provision, but note that if for example, the surviving spouse has a separate estate that is only two-thirds of the elective share, then she is entitled to one-third of the realty and one-third of the personalty. (§91-5-29) Note the right to a percentage of realty *and* personalty.
Missouri	Homestead offsets the elective share. (§474.160(2)) Furthermore, the elective share is "reduced by funeral and administration expenses, exempt property, family allowance and enforceable claims, and increased by the aggregate value of all money and property derived by the surviving spouse from the decedent by any means other than testate or intestate succession." (§474.163(1) The meaning of "derived from the decedent" is set forth in §474.163(2) and includes a beneficial interest in a trust created by the decedent during his lifetime, property appointed by the decedent, insurance proceeds, annuity proceeds, pension, disability benefits, death benefit or retirement plan benefits of decedent exclusive of Social Security, and the value of the surviving spouse's own share of community property formerly owned by the decedent.	Commuted value is used for annuity contract proceeds under which the decedent was the primary annuitant, attributable to premiums paid by him. (§474.163.(2)(4)) Also, commuted value is utilized for amounts payable after decedent's death under pensions, disability compensation, death benefit or retirement plans, exclusive of the federal Social Security System, by reason of services performed, or disabilities incurred by the decedent. (Id. at 2.(5)) Income earned prior to decedent's death by included property owned or transferred by surviving spouse is not taken into account. (§474.163(2)(4)) Premiums paid by decedent's employer, partner, or creditor are deemed paid by decedent. (§474.163(2), flush language at end of section) If surviving spouse was a cotenant or remainderman, she includes whole value of property at decedent's death, except the proportion of value based on what she or ascendant or collateral relatives of the surviving spouse, other than the decedent contributes to acquire, create or establish the money, property, fund or account. (474.163(3))	Apparently, the traditional abatement by the residuary devisee, then the general and specific would occur. (§§473.620; 473.623)

Table 6.03, Part 3
Calculation of Elective Share

	Are Amounts That Pass to the Surviving Spouse or Owned by the Surviving Spouse Used to Satisfy the Elective Share?	Are These Interests Valued in a Special Way, e.g., Life Income Interest at One-Half Value of Trust Property in Which the Surviving Spouse has an Interest?	How is the Burden of the Elective Share Apportioned Among Estate and/or Nonprobate Beneficiaries?
Montana	First, amounts included in the augmented estate that pass or have passed to the surviving spouse by testate or intestate succession; then nonprobate transfers to spouse included in the augmented estate; then amounts that would have passed to the surviving spouse but were disclaimed; then property owned by the surviving spouse or which would have been included in her augmented estate up to the applicable percentage, which is twice the elective share percentage. (§72-2-227(1))	Yes. Commuted value is to be used for present or future interests or amounts payable under any trust, life insurance settlement option, annuity contract, pension, disability compensation, death benefit, retirement plan, or any similar arrangement, exclusive of the federal social security system. Commuted values of life and term interests are determined in accordance with U.S. Treasury Regulations. (§72-2-222(4)) If there is an overlap under various provisions, only one of the values is relied upon, but it is the highest one. (§72-2-222(5))	After taking account of values in the first column, liability is equitably apportioned among recipients of the amounts transferred by decedent's probate estate and by decedent's nonprobate transfers to others. If the elective share is still not fully satisfied, the remaining portion of the decedent's nonprobate transfers to others is applied so that the liability is equitably apportioned among recipients of decedent's nonprobate transfers. (§72-2-227(2)&(3))
Nebraska	"[P]roperty which is part of the augmented estate which passes or has passed to the surviving spouse by testate or intestate succession or by other means and which has not been renounced... is applied first." (§30-2319(a))	Commuted value is used for determining proceeds of annuities and amounts of pensions, disability benefits, compensation, death benefit, retirement plan, or similar payment, exclusive of Social Security. (§30-2314 (a)(2)(i))	After taking account of values in the first column, liability is "equitably apportioned among the recipients of the augmented estate in proportion to the value of their interests therein... A person liable to contribution [to the surviving spouse] may choose to give up the property transferred to him or to pay its value." (§30-2319(b)&(c))
Nevada		community property state—no quasi-community property	
New Hampshire	No provision.	No provision.	No provision.
New Jersey	Yes. "[V]alue of all property, estate or interest therein, owned by the surviving spouse or domestic partner in his own right at the time of [death of decedent] from whatever source acquired or succeeded to by surviving spouse or domestic partner as a result of decedent's death, even if such property has been renounced by surviving spouse; in addition, any property" derived from decedent by means other than testate or intestate succession; also, property described in the preceding clause which was transferred by the surviving spouse or domestic partner during marriage or domestic partnership without full consideration and which would have been included in his augmented estate had he died. (§§ 3B:8-18; 3B:8-6)	Electing spouse's total or proportional beneficial interest in any life estate in real or personal property or in any trust is valued at one half of the total value of the property or trust of the portion of the property or trust subject to the life estate. (§3B:8-17) There is no provision to prove a different value.	If the amount of elective share is not satisfied by property in § 3B:8-18(a) and (b), the remaining property is so applied that liability for the balance of the elective share "is equitably apportioned among recipients of the augmented estates in proportion to the value of their interests therein." (§3B:8-18(c))
New Mexico	Community property state with quasi-community property. Quasi-community property is defined in §40-3-8(C). It is treated as community property for purposes of division of property incident to a dissolution of marriage or a legal separation if both parties are New Mexico domiciliaries at the time of the dissolution or legal separation. (§40-3-8(D)) It is not mentioned in any provision dealing with distribution of an estate.	See prior column.	See prior column.

Table 6.03, Part 3
Calculation of Elective Share

	Are Amounts That Pass to the Surviving Spouse or Owned by the Surviving Spouse Used to Satisfy the Elective Share?	Are These Interests Valued in a Special Way, e.g., Life Income Interest at One-Half Value of Trust Property in Which the Surviving Spouse has an Interest?	How is the Burden of the Elective Share Apportioned Among Estate and/or Nonprobate Beneficiaries?
New York[4]	Yes. The elective share is reduced by capital value of any interest passing absolutely from decedent to the spouse, or which would have passed, but was renounced. Interests in trust and interests of less than the entire property are not deemed to pass "absolutely." (Est. Powers & Trusts §5-1.1-A(a)(4))	No provision.	"[R]atable contribution to the share to which the surviving spouse is entitled [is] made by the beneficiaries and distributees...under the decedent's will, by intestacy" and other instruments making testamentary provision. (Est. Powers & Trusts §5-1.1-A(c) (2)) "Testamentary provision" includes testamentary substitutes. (Est. Powers & Trusts §5-1.1-A(a)(3))
North Carolina	Yes. The elective share is reduced by one-half of joint tenancy property and tenancy by the entirety property with the spouse; (§30-3.2(3f)(c)(1) then any benefits, other than social security, passing to the surviving spouse outright, in trust, or by power of appointment or default of exercise of power by devise, intestacy, or by beneficiary, designation or testamentary exercise or default of power; (§30-3.2(3c)(a)) then year's allowance; (§30-3.2(3c)(b)) then the value of property renounced by surviving spouse; (§30-3.2(3c)(c)) then the value of surviving spouse's interest in life insurance proceeds on the decedent's life; (§30-3.2(3c)(d)) certain gifts to the surviving spouse during the decedent's life; (§30-3.2(3c)(e)) then property awarded to the surviving spouse pursuant to an equitable distribution claim (§30-3.2(3c)(e)) and property held in certain spousal trusts. (§30-3.2(3c)(f))	The property is valued based on the fair market value, (§30-3.3A(a)) with some exceptions. (§30-3.3A(b)) The method for valuing is determined by good faith agreement between the surviving spouse, personal representatives, and the trustees. (§30-3.3A(f)) If no such agreement can be made, the clerk will decide after a hearing where the parties present evidence regarding value (§30-3.3A(f)(4)) The value of partial interests commencing or terminating in the future will be based on a 6% rate of return. (§30-3.3A(e))	Pro rata. (§ 30-3.5(a1), (a2), (a3) and (b))
North Dakota	First, the net probate estate passing to the surviving spouse; then the nonprobate assets in the augmented estate passing to the surviving spouse; then the assets that would have been included in the surviving spouse's augmented estate if the surviving spouse had died. (§30.1-05-03(1)(a)-(b))	Reference is made to commuted values of any present or future interests and amounts payable under a trust, life insurance settlement option, annuity contract, pensions, or any similar arrangement, exclusive of Social Security. (§30.1-05-02(4)) "Commuted value" is not defined.	After taking account of values in the first column, liability is equitably apportioned among recipients of the amounts transferred by decedent's probate estate and by decedent's nonprobate transfers to others. If the elective share is not fully satisfied, the remaining portion of the decedent's nonprobate transfers to others is applied so that the liability is equitably apportioned among recipients of decedent's nonprobate transfers. (§30.1-05-03(2)&(3))
Ohio	No provision.	No provision.	No provision.
Oklahoma	Yes, in that the decedent cannot devise to others so that the surviving spouse receives less in value that a one-half interest in the property acquired by the joint industry of husband and wife during coverture. (84 §44(B)(1))	No provision.	Election by widow to take under statute rather than will does not invalidate will in its entirety. Its provisions shall be carried out as far as possible in the distribution of the remaining property. (Long v. Drumright, 375 P.2d 953, 955 (Okla. 1962))

Table 6.03, Part 3
Calculation of Elective Share

	Are Amounts That Pass to the Surviving Spouse or Owned by the Surviving Spouse Used to Satisfy the Elective Share?	Are These Interests Valued in a Special Way, e.g., Life Income Interest at One-Half Value of Trust Property in Which the Surviving Spouse has an Interest?	How is the Burden of the Elective Share Apportioned Among Estate and/or Nonprobate Beneficiaries?
Oregon	Yes, the following are applied first to satisfy the elective share: decedent's probate transfers to the surviving spouse; decedent's non-probate transfers to the surviving spouse and other property of the surviving spouse at the time of the decedent's death. (§114.700(1)) If the elective share is still not satisfied, the following shall satisfy the balance of the elective share: decedent's probate estate; decedent's non-probate estate. (§114.700(2))	No provision.	Proportionate liability is born between probate and nonprobate estates (§114.700(3)) and among the recipients within each of these categories based on the recipient's relative interest. (§114.700(4))
Pennsylvania	Any beneficial interest in §2204(a) property which is owned outright by the surviving spouse immediately after decedent's death is chargeable against the elective share. (20 §2204(c)) "Beneficial interest" refers to typical probate and augmented estate interests and includes any power of appointment or consumption and any benefit arising from a direction of the decedent regarding the source of payment of inheritance or estate taxes. (20 §2204(d))	No provision.	Generally, property which otherwise would pass by intestacy is first applied toward satisfaction of elective share. Balance of elective share is charged separately against each conveyance subject to the election, providing spouse a fractional interest in each conveyance. Items of property within each conveyance are then allocated between elective and nonelective share property to give maximum effect to decedent's intentions with respect to dispositions of particular items or kinds of property. (20 §2211(b)(1))
Rhode Island	No provision.	No provision.	No provision.
South Carolina	Yes. All property, including beneficial interests, which pass or has passed to the surviving spouse under the decedent's will, by intestacy, by any homestead allowance, by exempt property allowance, or by other specified means, or which "would have passed to the spouse but was renounced, is applied first to satisfy the elective share and to reduce any contributions due from other recipients of transfers included in the probate estate." (§62-2-207(a))	Yes. The value of the electing spouse's beneficial interest in any property which would qualify for the federal estate tax marital deduction pursuant to I.R.C. §2056 is computed at the full value of the qualifying property. (§62-2-207(c))	After property passing or that was passed to the surviving spouse, or that has been renounced, see first column, then liability for the elective share will be satisfied by the decedent's devises which will abate in accordance with the general abatement provision, §62-3-902, that is, without "preference or priority as between real and personal property, in the following order: (1) property not disposed of by will; (2) residuary devises; (3) general devises; (4) specific devises," unless contrary to the testator's intention. (§62-2-207(d))
South Dakota	First, amounts which pass or have passed to the surviving spouse by testate or intestate succession, as well as amounts otherwise included in the augmented estate and amounts included in the augmented estate and passing to the surviving spouse; then amounts included in the augmented estate, but which were disclaimed by the surviving spouse; then property included in the augmented estate which was owned by the surviving spouse and property that passed to the surviving spouse from the decedent, with certain exceptions, and certain nonprobate transfers to others by the surviving spouse that would have been included in her augmented estate if she had died, but not more than the "applicable percentage, which is twice the elective share percentage." (§29A-2-209(a))	Commuted value is to be used for present and future interests, and amounts payable under a life insurance settlement option, annuity contract, pensions, disability compensation, or similar arrangement, exclusive of federal Social Security. The calculation method is not specified. If there is an overlap under various provisions, only one of the values is relied upon, but it is the highest one. (§29A-2-208(b)&(c))	After taking account of values in the first column, liability is equitably apportioned among recipients of the amounts transferred by decedent's probate estate and by decedent's nonprobate transfers to others. If the elective share is still not fully satisfied, the remaining portion of the decedent's nonprobate transfers to others is applied so that the liability is equitably apportioned among recipients of decedent's nonprobate transfers. (§29A-2-209(b)&(c))

6088

Table 6.03, Part 3
Calculation of Elective Share

	Are Amounts That Pass to the Surviving Spouse or Owned by the Surviving Spouse Used to Satisfy the Elective Share?	Are These Interests Valued in a Special Way, e.g., Life Income Interest at One-Half Value of Trust Property in Which the Surviving Spouse has an Interest?	How is the Burden of the Elective Share Apportioned Among Estate and/or Nonprobate Beneficiaries?
Tennessee	The amount of the surviving spouse's elective share shall be reduced by the value of the assets within the decedent's gross estate which were transferred, to or for the benefit of the surviving spouse. (§31-4-101(c))	Yes. The value of the decedent's gross estate is determined by the court in the same manner as for inheritance tax purposes pursuant to T.C.A. §§67-8-301, et seq., except that the value of any life estate or trust for the lifetime benefit of the surviving spouse shall be actuarially determined. (§31-4-101(c))	Persons to whom property from the decedent's net estate was distributed may be liable for contribution to satisfy the elective share. The action for contribution may be maintained against fewer than all persons against whom relief could be sought, but no person is subject to contribution in any greater amount than the person would have been if relief had been secured against all persons subject to contribution. (§31-4-102(d))
Texas		community property state—no quasi-community property	
Utah	Yes. First, amounts included in the augmented estate that pass or have passed by intestate or testate succession to the surviving spouse, other than the decedent's "separate property" (see next column); then decedent's nonprobate transfers to the spouse; then the surviving spouse's property and nonprobate transfers to others; then the value of the decedent's "separate property" that passes to the surviving spouse; then the surviving spouse's homestead allowance, exempt property, and family allowance. (§75-2-209(1))	"Separate property," such as premarital property owned by one of the spouses, property subject to a presently exercisable power of appointment not created by either spouse and which is exempt from creditors, gifts or inheritance from a third party, certain personal injury property, property "acquired in exchange for or with the proceeds of other separate property," and separate property created by waiver, as well as appreciation or income thereon during marriage, are not taken into account in determining the augmented estate. (§75-2-208(1)-(4)) Commuted value is to be used for present and future interests, and amounts payable under a life insurance settlement option, annuity contract, pensions, disability compensation, or similar arrangement. The calculation method is not specified, exclusive of federal Social Security. If there is an overlap under various provisions, only one of the values is relied upon, but it is the highest one. (§75-2-208(7)(b)&(8))	After taking account of values in the first column, liability is equitably apportioned among recipients of the amounts transferred by decedent's probate estate and by decedent's nonprobate transfers to others. If the elective share is still not fully satisfied, the remaining portion of the decedent's nonprobate transfers to others is applied so that the liability is equitably apportioned among recipients of decedent's nonprobate transfers. (§75-2-209(2)&(3))
Vermont	No provision.	No provision.	No provision.
Virginia	The value of property included in the augmented estate that passes or has passed to the surviving spouse, or that would have passed to the spouse but was disclaimed, is first applied to satisfy the elective share. (§64.2-306(a))	"Property" included in the augmented estate is valued as of the decedent's death, except that property transferred irrevocably during the lifetime of the decedent is valued as of the date the transferee came into possession or enjoyment if that event occurs first. Life estates and remainder interests are valued according to §55-269.1 et seq., and deferred payments and estates for years are discounted to present value using the interest rate specified in §55-269.1. (§64.2-305) The valuation of certain other property interests is outlined in §64.2-305(c)(3).	After taking into account the values in the first column, the recipients of the remaining property are liable to contribute the balance of the elective share and any interest thereon in proportion to the value of their interests. (§64.2-306(b))
Washington		Community Property state—no quasi-community property	

Table 6.03, Part 3
Calculation of Elective Share

	Are Amounts That Pass to the Surviving Spouse or Owned by the Surviving Spouse Used to Satisfy the Elective Share?	Are These Interests Valued in a Special Way, e.g., Life Income Interest at One-Half Value of Trust Property in Which the Surviving Spouse has an Interest?	How is the Burden of the Elective Share Apportioned Among Estate and/ or Nonprobate Beneficiaries?
West Virginia	First, amounts which pass or have passed to the surviving spouse by testate or intestate succession, as well as amounts otherwise included in the augmented estate and passing to the surviving spouse; then amounts included in the augmented estate, but which were disclaimed by the surviving spouse; then property included in the augmented estate which was owned by the surviving spouse and property that passed to the surviving spouse from the decedent, with certain exceptions, and certain nonprobate transfers to others by the surviving spouse that would have been included in the spouse's augmented estate if the spouse had died, but not more than the "applicable percentage, which is twice the elective share percentage." (§ 42-3-6(a))	Commuted value is used with regard to any present/ future interest, trust, and amounts payable under a life insurance settlement option, annuity, pension, retirement plan, death benefit, or similar arrangement, exclusive of federal Social Security. The statute does not specify how to determine commuted value or what value to use if different provisions apply but dictate different values. (§ 42-3-2(a)(1)(vi))	After taking account of values in the first column, liability is equitably apportioned among recipients of the amounts transferred by decedent's probate estate and by decedent's reclaimable estate to others except for property irrevocably transferred within two years before death. If the elective share is still not fully satisfied, the remaining portion of the decedent's eligible reclaimable estate to others is applied so that the liability is equitably apportioned among recipients of decedent's reclaimable estate. (§ 42-3-6(b)&(c))
Wisconsin	*Community Property state—quasi-community property known as deferred marital property estate is available to the surviving spouse*		
Wyoming	No provision.	No provision.	Court discretion. (§ 2-5-105(c))

[1] Community property state with quasi-community property.
[2] Georgia Year's Support—No elective share, however, the year's support is like the elective share because if the decedent makes a provision in lieu of year's support in the will, then the spouse may elect to take the year's support rather than the provision under the will. (§ 53-3-3)
[3] Community property state with quasi-community property.
[4] These answers assume that the decedent died after September 1, 1992.

Table 6.04
Waiver of Spousal Rights, Including Antenuptial Agreements

	Can Rights of Surviving Spouse Be Waived:			Special Conditions of Any Waiver		
	Before Marriage?	During Marriage?	Writing	Express Reference to Rights	Full Disclosure of Financial Status	Partial Waiver Allowed
Alabama	Yes. (§ 43-8-72)	Yes. (§ 43-8-72)	Yes. (§ 43-8-72)	Waiver of "all rights" or a property settlement (divorce) will constitute such a waiver. (§ 43-8-72)	Only requires "fair" disclosure. (§ 43-8-72)	Yes. (§ 43-8-72)
Alaska	Yes. (§ 13.12.213(a))	Yes. (§ 13.12.213(a))	Yes—written contract, agreement, waiver signed by surviving spouse. (§ 13.12.213(a))	Waiver of "all rights" or property settlement (divorce) will suffice. (§ 13.12.213(d))	A fair and reasonable disclosure of the property or financial obligations of the decedent is necessary, unless the person voluntarily and expressly waived, in writing, any right to disclosure of the property or financial obligations of the decedent beyond the disclosure provided. Also if the person had, or reasonably could have had, an adequate knowledge of the property or financial obligations of the decedent, no disclosure is necessary. (§ 13.12.213(b)(2))	Yes. (§ 13.12.213(a))
Arizona	Community Property—no quasi-community property. Note, prenuptial agreements are enforced with respect to divorce.					
Arkansas	Yes.[1] (§ 9-11-402)	No provision.	Yes.[2] (§ 9-11-402)	No provision.	Yes.[3] A fair and reasonable disclosure of the property or financial obligations of the decedent is necessary, unless the person voluntarily and expressly waived, in writing, any right to disclosure of the property or financial obligations of the decedent beyond the disclosure provided. Also if the person had, or reasonably could have had, an adequate knowledge of the property or financial obligations of the decedent, no disclosure is necessary. (§ 9-11-406)	Yes.[4] (§ 9-11-403)

Table 6.04
Waiver of Spousal Rights, Including Antenuptial Agreements

	Can Rights of Surviving Spouse Be Waived:		Writing	Special Conditions of Any Waiver		
	Before Marriage?	During Marriage?		Express Reference to Rights	Full Disclosure of Financial Status	Partial Waiver Allowed
California[5]	Yes. (Prob. §§ 140, 141(a)(7))	Yes. (Prob. §§ 140, 141(a)(7))	Yes. (Prob. § 142(a))	Is advisable (Prob. §§ 144, 145) but not necessary (Prob. § 143).	Fair and reasonable disclosure or a waiver of such disclosure, or knowledge of such statutes. (Prob. §§ 143, 144)	Yes. (Prob. § 141)
Colorado	Yes, if right is waived in a premarital or marital agreement defined in § 14-2-302 (§ 15-11-213(1)) or before July 1, 2014 under prior law. (§ 15-11-213(2))	Yes. (§ 15-11-207(1))	Yes. (§ 15-11-213(1))	Yes. (§§ 15-11-213(1), 14-2-309(3))	Must have adequate disclosure through a reasonably accurate description and good-faith estimate of value of the property, liabilities, and income or has adequate knowledge or a reasonable basis for having adequate knowledge of such information. (§ 14-2-309(4))	Yes. (§ 15-11-207(1))
Connecticut	Yes. (§ 46b-36d)	Yes, if provision is made in the agreement for the spouse. (§ 45a-436(f)) Also, a postnuptial agreement may be approved if "fair and equitable" in accordance with § 46b-66 and in compliance with its other terms. See Oliver v. Oliver, 1999 Conn. Super. Lexis 457, *10-11 (Feb. 17, 1999).	Yes. (§§ 45a-436(f), 46b-36c)	References to spousal support, as well as "[a]ny other matter, including . . . personal rights and obligations." (§ 46b-36d) It must not be unconscionable and the person must be afforded a reasonable opportunity to consult with independent counsel. (§ 46b-36g(a)(2)&(4))	Fair and reasonable disclosure required. (§ 46b-36g(a)(3))	Yes. (§ 46b-36d)
Delaware	Yes. (12 § 905)	Yes. (12 § 905)	Yes, "written contract, agreement, or waiver signed by the party waiving." (12 § 905)	Not required, but recommended. A reference to "all rights" or to "property settlement" in the event of divorce will suffice. The waiver cannot be unconscionable. (12 § 905, 13 § 326)	Fair and reasonable disclosure required. (13 § 326)	Yes. (12 § 905)
District of Columbia	Yes. (§ 19-113(f))	Yes. (§ 19-113(f))	Valid agreement. (§ 19-113(f))	No provision.	Yes. See Burtoff v. Burtoff, 418 A.2d 1085, 1089 (D.C. 1980).	No provision, but implied. (§ 19-113(f))
Florida	Yes. (§ 732.702(1))	Yes. (§ 732.702(1))	Yes, written contract, agreement, or waiver signed by the waiving party in the presence of two subscribing witnesses. (§ 732.702(1))	Waiver of "all rights" or equivalent language. (§ 732.702(1))	Before marriage—no disclosure. After marriage—fair disclosure. (§ 732.702(2))	Yes. (§ 732.702(1))

Table 6.04
Waiver of Spousal Rights, Including Antenuptial Agreements

	Can Rights of Surviving Spouse Be Waived:		Special Conditions of Any Waiver:			
	Before Marriage?	During Marriage?	Writing	Express Reference to Rights	Full Disclosure of Financial Status	Partial Waiver Allowed
Georgia[6]	Yes. (§ 19-3-63)	Yes, but not statutory authority. See, e.g., Sanders v. Colwell, 283 S.E.2d 461, 462 (Ga. 1981): "Agreements in contemplation of divorce settling issues of . . . property division . . . are not invalid."	Required, and the writing must be attested by two witnesses. (§ 19-3-63)	No technical expression required. Construed liberally to carry out intent of parties. (§ 19-3-63)	No provision.	No provision.
Hawaii	Yes. (§ 560:2-213(a))	Yes. (§ 560:2-213(a))	Yes, "written contract, agreement, or waiver signed by the surviving spouse or reciprocal beneficiary." (§ 560:2-213(a))	An express reference to rights is not necessary; a waiver of "all rights" is sufficient to imply a waiver of all rights of elective share, homestead allowance, exempt property, and family allowances. (§ 560:2-213(d))	A fair and reasonable disclosure of the property or financial obligations of the decedent is necessary, unless the person voluntarily and expressly waived, in writing, any right to disclosure of the property or financial obligations of the decedent beyond the disclosure provided. Also if the person had, or reasonably could have had, an adequate knowledge of the property or financial obligations of the decedent, no disclosure is necessary. (§ 560: 2-213(b)(2)(A)-(C))	Yes. (§ 560:2-213(a))
Idaho[7]	Yes. (§ 15-2-208)	Yes. (§ 15-2-208)	Yes, "written contract, agreement, or waiver signed by the party waiving." (§ 15-2-208)	A waiver of "all rights" (or equivalent language) is sufficient to waive the right of election. (§ 15-2-208)	Only fair disclosure is required. (§ 15-2-208)	Yes. (§ 15-2-208)

Table 6.04
Waiver of Spousal Rights, Including Antenuptial Agreements

	Can Rights of Surviving Spouse Be Waived:		Special Conditions of Any Waiver			Partial Waiver Allowed
	Before Marriage?	During Marriage?	Writing	Express Reference to Rights	Full Disclosure of Financial Status	
Illinois	Yes. (750 ILCS §10/4)	Yes. (In re Estate of Brosseau, 531 N.E.2d 158, 161 (App. Ct. 1988))	Must be in writing and signed by both parties. (750 ILCS §10/3)	Express reference to rights is necessary; however, exact language such as "surviving spouse's award" is not necessary. (In re Estate of Brosseau, 531 N.E.2d 158, 161 (App. Ct. 1988))	A fair and reasonable disclosure of the property or financial obligations of the decedent is necessary, unless, the person voluntarily and expressly waived, in writing, any right to disclosure of the property or financial obligation of the decedent beyond the disclosure provided. Also if the person had, or reasonably could have had, an adequate knowledge of the property or financial obligations of the decedent, no disclosure is necessary. (750 ILCS §10/7(a)(2)(i)-(iii))	No specific provision. Implied. (750 ILCS §10/4(a))
Indiana	Yes. (§§ 29-1-2-13, 29-1-3-6) See also §31-11-3-8.	Yes. (§§ 29-1-2-13, 29-1-3-6)	Written contract, agreement, or waiver is necessary and must be signed by party waiving. (§§ 29-1-2-13, 29-1-3-6(a)) See also §31-11-3-4 (prenuptial agreement)	Even if the waiver includes a clause referring to the specific statutory provision entitling the spouse to elect to take against the will, the spouse still must be informed of the nature and extent of her statutory rights before signing the waiver. (Bohnke v. Estate of Bohnke, 454 N.E.2d 446, 449 (Ct. App. 1983); §§ 29-1-2-13, 29-1-3-6); Boetsma v. Boetsma, 768 N.E.2d 1016, 1022 (Ct. App. 2002) (distinguishing Bohnke on the grounds that the waiver was more precise in terms of rights being waived, and the spouse contacted an attorney who fully explained the agreement to her); See also §31-11-3-8 (prenuptial agreement).	Full disclosure of the nature and extent of the right is required. (§§ 29-1-2-13, 29-1-3-6) The agreement must also not be unconscionable when it was executed. (§31-11-3-8(a)(2)) (prenuptial agreement).	No provision.

Table 6.04
Waiver of Spousal Rights, Including Antenuptial Agreements

	Can Rights of Surviving Spouse Be Waived:			Special Conditions of Any Waiver		
	Before Marriage?	During Marriage?	Writing	Express Reference to Rights	Full Disclosure of Financial Status	Partial Waiver Allowed
Iowa	Yes. (§596.5)	No provision.	A premarital agreement must be in writing and signed by both prospective spouses. (§596.4)	No provision, but contract cannot be unconscionable. (§596.8) Mentions ability to contract with regard to "[t]he disposition of property upon . . .death" and other "personal rights and obligations" of the parties. (§596.5)	The spouse must be provided a fair and reasonable disclosure of the property or financial obligations of the other spouse, unless the spouse has, or could reasonably have, an adequate knowledge of the property or financial obligations of the other spouse. (§596.8(1)(c))	No provision.
Kansas	Yes. (§59-6a213(a))	Yes. (§59-6a213(a))	Yes, written contract, agreement, consent to any instrument, or waiver signed by the surviving spouse. (§59-6a213(a))	An express reference to rights is not necessary; a waiver of "all rights" is sufficient to imply a waiver of all rights of elective share. (§59-6a213(d)) However, the waiver cannot be unconscionable. (§59-6a213(b)(2)) On or after July 1, 2002, the homestead, the homestead allowance, the family allowance, or all of them must be referred to in the document as having been waived by the spouse understandably and knowledgeably. (§59-6a213(d))	A fair and reasonable disclosure of the property or financial obligations of the decedent is necessary, unless, the person voluntarily and expressly waived, in writing, any right to disclosure of the property or financial obligation of the decedent beyond the disclosure provided. Also if the person had, or reasonably could have had, an adequate knowledge of the property or financial obligations of the decedent, no disclosure is necessary. (§59-6a213(b)(2)(A)–(C))	Yes. (§59-6a213(a))
Kentucky	Yes. (Gaines v. Gaines' Adm'r, 173 S.W.2d 774, 777 (Ky. Ct. App.1915); §392.020)	Yes. (Campbell v. Campbell, 377 S.W.2d 93, 94 (Ky. Ct. App. 1964); §392.020)	No specific authority.	No specific authority.	A full disclosure of financial condition is necessary. (See generally Lawson v. Loid, 896 S.W.2d 1, 7 (Ky. 1995))	No provision.
Louisiana	*Community property state—no quasi-community property*					
Maine	Yes. (18-A §2-204)	Yes. (18-A §2-204)	Yes, "written contract, agreement, or waiver signed by the party waiving." (18-A §2-204)	"All rights" or equivalent language is sufficient. (18-A §2-204)	"Fair disclosure." (18-A §2-204)	Yes. (18-A §2-204)

Table 6.04
Waiver of Spousal Rights, Including Antenuptial Agreements

| | Can Rights of Surviving Spouse Be Waived: | | Writing | Special Conditions of Any Waiver | | |
	Before Marriage?	During Marriage?		Express Reference to Rights	Full Disclosure of Financial Status	Partial Waiver Allowed
Maryland	Yes. (Est. & Trusts §3-205)	Yes. (Est. & Trusts §3-205)	Yes, written contract, agreement, or waiver signed by the party waiving election. (Est. & Trusts §3-205)	"All rights" is sufficient as is the parties entering into a "complete property settlement." (Est. & Trusts §3-205)	Yes. See, e.g., Hartz v. Hartz, 234 A.2d 865, 870-71 (Md. 1967) (requiring "frank, full and truthful disclosure of worth of property, real and personal, as to which there is wavier of rights in whole or in part") Unconscionability, determined at the time the agreement is entered into, nevertheless, can invalidate it. (Martin v. Farber, 510 A.2d 608, 610, 611 (Ct. Spec. App. 1986))	Yes, it is implied. (Est. & Trusts §3-205)
Massachusetts	Yes. (209 §25)	Uncertain. The Massachusetts Supreme Judicial Court expressly put off deciding the issue. See Fogg v. Fogg, 567 N.E.2d 921, 922 n. 2 (Mass. 1991).	Yes, written contract (209 §25)	Schedule of affected property is required and must be recorded if protection desired against creditors, but the contract will still be valid as between the parties. (209 §26)	"Fair disclosure" is required. See Osborne v. Osborne, 428 N.E.2d 810, 816 (Mass. 1981), citing to the rules in Rosenberg v. Lipnick, 389 N.E.2d 385 (Mass. 1979).	Yes. (209 §25) The statute refers to "any designated part of the real or personal property . . ."
Michigan	Yes. (§700.2205)	Yes. (§700.2205)	Yes, by a "written contract, agreement or waiver signed by the party waiving." (§700.2205)	"All rights" is sufficient to waive every thing. (§700.2205)	"Fair disclosure" is required. (§700.2205)	Yes. (§700.2205)
Minnesota	Spouse may waive right to election prior to marriage, but waiver must be made pursuant to §519.11. (§524.2-213)	Yes. (§§519.11(1)(a), 524.2-213)	Writing executed in the presence of two witnesses and acknowledged by the parties. (§519.11(2)) After marriage "by a written contract, agreement or waiver signed by the party waiving." (§524.2-213)	A waiver of "all rights" is only a waiver of the right to elective share. (§524.2-213)	"Full and fair disclosure." (§519.11(1)) But see §524.2-213: "fair disclosure."	Yes. (§524.2-213)
Mississippi	Yes; agreement is enforceable like any other contract. See Smith v. Smith, 656 So. 2d 1143, 1147 (Miss. 1995).	Yes; agreement is enforceable like any other contract. See Roberts v. Roberts, 381 So. 2d 1333, 1335 (Miss. 1980).	Yes, to the extent required by the statute of frauds. (§15-3-1)	No provision.	Yes. See Smith v. Smith, 656 So. 2d 1143, 1147 (Miss. 1995).	No provision.

Table 6.04
Waiver of Spousal Rights, Including Antenuptial Agreements

| | Can Rights of Surviving Spouse Be Waived: | | Special Conditions of Any Waiver | | | |
	Before Marriage?	During Marriage?	Writing	Express Reference to Rights	Full Disclosure of Financial Status	Partial Waiver Allowed
Missouri	Yes. (§ 474.220)	Yes. (§ 474.220)	Yes, written contract, agreement, or waiver signed by the waiving party. (§ 474.220) See also § 451.220.	No provision.	Full disclosure of nature and extent of right with fair consideration. (§ 474.220) Nevertheless, the agreement can be invalidated on the grounds of unconscionability, but not certain whether only at signing or at time of enforcement. (Darr v. Darr, 950 S.W.2d 867, 871 (Ct. App. 1997))	No provision.
Montana	Yes. (§ 72-2-224(1))	Yes. (§ 72-2-224(1))	Yes, written contract, agreement, or waiver, signed by the surviving spouse (§ 72-2-224(1))	A waiver of "all rights" or equivalent language waives elective share, homestead, exempt property, family allowance, and rights by testate or intestate succession. (§ 72-2-224(4))	A fair and reasonable disclosure of the property or financial obligations of the decedent is necessary, unless the person voluntarily and expressly waived, in writing, any right to disclosure of the property or financial obligations of the decedent beyond the disclosure provided. Also if the person had, or reasonably could have had, an adequate knowledge of the property or financial obligations of the decedent, no fair and reasonable disclosure is necessary. (§ 72-2-224(2)(b)(i)-(iii)) The waiver must not be unconscionable at the time of execution. (Id.)	Yes. (§ 72-2-224(1))

Table 6.04
Waiver of Spousal Rights, Including Antenuptial Agreements

| | Can Rights of Surviving Spouse Be Waived: | | Writing | Special Conditions of Any Waiver | | Partial Waiver Allowed |
	Before Marriage?	During Marriage?		Express Reference to Rights	Full Disclosure of Financial Status	
Nebraska	Yes. (§ 30-2316(a))	Yes. (§ 30-2316(a))	Yes, "written contract, agreement, or waiver signed by the surviving spouse." (§ 30-2316(a))	A waiver of "all rights" or equivalent language waives elective share, homestead, exempt property, family allowance, and rights by testate or intestate succession. (§ 30-2316(d))	A fair and reasonable disclosure of the property or financial obligations of the decedent is necessary, unless the person voluntarily and expressly waived, in writing, any right to disclosure of the property or financial obligations of the decedent beyond the disclosure provided. Also if the person had, or reasonably could have had, an adequate knowledge of the property or financial obligations of the decedent, no disclosure is necessary. However, the waiver cannot be unconscionable when executed. (§ 30-2316(b)(2)(i)-(iii))	Yes. (§ 30-2316(a))
Nevada	Yes. (§ 123A.050)	Unsettled. See Cord v. Neuhoff, 573 P.2d 1170, 1172 (Nev. 1978) (since the postnuptial agreement was viewed as integrated, an invalid limitation in it as to one spouse's support obligation had the result of invalidating the entire agreement).	Yes. "A premarital agreement must be in writing and signed by both parties." (§ 123A.040)	No provision.	Yes. Where spouse has not voluntarily and expressly waived, in writing, any right to disclosure of the property or financial obligations of the other party beyond the disclosure provided and did not have, or reasonably could not have had, an adequate knowledge of the property or financial obligations of the other party, fair and reasonable disclosure of the property or financial obligations of the other party is necessary (§ 123A.080(1)) See also Matley v. Matley, 701 P.2d 749, 750-51 (Nev. 1985).	Yes. See Jensen v. Jensen, 753 P.2d 342 (Nev. 1988) (relating to modification of existing agreement).

Table 6.04
Waiver of Spousal Rights, Including Antenuptial Agreements

	Can Rights of Surviving Spouse Be Waived:		Special Conditions of Any Waiver:			
	Before Marriage?	During Marriage?	Writing	Express Reference to Rights	Full Disclosure of Financial Status	Partial Waiver Allowed
New Hampshire	Yes. (§ 460:2-a)[8]	No provision.	Yes. (§ 460:2-a)	No provision.	Yes. See In re Yannalfo, 794 A.2d 795 (N.H. 2002) (dictum). The agreement can be invalidated on the ground of unconscionability at the time of execution or enforcement. (Id. See also MacFarlane v. Rich, 567 A.2d 585, 616 (N.H. 1989))	Yes. Since may "be in lieu of homestead right, distributive share, or either of them . . ." (§ 560:15)
New Jersey	Yes. (§ 3B:8-10)	Yes. (§ 3B:8-10)	Yes. "Written contract, agreement, or waiver signed by the party waiving." (§ 3B:8-10)	No, unless it provides to the contrary, a waiver of "all rights" (or equivalent language) waives everything. (§ 3B:8-10)	"Fair disclosure." (§ 3B:8-10)	Yes. (§ 3B:8-10)
New Mexico	Yes. (§ 45-2-407), but limited to family allowance and personal allowance. Other rights can be waived by contract. See also Lebeck, 881 P.2d 727 (N.M. Ct. App. 1994).	Yes. (§ 45-2-407) Generally, Christiansen v. Christiansen, 666 P.2d 781 (N.M. 1983).	Yes. "Written contract, agreement or waiver signed by the surviving spouse." (§§ 45-2-407, 40-2-4)	Unless it provides to the contrary, a waiver of "all rights" or equivalent language... is a waiver of all rights of family allowance and personal property allowance by each spouse in the property of the other and a renunciation by each of all benefits that would otherwise pass to each from the other by intestate succession or by virtue of any will. (§ 45-2-407)	A fair and reasonable disclosure of the property or financial obligations of the decedent is necessary, unless the person voluntarily and expressly waived, in writing, any right to disclosure of the property or financial obligations of the decedent beyond the disclosure provided. Also if the person had, or reasonably could have had, an adequate knowledge of the property or financial obligations of the decedent, no disclosure is necessary. (§ 45-2-407(B)(2))	Yes. (§ 45-2-407) See also Lebeck v. Lebeck, 881 P.2d 727, 734 (Ct. App. 1994).
New York[9]	Yes. (Est. Powers &Trusts § 5-1.1-A(e)(3)(A) (waiver of right of election); Gen. Oblig. L. § 3-303 (antenuptial agreement))	Yes. (Est. Powers &Trusts § 5-1.1-A(e)(3)(A)) A postnuptial agreement is valid under case law, and not statute. See, e.g., Kosovsky v. Zahl, 684 N.Y.S.2d 524 (App. Div. 1999)	Yes. (Est. Powers & Trusts § 5-1.1-A(e)(2) (waiver of elective share rights)) See, e.g., Dygert v. Remerschnider, 32 N.Y. 629, 630 (N.Y. 1865) (antenuptial agreement).	No. (Est. Powers & Trusts § 5-1.1-A(e)(1)) However, In re Greif, 680 N.Y.S.2d 894, 897 (N.Y. 1998), holds that if the surviving spouse shows "a fact-based particularized inequality" between the parties, then the burden of going forward shifts to the proponent of the antenuptial agreement.	No, if in the form of antenuptial agreement and regardless of fairness and reasonableness. The signatories were not in a confidential relationship when they entered into the agreement (Eckstein v. Eckstein, 514 N.Y.S.2d 47, 48-49 (App. Div. 1987))	Yes. (Est. Powers & Trusts § 5-1.1-A(e)(1)); no specific provision as to marital agreement.

Table 6.04
Waiver of Spousal Rights, Including Antenuptial Agreements

	Can Rights of Surviving Spouse Be Waived:		Special Conditions of Any Waiver			
	Before Marriage?	During Marriage?	Writing	Express Reference to Rights	Full Disclosure of Financial Status	Partial Waiver Allowed
North Carolina	Yes. (§52-10(a))	Yes. (§52-10(a))	"A premarital agreement must be in writing and signed by both parties." (§52B-3) As to other waivers, the same requirements as for any other contract. See, e.g., Loftin v. Loftin, 208 S.E.2d 670, 672 (N.C. 1974). Under §52-10(a) the contract or release must be in writing if entered into during coverture and affecting real estate of either spouse or the income there of for more than three years next ensuring the making of the contract or release. (§52-10(a))	No. (In re Estate of Tucci, 380 S.E.2d 782, 785 (Ct. App. 1989), cert. denied as to additional issues, 384 S.E.2d 514 (1989), aff'd, 388 S.E.2d 768 (1990))	A fair and reasonable disclosure of the property or financial obligations of the decedent is necessary, unless the person voluntarily and expressly waived, in writing, any right to disclosure of the property or financial obligations of the decedent beyond the disclosure provided. Also if the person had, or reasonably could have had, an adequate knowledge of the property or financial obligations of the decedent, no disclosure is necessary. (§52B-7) (for antenuptial agreements)	No provision.
North Dakota	Yes. (§14-03.2-06)	Yes. (§14-03.2-06)	"Written contract must be in a record and signed by both parties." (§14-03.2-05)	The agreement must have a "conspicuously displayed" reference to the particular rights being waived, unless the waiving party had adequate legal representation. (§14-03.2-08)	An agreement is unenforceable if consent was involuntary or obtained through duress; the party did not have "access to independent legal representation"; the agreement does not follow the form outlined in the prior column; or there was not "adequate financial disclosure." (§14.032-08). The waiver may not be enforced if it is unconscionable or if enforcement would result in substantial hardship . . . because of a material change in circumstances." (Id.)	No provision.
Ohio	Yes. (Hook v. Hook, 431 N.E.2d 667, 668-69 (Ohio 1982); §2106.01)	Yes. (Carnahan v. Carnahan, 159 N.E.2d 795 (Ohio Ct. App. 1959) (contract after decedent's death made with other beneficiaries); §2106.01)	No provision.	Yes. (In re Estate of Mowery, No. 10813, 1982 WL 5164 (Ohio Ct. App. 1982); §2106.01)	Full disclosure or full knowledge of effects. (Hook v. Hook, 431 N.E.2d 667, 670 (Ohio, 1982); §2106.01)	Seemingly so under In re Estate of Mowery, No. 10813, 1982 WL 5164 (Ohio Ct. App. 1982)

Table 6.04
Waiver of Spousal Rights, Including Antenuptial Agreements

| | Can Rights of Surviving Spouse Be Waived: | | | Special Conditions of Any Waiver | | |
	Before Marriage?	During Marriage?	Writing	Express Reference to Rights	Full Disclosure of Financial Status	Partial Waiver Allowed
Oklahoma	Yes. Washington and Lee Univ. v. Dist. Ct. of Okla. Cnty., 492 P. 2d 320, 321 (Okla. 1971); 84 § 44(B)(1))	No. A post-nuptial agreement of husband and wife waiving the right of survivor to take the other's estate under law of intestate succession, is not authorized by statute and is invalid and unenforceable. (Atkinson v. Barr, 428 P.2d 316, 320-21 (Okla. 1967); 84 §44)	Yes. (84 § 44(B)(1))	No provision.	Full and fair disclosure required. (In re Cobb's Estate, 305 P.2d 1028, 1032 (Okla. 1956)	No provision.
Oregon	Yes. (§ 114.620(1))	Yes. (§ 114.620(1))	Yes, written contract agreement or waiver signed by the surviving spouse. (§ 114.620(1))	A waiver of "all rights" waives all rights to an elective share and a renunciation of all benefits by intestacy, or under a will. (§ 114.620(2))	A fair and reasonable disclosure of the property or financial obligations of the decedent is necessary, unless the person voluntarily and expressly waived, in writing, any right to disclosure of the property or financial obligations of the decedent beyond the disclosure provided. Also if the person had, or reasonably could have had, an adequate knowledge of the property or financial obligations of the decedent, no disclosure is necessary. (§ 108.725(1)) (with respect to prenuptial agreement); (Day v. Vitus, 792 P.2d 1240, 1242 (Or. Ct. App. 1990) (postnuptial agreement))	Yes. (§ 114.620(1))
Pennsylvania	Yes (20 § 2207 (waiver of right of election)); antenuptial agreements are valid under common-law contracts. See, e.g., Simeone v. Simeone, 581 A.2d 162, 165 (Pa. 1990).	Yes, as to a waiver (20 § 2207); a postnuptial marital agreement is valid. See, e.g., Stoner v. Stoner, 819 A.2d 529, 533 n.5 (Pa. 2003)	As required by contract law. (Stoner v. Stoner, 819 A.2d 529, 533 (Sup. Ct. 2003); Simeone v. Simeone, 581 A.2d 162, 165-66 (Pa. 1990))	No provision.	"Full and fair disclosure" for antenuptial and postnuptial agreements. (Simeone v. Simeone, 581 A.2d 162, 166-67 (Pa.1990); Stoner v. Stoner, 819 A.2d 529, 533 (Pa. 2003) only refers to "full disclosure")	Yes, for waiver. (20 § 2207) No apparent obstacle with regard to marital agreement.

Table 6.04
Waiver of Spousal Rights, Including Antenuptial Agreements

	Can Rights of Surviving Spouse Be Waived:		Special Conditions of Any Waiver			
	Before Marriage?	During Marriage?	Writing	Express Reference to Rights	Full Disclosure of Financial Status	Partial Waiver Allowed
Rhode Island	Yes. (§15-17-1 et seq.)	No substantial statutory or case law.	Yes, in writing and signed by both parties (§15-17-2(1))	Yes. (Carr v. Carr, 1993 WL 853807, at *5-6 (R. I. Super. Ct. Apr. 22, 1993)	A fair and reasonable disclosure of the property or financial obligations of the decedent is necessary, unless the person voluntarily and expressly waived, in writing, any right to disclosure of the property or financial obligations of the decedent beyond the disclosure provided. Also if the person had, or reasonably could have had, an adequate knowledge of the property or financial obligations of the decedent, no disclosure is necessary. (§15-17-6(a)(2)(i)-(iii))	Yes. A waiver is allowed with regard to "any of the property of either or both" spouses. (§15-17-3(a))
South Carolina	Yes. (§62-2-204)	Yes. (§62-2-204)	Yes, written contract, agreement, or waiver, signed by the party waiving. (§62-2-204)	A waiver of all rights waives everything. (§62-2-204)	Fair and reasonable disclosures to the waiving party of the other party's property and financial obligations [must be] given in writing. (§62-2-204(A))	Yes. (§62-2-204)
South Dakota	Yes. (§29A-2-213(a))	Yes. (§29A-2-213(a))	Yes, written contract, agreement, or waiver signed by the surviving spouse. (§29A-2-213(a))	A waiver of "all rights" waives everything. (§29A-2-213(d))	A fair and reasonable disclosure of the property or financial obligations of the decedent is necessary, unless the person voluntarily and expressly waived, in writing, any right to disclosure of the property or financial obligations of the decedent beyond the disclosure provided. Also if the person had, or reasonably could have had, an adequate knowledge of the property or financial obligations of the decedent, no disclosure is necessary. (§29A-2-213(b)(2)(i)-(iii))	Yes. (§29A-2-213(a))
Tennessee	Yes. (§36-3-501)	Yes. (Bratton v. Bratton, 136 S.W.3d 595, 600 (Tenn. 2004))	No provision.	No provision.	Inferred. (§31-4-103)	Allowed. (In re Estate of Gray, 729 S.W.2d 668 (Tenn. Ct. App. 1987))

Table 6.04
Waiver of Spousal Rights, Including Antenuptial Agreements

	Can Rights of Surviving Spouse Be Waived: Before Marriage?	During Marriage?	Writing	Special Conditions of Any Waiver: Express Reference to Rights	Full Disclosure of Financial Status	Partial Waiver Allowed
Texas	Yes. (Fam. Code §4.002)	Yes. See Marsh v. Marsh, 949 S.W.2d 734, 739 n.4 (Tex. Ct. App. 1997), but not by statute and higher standard than antenuptial agreement due to fiduciary duty of spouses. See also Fam. Code §4.102 as to partition and exchange of community property.	Yes, in writing and if signed by both parties. (Fam. Code §4.002)	No provision.	Yes. See, e.g., Williams v. Williams, 569 S.W.2d 867, 870 (Tex. 1978), superseded by constitutional amendment on other grounds, Beck v. Beck, 814 S.W.2d 745 (Tex. 1991) (full disclosure of the nature and extent of the property interest involved)	Yes. (Fam. Code §4.003)
Utah	Yes. (§75-2-213(1))	Yes. (§75-2-213(1))	Yes, written contract, agreement, or waiver signed by the surviving spouse. (§75-2-213(1))	A waiver of "all rights" or equivalent language waives everything. (§75-2-213(4))	A fair and reasonable disclosure of the property or financial obligations of the decedent is necessary, unless the person voluntarily and expressly waived, in writing, any right to disclosure of the property or financial obligations of the decedent beyond the disclosure provided. Also if the person had, or reasonably could have had, an adequate knowledge of the property or financial obligations of the decedent, no disclosure is necessary. (§75-2-213(2)(b)(i)-(iii))	Yes. (§75-2-213(1))
Vermont	Yes. (Bassler v. Bassler, 593 A.2d 82, 87 (Vt. 1991))	Yes. (Bassler v. Bassler, 593 A.2d 82 (Vt. 1991) (general holding based on contracts though no express approval of postnuptial agreements))	Yes, but part performance can remove a contract from the Statute of Frauds. (Bassler v. Bassler, 593 A.2d 82, 86 (Vt. 1991))	Not required. (Bassler v. Bassler, 593 A.2d 82 (Vt. 1991))	Fair and reasonable disclosure. (Bassler v. Bassler, 593 A.2d 82, 87 (Vt. 1991)) The agreement must not be unconscionable. (Id.)	Yes. (Bassler v. Bassler, 593 A.2d 82, 84 (Vt. 1991))
Virginia	Yes. (§§20-149, 20-150)	Yes. (§20-155)	Required and must be signed by both parties. (§20-149)	No provision. (§20-151)	Fair and reasonable disclosure assuming no voluntary and express waiver in writing of the right to disclosure. (§20-151(A)(2)(i)-(ii))	Yes. (§20-150)

Table 6.04
Waiver of Spousal Rights, Including Antenuptial Agreements

	Can Rights of Surviving Spouse Be Waived:		Special Conditions of Any Waiver			
	Before Marriage?	During Marriage?	Writing	Express Reference to Rights	Full Disclosure of Financial Status	Partial Waiver Allowed
Washington	Yes, (1) if there was a full and frank disclosure of all the other spouse's property and its value and (2) the agreement was signed freely and voluntarily on competent independent advice with full knowledge of rights. See In re Estate of Crawford 730 P.2d 675, 678-79 (Wash. 1986) (en banc).	Yes, as to community property. (§ 26.16.120)	Yes, and signed by party to be charged therewith or a person authorized by that person to sign. (§§ 19.36.010(3) (separate property); 26.16.120 (community property)); status or disposition of spouses, which must be under their hands and seals, and witnessed, acknowledged, and certified in the same manner as deeds or real estate)	No provision.	Yes. "Full disclosure" is required. See In re Estate of Crawford, 730 P.2d 675, 678 (Wash. 1986) (en banc).	Yes. Cf. In re Marriage of Fox, 795 P.2d 1170 (Wash. Ct. App. 1990).
West Virginia	Yes. (§ 42-3-3a(a))	Yes. (§ 42-3-3a(a))	Yes, "written contract, agreement, or waiver signed by the surviving spouse." (§ 42-3-3a(a))	Waiver of "all rights" or equivalent language waives the elective share. (§ 42-3-3a(d))	A fair and reasonable disclosure of the property or financial obligations of the decedent is necessary, unless the person voluntarily and expressly waived, in writing, any right to disclosure of the property or financial obligations of the decedent beyond the disclosure provided. Also if the person had, or reasonably could have had, an adequate knowledge of the property or financial obligations of the decedent, no disclosure is necessary. (§ 42-3-3a(b)(2)(i)-(iii))	Yes. (§ 42-3-3a(a))

Table 6.04

Waiver of Spousal Rights, Including Antenuptial Agreements

	Can Rights of Surviving Spouse Be Waived:		Special Conditions of Any Waiver			
	Before Marriage?	During Marriage?	Writing	Express Reference to Rights	Full Disclosure of Financial Status	Partial Waiver Allowed
Wisconsin	Yes. (§767.61(3)(L))	Yes. (§767.61(3)(L)) Rules of antenuptial apply as well to postnuptial. See In re Beat's Estate, 130 N.W.2d 739, 742 n.4 (Wis. 1964).	Not always required. See, e.g., Bibelhausen v. Bibelhausen, 150 N.W. 516, 520-21 (Wis. 1915).	No provision. §767.61(3)(L) recognizes an agreement's effectiveness if it is in writing but does not specifically bar oral agreements.	Full disclosure or knowledge is required, and second marriages where the parties have independent wealth may affect the necessity of disclosure. See, e.g., In re Beat's Estate, 130 N.W.2d 739, 742-745 (Wis. 1964). More generally, however, "the widow, in asserting fraud, has the burden of proving it. In meeting this burden she may be aided by a presumption of fraud that arises in those instances where she is not adequately provided for by the terms of the agreement and where there has not been a full and fair disclosure to her of the husband's worth" (*Id.* at 742) (footnotes omitted).	Probably. The statute applies to "any arrangement for property distribution …" and this, presumably, does not require an arrangement for the distribution of *all* property. (§767.61(3)(L))
Wyoming	Yes. (§2-5-102)	Yes. (§2-5-102)	Yes, "written contract, agreement, or waiver signed by the party waiving." (§2-5-102)	A waiver of "all rights" waives everything. (§2-5-102)	Fair disclosure. (§28-11-403)	Yes. (§2-5-102)

[1] Taking land under will will waive dower or curtesy rights. (§28-11-404) Taking of other property that is expressly "in lieu of," will waive. (§28-11-403) If spouse joins decedent in conveying property, this will result in the waiving of dower rights with regard to that property. (§28-11-201(a)) Also rights and interests can be waived partially or wholly by antenuptial agreement in writing, with financial disclosure. (§§9-11-403, 9-11-406)

[2] Id.

[3] Id.

[4] Id.

[5] Community property state with quasi-community property.

[6] Georgia Year's Support—No elective share. However, the year's support is like the elective share in that if the decedent makes a provision in lieu of year's support in the will, then the spouse may elect to take the year's support rather than the provision under the will. (§53-3-3)

[7] Community property state with quasi-community property.

[8] §460:2-a authorizes the prenuptial; §560:15 relates to what rights can be waived; and §560:16 makes §560:15 applicable to waivers by husbands.

[9] These answers assume that the decedent died after Sept. 1, 1966 (§5-1.1-A(e)(3)(B)).

Table 7
Intestate Succession
(current through 5/1/17)

Although the expectation is that all wealth of an individual will be properly disposed of, the situation may arise with respect to at least a portion of the estate, in which this is not, in fact, the case. In such situation, the particular state's rules of intestate succession will control the disposition of the property. Furthermore, the majority of individuals actually die without a will or other dispositive instrument. A family member may seek an estate planner's advice as to whether he or she is entitled to a share of the deceased relative's estate.

Ordinarily, in the described situation, an attorney will be familiar with the parameters of the local law of descent and distribution. However, the estate at issue may also have real property situated in another state. Furthermore, the intestate may have died a domiciliary of another state, thus making its law pertinent to the disposition of all of the intestate's personal property. The analysis contained in this Table 7 details the intestacy laws of each of the states.

From an academic standpoint, this Table affords an up-to-date comparison of the way in which different states approach the topic of descent and distribution. Wide differences from state to state are readily apparent in terms of the share afforded a surviving spouse when there are no issue and also when there are issue, some of who are only the children or descendants of the surviving spouse or the intestate. Sharp distinctions in approach are also revealed on such matters as the precise order of succession with respect to collateral levels. Likewise, the cut-off of rights of inheritance due to remoteness is at the grandparent parentela in some states but in others is not so limited. Indeed, in certain states, escheat is avoided by granting rights to the heirs of a predeceasing spouse of the decedent.

One area of particular disagreement among the states relates to representation. When a person entitled to take is deceased, the descendants of such person may be entitled to take in his or her place. One issue that divides the states is the question when representation is available to the descendants at all. A second issue concerns what method should be employed in determining who should take. There are four principal approaches:

1. *Per capita at each generation.* The property subject to intestacy is divided into as many shares as there are descendants in the nearest degree living and deceased descendants in that degree who are survived by descendants. The living descendants take a single share. The shares of the deceased descendants are aggregated and the process is repeated at the next generation level, while treating those who have already received shares, along with their descendants, as being deceased and as if that line does not exist. This approach is repeated at each generation level, until all the property is distributed.

2. *Per capita with representation.* The first generation level at which there are descendants surviving is identified. The property subject to intestacy is divided into as many shares as there are living descendants at that generation level and deceased descendants leaving descendants of their own. The share of each deceased descendant is distributed within his or her line by following the same procedure at the next generation level and so on.

3. *Per stirpes.* The property subject to intestacy is divided into as many shares as there are children of the intestate or other relevant person who are either alive or are deceased but are survived by descendants. The division occurs at the child level even if *no* children survive the intestate or other relevant person. The share allocated to a child's line is subdivided among grandchildren taking by representation. If a grandchild is also deceased but survived by children of his or her own, then they take by representation the grandchild's share. This procedure is repeated down the generations until the entire share is apportioned.

4. *Per capita if of equal degree, otherwise per stirpes.* In certain states, a per stirpital approach is ordinarily applied. However, if all of the takers are of the same degree they are treated equally by

utilizing a per capita distributional scheme, notwithstanding that a per stirpital approach would have yielded a different outcome.

The foregoing approaches and their potentially different outcomes are revealed by the following example:

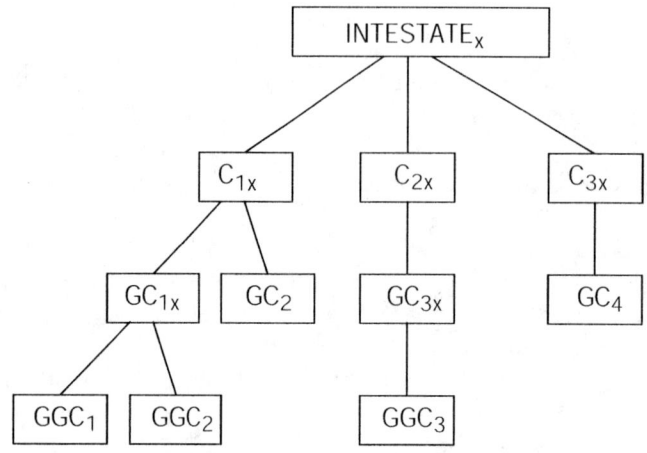

An x indicates that a person is deceased.

1. Per capita at each generation level: $GC_2 = 1/4$, $GC_4 = 1/4$, $GGC_1 = 1/6$, $GGC_2 = 1/6$, $GGC_3 = 1/6$

2. Per capita with representation: $GC_2 = 1/4$, $GC_4 = 1/4$, $GGC_1 = 1/8$, $GGC_2 = 1/8$, $GGC_3 = 1/4$

3. Per stirpes: $GC_2 = 1/6$, $GC_4 = 1/3$, $GGC_1 = 1/12$, $GGC_2 = 1/12$, $GGC_3 = 1/3$

4. Per capita if of equal degree, otherwise per stirpes. The result is the same as per stirpes, since the takers are not all of the same degree. If the example were changed so that GC_2 and GC_4 were also deceased and each were survived respectively by GGC_4 and GGC_5, then all of the GGCs would take $1/5$, even though a per stirpital distribution would result in GGC_1 and GGC_2 taking $1/12$, GGC_3 taking $1/3$, GGC_4 taking $1/6$, and GGC_5 taking $1/3$.

As the foregoing example indicates, a clear understanding of the divisional rules are of the utmost importance in determining what each heir takes. Care must also be exercised to assure that the descriptive words used in the statute, such as "per stirpes," really encompass the traditional meaning or are defined elsewhere in the law to mean a different divisional scheme, such as per capita if of equal degree, or even per capita with representation.

Alabama
Who Takes by Intestate Succession?

A. Surviving spouse takes:

1.	*If no surviving issue or parent*	100% (§ 43-8-41(1))
2.	*If no surviving issue, but parent or parents survive*	$100,000, plus ¹/₂ of balance of the interstate estate (§ 43-8-41(2))
3.	*If there are surviving issue all of whom are issue of the surviving spouse*	$50,000, plus ¹/₂ of balance of the interstate estate (§ 43-8-41(3))
4.	*If there are surviving issue, one of whom is not issue of the surviving spouse*[1]	¹/₂ of the intestate estate (§ 43-8-41(4))

B. All the estate, or the surplus if there is a surviving spouse, passes to:

1.	*Issue*	100% equally if of same degree of kinship, and otherwise by representation (§ 43-8-42(1))
2.	*Parent, or parents equally, if no issue*	100% (§ 43-8-42(2))
3.	*Issue of parents*	100%, by representation[2] (§ 43-8-42(3))
4.	*Grandparents, if no issue of parents*	50% to the paternal and 50% to the maternal side. The grandparents on either side share equally in the 50% share, and if only one, that grandparent takes the entire 50% share (§ 43-8-42(4))
5.	*Issue of grandparents, if no grandparents on one side*	Issue take equally 50% share if of the same degree, or otherwise by representation (§ 43-8-42(4))
6.	*Grandparents and issue of grandparents on the other side, if no grandparents or issue of grandparents on one side*	The 50% share is added to the other 50% share and distributed as per 4. and 5. above
7.	*Person related to the decedent through two lines of relation*	Only one share, based on the relation entitling him to the larger share (§ 43-8-58)
8.	*State, if no grandparents or issue of grandparents*	100% (§ 43-8-44)

---

[1] If the estate is in 2 or more states, the amount in the aggregate cannot exceed the preceding amounts. See § 43-8-41(5).

[2] "Representation" means per capita with representation. (§ 43-8-45(cmt.))

Alaska
Who Takes by Intestate Succession?

A. Surviving spouse takes:

1.	If no surviving descendants or parents	100% (§ 13.12.102(a)(1)(A))
2.	If all descendants are descendants of decedent and spouse	100% (§ 13.12.102(a)(1)(B))
3.	If no surviving descendant but a parent(s) survives	$200,000 plus 75% of balance of the interstate estate (§ 13.12.102(a)(2))
4.	If surviving descendants are also those of spouse but spouse has at least one other descendant	$150,000 plus 50% of balance of the interstate estate (§ 13.12.102(a)(3))
5.	If a surviving descendant of the decedent is not also a descendant of surviving spouse	$100,000 plus 50% of balance of the interstate estate of the interstate estate(§ 13.12.102(a)(4))
6.	Stock under Alaska Native Claims Settlement Act	If no surviving issue—100% If issue—50% (§§ 13.12.102(b)(1)&(2))

B. All the estate, or the surplus if there is a surviving spouse, passes to:

1.	Descendants by representation[3]	100% (§ 13.12.103(1))
2.	Parent, or parents equally, if no descendants	100% (§ 13.12.103(2))
3.	Descendants of parents by representation,[3] if no parents	100% (§ 13.12.103(3))
4.	Grandparents or their descendants, if no descendants of parents	50% to paternal and 50% to maternal grandparents or their surviving descendants by representation[3] (§ 13.12.103(4))
5.	Person related to decedent through two lines of relation	Only one share based on the relation entitling him to the larger share (§ 13.12.113)
6.	State, if no grandparents or their descendants	100% (§ 13.12.105)

[3] Representation: per capita at each generation level (§ 13.12.106).

Arizona
Who Takes by Intestate Succession?

A. Surviving spouse takes:

1.	If no surviving issue	100% (§ 14-2102(1))
2.	If surviving issue but all are issue of surviving spouse as well	100% (§ 14-2102(1))
3.	If any issue of decedent not also issue of surviving spouse	50% of separate property and none of decedent's portion of community property (§ 14-2102(2))

B. All the estate, or the surplus if there is a surviving spouse, passes to:

1.	Issue by representation:[4]	100% (§ 14-2103(1))
2.	Parent, or parents equally, if no descendants	100% (§ 14-2103(2))
3.	Descendants of parents, if no parents	100% to the descendants of decedent's parents or either of them by representation (§ 14-2103(3))
4.	Grandparents, if no issue of parents	50% to the paternal and 50% to the maternal side. The grandparents on either side share equally in the 50% share, and if only one, that grandparent takes the entire 50% share (§ 14-2103(4))
5.	Issue of grandparents, if no grandparents on one side	Issue take equally 50% share if of the same degree, or otherwise by representation (§ 14-2103(4))
6.	Grandparents and issue of grandparents on the other side, if no grandparents or issue of grandparents on one side	The 50% share is added to the other 50% share and distributed as per 4. and 5. above (§ 14-2103(4))
7.	Person related to the decedent through two lines of relation	Only one share based on the relation entitling him to the larger share (§ 14-2113)
8.	State, if no grandparents or their descendants	100% (§ 14-2105)

---

[4] Representation: per capita at each generation level (§ 14-2106).

Arkansas
Who Takes by Intestate Succession?

1.	Children and descendants of a deceased child	100%, per capita or per stirpes pursuant to §§ 28-9-204 and 28-9-205 (§ 28-9-214(1))
2.	Surviving spouse, if no children or descendants:	
	a. If married continuously for at least 3 years prior to death	100% (§ 28-9-214(2))
	b. If married less than 3 years prior to death	50% (§ 28-9-214(2))
3.	Parent or parents, if no spouse or descendants	100%, with parents taking equally if both survive (§ 28-9-214(3)); same result with respect to portion not passing to surviving spouse due to brevity of marriage (§ 28-9-214(4))
4.	Siblings and issue of predeceased siblings, if no parent	100% of portion not passing to surviving spouse, per capita or per stirpes pursuant to §§ 28-9-204 and 28-9-205[5] (§ 28-9-214(5))
5.	Grandparents, uncles, and aunts, and issue of predeceasing uncles and aunts, with respect to amounts not covered by 1.–4. above	100%, without regard to whether on the maternal or paternal side, whether any such deceased person is survived by descendants or whether a person is a grandparent, uncle, or aunt. If an uncle or aunt is deceased, the issue of such person takes per capita or per stirpes, pursuant to §§ 28-9-204 and 28-9-205 (§ 28-9-214(6))
6.	Great-grandparents, great-uncles, and great-aunts, if none of the persons in 5. above survive	100%, without regard to whether on the maternal or paternal side, or any such person's descendants or whether a person is a great-grandparent, great-uncle, or great-aunt. However, if a great-uncle or great-aunt is deceased, the issue of such person takes per capita or per stirpes, pursuant to §§ 28-9-204 and 28-9-205[5] (§ 28-9-214(7))
7.	Surviving spouse, if married less than 3 years and if none of the persons in 6. survive	100% (§ 28-9-215(1))
8.	Heirs of last spouse, if there is no spouse surviving and the marriage did not terminate in divorce	100%, with pattern the same as if decedent's own heirs (§ 28-9-215(2)(a))
9.	Escheat to county where decedent last "resided at death," if no other takers[6]	100% (§ 28-9-215(3))

[5] If of the same degree, the persons take per capita. If they are of different degree, they take "per stirpes," which, as defined in § 28-9-205(a)(3), actually is what is described generally as per capita with representation. In the case of 5. above, the living persons who qualify for the designated *relationships to the decedent* take per capita.

[6] This could, presumably, be a county in another state.

California
Who Takes by Intestate Succession?

A. Surviving spouse or surviving domestic partner (as defined in Prob. Code §37(a) and Fam. Code §297) takes:

1.	*Community property (Prob. Code §100) and quasi-community property (Prob. Code §101)*	the decedent's 50% share (Prob. Code §6401(a)&(b))	
2.	*Separate property:*		
	a.	*if no surviving issue, parent, sibling, or issue of sibling*	100% (Prob. Code §6401(c)(1))
	b.	*if one child or the issue of one deceased child*	50% (Prob. Code §6401(c)(2)(A))
	c.	*If no child or issue, but parent or issue of parent*	50% (Prob. Code §6401(c)(2)(B))
	d.	*If more than one child*	33.33% (Prob. Code §6401(c)(3)(A))
	e.	*If one child and issue of one or more deceased children*	33.33% (Prob. Code §6401(c)(3)(B))
	f.	*If issue of two or more deceased children*	33.33% (Prob. Code §6401(c)(3)(C))

B. All the estate, or the surplus if there is a surviving spouse, passes to:

1.	*Issue*	100%, with issue of same degree taking equally and if not of same degree then per capita with representation under Prob. Code §240 (Prob. Code §6402(a))
2.	*Parent, or parents equally, if no issue*	100% (Prob. Code §6402(b))
3.	*Issue of parents, if no parent or parents*	100% with issue of same degree taking equally and if not of same degree then per capita with representation under Prob. Code §240 (Prob. Code §6402(c))
4.	*Grandparents, or issue of grandparents if no surviving grandparents*	100%, with no distinction as to paternal or maternal. If more than one grandparent, they take equally. If no grandparents, issue take. If all of same degree, they take equally, and if not of same degree then per capita with representation under Prob. Code §240 (Prob. Code §6402(d))
5.	*Issue of a predeceased spouse (as defined in Prob. Code §6402.5), if no grandparents or issue of grandparents*	100% and the issue take equally if of same degree and if not of same degree then per capita with representation under Prob. Code §240 (Prob. Code §6402(e))
6.	*Next of kin by degree, if no grandparents, no issue of grandparents, and no issue of a predeceased spouse where two or more in equal degree claim through different ancestors, those who claim through nearest ancestor are preferred to those claiming through an ancestor more remote.*	100% to the next of kin in equal degree and if not of equal degree then per capita with representation under Prob. Code §240 (Prob. Code §6402(f))

7.	Parent or parents of predeceased spouse, if no next of kin and no surviv ing issue of a predeceased spouse	Parents take equally. If none survive decedent, issue take equally if of same degree, and if not of same degree, then per capita with representation under Prob. Code § 240 (Prob. Code § 6402(g))
8.	Person related to decedent through two lines of relation	Only one share, based on the relation entitling him to the larger share (Prob. Code § 6413)
9.	Person abusing, neglecting, or financially abusing, and acting in bad faith toward an elder or dependent adult who has been malicious, fraudulent, oppressive, or reckless in the above acts	Presumed to have predeceased decedent (Prob. Code § 259)
10.	Escheat, if no other taker	100%, as provided in Prob. Code § 6800 et seq.

Special Rule Regarding a Predeceasing Spouse For Purposes of Distributing Real Property: If predeceasing spouse died within last 15 years, and there is no surviving spouse or issue of decedent at decedent's death, then special rules apply for the portion of the estate attributable to the decedent's predeceased spouse. (Prob. Code § 6402.5)

Colorado
Who Takes by Intestate Succession?

A. Surviving spouse takes:

1.	If no descendant or parent	100% (§ 15-11-102(1)(a))[7]
2.	If all of decedent's descendants are also descendants of surviving spouse and the surviving spouse has no other descendants	100% (§ 15-11-102(1)(b))
3.	If no descendant of decedent survives, but a parent survives	First $300,000, plus $3/4$ of the balance (§ 15-11-102(2))
4.	If all of decedent's surviving descendants are also descendants of the surviving spouse and the surviving spouse has at least one descendant who is not a descendant of the decedent	First $225,000, plus $1/2$ of the balance (§ 15-11-102(3))
5.	If at least one of decedent's surviving descendants is not a surviving descendant of the surviving spouse	First $150,000, plus $1/2$ of the balance (§ 15-11-102(4))

If two or more of the above situations apply, the one yielding the largest amount for the surviving spouse governs. (§ 15-11-102)

B. All the estate, or the surplus if there is a surviving spouse, passes to:

1.	Descendants	100%, per capita at each generation (§ 15-11-103(2))
2.	Parent or parents, if no descendants[8]	100%, in equal shares if both survive (§ 15-11-103(3))
3.	Descendants of parents, or either of them, if no parents	100%, per capita at each generation (§ 15-11-103(4))
4.	Grandparents, if no descendants of parents	100%, divided $1/2$ paternal, $1/2$ maternal (§ 15-11-103(5))
5.	Descendants of grandparents, if no grandparents	100%, per capita at each generation on the paternal and maternal side, and if no descendants on one side, that $1/2$ share is added to the other and distributed likewise per capita at each generation (§ 15-11-103(6))
6.	Person related to decedent through two lines of relation	Only one share, based on the relation entitling him to the larger share (§ 15-11-113)
7.	State, if no other takers	100% (§ 15-11-105)

---

[7] The dollar amounts set forth in § 15-11-102 are required to be adjusted based on cost of living. (§§ 15-11-102(6), 15-10-112)

[8] A parent cannot take from child decedent if parental rights were terminated and not re-established, or could have been terminated at the time of the decedent's death (§ 15-11-114)

Connecticut
Who Takes by Intestate Succession?

A.	*Surviving spouse takes:*	
	1.	*If there are no surviving issue or parent of the decedent*
		100% (§ 45a-437(a)(1))
	2.	*If there are no surviving issue of the decedent but the decedent is survived by a parent or parents*
		First one hundred thousand dollars plus 75% of the balance of the interstate estate (§ 45a-437(a)(2))
	3.	*If there are surviving issue of the decedent all of whom are also issue of the surviving spouse*
		First one hundred thousand dollars plus 50% of the balance of the interstate estate (§ 45a-437(a)(3))
	4.	*If there are surviving issue of the decedent one or more of whom are not issue of the surviving spouse*
		50% of interstate estate (§ 45a-437(a)(4))
B.	*All the estate, or the surplus if there is a surviving spouse, passes to:*	
	1.	Descendants
		100% (§ 45a-438(a))
	2.	*Parent or parents equally, if there is no spouse or children*
		100% (§ 45a-439(a)(1))
	3.	*Parent who has abandoned decedent child and continued abandonment until time of child's death*
		No share (§ 45a-439)
	4.	*Brothers or sisters of the intestate and those who legally represent them[7] equally, if there is no parent*
		100% (§ 45a-439(a)(2))
	5.	*Next of kin in equal degree under the civil law rule (§ 45a-439(d)), if there are no brothers or sisters or those who legally represent them*
		100% (§ 45a-439(a)(3)) Limited to collaterals and not their representatives (Id.)
	6.	Stepchildren and those who legally represent them[9], if there is no next of kin
		100% (§ 45a-439(a)(4))
	7.	*State, if no other takers*
		100% (§ 45a-452)

[9] "Those who legally represent them" means a per stirpital distribution. See, *e.g.*, Daniels v. Daniels, 115 Conn. 239, 161 A. 94 (1932).

Delaware
Who Takes by Intestate Succession?

A.	Surviving spouse takes:	
	1. If there are no surviving issue or parents of the decedent	100% (12 § 502(1))
	2. If there are no surviving issue but the decedent is survived by a parent or parents	First $50,000.00 of the intestate personal estate, plus 50% of the balance of the intestate personal estate, plus a life estate in the intestate real estate (12 § 502(2))
	3. If there are surviving issue all of whom are issue of the surviving spouse also	First $50,000.00 of the intestate personal estate, plus 50% of the balance of the intestate personal estate, plus a life estate in the intestate real estate (12 § 502(3))
	4. If there are surviving issue, one or more of whom are not issue of the surviving spouse	50% of the intestate personal estate, plus a life estate in the intestate real estate (12 § 502(4))
B.	All the estate, or the surplus if there is a surviving spouse, passes to:	
	1. Issue of the decedent	100%, per stirpes[10] (12 § 503(1))
	2. Parents, if there is no surviving issue	100% equally[10] (12 § 503(2))
	3. Brothers and sisters and the issue of each deceased brother or sister, if there is no surviving parent	100% per stirpes[10] (12 § 503(3))
	4. Next of kin of the decedent, and to the issue of deceased next of kin, if there is no issue of a parent	100% per stirpes[10] (12 § 503(4))
	5. State, if no next of kin	(12 § 1101)

[10] Any property passing under 12 § 503 to two or more persons passes to such persons as tenants in common. (12 § 503(5))

District of Columbia
Who Takes by Intestate Succession?

A. *Surviving spouse or surviving domestic partner takes:*

1.	*If no descendant or parent of the decedent survives the decedent*	100% (§ 19-302(1))
2.	*If the decedent's surviving descendants are also descendants of the surviving spouse or surviving domestic partner and there is no other descendant of the surviving spouse or surviving domestic partner who survives the decedent*	$^2/_3$ of any balance of the intestate estate (§ 19-302(2))
3.	*If no descendant of the decedent survives the decedent, but a parent of the decedent survives the decedent*	$^3/_4$ of any balance of the intestate estate (§ 19-302(3))
4.	*If all of the decedent's surviving descendants are also descendants of the surviving spouse or surviving domestic partner and the surviving spouse or surviving domestic partner has one or more surviving descendants who are not descendants of the decedent*	One-half of any balance of the intestate estate (§ 19-302(4))
5.	*If one or more of the decedent's surviving descendants are not descendants of the surviving spouse or surviving domestic partner*	One-half of any balance of the intestate estate (§ 19-302(5))

B. *All the estate, or the surplus if there is a surviving spouse or surviving domestic partner, passes to (§ 19-305):*

1.	*Children, if no other descendants*	100% divided equally (§ 19-306)
2.	*Children and the children of deceased children, if not just living children*	100% divided equally among children, with children of deceased children taking their parent's share equally if of equal degree (§ 19-307(a)&(b))
3.	*Parents, if there is no surviving child or descendant[11]*	100% divided equally between the father and mother "or their survivor" (§ 19-308)
4.	*Brother and sister or their descendants, if no parent*	100% (§ 19-309) divided equally, with descendants "stand[ing] in the place"[12] of deceased parents (§ 19-310)
5.	*Collaterals in closest equal degree only, if no siblings or descendants of siblings*	100%, divided equally with representation not allowed[13] (§ 19-311)
6.	*Grandparents, if no collaterals*	100%, share alike (§ 19-312)
7.	*District of Columbia, if no relations within fifth degree*	100% (§ 19-701) ("for the benefit of the poor")

---

[11] The reference to descendant is confusing, because B2. above only anticipates inheritance as far down as grandchildren, but no further.

[12] "Standing in the place" remains undefined.

[13] Section 19-701 is also confusing because grandparents would take if there are no collaterals, see § 19-312, notwithstanding § 19-701, which provides for escheat if there are no descendants of a common ancestor of the decedent within the fifth degree.

Florida
Who Takes by Intestate Succession?

A. *Surviving spouse takes:*	
1. *If there is no surviving descendant of the decedent*	100% (§ 732.102(1))
2. *If there are surviving descendants of the decedent, all of whom are also lineal descendants of the surviving spouse*	100% (§ 732.102(2))
3. *If there are surviving descendants, one or more of whom are not lineal descendants of the surviving spouse*	50% of the intestate estate (§ 732.102(3))
4. *If there are surviving descendants, all of whom are descendants of the surviving spouse, and the surviving spouse has one or more descendants who are not descendants of the decedent*	50% (§ 732.102 (4))

B. *All the estate, or the surplus if there is a surviving spouse, passes to:*	
1. *Descendants of the decedent*	100% (§ 732.103(1))[14]
2. *Parents equally, or to the survivor of them, if no descendants survive*	100% (§ 732.103(2))
3. *Siblings and the descendants of a deceased sibling, if no lineal descendants*	100% (§ 732.103(3))[14]
4. *Grandparents*	100%, with 50% share to the paternal side and 50% share to the maternal side. The grandparents on each side share equally, or if only one, that grandparent takes the entire 50% share. (§ 732.103(4)(a))
a. *Uncles and aunts and descendants of deceased uncles and aunts of the decedent, if there are no grandparents on that side*	100% (§ 732.103(4)(b))[14]
b. *The kindred on the other side, if there is no kindred on one side*	100% (§ 732.103(4)(c)) The one side's share is combined with the other side's share and distributed as in 4. and 4.a. above[13]
5. *The kindred of the last deceased spouse of the decedent, as if the deceased spouse had survived the decedent and then died intestate entitled to the estate, if there is no kindred of either side*	100% (§ 732.103(5))[14]

6. *Descendants of the decedent's great grandparents, if any descendants of the decedent's great grandparents were Holocaust victims as defined in §626.9543(3)(a). [Provision ceases to be effective for proceedings filed after December 31, 2004.]*	100% (§ 732.103(6))
7. *State, if there are no other takers*	100% (§ 732.107(1))

[14] Distributions are made per stripes. See § 732.104.

Georgia
Who Takes by Intestate Succession?

A. *Surviving spouse or reciprocal beneficiary takes:*		
1.	*If there are no children or other descendants*	100% (§ 53-2-1(c)(1))
2.	*If there is any child or other descendant who survives the decedent*	Equally with the children or descendants taking a deceased child's share, but no less than $^1/_3$ (§ 53-2-1(c)(1))
B. *All the estate, or the surplus if there is a surviving spouse, passes to:*		
1.	*Children and descendants of deceased children*	100%, with descendants of deceased children taking per stirpes (§ 53-2-1(c)(3))
2.	*Parent, or parents equally, if no child or other descendants*	100% (§ 53-2-1(c)(4))
3.	*Siblings, if no parents*	100%, equally (§ 53-2-1(c)(5))
4.	*Nieces and nephews or their descendants, if no siblings*	100%, equally with descendants of a niece or nephew taking per stirpes (§ 53-2-1(c)(5))
5.	*Grandparents, if no nieces, nephews, or their descendants*	100%, equally (§ 53-2-1(c)(6))
6.	*Uncles and aunts, and the descendants of a deceased uncle or aunt*	100%, equally, with descendants taking per stirpes (§ 53-2-1(c)(7))
7.	*First cousins, if no uncles and aunts, even if there are surviving other descendants of uncles and aunts*	100%, equally (§ 53-2-1(c)(7))
8.	Surviving relatives nearest in degree by counting degrees of kinship by civil law method set forth in § 53-2-1(c)(8), if 1-7 do not apply	100%, equally. (§ 53-2-1(c)(8))
9.	*Person related to decedent through two lines of relation*	Only one share based on the relation entitling him to the larger share (§ 53-2-6)
10.	*Escheat, if no other taker*	100% (§ § 53-2-50 & 53-2-51)[15]

[15] If surviving spouse dies intestate and within 6 months, without heirs, undistributed property to which she was entitled from the first-to- die spouse, under intestacy, does not escheat but is distributed to the heirs of the first-to-die. (§ 53-2-8(a))

Hawaii
Who Takes by Intestate Succession?

A.		*Surviving spouse or reciprocal beneficiary takes:*	
	1.	*If no descendant or parent of the decedent survives the decedent*	100% (§ 560:2-102(1)(A))
	2.	*If all of the decedent's surviving descendants are also descendants of the surviving spouse or reciprocal beneficiary and there is no other descendant of the surviving spouse or reciprocal beneficiary who survives the decedent*	100% (§ 560:2-102(1)(B))
	3.	*If no descendant of the decedent survives the decedent, but a parent of the decedent survives the decedent*	First $200,000, plus 3/4 of any balance of the intestate estate (§ 560:2-102(2))
	4.	*If all of the decedent's surviving descendants are also descendants of the surviving spouse or reciprocal beneficiary and the surviving spouse or reciprocal beneficiary has one or more surviving descendants who are not descendants of the decedent*	First $150,000, plus 50% of any balance of the intestate estate (§ 560:2-102(3))
	5.	*If one or more of the decedent's surviving descendants are not descendants of the surviving spouse or reciprocal beneficiary*	First $100,000.00, plus 50% of any balance of the intestate estate (§ 560:2-102(4))
B.		*All the estate, or the surplus if there is a surviving spouse, passes to:*[16]	
	1.	*Descendants by representation*[17]	100% (§ 560:2-103(1))
	2.	*Decedent's parents if both survive, or to the surviving parent; provided, however, if the decedent is a minor, and if it is shown by clear and convincing evidence that any parent has deserted the child for at least 90 days, failed to communicate with child when able to do so for at least one year when the child is in custody of another, or failed to provide for care and support of the child when able to do so for at least one year when the child is in the custody of another despite a child support order requiring such support*	100% (§ 560:2-103(2)), but nothing if proviso not satisfied (§ 560:2-103(2)(A)–(C))
	3.	*Descendants of the decedent's parents or either of them by representation,*[17] *if there is no parent entitled to inherit*	100% (§ 560:2-103(3))

4.	*Grandparents or their descendants, if there are no descendants of decedent's parents*	50% of the estate to the decedent's paternal grandparents equally if both survive, or to the surviving paternal grandparent, or to the descendants of the decedent's paternal grandparents or either of them if both are deceased, the descendants taking by representation, and the other 50% passes to the decedent's maternal relatives in the same manner; but if there is no surviving grandparent or descendant of a grandparent on either the paternal or the maternal side, the entire estate passes to the decedent's relatives on the other side in the same manner as the half. (§ 560:2-103(4))
5.	*Person related to decedent through two lines of relation*	Only one share, based on the relation entitling him to the larger share (§ 560:2-113)
6.	*State, if no grandparents or their descendants*	100% (§ 560:2-105)

[16] Any intestate Kuleana lands escheat to the state Department of Land and Natural Resources until it approves a plan by the Office of Hawaiian Affairs for the disposition of these lands (§ 560:2-105.5)

[17] "Representation" means per capita at each generation. See § 560:2-106(b).

Idaho
Who Takes by Intestate Succession?

A.	Surviving spouse takes:	
1.	Separate Property: If there is no surviving issue or parent of the decedent	100% (§ 15-2-102(a)(1))
2.	Separate Property: If there is no surviving issue but the decedent is survived by a parent or parents	50% of the estate (§ 15-2-102(a)(2))
3.	Separate Property: If there is surviving issue of the deceased spouse	50% of the estate (§ 15-2-102(a)(3))
4.	Community property	The decedent's portion passes 100% to the surviving spouse (§ 15-2-102(b)(1))

B.	All the estate, or the surplus if there is a surviving spouse, passes to:	
1.	Issue	100% if they are all of the same degree of kinship to the decedent they take equally, but if of unequal degree, then those of more remote degree take by representation[18] (§ 15-2-103(a))
2.	Parent, or parents equally, if there is no surviving issue	100% (§ 15-2-103(b))
3.	Issue of the parents or either of them by representation, if there is no parent	100% (§ 15-2-103(c))
4.	Grandparents or issue of grandparents, if there is no surviving issue, parent or issue of a parent	50% to paternal grandparents and 50% to maternal grandparents, with the grandparents on one side sharing equally if they both survive. If neither grandparent on that side survives, to the issue of the grandparents or grandparent on that side by representation. If no issue survive on that side either, then the 50% share is added to the 50% share on the other side and the grandparents or their issue on the other side take the entire 100% in the manner described herein. (§ 15-2-103(d))
5.	Person related to decedent through two lines of relation	Only one share based on the relation entitling him to the larger share (§ 15-2-114)
6.	State, if there are no other takers	100% for public school permanent endowment fund. (§ 14-113) The provision refers alternatively to "property" and, in some instances, to "money or property" raising an issue as to coverage. See also § 14-503, which addresses taking custody of intangible unclaimed property but not real property.

[18] "Representation" means per capita with representation. See § 15-2-106.

Illinois
Who Takes by Intestate Succession?

A.		*Surviving spouse takes:*	
	1.	*If no descendant*	100% (755 ILCS § 5/2-1(c))
	2.	*If a descendant survives as well*	50% (755 ILCS § 5/2-1(a))
B.		*All the estate, or the surplus if there is a surviving spouse, passes to:*[19]	
	1.	*Descendant, if no surviving spouse*	100% per stirpes (755 ILCS § 5/2-1(b))
	2.	*Descendant and surviving spouse*	50% to spouse and 50% to descendants per stirpes (755 ILCS § 5/2-1(a))
	3.	*Parent, sibling, or descendants of a deceased sibling*	100%, in equal parts, with descendants of deceased siblings taking per stirpes. If there is only one parent surviving, that parent takes a double portion. (755 ILCS § 5/2-1(d)) But if a parent has for one year or more prior to the death of a minor or dependent child willfully neglected or failed to perform any duty of support to the child, or willfully deserted the child, the parent cannot take unless a court reduces the amount inherited by the parent as the interests of justice require. However, the reduction cannot be less than the child support owed. (755 ILCS § 5/2-6.5)
	4.	*Grandparents, if no parents, siblings, or descendants of siblings*	50% to the paternal side and 50% to the maternal side. The grandparents on one side share equally, and if only one survives, that grandparent takes the entire 50% share. (755 ILCS § 5/2-1(e))
	5.	*Descendants of grandparents, if no grandparents on that side*	The entire share is distributed per stirpes (755 ILCS § 5/ 2-1(e))
	6.	*Grandparents or descendants of grandparents on one side, if no descendants of grandparents on the other side*	The 50% share is combined with the other side's 50% share and the entire amount is distributed as per 4. and 5. above (755 ILCS § 5/2-1(e))
	7.	*Greatgrandparents or their descendants, if no grandparents or their descendants on either the maternal or paternal side*	50% share to paternal greatgrandparents and 50% to maternal greatgrandparents in equal parts of the 50% share on each side or to the descendants of a predeceased greatgrandparent per stirpes (755 ILCS § 5/2-1(f)) If no greatgrandparents or descendants of greatgrandparents on one side, then added to the share on the other side and distributed as described above in 4-6.
	8.	*Nearest kindred, if no greatgrandparents or descendants of greatgrandparents*	100%, in equal shares for those of nearest degree by civil law method of counting and without representation (755 ILCS § 5/2-1(g))

9. *Escheat, if no kindred*	Real estate escheats to county in which it is physically located. Personal estate escheats to county in which it is physically located. If property is located outside state and is subject to Illinois administration and ancillary administration elsewhere, then it passes to county in which decedent "was a resident," and if not a resident, the county in which the property was located. All other personal property or proceeds therefrom, wherever situated, passes to state, specifically State Treasurer pursuant to Uniform Disposition of Unclaimed Property Act. (755 §5/2-1(h))

[19] A person may not receive any property or benefit by reason of the death of an elderly or disabled person whom the person is convicted of exploiting, abusing, or neglecting, unless the decedent is shown to have been aware of the conviction and, after the conviction, ratified his or her intent to transfer to the person. (755 ILCS § 5/2-6.2(b))

Indiana
Who Takes by Intestate Succession?

A.	Surviving spouse takes:[20]	
	1. If the intestate is survived by at least one child or by the issue of at least one deceased child	50% (§ 29-1-2-1(b)(1))
	2. If there is no surviving issue but the intestate is survived by one or both of the intestate's parents	75% (§ 29-1-2-1(b)(2))
	3. If there is no surviving issue or parent	100% (§ 29-1-2-1(b)(3))
	4. If the surviving spouse is a second or other subsequent spouse who did not at any time have children by the decedent, and the decedent left surviving the decedent a child or children or the descendants of a child or children by a previous spouse	Life estate in 25% of the lands of the deceased spouse, and the fee vests, at the decedent's death, at once in such child or children, or the descendants of such as may be dead, subject only to the life estate of the surviving spouse. Such second or subsequent childless spouse, however, receives the same share of the personal property of the decedent with respect to surviving spouses generally. (§ 29-1-2-1(c))

B.	All the estate, or the surplus if there is a surviving spouse, passes to:	
	1. Issue	Equally; or if of unequal degree, then those of more remote degree take by representation[21] (§ 29-1-2-1(d)(1))
	2. Surviving parents, if there is a surviving spouse but no surviving issue of the decedent	100%. (§ 29-1-2-1(d)(2)) But a parent may not take if convicted of killing the other parent through criminal act. (§ 29-1-2-1(e))
	3. Surviving parents, brothers, and sisters, and the issue of deceased brothers and sisters of the intestate, if there is no surviving spouse or issue of the intestate	Each living parent of the intestate is treated as of the same degree as a brother or sister and is entitled to the same share as a brother or sister. However, the share of each parent is not to be less than one-fourth of the net estate. Issue of deceased brothers and sisters take by representation.[21] (§ 29-1-2-1(d)(3))
	4. Surviving grandparents, if there are no surviving issue, or parent of the intestate, or issue of a parent	100%, shared equally (§ 29-1-2-1(d)(5))
	5. Aunts and uncles and issue of deceased aunts and uncles, if no grandparents	100%; one share passes to each of the aunts and uncles, as well as deceased aunts and uncles who leave issue. The latter take per stirpes. (§ 29-1-2-1(d)(6))

6.	*Person related to the decedent through two lines of relation*	Only one share, based on the relation entitling him to the larger share (§ 29-1-2-9)
7.	*State, if no one mentioned in 1. through 5. above*	100% (§ 29-1-2-1(d)(8))

[20] A surviving spouse cannot take if he or she abandoned the decedent without just cause, or at the time of the decedent's death had left the decedent and was living in adultery (§§ 29-1-2-14, 29-1-2-15)

[21] "Representation" means per stirpes. See, e.g., Brown v. Taylor, 62 Ind. 295 (1878). Note also that if interests in real property go to a husband and wife, e.g., parents or grandparents, the aggregate interests so descending are owned by them as tenants by the entireties. Interests in personal property so descending are owned as tenants in common. (§ 29-1-2-1(d)(7))

Iowa
Who Takes by Intestate Succession?

A.	Surviving spouse takes:	
	1. If no issue or issue are also the issue of the surviving spouse	100% (§ 633.211)
	2. If issue some of whom are not the issue of the surviving spouse	a. 50% real property possessed during marriage and regarding which surviving spouse did not relinquish rights (§ 633.212(1)) b. 100% exempt personal property of decedent as "head of a family" (§ 633.212(2)) c. 50% of all other personal property not necessary for payment of debts and charges (§ 633.212(3)) d. if a.–c. is less than $50,000, additional homestead interest and other property subject to debts and charges is given to the surviving spouse, even to the extent of the whole net estate, as necessary to make the $50,000 (§ 633.212(4))

B.	All the estate, or the surplus if there is a surviving spouse, passes to:	
	1. Issue	100%, per stirpes (§ 633.219(1))
	2. Parents, if there is no surviving issue	100% (§ 633.219(2))
	3. Issue of decedent's parents, if no parents	50%, per stirpes, on the maternal and paternal side. If there are no surviving issue of one deceased parent, the entire estate passes to the issue of the other deceased parent per stirpes. (§ 633.219(3))
	4. Grandparents, if no issue of decedent's parents	50% per stirpes on the maternal and paternal sides. The paternal or maternal share is further divided among issue if neither grandparent on the particular side survives. One share passes per stirpes to the issue of the grandfather and one share passes per stirpes to the issue of the grandmother. If there are no issue, then to the issue of the other grandparent per stirpes. If there are no issue of either grandparent, then both of these subshares pass to the grandparents or their issue on the other side and are distributed in the same manner described above. (§ 633.219(4))
	5. Great grandparents or issue of great grandparents, if no grandparents or issue of grandparents	Estate passes equally to each set of great grandparents or their issue, per stirpes (§ 633.219(5))[22]
	6. Issue of deceased spouse, if no great grandparents or their issue	100%, per stirpes (§ 633.219(6)) If there is more than one predeceasing former spouse who died in lawful wedlock, then the estate passes equally among issue per stirpes of all such spouses. (Id.)
	7. State, if none of the above	100% (§ 633.219(7))

[22] Although the language of the statute is not clear, presumably a surviving great grandparent would take before issue of the other deceased great grandparent could take.

Kansas
Who Takes by Intestate Succession?

A.	*Surviving spouse takes:*		
	1.	*If no children or issue of children*	100% (§ 59-504)
	2.	*If a child or issue of a predeceased child*	50% (§ 59-504)
B.	*All the estate, or the surplus if there is a surviving spouse, passes to:*		
	1.	Children and issue of children	100%, with issue taking "collectively" what predeceasing child would have taken (§ 59-506)
	2.	Parents, or parents equally, if no children or issue	100% (§ 59-507)
	3.	Heirs (other than spouses) of parents, as if parents died at time of intestate's death, if no parents	100%, equally divided between paternal and maternal sides, but if no heirs on one side, then all to the heirs on the other side (§ 59-508)
	4.	Heirs of last spouse of intestate predeceasing intestate, if no heirs of parents	100% (§ 59-514)
	5.	State, if no heirs of last spouse who predeceased intestate	100% (§ 59-514)

Note: Pursuant to Section 59-505, the surviving spouse is entitled to 50% of all real estate decedent was "seized or possessed" at any time during the marriage if the surviving spouse did not consent to the disposition in writing, by will, or by election under the law. Exceptions exist for executions and judicial sales, and when the surviving spouse has not been a resident of Kansas during the marriage.

Note. None of the intestate's "property shall pass except by lineal descent to a person further removed from the decedent than the sixth degree." (§ 59-509)

Kentucky
Who Takes by Intestate Succession?

1.	*Children and descendants*	100% (§ 391.010(1))[23]
2.	*Parents, or parents equally, if no children or descendants*	100% (§ 391.010(2)) If a parent has given real estate and is still alive, that parent inherits the real estate. (§ 391.020(1)) If a person under age 18 dies without issue, any real property received gratuitously from a parent passes to that parent or the parent's kindred, and if none, then to the other parent and that parent's kindred. The kindred of one parent are not to be excluded if the kindred of the other is more remote than grandparents or aunts and uncles or their descendants. (§ 391.020(2)) But a parent cannot take from or administer the estate of a child whose care or maintenance he or she has willfully abandoned, unless the parent has resumed and continued this care and maintenance for one year prior to the child's death and substantially complied with all court orders regarding the child's support. (§ 391.033 (1))
3.	*Siblings and their descendants, if no parents*	100% (§ 391.010(3))
4.	*Surviving spouse, if no siblings or descendants of them*	100% (§ 391.010(4))
5.	*Grandparents, if no surviving spouse*	50% to the paternal side and 50% to the maternal side; with respect to each of these moieties, it is shared by grandfather and grandmother, or if only one survives, the entire moiety passes to that grandparent (§ 391.010(5)(a))
6.	*Aunts and uncles, or their descendants, if no grandparents with respect to the moiety*	100% (§ 391.010(5)(b))[24]
7.	*Great grandparents, if no aunts, uncles, or their descendants with respect to the moiety*	100%, in same manner as in 5. above (§ 391.010(5)(c))[24]
8.	*Siblings of grandparents, or their descendants, if no great grandparents with respect to the moiety*	100% (§ 391.010(5)(d))[24]
9.	*Nearest lineal ancestors and their descendants, if no siblings of grandparents or descendants of such siblings*	100% (§ 391.010(5)(d))[24]
10.	*Kindred of the other side, if no kindred on the one side (either paternal or maternal) as divided in 5. above*	100% (§ 391.010(6))
11.	*Kindred of the husband or wife, if there is neither paternal or maternal kindred.*	100% (§ 391.010(6))
12.	*State, if no kindred on the other side either*	100% (§ 393.020)

[23] Section 391.010 refers to real property. The same pattern of distribution with respect to personal property is adopted by section 391.030(1).
[24] Section 391.040 provides for a per stirpital distribution.

Louisiana
Who Takes by Intestate Succession?

A.	*Surviving spouse takes:*[25]	
	1. *If no descendants*	100% of decedent's share of community property (Civ. Code art. 889)
	2. *If descendants*	Usufruct in decedent's share of community property until death or remarriage (Civ. Code art. 890)
	3. *If no descendants, parents, siblings, or descendants, and the surviving spouse was not judicially separated from him*	100% (Civ. Code art. 894)
B.	*All the estate, or the surplus if there is a surviving spouse, passes to:*	
	1. *Descendants*	100% (Civ. Code art. 888)
	2. *Parents and siblings or descendants of sibling*	Siblings or their descendants by representation subject to usufruct in favor of surviving parent or parents, which is joint and successive if both parents survive (Civ. Code art. 891)
	3. *Siblings or descendants of sibling, if no parents*	100%, equally to siblings and descendants of siblings by representation (Civ. Code art. 893) If born of different parents, then equal shares are created on paternal and maternal side (Civ. Code art. 893)
	4. *Parents, or sole surviving parent, if no siblings or descendants of sibling*	100% (Civ. Code art. 892)
	5. *Grandparents, and if not, more removed ascendants, where no parents, siblings, or descendants of siblings*	If ascendants in maternal and paternal lines are of same degree, then equal shares to maternal and paternal lines. Ascendants on each side divide their share per capita. If the ascendant on one line is of nearer degree all passes to that ascendant, even if this excludes the other line. (Civ. Code art. 895)
	6. *Collaterals, if no ascendants*	100% to the one in the nearest degree. If more than one in that degree, then they take per capita. (Civ. Code art. 896)
	7. *State, if there are no other takers*	100% (Civ. Code art. 902)

[25] With respect to immovables, ascendants inherit real property originally given by them to their children. (Civ. Code art. 897) If property has been alienated, the ascendant is entitled to receive the remaining unpaid price as well as any right of reversion upon condition. (Id.)

Maine
Who Takes by Intestate Succession?

A.	Surviving spouse or registered domestic partner takes:	
	1.	If there is no surviving issue or parent of the decedent	100% (18-A § 2-102(1))
	2.	If there is no surviving issue but the decedent is survived by a parent or parents	First $50,000, plus 50% of the balance of the interstate estate (18-A § 2-102(2))
	3.	If there are surviving issue, all of whom are issue of the surviving spouse or registered domestic partner also	First $50,000, plus 50% of the balance of the interstate estate (18-A § 2-102(3))
	4.	If there are surviving issue one or more of whom are not issue of the surviving spouse	50% (18-A § 2-102(4))

B.	All the estate, or the surplus if there is a surviving spouse or surviving registered domestic partner, passes to:	
	1.	Issue	100%, per capita, at each generation (18-A § 2-103(1))
	2.	Parents, or parents equally, if no descendants	100%, equally (18-A § 2-103(2))
	3.	Issue of parents or either of them, if there is no surviving parent	100%, per capita at each generation (18-A § 2-103(3))
	4.	Grandparents or issue of grandparents, if there is no surviving issue of a parent	50% paternal side, 50% maternal side (18-A § 2-103(4)) Grandparents share equally, or all to one if just one survives. If no grandparents on one side, then to the issue per capita at each generation. If no grandparents or issue of grandparents on one side, then 100% to the other side. (Id.)
	5.	Great-grandparent or issue of great grandparent	50% paternal, 50% maternal (18-A § 2-103(5)) If no great grandparents on one side, then to the issue per capita at each generation. If no great-grandparents or issue of great-grandparents on one side, then 100% to the other side. (Id.)
	6.	State, if no great-grandparents or issue of great-grandparents	100% (18-A § 2-105)

Maryland
Who Takes by Intestate Succession?

A. *Surviving spouse takes:*

1.	*If there is a surviving minor child*	50% (Est. & Trusts § 3-102(b))
2.	*If there is no surviving child, but there is surviving issue*	First $40,000 plus 50% residue (Est. & Trusts § 3-102(c))
3.	*If there is no surviving issue but a surviving parent*	First $40,000 plus 50% residue (Est. & Trusts § 3-102(d))
4.	*If no surviving issue or parent*	100% (Est. & Trusts § 3-102(e))

B. *All the estate, or the surplus if there is a surviving spouse, passes to:*

1.	*Issue*	Divided equally by representation as defined in § 1-210 (Est. & Trusts § 3-103)
2.	*Parents, or parents equally, if no issue[26]*	100% (Est. & Trusts § 3-104(b))
3.	*Issue of parents, if no parents*	100%, by representation (Est. & Trusts § 3-104(b))
4.	*Grandparents and their issue, if no surviving issue of a parent*	50% to surviving paternal grandparents equally or all to the survivor (or if neither survives then to their issue by representation); 50% likewise to surviving maternal grandparents equally or all to the survivor (or if neither survives then to their issue by representation). If there are no grandparents or issue of grandparents on one side, then the 50% share is added to the 50% share to the other side, and the entire amount is distributed as provided above. (Est. & Trusts § 3-104(c))
5.	*Great-Grandparents and their issue, if no surviving issue of a grandparent*	25% to each pair of great-grandparents equally or all to the survivor, or if neither survives, all to the issue of either or of both of that pair of great-grandparents, by representation. In the event that neither member of a pair of great-grandparents nor any issue of either of that pair survives, the quarter share applicable is to be distributed equally among the remaining pairs of great-grandparents or the survivor of a pair or issue of either of a pair of great-grandparents, in the same manner as prescribed for a quarter share. (Est. & Trusts § 3-104(d))
6.	*Stepchildren, if no surviving blood relative*	100% equally to surviving stepchildren and to issue of predeceasing stepchildren by representation (Est. & Trusts § 3-104(e))
7.	*State[27], if no stepchildren*	100% (Est. & Trusts § 3-105(a))

[26] Under § 3-112 the surviving parent's inheritance rights may be denied in the case of an abandonment or failure to support a minor child.

[27] If an individual was a recipient of long-term care benefits under the Maryland Medical Assistance Program at the time of the individual's death, the net estate shall be converted to cash and paid to the Department of Health & Mental Hygiene, and shall be applied for the administration of the program. (§ 3-105(a)(2)(i)) If the provisions of subparagraph (i) of this paragraph are not applicable, the net estate shall be converted to cash and paid to the board of education in the county in which the letters were granted, and shall be applied for the use of the public schools in the county. (§ 3-105(a)(2)(ii))

Massachusetts
Who Takes by Intestate Succession?
(Effective March 31, 2012)

A. Surviving spouse takes:

1.	*If no descendant or parent of the decedent survives the decedent*	100% (190B § 2-102(1)(i))
2.	*If all of the decedent's surviving descendants are also descendants of the surviving spouse and there is no other descendant of the surviving spouse who survives the decedent*	100% (190B § 2-102(1)(ii))
3.	*If no descendant of the decedent survives the decedent, but a parent of the decedent survives the decedent*	The first $200,000, plus 3/4 of any balance of the intestate estate (190B § 2-102(2))
4.	*If all of the decedent's surviving descendants are also descendants of the surviving spouse and the surviving spouse has 1 or more surviving descendants who are not descendants of the decedent*	The first $100,000 plus 1/2 of any balance of the intestate estate (190B § 2-102(3))
5.	*If 1 or more of the decedent's surviving descendants are not descendants of the surviving spouse*	The first $100,000 plus 1/2 of any balance of the intestate estate (190B § 2-102(4))

B. All the estate, or the surplus if there is a surviving spouse, passes to:

1.	*Descendants*	100%, per capita at each generation. (190B § 2-103(1))
2.	*Parents equally if both survive, or to the surviving parent, if there is no surviving descendant*	100% (190B § 2-103(2))
3.	*To the descendants of the decedent's parents or either of them, if there is no surviving descendant or parent*	100%, per capita at each generation (190B § 2-103(3))
4.	*Equally to the decedent's next of kin in equal degree; but if there are 2 or more descendants of deceased ancestors in equal degree claiming through different ancestors, those claiming through the nearest ancestor shall be preferred to those claiming through an ancestor more remote, if there is no surviving descendant, parent, or descendant of a parent.*	100%, Degrees of kindred shall be computed according to the rules of civil law. (190B § 2-103(4))
5.	*State[28], if there is no taker.*	100% (190B § 2-105)

---

[28] If the intestate was a veteran who died a member of Soldier's Home, the estate shall inure to the legacy of the relevant home. (190B § 2-105)

Michigan
Who Takes by Intestate Succession?

A. *Surviving spouse takes:*

1.	*If no descendant or parent of decedent*	100% (§ 700.2102(1)(a))
2.	*If all of the decedent's surviving descendants are also descendants of surviving spouse and there are no other descendants of the surviving spouse*	First $150,000[29], plus $^1/_2$ of the balance (§ 700.2102(1)(b))
3.	*If no descendant of the decedent survives but a parent survives*	First $150,000[29], plus $^3/_4$ of the balance (§ 700.2102(1)(c))
4.	*If all of decedent's surviving descendants are also descendants of the surviving spouse and she has at least one descendant who is not a descendant of the decedent*	First $150,000[29], plus $^1/_2$ of the balance (§ 700.2102(1)(d))
5.	*If at least one but not all of decedent's surviving descendants is not also descendant of surviving spouse*	First $150,000[29], plus $^1/_2$ of the balance (§ 700.2102(1)(e))
6.	*If all of decedent's surviving descendants are not descendants of the surviving spouse*	First $100,000[29], plus $^1/_2$ of the balance (§ 700.2102(1)(f))

B. *All the estate, or the surplus if there is a surviving spouse, passes to:*

1.	*Descendants*	100%, by representation[30] (§ 700.2103(a))
2.	*Parents, or parents equally, if no descendants*	100% (§ 700.2103(b))
3.	*Descendants of parents, or either of them, if no parents*	100%, by representation[30] (§ 700.2103(c))
4.	*Grandparents, if no descendants of parents*	50% to the paternal side and 50% to the maternal side. On each side, the grandparents share equally, and if only one, he or she takes the entire share (§ 700.2103(d))
5.	*Descendants of grandparents, if no grandparents on one side*	The 50% share passes by representation[30] (§ 700.2103(d))
6.	*The other side, if no descendants of grandparents on one side*	The 50% share is added to the 50% share passing to the grandparents or their descendants on the other side and the entire amount is distributed as per B.4. and B.5. above (§ 700.2103(d))
7.	*Person related to decedent through two lines of relation*	Only one share, based on the relation entitling him to the larger share (§ 700.2113)
8.	*State, if no grandparents or descendants of grandparents on either side*	100% (§ 700.2105)

---

[29] Each dollar amount listed in § 700.2102(1) shall be adjusted for inflation based on § 700.1210. The $150,000 figure above is adjusted for 2016 to $222,000. The $100,000 figure above is adjusted for 2016 to $148,000. (See Mich. Dept. Treas., Estates and Protected Individuals Code Cost-of-Living Adjustments to Specific Dollar Amounts (Jan. 25, 2016))

[30] "Representation" means per capita at each generation. See § 700.2106.

Minnesota
Who Takes by Intestate Succession?

A.	*Surviving spouse takes:*		
	1.	If no descendant of decedent	100% (§ 524.2-102(1)(i))
	2.	If all of decedent's descendants are descendants of surviving spouse and the surviving spouse has no other descendants	100% (§ 524.2-102(1)(ii))
	3.	If one of the surviving spouse's descendants is not a descendant of the decedent or one of the decedent's descendants is not a descendant of the surviving spouse	First $150,000, plus $1/2$ of balance of the interstate estate (§ 524.2-102(2))
B.	*All the estate, or the surplus if there is a surviving spouse, passes to:*		
	1.	Descendants	100%, by representation[30] (§ 524.2-103(1))
	2.	Parents, or parents equally, if no descendants	100% (§ 524.2-103(2))
	3.	Descendants of parents, or of either of them, if no parents	100%, by representation[30] (§ 524.2-103(3))
	4.	Grandparents, if no descendants of parents	50% to the paternal side and 50% to the maternal side. On each side, the grandparents share equally, and if only one, he or she takes the entire share (§ 524.2-103(4))
	5.	Descendants of grandparents, if no grandparents on one side	The 50% share passes by representation[30] (§ 524.2-103(4))
	6.	The other side, if no descendants of grandparents on one side	The 50% share is added to the 50% share passing to the grandparents or their descendants on the other side (§ 524.2-103(4))
	7.	Next of kin, if no descendants of grandparents on either side	100%, but if more than one, then equally if in equal degree. However, if in equal degree, but claiming through different ancestors, those claiming through the nearest ancestor take to the exclusion of those claiming through a more remote ancestor (§ 524.2-103(5))
	8.	Person related to decedent through two lines of relation	Only one share, based on the relation entitling him to the larger share (§ 524.2-113)
	9.	State, if no grandparents or descendants of grandparents on either side and no next of kin	100% (§ 524.2-105)

---

[31] "Representation" means in the case of descendants of decedent a per stirpital distribution. See § 524.2-106(b). However, in the case of descendants of parents and grandparents, it means per capita with representation. See § 524.2-106(c)(1)&(2).

Mississippi
Who Takes by Intestate Succession?

A.		*Surviving spouse takes:*	
	1.	*If no children or descendants of children*	100% (§ 91-1-7)
	2.	*If any children or descendants of children*	A child's part (§ 91-1-7)
B.		*All the estate, or the surplus if there is a surviving spouse, passes to:*	
	1.	*Children and descendants of deceased children*	100% equally, but with descendants of deceased children taking by representation (§ 91-1-3)[31]
	2.	*Parents, siblings, and descendants of siblings, if no children or descendants of children*	100% in equal parts, with the "descendants of a sister or brother of the intestate to have in equal parts among them their deceased parent's share" (§ 91-1-3)
	3.	*Grandparents, uncles, and aunts, if no parents, siblings, or descendants of siblings*	100% in equal parts (§ 91-1-3)
	4.	*Next of kin, if no grandparents, uncles, and aunts*	100% in equal shares to those of equal degree under the civil law method of counting, but without representation (§ 91-1-3)
	5.	*State, if no other takers*	100% (§ 89-11-1)

[32] The statute refers only to real estate. However, § 91-1-11 applies the same rules to personal property. "Representation" is not defined, although there is some authority indicating that it means per stirpes. See, e.g., In re Griffin's Will, 411 So. 2d 766, 769-70 (1982).

Missouri
Who Takes by Intestate Succession?

A.		*Surviving spouse takes:*	
	1.	*If there is no surviving issue of the decedent*	100% (§ 474.010(1)(a))
	2.	*If there are surviving issue, all of whom are also issue of the surviving spouse*	First $20,000.00, plus 50% of the interstate estate (§ 474.010(1)(b))
	3.	*If there are surviving issue, one or more of whom are not issue of the surviving spouse*	50% of the interstate estate (§ 474.010(1)(c))
B.		*All the estate, or the surplus if there is a surviving spouse, passes to:*	
	1.	*Decedent's children or their descendants*	100%, in equal parts (§ 474.010(2)(a))
	2.	*Decedent's father, mother, brother and sisters or their descendants, if there are no children, or their descendants*	100%, in equal parts (§ 474.010(2)(b))
	3.	*Grandfathers, grandmothers, uncles and aunts or their descendants,[32] if no father, mother, brother or sister, or their descendants[33]*	100%, in equal parts (§ 474.010(2)(c))
	4.	*Great-grandfathers, great-grandmothers, or their descendants and so on passing to the nearest lineal ancestors and their children, or their descendants (provided, however, that collateral relatives, that is relatives who are neither ancestors nor descendants of the decedent, may not inherit unless they are related to the decedent at least as closely as the ninth degree), if there are no grandfather, grandmother, uncles, aunts, nor their descendants*	100%, in equal parts (§ 474.010(2)(d))
	5.	*Kindred of each predeceased spouse who was married to the decedent at the spouse's death, if there is no surviving spouse or kindred of the decedent entitled to inherit*	100%, in "equal shares" to the kindred of each predeceasing spouse. Each such share passes as described in B.1.-B.4. above. (§ 474.010(3))
	6.	*Escheat as provided by the law, if no other takers*	(§ 474.010(4))

---

[33] Generally, if takers are of the same lineal degree they take per capita. Otherwise, they take per stirpes. See § 474.020.

[34] There is no indication whether descendants of a deceased aunt or uncle take if there are surviving aunts or uncles. It would seem however, to be the case. Furthermore, the reference to descendants would appear to be referring to uncles and aunts, rather than grandparents. However, these matters are unresolved.

Montana
Who Takes by Intestate Succession?

A.	*Surviving spouse takes:*	
	1. *If no descendant or parent of the decedent survives the decedent*	100% (§ 72-2-112(1)(a))
	2. *If all of the decedent's surviving descendants are also descendants of the surviving spouse and there is no other descendant of the surviving spouse who survives the decedent*	100% (§ 72-2-112(1)(b))
	3. *If no descendant of the decedent survives the decedent but a parent of the decedent survives the decedent*	First $200,000.00, plus 75% of the balance of the interstate estate (§ 72-2-112(2))
	4. *If all of decedent's descendants are also surviving spouse's descendants and one or more of the spouse's descendants are not decedent's descendants*	First $150,000, plus 50% of the balance of the interstate estate (§ 72-2-112(3))
	5. *If one or more of the decedent's surviving descendants are not descendants of the surviving spouse*	First $100,000, plus 50% of the balance of the interstate estate (§ 72-2-112(4))
B.	*All the estate, or the surplus if there is a surviving spouse, passes to:*	
	1. *Decedent's descendants*	100% by representation (§ 72-2-113(1)(a))
	2. *Decedent's parents equally if both survive or to the surviving parent, if there is no surviving descendant*	100% (§ 72-2-113(1)(b))
	3. *Descendants of the decedent's parents or either of them, if there is no surviving parent*	100%, by representation[34] (§ 72-2-113(1)(c))
	4. *Grandparents or descendants of grandparents, if there is no descendant of a parent*	One-half to the decedent's paternal/maternal grandparents or descendants of the decedent's paternal/maternal grandparents, with each surviving grandparent on that side taking an equal portion if both survive. If not survived by a grandparent, then to descendants of grandparents on either the paternal or the maternal side (§ 72-2-113(d)(i))
	5. *The other side if no grandparents or descendants of grandparents on the one side*	100%, in same manner as B.4. above (§ 72-2-113(d)(ii))
	6. *The person or persons of the closest degree of kinship with the decedent, if no grandparents or descendants of grandparents*	100% (§ 72-2-113(1)(e)); if persons are of same degree but have different common ancestors with the decedent, the one(s) with the nearest ancestor takes exclusively (§ 72-2-113(2))
	7. *Person related to decedent through two lines of relation*	Only one share, based on the relation entitling him to the larger share (§ 72-2-123)
	8. *State, if there is no other taker*	100% (§ 72-2-115)

---

[35] "Representation" means per capita with representation. See § 72-2-116(2).

Nebraska
Who Takes by Intestate Succession?

A.	Surviving spouse takes:	
	1. If there is no surviving issue or parent of the decedent	100% (§ 30-2302(1))
	2. If there is no surviving issue but the decedent is survived by a parent or parents	First $100,000.00, plus 50% of the balance of the interstate estate (§ 30-2302(2))
	3. If there are surviving issue all of whom are issue of the surviving spouse also	First $100,000.00, plus 50% of the balance of the interstate estate (§ 30-2302(3))
	4. If there are surviving issue one or more of whom are not issue of the surviving spouse	50% of the balance of the interstate estate (§ 30-2302(4))
B.	All the estate, or the surplus if there is a surviving spouse, passes to:	
	1. Issue of the decedent	If they are all of the same degree of kinship to the decedent they take equally, but if of unequal degree, then those of more remote degree take by representation[35] (§ 30-2303(1))
	2. Parents, or parents equally, if no surviving issue	100% (§ 30-2303(2))
	3. Issue of the parents or either of them by representation, if there is no surviving issue or parent	100% (§ 30-2303(3))
	4. Grandparents, if there is no surviving issue of a parent	50% paternal side to be shared equally if both grandparents survive or otherwise all to sole surviving grandparent; 50% share for maternal side to be distributed in same manner (§ 30-2303(4))
	5. Issue of grandparents on one side, if there are no surviving grandparents on that side	100%, taking equally if issue are of same degree or, otherwise, taking by representation[35] (§ 30-2303(4))
	6. The other side if no grandparents or issue of grandparents on the one side	100%, in same manner as B.4. above (§ 30-2303(4))
	7. Next of kin, if there is no surviving grandparent or issue of any grandparent	100% in equal degree, excepting that when there are two or more collateral kindred in equal degree, but claiming through different ancestors, those who claim through the nearest ancestor are preferred to those claiming through a more remote ancestor (§ 30-2303(5))
	8. State, if no other taker	100% (§ 30-2305)

---

[36] "Representation" means per capita with representation.

Nevada
Who Takes by Intestate Succession?

A. *Surviving spouse takes:*

1.	If the decedent leaves a surviving spouse and only one child, or the lawful issue of one child	50% surviving spouse and 50% to the child or the issue of the child (§ 134.040(1))
2.	If the decedent leaves a surviving spouse and more than one child living, or a child and the lawful issue of one or more deceased children	One-third to the surviving spouse and the remainder in equal shares to the children and the lawful issue of any deceased child by right of representation (§ 134.040(2))
3.	If the decedent leaves no issue nor parents	50% of the separate property of the decedent goes to the surviving spouse and the other 50% goes in equal shares to the brothers and sisters of the decedent (§ 134.050(2))
4.	If the decedent leaves no issue	50% to the surviving spouse, 25% to the father of the decedent and 25% to the mother of the decedent, if both are living. If both parents are not living, 50% to either the father or the mother then living (§ 134.050(1))
5.	If the decedent leaves no issue, parent, sibling, or children of issue	100% of the separate property(§ 134.050(4))

B. *All the estate, or the surplus if there is a surviving spouse, passes to:*

1.	Child or children but no children of issue	100%, share and share alike (§ 134.090)
2.	Children and the issue of a deceased child	100%, with the issue taking by representation[36] (§ 134.100)
3.	Issue of children but no children	100%, by representation (§ 134.110)
4.	Parents, if there is no surviving issue or surviving spouse	50% to the father of the decedent and 50% to the mother of the decedent, if both are living. If both parents are not living, 100% to either the father or the mother then living. (§ 134.050(3))
5.	Siblings and the children of deceased siblings, if no issue, parent, children of issue, of spouse	100% to the siblings in equal shares and if a sibling is deceased then to the sibling's issue by right of representation. (§ 134.060)
6.	Next of kin if no issue, spouse, parent, or sibling	100%, equally, if in equal degree, but if claiming through different ancestors, the one(s) claiming through the nearest ancestor takes (§ 134.070)
7.	State, if no kindred	100% to state for educational purposes (§ 134.120)

Note: The decedent's share of community property with right of survivorship passes to the surviving spouse. (§ 134.010(1)) If there is no right of survivorship and it is not disposed of by will, it also passes to the surviving spouse. (§ § 134.010(2); 123.250(b)(1)) In the case of the death of a minor who has not been married and is childless and whose parents are deceased, the estate that came to the child by inheritance from the parent passes to the issue of the parent equally if they are of the same degree and otherwise they are entitled to take by representation. (§ 134.080)

---

[37] "Representation" is not defined in the statute or case law.

New Hampshire
Who Takes by Intestate Succession?

A. *Surviving spouse takes:*

1.	*If there is no surviving issue or parent*	100% (§ 561:1(I)(a))
2.	*If there is no surviving issue, but parent or parents*	First $250,000, plus ³/₄ of the balance (§ 561:1(I)(c))
3.	*If there are surviving issue all of whom are also issue of surviving spouse and there are no other issue of the surviving spouse who survive the decedent*	First $250,000, plus ¹/₂ of the balance (§ 561:1(I)(b))
4.	*If there is any surviving issue not also issue of surviving spouse*	$100,000 plus ¹/₂ of intestate estate. (§ 561:1(I)(e)) Query whether this should be "balance of the intestate estate "rather than" intestate estate."
5.	*If there are surviving issue of the decedent, all of whom are issue of the surviving spouse, and the surviving spouse has one or more surviving issue who are not issue of the decedent*	First $150,000, plus ¹/₂ of the balance (§ 561:1(I)(d))

B. *All the estate, or the surplus if there is a surviving spouse, passes to:*

1.	*Issue*	100%, equally if of same degree of kinship and if not, then by representation[37] (§ 561:1(II)(a))
2.	*Parents, if no issue*	100%, equally (§ 561:1(II)(b))
3.	*Siblings, if no parents*	100%, by representation (§ 561:1(II)(c))
4.	*Issue of siblings, if no siblings*	100%, equally if of same degree, but if not, then by representation[37] (§ 561:1(II)(c))
5.	*Grandparents, if no issue of siblings*	50% to the paternal grandparents or surviving grandparent and the same on the maternal side (§ 561:1(II)(d))
6.	*Issue of grandparents, if no grandparents on that side*	100%, equally if of same degree of kinship, but if not, then those of more remote degree take by representation. (§ 561:1(II)(e)) The issue of grandparents only take if they are not beyond the fourth degree of kinship to the decedent. If there are no issue within the fourth degree on either the paternal or maternal grandparent side, then those issue on the other side take in full.
7.	*Grandparents or issue of grandparents on one side, if no grandparents or issue of grandparents on the other side*	Entire share added to the other side's 50% share and then distributed as in B.5. and B.6. above (§ 561:1(II)(d))
8.	*State, if no other taker*	100% (§ 561:1(II)(g))

---

[38] "Representation" means per capita with representation. See Colony v. Colony, 97 N.H. 386, 394-96, 89 A.2d 909, 914-15 (1952); Preston v. Cole, 64 N.H. 459, 13 A. 788 (1888); Merrow v. Merrow, 105 N.H. 103, 193 A.2d 19 (1963).

New Jersey
Who Takes by Intestate Succession?

A. *Surviving spouse or domestic partner takes:*

1.	*If no descendant or parent of the decedent survives the decedent*	100% (§ 3B:5-3(a)(1))
2.	*If all of the decedent's surviving descendants are also descendants of the surviving spouse and there is no other descendant of the surviving spouse who survives the decedent*	100% (§ 3B:5-3(a)(2))
3.	*If no descendant of the decedent survives the decedent, but a parent of the decedent survives the decedent*	The first 25% of the intestate estate, but not less than $50,000.00 nor more than $200,000.00, plus 3/4 of any balance of the intestate estate. (§ 3B:5-3(b))
4.	*If all of the decedent's surviving descendants are also descendants of the surviving spouse and the surviving spouse has one or more surviving descendants who are not descendants of the decedent*	The first 25% of the intestate estate, but not less than $50,000.00 nor more than $200,000.00, plus 1/2 of the balance of the intestate estate. (§ 3B:5-3(c)(1))
5.	*If one or more of the decedent's surviving descendants is not a descendant of the surviving spouse*	The first 25% of the intestate estate, but not less than $50,000.00 nor more than $200,000.00, plus one-half of the balance of the intestate estate. (§ 3B:5-3(c)(2))

B. *All the estate, or the surplus if there is a surviving spouse or domestic partner, passes to:*

1.	*Descendants of decedent*	100%, by representation.[38] (§ 3B:5-4(a))
2.	*Parent, or parents equally, if no surviving descendant*[39]	100% (§ 3B:5-4(b))
3.	*Descendants of decedent's parents, if there are no surviving parents*	100%, descendants of parents or either of them taking by representation.[38] (§ 3B:5-4(c))
4.	*Grandparents, if there is no surviving descendant, parent, or descendant of a parent*	50% of the estate passes to the paternal grandparents equally if both survive, or to the surviving paternal grandparent; the same is true of the maternal grandparents. If both are deceased, then to the descendants of the grandparents or either of them, the descendants taking equally if they are all of the same degree of kinship to the decedent, but if of unequal degree those of more remote degree take by representation.[38] (§ 3B:5-4(d)&(e))
5.	*Grandparents, and descendants of grandparents on the other side, if there are no grandparents or descendants of grandparents on one side*	100%, adding the 50% share on one side to the 50% share on the other side and then distributing the whole as in B.4. above. (§ 3B:5-4(d))
6.	*Decedent's step-children or their descendants, if no surviving descendants of grandparents*	100%, taking by representation.[38] (§ 3B:5-4(f))

7. *State, if there are no other takers*	a. Use and custody by state in case of certain safe deposit contents constituting tangible personal property and most intangible personal property (§§46:30B-37.1; 46:30B-6(r) ("property" defined for purposes of Uniform Disposition of Unclaimed Property Act))
	b. 100% escheat in the case of most tangible personal and real property (§2A:37-1; Van Kleek v. O' Hanlon, 21 N.J.L. 582 (1845); In re Mill's Estate, 212 A.2d 799 (Ch. 1965))

---

[39] "Representation" means per capita at each generation level. See §3B:1-2.

[40] Parent of decedent loses any right to intestate succession by refusing to acknowledge, or abandoning the decedent by willfully forsaking the decedent; failing to care for and keep control and custody of the decedent such that the decedent is exposed to physical or moral risk without proper protection, or such that the decedent was in state custody at the time of death; having sexually assaulted the decedent; having had criminal sexual contact with the decedent; endangering the welfare of the decedent as a child; attempting or conspiring to murder the decedent; contributing to the decedent's death by abuse or neglect. (§3B:5-14.1)

New Mexico
Who Takes by Intestate Succession?

A.	*Surviving spouse takes:*	
	1. *If no surviving issue of the decedent*	100%, as to separate property (§ 45-2-102(A)(1))
	2. *If there is surviving issue of the decedent*[40]	25%, as to separate property (§ 45-2-102(A)(2))
	3. *Community property as to which the decedent could have exercised the power of testamentary disposition*	50% (§ 45-2-102)(B)
B.	*All the estate, or the surplus if there is a surviving spouse, passes to:*	
	1. *Descendants, if there is no surviving spouse*	100%, by representation (§ 45-2-103(A)(1))
	2. *Parents, if there is no surviving descendant*	100%, to the decedent's parents equally if both survive, or to the surviving parent (§ 45-2-103(A)(2))
	3. *Descendants of the decedent's parents or either one of them, if there is no surviving descendant or parent*	100%, by representation (§ 45-2-103(A)(3))
	4. *Grandparents or descendants of the grandparents, if there is no descendant of a parent*	50% of the estate to the decedent's paternal grandparents equally if both survive, or to the surviving paternal grandparent, or to the descendants of the decedent's paternal grandparents or either of them if both are deceased, the descendants taking by representation, and the other 50% passes to the decedent's maternal relatives in the same manner; but if there is no surviving grandparent or descendant of a grandparent on either the paternal or the maternal side, the entire estate passes to the decedent's relatives on the other side in the same manner as the half (§ 45-2-103(A)(4)–(5))
	5. *Person related to decedent through two lines of relation*	Only one share based on the relation entitling him to the larger share (§ 45-2-113)
	6. *State, if there is no other taker*	100% (§ 45-2-105)

[41] A parent is barred from inheriting if parental rights were terminated and not reestablished at the time the decedent died, or if the child died before reaching 18 years of age, and there is clear and convincing evidence to show parental rights could have been terminated on the basis of any action or inaction toward the decedent. (§ 45-2-114)

New York
Who Takes by Intestate Succession?

A.	*Surviving spouse takes:*	
	1. *If there is issue*	$50,000 and 50% of the residue (EPTL § 4-1.1(a)(1))
	2. *If there is no issue*[41]	100% (EPTL § 4-1.1(a)(2))
B.	*All the estate, or the surplus if there is a surviving spouse, passes to:*	
	1. *Issue, if there is no spouse*	100%, by representation (EPTL § 4-1.1(a)(3))
	2. *One or both parents, if there is no issue*	100% (EPTL § 4-1.1(a)(4))
	3. *Issue of parents, if there is no spouse, issue or parent*	100%, by representation (EPTL § 4-1.1(a)(5))
	4. *Grandparents or the issue of grandparents, but only so far as grandchildren, if no spouse, issue, parent or issue of parents*	50% to the surviving paternal grandparent or grandparents, or if neither of them survives the decedent, to their issue, by representation, and the other 50% to the surviving maternal grandparent or grandparents, or if neither of them survives the decedent, to their issue, by representation; provided that if the decedent was not survived by a grandparent or grandparents on one side or by the issue of such grandparents, the whole to the surviving grandparent or grandparents on the other side, or if neither of them survives the decedent, to their issue, by representation, in the same manner as the one-half (EPTL § 4-1.1(a)(6))
	5. *Great-grandchildren of grandparents, if no spouse, issue, parent, issue of parents, grandparent, children of grandparents or grandchildren of grandparents*	50% to the great-grandchildren of the paternal grandparents, per capita, and the other 50% to the great-grandchildren of the maternal grandparents, per capita; provided that if the decedent was not survived by great-grandchildren of grandparents on one side, the whole to the great-grandchildren of grandparents on the other side, in the same manner as the one-half (EPTL § 4-1.1(a)(7))
	6. *Escheat as abandoned property, if no other takers*	100% (EPTL § 4-1.5)

---

[42] A parent cannot inherit from a decedent child if, before the child reaches 21 years, the parent has failed or refused to provide for or abandoned the child, unless these relationships and duties were resumed and continued until the death of the child (§ 4-1.4(a)(1)). A parent also shall not inherit from a child if his or her parental rights were terminated (§ 4-1.4(a)(2)(A)), or if there has been a suspended judgment as to whether such rights should be revoked, and surrogate court finds by a preponderance of the evidence that the parent failed to comply with a court order to restore the parent-child relationship (§ 4-1.4(a)(2)(B)). But a parent is not so barred to a biological parent who places a child for adoption based on a fraudulent promise to complete such adoption (§ 4-1.4(b)(1)) or other fraud or deceit by a person or agency who fails to arrange or timely meet conditions for an adoption (§ 4-1.4(b)(2)).

North Carolina
Who Takes by Intestate Succession?

A. *Surviving spouse takes:*

1.	real property: if the intestate is survived by only one child or by any lineal descendant of only one deceased child	One-half undivided interest (§ 29-14(a)(1))
2.	real property: if the intestate is survived by two or more children, or by one child and any lineal descendant of one or more deceased children or by lineal descendants of two or more deceased children	One-third undivided interest (§ 29-14(a)(2))
3.	real property: if the intestate is not survived by a child, children or any lineal descendant of a deceased child or children, but is survived by one or more parents	One-half undivided interest (§ 29-14(a)(3))
4.	real property: if the intestate is not survived by a child, children or any lineal descendant of a deceased child or children, or by a parent	100% (§ 29-14(a)(4))
5.	personal property: if the intestate is survived by only one child or by any lineal descendant of only one deceased child	100%; if the net personal property does not exceed $60,000 in value; if the net personal property exceeds $60,000 in value, the sum of $60,000 plus one-half of the balance of the personal property. (§ 29-14(b)(1))
6.	personal property: if the intestate is survived by two or more children, or by one child and any lineal descendant of one or more deceased children or by lineal descendants of two or more deceased children	100%; if the net personal property does not exceed $60,000; if net personal property exceeds $60,000 in value, the sum of $60,000 plus one-third of the balance of personal property. (§ 29-14(b)(2))
7.	personal property: if the intestate is not survived by a child, children or any lineal descendant of a deceased child or children, but is survived by one or more parents	100%; if the net personal property exceeds $100,000 in value, the sum of $100,000 plus 50% of the balance of the personal property (§ 29-14(b)(3))
8.	personal property: if the intestate is not survived by a child, children, or any lineal descendant of a deceased child or children, or by a parent	100% (§ 29-14(b)(4))

Note: § 29-14(c) provides that the amount a surviving spouse receives under § 29-14(a)-(b) is offset by the net value of any equitable distribution awarded to the surviving spouse pursuant to § 50-20 subsequent to the death of the decedent spouse.

B. *All the estate, or the surplus if there is a surviving spouse, passes to:*

1.	If the intestate is survived by only one child or by only one lineal descendant of only one deceased child	100%, by representation[42] (§ 29-15(1))
2.	If the intestate is survived by two or more children or by one child and any lineal descendant of one or more deceased children, or by lineal descendants of two or more deceased children	100%, by representation[42] (§ 29-15(2))

3.	*Parents, if the intestate is not survived by a child, children or any lineal descendant of a deceased child or children*	100% to be shared equally if both survive and if only one, then the entire estate (§ 29-15(3))
4.	*Siblings of the intestate, and the lineal descendants of the deceased siblings, if the intestate is not survived by a parent*	100%, by representation[42] (§ 29-15(4))
5.	*Paternal/maternal grandparents, if no siblings or lineal descendants of siblings*	50% of the net estate in equal shares to each side. Within each side, each grandparent takes 50%, or, if either is dead, the survivor takes the entire 50% of the net estate, and if neither grandparent survives, the uncles and aunts of the decedent on that side or the descendants of an uncle or aunt by representation share in said 50%. If there is no grandparent and no uncle or aunt, or lineal descendant of a deceased uncle or aunt, on that side, then those of the other side who otherwise would be entitled to take 50% as hereinbefore provided take the whole. (§ 29-15(5)(a-d))
6.	*The state*	100% if no one entitled to take under § § 29-14, 29-15, 29-21, or 29-22 (§ 29-12)

[43] "Representation" means per capita at each generation. See § 29-16. In the case of descendants of siblings, no descendants removed beyond the fifth degree are entitled to take. See § 29-16(b)(5).

North Dakota
Who Takes by Intestate Succession?

A.	*Surviving spouse takes:*	
1.	no descendant or parent of the decedent survives the decedent	100% (§ 30.1-04-02(1)(a))
2.	all of the decedent's surviving descendants are also descendants of the surviving spouse and there is no other descendant of the surviving spouse who survives the decedent	100% (§ 30.1-04-02(1)(b))
3.	If no descendant of the decedent survives the decedent, but a parent of the decedent survives the decedent	First three hundred thousand dollars, plus 75% of any balance of the intestate estate (§ 30.1-04-02(2))
4.	If all of the decedent's surviving descendants are also descendants of the surviving spouse and the surviving spouse has one or more descendants who are not descendants of the decedent	First two hundred and twenty-five thousand dollars, plus one-half of any balance of the intestate estate (§ 30.1-04-02(3))
5.	If one or more of the decedent's surviving descendants are not descendants of the surviving spouse	First one hundred fifty thousand dollars, plus 50% of any balance of the intestate estate (§ 30.1-04-02(4))

B.	*All the estate, or the surplus if there is a surviving spouse, passes to:*	
1.	Decedent's descendants	100%, by representation (§ 30.1-04-03(1))
2.	Decedent's parents, if there is no surviving descendant	100% divided equally, or all if only one survives the decedent (§ 30.1-04-03(2))
3.	Descendants of the decedent's parents or either of them, if there is no surviving parent	100%, by representation (§ 30.1-04-03(3))
4.	Decedent's grandparents, if there is no surviving descendant of a parent	50% of the net estate in equal shares to the paternal and maternal sides. On each side, the grandparents share equally, or if either is deceased, the survivor takes the entire 50% share. If neither grandparent survives, the descendants of the grandparents on that side or of either one share in said 50%. If there is no grandparent or the descendant of deceased grandparents, on that side, then those on the other side who otherwise would be entitled to take 50% as hereinbefore provided take the whole by the same rules. (§§ 30.1-04-03(4), 30.1-04-03(5))
5.	Descendants of deceased spouse(s) of decedent	Equal shares for each deceased spouse and then such share divided among the deceased spouse's descendants by representation. (§ 30.1-04-03(6))
6.	Person related to decedent through two lines of relation	Only one share based on the relation entitling him to the larger share (§ 30.1-04-03.1)
7.	State[43], if there is no other taker	100% (§ 30.1-04-05)

[44] The intestate estate passes to the state for the support of the common schools. (§ 30.1-04-05)

Ohio
Who Takes by Intestate Succession?

A.	Surviving spouse takes:	
	1. If one or more children of the decedent or their lineal descendants are surviving and all of the decedent's children who survive or have lineal descendants surviving also are children of the surviving spouse	100% (§ 2105.06(B))[44]
	2. If one child of the decedent or the child's lineal descendants survive and the surviving spouse is not the natural or adoptive parent of the decedent's child	First twenty thousand dollars and 50% of the balance of the intestate estate if the spouse and the remainder to the child or the child's lineal descendants (§ 2105.06(C))[44]
	3. If more than one child or their lineal descendants survive and the spouse is the natural or adoptive parent of one, but not all, of the children	First $60,000 plus 1/3 of the balance (§ 2105.06(D))[44]
	4. If more than one child or their lineal descendants surviving and the spouse is the natural or adoptive parent of none of the children	$20,000 plus 1/3 of the balance (§ 2105.06(D))
	5. If there are no children or their lineal descendants	100% (§ 2105.06(E))
B.	All the estate, or the surplus if there is a surviving spouse, passes to:	
	1. Children or their lineal descendants	100%, equally if only children, but if there are any lineal descendants of deceased children, then per stirpes (§§ 2105.06(A), 2105.11, 2105.13) However, if there are only lineal descendants all of the same degree, then they share equally per capita (§ 2105.12)
	2. Parents of the intestate share equally, or the whole to the surviving parent, if no spouse and no children or their lineal descendants	100% (§ 2105.06 (F))
	3. Brothers and sisters, whether of the whole or of the half blood of the intestate, or their lineal descendants	100%, per stirpes (§ 2105.06 (G))
	4. Grandparents, if there are no brothers or sisters or their lineal descendants	50% to the paternal grandparents of the intestate equally, or to the survivor of them, and 50% to the maternal grandparents of the intestate equally, or to the survivor of them (§ 2105.06 (H))
	5. Lineal descendants of the deceased grandparents, if there is no paternal grandparent or no maternal grandparent	50% distributed among the lineal descendants on each side, per stirpes[45] (§ 2105.06 (I))
	6. The surviving grandparents on the other side or their lineal descendants, if there are no such lineal descendants on the other side	100%, as per B.4. and B.5. above (§ 2105.06 (I))
	7. The next of kin of the intestate,[46] if there are no surviving grandparents or their lineal descendants	100%, but without representation (§ 2105.06 (I))

8.	*The stepchildren or their lineal descendants, if there are no next of kin*	100%, per stirpes (§ 2105.06 (J))
9.	*State, if there are no stepchildren or their lineal descendants*	100% (§ 2105.06 (K))

[45] Real property is made subject to the foregoing rules by § 2105.061 and passes in parcenary subject to the monetary charge of the surviving spouse.

[46] Notwithstanding the use of the term "per stirpes" in § 2105.06, § 2105.13 provides for a distribution in this case per capita with representation. Note that it refers to "descendants of the intestate," but then states "not more remote than lineal descendants of grandparents." Presumably, the statute intends to refer to heirs other than descendants who share a common ancestor in "grandparents" of the intestate, but the language is poorly drafted.

[47] Next of kin is determined by the civil degree method of counting. See § 2105.03. There does not appear to be any cut-off for laughing heirs.

Oklahoma
Who Takes by Intestate Succession?

A. *Surviving spouse takes:*

1.	If no surviving issue, parent, or sibling	100% (84 § 213(B)(1)(a))
2.	If no surviving issue, but parent or parents, or siblings	100% of property acquired "by joint industry" of spouses during coverture (84 § 213(B)(1)(b)(1)), and an undivided $^1/_3$ interest in the balance (84 § 213(B)(1)(b)(2))
3.	If there are issue who are all issue of surviving spouse	$^1/_2$ of the estate (84 § 213(B)(1)(c))
4.	If there are surviving issue, one of whom is not issue of surviving spouse	An undivided $^1/_2$ interest in property acquired "by joint industry" of spouses during coverture (84 § 213(B)(1)(d)(1)), and an undivided equal part with each of the living children of the decedent and the lawful issue of any deceased child by right of representation in the balance (84 § 213(B)(1)(d)(2))
5.	Regardless of any other heirs	If one automobile in the estate, spouse takes it; if more than one automobile in the estate, spouse may choose one to take (84 § 232)

B. *All the estate, or the surplus if there is a surviving spouse, passes to:*

1.	Issue and their descendants	100%, in undivided equal shares by right of representation.[47] (84 § 213(B)(2)(a))
2.	Parent or parents, if no issue and their descendants	100% in undivided equal shares (84 § 213(B)(2)(b))
3.	Issue of parents, if no parents	100% in undivided equal shares by right of representation[47] (84 § 213(B)(2)(c))
4.	Grandparents, if no issue of parents	50% to paternal grandparents and 50% to maternal grandparents, with the grandparents on each side taking equally if both survive; otherwise, the survivor takes the entire 50% share (84 § 213(B)(2)(d))
5.	Issue of grandparent or grandparents if neither grandparent on one side survives	The 50% share is distributed to issue of same degree equally, and if not of equal degree, then by representation[47] (84 § 213(B)(2)(d))
6.	Grandparents or issue of grandparents on the other side, if no issue of grandparents on one side	100%, as per B.4.–5. above (84 § 213(B)(2)(d))
7.	Next of kin if no grandparent or issue on the other side	100% to next of kin in nearest equal degree (84 § 213(B)(2)(e))
8.	State for support of common schools, if no next of kin	100% (84 § 213(B)(3))

[48] "Representation" defined as per capita with representation by 84 § 213(B)(4). See In the Matter of Estate of Kendall, 968 P.2d 364, 366 (1998).

Oregon
Who Takes by Intestate Succession?

A.	*Surviving spouse takes:*	
	1. *If there are one or more surviving descendants of the decedent all of whom are issue of the surviving spouse also*	100% (§ 112.025(1))
	2. *If there are one or more surviving descendants of the decedent one or more of whom are not issue of the surviving spouse*	50% (§ 112.025(2))
	3. *If the decedent leaves a surviving spouse and no descendant*	100% (§ 112.035)
B.	*All the estate, or the surplus if there is a surviving spouse, passes to:*	
	1. *Descendant of the decedent*	100%. If the descendants are all of the same degree of kinship to the decedent, they take equally, but if of unequal degree, then those of more remote degrees take by representation.[48] (§ 112.045(1))
	2. *Surviving parents, if no descendants of the decedent*[49]	100% (§ 112.045(2)) If, at the time of taking, surviving parents are married to each other, they take real property as tenants by the entirety and personal property as joint owners with the right of survivorship (§ 112.045(5))
	3. *Brothers and sisters of the decedent and the descendants of any deceased brother or sister of the decedent, if no surviving parents*	100%, equally if siblings only, and by representation[48] to the extent of any descendants of deceased siblings of the decedent (§ 112.045(3))
	4. *Descendants of brothers and sisters, if there is no surviving brother or sister*	100%. If they are all of the same degree of kinship to the decedent, they take equally, but if of unequal degree, then those of more remote degree take by representation[48] (§ 112.045(3))
	5. *Grandparents of the decedent and the descendants of any deceased grandparent of the decedent, if there is no surviving descendant of a brother or sister of the decedent*	100%, with the descendant of a deceased grandparent taking by representation[48] (§ 112.045(4)) If, at the time of taking, surviving grandparents are married to each other, they take real property as tenants by the entirety and personal property as joint owners with the right of survivorship (§ 112.045(5))
	6. *Descendants of grandparents, if there is no surviving grandparent*	100%. If they are all of the same degree of kinship to the decedent, they take equally, but if of unequal degree, then those of more remote degrees take by representation[48] (§ 112.045(4))

7.	*Person related to the decedent through two lines of relation*	Only one share, based on the relation entitling him to the larger share (§ 112.115)
8.	*State, if there are no other takers*	100% (§ 112.055)

---

[49] "Representation" means per capita with representation. See § 112.065.

[50] Parent is treated as having predeceased the decedent if the parent (a) willfully deserted the decedent or (b) neglected without just and sufficient cause to provide proper care and maintenance for the decedent. This provision applies if the parent has performed either act for (a) the ten years immediately before an adult decedent became an adult, or (b) the ten years immediately before a minor decedent died. (§§ 112.047(1-2)) A court may disregard incidental visitations, communications, and contributions. (§ 112.047(2))

Pennsylvania
Who Takes by Intestate Succession?

A.	Surviving spouse takes:[50]	
	1. If there is no surviving issue or parent of the decedent	100% (20 § 2102(1))
	2. If there is no surviving issue of the decedent but he is survived by a parent or parents	The first $30,000 plus 50% of the balance of the intestate estate. (20 § 2102(2)) However, in the case of a decedent who died as a result of the terrorist attacks on September 11, 2001, a surviving spouse shall be entitled to 100% of any compensation award paid pursuant to the Air Transportation Safety and System Stabilization Act. (Id.)
	3. If there are surviving issue of the decedent all of whom are issue of the surviving spouse also	The first $30,000 plus 50% of the balance of the intestate estate (20 § 2102(3))
	4. If there are surviving issue of the decedent one or more of whom are not issue of the surviving spouse	50% (20 § 2102(4))
B.	All the estate, or the surplus if there is a surviving spouse, passes to:	
	1. Issue	100% (20 § 2103(1))
	2. Parents, if no issue survives[51]	100% (20 § 2103(2))
	3. Brothers, sisters, or their issue, if no parent survives	100% (20 § 2103(3))[52]
	4. Grandparents, if no issue of either of the decedent's parents but at least one grandparent survives the decedent	50% to the paternal grandparents or grandparent, or if both are deceased, to the children of each of them and the children of the deceased children of each of them,[52] and 50% to the maternal grandparents or grandparent, or if both are deceased to the children of each of them and the children of the deceased children of each of them.[52] If both of the paternal grandparents or both of the maternal grandparents are deceased leaving no child or grandchild surviving the decedent, the half which would have passed to them or to their children and grandchildren are added to the half passing to the grandparents or grandparent or to their children and grandchildren on the other side (20 § 2103(4))

5.	Uncles, aunts, their children, and grandchildren, if no grandparent survives the decedent	100% to uncles and aunts equally, and children or grandchildren of a deceased uncle or aunt. However, no share for any grandchild of an uncle or an aunt if there are any children of any other uncle or aunt, the latter taking exclusively. If there are no children, then grandchildren of uncles and aunts take, but no issue of a grandchild of an uncle or aunt is entitled to take under any circumstances. (20 §§ 2103(5) & 2104(1))
6.	State, in default of all other persons	100% (20 § 2103(6))

[51] A spouse's share is forfeit where, for one year or more previous to the decedent's death, the surviving spouse has neglected or refused to perform a duty of support owed to the decedent, or willfully and maliciously deserted the other spouse, or where the decedent dies domiciled in the Commonwealth during divorce proceedings where grounds for divorce are established. (20 § 2106 (a))

[52] A parent's share is forfeit if, for one year or more prior to the death of the parent's minor child or dependent child, the parent has deserted the child; failed to perform the duty of support to the child; been convicted of endangering the welfare of children; or been convicted of sexual abuse of children. (20 § 2106(b))

[53] "Representation" means per capita with representation. See 20 § 2104(1). However, if all takers are of the same degree, they take equally. See 20 § 2104(2).

Rhode Island
Who Takes by Intestate Succession?

A.	Surviving spouse takes:[53]	
	1. If no issue[53]	Real property: Life interest in real estate (§ 33-1-5)[54] Personal property: $50,000, plus ¹/₂ of the remainder (§ 33-1-10(1))
	2. If issue	¹/₂ of the personal property (§ 33-1-10(2))
B.	All the estate, or the surplus if there is a surviving spouse, passes to:[55]	
	1. Children or their descendants	100% (§ 33-1-1(1))
	2. Parents, equally, or the surviving parent of the intestate, if there are no children nor their descendants	100%, in equal shares (§ 33-1-1(2))
	3. Brothers and sisters of the intestate and their descendants, if there is no parent	100% (§ 33-1-1(3))
	4. Grandparents, if there is no brother, sister, nor their descendants	50% to the paternal grandparents and 50% to the maternal grandparents, to be divided equally between the grandparents on each side, if they both survive (§ 33-1-2(1))
	5. Uncles and aunts or their descendants, if there be no grandparents on that side	100%, with representation[56] in the case of descendants of deceased uncles and aunts (§ 33-1-2(2))
	6. Great grandparents, if no uncle, aunt, or their descendants on that side	100%, in equal shares (§ 33-1-2(3))
	7. Great uncles and great aunts or their descendants, if no great grandparent on that side	100%, with descendants of deceased great aunts or great uncles taking by representation[56] (§ 33-1-2(4))
	8. Nearest lineal ancestors and their descendants, if there are no great uncles, aunts, or descendants on that side	100%, with descendants of deceased nearest lineal descendants taking by representation[56] (§ 33-1-2(4))
	9. Grandparents or other kindred on the other side, if no lineal ancestors or their descendants on the one side	The 50% share of the one side is added to the other side's moiety, and the entire estate is distributed as per B.4.-B.8. above (§ 33-1-3)
	10. Surviving spouse, if no kindred of the intestate on either the paternal nor maternal sides	100%, in like manner as per B.4.-B.9. above (§ 33-1-3)
	11. Treated as unclaimed property, belonging to state and with respect to real property, town council takes possession, if no other takers	100% (§§ 33-21-1 et seq. (real property) & 33-21.1-2 et seq. (personal property) See also City of Providence v. Solomon, 444 A.2d 870 (1982)

[54] The surviving spouse, or, if deceased, the kindred of the surviving spouse, take if there are no kindred of the intestate to take on the paternal or maternal sides, as set forth in B.10. below.

[55] The surviving spouse may also petition, if there are no issue, for a set-off of an amount not exceeding $50,000 in value of real estate, which may be allowed in the discretion of the court. (§ 33-1-6)

[56] The personal property is distributed in accordance with the descent of real property, as set forth below. See § 33-1-10.

[57] "Representation" means per stirpes. See, e.g., Daboll v. Field, 9 R.I. 266 (1869); Kelaghan v. Lewis, 98 R.I. 458, 466, 204 A.2d 633, 637 (1964). See also B.M.C. Durfee Trust Co. v. Franzheim, 349 Mass. 335, 207 N.E.2d 913, 916 (1965). See generally § 33-1-7, which is not particularly helpful.

South Carolina
Who Takes by Intestate Succession?

A.		*Surviving spouse takes:*	
	1.	*If there is no surviving issue of the decedent*	100% (§ 62-2-102(1))
	2.	*If there are surviving issue of the decedent*	50% (§ 62-2-102(2))
B.		*All the estate, or the surplus if there is a surviving spouse, passes to:*	
	1.	*Issue, if there is no surviving spouse*	100%; if they are all of the same degree of kinship to the decedent they take equally, but if of unequal degree then those of more remote degree take by representation[57] (§ 62-2-103(1))
	2.	*Parent, or parents equally, if there is no surviving issue*[58]	100% (§ 62-2-103(2))
	3.	*Issue of the parents or either of them by representation, if there is no surviving parent*	100% (§ 62-2-103(3))
	4.	*Grandparents or issue of grandparents, if there is no surviving issue of a parent*	50% to the paternal grandparents if both survive, or to the surviving paternal grandparent, or to the issue of the paternal grandparents if both are deceased, the issue taking equally if they are all of the same degree of kinship to the decedent, but if of unequal degree those of more remote degree take by representation;[57] 50% to the maternal relatives in the same manner (§ 62-2-103(4))
	5.	*Relatives on the other side, if there be no surviving grandparent or issue of grandparent on one side*	In the same manner as B.4. above (§ 62-2-103(4))
	6.	*Greatgrandparents or issue of greatgrandparents, if there are no grandparents or issue of grandparents*	50% to the surviving paternal great grandparents in equal shares, or to the surviving paternal great grandparent if only one survives, or to the issue of the paternal great grandparents if none of the great grandparents survive, the issue taking equally if they are all of the same degree of kinship to the decedent, but if of unequal degree those of more remote degree take by representation;[57] 50% to the maternal relatives in the same manner (§ 62-2-103(5))
	7.	*Relatives on the other side, if there be no surviving greatgrandparent or issue of a greatgrandparent on either the paternal or the maternal side*	In the same manner as B.6. above (§ 62-2-103(5))
	8.	*Person related to decedent through two lines of relation*	Only one share, based on the relation entitling him to the larger share (§ 62-2-113)
	9.	*State, if there is no other taker*	100% (§ 62-2-105)

[58] "Representation" means per capita with representation. See § 62-2-106.

[59] Parents are disqualified from inheriting if, on petition by an interested person, with service of summons and notice to the parent, the Probate Court determines by a preponderance of the evidence that the parent failed to reasonably provide support for the decedent and did not otherwise meet the needs of the decedent during his minority. (§ 62-2-114)

South Dakota
Who Takes by Intestate Succession?

A. *Surviving spouse takes:*

  1. *If no descendant of the decedent survives the decedent* — 100% (§ 29A-2-102(1)(i))

  2. *If all of the decedent's surviving descendants are also descendants of the surviving spouse* — 100% (§ 29A-2-102(1)(ii))

  3. *If one or more of the decedent's surviving descendants are not descendants of the surviving spouse* — The first $100,000, plus one-half of any balance of the intestate estate (§ 29A-2-102(2))

B. *All the estate, or the surplus if there is a surviving spouse, passes to:*

  1. Descendants — 100% by representation[59] (§ 29A-2-103(1))

  2. Parents equally if both survive, or the surviving parent, if there is no surviving descendant — 100% (§ 29A-2-103(2))

  3. Descendants of the decedent's parents or either of them by representation, if there is no surviving parent — 100% by representation (§ 29A-2-103(3))

  4. Grandparents, if there is no surviving descendant of a parent — 50% to the decedent's paternal grandparents equally if both survive, or the whole of the share to the surviving paternal grandparent, or by representation[59] to the descendants of the decedent's paternal grandparents or either of them if both paternal grandparents are deceased; 50% passes to the decedent's maternal relatives in the same manner (§ 29A-2-103(4))

  5. Decedent's relatives on the other side, if there is no surviving grandparent or descendant of a grandparent on one side — In the same manner as B.4. above (§ 29A-2-103(4))

  6. Person related to decedent through two lines of relation — Only one share, based on the relation entitling him to the larger share (§ 29A-2-113)

  7. State, if there are no other takers — 100% (§ 29A-2-105)

[60] "Representation" means per capita with representation. See § 29A-2-106.

Tennessee
Who Takes by Intestate Succession?

A.		Surviving spouse takes:	
	1.	If there is no surviving issue of the decedent	100% (§ 31-2-104(a)(1))
	2.	If there are surviving issue of the decedent	Greater of ⅓ or a child's share of the entire intestate estate (§ 31-2-104(a)(2))
B.		All the estate, or the surplus if there is a surviving spouse, passes to:	
	1.	Issue	100%; if the issue are all of the same degree of kinship to the decedent they take equally, but if of unequal degree, then those of more remote degree take by representation.[60] (§ 31-2-104(b)(1))
	2.	Parent or parents equally, if there is no surviving issue	100% (§ 31-2-104(b)(2))
	3.	Brothers and sisters and the issue of each deceased brother and sister, if there is no parent	100%, by representation[60] (§ 31-2-104(b)(3))
	4.	Issue of brothers and sisters, if there is no surviving brother or sister	100%, by representation[60] (§ 31-2-104(b)(3))
	5.	Grandparents or issue of grandparents, if there is no surviving issue of a parent	50% to the paternal grandparents if both survive, or to the surviving paternal grandparent or to the issue of the paternal grandparents if both are deceased, the issue taking equally if they are all of the same degree of kinship to the decedent, but if of unequal degree those of more remote degree take by representation;[60] 50% to the maternal relatives in the same manner; but if there are no surviving grandparent or issue of grandparent on either the paternal or maternal side, the entire estate passes to the relatives on the other side in the same manner as the half. (§ 31-2-104(b)(4))
	6.	State, if there are no other takers	100% (§ 31-2-110)

[61] "Representation" means per stirpes. See § 31-2-106.

Texas
Who Takes by Intestate Succession?

A.	*Surviving spouse takes:*	
	1.	*If the deceased is survived by a child or children, or their descendants*	33% of the personal estate and an estate for life, in one-third of the land of the intestate, with remainder to the child or children of the intestate and their descendants; the balance of the personal estate passes to the child or children of the deceased and their descendants. (Estates Code § 201.002(b)(1)-(3)); all of the decedent's community estate, but only if all surviving children and surviving descendants of children are also children and descendants of the surviving spouse or no child or descendant of the deceased spouse survives the deceased spouse. (Estates Code § 201.003(b)); if a child or descendant of the deceased spouse is not a child or descendant of the surviving spouse, then the surviving spouse retains $^1/_2$ of the community estate and the other $^1/_2$ passes to the children or descendants of the deceased spouse. (Estates Code § 201.003(c))
	2.	*If the deceased is not survived by a child or children, or their descendants*	100% of the personal estate and 50% of the lands of the intestate, without remainder to any person, and the other 50% passes according to the rules of descent and distribution; provided, however, that if the deceased has neither surviving father nor mother nor surviving brothers or sisters, or their descendants, then the surviving husband or wife is entitled to the whole of the estate of such intestate (Estates Code § 201.002(c)(1)-(3)); all of the decedent's community estate (Estates Code § 201.001(b))

B.	*The children and their descendants, if no spouse*	100% (Estates Code § 201.001(6))

C.	*Parents take, if there are no children nor their descendants:*	
	1.	*If both survive*	50% each (Estates Code § 201.001(c))
	2.	*If only the father or mother survive the intestate*	50% to such survivor, and 50% to the brothers and sisters of the decedent, and to their descendants; but if there be none such, then the whole estate passes to the surviving father or mother (Estates Code § 201.001(d))
	3.	*The brothers and sisters of the intestate and their descendants if there is neither father nor mother surviving*	100% (Estates Code § 201.001(e))

4.	*Grandparents and descendants of deceased grandparents if no siblings or descendants of siblings*	Divided into two moieties, one of which passes to the paternal and the other to the maternal kindred, in the following course: To the grandfather and grandmother in equal portions, but if only one of them survives, then the estate is divided into two equal parts, one of which goes to such survivor, and the other goes to the descendant or descendants of such deceased grandfather or grandmother. If the grandparent has no descendants then all of the moiety to the surviving grandparent or descendants of that grandparent (Estates Code § 201.001(f)-(h)) If there are no grandparents or descendants of grandparents with respect to one of the moieties, it is added to the other moiety. (State v. Estate of Loomis, 553 S.W.2d 166, 169 (Ct. App. 1977))[61]
5.	*State, if there are no other takers*	100% (Prop. Code § 71.001(a))

---

[62] If in the first or same degree, relatives take per capita. Otherwise, they take per stirpes, (Estates Code § 201.101(a)-(b)) which, as interpreted, actually means per capital with representation. See, e.g., Welder v. Hitchcock, 617 S.W.2d 294, 297 (Civ. App. 1981).

Utah
Who Takes by Intestate Succession?

A.	*Surviving spouse takes:*	
1.	*If no descendant of the decedent survives the decedent*	100% (§ 75-2-102(1)(a)(i))
2.	*If all of the decedent's surviving descendants are also descendants of the surviving spouse*	100% (§ 75-2-102(1)(a)(ii))
3.	*If one or more of the decedent's surviving descendants are not descendants of the surviving spouse*	$75,000 plus 50% of any balance of the intestate estate (§ 75-2-102(1)(b)) If the intestate estate passes to the surviving spouse and decedent's heirs, any nonprobate transfer received by the surviving spouse is chargeable against the surviving spouse's intestate share. (§ 75-2-102(2))
B.	*All the estate, or the surplus if there is a surviving spouse, passes to:*	
1.	*Decedent's descendants*	100%, per capita at each generation (§ 75-2-103(1)(a))
2.	*Parents equally if both survive, or all to the surviving parent, if there is no surviving descendant*	100% (§ 75-2-103(1)(b))
3.	*The descendants of the decedent's parents, if no surviving parent*	100% per capita at each generation (§ 75-2-103(1)(c))
4.	*Grandparents or descendants of grandparents, if no descendants of parents*	50% passes to the decedent's paternal grandparents equally if both survive, or to the surviving paternal grandparent, or to the descendants of the decedent's paternal grandparents or either of them if both are deceased, per capita at each generation; 50% to the decedent's maternal relatives in the same manner. If there is no surviving grandparent or descendant of a grandparent on one side, the entire estate passes to the decedent's relatives on the other side as is distributed in the same manner as the half (§ § 75-2-103(1)(d), 75-2-103(1)(e))
5.	*Descendants of decedent's deceased spouse, if no surviving descendants of grandparent*	100%, per capita at each generation, with equal shares divided first to the number of deceased spouses with descendants of each set, then taking per capita at each generation (§ 75-2-103(1)(f)
6.	*State[62], if there are no other takers*	100% (§ 75-2-105)

[63] The intestate estate passes to the state for the benefit of the state school fund. (§ 75-2-105)

Vermont
Who Takes by Intestate Succession?

A. Surviving spouse takes:

1.	If no descendant of the decedent survives the decedent	100% (14 § 311(1))
2.	If all of the decedent's surviving descendants are also descendants of the surviving spouse	100% (14 § 311(1))
3.	If one or more descendants of the decedent are not descendants of the surviving spouse and are not excluded by the decedent's will from inheriting from the decedent	50% of the intestate estate (14 § 311(2))
4.	If no descendants object, or if another descendant objects but court allows	All furniture/furnishings in decedent's household, in addition to any other share (14 § 312)

B. All of the estate, or the surplus if there is a surviving spouse, passes to:

1.	Decedent's descendants	100%, by right of representation (14 § 314 (a))
2.	Parents equally if both survive or to the surviving parent	100% (14 § 314(b)(1))
3.	Siblings and the descendants of any deceased siblings[63]	100% by right of representation (14 § 314(b)(2))
4.	Grandparents	100%, one-half of the intestate estate to the decedent's paternal grandparents equally if they both survive or to the surviving paternal grandparent and one-half of the intestate estate to the decedent's maternal grandparents equally if they both survive or to the surviving maternal grandparent and if decedent is survived by a grandparent, or grandparents on only one side, to that grandparent or those grandparents (14 § 314 (b)(3))

5.	*Next of kin*[64]	100%, in equal shares to the next of kin in equal degree (14 § 314(b)(4))
6.	State, if "a person dies testate or intestate, seised of real or personal property in this state, leaving no heir nor person entitled to the same . . . "	100%, for the use of schools (14 § § 681, 683)

[64] The meaning of "representation" is uncertain. Historically, the right of inheritance was given to the "representatives" of the deceased ancestor. This was interpreted to mean per capita if they were all of the same degree. See In re Martin's Estate 120 A. 862 (1923). For example, if the intestate is survived by three grandchildren, one the child of one of the intestate's children and the other two the children of a second child of the intestate, they all took equally as a class, rather than $1/2$, $1/4$, $1/4$. When the descendants were not all of the same degree, "representation" would apply and this was held to be per stirpes. See Gaines v. Strong's Estate, 40 Vt. 354, 357-58 (1867); In re Martin's Estate, 120 A. 862, 862 (1923). The current statute refers to "representation" with respect to descendants of the intestate and descendants of siblings of the intestate. The statute appears, by the use of the term "representation" without more, thereby, to be adopting a per stirpital approach in these situations. On the other hand, one might argue that the statute overrides former precedent and adopts a newer approach to "representation," such as per capita with representation or per capita at each generation. However, there is no actual language in the statute supporting this shift in meaning. The statute also does not address whether "representation" still applies only if the descendants of the intestate or the siblings of the intestate are all of the same degree, as has been the case in the past. Certainly, nothing in the language of the statute indicates such a limitation.

[65] The statute provides for "equal shares to the next of kin in equal degree." The prior statute also explicitly provided: "but a person shall not be entitled, by right of representation, to the share of such next of kin who has died." Presumably, the omission of this language in the current statute was not intended to alter the outcome, which is to not apply representation, but to award shares solely to the person who is next of kin by proximity of degree to the intestate and, if more than one person of that proximate degree, to divide the net estate between or among such persons equally.

Virginia
Intestate Succession
(Post-September 30, 2012)

A.		Surviving spouse takes:	
	1.	If no children or their descendants, or if children or their descendants and the children of the decedent are also children of the surviving spouse	100% (§ 64.2-200(A)(1))
	2.	If intestate is survived by children or their descendants, one or more of whom are not children of their descendants of the surviving spouse	$2/3$ of the estate to the decedent's children and their descendant and $1/3$ of the estate to the surviving spouses (§ 64.2-200(A)(1))
B.		If no surviving spouse:	
	1.	Decedent's children and their descendants	100% (§ 64.2-200(A)(2))[65]
	2.	Parents or to the surviving parent	100% (§ 64.2-200(A)(3))
	3.	Brothers and sisters and their descendants	100% (§ 64.2-200(A)(4))[66]
	4.	Grandparents or surviving grandparent	50% of the estate to paternal kindred and 50% to the maternal kindred. (§ 64.2- 200(A)(5)(a))
	5.	Aunts and uncles and their descendant if no grandparents	50% of the estate to paternal kindred and 50% to the maternal kindred. (§ 64.2- 200(A)(5)(b))[67]
	6.	Decedent's great-grandparents	50% of the estate to paternal kindred and 50% to the maternal kindred. (§ 64.2- 200(A)(5)(c))
	7.	Brothers and sisters of decedent's grandparents and their descendants	50% of the estate to paternal kindred and 50% to the maternal kindred. (§ 64.2- 200(A)(5)(d))
	8.	The same procedure in B.4- B.7 above with respect to the identification of next nearest lineal ancestors and descendants of such ancestors	See above.
	9.	Paternal, if no maternal kindred, and vice versa	100% (§ 64.2-200(B))
	10.	If neither maternal or paternal kindred, the kindred of the decedent's most recent spouse, provided decedent and the spouse were married at the time spouse's death, as if such spouse had died intestate entitled to the state	100% (§ 64.2-200(B))
	11.	State, if there are no other takers	100% (§ 64.2-200(C))

[66] The statutory citations herein deal with the descent of real property. The same pattern is followed with respect to the distribution of personal property. (§ 64.2-201(A)(B))

[67] Except as otherwise specified in A.1 the division of shares is among heirs and distributees in the closest degree of kinship and deceased heirs and distributees in that degree survived by descendants at the time of the decedent's death. One share descends or passes to the heir or distributee, and one share to the descendants per stirpes. (§ 64.2-202(A))

[68] Collaterals of the half blood inherit only half as much as those of the whole blood. (§ 64.2-202(B))

Washington
Who Takes by Intestate Succession?

A.	*Surviving spouse or state-registered domestic partner, takes:*	
	1. *If no surviving issue nor parent nor issue of parent*	100% plus all of decedent's net community estate (§ 11.04.015(1)(a)&(d))
	2. *If surviving issue*	$^1/_2$ net separate estate plus all of decedent's net community estate (§ 11.04.015(1)(a)&(b))[68]
	3. *If no surviving issue but a parent survives or issue of parent survives*	$^3/_4$ of net separate estate plus all of decedent's net community estate (§ 11.04.015(1)(a)&(c))
B.	*All the estate, or the surplus if there is a surviving spouse, passes to:*	
	1. *Issue if no surviving spouse*	100% equally if in same degree, otherwise by representation[69] (§ 11.04.015(2)(a))
	2. *Parents, or parents equally, if no issue*	100% (§ 11.04.015(2)(b))
	3. *Issue of parents, if no parents*	100% equally if in same degree, otherwise by representation[69] (§ 11.04.015(2)(c))
	4. *Grandparents, if no issue of parents*	50% to paternal and 50% to maternal grandparents. If both survive on one side they take equal portions of the 50% share, and if not the surviving one takes the whole 50% (§ 11.04.015(2)(d))
	5. *Issue of grandparents, if no grandparents on that side*	100%, with those on the maternal grandparents' side and paternal grandparents' side taking 50% as a group. Within the group, those issue of the same degree of kinship take equally and those of more remote degree take by representation (§ 11.04.015(2)(e))[69] Implication, even though not explicitly set forth in the statute, that if there are no issue of grandparents on one side, the issue on the other side take 100%.[70]
	6. *State, if there is no other taker*	100% (§ 11.08.140)

[69] If decedent leaves a surviving spouse and surviving issue who are not the issue of the surviving spouse, and if all or substantially all of decedent's property passes to the surviving spouse, and if, at surviving spouse's death, the property would otherwise escheat, the property which passed from the first deceased spouse will pass to that spouse's surviving issue. (§ 11.04.095)

[70] "Representation" means per capita with representation. (§ 11.02.005(13))

[71] There does not appear to be any provision for adding the share of one side to the other side if there are no issue of grandparents on one side.

West Virginia
Who Takes by Intestate Succession?

A.		*Surviving spouse takes:*	
	1.	*If no descendant of the decedent survives*	100% (§ 42-1-3(a)(1))
	2.	*If all of the decedent's surviving descendants are also descendants of the surviving spouse and there is no other descendant of the surviving spouse who survives the decedent*	100% (§ 42-1-3(a)(2))
	3.	*If any of the decedent's surviving descendants are not descendants of the surviving spouse*	1/2 (§ 42-1-3(c))
	4.	*If all the decedent's surviving descendants are also descendants of the surviving spouse and the surviving spouse has one or more surviving descendants who are not descendants of the decedent*	3/5 (§ 42-1-3(b))
B.		*All the estate, or the surplus if there is a surviving spouse, passes to:*	
	1.	*Descendants*	100% by representation[71] (§ 42-1-3a(a))
	2.	*Parents, or parents equally, if no descendants*	100% (§ 42-1-3a(b))
	3.	*Descendants of parents, if no parents*	100% by representation[71] (§ 42-1-3a(c))
	4.	*Grandparents or their descendants, if no surviving descendant of a parent*	50% to paternal grandparents and 50% to maternal grandparents, with the grandparents on one side sharing equally if they both survive. If neither grandparent on that side survives, to the issue of the grandparents or grandparent on that side by representation. If no issue survive on that side either, then the 50% share is added to the 50% share on the other side and the grandparents or their issue on the other side take the entire 100% in the manner described herein. (§ 42-1-3a(d))
	5.	*State, if no surviving grandparents or their descendants*	100% (§ 42-1-3c) Real property passes to the state auditor and personal property passes to the state treaurer for disposition by public sale (*Id*).

[72] "Representation" means per capita at each generation. See § 42-1-3d(b).

Wisconsin
Who Takes by Intestate Succession?

A. *Surviving spouse or domestic partner takes:*

1.	*If no surviving issue of the decedent*	100% (§ 852.01(1)(a)(1))
2.	*If surviving issue are all issue of the surviving spouse*	100% (§ 852.01(1)(a)(1))
3.	*If there are surviving issue one or more of whom are not issue of the surviving spouse*	50% of the decedent's property, other than the decedent's interest in marital property or the decedent's interest in property held equally or exclusively with the surviving spouse or domestic partner as tenants in common (§ 852.01(1)(a)(2))

B. *All the estate, or the surplus if there is a surviving spouse, passes to:*

1.	*Issue, if no surviving spouse*	100%, per stirpes (§ 852.01(1)(b))
2.	*Parents, if no surviving spouse or issue*	100% (§ 852.01(1)(c))
3.	*Brothers and sisters and the issue of any deceased brother or sister if no surviving parent*	100%, with any issue taking per stirpes (§ 852.01(1)(d))
4.	*Grandparents and their issue, if no parent or issue of a parent*	50% to paternal and 50% to maternal grandparents. If both grandparents on one side survive, they take equally. If only one survives, that one takes the entire 50% share. (§§ 852.01(1)(f)(1)&(2)) If both grandparents on one side are deceased, then to their issue per stirpes (§ 852.01(1)(f)(1))
5.	*Grandparents and issue of grand-parents on the other side, if no grandparents or their issue survive on one side*	The 50% share of the one side is added to the 50% share of the other side and the whole is distributed as set forth in B.4. and 5. above (§ 852.01(1)(f)(3))
6.	*State, if no grandparents or their descendants*	100%, to the state school fund (§ 852.01(3))

Note: If marital property is held as "survivorship marital property," it vests in the surviving spouse as a nontestamentary disposition at death. (§ 766.60(5)(a))

Wyoming
Who Takes by Intestate Succession?

A.		*Surviving spouse takes:*	
	1.	*If no surviving children or descendants of any child*	100% (§ 2-4-101(a)(ii))
	2.	*If surviving children*	50% (§ 2-4-101(a)(i))
B.		*All the estate, or the surplus if there is a surviving spouse, passes to:*	
	1.	*Children and the descendants of deceased children*	100% equally, and descendants of deceased child "collectively" taking that child's share (§ 2-4-101(c)(i))[72]
	2.	*Mother, father, brothers, sisters, and the descendants of brothers and sisters who are deceased, if no children or their descendants*	100%, shared equally, with descendants of a deceased sibling taking "collectively"[72] the sibling's share (§ 2-4-101(c)(ii))
	3.	*Grandfather, grandmother, uncles, aunts and their descendants, if no father, mother, brothers, sisters, or descendants of deceased brothers and sisters*	100%, shared equally, with descendants of one of the mentioned relatives taking "collectively"[72] the relative's share In equal parts (§ 2-4-101(c)(iii))
	4.	*State, if there are no other takers*	100% (§ 9-5-202) See also Kirby Royalties, Inc. v. Texaco, Inc., 458 P.2d 101 (1969)

[73] "Collectively" appears to mean per stirpes. See Fosler v. Collins, 13 P.3d 686 (2000).

Table 8
Asset Protection
(current through 5/1/18)

The objectives of conserving, enhancing, and ultimately transmitting wealth cannot be accomplished if the owner of the property is subject to catastrophic judgments that deplete the estate. Many persons with substantial resources are standard prey for enterprising plaintiffs and their attorneys. Since successful persons are often in professions or businesses in which the potential for lawsuits and favorable jury verdicts is high, there has been much interest in insulating assets from these claims. While a great deal of attention has been paid to trusts, far less consideration has been given to the ability of creditors of insureds, owners of policies, plans, and accounts, as well as beneficiaries of life insurance, annuities, pension plans, and IRA's to reach these debtor assets.

Table 8 is subdivided into four subparts. Table 8.01 addresses life insurance. It explores initially whether the beneficiaries of proceeds have a superior claim to those proceeds than do creditors. The table then considers such vital issues as whether payments to the estate of the insured, an owner other than the insured, an owner retaining the right to change beneficiaries, and a spouse of the insured or any other beneficiary are insulated from creditors' claims. The table proceeds to detail the dollar amount of the protection, when available. It also includes coverage as to the exposure of the policy to creditors in the premortem period as well as in bankruptcy.

Table 8.02 takes a similar approach to annuities. In particular, an inquiry is made on a state-by-state comparative basis as to whether the annuitant's rights can be reached. This question is also considered in the context of bankruptcy. In addition, certain tax-exempt annuities under IRC § 403(b) for employees of public schools or universities or certain other of 501(c)(3) organizations and ministers are considered independently. There has been much controversy over § 403(b) annuities—whether they qualify for ERISA protection against creditors, especially in view of the requirement under ERISA that assets be held in "trust."

Table 8.03 looks more specifically at pension plans. A variety of questions are explored. To begin with, consideration is given to whether IRC § 401 federally exempt retirement plans are insulated from the reach of creditors. The same is considered with regard to IRC § 403(a) annuity plans. The analysis then proceeds to IRC § 408 tax-sheltered IRAs. While states may have their own statutes providing only limited protection in the case of retirement plans, and these are analyzed, the fact is that 401(a) plans remain completely protected at the federal level, which preempts these state laws. The situation is far less certain with respect to other employer-sponsored plans. Nevertheless, if any such plan meets certain tax qualifications and a determination letter has been obtained from the IRS, it will be protected in bankruptcy. IRAs that are employer-provided also have unlimited protection in bankruptcy. However, individual IRAs are limited to a $1,000,000 exemption in bankruptcy. Importantly, outside of bankruptcy, these non-401(a) plans, annuities and IRAs are not protected from creditors at the federal level; nor are SEP and Keough plans and plans that do not benefit employees who are not owners, such as sole-owner LLCs. Finally, even with respect to protected § 401(a) plans, once the distribution has been made, the beneficiary is not protected under ERISA, although state law may provide the protection. Accordingly, the state laws are critical to understanding the level of debtor protection available depending on the plan, annuity, or account.

The final question considered concerns whether transfers to a plan shortly before bankruptcy can be brought back into the bankruptcy estate. Some states will not afford protection if the transfers are too close in time to the bankruptcy. Other states have no such restrictions, thereby affording certain debtors a major opportunity, subject, of course, to fraudulent conveyance laws and the like.

Table 8.04 deals with jointly-owned property. The term is used in its broadest sense, so as to refer as well to tenancies in common. The first issue dealt with by the table is whether, in the use of a joint tenancy with a right of survivorship, the creditors of the first joint tenant to die can reach his interest. At common law, there was no such right, since on death, the interest of the surviving joint tenant(s) automatically became a whole interest, with the deceased's interest consumed. While most states maintain this position by statute or case law, this is not true in all states.

The second question considered in Table 8.04 is the form of ownership that will be presumed when there are interests of several persons. In other words, if ownership is in the form of ''A or B'' or ''A and B,'' and no right of survivorship is indicated, will the presumption be that a joint tenancy or tenancy in common has been established?

Table 8.01
Life Insurance

	Are Payments of Proceeds Protected from Beneficiary's Creditors?	Are Payments to Beneficiaries Other Than the Insured or Owner Protected from Creditors of the Person "Effecting" the Insurance," Even if Not the Insured?	Are Payments to the Insured's Estate Protected?	Are Payments to the Owner, If Not the Insured, Protected?	Is There a Limit on the Protection?	Can Policies Be Reached Prior to Death by Creditors of Person "Effecting Insurance?"	Does It Matter Whether the Debtor Is in Bankruptcy?
Alabama	Personal property exemption up to $7,500. (§6-10-6)	Yes. (§6-10-8)	No definite authority.	No, with respect to the person "effecting" the life insurance policy. (§6-10-8) However, there is an exception for a spouse or child of the insured. (Id.)	No. (Shepard v. Morris, 30 Bankr. 392 (Bankr. N.D. Ala. 1983))	No, unless intent to defraud creditors, in which case premiums and interest thereon can be reached. (§27-14-29(a))	No. (§27-14-29(a))
Alaska	Yes, to the extent of earnings, income, cash, or other liquid assets. (§09.38.030(a), (b) & (e)(4)) This is a limited amount. (See also §09.38.025(a))	Yes. (§13.33.101(d) & (e)) However, the protection does not apply to a person other than the insured nor to the extent of spousal or child support arrearages. (§13.33.101(e))	Yes. This is the case even if paid to a testamentary or revocable trust or irrevocable inter vivos trust. (§13.33.101(e)(2)) However, the protection does not apply to the extent of spousal or child support arrearages. Id.	Yes. Implied. (§13.33.101(e)(4))	No. However, with respect to an owner's interest in unmatured life insurance, a creditor may reach accrued dividends and loan values in an amount greater than $500,000. (§09.38.025(a)) Section 09.38.115 periodically adjusts this for cost-of-living increases.	No, unmatured life insurance policies are exempted. (§09.38.025(a))	No, the exemption applies. (§09.38.055)
Arizona	Yes, up to $20,000 and only if to a spouse or child of the insured. (§33-1126(A)(1))	Yes. (§20-1131(A))	Uncertain. Life insurance must be in favor of another person (§20-1131(A)). A "person" does not include an estate. (§20-105)	Yes. (§20-1131(A))	No. (§20-1131)	No. If owned by debtor continuously for two years, and payable to spouse, child, parent, sibling, or dependent; only the portion designated to these beneficiaries (if others exist) is exempt, unless the policy was pledged or assigned to a creditor by the insured. (§20-1131(D))	No. See prior col.

Table 8.01
Life Insurance

	Are Payments of Proceeds Protected from Beneficiary's Creditors?	Are Payments to Beneficiaries Other Than the Insured or Owner Protected from Creditors of the Person "Effecting the Insurance," Even if Not the Insured?	Are Payments to the Insured's Estate Protected?	Are Payments to the Owner, If Insured, Protected?	Is There a Limit on the Protection?	Can Policies Be Reached Prior to Death by Creditors of Person "Effecting Insurance?"	Does It Matter Whether the Debtor Is in Bankruptcy?
Arkansas	Yes, if beneficiary is a resident. (§16-66-209(a)) However, the provision only applies "to the extent permitted by the Arkansas Constitution . . ." Quaere whether this means there has to be a specific allowance in the Constitution or there need only be no prohibition of the exemption. Note that the Constitution provides that personal property of a resident is exempt from seizure and attachment to a maximum of $200 (single) or $500 (married) in "specific articles," other than wearing apparel. (Ark. Const. Art. 9, §§1, 2)	Yes. (§23-79-131(a)(1))	No, the "executors" of the insured are not protected. (§23-79-131(a)(1))	No, with respect to the person "effecting" the life insurance policy. (§23-79-131(a)(1))	See col. 1. There is likely a limit on protection imposed by the Arkansas Constitution. (See Fed. Sav. & Loan Ins. Co. v. Holt, 894 F.2d 1005, 1008 (8th Cir. 1990))	Yes. Any portion of a policy above the capped exemption amounts listed in the Arkansas Constitution (Art. 9, §2) can likely be reached by creditors of person "effecting insurance." (See Fed. Sav. & Loan Ins. Co. v. Holt, 894 F.2d 1005, 1008 (8th Cir. 1990)) For federal bankruptcy, see next col.	There is no direct authority in case of bankruptcy of person effecting the insurance. It may be governed though, by rule re bankruptcy of beneficiary. In Fed. Sav. & Loan Ins. Co. v. Holt, 894 F.2d 1005, 1008 (8th Cir. 1990), the court held that an unlimited exemption in §16-66-209 did not apply to bankruptcy debtors in light of monetary limits in Art. 9 §2 of the Arkansas Constitution. In response, the Arkansas legislature enacted §16-66-217, allowing an individual to opt for the limited $500 exemption of the Arkansas Constitution or the unlimited federal exemption in 11 U.S.C. §522(d)(7). This was held constitutional in In re Criswell, 152 B.R. 264, 266 (Bankr. E.D. Ark. 1992)

Table 8.01
Life Insurance

	Are Payments of Proceeds Protected from Beneficiary's Creditors?	Are Payments to Beneficiaries Other Than the Insured or Owner Protected from Creditors of the Person "Effecting the Insurance," Even if Not the Insured?	Are Payments to the Insured's Estate Protected?	Are Payments to the Owner, If Not the Insured, Protected?	Is There a Limit on the Protection?	Can Policies Be Reached Prior to Death by Creditors of Person "Effecting Insurance?"	Does It Matter Whether the Debtor Is in Bankruptcy?
California	"[T]o the extent reasonably necessary for support of the judgment debtor and [his or her] spouse and dependents." (Civ. Proc. §704.100(c))	Apparently not, unless beneficiary is spouse or dependent and payment is reasonably necessary for support. (Civ. Proc. §704.100(c))	Uncertain. May depend on who takes the estate.	Depends if owner is spouse or dependent of insured and payments are reasonably necessary for support. (Civ. Proc. §704.100(c))	$9,700, with respect to a money judgment against the loan value of unmatured life insurance. (Civ. Proc. §704.100(b)) This can be doubled if married, even if the spouse has no interest in policy and is not a judgment debtor. (Id.) There is no other monetary limit on protection for unmatured life insurance policies. (Civ. Proc. §704.100(a)) Benefits from matured policies are exempt to the extent reasonably necessary for support of the judgment debtor and the spouse and dependents of the debtor. (Civ. Proc. §704.100(c))	No, except for the loan value of an unmatured policy. (Civ. Proc. §704.100(a) (Legislative Comm. Comment))	Yes. A debtor may elect to exempt the following from the bankruptcy estate: (a) "unmatured life insurance contract owned by debtor, other than a credit life insurance contract" (Civ. Proc. §703.140(b)(7); (b), debtor's interest, subject to $12,860 limitation, in accrued dividend or interest, or loan value, of unmatured life insurance contract where debtor is owner and insured, or where debtor owns and dependent is insured (Civ. Proc. §703.140(b)(8)); and (c) debtor's right to receive payment of life insurance contract where debtor was dependent of insured, to the extent reasonably necessary for support of debtor and any dependent of debtor. (Civ. Proc. §703.140(b)(11)(C))

Table 8.01
Life Insurance

	Are Payments of Proceeds Protected from Beneficiary's Creditors?	*Are Payments to Beneficiaries Other Than the Insured or Owner Protected from Creditors of the Person "Effecting the Insurance," Even if Not the Insured?*	*Are Payments to the Insured's Estate Protected?*	*Are Payments to the Owner, If Not the Insured, Protected?*	*Is There a Limit on the Protection?*	*Can Policies Be Reached Prior to Death by Creditors of Person "Effecting Insurance?"*	*Does It Matter Whether the Debtor Is in Bankruptcy?*
Colorado	No. (§ 13-54-102(1)(*l*)(II)) However, there is an exception for group insurance proceeds, which have unlimited protection. (§ 10-7-205)	Beneficiaries appear to be protected only from creditors of the insured. (§ 13-54-102(1)(*l*)(I)(B))	No. (§ 13-54-102(1)(*l*)(III))	Yes, if owner is a designated beneficiary. (§ 13-54-102(1)(*l*)(I)(B)) This protection is only from creditors of the insured. (Id.)	$250,000, unless contributed more than four years prior to writ of attachment or writ of execution (only applies to cash surrender value); (§ 13-54-102(1)(*l*)(I)(A)) if proceeds go to the designated beneficiary, no limit. (§ 13-54-102(1)(*l*)(I)(B))	See prior col.	Yes. If debtor has right to cash surrender value in the event of default on policy, bankruptcy trustee may exercise the right. (Travelers' Ins. Co. v. Middlekamp, 185 P. 335, 337 (Colo. 1919))
Connecticut	No Provision	Yes, unless there is intent to defraud. (§ 38a-453(a))	Probably not, as payments to the insured are not protected. (§ 38a-453(a))	Yes. (§ 38a-453(a))	No. But see next col.	Yes, in excess of $4,000 of interest in accrued dividend or interest under, or loan value of, unmatured policy owned by debtor or person of whom debtor is a dependent. (§ 52-352b(s))	Exemption applies to claims of insured's creditors against beneficiaries as well as claims against insured for cash surrender value. See Klebanoff v. Mutual Life Ins. Co., 246 F. Supp. 935, 941, 942 (D. Conn. 1965) (the opinion did not consider § 52-352b(s) and its $4,000 limited exemption).
Delaware	Yes, with respect to any debt existing at the time the proceeds are made available for use. (18 § 2725(a))	Yes, except premiums paid with intent to defraud and interest thereon. (18 § 2725(a))	No. (18 § 2725(a)) In case of group life insurance, protection is afforded. (18 § 2727(a))	No, with respect to the person "effecting" the life insurance policy. (18 § 2725(a))	If made with intent to defraud creditors, they get premiums paid plus interest. (18 § 2725(a))	No provision. But see col. 3.	There is no statutory provision or definite case authority on point. However, 18 § 2725(a) does not specify a limit on the protection for proceeds and avails.

Table 8.01
Life Insurance

	Are Payments of Proceeds Protected from Beneficiary's Creditors?	Are Payments to Beneficiaries Other Than the Insured or Owner Protected from Creditors of the Person "Effecting the Insurance," Even if Not the Insured?	Are Payments to the Insured's Estate Protected?	Are Payments to the Owner, If Not the Insured, Protected?	Is There a Limit on the Protection?	Can Policies Be Reached Prior to Death by Creditors of Person "Effecting Insurance?"	Does It Matter Whether the Debtor Is in Bankruptcy?
District of Columbia	Yes, if traceable to a life insurance contract insuring life of individual of whom debtor was a dependent on date of death, but only to extent reasonably necessary for support of debtor and any dependent of the debtor. (§15-501(a)(11)(C))	Yes, except premiums paid with intent to defraud and interest thereon. (§31-4716(a))	No. (§31-4716(a)) In case of group life insurance, protection is afforded. (§31-4717)	No, with respect to the person "effecting" the life insurance policy. (§31-4716(a))	If made with intent to defraud creditors, they get premiums paid plus interest. (§31-4716(a))	No, as long as the policy is payable to a beneficiary other than the debtor-insured and the debtor does not change the beneficiary designation to his own advantage. See In re Davis, 275 B.R. 134, 137-38 (Bankr. D.D.C. 2002), interpreting §31-4716. See also §15-501(a)(5) (any unmatured life insurance policy owned by the debtor other than a credit life insurance contract)	There is no statutory provision or definite case authority on point. Does not specify a limit on the protection for proceeds and avails. (§31-4716(a))
Florida	No provision.	Beneficiaries appear to be protected from creditors of the insured. (§222.13)	No, the payments become part of the estate. (§222.13(1))	Yes. (§222.13(1))	No. "The proceeds thereof shall be exempt." (§222.13(1))	No. (§222.14) Cash surrender value is exempt, unless the policy was effected for the benefit of a creditor.	Not exempt if the debtor is the insured. (Morgan v. McCaffrey, 286 F. 922 (5th Cir. 1923)); In re D.F. & C.P. Long, 282 F. 383 (S.D. Fla. 1918)
Georgia	Yes, if traceable to a life insurance contract insuring life of individual of whom debtor was a dependent at date of death, but only to extent reasonably necessary for support of debtor and any dependent of the debtor. (§44-13-100(a)(11)(C))	Beneficiaries appear to be protected only from creditors of the insured. (§33-25-11(a))	No. (§33-25-11(a))	Yes, so long as a beneficiary. (§33-25-11(a))	No limit on protection for proceeds payable due to death of insured. (§33-25-11(a) This can be amended through the insurance agreement. (Id.)	No, if the person effecting the insurance is the insured. (§33-25-11(c)) If intent to defraud creditors, then no longer exempt from creditors of insured. (Id.)	Yes, since in the case of bankruptcy only, there is an exemption for an unmatured life insurance contract owned by debtor other than credit life insurance contract. (§44-13-100(a)(8))

Table 8.01
Life Insurance

	Are Payments of Proceeds Protected from Beneficiary's Creditors?	Are Payments to Beneficiaries Other Than the Insured or Owner Protected from Creditors of the Person "Effecting the Insurance," Even if Not the Insured?	Are Payments to the Insured's Estate Protected?	Are Payments to the Owner, If Not the Insured, Protected?	Is There a Limit on the Protection?	Can Policies Be Reached Prior to Death by Creditors of Person "Effecting Insurance?"	Does It Matter Whether the Debtor Is in Bankruptcy?
Hawaii	Yes, if spouse, children, parent, or other dependent of insured under a settlement plan where insurer retains proceeds. (§431:10-232(b)) In addition, provision is made for agreement between the insurer and the policyholder or the beneficiaries exempting the proceeds from claims of creditors of the beneficiaries (§431:10D-112) while the proceeds are held by the insurer.	No. The exemption in §431:10-232(a) only extends to debts of the insured.	The implication is in the negative. (§431:10-232(a))	Yes. (§431:10-232(b)) On the other hand, an agreement with the insurer to accomplish this by the insurer holding the proceeds for the owner will not be given effect. (§431:10D-112)	If intent to defraud, then no protection to extent of premiums, assuming recovery period has not expired. (§431:10-232(a)) Otherwise, no limits on protection. Id.	No, if the debtor is the insured and the policy beneficiary is a spouse, child, parent, or other person dependent upon insured. (§431:10-232(a))	There is no statutory provision or definite case authority on point.
Idaho	Yes, if the debtor-beneficiary is the spouse or dependent of the insured and the proceeds are reasonably necessary for support of the debtor-beneficiary or such person's dependents. (§11-604(1)(d)(3))	Yes. (§41-1833(1))	No. (§41-1833(1))	No, with respect to the person "effecting" the life insurance policy. (§41-1833(1))	If made with intent to defraud creditors, they get premiums paid plus interest. (§41-1833(1)) Otherwise, no limit on protection. Id.	There is no statutory provision or definite case authority on point.	There is no statutory provision or definite case authority on point.

Table 8.01
Life Insurance

	Are Payments of Proceeds from Protected from Beneficiary's Creditors?	Are Payments to Beneficiaries Other Than the Insured or Owner Protected from Creditors of the Person "Effecting the Insurance," Even if Not the Insured?	Are Payments to the Insured's Estate Protected?	Are Payments to the Owner, If Not the Insured, Protected?	Is There a Limit on the Protection?	Can Policies Be Reached Prior to Death by Creditors of Person "Effecting Insurance?"	Does It Matter Whether the Debtor Is in Bankruptcy?
Illinois	Yes, if debtor was dependent of the insured. (735 ILCS §5/12-1001(f))	Yes, if beneficiaries are the spouse, child, parent, and/or dependent person. (735 ILCS §5/12-1001(f))	No. (735 ILCS §5/12-1001(f))	Yes, if the owner is the spouse, child, parent, or dependent person of insured. (735 ILCS §5/12-1001(f))	No. (735 ILCS §5/12-1001(f))	No. (735 ILCS §5/12-1001(f) (cash value))	If insurance acquired within six months of the filing for bankruptcy, presumed to have been acquired in contemplation of bankruptcy. (735 ILCS §5/12-1001(j) (second flush paragraph after (j)))
Indiana	If debtor beneficiary is insured's spouse, then payments of proceeds are protected from the spouse's creditors. (§27-1-12-14(e)) Otherwise, no provision.	If beneficiary is a spouse, child, dependent, or creditor of insured, then the proceeds are free and clear of claims of creditors of insured or insured's spouse. (§27-1-12-14(e))	No provision.	Depends. See col. 2	There is no statutory limit on protection. (See §27-1-12-14(e)) However, in Citizens Nat'l Bank of Evansville v. Foster (668 N.E. 2d 1236 (Ind. 1996)), the Indiana Supreme Court stated that a claimant wishing to exempt life insurance proceeds must establish that the exempted amount comports with the language of the Indiana Constitution. Section 22 only allows exemptions for the "necessary comports of life." (Foster, 668 N.E. 2d at 1239-40) Further, the policy must not have had the intent to defraud. (§27-1-12-14(f)) Premiums paid with intent to defraud are not exempt. (Id.)	No, if the debtor is the insured or the insured's spouse, and the named beneficiaries are the insured's spouse, children or dependent relatives. (§27-1-12-14(e)) Creditors can presumably reach the interest of non-dependent beneficiaries. (Id.)	Premiums must be paid one year prior to bankruptcy. (§27-1-12-14(f))

Table 8.01
Life Insurance

	Are Payments of Proceeds Protected from Beneficiary's Creditors?	Are Payments to Beneficiaries Other Than the Insured or Other Protected from Creditors of the Person "Effecting" the Insurance," Even if Not the Insured?	Are Payments to the Insured's Estate Protected?	Are Payments to the Owner, If Not the Insured, Protected?	Is There a Limit on the Protection?	Can Policies Be Reached Prior to Death by Creditors of Person "Effecting Insurance?"	Does It Matter Whether the Debtor Is in Bankruptcy?
Iowa	Exempt from debts of beneficiary contracted prior to death of insured, but not in excess of $15,000 and so long as beneficiary is surviving spouse, child, or dependent. (§ 627.6(c))	No provision.	No. (§ 627.6(6)) An exception may exist for "reasonable costs, fees, and expenses of administration" out of life insurance proceeds paid to decedent's estate. These expenditures are distinguishable from "debts of a decedent." (In re Wilson's Estate, 202 N.W.2d 41, 43-44 (Iowa 1972))	Only if a dependent, surviving spouse, or child of insured and then not in excess of $15,000. (§ 627.6(6))	Yes, $10,000 for interest acquired within two years of the date of execution is claimed, or for additions within the period for prior existing policies. (§ 627.6(6)) Matured policies are exempt only up to $15,000 and so long as beneficiary is surviving spouse, child, or dependent. (§ 627.6(6)(c))	There is no statutory provision or definite case authority on point.	(See § 627.6(6)) There is no statutory provision or definite case authority on point.
Kansas	Yes. (§ 40-414(a)(4))	Yes. (§ 40-414(a)(1), (2))	No. (Shawnee State Bank v. Royal Union Life Ins. Co., 274 P. 132 (Kan. 1929))	Yes, if owner has insurable interest in life of the insured. (§ 40-414(a))	No, other than with respect to bankruptcy or if execution on judgment is issued within one year after the policy is issued. (§ 40-414(b)(1)-(2))	No. (§ 40-414(a) & (b))	Yes, nonforfeiture value not exempt if policy purchased within one year of bankruptcy. (§ 40-414(b)(1))
Kentucky	Yes, with respect to any debts existing at the time the policy is made available for the beneficiary's use. (§ 304.14-300(1))	Yes. (§ 304.14-300(1))	No. (§ 304.14-300(1))	No, with respect to the person "effecting" the life insurance policy. (§ 304.14-300(1))	No. (Proceeds and avails exempt) (§ 304.14-300(1))	No. (§ 427.110(1); See in re Worthington, 28 B.R. 736, 737-38 (Bankr. W.D. Ky. 1983))	No. (In re Daly, 2004 Bankr. LEXIS 803 (E.D. Ky. 2004) (discussing the inclusion of a life insurance policy in a bankruptcy schedule of assets))
Louisiana	Yes, with respect to any debts existing at the time the policy is made available for the beneficiary's use. (Rev. Stat. § 22:912(A)(1))	Yes. (Rev. Stat. § 22:912(A)(1))	Yes. (Rev. Stat. § 22:912(A)(1))	Probably so, to the extent a "payee." (Rev. Stat. § 22:912(A)(1))	Yes. Limited to $35,000 if policy was issued within nine months of the attempted seizure. (Rev. Stat. § 22:912(A)(2))	Yes, if more than $35,000. Cash surrender value over $35,000 is not exempt if policy issued within nine months of the writ, mandate, or filing of a bankruptcy petition. (Rev. Stat. § 22:912(A)(2))	Yes. Exemption limited to $35,000 if policy issued within nine months of bankruptcy. (Rev. Stat. § 22:912(A)(2))

Table 8.01
Life Insurance

	Are Payments of Proceeds Protected from Beneficiary's Creditors?	Are Payments to Beneficiaries Other Than the Insured or Owner Protected from Creditors of the Person "Effecting" the Insurance," Even if Not the Insured?	Are Payments to the Insured's Estate Protected?	Are Payments to the Owner, If Not the Insured, Protected?	Is There a Limit on the Protection?	Can Policies Be Reached Prior to Death by Creditors of Person "Effecting Insurance?"	Does It Matter Whether the Debtor Is in Bankruptcy?
Maine	Yes, with respect to any debts existing at the time the policy is made available for the beneficiary's use. (24-A § 2428(2))	Yes. (24-A § 2428(2))	No. (24-A § 2428(2))	No, with respect to the person "effecting" the life insurance policy. (24-A § 2428(2))	If made with intent to defraud creditors, they get premiums paid plus interest. (24-A § 2428(2))	"[U]nmatured life insurance contract owned by the debtor, other than a credit life insurance contract," is exempt (14 § 4422(10)) Debtor's interest, up to $4,000, in any accrued dividend or interest under any unmatured life insurance contract owned by the debtor or interest under which the insured is the debtor or debtor's dependent is exempt. (14 § 4422(11))	There is no statutory provision or definite case authority on point.
Maryland	There is a broad provision that exempts from execution on a judgment "money payable in the event of . . . death of any person." (Cts. & Jud. Proceedings § 11-504(b)(2); see In re Kleinman, 274 B.R. 171, 172 (Bankr. D. Md. 2002))	Protection only applies when the beneficiary is a spouse, child, or dependent relative of the insured. (Ins. § 16-111(a)) But see also Cts. & Jud. Proceedings § 11-504(b)(2), which is not limited to specific beneficiaries.	No. (Ins. § 16-111(a))	Protection is limited to the spouse, child, or dependent relative of insured. (Ins. § 16-111(a)) But see also Cts. & Jud. Proceedings § 11-504(b)(2), which is not limited to specific beneficiaries.	Creditors can reach proceeds if pledged as security of a debt. (Ins. § 16-111(c)) "A change of beneficiary, assignment, or other transfer is" not protected "if intent to hinder, delay, or defraud creditors" (Ins. § 16-111(d)) Otherwise, no limit. (Id.)	There is no statutory provision or definite case authority on point.	No. (In re Kleinman, 274 B.R. 171, 172 (Bankr. D. Md. 2002))
Massachusetts	No provision.	Yes, but only if named as original beneficiary when the insurance was effected. (In re Sloss, 279 B.R. 6, 14 (Bankr. D. Mass. 2002))	No. (175 § 125)	No, with respect to the person "effecting" the life insurance policy. (175 § 125)	If made with intent to defraud creditors, they get premiums paid plus interest. (175 § 125) Otherwise, no limit. (Id.)	No (proceeds). (175 § 125)	No. (175 § 125; In re Beach, 8 F. Supp. 910 (D. Mass. 1934))

Table 8.01
Life Insurance

	Are Payments of Proceeds Protected from Beneficiary's Creditors?	Are Payments to Beneficiaries Other Than the Insured or Owner Protected from Creditors of the Person "Effecting the Insurance," Even if Not the Insured?	Are Payments to the Insured's Estate Protected?	Are Payments to the Owner, If Not the Insured, Protected?	Is There a Limit on the Protection?	Can Policies Be Reached Prior to Death by Creditors of Person "Effecting Insurance?"	Does It Matter Whether the Debtor Is in Bankruptcy?
Michigan	No provision.	Yes, but only if beneficiaries are spouse or children of insured and their assigns. (§ 500.2207(1)) However, § 500.2207(2) is not limited to specific persons, and also covers creditors of person effecting insurance, though not insured, thus introducing ambiguity.	No. (§ 500.2207(2))	No. Protection limited to spouse and child of insured and their assigns. Where owner is an assignee of spouse and/or child, payments to owner may be protected. (§ 500.2207(1)) On the other hand, 500.2207(2) does not allow such protection.	If made with intent to defraud creditors, they get premiums paid plus interest. (§500.2207(2)) Otherwise, no limit. (Id.)	No. Cash value is exempt to same extent as proceeds. (§ 500.2207(1)); See also In re Johnson, 274 B.R. 473 (Bankr. E.D. Mich. 2002))	No. (In re Johnson, 274 B.R. 473 (Bankr. E.D. Mich. 2002))
Minnesota	No. (§ 61A.12 (Subd. 1)) But see § 550.37 (Subd. 10): Up to $46,000 in the case of a surviving spouse or child payable at the death of a spouse or parent, with an increase of "$11,500 for each dependent of the surviving spouse or child" payee.	Yes. (§ 61A.12(Subd. 1))	No. (§ 61A.12(Subd. 1))	No, with respect to the person "effecting" the life insurance policy. (§61A.12(Subd. 1))	If made with intent to defraud creditors, they get premiums paid plus interest. (§61A.12(Subd. 1)) Otherwise, the limit on protection is $46,000 in the case of a surviving spouse or child, with an $11,500 increase for each dependent of the beneficiary. (§ 550.37(Subd.10))	Yes, but only in excess of $9,200 of accrued dividend, interest, or loan value on contract owned by debtor where debtor is insured or insured is person of whom debtor is a dependent. (§ 550.37(Subd. 23)) Fraternal contracts cannot be favored in this regard. (In re Haggerty, 448 N.W. 2d 363, 365–66 (Minn. 1989); In re Tveten, 402 N.W.2d 551 (Minn. 1987)) As there is no exemption for policies where neither a spouse nor a child is a listed beneficiary, such policies are presumptively reachable.	There is no statutory provision or case law on point.

Table 8.01
Life Insurance

	Are Payments of Proceeds Protected from Beneficiary's Creditors?	Are Payments to Beneficiaries Other Than the Insured or Owner Protected from Creditors of the Person "Effecting the Insurance," Even if Not the Insured?	Are Payments to the Insured's Estate Protected?	Are Payments to the Owner, If Not the Insured, Protected?	Is There a Limit on the Protection?	Can Policies Be Reached Prior to Death by Creditors of Person "Effecting Insurance?"	Does It Matter Whether the Debtor Is in Bankruptcy?
Mississippi	Only while retained in hands of insurer, and then only if so provided in policy or supplemental agreement issued by insurer. (§ 83-7-5)	Beneficiaries appear to be protected only from creditors of the insured. (§ 85-3-11(1))	Yes, up to $50,000. (§ 85-3-13)	Yes. (§ 85-3-11(1)), as long as owner has insurable interest (§ 83-5-251)	Yes. See the first two columns.	Yes. Any portion of cash surrender value or loan value of any life insurance policy which exceeds the sum of $50,000 as a result of any payments made within 12 months of issuance of a writ of seizure, attachment garnishment, or other process, or the filing of a bankruptcy petition. (§ 85-3-11(2)(a)) Also, any premiums paid with intent to defraud creditors, plus interest are reachable (§ 85-3-11(2)(b)).	Yes. Any portion of cash surrender value or loan value of any life insurance policy which exceeds the sum of $50,000 as a result of any payments made within 12 months of issuance of a writ of seizure, attachment garnishment, or other process, or the filing of a bankruptcy petition is not exempt from creditor's claims against the insured. (§ 85-3-11(2)(a))
Missouri	No provision.	There is no statutory provision or definite case authority on point. (See Judson v. Walker, 55 S.W. 1083, 1086-87 (Mo. 1900) (proceeds protected if insured not insolvent at time premium payment made)).	There is no statutory provision or definite case authority on point.	There is no statutory provision or definite case authority on point.	If premiums are paid with intent to defraud, this cannot affect creditors. (Kansas City v. Halvorson, 180 S.W.2d 710, 711 (Mo. 1944))	No, except for any claim for child support. (§ 513.430(1)(8))	Yes. Exemption limited to $150,000 in any bankruptcy proceeding and exemption is limited to owner-insured or where owner-debtor is dependent of insured. (§ 513.430(1)(8)) If purchased within one year prior to commencement of proceedings, no exemption at all. (Id.)
Montana	No provision.	Yes. (§ 33-15-511(1))	No. (§ 33-15-511(1))	No, with respect to the person "effecting" the life insurance policy. (§ 33-15-511(1))	If intent to defraud creditors, they get amount paid in premiums plus interest. (§ 33-15-511(1)) Otherwise, no limit on protection. (Id.)	No. The interest in an "unmatured life insurance contract" owned by debtor is exempted. (§ 25-13-608(1)(k))	Yes. If the debtor is in bankruptcy, the policy is not exempt. (§§ 31-2-106(1), 33-15-511(1))

Table 8.01
Life Insurance

	Are Payments of Proceeds Protected from Beneficiary's Creditors?	Are Payments to Beneficiaries Other Than the Insured or Owner Protected from Creditors of the Person "Effecting the Insurance," Even if the Insured or Owner Is Not the Insured?	Are Payments to the Insured's Estate Protected?	Are Payments to the Owner, If Not the Insured, Protected?	Is There a Limit on the Protection?	Can Policies Be Reached Prior to Death by Creditors of Person "Effecting Insurance?"	Does It Matter Whether the Debtor Is in Bankruptcy?
Nebraska	Yes, if related to the insured "by blood or marriage." (§ 44-371(1)(a))	Unclear. Statute only mentions protections from creditors of insured or beneficiaries related to insured "by blood or marriage." (§ 44-371(1)(a))	No. (§ 44-371(1)(a), ("other than the estate of the insured"))	No. Protection limited to persons related "by blood or marriage" to insured. (§ 44-371(1)(a))	Protection is limited to aggregate value of $100,000. (§ 44-371(1)(b)(i)) Also note that there is no exemption for a judgment against the beneficiary if the judgment was based on criminal conduct of the beneficiary for which the beneficiary was convicted and was punishable by death or life imprisonment. (§ 44-371(2)) Also, no exemption if "a written assignment to the contrary has been obtained by the claimant." (§ 44-371(1)(a))	Yes, for example cash values in a bankruptcy proceeding. (§ 44-371(1)(b)(ii))	Protections "shall not apply to . . . proceeds, cash values, or benefits accruing . . . within three years prior to bankruptcy." (§ 44-371(1)(b)(iii))
Nevada	Yes, with respect to any debt existing at the time proceeds are made available for the beneficiary's use. (§ 687B.260(1))	Yes. (§ 687B.260(1))	No. (§ 687B.260(1))	No, with respect to the person "effecting" the life insurance policy. (§ 687B.260(1))	Generally not. However, if made with intent to defraud creditors, they get premiums paid plus interest. (§ 687B.260(1))	No, subject to some exceptions. See prior col.	No. (§ 21.090(3))
New Hampshire	No provision, but exclusion from statute implies no. (See § 408:2)	Yes.	No. (§ 408:2) State exemption does not protect an owner-insured, but only a third-party beneficiary. (Caron v. Farmington Nat'l Bank, 82 F.3d 7, 10-11 (1st Cir. 1996))	No, with respect to the person "effecting" the life insurance policy. (§ 408:2)	Generally, not. However, if made with intent to defraud creditors, they get premiums paid plus interest. (§§ 408:2, 408:3)	Yes, cash surrender value is not exempt. (In re Monahan, 171 B.R. 710, 718-19 (Bankr. D.N.H. 1994))	State exemption does not protect an owner insured, but only a third-party beneficiary. (Caron v. Farmington Nat'l Bank, 82 F.3d 7, 10-11 (1st Cir. 1996))

Table 8.01
Life Insurance

	Are Payments of Proceeds Protected from Beneficiary's Creditors?	Are Payments to Beneficiaries Other Than the Insured or Other Person Protected from Creditors of the Person "Effecting the Insurance," Even if Not the Insured?	Are Payments to the Insured's Estate Protected?	Are Payments to the Owner, If Not the Insured, Protected?	Is There a Limit on the Protection?	Can Policies Be Reached Prior to Death by Creditors of Person "Effecting Insurance?"	Does It Matter Whether the Debtor Is in Bankruptcy?
New Jersey	Yes, with respect to any debt existing at the time proceeds are made available for the beneficiary's use. (§17B:24-6(b))	Yes. (§17B:24-6(a))	No. (§17B:24-6(a)(3))	No, with respect to the person "effecting" the life insurance policy. (§§17B:24-6(a), 17B:24-6(a)(2))	Generally, not. However, if made with intent to defraud creditors, they get premiums paid plus interest. (§17B:24-6(b)) Also subject to child support obligations of decedent. (Deceglia v. Estate of Colleti, 625 A.2d 590, 592-93 (N.J. 1993))	No provision.	No. However, there is no protection to the extent of premiums paid with intent to defraud, and interest thereon. (§17B:24-6(b))
New Mexico	Yes, (§42-10-3) without limit, except in the case of taxes due or a garnishment. (§42-10-7) Garnishment is described in §35-12-1 et seq.	Yes, for the "debts of the deceased" unless there is a special contract or arrangement to the contrary in writing. (§42-10-5) Also, no exemption for taxes or garnishment. (§42-10-7)	Yes. (§42-10-5)	Yes. (§42-10-5)	Only if special contract or agreement in writing. (§42-10-5)	No, unless made or assigned in writing for benefit of such creditor; even protected from garnishment. (§42-10-3)	No, unless fraudulent. (In re Zouhar, 10 B.R. 154 (Bankr. D.N.M. 1981))
New York	Yes, if the beneficiary effected the policy and is the spouse of the insured. (Ins. §3212(b)(2))	Yes. (Ins. §3212(b)(3))	No. (In re Will of Adas, 335 N.Y.S.2d 128, 129-30 (N.Y. Surr. Ct. 1972))	Yes. (Ins. §3212(b)(1)-(2))	There is no statutory provision or definite case authority on point.	No (§3212(b)(1)-(3)), except to satisfy a judgment for unpaid alimony. (Rubenstein v. Rubenstein, 105 N.Y.S.2d 24, 27 (N.Y. Supp. Ct. 1951); see also CPLR §5205(i))	No. (Debt. & Cred. Law §282)
North Carolina	Yes, if the beneficiary was a dependent of the insured. Note that in the case of lifetime claims where there is cash value, there is protection if the policy is "for the sole use and benefit of that person's spouse, or children, or both ..." (§58-58-95)	Yes. (§58-58-95)	No. (§58-58-115)	No, with respect to the person "effecting" the life insurance policy. (§58-58-115)	If made with intent to defraud, creditors get premiums paid plus interest. (§58-58-115)	No. (§58-58-115)	If debtor reserves right to change beneficiaries, then cash surrender value of policy on debtor's life is property vested in the trustee in bankruptcy. (In re Wolfe, 249 F. Supp. 784 (M.D. N.C. 1966))

Table 8.01
Life Insurance

	Are Payments of Proceeds Protected from Beneficiary's Creditors?	Are Payments to Beneficiaries Other Than the Insured or Owner Protected from Creditors of the Person "Effecting the Insurance," Even if Not the Insured?	Are Payments to the Insured's Estate Protected?	Are Payments to the Owner, If Not the Insured, Protected?	Is There a Limit on the Protection?	Can Policies Be Reached Prior to Death by Creditors of Person "Effecting Insurance?"	Does It Matter Whether the Debtor Is in Bankruptcy?
North Dakota	Maybe. If the debtor was a dependent of the insured on the date of the insured's death, to the extent reasonably necessary for the support of the debtor and any dependent of the debtor. (§28-22–03.1(9)(c))	There is no statutory provision or definite case authority on point.	There is no statutory provision or definite case authority on point.	See col. 1	See col. 1	No, with respect to policies owned by the debtor other than a credit life insurance contract. (§28-22–03.1(4))	There is no statutory provision or definite case authority on point.
Ohio	If group life insurance, then yes. (§3917.05) Otherwise, no provision.	Yes, if the beneficiary is a person or entity within class of beneficiaries named in §3911.09(B)(1) (spouse, child, or dependent relative of insured, any creditor, certain charities, or to trustee of such beneficiaries). (§3911.10)	No, because insured's estate is not an exempted class of beneficiaries. (§3911.10)	Yes. (§3911.10)	If made with intent to defraud, creditors get premiums paid plus interest. (§3911.10) Otherwise, there is no limit on the offered protection. (Id.)	No. Cash surrender value of unmatured life insurance policies cannot be garnished, as long as policy condition precedent to right of surrender value is unperformed. (Marquis v. New York Life Ins. Co., 92 Ohio App. 389, 108 N.E.2d 227 (Ct. App. 1952))	No. (§2329.66(A)(6)(b))
Oklahoma	Yes. (36 §3631.1(A))	Yes. (36 §3631.1(A))	Yes. (36 §3631.1(A))	Yes. (36 §3631.1(A))	If made with intent to defraud, exemptions do not apply. (36 §3631.1(C)(1)) Otherwise, there is no limit on protection. (36 §3631.1(A))	No (36 §3631.1(A)), except for premium payments made in fraud on creditors, fines imposed by violation of state or federal statutes, or a debt of the insured secured by a pledge of the policy. (36 §3631.1(C)(1)–(3))	No. (36 §3631.1(A)(4))
Oregon	No provision.	Yes. (§743.046(1))	No. (§743.046(1)) (other than insured's person "effecting" the "legal representative")	No, with respect to the person "effecting" the life insurance policy. (§743.046(1))	Yes. If fraud, creditors get premiums and interest. (§743.046(4)) Annuity policies are not included. (§743.046(6))	No, so long as the policy is payable to a beneficiary other than the estate of the insured. (§743.046(3))	No, so long as the policy is payable to a beneficiary other than the estate of the insured. (§743.046(3))

Table 8.01
Life Insurance

	Are Payments of Proceeds Protected from Beneficiary's Creditors?	Are Payments to Beneficiaries Other Than the Insured or Owner Protected from Creditors of the Person "Effecting the Insurance," Even if Not the Insured?	Are Payments to the Insured's Estate Protected?	Are Payments to the Owner, If Not the Insured, Protected?	Is There a Limit on the Protection?	Can Policies Be Reached Prior to Death by Creditors of Person "Effecting Insurance?"	Does It Matter Whether the Debtor Is in Bankruptcy?
Pennsylvania	Amounts retained by the insurer that the policy or a supplemental agreement makes nonassignable. (42 §8124(c)(4)	Yes, if beneficiary is the spouse, child, or dependent relative of insured. (42 §8124(c)(6)	No. (42 §8124(c)(6)) But see 42 §8124, which seems to exempt a policy issued to a solvent insured, who is also the beneficiary.	Yes, if the owner is the spouse, child, or dependent relative of insured. (42 §8124(c)(6))	Exemption will not apply if the judgment debtor is spouse, child, or dependent relative. (42 §8124(c)(6))	No. (See In re Himel, 190 B.R. 59, 61-62 (Bankr. W.D.Pa. 1995) (Citing Schmitz v. Schmitz, 451 A. 2d 555, 556-57 (Pa. 1882) for the proposition that cash surrender values of life insurance are exempt under §8124(c)(4))	There is no statutory provision or definite case authority on point.
Rhode Island	No provision.	Yes, except in cases of intent to defraud. (§27-4-11)	No. (§27-4-11)	No, with respect to the person "effecting" the life insurance policy. (§27-4-11)	If made with intent to defraud, creditors get premiums paid plus interest. (§27-4-11) Otherwise, no limit on protection. (Id.)	There is no statutory provision or definite case authority on point.	There is no statutory provision or definite case authority on point.
South Carolina	Yes, if the insured is an individual of whom the debtor was a dependent, to the extent reasonably necessary for the support of the debtor and any dependent of the debtor. (§15-41-30(A)(12)(c))	Yes, if beneficiaries are insured's spouse, child, or dependent, it is protected from the creditors of the insured. (§38-63-40(A)) No mention of person "effecting.". (§38-63-40(A))	No. (38-63-40(A))	Yes, if the owner is the spouse, child, or dependent of insured. (§38-63-40(A))	Yes, up to $4,000 in any unmatured life insurance dividend, interest or loan value. (§15-41-30(A)(9)) For matured life insurance policies, the statute contains no limit on protection from insured's creditors. (§38-63-40(A)) Also, no exemption to the extent of premiums and interest if attempt to defraud creditors. (§38-63-40(A)(2))	No, unless credit life insurance contract. (§15-41-30(A)(8))	Yes. Cash surrender value or payments are not exempt if insured has filed bankruptcy petition within two years of purchasing insurance. (§§38-63-40(A)(1), 15-41-30)
South Dakota	Yes, if beneficiary is surviving spouse or child, up to $20,000. (§58-12-4)	Yes, if beneficiary is surviving spouse or child of insured. (§58-12-4)	Yes, if for use of surviving spouse or minor children. (§43-45-6)	Yes, in the absence of an agreement or assignment, but only if the owner is a spouse or child of the insured. (§58-12-4)	Yes, $20,000 if payments to beneficiaries, or $10,000 if payments to insured's estate. (§§58-12-4, 43-45-6)	Yes, to the extent over limits on protection. (§§58-12-4, 43-45-6)	There is no statutory provision or definite case authority on point.

Table 8.01
Life Insurance

	Are Payments of Proceeds Protected from Beneficiary's Creditors?	Are Payments to Beneficiaries Other Than the Insured or Owner Protected from Creditors of the Person "Effecting the Insurance," Even if Not the Insured?	Are Payments to the Insured's Estate Protected?	Are Payments to the Owner, If Not the Insured, Protected?	Is There a Limit on the Protection?	Can Policies Be Reached Prior to Death by Creditors of Person "Effecting Insurance?"	Does It Matter Whether the Debtor Is in Bankruptcy?
Tennessee	No. If the beneficiary has creditors, the protections do not apply to their claims. (See, e.g., In re Huffines, 57 B.R. 740, 742 (M.D. Tenn. 1985))	Yes, if the beneficiary or assignee of the policy is the spouse, child, or dependent relative of insured, claims will be exempt from the insured's creditors. (§56-7-203)	Yes, but only if for use of surviving spouse or children and debts are not specifically charged in the will. (§56-7-201)	Yes, if the owner is the spouse, child, or dependent relative of insured. (§56-7-203)	No. (§56-7-203)	No, as long as the beneficiary is surviving spouse, child, or dependent relative. (§56-7-203; In re Thurman, 127 B.R. 401 (M.D. Tenn. 1991))	No, as long as the beneficiary is the surviving spouse, a child, or a dependent relative. (§56-7-203; In re Thurman, 120 B.R. 99 (Bankr. M.D. Tenn. 1990)) Protection is afforded even if surviving spouse, child, or dependent relative was named as a contingent beneficiary. (In re Billington, 376 B.R. 239, 241 (Bankr. M.D. Tenn. 2007)
Texas	Yes. (Ins. Code §1108.051(b)(2)(B))	Not specified, but is implied. Proceeds are fully exempt from "garnishment, attachment, execution or other seizure." (Ins. Code §1108.051(b)(2)(A))	Yes. (Ins. Code §1108.052(2))	Yes, as beneficiary. (Ins. Code §1108.051(b))	No. (Ins. Code §1108.051)	No. (Ins. Code §1108.051(a))	No. (Ins. Code §1108.051(b)(2)(C))
Utah	Yes, if payable on death of spouse or children of debtor-beneficiary, and if "policy has been in existence for a continuous unexpired period of one year." (§78B-5-505(1)(a)(xiii))	Yes, but only if (1) decedent was the spouse or child of the debtor, or the beneficiary is the spouse or child of the decedent-debtor; and (2) the policy has been in existence for a continuous unexpired period of one year. (§78B-5-505(1)(a)(xi)-(xii))	No provision.	Yes, if owner is the spouse or children of insured. (§78B-5-505 (1)(a)(xi)(xiii))	No. (§78B-5-505(1)(a)(xi)-(xiii)), unless the proceeds or avails were pledged as collateral. (§78B-5-505(2))	Yes, but only payments made on the contract during the one year immediately preceding a creditor's levy are reachable. (§78B-5-505(1)(a)(xiii))	There is no statutory provision or definite case authority on point.

Table 8.01
Life Insurance

	Are Payments of Proceeds Protected from Beneficiary's Creditors?	Are Payments to Beneficiaries Other Than the Insured or Owner Protected from Creditors of the Person "Effecting the Insurance," Even if Not the Insured?	Are Payments to the Insured's Estate Protected?	Are Payments to the Owner, If Not the Insured, Protected?	Is There a Limit on the Protection?	Can Policies Be Reached Prior to Death by Creditors of Person "Effecting Insurance?"	Does It Matter Whether the Debtor Is in Bankruptcy?
Vermont	Generally, no. 8 §3709(a) However, there are three exceptions: (1) Creditors can reach premiums paid with intent to defraud creditors. (8 §3709(a)(1)) (2) Annuity benefit payments presently due and payable that exceed a combined $350/month shall be subject to garnishee execution. (8 §3709(a)(2))	Yes, except in cases of transfer with intent to defraud. (8 §3706(a))	No. (8 §3706(a))	No, with respect to the person "effecting" the life insurance policy. (8 §3706(a))	No. However, if intent to defraud creditors, they are entitled to the amount of premiums paid plus interest thereon. (8 §3706(a))	No, unless it is a credit life insurance contract. (12 §2740(18))	No. (12 §2740(18))

Table 8.01
Life Insurance

Are Payments of Proceeds Protected from Beneficiary's Creditors?	Are Payments to Beneficiaries Other Than the Insured or Owner Protected from Creditors of the Person "Effecting the Insurance," Even if Not the Insured?	Are Payments to the Insured's Estate Protected?	Are Payments to the Owner, If Not the Insured, Protected?	Is There a Limit on the Protection?	Can Policies Be Reached Prior to Death by Creditors of Person "Effecting Insurance?"	Does It Matter Whether the Debtor Is in Bankruptcy?
				(3) Courts can apply annuity benefits presently due to an annuitant that exceed a combined payment at the rate of $350/month to judgments against the annuitant, but only "after due regard for the reasonable requirements of the judgment debtor [and the debtor's dependent family members]." (8 §3709(a)(3))		

Table 8.01
Life Insurance

	Are Payments of Proceeds Protected from Beneficiary's Creditors?	Are Payments to Beneficiaries Other Than the Insured or Owner Protected from Creditors of the Person "Effecting the Insurance," Even if Not the Insured?	Are Payments to the Insured's Estate Protected?	Are Payments to the Owner, If Not the Insured, Protected?	Is There a Limit on the Protection?	Can Policies Be Reached Prior to Death by Creditors of Person "Effecting Insurance?"	Does It Matter Whether the Debtor Is in Bankruptcy?
Virginia	Yes, if beneficiary is owner, insured, or is a spouse, intended spouse, dependent child, or any other person dependent on the insured or owner. (§ 38.2-3122(B)) Also, if proceeds retained by insurer, and also, if the policy or a supplemental agreement to the policy provides that no payments of income or principal will be subject to creditor's claims. (§ 38.2-3118) Group insurance is fully exempt, except with respect to a child or spousal support obligation. (§ 51.1-510(A))	Yes, except in cases of transfer with intent to defraud. (§ 38.2-3122(B)(4))	Not addressed, but implied. (§ 38.2-3122(B)(1) (proceeds that are payable to person whose life is insured))	Yes. (§ 38.2-3122(B)(2))	If made with intent to defraud, creditors get premiums paid plus interest. (§ 38.2-3122(D); White v. Pac. Mut. 143 S.E. 340 (Va. 1928)) However, this does not apply to unmatured life insurance policy without cash surrender value as such policies are not deemed to be property. (Coulter v. Willard, 158 S.E. 724 (Va. 1931)) No protection if person claiming exemption if in 6 months before insurance item issued or effected, the person claiming exemption (i) filed for bankruptcy, (ii) becomes subject of an order for relief or declared insolvent in a bankruptcy or insolvency proceeding, or (iii) filed for reorganization, liquidation and the like under any statute, law, or regulation. (§ 38.2-3122(E))	There is no statutory provision or definite case authority on point.	There is no statutory provision or definite case authority on point.

Table 8.01
Life Insurance

	Are Payments of Proceeds Protected from Beneficiary's Creditors?	Are Payments to Beneficiaries Other Than the Insured or Owner Protected from Creditors of the Person "Effecting the Insurance," Even if Not the Insured?	Are Payments to the Insured's Estate Protected?	Are Payments to the Owner, If Not the Insured, Protected?	Is There a Limit on the Protection?	Can Policies Be Reached Prior to Death by Creditors of Person "Effecting Insurance?"	Does It Matter Whether the Debtor Is in Bankruptcy?
Washington	Yes, with respect to any debts existing at the time the policy is made available for his or her use. (§48.18.410(1)) Proceeds of a group policy are exempt without the requirement that the debt has to exist at the time the policy is made available for use, as in the case of an individual policy. (§48.18.420(1))	Yes. (§48.18.410(1))	No. (§48.18.410(3)(a))	No, with respect to the person "effecting" the insurance. (§§48.18.410(1), 410(3)(a))	No. (§48.18.410(1)) There is no exemption if there is intent to defraud creditors. (§48.18.410(3)(b)) Spouse is entitled to his half community property interest in the proceeds regardless of beneficiary designation. (In re Towey's Estate, 22 Wash. 2d 212, 155 P.2d 273, 275 (Wash. 1945))	"Proceeds and avails [protected under §48.18.410(1) have] been interpreted to include cash surrender value." (In re Mehrer, 2 B.R. 309, 311 (Bankr. E.D.Wash. 1980))	Probably not. (See Turner v. Bovee, 92 F.2d 791 (9th Cir. 1937))
West Virginia	Yes, if the insured is an individual of whom the debtor-beneficiary was a dependent, to the extent reasonably necessary for the support of the debtor-beneficiary or a dependent of the debtor-beneficiary. (§38-10-4(k)(3)) Proceeds of group life insurance are exempt, without the relationship and dependency requirements of the exemption with respect to an individual policy. (§33-6-28(a))	Yes, except in cases of transfer with intent to defraud. (§33-6-27(a))	No. (§33-6-27(a))	No, with respect to the person "effecting" the life insurance policy. (§33-6-27(a))	If made with intent to defraud, creditors get premiums paid plus interest. (§33-6-27(b))	No. (In re White, 185 F.Supp. 609, 612 (D.W.Va. 1960))	Can exempt unmeasured life insurance contract owned by the debtor, other than a credit life insurance contract from bankruptcy estate (§38-10-4(g)), and debtor's interest, not in excess of $8,000, in dividend or interest under, or loan value in, any unmeasured life insurance contract owned by debtor where "insured is the debtor or an individual of whom the debtor is a dependent" (§38-10-4(h)).

Table 8.01
Life Insurance

	Are Payments of Proceeds Protected from Beneficiary's Creditors?	Are Payments to Beneficiaries Other Than the Insured or Owner Protected from Creditors of the Person "Effecting the Insurance," Even if Not the Insured?	Are Payments to the Insured's Estate Protected?	Are Payments to the Owner, If Not the Insured, Protected?	Is There a Limit on the Protection?	Can Policies Be Reached Prior to Death by Creditors of Person "Effecting Insurance?"	Does It Matter Whether the Debtor Is in Bankruptcy?
Wisconsin	Yes, if beneficiary was a dependent of the insured on the date of the insured's death, to the extent the proceeds are reasonably necessary for the support of the debtor-beneficiary and the debtor-beneficiary's dependents. (§815.18(3)(i)(1)(a))	Yes, if the beneficiary is the spouse of the deceased spouse who owed the obligation. (§859.18(4)(a)(4))	No. (§859.18(4)(a)(4))	Yes, under circumstances set forth in the second col.	There is no limit where the beneficiary is the spouse. (§859.18(4)(a)(4)) In other cases, see the next col.	Unmatured life insurance contracts are exempt, but may be limited to as little as $4,000 if the policy was acquired or first funded 24 months or less before a cause of action is filed resulting in a judgment or an exemption claim is made. (§815.18(3)(f)(1),(3)) There is no exemption for credit insurance subject to the 24 month condition; (§815.18(3)(f)(3)(D)) protection is also limited to $150,000 in value of any accrued dividends, interest, or loan value on all unmatured policies owned by the debtor and insuring the debtor, the debtor's dependent, or an individual of whom the debtor is a dependent. (§815.18(3)(f)(2))	No. (Cannon v. Lincoln Nat. Life Ins. Co., 243 N.W. 320 (1932))
Wyoming	Yes, with respect to any debts existing at the time the policy is made available for his use. (§26-15-129(a)) Proceeds of a group policy are exempt without the requirement that the debt exist at the time the policy is made available for use, as in the case of an individual policy. (§26-15-131)	Yes, except in cases of transfer with intent to defraud. (§26-15-129(a)); See also §26-15-131 for group life insurance proceeds)	No. (§26-15-129(a))	No, with respect to the person "executing" the life insurance policy. (§26-15-129(a))	If made with intent to defraud, creditors get premiums paid plus interest. (§26-15-129(b))	No (§26-15-129(a)), including cash surrender value. Values are included. (§26-15-129(a)) But see In re Evans, 2000 U.S. Dist. LEXIS 21893, *8 (D. Wyo. 2000), which suggests a different result in the case of bankruptcy.	Yes. At least benefits available at date of filing can be reached. (In re Evans, 2000 U.S. Dist. LEXIS 21893 (D. Wyo. 2000))

Table 8.02
Annuities

	Can the Rights of the Annuitant Be Reached?	Are Tax-Exempt Annuities Under §403(b), Protected?	Does It Matter Whether the Debtor Is in Bankruptcy?
Alabama	No, unless intent to defraud creditors or for amount over $250/month. (§27-14-32(a)(1)-(2))	Yes. (§ 19-3B-508(b) & (e)(4))	No. (§19-3B-508(d))
Alaska	No, but subject to $500,000 dollar limit. (§09.38.025(a))	Yes. (§09.38.017(a) & (e)(5)(A))	No. (§09.38.055)
Arizona	No, so long as the annuity contract has been owned by the debtor for two years continuously and the beneficiary is the spouse, child, parent, sibling, or other dependent family member. (§33-1126(A)(7))	Yes. (§33-1126(B))	Amounts contributed to § 403(b) annuity plans within 120 days of a bankruptcy petition are not protected. (§33-1126(B)(2))
Arkansas	No, unless payment to annuitant with intent to defraud creditors, or in excess of reasonable requirements of annuitant and dependent family members. (§23-79-134(a))	Yes. (§ 16-66-220(a))	No. § 23-79-134(a) speaks of creditors generally, yet does not specifically mention bankruptcy.
California	No, subject to $9,700 limit. (Civ. Proc. § 704.100(a)-(c)) Must qualify as or function like life insurance. (In re Turner, 186 B.R. 108, 119 (9th Cir. BAP 1995)) If matured, then "exempt to the extent reasonably necessary for the support of the debtor and the spouse and dependents of the debtor." (In re Moffat, 959 F.2d 740,742 (9th Cir. 1992) (internal quotation marks omitted))	Yes. (Civ. Proc. § 704.115(b))	Yes. If the debtor is in bankruptcy, the debtor can elect to use the exemption provided in §703.140(b)(10)(E). This exemption covers only payments reasonably necessary for support of the debtor and debtor's dependents, and certain employment-related annuities are not protected. (Id.)
Colorado	No. (§§ 10-7-106; 13-54-102(1)(s))	Yes. (§ 13-54-102(1)(s))	No. (§10-7-106)
Connecticut	No. Retirement annuities are exempt from the claims of creditors to the same extent as "ERISA qualified" retirement plans. (§§ 52-352b, 52-321a)	Yes. (§52-321a(1))	There is no statutory provision or definite case authority on point.
Delaware	Generally, no. (18 § 2728(a)) However, there are three exceptions: (1) Creditors can reach premiums paid with intent to defraud creditors. (18 § 2728(a)(1) (2) Annuity benefit payments presently due and payable that exceed a combined $350/month are subject to garnishee execution to the same extent as wages and salaries. (18 § 2728(a)(2)) (3) Courts can apply annuity benefits presently due to an annuitant that exceed a combined payment at the rate of $350/month to judgments against the annuitant, but only "after due regard for the reasonable requirements of the judgment debtor [and the debtor's dependent family members]." (18 § 2728(a)(3))	See Table 8.03.	There is no statutory provision or definite case authority on point.
District of Columbia	Yes, if certain requirements are not met. (§15-501(a)(7)(E)) First $200/month exempt if principal supporter of family for two months preceding the issuance of a writ. (§15-503(a)) $60/month for people who do not provide support for a family for the two months preceding the issuance of a writ. (§15-503(b))	Yes. (§ 15-501(a)(9))	There is no statutory provision or definite case authority on point.

Table 8.02
Annuities

	Can the Rights of the Annuitant Be Reached?	Are Tax-Exempt Annuities Under §403(b), Protected?	Does It Matter Whether the Debtor Is in Bankruptcy?
Florida	No, unless effected for the benefit of the creditor. (§222.14)	Yes (§222.21(2)(a)(1)), unless subject to qualified domestic relations order. (§222.21(2)(d))	In addition to any available state exemptions, debtors in bankruptcy can elect to exempt property pursuant to §522(d)(10) of the bankruptcy code. (§222.201)
Georgia	No, unless assigned to or effected for the benefit of the creditor or transfer is made with intent to defraud creditor. (§33-28-7)	Yes, but this protection likely only extends up to the general constitutional exemption of $5,000. (§44-13-1)	Yes, exemption for support of debtor or dependent, as an alternative to the §44-13-100(a)(1) personal property exemption. (§44-13-100(a)(2)(E)) In bankruptcy, there is a right to receive a payment to the extent reasonably necessary for the support of the debtor and any dependent (§44-13-100(a)(2)(F) (any individual retirement account, which includes a retirement annuity under IRC §408)) or with respect to an interest held on behalf of the debtor, but not yet distributed to him. (§44-13-100(a)(2.1) (any retirement or pension plan or system))
Hawaii	No, unless subject to qualified domestic relations order. (§651-124)	Yes, unless subject to qualified domestic relations order. (§651-124)	No, unless contribution is made within three years of filing. (§651-124)
Idaho	Generally, no. (§41-1836(1)) However, there are three exceptions: (1) Creditors can reach premiums paid with intent to defraud creditors. (§41-1836(1)(a)) (2) Annuity benefit payments presently due and payable that exceed a combined $1,250/month are subject to garnishee execution to the same extent as wages and salaries. (§41-1836(1)(b)) (3) Courts can apply annuity benefits presently due to an annuitant that exceed a combined payment at the rate of $1,250/month to judgments against the annuitant, but only "after due regard for the reasonable requirements of the judgment debtor [and the debtor's dependent family members]." (§41-1836(1)(c))	Yes, if claim arises out of a negligent or otherwise wrongful act or omission of the beneficiary or participant resulting in monetary damages to the judgment creditor. (§55-1011(1)) There is no protection, however, in the event of a qualified domestic relations order. (§55-1011(2)) See also col. 1 for annuity generally.	Yes. The cash surrender value of a deferred annuity contract up to the value of premiums paid within the six months preceding bankruptcy filing are not exempt. (§41-1836(1)(d))
Illinois	No, so long as plan is intended to be a retirement plan or the plan is a public employee pension plan.. (735 ILCS §5/12-1006(a) & (b)(3))	Yes. (735 ILCS §5/12-1006(a) & (b))	There is no statutory provision or definite case authority on point.
Indiana	Only certain annuities are exempt. (§§34-6-2-131(1); 34-55-10-2(c)(6))	Yes. (§§34-6-2-131(1), 34-55-10-2(c)(6))	There is no statutory provision or definite case authority on point.
Iowa	No. (§627.6(8)(e)) In the case of a Roth annuity, the exemption is limited to the lesser of the maximum allowed in a taxable year or the actual amount contributed. Accumulated earnings and increases are likewise exempt on the basis of a fraction, the numerator being exempt contributions and the denominator being all exempt and nonexempt contributions. (§627.6(8)(e)) However, in the two years prior to exemption claim or bankruptcy, the maximum contribution is limited to the maximum deductible contribution to an IRA under §408(a). (§627.6(8)(f))	Yes. (§627.6(8)(f))	As for a payment or portion of payment resulting from contributions within one year of bankruptcy, which contributions are above the normal and customary contributions under the plan or contract, the excess contributions are not exempt. (§627.6(8)(e))

Table 8.02
Annuities

	Can the Rights of the Annuitant Be Reached?	Are Tax-Exempt Annuities Under § 403(b), Protected?	Does It Matter Whether the Debtor Is in Bankruptcy?
Kansas	Only certain annuities are exempt. (§ 60-2308)	Yes. (§ 60-2308(b))	Not mentioned.
Kentucky	Generally, no. (§ 304.14-300(1)) However, there are four exceptions: (1) Creditors can reach premiums paid with intent to defraud creditors. (§ 304.14-300(1)) (2) Annuity benefit payments presently due and payable that exceed a combined $350/month are subject to garnishee execution to the same extent as wages and salaries. (§ 304.14-300(1)) (3) Courts can apply annuity benefits presently due to an annuitant that exceed a combined payment at the rate of $350/month to judgments against the annuitant, but only "after due regard for the reasonable requirements of the judgment debtor [and the debtor's dependent family members]." (§ 304.14-300(1)) (4) The cash surrender value of deferred annuity contracts for which no periodic payments are being made can be reached, but only to the extent of premiums paid within six months prior to a bankruptcy petition filing or the date of attachment or levy on execution. (§ 41-1836(1))	Yes, subject to court order for payment of "maintenance" or "child support." (§ 427.150(2)(f))	Funds contributed to the plan within 120 days of bankruptcy are not exempt. (§ 427.150(2)(f))
Louisiana	No. (Rev. Stat. § 22:912(B))	Yes, except from alimony and child support. (Rev. Stat. § 20:33(1))	No provision.
Maine	Generally, no. (24-A § 2431(1)) However, there are three exceptions: (1) Creditors can reach premiums paid with intent to defraud creditors. (24-A § 2431(1)(A)) (2) Annuity benefit payments presently due and payable that exceed a combined $450/month are subject to garnishee execution to the same extent as wages and salaries. (24-A § 2431(1)(B)) (3) Courts can apply annuity benefits presently due to an annuitant that exceed a combined payment at the rate of $450/month to judgments against the annuitant, but only "after due regard for the reasonable requirements of the judgment debtor [and the debtor's dependent family members]." (24-A § 2431(1)(C))	Yes. (14 § 4422(13)(E))	There is no statutory provision or definite case authority on point.
Maryland	No, if proceeds benefit spouse, child, or dependent relative. (Ins. § 16-111(a))	Yes, except for claims by the Department of Health and Mental Hygiene. (Cts. & Jud. Proc. § 11-504(h)(1))	No. Further, a debtor is not entitled to the federal exemptions provided by § 522(d)(E) of the U.S. Bankruptcy Code. (Ct. & Jud. Proc. § 11-504(g))
Massachusetts	No, unless there is (1) divorce, separate maintenance or child support court order or (2) a court order requiring payment of monetary penalty or restitution in the case of a crime. (235 § 34A)	Yes. (235 § 34A)	There is also a limitation for non-rollover individual plans for sums deposited in the 5 years prior to a declaration of bankruptcy or entry of judgment in excess of 7% of the total income of the individual during the 5-year period. (235 § 34A)

Table 8.02
Annuities

	Can the Rights of the Annuitant Be Reached?	Are Tax-Exempt Annuities Under §403(b), Protected?	Does It Matter Whether the Debtor Is in Bankruptcy?
Michigan	No, unless there is an order of divorce, separate maintenance, or child support. (§600.6023(1)(i))	Yes. (§600.6023(1)(k))	Yes, does not exempt contributions within 120 days before filing bankruptcy. (§§600.6023(1)(j) & (k))
Minnesota	Yes, up to a present value of $69,000 in the aggregate of all plans and contracts, plus additional amounts under all plans and contracts to the extent reasonably necessary for support of debtor, debtor's spouse, or dependent of debtor. However, the exemptions do not apply when the debt is owed under a support order as defined in §518A.26 (Subd. 21). (§550.37(Subd.24))	Yes, up to a present value of $69,000 in the aggregate of all plans and contracts, plus additional amounts under all plans and contracts to the extent reasonably necessary for support of debtor, debtor's spouse, or dependent of debtor. However, the exemptions do not apply when the debt is owed under a support order as defined in §518A.26(Subd. 21). (§550.37(Subd. 24))	Protection is the same in bankruptcy. (In re Walsh, 19 F. Supp. 567, 569-70 (D. Minn. 1937))
Mississippi	No, with respect to specified particular plans—(i) under IRC §§401(a), 403(a), or 403(b), (ii) a deferred compensation plan under IRC §457(b), or (iii) an individual retirement annuity under IRC §408. (§85-3-1(e))	Yes. (§85-3-1(e))	No. Mississippi has elected to "opt-out" of federal exemptions under §522(d), (see §85-3-2) state exemptions for annuities are essentially the same and regardless of whether the debtor is in bankruptcy. (See Cols 1 & 2)
Missouri	No. Exempt to the extent reasonably necessary for the support of the debtor and any dependent of debtor. (§513.430(1)(10)(e))	Yes. (§513.430(1)(10)(f))	Yes. Funds not exempt if fraudulent, and for three year-period prior to commencement of the proceedings. (§513.430(1)(10)(f))
Montana	Generally, no. (§33-15-514(1)) However, there are three exceptions: (1) Creditors can reach premiums paid with intent to defraud creditors. (§33-15-514(1)(a)) (2) Annuity benefit payments presently due and payable that exceed a combined $350/month must be subject to garnishee execution. (§33-15-514(1)(b)) (3) Courts can apply annuity benefits presently due to an annuitant that exceed a combined payment at the rate of $350/month to judgments against the annuitant, but only "after due regard for the reasonable requirements of the judgment debtor [and the debtor's dependent family members]." (§33-15-514(1)(c))	Yes. (§25-13-608(1)(e))	Yes, contributions within one year before filing of bankruptcy which exceed 15% of individual's income for such year. (§31-2-106(4))
Nebraska	Yes. Funds are protected only if beneficiary is related by blood or marriage to insured (§44-371(1)(a)) and only up to $100,000. (§44-371(1)(b))	Yes, to the extent reasonably necessary for the support of the debtor. (§25-1563.01)	Yes. The 403(b) annuity trust is not exempt if, within two years prior to bankruptcy, plan was established or amended to increase contribution. (§25-1563.01(1))
Nevada	No, except as to premiums paid with intent to defraud. (§687B.290(1))	Yes, up to $500,000. (§21.090(1)(r)(4))	No. (§§21.090(3), 21.090(1)(n))
New Hampshire	Tax-exempt retirement plan annuities are protected from creditors. (§511:2(XIX))	Yes. (§511:2(XIX))	There is no statutory provision or definite case authority on point.
New Jersey	Generally, no. (§17B:24-7(a)) However, there are three exceptions: (1) Creditors can reach premiums paid with intent to defraud creditors. (§17B:24-7(a)(1)) (2) Annuity benefit payments presently due and payable that exceed a combined $500/month are subject to garnishee execution to the same extent as wages and salaries. (§17B:24-7(a)(2))	Yes, (§25:2-1(b)), unless there is an order for child or spousal support. (§25:2-1(b)(2))	No. Only subject to "intent to defraud" exception preference or fraudulent conveyance. (§§17B:24-7(a)(1), 25:2-1(b)(1))

Table 8.02
Annuities

	Can the Rights of the Annuitant Be Reached?	Are Tax-Exempt Annuities Under § 403(b), Protected?	Does It Matter Whether the Debtor Is in Bankruptcy?
New Mexico	No. (§ 42-10-3). (3) Courts can apply annuity benefits presently due to an annuitant that exceed a combined payment at the rate of $500/month to judgments against the annuitant, but only "after due regard for the reasonable requirements of the judgment debtor [and the debtor's dependent family members]." (§ 17B-24-7(a)(2))	No provision.	No. (§§ 42-10-1, 42-10-2).
New York	No. (N.Y. Civ. Pract. L&R § 5205(c)(3) & (d)(1))	Yes. (N.Y. Civ. Pract. L&R § 5205(c)(2) & (d)(1))	No (N.Y. Civ. Pract. L&R § 5205(c)(3)&(d)(1)), except that the aggregate amount that may be exempted from annuity contract is $10,000. (NY Debt. & Cred. Law § 283(1))
North Carolina	No, but only if it is an individual retirement plan as defined in the Internal Revenue Code or any plan treated in the same manner as an individual retirement plan under the Code. (§1C-1601(a)(9))	Yes. (§1C-1601(a)(9))	No statutory provision or case authority on point.
North Dakota	No, so long as (1) annuity was not established by an employer of debtor, (2) annuity payment is not figured by age/length of service, and (3) plan qualifies under the IRC. (§28-22-03.1(8)(e))	Yes, up to $100,000 individually and $200,000 in combination with other accounts, pensions, IRAs, life insurance, and retirement plans. (§ 28-22-03.1(7)-(8)) Exemption covers plans in effect for longer than a period of one year. (§ 28-22-03.1(7))	There is no statutory provision or definite case authority on point.
Ohio	No, as long as annuitant is a member of an exempted class under § 3911.10. (§ 2329.66(A)(6)(b))	Yes, to extent payments are reasonably necessary for support. (§2329.66(A)(10)(b), (c)(iii))	No. (§ 2329.66(A)(6)(b))
Oklahoma	No, except for (1) premium payments made in fraud on creditors, (2) "fines imposed for violation of state or federal statutes," or (3) "a debt of the insured secured by a pledge of the policy." (36 § 3631.1(A) & (C))	Yes, to extent that contributions by or on behalf of a participant were not subject to federal income tax at the time of such contributions. (implied by 36 § 3631.1(A))	No. (36 § 3631.1(A)(4))
Oregon	Generally, no. (§743.049(1)) However, there are three exceptions: (1) Creditors can reach premiums paid with intent to defraud creditors. (§743.049(1)(a)) (2) Annuity benefit payments presently due and payable that exceed a combined $500/month are subject to garnishee execution to the same extent as wages and salaries. (§743.049(1)(b)) (3) Courts can apply annuity benefits presently due to an annuitant that exceed a combined payment at the rate of $500/month to judgments against the annuitant, but only "after due regard for the reasonable requirements of the judgment debtor [and the debtor's dependent family members]." (§743.049(1)(c))	Yes, except for certain claims regarding fraudulent transfers and support. (§18.358)	No. (In re Thompson, 197 B.R. 326 (Bankr. D. Or. 1996))

Table 8.02
Annuities

	Can the Rights of the Annuitant Be Reached?	Are Tax-Exempt Annuities Under §403(b) Protected?	Does It Matter Whether the Debtor Is in Bankruptcy?
Pennsylvania	Yes, $100/month is exempt. (42 §8124(c)(3)). Proceeds to spouse, child, or dependent relative are wholly exempt. (42 §8124(c)(6)) In the case of a federal, e.g. ERISA authorized annuity, protections are limited and do not apply to amounts contributed within one year of bankruptcy, amounts contributed in excess of $15,000 in one year, and amounts deemed fraudulent conveyances.	Yes. (42 §8124(b)(1)(ix))	Will not protect amounts contributed to a federal, e.g. ERISA authorized annuity, within one year of bankruptcy. (42 §8124(b)(1)(ix)(A))
Rhode Island	Yes, if protected by ERISA or if there is an order of the court pursuant to spousal or child support. (§9-26-4(12))	Yes. (§9-26-4(12))	No. (§9-26-4(12))
South Carolina	No, so long as (1) annuity was not established by an employer of debtor, (2) annuity payment is not figured by age/length of service, and (3) plan qualifies under the Internal Revenue Code. (§15-41-30(A)(11)(e))	Yes. (§15-41-30(A)(11)(e)(iii))	There is no statutory provision or definite case authority on point.
South Dakota	Yes. If total annuity payments exceed $250/month, only $250 is exempt. (§§58-12-6, 58-12-8)	Yes, up to total of $1,000,000 principal and income and distributions related thereto, in aggregate for all employee benefit plans. (§§43-45-16, 43-45-17)	There is no statutory provision or definite case authority on point.
Tennessee	No, so long as (1) annuity was not established by an employer of debtor, (2) annuity payment is not figured by age/length of service, and (3) plan qualifies under the Internal Revenue Code. (§26-2-111)	Yes. (§26-2-111(1)(D)(iii))	There is no statutory provision or definite case authority on point.
Texas	Generally, no. (Ins. Code §1108.051(a)(2)) However, exemptions do not apply to payments made in fraud of creditors, debts secured by a pledge of the policy or its proceeds, or child support liens and levies. (Ins. Code §1108.053)	Yes. (Prop. §42.0021)	No. (Ins. Code §1108.051(b)(2)(C))
Utah	No, if for disability, illness or unemployment (§78B-5-505(1)(a)(iii)(A)–(B)) or pursuant to certain types of qualified plans. (§78B-5-505(1)(a)(xiv))	Yes, unless the creditor is an alternative payee under a domestic relations order. (§78B-5-505(1)(a)(xiv))	If it is a §403(b) trust, amounts contributed or benefits accrued on or on behalf of a debtor, within one year before the debtor files for bankruptcy are not exempt. (§78B-5-505(1)(b)(ii))
Vermont	Generally, no. (8 §3709(a)) However, there are three exceptions: (1) Creditors can reach premiums paid with intent to defraud creditors. (8 §3709(a)(1)) (2) Annuity benefit payments presently due and payable that exceed a combined $350/month shall be subject to garnishee execution to the same extent as wages and salaries. (8 §3709(a)(2)) (3) Courts can apply annuity benefits presently due to an annuitant that exceed a combined payment at the rate of $350/month to judgments against the annuitant, but only "after due regard for the reasonable requirements of the judgment debtor [and the debtor's dependent family members]" (8 §3709(a)(3))	Yes. (12 §2740(16))	Section 403(b) contributions made within one year of filing for bankruptcy are not exempt. (12 §2740(16))

Table 8.02
Annuities

	Can the Rights of the Annuitant Be Reached?	Are Tax-Exempt Annuities Under §403(b), Protected?	Does It Matter Whether the Debtor Is in Bankruptcy?
Virginia	No. The protection offered to a retirement plan is the same protection afforded to such plan under federal bankruptcy law. (§34-34(B))	Yes. See prior col. (§34-34(B))	No. (§34-34(B))
Washington	Generally, no. (§48.18.430(1)) However, there are three exceptions: (1) Creditors can reach premiums paid with intent to defraud creditors. (§48.18.430(1)(a)) (2) Annuity benefit payments presently due and payable that exceed a combined $3,000/month are subject to garnishee execution to the same extent as wages and salaries. (§48.18.430(1)(b)) (3) Courts can apply annuity benefits presently due to an annuitant that exceed a combined payment at the rate of $1,000/month to judgments against the annuitant, but only "after due regard for the reasonable requirements of the judgment debtor [and the debtor's dependent family members]." (§48.18.430(1)(c))	Yes. (§6.15.020(3))	No. (§6.15.020(3))
West Virginia	Yes, unless in bankruptcy, then exempt as reasonably necessary for support of the debtor or a dependent of the debtor. (§38-10-4(j)(5))	Yes, for amount reasonably necessary for support of debtor and dependents, but the provision only refers to bankruptcy proceedings. (§38-10-4(j)(5))	Can exempt annuity payments to the extent reasonably necessary for support of the debtor and any dependents. (§38-10-4(j)(5))
Wisconsin	No, (§815.18(3)(j)(1) if under a plan that complies with the Internal Revenue Code or the employer created the plan or contract for the exclusive benefit of the employer if self-employed, or of some of all of the employees, or their dependents or beneficiaries and that plan or contract requires the employer or employees or both to make contributions for the ultimate and exclusive distribution to any of the foregoing persons. With respect to other annuities, there is protection as to an unmatured contract in the amount of $150,000 in any accrued dividends, interest, or loan value. (§815.18(3)(f)(2)) Furthermore, if the annuity contract was issued or funded less than 24 months prior to the claim of exemption the exemption must not exceed $4,000. (§815.18(3)(f)(3)(a)-(b))	Yes. (§815.18(3)(j)(1))	There is no statutory provision or definite case authority on point.
Wyoming	Yes, if (1) premium paid with intent to defraud, (2) total exemption benefits exceed $350/month, or (3) total exemption benefits exceed $350/month and the court ordered to pay creditors after taking account reasonable requirements of the judgment debtor and his family if dependent upon him. (§26-15-132(a)(i)-(iii))	Yes. (§1-20-110)	Yes. Exemption for Section 403(b) annuities does not apply to payments made within 90 days of a filing for bankruptcy. (§1-20-110(b))

Table 8.03
Pension Plans

	Are Federally Qualified §401 Pension Plans Exempt?	Are §403(a) Annuity Plans Exempt?	Are §408 IRAs Exempt?*	Is There an Income Exemption for Payments Not Covered by the Pension Plan Exemption?	Are Contributions Within a Certain Period of Bankruptcy Exempt?
Alabama	Yes, unless to satisfy a qualified domestic relations order. (§19-3B-508(a)(4)).	Yes. (§19-3B-508(b))	Yes. (§19-3B-508(a)(4))	There is no statutory provision or definite case authority on point.	Yes. (§19-3B-508(c)) Statute does not provide a time limit; In re Hyde (200 B.R. 694 (Bankr. N.D. Ala. 1996)) exempts these plans from bankruptcy.
Alaska	Yes. (§09.38.017(a)(1), (e)(5)(A))	Yes. (§09.38.017(e)(5)(A))	Yes. (§09.38.017(e)(3))	No. §09.38.030(e) treats the payments as earnings.	Contributions made within 120 days before filing for bankruptcy are not exempt. (§09.38.017(b))
Arizona	Yes. (§33-1126(B))	Yes. (§33-1126(B))	Yes. (§33-1126(B))	No. §12-1598(4) treats as earnings.	Yes. Contributions made before 120 days of filing for bankruptcy are not exempt. (§33-1126(B)(2))
Arkansas	Yes. (§16-66-220(a))	Yes. (§16-66-220(a))	Yes. (§16-66-220(a))	There is no statutory provision or definite case authority on point.	There is no statutory provision or definite case authority on point.
California[1]	Yes. (Civ. Proc. §704.115(a)(3))	Yes. (Civ. Proc. §704.115(a)(3))	Yes. (Civ. Proc. §704.115(a)(3))	Exempt from garnishment to the same extent as wages in private plans (Civ. Pro. §704.115(f)), public plans (Civ. Pro. §704.110(c)(2)).	The status of pension in bankruptcy is determined as of the date of bankruptcy filing. If non-exempt assets from an IRA are transferred into a retirement plan that is protected by a state bankruptcy exemption, and there was no fraudulent intent, then the IRA is protected, though transferred to protected status after the bankruptcy filing. (Gill v. Stern, 345 F.3d 1036 (9th Cir. 2003))
Colorado[1]	Yes. (§13-54-102(1)(s))	No, not expressly listed as exempt. (§13-54-102(1)(s))	Yes. (§13-54-102(1)(s))	No. (§13-54-102(1)(s))	There is no statutory provision or definite case authority on point.
Connecticut	Yes. (§52-321a(a)(1))	Yes. (§52-321a(a)(1))	Yes. (§52-321a(a)(1); Central Bank v. Hickey, 680 A.2d 298, 300 (Conn. 1996))	No. (§52-321a)	There is no statutory provision or definite case authority on point.
Delaware	Yes. (10 §4915(a), (f))	Yes. (10 §4915(a), (f))	Yes. (10 §4915(a), (f))	Amounts payable under a retirement plan are exempt. (10 §4915(a))	There is no statutory provision or definite case authority on point.

Table 8.03
Pension Plans

	Are Federally Qualified §401 Pension Plans Exempt?	Are §403(a) Annuity Plans Exempt?	Are §408 IRAs Exempt?*	Is There an Income Exemption for Payments Not Covered by the Pension Plan Exemption?	Are Contributions Within a Certain Period of Bankruptcy Exempt?
District of Columbia[1]	Yes. (§15-501(a)(9))	Yes. (§15-501(a)(9))	Yes. (§15-501(a)(9))	Yes. $200/month exempt if principal supporter of family for two months preceding the issuance of a writ. (§15-503(a)) $60/month for people who do not provide support for a family for the two months preceding the issuance of a writ. (§15-503(b))	There is no statutory provision or definite case authority on point.
Florida	Yes (§222.21(2)(a)), unless subject to qualified domestic relations order. (§222.21(2)(d))	Yes (§222.21(2)(a)), unless subject to qualified domestic relations order. (§222.21(2)(d))	Yes (§222.21(2)(a)), unless subject to qualified domestic relations order. (§222.21(2)(d))	There is no statutory provision or definite case authority on point.	There is no statutory provision or definite case authority on point.
Georgia[1]	Yes. Exempt from bankruptcy "to the extent reasonably necessary for the support of the debtor and any dependent." (§44-13-100(a)(2)(E))	Yes. Exempt from bankruptcy to the extent reasonably necessary for the support of the debtor and any dependent. (§44-13-100(a)(2)(E))	Yes. Exempt from bankruptcy to the extent reasonably necessary for the support of the debtor and dependent. (§44-13-100(a)(2)(F))	There is no statutory provision or definite case authority on point.	There is no statutory provision or definite case authority on point.
Hawaii	Yes, unless subject to a qualified domestic relations order. (§651-124)	Yes, unless subject to a qualified domestic relations order. (§651-124)	Yes, unless subject to a qualified domestic relations order. (§651-124)	There is no statutory provision or definite case authority on point.	Contributions made within three years of filing for bankruptcy are not exempt. (§651-124)
Idaho	Yes, unless subject to a qualified domestic relations order under 26 U.S.C. §414(p). (§55-1011)	Yes, unless subject to a qualified domestic relations order under 26 U.S.C. §414(p). (§55-1011)	Yes, unless subject to a qualified domestic relations order under 26 U.S.C. §414(p). (§55-1011)	Exempt to the extent reasonably necessary for the support of the debtor and dependents. (§11-604(2))	There is no statutory provision or definite case authority on point.
Illinois[1]	Yes. Plans intended in good faith to be IRC-exempt are also exempted. (735 ILCS §5/12-1006(a))	Yes. (735 ILCS §5/12-1006(a))	Yes. (735 ILCS §5/12-1006(a))	There is no statutory provision or definite case authority on point.	There is no statutory provision or definite case authority on point.

Table 8.03
Pension Plans

	Are Federally Qualified § 401 Pension Plans Exempt?	Are § 403(a) Annuity Plans Exempt?	Are § 408 IRAs Exempt?*	Is There an Income Exemption for Payments Not Covered by the Pension Plan Exemption?	Are Contributions Within a Certain Period of Bankruptcy Exempt?
Indiana	Yes. (§§ 34-6-2-131, 34-55-10-2(c)(6))	Yes. (§§ 34-6-2-131, 34-55-10-2(c)(6))	Yes. (§§ 34-6-2-131, 34-55-10-2(c)(6)(A)(ii))	There is no statutory provision or definite case authority on point.	There is no statutory provision or definite case authority on point. One case has held, however, that an ERISA-qualified pension is a spendthrift trust under state law and is not included in bankruptcy estate where the plan contains an absolute restriction on alienation of at least 90% of benefits. (In re LeFeber, 906 F.2d 330, 331 (7th Cir. 1990))
Iowa	Yes. (§ 627.6(8)(f))	Yes, either all or a portion. (§ 627.6(8)(e))	Yes. (§ 627.6(8)(f))	There is no statutory provision or definite case authority on point.	Payments made within one year of a bankruptcy petition filing are not exempt. (§ 627.6(8)(e)). This does not apply to subsection (f).
Kansas	Yes. (§ 60-2308(b))	Yes. (§ 60-2308(b))	Yes. (§ 60-2308(b))	There is no statutory provision or definite case authority on point.	There is no statutory provision or definite case authority on point.
Kentucky[1]	Yes. (§ 427.150(2)(f))	Yes. (§ 427.150(2)(f))	Yes. (§ 427.150(2)(f))	There is no statutory provision or definite case authority on point.	Funds contributed within 120 days of filing for bankruptcy are not exempt. (§ 427.150(2)(f))
Louisiana[1]	Yes, except subject to alimony and child support. (Rev. Stat. § 20:33(1))	Yes, except subject to alimony and child support. (Rev. Stat. § 20:33(1))	Yes, except subject to alimony and child support. (Rev. Stat. § 20:33(1))	Yes. Gratuitous payments from an employer are exempt. (Rev. Stat. § 20:33(2)	Not exempt if made "less than one calendar year of the date of filing for bankruptcy whether, voluntary or involuntary. . . ." (Rev. Stat. 13:3881(D)(2))
Maine	Yes, to the extent reasonably necessary for the support of the debtor and his or her dependents. (14 § 4422(13)(E)).	Yes, to the extent reasonably necessary for the support of the debtor and his or her dependents. (14 § 4422(13)(E)).	Yes, to the extent reasonably necessary for the support of the debtor and his or her dependents. (14 § 4422(13)(E)).	There is no statutory provision or definite case authority on point.	There is no statutory provision or definite case authority on point.
Maryland	Yes. (Cts. & Jud. Proc. § 11-504(h))	Yes. (Cts. & Jud. Proc. § 11-504(h))	Yes. (Cts. & Jud. Proc. § 11-504(h))	There is no statutory provision or definite case authority on point.	There is no statutory provision or definite case authority on point.

Table 8.03
Pension Plans

	Are Federally Qualified §401 Pension Plans Exempt?	Are §403(a) Annuity Plans Exempt?	Are §408 IRAs Exempt?*	Is There an Income Exemption for Payments Not Covered by the Pension Plan Exemption?	Are Contributions Within a Certain Period of Bankruptcy Exempt?
Massachusetts	Yes, except to enforce divorce, separate maintenance, or child support upon order of court. (235 §34A)	Yes, subject to the limitations in col. 1. (235 §34A)	Yes. (235 §34A)	There is no statutory provision or definite case authority on point.	Generally, yes. However, in the case of IRAs of a non-roll over kind, only contributions in the 5 years prior to bankruptcy not in excess of 7 percent of the total income of the individual for such period are protected. (235 §34A)
Michigan	Yes. (§600.6023(1)(k))	There is no statutory provision or definite case authority on point.	Yes. (§600.6023(1)(j))	There is no statutory provision or definite case authority on point.	Contributions are generally not exempt if made within 120 days of filing for bankruptcy by the debtor. (§600.6023(1)(j) & (k))
Minnesota[1]	Yes, up to $69,000 (§550.37(Subd. 24)) The exemption can be raised "to the extent reasonably necessary for the support of the debtor and any spouse or dependent of the debtor." (Id.)	Yes, up to $69,000 (§550.37(Subd. 24)) The exemption can be raised "to the extent reasonably necessary for the support of the debtor and any spouse or dependent of the debtor." (Id.)	Yes, up to $69,000 (§550.37(Subd. 24)) The exemption can be raised "to the extent reasonably necessary for the support of the debtor and any spouse or dependent of the debtor." (Id.)	Yes. (§571.922)	There is no statutory provision or definite case authority on point.
Mississippi	Yes. (§85-3-1(e)(i))	Yes. (§85-3-1(e)(i))	Yes. (§85-3-1(e)(iii)) See also In re Henderson, 167 B.R. 67, 70-71 (Bankr. N.D. Miss. 1993), in which bankruptcy debtors' exemption claims in their SEP-IRAs extended only to amounts reasonably necessary for support of debtors as well as any dependents.	There is no statutory provision or definite case authority on point.	There is no statutory provision or definite case authority on point.
Missouri	Yes, but not from qualified domestic relations order. (§513.430(1)(10))	Yes, but not from qualified domestic relations order. (§513.430(1)(10))	Yes, but not from qualified domestic relations order. (§513.430(1)(10))	There is no statutory provision or definite case authority on point.	Yes. Funds are not exempt for the three year period prior to commencement of bankruptcy proceedings. (§513.430(10)(f))
Montana	Yes. (§31-2-106(4))	Yes. (§31-2-106(4))	Yes. (§31-2-106(4))	There is no statutory provision or definite case authority on point.	Yes, contributions within one year before filing of bankruptcy which exceed 15% of individual's income for such year are not exempt. (§31-2-106(4))

Table 8.03
Pension Plans

	Are Federally Qualified §401 Pension Plans Exempt?	Are §403(a) Annuity Plans Exempt?	Are §408 IRAs Exempt?*	Is There an Income Exemption for Payments Not Covered by the Pension Plan Exemption?	Are Contributions Within a Certain Period of Bankruptcy Exempt?
Nebraska	Yes, to extent reasonably necessary for the support of the debtor. (§25-1563.01)	Yes, to extent reasonably necessary for the support of the debtor. (§25-1563.01)	Yes, to extent reasonably necessary for the support of the debtor. (§25-1563.01)	There is no statutory provision or definite case authority on point.	Exempt unless, within two years prior to bankruptcy, plan was established or amended to increase contributions. (§25-1563.01(1))
Nevada[1]	Yes, up to $500,000. (§21.090(1)(r)(4))	Yes, up to $500,000. (§21.090(1)(r)(3))	Yes, up to $500,000. (§21.090(1)(r)(1) (2))	There is no statutory provision or definite case authority on point.	No statutory provision.
New Hampshire[1]	Yes. No exemption, however, for claims of spousal or child support or a qualified domestic relations order. (§511:2(XIX))	Yes. No exemption, however, for claims of spousal or child support or a qualified domestic relations order. (§511:2(XIX))	Yes. No exemption, however, for claims of spousal or child support or a qualified domestic relations order. (§511:2(XIX))	Yes. (§512:21)	There is no statutory provision or definite case authority on point.
New Jersey	Yes, unless there is an order for child or spousal support or a qualified domestic relations order. (§25:2-1(b))	Yes, unless there is an order for child or spousal support. (§25:2-1(b))	Yes, unless there is an order for child or spousal support. (§25:2-1(b))	There is no statutory provision or definite case authority on point.	Yes, unless preference or fraudulent conveyance. (§25:2-1(b)(1))
New Mexico[1]	Yes. No exemption, however, for claims of spousal or child support or a qualified domestic relations order. (§§42-10-1, 42-10-2)	Yes. No exemption, however, for claims of spousal or child support or a qualified domestic relations order. (§§42-10-1, 42-10-2)	Yes. No exemption, however, for claims of spousal or child support or a qualified domestic relations order. (§§42-10-1, 42-10-2)	There is no statutory provision or definite case authority on point.	No particular provision, but fraudulent contributions are not exempt. (Dona Ana Sav. & Loan, F.A. v. Dofflemeyer, 855 P.2d 1054 (N.M. 1993))
New York	Yes. (N.Y. Civ. Pract. L&R §5205(c) & (d)(1))	Yes. (N.Y. Civ. Pract. L&R §5205(c) & (d)(1))	Yes. (N.Y. Civ. Pract. L&R §5205(c) & (d)(1))	There is no statutory provision or definite case authority on point.	There is no statutory provision or definite case authority on point.
North Carolina	Yes, as to individual retirement plans under the Internal Revenue Code, and any plan treated in the same manner as an individual retirement plan under the Code. No exemption, however, for claims of spousal or child support or a qualified domestic relations order. (§1C-1601(a)(9))	Yes, as to individual retirement plans under the Internal Revenue Code, and any plan treated in the same manner as an individual retirement plan under the Code. No exemption, however, for claims of spousal or child support or a qualified domestic relations order. (§1C-1601(a)(9))	Yes. No exemption, however, for claims of spousal or child support or a qualified domestic relations order. (§1C-1601(a)(9))	There is no statutory provision or definite case authority on point.	They may generally be exempt. (In re Hare, 32 B.R. 16 (Bankr. G.D.N.C. 1983))

Table 8.03
Pension Plans

	Are Federally Qualified §401 Pension Plans Exempt?	Are §403(a) Annuity Plans Exempt?	Are §408 IRAs Exempt?*	Is There an Income Exemption for Payments Not Covered by the Pension Plan Exemption?	Are Contributions Within a Certain Period of Bankruptcy Exempt?
North Dakota	Yes, residents can exempt up to $100,000 for each plan and $200,000 for all plans, policies, and pensions combined; however, this can be increased to situations where this property "is reasonably necessary for the support of the resident and the resident's dependents." (§28-22-03.1(7))	Yes, residents can exempt up to $100,000 for each plan and $200,000 for all plans, policies, and pensions combined; however, this can be increased to situations where this property "is reasonably necessary for the support of the resident and the resident's dependents." (§28-22-03.1(7))	Yes, residents can exempt up to $100,000 for each plan and $200,000 for all plans, policies, and pensions combined; however, this can be increased to situations where this property "is reasonably necessary for the support of the resident and the resident's dependents." (§28-22-03.1(7))	There is no statutory provision or definite case authority on point.	Exemption covers plans in effect for a period of at least one year. (§28-22-03.1(7))
Ohio	Yes, to extent payments are reasonably necessary for support. No exemption, however, for claims of spousal or a qualified domestic relations order. (§2329.66(A)(10)(b))	Yes, to extent payments are reasonably necessary for support. No exemption, however, for claims of spousal or child support or a qualified domestic relations order. (§2329.66(A)(10)(b))	Yes, except for any assets deposited for the purpose of evading debts and certain other exceptions. No exemption, however, for claims of spousal or child support or a qualified domestic relations order. (§2329.66(A)(10)(c) & (d))	There is no statutory provision or definite case authority on point.	There is no statutory provision or definite case authority on point.
Oklahoma	Yes, to extent that contributions by or on behalf of a participant were not subject to federal income tax at the time of such contributions. No exemption, however, for claims of spousal or child support or a qualified domestic relations order. (31 §1(A)(20))	Yes, to extent that contributions by or on behalf of a participant were not subject to federal income tax at the time of such contributions. No exemption, however, for claims of spousal or a qualified domestic relations order. (31 §1(A)(20))	Yes, to extent that contributions by or on behalf of a participant were not subject to federal income tax at the time of such contributions. No exemption, however, for claims of spousal or child support or a qualified domestic relations order. (31 §1(A)(20))	There is no statutory provision or definite case authority on point.	No time requirement. Section exempts all these accounts from attachment, execution or other forced sale in a bankruptcy proceeding. (31 §1(A)(20))
Oregon	Yes, except for certain claims regarding fraudulent transfers and support. (§18.358)	Yes, except for certain claims regarding fraudulent transfers and support. (§18.358)	Yes, except for certain claims regarding fraudulent transfers and support. (§18.358)	There is no statutory provision or definite case authority on point.	There is no statutory provision or definite case authority on point.
Pennsylvania	Yes. (42 §8124(b)(1)(ix)) However, amounts over $15,000 contributed within a one-year period are not exempt. (42 §8124(b)(1)(ix)(B))	Yes. (42 §8124(b)(1)(ix)) However, $15,000 contributed within a one-year period are not exempt. (42 §8124(b)(1)(ix)(B))	Yes. (42 §8124(b)(1)(ix)) However, amounts over $15,000 contributed within a one-year period are not exempt. (42 §8124(b)(1)(ix)(B))	There is no statutory provision or definite case authority on point.	Amounts contributed within one year of bankruptcy are not exempt. (42 §8124(b)(1)(ix)(A))

Table 8.03
Pension Plans

	Are Federally Qualified § 401 Pension Plans Exempt?	Are § 403(a) Annuity Plans Exempt?	Are § 408 IRAs Exempt?*	Is There an Income Exemption for Payments Not Covered by the Pension Plan Exemption?	Are Contributions Within a Certain Period of Bankruptcy Exempt?
Rhode Island[1]	Yes, but not to the extent subject to an order of divorce, separate maintenance or child support. Fraudulent conveyances are not exempt. (§ 9-26-4(12))	Yes, if it is protected by ERISA, except for fraudulent conveyances. (§ 9-26-4(12))	Yes, except for fraudulent conveyances. (§ 9-26-4(11))	There is no statutory provision or definite case authority on point.	There is no statutory provision or definite case authority on point.
South Carolina	Yes. (§ 15-41-30(A)(11)(e))	Yes. (§ 15-41-30(A)(11)(e)(iii))	Yes. (§ 15-41-30(A)(13))	There is no statutory provision or definite case authority on point.	There is no statutory provision or definite case authority on point.
South Dakota	Yes, up to total of $1 million principal and income, and distributions related thereto, in aggregate for all employee benefit plans. (§ 43-45-16)	Yes, up to total of $1 million principal and income, and distributions related thereto, in aggregate for all employee benefit plans. (§§ 43-45-16 to 43-45-17)	Yes, up to total of $1 million principal and income, and distributions related thereto, in aggregate for all employee benefit plans. (§§ 43-45-16 to 43-45-17)	Yes. (§§ 21-18-51 to 21-18-53)	"Absolute exemption." (§ 43-45-15)
Tennessee	Yes, in the case of a resident if payable on or after age 58, on a periodic basis and there is no option to accelerate so as to receive in a lump sum or over a period of 60 months or less. (§ 26-2-111(1)(D))	Yes, in the case of a resident if payable on or after age 58, on a periodic basis and there is no option to accelerate so as to receive in a lump sum or over a period of 60 months or less. (§ 26-2-111(1)(D))	Yes, in the case of a resident if payable on or after age 58, on a periodic basis and there is no option to accelerate so as to receive in a lump sum or over a period of 60 months or less. (§ 26-2-111(1)(D))	Yes. (§ 26-2-106)	There is no statutory provision or definite case authority on point.
Texas	Yes, to extent contributions are deductible and not subject to a child support lien. (Prop. §§ 42.0021(a), 42.005)	Yes, to extent contributions are deductible and not subject to a child support lien. (Prop. §§ 42.0021(a), 42.005)	Yes, to extent contributions are deductible and not subject to a child support lien. (Prop. §§ 42.0021(a), 42.005)	There is no statutory provision or definite case authority on point.	There is no statutory provision or definite case authority on point.
Utah	Yes, unless the creditor is an alternative payee under a domestic relations order. (§ 78B-5-505(1)(a)(xiv))	Yes, unless the creditor is an alternative payee under a domestic relations order. (§ 78B-5-505(1)(a)(xiv))	Yes, unless the creditor is an alternative payee under a domestic relations order. (§ 78B-5-505(1)(a)(xiv))	There is no statutory provision or definite case authority on point.	"[A]mounts contributed or benefits accrued by or on behalf of a debtor within one year before the debtor files bankruptcy" are not exempt. (§ 78B-5-505(1)(b)(ii))

Table 8.03
Pension Plans

	Are Federally Qualified §401 Pension Plans Exempt?	Are §403(a) Annuity Plans Exempt?	Are §408 IRAs Exempt?*	Is There an Income Exemption for Payments Not Covered by the Pension Plan Exemption?	Are Contributions Within a Certain Period of Bankruptcy Exempt?
Vermont	Yes, to extent reasonably necessary for support in the case of a debtor entitled to receive payments. (12 §2740(19)(J)) Otherwise, in the case of self-directed accounts, there is a general exemption regarding a debtor's interest in an account, but only to the extent of tax-deductible and exempt contributions, as well as interest, dividends or other earnings on these contributions and all growth thereon. (12 §2740(16)) In the case of attachment for child support, the exemption is limited to $5,000. (*Id.*)	See col. 1.	Yes, to extent reasonably necessary for support. (12 §2740(16)) There is a general exemption regarding a debtor's interest in a Roth IRA, but only to extent of contribution limits under IRC §408A and interest, dividends or other earnings on these contributions and all growth thereon. (*Id.*) In the case of attachment for child support, the exemption is limited to $5,000. (*Id.*)	No provision.	No protection for a contribution to a self-directed plan or account within one year before debtor files for bankruptcy. (12 §2740(16))
Virginia	Yes, "to the same extent permitted under federal bankruptcy law for such a plan." (§34-34(B)). However, there is no exemption from claims by an alternate payee or claims by the state under chapter 19 of Title 632. (§34-34(C)) Similarly, there is no exemption from child or spousal support obligations. (*Id.*)	See col. 1.	See col. 1.	Yes. (§34-29)	No provision.
Washington	Yes. (§6.15.020(3)-(4))	Yes. (§6.15.020(3)-(4))	Yes. (§6.15.020(3))	There is no statutory provision or definite case authority on point.	There is no statutory provision or definite case authority on point.
West Virginia	Yes. (§38-8-1(a)(5)). If in bankruptcy, exempt only for amount reasonably necessary for support of debtor and dependents. (§38-10-4(j)(5)).	Yes. (§38-8-1(a)(5)). If in bankruptcy, exempt only for amount reasonably necessary for support of debtor and dependents. (§38-10-4(j)(5)).	Yes. (§38-8-1(a)(5)). If in bankruptcy, exempt only for amount reasonably necessary for support of debtor and dependents. (§38-10-4(j)(5)).	There is no statutory provision or definite case authority on point.	There is no statutory provision or definite case authority on point.

Table 8.03
Pension Plans

	Are Federally Qualified §401 Pension Plans Exempt?	Are §403(a) Annuity Plans Exempt?	Are §408 IRAs Exempt?*	Is There an Income Exemption for Payments Not Covered by the Pension Plan Exemption?	Are Contributions Within a Certain Period of Bankruptcy Exempt?
Wisconsin[1]	Yes, except for claims "concerning child support, family support or maintenance payments, or any judgment of annulment, divorce, or legal separation." (§815.18(3)(j)(1), (5))	See col. 1.	See col. 1.	There is no statutory provision or definite case authority on point.	There is no statutory provision or definite case authority on point.
Wyoming[1]	Yes. (§1-20-110(a))	Yes. (§1-20-110(a))	Yes. (§1-20-110(a))	There is no statutory provision or definite case authority on point.	Contributions made within 90 days of filing a bankruptcy petition are not exempt. (§1-20-110(b))

* A number of state statutes keyed non-exemption to the assumption that IRAs had no federal bankruptcy exemption. In Rousey v. Jacoway, 544 U.S. 320 (2005), the U.S. Supreme Court held that IRAs did qualify for federal bankruptcy exemption. This may alter the outcome in a number of states in affording more protection against creditor claims to IRAs.

[1] The statute does not refer to specific provisions of the Internal Revenue Code, but affords a general exemption with respect to pension or retirement arrangements and annuity contracts.

Table 8.04
Jointly-Owned Property

	Upon the Death of Joint Tenant, Can Creditors Reach His Interest?	If Not Specified, Is Joint Tenancy or Tenancy in Common Presumed?
Alabama	No definitive authority.	Tenancy in common. (§35-4-7)
Alaska	§34.15.130 abolishes the joint tenancy in Alaska with respect to real property, although tenancy by the entirety is preserved. See also §34.15.110(b) With respect to tenants by the entirety, a creditor takes subject to right of survivorship. (Pilip v. U.S., 186 F. Supp. 397, 402 (D. Alaska 1960))	Tenancy in common. (§34.15.110(a)) Husband and wife, who acquire title to real property, hold it as tenants by the entirety, unless declared otherwise in the conveyance or devise. (§34.15.110(b)
Arizona	No specific authority, although dictum that on death property is solely that of survivor. (Graham v. Allen, 463 P.2d 102, 103 (Ct. App. 1970))	Tenancy in common. (§33-431(A) (real property); In re Baldwin's Estate, 71 P. 2d 791, 793 (Ariz. 1937) (personal property); but, if multiple party account with a financial institution, the account belongs to a survivor on death of a party. (§14-6212)
Arkansas	No explicit authority.	Tenancy in common. (§18-12-603)
California	No. (Ziegler v. Bonnell, 126 P.2d 118, 119-20 (Dist. Ct. App. 1942) (judgment debtor died prior to levy of execution)	Tenancy in common. (Civ. Code §686)
Colorado	No explicit authority, but implied by First Nat'l Bank v. Energy Fuels Corp., 618 P.2d 1115, 1118-19 (Colo. 1980)	Personal property: Tenancy in common. (§38-11-101) Real property: Tenancy in common. (§38-31-101(1)) However, with respect to real property, a joint tenancy is presumed if a conveyance or devise is made to two or more personal representatives, trustees, or other fiduciaries. (§38-31-101(3)) An estate in joint tenancy in real property can only be created in natural persons, with an exemption for conveyances or devises to two or more personal representatives, trustees, or other fiduciaries. (§38-31-101(4))
Connecticut	Yes, to the extent of an existing, valid attachment, lien, or execution. (§47-14f; In re Bernier, 176 B.R. 976, 982 (Bankr. D. Conn. 1995))	Tenancy in common. (Dennen v. Searle, 176 A.2d 561, 565 (Sup. Ct. Err. 1961))
Delaware	There is no statutory provision or definite case authority on point.	Tenancy in common. (25 §701) (real property); tenancy in common (personal property unless language to contrary) (In re McCracken's Estate, 219 A.2d 908, 911 (Ch. 1966))
District of Columbia	No. (Dist. of Columbia v. Riggs Nat'l Bank, 335 A.2d 238, 244 (D.C. 1975)) However, there is an exception for real estate owned by common law partnership. (Id.)	Tenancy in common. (§42-516(a))
Florida	No, if tenant by entirety; yes, if solely right of survivorship. (Hurlbert v. Shackleton, 560 So. 2d 1276, 1278 (Fla. Dist. Ct. App. 1990))	Tenancy in common. (§689.15)
Georgia	No. (Taylor v. Taylor, 394 S.E.2d 628, 629 (Ct. App. 1990))	Tenancy in common. (§44-6-120)
Hawaii	No. (U.S. v. Property Entitled in the Names of Alexander Morio Toki & Elizabeth Mila Toki, 779 F. Supp. 1272, 1281 (D. Haw. 1991) (tenancy by the entirety))	Tenancy in common. (§509-1) (real property) As to personal property, the result turns on intent and there does not appear to be a presumption. (In re Estate of Au, 583 P.2d 966, 969 (Haw. 1978)) (in the case of real property, it is a rule of construction; in the case of personal property there is no presumption)
Idaho	No. (Ogilvie v. Idaho Bank & Trust Co., 582 P.2d 215, 220 (1978))	Tenancy in common. (§§55-104, 55-508)
Illinois	No. (People's Tr. & Sav. Bank v. Haas, 160 N.E. 85 (Ill. 1927))	Tenancy in common. (765 ILCS 1005/1 with respect to real property) As for personal property, tenancy in common is presumed, unless there is a written instrument with appropriate language establishing joint tenancy. (O'Vadka v. Rend Lake Bank, 561 N.E.2d 360 (App. Ct. 1990))
Indiana	Uncertain. May be reachable if there is lien. (Wilken v. Young, 41 N.E. 68, 70 (Ind. 1895)	Tenancy in common. (§32-17-2-1(c) (to real property, but not re spouses); §32-17-11-29 (personal property, but not re spouses upon death of a spouse for listed property type)
Iowa	No, but if attachment occurs prior to death, then it survives the death of joint tenant. (Frederick v. Shorman, 147 N.W.2d 478, 484 (Iowa 1966))	Tenancy in common. (§557.15) (with respect to real property, although joint tenancy if indication grantees are married) (In re Estate of Miller, 79 N.W.2d 315, 318 (Iowa 1956) with respect to personal property

Table 8.04
Jointly-Owned Property

State	Upon the Death of Joint Tenant, Can Creditors Reach His Interest?	If Not Specified, Is Joint Tenancy or Tenancy in Common Presumed?
Kansas	No. (Simons v. McLain, 32 P. 919, 920 (Kan. 1893))	Tenancy in common. (§ 58-501)
Kentucky	No. (Stambaugh v. Stambaugh, 156 S.W.2d 827, 831 Ky. 1941))	No provision.
Louisiana	N/A. Joint tenancy laws have no application in determining ownership of property. (Gathright v. Smith, 352 So. 2d 282, 286 (Ct. App. 1977), aff'd and remanded, 368 So. 2d 679 (La. 1978))	"Ownership is indivision." (Civil Code §§ 480, 497) Most like tenancy in common.
Maine	No. (Irvin L. Young Foundation v. Damrell, 511 A.2d 1069, 1070 (Me. 1986))	For real property, tenancy in common (33 § 159); no definitive authority as to personal property.
Maryland	No. (Eastern Shore Bldg. & Loan Corp. v. Bank of Somerset, 253 A.2d 367, 370 (Md. 1969))	Tenancy in common. (Real Prop. § 2-117)
Massachusetts	No. (Weaver v. City of New Bedford, 140 N.E.2d 309, 310 (Mass. 1957))	For real property, tenancy in common (184 § 7); no definitive authority as to personal property.
Michigan	No. (Guilds v. Monroe County Bank, 200 N.W.2d 769 (Ct. App. 1972))	For real property, tenancy in common (§ 554.44); no definitive authority as to personal property.
Minnesota	No definitive authority.	Tenancy in common. (§ 500.19 (subd.2) ("All grants and devises of lands . . ."); (personal property) Farmers Security St. Bank v. Voegele, 386 N.W.2d 760 (Ct. App. 1986)
Mississippi	No. (Wallace v. United Miss. Bank, 726 So.2d 578, 584 (Miss. 1998))	Tenancy in common. (§ 89-1-7)
Missouri	No. (Heintz v. Hudkins, 824 S.W.2d 139, 142 (Ct. App. 1992))	For real property, tenancy in common for grants or devises made to two or more persons other than executors, trustees and husband and wife (§ 442.450); no definitive authority as to personal property.
Montana	No definitive authority.	Tenancy in common (§ 70-1-314), except motor vehicles, which is joint tenancy (§ 61-3-202(4)).
Nebraska	No. (DeForge v. Patrick, 76 N.W.2d 733, 737 (Neb. 1956))	Tenancy in common. (§ 76-275.07)
Nevada	No definitive authority.	Tenancy in common, other than devises to executors or trustees. (§ 111.060)
New Hampshire	No definitive authority.	Tenancy in common. (§ 477:18)
New Jersey	No definitive authority.	Tenancy in common. (§ 46:3-17)
New Mexico	No definitive authority.	Tenancy in common, other than those granted or bequeathed to executors or trustees. (§ 47-1-15)
New York	Yes, if gratuitous transfer creates joint tenancy and estate thereby becomes insolvent. (In re Estate of Granwell, 228 N.E.2d 779, 781 (Ct. App. 1967) But no clear rule if estate of debtor is not insolvent and there is, therefore, not a presumed fraudulent conveyance. No, if a tenancy by the entireties is involved. (In re Dickie's Will, 286 N.Y.S.2d 893 (Sur. Ct. 1968))	Tenancy in common. (Est., Powers & Tr. Law § 6-2.2(a)) In the case of dispositions of real property to spouses, they take by tenants by the entirety. (Id. at (b.)) The same is true of a co-op apartment. (Id. at (c.)) If persons take title to real property or co-op as spouses, but are not, in fact, married, then they are deemed to have a joint tenancy. (Id. at (d.)) A disposition of property to executors or trustees creates a joint tenancy. (Id. at (e)
North Carolina	No. (Wilson Cty. v. Wooten, 111 S.E.2d 875, 877 (N.C. 1960))	Tenancy in common. (§§ 41-2, 41-2.2 (securities))
North Dakota	No, except payment of estate taxes. (Schlichenmayer v. Luithle, 221 N.W.2d 77, 82-83 (N.D. 1974))	Tenancy in common. (§ 47-02-08)
Ohio	No. (In re Certificates of Deposit Issued by Hocking Valley Bank of Athens Co, 569 N.E.2d 484, 486 (Ohio 1991))	Tenancy in common. (§ 5302.19) (real property); as to personal property, no definitive authority.

Table 8.04
Jointly-Owned Property

	Upon the Death of Joint Tenant, Can Creditors Reach His Interest?	If Not Specified, Is Joint Tenancy or Tenancy in Common Presumed?
Oklahoma	No. (Ladd v. State ex rel. Okla. Tax Comm'n, 688 P.2d 59, 61 (Okla. 1989))	Tenancy in common. (84 §184 (when devise or legacy given to more than one person); Clinton v. Clinton, 101 P.2d 609, 613-14 (Okla. 1940)) No definitive authority regarding inter vivos conveyances or gifts.
Oregon	No definitive authority.	Tenancy in common, when conveyance or devise of real property, unless between husband and wife, in which case treated as tenancy by entirety. (§93.180) As to personal Property, no definitive authority.
Pennsylvania	No. (In re Jones, 2004 WL 1924888, (Bankr. E.D. Pa. July 27, 2004) Joint bank accounts go to surviving joint tenant rather than the estate of the decedent. (20 Pa. CSA §6304)	Tenancy in common with respect to eliminating right of survivorship at death. (68 P.S. §110) Goodheart Estate, 12 Pa. D.C. 2d 403 (1957), Zomisky v. Zamiska, 296 A.2d 722, 723 (Pa. 1972)
Rhode Island	No. (Knibb v. Sec. Ins. Co. of New Haven, 399 A.2d 1214, 1216 (R.I. 1979))	Tenancy in common. (§34-3-1)
South Carolina	No definitive authority.	Tenancy in common. (Telfair v. Howe, 24 S.C. Eq. (3 Rich. Eq.) 235 (1851); Free v. Sandifer, 126 S.E. 521 (S.C. 1925))
South Dakota	Yes, to extent of the value of the amount contributed by deceased joint owner subject to all homestead and legal exemptions in such debtor's jointly owned property. (§§43-46-1 to 43-46-5) Creditors must initiate a legal action to recover the debt within six months of death. (§43-46-2)	Tenancy in common unless acquired by a partnership. (§43-2-17)
Tennessee	No definitive authority.	Tenancy in common in that right of survivorship in joint tenancy eliminated. (§66-1-107)
Texas	No definitive authority.	Tenancy in common. (Chandler v. Kountze, 130 S.W.2d 327 (Tex. Civ. App. 1939))
Utah	No definitive authority, although "yes" implied in Beehive State Bank v. Rosquist, 439 P.2d 468 (Utah 1968).	Tenancy in common, unless real property interest is between husband and wife, in which case a joint tenancy is presumed. (§57-1-5(1)(a), (1)(b)) Also, tenants holding title as tenants by the entirety (§57-1-5(7)) or community property are joint tenants. (See amended §57-1-5(8))
Vermont	No definitive authority.	Tenancy in common. (27 §2) (real property); does not apply to devises or conveyances made in trust or made to spouses; no definitive authority as to personal property.
Virginia	No definitive authority.	Tenancy in common. (§55-20)
Washington	No. (Kalk v. Security Pac. Bank Washington NA, 894 P.2d 559 (Wash. 1995) (en banc))	Tenancy in common unless acquired by them in partnership, for partnership purposes. (§64.28.020(1))
West Virginia	No. (In re DeMarco, 114 B.R. 121, 125 (Bankr. N.D. W. Va. 1990))	Tenancy in common (§36-1-19) (no right of survivorship, even if declared to be a joint tenancy or tenancy by the entireties); however, may be joint tenancy with right of survivorship if "it manifestly appears from the tenor of the instrument that it was intended." (§36-1-20(a)), or if multiple owners are linked with the disjunctive word "or." (§36-1-20(b))
Wisconsin	If unsecured, no. Yes, however, if the interest was subject to a judgment lien on which execution was issued before the spouse's death. (§859.18(4)(a)(2)) If interest secured by a mortgage, security interest, or statutory lien, the joint tenant takes the decedent's interest subject to the mortgage, security interest, or statutory lien. (§700.24)	Tenancy in common (§700.18), unless owners or buyers are described as (or are) husband and wife or domestic partners, in which case joint tenancy is presumed. (§700.19)
Wyoming	While there is no controlling authority, the answer probably is no. (Wightman v. Am. Nat'l Bank, 591 P.2d 903, 906 (Wyo. 1979), vacated by Supreme Court on rehearing, 610 P.2d 1001 (Wyo. 1980) (emphasizing a different result when there is a preexisting security interest held by the creditor)).	Tenancy in common. (Choman v. Epperley, 592 P.2d 714, 717 (Wyo. 1970); In re Anselmi, 52 B.R. 479, 487-88 (Bankr. D. Wyo. 1985))

Table 9
Rule Against Perpetuities
(current through 5/1/18)

The rule against perpetuities is in flux. The traditional rule is dead—not observed in any state. In all, two camps have emerged: states that have adopted the Uniform Statutory Rule Against Perpetuities (USRAP), and states abolishing the rule altogether or adopting a perpetuities period several hundred years in length coupled with novel and flexible statutory provisions. Differences exist even among states within a particular camp, so that careful analysis of a relevant state's law is essential.

The question whether the rule applies and, if so, what are its components, is not simply an academic inquiry. The common law rule has serious, even severe consequences *ab initio* if violated. On the other hand, there are a number of valuable planning opportunities in states where the rule has been abolished. First, dead hand control can be perpetuated for many generations via a dynastic trust. Second, substantial tax advantages can be achieved in connection with generation-skipping transfer tax (GST) exemption. Property sheltered by the GST exemption (at least through 2012) is not subject to tax. In addition, the appreciation experienced by such exempt property is sheltered as well. Ordinarily, when this exempt property is distributed, a beneficiary may receive an asset that has appreciated significantly over several decades and, thus, presents him with a severe estate planning/tax problem of his own. However, if the rule has been abolished, there is no requirement to ever make a substantial, final distribution to a younger generation beneficiary. By drafting for successive life interests, the death of any beneficiary does not trigger estate tax. Of course, the sheltered principal also remains exempt from generation-skipping transfer tax.

States that have enacted USRAP typically provide a variety of benefits as well, even if somewhat less dramatic. The centerpiece of USRAP is the wait-and-see rule, which eliminates the harshness of the common law rule's invalidating an interest solely on the hypothetical possibility that it may violate the perpetuities period in the future. In addition, through careful planning and the use of special powers of appointment, the perpetuities period can be extended well beyond the common law rule, albeit not in perpetuity.

The accompanying table analyzes in detail many of the critical questions associated with the rule against perpetuities through a series of 26 questions. It does so on a state-by-state basis. Since this is a volatile area, the reader should confirm that the authority cited in support of an answer to a particular question has not changed since the date indicated above. Care should also be exercised in simply adopting the law of a state that appears to take a favorable stance on the perpetuities issue. There are highly complex choice-of-law issues that may undermine the attempt to adopt the law of a particular state on this subject. See 1 Jeffrey A. Schoenblum, *Multistate And Multinational Estate Planning* § 13.03.

9002

Table 9
Rule Against Perpetuities

	ALABAMA	ALASKA	ARIZONA
1. *Which rule is in effect: the common law rule, the Uniform Statutory Rule Against Perpetuities (USRAP), other law, or none?*	USRAP is in effect as of Jan. 1, 2012. (Ala. Code §§ 35-4A-1–35-4A-8) However, see #2.b.3 & 3.9, specifying that the rule does not apply to a trust in existence not in excess of 360 years; it is governed by the laws of the state and the trustee has the power to sell, lease, and mortgage property held in trust.)	Other. (Alaska Stat. §§ 34.27.051–34.27.053)	USRAP. (Ariz. Rev. Stat. §§ 14-2901–14-2906) However, see #2.b.3., which allows the drafter effectively to opt out of the rule by providing for a power in a trustee to sell the trust assets, and at least one person alive when the trust is created has an unlimited power to terminate the interest in question.
2. a. *Is the common law rule relevant to any interests?*	Yes, but only as the starting point of the analysis. (§35-4A-2)	The common law is superseded and does not apply in the state. (§34.27.075) However, there is a 1,000 year limitation with respect to powers of appointment, largely intended to avoid the "Delaware Tax Trap." (§34.27.051)	Yes, but only as the starting point of the analysis. (§14-2901(A))
b. *What is the relevant rule?*	A nonvested property interest is invalid unless at least one of the following is true: 1. At the time the interest is created it is certain to vest or to terminate not later than twenty-one years after the death of a person who is then alive. 2. The interest either vests or terminates within 100 years after its creation. (§35-4A-2)	See #2a.	A nonvested property interest is invalid unless at least one of the following is true: 1. At the time the interest is created it is certain to vest or to terminate not later than twenty-one years after the death of a person who is then alive. 2. The interest either vests or terminates within ninety years after its creation.

Table 9
Rule Against Perpetuities

	ALABAMA	ALASKA	ARIZONA
	3. The rule does not apply to a trust (i) which in its terms does not exceed 360 years in duration, (ii) which is governed by the laws of [Alabama], and (iii) the instrument governing which includes a power of the trustee to sell, lease, and mortgage all property held in trust. (§35-4A-5 (a))		3. The interest is under a trust whose trustee has the expressed or implied power to sell the trust assets and at one or more times after the creation of the interest one or more persons who are living when the trust is created have an unlimited power to terminate the interest. (§14-2901(A))
3. *Does the rule apply to other than private trusts?*	Yes. The rule applies except to: 1. A nonvested property interest or a power of appointment arising out of a nondonative transfer, except for a nonvested property interest or a power of appointment arising out of any of the following: (a) A premarital or postmarital agreement. (b) A separation or divorce settlement. (c) A spouse's election. (d) A similar arrangement arising out of a prospective, existing or previous marital relationship between the parties. (e) A contract to make or not revoke a will or trust.	N/A	Yes. The rule applies except to: 1. A nonvested property interest or a power of appointment arising out of a nondonative transfer, except for a nonvested property interest or a power of appointment arising out of any of the following: (a) A premarital or postmarital agreement. (b) A separation or divorce settlement. (c) A spouse's election. (d) A similar arrangement arising out of a prospective, existing or previous marital relationship between the parties. (e) A contract to make or not to revoke a will or trust.

Table 9
Rule Against Perpetuities

ALABAMA	ALASKA	ARIZONA
(f) A contract to exercise or not to exercise a power of appointment.		(f) A contract to exercise or not to exercise a power of appointment.
(g) A transfer in satisfaction of a duty of support.		(g) A transfer in satisfaction of a duty of support.
(h) A reciprocal transfer.		(h) A reciprocal transfer.
2. A fiduciary's power relating to the administration or management of assets, including the power of a fiduciary to sell, lease, or mortgage property, and the power of a fiduciary to determine principal and income.		2. A fiduciary's power relating to the administration or management of assets, including the power of a fiduciary to sell, lease or mortgage property, and the power of a fiduciary to determine principal and income.
3. A power to appoint a fiduciary.		3. A power to appoint a fiduciary.
4. A discretionary power of a trustee to distribute principal before termination of a trust to a beneficiary who has an indefeasibly vested interest in the income and principal.		4. A discretionary power of a trustee to distribute principal before termination of a trust to a beneficiary who has an indefeasibly vested interest in the income and principal.
5. A nonvested property interest held by a charity, government or governmental agency or subdivision, if the nonvested property interest is preceded by an interest held by another charity, government or governmental agency or subdivision.		5. A nonvested property interest held by a charity, government or governmental agency or subdivision, if the nonvested property interest is preceded by an interest held by another charity, government or governmental agency or subdivision.

Table 9
Rule Against Perpetuities

ALABAMA	ALASKA	ARIZONA
6. "A nonvested property interest in a trust or other property arrangement, which trust or other property arrangement is exclusively for the benefit of one or more charities, governments, or government agencies or subdivisions." The editor's notes state that this was added to make clear that charitable trusts are excluded from the statutory rule USRAP.		6. A nonvested property interest in or a power of appointment with respect to a trust or any other property arrangement forming part of any pension, profit sharing, stock bonus, health, disability, death benefit, income deferral or other current or deferred benefit plan for one or more employees, independent contractors or their beneficiaries or spouses, to which contributions are made for the purpose of distributing to or for the benefit of the participants or their beneficiaries or spouses the property, income or principal in the trust or other property arrangement, except a nonvested property interest or a power of appointment that is created by an election of a participant or a beneficiary or spouse.

Table 9
Rule Against Perpetuities

ALABAMA	ALASKA	ARIZONA
7. A nonvested property interest in or a power of appointment with respect to a trust or any other property arrangement forming part of any pension, profit sharing, stock bonus, health, disability, death benefit, income deferral or other current or deferred benefit plan for one or more employees, independent contractors or their beneficiaries or spouses, to which contributions are made for the purpose of distributing to or for the benefit of the participants or their beneficiaries or spouses the property, income or principal in the trust or other property arrangement, except a nonvested property interest or a power of appointment that is created by an election of a participant or a beneficiary or spouse. 8. A property interest, power of appointment or arrangement that was not subject to the common law rule against perpetuities or is excluded by another statute of this state.		7. A property interest, power of appointment or arrangement that was not subject to the common law rule against perpetuities or is excluded by the laws of this state. (§ 14-2904)

Table 9
Rule Against Perpetuities

	ALABAMA	ALASKA	ARIZONA
	9. A trust, (i) which on its terms does not exceed 360 years by the laws of this state, (ii) which is governed by the laws of this State, and (iii) the power of the trust to sell, lease, and mortgage all property held in trust. (§ 35-4A-5)		
4. *Does the rule invalidate the interest at its creation, or is the rule revised by a wait-and-see approach?*	Wait-and-see. (§ 35-4A-2)	There is no rule against perpetuities, but a wait-and-see approach applies to powers of appointment and certain interests created by powers. (§ 34.27.051)	Wait-and-see. (§ 14-2901(A)(2))
5. *Can the trust be reformed?*	Yes, but only if: 1. A nonvested property interest or a power of appointment becomes invalid under § 35-4A-2. 2. A class gift is not but might become invalid under § 35-4A-2(a)(1) and the time has arrived when the share of any class member is to take effect in possession or enjoyment.	Yes, but only "[i]f a nonvested property interest or a power of appointment was created before January 1, 1996, and is determined in a judicial proceeding, commenced on or after that date, to violate this state's rule against perpetuities as that rule existed before January 1, 1996, or if a nonvested	Yes, but only if: 1. A nonvested property interest or a power of appointment becomes invalid under section 14-2901. (See #2b). 2. A class gift is not but might become invalid under section 14-2901 and the time has arrived when the share of any class member is to take effect in possession or enjoyment.

Table 9
Rule Against Perpetuities

	ALABAMA	ALASKA	ARIZONA
	3. A nonvested property interest that is not validated by § 35-4A-2, that is, the traditional common rule, can vest but not within 100 years after its creation or in the case of a trust under § 35-4A-5(9), not within 360 years of its creation. (§ 35-4A-4)	property interest or a power of appointment was created on or after January 1, 1996, but before April 2, 1997, and is determined in a judicial proceeding, commenced on or after that date, to violate this state's rule against perpetuities as that rule existed, on or after January 1, 1996, and before April 2, 1997." (§ 34.27.070(b))	3. A nonvested property interest that is not validated by section 14-2901, subsection A, paragraph 1, that is, the traditional common rule, can vest but not within ninety years after its creation. (§ 14-2903)
6. *If yes to 5., under what theory?*	A circuit court, on the petition of an interested person, may reform the disposition in the manner that most closely approximates the transferor's manifested plan of distribution and that is within the 100 years allowed under § 35-4A-2 (a)(2), (b)(2), or (c)(2) or the 360 years allowed by § 35-4A-5(9). (§ 35-4A-4)	A court, upon the petition of an interested person, may reform the disposition in the manner that most closely approximates the transferor's manifested plan of distribution and is within the limits of the rule against perpetuities applicable when the nonvested property interest or power of appointment was created. (§ 34.27.070(b))	A court, on the petition of an interested person, may reform the disposition in the manner that most closely approximates the transferor's manifested plan of distribution and that is within the ninety years allowed under section 14-2901. (§ 14-2903) *See also* § 14-2905(B) (If a nonvested property interest or a power of appointment was created before December 31, 1994 and is determined in a judicial proceeding, commenced on or after December 31, 1994, to violate this state's rule against perpetuities as that rule existed before December 31, 1994, a court may also make a reformation.)

Table 9
Rule Against Perpetuities

	ALABAMA	ALASKA	ARIZONA
7. *When is a general testamentary power of appointment invalid?*	A general testamentary power of appointment is invalid unless: 1. At the time the power is created it is certain to be irrevocably exercised or otherwise to terminate not later than twenty-one years after the death of a person who is then alive, or 2. The power is irrevocably exercised or otherwise terminates within 100 years after its creation. (§ 35-4A-2(c)) Note that the requirements set forth in #9 also appear to apply to a general testamentary power. (§ 35-4A-2(b))	A general or nongeneral power of appointment not presently exercisable because of a condition precedent is invalid unless, within a period of 1,000 years after its creation, either the power is irrevocably exercised or the power terminates. (§ 34.27.051(a))	A general testamentary power of appointment is invalid unless: 1. At the time the power is created it is certain to be irrevocably exercised or otherwise to terminate not later than twenty-one years after the death of a person who is then alive, or 2. The power is irrevocably exercised or otherwise terminates within ninety years after its creation. (§ 14-2901(C)) Note that the requirements set forth in #9 also appear to apply to a general testamentary power. (§ 14-2901(B))
8. *Same, but nongeneral testamentary power.*	A nongeneral power of appointment . . . is invalid unless: 1. At the time the power is created it is certain to be irrevocably exercised or otherwise to terminate not later than twenty-one years after the death of a person who is then alive, or 2. The power is irrevocably exercised or otherwise terminates within 100 years after its creation. (§ 35-4A-2(c))	See #7.	A nongeneral power of appointment . . . is invalid unless: 1. At the time the power is created it is certain to be irrevocably exercised or otherwise to terminate not later than twenty-one years after the death of a person who is then alive. 2. The power is irrevocably exercised or otherwise terminates within ninety years after its creation. (§ 14-2901(C))

Table 9
Rule Against Perpetuities

	ALABAMA	*ALASKA*	*ARIZONA*
9. *Same, but general power, whether testamentary or inter vivos, not presently exercisable because of a condition precedent.*	A general power of appointment that is not presently exercisable because of a condition precedent is invalid unless either of the following is true: 1. At the time the power is created the condition precedent is certain to be satisfied or becomes impossible to satisfy no later than twenty-one years after the death of a person who is then alive. 2. The condition precedent either is satisfied or becomes impossible to satisfy within 100 years after its creation. (§ 35-4A-2(b))	See #7.	A general power of appointment that is not presently exercisable because of a condition precedent is invalid unless either of the following is true: 1. At the time the power is created the condition precedent is certain to be satisfied or becomes impossible to satisfy no later than twenty-one years after the death of a person who is then alive. 2. The condition precedent either is satisfied or becomes impossible to satisfy within ninety years after its creation. (§ 14-2901(B))
10. *Same, but nongeneral inter vivos power.*	See #8.	See #7.	See #8.

Table 9
Rule Against Perpetuities

	ALABAMA	ALASKA	ARIZONA
11. Is a period of gestation added to the perpetuity period?	No. The possibility that a child will be born to a person after that person's death is disregarded. (§ 35-4A-2(d)) *See also* Unif. Statutory Rule Against Perpetuities §1, 8B U.L.A. 243, 243 (amended 1990) ("[T]he possibility that a child will be born to [a testator] after his death must be disregarded; and the possibility that a child will be born to any of [the testator's] descendants after their deaths must also be disregarded. Note, however, that the rule of subsection (d) does not apply to the question of the entitlement of an after-born child to take a beneficial interest in the trust".)	N/A	No. The possibility that a child will be born to a person after that person's death is disregarded. (§ 14-2901(D)) *See also* Unif. Statutory Rule Against Perpetuities §1, 8B U.L.A. 243, 243 (amended 1990) ("[T]he possibility that a child will be born to [a testator] after his death must be disregarded; and the possibility that a child will be born to any of [the testator's] descendants after their deaths must also be disregarded. Note, however, that the rule of subsection (d) does not apply to the question of the entitlement of an after-born child to take a beneficial interest in the trust").
12. What is the treatment of a "later of the traditional rule or 90 years" clause? *See* UPC 2-901(e).	That language is inoperative to the extent that it produces a period of time that exceeds 21 years after the death of the survivor. (§ 35-4A-2(e))	N/A	That language is inoperative to the extent that it produces a period of time that exceeds 21 years after the death of the survivor. (§ 14-2901(E))

Table 9
Rule Against Perpetuities

	ALABAMA	*ALASKA*	*ARIZONA*
13. *When is an interest created by the exercise of a general testamentary power deemed created?*	"Except as provided in subsections (b), (c), and (d), and in § 35-4A-5, the time of creation of a nonvested property interest or a power of appointment is determined under general principles of property law." (§ 35-4A-3(a)) The first of the excepted provisions states that, as long as a person with a general power to become the unqualified beneficial owner has that power, the nonvested interest is created when the power terminates. The second of the excepted provisions states that a nonvested property interest, which arises from a transfer to an existing trust, is created when the nonvested property interest in the trust was created. The third of the excepted provisions states that if a testamentary power of appointment is exercised to create another testamentary power of appointment, every nonvested property interest or power of appointment created through the exercise of such testamentary power is considered to have been created at the time of the creation of the testamentary power of appointment.	No provision. However, if a nongeneral power is exercised to create a new presently exercisable general power, property interests subject to the new power either vest or terminate within 1,000 years of the creation of the new power. (§ 34.27.051(b))	"Except as provided in subsections B and C of this section and section 14-2905, subsection A, the time of creation of a nonvested property interest or a power of appointment is determined under general principles of property law." (§ 14-2902(A)) The first two of the excepted provisions state that as long as a person with a general power to become the unqualified beneficial owner has that power, the nonvested interest is created when the power terminates. The third of the excepted provisions states that a nonvested property interest, which arises from a transfer to an existing trust, is created when the nonvested property interest in the trust was created. *See also* Unif. Statutory Rule Against Perpetuities § 2, 8B U.L.A. 268 (amended 1990) (explaining that "general principles of property law determine that the time . . . [of creation] is at the decedent's death.") *See generally* § 14-2905(C) ("a nonvested property interest or a power of appointment created by the exercise of a power of appointment is created when the power is irrevocably exercised or when a revocable exercise becomes irrevocable.")

Table 9
Rule Against Perpetuities

	ALABAMA	ALASKA	ARIZONA
14. *Same, but nongeneral testamentary power.*	See #13.	No provision. However, if a nongeneral power is exercised to create a new or successive nongeneral or general testamentary power, all property interests created by the exercise of the new or successive power must vest or terminate within 1,000 years after the creation of the original instrument creating the nongeneral power. (§ 34.27.051(c))	See #13.

Table 9
Rule Against Perpetuities

	ALABAMA	ALASKA	ARIZONA
15. *Same, but general inter vivos power.*	Except as provided in subsections (b) and (c), and §35-4A-5, the time of creation of a nonvested property interest or a power of appointment is determined under general principles of property law. (§35-4A-5) The first excepted provision states that as long as a person with a general power to become the unqualified beneficial owner has that power, the nonvested interest is created when the power terminates. The second of the excepted provisions states that a nonvested property interest, or a power of appointment, which arises from a transfer to an existing trust or other existing property arrangement is created when the nonvested property interest or power of appointment in the original contribution was created. *See also* Unif. Statutory Rule Against Perpetuities §2, 8B U.L.A. 268 (amended 1990) (explaining that "general principles of property law determine that the time . . . [of creation] is at the decedent's death.")	If the power is the original power creating an interest, there is no provision. If the power creating an interest is itself created by an earlier nongeneral power's exercise, see #13 or #14.	Except as provided in subsections B and C of this section and section 14-2905, subsection A, the time of creation of a nonvested property interest or a power of appointment is determined under general principles of property law (§14-2902(A)) The first two of the excepted provisions states that as long as a person with a general power to become the unqualified beneficial owner has that power, the nonvested interest is created when the power terminates. The third of the excepted provisions states that a nonvested property interest, which arises from a transfer to an existing trust, is created when the nonvested property interest in the trust was created. *See also* Unif. Statutory Rule Against Perpetuities §2, 8B U.L.A. 268 (amended 1990) (explaining that "the time when the interest or power is created is the date the transfer becomes effective for purposes of property law generally, normally the date of delivery of the deed"); Comment to Unif. Probate Code §2-902(a) (stating same and adding "the funding of the trust" as "normally" the time when the interest is created). *See generally* §14-2905(C) ("For purposes of this section, a nonvested

Table 9
Rule Against Perpetuities

	ALABAMA	ALASKA	ARIZONA
			property interest or a power of appointment created by the exercise of a power of appointment is created when the power is irrevocably exercised or when a revocable exercise becomes irrevocable.")
16. *Same, but nongeneral inter vivos power.*	See #15.	If the power was the original power creating the interest, there is no provision. If the power created another power which then created an interest or if the power itself was created by an earlier nongeneral power's exercise, see #13 or #14.	See #15.

Table 9
Rule Against Perpetuities

	ALABAMA	ALASKA	ARIZONA
17. *When is an interest created if the grantor of a trust has a power to revoke?*	If there is a person who alone can exercise a power created by a governing instrument to become the unqualified beneficial owner of a nonvested property interest or a property interest subject to a power of appointment described in § 35-4A-2(b) or (c), the nonvested property interest or power of appointment is created when that person's power to become the unqualified beneficial owner terminates. (§ 35-4A-3(b)) *See also* Unif. Statutory Rule Against Perpetuities § 2, 8B U.L.A. 268 (amended 1990) (explaining that "any nonvested property interest subject to [a power to revoke] is not created … until the power terminates (by release, expiration at the death of the donee, or otherwise")); Comment to Unif. Probate Code § 2-902(b) (noting that "nonvested property interests and powers of appointment created in [a revocable inter-vivos trust] are created when the power to revoke expires, usually at the settlor's death").	There is no statute or case law. Statutory provisions addressing the matter were repealed by § 9, Ch.17 SLA 2000. These previously appeared as sections 34.27.055-34.27.065.	If there is a person who alone can exercise a power created by a governing instrument to become the unqualified beneficial owner of a nonvested property interest or a property interest subject to a power of appointment described in section 14-2901, subsection B or C, the nonvested property interest or power of appointment is created when that person's power to become the unqualified beneficial owner terminates. (§ 14-2902(B)) *See also* Unif. Statutory Rule Against Perpetuities § 2, 8B U.L.A. 268 (amended 1990) (explaining that "any nonvested property interest subject to [a power to revoke] is not created … until the power terminates (by release, expiration at the death of the donee, or otherwise")); Comment to Unif. Probate Code § 2-902(b) (noting that "nonvested property interests and powers of appointment created in [a revocable inter-vivos trust] are created when the power to revoke expires, usually at the settlor's death"). *See generally* § 14-2905(C) ("A nonvested property interest or a power of appointment created by the exercise of a power of appointment is created when the power is irrevocably exercised or when a revocable exercise becomes irrevocable.").

Table 9
Rule Against Perpetuities

	ALABAMA	ALASKA	ARIZONA
18. *When does the period of the rule start re an interest contributed to an irrevocable trust?*	A nonvested property interest or power of appointment arising from a transfer of property to a previously funded trust or any other existing property arrangement is created when the nonvested property interest or power of appointment in the original contribution was created. (§35-4A-3(c))	N/A	A nonvested property interest or a power of appointment arising from a transfer of property to a previously funded trust or any other existing property arrangement is created when the nonvested property interest or power of appointment in the original contribution was created. (§14-2902(C))
19. *Is there a conclusive presumption of fertility, that is, the "fertile octogenarian" rule?*	No specific state case or statute.[1] See Unif. Statutory Rule Against Perpetuities §1, 8B U.L.A. 256 (amended 1990) (holding that "[t]his principle is not superseded by this Act, and in view of new advances in medical science . . . [this] is not unrealistic"). But see C.P. Jhong, Annotation, Modern Status of Presumption Against Possibility of Issue Being Extinct, 98 A.L.R.2d 1285 (2003) (noting "a trend toward denying the conclusive or absolute nature of the presumption against the possibility of issue being extinct where there is competent evidence to the contrary has developed in the decisions, although some courts still adhere to the traditional view treating the presumption as conclusive or absolute").	N/A	No specific state case or statute.[1] See Unif. Statutory Rule Against Perpetuities §1, 8B U.L.A. 256 (amended 1990) (holding that "[t]his principle is not superseded by this Act, and in view of new advances in medical science . . . [this] is not unrealistic"). But see C. P. Jhong, Annotation, Modern Status of Presumption of Possibility of Issue Being Extinct, 98 A.L.R.2d 1285 (2003) (noting "a trend toward denying the conclusive or absolute nature of the presumption against the possibility of issue being extinct where there is competent evidence to the contrary has developed in the decisions, although some courts still adhere to the traditional view treating the presumption as conclusive or absolute").

Table 9
Rule Against Perpetuities

	ALABAMA	*ALASKA*	*ARIZONA*
20. *What is the earliest age a child is deemed capable of bearing a child? What is the impact of illegitimacy?*	Not specifically addressed by USRAP, but the reasoning is the same as set forth in the comment to section 1 of USRAP, 2, Comment, Technical Violations of the Common Law Rule. Wait-and-see will typically result in no violation. Nevertheless, the common law rule ordinarily will be applied initially. "Under the rule, courts must presume that living persons are capable of having or fathering children, no matter how young they are. See In re Graite's Will Trusts, [1949] 1 All E.R. 459, 460 (Ch.). Thus, the rule strikes down any interest whose vesting depends on the assertion that, for example, a toddler will not have children." (Keith L. Butler, Notes & Comments, *Long Live the Dead Hand: A Case for Repeal of the Rule Against Perpetuities in Washington*, 75 Wash. L. Rev. 1237, 1246 n. 78 (2000)).	N/A	Not specifically addressed by USRAP, but the reasoning is the same as set forth in the comment to section 1 of USRAP, 2, Comment, Technical Violations of the Common Law Rule. Wait and see will typically result in no violation. Nevertheless, the [common law] rule ordinarily will be applied initially. "Under the rule, courts must presume that living persons are capable of having or fathering children, no matter how young they are. See In re Graite's Will Trusts, [1949] 1 All E.R. 459, 460 (Ch.). Thus, the rule strikes down any interest whose vesting depends on the assertion that, for example, a toddler will not have children." (Keith L. Butler, Notes & Comments, *Long Live the Dead Hand: A Case for Repeal of the Rule Against Perpetuities in Washington*, 75 Wash. L. Rev. 1237, 1246 n.78 (2000)).

Table 9
Rule Against Perpetuities

	ALABAMA	ALASKA	ARIZONA
21. *Is the "unborn widow" rule observed?*	No specific state statute or case. See Unif. Statutory Rule Against Perpetuities §1, 8B U.L.A. 246 (amended 1990) (explaining that "[t]he chance that [an] interest will become invalid under the Statutory Rule is small" and so the unborn widow rule would rarely invalidate an interest); *see also* 61 Am. Jur. 2d *Perpetuities and Restraints on Alienation* §39 (2013) (noting the same).	N/A	No specific state statute or case. See Unif. Statutory Rule Against Perpetuities §1, 8B U.L.A. 246 (amended 1990) (explaining that "[t]he chance that [an] interest will become invalid under the Statutory Rule is small" and so the unborn widow rule would rarely invalidate an interest); *see also* 61 Am. Jur. 2d Perpetuities and Restraints on Alienation §39 (2013) (noting the same).
22. *Does the "slothful executor" rule apply, i.e., an administrative contingency clause providing for a "distribution to, e.g., those issue living at the time of the satisfaction of the administrative condition precedent?"*	Unclear. Unif. Statutory Rule Against Perpetuities §1, 8B U.L.A. 245 (amended 1990) (Under USRAP an "interest becomes invalid only if it remains in existence and nonvested 90 years after [the testator's] death. Since it is almost certain that the final distribution of [an] estate will occur well within this 90-year period, the chance that [an] interest will be invalid is negligible.")	N/A	Unclear. See In re Estate of Johnson, 811 P.2d 360, 363 (Ariz. Ct. App. 1991) (holding that a clause in a will was not an "administrative contingency" violation.); *see also* Unif. Statutory Rule Against Perpetuities §1, 8B U.L.A. 245 (amended 1990) (Under USRAP an "interest becomes invalid only if it remains in existence and nonvested 90 years after [the testator's] death. Since it is almost certain that the final distribution of [an] estate will occur well within this 90-year period, the chance that [an] interest will be invalid is negligible.")

Table 9
Rule Against Perpetuities

	ALABAMA	*ALASKA*	*ARIZONA*
23. *Does the all-or-nothing rule apply to class gifts?*	Yes. *See* Unif. Statutory Rule Against Perpetuities § 1, 8B U.L.A. 257 (amended 1990) ("Although this Act does not supersede the basic idea of the much-maligned 'all-or-nothing' rule, the evils sometimes attributed to it are substantially if not entirely eliminated by the wait-and-see feature of the Statutory Rule and by the availability of reformation under Section 3.")	N/A	No specific state case or statute. See Unif. Statutory Rule Against Perpetuities § 1, 8B U.L.A. 257 (amended 1990) ("Although this Act does not supersede the basic idea of the much-maligned 'all-or-nothing' rule, the evils sometimes attributed to it are substantially if not entirely eliminated by the wait-and-see feature of the Statutory Rule and by the availability of reformation under Section 3.")

Table 9
Rule Against Perpetuities

	ALABAMA	ALASKA	ARIZONA
24. *Is there an exception to the all-or-nothing rule in the case of subclasses or specific sums to each member of the class?*	See First Alabama Bank of Montgomery v. Adams, 382 So. 2d 1104, 1109 (1980) (noting that "the fact that this gift to a subclass would fail . . . does not mean that the gift to the subclasses of the 'descendants' of Andrea and Wayne must fail"). *See also* Unif. Statutory Rule Against Perpetuities §1, 8B U.L.A. 257 ("The common law also recognizes a doctrine called the specific-sum doctrine which is derived from Storrs v. Benbow, 3 De G.M. & G. 390, 43 Eng. Rep 153 (Ch. 1853), and states: If a specified sum of money is to be paid to each member of a class, the interest of each class member is entitled to separate treatment and is valid or invalid under the Rule on its own. The common law also recognizes a doctrine called the sub-class doctrine, which is derived from Cattlin v. Brown, 11 Hare 372, 68 Eng. Rep. 1318 (Ch. 1853), and states: If the ultimate takers are not described as a single class but rather as a group of subclasses, and if the share to which each separate subclass is entitled will finally be determined within the period of the Rule, the gifts to the different subclasses are separable for the purpose of the Rule.").	N/A	No specific case or statute. See Unif. Statutory Rule Against Perpetuities §1, 8B U.L.A. 257 (amended 1990) ("The specific-sum and sub-class doctrines are not superseded by this Act.").

Table 9
Rule Against Perpetuities

	ALABAMA	ALASKA	ARIZONA
25. *Is the infectious invalidity rule followed outside class gifts?*	No specific case or statute. See Unif. Statutory Rule Against Perpetuities § 1, 8B U.L.A. 256 (amended 1990) (explaining that "[t]he doctrine of infectious invalidity is superseded by this Act by Section 3, under which courts . . . are required to reform the disposition to approximate as closely as possible the transferor's . . . plan of distribution.")	N/A	No specific state case or statute. See Unif. Statutory Rule Against Perpetuities § 1, 8B U.L.A. 256 (amended 1990) (explaining that "[t]he doctrine of infectious invalidity is superseded by this Act by Section 3, under which courts . . . are required to reform the disposition to approximate as closely as possible the transferor's . . . plan of distribution.") *But see* In re Olsen (there is no violation of rule because after 21 years a trustee has the power to convey an absolute fee in possession or absolute ownership of the trust property).
26. *Is there a rule against the suspension of the power of alienation? If so, how is it stated?*	Prohibition against absolute restraint on alienation. Pritchett v. Turner, 437 So. 2d 104, 108 (Ala. 1983).	A future interest or trust is void if, as to property subject to the future interest or trust,	No specific state statute. Case law unclear. See Tovrea v. Umphress, 556 P.2d 814 (Ariz. Ct. App. 1976) (holding that an option agreement that could be exercised up to one year after the death of one of the parties did not constitute a restraint on alienation).

Table 9
Rule Against Perpetuities

ALABAMA	ALASKA	ARIZONA
	(1) the future interest or trust suspends the power of alienation of the property, the suspension of the power of alienation is for a period of at least 30 years after the death of an individual alive at the time of the creation of the future interest or trust, and the suspension of the power of alienation occurs in the document creating the future interest or trust;	
	(2) the future interest or trust suspends the power of alienation of the property and the suspension of the power of alienation is for a period of at least 30 years after the death of an individual alive at the time of the creation of the future interest or trust as computed from the time of the termination of a settlor's power to revoke the trust;	

Table 9
Rule Against Perpetuities

ALABAMA	ALASKA	ARIZONA
	(3) the future interest or trust suspends the power of alienation of the property, the future interest or trust is created by the exercise of a presently exercisable general power of appointment, whether by will or otherwise, and the suspension of the power of alienation is for a period of at least 30 years after the death of an individual alive at the time of the creation of the future interest or trust as computed from the time of creation of the presently exercisable power of appointment; or	

Table 9
Rule Against Perpetuities

ALABAMA	ALASKA	ARIZONA
	(4) the future interest or trust suspends the power of alienation of the property, the future interest or trust is created by the exercise of a nongeneral or testamentary general power of appointment, and the suspension of the power of alienation is for a period of at least 30 years after the death of an individual alive at the time of the creation of the future interest or trust as computed from the time of creation of the original instrument or conveyance creating the original power of appointment that was exercised to create a new or successive nongeneral or testamentary general power of appointment.

(§ 34.27.100(a))

For exceptions to the rule, *see* § 34.27.100(c) | |

Table 9
Rule Against Perpetuities

	ALABAMA	ALASKA	ARIZONA
27. *Effective date.*	Jan. 1, 2012	April 2, 1997. Separate statutory provisions apply to nonvested interests and powers created on or after January 1, 1996 and before April 2, 1997. (§ 34.27.070) Prior interests and powers can be reformed. See #5. (§ 34.27.070(b)) The 1,000 year rule of section 34.27.051, respecting powers of appointment, only applies to a trust instrument or conveyance executed on or after April 2, 1997, if the trust instrument or conveyance creates a contingent power of appointment or nonvested property interest subject to the exercise of a power of appointment creating a new or successive power of appointment. (§ 34.27.070(c))	January 1, 1995. See #6.

---

[1] For questions #19-25, *see* Ala. Code § 35-4a-8 and Ariz. Rev. Stat. § 14.2906 (noting that the state's USRAP "applies notwithstanding the common law rule against perpetuities . . .").

Table 9
Rule Against Perpetuities

	ARKANSAS	CALIFORNIA	COLORADO
1. *Which rule is in effect: the common law rule, the Uniform Statutory Rule Against Perpetuities (USRAP), other law, or none?*	USRAP (Ark. Code Ann. § 18-3-101). However, the Dynasty Trust Act of 2017 has added an exception for trusts administered in the state if the trust has (i) one or more trustees able to convey an absolute fee ownership in land or fee ownership of personal property; or (ii) one or more trustees with express or implied power to sell trust assets; or (iii) vests in one or more persons in being the unlimited power to terminate the trust. (§ 18-3-104(8)(A))	USRAP. (Cal. Prob. Code §§ 21200 - 21225)	There are several rules in effect: 1. With respect to an interest in trust or power of appointment with respect to a trust created after May 31, 2001, (i) a nonvested property interest must vest or terminate within 1,000 years of its creation; (ii) in the case of a general power of appointment subject to a condition precedent, the condition precedent must be satisfied or be impossible to satisfy within 1,000 years after its creation; (iii) a nongeneral power of appointment or a general testamentary power must be irrevocably exercised or otherwise terminate within 1,000 years after its creation. (Colo. Rev. Stat. Ann. § 15-11-1102.5(1)(a)-(b)) Furthermore, reformation is allowed on petition to assure

Table 9
Rule Against Perpetuities

ARKANSAS	CALIFORNIA	COLORADO
		compliance with the 1,000-year rule. (§ 15-11-1104.5(1)) **Note:** The use of the 1,000 year timeframe for the rule against perpetuities, rather than no time limit at all, is intended to avoid the Delaware Tax Trap. **Note:** With a few exceptions for the rules as to when a power of appointment is created, general principles of property law apply. (§ 15-11-1103(1)) **Note:** For when the period begins for an interest contributed to an existing irrevocable trust, see #18. 2. Interests in trusts and powers of appointment created on or after June 1, 1991, but before May 31, 2001, remain governed by a modified USRAP. (§ 15-11-1102.5(2)(a)-(b)) Nontrust interests in a will, such as a testamentary power of appointment not with respect to a trust, executory devises of real estate, or the "slothful executor" situation, though occurring after May 31, 2001, are also governed by a modified USRAP. (§ 15-11-1102.5(2)(a)-(b))

Table 9
Rule Against Perpetuities

ARKANSAS	CALIFORNIA	COLORADO
		3. Interests and powers created by the exercise of a nongeneral power over all or part of a trust that was irrevocable on September 25, 1985, do not qualify under 1. above, but will qualify under 2. above. (§15-11-1102.5(3)(c)(I)-(II)) However, for pre-June 1, 1991 trusts not irrevocable on Sept. 25, 1985, the exercise of a power after June 30, 2006 would give rise to the rule in 1. above. In other respects, these pre-June 1, 1991 trusts are governed by the common law rule and not even a modified USRAP. (§15-11-1107) Nevertheless, judicial reformation, as per cy pres, is allowed. (§15-11-1106(2))

Table 9
Rule Against Perpetuities

	ARKANSAS	CALIFORNIA	COLORADO
			4. With respect to any interest or power of appointment created before July 1, 2006, the owner or holder of the interest or power had to deliver a written notice that 1. above should not apply retroactively. (§ 15-11-1106.5(1)) If this was done, then the modified USRAP explained below, and referred to in 2. above, applies instead. (§ 15-11-1106.5) Notice must have been delivered to a trustee, or, if none then serving, to a person authorized to appoint a successor trustee, on or before July 1, 2008. (§ 15-11-1106.5(2)(b)) **CAUTION:** The analysis below, ##2-27, pertains primarily to the interests created post-May 31, 1991, and prior to June 1, 2001, and also trust interests and powers of appointment post-May 31, 2001 and prior to July 1, 2006 in which the election to apply a modified USRAP was made on or before July 1, 2008. (Colo. Rev. Stat. §§ 15-11-1101-15-11-1107)
2. *Is the common law rule relevant to any interests?*	The common law rule is superseded (§ 18-3-109) but has to be taken into account all the same. See 2.b.(1). It is not relevant at all if the Dynasty Trust Act of 2017 applies. *See* 1 above.	Yes, but only as the starting point of the analysis. The common law rule is superseded. (§ 21201)	Yes, but only as the starting point of the analysis. See above.
a.			

Table 9
Rule Against Perpetuities

	ARKANSAS	CALIFORNIA	COLORADO
b. *What is the relevant rule?*	A nonvested property interest is invalid unless: (1) When the interest is created, it is certain to vest or terminate no later than 21 years after the death of an individual then alive; or (2) The interest either vests or terminates within 90 years after its creation. (§ 18-3-101(a))	A nonvested property interest is invalid unless one of the following conditions is satisfied: (a) When the interest is created, it is certain to vest or terminate no later than 21 years after the death of an individual then alive. (b) The interest either vests or terminates within 90 years after its creation. (§ 21205)	A nonvested property interest is invalid unless: (a) When the interest is created, it is certain to vest or terminate no later than twenty-one years after the death of an individual then alive; or (b) The interest either vests or terminates within ninety years after its creation. (§ 15-11-1102.5(2)(b)(I)(A)-(B))
3. *Does the rule apply to other than private trusts?*	Yes. The rule applies except to: (1) A nonvested property interest or a power of appointment arising out of a nondonative transfer, except a nonvested property interest or a power of appointment arising out of any of the following: (i) A premarital or postmarital agreement; (ii) A separation or divorce settlement; (iii) A spouse's election; (iv) A similar arrangement arising out of a prospective, an existing, or a previous marital relationship between the parties;	Yes. The rule applies except to: (a) A nonvested property interest or a power of appointment arising out of a nondonative transfer, except a nonvested property interest or a power of appointment arising out of (1) a premarital or postmarital agreement, (2) a separation or divorce settlement, (3) a spouse's election, (4) or a similar arrangement arising out of a prospective, existing, or previous marital relationship between the parties, (5) a contract to make or not to revoke a will or trust, (6) a contract to exercise or not to exercise a power of	Yes. The rule applies except to: (a) A nonvested property interest or a power of appointment arising out of a nondonative transfer, except a nonvested property interest or a power of appointment arising out of: (I) A premarital or postmarital agreement; (II) A separation or divorce settlement; (III) A spouse's election; (IV) A similar arrangement arising out of a prospective, existing, or previous marital relationship between the parties;

Table 9
Rule Against Perpetuities

ARKANSAS	CALIFORNIA	COLORADO
(v) A contract to make or not to revoke a will or trust;		(V) A contract to make or not to revoke a will or trust;
(vi) A contract to exercise or not to exercise a power of appointment;		(VI) A contract to exercise or not to exercise a power of appointment; or
(vii) A transfer in satisfaction of a duty of support;	appointment, (7) a transfer in satisfaction of a duty of support, or (8) a reciprocal transfer.	(VII) A transfer in satisfaction of a duty of support.
(viii) A reciprocal transfer.		
(2) A fiduciary's power relating to the administration or management of assets, including the power of a fiduciary to sell, lease, or mortgage property, and the power of a fiduciary to determine principal and income.	(b) A fiduciary's power relating to the administration or management of assets, including the power of a fiduciary to sell, lease, or mortgage property, and the power of a fiduciary to determine principal and income.	(b) A fiduciary's power relating to the administration or management of assets, including the power of a fiduciary to sell, lease, or mortgage property, and the power of a fiduciary to determine principal and income;
(3) A power to appoint a fiduciary.	(c) A power to appoint a fiduciary.	(c) A power to appoint a fiduciary;
(4) A discretionary power of a trustee to distribute principal before termination of a trust to a beneficiary having an indefeasibly vested interest in the income and principal.	(d) A discretionary power of a trustee to distribute principal before termination of a trust to a beneficiary having an indefeasibly vested interest in the income and principal.	(d) A discretionary power of a trustee to distribute principal before termination of a trust to a beneficiary having an indefeasibly vested interest in the income and principal;
(5) A nonvested property interest held by a charity, government, or governmental agency or subdivision, if the nonvested property interest is preceded by an interest held by another charity, government, or governmental agency or subdivision.	(e) A nonvested property interest held by a charity, government, or governmental agency or subdivision, if the nonvested property interest is preceded by an interest held by another charity, government, or governmental agency or subdivision.	(e) A nonvested property interest held by a charity, government, or governmental agency or subdivision, if the nonvested property interest is preceded by an interest held by another charity, government, or governmental agency or subdivision;

Table 9
Rule Against Perpetuities

ARKANSAS	CALIFORNIA	COLORADO
(6) A nonvested property interest in or a power of appointment with respect to a trust or other property arrangement forming part of a pension, a profit sharing, a stock bonus, a health, a disability, a death benefit, an income deferral, or other current or deferred benefit plan for one (1) or more employees, independent contractors, or their beneficiaries or spouses, to which contributions are made for the purpose of distributing to or for the benefit of the participants or their beneficiaries or spouses the property, income, or principal in the trust or other property arrangement, except a nonvested property interest or a power of appointment that is created by an election of a participant or a beneficiary or spouse.	(f) A nonvested property interest in or a power of appointment with respect to a trust or other property arrangement forming part of a pension, profit-sharing, stock bonus, health, disability, death benefit, income deferral, or other current or deferred benefit plan for one or more employees, independent contractors, or their beneficiaries or spouses, to which contributions are made for the purpose of distributing to or for the benefit of the participants or their beneficiaries or spouses the property, income, or principal in the trust or other property arrangement, except a nonvested property interest or a power of appointment that is created by an election of a participant or a beneficiary or spouse. (g) A property interest, power of appointment, or arrangement that was not subject to the common law rule against perpetuities or is excluded by another statute of this state.	(f) A nonvested property interest in or a power of appointment with respect to a trust or other property arrangement forming part of a pension, profit-sharing, stock bonus, health, disability, death benefit, income deferral, or other current or deferred benefit plan for one or more employees, independent contractors, or their beneficiaries or spouses, to which contributions are made for the purpose of distributing to or for the benefit of the participants or their beneficiaries or spouses the property, income, or principal in the trust or other property arrangement, except a nonvested property interest or a power of appointment that is created by an election of a participant or a beneficiary or spouse; or (g) A property interest, power of appointment, or arrangement that was not subject to the common law rule against perpetuities or is excluded by another statute of this state.

Table 9
Rule Against Perpetuities

	ARKANSAS	CALIFORNIA	COLORADO
	(7) A property interest, power of appointment, or arrangement that was not subject to the common law rule against perpetuities or is excluded by another Arkansas statute.	(h) A trust created for the purpose of providing for its beneficiaries under hospital service contracts, group life insurance, group disability insurance, group annuities, or any combination of such insurance, as defined in the Insurance Code.	(§15-11-1105)
	(8) A qualifying trust. *See* 1 above. (§18-3-104)	(§21225)	
4. *Does the rule invalidate the interest at its creation, or is the rule revised by a wait-and-see approach?*	Wait-and-see. (§18-3-101)	Wait-and-see. (§21205(b))	Wait-and-see. (§§15-11-1102.5(2)(B), 15-11-1104.5(2))
5. *Can the trust be reformed?*	Yes, but only if one of the following conditions is met: (1) a nonvested property interest or a power of appointment becomes invalid under §18-3-101; (2) a class gift is not but might become invalid under §18-3-101 and the time has arrived when the share of any class member is to take effect in possession or enjoyment; or	Yes, but only if any of the following conditions is satisfied: (a) A nonvested property interest or a power of appointment becomes invalid under the statutory rule against perpetuities provided in Article 2 (commencing with Section 21205). (b) A class gift is not but might become invalid under the statutory rule against	Yes, but only if one of the following conditions is satisfied: (a) A nonvested property interest or a power of appointment becomes invalid under the statutory rule against perpetuities of section 15-11-1102.5(2)(b); (b) A class gift is not but might become invalid under section 15-11-1102.5(2)(b) and the time has arrived when the share of any class member is to take effect in possession or enjoyment. (§15-11-1104.5(2))

Table 9
Rule Against Perpetuities

ARKANSAS	CALIFORNIA	COLORADO
(3) a nonvested property interest that is not validated by §18-3-101(a)(1), that is, the traditional common law rule, can vest but not within ninety (90) years after the interest's creation. (§18-3-103)	perpetuities provided in Article 2 (commencing with Section 21205), and the time has arrived when the share of any class member is to take effect in possession or enjoyment. (c) A nonvested property interest that is not validated by subdivision (a) of Section 21205, that is, the traditional common law rule, can vest but not within 90 years after its creation. (§21220) *See also* #27.	*See also* #27.

Table 9
Rule Against Perpetuities

	ARKANSAS	CALIFORNIA	COLORADO
6. *If yes to 5., under what theory?*	Upon the petition of an interested person, a court shall reform a disposition in the manner that most closely preserves the transferor's plan of distribution and is within the ninety (90) years allowed by §§ 18-3-101(a)(2), 18-3-101(b)(2), or 18-3-101(c)(2). (§ 18-3-103). *See also* § 18-3-105(b) (If a nonvested property interest or a power of appointment was created before the effective date of this chapter, and is determined in a judicial proceeding commenced on or after the effective date of this chapter, to violate this state's rule against perpetuities as that rule existed before the effective date of this chapter, a court upon the petition of an interested person may reform the disposition in the manner that most closely approximates the transferor's manifested plan of distribution and is within the limits of the rule against perpetuities applicable when the nonvested property interest or power of appointment was created.)	On petition of an interested person, a court shall reform a disposition in the manner that most closely approximates the transferor's manifested plan of distribution and is within the 90 years allowed by the applicable provision in Article 2 (commencing with Section 21205). (§ 21220)	Upon the petition of an interested person, a court shall reform a disposition in the manner that most closely approximates the transferor's manifested plan of distribution and is within the ninety years allowed by section 15-11-1102.5(2)(b)(I)-(III). (§ 15-11-1104.5(2) *See also* § 15-11-1106(2) ("If a nonvested property interest or a power of appointment was created before May 31, 1991, and is determined in a judicial proceeding, commenced on or after May 31, 1991, to violate this state's rule against perpetuities as that rule existed before May 31, 1991, a court upon the petition of an interested person shall reform the disposition by inserting a savings clause that preserves most closely the transferor's manifested plan of distribution and that brings that plan within the limits of the rule against perpetuities applicable when the nonvested property interest or power of appointment was created.")

Table 9
Rule Against Perpetuities

	ARKANSAS	CALIFORNIA	COLORADO
7. *When is a general testamentary power of appointment invalid?*	A general testamentary power of appointment is invalid unless one of the following conditions is satisfied: (1) When the power is created, it is certain to be irrevocably exercised or otherwise to terminate no later than 21 years after the death of an individual then alive; (2) The power is irrevocably exercised or otherwise terminates within 90 years after its creation. (§ 18-3-101(c))	A general testamentary power of appointment is invalid unless one of the following conditions is satisfied: (a) When the power is created, it is certain to be irrevocably exercised or otherwise to terminate no later than 21 years after the death of an individual then alive. (b) The power is irrevocably exercised or otherwise terminates within 90 years after its creation. (§ 21207)	A general testamentary power of appointment is invalid unless one of the following conditions is satisfied: (a) When the power is created, it is certain to be irrevocably exercised or otherwise to terminate no later than 21 years after the death of an individual then alive. (b) The power is irrevocably exercised or otherwise terminates within 90 years after its creation. (§ 15-11-1102.5(2)(b)(III)(A)–(B))
8. *Same, but nongeneral testamentary power.*	A nongeneral power of appointment is invalid unless one of the following conditions is satisfied: (1) When the power is created, it is certain to be irrevocably exercised or otherwise to terminate no later than 21 years after the death of an individual then alive; (2) The power is irrevocably exercised or otherwise terminates within 90 years after its creation. (§ 18-3-101(c))	A nongeneral power of appointment . . . is invalid unless one of the following conditions is satisfied: (a) When the power is created, it is certain to be irrevocably exercised or otherwise to terminate no later than 21 years after the death of an individual then alive. (b) The power is irrevocably exercised or otherwise terminates within 90 years after its creation. (§ 21207)	A nongeneral power of appointment . . . is invalid unless one of the following conditions is satisfied: (a) When the power is created, it is certain to be irrevocably exercised or otherwise to terminate no later than 21 years after the death of an individual then alive. (b) The power is irrevocably exercised or otherwise terminates within 90 years after its creation. (§ 15-11-1102.5(2)(b)(III)(A)–(B))

Table 9
Rule Against Perpetuities

	ARKANSAS	CALIFORNIA	COLORADO
9. *Same, but general power, whether testamentary or inter vivos, not presently exercisable because of a condition precedent.*	A general power of appointment not presently exercisable because of a condition precedent is invalid unless one of the following conditions is satisfied: (1) When the power is created, the condition precedent is certain to be satisfied or become impossible to satisfy no later than 21 years after the death of an individual then alive; (2) The condition precedent either is satisfied or becomes impossible to satisfy within 90 years after its creation. (§ 18-3-101(b))	A general power of appointment not presently exercisable because of a condition precedent is invalid unless one of the following conditions is satisfied: (a) When the power is created, the condition precedent is certain to be satisfied or become impossible to satisfy no later than 21 years after the death of an individual then alive. (b) The condition precedent either is satisfied or becomes impossible to satisfy within 90 years after its creation. (§ 21206)	A general power of appointment not presently exercisable because of a condition precedent is invalid unless one of the following conditions is satisfied: (a) When the power is created, the condition precedent is certain to be satisfied or become impossible to satisfy no later than 21 years after the death of an individual then alive. (b) The condition precedent either is satisfied or becomes impossible to satisfy within 90 years after its creation. (§ 15-11-1102.5(2)(b)(II)(A)-(B))
10. *Same, but nongeneral inter vivos power.*	See #8.	See #8.	See #8.

Table 9
Rule Against Perpetuities

	ARKANSAS	CALIFORNIA	COLORADO
11. *Is a period of gestation added to the perpetuity period?*	No. The possibility that a child will be born to a person after that person's death is disregarded. (§ 18-3-101(d)) *See also* Unif. Statutory Rule Against Perpetuities § 1, 8B U.L.A. 243, 243 (amended 1990) ("[T]he possibility that a child will be born to [a testator] after his death must be disregarded; and the possibility that a child will be born to any of [the testator's] descendants after their deaths must also be disregarded. Note, however, that the rule of subsection (d) does not apply to the question of the entitlement of an after-born child to take a beneficial interest in the trust").	No. The possibility that a child will be born to a person after that person's death is disregarded. (§ 21208) *See also* Unif. Statutory Rule Against Perpetuities § 1, 8B U.L.A. 243, 243 (amended 1990) ("[T]he possibility that a child will be born to [a testator] after his death must be disregarded; and the possibility that a child will be born to any of [the testator's] descendants after their deaths must also be disregarded. Note, however, that the rule of subsection (d) does not apply to the question of the entitlement of an after-born child to take a beneficial interest in the trust").	No. The possibility that a child will be born to a person after that person's death is disregarded. (§ 15-11-1102.5(2)(b)(IV)) *See also* Unif. Statutory Rule Against Perpetuities § 1, 8B U.L.A. 243, 243 (amended 1990) ("[T]he possibility that a child will be born to [a testator] after his death must be disregarded; and the possibility that a child will be born to any of [the testator's] descendants after their deaths must also be disregarded. Note, however, that the rule of subsection (d) does not apply to the question of the entitlement of an after-born child to take a beneficial interest in the trust").
12. *What is the treatment of a "later of the traditional rule or 90 years" clause? See UPC 2-901(e).*	It is not allowed to extend the perpetuities period beyond the traditional rule. The language is inoperative. (§ 18-3-101(e))	That language is inoperative to the extent it produces a period that exceeds 21 years after the death of the survivor of the specified lives. (§ 21209)	That language is inoperative to the extent it produces a period of time that exceeds 21 years after the death of the survivor of the specified lives. (§ 15-11-1102.5(2)(b)(V))

Table 9
Rule Against Perpetuities

	ARKANSAS	CALIFORNIA	COLORADO
13. *When is an interest created by the exercise of a general testamentary power deemed created?*	The Dynasty Trust Act of 2017 provides that a nonvested property interest or power of appointment created through exercise of a general testamentary power of appointment is considered created when the first power of appointment was created. (§ 18-3-102(d)) *Note:* There are numerous construction issues with this provision. Apparently, when the new subsection (d) does not apply the following are the controlling provisions: Except as provided in subsections (b) and (c) of § 18-3-102 and in § 18-3-105, the time of creation of a nonvested property interest or a power of appointment is determined under general principles of property law. (§ 18-3-102(a)) The first two of the excepted provisions state that as long as a person with a general power to become the unqualified beneficial owner has that power, the nonvested interest is created when the power terminates. The third of the excepted provisions states that a nonvested property interest, which arises from a transfer to a previously funded trust or other existing property arrangement, is created when the nonvested property interest in the original contribution was created. *See also* Unif. Statutory Rule Against Perpetuities § 2, 8B U.L.A. 268	Except as provided in Sections 21211 and 21212, the time of creation of a nonvested property interest or a power of appointment is determined by other applicable statutes or, if none, under general principles of property law. (§ 21210) The first of the excepted provisions states that as long as a person with a general power to become the unqualified beneficial owner has that power, the nonvested interest is created when the power terminates. (§ 21211(a)) The second of the excepted provisions states that a nonvested property interest, which arises from a transfer to a previously funded trust or other existing property arrangement, is created when the nonvested property interest in the original contribution was created. *See also* Unif. Statutory Rule Against Perpetuities § 2, 8B U.L.A. 268 (amended 1990) (explaining that "general principles of property law determine that the time . . . [of creation] is at the decedent's death.")	The time of creation of a nonvested property interest or a power of appointment created by the exercise of a power of appointment is created when the power is irrevocably exercised or when a revocable exercise becomes irrevocable, that is, at death. (§ 15-11-1106(1)) *See also* § 15-11-1103(1), which indicates that if the foregoing does not apply, then the general principles of property law apply. *See also* Unif. Statutory Rule Against Perpetuities § 2, 8B U.L.A. 268 (amended 1990) (explaining that "general principles of property law determine that the time . . . [of creation] is at the decedent's death.")

Table 9
Rule Against Perpetuities

	ARKANSAS	CALIFORNIA	COLORADO
	(amended 1990) (explaining that "general principles of property law determine that the time . . . [of creation] is at the decedent's death.") *See generally* § 18-3-105(a) ("A nonvested property interest or a power of appointment created by the exercise of a power of appointment is created when the power is irrevocably exercised or when a revocable exercise becomes irrevocable.")		
14. *Same, but nongeneral testamentary power.*	Same as 13. above, but applies when nongeneral power is used instead of general testamentary power of appointment.	See #13.	See #13.

Table 9
Rule Against Perpetuities

	ARKANSAS	CALIFORNIA	COLORADO
15. *Same, but general inter vivos power.*	Except as provided in subsections (b) and (c) of § 18-3-102 and in § 18-3-105(a), the time of creation of a nonvested property interest or a power of appointment is determined under general principles of property law. (§ 18-3-102(a)) The first two of the excepted provisions state that as long as a person with a general power to become the unqualified beneficial owner has that power, the nonvested interest is created when the power terminates. The third of the excepted provisions states that a nonvested property interest, which arises from a transfer to a previously funded trust or other existing property arrangement, is created when the nonvested property interest in the original contribution was created. *See also* Unif. Statutory Rule Against Perpetuities § 2, 8B U.L.A. 268 (amended 1990) (explaining that "the time when the interest or power is created is the date the transfer becomes effective for purposes of property law generally, normally the date of delivery of the deed"); Comment to Unif. Probate Code § 2-902(a) (stating same and adding "the funding of the trust" as "normally" the time when the interest is created). *See generally* § 18-3-105(a) ("A	Except as provided in Sections 21211 and 21212, the time of creation of a nonvested property interest or a power of appointment is determined by other applicable statutes or, if none, under general principles of property law. (§ 21210) The first of the excepted provisions states that as long as a person with a general power to become the unqualified beneficial owner has that power, the nonvested interest is created when the power terminates. The second of the excepted provisions states that a nonvested property interest, which from a transfer to an existing trust, is created when the nonvested property interest in the trust was created. *See also* Unif. Statutory Rule Against Perpetuities § 2, 8B U.L.A. 268 (amended 1990) (explaining that "the time when the interest or power is created is the date the transfer becomes effective for purposes of property law generally, normally the date of delivery of the deed"); Comment to Unif. Probate Code § 2-902(a) (stating same and adding "the funding of the trust" as "normally" the time when the interest is created).	Except as provided in subsections (2) and (3) of this section and in sections 15-11-1102.5(3)(a) and 15-11-1106(1), the time of creation of a nonvested property interest or a power of appointment is determined under general principles of property law. (§ 15-11-1103(1)) The first of the excepted provisions states that as long as a person with a general power to become the unqualified beneficial owner has that power, the nonvested interest is created when the power terminates. The second of the excepted provisions states that a nonvested property interest, which arises from a transfer to an existing trust, is created when the nonvested property interest in the trust was created. *See also* Unif. Statutory Rule Against Perpetuities § 2, 8B U.L.A. 268 (amended 1990) (explaining that "the time when the interest or power is created is the date the transfer becomes effective for purposes of property law generally, normally the date of delivery of the deed"); Comment to Unif. Probate Code § 2-902(a) (stating same and adding "the funding of the trust" as "normally" the time when the interest is created). *See generally* § 15-11-1106(1) ("a nonvested property interest or a power

Table 9
Rule Against Perpetuities

	ARKANSAS	CALIFORNIA	COLORADO
	nonvested property interest or a power of appointment created by the exercise of a power of appointment is created when the power is irrevocably exercised or when a revocable exercise becomes irrevocable.")		of appointment created by the exercise of a power of appointment is created when the power is irrevocably exercised or when a revocable exercise becomes irrevocable.")
16. *Same, but nongeneral inter vivos power.*	See #15.	See #15.	See #13.
17. *When is an interest created if the grantor of a trust has a power to revoke?*	If there is a person who alone can exercise a power created by a governing instrument to become the unqualified beneficial owner of: (1) a nonvested property interest; or (2) a property interest subject to a power of appointment described in § 18-3-101(b) or § 18-3-101(c);	If there is a person who alone can exercise a power created by a governing instrument to become the unqualified beneficial owner of (1) a nonvested property interest or (2) a property interest subject to a power of appointment described in Section 21206 or 21207, the nonvested property interest or power of appointment is created when the power to become the unqualified beneficial owner terminates. (§ 21211(a)).	If there is a person who alone can exercise a power created by a governing instrument to become the unqualified beneficial owner of either a nonvested property interest or a property interest subject to a power of appointment described in section 15-11-1102(2) or (3), the nonvested property interest or power of appointment is created when the power to become the unqualified beneficial owner terminates. (§ 15-11-1103(2)) The problem is that the cross-reference to § 15-11-1102(2) or (3) is problematic since these provisions have been repealed.

Table 9
Rule Against Perpetuities

ARKANSAS	CALIFORNIA	COLORADO
the nonvested property interest or power of appointment is created when the power to become the unqualified beneficial owner terminates. (§ 18-3-102(b)) *See also* Unif. Statutory Rule Against Perpetuities § 2, 8B U.L.A. 268 (amended 1990) (explaining that "any nonvested property interest subject to [a power to revoke] is not created . . . until the power terminates (by release, expiration at the death of the donee, or otherwise)"; Comment to Unif. Probate Code § 2-902(b) (noting that "nonvested property interests and powers of appointment created in [a revocable inter-vivos trust] are created when the power to revoke expires, usually at the settlor's death"). *See generally* § 18-3-105(a) [prospective application to nonvested property interest or a power of appointment created on or after the effective date] ("A nonvested property interest or a power of appointment created by the exercise of a power of appointment is created when the power is irrevocably exercised or when a revocable exercise becomes irrevocable.")	*See also* Unif. Statutory Rule Against Perpetuities § 2, 8B U.L.A. 268 (amended 1990) (explaining that "any nonvested property interest subject to [a power to revoke] is not created . . . until the power terminates (by release, expiration at the death of the donee, or otherwise)"; Comment to Unif. Probate Code § 2-902(b) (noting that "nonvested property interests and powers of appointment created in [a revocable inter-vivos trust] are created when the power to revoke expires, usually at the settlor's death").	*See also* Unif. Statutory Rule Against Perpetuities § 2, 8B U.L.A. 268 (amended 1990) (explaining that "any nonvested property interest subject to [a power to revoke] is not created . . . until the power terminates (by release, expiration at the death of the donee, or otherwise)"; Comment to Unif. Probate Code § 2-902(b) (noting that "nonvested property interests and powers of appointment created in [a revocable inter-vivos trust] are created when the power to revoke expires, usually at the settlor's death"). *See generally* § 15-11-1106(1) ("a nonvested property interest or a power of appointment created by the exercise of a power of appointment is created when the power is irrevocably exercised or when a revocable exercise becomes irrevocable.")

Table 9
Rule Against Perpetuities

	ARKANSAS	CALIFORNIA	COLORADO
18. *When does the period of the rule start re an interest contributed to an irrevocable trust? See UIPC 2-902(c).*	A nonvested property interest or a power of appointment arising from a transfer of property to a previously funded trust or other existing property arrangement is created when the nonvested property interest or power of appointment in the original contribution was created. (§ 18-3-102(c))	A nonvested property interest or a power of appointment arising from a transfer of property to a previously funded trust or other existing property arrangement is created when the nonvested property interest or power of appointment in the original contribution was created. (§ 21212)	A nonvested property interest or a power of appointment arising from a transfer of property to a previously funded trust or other existing property arrangement is created when the nonvested property interest or power of appointment in the original contribution was created. (§ 15-11-1103(3))
19. *Is there a conclusive presumption of fertility, that is, the "fertile octogenarian" rule?*	Yes. (Love v. McDonald, 148 S.W.2d 170, 171 n.3 (Ark. 1941) ("'the presumption being that there may be issue so long as life continues'") (citations omitted)) See also Unif. Statutory Rule Against Perpetuities § 1, 8B U.L.A. 256 (amended 1990) (holding that "[t]his principle is not superseded by this Act, and in view of new advances in medical science . . . [this] is not unrealistic."). But see C. P. Jhong, Annotation, *Modern Status of Presumption Against Possibility of Issue Being Extinct,* 98 A.L.R.2d 1285 (2003) (noting "a trend toward denying the conclusive or absolute nature of the presumption against the possibility of issue being extinct where there is competent evidence to the contrary has developed in the decisions, although some courts still adhere to the traditional view treating the presumption as conclusive or absolute").	Yes. Fletcher v. Los Angeles T. & Sav. Bank, 187 P. 425, 428 (Cal. 1920); In re Sahlender's Estate 201 P. 2d 69, 81 (Cal. Ct. App. 1948).[1] *See also* Unif. Statutory Rule Against Perpetuities § 1, 8B U.L.A. 256 (amended 1990) (holding that "[t]his principle is not superseded by this Act, and in view of new advances in medical science . . . [this] is not unrealistic."). But see C. P. Jhong, Annotation, Modern Status of Presumption Against Possibility of Issue Being Extinct, 98 A.L.R.2d 1285 (2003) (noting "a trend toward denying the conclusive or absolute nature of the presumption against the possibility of issue being extinct where there is competent evidence to the contrary has developed in the decisions, although some courts still adhere to the traditional view treating the presumption as conclusive or absolute").	No specific state case or statute. *See Unif.* Statutory Rule Against Perpetuities § 1, 8B U.L.A. 256 (amended 1990) (holding that "[t]his principle is not superseded by this Act, and in view of new advances in medical science . . . [this] is not unrealistic."). But see C. P. Jhong, Annotation, Modern Status of Presumption Against Possibility of Issue Being Extinct, 98 A.L.R.2d 1285 (2003) (noting "a trend toward denying the conclusive or absolute nature of the presumption against the possibility of issue being extinct where there is competent evidence to the contrary has developed in the decisions, although some courts still adhere to the traditional view treating the presumption as conclusive or absolute").

Table 9
Rule Against Perpetuities

	ARKANSAS	CALIFORNIA	COLORADO
20. *What is the earliest age a child is deemed capable of bearing a child? What is the impact of illegitimacy?*	Not specifically addressed by USRAP, but the reasoning is the same as set forth in the comment to section 1 of USRAP, 2, Technical Violations of the Common Law Rule. Wait and see will typically result in no violation. Nevertheless, the common law rule ordinarily will be applied initially. "Under the rule, courts must presume that living persons are capable of having or fathering children, no matter how young they are. See In re Graite's Will Trusts, [1949] 1 All E.R. 459, 460 (Ch.). Thus, the rule strikes down any interest whose vesting depends on the assertion that, for example, a toddler will not have children." (Keith L. Butler, Notes & Comments, *Long Live the Dead Hand: A Case for Repeal of the Rule Against Perpetuities in Washington,* 75 Wash. L. Rev. 1237, 1246 n.78 (2000)).	Not specifically addressed by USRAP, but the reasoning is the same as set forth in the comment to section 1 of USRAP, 2, Technical Violations of the Common Law Rule. Wait and see will typically result in no violation. Nevertheless, the common law rule ordinarily will be applied initially. "Under the rule, courts must presume that living persons are capable of having or fathering children, no matter how young they are. See In re Graite's Will Trusts, [1949] 1 All E.R. 459, 460 (Ch.). Thus, the rule strikes down any interest whose vesting depends on the assertion that, for example, a toddler will not have children." (Keith L. Butler, Notes & Comments, *Long Live the Dead Hand: A Case for Repeal of the Rule Against Perpetuities in Washington,* 75 Wash. L. Rev. 1237, 1246 n.78 (2000)).	Not specifically addressed by USRAP, but the reasoning is the same as set forth in the comment to section 1 of USRAP, 2, Technical Violations of the Common Law Rule. Wait and see will result in no violation. Nevertheless, the common law rule ordinarily will be applied initially. "Under the rule, courts must presume that living persons are capable of having or fathering children, no matter how young they are. See In re Graite's Will Trusts, [1949] 1 All E.R. 459, 460 (Ch.). Thus, the rule strikes down any interest whose vesting depends on the assertion that, for example, a toddler will not have children." (Keith L. Butler, Notes & Comments, *Long Live the Dead Hand: A Case for Repeal of the Rule Against Perpetuities in Washington,* 75 Wash. L. Rev. 1237, 1246 n.78 (2000)).

Table 9
Rule Against Perpetuities

	ARKANSAS	CALIFORNIA	COLORADO
21. *Is the "unborn widow" rule observed?*	Yes. Dickerson v. Union Nat'l Bank, 595 S.W.2d 677, 680 (Ark. 1980) *See also* Unif. Statutory Rule Against Perpetuities § 1, 8B U.L.A. 246 (amended 1990) (explaining that "[t]he chance that [an] interest will become invalid under the Statutory Rule is small" and so the unborn widow rule would rarely invalidate an interest); 61 Am. Jur. 2d *Perpetuities and Restraints on Alienation* § 39 (2013) (noting the same).	No specific state case or statute. *See* Unif. Statutory Rule Against Perpetuities § 1, 8B U.L.A. 246 (amended 1990) (explaining that "[t]he chance that [an] interest will become invalid under the Statutory Rule is small" and so the unborn widow rule would rarely invalidate an interest); *see also* 61 Am. Jur. 2d *Perpetuities and Restraints on Alienation* § 39 (2013) (noting the same).	No specific state case or statute. *See* Unif. Statutory Rule Against Perpetuities § 1, 8B U.L.A. 246 (amended 1990) (explaining that "[t]he chance that [an] interest will become invalid under the Statutory Rule is small" and so the unborn widow rule would rarely invalidate an interest); *see also* 61 Am. Jur. 2d *Perpetuities and Restraints on Alienation* § 39 (2013) (noting the same).
22. *Does the "slothful executor" rule apply, i.e., an administrative contingency clause providing for a "distribution to, e.g., those issue living at the time of the satisfaction of the administrative condition precedent?"*	No specific state case or statute. *See* Unif. Statutory Rule Against Perpetuities § 1, 8B U.L.A. 245 (amended 1990) (Under USRAP, an "interest becomes invalid only if it remains in existence and nonvested 90 years after [the testator's] death. Since it is almost certain that the final distribution of [an] estate will occur well within this 90-year period, the chance that [an] interest will be invalid is negligible.")	No. Estate of Taylor, 428 P.2d 301, 303 (Cal. 1967) ("In the absence of any indication to the contrary a testator contemplates prompt distribution. His intention is substantially complied with if a beneficiary who is alive at the time distribution could and should have occurred is allowed to take under the will.") See also Unif. Statutory Rule Against Perpetuities § 1, 8B U.L.A. 245 (amended 1990) (Under USRAP an "interest becomes invalid only if it remains in existence and nonvested 90 years after [the testator's] death. Since it is almost certain that the final distribution of [an] estate will occur well within this 90-year period, the chance that [an] interest will be invalid is negligible.")	No. Miller v. Weston, 189 P. 610, 612-613 (Colo. 1920) (validating a will despite an administrative contingency clause). *See also* Unif. Statutory Rule Against Perpetuities § 1, 8B U.L.A. 245 (amended 1990) (Under USRAP an "interest becomes invalid only if it remains in existence and nonvested 90 years after [the testator's] death. Since it is almost certain that the final distribution of [an] estate will occur well within this 90-year period, the chance that [an] interest will be invalid is negligible.")

Table 9
Rule Against Perpetuities

	ARKANSAS	CALIFORNIA	COLORADO
23. *Does the all-or-nothing rule apply to class gifts?*	No specific state case or statute. *See* Unif. Statutory Rule Against Perpetuities §1, 8B U.L.A. 257 (amended 1990) ("Although this Act does not supersede the basic idea of the much-maligned 'all-or-nothing' rule, the evils sometimes attributed to it are substantially if not entirely eliminated by the wait-and-see feature of the Statutory Rule and by the availability of reformation under Section 3.").	Sometimes. Estate of Ghiglia, 116 Cal. Rptr. 827, 832 (Cal. Ct. App. 1974) (citations omitted) (explaining that the test to sever an invalid part of a class gift from the valid "is 'whether the two (plans) are so parts of a single plan or scheme or otherwise so dependent one upon the other, that by avoiding the invalid provisions and allowing the valid to stand there will result a disposition of the estate so different from what the testator contemplated or so unreasonable that it must be presumed that [he] would not have made the valid provisions if he had been aware of the invalidity of the others'"). *See also* Unif. Statutory Rule Against Perpetuities §1, 8B U.L.A. 257 (amended 1990) ("Although this Act does not supersede the basic idea of the much-maligned "all-or-nothing" rule, the evils sometimes attributed to it are substantially if not entirely eliminated by the wait-and-see feature of the Statutory Rule and by the availability of reformation under Section 3.").	No specific state case or statute. *See* Unif. Statutory Rule Against Perpetuities §1, 8B U.L.A. 257 (amended 1990) ("Although this Act does not supersede the basic idea of the much-maligned 'all-or-nothing' rule, the evils sometimes attributed to it are substantially if not entirely eliminated by the wait-and-see feature of the Statutory Rule and by the availability of reformation under Section 3.").

Table 9
Rule Against Perpetuities

	ARKANSAS	CALIFORNIA	COLORADO
24. *Is there an exception to the all-or-nothing rule in the case of subclasses or specific sums to each member of the class?*	No specific state case or statute. See Unif. Statutory Rule Against Perpetuities §1, 8B U.L.A. 257 (amended 1990) ("The specific-sum and sub-class doctrines are not superseded by this Act.")	No specific state case or statute. See Unif. Statutory Rule Against Perpetuities §1, 8B U.L.A. 257 (amended 1990) ("The specific-sum and sub-class doctrines are not superseded by this Act.")	No specific state case or statute. See Unif. Statutory Rule Against Perpetuities §1, 8B U.L.A. 257 (amended 1990) ("The specific-sum and sub-class doctrines are not superseded by this Act.")
25. *Is the infectious invalidity rule followed outside class gifts?*	No specific state case or statute. See Unif. Statutory Rule Against Perpetuities §1, 8B U.L.A. 256 (amended 1990) (explaining that "[t]he doctrine of infectious invalidity is superseded by this Act by Section 3, under which courts … are required to *reform* the disposition to approximate as closely as possible the transferor's … plan of distribution.")	No specific state case or statute. See Unif. Statutory Rule Against Perpetuities §1, 8B U.L.A. 256 (amended 1990) (explaining that "[t]he doctrine of infectious invalidity is superseded by this Act by Section 3, under which courts … are required to *reform* the disposition to approximate as closely as possible the transferor's … plan of distribution.")	Yes. Perry v. Brundage, 614 P.2d 362, 366 (Colo. 1980). But see Unif. Statutory Rule Against Perpetuities §1, 8B U.L.A. 256 (amended 1990) (explaining that "[t]he doctrine of infectious invalidity is superseded by this Act by Section 3, under which courts … are required to *reform* the disposition to approximate as closely as possible the transferor's … plan of distribution.")
26. *Is there a rule against the suspension of the power of alienation? If so, how is it stated?*	Yes, as to restraints on alienation of property. Such restraints are void. See Casey v. Casey, 700 S.W.2d 46, 48 (Ark. 1985); Broach v. City of Hampton, 677 S.W.2d 851, 855 (Ark. 1984). Pursuant to the Dynasty Trust Act 2017, if the power of alienation is suspended during the life of "the trust," the rule against perpetuities under USRAP will begin to run from the date of the suspension. (§ 118-3-104(8)(B). The reference to "the trust" in the statute is ambiguous.	Cal. Civ. Code §715, which provided a rule against the suspension of the power of alienation was repealed in 1991. *See also* Cal. Civ. Code §711 ("Conditions [of ownership] restraining alienation, when repugnant to the interest created, are void.")	Reasonableness standard. Perry v. Brundage, 614 P. 2d 362, 366-67 (Colo. 1980) ("The common law doctrine of restraints on alienation is part of the common law in Colorado and prohibits 'unreasonable restraints.'") (citations omitted)

Table 9
Rule Against Perpetuities

	ARKANSAS	CALIFORNIA	COLORADO
27. *Effective date.*	March 9, 2007. *See* Act 240, H.B. 1130, § 1. With respect to the trusts exempted from the rule against perpetuities, *see* 1. Above. It applies to a trust created in Arkansas on or after the effective date of the Dynasty Trust Act of 2017 and to any trust whose principal place of administration is transferred to Arkansas on or after the effective date of the Dynasty Trust Act 2017, regardless of when the trust was created. This is also the effective date for the change in the rule against the suspension of the power of alienation described in 26 above. However, no effective date appears to have been prescribed for the changes in 13., 14., and 16 above, introduced by the Dynasty Trust Act 2017. Also, the Dynasty Trust Act of 2017 does not set forth an effective date, although it was "approved" on April 5, 2017.	Effective for all interests and powers whenever created, except if validity determined in a judicial proceeding or settlement. (§ 21202)	A modified USRAP applies to nonvested interests and powers created on or after May 31, 1991. (§§ 15-11-1106(1), 15-11-1102.5(2)) For pre-June 1, 1991 interests and powers, the common law rule applies, except to the extent judicially reformed after May 31, 1991. (§ 15-11-1106(2)) For interests in trust and powers of appointment *with respect to all or any part of a trust* created after May 31, 2001, the 1000-year rule against perpetuities (§ 15-11-1102.5(1)) and the 1,000-year reform rule apply. (§ 15-11-1104.5(1))

---

[1] For questions #19-25, *see also* § 21201 (noting that the state's USRAP supersedes the common law rule against perpetuities). This does not mean the common law is neglected, but only that it is the starting point in the analysis.

Table 9
Rule Against Perpetuities

		CONNECTICUT	DELAWARE	DISTRICT OF COLUMBIA
1.	*Which rule is in effect: the common law rule, the Uniform Statutory Rule Against Perpetuities (USRAP), other law, or none?*	USRAP. (Conn. Gen. Stat. §§ 45a-490 - 45a-496; §§ 45a-502 - 45a-508)	Other. (Del. Code Ann. 25 §§ 501; 503)	USRAP. (D.C. Code Ann. §§ 19-901 - 19-907)
2. a.	*Is the common law rule relevant to any interests?*	Yes, but only as the starting point of the analysis.	Yes, other than interests in trust. "The rule against perpetuities is defined in Taylor v. Crosson, 11 Del. Ch. 145, 98 A. 375 (1916) as follows: "No interest is good unless it must vest, if at all, not later than twenty-one years after some life in being at the creation of the interest.'" In re Will of Greenwood, 268 A.2d 867, 868 (Del. 1970).	Yes, but only as the starting point of the analysis.
b.	*What is the relevant rule?*	A nonvested property interest is invalid unless: (1) When the interest is created, it is certain to vest or terminate no later than twenty-one years after the death of an individual then alive; or (2) the interest either vests or terminates within ninety years after its creation. (§ 45a-491(a))	With respect to trusts, the rule is: (a) No interest created in real property held in trust shall be void by reason of the common law rule against perpetuities and no interest created in personal property held in trust shall be void by reason of any rule against perpetuities whether the common law rule or otherwise. (25 § 503)	A nonvested property interest is invalid unless: (1) When the interest is created, it is certain to vest or terminate no later than twenty-one years after the death of an individual then alive; or (2) the interest either vests or terminates within ninety years after its creation.

Table 9
Rule Against Perpetuities

CONNECTICUT	DELAWARE	DISTRICT OF COLUMBIA
	(b) In this State, the rule against perpetuities for real property held in trust is that at the expiration of 110 years from the later of the date on which a parcel of real property or an interest in real property is added to or purchased by a trust or the date the trust became irrevocable, such parcel or interest, if still held in such trust, shall be distributed in accordance with the trust instrument regarding distribution of such property upon termination of the trust as though termination occurred at that time, or if no such provisions exist, to the persons then entitled to receive the income of the trust in proportion to the amount of the income so receivable by such beneficiaries, or in equal shares if specific proportions are not specified in the trust instrument. (25 § 503(b)) Note that real property does not include intangible personal property such as an interest in a corporation, limited liability company, partnership, statutory trust, business trust or other entity, regardless whether the entity owns real property or an interest therein. (25 § 503(e))	(§ 19-901(a))

Table 9
Rule Against Perpetuities

	CONNECTICUT	DELAWARE	DISTRICT OF COLUMBIA
3. *Does the rule apply to other than private trusts?*	Yes. The rule applies except to: (1) A nonvested property interest or a power of appointment arising out of a nondonative transfer, except a nonvested property interest or a power of appointment arising out of: (A) a premarital or postmarital agreement; (B) a separation or divorce settlement; (C) a spouse's election; (D) a similar arrangement arising out of a prospective existing or previous marital relationship between the parties; (E) a contract to make or not to revoke a will or trust; (F) a contract to exercise or not to exercise a power of appointment; (G) a transfer in satisfaction of a duty of support; or (H) a reciprocal transfer;	The rule does not apply to the following trusts, all of which may be perpetual: (1) A trust for the benefit of 1 or more charitable organizations; (2) A trust created by an employer as part of a stock bonus plan, pension plan, disability or death benefit plan or profit sharing plan for the exclusive benefit of some or all of its employees, to which contributions are made by such employer or employees, or both, for the purpose of distributing to such employees the earnings or the principal, or both earnings and principal, of the fund held in trust; (3) A statutory trust formed under Chapter 38 of Title 12 for which a certificate of statutory trust (akin to a Massachusetts business trust) is on file in the office of the Secretary of State; or	The rule applies except to: (1) A nonvested property interest or a power of appointment arising out of a nondonative transfer, except a nonvested property interest or a power of appointment arising out of: (A) A premarital or postmarital agreement; (B) A separation or divorce settlement; (C) A domestic partnership or spouse's election under section 19-113; (D) A similar arrangement arising out of a prospective existing or previous marital relationship or domestic partnership between the parties; (E) A contract to make or not to revoke a will or trust; (F) A contract to exercise or not to exercise a power of appointment;

Table 9
Rule Against Perpetuities

CONNECTICUT	DELAWARE	DISTRICT OF COLUMBIA
(2) A fiduciary's power relating to the administration or management of assets, including the power of a fiduciary to sell, lease or mortgage property, and the power of a fiduciary to determine principal and income;	(4) A trust of real or personal property created for the perpetual care of cemeteries pursuant to the provisions of subchapter IV of Chapter 35 of Title 12.	(G) A transfer in satisfaction of a duty of support; or
(3) A power to appoint a fiduciary;	(25 § 503(b))	(H) A reciprocal transfer;
(4) A discretionary power of a trustee to distribute principal before termination of a trust to a beneficiary having an indefeasibly vested interest in the income and principal;		(2) A fiduciary's power relating to the administration or management of assets, including the power of a fiduciary to sell, lease or mortgage property, and the power of a fiduciary to determine principal and income;
(5) A nonvested property interest held by a charity, government or governmental agency or subdivision, if the nonvested property interest is preceded by an interest held by another charity, government or governmental agency or subdivision;		(3) A power to appoint a fiduciary;
		(4) A discretionary power of a trustee to distribute principal before termination of a trust to a beneficiary having an indefeasibly vested interest in the income and principal;
		(5) A nonvested property interest held by a charity, government, or governmental agency or subdivision;

Table 9
Rule Against Perpetuities

CONNECTICUT	DELAWARE	DISTRICT OF COLUMBIA
(6) A nonvested property interest in or a power of appointment with respect to a trust or other property arrangement forming part of a pension, profit sharing, stock bonus, health, disability, death benefit, income deferral or other current or deferred benefit plan for one or more employees, independent contractors or their beneficiaries or spouses, to which contributions are made for the purpose of distributing to or for the benefit of the participants or their beneficiaries or spouses the property, income or principal in the trust or other property arrangement, except a nonvested property interest or a power of appointment that is created by an election of a participant or a beneficiary or spouse; or		(6) A nonvested property interest in or a power of appointment with respect to a trust or other property arrangement forming part of a pension, profit-sharing, stock bonus, health, disability, death benefit, income deferral, or other current or deferred benefit plan for one or more employees, independent contractors, or their beneficiaries, spouses or domestic partners to which contributions are made for the purpose of distributing to or for the benefit of the participants or their beneficiaries, spouses or domestic partners the property, income, or principal in the trust or other property arrangement, except a nonvested property interest or a power of appointment that is created by an election of a participant or a beneficiary, spouse or domestic partner;
(7) A property interest, power of appointment or arrangement that was not subject to the common-law rule against perpetuities or is excluded by another statute of this state.		(7) A property interest, power of appointment, or arrangement that was not subject to the common-law rule against perpetuities or is excluded by another statute of the District of Columbia;

(§ 45a-494)

Table 9
Rule Against Perpetuities

CONNECTICUT	DELAWARE	DISTRICT OF COLUMBIA
		(8) A gift of a present interest or devise to charitable uses;
		(9) In accordance with section 43-113, a grant, donation, or bequest for the embellishment, preservation, renewal, or repair of any tomb, monument, gravestone, or other structure, fence, railing, or other enclosure in or around any cemetary lot, or for the planting and cultivation of any trees, shrubs, flowers, or plants in or around any cemetery lot, according to the terms of such grant, donation, or bequest; or
		(10) A trust in which the governing instrument states that the provisions of this chapter do not apply to the trust and under which the trustee, or other person to whom the power is properly granted or delegated, has the power under the governing instrument, applicable statute, or common law to hold, sell, lease, or mortgage property for any period of time beyond the period that is required for an interest created under the governing instrument to vest.
		(§ 19-904(a))

Table 9
Rule Against Perpetuities

	CONNECTICUT	DELAWARE	DISTRICT OF COLUMBIA
4. *Does the rule invalidate the interest at its creation, or is the rule revised by a wait-and-see approach?*	Wait-and-see. (§ 45a-491(a)(2))	Wait-and-see for real property held in trust (25 § 503b) and for interests created by the exercise of a power of appointment (25 § 501). Otherwise, the rule does not apply at all for interests in trust. For provisions subject to the common law rule, there is no wait-and-see provision.	Wait-and-see. (§ 19-901(a)(2))
5. *Can the trust be reformed?*	Yes, but only if one of the following conditions is satisfied: (1) A nonvested property interest or a power of appointment becomes invalid under section 45a-491 (see #2b); (2) A class gift is not but might become invalid under section 45a-491 and the time has arrived when the share of any class member is to take effect in possession or enjoyment; or (3) A nonvested property interest that is not validated by subdivision (1) of subsection (a) of section 45a-491, that is, the traditional common law rule, can vest but not within ninety years after its creation. (§ 45a-493) *See also* #27.	No specific state case or statute.	Yes, but only if one of the following conditions is satisfied: (1) A nonvested property interest or a power of appointment becomes invalid under section 19-901; (see #2b); (2) A class gift is not but might become invalid under section 19-901 and the time has arrived when the share of any class member is to take effect in possession or enjoyment; or (3) A nonvested property interest that is not validated by section 19-901(a)(1), that is, the traditional common law rule, can vest but not within 90 years after its creation. (§ 19-903) *See also* #27.

Table 9
Rule Against Perpetuities

	CONNECTICUT	DELAWARE	DISTRICT OF COLUMBIA
6. *If yes to 5., under what theory?*	Upon the petition of an interested person, a court shall reform a disposition in the manner that most closely approximates the transferor's manifested plan of distribution and is within the ninety years allowed by subdivision (2) of subsection (a), (b) or (c) of section 45a-491. (§ 45a-493) However, if a nonvested property interest or a power of appointment that was created before October 1, 1989, and is determined in a judicial proceeding, commenced on or after October 1, 1989, to violate this state's rule against perpetuities as that rule existed before October 1, 1989, a court upon the petition of an interested person may reform the disposition in the manner that most closely approximates the transferor's manifested plan of distribution and is within the limits of the rule against perpetuities applicable when the nonvested property interest or power of appointment was created. (§ 45a-495(b))	See #5.	Upon the petition of an interested person, a court shall reform a disposition in the manner that most closely approximates the transferor's manifested plan of distribution and is within the 90 years allowed by section 19-901(a)(2), (b)(2), or (c)(2). (§ 19-903) However, if a nonvested property interest or a power of appointment was created before the effective date of this chapter [April 27, 2001] and is determined in a judicial proceeding, commenced on or after the effective date of this chapter, to violate the District of Columbia's rule against perpetuities as that rule existed before the effective date of this chapter [April 27, 2001], a court, upon the petition of an interested person, may reform the disposition in the manner that most closely approximates the transferor's manifested plan of distribution and is within the limits of the rule against perpetuities applicable when the nonvested property interest or power of appointment was created. (§ 19-905(b))

Table 9
Rule Against Perpetuities

	CONNECTICUT	DELAWARE	DISTRICT OF COLUMBIA
7. *When is a general testamentary power of appointment invalid?*	A general testamentary power of appointment is invalid unless: (1) When the power is created, it is certain to be irrevocably exercised or otherwise to terminate no later than 21 years after the death of an individual then alive. (2) The power is irrevocably exercised or otherwise terminates within 90 years after its creation. (§ 45a-491(c))	With respect to wills, see Unif. Statutory Rule Against Perpetuities §1, 8B U.L.A. 248 (amended 1990) ("Under the Common-law Rule . . . a *nongeneral power* (whether or not presently exercisable) or a *general testamentary power* is invalid as of the time of its creation if it *might* not terminate (by irrevocable exercise or otherwise) within a life in being plus 21 years.") With respect to trusts, *see* #2b above.	A general testamentary power of appointment is invalid unless: (1) When the power is created, it is certain to be irrevocably exercised or otherwise to terminate no later than 21 years after the death of an individual then alive. (2) The power is irrevocably exercised or otherwise terminates within 90 years after its creation. (§ 19-901(c))
8. *Same, but nongeneral testamentary power.*	A nongeneral power of appointment . . . is invalid unless: (1) When the power is created, it is certain to be irrevocably exercised or otherwise to terminate no later than 21 years after the death of an individual then alive. (2) The power is irrevocably exercised or otherwise terminates within 90 years after its creation. (§ 45a-491(c))	See #7.	A nongeneral power of appointment . . . is invalid unless: (1) When the power is created, it is certain to be irrevocably exercised or otherwise to terminate no later than 21 years after the death of an individual then alive. (2) The power is irrevocably exercised or otherwise terminates within 90 years after its creation. (19-901(c))

Table 9
Rule Against Perpetuities

	CONNECTICUT	DELAWARE	DISTRICT OF COLUMBIA
9. *Same, but general power, whether testamentary or inter vivos, not presently exercisable because of a condition precedent.*	A general power of appointment not presently exercisable because of a condition precedent is invalid unless: (1) When the power is created, the condition precedent is certain to be satisfied or become impossible to satisfy no later than 21 years after the death of an individual then alive. (2) The condition precedent either is satisfied or becomes impossible to satisfy within 90 years after its creation. (§ 45a-491(b))	With respect to wills, see Unif. Statutory Rule Against Perpetuities § 1, 8B U.L.A. 248 (amended 1990) ("Under the Common-law Rule, *a general power not presently exercisable because of a condition precedent* is invalid as of the time of its creation if the condition might neither be satisfied nor become impossible to satisfy with a life in being plus 21 years.") With respect to trusts, *see* #2b above.	A general power of appointment not presently exercisable because of a condition precedent is invalid unless: (1) When the power is created, the condition precedent is certain to be satisfied or become impossible to satisfy no later than 21 years after the death of an individual then alive. (2) The condition precedent either is satisfied or becomes impossible to satisfy within 90 years after its creation. (§ 19-901(b))
10. *Same, but nongeneral inter vivos power.*	See #8.	See #7.	See #8.

Table 9
Rule Against Perpetuities

	CONNECTICUT	DELAWARE	DISTRICT OF COLUMBIA
11. *Is a period of gestation added to the perpetuity period?*	No. The possibility that a child will be born to a person after that person's death is disregarded. (§ 45a-491(d)) *See also* Unif. Statutory Rule Against Perpetuities §1, 8B U.L.A. 243, 243 (amended 1990) ("[T]he possibility that a child will be born to [a testator] after his death must be disregarded; and the possibility that a child will be born to any of [the testator's] descendants after their deaths must also be disregarded. Note, however, that the rule of subsection (d) does not apply to the question of the entitlement of an after-born child to take a beneficial interest in the trust").	Yes. (See *Wilmington Trust Co. v. Sloane*, 54 A.2d 544, 548 (Del. 1947)).[1]	No. The possibility that a child will be born to a person after that person's death is disregarded. (§ 19-901(d)) *See also* Unif. Statutory Rule Against Perpetuities §1, 8B U.L.A. 243, 243 (amended 1990) ("[T]he possibility that a child will be born to [a testator] after his death must be disregarded; and the possibility that a child will be born to any of [the testator's] descendants after their deaths must also be disregarded. Note, however, that the rule of subsection (d) does not apply to the question of the entitlement of an after-born child to take a beneficial interest in the trust").
12. *What is the treatment of a "later of the traditional rule or 90 years" clause?* See UPC 2-901(e).	That language is inoperative to the extent it produces a period of time that exceeds 21 years after the death of the survivor. (§ 45a-491(e))	N/A	The language is inoperative to the extent it produces a period of time that exceeds 21 years after the death of the survivor. (§ 19-901(e))

Table 9
Rule Against Perpetuities

	CONNECTICUT	DELAWARE	DISTRICT OF COLUMBIA
13. *When is an interest created by the exercise of a general testamentary power deemed created?*	Except as provided in subsections (b) and (c) of this section and in subsection (a) of section 45a-495, the time of creation of a nonvested property interest or a power of appointment is determined under general principles of property law. (§ 45a-492(a)) The first of the excepted provisions states that as long as a person with a general power to become the unqualified beneficial owner has that power, the nonvested interest is created when the power terminates. The second of the excepted provisions states that a nonvested property interest, or a power of appointment, which arises from a transfer to an existing trust, is created when the nonvested property interest in the original contribution was created. (§ 45a-492(b)–(c)) *See also* Unif. Statutory Rule Against Perpetuities § 2, 8B U.L.A. 268 (amended 1990) (explaining that "general principles of property law determine that the time . . . [of creation] is at the decedent's death.") *See generally* § 45a-495(a) ("a nonvested property interest or a power of appointment created by the exercise of a power of appointment is created when the power is irrevocably exercised or when a revocable exercise becomes irrevocable.")	Every estate or interest in property, real or personal, created through the exercise, by will, deed or other instrument, of a power of appointment . . . shall, for the purpose of any rule of law against perpetuities, remoteness in vesting, restraint upon the power of alienation or accumulations now in effect or hereafter enacted be deemed to have been created at the time of the exercise and not at the time of the creation of such power of appointment unless the instrument of exercise makes express reference to § 501 and expressly states that the provisions of § 501(b) apply. (25 § 501)	Except as provided in subsections (b) and (c) of this section and in section 19-905(a), the time of creation of a nonvested property interest or a power of appointment is determined under general principles of property law. (§ 19-902(a)) The first two of the excepted provisions states that as long as a person with a general power to become the unqualified beneficial owner has that power, the nonvested interest is created when the power terminates. The third of the excepted provisions states that a nonvested property interest, which arises from a transfer to an existing trust, is created when the nonvested property interest in the trust was created. (§ 19-902(b)–(c)) *See also* Unif. Statutory Rule Against Perpetuities § 2, 8B U.L.A. 268 (amended 1990) (explaining that "general principles of property law determine that the time . . . [of creation] is at the decedent's death.") *See generally* § 19-905(a) ("[A] nonvested property interest or a power of appointment created by the exercise of a power of appointment is created when the power is irrevocably exercised or when a revocable exercise becomes irrevocable.")

Table 9
Rule Against Perpetuities

	CONNECTICUT	DELAWARE	DISTRICT OF COLUMBIA
14. Same, but nongeneral testamentary power.	See #13.	See #13. However, if the power is over a trust that is not subject to the generation-skipping transfer tax or has a zero inclusion ratio, then the estate or interest created by the exercise of the power is deemed created at the creation of the power and not at its exercise. As for any power created by the exercise of the initial power, said power and any estate or interest created by its exercise are deemed created at the creation of the initial power. (25 § 504)	See #13.

Table 9
Rule Against Perpetuities

	CONNECTICUT	DELAWARE	DISTRICT OF COLUMBIA
15. *Same, but general inter vivos power.*	Except as provided in subsections (b) and (c) of this section and in subsection (a) of section 45a-495, the time of creation of a nonvested property interest or a power of appointment is determined under general principles of property law. (§ 45a-492(a)) *See also* Unif. Statutory Rule Against Perpetuities § 2, 8B U.L.A. 268 (amended 1990) (explaining that "the time when the interest or power is created is the date the transfer becomes effective for purposes of property law generally, normally the date of delivery of the deed"); Comment to Unif. Probate Code § 2-902(a) (stating same and adding "the funding of the trust" as "normally" the time when the interest is created). *See generally* § 45a-495(a) ("A nonvested property interest or a power of appointment created by the exercise of a power of appointment is created when the power is irrevocably exercised or when a revocable exercise becomes irrevocable.")	See #13.	Except as provided in subsections (b) and (c) of this section and in section 19-905(a), the time of creation of a nonvested property interest or a power of appointment is determined under general principles of property law. (§ 19-902(a)) *See also* Unif. Statutory Rule Against Perpetuities § 2, 8B U.L.A. 268 (amended 1990) (explaining that "the time when the interest or power is created is the date the transfer becomes effective for purposes of property law generally, normally the date of delivery of the deed"); Comment to Unif. Probate Code § 2-902(a) (stating same and adding "the funding of the trust" as "normally" the time when the interest is created). *See generally* § 19-905(a) ("[A] nonvested property interest or a power of appointment created by the exercise of a power of appointment is created when the power is irrevocably exercised or when a revocable exercise becomes irrevocable.")

Table 9
Rule Against Perpetuities

	CONNECTICUT	DELAWARE	DISTRICT OF COLUMBIA
16. *Same, but nongeneral inter vivos power.*	See #15.	See #13. However, if the power is over a trust that is not subject to the generation-skipping transfer tax or has a zero inclusion ratio, then the estate or interest created by the exercise of the power is deemed created at the creation of the power and not at its exercise. As for any power created by the exercise of the initial power, said power and any estate or interest created by its exercise are deemed created at the creation of the initial power. (25 §504)	See #15.

Table 9
Rule Against Perpetuities

	CONNECTICUT	DELAWARE	DISTRICT OF COLUMBIA
17. *When is an interest created if the grantor of a trust has a power to revoke?*	For purposes of sections 45a-490 to 45a-496, inclusive, if there is a person who alone can exercise a power created by a governing instrument to become the unqualified beneficial owner of (1) a nonvested property interest or (2) a property interest subject to a power of appointment described in subsection (b) or (c) of section 45a-491, the nonvested property interest or power of appointment is created when the power to become the unqualified beneficial owner terminates. (§ 45a-492(b)) *See also* Unif. Statutory Rule Against Perpetuities § 2, 8B U.L.A. 268 (amended 1990) (explaining that "any nonvested property interest subject to [a power to revoke] is not created . . . until the power terminates (by release, expiration at the death of the donee, or otherwise)"; Comment to Unif. Probate Code § 2-902(b) (noting that "nonvested property interest and powers of appointment created in [a revocable inter-vivos trust] are created when the power to revoke expires, usually at the settlor's death.") *See generally* § 45a-495(a) ("[A] nonvested property interest or a power of appointment created by the exercise	Trusts created by the exercise of a power of appointment, whether limited or general, and whether by will, deed or other instrument, shall be deemed to have become irrevocable by the trustor or testator on the date on which such exercise became irrevocable. (25 § 503(c)) The donors of nongeneral powers are deemed the settlor or testator and the donees of general powers are likewise deemed the settlors and testators. (25 § 503(c)) If a trust is created by a nongeneral exercise of a power, the trust is deemed to have become irrevocable on the date the power was created. (25 § 503(c))	For purposes of this chapter, if there is a person who alone can exercise a power created by a governing instrument to become the unqualified beneficial owner of a nonvested property interest or a property interest subject to a power of appointment described in section 19-901(b) or (c), the nonvested property interest or power of appointment is created when the power to become the unqualified beneficial owner terminates. (§ 19-902(b)) *See also* Unif. Statutory Rule Against Perpetuities § 2, 8B U.L.A. 268 (amended 1990) (explaining that "any nonvested property interest subject to [a power to revoke] is not created . . . until the power terminates (by release, expiration at the death of the donee, or otherwise)"; Comment to Unif. Probate Code § 2-902(b) (noting that "nonvested property interest and powers of appointment created in [a revocable inter-vivos trust] are created when the power to revoke expires, usually at the settlor's death.") *See generally* § 19-905(a) ("[A] nonvested property interest or a power of appointment created by the exercise of a power of appointment is created when the power is irrevocably

Table 9
Rule Against Perpetuities

	CONNECTICUT	DELAWARE	DISTRICT OF COLUMBIA
	of a power of appointment is created when the power is irrevocably exercised or when a revocable exercise becomes irrevocable.")		exercised or when a revocable exercise becomes irrevocable.")
18. *When does the period of the rule start re an interest contributed to an irrevocable trust? See UPC 2-902(c).*	A nonvested property interest or a power of appointment arising from a transfer of property to a previously funded trust or other existing property arrangement is created when the nonvested property interest or power of appointment in the original contribution was created. (§ 45a-492(c))	No statute or case law generally. However, see questions #13-17 with regard to powers of appointment.	A nonvested property interest or a power of appointment arising from a transfer of property to a previously funded trust or other existing property arrangement is created when the nonvested property interest or power of appointment in the original contribution was created. (§ 19-902(c))

Table 9
Rule Against Perpetuities

	CONNECTICUT	DELAWARE	DISTRICT OF COLUMBIA
19. Is there a conclusive presumption of fertility, that is, the "fertile octogenarian" rule?	Yes. Willimantic Investors, Inc. v. Covell, 156 A.2d 473, 475 (Conn. 1959) ("The presumption that the possibility of issue is never extinct so long as a person lives is settled law in this country as it pertains to the validity of titles and the distribution of property.") (citations omitted). See Unif. Statutory Rule Against Perpetuities §1, 8B U.L.A. 256 (amended 1990) (holding that "[t]his principle is not superseded by this Act, and in view of new advances in medical science . . . [this] is not unrealistic."). But see C. P. Jhong, Modern Status of Presumption Against Possibility of Issue Being Extinct, 98 A.L.R.2d 1285 (2003) (noting "a trend toward denying the conclusive or absolute nature of the presumption against the possibility of issue being extinct where there is competent evidence to the contrary has developed in the decisions, although some courts still adhere to the traditional view treating the presumption as conclusive or absolute").	Yes. P v. Wilmington Trust Co., 188 A.2d 361, 364 (Del. Ch. 1962) (noting the "common law doctrine, usually applied in determining questions of remoteness of vesting but nonetheless clearly recognized in Delaware, that human beings are presumed to be capable of getting and bearing children regardless of age").[2]	Apparently not, even under the common law. See Whitney v. Groo, 40 App. D.C. 496-97 (D.C. Cir. 1913) (finding that a title did not have a defect nor was it not marketable because of the remote contingency that a widow may have children after 70 years of age).[3] See also Unif. Statutory Rule Against Perpetuities §1, 8B U.L.A. 256 (amended 1990) (holding that "[t]his principle is not superseded by this Act, and in view of new advances in medical science . . . [this] is not unrealistic."). But see C. P. Jhong, Modern Status of Presumption Against Possibility of Issue Being Extinct, 98 A.L.R.2d 1285 (2003) (noting "a trend toward denying the conclusive or absolute nature of the presumption against the possibility of issue being extinct where there is competent evidence to the contrary has developed in the decisions, although some courts still adhere to the traditional view treating the presumption as conclusive or absolute").

Table 9

Rule Against Perpetuities

	CONNECTICUT	DELAWARE	DISTRICT OF COLUMBIA
20. *What is the earliest age a child is deemed capable of bearing a child? What is the impact of illegitimacy?*	Not specifically addressed by USRAP, but the reasoning is the same as set forth in the comment to section 1 of USRAP, 2, Technical Violations of the Common Law Rule. Wait and see will typically result in no violation. Nevertheless, the common law rule ordinarily will be applied initially. "Under the rule, courts must presume that living persons are capable of having or fathering children, no matter how young they are. *See In re Graite's Will Trusts*, [1949] 1 All E.R. 459, 460 (Ch.). Thus, the rule strikes down any interest whose vesting depends on the assertion that, for example, a toddler will not have children." (Keith L. Butler, Notes & Comments, *Long Live the Dead Hand: A Case for Repeal of the Rule Against Perpetuities in Washington*, 75 Wash. L. Rev. 1237, 1246 n.78 (2000)).	"Under the rule, courts must presume that living persons are capable of having or fathering children, no matter how young they are. *See* 19. above. *See also In re Graite's Will Trusts*, [1949] 1 All E.R. 459, 460 (Ch.). Thus, the rule strikes down any interest whose vesting depends on the assertion that, for example, a toddler will not have children." (Keith L. Butler, Notes & Comments, *Long Live the Dead Hand: A Case for Repeal of the Rule Against Perpetuities in Washington*, 75 Wash. L. Rev. 1237, 1246 n.78 (2000)).	Not specifically addressed by USRAP, but the reasoning is the same as set forth in the comment to section 1 of USRAP, 2, Technical Violations of the Common Law Rule. Wait and see will typically result in no violation. Nevertheless, the common law rule ordinarily will be applied initially. "Under the rule, courts must presume that living persons are capable of having or fathering children, no matter how young they are. *See In re Graite's Will Trusts*, [1949] 1 All E.R. 459, 460 (Ch.). Thus, the rule strikes down any interest whose vesting depends on the assertion that, for example, a toddler will not have children." (Keith L. Butler, Notes & Comments, *Long Live the Dead Hand: A Case for Repeal of the Rule Against Perpetuities in Washington*, 75 Wash. L. Rev. 1237, 1246 n.78 (2000)).
21. *Is the "unborn widow" rule observed?*	No specific state case or statute. See Unif. Statutory Rule Against Perpetuities § 1, 8B U.L.A. 246 (amended 1990) (explaining that "[t]he chance that [an] interest will become invalid under the Statutory Rule is small" and so the unborn widow rule would rarely invalidate an interest); see also 61 Am. Jur. 2d *Perpetuities and Restraints on Alienation* § 39 (2013) (noting the same).	*See, e.g.*, Arkansas, question #21.	No specific state case or statute. See Unif. Statutory Rule Against Perpetuities § 1, 8B U.L.A. 246 (amended 1990) (explaining that "[t]he chance that [an] interest will become invalid under the Statutory Rule is small" and so the unborn widow rule would rarely invalidate an interest); *see also* 61 Am. Jur. 2d *Perpetuities and Restraints on Alienation* § 39 (2013) (noting the same).

Table 9
Rule Against Perpetuities

	CONNECTICUT	DELAWARE	DISTRICT OF COLUMBIA
22. Does the "slothful executor" rule apply, i.e., an administrative contingency clause providing for a "distribution to e.g., those issue living at the time of the satisfaction of the administrative condition precedent?"	No. Belfield v. Booth, 27 A. 585, 588 (Conn. 1893) (validating a will despite an administrative contingency clause and noting that "wills are not defeated by informality in the expression of the testator's wishes, where his substantial intent is apparent, and the estate which he seeks to create is not an unlawful one"). See also Unif. Statutory Rule Against Perpetuities § 1, 8B U.L.A. 245 (amended 1990) (Under USRAP an "interest becomes invalid only if it remains in existence and nonvested 90 years after [the testator's] death. Since it is almost certain that the final distribution of [an] estate will occur well within this 90-year period, the chance that [an] interest will be invalid is negligible.")	No. Asche v. Asche, 216 A.2d 272, 279 (Del. Ch. 1966) (affirming the Restatement rule that "when a will directs distribution to be made to persons to be ascertained 'on the probate of this will,' or 'on the conclusion of the administration of this estate', it is reasonable to infer that the testator has merely envisioned those preliminaries required by law prior to the time when distribution first becomes practicable and that the quoted language was not intended to postpone the ascertainment of the distributees by the injecting of a period of indefinite length.")	No specific state case or statute. See Unif. Statutory Rule Against Perpetuities § 1, 8B U.L.A. 245 (amended 1990) (Under USRAP an "interest becomes invalid only if it remains in existence and nonvested 90 years after [the testator's] death. Since it is almost certain that the final distribution of [an] estate will occur well within this 90-year period, the chance that [an] interest will be invalid is negligible.")

Table 9
Rule Against Perpetuities

	CONNECTICUT	DELAWARE	DISTRICT OF COLUMBIA
23. *Does the all-or-nothing rule apply to class gifts?*	Yes. Warren v. Daval, 200 A. 804, 806 (Conn. 1938). See also Unif. Statutory Rule Against Perpetuities §1, 8B U.L.A. 257 (amended 1990) ("Although this Act does not supersede the basic idea of the much-maligned 'all-or-nothing' rule, the evils sometimes attributed to it are substantially if not entirely eliminated by the wait-and-see feature of the Statutory Rule and by the availability of reformation under Section 3.")	Yes. Stuart v. Stuart, 106 A.2d 771, 773 (Del. Ch. 1953) ("If the gift is bad as to the class, even though some of the class are within the rule or even though, as it may later develop, all of the class may be within the rule, the gift is still bad.")	No specific case or statute. See Unif. Statutory Rule Against Perpetuities §1, 8B U.L.A. 257 (amended 1990) ("Although this Act does not supersede the basic idea of the much-maligned 'all-or-nothing' rule, the evils sometimes attributed to it are substantially if not entirely eliminated by the wait-and-see feature of the Statutory Rule and by the availability of reformation under Section 3.")

Table 9
Rule Against Perpetuities

	CONNECTICUT	DELAWARE	DISTRICT OF COLUMBIA
24. *Is there an exception to the all-or-nothing rule in the case of subclasses or specific sums to each member of the class?*	No specific state case or statute. *See* Unif. Statutory Rule Against Perpetuities §1, 8B U.L.A. 257 (amended 1990) ("The specific-sum and sub-class doctrines are not superseded by this Act.")	No specific case or statute. See Unif. Statutory Rule Against Perpetuities §1, 8B U.L.A. 257 ("The common law also recognizes a doctrine called the specific-sum doctrine which is derived from Storrs v. Benbow, 3 De G.M. & G. 390, 43 Eng. Rep 153 (Ch. 1853), and states: If a specified sum of money is to be paid to each member of a class, the interest of each class member is entitled to separate treatment and is valid or invalid under the Rule on its own. The common law also recognizes a doctrine called the sub-class doctrine, which is derived from Cattlin v. Brown, 11 Hare 372, 68 Eng. Rep. 1318 (Ch. 1853), and states: If the ultimate takers are not described as a single class but rather as a group of separate subclasses, and if the share to which each separate subclass is entitled will finally be determined within the period of the Rule, the gifts to the different subclasses are separate for the purpose of the Rule.").	No specific case or statute. See Unif. Statutory Rule Against Perpetuities §1, 8B U.L.A. 257 (amended 1990) ("The specific-sum and sub-class doctrines are not superseded by this Act.")

Table 9
Rule Against Perpetuities

	CONNECTICUT	DELAWARE	DISTRICT OF COLUMBIA
25. Is the infectious invalidity rule followed outside class gifts?	No specific state case or statute. See Unif. Statutory Rule Against Perpetuities §1, 8B U.L.A. 256 (amended 1990) (explaining that "[t]he doctrine of infectious invalidity is superseded by this Act by Section 3, under which courts . . . are required to *reform* the disposition to approximate as closely as possible the transferor's . . . plan of distribution.")	*See, e.g.,* Colorado, question #25.	No specific case or statute. See Unif. Statutory Rule Against Perpetuities §1, 8B U.L.A. 256 (amended 1990) (explaining that "[t]he doctrine of infectious invalidity is superseded by this Act by Section 3, under which courts . . . are required to *reform* the disposition to approximate as closely as possible the transferor's . . . plan of distribution.")
26. *Is there a rule against the suspension of the power of alienation? If so, how is it stated?*	No specific state statute. Case law is unclear. See Tappan's Appeal, 52 Conn. 412, 420 (1885) (stating that a statute at that time provided that "suspension may be made during any number of lives in being when the will is made creating the suspension, and during such a period afterwards as will leave it impossible for the estate to be carried by the terms of the will to parties not in being when the will was made and not the immediate issue of parties then in being").	No specific case on real property. See Tracey v. Franklin, 67 A.2d 56, 59 (Del. 1949) (explaining in the case of personal property, "arbitrary restraints on alienation are forbidden and unless restraints are imposed for purposes recognized as sufficient, they will be held invalid.") Note also that provisions directing or authorizing accumulations are valid. (25 §506)	D.C. Code Ann. §42-302, which provided a rule against the suspension of the power of alienation, was repealed in 2001.

Table 9
Rule Against Perpetuities

	CONNECTICUT	DELAWARE	DISTRICT OF COLUMBIA
27. *Effective date.*	October 1, 1989. (§ 45a-495(a)) *See also* #6.	The exemption from the rule against perpetuities is effective with respect to trusts becoming irrevocable on or after July 7, 1995. The provisions relating to powers of appointment and the Delaware Tax Trap, *see* #14 & 16, are effective with respect to powers exercised after July 6, 2000, regardless of when the power was created.	April 27, 2001. (§ 19-905(a)) *See also* #6.

---

[1] The USRAP provision stating that the common law rule against perpetuities has been superseded is omitted in the Delaware law.

[2] The answers to questions #19-25 are not likely to apply in most cases because of the abolition of the rule with respect to the vast majority of trusts.

[3] For questions, #19-25, *see also* § 19-906 (noting that the state's USRAP supersedes the common law rule against perpetuities). This does not mean that the common law is neglected, only that it is the starting point in the analysis.

Table 9
Rule Against Perpetuities

		FLORIDA	GEORGIA	HAWAII
1.	*Which rule is in effect: the common law rule, the Uniform Statutory Rule Against Perpetuities (USRAP), other law, or none?*	USRAP. (Fla. Stat. § 689.225)	USRAP. (Ga. Code Ann. §§ 44-6-200 - 44-6-206)	USRAP. (Haw. Rev. Stat. Ann. §§ 525-1—525-6)
2. a.	*Is the common law rule relevant to any interests?*	Yes, but only as the starting point of the analysis.	Yes, but only as the starting point of the analysis.	Yes, but only as the starting point of the analysis.
b.	*What is the relevant rule?*	A nonvested property interest in real or personal property is invalid unless: (1) When the interest is created, it is certain to vest or terminate no later than 21 years after the death of an individual then alive; or (2) The interest either vests or terminates within 90 years after its creation. (§ 689.225(2)(a)) *However, as to any trust created after December 31, 2000, 90 years is changed to 360 years with respect to any nonvested property interest or power of appointment contained in the trust. (§ 689.225(2)(f)) All subsequent references in the Table to "90 years" should be read as "360 years" if involving a post-December 31, 2000 trust.*	A nonvested property interest is invalid unless: (1) When the interest is created, it is certain either to vest or to terminate within the lifetime of an individual then alive or within 21 years after the death of that individual; or (2) The interest either vests or terminates within 90 years after its creation. (§ 44-6-201(a))	A nonvested property interest is invalid unless: (1) When the interest is created, it is certain to vest or terminate no later than 21 years after the death of an individual then alive; or (2) The interest either vests or terminates within 90 years after its creation. (§ 525-1(a))

9075

Table 9
Rule Against Perpetuities

	FLORIDA	GEORGIA	HAWAII
3. *Does the rule apply to other than private trusts?*	Yes. The rule applies except to:	Yes. The rule applies except to:	Yes. The rule applies except to:
	(a) A nonvested property interest or a power of appointment arising out of a nondonative transfer, except a nonvested property interest or a power of appointment arising out of:	(1) A nonvested property interest or a power of appointment arising out of a nondonative transfer, except a nonvested property interest or a power of appointment arising out of:	(1) A fiduciary's power to sell, lease, or mortgage property, and the power of a fiduciary to determine principal and income;
	1. A premarital or postmarital agreement;	(A) A premarital or postmarital agreement;	(2) A discretionary power of a trustee to distribute principal before termination of a trust;
	2. A separation or divorce settlement;	(B) A separation or divorce settlement;	(3) A nonvested property interest held by a charity, government or governmental agency or subdivision, if the nonvested property interest is preceded by an interest held by another charity, government or governmental agency or subdivision;
	3. A spouse's election;	(C) A spouse's election;	
	4. A similar arrangement arising out of a prospective existing or previous marital relationship between the parties;	(D) A similar arrangement arising out of a prospective existing or previous marital relationship between the parties;	(4) A property interest in or a power of appointment with respect to a pension, profit-sharing, stock bonus, health, disability, death benefit, income deferral, or other current or deferred benefit plan for one or more employees, independent
	5. A contract to make or not to revoke a will or trust;	(E) A contract to make or not to revoke a will or trust;	
	6. A contract to exercise or not to exercise a power of appointment;	(F) A contract to exercise or not to exercise a power of appointment;	
	7. A transfer in satisfaction of a duty of support; or	(G) A transfer in satisfaction of a duty of support; or	
	8. A reciprocal transfer;	(H) A reciprocal transfer;	
	(b) A fiduciary's power relating to the administration or		

Table 9
Rule Against Perpetuities

FLORIDA	GEORGIA	HAWAII
management of assets, including the power of a fiduciary to sell, lease, or mortgage property, and the power of a fiduciary to determine principal and income;	(2) A fiduciary's power relating to the administration or management of assets, including the power of a fiduciary to sell, lease, or mortgage property, and the power of a fiduciary to determine principal and income;	contractors, or their beneficiaries or spouses;
(c) A power to appoint a fiduciary;	(3) A power to appoint a fiduciary;	(5) A property interest, power of appointment, or arrangement that was not subject to the common-law rule against perpetuities or is excluded by any other applicable law; or
(d) A discretionary power of a trustee to distribute principal before termination of a trust to a beneficiary having an indefeasibly vested interest in the income and principal;	(4) A discretionary power of a trustee to distribute principal before termination of a trust to a beneficiary having an indefeasibly vested interest in the income and principal. Nothing contained in paragraphs (2) and (3) of this Code section and this paragraph shall be construed to permit the fiduciary to continue the administration or management of assets once the nonvested property interest becomes invalid as described in subsection (a) of 44-6-201;	(6) A trust described in Chapter 554G, essentially a domestic asset protection trust. (§525-4)
(e) A nonvested property interest held by a charity, government or governmental agency or subdivision, if the nonvested property interest is preceded by an interest held by another charity, government or governmental agency or subdivision;		
(f) A nonvested property interest in or a power of appointment with respect to a trust or other property arrangement forming		

Table 9
Rule Against Perpetuities

FLORIDA	GEORGIA	HAWAII
part of a pension, profit sharing, stock bonus, health, disability, death benefit, income deferral or other current or deferred benefit plan for one or more employees, independent contractors or their beneficiaries or spouses, to which contributions are	(5) A nonvested property interest held by a charity, government or governmental agency or subdivision, if the nonvested property interest is preceded by an interest held by another charity, government or governmental agency or subdivision;	
made for the purpose of distributing to or for the benefit of the participants or their beneficiaries or spouses the property, income or principal in the trust or other property arrangement, except a nonvested property interest or a power of appointment that is created by an election of a participant or a beneficiary or spouse; or	(6) A nonvested property interest in or a power of appointment with respect to a trust or other property arrangement forming part of a pension, profit sharing, stock bonus, health, disability, death benefit, income deferral or other current or deferred benefit plan for one or more employees, independent contractors or their	
(g) A property interest, power of appointment or arrangement that was not subject to the common-law rule against perpetuities or is excluded by another statute of this state. (§689.225(5))	beneficiaries or spouses, to which contributions are made for the purpose of distributing to or for the benefit of the participants or their beneficiaries or spouses the	
	property, income or principal in the trust or other property arrangement, except a nonvested property interest or a power of appointment that is created by an election of a participant or a beneficiary or spouse; or	

Table 9
Rule Against Perpetuities

	FLORIDA	GEORGIA	HAWAII
		(7) A property interest, power of appointment or arrangement that was not subject to the common-law rule against perpetuities or is excluded by another statute of this state. (§ 44-6-204)	
4. *Does the rule invalidate the interest at its creation, or is the rule revised by a wait-and-see approach?*	Wait-and-see. (§ 689.225(2)(a)(2))	Wait-and-see. (§ 44-6-201(a)(2))	Wait-and-see. (§ 525-1(a)(2))
5. *Can the trust be reformed?*	Yes, but only if one of the following conditions applies: (a) A nonvested property interest or a power of appointment becomes invalid under subsection (2) (see #2b); (b) A class gift is not but might become invalid under subsection (2) and the time has arrived when the share of any class member is to take effect in possession or enjoyment; or (c) A nonvested property interest that is not validated by subparagraph (2)(a), that is, the traditional common law rule, can vest but not within 90 years after its creation. (§ 689.225(4)) *See also #27.*	Yes, but only if one of the following conditions applies: (1) A nonvested property interest or a power of appointment becomes invalid under Code Section 44-6-201 (*see #2b*); (2) A class gift is not but might still become invalid under Code Section 44-6-201 and the time has arrived when the share of any class member is to take effect in possession or enjoyment; or (3) A nonvested property interest that is not validated by paragraph (1) of subsection (a) of Code Section 44-6-201, that is, the traditional common law rule, can vest, but not within 90 years after its creation. (§ 44-6-203) *See also #27.*	Yes, but only if one of the following conditions applies: (1) A nonvested property interest or a power of appointment becomes invalid under section 525-1 (see #2b); (2) A class gift is not but might become invalid under section 525-1 and the time has arrived when the share of any class member is to take effect in possession or enjoyment; or (3) A nonvested property interest that is not validated by section 525-1(a)(1), that is, the traditional common law rule, can vest but not within 90 years after its creation. (§ 525-3) *See also #27.*

Table 9
Rule Against Perpetuities

	FLORIDA	GEORGIA	HAWAII
6. *If yes to 5., under what theory?*	Upon the petition of an interested person, a court shall reform a disposition in the manner that most closely approximates the transferor's manifested plan of distribution and is within the 90 years allowed by subparagraph (2)(a)2., subparagraph (2)(b)2., or subparagraph (2)(c)2. (§ 689.225(4)) See also § 689.225(6)(c) ("If a nonvested property interest or a power of appointment was created before October 1, 1988, and is determined in a judicial proceeding commenced on or after October 1, 1988, to violate this state's rule against perpetuities as that rule existed before October 1, 1988, a court, upon the petition of an interested person, may reform the disposition in the manner that most closely approximates the transferor's manifested plan of distribution and is within the limits of the rule against perpetuities applicable when the nonvested property interest or power of appointment was created.")	Upon the petition of an interested person, a court shall reform a disposition in the manner that most closely approximates the transferor's manifested plan of distribution and is within the 90 years allowed by paragraph (2) of subsection (a), paragraph (2) of subsection (b), or paragraph (2) of subsection (c) of Code Section 44-6-201. (§ 44-6-203) See also § 44-6-205(b) ("With respect to a nonvested property interest or a power of appointment that was created before May 1, 1990, and that violates this state's rule against perpetuities as that rule existed before May 1, 1990, a court upon the petition of an interested party may exercise its equitable power to reform the disposition in the manner that most closely approximates the transferor's manifested plan of distribution and is within the limits of the rule against perpetuities applicable when the nonvested property interest or power of appointment was created.")	Upon the petition of an interested person, a court shall reform a disposition in the manner that most closely approximates the transferor's manifested plan of distribution and is within the ninety years allowed by section 525-1(a)(2), (b)(2), or (c)(2). (§ 525-3) See also § 525-5(b) ("If a nonvested property interest or a power of appointment was created before June 18, 1992, and is determined in a judicial proceeding, commenced on or after June 18, 1992, to violate this State's common law rule against perpetuities as that rule existed before June 18, 1992, a court upon the petition of an interested person may reform the disposition in the manner that most closely approximates the transferor's manifested plan of distribution and is within the limits of the rule against perpetuities applicable when the nonvested property interest or power of appointment was created.")

Table 9
Rule Against Perpetuities

	FLORIDA	GEORGIA	HAWAII
7. When is a general testamentary power of appointment invalid?	A general testamentary power of appointment is invalid unless one of the following conditions is satisfied: (1) When the power is created, it is certain to be irrevocably exercised or otherwise to terminate no later than 21 years after the death of an individual then alive. (2) The power is irrevocably exercised or otherwise terminates within 90 years after its creation. (§ 689.225(2)(c))	A general testamentary power of appointment is invalid unless: (1) When the power is created, it is certain to be irrevocably exercised or otherwise to terminate within the lifetime of an individual then alive or within 21 years after the death of that individual; or (2) The power is irrevocably exercised or otherwise terminates within 90 years after its creation. (§ 44-6-201(c))	A general testamentary power of appointment is invalid unless one of the following conditions is satisfied: (1) When the power is created, it is certain to be irrevocably exercised or otherwise to terminate no later than 21 years after the death of an individual then alive. (2) The power is irrevocably exercised or otherwise terminates within 90 years after its creation. (§ 525-1-1(c))
8. Same, but nongeneral testamentary power.	A nongeneral power of appointment . . . is invalid unless one of the following conditions is satisfied: (1) When the power is created, it is certain to be irrevocably exercised or otherwise to terminate no later than 21 years after the death of an individual then alive. (2) The power is irrevocably exercised or otherwise terminates within 90 years after its creation. (§ 689.225(2)(c))	A nongeneral power of appointment . . . is invalid unless: (1) When the power is created, it is certain to be irrevocably exercised or otherwise to terminate within the lifetime of an individual then alive or within 21 years after the death of that individual; or (2) The power is irrevocably exercised or otherwise terminates within 90 years after its creation. (§ 44-6-201(c))	A nongeneral power of appointment . . . is invalid unless one of the following conditions is satisfied: (1) When the power is created, it is certain to be irrevocably exercised or otherwise to terminate no later than 21 years after the death of an individual then alive. (2) The power is irrevocably exercised or otherwise terminates within 90 years after its creation. (§ 525-1-1(c))

Table 9
Rule Against Perpetuities

	FLORIDA	GEORGIA	HAWAII
9. Same, but general power, whether testamentary or inter vivos, not presently exercisable because of a condition precedent.	A general power of appointment not presently exercisable because of a condition precedent is invalid unless one of the following conditions is satisfied: (1) When the power is created, the condition precedent is certain to be satisfied or become impossible to satisfy no later than 21 years after the death of an individual then alive. (2) The condition precedent either is satisfied or becomes impossible to satisfy within 90 years after its creation. (689.225(2)(b))	A general power of appointment not presently exercisable because of a condition precedent is invalid unless: (1) When the power is created, the condition precedent is certain either to be satisfied or to become impossible to satisfy within the lifetime of an individual then alive or within 21 years after the death of that individual; or (2) The condition precedent either is satisfied or becomes impossible to satisfy within 90 years after its creation. (§ 44-6-201(b))	A general power of appointment not presently exercisable because of a condition precedent is invalid unless one of the following conditions is satisfied: (1) When the power is created, the condition precedent is certain to be satisfied or becomes impossible to satisfy no later than 21 years after the death of an individual then alive. (2) The condition precedent either is satisfied or becomes impossible to satisfy within 90 years after its creation. (§ 525-1(b))
10. Same, but nongeneral inter vivos power.	See #8.	See #8.	See #8.

Table 9
Rule Against Perpetuities

	FLORIDA	GEORGIA	HAWAII
11. *Is a period of gestation added to the perpetuity period?*	No. The possibility that a child will be born to a person after that person's death is disregarded. (§ 689.225(2)(d)) See also Unif. Statutory Rule Against Perpetuities § 1, 8B U.L.A. 243, 243 (amended 1990) ("[T]he possibility that a child will be born to [a testator] after his death must be disregarded; and the possibility that a child will be born to any of [the testator's] descendants after their deaths must also be disregarded. Note, however, that the rule of subsection (d) does not apply to the question of the entitlement of an after-born child to take a beneficial interest in the trust").	No. The possibility that a child will be born to a person after that person's death is disregarded (§ 44-6-201(d)) See also Unif. Statutory Rule Against Perpetuities § 1, 8B U.L.A. 243, 243 (amended 1990) ("[T]he possibility that a child will be born to [a testator] after his death must be disregarded; and the possibility that a child will be born to any of [the testator's] descendants after their deaths must also be disregarded. Note, however, that the rule of subsection (d) does not apply to the question of the entitlement of an after-born child to take a beneficial interest in the trust").	No. The possibility that a child will be born to a person after that person's death is disregarded (§ 525-1(d)) See also Unif. Statutory Rule Against Perpetuities § 1, 8B U.L.A. 243, 243 (amended 1990) ("[T]he possibility that a child will be born to [a testator] after his death must be disregarded; and the possibility that a child will be born to any of [the testator's] descendants after their deaths must also be disregarded. Note, however, that the rule of subsection (d) does not apply to the question of the entitlement of an after-born child to take a beneficial interest in the trust").
12. *What is the treatment of a "later of the traditional rule or 90 years" clause? See UIPC 2-901(e).*	The language is inoperative to the extent it produces a period of time that exceeds 21 years after the death of the survivor. (§ 689.225(2)(e))	Georgia's USRAP does not specify how it will treat "later of" clauses.	The language is inoperative to the extent it produces a period of time that exceeds 21 years after the death of the survivor of the specified lives. (§ 525-1(e))

Table 9
Rule Against Perpetuities

	FLORIDA	GEORGIA	HAWAII
13. *When is an interest created by the exercise of a general testamentary power deemed created?*	Except as provided in paragraphs (b), (d), and (e) of this subsection and in paragraph (a) of subsection (6), the time of creation of a nonvested property interest or a power of appointment is determined under general principles of property law. (§ 689.225(3)(a)) The first of the excepted provisions states that as long as a person with a general power to become the unqualified beneficial owner has that power, the nonvested interest is created when the power terminates. (§ 689.225(3)(b)) The second of the excepted provisions states that a nonvested property interest, which arises from a transfer to an existing trust, is created when the nonvested property interest in the trust was created. (§ 689.225(3)(d)) *See also* Unif. Statutory Rule Against Perpetuities § 2, 8B U.L.A. 268 (amended 1990) (explaining that general principles of property law determine that the time [of creation] is at the decedent's death). *See generally* § 689.225(3)(e) ("[I]f a nongeneral or testamentary power of appointment is exercised to create another nongeneral or testamentary power of appointment, every nonvested property interest or power of appointment created through the exercise of such other nongeneral or	Except as provided in subsections (b) and (c) of this Code section and in subsection (a) of Code Section 44-6-205, the time of creation of a nonvested property interest or a power of appointment is determined under general principles of property law. (§ 44-6-202(a)) The first of the excepted provisions states that as long as a person with a general power to become the unqualified beneficial owner has that power, the nonvested interest is created when the power terminates. The second of the excepted provisions states that a nonvested property interest, which arises from a transfer to an existing trust, is created when the nonvested property interest in the trust was created. (§ 44-6-202(b)-(c)) *See also* Unif. Statutory Rule Against Perpetuities § 2, 8B U.L.A. 268 (amended 1990) (explaining that "general principles of property law determine that the time . . . [of creation] is at the decedent's death.") *See generally* § 44-6-205(a) ("[A] nonvested property interest or a power of appointment created by the exercise of a power of appointment is created when the power is irrevocably exercised or when a revocable exercise becomes irrevocable.")	Except as provided in subsections (b) and (c) and in section 525-5(a), the time of creation of a nonvested property interest or a power of appointment is determined under general principles of property law. (§ 525-2(a)) The first of the excepted provisions states that as long as a person with a general power to become the unqualified beneficial owner has that power, the nonvested interest is created when the power terminates. The second of the excepted provisions states that a nonvested property interest, which arises from a transfer to an existing trust, is created when the nonvested property interest in the trust was created. (§ 525-2(b)-(c)) *See also* Unif. Statutory Rule Against Perpetuities § 2, 8B U.L.A. 268 (amended 1990) (explaining that "general principles of property law determine that the time . . . [of creation] is at the decedent's death.") *See generally* § 525-5(a) ("[A] nonvested property interest or a power of appointment created by the exercise of a power of appointment is created when the power is irrevocably exercised or when a revocable exercise becomes irrevocable.")

Table 9
Rule Against Perpetuities

	FLORIDA	GEORGIA	HAWAII
	testamentary power is considered to have been created at the time of the creation of the first nongeneral or testamentary power of appointment"). *See generally* § 689.225(6)(a) ("For the purposes of this subsection, a nonvested property interest or a power of appointment created by the exercise of a power of appointment is created when the power is irrevocably exercised or when a revocable exercise becomes irrevocable.")		
14. *Same, but nongeneral testamentary power.*	See #13.	See #13.	See #13.

Table 9
Rule Against Perpetuities

	FLORIDA	GEORGIA	HAWAII
15. *Same, but general inter vivos power.*	Except as provided in paragraphs (b), (d), and (e) of this subsection and in paragraph (a) of subsection (6), the time of creation of a nonvested property interest or a power of appointment is determined under general principles of property law. (§ 689.225(3)(a)) The first of the excepted provisions states that as long as a person with a general power to become the unqualified beneficial owner has that power, the nonvested interest is created when the power terminates. (§ 689.225(3)(b)) The second of the excepted provisions states that a nonvested property interest, which arises from a transfer to an existing trust, is created when the nonvested property interest in the trust was created. (§ 689.225(3)(d)) See also § 689.225(3)(e) ("For purposes of this section, if a nongeneral or testamentary power of appointment is exercised to create another nongeneral or testamentary power of appointment, every nonvested property interest or power of appointment created through the exercise of such other nongeneral or testamentary power is considered to have been created at the time of the creation of the first nongeneral or testamentary power of appointment"); Unif. Statutory Rule Against	Except as provided in subsections (b) and (c) of this Code section and in subsection (a) of Code Section 44-6-205, the time of creation of a nonvested property interest or a power of appointment is determined under general principles of property law. (§ 44-6-202(a)) The first of the excepted provisions states that as long as a person with a general power to become the unqualified beneficial owner has that power, the nonvested interest is created when the power terminates. The second of the excepted provisions states that a nonvested property interest, which arises from a transfer to an existing trust, is created when the nonvested property interest in the trust was created. (§ 44-6-202(b)-(c)) See also Unif. Statutory Rule Against Perpetuities § 2, 8B U.L.A. 268 (amended 1990) (explaining that "the time when the interest or power is created is the date the transfer becomes effective for purposes of property law generally, normally the date of delivery of the deed"); Comment to Unif. Probate Code § 2-902(a) (stating same and adding "the funding of the trust" as "normally" the time when the interest is created). See generally § 44-6-205(a) ("[A]	Except as provided in subsections (b) and (c) and in section 525-5(a), the time of creation of a nonvested property interest or a power of appointment is determined under general principles of property law. (§ 525-2(a)) The first of the excepted provisions states that as long as a person with a general power to become the unqualified beneficial owner has that power, the nonvested interest is created when the power terminates. The second of the excepted provisions states that a nonvested property interest, which arises from a transfer to an existing trust, is created when the nonvested property interest in the trust was created. (§ 525-2(b)-(c)) See also Unif. Statutory Rule Against Perpetuities § 2, 8B U.L.A. 268 (amended 1990) (explaining that "the time when the interest or power is created is the date the transfer becomes effective for purposes of property law generally, normally the date of delivery of the deed"); Comment to Unif. Probate Code § 2-902(a) (stating same and adding "the funding of the trust" as "normally" the time when the interest is created). See generally § 525-5(a) ("[A] nonvested property interest or a power of appointment created by the exercise

Table 9
Rule Against Perpetuities

	FLORIDA	GEORGIA	HAWAII
	Perpetuities §2, 8B U.L.A. 268 (amended 1990) (explaining that "the time when the interest or power is created is the date the transfer becomes effective for purposes of property law generally, normally the date of delivery of the deed"); Comment to Unif. Probate Code §2-902(a) (stating same and adding "the funding of the trust" as "normally" the time when the interest is created). See generally §689.225(6)(a) ("[A] nonvested property interest or a power of appointment created by the exercise of a power of appointment is created when the power is irrevocably exercised or when a revocable exercise becomes irrevocable.")	nonvested property interest or a power of appointment created by the exercise of a power of appointment is created when the power is irrevocably exercised or when a revocable exercise becomes irrevocable.")	of a power of appointment is created when the power is irrevocably exercised or when a revocable exercise becomes irrevocable.")
16. *Same, but nongeneral inter vivos power.*	See #15.	See #15.	See #15.
17. *When is an interest created if the grantor of a trust has a power to revoke?*	If there is a person who alone can exercise a power created by a governing instrument to become the unqualified beneficial owner of a nonvested property interest or a property interest subject to a power of appointment described in	If there is a person who alone can exercise a power created by a governing instrument to become the unqualified beneficial owner of: (1) A nonvested property interest; or	If there is a person who alone can exercise a power created by a governing instrument to become the unqualified beneficial owner of a nonvested property interest or a property interest subject to a power of appointment described in

Table 9
Rule Against Perpetuities

FLORIDA	GEORGIA	HAWAII
paragraph (b) or paragraph (c) of subsection (2), the nonvested property interest or power of appointment is created when the power to become the unqualified beneficial owner terminates. (§ 689.225(3)(b)) See also Unif. Statutory Rule Against Perpetuities § 2, 8B U.L.A. 268 (amended 1990) (explaining that "any nonvested property interest subject to [a power to revoke] is not created ... until the power terminates (by release, expiration at the death of the donee, or otherwise)"; Comment to Unif. Probate Code § 2-902(b) (noting that "nonvested property interests and powers of appointment created in [a revocable inter-vivos trust] are created when the power to revoke expires, usually at the settlor's death"). See generally § 689.225(6)(a) ("A nonvested property interest or a power of appointment created by the exercise of a power of appointment is created when the power is irrevocably exercised or when a revocable exercise becomes irrevocable.")	(2) A property interest subject to a power of appointment described in subsection (b) or (c) of Code Section 44-6-201, the nonvested property interest or power of appointment is created when the power to become the unqualified beneficial owner terminates. (§ 44-6-202(b)) See also Unif. Statutory Rule Against Perpetuities § 2, 8B U.L.A. 268 (amended 1990) (explaining that "any nonvested property interest subject to [a power to revoke] is not created ... until the power terminates (by release, expiration at the death of the donee, or otherwise"); Comment to Unif. Probate Code § 2-902(b) (noting that "nonvested property interests and powers of appointment created in [a revocable inter-vivos trust] are created when the power to revoke expires, usually at the settlor's death"). See generally § 44-6-205(a) ("A nonvested property interest or a power of appointment created by the exercise of a power of appointment is created when the power is irrevocably exercised or when a revocable exercise becomes irrevocable.")	section 525-1(b) or (c), the nonvested property interest or power of appointment is created when the power to become the unqualified beneficial owner terminates. (§ 525-2(b)) See also Unif. Statutory Rule Against Perpetuities § 2, 8B U.L.A. 268 (amended 1990) (explaining that "any nonvested property interest subject to [a power to revoke] is not created ... until the power terminates (by release, expiration at the death of the donee, or otherwise"); Comment to Unif. Probate Code § 2-902(b) (noting that "nonvested property interests and powers of appointment created in [a revocable inter-vivos trust] are created when the power to revoke expires, usually at the settlor's death"). See generally § 525-5(a) ("A nonvested property interest or a power of appointment created by the exercise of a power of appointment is created when the power is irrevocably exercised or when a revocable exercise becomes irrevocable.")

Table 9
Rule Against Perpetuities

	FLORIDA	GEORGIA	HAWAII
18. *When does the period of the rule start re an interest contributed to an irrevocable trust? See UPC 2-902(c).*	A nonvested property interest or a power of appointment arising from a transfer of property to a previously funded trust or other existing property arrangement is created when the nonvested property interest or power of appointment in the original contribution was created. (§ 689.225(3)(d))	A nonvested property interest or a power of appointment arising from a transfer of property to a previously funded trust or other existing property arrangement is created when the nonvested property interest or power of appointment in the original contribution was created. (§ 44-6-202(c))	A nonvested property interest or a power of appointment arising from a transfer of property to a previously funded trust or other existing property arrangement is created when the nonvested property interest or power of appointment in the original contribution was created. (§ 525-2(c))
19. *Is there a conclusive presumption of fertility, that is, the "fertile octogenarian" rule?*	Yes. Byers v. Beddow, 142 So. 894, 897 (Fla. 1932).[1] *See also* Unif. Statutory Rule Against Perpetuities § 1, 8B U.L.A. 256 (amended 1990) (holding that "[t]his principle is not superseded by this Act, and in view of new advances in medical science . . . [this] is not unrealistic."). But see C. P. Jhong, Annotation, Modern Status of Presumption Against Possibility of Issue Being Extinct, 98 A.L.R.2d 1285 (2003) (noting "a trend toward denying the conclusive or absolute nature of the presumption against the possibility of issue being extinct where there is competent evidence to the contrary has developed in the decisions, although some courts still adhere to the traditional view treating the presumption as conclusive or absolute").	Yes. Haley v. Regions Bank, 586 S.E.2d 633, 636 (Ga. 2003) ("Georgia law conclusively presumes that the possibility of issue is not extinct until death.")	No specific state case or statute. See Unif. Statutory Rule Against Perpetuities § 1, 8B U.L.A. 256 (amended 1990) (holding that "[t]his principle is not superseded by this Act, and in view of new advances in medical science . . . [this] is not unrealistic."). But see C. P. Jhong, Annotation, Modern Status of Presumption Against Possibility of Issue Being Extinct, 98 A.L.R.2d 1285 (2003) (noting "a trend toward denying the conclusive or absolute nature of the presumption against the possibility of issue being extinct where there is competent evidence to the contrary has developed in the decisions, although some courts still adhere to the traditional view treating the presumption as conclusive or absolute").

Table 9
Rule Against Perpetuities

	FLORIDA	GEORGIA	HAWAII
20. *What is the earliest age a child is deemed capable of bearing a child? What is the impact of illegitimacy?*	Not specifically addressed by USRAP, but the reasoning is the same as set forth in the comment to section 1 of USRAP, 2, Technical Violations of the Common Law Rule. Wait and see will typically result in no violation. Nevertheless, the common law rule ordinarily will be applied initially. "Under the rule, courts must presume that living persons are capable of having or fathering children, no matter how young they are. *See In re* Graite's Will Trusts, [1949] 1 All E.R. 459, 460 (Ch.). Thus, the rule strikes down any interest whose vesting depends on the assertion that, for example, a toddler will not have children." (Keith L. Butler, Notes & Comments, *Long Live the Dead Hand: A Case for Repeal of the Rule Against Perpetuities in Washington,* 75 Wash. L. Rev. 1237, 1246 n.78 (2000)).	Not specifically addressed by USRAP, but the reasoning is the same as set forth in the comment to section 1 of USRAP, 2, Technical Violations of the Common Law Rule. Wait and see will typically result in no violation. Nevertheless, the common law rule ordinarily will be applied initially. "Under the rule, courts must presume that living persons are capable of having or fathering children, no matter how young they are. *See In re* Graite's Will Trusts, [1949] 1 All E.R. 459, 460 (Ch.). Thus, the rule strikes down any interest whose vesting depends on the assertion that, for example, a toddler will not have children." (Keith L. Butler, Notes & Comments, *Long Live the Dead Hand: A Case for Repeal of the Rule Against Perpetuities in Washington,* 75 Wash. L. Rev. 1237, 1246 n.78 (2000)).	Not specifically addressed by USRAP, but the reasoning is the same as set forth in the comment to section 1 of USRAP, 2, Technical Violations of the Common Law Rule. Wait and see will typically result in no violation. Nevertheless, the common law rule ordinarily will be applied initially. "Under the rule, courts must presume that living persons are capable of having or fathering children, no matter how young they are. *See In re* Graite's Will Trusts, [1949] 1 All E.R. 459, 460 (Ch.). Thus, the rule strikes down any interest whose vesting depends on the assertion that, for example, a toddler will not have children." (Keith L. Butler, Notes & Comments, *Long Live the Dead Hand: A Case for Repeal of the Rule Against Perpetuities in Washington,* 75 Wash. L. Rev. 1237, 1246 n.78 (2000)).

Table 9
Rule Against Perpetuities

	FLORIDA	GEORGIA	HAWAII
21. *Is the "unborn widow" rule observed?*	No specific state case or statute. See Unif. Statutory Rule Against Perpetuities § 1, 8B U.L.A. 246 (amended 1990) (explaining that "[t]he chance that [an] interest will become invalid under the Statutory Rule is small" and so the unborn widow rule would rarely invalidate an interest); *see also* 61 Am. Jur. 2d *Perpetuities and Restraints on Alienation* § 39 (2013) (noting the same).	Yes. Lanier v. Lanier, 126 S.E.2d 776, 780 (Ga. 1962) *See also* Unif. Statutory Rule Against Perpetuities § 1, 8B U.L.A. 246 (amended 1990) (explaining that "[t]he chance that [an] interest will become invalid under the Statutory Rule is small" and so the unborn widow rule would rarely invalidate an interest); *see also* 61 Am. Jur. 2d *Perpetuities and Restraints on Alienation* § 39 (2013) (noting the same).	No specific state case or statute. See Unif. Statutory Rule Against Perpetuities § 1, 8B U.L.A. 246 (amended 1990) (explaining that "[t]he chance that [an] interest will become invalid under the Statutory Rule is small" and so the unborn widow rule would rarely invalidate an interest); *see also* 61 Am. Jur. 2d *Perpetuities on Alienation* § 39 (2013) (noting the same).
22. *Does the "slothful executor" rule apply, i.e., an administrative contingency clause providing for a "distribution to, e.g., those issue living at the time of the satisfaction of the administrative condition precedent?"*	No specific state case or statute. See Unif. Statutory Rule Against Perpetuities § 1, 8B U.L.A. 245 (amended 1990) (Under USRAP an "interest becomes invalid only if it remains in existence and nonvested 90 years after [the testator's] death. Since it is almost certain that the final distribution of [an] estate will occur well within this 90-year period, the chance that [an] interest will be invalid is negligible.")	No specific state case or statute. See Unif. Statutory Rule Against Perpetuities § 1, 8B U.L.A. 245 (amended 1990) (Under USRAP an "interest becomes invalid only if it remains in existence and nonvested 90 years after [the testator's] death. Since it is almost certain that the final distribution of [an] estate will occur well within this 90-year period, the chance that [an] interest will be invalid is negligible.")	No specific state case or statute. See Unif. Statutory Rule Against Perpetuities § 1, 8B U.L.A. 245 (amended 1990) (Under USRAP an "interest becomes invalid only if it remains in existence and nonvested 90 years after [the testator's] death. Since it is almost certain that the final distribution of [an] estate will occur well within this 90-year period, the chance that [an] interest will be invalid is negligible.")

Table 9
Rule Against Perpetuities

	FLORIDA	GEORGIA	HAWAII
23. *Does the all-or-nothing rule apply to class gifts?*	No specific state case or statute. See Unif. Statutory Rule Against Perpetuities § 1, 8B U.L.A. 257 (amended 1990) ("Although this Act does not supersede the basic idea of the much-maligned 'all-or-nothing' rule, the evils sometimes attributed to it are substantially if not entirely eliminated by the wait-and-see feature of the Statutory Rule and by the availability of reformation under Section 3.")	Yes. Landrum v. Nat'l City Bank, 80 S.E.2d 300, 302 (Ga. 1954) (invalidating a class gift to "nieces" because there were living sisters of the testator so more nieces could have later been born to the class). *See also* Unif. Statutory Rule Against Perpetuities § 1, 8B U.L.A. 257 (amended 1990) ("Although this Act does not supersede the basic idea of the much-maligned 'all-or-nothing' rule, the evils sometimes attributed to it are substantially if not entirely eliminated by the wait-and-see feature of the Statutory Rule and by the availability of reformation under Section 3.")	No specific state case or statute. See Unif. Statutory Rule Against Perpetuities § 1, 8B U.L.A. 257 (amended 1990) ("Although this Act does not supersede the basic idea of the much-maligned 'all-or-nothing' rule, the evils sometimes attributed to it are substantially if not entirely eliminated by the wait-and-see feature of the Statutory Rule and by the availability of reformation under Section 3.")
24. *Is there an exception to the all-or-nothing rule in the case of subclasses or specific sums to each member of the class?*	No specific state case or statute. See Unif. Statutory Rule Against Perpetuities § 1, 8B U.L.A. 257 (amended 1990) ("The specific-sum and sub-class doctrines are not superseded by this Act.")	No specific state case or statute. See Unif. Statutory Rule Against Perpetuities § 1, 8B U.L.A. 257 (amended 1990) ("The specific-sum and sub-class doctrines are not superseded by this Act.")	No specific state case or statute. See Unif. Statutory Rule Against Perpetuities § 1, 8B U.L.A. 257 (amended 1990) ("The specific-sum and sub-class doctrines are not superseded by this Act.")

Table 9
Rule Against Perpetuities

	FLORIDA	GEORGIA	HAWAII
25. *Is the infectious invalidity rule followed outside class gifts?*	No specific state case or statute. See Unif. Statutory Rule Against Perpetuities §1, 8B U.L.A. 256 (amended 1990) (explaining that "[t]he doctrine of infectious invalidity is superseded by this Act by Section 3, under which courts … are required to reform the disposition to approximate as closely as possible the transferor's … plan of distribution.")	Yes. Walker v. Bogle, 260 S.E.2d 338, 342 (Ga. 1979) (reversing a lower court decision that found a testatrix' dispositive plan void through the doctrine of "infectious invalidity" because the court only invalidated two, less important, parts of the will). But see Unif. Statutory Rule Against Perpetuities §1, 8B U.L.A. 256 (amended 1990) (explaining that "[t]he doctrine of infectious invalidity is superseded by this Act by Section 3, under which courts … are required to reform the disposition to approximate as closely as possible the transferor's … plan of distribution.")	No specific state case or statute. See Unif. Statutory Rule Against Perpetuities §1, 8B U.L.A. 256 (amended 1990) (explaining that "[t]he doctrine of infectious invalidity is superseded by this Act by Section 3, under which courts … are required to reform the disposition to approximate as closely as possible the transferor's … plan of distribution.")

Table 9
Rule Against Perpetuities

	FLORIDA	GEORGIA	HAWAII
26. *Is there a rule against the suspension of the power of alienation? If so, how is it stated?*	See Harbour Watch Homeowners Ass'n v. Derderian, 618 So. 2d 315, 316 (Fla. Dist. Ct. App. 1993) (discussing the rule against the restraint on alienation as precluding "only unlimited or absolute restraints on alienation")	Yes. Floyd v. Hoover, 234 S.E.2d 89, 92 (Ga. Ct. App. 1977). ("The power of alienation is necessarily incident to every estate in fee simple absolute and no one can create what is intended in law to be a fee simple absolute and at the same time deprive the owner of those rights and privileges which the law attaches to that estate.")	No specific state case or statute.
27. *Effective date.*	October 1, 1988, (§ 689.225(6)(c)), including powers unexercised on October 1, 1988, though created earlier (§ 689.225(6)(b)), *see also* #6, but the extension of the rule to trusts for 360 years only applies to trusts created after December 31, 2000. (§ 689.225(2)(f)) In Old Port Cove Condominium Ass'n One, Inc. v. Old Port Cove Holdings, Inc., 954 So. 2d 742, 745 (Fla. Dist. Ct. App. 2007), the court of appeals held that the current statute is fully retroactive in abrogating the common law rule against perpetuities. Quaere as to the 360-year provision for trusts.	May 1, 1990. *See also* #6.	June 18, 1992. *See also* #6.

[1] For questions #19-25, *see also* § 689.225(7) (noting that "no common-law rule against perpetuities or remoteness in vesting shall exist with respect to any interest or power").

Table 9
Rule Against Perpetuities

	IDAHO	ILLINOIS	INDIANA
1. *Which rule is in effect: the common law rule, the Uniform Statutory Rule Against Perpetuities (USRAP), other law, or none?*	None. Idaho Code § 55-111 ("[T]here shall be no rule against perpetuities applicable to real or personal property.")	Other. Qualified perpetual trusts as described in #3.(8) below allow for total avoidance of the rule. There are also other exceptions to the common law rule. (765 ILCS §§ 305/1 - 305/6)) Otherwise, the rule described in #2.b below applies.	USRAP. (§§ 32-17-8-1 - 32-17-8-6)
2. *a. Is the common law rule relevant to any interests?*	N/A	Yes.	Yes, but only as the starting point of the analysis.
b. What is the relevant rule?	N/A	"The rule against perpetuities as established for many years is that no interest in real estate is good unless it must vest, if at all, not later than twenty-one years and nine months after some life in being at the creation of the interest." (Spicer v. Moss, 100 N.E.2d 761, 771 (Ill. 1951); *see also* 305/2 ("This Act modifies the	A nonvested property interest is invalid unless: (1) When the interest is created, it is certain to vest or terminate no later than 21 years after the death of an individual then alive; or (2) The interest either vests or terminates within 90 years after its creation.

Table 9
Rule Against Perpetuities

IDAHO	ILLINOIS	INDIANA
	common law rule of property known as the rule against perpetuities, which, except as modified by statutes in force at the effective date of this Act and by this Act, shall remain in full force and effect.") As a general matter, a trust containing any limitation which, but for paragraph 30515(a), would violate the rule against perpetuities (as modified by statute) shall terminate at the expiration of a period of (A) 21 years after the death of the last to die of all of the beneficiaries of the instrument who were living at the date when the period of the rule against perpetuities commenced to run or (B) 21 years after that date if no beneficiary of the instrument was then living, unless events occur which cause an earlier termination in accordance with the terms of the instrument and then the principal shall be distributed as provided by the instrument. (305/5(a)) The rule does not apply to perpetual trusts. See #3. Based on 765 ILCS 305/5(a), (f), the violation of the rule does not void the trust ab initio. Other provisions establish the method for determining who receives what upon the termination of the trust. (765 ILCS 305/5(b)-(d))	(§32-17-8-3(a))

Table 9
Rule Against Perpetuities

	IDAHO	ILLINOIS	INDIANA
3. *Does the rule apply to other than private trusts?*	N/A	(a) The rule against perpetuities does not apply: (1) to any disposition of property or interest therein which, at the effective date of this Act, does not violate, or is exempted by statute from the operation of, the common law rule against perpetuities; (2) to powers of a trustee to sell, lease or mortgage property or to powers which relate to the administration or management of trust assets, including, without limitation, discretionary powers of a trustee to determine what receipts constitute principal and what receipts constitute income and powers to appoint a successor trustee; (3) to mandatory powers of a trustee to distribute income, or to discretionary powers of a trustee to distribute principal prior to termination of a trust, to a beneficiary having an interest in the principal which is irrevocably vested in quality and quantity;	Yes. The rule applies except to: (1) A nonvested property interest or a power of appointment arising out of a nondonative transfer, except a nonvested property interest or a power of appointment arising out of any of the following: (A) A premarital or postmarital agreement; (B) A separation or divorce settlement; (C) A spouse's election; (D) A similar arrangement arising out of a prospective, an existing, or a previous marital relationship between the parties; (E) A contract to make or not to revoke a will or trust; (F) A contract to exercise or not to exercise a power of appointment; (G) A transfer in satisfaction of a duty of support; (H) A reciprocal transfer. (2) A fiduciary's power relating to the administration or

Table 9

Rule Against Perpetuities

IDAHO	ILLINOIS	INDIANA
	(4) to discretionary powers of a trustee to allocate income and principal among beneficiaries, but no exercise of any such power after the expiration of the period of the rule against perpetuities is valid;	management of assets, including the power of a fiduciary to sell, lease, or mortgage property, and the power of a fiduciary to determine principal and income;
	(5) to leases to commence in the future or upon the happening of a future event, but no such lease shall be valid unless the term thereof actually commences in possession within 40 years from the date of execution of the lease;	(3) A power to appoint a fiduciary;
		(4) A discretionary power of a trustee to distribute principal before termination of a trust to a beneficiary having an indefeasibly vested interest in the income and principal;
	(6) to commitments (A) by a lessor to enter into a lease with a subtenant or with the holder of a leasehold mortgage or (B) by a lessee or sublessee to enter into a lease with the holder of a mortgage;	(5) A nonvested property interest held by a charity, government or governmental agency or subdivision, if the nonvested property interest is preceded by an interest held by another charity, government or governmental agency or subdivision;
	(7) to options in gross or to preemptive rights in the nature of a right of first refusal, but no option in gross shall be valid for more than 40 years from the date of its creation; or	(6) A nonvested property interest in or a power of appointment with respect to a trust or other property arrangement forming part of a pension, a profit

Table 9
Rule Against Perpetuities

IDAHO	ILLINOIS	INDIANA
	(8) to qualified perpetual trusts as defined in 765 ILCS 305/3. Qualified perpetual trusts are trust created by written instrument executed on or after January 1, 1998, including amendments to a prior-executed instrument or by way of the exercise of a power of appointment granted or amended after that date. The trust, by its terms, provides that the rule does not apply and the trustee or other person "to whom the power is granted" has the power to sell property, where this required power of sale is not limited by the trust instrument or law for any period of time beyond the period of the rule against perpetuities. (305(3)) (305/4(a))	sharing, a stock bonus, a health, a disability, a death benefit, an income deferral, or other current or deferred benefit plan for one (1) or more employees, independent contractors, or their beneficiaries or spouses, to which contributions are made for the purpose of distributing to or for the benefit of the participants or their beneficiaries or spouses the property, income, or principal in the trust or other property arrangement, except a nonvested property interest or a power of appointment that is created by an election of a participant or a beneficiary or spouse. (7) A property interest, power of appointment or arrangement that was not subject to the common-law rule against perpetuities or is excluded by another Indiana statute. (8) A:

Table 9
Rule Against Perpetuities

Top of INDIANA column (continued):

(A) provision for the accumulation of an amount of the income of a trust estate reasonably necessary for the upkeep, repair, or proper management of the subject of the estate;

(B) direction in a trust that provides for the allocation wholly or in part to the principal of the trust of stock dividends or stock rights derived from shares held in a trust;

(C) provision for a sinking or reserve fund; or

(D) statutory provision directing an accumulation.

(§32-17-8-2)

	IDAHO	ILLINOIS	INDIANA
4. Does the rule invalidate the interest at its creation, or is the rule revised by a wait-and-see approach?	N/A	At its creation for wills (Spicer v. Moss, 100 N.E.2d 761, 771 (Ill. 1951).) Wait-and-see for trusts. (305/5(a))	Wait-and-see. (§32-17-8-3(a))
5. Can the trust be reformed?	Yes. [N]o trust heretofore or hereafter created, either testamentary or inter vivos, shall be declared void, but shall be so construed as to eliminate parts violating the above provisions	No general reformation, but see #2b.	Yes, but only if one of the following conditions is met: (1) a nonvested property interest or a power of appointment becomes invalid under section 3 of this chapter (see #2);

Table 9
Rule Against Perpetuities

	IDAHO	ILLINOIS	INDIANA
	[rule against perpetuities or rule against the suspension of power of alienation]. (§ 55-111A(1))		(2) a class gift is not but might become invalid under section 3 of this chapter and the time has arrived when the share of any class member is to take effect in possession or enjoyment; or (3) a nonvested property interest that is not validated by section 3(a)(1) of this chapter, that is, the traditional common law rule, can vest but not within ninety (90) years after the interest's creation. (§ 32-17-8-6) *See also* #27.
6. *If yes to 5., under what theory?*	[I]n such a way that the testators or trustors wishes are carried out to the greatest extent permitted by this section. (§ 55-111A(1))	See #5.	A court shall reform a disposition in the manner that most closely preserves the transferor's plan of distribution and is within the ninety (90) years allowed by section 3(a)(2), 3(b)(2), or 3(c)(2) of this chapter. (§ 32-17-8-6) *See also* § 32-17-8-1(b) ("If a nonvested property interest or a power of appointment was created before May 8, 1991, and: (1) is determined in a judicial proceeding commenced on or after May 8, 1991, to violate this state's rule against perpetuities as that rule existed before May 8, 1991; or (2) may violate this state's rule against perpetuities as that rule existed before May 8, 1991;

Table 9
Rule Against Perpetuities

	IDAHO	ILLINOIS	INDIANA
			a court upon the petition of an interested person shall reform the disposition by inserting a savings clause that most closely preserves the transferor's plan of distribution and is within the limits of the rule against perpetuities applicable when the nonvested property interest or power of appointment was created.")
7. *When is a general testamentary power of appointment invalid?*	N/A	With respect to wills, see Unif. Statutory Rule Against Perpetuities §1, 8B U.L.A. 248 (amended 1990) ("Under the Common-law Rule . . . a nongeneral power (whether or not presently exercisable) or a general testamentary power is invalid as of the time of its creation if it might not terminate (by irrevocable exercise or otherwise) within a life in being plus 21 years.")	A general testamentary power of appointment is invalid unless one of the following conditions is satisfied: (1) When the power is created, it is certain to be irrevocably exercised or otherwise to terminate no later than 21 years after the death of an individual then alive. (2) The power is irrevocably exercised or otherwise terminates within 90 years after its creation. (§32-17-8-3(c))

Table 9
Rule Against Perpetuities

	IDAHO	ILLINOIS	INDIANA
8. *Same, but nongeneral testamentary power.*	N/A	See #7.	A nongeneral power of appointment . . . is invalid unless one of the following conditions is satisfied: (1) When the power is created, it is certain to be irrevocably exercised or otherwise to terminate no later than 21 years after the death of an individual then alive. (2) The power is irrevocably exercised or otherwise terminates within 90 years after its creation. (§ 32-17-8-3(c))
9. *Same, but general power, whether testamentary or inter vivos, not presently exercisable because of a condition precedent.*	N/A	*See* Unif. Statutory Rule Against Perpetuities § 1, 8B U.L.A. 248 (amended 1990) ("Under the Common-law Rule, a *general power not presently exercisable because of a condition precedent* is invalid as of the time of its creation if the condition *might* neither be satisfied nor become impossible to satisfy with a life in being plus 21 years.")	A general power of appointment not presently exercisable because of a condition precedent is invalid unless one of the following conditions is satisfied: (1) When the power is created, the condition precedent is certain to be satisfied or become impossible to satisfy no later than 21 years after the death of an individual then alive. (2) The condition precedent either is satisfied or becomes impossible to satisfy within 90 years after its creation. (§ 32-17-8-3(b))

Table 9
Rule Against Perpetuities

	IDAHO	ILLINOIS	INDIANA
10. *Same, but nongeneral inter vivos power.*	N/A	See #7.	See #8.
11. *Is a period of gestation added to the perpetuity period?*	N/A	Yes. (See #2a.)	No. The possibility that a child will be born to a person after that person's death is disregarded. (§32-17-8-3(d)) *See also* Unif. Statutory Rule Against Perpetuities §1, 8B U.L.A. 243, 243 (amended 1990) ("[T]he possibility that a child will be born to [a testator] after his death must be disregarded; and the possibility that a child will be born to any of [the testator's] descendants after their deaths must also be disregarded. Note, however, that the rule of subsection (d) does not apply to the question of the entitlement of an after-born child to take a beneficial interest in the trust").

Table 9
Rule Against Perpetuities

	IDAHO	ILLINOIS	INDIANA
12. *What is the treatment of a "later of the traditional rule or 90 years" clause? See UPC 2-901(e).*	N/A	N/A	Indiana's USRAP applies to clauses that contain that language. (§ 32-17-8-5(a)). But *see* § 32-17-8-5(b) ("[T]he portion of the clause that pertains to the period that exceeds twenty-one (21) years or that might exceed twenty-one (21) years after the death of the survivor of lives in being at the creation of the trust or other property arrangement is not valid. The court shall construe the clause as becoming effective upon: (1) the death of; or (2) the expiration of the period not exceeding twenty-one (21) years after the death of; the survivor of the specified lives in being at the creation of the trust or other property arrangement."

Table 9
Rule Against Perpetuities

	IDAHO	ILLINOIS	INDIANA
13. *When is an interest created by the exercise of a general testamentary power deemed created?*	N/A	Northern Trust Co. v. Porter, 13 N.E.2d 487, 491 (Ill. 1938) ("[T]he validity of an appointment, under a general testamentary power, must be determined by considering the donee's appointment as part of the instrument created by the donor. Thus, we must look to see whether or not the remainders will vest in interest (although not necessarily in possession) within the period measured from the time of the creation of the power by the donor."). *See also* comment to Unif. Probate Code § 2-902(a) ("general principles of property law determine that a nonvested property interest or power of appointment created by will is created at the decedent's death"); Unif. Statutory Rule Against Perpetuities § 2, 8B U.L.A. 268 (amended 1990) (stating the same).	Except as provided in subsections (b) and (c) and in section 1(a) of this chapter, the time of creation of a nonvested property interest or a power of appointment is determined under general principles of property law. (§ 32-17-8-4(a)) The first of the excepted provisions states that as long as a person with a general power to become the unqualified beneficial owner has that power, the nonvested interest is created when the power terminates. The second of the excepted provisions states that a nonvested property interest, which arises from a transfer to an existing trust, is created when the nonvested property interest in the trust was created. (§ 32-17-8-4(b)–(c)) *See also* Unif. Statutory Rule Against Perpetuities § 2, 8B U.L.A. 268 (amended 1990) (explaining that "general principles of property law determine that the time . . . [of creation] is at the decedent's death.") *See generally* § 32-17-8-1(a) ("[A] nonvested property interest or a power of appointment created by the exercise of a power of appointment is created when the power is irrevocably exercised or when a revocable exercise becomes irrevocable.")

Table 9
Rule Against Perpetuities

	IDAHO	ILLINOIS	INDIANA
14. Same, but nongeneral testamentary power.	N/A	See #13.	See #13.

Table 9
Rule Against Perpetuities

	IDAHO	ILLINOIS	INDIANA
15. *Same, but general inter vivos power.*	N/A	*See* comment to Unif. Probate Code § 2-902(a) ("With respect to an intervivos transfer, an interest or power is created on the date the transfer becomes effective for purpose of property law generally, normally the date of delivery of the deed or funding of the trust."); Unif. Statutory Rule Against Perpetuities § 2, 8B U.L.A. 268 (stating the same).	Except as provided in subsections (b) and (c) and in section 1(a) of this chapter, the time of creation of a nonvested property interest or a power of appointment is determined under general principles of property law. (§ 32-17-8-4(a)) The first of the excepted provisions states that as long as a person with a general power to become the unqualified beneficial owner has that power, the nonvested interest is created when the power terminates. The second of the excepted provisions states that a nonvested property interest, which arises from a transfer to an existing trust, is created when the nonvested property interest in the trust was created. (§ 32-17-8-4(b)-(c)) *See also* Unif. Statutory Rule Against Perpetuities § 2, 8B U.L.A. 268 (amended 1990) (explaining that "the time when the interest or power is created is the date the transfer becomes effective for purposes of property law generally, normally the date of delivery of the deed"); Comment to Unif. Probate Code § 2-902(a) (stating same and adding "the funding of the trust" as "normally" the time when the interest is created). *See generally* § 32-17-8-1(a) ("For the purposes of this section, a nonvested

Table 9
Rule Against Perpetuities

	IDAHO	ILLINOIS	INDIANA
			property interest or a power of appointment created by the exercise of a power of appointment is created when the power is irrevocably exercised or when a revocable exercise becomes irrevocable.")
16. *Same, but nongeneral inter vivos power.*	N/A	See #15.	See #15.
17. *When is an interest created if the grantor of a trust has a power to revoke?*	N/A	When the maker of the instrument no longer has the power to revoke or to transfer or direct to be transferred to himself the entire legal or equitable ownership of the property or interest therein. (765 ILCS 305/4(b))	If there is a person who alone can exercise a power created by a governing instrument to become the unqualified beneficial owner of: (1) a nonvested property interest; or (2) a property interest subject to a power of appointment described in section 3(b) or 3(c) of this chapter;

Table 9
Rule Against Perpetuities

IDAHO	ILLINOIS	INDIANA
		the nonvested property interest or power of appointment is created when the power to become the unqualified beneficial owner terminates. (§ 32-17-8-4(b)) *See also* Unif. Statutory Rule Against Perpetuities § 2, 8B U.L.A. 268 (amended 1990) (explaining that "any nonvested property interest subject to [a power to revoke] is not created . . . until the power terminates (by release, expiration at the death of the donee, or otherwise"); Comment to Unif. Probate Code § 2-902(b) (noting that "nonvested property interest and powers of appointment created in [a revocable inter-vivos trust] are created when the power to revoke expires, usually at the settlor's death"). *See generally* § 32-17-8-1(a) ("[A] nonvested property interest or a power of appointment created by the exercise of a power of appointment is created when the power is irrevocably exercised or when a revocable exercise becomes irrevocable.")

Table 9
Rule Against Perpetuities

	IDAHO	ILLINOIS	INDIANA
18. *When does the period of the rule start re an interest contributed to an irrevocable trust? See UPC 2-902(c).*	N/A	*See* comment to Unif. Probate Code 2-902(c) ("Arguably, at common law, each transfer [to an existing irrevocable inter-vivos trust] starts the period of the Rule running anew as to each transfer.");	A nonvested property interest or a power of appointment arising from a transfer of property to a previously funded trust or other existing property arrangement is created when the nonvested property interest or power of appointment in the original contribution was created. (§32-17-8-4(c))
19. *Is there a conclusive presumption of fertility, that is, the "fertile octogenarian" rule?*	[T]here shall be no presumption that a person is capable of having children at any stage of adult life. (§55-111A(1))	No. Any person who has attained the age of 65 is deemed not capable of having a child. Evidence shall be admissible as to the capacity of having a child by a living person who has attained the age of 65 years. The possibility of adoption is disregarded. (305/4(c)(3))	No specific state case or statute. *See* Unif. Statutory Rule Against Perpetuities §1, 8B U.L.A. 256 (amended 1990) (holding that "[t]his principle is not superseded by this Act, and in view of new advances in medical science … [this] is not unrealistic."). *But see* C. P. Jhong, Annotation, *Modern Status of Presumption Against Possibility of Issue Being Extinct*, 98 A.L.R.2d 1285 (2003) (noting "a trend toward denying the conclusive or absolute nature of the presumption against the possibility of issue being extinct where there is competent evidence to the contrary has developed in the decisions, although some courts still adhere to the traditional view treating the presumption as conclusive or absolute").

Table 9
Rule Against Perpetuities

	IDAHO	ILLINOIS	INDIANA
20. *What is the earliest age a child is deemed capable of bearing a child? What is the impact of illegitimacy?*	Not specifically addressed. "Under the rule, courts must presume that living persons are capable of having or fathering children, no matter how young they are. See In re Graite's Will Trusts, [1949] 1 All E.R. 459, 460 (Ch.). Thus, the rule strikes down any interest whose vesting depends on the assertion that, for example, a toddler will not have children." (Keith L. Butler, Notes & Comments, *Long Live the Dead Hand: A Case for the Repeal of the Rule Against Perpetuities in Washington,* 75 Wash. L. Rev. 1237, 1246 n.78 (2000)).	13 years. (305/4(c)(3)(A))	Not specifically addressed by USRAP, but the reasoning is the same as set forth in the comment to section 1 of USRAP, 2, Technical Violations of the Common Law Rule. Wait and see will typically result in no violation. Nevertheless, the common law rule ordinarily will be applied initially. "Under the rule, courts must presume that living persons are capable of having or fathering children, no matter how young they are. *See* In re Graite's Will Trusts, [1949] 1 All E.R. 459, 460 (Ch.). Thus, the rule strikes down any interest whose vesting depends on the assertion that, for example, a toddler will not have children." (Keith L. Butler, Notes & Comments, *Long Live the Dead Hand: A Case for Repeal of the Rule Against Perpetuities in Washington,* 75 Wash. L. Rev. 1237, 1246 n.78 (2000)).
21. *Is the "unborn widow" rule observed?*	N/A	In determining whether an interest violates the rule against perpetuities: (1) it shall be presumed . . . (C) where the instrument creates an interest in the "widow," "widower," or "spouse" of another person, that the maker of the instrument intended to refer to a person who was living at the date that the period of the rule against perpetuities commences to run (305/4(c)(1)(C))	No specific state case or statute. See Unif. Statutory Rule Against Perpetuities §1, 8B U.L.A. 246 (amended 1990) (explaining that "[t]he chance that [an] interest will become invalid under the Statutory Rule is small" and so the unborn widow rule would rarely invalidate an interest); *see also* 61 Am Jur 2d *Perpetuities and Restraints on Alienation* §39 (2013) (noting the same).

Table 9
Rule Against Perpetuities

	IDAHO	ILLINOIS	INDIANA
22. *Does the "slothful executor" rule apply, i.e. an administrative contingency clause providing for a "distribution to, e.g., those issue living at the time of the satisfaction of the administrative condition precedent?"*	N/A	In determining whether an interest violates the rule against perpetuities: (1) it shall be presumed . . . (B) in the case of an interest conditioned upon the probate of a will, the appointment of an executor, administrator or trustee, the completion of the administration of an estate, the payment of debts, the sale or distribution of property, the determination of federal or state tax liabilities or the happening of any administrative contingency, that the contingency must occur, if at all, within the period of the rule against perpetuities (305/4(c)(1)(B)) *See also* 310/1, providing that the vesting of any limitation of property is not deemed deferred for purposes of the rule against perpetuities merely because the limitation is made to the estate of a person or to a personal representative, or to a trustee under a will, or to take effect on the probate of a will. The provision only applies to limitations created after the effective date, 1951.	No specific state case or statute. *See* Unif. Statutory Rule Against Perpetuities §1, 8B U.L.A. 245 (amended 1990) (Under USRAP, an "interest becomes invalid only if it remains in existence and nonvested 90 years after [the testator's] death. Since it is almost certain that the final distribution of [an] estate will occur well within this 90-year period, the chance that [an] interest will be invalid is negligible.")

Table 9
Rule Against Perpetuities

	IDAHO	ILLINOIS	INDIANA
23. *Does the all-or-nothing rule apply to class gifts?*	N/A	Case law unclear. *See generally* Aldendifer v. Wylie, 138 N.E. 143, 146 (Ill. 1923) ("Where a will contains separate provisions, some of which are valid and others invalid, the valid ones will be upheld if they can be separated from the invalid and still give effect to the intention of the testator and not interfere with the general testamentary scheme.")	No specific state case or statute. *See* Unif. Statutory Rule Against Perpetuities §1, 8B U.L.A. 257 (amended 1990) ("Although this Act does not supersede the basic idea of the much-maligned 'all-or-nothing' rule, the evils sometimes attributed to it are substantially if not entirely eliminated by the wait-and-see feature of the Statutory Rule and by the availability of reformation under Section 3.").

Table 9
Rule Against Perpetuities

	IDAHO	ILLINOIS	INDIANA
24. *Is there an exception to the all-or-nothing rule in the case of subclasses or specific sums to each member of the class?*	N/A	*See* Unif. Statutory Rule Against Perpetuities §2, 8B U.L.A. 257 ("The common law also recognizes a doctrine called the specific-sum doctrine which is derived from Storrs v. Benbow, 3 De G.M. & G. 390, 43 Eng. Rep 153 (Ch. 1853), and states: If a specified sum of money is to be paid to each member of a class, the interest of each class member is entitled to separate treatment and is valid or invalid under the Rule on its own. The common law also recognizes a doctrine called the sub-class doctrine, which is derived from Cattlin v. Brown, 11 Hare 372, 68 Eng. Rep. 1318 (Ch. 1853), and states: If the ultimate takers are not described as a single class but rather as a group of separate subclasses, and if the share to which each separate subclass is entitled will finally be determined within the period of the Rule, the gifts to the different subclasses are separate for the purpose of the Rule.").	No specific state case or statute. *See* Unif. Statutory Rule Against Perpetuities §1, 8B U.L.A. 257 (amended 1990) ("The specific-sum and sub-class doctrines are not superseded by this Act.").

Table 9
Rule Against Perpetuities

	IDAHO	ILLINOIS	INDIANA
25. *Is the infectious invalidity rule followed outside class gifts?*	N/A	*See* 1. above.	No specific state case or statute. *See* Unif. Statutory Rule Against Perpetuities §1, 8B U.L.A. 256 (amended 1990) (explaining that "[t]he doctrine of infectious invalidity is superseded by this Act by Section 3, under which courts . . . are required to *reform* the disposition to approximate as closely as possible the transferor's . . . plan of distribution.")
26. *Is there a rule against the suspension of the power of alienation? If so, how is it stated?*	Yes. The absolute power of alienation of property cannot be suspended by any limitation or condition whatever, for a longer period than during the continuance of the lives of the persons in being at the creation of the limitation or condition, and 25 years thereafter (§55-111A(1)). However, subsection (1) does "not limit transfers, outright or in trust, for charitable purposes or transfers to charitable entit ies." (§55-111A(4)) *See also* Estate of Kirk v. Seideman, 907 P.2d 794, 805 (Idaho 1995) (the rule against the suspension of power of alienation does not apply to charitable trusts).	Case law unclear. *See* Green v. Gawne, 47 N.E.2d 86, 93 (Ill. 1943) (suggesting that restraints on alienation will be invalidated depending on the circumstances of each particular case or instrument).	Yes. *See* Quilliam v. Union Trust Co., 142 N.E. 214, 216 (Ind. 1924) (invaliding part of a will that suspended the power of alienation of real estate for 50 years).

Table 9
Rule Against Perpetuities

	IDAHO	ILLINOIS	INDIANA
27. *Effective date.*	N/A	September 22, 1969. Qualified perpetual trusts that avoid the rule against perpetuities must have been created by instrument executed on or after Jan. 1, 1998, or by an exercise of a power granted after that date. See #3.(8) above.	May 8, 1991 (§ 32-17-8-1(a)) *See also #6.*

Table 9
Rule Against Perpetuities

	IOWA	KANSAS	KENTUCKY
1. *Which rule is in effect: the common law rule, the Uniform Statutory Rule Against Perpetuities (USRAP), other law, or none?*	Variation of wait-and-see. (Iowa Code § 558.68)	USRAP. (Kan. Stat. Ann. §§ 59-3401 - 59-3408)	None. (Kan. Rev. Stat. Ann. § 381.224 ("An interest created in real or personal property shall not be void by reason of any rule against perpetuities, whether the common law rule or otherwise. The common law rule against perpetuities shall not be in force in this commonwealth.")) The rule against perpetuities is no longer in force with respect to future property interests or powers of appointment created on or after July 15, 2010, including a property interest or power of appointment created pursuant to the exercise of a power of appointment under an instrument executed prior to July 15, 2010. The rule against perpetuities also does not apply to a future property interest or power of appointment that is created pursuant to the laws of any state that does not have a rule against perpetuities in force, that is not covered by any previously existing rule against perpetuities, and to which, after July 15, 2010, the laws of Kentucky are made applicable by transfer of the situs of the trust to Kentucky, by a change of "law governing a trust instrument" to Kentucky law, or otherwise. In addition, a procedure is established for reforming interests and powers to qualify under the applicable law if the new law does not apply.

Table 9
Rule Against Perpetuities

		IOWA	KANSAS	KENTUCKY
2.	a.	*Is the common law rule relevant to any interests?*	Yes, but only as the starting point of the analysis.	Yes, but only as the starting point of the analysis.	No.
	b.	*What is the relevant rule?*	(1) A nonvested interest in property is not valid unless it must vest, if at all, within twenty-one years after one or more lives in being at the creation of the interest and any relevant period of gestation.	A nonvested property interest is invalid unless: (1) When the interest is created, it is certain to vest or terminate no later than 21 years after the death of an individual then alive; or	See the beginning of question 1 for the statement of the statute. The common law rule against perpetuities has been abrogated. (§ 381.215) Specifically, section 381.216 introduces a wait and-see rule to the extent that a non-vested property interest or power of appointment violates the rule against perpetuities at its creation. See #6.

Finally, if an instrument provides for vesting within the "common law rule against perpetuities," the provision shall be construed as having the new law described above apply unless the provision is determined "by the court" to have been included for reasons other than protecting the interest against a violation of the rule against perpetuities. The term "common law rule against perpetuities" includes KRS 381.215, 381.216 and 381.217 prior to their repeal on July 15, 2010. (Ky. Rev. Stat. Ann. § 321.226)

Table 9
Rule Against Perpetuities

	IOWA	KANSAS	KENTUCKY
	(2) In determining whether a nonvested interest would violate the rule against perpetuities in 1, the period of the rule is measured by actual events rather than by possible events, in any case in which that would validate the interest. (§ 558.68)	(2) The interest either vests or terminates within 90 years after its creation. (§ 59-3401(a))	
3. *Does the rule apply to other than private trusts?*	No. The rule does not apply to charitable trusts. Kositzky v. Monfore (In re Estate of Keenan), 519 N.W.2d 376 (Iowa 1994).	Yes. The rule applies except to: (1) A nonvested property interest or a power of appointment arising out of a nondonative transfer, except a nonvested property interest or a power of appointment arising out of (i) a premarital or post-marital agreement, (ii) a separation or divorce settlement, (iii) a spouse's election, (iv) a similar arrangement arising out of a prospective, existing or previous marital relationshi between the parties, (v) a contract to make or not to revoke a will or trust, (vi) a contract to exercise or not to exercise a power of appointment, (vii) a transfer in satisfaction of a duty of support, or (viii) a reciprocal transfer;	Not applicable.

Table 9
Rule Against Perpetuities

IOWA	KANSAS	KENTUCKY
	(2) A fiduciary's power relating to the administration or management of assets, including the power of a fiduciary to sell, lease or mortgage property, and the power of a fiduciary to determine principal and income;	
	(3) A power to appoint a fiduciary;	
	(4) A discretionary power of a trustee to distribute principal before termination of a trust to a beneficiary having an indefeasibly vested interest in the income and principal;	
	(5) A nonvested property interest held by a charity, government or governmental agency or subdivision, if the nonvested property interest is preceded by an interest held by another charity, government or governmental agency or subdivision;	

Table 9
Rule Against Perpetuities

	IOWA	KANSAS	KENTUCKY
		(6) A nonvested property interest in or a power of appointment with respect to a trust or other property arrangement forming part of a pension, profit sharing, stock bonus, health, disability, death benefit, income deferral or other current or deferred benefit plan for one or more employees, independent contractors or the beneficiaries or spouses, to which contributions are made for the purpose of distributing to or for the benefit of the participants or their beneficiaries or spouses the property, income or principal in the trust or other property arrangement, except a nonvested property interest or a power of appointment that is created by an election of a participant or a beneficiary or spouse; or (7) A property interest, power of appointment or arrangement that was not subject to the common-law rule against perpetuities or is excluded by another statute of this state. (§ 59-3404)	
4. *Does the rule invalidate the interest at its creation, or is the rule revised by a wait-and-see approach?*	Wait-and-see. (§ 558.68(2)(a))	Wait-and-see. (§ 59-3401(a)(2))	Not applicable.

Table 9
Rule Against Perpetuities

	IOWA	KANSAS	KENTUCKY
5. *Can the trust be reformed?*	Yes. (§ 558.68(3)) *See also #27.*	Yes, but only if one of the following conditions applies: (1) A nonvested property interest or a power of appointment becomes invalid under K.S.A. 59-3401, statutory rule against perpetuities; (2) a class gift is not but might become invalid under K.S.A. 59-3401, statutory rule against perpetuities, and the time has arrived when the share of any class member is to take effect in possession or enjoyment; or (3) a nonvested property interest that is not validated by subsection (a)(1)of K.S.A. 59-3401, that is, the traditional common law rule, can vest but not within 90 years after its creation. (§ 59-3403)	Yes. (§ 381.216) *See also #6 and 27.*

Table 9
Rule Against Perpetuities

	IOWA	*KANSAS*	*KENTUCKY*
6. *If yes to 5., under what theory?*	[J]udicially reformed to most closely approximate the intention of the creator of the interest in order that the nonvested interest will vest, even though it may not become possessory, within the period of the rule. (§ 558.68(3))	A court shall reform a disposition in the manner that most closely approximates the transferor's manifested plan of distribution and is within the 90 years allowed by subsections (a)(2), (b)(2) or (c)(2) of K.S.A. 59-3401. (§ 59-3403) *See also* § 59-3405(b) ("If a nonvested property interest or a power of appointment was created before the effective date of this act and is determined in a judicial proceeding, commenced on or after the effective date of this act, to violate this state's rule against perpetuities as that rule existed before the effective date of this act, a court upon the petition of an interested person may reform the disposition in the manner that most closely approximates the transferor's manifested plan of distribution and is within the limits of the rule against perpetuities applicable when the nonvested property interest or power of appointment was created.")	With respect to a nonvested property interest or a power of appointment created before or after July 15, 2010, which is determined in a judicial proceeding commenced on or after July 15, 2010, to violate Kentucky's rule against perpetuities as that rule existed at the time of creation, a court upon the petition of an interested person may reform the disposition in the manner that most closely approximates the transferor's manifested plan of disposition and is within the limits of the rule against perpetuities applicable when the nonvested property interest or power of appointment was created. (§ 381.226(2))

Table 9
Rule Against Perpetuities

	IOWA	KANSAS	KENTUCKY
7. *When is a general testamentary power of appointment invalid?*	*See* Unif. Statutory Rule Against Perpetuities §1, 8B U.L.A. 248 (amended 1990) ("Under the Common-law Rule . . . a *nongeneral power* (whether or not presently exercisable) or a *general testamentary power* is invalid as of the time of its creation if it *might* not terminate (by irrevocable exercise or otherwise) within a life in being plus 21 years.")	A general testamentary power of appointment is invalid unless one of the following conditions is satisfied: (1) When the power is created, it is certain to be irrevocably exercised or otherwise to terminate no later than 21 years after the death of an individual then alive. (2) The power is irrevocably exercised or otherwise terminates within 90 years after its creation. (§ 59-3401(c))	Not applicable.
8. *Same, but nongeneral testamentary power.*	*See* #7.	A nongeneral power of appointment . . . is invalid unless one of the following conditions is satisfied: (1) When the power is created, it is certain to be irrevocably exercised or otherwise to terminate no later than 21 years after the death of an individual then alive. (2) The power is irrevocably exercised or otherwise terminates within 90 years after its creation. (§ 59-3401(c))	Not applicable.

Table 9
Rule Against Perpetuities

	IOWA	KANSAS	KENTUCKY
9. *Same, but general power, whether testamentary or inter vivos, not presently exercisable because of a condition precedent.*	*See* Unif. Statutory Rule Against Perpetuities § 1, 8B U.L.A. 248 (amended 1990) ("Under the Common-law Rule, a *general power not presently exercisable because of a condition precedent* is invalid if the condition *might* neither be satisfied nor become impossible to satisfy with a life in being plus 21 years.")	A general power of appointment not presently exercisable because of a condition precedent is invalid unless one of the following conditions is satisfied: (1) When the power is created, the condition precedent is certain to be satisfied or become impossible to satisfy no later than 21 years after the death of an individual then alive. (2) The condition precedent either is satisfied or becomes impossible to satisfy within 90 years after its creation. (§ 59-3401(b))	Not applicable.
10. *Same, but nongeneral inter vivos power.*	See #7.	See #8.	See #7.

Table 9
Rule Against Perpetuities

	IOWA	KANSAS	KENTUCKY
11. *Is a period of gestation added to the perpetuity period?*	Yes, any relevant period of gestation is added. (§ 558.68(1))	No. The possibility that a child will be born to a person after that person's death is disregarded. (§ 59-3401(d)) *See also* Unif. Statutory Rule Against Perpetuities § 1, 8B U.L.A. 243, 243 (amended 1990) ("[T]he possibility that a child will be born to [a testator] after his death must be disregarded; and the possibility that a child will be born to any of [the testator's] descendants after their deaths must also be disregarded. Note, however, that the rule of subsection (d) does *not* apply to the question of the entitlement of an after-born child to take a beneficial interest in the trust").	Not applicable.
12. *What is the treatment of a "later of the traditional rule or 90 years" clause? See UPC 2-901(e).*	N/A	That language is inoperative to the extent it produces a period of time that exceeds 21 years after the death of the survivor of the specified lives. (§ 59-3401(e))	N/A

Table 9
Rule Against Perpetuities

	IOWA	KANSAS	KENTUCKY
13. *When is an interest created by the exercise of a general testamentary power deemed created?*	*See* comment to Unif. Probate Code § 2-902(a) ("general principles of property law determine that a nonvested property interest or power of appointment created by will is created at the decedent's death"); Unif. Statutory Rule Against Perpetuities § 2, 8B U.L.A. 268 (amended 1990) (stating the same).	Except as provided in subsections (b) and (c) and in subsection (a) of K.S.A. 59-3405, the time of creation of a nonvested property interest or a power of appointment is determined under general principles of property law (§ 59-3402(a)) The first of the excepted provisions states that as long as a person with a general power to become the unqualified beneficial owner has that power, the nonvested interest is created when the power terminates. The second of the excepted provisions states that a nonvested property interest, which arises from a transfer to an existing trust, is created when the nonvested property interest in the trust is created. (§ 59-3402(b)-(c)) *See also* Unif. Statutory Rule Against Perpetuities § 2, 8B U.L.A. 268 (amended 1990) (explaining that "general principles of property law determine that the time … . [of creation] is at the decedent's death.") *See generally* § 59-3405(a) ("[A] nonvested property interest or a power of appointment created by the exercise of a power of appointment is created when the power is irrevocably exercised or when a revocable exercise becomes irrevocable.")	For purposes of this section only, a future property interest or a power of appointment is created when the power is irrevocably exercised or when a revocable exercise becomes irrevocable. (§ 381.226(3))

Table 9
Rule Against Perpetuities

	IOWA	KANSAS	KENTUCKY
14. *Same, but nongeneral testamentary power.*	See #13.	See #13.	See #13.

Table 9
Rule Against Perpetuities

IOWA	KANSAS	KENTUCKY
15. *Same, but general inter vivos power.*		
See comment to Unif. Probate Code §2-902(a) ("With respect to an intervivos transfer, an interest or power is created on the date the transfer becomes effective for purpose of property law generally, normally the date of delivery of the deed or funding of the trust."); Unif. Statutory Rule Against Perpetuities §2, 8B U.L.A. 268 (stating the same).	Except as provided in subsections (b) and (c) and in subsection (a) of K.S.A. 59-3405, the time of creation of a nonvested property interest or a power of appointment is determined under general principles of property law (§59-3402(a)) The first of the excepted provisions states that as long as a person with a general power to become the unqualified beneficial owner has that power, the nonvested interest is created when the power terminates. The second of the excepted provisions states that a nonvested property interest, which arises from a transfer to an existing trust, is created when the nonvested property interest in the trust was created. (§59-3402(b)-(c)) *See also* Unif. Statutory Rule Against Perpetuities §2, 8B U.L.A. 268 (amended 1990) (explaining that "the time when the interest or power is created is the date the transfer becomes effective for purposes of property law generally, normally the date of delivery of the deed"); Comment to Unif. Probate Code §2-902(a) (stating same and adding "the funding of the trust" as "normally" the time when the interest is created). *See generally* §59-3405(a) ("For the purposes of this section, a nonvested	*See* 13. above.

Table 9
Rule Against Perpetuities

IOWA	KANSAS	KENTUCKY
	property interest or a power of appointment created by the exercise of a power of appointment is created when the power is irrevocably exercised or when a revocable exercise becomes irrevocable.").	
See #15.	See #15.	See #13.
16. *Same, but nongeneral inter vivos power.*		

Table 9
Rule Against Perpetuities

	IOWA	KANSAS	KENTUCKY
17. *When is an interest created if the grantor of a trust has a power to revoke?*	*See* comment to Unif. Probate Code § 2-902(b) (noting that "nonvested property interests and powers of appointment created in [a revocable inter-vivos trust] are created when the power to revoke expires, usually at the settlor's death"); Unif. Statutory Rule Against Perpetuities § 2, 8B U.L.A. 268 (amended 1990) (explaining that "any nonvested property interest subject to [a power to revoke] is not created . . . until the power terminates (by release, expiration at the death of the donee, or otherwise").	For purposes of this act, if there is a person who alone can exercise a power created by a governing instrument to become the unqualified beneficial owner of (i) a nonvested property interest or (ii) a property interest subject to a power of appointment described in subsection (b) or (c) of K.S.A. 59-3401, the nonvested property interest or power of appointment is created when the power to become the unqualified beneficial owner terminates. For purposes of this act, a joint power with respect to community property or to marital property under the uniform marital property act held by individuals married to each other is a power exercisable by one person alone. (§ 59-3402(b)) *See also* Unif. Statutory Rule Against Perpetuities § 2, 8B U.L.A. 268 (amended 1990) (explaining that "any nonvested property interest subject to [a power to revoke] is not created . . . until the power terminates (by release, expiration at the death of the donee, or otherwise"); Comment to Unif. Probate Code § 2-902(b) (noting that "nonvested property interest and powers of appointment created in [a revocable inter-vivos trust] are created when the power to revoke expires, usually at the settlor's death"). *See generally* § 59-3405(a) ("A	*See* #13.

Table 9
Rule Against Perpetuities

	IOWA	KANSAS	KENTUCKY
		nonvested property interest or a power of appointment created by the exercise of a power of appointment is created when the power is irrevocably exercised or when a revocable exercise becomes irrevocable.")	Not applicable.
18. *When does the period of the rule start re an interest contributed to an irrevocable trust? See UPC 2-902(c).*	*See* comment to Unif. Probate Code 2-902(c) ("Arguably, at common law, each transfer [to an existing irrevocable inter-vivos trust] starts the period of the Rule running anew as to each transfer.").	A nonvested property interest or a power of appointment arising from a transfer of property to a previously funded trust or other existing property arrangement is created when the nonvested property interest or power of appointment in the original contribution was created. (§ 59-3402(c))	

Table 9
Rule Against Perpetuities

	IOWA	KANSAS	KENTUCKY
19. Is there a conclusive presumption of fertility that is, the "fertile octogenarian" rule?	See, e.g., Arkansas, question #19.	No specific state case or statute.[1] See Unif. Statutory Rule Against Perpetuities §1, 8B U.L.A. 256 (amended 1990) (holding that "[t]his principle is not superseded by this Act, and in view of new advances in medical science . . . [this] is not unrealistic."). But see C. P. Jhong, Annotation, Modern Status of Presumption Against Possibility of Issue Being Extinct, 98 A.L.R.2d 1285 (2003) (noting "a trend toward denying the conclusive or absolute nature of the presumption against the possibility of issue being extinct where there is competent evidence to the contrary has developed in the decisions, although some courts still adhere to the traditional view treating the presumption as conclusive or absolute").	Not applicable.

Table 9
Rule Against Perpetuities

	IOWA	KANSAS	KENTUCKY
20. *What is the earliest age a child is deemed capable of bearing a child? What is the impact of illegitimacy?*	"Under the rule, courts must presume that living persons are capable of having or fathering children, no matter how young they are. See In re Graite's Will Trusts, [1949] 1 All E.R. 459, 460 (Ch.). Thus, the rule strikes down any interest whose vesting depends on the assertion that, for example, a toddler will not have children." (Keith L. Butler, Notes & Comments, *Long Live the Dead Hand: A Case for Repeal of the Rule Against Perpetuities in Washington*, 75 Wash. L. Rev. 1237, 1246 n.78 (2000)).	Not specifically addressed by USRAP, but the reasoning is the same as set forth in the comment to section 1 of USRAP, 2, Technical Violations of the Common Law Rule. Wait and see will typically result in no violation. Nevertheless, the common law rule ordinarily will be applied initially. "Under the rule, courts must presume that living persons are capable of having or fathering children, no matter how young they are. See In re Graite's Will Trusts, [1949] 1 All E.R. 459, 460 (Ch.). Thus, the rule strikes down any interest whose vesting depends on the assertion that, for example, a toddler will not have children." (Keith L. Butler, Notes & Comments, *Long Live the Dead Hand: A Case for Repeal of the Rule Against Perpetuities in Washington*, 75 Wash. L. Rev. 1237, 1246 n.78 (2000)).	Not applicable.
21. *Is the "unborn widow" rule observed?*	*See, e.g.,* Arkansas, question #21.	No specific state case or statute. *See* Unif. Statutory Rule Against Perpetuities § 1, 8B U.L.A. 246 (amended 1990) (explaining that "[t]he chance that [an] interest will become invalid under the Statutory Rule is small" and so the unborn widow rule would rarely invalidate an interest); *see also* 61 Am. Jur.2d *Perpetuities and Restraints on Alienation* § 39 (2013) (noting the same).	Not applicable.

Table 9
Rule Against Perpetuities

	IOWA	KANSAS	KENTUCKY
22. Does the "slothful executor" rule apply, i.e., an administrative contingency clause providing for a "distribution to, e.g., those issue living at the time of the satisfaction of the administrative condition precedent?"	See, e.g., California, question #22.	No specific state case or statute. See Unif. Statutory Rule Against Perpetuities § 1, 8B U.L.A. 245 (amended 1990) (Under USRAP, an "interest becomes invalid only if it remains in existence and nonvested 90 years after [the testator's] death. Since it is almost certain that the final distribution of [an] estate will occur well within this 90-year period, the chance that [an] interest will be invalid is negligible.")	Not applicable.
23. Does the all-or-nothing rule apply to class gifts?	See, e.g., California, question #23.	Yes. Beverlin v. First Nat'l Bank, 98 P.2d 200, 204 (Kan. 1940) (upholding the principle that "if the interest of any potential member of a class can by any possibility vest too remotely the entire class gift fails"). See also Unif. Statutory Rule Against Perpetuities § 1, 8B U.L.A. 257 (amended 1990) ("Although this Act does not supersede the basic idea of the much-maligned 'all-or-nothing' rule, the evils sometimes attributed to it are substantially if not entirely eliminated by the wait-and-see feature of the Statutory Rule and by the availability of reformation under Section 3.")	Not applicable.

Table 9
Rule Against Perpetuities

	IOWA	KANSAS	KENTUCKY
24. Is there an exception to the all-or-nothing rule in the case of subclasses or specific sums to each member of the class?	*See* Unif. Statutory Rule Against Perpetuities §2, 8B U.L.A. 257 ("The common law also recognizes a doctrine called the specific-sum doctrine which is derived from Storrs v. Benbow, 3 De G.M. & G. 390, 43 Eng. Rep. 153 (Ch. 1853), and states: If a specified sum of money is to be paid to each member of a class, the interest of each class member is entitled to separate treatment and is valid or invalid under the Rule on its own. The common law also recognizes a doctrine called the sub-class doctrine, which is derived from Cattlin v. Brown, 11 Hare 372, 68 Eng. Rep. 1318 (Ch. 1853), and states: If the ultimate takers are not described as a single class but rather as a group of separate subclasses, and if the share to which each separate subclass is entitled will finally be determined within the period of the Rule, the gifts to the different subclasses are separate for the purpose of the Rule.").	*See* Unif. Statutory Rule Against Perpetuities §1, 8B U.L.A. 257 (amended 1990) ("The specific-sum and sub-class doctrines are not superseded by this Act.")	Not applicable.

9138

Table 9
Rule Against Perpetuities

	IOWA	KANSAS	KENTUCKY
25. Is the *infectious invalidity rule* followed outside class gifts?	*See, e.g.,* Colorado, question #25.	Unclear. Singer Co. v. Makad, Inc. 518 P.2d 493, 497 (Kan. 1974) (noting the Supreme Court of Kansas's "reluctance to extend the infectious invalidity rule to situations where its use is not necessary to prevent a disposition tying up property for a remote period"). *But see* Unif. Statutory Rule Against Perpetuities § 1, 8B U.L.A. 256 (amended 1990) (explaining that "[t]he doctrine of infectious invalidity is superseded by this Act by Section 3, under which courts . . . are required to *reform* the disposition to approximate as closely as possible the transferor's . . . plan of distribution.")	Not applicable.
26. Is there a rule against the suspension of the power of alienation? If so, how is it stated?	Reasonableness standard. *See* In re Estate of Claussen, 482 N.W.2d 381, 385 (Iowa 1992) (characterizing the rule as "the rule against unreasonable restraints on alienation.")	Case law unclear. *See* Ehrhart v. Spencer, 263 P.2d 246, 250 (Kan. 1953) (explaining that perpetual leases are not violative of the rule against the suspension of the power of alienation). *But see* Metropolitan Life Ins. Co. v. Strnad, 876 P.2d 1362, 1370 (Kan. 1994) ("Kansas courts recognize that restraints on alienation, even indirect restraints, are not favored by the law.")	§ 381.225(1)(a): A future interest or trust is void if it suspends the power of alienation for longer than the permissible period. The permissible period is within 21 years after the death of an individual or individuals then alive. There is no suspension of the power of alienation by a trust or by equitable interests under a trust if the trustee has power to sell, either expressed or implied, or if there is a power to terminate the trusts by distributing the property subject to the trust to the beneficiaries in fee simple in one or more persons then living. (§ 381.225(3))

Table 9
Rule Against Perpetuities

	IOWA	*KANSAS*	*KENTUCKY*
27. *Effective date.*	July 1, 1983. (§ 558.68(4))	Apparently July 1, 1992. *See also* #6. The law applies "on or after the effective date." (§ 59-3405(a)). Session Laws 1992, ch. 302, § 5, (S.B.624) Section 20 states the law is effective after publication in the statute book. West provides a July 1, 1992 date as does LEXIS.	July 15, 2010. See #1.

[1] For questions, #19-25, *see also* § 59-3408 (noting that the state's USRAP supersedes the common law rule against perpetuities). The answers to questions #19-25 are not like to apply in most cases because of the abolition of the rule with respect to the vast majority of trusts.

Table 9
Rule Against Perpetuities

	LOUISIANA	MAINE	MARYLAND
1. Which rule is in effect: the common law rule, the Uniform Statutory Rule Against Perpetuities (USRAP), other law, or none?	Other.	Common law rule with major exceptions. In particular, see #2.b. for trusts that are exempt from the rule against perpetuities much like Illinois Qualified Perpetual Trusts. (Me. Rev. Stat. Ann. 33, §§ 101 - 106)	Common law rule with major exceptions. In particular, see #2.b. for trusts that are exempt from the rule against perpetuities much like Illinois Qualified Perpetual Trusts. (Md. Code Ann. Est. & Trusts § 11-102)
2. a. Is the common law rule relevant to any interests?	La. Rev. Stat. Ann. 9 § 1721 et seq. (sets out the trust code only); Crichton v. Succession of Gredler, 220 So. 2d 714, 719 (La. Ct. App. 1969) (explaining that Louisiana does not follow the common law rule against perpetuities). Rather, a limit on the term of a trust is imposed. (9 § 1833) See also the Comment to 9 § 1831: "The Rule Against Perpetuities is foreign to the legal tradition of this state. This Code applies instead the Rules of this Sub-part, which are based upon termination of interests."	Yes, but only as a starting point of the analysis.	Yes, but only as a starting point of the analysis.
b. What is the relevant rule?	If the trust instrument stipulates a term and unless an earlier termination is required by the trust instrument, or by the proper court, a trust shall terminate at:	The interest must vest, if at all, within twenty-one years after some life in being at the creation of the interest. (White v. Fleet Bank, 739 A.2d 373, 377 (Me. 1999))	[T]he common law rule against perpetuities as now recognized in the State is preserved (§ 11-102) The object of [the] rule is to prevent the future vesting of an

Table 9
Rule Against Perpetuities

LOUISIANA	MAINE	MARYLAND
(1) the death of the last surviving income beneficiary or the expiration of twenty years from the death of the settlor last to occur, whichever last occurs, of at least one settlor and one income beneficiary are natural persons;	In applying the rule against perpetuities to an interest in real or personal property limited to take effect at or after the termination of one or more life estates in, or lives of, persons in being when the period of said rule commences to run, the validity of the interest	estate upon a contingency which is not certain to happen within 21 years, and a fraction of a year beyond to cover the period of gestation, after some life or lives in being at the creation of the estate. (Ringgold v. Carvel, 76 A.2d 327, 330 (Md. 1950)) The statute applies to legal, as well as equitable interests. (§ 11-103(c))
(2) the death of the last surviving income beneficiary or the expiration of twenty years from the creation of the trust, whichever last occurs, if none of the settlers is a natural person but at least one income beneficiary is a natural person;	shall be determined on the basis of facts existing at the termination of such one or more life estates or lives. In this section, an interest which must terminate not later than the death of one or more persons is a "life estate" even though it may terminate at an earlier time. (33 § 101)	But see § 11-102(b)(5) (the common-law rule against perpetuities does not apply to "a trust in which the governing instrument states that the rule against perpetuities does not apply
(3) the expiration of twenty years from the death of the settlor last to die, if at least one settlor is a natural person but none of the income beneficiaries is a natural person;	**But see** 33 § 101-A "The rule against perpetuities does not apply to a trust created after the effective date of this section if:	to the trust and under which the trustee, or other person to whom the power is properly granted or delegated, has the power under the governing instrument, applicable statute, or common law to sell,
(4) the expiration of fifty years from the creation of the trust, if none of the settlers and none of the income beneficiaries is a natural person.	1. DECLARATION IN INSTRUMENT. The instrument creating the trust states that the rule against perpetuities does not apply to the trust; and	lease, or mortgage property for any period of time beyond the period that is required for an interest created under the governing instrument to vest, so as to be good under the rule against perpetuities.")

9142

Table 9
Rule Against Perpetuities

	LOUISIANA	MAINE	MARYLAND
	(9 §1831) If the trust instrument does not stipulate a term, the trust shall terminate (1) upon the death of the last income beneficiary who is a natural person; or (2) at the end of the term prescribed in (3) or (4) as if a term had been stipulated. (9 §1833)	2. POWER TO SELL, LEASE OR MORTGAGE. The trustee or other person to whom the power is properly granted or delegated has the power under the governing instrument, applicable statute or common law to sell or mortgage property or to lease property for any period of time beyond the period that is required for an interest created under the governing instrument to vest in order to be valid under the rule against perpetuities."	
3. *Does the rule apply to other than private trusts?*	No. *See* 9 §1834 ("The provisions of [§ 1831] shall not apply to class trusts, to trusts by employers for the benefit of employees, or to charitable dispositions contained in trusts for mixed private and charitable purposes.")	No. This rule does not apply to charitable trusts. (Snow v. President & Trustees of Bowdoin College, 175 A. 268, 270 (Me. 1934))	No. The rule does not apply to:

Table 9
Rule Against Perpetuities

LOUISIANA	MAINE	MARYLAND
		(1) A legacy or inter vivos conveyance having a value of $5,000 or less, or of any burial lot of any value, in trust or otherwise, for the purpose of providing for the perpetual care or keeping in good order and condition, or making repairs to, any lot, vault, mausoleum, or other place of sepulture belonging to any individual or several individuals in any cemetery or graveyard, the lots in which are intended for the burial of members of the family, family connections, relatives, or friends of the owners, or their successors in ownership.
		(2) A legacy or inter vivos conveyance intended to transfer assets from any corporation incorporated for charitable objects, to any other charitable corporation on a contingency or future event.

Table 9
Rule Against Perpetuities

LOUISIANA	MAINE	MARYLAND
		(3) A trust created by an employer as part of a pension, stock bonus, disability, death benefit, profit-sharing, retirement, welfare, or other plan for the exclusive benefit of some or all of the employees of the employer or their beneficiaries, to which contributions are made by the employer or employees, or both the employer and employees, for the purpose of making distributions to or for the benefit of employees or their beneficiaries out of the income or principal or both the income and principal of the trust, or for any other purposes set out in the plan.
		(4) A trust for charitable purposes, which shall include all purposes as are within the spirit or letter of the statute of 43 Elizabeth Ch. 4 (1601), commonly known as the statute of charitable uses.

Table 9
Rule Against Perpetuities

LOUISIANA	MAINE	MARYLAND
		(5) A trust in which the governing instrument states that the rule against perpetuities does not apply to the trust and under which the trustee, or other person to whom the power is properly granted or delegated, has the power under the governing instrument, applicable statute, or common law to sell, lease, or mortgage property for any period of time beyond the period that is required for an interest created under the governing instrument to vest, so as to be good under the rule against perpetuities.
		(6) An option of a tenant to renew a lease.
		(7) An option of a tenant to purchase all or part of the premises leased by the tenant.
		(8) An option of a usufructuary to extend the scope of an easement for profit.
		(9) The right of a county, a municipality, a person from whom land is acquired, or the successor-in-interest of a person from whom land is acquired, to acquire land from the State in accordance with §8-309 of the Transportation Article.

Table 9
Rule Against Perpetuities

LOUISIANA	MAINE	MARYLAND
		(10) A right or privilege, including an option, warrant, pre-emptive right, right of first refusal, right of first option, right of first negotiation, call right, exchange right, or conversion right, to acquire an interest in a domestic or foreign joint venture, partnership, limited liability partnership, limited partnership, limited liability limited partnership, corporation, cooperative, limited liability company, business trust, or similar enterprise, whether the interest is characterized as a joint venture interest, partnership interest, limited partnership interest, membership interest, security, stock, or otherwise.
		(11) A nondonative property interest as described in § 11-102.1 of this subtitle.
		(12) A trust created under Md. Est. & Tr. § 14.5-407 to provide for the care of an animal alive during the lifetime of the settlor, or
		(13) An affordable housing land trust agreement executed under Title 14, Subtitle 5 of the Real Property Article.
		(§ 11-102)

Table 9
Rule Against Perpetuities

	LOUISIANA	MAINE	MARYLAND
4. *Does the rule invalidate the interest at its creation, or is the rule revised by a wait-and-see approach?*	Wait-and-see. (9 § 1831)	Wait-and-see. (33 § 101; White v. Fleet Bank, 739 A.2d 373, 378 (Me. 1999))	It appears that the rule applies a wait-and-see approach. "In applying the rule against perpetuities to an interest limited to take effect at or after the termination of one or more life estates in, or lives of, persons in being when the period of the rule commences to run, the validity of the interest *shall be determined on the basis of facts existing at the termination of one or more life estates or lives."* (§ 11-103(a)) (emphasis added)

Table 9
Rule Against Perpetuities

	LOUISIANA	MAINE	MARYLAND
5. *Can the trust be reformed?*	No specific state case or statute. However, 9 § 1832 provides that if the term is too exclusive, then the trust "shall be enforced as though the maximum allowable term had been stipulated." See also 9 § 1891 with respect to "class trusts."	No specific state case or statute.	Yes, but only "[i]f an interest would violate the rule against perpetuities … because the interest is contingent upon any person attaining or failing to attain an age in excess of 21." (§ 11-103(b))
6. *If yes to 5., under what theory?*	See #5.	See #5.	"[T]he age contingency shall be reduced to 21 as to all persons subject to the same age contingency." (§ 11-103(b))
7. *When is a general testamentary power of appointment invalid?*	See #5.	*See* Unif. Statutory Rule Against Perpetuities § 1, 8B U.L.A. 248 (amended 1990) ("Under the Common-law Rule … a *nongeneral power* (whether or not presently exercisable) or a *general testamentary power* is invalid as of the time of its creation if it *might* not terminate (by irrevocable exercise or otherwise) within a life in being plus 21 years.")	*See* Unif. Statutory Rule Against Perpetuities § 1, 8B U.L.A. 248 (amended 1990) ("Under the Common-law Rule … a *nongeneral power* (whether or not presently exercisable) or a *general testamentary power* is invalid as of the time of its creation if it *might* not terminate (by irrevocable exercise or otherwise) within a life in being plus 21 years.")
8. *Same, but nongeneral testamentary power.*	See #5.	See #7.	See #7.

Table 9
Rule Against Perpetuities

	LOUISIANA	MAINE	MARYLAND
9. *Same, but general power, whether testamentary or inter vivos, not presently exercisable because of a condition precedent.*	See #5.	*See* Unif. Statutory Rule Against Perpetuities § 1, 8B U.L.A. 248 (amended 1990) ("Under the Common-law Rule, a general power not presently exercisable because of a condition precedent is invalid as of the time of its creation if the condition might neither be satisfied nor become impossible to satisfy with a life in being plus 21 years.")	*See* Unif. Statutory Rule Against Perpetuities § 1, 8B U.L.A. 248 (amended 1990) ("Under the Common-law Rule, a general power not presently exercisable because of a condition precedent is invalid as of the time of its creation if the condition might neither be satisfied nor become impossible to satisfy with a life in being plus 21 years.")
10. *Same, but nongeneral inter vivos power.*	See #5.	See #7.	See #7.
11. *Is a period of gestation added to the perpetuity period?*	N/A	Yes. First Portland Nat'l Bank v. Rodrique, 172 A.2d 107, 114 (Me. 1961) (citing with approval the Model Rule Against perpetuities which holds that "'no interest in real or personal property shall be good unless it must vest not later than twenty-one years after some life in being at the creation of the interest and any period of gestation involved in the situation to which the limitation applies.'")	Yes. (See #2a.)
12. *What is the treatment of a "later of the traditional rule or 90 years" clause?* See UPC 2-901(e).	N/A	N/A	N/A

Table 9
Rule Against Perpetuities

	LOUISIANA	MAINE	MARYLAND
13. *When is an interest created by the exercise of a general testamentary power deemed created?*	See #5.	*See* comment to Unif. Probate Code §2-902(a) ("general principles of property law determine that a nonvested property interest or power of appointment created by will is created at the decedent's death"); Unif. Statutory Rule Against Perpetuities §2, 8B U.L.A. 268 (amended 1990) (stating the same).	It is a settled rule that in order to test the validity of such appointments they must be construed as if they were inserted in the instrument creating the power. (Gambrill v. Gambrill, 89 A. 1094, 1095 (Md. 1914)) *See also* comment to Unif. Probate Code §2-902(a) ("general principles of property law determine that a nonvested property interest or power of appointment created by will is created at the decedent's death"); Unif. Statutory Rule Against Perpetuities §2, 8B U.L.A. 268 (amended 1990) (stating the same).
14. *Same, but nongeneral testamentary power.*	See #13.	See #13.	See #13.
15. *Same, but general inter vivos power.*	See #5.	*See* comment to Unif. Probate Code §2-902(a) ("With respect to an intervivos transfer, an interest or power is created on the date the transfer becomes effective for purposes of property law generally, normally the date of delivery of the deed or funding of the trust."); Unif. Statutory Rule Against Perpetuities §2, 8B U.L.A. 268 (stating the same).	*See* comment to Unif. Probate Code §2-902(a) ("With respect to an intervivos transfer, an interest or power is created on the date the transfer becomes effective for purposes of property law generally, normally the date of delivery of the deed or funding of the trust."); Unif. Statutory Rule Against Perpetuities §2, 8B U.L.A. 268 (stating the same).
16. *Same, but nongeneral inter vivos power.*	See #15.	See #15.	See #15.

Table 9
Rule Against Perpetuities

	LOUISIANA	MAINE	MARYLAND
17. *When is an interest created if the grantor of a trust has a power to revoke?*	See #5.	*See* comment to Unif. Probate Code §2-902(b) (noting that "nonvested property interests and powers of appointment created in [a revocable inter-vivos trust] are created when the power to revoke expires, usually at the settlor's death"); Unif. Statutory Rule Against Perpetuities §2, 8B U.L.A. 268 (amended 1990) (explaining that "any nonvested property interest subject to [a power to revoke] is not created …. until the power terminates (by release, expiration at the death of the donee, or otherwise").	*See* comment to Unif. Probate Code §2-902(b) (noting that "nonvested property interests and powers of appointment created in [a revocable inter-vivos trust] are created when the power to revoke expires, usually at the settlor's death"); Unif. Statutory Rule Against Perpetuities §2, 8B U.L.A. 268 (amended 1990) (explaining that "any nonvested property interest subject to [a power to revoke] is not created …. until the power terminates (by release, expiration at the death of the donee, or otherwise").
18. *When does the period of the rule start re an interest contributed to an irrevocable trust? See UPC 2-902(c).*	See #5.	*See* comment to Unif. Probate Code 2-902(c) ("Arguably, at common law, each transfer [to an existing irrevocable inter-vivos trust] starts the period of the Rule running anew as to each transfer.")	*See* comment to Unif. Probate Code 2-902(c) ("Arguably, at common law, each transfer [to an existing irrevocable inter-vivos trust] starts the period of the Rule running anew as to each transfer.")
19. *Is there a conclusive presumption of fertility, that is, the "fertile octogenarian" rule?*	N/A	*See, e.g.,* Arkansas, question #19.	Yes. Marty v. First Nat'l Bank, 120 A.2d 841, 845 (Md. 1956) (noting that "it is considered always possible that a living person may have a child.")

Table 9
Rule Against Perpetuities

	LOUISIANA	MAINE	MARYLAND
20. *What is the earliest age a child is deemed capable of bearing a child? What is the impact of illegitimacy?*	N/A	"Under the rule, courts must presume that living persons are capable of having or fathering children, no matter how young they are. See In re Graite's Will Trusts, [1949] 1 All E.R. 459, 460 (Ch.). Thus, the rule strikes down any interest whose vesting depends on the assertion that, for example, a toddler will not have children." (Keith L. Butler, Notes & Comments, *Long Live the Dead Hand: A Case for Repeal of the Rule Against Perpetuities in Washington*, 75 Wash. L. Rev. 1237, 1246 n.78 (2000)).	"Under the rule, courts must presume that living persons are capable of having or fathering children, no matter how young they are. See In re Graite's Will Trusts, [1949] 1 All E.R. 459, 460 (Ch.). Thus, the rule strikes down any interest whose vesting depends on the assertion that, for example, a toddler will not have children." (Keith L. Butler, Notes & Comments, *Long Live the Dead Hand: A Case for Repeal of the Rule Against Perpetuities in Washington*, 75 Wash. L. Rev. 1237, 1246 n.78 (2000)).
21. *Is the "unborn widow" rule observed?*	N/A	*See, e.g.,* Arkansas, question #21.	Yes. Perkins v. Iglehart, 183 Md. 520, 537 (Md. 1944).
22. *Does the "slothful executor" rule apply, i.e., an administrative contingency clause providing in the case of a "distribution to those of issue living at the time of distribution?"*	N/A	*See, e.g.,* California, question #22.	*See, e.g.,* California, question #22.
23. *Does the all-or-nothing rule apply to class gifts?*	N/A	*See, e.g.,* Alabama, question #23.	Yes. Snyder's Estate v. Denit, 72 A.2d 757, 760 (Md. 1950) ("If [a gift to a class] might not be good as to some members of the class, the entire gift to the class would fail.")

Table 9
Rule Against Perpetuities

	LOUISIANA	MAINE	MARYLAND
24. *Is there an exception to the all-or-nothing rule in the case of subclasses or specific sums to each member of the class?*	N/A	*See* Unif. Statutory Rule Against Perpetuities § 2, 8B U.L.A. 257 ("The common law also recognizes a doctrine called the specific-sum doctrine which is derived from Storrs v. Benbow, 3 De G.M. & G. 390, 43 Eng. Rep 153 (Ch. 1853), and states: If a specified sum of money is to be paid to each member of a class, the interest of each class member is entitled to separate treatment and is valid or invalid under the Rule on its own. The common law also recognizes a doctrine called the sub-class doctrine, which is derived from Cattlin v. Brown, 11 Hare 372, 68 Eng. Rep. 1318 (Ch. 1853), and states: If the ultimate takers are not described as a single class but rather as a group of separate subclasses, and if the share to which each separate subclass is entitled will finally be determined within the period of the Rule, the gifts to the different subclasses are separate for the purpose of the Rule.").	*See* Unif. Statutory Rule Against Perpetuities § 2, 8B U.L.A. 257 ("The common law also recognizes a doctrine called the specific-sum doctrine which is derived from Storrs v. Benbow, 3 De G.M. & G. 390, 43 Eng. Rep. 153 (Ch. 1853), and states: If a specified sum of money is to be paid to each member of a class, the interest of each class member is entitled to separate treatment and is valid or invalid under the Rule on its own. The common law also recognizes a doctrine called the sub-class doctrine, which is derived from Cattlin v. Brown, 11 Hare 372, 68 Eng. Rep. 1318 (Ch. 1853), and states: If the ultimate takers are not described as a single class but rather as a group of separate subclasses, and if the share to which each separate subclass is entitled will finally be determined within the period of the Rule, the gifts to the different subclasses are separate for the purpose of the Rule.").
25. *Is the infectious invalidity rule followed outside class gifts?*	N/A	*See, e.g.,* Colorado, question #25.	*See, e.g.,* Colorado, question #25.

Table 9
Rule Against Perpetuities

	LOUISIANA	MAINE	MARYLAND
26. *Is there a rule against the suspension of the power of alienation? If so, how is it stated?*	The general rule is that: "A beneficiary may transfer or encumber the whole or any part of his interest unless the trust instrument provides to the contrary." The trust instrument may provide that the interest of a beneficiary shall not be subject to voluntary or involuntary alienation by a beneficiary. A restraint upon voluntary alienation by a beneficiary is valid. But a restraint upon involuntary alienation by a beneficiary is subject to the limitations prescribed by this sub-part. (9 § 2002)	Reasonableness standard. Estate of Plummer, 666 A.2d 116, 118 (Me. 1995) ("[W]e addressed three factors to be considered in evaluating the reasonableness of a restraint on alienation. Specifically, we considered (1) the method of determining the price; (2) the duration of the restraint; and (3) the purpose of the restraint.")	Standard unclear. With respect to leases, see Julian v. Christopher, 575 A.2d 735, 738-39 (Md. 1990) ("because there is a public policy against restraints on alienation, if a lease is silent on the subject, a tenant may freely sublease or assign. Restraints on alienation are permitted in leases, but are looked upon with disfavor and are strictly construed").
27. *Effective date.*	The law has prospective and retroactive effect, except if, with respect to a trust created prior to August 1, 1987, a settlor, trustee or beneficiary makes written objection prior to February 1, 1988. See Acts of 1987. No. 164, §3.	Instruments taking effect after August 20, 1955, including appointments after that date by inter vivos instruments or wills under powers created before August 20, 1955. (33 § 106) The revised Maine rule applies only to "inter vivos" instruments taking effect after August 20, 1955, to wills where the testator dies after August 20, 1955, and to appointments made after August 20, 1955, including appointments made by inter vivos instruments or wills under powers created before said August 20. (33 § 106) Prior valid interests are not affected by the law. (33 § 105)	October 1, 1998. See Acts 1998, Ch. 694, § 1.

Table 9
Rule Against Perpetuities

	MASSACHUSETTS	*MICHIGAN*	*MINNESOTA*
1. *Which rule is in effect: the common law rule, the Uniform Statutory Rule Against Perpetuities (USRAP), other law, or none?*	USRAP. (Mass. Gen. Law. Ann. Ch.-190B, §§ 2-901 - 2-906)	USRAP. (Mich. Comp. Laws §§ 554.71-554.78) No interest in or power of appointment over personal property held in trust is invalidated by the rule against perpetuities, as well as by the suspension of absolute ownership, the suspension of the power of alienation, or accumulations of income. (§ 554.93(1)) This law is known as the "personal property trust perpetuities act" (§ 554.91) and is effective for a nonvested interest in or power of appointment over personal property held in a trust that is either revocable on, or created after, May 29, 2008 (§ 554.94) and is not a "special appointee trust." A special appointee trust is a trust to the extent it includes assets that were held in a trust that was irrevocable on Sept. 25, 1985 if (a) the assets have continuously been held in trust since that date and (b) the assets have not become subject to a general power of appointment since Sept. 25, 1985. (§ 554.94 eff. Mar. 24, 2011)) Note: If a first power of appointment is exercised so as to subject the personal property to, or create, a second power, the period during which vesting may be postponed by the exercise of the second power is determined under USRAP by reference to the time the first power was created. (§ 554.93(3))	USRAP. (Minn. Stat. Ann. §§ 501A.01-501A.07)

Table 9
Rule Against Perpetuities

	MASSACHUSETTS	MICHIGAN	MINNESOTA
2. a. *Is the common law rule relevant to any interests?*	Yes, but only as a starting point of the analysis.	The period used is 360 years, however, rather than 90 years. (§ 554.75(2)) **Note**: The subsequent analysis, ##2-29, applies to interests and powers not governed by the personal property trust perpetuities act. With respect to nonvested property interests created after September 23, 1949 and before December 24, 1988, the common law rule against perpetuities applies (§ 554.51). Prior to September 23, 1949, § 14-20 of the Revised Statutes of 1846 applied, being § 554.14 et. seq. of the Compiled Laws of 1948.	Yes, but only as a starting point of the analysis.

Table 9
Rule Against Perpetuities

	MASSACHUSETTS	*MICHIGAN*	*MINNESOTA*
b. *What is the relevant rule?*	A nonvested property interest is invalid unless: (1) When the interest is created, it is certain to vest or terminate no later than 21 years after the death of an individual then alive; or (2) The interest either vests or terminates within 90 years after its creation. (§ 2-901(a))	A nonvested property interest is invalid unless 1 or more of the following are applicable to the interest: (a) When the interest is created, it is certain to vest or terminate no later than 21 years after the death of an individual then alive; or (b) The interest either vests or terminates within 90 years after its creation. **But see** #1 above regarding the personal property trust perpetuities act. But *see also* § 554.72(5), which provides that in measuring a period from the creation of a trust or other property arrangement irrevocable on Sept. 25, 1985, if language in an instrument governing the exercise of a power purports to disallow vesting, or to have a similar effect, beyond 21 years after the death of survivor of specified lives in being at the creation of trust or other property arrangement, the language is inoperative.	A nonvested property interest is invalid unless: (1) When the interest is created, it is certain to vest or terminate no later than 21 years after the death of an individual then alive; or (2) The interest either vests or terminates within 90 years after its creation. (§ 501A.01(a))

Table 9
Rule Against Perpetuities

	MASSACHUSETTS	MICHIGAN	MINNESOTA
3. Does the rule apply to other than private trusts?	Yes. The rule applies except to:	Yes. The rule applies except to:	Yes. The rule applies except to:
	(1) a nonvested property interest or a power of appointment arising out of a nondonative transfer, except a nonvested property interest or a power of appointment arising out of (i) a premarital or postmarital agreement, (ii) a separation or divorce settlement, (iii) a spouse's election, (iv) a similar arrangement arising out of a prospective, existing, or previous marital relationship between the parties, (v) a contract to make or not to revoke a will or trust, (vi) a contract to exercise or not to exercise a power of appointment, (vii) a transfer in satisfaction of a duty of support, or (viii) a reciprocal transfer;	(a) A nonvested property interest or a power of appointment arising out of a nondonative transfer, except a nonvested property interest or a power of appointment arising out of a premarital or postmarital agreement; a separation or divorce settlement; a spouse's election; a similar arrangement arising out of a prospective, existing, or previous marital relationship between the parties; a contract to make or not to revoke a will or trust; a contract to exercise or not to exercise a power of appointment; a transfer in satisfaction of a duty of support; or a reciprocal transfer.	(1) a nonvested property interest or a power of appointment arising out of a nondonative transfer, except a nonvested property interest or a power of appointment arising out of (i) a premarital or postmarital agreement, (ii) a separation or divorce settlement, (iii) a spouse's election, (iv) a similar arrangement arising out of a prospective, existing, or previous marital relationship between the parties, (v) a contract to make or not to revoke a will or trust, (vi) a contract to exercise or not to exercise a power of appointment, (vii) a transfer in satisfaction of a duty of support, or (viii) a reciprocal transfer;
	(2) a fiduciary's power relating to the administration or management of assets, including the power of a fiduciary to sell, lease or mortgage property, and the power of a fiduciary to determine principal and income;	(b) A fiduciary's power relating to the administration or management of assets, including the power of a fiduciary to sell, lease or mortgage property, and the power of a fiduciary to determine principal and income.	(2) a fiduciary's power relating to the administration or management of assets, including the power of a fiduciary to sell, lease or mortgage property, and the power of a fiduciary to determine principal and income;
	(3) a power to appoint a fiduciary;	(c) A power to appoint a fiduciary.	(3) a power to appoint a fiduciary;

Table 9
Rule Against Perpetuities

MASSACHUSETTS	MICHIGAN	MINNESOTA
(4) a discretionary power of a trustee to distribute principal before termination of a trust to a beneficiary having an indefeasibly vested interest in the income and principal;	(d) A discretionary power of a trustee to distribute principal before termination of a trust to a beneficiary having an indefeasibly vested interest in the income and principal.	(4) a discretionary power of a trustee to distribute principal before termination of a trust to a beneficiary having an indefeasibly vested interest in the income and principal;
(5) a nonvested property interest held by a charity, government or governmental agency or subdivision, if the nonvested property interest is preceded by an interest held by another charity, government or governmental agency or subdivision;	(e) A property interest, power of appointment, or any other arrangement that was not subject to the common-law rule against perpetuities or is excluded by another statute.	(5) a nonvested property interest held by a charity, government, or governmental agency or subdivision, if the nonvested property interest is preceded by an interest held by another charity, government or governmental agency or subdivision;
(6) a nonvested property interest in or a power of appointment with respect to a trust or other property arrangement forming part of a pension, profit	(f) Except as provided in § 554.75(2), an interest in, or power of appointment over, personal property held in a trust that is either revocable on or created after the effective date of the personal property trust perpetuities act (May 18, 2008). See #1 above. (§ 554.75)	(6) a nonvested property interest in or a power of appointment with respect to a trust or other property arrangement forming part of a pension, profit sharing, stock bonus, health,
disability, death benefit,		sharing, stock bonus, health,

Table 9

Rule Against Perpetuities

	MASSACHUSETTS	MICHIGAN	MINNESOTA
	income deferral or other current or deferred benefit plan for one or more employees, independent contractors or their beneficiaries or spouses, to which contributions are made for the purpose of distributing to or for the benefit of the participants or their beneficiaries or spouses the property, income or principal in the trust or other property arrangement, except a nonvested property interest or a power of appointment that is created by an election of a participant or a beneficiary or spouse; or (7) a property interest, power of appointment or arrangement that was not subject to the common-law rule against perpetuities or is excluded by another statute of the commonwealth. (§2-904)	*See also* §554.381 ("No statutory or common law rule of this state against perpetuities or restraint of alienation shall hereafter invalidate any gift, grant, devise or bequest, in trust or otherwise, for public welfare purposes.")	disability, death benefit, income deferral, or other current or deferred benefit plan for one or more employees, independent contractors, or their beneficiaries or spouses, to which contributions are made for the purpose of distributing to or for the benefit of the participants or their beneficiaries or spouses the property, income, or principal in the trust or other property arrangement, except a nonvested property interest or a power of appointment that is created by an election of a participant or a beneficiary or spouse; or (7) a property interest, power of appointment or arrangement that was not subject to the common-law rule against perpetuities or is excluded by another statute of this state. (§501A.04)
4. *Does the rule invalidate the interest at its creation, or is the rule revised by a wait-and-see approach?*	Wait-and-see. (§2-901(a)(2))	Wait-and-see. (§554.72(1))	Wait-and-see. (§501A.01(a))

Table 9
Rule Against Perpetuities

	MASSACHUSETTS	MICHIGAN	MINNESOTA
5. *Can the trust be reformed?*	Yes, but only if one of the following conditions is satisfied:	Yes, but only if one of the following conditions is satisfied:	Yes but only if one of the following conditions is satisfied:
	(1) a nonvested property interest or power of appointment becomes invalid under Section 1 (see #2b).	(a) A nonvested property interest or a power of appointment becomes invalid under Section 2 (see #2b).	(1) a nonvested property interest or a power of appointment becomes invalid under Section 501A.01 (statutory rule against perpetuities);
	(2) a class gift is not, but might become, invalid under Section 2-901 and the time has arrived when the share of any class member is to take effect in possession or enjoyment; or	(b) A class gift is not but might become invalid under Section 2 and the time has arrived when the share of any class member is to take effect in possession or enjoyment.	(2) a class gift is not but might become invalid under Section 501A.01 (statutory rule against perpetuities) and the time has arrived when the share of any class member is to take effect in possession or enjoyment; or
	(3) a nonvested property interest that is not validated by section 2-901(a)(1), that is, the traditional common law rule, can vest but not within ninety years after its creation.	(c) A nonvested property interest that is not validated by Section 2(1)(a), that is, the traditional common law rule, can vest but not within 90 years after its creation.	(3) a nonvested property interest that is not validated by Section 501A.01, subsection (a)(1), that is, the traditional common law rule, can vest but not within 90 years after its creation.
	(§ 2-903)	(§ 554.74)	(§ 501A.03)

Table 9
Rule Against Perpetuities

	MASSACHUSETTS	*MICHIGAN*	*MINNESOTA*
6. *If yes to 5., under what theory?*	Upon the petition of an interested person, a court shall reform a disposition that most closely approximates the trans-feror's manifested plan of distribution and is within the ninety years allowed by section 2-901(a)(2), 2-901(b)(2), or 2-901(c)(2). (§2-903) *See also* §2-905(b) ("If a nonvested property interest or a power of appointment was created before the effective date of this part and is determined in a judicial proceeding, commenced on or after the effective date of this part, to violate the commonwealth's rule against perpetuities as that rule existed before the effective date of this part, a court upon the petition of an interested person may reform the disposition in the manner that most closely approximates the transferor's manifested plan of distribution and is within the limits of the rule against perpetuities applicable when the nonvested property interest or power of appointment was created.")	Upon the petition of an interested person, a court shall reform a disposition in the manner most closely approximates the transferor's manifested plan of distribution and is within the 90 years allowed by §554.72 (§554.74) *See also* §555.76(2) ("If a nonvested property interest or a power of appointment was created before the effective date of this act and is determined in a judicial proceeding, commenced on or after the effective date of this act, to violate the rule against perpetuities as it existed before the effective date of this act, a court, upon the petition of an interested person, may reform the disposition in the manner that most closely approximates the transferor's manifested plan of distribution and is within the limits of the rule against perpetuities applicable when the nonvested property interest or power of appointment was created.")	Upon the petition of an interested person, a court shall reform a disposition in the manner that most closely approximates the transferor's manifested plan of distribution and is within the 90 years allowed by §501A.01 (§501A.03) *See also* §501A.05(b) ("If a nonvested property interest or a power of appointment was created before January 1, 1992, and is determined in a judicial proceeding, commenced after December 31, 1991, to violate this state's rule against perpetuities as that rule existed before January 1, 1992, a court upon the petition of an interested person may reform the disposition in the manner that most closely approximates the transferor's manifested plan of distribution and is within the limits of the rule against perpetuities applicable when the nonvested property interest or power of appointment was created.")

Table 9
Rule Against Perpetuities

	MASSACHUSETTS	MICHIGAN	MINNESOTA
7. *When is a general testamentary power of appointment invalid?*	A general testamentary power of appointment is invalid unless: (1) When the power is created, it is certain to be irrevocably exercised or otherwise to terminate no later than 21 years after the death of an individual then alive; or (2) The power is irrevocably exercised or otherwise terminates within 90 years after its creation. (§ 2-901(c))	A general testamentary power of appointment is invalid unless: (a) When the power is created, it is certain to be irrevocably exercised or otherwise to termination no later than 21 years after the death of an individual then alive; or (b) The power is irrevocably exercised or otherwise terminates within 90 years after its creation. (§ 554.72(3))	A general testamentary power of appointment is invalid unless: (1) When the power is created, it is certain to be irrevocably exercised or otherwise to terminate no later than 21 years after the death of an individual then alive; or (2) The power is irrevocably exercised or otherwise terminates within 90 years after its creation. (§ 501A.01(c))
8. *Same, but nongeneral testamentary power.*	A nongeneral testamentary power of appointment is invalid unless: (1) When the power is created, it is certain to be irrevocably exercised or otherwise to terminate no later than 21 years after the death of an individual then alive; or (2) The power is irrevocably exercised or otherwise terminates within 90 years after its creation. (§ 2-901(c))	A nongeneral testamentary power of appointment is invalid unless: (a) When the power is created, it is certain to be irrevocably exercised or otherwise to terminate no later than 21 years after the death of an individual then alive; or (b) The power is irrevocably exercised or otherwise terminates within 90 years after its creation. (§ 554.72(3))	A nongeneral testamentary power of appointment is invalid unless: (1) When the power is created, it is certain to be irrevocably exercised or otherwise to terminate no later than 21 years after the death of an individual then alive; or (2) The power is irrevocably exercised or otherwise terminates within 90 years after its creation. (§ 501A.01(c))

Table 9
Rule Against Perpetuities

	MASSACHUSETTS	MICHIGAN	MINNESOTA
9. Same, but general power, whether testamentary or inter vivos, not presently exercisable because of a condition precedent.	A general power of appointment not presently exercisable because of a condition precedent is invalid unless:	A general power of appointment not presently exercisable because of a condition precedent is invalid unless:	A general power of appointment not presently exercisable because of a condition precedent is invalid unless:
	(1) When the power is created, the condition precedent is certain to be satisfied or becomes impossible to satisfy no later than 21 years after the death of an individual then alive; or	(a) When the power is created, the condition precedent is certain to be satisfied or becomes impossible to satisfy no later than 21 years after the death of an individual then alive; or	(1) When the power is created, the condition precedent is certain to be satisfied or becomes impossible to satisfy no later than 21 years after the death of an individual then alive; or
	(2) The condition precedent either is satisfied or becomes impossible to satisfy within 90 years after its creation.	(b) the condition precedent either is satisfied or becomes impossible to satisfy within 90 years after its creation.	(2) The condition precedent either is satisfied or becomes impossible to satisfy within 90 years after its creation.
	(§ 2-901(b))	(§ 554.72(2))	(§ 501A.01(b))
10. Same, but nongeneral inter vivos power.	See #8.	See #8.	See #8.

Table 9
Rule Against Perpetuities

	MASSACHUSETTS	MICHIGAN	MINNESOTA
11. *Is a period of gestation added to the perpetuity period?*	No. The possibility that a child will be born to a person after that person's death is disregarded. (§ 2-901(d)) *See also* Unif. Statutory Rule Against Perpetuities § 1, 8B U.L.A. 243, 243 (amended 1990) ("[T]he possibility that a child will be born to [a testator] after his death must be disregarded; and the possibility that a child will be born to any of [the testator's] descendants after their deaths must also be disregarded. Note, however, that the rule of subsection (d) does *not* apply to the question of the entitlement of an after-born child to take a beneficial interest in the trust").	No. The possibility that a child will be born to a person after that person's death is disregarded. (§ 554.72(4)) *See also* Unif. Statutory Rule Against Perpetuities § 1, 8B U.L.A. 243, 243 (amended 1990) ("[T]he possibility that a child will be born to [a testator] after his death must be disregarded; and the possibility that a child will be born to any of [the testator's] descendants after their deaths must also be disregarded. Note, however, that the rule of subsection (d) does *not* apply to the question of the entitlement of an after-born child to take a beneficial interest in the trust").	No. The possibility that a child will be born to a person after that person's death is disregarded. (§ 501A.01(d)) *See also* Unif. Statutory Rule Against Perpetuities § 1, 8B U.L.A. 243, 243 (amended 1990) ("[T]he possibility that a child will be born to [a testator] after his death must be disregarded; and the possibility that a child will be born to any of [the testator's] descendants after their deaths must also be disregarded. Note, however, that the rule of subsection (d) does *not* apply to the question of the entitlement of an after-born child to take a beneficial interest in the trust").
12. *What is the treatment of a "later of the traditional rule or 90 years" clause? See* UIPC 2-901(e).	That language is inoperative to the extent it produces a period of time that exceeds 21 years after the death of the survivor of the specified lives. (§ 2-901(e))	That language is inoperative to the extent it produces a period of time that exceeds 21 years after the death of the survivor of the specified lives. (§ 554.72(5))	That language is inoperative to the extent it produces a period of time that exceeds 21 years after the death of the survivor of the specified lives. (§ 501A.01(e))

Table 9
Rule Against Perpetuities

	MASSACHUSETTS	MICHIGAN	MINNESOTA
13. *When is an interest created by the exercise of a general testamentary power deemed created?*	Except as provided in subsections (b) and (c) and in section 2-905(a), the time of creation of a nonvested property interest or a power of appointment is determined under general principles of property law. The first of the excepted provisions states that as long as a person with a general power to become the unqualified beneficial owner has that power, the nonvested interest is created when the power terminates. The second of the excepted provisions states that a nonvested property interest, which arises from a transfer to an existing trust, is created when the nonvested property interest in the trust was created. (§2-902(b)(c)) *See also* Unif. Statutory Rule Against Perpetuities §2, 8B U.L.A. 268 (amended 1990) (explaining that "general principles of property law determine that the time . . . [of creation] is at the decedent's death"). *See generally* §62-905(a) ("For purposes of this section, a nonvested property interest or a power of appointment created by the exercise of a power of appointment is created when the power is irrevocably exercised or when a revocable exercise becomes irrevocable.")	Except as provided in subsections (2), (3), and section 6(1), the time of creation of a nonvested property interest or a power of appointment shall be determined by statutory or common law. (§554.73(1)) The first of the excepted provisions states that as long as a person with a general power to become the unqualified beneficial owner has that power, the nonvested interest is created when the power terminates. The second of the excepted provisions states that a nonvested property interest, which arises from a transfer to an existing trust, is created when the nonvested property interest in the trust was created. (§554.73(2)(3)) *See also* Unif. Statutory Rule Against Perpetuities §2, 8B U.L.A. 268 (amended 1990) (explaining that "general principles of property law determine that the time . . . [of creation] is at the decedent's death"). *See generally* §554.76(1) ("For purposes of this section, a nonvested property interest or a power of appointment created by the exercise of a power of appointment is created when the power is irrevocably exercised or when a revocable exercise becomes irrevocable.")	Except as provided in subsections (b) and (c) and in section 501A.05, subsection (a), the time of creation of a nonvested property interest or a power of appointment is determined under general principles of property law. (§501A.02(a)) The first of the excepted provisions states that as long as a person with a general power to become the unqualified beneficial owner has that power, the nonvested interest is created when the power terminates. (§501A.02(b)-(c)) The second of the excepted provisions states that a nonvested property interest, which arises from a transfer to an existing trust, is created when the nonvested property interest in the trust was created. *See also* Unif. Statutory Rule Against Perpetuities §2, 8B U.L.A. 268 (amended 1990) (explaining that "general principles of property law determine that the time . . . [of creation] is at the decedent's death"). *See generally* §501A.05(a) ("For purposes of this section, a nonvested property interest or a power of appointment created by the exercise of a power of appointment is created when the power is irrevocably exercised or when a revocable exercise becomes irrevocable.")

Table 9
Rule Against Perpetuities

	MASSACHUSETTS	MICHIGAN	MINNESOTA
14. *Same, but nongeneral testamentary power.*	See #13.	See #13.	See #13.

Table 9
Rule Against Perpetuities

	MASSACHUSETTS	MICHIGAN	MINNESOTA
15. *Same, but general inter vivos power.*	Except as provided in subsections (b) and (c) and in section 2-905(a), the time of creation of a nonvested property interest or a power of appointment is determined under general principles of property law. (184A, § 2(a)) The first of the excepted provisions states that as long as a person with a general power to become the unqualified beneficial owner has that power, the nonvested interest is created when the power terminates. The second of the excepted provisions states that a nonvested property interest, which arises from a transfer to an existing trust, is created when the nonvested property interest in the trust was created. (§ 2-902(b)(c)) *See also* Unif. Statutory Rule Against Perpetuities § 2, 8B U.L.A. 268 (amended 1990) (explaining that "the time when the interest or power is created is the date the transfer becomes effective for purposes of property law generally, normally the date of delivery of the deed"); Comment to Unif. Probate Code § 2-902(a) (stating same and adding "the funding of the trust" as "normally" the time when the interest is created). *See generally* § 2-905(a) ("For purposes of this section, a nonvested property interest or a power of appointment	Except as provided in subsections (2), (3), and section 6(1), the time of creation of a nonvested property interest or a power of appointment shall be determined by statutory or common law. (§ 554.73(1) The first of the excepted provisions states that as long as a person with a general power to become the unqualified beneficial owner has that power, the nonvested interest is created when the power terminates. The second of the excepted provisions states that a nonvested property interest, which arises from a transfer to an existing trust, is created when the nonvested property interest in the trust was created. *See also* Unif. Statutory Rule Against Perpetuities § 2, 8B U.L.A. 268 (amended 1990) (explaining that "the time when the interest or power is created is the date the transfer becomes effective for purposes of property law generally, normally the date of delivery of the deed"); Comment to Unif. Probate Code § 2-902(a) (stating same and adding "the funding of the trust" as "normally" the time when the interest is created). (§ 554.73(2)-(3)) *See generally* § 554.76(1) ("For purposes of this section, a nonvested property interest or a power of appointment	Except as provided in subsections (b) and (c) and in § 501A.05, subsection (a), the time of creation of a nonvested property interest or a power of appointment is determined under general principles of property law. The first of the excepted provisions states that as long as a person with a general power to become the unqualified beneficial owner has that power, the nonvested interest is created when the power terminates. The second of the excepted provisions states that a nonvested property interest, which arises from a transfer to an existing trust, is created when the nonvested property interest in the trust was created. (§ 501A.02(b)-(c)) *See also* Unif. Statutory Rule Against Perpetuities § 2, 8B U.L.A. 268 (amended 1990) (explaining that "the time when the interest or power is created is the date the transfer becomes effective for purposes of property law generally, normally the date of delivery of the deed"); Comment to Unif. Probate Code § 2-902(a) (stating same and adding "the funding of the trust" as "normally" the time when the interest is created). *See generally* § 501A.05(a) ("For purposes of this section, a nonvested property interest or a power of

Table 9
Rule Against Perpetuities

	MASSACHUSETTS	MICHIGAN	MINNESOTA
	created by the exercise of a power of appointment is created when the power is irrevocably exercised or when a revocable exercise becomes irrevocable.")	created by the exercise of a power of appointment is created when the power is irrevocably exercised or when a revocable exercise becomes irrevocable.")	appointment created by the exercise of a power of appointment is created when the power is irrevocably exercised or when a revocable exercise becomes irrevocable.")
16. *Same, but nongeneral inter vivos power.*	See #15.	See #15.	See #15.

Table 9
Rule Against Perpetuities

	MASSACHUSETTS	MICHIGAN	MINNESOTA
17. *When is an interest created if the grantor of a trust has a power to revoke?*	"If there is a person who alone can exercise a power created by a governing instrument to become the unqualified beneficial owner of (i) a nonvested property interest or (ii) a property interest subject to a power of appointment described in section 2-901(b) or (c), the nonvested property interest or power of appointment is created when the power to become the unqualified beneficial owner terminates." (§2-902(b)) *See also* Unif. Statutory Rule Against Perpetuities §2, 8B U.L.A. 268 (amended 1990) (explaining that "any nonvested property interest subject to [a power to revoke] is not created . . . until the power terminates (by release, expiration at the death of the donee, or otherwise"); Comment to Unif. Probate Code §2-902(b) (noting that "nonvested property interests and powers of appointment created in [a revocable inter-vivos trust] are created when the power to revoke expires, usually at the settlor's death"). *See generally* §2-905(a) ("[A] nonvested property interest or a power of appointment created by the exercise of a power of appointment is created when the power is irrevocably	For purposes of this act, if there is a person who alone can exercise a power created by a governing instrument to become the unqualified beneficial owner of a nonvested property interest or a property interest subject to a power of appointment described in section 2(2) or (3), the nonvested property interest or power of appointment is created when the power to become the unqualified beneficial owner terminates. (§554.73(2)) *See also* Unif. Statutory Rule Against Perpetuities §2, 8B U.L.A. 268 (amended 1990) (explaining that "any nonvested property interest subject to [a power to revoke] is not created . . . until the power terminates (by release, expiration at the death of the donee, or otherwise"); Comment to Unif. Probate Code §2-902(b) (noting that "nonvested property interests and powers of appointment created in [a revocable inter-vivos trust] are created when the power to revoke expires, usually at the settlor's death"). *See generally* §554.76(1) ("a nonvested property interest or a power of appointment created by the exercise of a power of appointment is created	"If there is a person who alone can exercise a power created by a governing instrument to become the unqualified beneficial owner of (i) a nonvested property interest or (ii) a property interest subject to a power of appointment described in section 501A.01, subsection (b) or (c), the nonvested property interest or power of appointment is created when the power to become the unqualified beneficial owner terminates. (§501A.02(b)) *See also* Unif. Statutory Rule Against Perpetuities §2, 8B U.L.A. 268 (amended 1990) (explaining that "any nonvested property interests subject to [a power to revoke] is not created . . . until the power terminates (by release, expiration at the death of the donee, or otherwise"); Comment to Unif. Probate Code §2-902(b) (noting that "nonvested property interest and powers of appointment created in [a revocable inter-vivos trust] are created when the power to revoke expires, usually at the settlor's death"). *See generally* §501A.05(a) ("[A] nonvested property interest or a power of appointment created by the exercise of a power of appointment is created

---

Table 9
Rule Against Perpetuities

	MASSACHUSETTS	MICHIGAN	MINNESOTA
	exercised or when a revocable exercise becomes irrevocable.")	when the power is irrevocably exercised or when a revocable exercise becomes irrevocable.")	when the power is irrevocably exercised or when a revocable exercise becomes irrevocable.")
18. *When does the period of the rule start re an interest contributed to an irrevocable trust? See UIPC 2-902(c).*	A nonvested property interest or power of appointment arising from a transfer of property to a previously funded trust or other existing property arrangement is created when the nonvested property interest or power of appointment in the original contribution was created. (§2-902(c))	A nonvested property interest or power of appointment arising from a transfer of property to a previously funded trust or other existing arrangement is created when the nonvested property interest or power of appointment in the original contribution was created. (§554.73(3))	A nonvested property interest or power of appointment arising from a transfer of property to a previously funded trust or other existing arrangement is created when the nonvested property interest or power of appointment in the original contribution was created. (§501A.02(c))

Table 9
Rule Against Perpetuities

	MASSACHUSETTS	MICHIGAN	MINNESOTA
19. *Is there a conclusive presumption of fertility, that is, the "fertile octogenarian" rule?*	Unclear. *See Commissioner of Corps. & Taxation v. Bullard*, 46 N.E.2d 557, 565 (Mass. 1943) ("It is clear . . . that this court has never laid down expressly or by implication the general proposition applicable to all kinds of cases that there is an "irrebuttable presumption" or rule of substantive law that a woman is capable of bearing children throughout her life.")[1] *See also* Unif. Statutory Rule Against Perpetuities §1, 8B U.L.A. 256 (amended 1990) (holding that "[t]his principle is not superseded by this Act, and in view of new advances in medical science . . . [this] is not unrealistic."). *But see* C. P. Jhong, *Annotation, Modern Status of Presumption Against Possibility of Issue Being Extinct*, 98 A.L.R.2d 1285 (2003) (noting "a trend toward denying the conclusive or absolute nature of the presumption against the possibility of issue being extinct where there is competent evidence to the contrary has developed in the decisions, although some courts still adhere to the traditional view treating the presumption as conclusive or absolute").	Yes. *Gettins v. Grand Rapids Trust Co.*, 228 N.W. 703, 704 (Mich. 1930). *See also* Unif. Statutory Rule Against Perpetuities §1, 8B U.L.A. 256 (amended 1990) (holding that "[t]his principle is not superseded by this Act, and in view of new advances in medical science . . . [this] is not unrealistic."). *But see* C. P. Jhong, *Annotation, Modern Status of Presumption Against Possibility of Issue Being Extinct*, 98 A.L.R.2d 1285 (2003) (noting "a trend toward denying the conclusive or absolute nature of the presumption against the possibility of issue being extinct where there is competent evidence to the contrary has developed in the decisions, although some courts still adhere to the traditional view treating the presumption as conclusive or absolute").	No specific state case or statute.[2] *See* Unif. Statutory Rule Against Perpetuities §1, 8B U.L.A. 256 (amended 1990) (holding that "[t]his principle is not superseded by this Act, and in view of new advances in medical science . . . [this] is not unrealistic."). *But see* C. P. Jhong, *Annotation, Modern Status of Presumption Against Possibility of Issue Being Extinct*, 98 A.L.R.2d 1285 (2003) (noting "a trend toward denying the conclusive or absolute nature of the presumption against the possibility of issue being extinct where there is competent evidence to the contrary has developed in the decisions, although some courts still adhere to the traditional view treating the presumption as conclusive or absolute").

Table 9
Rule Against Perpetuities

	MASSACHUSETTS	MICHIGAN	MINNESOTA
20. *What is the earliest age a child is deemed capable of bearing a child? What is the impact of illegitimacy?*	Not specifically addressed by USRAP, but the reasoning is the same as set forth in the comment to section 1 of USRAP, 2, Technical Violations of the Common Law Rule. Wait and see will typically result in no violation. Nevertheless, the common law rule ordinarily will be applied initially. "Under the rule, courts must presume that living persons are capable of having or fathering children, no matter how young they are. See In re Graite's Will Trusts, [1949] 1 All E.R. 459, 460 (Ch.). Thus, the rule strikes down any interest whose vesting depends on the assertion that, for example, a toddler will not have children." (Keith L. Butler, Notes & Comments, *Long Live the Dead Hand: A Case for Repeal of the Rule Against Perpetuities in Washington*, 75 Wash. L. Rev. 1237, 1246 n.78 (2000)).	Not specifically addressed by USRAP, but the reasoning is the same as set forth in the comment to section 1 of USRAP, 2, Technical Violations of the Common Law Rule. Wait and see will typically result in no violation. Nevertheless, the common law rule ordinarily will be applied initially. "Under the rule, courts must presume that living persons are capable of having or fathering children, no matter how young they are. See In re Graite's Will Trusts, [1949] 1 All E.R. 459, 460 (Ch.). Thus, the rule strikes down any interest whose vesting depends on the assertion that, for example, a toddler will not have children." (Keith L. Butler, Notes & Comments, *Long Live the Dead Hand: A Case for Repeal of the Rule Against Perpetuities in Washington*, 75 Wash. L. Rev. 1237, 1246 n.78 (2000)).	Not specifically addressed by USRAP, but the reasoning is the same as set forth in the comment to section 1 of USRAP, 2, Technical Violations of the Common Law Rule. Wait and see will typically result in no violation. Nevertheless, the common law rule ordinarily will be applied initially. "Under the rule, courts must presume that living persons are capable of having or fathering children, no matter how young they are. See In re Graite's Will Trusts, [1949] 1 All E.R. 459, 460 (Ch.). Thus, the rule strikes down any interest whose vesting depends on the assertion that, for example, a toddler will not have children." (Keith L. Butler, Notes & Comments, *Long Live the Dead Hand: A Case for Repeal of the Rule Against Perpetuities in Washington*, 75 Wash. L. Rev. 1237, 1246 n.78 (2000)).
21. *Is the "unborn widow" rule observed?*	No specific state case or statute. *See* Unif. Statutory Rule Against Perpetuities § 1, 8B U.L.A. 246 (amended 1990) (explaining that "[t]he chance that [an] interest will become invalid under the Statutory Rule is small" and so the unborn widow rule would rarely invalidate an interest); *see also* 61 Am. Jur. 2d *Perpetuities and Restraints on Alienation* § 39 (2013) (noting the same).	No specific state case or statute. *See* Unif. Statutory Rule Against Perpetuities § 1, 8B U.L.A. 246 (amended 1990) (explaining that "[t]he chance that [an] interest will become invalid under the Statutory Rule is small" and so the unborn widow rule would rarely invalidate an interest); *see also* 61 Am. Jur. 2d *Perpetuities and Restraints on Alienation* § 39 (2013) (noting the same).	No specific state case or statute. *See* Unif. Statutory Rule Against Perpetuities § 1, 8B U.L.A. 246 (amended 1990) (explaining that "[t]he chance that [an] interest will become invalid under the Statutory Rule is small" and so the unborn widow rule would rarely invalidate an interest); *see also* 61 Am. Jur. 2d *Perpetuities and Restraints on Alienation* § 39 (2013) (noting the same).

Table 9
Rule Against Perpetuities

	MASSACHUSETTS	MICHIGAN	MINNESOTA
22. Does the "slothful executor" rule apply, i.e., an administrative contingency clause providing for a "distribution to, e.g., those issue living at the time of the satisfaction of the administrative condition precedent?"	No. Brandenburg v. Thorndike, 28 N.E. 575, 576 (Mass. 1885) (explaining that it is not within the "unlimited discretion of the [executors] to delay the vesting or enjoyment of the estates to such time as they think expedient.") See also Unif. Statutory Rule Against Perpetuities § 1, 8B U.L.A. 245 (amended 1990) (Under USRAP, an "interest becomes invalid only if it remains in existence and nonvested 90 years after [the testator's] death. Since it is almost certain that the final distribution of [an] estate will occur well within this 90-year period, the chance that [an] interest will be invalid is negligible.")	No specific state case or statute. See Unif. Statutory Rule Against Perpetuities § 1, 8B U.L.A. 245 (amended 1990) (Under USRAP, an "interest becomes invalid only if it remains in existence and nonvested 90 years after [the testator's] death. Since it is almost certain that the final distribution of [an] estate will occur well within this 90-year period, the chance that [an] interest will be invalid is negligible.")	No specific state case or statute. See Unif. Statutory Rule Against Perpetuities § 1, 8B U.L.A. 245 (amended 1990) (Under USRAP, an "interest becomes invalid only if it remains in existence and nonvested 90 years after [the testator's] death. Since it is almost certain that the final distribution of [an] estate will occur well within this 90-year period, the chance that [an] interest will be invalid is negligible.")

Table 9
Rule Against Perpetuities

	MASSACHUSETTS	MICHIGAN	MINNESOTA
23. *Does the all-or-nothing rule apply to class gifts?*	Yes. Springfield Safe Deposit & Trust Co. v. Ireland, 167 N.E. 261, 263 (Mass. 1929) ("When the gift is of the whole estate to a class of persons answering a given description, and not separately to its members, and any member of that class may have to be ascertained at a period beyond the limit allowed by law, the whole gift is void.") *See also* Unif. Statutory Rule Against Perpetuities §1, 8B U.L.A. 257 (amended 1990) ("Although this Act does not supersede the basic idea of the much-maligned 'all-or-nothing' rule, the evils sometimes attributed to it are substantially if not entirely eliminated by the wait-and-see feature of the Statutory Rule and by the availability of reformation under Section 3.")	No specific state case or statute. *See* Unif. Statutory Rule Against Perpetuities §1, 8B U.L.A. 257 (amended 1990) ("Although this Act does not supersede the basic idea of the much-maligned 'all-or-nothing' rule, the evils sometimes attributed to it are substantially if not entirely eliminated by the wait-and-see feature of the Statutory Rule and by the availability of reformation under Section 3.")	No specific state case or statute. *See* Unif. Statutory Rule Against Perpetuities §1, 8B U.L.A. 257 (amended 1990) ("Although this Act does not supersede the basic idea of the much-maligned 'all-or-nothing' rule, the evils sometimes attributed to it are substantially if not entirely eliminated by the wait-and-see feature of the Statutory Rule and by the availability of reformation under Section 3.")
24. *Is there an exception to the all-or-nothing rule in the case of subclasses or specific sums to each member of the class?*	No specific state case or statute. *See* Unif. Statutory Rule Against Perpetuities §1, 8B U.L.A. 257 (amended 1990) ("The specific-sum and sub-class doctrines are not superseded by this Act.")	No specific state case or statute. *See* Unif. Statutory Rule Against Perpetuities §1, 8B U.L.A. 257 (amended 1990) ("The specific-sum and sub-class doctrines are not superseded by this Act.")	No specific state case or statute. *See* Unif. Statutory Rule Against Perpetuities §1, 8B U.L.A. 257 (amended 1990) ("The specific-sum and sub-class doctrines are not superseded by this Act.")

Table 9
Rule Against Perpetuities

	MASSACHUSETTS	MICHIGAN	MINNESOTA
25. *Is the infectious invalidity rule followed outside class gifts?*	Yes, but only in "circumstances where the failure of a gift may so disrupt the dispositive scheme of the settlor or testator that he would prefer that valid prior gifts should also be struck down." New England Trust Co. v. Sanger, 149 N.E.2d 598, 605 (Mass. 1958). *But see* Unif. Statutory Rule Against Perpetuities §1, 8B U.L.A. 256 (amended 1990) (explaining that "[t]he doctrine of infectious invalidity is superseded by this Act by Section 3, under which courts . . . are required to *reform* the disposition to approximate as closely as possible the transferor's . . . plan of distribution.")	No specific state case or statute. *See* Unif. Statutory Rule Against Perpetuities §1, 8B U.L.A. 256 (amended 1990) (explaining that "[t]he doctrine of infectious invalidity is superseded by this Act by Section 3, under which courts . . . are required to *reform* the disposition to approximate as closely as possible the transferor's . . . plan of distribution.")	No specific state case or statute. *See* Unif. Statutory Rule Against Perpetuities §1, 8B U.L.A. 256 (amended 1990) (explaining that "[t]he doctrine of infectious invalidity is superseded by this Act by Section 3, under which courts . . . are required to *reform* the disposition to approximate as closely as possible the transferor's . . . plan of distribution.") *But see* In re Olson, File No. 75-PR-06-445 (Minnesota Court of Appeals Sept. 3, 2013) (unpublished opinion) (there is no violation of rule because after 21 years a trustee has the power to convey an absolute fee in possession or absolute ownership of the trust property)

Table 9
Rule Against Perpetuities

	MASSACHUSETTS	MICHIGAN	MINNESOTA
26. *Is there a rule against the suspension of the power of alienation? If so, how is it stated?*	No specific state statute. *See Franklin* v. Spadafora, 447 N.E.2d 1244, 1246 (Mass. 1983) (explaining that the court will enforce "reasonable" restraints on alienation and listing five factors that support the conclusion of reasonableness.)	Michigan's § 554.52, which provided a rule against the suspension of the power of alienation, was repealed. *See also* #1 above.	*Pre-2016:* The power of alienation of property held in trust may be suspended, by terms of a trust, for a period of not more than 21 years. (§ 501B.09 (subd. 2)) *Post-2015:* The rule is still in effect. (§ 201C.1202 (subd. 2)) However, there is no suspension of the power if there is an unlimited power in a person to eliminate the trust and to acquire an absolute fee or ownership, such as by revocation. There is also no suspension if the trustee has power to sell an absolute fee in possession or absolute ownership of property. (§ 501C.1202 (subd. 2)) (eff. Jan. 1, 2016)
27. *Effective date.*	March 31, 2012. *See also* #6.	December 27, 1988. *See also* #1 with respect to the personal property trust perpetuities act abolishing the rule against perpetuities and related rules in certain instances.	January 1, 1992. *See also* #6.

---

[1] For questions, #19-25, *see also* § 2-906 (noting that the state's USRAP supersedes the common law rule against perpetuities). The answers to questions #19-25 are not likely to apply in most cases because of the abolition of the rule with respect to the vast majority of trusts.

[2] For questions, #19-25, *see also* § 501A.06 (noting that the state's USRAP supersedes the common law rule against perpetuities). The answers to questions #19-25 are not likely to apply in most cases because of the abolition of the rule with respect to the vast majority of trusts.

Table 9
Rule Against Perpetuities

	MISSISSIPPI	MISSOURI	MONTANA
1. *Which rule is in effect: the common law rule, the Uniform Statutory Rule Against Perpetuities (USRAP), other law, or none?*	USRAP	Common law rule with major exceptions. In particular, see #2b for trusts that are exempt much like Illinois Qualified Perpetual Trusts. (§ 456.025)	USRAP (Mont. Code Ann. §§ 72-2-1001 - 72-2-1007)
2. a. *Is the common law rule relevant to any interests?*	Yes.	Yes, for some interests.	Yes, but only as the starting point of the analysis.
b. *What is the relevant rule?*	The rule against perpetuities requires that [an interest] must either definitely vest or definitely fail within 21 years of some life in being at the time of the instrument. (C&D Inv. Co. v. Gulf Transport Co., 526 So. 2d 526, 528 (Miss. 1988))	"'The rule against perpetuities is that no interest within its scope is good unless it must vest, if at all, not later than twenty-one years after some life or lives in being at the creation of the interest, to which period is added the period of gestation, if gestation exists.'" (St. Louis Union Trust Co. v. Kelley, 199 S.W.2d 344, 350 (Mo. 1947)	A nonvested property interest is invalid unless: (a) When the interest is created, it is certain to vest or terminate no later than 21 years after the death of an individual then alive; or (b) The interest either vests or terminates within 90 years after its creation.

Table 9
Rule Against Perpetuities

	MISSISSIPPI	MISSOURI	MONTANA
		(citations omitted) *See also* §456.025(1) ("The rule against perpetuities shall not apply to and any rule prohibiting unreasonable restraints on or suspension of the power of alienation shall not be violated by a trust if a trustee, or other person or persons to whom the power is properly granted or delegated, has the power pursuant to the terms of the trust or applicable law to sell the trust property during the period of time the trust continues beyond the period of the rule against perpetuities that would apply to the trust but for this subsection.")	(§72-2-1002(1))
3. *Does the rule apply to other than private trusts?*	Yes. The rule applies to everything except: §79-15-21 (inapplicable to investment trusts); § 41-43-51 (inapplicable to cemeteries); *see, e.g.,* Alabama, question #3 (noting that the Rule generally does not apply to charitable trusts)	Yes. The rule applies except to: - "a trust of real or personal property, or both, created as part of a stock bonus plan, pension plan, disability or death benefit plan, medical benefit plan, profit-sharing plan or retirement plan, for the exclusive benefit of employees or self-employed persons, to which contributions are made by an employer, or employees, or	Yes. The rule applies except to: (1) a nonvested property interest or a power of appointment arising out of a nondonative transfer, except a nonvested property interest or a power of appointment arising out of a: (a) premarital or postmarital agreement; (b) separation or divorce settlement; (c) spouse's election;

Table 9
Rule Against Perpetuities

MISSISSIPPI	MISSOURI	MONTANA
	both, or by self-employed persons, for the purpose of distributing to such employees or self-employed persons the earnings or the principal, or both earnings and principal of the fund so held in trust." (§ 456.011) - a trust for charitable purposes. (Mercantile Trust Co. v. Shriners' Hospital, 551 S.W.2d 864, 867 (Mo. Ct. App. 1977) - a qualifying trust. See #2b. The exception to the rule with respect to qualifying trusts applies to such trusts created by instrument or exercise of a nongeneral power executed or amended on or after August 28, 2001; a trust created by exercise of a general power on or after August 28, 2001; or the laws of Missouri become applicable to the trust on or after August 28, 2001, the laws of any other state applied to the trust before August 28, 2001, and the rule did not apply to the trust pursuant to the law of the other state.	(d) similar arrangement arising out of a prospective existing or previous marital relationship between the parties; (e) contract to make or not to revoke a will or trust; (f) contract to exercise or not to exercise a power of appointment; (g) transfer in satisfaction of a duty of support; or (h) reciprocal transfer; (2) a fiduciary's power relating to the administration or management of assets, including the power of a fiduciary to sell, lease, or mortgage property, and the power of a fiduciary to determine principal and income; (3) the power to appoint a fiduciary; (4) a discretionary power of a trustee to distribute principal before termination of a trust to a beneficiary having an indefeasibly vested interest in the income and principal;

Table 9
Rule Against Perpetuities

MISSISSIPPI	MISSOURI	MONTANA
	(§ 456.025(3)(3))	(5) a nonvested property interest held by a charity, government or governmental agency or subdivision, if the nonvested property interest is preceded by an interest held by another charity, government or governmental agency or subdivision; (6) a nonvested property interest in or a power of appointment with respect to a trust or other property arrangement forming part of a pension, profit sharing, stock bonus, health, disability, death benefit, income deferral or other current or deferred benefit plan for one or more employees, independent contractors or their beneficiaries or spouses, to which contributions are made for the purpose of distributing to or for the benefit of the participants or their beneficiaries or spouses the property, income or principal in the trust or other property arrangement, except a nonvested property interest or a power of appointment that is created by an election of a participant or a beneficiary or spouse; or

Table 9
Rule Against Perpetuities

	MISSISSIPPI	MISSOURI	MONTANA
			(7) a property interest, power of appointment or arrangement that was not subject to the common-law rule against perpetuities or is excluded by another statute of this state. §72-2-1005
4. *Does the rule invalidate the interest at its creation, or is the rule revised by a wait-and-see approach?*	Wait-and-see. (C&D Inv. Co. v. Gulf Transport Co., 526 So. 2d 526, 530 (Miss. 1988))	At its creation. (Davies v. McDowell, 549 S.W.2d 619, 623 (Mo. 1977))	Wait-and-see (§72-2-1002(1)(b))
5. *Can the trust be reformed?*	N/A	No statutory provision.	Yes but only if one of the following conditions is satisfied: (1) a nonvested property interest or power of appointment becomes invalid under §72-2-1002 see #2b; (2) a class gift is not but might become invalid under 72-2-1002 and the time has arrived when the share of any class member is to take effect in possession or enjoyment; or (3) a nonvested property interest that is not validated by §72-2-1002(1)(a), that is, the traditional common law rule, can vest but not within 90 years after its creation. (§72-2-1004)

Table 9
Rule Against Perpetuities

	MISSISSIPPI	MISSOURI	MONTANA
6. *If yes to 5., under what theory?*	N/A	No statutory provision.	[A] court shall reform a disposition in the manner most closely approximates the transferor's manifested plan of distribution and is within the 90 years allowed by §72-2-1002 (§72-2-1004) *See also* §72-2-1006 ("If a nonvested property interest or a power of appointment was created before October 1, 1989, and is determined in a judicial proceeding commenced on or after October 1, 1989, to violate this state's rule against perpetuities as that rule existed before October 1, 1989, a court, upon the petition of an interested person, may reform the disposition in the manner that most closely approximates the transferor's manifested plan of distribution and that is within the limits of the rule against perpetuities applicable when the nonvested property interest or power of appointment was created.")

Table 9
Rule Against Perpetuities

	MISSISSIPPI	MISSOURI	MONTANA
7. *When is a general testamentary power of appointment invalid?*	*See* Unif. Statutory Rule Against Perpetuities § 1, 8B U.L.A. 248 (amended 1990) ("Under the Common-law Rule . . . a *nongeneral power* (whether or not presently exercisable) or a *general testamentary power* is invalid as of the time of its creation if it *might* not terminate (by irrevocable exercise or otherwise) within a life in being plus 21 years.")	*See* Unif. Statutory Rule Against Perpetuities § 1, 8B U.L.A. 248 (amended 1990) ("Under the Common-law Rule . . . a *nongeneral power* (whether or not presently exercisable) or a *general testamentary power* is invalid as of the time of its creation if it *might* not terminate (by irrevocable exercise or otherwise) within a life in being plus 21 years.")	A general testamentary power of appointment is invalid unless: (a) when the power is created, it is certain to be irrevocably exercised or otherwise to terminate no later than 21 years after the death of an individual then alive; or (b) the power is irrevocably exercised or otherwise terminates within 90 years after its creation. (§72-2-1002(3))
8. *Same, but nongeneral testamentary power.*	See #7.	See #7.	A nongeneral testamentary power of appointment is invalid unless: (a) when the power is created, it is certain to be irrevocably exercised or otherwise to termination no later than 21 years after the death of an individual then alive; or (b) the power is irrevocably exercised or otherwise terminates within 90 years after its creation. (§72-2-1002(3))

Table 9
Rule Against Perpetuities

	MISSISSIPPI	*MISSOURI*	*MONTANA*
9. *Same, but general power, whether testamentary or inter vivos, not presently exercisable because of a condition precedent.*	*See* Unif. Statutory Rule Against Perpetuities § 1, 8B U.L.A. 248 (amended 1990) ("Under the Common-law Rule, a general power not presently exercisable because of a condition precedent is invalid as of the time of its creation if the condition might neither be satisfied nor become impossible to satisfy with a life in being plus 21 years.")	*See* Unif. Statutory Rule Against Perpetuities § 1, 8B U.L.A. 248 (amended 1990) ("Under the Common-law Rule, a general power not presently exercisable because of a condition precedent is invalid as of the time of its creation if the condition might neither be satisfied nor become impossible to satisfy with a life in being plus 21 years.")	A general power of appointment not presently exercisable because of a condition precedent is invalid unless: (a) when the power is created, the condition precedent is certain to be satisfied or becomes impossible to satisfy no later than 21 years after the death of an individual then alive; or (b) the condition precedent either is satisfied or becomes impossible to satisfy within 90 years after its creation. (§72-2-1002(2))
10. *Same, but nongeneral inter vivos power.*	See #7.	See #7.	See #8.

Table 9
Rule Against Perpetuities

	MISSISSIPPI	MISSOURI	MONTANA
11. *Is a period of gestation added to the perpetuity period?*	Yes. Carter v. Berry, 136 So. 2d 871, 877 (Miss. 1962) (stating that a period of gestation of 9 months may be applied, if necessary.)	Yes. (St. Louis Union Trust Co. v. Kelley, 199 S.W.2d 344, 350 (Mo. 1947))	No. The possibility that a child will be born to a person after that person's death is disregarded. (§72-2-1002(4)) *See also* Unif. Statutory Rule Against Perpetuities §1, 8B U.L.A. 243, 243 (amended 1990) ("[T]he possibility that a child will be born to [a testator] after his death must be disregarded; and the possibility that a child will be born to any of [the testator's] descendants after their deaths must also be disregarded. Note, however, that the rule of subsection (d) does *not* apply to the question of the entitlement of an after-born child to take a beneficial interest in the trust").
12. *What is the treatment of a "later of the traditional rule or 90 years" clause? See UPC 2-901(e).*	N/A	N/A	That language must be disregarded to the extent it produces a period of time that exceeds 21 years after the death of the survivor of the specified lives. (§72-2-1002(5))

Table 9
Rule Against Perpetuities

	MISSISSIPPI	MISSOURI	MONTANA
13. *When is an interest created by the exercise of a general testamentary power deemed created?*	*See* comment to Unif. Probate Code §2-902(a) ("general principles of property law determine that a nonvested property interest or power of appointment created by will is created at the decedent's death"); Unif. Statutory Rule Against Perpetuities §2, 8B U.L.A. 268 (amended 1990) (stating the same).	*See* §442.557 ("In determining the validity of limitations appointed in the exercise of a general power of appointment exercisable only at the death of the donee of the power by will or other instrument, or of limitations in default of such appointment, the perpetuities period and any similar period shall run from the death of the donee of the power and not from the time of creation of the power.") *See also* comment to Unif. Probate Code §2-902(a) ("general principles of property law determine that a nonvested property interest or power of appointment created by will is created at the decedent's death"); Unif. Statutory Rule Against Perpetuities §2, 8B U.L.A. 268 (amended 1990) (stating the same).	Except as provided in 72-2-1005 and subsections (2) and (3) of this section, the time of creation of a nonvested property interest or a power of appointment is determined under general principles of property law. (§72-2-1003(1)) The first of the excepted provisions states that as long as a person with a general power to become the unqualified beneficial owner has that power, the nonvested interest is created when the power terminates. The second of the excepted provisions states that a nonvested property interest, which arises from a transfer to an existing trust, is created when the nonvested property interest in the trust was created. (§72-2-1003(2)(3)) *See also* Unif. Statutory Rule Against Perpetuities §2, 8B U.L.A. 268 (amended 1990) (explaining that "general principles of property law determine that the time … [of creation] is at the decedent's death.") *See generally* §72-2-1006(a) ("For purposes of this section, a nonvested property interest or a power of appointment created by the exercise of a power of appointment is created when the power is irrevocably exercised or when a revocable exercise becomes irrevocable.")

Table 9
Rule Against Perpetuities

	MISSISSIPPI	MISSOURI	MONTANA
14. *Same, but nongeneral testamentary power.*	See #13.	*See also* comment to Unif. Probate Code § 2-902(a) ("general principles of property law determine that a nonvested property interest or power of appointment created by will is created at the decedent's death"); Unif. Statutory Rule Against Perpetuities § 2, 8B U.L.A. 268 (amended 1990) (stating the same).	See #13.

Table 9
Rule Against Perpetuities

MISSISSIPPI	MISSOURI	MONTANA
15. *Same, but general inter vivos power.*	*See* comment to Unif. Probate Code §2-902(a) ("With respect to an inter vivos transfer, an interest or power is created on the date the transfer becomes effective for purposes of property law generally, normally the date of delivery of the deed or funding of the trust."); Unif. Statutory Rule Against Perpetuities §2, 8B U.L.A. 268 (stating the same).	*See* comment to Unif. Probate Code §2-902(a) ("With respect to an inter vivos transfer, an interest or power is created on the date the transfer becomes effective for purposes of property law generally, normally the date of delivery of the deed or funding of the trust."); Unif. Statutory Rule Against Perpetuities §2, 8B U.L.A. 268 (stating the same).	Except as provided in 72-2-1005 and subsections (2) and (3) of this section, the time of creation of a nonvested property interest or a power of appointment is determined under general principles of property law. (§72-2-1003(1)) The first of the excepted provisions states that as long as a person with a general power to become the unqualified beneficial owner has that power, the nonvested interest is created when the power terminates. The second of the excepted provisions states that a nonvested property interest, which arises from a transfer to an existing trust, is created when the nonvested property interest in the trust was created. (§72-2-1003(2)-(3)) *See also* Unif. Statutory Rule Against Perpetuities §2, 8B U.L.A. 268 (amended 1990) (explaining that "the time when the interest or power is created is the date the transfer becomes effective for purposes of property law generally, normally the date of delivery of the deed"); Comment to Unif. Probate Code §2-902(a) (stating same and adding "the funding of the trust" as "normally" the time when the interest is created). *See generally* §72-2-1006(1) ("For purposes of this section, a nonvested

Table 9
Rule Against Perpetuities

	MISSISSIPPI	MISSOURI	MONTANA
			property interest or a power of appointment created by the exercise of a power of appointment is created when the power is irrevocably exercised or when a revocable exercise becomes irrevocable.")
16. *Same, but nongeneral inter vivos power.*	See #15.	See #15.	See #15.

Table 9
Rule Against Perpetuities

	MISSISSIPPI	MISSOURI	MONTANA
17. *When is an interest created if the grantor of a trust has a power to revoke?*	*See* comment to Unif. Probate Code § 2-902(b) (noting that "nonvested property interests and powers of appointment created in [a revocable inter-vivos trust] are created when the power to revoke expires, usually at the settlor's death"); Unif. Statutory Rule Against Perpetuities § 2, 8B U.L.A. 268 (amended 1990) (explaining that "any nonvested property interest subject to [a power to revoke] is not created . . . until the power terminates (by release, expiration at the death of the donee, or otherwise").	*See* comment to Unif. Probate Code § 2-902(b) (noting that "nonvested property interests and powers of appointment created in [a revocable inter-vivos trust] are created when the power to revoke expires, usually at the settlor's death"); Unif. Statutory Rule Against Perpetuities § 2, 8B U.L.A. 268 (amended 1990) (explaining that "any nonvested property interest subject to [a power to revoke] is not created . . . until the power terminates (by release, expiration at the death of the donee, or otherwise").	For purposes of this part, if there is a person who alone can exercise a power created by a governing instrument to become the unqualified beneficial owner of a nonvested property interest or a property interest subject to a power of appointment described in 72-2-1002(2) or (3), the nonvested property interest or power of appointment is created when the power to become the unqualified beneficial owner terminates. (§72-2-1003(2) *See also* Unif. Statutory Rule Against Perpetuities § 2, 8B U.L.A. 268 (amended 1990) (explaining that "any nonvested property interest subject to [a power to revoke] is not created . . . until the power terminates (by release, expiration at the death of the donee, or otherwise"); Comment to Unif. Probate Code § 2-902(b) (noting that "nonvested property interests and powers of appointment created in [a revocable inter-vivos trust] are created when the power to revoke expires, usually at the settlor's death"). *See generally* §72-2-1006(1) ("A nonvested property interest or a power of appointment created by the exercise of a power of appointment is created when the power is irrevocably

Table 9
Rule Against Perpetuities

	MISSISSIPPI	*MISSOURI*	*MONTANA*
			exercised or when a revocable exercise becomes irrevocable.")
18. *When does the period of the rule start re an interest contributed to an irrevocable trust? See UPC 2-902(c).*	*See* comment to Unif. Probate Code 2-902(c) ("Arguably, at common law, each transfer [to an existing irrevocable inter-vivos trust] starts the period of the Rule running anew as to each transfer.")	*See* comment to Unif. Probate Code 2-902(c) ("Arguably, at common law, each transfer [to an existing irrevocable inter-vivos trust] starts the period of the Rule running anew as to each transfer.")	A nonvested property interest or power of appointment arising from a transfer of property to a previously funded trust or other existing arrangement is created when the nonvested property interest or power of appointment in the original contribution was created. (§ 72-2-1003(3))
19. *Is there a conclusive presumption of fertility, that is, the "fertile octogenarian" rule?*	Probably not. *See* Citizens Nat'l Bank v. Longshore, 304 So. 2d 287, 289 (Miss. 1974) ("The common law presumption of the possibility of issue regardless of the age of husband and wife, did not envision modern surgery (e.g., hysterectomy here) rendering procreation impossible.")	Yes. Loud v. St. Louis Union Trust Co., 249 S.W. 629, 634 (Mo. 1923) ("And in applying the rule it should not be forgotten that a woman is legally presumed to be capable of bearing children so long as she lives.")	No specific state case or statute. *See* Unif. Statutory Rule Against Perpetuities § 1, 8B U.L.A. 256 (amended 1990) (holding that "[t]his principle is not superseded by this Act, and in view of new advances in medical science . . . [this] is not unrealistic.")). *But see* C. P. Jhong, Annotation, *Modern Status of Presumption Against Possibility of Issue Being Extinct*, 98 A.L.R.2d 1285 (2003) (noting "a trend toward denying the conclusive or absolute nature of the presumption against the possibility of issue being extinct where there is competent evidence to the contrary has developed in the decisions, although some courts still adhere to the traditional view treating the presumption as conclusive or absolute").

Table 9
Rule Against Perpetuities

	MISSISSIPPI	MISSOURI	MONTANA
20. *What is the earliest age a child is deemed capable of bearing a child? What is the impact of illegitimacy?*	"Under the rule, courts must presume that living persons are capable of having or fathering children, no matter how young they are. See In re Graite's Will Trusts, [1949] 1 All E.R. 459, 460 (Ch.). Thus, the rule strikes down any interest whose vesting depends on the assertion that, for example, a toddler will not have children." (Keith L. Butler, Notes & Comments, *Long Live the Dead Hand: A Case for Repeal of the Rule Against Perpetuities in Washington,* 75 Wash. L. Rev. 1237, 1246 n.78 (2000)).	"Under the rule, courts must presume that living persons are capable of having or fathering children, no matter how young they are. See In re Graite's Will Trusts, [1949] 1 All E.R. 459, 460 (Ch.). Thus, the rule strikes down any interest whose vesting depends on the assertion that, for example, a toddler will not have children." (Keith L. Butler, Notes & Comments, *Long Live the Dead Hand: A Case for Repeal of the Rule Against Perpetuities in Washington,* 75 Wash. L. Rev. 1237, 1246 n.78 (2000)).	Not specifically addressed by USRAP, but the reasoning is the same as set forth in the comment to section 1 of USRAP, 2, Technical Violations of the Common Law Rule. Wait and see will typically result in no violation. Nevertheless, the common law rule ordinarily will be applied initially. "Under the rule, courts must presume that living persons are capable of having or fathering children, no matter how young they are. See In re Graite's Will Trusts, [1949] 1 All E.R. 459, 460 (Ch.). Thus, the rule strikes down any interest whose vesting depends on the assertion that, for example, a toddler will not have children." (Keith L. Butler, Notes & Comments, *Long Live the Dead Hand: A Case for Repeal of the Rule Against Perpetuities in Washington,* 75 Wash. L. Rev. 1237, 1246 n.78 (2000)).
21. *Is the "unborn widow" rule observed?*	*See, e.g.,* Arkansas, question #21.	*See, e.g.,* Arkansas, question #21.	No specific state case or statute. *See* Unif. Statutory Rule Against Perpetuities §1, 8B U.L.A. 246 (amended 1990) (explaining that "[t]he chance that [an] interest will become invalid under the Statutory Rule is small" and so the unborn widow rule would rarely invalidate an interest); *see also* 61 Am. Jur. 2d *Perpetuities and Restraints on Alienation* § 39 (2013) (noting the same).

Table 9
Rule Against Perpetuities

	MISSISSIPPI	MISSOURI	MONTANA
22. Does the "slothful executor" rule apply, i.e., an administrative contingency clause providing for a "distribution to, e.g., those issue living at the time of the satisfaction of the administrative condition precedent?"	See, e.g., California, question #22.	See, e.g., California, question #22.	No specific state case or statute. See Unif. Statutory Rule Against Perpetuities §1, 8B U.L.A. 245 (amended 1990) (Under USRAP, an "interest becomes invalid only if it remains in existence and nonvested 90 years after [the testator's] death. Since it is almost certain that the final distribution of [an] estate will occur well within this 90-year period, the chance that [an] interest will be invalid is negligible.")

Table 9
Rule Against Perpetuities

	MISSISSIPPI	MISSOURI	MONTANA
23. *Does the all-or-nothing rule apply to class gifts?*	Carter v. Berry, 140 So. 2d 843, 848 (Miss. 1962) (appearing to reject the all-or-nothing rule with respect to class gifts; instead favoring a case by case analysis to see if the valid portion of the trust can be separated and saved from the invalid portion of the trust.)	No. § 442.555(1) ("When any limitation or provision violates the rule against perpetuities or a rule or policy corollary thereto and the instrument containing the limitation or provision also contains other limitations or provisions which do not in themselves violate the rule against perpetuities or any such rule or policy, the other limitations or provisions shall be valid and effective in accordance with their terms unless the limitation or provision which violates the rule against perpetuities or such rule or policy is manifestly so essential to the dispositive scheme of the grantor, settlor or testator that it is inferable that he would not wish the limitations or provisions which do not in themselves violate the rule against perpetuities to stand alone. Doubts as to the probable wishes of the grantor, settlor or testator shall be resolved in favor of the validity of limitations and provisions.")	No specific state case or statute. *See* Unif. Statutory Rule Against Perpetuities § 1, 8B U.L.A. 257 (amended 1990) ("Although this Act does not supersede the basic idea of the much-maligned 'all-or-nothing' rule, the evils sometimes attributed to it are substantially if not entirely eliminated by the wait-and-see feature of the Statutory Rule and by the availability of reformation under Section 3.")

Table 9
Rule Against Perpetuities

	MISSISSIPPI	*MISSOURI*	*MONTANA*
24. *Is there an exception to the all-or-nothing rule in the case of subclasses or specific sums to each member of the class?*	*See* Unif. Statutory Rule Against Perpetuities §2, 8B U.L.A. 257 ("The common law also recognizes a doctrine called the specific-sum doctrine which is derived from Storrs v. Benbow, 3 De G.M. & G. 390, 43 Eng. Rep 153 (Ch. 1853), and states: If a specified sum of money is to be paid to each member of a class, the interest of each class member is entitled to separate treatment and is valid or invalid under the Rule on its own. The common law also recognizes a doctrine called the sub-class doctrine, which is derived from Cattlin v. Brown, 11 Hare 372, 68 Eng. Rep. 1318 (Ch. 1853), and states: If the ultimate takers are not described as a single class but rather as a group of separate subclasses, and if the share to which each separate subclass is entitled will finally be determined within the period of the Rule, the gifts to the different subclasses are separate for the purpose of the Rule.").	*See* Unif. Statutory Rule Against Perpetuities §2, 8B U.L.A. 257 ("The common law also recognizes a doctrine called the specific-sum doctrine which is derived from Storrs v. Benbow, 3 De G.M. & G. 390, 43 Eng. Rep 153 (Ch. 1853), and states: If a specified sum of money is to be paid to each member of a class, the interest of each class member is entitled to separate treatment and is valid or invalid under the Rule on its own. The common law also recognizes a doctrine called the sub-class doctrine, which is derived from Cattlin v. Brown, 11 Hare 372, 68 Eng. Rep. 1318 (Ch. 1853), and states: If the ultimate takers are not described as a single class but rather as a group of separate subclasses, and if the share to which each separate subclass is entitled will finally be determined within the period of the Rule, the gifts to the different subclasses are separate for the purpose of the Rule.").	No specific state case or statute. *See* Unif. Statutory Rule Against Perpetuities §1, 8B U.L.A. 257 (amended 1990) ("The specific-sum and sub-class doctrines are not superseded by this Act.").

Table 9
Rule Against Perpetuities

	MISSISSIPPI	MISSOURI	MONTANA
25. *Is the infectious invalidity rule followed outside class gifts?*	Carter v. Berry, 140 So. 2d 843, 850 (Miss. 1962) ("Infectious invalidity is not a universal doctrine, as will be hereinafter noted. Where part of the testator's plan is valid and part invalid, the normal procedure is to examine the total plan of testator, and determine whether that part which is invalid is so integral to the total plan that it can be inferred testator would have preferred all to fail, rather than to have the valid part stand alone. If the valid part actually accomplishes most of testator's desires, then that portion should stand.")	See #23 and Cole v. Peters, 3 S.W.3d 846, 852 (Mo. Ct. App. 1999).	No specific state case or statute. *See* Unif. Statutory Rule Against Perpetuities §1, 8B U.L.A. 256 (amended 1990) (explaining that "[t]he doctrine of infectious invalidity is superseded by this Act by Section 3, under which courts . . . are required to *reform* the disposition to approximate as closely as possible the transferor's . . . plan of distribution.")
26. *Is there a rule against the suspension of the power of alienation? If so, how is it stated?*	Reasonableness standard. Sanders v. Hicks, 317 So. 2d 61, 64 (1975) (overruled on other grounds) (finding that restraints will be upheld only if reasonable under the circumstances). *See also* Estate of Kelly, 193 So. 2d 575, 578 (1967). ("[A] restraint on alienation may not exceed the life of the life tenant or a succession of life tenants living at the time the life estate is created.")	The rule does not apply with respect to qualifying trusts. See #2a. (§456.025(1)) Reasonableness standard. Cole v. Peters, 3 S.W.3d 846, 850-51 (Mo. Ct. App. 1999) (considering four factors to determine reasonableness including purpose and duration of restraint).	"Reasonableness" standard. Edgar v. Hunt, 706 P.2d 120, 122 (Mont. 1985) (interpreting section 70-1-405, which states "conditions restraining alienation, when repugnant to the interest created, are void" as applying "the majority common law rule that restraints on alienation, when reasonable, are valid.")

Table 9
Rule Against Perpetuities

	MISSISSIPPI	MISSOURI	MONTANA
27. *Effective date.*	N/A	August 28, 2001. *See also #3.*	October 1, 1989. *See also #6.*

Table 9
Rule Against Perpetuities

	NEBRASKA	NEVADA	NEW HAMPSHIRE
1. Which rule is in effect: the common law rule, the Uniform Statutory Rule Against Perpetuities (USRAP), other law, or none?	USRAP. (Neb. Rev. Stat. §§ 76-2001 - § 76-2008) However, note the exception when the trust instrument states that the rule does not apply. See #3.(a).	USRAP with an extended 365-year rule. (Nev. Rev. Stat. §§ 111.103 - 111.1039) Attempt to repeal constitutional prohibition of perpetuities, art. 15, § 4, was rejected by voters in 2002. In Bullion Monarch v. Barrick Goldstrike, 345 P.3d 1040 (Sup. Ct. 2015), the Nevada Supreme Court appears to have construed the term "perpetuities" in the constitution as a general principle to be defined more precisely by the legislature and not locked into the common law meaning of the "rule against perpetuities." However, the constitutional bar regarding perpetuities was declared by court not the same as the common law rule. Thus, the permissible 365-year term, enacted by statute, is constitutional. (Bullion Monarch Mining, Inc. v. Barrick Goldstrike Mines, Inc., 345 P.3d 1040, 1041-42 (Nev. 2015)).	Common law rule with major exceptions. (N.H. Rev. Stat. § 547:3-k) See #2.b.
2. a. Is the common law rule relevant to any interests?	Yes, but only as the starting point of the analysis. However, § 76-2001 supersedes the rule of common law. (§ 76-2008)	Yes, but only as the starting point of the analysis.	Yes, for some interests.

Table 9
Rule Against Perpetuities

	NEBRASKA	*NEVADA*	*NEW HAMPSHIRE*
b. What is the relevant rule?	A nonvested property interest is invalid unless: (1) When the interest is created, it is certain to vest or terminate no later than 21 years after the death of an individual then alive; or (2) The interest either vests or terminates within 90 years after its creation. (§76-2002(a))	A nonvested property interest is invalid unless: (a) When the interest is created, it is certain to vest or terminate no later than 21 years after the death of an individual then alive; or (b) The interest either vests or terminates within 365 years after its creation. (§111.1031(1))	The Rule Against Perpetuities provides that no interest in property is good "'unless it must vest, if at all, not later than twenty-one years after some life in being at the creation of the interest'." (Emerson v. King, 394 A.2d 51, 54 (N.H. 1978)) However the rule does not apply to any disposition of property or interest therein created after the effective date of this section, if (i) the instrument making the disposition or creating the interest contains a provision which expressly exempts the instrument from the application of the rule and (ii) the trustee or other person to whom the power is granted or delegated has the power to sell, mortgage, or lease the property for any period of time beyond the period required for an interest created under the instrument to be valid under the rule against perpetuities. (§547:3-k) This provision is broader than that of a number of other states because it applies to interests in trust as well as otherwise.

Table 9
Rule Against Perpetuities

	NEBRASKA	NEVADA	NEW HAMPSHIRE
3. *Does the rule apply to other than private trusts?*	Yes. The rule applies except to: (1) A nonvested property interest or a power of appointment arising out of a nondonative transfer, except a nonvested property interest or a power of appointment arising out of (i) a premarital or postmarital agreement, (ii) a separation or divorce settlement, (iii) a spouse's election, (iv) a similar arrangement arising out of a prospective, existing, or previous marital relationship between the parties, (v) a contract to make or not to revoke a will or trust, (vi) a contract to exercise or not to exercise a power of appointment, (vii) a transfer in satisfaction of a duty of support, or (viii) a reciprocal transfer; (2) A fiduciary's power relating to the administration or management of assets, including the power of a	Yes. The rule applies except to: (1) A nonvested property interest or a power of appointment arising out of a nondonative transfer, except a nonvested property interest or a power of appointment arising out of: (a) A premarital or postmarital agreement; (b) A separation or divorce settlement; (c) A spouse's election; (d) A similar arrangement arising out of a prospective existing or previous marital relationship between the parties; (e) A contract to make or not to revoke a will or trust; (f) A contract to exercise or not to exercise a power of appointment; (g) A transfer in satisfaction of a duty of support; or (h) A reciprocal transfer;	Yes. See #2b. In addition: A trust created by an employer as part of a stock bonus, pension, disability, death benefit or profit sharing plan for the exclusive benefit of some or all of his employees, to which contributions are made by the employer or employees, or both, for the purpose of distributing to the employees the earnings or the principal of the fund held in trust, may continue in perpetuity. (§ 275:48-a) Charitable trusts are not subject to the rule against perpetuities. (Smart v. Town of Durham, 86 A. 821, 823 (N.H. 1913))

Table 9
Rule Against Perpetuities

NEBRASKA	NEVADA	NEW HAMPSHIRE
fiduciary to sell, lease or mortgage property, and the power of a fiduciary to determine principal and income;	(2) A fiduciary's power relating to the administration or management of assets, including the power of a fiduciary to sell, lease or mortgage property, and the power of a fiduciary to determine principal and income;	
(3) A power to appoint a fiduciary;	(3) A power to appoint a fiduciary;	
(4) A discretionary power of a trustee to distribute principal before termination of a trust to a beneficiary having an indefeasibly vested interest in the income and principal;	(4) A discretionary power of a trustee to distribute principal before termination of a trust to a beneficiary having an indefeasibly vested interest in the income and principal;	
(5) A nonvested property interest held by a charity, government or governmental agency or subdivision, if the nonvested property interest is preceded by an interest held by another charity, government or governmental agency or subdivision;	(5) A nonvested property interest held by a charity, government or governmental agency or subdivision, if the nonvested property interest is preceded by an interest held by another charity, government or governmental agency or subdivision;	
(6) A nonvested property interest in or a power of appointment with respect to a trust or other property arrangement forming		

Table 9
Rule Against Perpetuities

NEBRASKA	NEVADA	NEW HAMPSHIRE
part of a pension, profit-sharing, stock bonus, health, disability, death benefit, income deferral, or other current or deferred benefit plan for one or more employees, independent contractors, or their beneficiaries or spouses, to which contributions are made for the purpose of distributing to or for the benefit of the participants or their beneficiaries or spouses the property, income or principal in the trust or other property arrangement, except a nonvested property interest or a power of appointment that is created by an election of a participant or a beneficiary or spouse;	(6) A nonvested property interest in or a power of appointment with respect to a trust or other property arrangement forming part of a pension, profit sharing, stock bonus, health, disability, death benefit, income deferral or other current or deferred benefit plan for one or more employees, independent contractors or their beneficiaries or spouses, to which contributions are made for the purpose of distributing to or for the benefit of the participants or their beneficiaries or spouses the property, income or principal in the trust or other property arrangement, except a nonvested property interest or a power of appointment that is created by an election of a participant or a beneficiary or spouse; or	
(7) A property interest, power of appointment, or arrangement that was not subject to the common-law rule against perpetuities or is excluded by another law of this state;	(7) A property interest, power of appointment or arrangement that was not subject to the common-law rule against perpetuities or is expressly excluded by another statute of this state.	
(8) A property interest, ownership, or a power of appointment transferred in trust for charitable purposes by whose terms such trust is to continue for an indefinite or unlimited		

Table 9
Rule Against Perpetuities

NEBRASKA

period or arrangement of like import; or

(9) A trust in which the governing instrument states that the rule against perpetuities does not apply to the trust and under which the trustee or other person to whom the power is properly granted or delegated has power under the governing instrument, any applicable statute, or the common law to sell, lease, or mortgage property for any period of time beyond the period which would otherwise be required for an interest created under the governing instrument to vest. This subdivision shall apply to all trusts created by will or inter vivos agreement executed or amended on or after July 20, 2002, and to all trusts created by exercise of power of appointment granted under instruments executed or amended on or after July 20, 2002.

(§ 76-2005)

NEVADA

(§ 111.1037) The rule also does not apply to area-of-interest royalties created by commercial mining agreements. This is consistent with the statutory exemption of commercial, nondonative transfers from the rule against perpetuities. (Bullion Monarch v. Barrick Goldstrike, 345 P.3d 1040 (Sup. Ct. 2015))

NEW HAMPSHIRE

Table 9
Rule Against Perpetuities

	NEBRASKA	NEVADA	NEW HAMPSHIRE
4. *Does the rule invalidate the interest at its creation, or is the rule revised by a wait-and-see approach?*	Wait-and-see. (§76-2002(a)(2))	Wait-and-see. (§111.1031(1)(b))	Wait-and-see. (Merchants Nat'l Bank v. Curtis, 97 A.2d 207, 212 (N.H. 1953))
5. *Can the trust be reformed?*	Yes, but only if one of the following conditions applies: (1) a nonvested property interest or power of appointment becomes invalid under §76-2002 (see #2b); (2) a class gift is not but might become invalid under 76-2002 and the time has arrived when the share of any class member is to take effect in possession or enjoyment; or (3) a nonvested property interest that is not validated by subdivision (a)(1) of §76-2002, that is, the traditional common law rule, can vest but not within 90 years after its creation. (§76-2004 - only operative after Jan. 1, 2005) (Laws 2003, LB 130, §140)	Yes, but only if one of the following conditions applies: (1) a nonvested property interest or power of appointment becomes invalid under §111.1031 (see #2b); (2) a class gift is not but might become invalid under 111.1031 and the time has arrived when the share of any class member is to take effect in possession or enjoyment; or (3) a nonvested property interest that is not validated by paragraph (a) of subsection 1, §111.1031, that is, the traditional common law rule, can vest but not later than 365 years after its creation. (§111.1035)	No specific state case or statute.

Table 9
Rule Against Perpetuities

	NEBRASKA	NEVADA	NEW HAMPSHIRE
6. *If yes to 5., under what theory?*	[A] court shall reform a disposition in the manner that most closely approximates the transferor's manifested plan of distribution and is within the 90 years allowed by subdivision (a)(2), (b)(2), or (c)(2) of section 76-2002. (§76-2004 - only operative after Jan 1, 2005) *See also* §76-2006(b) - only operative after Jan 1, 2005 ("If a nonvested property interest or a power of appointment was created before August 25, 1989, and is determined in a judicial proceeding, commenced on or after such date, to violate this state's rule against perpetuities as that rule existed before such date, a county court in a proceeding described in section 30-2211 or 30-3812 or a district court upon the petition of an interested person may reform the disposition in the manner that most closely approximates the transferor's manifested plan of distribution and is within the limits of the rule against perpetuities applicable when the nonvested property interest or power of appointment was created.")	[A] court shall reform a disposition in the manner that most closely approximates the transferor's manifested plan of distribution and is within the 365 years allowed by paragraph (b) of subsection 1, paragraph (b) of subsection 2 or paragraph (b) of subsection 3 of NRS § 111.1031. (§111.1035) *See also* § 111.1039 ("With respect to a nonvested property interest or a power of appointment that was created before July 1, 1987, and that violates the rule against perpetuities as that rule existed before that date, a court upon the petition of an interested person may exercise its equitable power to reform the disposition in the manner that most closely approximates the transferor's manifested plan of distribution and is within the limits of the rule against perpetuities applicable when the nonvested property interest or power of appointment was created.")	N/A

Table 9
Rule Against Perpetuities

	NEBRASKA	NEVADA	NEW HAMPSHIRE
7. *When is a general testamentary power of appointment invalid?*	A general testamentary power of appointment is invalid unless: (1) when the power is created, it is certain to be irrevocably exercised or otherwise to terminate no later than 21 years after the death of an individual then alive; or (2) The power is irrevocably exercised or otherwise terminates within 90 years after its creation. (§ 76-2002(c))	A general testamentary power of appointment is invalid unless: (a) When the power is created, it is certain to be irrevocably exercised or otherwise to terminate no later than 21 years after the death of a natural person then alive; or (b) the power is irrevocably exercised or otherwise terminates within 365 years after its creation. (§ 111.1031(3))	*See* Unif. Statutory Rule Against Perpetuities § 1, 8B U.L.A. 248 (amended 1990) ("Under the Common-law Rule . . . a *nongeneral power* (whether or not presently exercisable) or a *general testamentary power* is invalid as of the time of its creation if it *might* not terminate (by irrevocable exercise or otherwise) within a life in being plus 21 years.")
8. *Same, but nongeneral testamentary power.*	A nongeneral testamentary power of appointment is invalid unless: (1) When the power is created, it is certain to be irrevocably exercised or otherwise to terminate no later than 21 years after the death of an individual then alive; or (2) The power is irrevocably exercised or otherwise terminates within 90 years after its creation. (§ 76-2002(c))	A nongeneral testamentary power of appointment is invalid unless: (a) when the power is created, it is certain to be irrevocably exercised or otherwise to terminate no later than 21 years after the death of an individual then alive; or (b) the power is irrevocably exercised or otherwise terminates within 365 years after its creation. (§ 111.1031(3))	*See* #7.

Table 9
Rule Against Perpetuities

	NEBRASKA	NEVADA	NEW HAMPSHIRE
9. *Same, but general power, whether testamentary or inter vivos, not presently exercisable because of a condition precedent.*	A general power of appointment not presently exercisable because of a condition precedent is invalid unless: (1) When the power is created, the condition precedent is certain to be satisfied or becomes impossible to satisfy no later than 21 years after the death of an individual then alive; or (2) The condition precedent either is satisfied or becomes impossible to satisfy within 90 years after its creation. (§ 76-2002(b))	A general power of appointment not presently exercisable because of a condition precedent is invalid unless: (a) When the power is created, the condition precedent is certain to be satisfied or becomes impossible to satisfy no later than 21 years after the death of an individual then alive; or (b) The condition precedent either is satisfied or becomes impossible to satisfy within 365 years after its creation. (§ 111.1031(2))	*See* Unif. Statutory Rule Against Perpetuities § 1, 8B U.L.A. 248 (amended 1990) ("Under the Common-law Rule, a *general power not presently exercisable because of a condition precedent* is invalid as of the time of its creation if the condition *might* neither be satisfied nor become impossible to satisfy with a life in being plus 21 years.")
10. *Same, but nongeneral inter vivos power.*	See #8.	See #8.	See #7.

Table 9
Rule Against Perpetuities

	NEBRASKA	NEVADA	NEW HAMPSHIRE
11. *Is a period of gestation added to the perpetuity period?*	No. The possibility that a child will be born to a person after that person's death is disregarded. (§76-2002(d)) *See also* Unif. Statutory Rule Against Perpetuities § 1, 8B U.L.A. 243, 243 (amended 1990) ("[T]he possibility that a child will be born to [a testator] after his death must be disregarded; and the possibility that a child will be born to any of [the testator's] descendants after their deaths must also be disregarded. Note, however, that the rule of subsection (d) does *not* apply to the question of the entitlement of an after-born child to take a beneficial interest in the trust").	No. The possibility that a child will be born to a person after that person's death is disregarded. (§ 111.1031(4)) *See also* Unif. Statutory Rule Against Perpetuities § 1, 8B U.L.A. 243, 243 (amended 1990) ("[T]he possibility that a child will be born to [a testator] after his death must be disregarded; and the possibility that a child will be born to any of [the testator's] descendants after their deaths must also be disregarded. Note, however, that the rule of subsection (d) does *not* apply to the question of the entitlement of an after-born child to take a beneficial interest in the trust").	In one case, Rolfe & Rumford Asylum v. Lefebre, 45 A. 1087, 1089 (N.H. 1898), the court states: "The present case furnishes no occasion for deciding . . . whether an additional period of nine months can be allowed without gestation."
12. *What is the treatment of a "later of the traditional rule or 90 years" clause?* *See* UIPC 2-901(e).	Nebraska's USRAP does not specify how it will treat "later of" clauses.	That language is inoperative to the extent it produces a period of time that exceeds 21 years after the death of the survivor of the specified lives. (§ 111.1031(5))	N/A

Table 9
Rule Against Perpetuities

	NEBRASKA	*NEVADA*	*NEW HAMPSHIRE*
13. *When is an interest created by the exercise of a general testamentary power deemed created?*	Except as provided in subsections (b) and (c) of this section and subsection (a) of section 76-2006, the time of creation of a nonvested property interest or a power of appointment is determined under general principles of property law. (§ 76-2003(a)) The first of the excepted provisions states that as long as a person with a general power to become the unqualified beneficial owner has that power, the nonvested interest is created when the power terminates. The second of the excepted provisions states that a nonvested property interest, which arises from a transfer to an existing trust, is created when the nonvested property interest in the trust was created. (§ 76-2003(b)-(c)) *See also* Unif. Statutory Rule Against Perpetuities § 2, 8B U.L.A. 268 (amended 1990) (explaining that "general principles of property law determine that the time . . . [of creation] is at the decedent's death.") *See generally* § 76-2006(a) ("[A] nonvested property interest or a power of appointment created by the exercise of a power of appointment is created when the power is irrevocably exercised or when a revocable exercise becomes irrevocable.")	Except as provided in subsections 2 and 3 and in subsection 1 of NRS 111.1039, the time of creation of a nonvested property interest or a power of appointment is determined under general principles of property law. (§ 111.1033(1)) The first of the excepted provisions states that as long as a person with a general power to become the unqualified beneficial owner has that power, the nonvested interest is created when the power terminates. The second of the excepted provisions states that a nonvested property interest, which arises from a transfer to an existing trust, is created when the nonvested property interest in the trust was created. (§ 111.1033(2)) *See also* Unif. Statutory Rule Against Perpetuities § 2, 8B U.L.A. 268 (amended 1990) (explaining that "general principles of property law determine that the time . . . [of creation] is at the decedent's death.") *See generally* § 111.1039(1) ("A nonvested property interest or a power of appointment created by the exercise of a power of appointment is created when the power is irrevocably exercised or when a revocable exercise becomes irrevocable.")	*See* comment to Unif. Probate Code § 2-902(a) ("general principles of property law determine that a nonvested property interest or power of appointment created by will is created at the decedent's death"); Unif. Statutory Rule Against Perpetuities § 2, 8B U.L.A. 268 (amended 1990) (stating the same).

Table 9
Rule Against Perpetuities

	NEBRASKA	NEVADA	NEW HAMPSHIRE
14. *Same, but nongeneral testamentary power.*	See #13.	See #13.	See #13.

Table 9
Rule Against Perpetuities

	NEBRASKA	NEVADA	NEW HAMPSHIRE
15. *Same, but general inter vivos power.*	Except as provided in subsections (b)and (c) of this section and subsection (a) of section 76-2006, the time of creation of a nonvested property interest or a power of appointment is determined under general principles of property law. (§76-2003(a)) The first of the excepted provisions states that as long as a person with a general power to become the unqualified beneficial owner has that power, the nonvested interest is created when the power terminates. The second of the excepted provisions states that a nonvested property interest, which arises from a transfer to an existing trust, is created when the nonvested property interest in the trust was created. (§76-2003(b)-(c)) *See also* Unif. Statutory Rule Against Perpetuities §2, 8B U.L.A. 268 (amended 1990) (explaining that "the time when the interest or power is created is the date the transfer becomes effective for purposes of property law generally, normally the date of delivery of the deed"); Comment to Unif. Probate Code §2-902(a) (stating same and adding "the funding of the trust" as "normally" the time when the interest is created). *See generally* §76-2006(a) ("a nonvested	Except as provided in subsections 2 and 3 and in subsection 1 of NRS 111.1039, the time of creation of a nonvested property interest or a power of appointment is determined under general principles of property law. (§111.1033(1)) The first of the excepted provisions states that as long as a person with a general power to become the unqualified beneficial owner has that power, the nonvested interest is created when the power terminates. The second of the excepted provisions states that a nonvested property interest, which arises from a transfer to an existing trust, is created when the nonvested property interest in the trust was created. (§111.1033(2)-(3)) *See also* Unif. Statutory Rule Against Perpetuities §2, 8B U.L.A. 268 (amended 1990) (explaining that "the time when the interest or power is created is the date the transfer becomes effective for purposes of property law generally, normally the date of delivery of the deed"); Comment to Unif. Probate Code §2-902(a) (stating same and adding "the funding of the trust" as "normally" the time when the interest is created). *See generally* §111.1039(1) ("A nonvested property interest or a power	*See* comment to Unif. Probate Code §2-902(a) ("With respect to an inter-vivos transfer, an interest or power is created on the date the transfer becomes effective for purposes of property law generally, normally the date of delivery of the deed or funding of the trust."); Unif. Statutory Rule Against Perpetuities §2, 8B U.L.A. 268 (stating the same).

Table 9
Rule Against Perpetuities

NEBRASKA	NEVADA	NEW HAMPSHIRE
property interest or a power of appointment created by the exercise of a power of appointment is created when the power is irrevocably exercised or when a revocable exercise becomes irrevocable.")	of appointment created by the exercise of a power of appointment is created when the power is irrevocably exercised or when a revocable exercise becomes irrevocable.")	
16. Same, but nongeneral inter vivos power. See #16.	See #16.	See #16.
17. When is an interest created if the grantor of a trust has a power to revoke? For purposes of the Uniform Statutory Rule Against Perpetuities Act, if there is a person who alone can exercise a power created by a governing instrument to become the unqualified beneficial owner of (i) a nonvested property interest or (ii) a property interest subject to a power of appointment described in subsection (a) or (b) of section 76-2002, the nonvested property interest or power of appointment is created when the power to become the unqualified beneficial owner terminates. (§76-2003(b)) *See also* Unif. Statutory Rule Against Perpetuities §2, 8B	For purposes of NRS 111.103 to 111.1039, inclusive, if there is a person who alone can exercise a power created by a governing instrument to become the unqualified beneficial owner of: (a) A nonvested property interest; or (b) a property interest subject to a power of appointment described in subsection 2 or 3 of NRS 111.1031, the nonvested property interest or power of appointment is created when the power to become the unqualified beneficial owner terminates.	*See* comment to Unif. Probate Code §2-902(b) (noting that "nonvested property interest and powers of appointment created in [a revocable inter-vivos trust] are created when the power to revoke expires, usually at the settlor's death"); Unif. Statutory Rule Against Perpetuities §2, 8B U.L.A. 268 (amended 1990) (explaining that "any nonvested property interest subject to [a power to revoke] is not created . . . until the power terminates (by release, expiration at the death of the donee, or otherwise").

Table 9
Rule Against Perpetuities

	NEBRASKA	NEVADA	NEW HAMPSHIRE
18. When does the period of the rule start re an interest contributed to an irrevocable trust? See UPC 2-902(c).	A nonvested property interest or power of appointment arising from a transfer of property to a previously funded trust or other existing arrangement is created when the nonvested property interest or power of appointment in the original contribution was created. (§76-2003(c))	U.L.A. 268 (amended 1990) (explaining that "any nonvested property interest subject to [a power to revoke] is not created . . . until the power terminates (by release, expiration at the death of the donee, or otherwise)"; Comment to Unif. Probate Code §2-902(b) (noting that "nonvested property interests and powers of appointment created in [a revocable inter-vivos trust] are created when the power to revoke expires, usually at the settlor's death"). *See generally* §76-2006(a) ("A nonvested property interest or a power of appointment created by the exercise of a power of appointment is created when the power is irrevocably exercised or when a revocable exercise becomes irrevocable.")	(§111.1033(2)) *See also* Unif. Statutory Rule Against Perpetuities §2, 8B U.L.A. 268 (amended 1990) (explaining that "any nonvested property interest subject to [a power to revoke] is not created . . . until the power terminates (by release, expiration at the death of the donee, or otherwise"); Comment to Unif. Probate Code §2-902(b) (noting that "nonvested property interest and powers of appointment created in [a revocable inter-vivos trust] are created when the power to revoke expires, usually at the settlor's death"). *See generally* §111.1039(a) ("A nonvested property interest or a power of appointment created by the exercise of a power of appointment is created when the power is irrevocably exercised or when a revocable exercise becomes irrevocable.")	A nonvested property interest or power of appointment arising from a transfer of property to a previously funded trust or other existing arrangement is created when the nonvested property interest or power of appointment in the original contribution was created. (§111.1033(3))	*See* comment to Unif. Probate Code 2-902(c) ("Arguably, at common law, each transfer [to an existing irrevocable inter-vivos trust] starts the period of the Rule running anew as to each transfer.")

Table 9
Rule Against Perpetuities

NEBRASKA	NEVADA	NEW HAMPSHIRE
19. *Is there a conclusive presumption of fertility, that is, the "fertile octogenarian" rule?*		

No specific state case or statute.[1] *See* Unif. Statutory Rule Against Perpetuities § 1, 8B U.L.A. 256 (amended 1990) (holding that "[t]his principle is not superseded by this Act, and in view of new advances in medical science ... [this] is not unrealistic.").

But see C. P. Jhong, Annotation, *Modern Status of Presumption Against Possibility of Issue Being Extinct*, 98 A.L.R.2d 1285 (2003) (noting "a trend toward denying the conclusive or absolute nature of the presumption against the possibility of issue being extinct where there is competent evidence to the contrary has developed in the decisions, although some courts still adhere to the traditional view treating the presumption as conclusive or absolute").

No specific state case or statute. *See* Unif. Statutory Rule Against Perpetuities § 1, 8B U.L.A. 256 (amended 1990) (holding that "[t]his principle is not superseded by this Act, and in view of new advances in medical science ... [this] is not unrealistic.").

But see C. P. Jhong, Annotation, *Modern Status of Presumption Against Possibility of Issue Being Extinct*, 98 A.L.R.2d 1285 (2003) (noting "a trend toward denying the conclusive or absolute nature of the presumption against the possibility of issue being extinct where there is competent evidence to the contrary has developed in the decisions, although some courts still adhere to the traditional view treating the presumption as conclusive or absolute").

No. In re Bassett's Estate, 190 A.2d 415, 417 (N.H. 1963) (rejecting the presumption).

9216

Table 9
Rule Against Perpetuities

NEBRASKA	NEVADA	NEW HAMPSHIRE
20. *What is the earliest age a child is deemed capable of bearing a child? What is the impact of illegitimacy?* Not specifically addressed by USRAP, but the reasoning is the same as set forth in the comment to section 1 of USRAP, 2, Technical Violations of the Common Law Rule. Wait and see will typically result in no violation. Nevertheless, the common law rule ordinarily will be applied initially. "Under the rule, courts must presume that living persons are capable of having or fathering children, no matter how young they are. See In re Graite's Will Trusts, [1949] 1 All E.R. 459, 460 (Ch.). Thus, the rule strikes down any interest whose vesting depends on the assertion that, for example, a toddler will not have children." (Keith L. Butler, Notes & Comments, *Long Live the Dead Hand: A Case for Repeal of the Rule Against Perpetuities in Washington*, 75 Wash. L. Rev. 1237, 1246 n.78 (2000)).	Not specifically addressed by USRAP, but the reasoning is the same as set forth in the comment to section 1 of USRAP, 2, Technical Violations of the Common Law Rule. Wait and see will typically result in no violation. Nevertheless, the common law rule ordinarily will be applied initially. "Under the rule, courts must presume that living persons are capable of having or fathering children, no matter how young they are. See In re Graite's Will Trusts, [1949] 1 All E.R. 459, 460 (Ch.). Thus, the rule strikes down any interest whose vesting depends on the assertion that, for example, a toddler will not have children." (Keith L. Butler, Notes & Comments, *Long Live the Dead Hand: A Case for Repeal of the Rule Against Perpetuities in Washington*, 75 Wash. L. Rev. 1237, 1246 n.78 (2000)).	"Under the rule, courts must presume that living persons are capable of having or fathering children, no matter how young they are. See In re Graite's Will Trusts, [1949] 1 All E.R. 459, 460 (Ch.). Thus, the rule strikes down any interest whose vesting depends on the assertion that, for example, a toddler will not have children." (Keith L. Butler, Notes & Comments, *Long Live the Dead Hand: A Case for Repeal of the Rule Against Perpetuities in Washington*, 75 Wash. L. Rev. 1237, 1246 n.78 (2000)).

Table 9
Rule Against Perpetuities

	NEBRASKA	NEVADA	NEW HAMPSHIRE
21. *Is the "unborn widow" rule observed?*	No specific state case or statute. *See* Unif. Statutory Rule Against Perpetuities § 1, 8B U.L.A. 246 (amended 1990) (explaining that "[t]he chance that [an] interest will become invalid under the Statutory Rule is small" and so the unborn widow rule would rarely invalidate an interest); *see also* 61 Am. Jur. 2d *Perpetuities and Restraints on Alienation* § 39 (2013) (noting the same).	No specific state case or statute. *See* Unif. Statutory Rule Against Perpetuities § 1, 8B U.L.A. 246 (amended 1990) (explaining that "[t]he chance that [an] interest will become invalid under the Statutory Rule is small" and so the unborn widow rule would rarely invalidate an interest); *see also* 61 Am. Jur. 2d *Perpetuities and Restraints on Alienation* § 39 (2013) (noting the same).	No explicit mention, *but see* Merchant's Nat'l Bank v. Curtis, 97 A.2d 207, 211 (noting that the rule has never been applied "remorselessly" in New Hampshire and the wait-and-see approach has "the salutary effect of avoiding the punitive and technical aspects of the rule but at the same time confirming the policy and purpose of the rule within reasonable limits"); *compare, e.g.*, Arkansas, question #21 (applying the common law "unborn widow" rule).
22. *Does the "slothful executor" rule apply, i.e., an administrative contingency clause providing for a "distribution to, e.g., those issue living at the time of satisfaction of the administrative condition precedent?"*	No specific state case or statute. *See* Unif. Statutory Rule Against Perpetuities § 1, 8B U.L.A. 245 (amended 1990) (Under USRAP, an "interest becomes invalid only if it remains in existence and nonvested 90 years after [the testator's] death. Since it is almost certain that the final distribution of [an] estate will occur well within this 90-year period, the chance that [an] interest will be invalid is negligible."")	No specific state case or statute. *See* Unif. Statutory Rule Against Perpetuities § 1, 8B U.L.A. 245 (amended 1990) (Under USRAP, an "interest becomes invalid only if it remains in existence and nonvested 90 years after [the testator's] death. Since it is almost certain that the final distribution of [an] estate will occur well within this 90-year period, the chance that [an] interest will be invalid is negligible."")	No explicit mention, *but see* Merchant's Nat'l Bank v. Curtis, 97 A.2d 207, 210-11 (noting that the rule has never been applied "remorselessly" in New Hampshire and the wait-and-see approach has "the salutary effect of avoiding the punitive and technical aspects of the rule but at the same time confirming the policy and purpose of the rule within reasonable limits"); *compare, e.g.*, California, question #22 (applying the common law "slothful executor" rule).

Table 9
Rule Against Perpetuities

	NEBRASKA	*NEVADA*	*NEW HAMPSHIRE*
23. *Does the all-or-nothing rule apply to class gifts?*	No specific state case or statute. *See* Unif. Statutory Rule Against Perpetuities § 1, 8B U.L.A. 257 (amended 1990) ("Although this Act does not supersede the basic idea of the much-maligned 'all-or-nothing' rule, the evils sometimes attributed to it are substantially if not entirely eliminated by the wait-and-see feature of the Statutory Rule and by the availability of reformation under Section 3.")	No specific state case or statute. *See* Unif. Statutory Rule Against Perpetuities § 1, 8B U.L.A. 257 (amended 1990) ("Although this Act does not supersede the basic idea of the much-maligned 'all-or-nothing' rule, the evils sometimes attributed to it are substantially if not entirely eliminated by the wait-and-see feature of the Statutory Rule and by the availability of reformation under Section 3.")	No explicit mention, *but see* Merchant's Nat'l Bank v. Curtis, 97 A.2d 207, 210-11 (noting that the rule has never been applied "remorselessly" in New Hampshire and the wait-and-see approach has "the salutary effect of avoiding the punitive and technical aspects of the rule but at the same time confirming the policy and purpose of the rule within reasonable limits"); *compare, e.g.,* Alabama, question #23 (applying the common law "all-or-nothing" rule).

Table 9
Rule Against Perpetuities

	NEBRASKA	NEVADA	NEW HAMPSHIRE
24. *Is there an exception to the all-or-nothing rule in the case of subclasses or specific sums to each member of the class?*	No specific state case or statute. *See* Unif. Statutory Rule Against Perpetuities §1, 8B U.L.A. 257 (amended 1990) ("The specific-sum and sub-class doctrines are not superseded by this Act.")	No specific state case or statute. *See* Unif. Statutory Rule Against Perpetuities §1, 8B U.L.A. 257 (amended 1990) ("The specific-sum and sub-class doctrines are not superseded by this Act.")	No specific state case or statute. *See* Unif. Statutory Rule Against Perpetuities §1, 8B U.L.A. 257 ("The common law also recognizes a doctrine called the specific-sum doctrine which is derived from Storrs v. Benbow, 3 De G.M. & G. 390, 43 Eng. Rep 153 (Ch. 1853), and states: If a specified sum of money is to be paid to each member of a class, the interest of each class member is entitled to separate treatment and is valid or invalid under the Rule on its own. The common law also recognizes a doctrine called the sub-class doctrine, which is derived from Cattlin v. Brown, 11 Hare 372, 68 Eng. Rep. 1318 (Ch. 1853), and states: If the ultimate takers are not described as a single class but rather as a group of separate subclasses, and if the share to which each separate subclass is entitled will finally be determined within the period of the Rule, the gifts to the different subclasses are separate for the purpose of the Rule.").

Table 9
Rule Against Perpetuities

	NEBRASKA	NEVADA	NEW HAMPSHIRE
25. *Is the infectious invalidity rule followed outside class gifts?*	No specific state case or statute. *See* Unif. Statutory Rule Against Perpetuities §1, 8B U.L.A. 256 (amended 1990) (explaining that "[t]he doctrine of infectious invalidity is superseded by this Act by Section 3, under which courts . . . are required to *reform* the disposition to approximate as closely as possible the transferor's . . . plan of distribution.")	No specific state case or statute. *See* Unif. Statutory Rule Against Perpetuities §1, 8B U.L.A. 256 (amended 1990) (explaining that "[t]he doctrine of infectious invalidity is superseded by this Act by Section 3, under which courts . . . are required to *reform* the disposition to approximate as closely as possible the transferor's . . . plan of distribution.")	No explicit mention, *but see* Merchant's Nat'l Bank v. Curtis, 97 A.2d 207, 210-11 (noting that the rule has never been applied "remorselessly" in New Hampshire and the wait-and-see approach has "the salutary effect of avoiding the punitive and technical aspects of the rule but at the same time confirming the policy and purpose of the rule within reasonable limits"); *compare, e.g.* Colorado, question #25 (applying the common law "infectious invalidity" rule).

Table 9
Rule Against Perpetuities

	NEBRASKA	NEVADA	NEW HAMPSHIRE
26. *Is there a rule against the suspension of the power of alienation? If so, how is it stated?*	Reasonable standard. Spanish Oaks, Inc. v. Hy-Vee, Inc., 655 N.W.2d 390, 399 (Neb. 2003) ("Indirect restraints historically have been restricted by the rule against perpetuities and related rules and have not been as harshly struck down as the classical direct restraints. Courts generally have upheld and enforced such nonclassical restraints if they are found reasonably necessary to protect a justifiable or legitimate interest of the parties.")	Good faith standard. Waters v. Harper, 250 P.2d 915, 916-17 (Nev. 1952) ("The general rule relative to the right of alienation in such cases is expressed in 57 Am. Jur. 479, Wills, §710, as follows: 'Whether testators who have executed a joint will, or separate wills, containing mutual and reciprocal provisions are restricted from disposing of the property during their respective lifetimes is a question primarily of the construction of the agreement under which the will or wills were executed. It may be stated generally that the courts do not consider that the parties to a joint and mutual will intended to restrict either party from disposing of property in good faith by transfers effective during his or her lifetime, unless a plain intention to this effect is expressed in the will or in the contract pursuant to which it was executed.' We have no quarrel with the rule as so expressed. The essential question in our view is whether the transfer here considered can be characterized as one in good faith.")	Reasonableness standard. Horse Pond Fish & Game Club, Inc. v. Cormier, 581 A.2d 478, 480 (N.H. 1990) ("to be enforceable, [restraints against alienation of property] must be reasonable in view of the justifiable interests of parties, and unreasonable restraints will be held invalid.")
27. *Effective date.*	July 20, 2002. *See also* #3.	July 1, 1987. *See also* #6.	January 1, 2004. *See also* #2b.

[1] For questions, #19-25, *see also* §76-2008 (noting that the state's USRAP supersedes the common law rule against perpetuities). The answers to questions #19-25 are not likely to apply in most cases because of the abolition of the rule with respect to the vast majority of many trusts.

Table 9
Rule Against Perpetuities

	NEW JERSEY	NEW MEXICO	NEW YORK
1. *Which rule is in effect: the common law rule, the Uniform Statutory Rule Against Perpetuities (USRAP), other law, or none?*	None. (N.J. Stat. Ann. § 46:2F-9) ("No interest created in real or personal property shall be void by reason of any rule against perpetuities, whether the common law rule or otherwise. The common law rule against perpetuities shall not be in force in this State."). New Jersey only has a power of alienation provision. See (§ 46:2F-10)	USRAP. (N.M. Stat. Ann. §§ 45-2-901 - 45-2-906)	Common Law Rule. (N.Y. Est. Powers & Trusts Law §§ 9-1.1 - 9-1.8) However, there are certain savings provisions that have been enacted.
2. a. *Is the common law rule relevant to any interests?*	No.	Yes, but only as the starting point of the analysis.	Yes.
b. *What is the relevant rule?*	N/A	A nonvested property interest is invalid unless: (1) When the interest is created, it is certain to vest or terminate no later than 21 years after the death of an individual then alive; or (2) The interest either vests or terminates within 90 years after its creation. (§ 45-2-901(A))	No estate in property shall be valid unless it must vest, if at all, not later than twenty-one years after one or more lives in being at the creation of the estate and any period of gestation involved. (§ 9-1.1(b))

Table 9
Rule Against Perpetuities

	NEW JERSEY	NEW MEXICO	NEW YORK
3. Does the rule apply to other than private trusts?	N/A	Yes. The rule applies except to: 1. a nonvested property interest or a power of appointment arising out of a nondonative transfer, except a nonvested property interest or a power of appointment arising out of: (a) a premarital or postmarital agreement; (b) a separation or divorce settlement; (c) spouse's election; (d) a similar arrangement arising out of a prospective, existing or previous marital relationship between the parties; (e) a contract to make or not to revoke a will or trust; (f) a contract to exercise or not to exercise a power of appointment; (g) a transfer in satisfaction of a duty of support; or (h) a reciprocal transfer;	Yes. The rule applies except to: Trusts with transferable certificates (§ 9-1.5) Trusts for employees (§ 9-1.6) Trusts created by national security exchanges to assist customers of members, member firms, or member corporations (§ 9-1.7) Charitable trusts (In re Estate of Wilson, 452 N.E. 2d 1228, 1232 (N.Y. 1983)

Table 9

Rule Against Perpetuities

NEW JERSEY	NEW MEXICO	NEW YORK
	2. a fiduciary's power relating to the administration or management of assets, including the power of a fiduciary to sell, lease or mortgage property and the power of a fiduciary to determine principal and income;	
	3. a power to appoint a fiduciary;	
	4. a discretionary power of a trustee to distribute principal before termination of a trust to a beneficiary having an indefeasibly vested interest in the income and principal;	
	5. a nonvested property interest held by preceded by an interest held by another charity, government or governmental agency or subdivision;	

Table 9
Rule Against Perpetuities

NEW JERSEY	NEW MEXICO	NEW YORK
	6. a nonvested property interest in or a power of appointment with respect to a trust or other property arrangement forming part of a pension, profit-sharing, stock bonus, health, disability, death benefit, income deferral or other current or deferred benefit plan for one or more employees, independent contractors or their beneficiaries or spouses, to which contributions are made for the purpose of distributing to or for the benefit of the participants or their beneficiaries or spouses the property, income or principal in the trust or other property arrangement, except a nonvested property interest or a power of appointment that is created by an election of a participant or a beneficiary or spouse; 7. a property interest, power of appointment or arrangement that was not subject to the common-law rule against perpetuities or that is excluded by another statute of New Mexico; or	

Table 9
Rule Against Perpetuities

	NEW JERSEY	NEW MEXICO	NEW YORK
		8. a property interest or arrangement subject to a time limit under the provisions of Section 45-2-907 NMSA 1978 (pertaining to honorary trusts and trusts for pets). (§ 45-2-904)	
4. *Does the rule invalidate the interest at its creation, or is the rule revised by a wait-and-see approach?*	N/A	Wait-and-see. (§ 45-2-901(A)(2))	At its creation. Symphony Space, Inc. v. Pergola Props., Inc., 669 N.E.2d 799, 808 (N.Y. 1996) ("This Court, however, has long refused to 'wait and see' whether a perpetuities violation in fact occurs.")
5. *Can the trust be reformed?*	Yes, but only [w]ith respect to a nonvested property interest or a power of appointment created before the effective date of this act, which is determined in a judicial proceeding commenced on or after the effective date of this act, to violate this State's rule against perpetuities as that rule existed before the effective date of this act. (§ 46:2F-11(b))	Yes, but only if one of the following conditions applies: (A) a nonvested property interest or power of appointment becomes invalid under § 45-2-901 (see #2b); (B) a class gift is not but might become invalid under 45-2-901 and the time has arrived when the share of any class member is to take effect in possession or enjoyment; or	Yes, to the extent of statutory authorization. See, e.g., § 9-1.2, allowing for a reduction of an age contingency to age 21, thereby avoiding a violation of the rule and compelling an outright distribution. See also In re BNY Mellon, N.A., 2 N.Y.S.3d 757 (Sur. Ct. Nassau Co. 2014)

Table 9
Rule Against Perpetuities

NEW JERSEY	NEW MEXICO	NEW YORK
Note also that the current law applies to a future property interest or power of appointment in a trust created before the effective date but valid pursuant to the laws of another state that does not have the rule, if the law of New Jersey is made applicable after the effective date by a change in the trusts situs, governing law or otherwise. (§ 46:2F-11(a)(2))	(C) a nonvested property interest that is not validated by § 45-2-901, that is, the traditional common law rule, can vest but not within 90 years after its creation. (§ 45-2-903)	

Table 9
Rule Against Perpetuities

	NEW JERSEY	NEW MEXICO	NEW YORK
6. *If yes to 5., under what theory?*	[A] court upon the petition of an interested person may reform the disposition in the manner that most closely approximates the transferor's manifested plan of distribution and is within the limits of the rule against perpetuities applicable when the nonvested property interest or power of appointment was created. (§ 46-2:F-11(b)). *See also* In re Estate of Passoff, 819 A.2d 26, 31-32 (N.J. 2002) (applying an equitable reformation, where modifying the will is necessary to give effect to the intent of the decedent).	Upon the petition of an interested person, a court shall reform a disposition in the manner that most closely approximates the transferor's manifested plan of distribution and is within the 90 years allowed by § 45-2-901. (§ 45-2-903) *See also* § 45-2-905(B) ("If a nonvested property interest or a power of appointment was created before July 1, 1992 and is determined in a judicial proceeding, commenced on or after July 1, 1992, to violate the New Mexico rule against perpetuities as that rule existed before July 1, 1992, a court, upon the petition of an interested person, may reform the disposition in the manner that most closely approximates the transferor's manifested plan of distribution and is within the limits of the rule against perpetuities applicable when the nonvested property interest or power of appointment was created.")	N/A
7. *When is a general testamentary power of appointment invalid?*	N/A	A general testamentary power of appointment is invalid unless:	*See* Unif. Statutory Rule Against Perpetuities § 1, 8B U.L.A. 248

Table 9
Rule Against Perpetuities

	NEW JERSEY	NEW MEXICO	NEW YORK
		(1) when the power is created, it is certain to be irrevocably exercised or otherwise to terminate no later than 21 years after the death of an individual then alive; or (2) the power is irrevocably exercised or otherwise terminates within 90 years after its creation. (§ 45-2-901(C))	(amended 1990) ("Under the Common-law Rule … a *nongeneral power* (whether or not presently exercisable) or a *general testamentary power* is invalid as of the time of its creation if it might not terminate (by irrevocable exercise or otherwise) within a life in being plus 21 years.")
8.	*Same, but nongeneral testamentary power.*	A nongeneral testamentary power of appointment is invalid unless: (1) when the power is created, it is certain to be irrevocably exercised or otherwise to terminate no later than 21 years after the death of an individual then alive; or (2) the power is irrevocably exercised or otherwise terminates within 90 years after its creation. (§ 45-2-901(C))	See #7.
9.	*Same, but general power, whether testamentary or inter vivos, not presently exercisable because of a condition precedent.*	A general power of appointment not presently exercisable because of a condition precedent is invalid unless: (1) when the power is created, the condition precedent is certain to be satisfied or become impossible to satisfy no later than 21 years after the death of an individual then alive; or	*See* Unif. Statutory Rule Against Perpetuities § 1, 8B U.L.A. 248 (amended 1990) ("Under the Common-law Rule, a *general power not presently exercisable because of a condition precedent* is invalid as of the time of its creation if the condition *might* neither be satisfied nor become impossible to satisfy with a life in being plus 21 years.")

Table 9
Rule Against Perpetuities

	NEW JERSEY	NEW MEXICO	NEW YORK
		(2) the condition precedent either is satisfied or becomes impossible to satisfy within 90 years after its creation. (§ 45-2-901(B))	
10. *Same, but nongeneral intervivos power.*	N/A	See #8.	See #7.
11. *Is a period of gestation added to the perpetuity period?*	N/A	No. The possibility that a child will be born to a person after that person's death is disregarded. (§ 45-2-901(D)) *See also* Unif. Statutory Rule Against Perpetuities § 1, 8B U.L.A. 243, 243 (amended 1990) ("[T]he possibility that a child will be born to [a testator] after his death must be disregarded; and the possibility that a child will be born to any of [the testator's] descendants after their deaths must also be disregarded. Note, however, that the rule of subsection (d) does not apply to the question of the entitlement of an after-born child to take a beneficial interest in the trust.")	Yes (§ 9-1.1(b))
12. *What is the treatment of a "later of the traditional rule or 90 years" clause?*	N/A	That language is inoperative to the extent it produces a period of time that exceeds 21 years after the death of the survivor of the specified lives. (§ 45-2-901(E))	N/A

Table 9
Rule Against Perpetuities

	NEW JERSEY	NEW MEXICO	NEW YORK
13. *When is an interest created by the exercise of a general testamentary power deemed created?*	N/A	Except as provided in Subsections B and C of this section and except as provided in Subsection A of Section 45-2-905 NMSA 1978, the time of creation of a nonvested property interest or a power of appointment is determined under general principles of property law. (§45-2-902(A)) The first of the excepted provisions states that as long as a person with a general power to become the unqualified beneficial owner has that power, the nonvested interest is created when the power terminates. The second of the excepted provisions states that a nonvested property interest, which arises from a transfer to an existing trust, is created when the nonvested property interest in the trust was created. (§45-2-902(B)–(C)) *See also* Unif. Statutory Rule Against Perpetuities §2, 8B U.L.A. 268 (amended 1990) (explaining that "general principles of property law determine that the time . . . [of creation] is at the decedent's death.") *See generally* §45-2-905(A) ("A nonvested property interest or a power of appointment created by the exercise of a power of appointment is created when the power is irrevocably exercised or when a revocable exercise becomes irrevocable.")	Where an estate is created by an instrument exercising a power of appointment, the permissible period of the rule against perpetuities begins: (1) In the case of an instrument exercising a general power which is presently exercisable, on the effective date of the instrument of exercise. (§10-8.1(a)(1))

Table 9
Rule Against Perpetuities

	NEW JERSEY	NEW MEXICO	NEW YORK
14. Same, but nongeneral testamentary power.	N/A	See #13.	See #13.

Table 9
Rule Against Perpetuities

	NEW JERSEY	NEW MEXICO	NEW YORK
15. *Same, but general intervivos power.*	N/A	Except as provided in Subsections B and C of this section and except as provided in Subsection A of Section 45-2-905 NMSA 1978, the time of creation of a nonvested property interest or a power of appointment is determined under general principles of property law. (§ 45-2-902(A)) The first of the excepted provisions states that as long as a person with a general power to become the unqualified beneficial owner has that power, the nonvested interest is created when the power terminates. The second of the excepted provisions states that a nonvested property interest, which arises from a transfer to an existing trust, is created when the nonvested property interest in the trust was created. (§ 45-2-902(B)–(C)) *See also* Unif. Statutory Rule Against Perpetuities § 2, 8B U.L.A. 268 (amended 1990) (explaining that "the time when the interest or power is created is the date the transfer becomes effective for purposes of property law generally, normally the date of delivery of the deed"); Comment to Unif. Probate Code § 2-902(a) (stating same and adding "the funding of the trust" as "normally" the time when the interest is created). *See generally* § 45-2-905(A) ("For	See #13.

Table 9
Rule Against Perpetuities

	NEW JERSEY	NEW MEXICO	NEW YORK
		purposes of this section, a nonvested property interest or a power of appointment created by the exercise of a power of appointment is created when the power is irrevocably exercised or when a revocable exercise becomes irrevocable.")	
16. *Same, but nongeneral inter vivos power.*	N/A	See #15.	See #13.

Table 9
Rule Against Perpetuities

	NEW JERSEY	NEW MEXICO	NEW YORK
17. *When is an interest created if the grantor of a trust has a power to revoke?*	N/A	Under Sections 45-2-901 through 45-2-905 NMSA 1978, if there is a person who alone can exercise a power created by a governing instrument to become the unqualified owner of either a nonvested property interest or a property interest subject to a power of appointment as described in Subsection B or C of Section 45-2-901 NMSA 1978, the nonvested property interest or power of appointment is created when the power to become the unqualified beneficial owner terminates. (§ 45-2-902(B)) *See also* Unif. Statutory Rule Against Perpetuities § 2, 8B U.L.A. 268 (amended 1990) (explaining that "any nonvested property interest subject to [a power to revoke] is not created … until the power terminates (by release, expiration at the death of the donee, or otherwise"); Comment to Unif. Probate Code § 2-902(b) (noting that "nonvested property interests and powers of appointment created in [a revocable inter-vivos trust] are created when the power to revoke expires, usually at the settlor's death"). *See generally* § 45-2-905(A) ("[A] nonvested property interest or a power of appointment created by the exercise of a power of appointment is created when the power is irrevocably	Where the creator of a trust reserves to himself an unqualified power to revoke, the permissible period of the rule against perpetuities begins when the power to revoke terminates by reason of the death of the creator, by a release of such power or otherwise. (§ 10-8.1(b))

Table 9
Rule Against Perpetuities

	NEW JERSEY	NEW MEXICO	NEW YORK
			exercised or when a revocable exercise becomes irrevocable.")
18. *When does the period of the rule start re an interest contributed to an irrevocable trust? See UIPC 2-902(c).*	N/A	A nonvested property interest or power of appointment arising from a transfer of property to a previously funded trust or other existing arrangement is created when the nonvested property interest or power of appointment in the original contribution was created. (§45-2-902(C))	*See* comment to Unif. Probate Code 2-902(c) ("Arguably, at common law, each transfer [to an existing irrevocable inter-vivos trust] starts the period of the Rule running anew as to each transfer.")
19. *Is there a conclusive presumption of fertility, that is, the "fertile octogenarian" rule?*	N/A	No specific state case or statute.[1] See Unif. Statutory Rule Against Perpetuities §1, 8B U.L.A. 256 (amended 1990) (holding that "[t]his principle is not superseded by this Act, and in view of new advances in medical science ... [this] is not unrealistic."). *But see* C. P. Jhong, Annotation, *Modern Status of Presumption Against Possibility of Issue Being Extinct,* 98 A.L.R.2d 1285 (2003) (noting "a trend toward denying the conclusive or absolute nature of the presumption against the	Subject to (2) below, a female is presumed not able to have a child over the age of fifty-five years. (2) In the case of a living person, evidence may be given to establish whether he or she is able to have a child at the time in question. (3) Where the validity of a disposition depends upon the ability of a person to have a child at some future time, the possibility that such person may have a child by adoption shall be disregarded.

Table 9
Rule Against Perpetuities

NEW JERSEY	NEW MEXICO	NEW YORK
	possibility of issue being extinct where there is competent evidence to the contrary has developed in the decisions, although some courts still adhere to the traditional view treating the presumption as conclusive or absolute").	(4) The provisions of subparagraphs (1), (2) and (3) shall not apply for any purpose other than that of determining the validity of a disposition under the rule against perpetuities where such validity depends on the ability of a person to have a child at some future time. A determination of validity or invalidity of a disposition under the rule against perpetuities by the application of subparagraph (1) or (2) or (3) shall not be affected by the later occurrence of facts in contradiction to the facts presumed or determined or the possibility of adoption disregarded under subparagraph (1) or (2) or (3). (§9-1.3(e))

Table 9
Rule Against Perpetuities

	NEW JERSEY	NEW MEXICO	NEW YORK
20. *What is the earliest age a child is deemed capable of bearing a child? What is the impact of illegitimacy?*	N/A	Not specifically addressed by USRAP, but the reasoning is the same as set forth in the comment to section 1 of USRAP, 2, Technical Violations of the Common Law Rule. Wait and see will typically result in no violation. Nevertheless, the common law rule ordinarily will be applied initially. "Under the rule, courts must presume that living persons are capable of having or fathering children, no matter how young they are. See In re Graite's Will Trusts, [1949] 1 All E.R. 459, 460 (Ch.). Thus, the rule strikes down any interest whose vesting depends on the assertion that, for example, a toddler will not have children." (Keith L. Butler, Notes & Comments, *Long Live the Dead Hand: A Case for Repeal of the Rule Against Perpetuities in Washington,* 75 Wash. L. Rev. 1237, 1246 n.78 (2000)).	Where the validity of a disposition depends upon the ability of a person to have a child at some future time, it shall be presumed, subject to subparagraph (2), that a male can have a child at fourteen years of age or over, but not under that age, and that a female can have a child at twelve years of age or over, but not under that age or over the age of fifty-five years. (§ 9-1.3(e)(1))
21. *Is the "unborn widow" rule observed?*	N/A	No specific state case or statute. *See* Unif. Statutory Rule Against Perpetuities § 1, 8B U.L.A. 246 (amended 1990) (explaining that "[t]he chance that [an] interest will become invalid under the Statutory Rule is small" and so the unborn	No.

(a) Unless a contrary intention appears, the rules of construction provided in this section govern with respect to any matter affecting the rule against perpetuities. |

Table 9
Rule Against Perpetuities

	NEW JERSEY	NEW MEXICO	NEW YORK
		widow rule would rarely invalidate an interest); *see also* 61 Am. Jur. 2d *Perpetuities and Restraints on Alienation* § 39 (2013) (noting the same).	(c) Where an estate would, except for this paragraph, be invalid because of the possibility that the person to whom it is given or limited may be a person not in being at the time of the creation of the estate, and such person is referred to in the instrument creating such estate as the spouse of another without other identification, it shall be presumed that such reference is to a person in being on the effective date of the instrument. (§ 9-1.3)
22. Does the "slothful executor" rule apply, i.e., an administrative contingency clause providing for a "distribution to, e.g., those issue living at the time of the satisfaction of the administrative condition precedent?"	N/A	No specific state case or statute. *See* Unif. Statutory Rule Against Perpetuities § 1, 8B U.L.A. 245 (amended 1990) (Under USRAP, an "interest becomes invalid only if it remains in existence and nonvested 90 years after [the testator's] death. Since it is almost certain that the final distribution of [an] estate will occur well within	No. (a) Unless a contrary intention appears, the rules of construction provided in this section govern with respect to any matter affecting the rule against perpetuities. (b) It shall be presumed that the creator intended the estate to be valid.

Table 9
Rule Against Perpetuities

	NEW JERSEY	NEW MEXICO	NEW YORK
		this 90-year period, the chance that [an] interest will be invalid is negligible.")	(c) Where the duration or vesting of an estate is contingent upon the probate of a will, the appointment of a fiduciary, the location of a distributee, the payment of debts, the sale of assets, the settlement of an estate, the determination of questions relating to an estate or transfer tax or the occurrence of any specified contingency, it shall be presumed that the creator of such estate intended such contingency to occur, if at all, within twenty-one years from the effective date of the instrument creating such estate. (§9-1.3)
23. *Does the all-or-nothing rule apply to class gifts?*	N/A	No specific state case or statute. *See* Unif. Statutory Rule Against Perpetuities § 1, 8B U.L.A. 257 (amended 1990) ("Although this Act does not supersede the basic idea of the much-maligned 'all-or-nothing' rule, the evils sometimes attributed to it are substantially if not entirely eliminated by the wait-and-see feature of the Statutory Rule and by the availability of reformation under Section 3.")	Yes. In applying the rule against perpetuities to class gifts, "a class gift must stand or fall as a unit and cannot be split for purposes of determining its viability." (Matter of Estate of Kreuzer, 243 A.D.2d 207, 209 (N.Y. App. Div. 1998))

Table 9
Rule Against Perpetuities

	NEW JERSEY	NEW MEXICO	NEW YORK
24. *Is there an exception to the all-or-nothing rule in the case of subclasses or specific sums to each member of the class?*	N/A	No specific state case or statute. *See* Unif. Statutory Rule Against Perpetuities § 1, 8B U.L.A. 257 (amended 1990) ("The specific-sum and sub-class doctrines are not superseded by this Act.")	See Unif. Statutory Rule Against Perpetuities § 1, 8B U.L.A. 257 ("The common law also recognizes a doctrine called the specific-sum doctrine which is derived from Storrs v. Benbow, 3 De G.M. & G. 390, 43 Eng. Rep 153 (Ch. 1853), and states: If a specified sum of money is to be paid to each member of a class, the interest of each class member is entitled to separate treatment and is valid or invalid under the Rule on its own. The common law also recognizes a doctrine called the sub-class doctrine, which is derived from Cattlin v. Brown, 11 Hare 372, 68 Eng. Rep. 1318 (Ch. 1853), and states: If the ultimate takers are not described as a group of separate subclasses, and if the share to which each separate subclass is entitled will finally be determined within the period of the Rule, the gifts to the different subclasses are separate for the purpose of the Rule.").

Table 9
Rule Against Perpetuities

	NEW JERSEY	NEW MEXICO	NEW YORK
25. *Is the infectious invalidity rule followed outside class gifts?*	N/A	No specific state case or statute. *See* Unif. Statutory Rule Against Perpetuities § 1, 8B U.L.A. 256 (amended 1990) (explaining that "[t]he doctrine of infectious invalidity is superseded by this Act by Section 3, under which courts . . . are required to reform the disposition to approximate as closely as possible the transferor's . . . plan of distribution.")	*See, e.g.,* Colorado, question #25.
26. *Is there a rule against the suspension of the power of alienation? If so, how is it stated?*	A future interest or trust is void if it suspends the power of alienation for longer than the permissible period. The power of alienation is the power to convey to another an absolute fee in possession of land, or full ownership of personalty. The permissible period is within 21 years after the death of an individual or individuals then alive. (§ 46:2F-10(a)(1)) For more detailed rules on calculating the "permissible period," *see* § 46:2F-10(a)(2)–(3).	Reasonableness standard. Gartley v. Ricketts, 760 P.2d 143, 145 (N.M. 1988) ("New Mexico has adopted and interpreted the common law rule against restrictions on alienation to mean that 'reasonable restraints upon the alienation of property are enforceable, but will be construed to operate within their exact limits.'")	(1) The absolute power of alienation is suspended when there are no persons in being by whom an absolute fee or estate in possession can be conveyed or transferred. (2) Every present or future estate shall be void in its creation which shall suspend the absolute power of alienation by any limitation or condition for a longer period than lives in being at the creation of the estate and a term of not more

Table 9

Rule Against Perpetuities

NEW JERSEY	NEW MEXICO	NEW YORK
For exceptions to the rule, see § 46:2F-10(d). Most importantly, there is no suspension of the power by a trust or by equitable interests under a trust if a trustee has power to sell, either expressed or implied, or if there is an unlimited power to terminate in one or more persons then alive. (§ 46:2F-10(c))		than twenty-one years. Lives in being shall include a child conceived before the creation of the estate but born thereafter. In no case shall the lives measuring the permissible period be so designated or so numerous as to make proof of their end unreasonably difficult. (§ 9-1.1(a)) Note that E.P.T.L. § 9-1.2 may cure the suspension problem by revising a provision requiring a distribution at a certain age to be at age 21. (In re BNY Mellon, N.A., 2 N.Y.S.3d 757 (Sur. Ct. Nassau Co. 2014))

Table 9
Rule Against Perpetuities

	NEW JERSEY	NEW MEXICO	NEW YORK
27. *Effective date.*	The first business day following July 8, 1999. See L.1999, Ch. 159, §17. In general, section 16 applied New Jersey's prior wait-and-see law to interests created prior to July 8, 1999.	July 1, 1992. *See also* #6.	N/A

---

[1] For questions, #19-25, *see also* § 45-2-906 (noting that the state's USRAP supersedes the common law rule against perpetuities). The answers to questions #19-25 are not likely to apply in most cases because of the abolition of the rule with respect to the vast majority of trusts.

Table 9
Rule Against Perpetuities

	NORTH CAROLINA	NORTH DAKOTA	OHIO
1. *Which rule is in effect: the common law rule, the Uniform Statutory Rule Against Perpetuities (USRAP), other law, or none?*	USRAP. (N.C. Gen. Stat. Ann. §§ 41-15 - 41-23)	USRAP. (N.D. § 47-02-27.1 - 47-02-27.5)	Common law rule with major exceptions. In particular, see #2b for trusts that are exempt much like Illinois Qualified Perpetual Trusts. Ohio Rev. Code Ann. (§§ 2131.08-2131.09)
2. a. *Is the common law rule relevant to any interests?*	Yes, but only as the starting point of the analysis. The common law rule itself does not apply to trusts created or administered in North Carolina. (§ 41-23(h); *see also* Brown Bros. Harriman Trust Co., N.A. v. Benson, 688 S.E.2d 752 (N.C. Ct. App. 2010) (upholding constitutionality of statute suspending common law rule despite constitutional provision barring "perpetuities." The common law rule still applies, for example, with respect to a tenant's preemptive right to purchase the underlying estate. (Khwaja v. Khan, 767 S.E.2d 901 (Ct. App. 2015))	Yes, but only as the starting point of the analysis.	Yes, for some interests.
b. *What is the relevant rule?*	A nonvested property interest is invalid unless: (1) When the interest is created, it is certain to vest or terminate no later than 21 years after the death of an individual then alive; or (2) The interest either vests or terminates within 90 years after its creation.	A contingent property interest is invalid unless: a. When the interest is created, it is certain to vest or terminate no later than twenty-one years after the death of an individual then alive; or b. The interest either vests or terminates within ninety years after its creation.	[N]o interest in real or personal property shall be good unless it must vest, if at all, not later than twenty-one years after a life or lives in being at the creation of the interest. (§ 2131.08(A)) *See also* § 2131.09(B)(1) "No rule of law against perpetuities . . . shall apply with respect to any interest

Table 9
Rule Against Perpetuities

	NORTH CAROLINA	NORTH DAKOTA	OHIO
	(§ 41-15(a))	(§ 47-02-27.1(1))	in real or personal property held in trust if the instrument creating the trust specifically states that the rule against perpetuities or the provisions of division (B) of section 2131.08 of the Revised Code shall not apply to the trust and if either the trustee of the trust has unlimited power to sell all trust assets or if one or more persons, one of whom may be the trustee, has the unlimited power to terminate the entire trust."
3. *Does the rule apply to other than private trusts?*	Yes. The rule applies except to:	Yes. The rule applies except to:	Yes. The rule applies except to:
	(1) A nonvested property interest or a power of appointment arising out of a nondonative transfer, except a nonvested property interest or a power of appointment arising out of:	1. A contingent property interest or a power of appointment arising out of a nondonative transfer, except a contingent property interest or a power of appointment arising out of a	Business Trusts (§ 1746.14), Real Estate Investment Trusts (§ 1747.09). A trust created by an employer as part of a stock bonus, or other listed, plan. § 2131.09 (A) Charitable trusts (Schreiner v.
	a. A premarital or postmarital agreement;	premarital or postmarital agreement, a separation or	Cincinnati Altenheim, 22 N.E.2d 587, 591 (Ohio Ct. App. 1939))
	b. A separation or divorce settlement;	divorce settlement, a spouse's election, a similar	Trusts that qualify under § 2131.09(B)(1). See #2b.
	c. A spouse's election;	arrangement arising out of a	
	d. A similar arrangement arising out of a prospective existing or previous marital relationship between the parties;	prospective, existing, or previous marital relationship between the parties, a contract to make or not to revoke a will or trust, a contract to exercise	

Table 9
Rule Against Perpetuities

NORTH CAROLINA	NORTH DAKOTA	OHIO
e. A contract to make or not to revoke a will or trust; f. A contract to exercise or not to exercise a power of appointment; g. A transfer in satisfaction of a duty of support; or h. A reciprocal transfer; (2) A fiduciary's power relating to the administration or management of assets, including the power of a fiduciary to sell, lease, or mortgage property, and the power of a fiduciary to determine principal and income; (3) A power to appoint a fiduciary; (4) A discretionary power of a trustee to distribute principal before termination of a trust to a beneficiary having an indefeasibly vested interest in the income and principal; (5) A nonvested property interest held by a charity, government or governmental agency or subdivision, if the nonvested property interest is preceded by an interest held by another	or not to exercise a power of appointment, a transfer in satisfaction of a duty of support, or a reciprocal transfer. 2. A fiduciary's power relating to the administration or management of assets, including the power of a fiduciary to sell, lease, or mortgage property, and the power of a fiduciary to determine principal and income. 3. A power to appoint a fiduciary. 4. A discretionary power of a trustee to distribute principal before termination of a trust to a beneficiary having an indefeasibly vested interest in the income and principal. 5. A contingent property interest held by a charity, government, or governmental agency or subdivision, if the contingent property interest is preceded by an interest held by another charity, government, or governmental agency or subdivision.	

Table 9
Rule Against Perpetuities

NORTH CAROLINA	NORTH DAKOTA	OHIO
charity, government or governmental agency or subdivision;	6. A property interest, power of appointment, or arrangement that was not subject to the common-law rule against perpetuities or excluded by another statute of this state.	
(6) A nonvested property interest in or a power of appointment with respect to a trust or other property arrangement forming part of a pension, profit sharing, stock bonus, health, disability, death benefit, income deferral or other current or deferred benefit plan for one or more employees, independent contractors or their beneficiaries or spouses, to which contributions are made for the purpose of distributing to or for the benefit of the participants or their beneficiaries or spouses the property, income or principal in the trust or other property arrangement, except a nonvested property interest or a power of appointment that is created by an election of a participant or a beneficiary or spouse;	(§ 47-02-27.4)	
(7) A property interest, power of appointment or arrangement that was not subject to the common-law rule against perpetuities or is excluded by another statute of this State.		

Table 9
Rule Against Perpetuities

	NORTH CAROLINA	*NORTH DAKOTA*	*OHIO*
	(8) A property interest or arrangement subjected to a time limit under Article 14 of Chapter 36A, "Honorary Trusts; Trusts for Pets; Trusts for Cemetery Lots;" or (9) A property interest or arrangement subjected to a time limit under Article 3 of this Chapter, "Time Limits on Options in Gross and Certain Other Interests in Land". (§ 41-18)		
4. *Does the rule invalidate the interest at its creation, or is the rule revised by a wait-and-see approach?*	Wait-and-see. (§ 41-15(a)(2))	Wait-and-see. (§ 47-02-27.1(1)(b))	Wait-and-see. (§ 2131.08(C)) ("In determining whether an interest would violate the rule and in reforming an interest, the period of perpetuities shall be measured by actual rather than possible events.")
5. *Can the trust be reformed?*	Yes, but only if one of the following conditions applies: (1) a nonvested property interest or power of appointment becomes invalid under § 41-15 (see #2b); (2) a class gift is not but might become invalid under 41-15 and the time has arrived when the share of any class member is to take effect in possession or enjoyment; or	Yes, but only if one of the following conditions applies: (1) a nonvested property interest or power of appointment becomes invalid under § 47-02-01.1 (see #2b); (2) a class gift is not but might become invalid under 47-02-27.1 and the time has arrived when the share of any class member is to take effect in possession or enjoyment; or	Yes. (§ 2131.08(C))

Table 9
Rule Against Perpetuities

	NORTH CAROLINA	NORTH DAKOTA	OHIO
	(3) a nonvested property interest that is not validated by § 41-15(a)(1), that is, the traditional common law rule, can vest but not within 90 years after its creation. (§ 41-17)	(3) a nonvested property interest that is not validated by subdivision a of subsection 1, § 47-02-27.1, that is, the traditional common law rule, can vest but not within 90 years after its creation. (§ 47-02-27.3)	
6. *If yes to 5., under what theory?*	[A] court shall reform a disposition in the manner most closely approximates the transferor's manifested plan of distribution and is within the 90 years allowed by § 41-15. (§ 41-17) *See also* § 41-19(b) ("If a nonvested property interest or a power of appointment was created prior to October 1, 1995, and is determined in a judicial proceeding, commenced on or after October 1, 1995, to violate this State's rule against perpetuities as that rule existed before October 1, 1995, a court upon the petition of an interested person may reform the disposition in the manner that most closely approximates the transferor's manifested plan of distribution and is within the limits of the rule against perpetuities applicable when the nonvested property interest or power of appointment was created.")	[A] court shall reform a disposition in the manner most closely approximates the transferor's manifested plan of distribution and is within the 90 years allowed by § 47-02-27.1. (§ 47-02-27.3) *See also* § 47-02-27.5(2)("If a contingent property interest or a power of appointment was created before July 1, 1991, and is determined in a judicial proceeding, commenced on or after July 1, 1991, to violate this state's rule against perpetuities as that rule existed before July 1, 1991, a court upon the petition of an interested person may reform the disposition in the manner that most closely approximates the transferor's manifested plan of distribution and is within the limits of the rule against perpetuities applicable when the contingent property interest or power of appointment was created.")	Any interest in real or personal property that would violate the rule against perpetuities, under division (A) of this section, shall be reformed, within the limits of the rule, to approximate most closely the intention of the creator of the interest. In determining whether an interest would violate the rule and in reforming an interest, the period of perpetuities shall be measured by actual rather than possible events. (§ 2131.08(C)) This provision applies to interests created after December 31, 1967, or powers under instruments created after that date exercising the power, even if the instrument creating the power was itself created prior to 1968. (§ 2131.08(E))

Table 9
Rule Against Perpetuities

	NORTH CAROLINA	NORTH DAKOTA	OHIO
7. *When is a general testamentary power of appointment invalid?*	A general testamentary power of appointment is invalid unless: (1) when the power is created, it is certain to be irrevocably exercised or otherwise to terminate no later than 21 years after the death of an individual then alive; or (2) the power is irrevocably exercised or otherwise terminates within 90 years after its creation. (§ 41-15(c))	A general testamentary power of appointment is invalid unless: (a) when the power is created, it is certain to be irrevocably exercised or otherwise to terminate no later than 21 years after the death of an individual then alive; or (b) the power is irrevocably exercised or otherwise terminates within 90 years after its creation. (§ 47-02-27.1(3))	Common law rule. (See Cleveland Trust Co. v. McQuade, 142 N.E.2d 249, 257-58 (Ohio Ct. App. 1957); Dollar Sav. & Trust Co. v. First Nat'l Bank, 285 N.E.2d 768, 778 (Ohio Misc. 1972) (applying the rule from *McQuade*); *see also* Unif. Statutory Rule Against Perpetuities § 1, 8B U.L.A. 248 (amended 1990) ("Under the Common-law Rule … a nongeneral power (whether or not presently exercisable) or a general testamentary power is invalid as of the time of its creation if it might not terminate (by irrevocable exercise or otherwise) within a life in being plus 21 years.")
8. *Same, but nongeneral testamentary power.*	A nongeneral testamentary power of appointment is invalid unless: (1) when the power is created, it is certain to be irrevocably exercised or otherwise to terminate no later than 21 years after the death of an individual then alive; or (2) the power is irrevocably exercised or otherwise terminates within 90 years after its creation. (§ 41-15(c))	A special testamentary power of appointment is invalid unless: (a) when the power is created, it is certain to be irrevocably exercised or otherwise to terminate no later than 21 years after the death of an individual then alive; or (b) the power is irrevocably exercised or otherwise terminates within 90 years after its creation. (§ 47-02-27.1(3))	See #7.

Table 9
Rule Against Perpetuities

	NORTH CAROLINA	NORTH DAKOTA	OHIO
9. *Same, but general power, whether testamentary or inter vivos, not presently exercisable because of a condition precedent.*	A general power of appointment not presently exercisable because of a condition precedent is invalid unless: (1) when the power is created, the condition precedent is certain to be satisfied or become impossible to satisfy no later than 21 years after the death of an individual then alive; or (2) the condition precedent either is satisfied or becomes impossible to satisfy within 90 years after its creation. (§ 41-15(b))	A general power of appointment not presently exercisable because of a condition precedent is invalid unless: (a) when the power is created, the condition precedent is certain to be satisfied or become impossible to satisfy no later than 21 years after the death of an individual then alive; or (a) the condition precedent either is satisfied or becomes impossible to satisfy within 90 years after its creation. (§ 47-02-27.1(2))	*See* Unif. Statutory Rule Against Perpetuities § 1, 8B U.L.A. 248 (amended 1990) ("Under the Common-law Rule, a general *power not presently exercisable because of a condition precedent is invalid as of the time of its creation if the condition might neither be satisfied nor become impossible to satisfy with a life in being plus 21 years.")
10. *Same, but nongeneral inter vivos power.*	See #8.	See #8.	See #7.

Table 9
Rule Against Perpetuities

	NORTH CAROLINA	NORTH DAKOTA	OHIO
11. *Is a period of gestation added to the perpetuity period?*	No. The possibility that a child will be born to a person after that person's death is disregarded. (§ 41-15(d)) *See also* comment to § 41-15 ("[T]he possibility that a child will be born to [a testator] after his death must be disregarded; and the possibility that a child will be born to any of [the testator's] descendants after their deaths must also be disregarded. Note, however, that the rule of subsection(d) does *not* apply to the question of the entitlement of an after-born child to take a beneficial interest in the trust").	No. The possibility that a child will be born to a person after that person's death is disregarded. (§ 47-02-27.1(4)) *See also* Unif. Statutory Rule Against Perpetuities § 1, 8B U.L.A. 243, 243 (amended 1990) ("[T]he possibility that a child will be born to [a testator] after his death must be disregarded; and the possibility that a child will be born to any of [the testator's] descendants after their deaths must also be disregarded. Note, however, that the rule of subsection (d) does *not* apply to the question of the entitlement of an after-born child to take a beneficial interest in the trust").	*Werling v. Sandy*, 476 N.E.2d 1053, 1055 (Ohio 1985) ("A child in gestation who is subsequently born alive may be considered a life in being throughout the gestation period for purposes of the now statutory rule against perpetuities.")
12. *What is the treatment of a "later of the traditional rule or 90 years" clause? See UIPC 2-901(e).*	That language is inoperative to the extent it produces a period of time that exceeds 21 years after the death of the survivor of the specified lives. (§ 41-15(e))	That language is inoperative to the extent it produces a period of time that exceeds 21 years after the death of the survivor of the specified lives. (§ 47-02-27.1(5))	N/A

Table 9
Rule Against Perpetuities

	NORTH CAROLINA	NORTH DAKOTA	OHIO
13. *When is an interest created by the exercise of a general testamentary power deemed created?*	Except as provided in subsections (b) and (c) of this section and in G.S. 41-19(a), the time for creation of a nonvested property interest or a power of appointment is determined under general principles of property law. (§ 41-16(a)) The first of the excepted provisions states that as long as a person with a general power to become the unqualified beneficial owner has that power, the nonvested interest is created when the power terminates. The second of the excepted provisions states that a nonvested property interest, which arises from a transfer to an existing trust, is created when the nonvested property interest in the trust was created. (§ 41-16(b)–(c)) *See also* comment to § 41-16 (explaining that "general principles of property law determine that the time . . . [of creation] is at the decedent's death.") *See generally* § 41-19(a) ("A nonvested property interest or a power of appointment created by the exercise of a power of appointment is created when the power is irrevocably exercised or when a revocable exercise becomes irrevocable.")	Except as provided in subsections 2 and 3 of this section and in subsection 1 of section 47-02-27.5, the time of creation of a contingent property interest or a power of appointment is determined under general principles of property law. (§ 47-02-27.2(1)) The first of the excepted provisions states that as long as a person with a general power to become the unqualified beneficial owner has that power, the nonvested interest is created when the power terminates. The second of the excepted provisions states that a nonvested property interest, which arises from a transfer to an existing trust, is created when the nonvested property interest in the trust was created. (§ 47-02-27.2(2)–(3)) *See also* Unif. Statutory Rule Against Perpetuities § 2, 8B U.L.A. 268 (amended 1990) (explaining that "general principles of property law determine that the time . . . [of creation] is at the decedent's death.") *See generally* § 47-02-27.5(1) ("[A] contingent property interest or a power of appointment created by the exercise of a power of appointment is created when the power is irrevocably exercised or when a revocable exercise becomes irrevocable.")	[W]e hold that the period for testing the validity of an exercise of a general testamentary power of appointment, under the common-law rule against perpetuities, is measured from the time of the creation of the power and not from its exercise. (Cleveland Trust Co. v. McQuade, 142 N.E.2d 249, 254 (Ohio Ct. App. 1957)) *See also* comment to Unif. Probate Code § 2-902(a) ("general principles of property law determine that a nonvested property interest or power of appointment created by will is created at the decedent's death"); Unif. Statutory Rule Against Perpetuities § 2, 8B U.L.A. 268 (amended 1990) (stating the same).

Table 9
Rule Against Perpetuities

	NORTH CAROLINA	NORTH DAKOTA	OHIO
14. *Same, but nongeneral testamentary power.*	See #13.	See #13.	See #13.

Table 9
Rule Against Perpetuities

	NORTH CAROLINA	NORTH DAKOTA	OHIO
15. *Same, but general inter vivos power.*	Except as provided in subsections (b) and (c) of this section and in G.S. 41-19(a), the time for creation of a nonvested property interest or a power of appointment is determined under general principles of property law. (§ 41-16(a)) The first of the excepted provisions states that as long as a person with a general power to become the unqualified beneficial owner has that power, the nonvested interest is created when the power terminates. The second of the excepted provisions states that a nonvested property interest, which arises from a transfer to an existing trust, is created when the nonvested property interest in the trust was created. (§ 41-16(b)–(c)) *See also* comment to § 41-16 (explaining that "the time when the interest or power is created is the date the transfer becomes effective for purposes of property law generally, normally the date of delivery of the deed"); Comment to Unif. Probate Code § 2-902(a) (stating same and adding "the funding of the trust" as "normally" the time when the interest is created). *See generally* § 41-19(a) ("For purposes of this section, a nonvested property interest or a power of appointment created by the exercise of a power of appointment is created when the	Except as provided in subsections 2 and 3 of this section and in subsection 1 of section 47-02-27.5, the time of creation of a contingent property interest or a power of appointment is determined under general principles of property law. (§ 47-02-27.2(1)) The first of the excepted provisions states that as long as a person with a general power to become the unqualified beneficial owner has that power, the nonvested interest is created when the power terminates. The second of the excepted provisions states that a nonvested property interest, which arises from a transfer to an existing trust, is created when the nonvested property interest in the trust was created. (§ 47-02-27.2(2)–(3)) *See also* Unif. Statutory Rule Against Perpetuities § 2, 8B U.L.A. 268 (amended 1990) (explaining that "the time when the interest or power is created is the date the transfer becomes effective for purposes of property law generally, normally the date of delivery of the deed"); Comment to Unif. Probate Code § 2-902(a) (stating same and adding "the funding of the trust" as "normally" the time when the interest is created). *See generally* § 47-02-27.5(1) ("For purposes of this section, a contingent	*See* comment to Unif. Probate Code § 2-902(a) ("With respect to an intervivos transfer, an interest or power is created on the date the transfer becomes effective for purposes of property law generally, normally the date of delivery of the deed or funding of the trust."); Unif. Statutory Rule Against Perpetuities § 2, 8B U.L.A. 268 (stating the same).

Table 9
Rule Against Perpetuities

	NORTH CAROLINA	NORTH DAKOTA	OHIO
	power is irrevocably exercised or when a revocable exercise becomes irrevocable.")	property interest or a power of appointment created by the exercise of a power of appointment is created when the power is irrevocably exercised or when a revocable exercise becomes irrevocable.")	
16. *Same, but nongeneral inter vivos power.*	See #15.	See #15.	See #15.

Table 9
Rule Against Perpetuities

	NORTH CAROLINA	NORTH DAKOTA	OHIO
17. *When is an interest created if the grantor of a trust has a power to revoke?*	For purposes of this Article, if there is a person who alone can exercise a power created by a governing instrument to become the unqualified beneficial owner of (i) a nonvested property interest or (ii) a property interest subject to a power of appointment described in G.S. 41-15(b) or (c), the nonvested property interest or power of appointment is created when the power to become the unqualified beneficial owner terminates. (§ 41-16(b)) *See also* comment to § 41-16 (explaining that "any nonvested property interest subject to [a power to revoke] is not created … until the power terminates (by release, expiration at the death of the donee, or otherwise"); Comment to Unif. Probate Code § 2-902(b) (noting that "nonvested property interests and powers of appointment created in [a revocable inter-vivos trust] are created when the power to revoke expires, usually at the settlor's death"). *See generally* § 41-19(a) ("A nonvested property interest or a power of appointment created by the exercise of a power of appointment is created when the power is irrevocably exercised or when a revocable exercise becomes irrevocable.")	For purposes of sections 47-02-27.1 through 47-02-27.5, if there is a person who alone can exercise a power created by a governing instrument to become an unqualified beneficial owner of a contingent property interest or a property interest subject to a power of appointment described in subsection 2 or 3 of section 47-02-27.1, the contingent property interest or power of appointment is created when the power to become the unqualified beneficial owner terminates. (§ 47-02-27.2(2)) *See also* Unif. Statutory Rule Against Perpetuities § 2, 8B U.L.A. 268 (amended 1990) (explaining that "any nonvested property interest subject to [a power to revoke] is not created … until the power terminates (by release, expiration at the death of the donee, or otherwise"); Comment to Unif. Probate Code § 2-902(b) (noting that "nonvested property interest and powers of appointment created in [a revocable inter-vivos trust] are created when the power to revoke expires, usually at the settlor's death"). *See generally* § 47-02-27.5(1) ("A nonvested property interest or a power of appointment created by the exercise of a power of appointment is created	The time of the creation of an interest in real or personal property subject to a power reserved by the grantor to revoke or terminate the interest shall be the time at which the reserved power expires by reason of the death of the grantor, by release of the power, or otherwise. (§ 2131.08(B)) *See also* comment to Unif. Probate Code § 2-902(b) (noting that "nonvested property interests and powers of appointment created in [a revocable inter-vivos trust] are created when the power to revoke expires, usually at the settlor's death"); Unif. Statutory Rule Against Perpetuities § 2, 8B U.L.A. 268 (amended 1990) (explaining that "any nonvested property interest subject to [a power to revoke] is not created … until the power terminates (by release, expiration at the death of the donee, or otherwise").

Table 9
Rule Against Perpetuities

	NORTH CAROLINA	NORTH DAKOTA	OHIO
18. *When does the period of the rule start re an interest contributed to an irrevocable trust? See UPC 2-902(c).*	A nonvested property interest or power of appointment arising from a transfer of property to a previously funded trust or other existing arrangement is created when the nonvested property interest or power of appointment in the original contribution was created. (§41-16(c))	A contingent property interest or power of appointment arising from a transfer of property to a previously funded trust or other existing arrangement is created when the nonvested property interest or power of appointment in the original contribution was created. (§47-02-27.2(3))	*See* comment to Unif. Probate Code 2-902(c) ("Arguably, at common law, each transfer [to an existing irrevocable inter-vivos trust] starts the period of the Rule running anew as to each transfer.")

when the power is irrevocably exercised or when a revocable exercise becomes irrevocable.")

Table 9
Rule Against Perpetuities

NORTH CAROLINA	*NORTH DAKOTA*	*OHIO*
19. *Is there a conclusive presumption of fertility, that is, the "fertile octogenarian" rule?*	Yes. Hicks v. Hicks, 130 S.E.2d 666, 667 (N.C. 1963) (explaining that there is a rebuttable presumption of fertility until death).[1] *See also* Unif. Statutory Rule Against Perpetuities §1, 8B U.L.A. 256 (amended 1990) (holding that "[t]his principle is not superseded by this Act, and in view of new advances in medical science . . . [this] is not unrealistic."). *But see* C. P. Jhong, Annotation, *Modern Status of Presumption Against Possibility of Issue Being Extinct*, 98 A.L.R.2d 1285 (2003) (noting "a trend toward denying the conclusive or absolute nature of the presumption against the possibility of issue being extinct where there is competent evidence to the contrary has developed in the decisions, although some courts still adhere to the traditional view treating the presumption as conclusive or absolute").	No specific state case or statute. *See* Unif. Statutory Rule Against Perpetuities §1, 8B U.L.A. 256 (amended 1990) (holding that "[t]his principle is not superseded by this Act, and in view of new advances in medical science . . . [this] is not unrealistic."). *But see* C. P. Jhong, Annotation, *Modern Status of Presumption Against Possibility of Issue Being Extinct*, 98 A.L.R.2d 1285 (2003) (noting "a trend toward denying the conclusive or absolute nature of the presumption against the possibility of issue being extinct where there is competent evidence to the contrary has developed in the decisions, although some courts still adhere to the traditional view treating the presumption as conclusive or absolute").	Yes. In re Estate of Herrick, 2003 WL 21361664 *3 (Ohio Ct. App. June 12, 2003) ("Although R.C. 2131.08(C) allows reformation of grants that violate the rule against perpetuities, the legislature has not expressly abrogated certain concepts associated with the rule and applicable in other contexts, among them the 'fertile octogenarian.' Therefore, even if [the beneficiaries] established that they were beyond normal child-bearing age, the law would not regard the class of beneficiaries as closed until their deaths.").

Table 9
Rule Against Perpetuities

	NORTH CAROLINA	NORTH DAKOTA	OHIO
20. *What is the earliest age a child is deemed capable of bearing a child? What is the impact of illegitimacy?*	Not specifically addressed by USRAP, but the reasoning is the same as set forth in the comment to section 1 of USRAP, 2, Technical Violations of the Common Law Rule. Wait and see will typically result in no violation. Nevertheless, the common law rule ordinarily will be applied initially. "Under the rule, courts must presume that living persons are capable of having or fathering children, no matter how young they are. See In re Graite's Will Trusts, [1949] 1 All E.R. 459, 460 (Ch.). Thus, the rule strikes down any interest whose vesting depends on the assertion that, for example, a toddler will not have children." (Keith L. Butler, Notes & Comments, *Long Live the Dead Hand: A Case for Repeal of the Rule Against Perpetuities in Washington*, 75 Wash. L. Rev. 1237, 1246 n.78 (2000)).	Not specifically addressed by USRAP, but the reasoning is the same as set forth in the comment to section 1 of USRAP, 2, Technical Violations of the Common Law Rule. Wait and see will typically result in no violation. Nevertheless, the common law rule ordinarily will be applied initially. "Under the rule, courts must presume that living persons are capable of having or fathering children, no matter how young they are. See In re Graite's Will Trusts, [1949] 1 All E.R. 459, 460 (Ch.). Thus, the rule strikes down any interest whose vesting depends on the assertion that, for example, a toddler will not have children." (Keith L. Butler, Notes & Comments, *Long Live the Dead Hand: A Case for Repeal of the Rule Against Perpetuities in Washington*, 75 Wash. L. Rev. 1237, 1246 n.78 (2000)).	"Under the rule, courts must presume that living persons are capable of having or fathering children, no matter how young they are. See In re Graite's Will Trusts, [1949] 1 All E.R. 459, 460 (Ch.). Thus, the rule strikes down any interest whose vesting depends on the assertion that, for example, a toddler will not have children." (Keith L. Butler, Notes & Comments, *Long Live the Dead Hand: A Case for Repeal of the Rule Against Perpetuities in Washington*, 75 Wash. L. Rev. 1237, 1246 n.78 (2000)).

Table 9
Rule Against Perpetuities

	NORTH CAROLINA	NORTH DAKOTA	OHIO
21. *Is the "unborn widow" rule observed?*	No specific state case or statue. *See* comment to § 41-15 (explaining that "[t]he chance that [an] interest will become invalid under the Statutory Rule is small" and so the unborn widow rule would rarely invalidate an interest); *see also* 61 Am. Jur. 2d *Perpetuities and Restraints on Alienation* § 39 (2013) (noting the same).	No specific state case or statue. *See* Unif. Statutory Rule Against Perpetuities § 1, 8B U.L.A. 246 (amended 1990) (explaining that "[t]he chance that [an] interest will become invalid under the Statutory Rule is small" and so the unborn widow rule would rarely invalidate an interest); *see also* 61 Am. Jur. 2d *Perpetuities and Restraints on Alienation* § 39 (2013) (noting the same).	*See, e.g.,* Arkansas, question #21.
22. *Does the "slothful executor" rule apply, i.e., an administrative contingency clause providing in the case of a "distribution to those of issue living at the time of distribution?"*	No specific state case or statute. *See* comment to § 41-15 (Under USRAP, an "interest becomes invalid only if it remains in existence and nonvested 90 years after [the testator's] death. Since it is almost certain that the final distribution of [an] estate will occur well within this 90-year period, the chance that [an] interest will be invalid is negligible.")	No specific state case or statute. *See* Unif. Statutory Rule Against Perpetuities § 1, 8B U.L.A. 245 (amended 1990) (Under USRAP, an "interest becomes invalid only if it remains in existence and nonvested 90 years after [the testator's] death. Since it is almost certain that the final distribution of [an] estate will occur well within this 90-year period, the chance that [an] interest will be invalid is negligible.")	*See, e.g.,* California, question # 22.

Table 9
Rule Against Perpetuities

	NORTH CAROLINA	NORTH DAKOTA	OHIO
23. *Does the all-or-nothing rule apply to class gifts?*	No specific state case or statute. *See* comment to § 41-15 ("Although this Act does not supersede the basic idea of the much-maligned 'all-or-nothing' rule, the evils sometimes attributed to it are substantially if not entirely eliminated by the wait-and-see feature of the Statutory Rule and by the availability of reformation under Section 3.")	No specific state case or statute. *See* Unif. Statutory Rule Against Perpetuities § 1, 8B U.L.A. 257 (amended 1990) ("Although this Act does not supersede the basic idea of the much-maligned 'all-or-nothing' rule, the evils sometimes attributed to it are substantially if not entirely eliminated by the wait-and-see feature of the Statutory Rule and by the availability of reformation under Section 3.")	Yes. (Dayton v Phillips, 28 WL Bull. 327, 5 (Ohio Super. Ct. 1892))

Table 9
Rule Against Perpetuities

	NORTH CAROLINA	*NORTH DAKOTA*	*OHIO*
24. *Is there an exception to the all-or-nothing rule in the case of subclasses or specific sums to each member of the class?*	No specific state case or statute. *See* comment to §41-15 ("The specific-sum and sub-class doctrines are not superseded by this Act.")	No specific state case or statute. *See* Unif. Statutory Rule Against Perpetuities §1, 8B U.L.A. 257 (amended 1990) ("The specific-sum and sub-class doctrines are not superseded by this Act.")	*See* Unif. Statutory Rule Against Perpetuities §1, 8B U.L.A. 257 ("The common law . . . recognizes a doctrine called the specific-sum doctrine which is derived from Storrs v. Benbow, 3 De G.M. & G. 390, 43 Eng. Rep 153 (Ch. 1853), and states: If a specified sum of money is to be paid to each member of a class, the interest of each class member is entitled to separate treatment and is valid or invalid under the Rule on its own. The common law also recognizes a doctrine called the sub-class doctrine, which is derived from Cattlin v. Brown, 11 Hare 372, 68 Eng. Rep. 1318 (Ch. 1853), and states: If the ultimate takers are not described as a single class but rather as a group of separate subclasses, and if the share to which each separate subclass is entitled will finally be determined within the period of the Rule, the gifts to the different subclasses are separate for the purpose of the Rule.").

Table 9
Rule Against Perpetuities

	NORTH CAROLINA	NORTH DAKOTA	OHIO
25. *Is the infectious invalidity rule followed outside class gifts?*	No specific state case or statute. *See* comment to § 41-15 (explaining that "[t]he doctrine of infectious invalidity is superseded by this Act by Section 3, under which courts . . . are required to *reform* the disposition to approximate as closely as possible the transferor's . . . plan of distribution.")	No specific state case or statute. *See* Unif. Statutory Rule Against Perpetuities § 1, 8B U.L.A. 256 (amended 1990) (explaining that "[t]he doctrine of infectious invalidity is superseded by this Act by Section 3, under which courts . . . are required to *reform* the disposition to approximate as closely as possible the transferor's . . . plan of distribution.")	Unclear. *See* Cleveland Trust Co. v. McQuade, 142 N.E.2d 249, 263 (Ohio Ct. App. 1957) (declining to apply the infectious invalidity rule in this instance but not answering whether the rule is to be applied in any case).

Table 9
Rule Against Perpetuities

	NORTH CAROLINA	NORTH DAKOTA	OHIO
26. *Is there a rule against the suspension of the power of alienation? If so, how is it stated?*	"21 years after the death of an individual then alive or lives then in being plus a period of 21 years." (§ 41-23(a)) The power is not suspended in the case of a trust if the trustee "has the power to sell, either express or implied, or if there exists an unlimited power to terminate the trust in one or more persons in being." (§ 41-23(e))	N.D. Cent. Code § 47-02-26 ("Conditions restraining alienation, when repugnant to the interest created, are void.")	With respect to trusts, *see* § 2131.09(B)(1) ("No . . . suspension of the power of alienation of the title to property, . . . shall apply with respect to any interest in real or personal property held in trust if the instrument creating the trust specifically states that the rule against perpetuities or the provisions of division (A) of section 2131.08 of the Revised Code shall not apply to the trust and if either the trustee of the trust has unlimited power to sell all trust assets or if one or more persons, one of whom may be the trustee, has the unlimited power to terminate the entire trust.") With respect to estates in fee, see Baker v. Alexander, 156 N.E. 223, 225 (Ohio App. 1926) ("The only safe rule of decision is to hold, as I understand the common law for ages to have been, that a condition or restriction which would suspend all power of alienation for a single day, is inconsistent with the estate granted, unreasonable and void.")
27. *Effective date.*	October 1, 1995. *See also* #6.	July 1, 1991. *See also* #6.	January 1, 1968. *See also* #6.

[1] For questions #19 - 25, *see also* § 41-22 (noting that the state's USRAP supersedes the common law rule against perpetuities). The answers to questions #19 - 25 are not likely to apply in most cases because of the abolition of the rule with respect to the vast majority of many trusts.

Table 9
Rule Against Perpetuities

	OKLAHOMA	OREGON	PENNSYLVANIA
1. *Which rule is in effect: the common law rule, the Uniform Statutory Rule Against Perpetuities (USRAP), other law, or none?*	The following responses address circumstances in which the common law rule applies. The common law rule against perpetuities no longer applies with respect "to a trust subject to the trust laws of this state." (60 § 175.47(c)) There is a constitutional prohibition against perpetuities. The term "perpetuities" in the constitution has been construed as meaning the common law rule against perpetuities. (Melcher v. Camp, 435 P.2d 107, 111-12 (Sup. Ct. 1967) The current legislation presumes the contrary to Melcher — that "perpetuities" in the constitution refers to the suspension of the power of alienation, thereby permitting a statutory repeal of the rule against perpetuities. The matter will likely be addressed by the Oklahoma courts eventually. Otherwise, the common law rule, with reform elements, applies. (Phillips v. Chambers, 51 P.2d 303, 306 (Okla. 1935))	USRAP. (Or. Rev. Stat. §§ 105.950-105.975)	The rule against perpetuities has been abolished with respect to all interests created after December 31, 2006. (20 Pa. Cons. Stat. Ann. § 6107.1) If a power of appointment is exercised to create a new power of appointment, any interest created by the new power is invalid if it does not vest within 360 years of the creation of the original power, unless the exercise of the new power of appointment expressly states that this statutory provision shall not apply to the interests created by the exercise. (20 § 6107.1(b)(3)) The common law rule with wait-and-see addition applies to interests created prior to 2007. (20 § 6107.1(a)(1)) The following analysis applies to interests created before 2007. (20 Pa. Cons. Stat. §§ 6104-6105)
2. a. *Is the common law rule relevant to any interests?*	Yes.	Yes, but only as the starting point of the analysis.	Yes, but only as the starting point of the analysis.

Table 9
Rule Against Perpetuities

	OKLAHOMA	OREGON	PENNSYLVANIA
b. *What is the relevant rule?*	No interest is good *unless it must vest,* if at all, no later than twenty-one years after some life in being at the creation of the interest. (In re Crowl, 737 P.2d 911, 915 (Okla. 1987) (citation omitted)) However, reformation is allowed. See #6.	A nonvested property interest is invalid unless: (a) When the interest is created, it is certain to vest or terminate no later than 21 years after the death of an individual then alive; or (b) The interest either vests or terminates within 90 years after its creation. (§ 105.950(1))	"The rule against perpetuities provides that an interest must vest, if it vests at all, within twenty-one years of a life in being, and is currently codified at Act of June 30, 1972, P.L. 508, No. 164, § 2, 20 Pa.C.S. § 6104." Central Del. County Auth. v. Greyhound Corp., 588 A.2d 485, 487 n.1 (Pa. 1991) Upon the expiration of the period allowed by the common law rule against perpetuities as measured by actual rather than possible events, any interest not then vested and any interest in members of a class the membership of which is then subject to increase shall be void. (20 § 6104(b))

Table 9
Rule Against Perpetuities

	OKLAHOMA	OREGON	PENNSYLVANIA
3. *Does the rule apply to other than private trusts?*	No. It does not apply to charitable trusts. (Phillips *v.* Chambers, 51 P.2d 303, 310 (Okla. 1935))	Yes. The rule applies except to: (1) A nonvested property interest or a power of appointment arising out of a nondonative transfer, except a nonvested property interest or a power of appointment arising out of: (a) A premarital or postmarital agreement; (b) A separation or divorce settlement; (c) A spouse's election; (d) A similar arrangement arising out of a prospective existing or previous marital relationship between the parties; (e) A contract to make or not to revoke a will or trust; (f) A contract to exercise or not to exercise a power of appointment; (g) A transfer in satisfaction of a duty of support; or (h) A reciprocal transfer; (2) A fiduciary's power relating to the administration or management of assets,	Yes. The rule applies except to: (1) Interest exempt at common law. Interests which would not have been subject to the common law rule against perpetuities. (2) Cemetery trusts. Interests which are directed to be used for the maintenance, care, or adornment of any cemetery, churchyard, or other place for the burial of the dead, or any portion thereof, or any grave therein or any improvement on or about the same, and which are subject to no condition precedent at the end of the period described in subsection (b). (3) Pension or profit-sharing plans. Interests created by a bona fide trust inter vivos primarily for the benefit of business employees, their families or appointees, under a stock bonus, pension, disability or death benefit, profit-sharing or other employee benefit plan.

Table 9
Rule Against Perpetuities

OKLAHOMA	OREGON	PENNSYLVANIA
	including the power of a fiduciary to sell, lease or mortgage property, and the power of a fiduciary to determine principal and income;	(4) Administrative powers. Powers which contribute to the effective management of trust assets, including powers to sell, mortgage, or lease trust assets, powers relating to
	(3) A power to appoint a fiduciary;	investment of trust assets, powers to determine what is
	(4) A discretionary power of a trustee to distribute principal before termination of a trust to a beneficiary having an indefeasibly vested interest in the income and principal;	principal and what is income, and powers to name successor trustees.
	(5) A nonvested property interest held by a charity, government or governmental agency or subdivision, if the nonvested property interest is preceded by an interest held by another charity, government or governmental agency or subdivision;	(20 § 6104(b))

Table 9
Rule Against Perpetuities

	OKLAHOMA	OREGON	PENNSYLVANIA
		(6) A nonvested property interest in or a power of appointment with respect to a trust or other property arrangement forming part of a pension, profit sharing, stock bonus, health, disability, death benefit, income deferral or other current or deferred benefit plan for one or more employees, independent contractors or their beneficiaries or spouses, to which contributions are made for the purpose of distributing to or for the benefit of the participants or their beneficiaries or spouses the property, income or principal in the trust or other property arrangement, except a nonvested property interest or a power of appointment that is created by an election of a participant or a beneficiary or spouse; or (7) A property interest, power of appointment or arrangement that was not subject to the common-law rule against perpetuities or is excluded by another statute of this state. (§ 105.965)	
4. *Does the rule invalidate the interest at its creation, or is the rule revised by a wait-and-see approach?*	At its creation (See #2a).	Wait-and-see. (§105.950(1)(b))	Wait-and-see. (20 §6104(b) (using actual events rather than possible events as the measuring device).

Table 9

Rule Against Perpetuities

	OKLAHOMA	OREGON	PENNSYLVANIA
5. *Can the trust be reformed?*	Yes. (60 Okl. St. §§ 75, 77)	Yes, but only if one of the following conditions applies: (1) A nonvested property interest or a power of appointment becomes invalid under ORS 105.950, statutory rule against perpetuities; (2) A class gift is not but might become invalid under ORS 105.950, statutory rule rule against perpetuities, and the time has arrived when the share of any class member is to take effect in possession or enjoyment; or (3) A nonvested property interest is not validated by ORS 105.950(1)(a), that is the traditional common law rule, can vest but not within ninety (90) years after its creation.	No specific provision. However, 20 § 6105 provides how interests are disposed of when invalidity occurs. If a valid interest follows a void income interest, the valid interest is accelerated. (20 §6105(a)). If a void interest follows a valid interest on condition subsequent or special limitation, it vests in the owner of the valid interest. (20 §6105(b)) Other void interests vest in the income beneficiary at the end of the permissible period as measured by actual rather than possible events. (20 §6105(c))

Table 9
Rule Against Perpetuities

OKLAHOMA	OREGON	PENNSYLVANIA
	(§ 105.960) *See also* § 105.970(2) ("If a nonvested property interest or a power of appointment was created before January 1, 1990, and is determined in a judicial proceeding, commenced on or after January 1, 1990, to violate this state's rule against perpetuities as that rule existed before January 1, 1990, a court may reform the disposition in the manner that most closely approximates the transferor's intent and is within the limits of the applicable rule against perpetuities.")	

Table 9
Rule Against Perpetuities

	OKLAHOMA	OREGON	PENNSYLVANIA
6. If yes to 5., under what theory?	Any interest in real or personal property that would violate the rule against perpetuities shall be reformed, or construed within the limits of the rule, to give effect to the general intent of the creator of that interest whenever that general intent can be ascertained. This provision shall be liberally construed and applied to validate such interest to the fullest extent consistent with such ascertained intent. (60, §75) If an instrument violates the rule against perpetuities, but can be reformed or construed in accordance with the provisions of this act, it shall not be declared totally invalid. Rather, the provisions thereof that do not offend the rule shall be enforced, and only the provisions thereof that do violate, or might violate, the rule shall be subject to reformation or construction under the doctrine of cy pres within the terms of this act. (60, §77)	[A] court shall reform a disposition in the manner that most closely approximates the transferor's manifested plan of distribution and is within the ninety years allowed by ORS 105.950 (1)(b), (2)(b) and (3)(b). (§ 105.960)	See #5.

Table 9
Rule Against Perpetuities

	OKLAHOMA	OREGON	PENNSYLVANIA
7. *When is a general testamentary power of appointment invalid?*	*See* Unif. Statutory Rule Against Perpetuities § 1, 8B U.L.A. 248 (amended 1990) ("Under the Common-law Rule . . . a *nongeneral power* (whether or not presently exercisable) or a *general testamentary power* is invalid as of the time of its creation if it *might* not terminate (by irrevocable exercise or otherwise) within a life in being plus 21 years.")	A general testamentary power of appointment is invalid unless one of the following conditions is satisfied: (a) When the power is created, it is certain to be irrevocably exercised or otherwise to terminate no later than 21 years after the death of an individual then alive. (b) The power is irrevocably exercised or otherwise terminates within 90 years after its creation. (§ 105.950(3))	*See* Unif. Statutory Rule Against Perpetuities § 1, 8B U.L.A. 248 (amended 1990) ("Under the Common-law Rule . . . a *nongeneral power* (whether or not presently exercisable) or a *general testamentary power* is invalid as of the time of its creation if it *might* not terminate (by irrevocable exercise or otherwise) within a life in being plus 21 years.")
8. *Same, but nongeneral testamentary power.*	See #7.	A nongeneral power of appointment . . . is invalid unless one of the following conditions is satisfied: (a) When the power is created, it is certain to be irrevocably exercised or otherwise to terminate no later than 21 years after the death of an individual then alive. (b) The power is irrevocably exercised or otherwise terminates within 90 years after its creation. (§ 105.950(3))	See #7.

Table 9
Rule Against Perpetuities

	OKLAHOMA	OREGON	PENNSYLVANIA
9.	*Same, but general power, whether testamentary or inter vivos, not presently exercisable because of a condition precedent.*	See Unif. Statutory Rule Against Perpetuities § 1, 8B U.L.A. 248 (amended 1990) ("Under the Common-law Rule, a *general power not presently exercisable because of a condition precedent* is invalid as of the time of its creation if the condition *might* neither be satisfied nor become impossible to satisfy with a life in being plus 21 years.")	A general power of appointment not presently exercisable because of a condition precedent is invalid unless one of the following conditions is satisfied: (1) When the power is created, the condition precedent is certain to be satisfied or become impossible to satisfy no later than 21 years after the death of an individual then alive. (2) The condition precedent either is satisfied or becomes impossible to satisfy within 90 years after its creation. (§ 105.950(2))	See Unif. Statutory Rule Against Perpetuities § 1, 8B U.L.A. 248 (amended 1990) ("Under the Common-law Rule, a *general power not presently exercisable because of a condition precedent* is invalid as of the time of its creation if the condition *might* neither be satisfied nor become impossible to satisfy with a life in being plus 21 years.")
10.	*Same, but nongeneral inter vivos power.*	See #7.	See #8.	See #7.

Table 9
Rule Against Perpetuities

	OKLAHOMA	OREGON	PENNSYLVANIA
11. *Is a period of gestation added to the perpetuity period?*	Yes. (Barnes v. Barnes, 280 P.2d 996, 999 (Okla. 1955))	No. The possibility that a child will be born to a person after that person's death is disregarded. (§ 105.950(4)) *See also* Unif. Statutory Rule Against Perpetuities § 1, 8B U.L.A. 243, 243 (amended 1990) ("[T]he possibility that a child will be born to [a testator] after his death must be disregarded; and the possibility that a child will be born to any of [the testator's] descendants after their deaths must also be disregarded. Note, however, that the rule of subsection (d) does *not* apply to the question of the entitlement of an after-born child to take a beneficial interest in the trust").	Yes. (In re Lewis' Estate, 37 A.2d 482, 484 (Pa. 1944))
12. *What is the treatment of a "later of the traditional rule or 90 years" clause? See UPC 2-901(e).*	N/A	The language in a governing instrument is inoperative to the extent it produces a period longer than 21 years after lives in being. (§ 105.950(5))	N/A

Table 9
Rule Against Perpetuities

OKLAHOMA	OREGON	PENNSYLVANIA
13. *When is an interest created by the exercise of a general testamentary power deemed created?*		
See comment to Unif. Probate Code § 2-902(a) ("general principles of property law determine that a nonvested property interest or power of appointment created by will is created at the decedent's death"); Unif. Statutory Rule Against Perpetuities § 2, 8B U.L.A. 268 (amended 1990) (stating the same).	Except as provided in subsections (2) and (3) of this section and ORS 105.970(1), the time of creation of a nonvested property interest or a power of appointment is determined under general principles of property law. (§ 105.955(1)) The first of the excepted provisions states that as long as a person with a general power to become the unqualified beneficial owner has that power, the nonvested interest is created when the power terminates. The second of the excepted provisions states that a nonvested property interest, which arises from a transfer to an existing trust, is created when the nonvested property interest in the trust was created. (§ 105.955(2)-(3)) *See also* Unif. Statutory Rule Against Perpetuities § 2, 8B U.L.A. 268 (amended 1990) (explaining that "general principles of property law determine that the time . . . [of creation] is at the decedent's death.") *See generally* subsection 91, § 105.970 ("A nonvested property interest or a power of appointment created by the exercise of a power of appointment is created when the power is irrevocably exercised or when a revocable exercise becomes irrevocable.")	The period allowed by the common law rule against perpetuities under subsection (b) of this section shall be measured from the expiration of any time during which one person while living has the unrestricted power to transfer to himself the entire legal and beneficial interest in the property. (§ 6104(c)) *See also* official comment to § 6104(c) ("The period would begin as of the death of a donee of a power who could appoint by deed or by will (Mifflin's Ap., 121 Pa. 205), but not where the power is to appoint by will alone: Lawrence's Est., 136 Pa. 354.")

Table 9
Rule Against Perpetuities

	OKLAHOMA	OREGON	PENNSYLVANIA
14. *Same, but nongeneral testamentary power.*	See #13.	See #13.	See #13.

Table 9
Rule Against Perpetuities

	OKLAHOMA	OREGON	PENNSYLVANIA
15. *Same, but general inter vivos power.*	*See* comment to Unif. Probate Code § 2-902(a) ("With respect to an intervivos transfer, an interest or power is created on the date the transfer becomes effective for purposes of property law generally, normally the date of delivery of the deed or funding of the trust."); Unif. Statutory Rule Against Perpetuities § 2, 8B U.L.A. 268 (stating the same).	Except as provided in subsections (2) and (3) of this section and ORS 105.970(1), the time of creation of a nonvested property interest or a power of appointment is determined under general principles of property law. (§ 105.955(1)) The first of the excepted provisions states that as long as a person with a general power to become the unqualified beneficial owner has that power, the nonvested interest is created when the power terminates. The second of the excepted provisions states that a nonvested property interest, which arises from a transfer to an existing trust, is created when the nonvested property interest in the trust was created. (§ 105.955(2)-(3)) *See also* Unif. Statutory Rule Against Perpetuities § 2, 8B U.L.A. 268 (amended 1990) (explaining that "the time when the interest or power is created is the date the transfer becomes effective for purposes of property law generally, normally the date of delivery of the deed"); Comment to Unif. Probate Code § 2-902(a) (stating same and adding "the funding of the trust" as "normally" the time when the interest is created). *See generally* § 105.970 ("[A] nonvested property interest or a power of	See #13.

Table 9
Rule Against Perpetuities

	OKLAHOMA	OREGON	PENNSYLVANIA
		appointment created by the exercise of a power of appointment is created when the power is irrevocably exercised or when a revocable exercise becomes irrevocable.")	
16. *Same, but nongeneral inter vivos power.*	See #15.	See #15.	See #13.

Table 9
Rule Against Perpetuities

	OKLAHOMA	OREGON	PENNSYLVANIA
17. *When is an interest created if the grantor of a trust has a power to revoke?*	*See* comment to Unif. Probate Code § 2-902(b) (noting that "nonvested property interest and powers of appointment created in [a revocable inter-vivos trust] are created when the power to revoke expires, usually at the settlor's death"); Unif. Statutory Rule Against Perpetuities § 2, 8B U.L.A. 268 (amended 1990) (explaining that "any nonvested property interest subject to [a power to revoke] is not created . . . until the power terminates (by release, expiration at the death of the donee, or otherwise)".	If there is a person who alone can exercise a power created by a governing instrument to become the unqualified beneficial owner of either a nonvested property interest or a property interest subject to a power of appointment described in ORS 105.950(2) or (3), the nonvested property interest or power of appointment is created when the power to become the unqualified beneficial owner terminates. (§ 105.955(2)) *See also* Unif. Statutory Rule Against Perpetuities § 2, 8B U.L.A. 268 (amended 1990) (explaining that "any nonvested property interest subject to [a power to revoke] is not created . . . until the power terminates (by release, expiration at the death of the donee, or otherwise"); Comment to Unif. Probate Code § 2-902(b) (noting that "nonvested property interests and powers of appointment created in [a revocable inter-vivos trust] are created when the power to revoke expires, usually at the settlor's death"). *See generally* § 105.970, subsection (1) ("[A] nonvested property interest or a power of appointment created by the exercise of a power of appointment is created when the power is irrevocably exercised or when a revocable exercise becomes irrevocable.")	The period allowed by the common law rule against perpetuities under subsection (b) of this section shall be measured from the expiration of any time during which one person while living has the unrestricted power to transfer to himself the entire legal and beneficial interest in the property. (§ 6104(c)) *See also* official comment to § 6104(c) ("For revocable trusts the period would begin as of the settlor's death.")

Table 9
Rule Against Perpetuities

	OKLAHOMA	OREGON	PENNSYLVANIA
18. When does the period of the rule start re an interest contributed to an irrevocable trust? See UPC 2-902(c).	See comment to Unif. Probate Code 2-902(c) ("Arguably, at common law, each transfer [to an existing irrevocable inter-vivos trust] starts the period of the Rule running anew as to each transfer.").	A nonvested property interest or a power of appointment arising from a transfer of property to a previously funded trust or other existing property arrangement is created when the nonvested property interest or power of appointment in the original contribution was created. (§ 105.955(3))	See comment to Unif. Probate Code 2-902(c) ("Arguably, at common law, each transfer [to an existing irrevocable inter-vivos trust] starts the period of the Rule running anew as to each transfer.").
19. Is there a conclusive presumption of fertility, that is, the "fertile octogenarian" rule?	See, e.g., Arkansas, question #19.	No specific state case or statute.[1] See Unif. Statutory Rule Against Perpetuities §1, 8B U.L.A. 256 (amended 1990) (holding that "[t]his principle is not superseded by this Act, and in view of new advances in medical science . . . [this] is not unrealistic."). But see C. P. Jhong, Annotation, Modern Status of Presumption Against Possibility of Issue Being Extinct, 98 A.L.R.2d 1285 (2003) (noting "a trend toward denying the conclusive or absolute nature of the presumption against the possibility of issue being extinct where there is competent evidence to the contrary has developed in the decisions, although some courts still adhere to the traditional view treating the presumption as conclusive or absolute").	No. In re Estate of Weaver, 572 A.2d 1249, 1254 (Pa. Super. Ct. 1990) ("The new rule required Pennsylvania courts to determine the validity of future interests in accordance with events which actually occurred during the period of the common law rule against perpetuities, . . . [and] eliminated some of the more improbable possibilities that determined the validity of some future interests under the old rule such as the fertile octogenarian and the unborn widow."); Estate of Weeks, 402 A.2d 657, 659 (Pa. 1979) ("This Court, however, has long held that distribution of trust funds is governed by principles of equity rather than the conclusive common law presumption of 'fertility unto death.'")

Table 9
Rule Against Perpetuities

	OKLAHOMA	OREGON	PENNSYLVANIA
20. *What is the earliest age a child is deemed capable of bearing a child? What is the impact of illegitimacy?*	No answer to either question is provided in case law or statutory law. "Under the [common law] rule, courts must presume that living persons are capable of having or fathering children, no matter how young they are. *See* In re Graite's Will Trusts, [1949] 1 All E.R. 459, 460 (Ch.). Thus, the rule strikes down any interest whose vesting depends on the assertion that, for example, a toddler will not have children." (Keith L. Butler, Notes & Comments, *Long Live the Dead Hand: A Case for Repeal of the Rule Against Perpetuities in Washington,* 75 Wash. L. Rev. 1237, 1246 n.78 (2000)). However, the reform approach of Oklahoma would appear to negate the application of the common law rule.	Not specifically addressed by USRAP, but the reasoning is the same as set forth in the comment to section 1 of USRAP, 2, Technical Violations of the Common Law Rule. Wait and see will typically result in no violation. Nevertheless, the common law rule ordinarily will be applied initially. "Under the rule, courts must presume that living persons are capable of having or fathering children, no matter how young they are. See In re Graite's Will Trusts, [1949] 1 All E.R. 459, 460 (Ch.). Thus, the rule strikes down any interest whose vesting depends on the assertion that, for example, a toddler will not have children." (Keith L. Butler, Notes & Comments, *Long Live the Dead Hand: A Case for Repeal of the Rule Against Perpetuities in Washington,* 75 Wash. L. Rev. 1237, 1246 n.78 (2000)).	"Under the rule, courts must presume that living persons are capable of having or fathering children, no matter how young they are. See In re Graite's Will Trusts, [1949] 1 All E.R. 459, 460 (Ch.). Thus, the rule strikes down any interest whose vesting depends on the assertion that, for example, a toddler will not have children." (Keith L. Butler, Notes & Comments, *Long Live the Dead Hand: A Case for Repeal of the Rule Against Perpetuities in Washington,* 75 Wash. L. Rev. 1237, 1246 n.78 (2000)).

Table 9
Rule Against Perpetuities

	OKLAHOMA	OREGON	PENNSYLVANIA
21. *Is the "unborn widow" rule observed?*	*See, e.g.,* Arkansas, question #21.	No specific state case or statute. *See* Unif. Statutory Rule Against Perpetuities § 1, 8B U.L.A. 246 (amended 1990) (explaining that "[t]he chance that [an] interest will become invalid under the Statutory Rule is small" and so the unborn widow rule would rarely invalidate an interest); *see also* 61 Am Jur 2d *Perpetuities and Restraints on Alienation* § 39 (2013) (noting the same).	No. In re Estate of Weaver, 572 A.2d 1249, 1254(Pa. Super. Ct. 1990) ("The new rule required Pennsylvania courts to determine the validity of future interests in accordance with events which actually occurred during the period of the common law rule against perpetuities, … [and] eliminated some of the more improbable possibilities that determined the validity of some future interests under the old rule such as the fertile octogenarian and the unborn widow.")
22. *Does the "slothful executor" rule apply, i.e., an administrative contingency clause providing for a "distribution to, e.g., those issue living at the time of the satisfaction of the administrative condition precedent?"*	*See, e.g.,* California, question #22.	No specific state case or statute. *See* Unif. Statutory Rule Against Perpetuities § 1, 8B U.L.A. 245 (amended 1990) (Under USRAP, an "interest becomes invalid only if it remains in existence and nonvested 90 years after [the testator's] death. Since it is almost certain that the final distribution of [an] estate will occur well within this 90-year period, the chance that [an] interest will be invalid is negligible.")	*See, e.g.,* California, question #22.

Table 9
Rule Against Perpetuities

	OKLAHOMA	OREGON	PENNSYLVANIA
23. *Does the all-or-nothing rule apply to class gifts?*	Yes. (McLaughlin v. Yingling, 213 P. 552, 562-63 (Okla. 1923))	Yes. Closset v. Burtchaell, 230 P. 554, 561 (Or. 1924) (affirming the all-or-nothing rule as stated in Gray on Perpetuities). *See also* Unif. Statutory Rule Against Perpetuities § 1, 8B U.L.A. 257 (amended 1990) ("Although this Act does not supersede the basic idea of the much-maligned 'all-or-nothing' rule, the evils sometimes attributed to it are substantially if not entirely eliminated by the wait-and-see feature of the Statutory Rule and by the availability of reformation under Section 3.")	Yes. Upon the expiration of the period allowed by the common law rule against perpetuities as measured by actual rather than possible events, . . . any interest in members of a class the membership of which is then subject to increase shall be void. (§ 6104(b)); *see also* In re Lockhart's Estate, 159 A. 874, 876 (Pa. 1932)

Table 9
Rule Against Perpetuities

	OKLAHOMA	OREGON	PENNSYLVANIA
24. *Is there an exception to the all-or-nothing rule in the case of subclasses or specific sums to each member of the class?*	*See* Unif. Statutory Rule Against Perpetuities §1, 8B U.L.A. 257 ("The common law also recognizes a doctrine called the specific-sum doctrine which is derived from Storrs v. Benbow, 3 De G.M. & G. 390, 43 Eng. Rep 153 (Ch. 1853), and states: If a specified sum of money is to be paid to each member of a class, the interest of each class member is entitled to separate treatment and is valid or invalid under the Rule on its own. The common law also recognizes a doctrine called the sub-class doctrine, which is derived from Cattlin v. Brown, 11 Hare 372, 68 Eng. Rep. 1318 (Ch. 1853), and states: If the ultimate takers are not described as a single class but rather as a group of separate subclasses, and if the share to which each separate subclass is entitled will finally be determined within the period of the Rule, the gifts to the different subclasses are separate for the purpose of the Rule.").	No specific state case or statute. *See* Unif. Statutory Rule Against Perpetuities §1, 8B U.L.A. 257 (amended 1990) ("The specific-sum and sub-class doctrines are not superseded by this Act.").	No specific state case or statute. *See* Unif. Statutory Rule Against Perpetuities §1, 8B U.L.A. 257 ("The common law also recognizes a doctrine called the specific-sum doctrine which is derived from Storrs v. Benbow, 3 De G.M. & G. 390, 43 Eng. Rep 153 (Ch. 1853), and states: If a specified sum of money is to be paid to each member of a class, the interest of each class member is entitled to separate treatment and is valid or invalid under the Rule on its own. The common law also recognizes a doctrine called the sub-class doctrine, which is derived from Cattlin v. Brown, 11 Hare 372, 68 Eng. Rep. 1318 (Ch. 1853), and states: If the ultimate takers are not described as a single class but rather as a group of separate subclasses, and if the share to which each separate subclass is entitled will finally be determined within the period of the Rule, the gifts to the different subclasses are separate for the purpose of the Rule.").

Table 9

Rule Against Perpetuities

	OKLAHOMA	OREGON	PENNSYLVANIA
25. *Is the infectious invalidity rule followed outside class gifts?*	*See, e.g.,* Colorado, question #25.	No specific state case or statute. *See* Unif. Statutory Rule Against Perpetuities §1, 8B U.L.A. 256 (amended 1990) (explaining that "[t]he doctrine of infectious invalidity is superseded by this Act by Section 3, under which courts . . . are required to *reform* the disposition to approximate as closely as possible the transferor's . . . plan of distribution.")	Morton Estate, 59 Pa. D. & C.2d 300, 318 (Pa. D. & C. 1972) (striking down provision of testamentary trust using the doctrine of infectious invalidity).

Table 9
Rule Against Perpetuities

	OKLAHOMA	OREGON	PENNSYLVANIA
26. *Is there a rule against the suspension of the power of alienation? If so, how is it stated?*	In 2015, the rule was amended. The absolute power of alienation is not deemed suspended if there is any person who has the power to sell, exchange or otherwise convey property. If the terms of a trust do not suspend the absolute power beyond the 21-year term set forth in 60 § 175.47(A), "the trust may not exist in perpetuity." (60 § 175.47(A)) There are also other exceptions to the rule: "when property is given, granted, bequeathed, or devised to: 1. A charitable use; 2. Literary, educational, scientific, religious, or charitable corporations for their sole use and benefit; 3. Any cemetery corporation, society or association; 4. The Department of Mental Health and Substance Abuse Services as provided in Section 1 of this act; or 5. Gifts absolute, limited, or in trust, for the advancement of medical science to an incorporated state society of physicians and surgeons."	Case law unclear. *See* Gange v. Hayes, 237 P.2d 196, 202 (Or. 1951) (finding that an option in a deed without any time limits was an invalid restraint on alienation); Friswold v. United States Nat'l Bank, 257 P. 818, 821 (Or. 1927) ("[A] restriction, . . . against any and all alienation whatever during a limited time, of an estate in fee, is . . . void.")	Reasonableness standard. Rice v. Rice, 359 A.2d 782, 784 (Pa. 1976) ("While the question whether a particular restraint on alienation is unreasonable and so invalid is basically a question of law, the answer depends upon factual considerations, such as the time within which the restraint may be exercised and whether it is supported by consideration.")

Table 9
Rule Against Perpetuities

	OKLAHOMA	OREGON	PENNSYLVANIA
27. *Effective date.*	October 1, 1971. The law is effective respecting instruments taking effect after the Act becomes effective and this includes both appointments afterwards and appointments created before the act became effective to remain consistent (60 §78).	January 1, 1990. *See also* #5.	The provisions of this section and of section 6105 (relating to rule against perpetuities; disposition when invalidity occurs) shall apply to all interests created before January 1, 2007. (§6104(d))

---

[1] For questions, #19 - 25, *see also* § 105.975(3) (noting that the state's USRAP supersedes the common law rule against perpetuities). The answers to questions #19 - 25 are not likely to apply in most cases because of the abolition of the rule with respect to the vast majority of many trusts.

Table 9
Rule Against Perpetuities

	RHODE ISLAND	SOUTH CAROLINA	SOUTH DAKOTA
1. Which rule is in effect: the common law rule, the Uniform Statutory Rule Against Perpetuities (USRAP), other law, or none?	None. (R.I. Gen. Laws §34-11-38) ("The common law rule against perpetuities shall no longer be deemed to be in force and/or of any effect in this state, provided, the provisions of this section shall not be construed to invalidate or modify the terms of any interest which would have been valid prior to the effective date of this act, and, provided further, that the provisions of this section shall apply to both legal and equitable interests.")	USRAP. (S.C. Code Ann. §§ 27-6-10 - 27-6-80)	None. (S.D. Codified Laws §43-5-8) ("The common-law rule against perpetuities is not in force in this state.") If a power is exercised to create a new trust, pursuant to §55-2-15, the power cannot suspend the power to alienate trust property or extend the first trust beyond the permissible period of any rule against perpetuities applicable to the first trust. (§55-2-20)
2. a. Is the common law rule relevant to any interests?	N/A	Yes, but only as a starting point in the analysis.	N/A
b. What is the relevant rule?	N/A	A nonvested property interest is invalid unless: (1) When the interest is created, it is certain to vest or terminate no later than 21 years after the death of an individual then alive; or (2) The interest either vests or terminates within ninety years after its creation. (§ 27-6-20(A))	N/A
3. Does the rule apply to other than private trusts?	N/A	Yes. The rule applies except to:	N/A

Table 9
Rule Against Perpetuities

RHODE ISLAND	SOUTH CAROLINA	SOUTH DAKOTA
	(1) a nonvested property interest or a power of appointment arising out of a nondonative transfer, except a nonvested property interest or a power of appointment arising out of (i) a premarital or postmarital agreement, (ii) a separation or divorce settlement, (iii) a spouse's election, (iv) a similar arrangement arising out of a prospective, existing, or previous marital relationship between the parties, (v) a contract to make or not to revoke a will or trust, (vi) a contract to exercise or not to exercise a power of appointment, (vii) a transfer in satisfaction of a duty of support, or (viii) a reciprocal transfer; (2) a fiduciary's power relating to the administration or management of assets, including the power of a fiduciary to sell, lease, or mortgage property, and the power of a fiduciary to determine principal and income; (3) a power to appoint a fiduciary; (4) a discretionary power of a trustee to distribute principal before termination of a trust to a beneficiary having an indefeasibly vested interest in the income and principal;	

Table 9
Rule Against Perpetuities

RHODE ISLAND	SOUTH CAROLINA	SOUTH DAKOTA
	(5) a nonvested property interest held by a charity, government, or governmental agency or subdivision, if the nonvested property interest is preceded by an interest held by another charity, government, or governmental agency or subdivision;	
	(6) a nonvested property interest in or a power of appointment with respect to a trust or other property arrangement forming part of a pension, profit-sharing, stock bonus, and health, disability, death benefit, income deferral, or other current or deferred benefit plan for one or more employees, independent contractors, or their beneficiaries or spouses, to which contributions are made for the purpose of distributing to or for the benefit of the participants or their beneficiaries or spouses the property, income, or principal in the trust or other property arrangement, except a nonvested property interest or a power of appointment that is created by an election of a participant or a beneficiary or spouse; or	

Table 9
Rule Against Perpetuities

	RHODE ISLAND	SOUTH CAROLINA	SOUTH DAKOTA
		(7) a property interest, power of appointment, or arrangement that was not subject to the common law rule against perpetuities or is excluded by another statute of this State, including, but not limited to, the interests, powers, and arrangements coming within §§ 13-7-30, 27-5-70, 27-5-80, 33-53-30, 39-55-135, and 62-7-409. (§ 27-6-50) The rule does not apply to business trusts, certain pension plans, and annuity trusts of employers. (§ 27-5-80)	
4. *Does the rule invalidate the interest at its creation, or is the rule revised by a wait-and-see approach?*	N/A	Wait-and-see. (§ 27-6-20(A)(2); Abrams v. Templeton, 465 S.E.2d 117, 120 (S.C. Ct. App. 1995))	N/A
5. *Can the trust be reformed?*	N/A	Yes, but only if one of the following conditions applies: (1) a nonvested property interest or a power of appointment becomes invalid under § 27-6-20 (see #2b); (2) a class gift is not but may become invalid under § 27-6-20 and the time has arrived when the share of any class member is to take effect in possession or enjoyment; or	N/A

Table 9
Rule Against Perpetuities

	RHODE ISLAND	SOUTH CAROLINA	SOUTH DAKOTA
		(3) a nonvested property interest that is not validated by § 27-6-20(A)(1), that is, the traditional common law rule, can vest but not within ninety years after its creation. (§ 27-6-40)	
6. *If yes to 5., under what theory?*	N/A	Upon the petition of an interested person, a court shall reform a disposition in the manner that most closely approximates the transferor's manifested plan of distribution and is within the ninety years permitted by this chapter. (§ 27-6-40) *See also* § 27-6-60(B) ("If a nonvested property interest or a power of appointment was created before July 1, 1987, and is determined in a judicial proceeding, commenced on or after July 1, 1987, to violate this State's rule against perpetuities as that rule existed before July 1, 1987, a court upon the petition of an interested person shall reform the disposition by inserting a savings clause that preserves most closely the transferor's plan of distribution and that brings that plan within the limits of the rule against perpetuities applicable when the nonvested property interest or power of appointment was created.")	N/A

Table 9

Rule Against Perpetuities

	RHODE ISLAND	SOUTH CAROLINA	SOUTH DAKOTA
7. When is a general testamentary power of appointment invalid?	N/A	A general testamentary power of appointment is invalid unless one of the following conditions is satisfied: (1) When the power is created, it is certain to be irrevocably exercised or otherwise to terminate no later than 21 years after the death of an individual then alive. (2) The power is irrevocably exercised or otherwise terminates within 90 years after its creation. (§ 27-6-20(C))	N/A
8. Same, but nongeneral testamentary power.	N/A	A nongeneral power of appointment . . . is invalid unless one of the following conditions is satisfied: (1) When the power is created, it is certain to be irrevocably exercised or otherwise to terminate no later than 21 years after the death of an individual then alive. (2) The power is irrevocably exercised or otherwise terminates within 90 years after its creation. (§ 27-6-20(C))	N/A

Table 9
Rule Against Perpetuities

	RHODE ISLAND	SOUTH CAROLINA	SOUTH DAKOTA
9. Same, but general power, whether testamentary or inter vivos, not presently exercisable because of a condition precedent.	N/A	A general power of appointment not presently exercisable because of a condition precedent is invalid unless one of the following conditions is satisfied: (1) When the power is created, the condition precedent is certain to be satisfied or become impossible to satisfy no later than 21 years after the death of an individual then alive. (2) The condition precedent either is satisfied or becomes impossible to satisfy within 90 years after its creation. (§ 27-6-20(B))	N/A
10. Same, but nongeneral inter vivos power.	N/A	See #8.	N/A

Table 9
Rule Against Perpetuities

	RHODE ISLAND	SOUTH CAROLINA	SOUTH DAKOTA
11. *Is a period of gestation added to the perpetuity period?*	N/A	No. The possibility that a child will be born to a person after that person's death is disregarded. (§ 27-6-20(D)) *See also* Unif. Statutory Rule Against Perpetuities § 1, 8B U.L.A. 243, 243 (amended 1990) ("[T]he possibility that a child will be born to [a testator] after his death must be disregarded; and the possibility that a child will be born to any of [the testator's] descendants after their deaths must also be disregarded. Note, however, that the rule of subsection (d) does *not* apply to the question of the entitlement of an after-born child to take a beneficial interest in the trust").	N/A
12. *What is the treatment of a "later of the traditional rule or 90 years" clause? See UPC 2-901(e).*	N/A	South Carolina's USRAP does not specify how it will treat "later of" clauses.	N/A

Table 9
Rule Against Perpetuities

	RHODE ISLAND	SOUTH CAROLINA	SOUTH DAKOTA
13. *When is an interest created by the exercise of a general testamentary power deemed created?*	N/A	Except as provided in subsections (B) and (C) and in §27-6-60(A), the time of creation of a nonvested property interest or a power of appointment is determined under general principles of property law. (§27-6-30(A)) The first of the excepted provisions states that as long as a person with a general power to become the unqualified beneficial owner has that power, the nonvested interest is created when the power terminates. The second of the excepted provisions states that a nonvested property interest, which arises from a transfer to an existing trust, is created when the nonvested property interest in the trust was created. *See also* Unif. Statutory Rule Against Perpetuities § 2, 8B U.L.A. 268 (amended 1990) (explaining that "general principles of property law determine that the time . . . . [of creation] is at the decedent's death."). *See generally* § 27-6-60(A) ("A nonvested property interest or a power of appointment created by the exercise of a power of appointment is created when the power is irrevocably exercised or when a revocable exercise becomes irrevocable.")	N/A

Table 9
Rule Against Perpetuities

	RHODE ISLAND	SOUTH CAROLINA	SOUTH DAKOTA
14. Same, but nongeneral testamentary power.	N/A	See #13.	N/A

Table 9
Rule Against Perpetuities

	RHODE ISLAND	SOUTH CAROLINA	SOUTH DAKOTA
15. *Same, but general inter vivos power.*	N/A	Except as provided in subsections (B) and (C) and in §27-6-60(A), the time of creation of a nonvested property interest or a power of appointment is determined under general principles of property law. (§27-6-30(A)) The first of the excepted provisions states that as long as a person with a general power to become the unqualified beneficial owner has that power, the nonvested interest is created when the power terminates. The second of the excepted provisions states that a nonvested property interest, which arises from a transfer to an existing trust, is created when the nonvested property interest in the trust was created. (§27-6-30(B)–(C)) *See also* Unif. Statutory Rule Against Perpetuities §2, 8B U.L.A. 268 (amended 1990) (explaining that "the time when the interest or power is created is the date the transfer becomes effective for purposes of property law generally, normally the date of delivery of the deed"); Comment to Unif. Probate Code §2-902(a) (stating same and adding "the funding of the trust" as "normally" the time when the interest is created). *See generally* §27-6-60(A) ("A nonvested property interest or a power of appointment created by the exercise	N/A

Table 9
Rule Against Perpetuities

	RHODE ISLAND	SOUTH CAROLINA	SOUTH DAKOTA
		of a power of appointment is created when the power is irrevocably exercised or when a revocable exercise becomes irrevocable.")	
16. *Same, but nongeneral inter vivos power.*	N/A	See #15.	N/A

Table 9
Rule Against Perpetuities

	RHODE ISLAND	SOUTH CAROLINA	SOUTH DAKOTA
17. *When is an interest created if the grantor of a trust has a power to revoke?*	N/A	If there is a person who alone can exercise a power created by a governing instrument to become the unqualified beneficial owner of (i) a nonvested property interest or (ii) a property interest subject to a power of appointment described in § 27-6-20(B) or 27-6-20(C), the nonvested property interest or power of appointment is created when the power to become the unqualified beneficial owner terminates. (§ 27-6-30(B)) *See also* Unif. Statutory Rule Against Perpetuities § 2, 8B U.L.A. 268 (amended 1990) (explaining that "any nonvested property interest subject to [a power to revoke] is not created . . . until the power terminates (by release, expiration at the death of the donee, or otherwise"); Comment to Unif. Probate Code § 2-902(b) (noting that "nonvested property interest and powers of appointment created in [a revocable inter-vivos trust] are created when the power to revoke expires, usually at the settlor's death"). *See generally* § 27-6-60(A) ("A nonvested property interest or a power of appointment created by the exercise of a power of appointment is created when the power is irrevocably exercised or when a revocable exercise becomes irrevocable.")	N/A

Table 9
Rule Against Perpetuities

	RHODE ISLAND	SOUTH CAROLINA	SOUTH DAKOTA
18. *When does the period of the rule start re an interest contributed to an irrevocable trust? See UPC 2-902(c).*	N/A	A nonvested property interest or a power of appointment arising from a transfer of property to a previously funded trust or other existing property arrangement is created when the nonvested property interest or power of appointment in the original contribution was created. (§ 27-6-30(C))	N/A
19. *Is there a conclusive presumption of fertility, that is, the "fertile octogenarian" rule?*	N/A	No specific state case or statute.[1] *See* Unif. Statutory Rule Against Perpetuities § 1, 8B U.L.A. 256 (amended 1990) (holding that "[t]his principle is not superseded by this Act, and in view of new advances in medical science . . . [this] is not unrealistic."). *But see* C. P. Jhong, Annotation, *Modern Status of Presumption Against Possibility of Issue Being Extinct*, 98 A.L.R.2d 1285 (2003) (noting "a trend toward denying the conclusive or absolute nature of the presumption against the possibility of issue being extinct where there is competent evidence to the contrary has developed in the decisions, although some courts still adhere to the traditional view treating the presumption as conclusive or absolute").	N/A

Table 9
Rule Against Perpetuities

	RHODE ISLAND	SOUTH CAROLINA	SOUTH DAKOTA
20. What is the earliest age a child is deemed capable of bearing a child? What is the impact of illegitimacy?	N/A	Not specifically addressed by USRAP, but the reasoning is the same as set forth in the comment to section 1 of USRAP, 2, Technical Violations of the Common Law Rule. Wait and see will typically result in no violation. Nevertheless, the common law rule ordinarily will be applied initially. "Under the rule, courts must presume that living persons are capable of having or fathering children, no matter how young they are. See In re Graite's Will Trusts, [1949] 1 All E.R. 459, 460 (Ch.). Thus, the rule strikes down any interest whose vesting depends on the assertion that, for example, a toddler will not have children." (Keith L. Butler, Notes & Comments, *Long Live the Dead Hand: A Case for Repeal of the Rule Against Perpetuities in Washington*, 75 Wash. L. Rev. 1237, 1246 n.78 (2000)).	N/A
21. Is the "unborn widow" rule observed?	N/A	No specific state case or statute. See Unif. Statutory Rule Against Perpetuities § 1, 8B U.L.A. 246 (amended 1990) (explaining that "[t]he chance that [an] interest will become invalid under the Statutory Rule is small" and so the unborn widow rule would rarely invalidate an interest); *see also* 61 Am. Jur. 2d *Perpetuities and Restraints on Alienation* § 39 (2013) (noting the same).	N/A

Table 9
Rule Against Perpetuities

	RHODE ISLAND	SOUTH CAROLINA	SOUTH DAKOTA
22. Does the "slothful executor" rule apply, i.e., an administrative contingency clause providing for a "distribution to, e.g., those issue living at the time of the satisfaction of the administrative condution precedent?"	N/A	No specific state case or statute. *See* Unif. Statutory Rule Against Perpetuities §1, 8B U.L.A. 245 (amended 1990) (Under USRAP, an "interest becomes invalid only if it remains in existence and nonvested 90 years after [the testator's] death. Since it is almost certain that the final distribution of [an] estate will occur well within this 90-year period, the chance that [an] interest will be invalid is negligible.")	N/A
23. Does the all-or-nothing rule apply to class gifts?	N/A	No specific state case or statute. *See* Unif. Statutory Rule Against Perpetuities §1, 8B U.L.A. 257 (amended 1990) ("Although this Act does not supersede the basic idea of the much-maligned 'all-or-nothing' rule, the evils sometimes attributed to it are substantially if not entirely eliminated by the wait-and-see feature of the Statutory Rule and by the availability of reformation under Section 3.")	N/A
24. Is there an exception to the all-or-nothing rule in the case of subclasses or specific sums to each member of the class?	N/A	No specific state case or statute. *See* Unif. Statutory Rule Against Perpetuities §1, 8B U.L.A. 257 (amended 1990) ("The specific-sum and sub-class doctrines are not superseded by this Act.")	N/A

Table 9
Rule Against Perpetuities

	RHODE ISLAND	SOUTH CAROLINA	SOUTH DAKOTA
25. *Is the infectious invalidity rule followed outside class gifts?*	N/A	No specific state case or statute. *See* Unif. Statutory Rule Against Perpetuities §1, 8B U.L.A. 256 (amended 1990) (explaining that "[t]he doctrine of infectious invalidity is superseded by this Act by Section 3, under which courts . . . are required to *reform* the disposition to approximate as closely as possible the transferor's . . . plan of distribution.")	N/A
26. *Is there a rule against the suspension of the power of alienation? If so, how is it stated?*	Substantiality test. *See* Chile v. Beck, 452 A.2d 626, 629 (R.I. 1982) ("Limited restraints that do not substantially diminish the whole power of alienation are not necessarily void. Here, our ultimate objective in measuring the scope and effect of the restraints on alienation is to arrive at the intent of the testator.")	No specific state case or statute. Limited restraints appear to be okay. *See* Lynch v. Lynch, 159 S.E. 26 (S.C. 1931) ("The weight of authority clearly supports the view that a limited restraint upon alienation for a particular purpose is not repugnant to the grant of a fee-simple estate.")	The absolute power of alienation may not be suspended by any limitation or condition whatever for a longer period than during the continuance of the lives of persons in being plus a period of thirty years at the creation of the limitation or condition, except in the single case mentioned in § 43-9-5 relating to contingent fee remainder on a prior fee remainder. (§ 43-5-1) For more specific rules calculating the period of the rule, *see* § 43-5-5. For additional rules relating to the suspension of the power of alienation, *see* § 43-5-2 - 43-5-9. Most importantly, there is no suspension of the power by a trust or by equitable interests under a trust if the trustee has power to sell, either expressed or implied, or there is an unlimited power to terminate in one or more persons then alive. (§ 43-5-4)

Table 9

Rule Against Perpetuities

	RHODE ISLAND	SOUTH CAROLINA	SOUTH DAKOTA
27. *Effective date.*	N/A	July 1, 1987. *See also* #6.	N/A

---

[1] For questions #19 - 25, *see also* § 27-6-80 (noting that the state's USRAP supersedes the common law rule against perpetuities). The answers to questions #19 - 25 are not likely to apply in most cases because of the abolition of the rule with respect to the vast majority of many trusts.

Table 9
Rule Against Perpetuities

	TENNESSEE	TEXAS	UTAH
1. Which rule is in effect: the common law rule, the Uniform Statutory Rule Against Perpetuities (USRAP), other law, or none?	USRAP. (Tenn. Code Ann. §§ 66-1-201 - 66-1-208) As to any trust created after June 30, 2007, or that becomes irrevocable after June 30, 2007, the terms of the trust shall require that all beneficial interests in the trust vest or terminate or the power of appointment is exercised within three hundred sixty (360) years.	Common Law Rule with possibility of reformation. (Tex. Prop. Code § 112.036)	Modified USRAP. (Utah Code Ann. §§ 75-2-1201 - 75-2-1209)
2. a. Is the common law rule relevant to any interests?	Yes, but only as the starting point of the analysis.	Yes, but revised.	Yes, but only as the starting point of the analysis.
b. What is the relevant rule?	A nonvested property interest is invalid unless one (1) of the following conditions is satisfied: (1) When the interest is created, it is certain to vest or terminate no later than twenty-one (21) years after the death of an individual then alive; or (2) The interest either vests or terminates within ninety (90) yearsafter its creation. (3) The interest satisfies the conditions set forth in #1 above. (§ 66-1-202(a))	The Rule states that no interest is valid unless it must vest, if at all, within twenty-one years after some life in being at the time of the creation of the interest, plus a period of gestation. (§ 112.036) The Rule requires that a challenged conveyance be viewed as of the date the instrument is executed, and it is void if by any possible contingency the grant or devise could violate the Rule. (Peveto v. Starkey, 645 S.W.2d 770, 772 (Tex. 1982) (citations omitted))	A nonvested property interest is invalid unless within 1,000 years after the interest's creation the interest vests or terminates. (§75-2-1203(1)) The language in the governing instrument cannot extend this for a longer period. (§75-2-1203(4))

Table 9
Rule Against Perpetuities

	TENNESSEE	TEXAS	UTAH
3. *Does the rule apply to other than private trusts?*	Yes. The rule applies except to:	The rule does not apply to charitable trusts. (§ 112.036) The rule also does not apply to pension trusts. (§ 121.004)	Yes. The rule applies except to:
	(1) nonvested property interest or a power of appointment arising out of a nondonative transfer, except a nonvested property interest or a power of appointment arising out of:		(1) a nonvested property interest or a power of appointment arising out of a nondonative transfer, except a nonvested property interest or a power of appointment arising out of:
	(A) A premarital or postmarital agreement;		(a) a premarital or postmarital agreement;
	(B) A separation or divorce settlement;		(b) a separation or divorce settlement;
	(C) A spouse's election;		(c) a spouse's election;
	(D) A similar arrangement arising out of a prospective, existing, or previous marital relationship between the parties;		(d) a similar arrangement arising out of a prospective, existing, or previous marital relationship between the parties;
	(E) A contract to make or not to revoke a will or trust;		(e) a contract to make or not to revoke a will or trust;
	(F) A contract to exercise or not to exercise a power of appointment;		(f) a contract to exercise or not to exercise a power of appointment;
	(G) A transfer in satisfaction of a duty of support; or		(g) a transfer in satisfaction of a duty of support; or
	(H) A reciprocal transfer;		(h) a reciprocal transfer;

Table 9
Rule Against Perpetuities

TENNESSEE	TEXAS	UTAH
(2) A fiduciary's power relating to the administration or management of assets, including the power of a fiduciary to sell, lease, or mortgage property, and the power of a fiduciary to determine principal and income;		(2) a fiduciary's power relating to the administration or management of assets, including the power of a fiduciary to sell, lease, or mortgage property, and the power of a fiduciary to determine principal and income;
(3) A power to appoint a fiduciary;		(3) a power to appoint a fiduciary;
(4) A discretionary power of a trustee to distribute principal before termination of a trust to a beneficiary having an indefeasibly vested interest in the income and principal;		(4) a discretionary power of a trustee to distribute principal before termination of a trust to a beneficiary having an indefeasibly vested interest in the income and principal;
(5) A nonvested property interest held by a charity, government, or governmental agency or subdivision, if the nonvested property interest is preceded by an interest held by another charity, government, or governmental agency or subdivision;		(5) a nonvested property interest held by a charity, government, or governmental agency or subdivision, if the nonvested property interest is preceded by an interest held by another charity, government, or governmental agency or subdivision;

Table 9
Rule Against Perpetuities

	TENNESSEE	*TEXAS*	*UTAH*
	(6) A nonvested property interest in or a power of appointment with respect to a trust or other property arrangement forming part of a pension, profit-sharing, stock bonus, health, disability, death benefit, income deferral, or other current or deferred benefit plan for one (1) or more employees, independent contractors, or their beneficiaries or spouses, to which contributions are made for the purpose of distributing to or for the benefit of the participants or their beneficiaries or spouses the property, income, or principal in the trust or other property arrangement, except a nonvested property interest or a power of appointment that is created by an election of a participant or a beneficiary or spouse; or		(6) a nonvested property interest in or a power of appointment with respect to a trust or other property arrangement forming part of a pension, profit-sharing, stock bonus, health, disability, death benefit, income deferral, or other current or deferred benefit plan for one or more employees, independent contractors, or their beneficiaries or spouses, to which contributions are made for the purpose of distributing to or for the benefit of the participants or their beneficiaries or spouses the property, income, or principal in the trust or other property arrangement, except a nonvested property interest or a power of appointment that is created by an election of a participant or a beneficiary or spouse;
	(7) A property interest, power of appointment, or arrangement that was not subject to the common law rule against perpetuities or is excluded by another statute of this state.		(7) a property interest, power of appointment, or arrangement that was not subject to the common law rule against perpetuities or is excluded by another statute of this state; or
	(§66-1-205)		(8) a property interest or arrangement subjected to a time limit under Section 75-2-1001.
			(§75-2-1206)

Table 9
Rule Against Perpetuities

	TENNESSEE	TEXAS	UTAH
4. Does the rule invalidate the interest at its creation, or is the rule revised by a wait-and-see approach?	Wait-and-see. (§ 66-1-202(a)(2))	At its creation. (See #2a)	Wait-and-see. (§75-2-1203)
5. Can the trust be reformed?	Yes, but only if any of the following conditions is satisfied: (1) A nonvested property interest or a power of appointment becomes invalid under the statutory rule against perpetuities provided in § 66-1-202 (see #2b); (2) A class gift is not but might become invalid under the statutory rule against perpetuities provided in § 66-1-202, and the time has arrived when the share of any class member is to take effect in possession or enjoyment; or (3) A nonvested property interest that is not validated by § 66-1-202(a)(1), that is, the traditional common law rule, can vest but not within ninety (90) years after its creation. (§ 66-1-204).	Yes. (§§ 112.036; 5.043)	Yes, but only if any of the following conditions is satisfied: (1) a nonvested property interest or a power of appointment becomes invalid under Section 75-2-1203 (see #2b); (2) a class gift is not but might become invalid under Section 75-2-1203 and the time has arrived when the share of any class member is to take effect in possession or enjoyment; or (3) a nonvested property interest that is not validated by Section 75-2-1203, that is, the traditional common law rule, can vest but not within 1,000 years after its creation. (§75-2-1205)

Table 9
Rule Against Perpetuities

	TENNESSEE	TEXAS	UTAH
6. *If yes to 5., under what theory?*	Upon the petition of an interested person, a court shall reform a disposition in the manner that most closely approximates the transferor's manifested plan of distribution and is within the ninety (90) years allowed by §§ 66-1-202(a)(2), (b)(2) or (c)(2). (§ 66-1-204)	Any interest in a trust may, however, be reformed or construed to the extent and as provided by Section 5.043. (§ 112.036) *See* § 5.043(a) ("Within the limits of the rule against perpetuities, a court shall reform or construe an interest in real or personal property that violates the rule to effect the ascertainable general intent of the creator of the interest. A court shall liberally construe and apply this provision to validate an interest to the fullest extent consistent with the creator's intent.") The court may reform or construe an interest according to the doctrine of cy pres by giving effect to the general intent and specific directive of the creator within the limits of the rule against perpetuities. (§ 5.043(b))	Upon the petition of an interested person, a court shall reform a disposition in the manner that most closely approximates the transferor's manifested plan of distribution and is within the 1,000 years allowed by Section 75-2-1203. (§ 75-2-1205) *See also* § 75-2-1207(2) ("If a nonvested property interest or a power of appointment was created before December 31, 2003, and is determined in a judicial proceeding, commenced on or after December 31, 2003, to violate Utah's rule against perpetuities as that rule existed before December 31, 2003, a court upon the petition of an interested person may reform the disposition: (a) in the manner that most closely approximates the transferor's manifested plan of distribution; and (b) that is within the limits of the rule against perpetuities applicable when the nonvested property interest or power of appointment was created.")

Table 9
Rule Against Perpetuities

	TENNESSEE	TEXAS	UTAH
7. *When is a general testamentary power of appointment invalid?*	A general testamentary power of appointment is invalid unless one of the following conditions is satisfied: (1) When the power is created, it is certain to be irrevocably exercised or otherwise to terminate no later than 21 years after the death of an individual then alive. (2) The power is irrevocably exercised or otherwise terminates within 90 years after its creation. (§ 66-1-202(c))	*See* Unif. Statutory Rule Against Perpetuities § 1, 8B U.L.A. 248 (amended 1990) ("Under the Common-law Rule . . . a *nongeneral power* (whether or not presently exercisable) or a *general testamentary power* is invalid as of the time of its creation if it *might* not terminate (by irrevocable exercise or otherwise) within a life in being plus 21 years.")	A general testamentary power of appointment is invalid unless within 1,000 years after its creation the power of appointment is irrevocably exercised or terminates. (§ 75-2-1203(3))
8. *Same, but nongeneral testamentary power.*	A nongeneral power of appointment . . . is invalid unless one of the following conditions is satisfied: (1) When the power is created, it is certain to be irrevocably exercised or otherwise to terminate no later than 21 years after the death of an individual then alive. (2) The power is irrevocably exercised or otherwise terminates within 90 years after its creation. (§ 66-1-202(c)) *But see* 1. above with respect to a 360-year period as an alternative.	*See* #7.	A nongeneral power of appointment . . . is invalid unless within 1,000 years after its creation the power of appointment is irrevocably exercised or terminates. (§ 75-2-1203(3))

Table 9
Rule Against Perpetuities

	TENNESSEE	TEXAS	UTAH
9. *Same, but general power, whether testamentary or inter vivos, not presently exercisable because of a condition precedent.*	A general power of appointment not presently exercisable because of a condition precedent is invalid unless one of the following conditions is satisfied: (1) When the power is created, the condition precedent is certain to be satisfied or become impossible to satisfy no later than 21 years after the death of an individual then alive. (2) The condition precedent either is satisfied or becomes impossible to satisfy within 90 years after its creation. (§ 66-1-202(b))	*See* Unif. Statutory Rule Against Perpetuities § 1, 8B U.L.A. 248 (amended 1990) ("Under the Common-law Rule, a *general power not presently exercisable because of a condition precedent* is invalid as of the time of its creation if the condition *might* neither be satisfied nor become impossible to satisfy with a life in being plus 21 years.")	A general power of appointment not presently exercisable because of a condition precedent is invalid unless within 1,000 years after the general power of appointment's creation the power of appointment is irrevocably exercised or terminates. (§ 75-2-1203(2))
10. *Same, but nongeneral inter vivos power.*	See #8.	See #7.	See #8.

Table 9
Rule Against Perpetuities

	TENNESSEE	TEXAS	UTAH
11. *Is a period of gestation added to the perpetuity period?*	No. The possibility that a child will be born to a person after that person's death is disregarded. (§66-1-202(d)) *See also* Unif. Statutory Rule Against Perpetuities §1, 8B U.L.A. 243, 243 (amended 1990) ("[T]he possibility that a child will be born to [a testator] after his death must be disregarded; and the possibility that a child will be born to any of [the testator's] descendants after their deaths must also be disregarded. Note, however, that the rule of subsection (d) does *not* apply to the question of the entitlement of an after-born child to take a beneficial interest in the trust").	Yes. (§112.036; Foshee v. Republic Nat'l Bank, 617 S.W.2d 675, 677 (Tex. 1981))	N/A
12. *What is the treatment of a "later of the traditional rule or 90 years" clause? See UPC 2-901(e).*	Such language is inoperative to the extent it produces a period of time that exceeds twenty-one (21) years after the death of the survivor of the specified lives. (§66-1-202(e))	N/A	Such language is inoperative to the extent it produces a period of time that exceeds 1,000 years after the death of the survivor of the specified lives. (§75-2-1203(4))

Table 9
Rule Against Perpetuities

	TENNESSEE	TEXAS	UTAH
13. *When is an interest created by the exercise of a general testamentary power deemed created?*	Except as provided in subsections (b) and (c) of this section and in § 66-1-206(a), the time of creation of a nonvested property interest or a power of appointment is determined by other applicable statutes or, if none, under general principles of property law. (§ 66-1-203(a)) The first of the excepted provisions states that as long as a person with a general power to become the unqualified beneficial owner has that power, the nonvested interest is created when the power terminates. The second of the excepted provisions states that a nonvested property interest, which arises from a transfer to an existing trust, is created when the nonvested property interest in the trust was created. (§ 66-1-203(b)-(c)) *See also* Unif. Statutory Rule Against Perpetuities § 2, 8B U.L.A. 268 (amended 1990) (explaining that "general principles of property law determine that the time . . . [of creation] is at the decedent's death.")	*See* comment to Unif. Probate Code § 2-902(a) ("general principles of property law determine that a nonvested property interest or power of appointment created by will is created at the decedent's death"); Unif. Statutory Rule Against Perpetuities § 2, 8B U.L.A. 268 (amended 1990) (stating the same).	Except as provided in Subsections (2) and (3) and in Section 75-2-1207, the time of creation of a nonvested property interest or a power of appointment is determined under general principles of property law. (§ 75-2-1204(1)) The first of the excepted provisions states that as long as a person with a general power to become the unqualified beneficial owner has that power, the nonvested interest is created when the power terminates. The second of the excepted provisions states that a nonvested property interest, which arises from a transfer to an existing trust, is created when the nonvested property interest in the trust was created. (§ 75-2-1204(2)-(3)) *See also* Unif. Statutory Rule Against Perpetuities § 2, 8B U.L.A. 268 (amended 1990) (explaining that "general principles of property law determine that the time . . . [of creation] is at the decedent's death.") *See generally* § 75-2-1207(1)(b) (A nonvested property interest or a power of appointment created by the exercise of a power of appointment is created when the power is irrevocably exercised or when a revocable exercise becomes irrevocable.)

Table 9
Rule Against Perpetuities

	TENNESSEE	TEXAS	UTAH
14. *Same, but nongeneral testamentary power.*	See #13.	See #13.	

Table 9
Rule Against Perpetuities

	TENNESSEE	TEXAS	UTAH
15. *Same, but general inter vivos power.*	Except as provided in subsections (b) and (c) of this section and in §66-1-206(a), the time of creation of a nonvested property interest or a power of appointment is determined by other applicable statutes or, if none, under general principles of property law. (§66-1-203(a)) The first of the excepted provisions states that as long as a person with a general power to become the unqualified beneficial owner has that power, the nonvested interest is created when the power terminates. The second of the excepted provisions states that a nonvested property interest, which arises from a transfer to an existing trust, is created when the nonvested property interest in the trust was created. (§66-1-203(b)-(c)) *See also* Unif. Statutory Rule Against Perpetuities §2, 8B U.L.A. 268 (amended 1990) (explaining that "the time when the interest or power is created is the date the transfer becomes effective for purposes of property law generally, normally the date of delivery of the deed"); Comment to Unif. Probate Code §2-902(a) (stating same and adding "the funding of the trust" as "normally" the time when the interest is created).	*See* comment to Unif. Probate Code §2-902(a) ("With respect to an inter-vivos transfer, an interest or power is created on the date the transfer becomes effective for purpose of property law generally, normally the date of delivery of the deed or funding of the trust."); Unif. Statutory Rule Against Perpetuities §2, 8B U.L.A. 268 (stating the same).	Except as provided in Subsections (2) and (3) and in Section 75-2-1207, the time of creation of a nonvested property interest or a power of appointment is determined under general principles of property law. (§75-2-1204(1)) The first of the excepted provisions states that as long as a person with a general power to become the unqualified beneficial owner has that power, the nonvested interest is created when the power terminates. The second of the excepted provisions states that a nonvested property interest, which arises from a transfer to an existing trust, is created when the nonvested property interest in the trust was created. *See also* Unif. Statutory Rule Against Perpetuities §2, 8B U.L.A. 268 (amended 1990) (explaining that "the time when the interest or power is created is the date the transfer becomes effective for purposes of property law generally, normally the date of delivery of the deed"); Comment to Unif. Probate Code §2-902(a) (stating same and adding "the funding of the trust" as "normally" the time when the interest is created). (§75-2-1204(2)-(3)) *See generally* §75-2-1207(1)(b) ("For the purposes of this section, a nonvested property interest or a power of

Table 9
Rule Against Perpetuities

	TENNESSEE	TEXAS	UTAH
			appointment created by the exercise of a power of appointment is created when the power is irrevocably exercised or when a revocable exercise becomes irrevocable.")
16. *Same, but nongeneral inter vivos power.*	See #15.	See #15.	See #15.
17. *When is an interest created if the grantor of a trust has a power to revoke?*	For purposes of this part, if there is a person who alone can exercise a power created by a governing instrument to become the unqualified beneficial owner of: (1) A nonvested property interest; or (2) A property interest subject to a power of appointment described in §§ 66-1-202(b) or (c); the nonvested property interest or power of appointment is created when the power to become the unqualified beneficial owner terminates. (§ 66-1-203(b))	*See* comment to Unif. Probate Code § 2-902(b) (noting that "nonvested property interest and powers of appointment created in [a revocable inter-vivos trust] are created when the power to revoke expires, usually at the settlor's death"); Unif. Statutory Rule Against Perpetuities § 2, 8B U.L.A. 268 (amended 1990) (explaining that "any nonvested property interest subject to [a power to revoke] is not created . . . until the power terminates (by release, expiration at the death of the donee, or otherwise").	For purposes of this part, if there is a person who alone can exercise a power created by a governing instrument to become the unqualified beneficial owner of: (a) a nonvested property interest; or (b) a property interest subject to a power of appointment described in Subsection 75-2-1203(2)(a) or (b), the nonvested property interest or power of appointment is created when the power to become the unqualified beneficial owner terminates. (§ 75-2-1204(2))

Table 9
Rule Against Perpetuities

	TENNESSEE	TEXAS	UTAH
	See also Unif. Statutory Rule Against Perpetuities §2, 8B U.L.A. 268 (amended 1990) (explaining that "any nonvested property interest subject to [a power to revoke] is not created . . . . until the power terminates (by release, expiration at the death of the donee, or otherwise"); Comment to Unif. Probate Code §2-902(b) (noting that "nonvested property interests and powers of appointment created in [a revocable inter-vivos trust] are created when the power to revoke expires, usually at the settlor's death").		See also §75-2-1207(1)(b) (A nonvested property interest or a power of appointment created by the exercise of a power of appointment is created when the power is irrevocably exercised or when a revocable exercise becomes irrevocable.) See generally Unif. Statutory Rule Against Perpetuities §2, 8B U.L.A. 268 (amended 1990) (explaining that "any nonvested property interest subject to [a power to revoke] is not created . . . until the power terminates (by release, expiration at the death of the donee, or otherwise"); Comment to Unif. Probate Code §2-902(b) (noting that "nonvested property interests and powers of appointment created in [a revocable inter-vivos trust] are created when the power to revoke expires, usually at the settlor's death").
18. *When does the period of the rule start re an interest contributed to an irrevocable trust? See UPC 2-902(c).*	A nonvested property interest or a power of appointment arising from a transfer of property to a previously funded trust or other existing property arrangement is created when the nonvested property interest or power of appointment in the original contribution was created. (§66-1-203(c))	*See* comment to Unif. Probate Code 2-902(c) ("Arguably, at common law, each transfer [to an existing irrevocable inter-vivos trust] starts the period of the Rule running anew as to each transfer.")	For purposes of this title, a nonvested property interest or a power of appointment arising from a transfer of property to a previously funded trust or other existing property arrangement is created when the nonvested property interest or power of appointment in the original contribution was created. (§75-2-1204(3))

Table 9
Rule Against Perpetuities

	TENNESSEE	TEXAS	UTAH
19. *Is there a conclusive presumption of fertility, that is, the "fertile octogenarian" rule?*	Yes. McCarley v. McCarley, 360 S.W.2d 27, 29 (Tenn. 1962) (affirming the statement: "'A possibility of issue is always supposed to exist, in law, unless extinguished by the death of the parties . . . .'")[1] *See also* Unif. Statutory Rule Against Perpetuities § 1, 8B U.L.A. 256 (amended 1990) (holding that "[t]his principle is not superseded by this Act, and in view of new advances in medical science . . . [this] is not unrealistic."). *But see* C. P. Jhong, Annotation, *Modern Status of Presumption Against Possibility of Issue Being Extinct*, 98 A.L.R.2d 1285 (2003) (noting "a trend toward denying the conclusive or absolute nature of the presumption against the possibility of issue being extinct where there is competent evidence to the contrary has developed in the decisions, although some courts still adhere to the traditional view treating the presumption as conclusive or absolute").	There is a presumption, but it is rebuttable. Frost Nat'l Bank v. Newton, 554 S.W.2d 149, 156 (Tex. 1977) (holding that there is a "presumption of fertility but 'this presumption can be rebutted by relevant evidence as to such person and by past experience concerning births to persons of like age and physical condition.'")	No specific state case or statute. *See* Unif. Statutory Rule Against Perpetuities § 1, 8B U.L.A. 256 (amended 1990) (holding that "[t]his principle is not superseded by this Act, and in view of new advances in medical science . . . [this] is not unrealistic."). *But see* C. P. Jhong, Annotation, *Modern Status of Presumption Against Possibility of Issue Being Extinct*, 98 A.L.R.2d 1285 (2003) (noting "a trend toward denying the conclusive or absolute nature of the presumption against the possibility of issue being extinct where there is competent evidence to the contrary has developed in the decisions, although some courts still adhere to the traditional view treating the presumption as conclusive or absolute").

Table 9
Rule Against Perpetuities

	TENNESSEE	TEXAS	UTAH
20. *What is the earliest age a child is deemed capable of bearing a child? What is the impact of illegitimacy?*	Not specifically addressed by USRAP, but the reasoning is the same as set forth in the comment to section 1 of USRAP, 2, Technical Violations of the Common Law Rule. Wait and see will typically result in no violation. Nevertheless, the common law rule ordinarily will be applied initially. "Under the rule, courts must presume that living persons are capable of having or fathering children, no matter how young they are. See In re Graite's Will Trusts, [1949] 1 All E.R. 459, 460 (Ch.). Thus, the rule strikes down any interest whose vesting depends on the assertion that, for example, a toddler will not have children." (Keith L. Butler, Notes & Comments, *Long Live the Dead Hand: A Case for Repeal of the Rule Against Perpetuities in Washington*, 75 Wash. L. Rev. 1237, 1246 n.78 (2000)).	No specific case or statute. "Under the rule, courts must presume that living or fathering children, no matter how young they are. See In re Graite's Will Trusts, [1949] 1 All E.R. 459, 460 (Ch.). Thus, the rule strikes down any interest whose vesting depends on the assertion that, for example, a toddler will not have children." (Keith L. Butler, Notes & Comments, *Long Live the Dead Hand: A Case for Repeal of the Rule Against Perpetuities in Washington*, 75 Wash. L. Rev. 1237, 1246 n.78 (2000)).	Not specifically addressed by USRAP, but the reasoning is the same as set forth in the comment to section 1 of USRAP, 2, Technical Violations of the Common Law Rule. Wait and see will typically result in no violation. Nevertheless, the common law rule ordinarily will be applied initially. "Under the rule, courts must presume that living persons are capable of having or fathering children, no matter how young they are. See In re Graite's Will Trusts, [1949] 1 All E.R. 459, 460 (Ch.). Thus, the rule strikes down any interest whose vesting depends on the assertion that, for example, a toddler will not have children." (Keith L. Butler, Notes & Comments, *Long Live the Dead Hand: A Case for Repeal of the Rule Against Perpetuities in Washington*, 75 Wash. L. Rev. 1237, 1246 n.78 (2000)).

Table 9
Rule Against Perpetuities

	TENNESSEE	TEXAS	UTAH
21. Is the "unborn widow" rule observed?	No specific state case or statute. *See* Unif. Statutory Rule Against Perpetuities § 1, 8B U.L.A. 246 (amended 1990) (explaining that "[t]he chance that [an] interest will become invalid under the Statutory Rule is small" and so the unborn widow rule would rarely invalidate an interest); *see also* 61 Am Jur 2d *Perpetuities and Restraints on Alienation* § 39 (2013) (noting the same).	*See, e.g.,* Arkansas, question #21.	No specific state case or statute. *See* Unif. Statutory Rule Against Perpetuities § 1, 8B U.L.A. 246 (amended 1990) (explaining that "[t]he chance that [an] interest will become invalid under the Statutory Rule is small" and so the unborn widow rule would rarely invalidate an interest); *see also* 61 Am Jur 2d *Perpetuities and Restraints on Alienation* § 39 (2013) (noting the same). This is even more poignant for Utah's 1000-year rule.
22. Does the "slothful executor" rule apply, i.e., an administrative contingency clause providing for a "distribution to, e.g., those issue living at the time of the satisfaction of the administrative condition precedent?"	No specific state case or statute. *See* Unif. Statutory Rule Against Perpetuities § 1, 8B U.L.A. 245 (amended 1990) (Under USRAP, an "interest becomes invalid only if it remains in existence and nonvested 90 years after [the testator's] death. Since it is almost certain that the final distribution of [an] estate will occur well within this 90-year period, the chance that [an] interest will be invalid is negligible.")	*See, e.g.,* California, question #22.	No specific state case or statute. *See* Unif. Statutory Rule Against Perpetuities § 1, 8B U.L.A. 245 (amended 1990) (Under USRAP, an "interest becomes invalid only if it remains in existence and nonvested 90 years after [the testator's] death. Since it is almost certain that the final distribution of [an] estate will occur well within this 90-year period, the chance that [an] interest will be invalid is negligible.") This is even more poignant for Utah's 1000-year rule.

Table 9

Rule Against Perpetuities

	TENNESSEE	TEXAS	UTAH
23. *Does the all-or-nothing rule apply to class gifts?*	Yes. Crockett v. Scott, 284 S.W.2d 289, 295 (Tenn. 1955) (affirming the statement that: "'[W]here the gift is to a class, the class must be such that all the members thereof must necessarily be ascertained and take absolutely vested interests within the period specified by the rule against perpetuities, and if, because of a violation of the rule, a gift or limitation is void as to any of the class to which it is given, it is void as to all.'") *But see* Unif. Statutory Rule Against Perpetuities §1, 8B U.L.A. 257 (amended 1990) ("Although this Act does not supersede the basic idea of the much-maligned 'all-or-nothing' rule, the evils sometimes attributed to it are substantially if not entirely eliminated by the wait-and-see feature of the Statutory Rule and by the availability of reformation under Section 3.")	Yes. Henderson v. Moore, 190 S.W.2d 800, 801-02 (Tex. 1945).	No specific state case or statute. *See* Unif. Statutory Rule Against Perpetuities §1, 8B U.L.A. 257 (amended 1990) ("Although this Act does not supersede the basic idea of the much-maligned 'all-or-nothing' rule, the evils sometimes attributed to it are substantially if not entirely eliminated by the wait-and-see feature of the Statutory Rule and by the availability of reformation.") This is even more poignant for Utah's 1000-year rule.

Table 9
Rule Against Perpetuities

	TENNESSEE	TEXAS	UTAH
24. *Is there an exception to the all-or-nothing rule in the case of subclasses or specific sums to each member of the class?*	No specific state case or statute. *See* Unif. Statutory Rule Against Perpetuities §1, 8B U.L.A. 257 (amended 1990) ("The specific-sum and sub-class doctrines are not superseded by this Act.")	No specific case or statute. *See* Unif. Statutory Rule Against Perpetuities §1, 8B U.L.A. 257 ("The common law also recognizes a doctrine called the specific-sum doctrine which is derived from Storrs v. Benbow, 3 De G.M. & G. 390, 43 Eng. Rep 153 (Ch. 1853), and states: If a specified sum of money is to be paid to each member of a class, the interest of each class member is entitled to separate treatment and is valid or invalid under the Rule on its own. The common law also recognizes a doctrine called the sub-class doctrine, which is derived from Cattlin v. Brown, 11 Hare 372, 68 Eng. Rep. 1318 (Ch. 1853), and states: If the ultimate takers are not described as a single class but rather as a group of separate subclasses, and if the share to which each separate subclass is entitled will finally be determined within the period of the Rule, the gifts to the different subclasses are separate for the purpose of the Rule.").	No specific state case or statute. *See* Unif. Statutory Rule Against Perpetuities §1, 8B U.L.A. 257 (amended 1990) ("The specific-sum and sub-class doctrines are not superseded by this Act.")

Table 9
Rule Against Perpetuities

	TENNESSEE	TEXAS	UTAH
25. *Is the infectious invalidity rule followed outside class gifts?*	No specific state case or statute. *See* Unif. Statutory Rule Against Perpetuities §1, 8B U.L.A. 256 (amended 1990) (explaining that "[t]he doctrine of infectious invalidity is superseded by this Act by Section 3, under which courts . . . are required to *reform* the disposition to approximate as closely as possible the transferor's . . . plan of distribution.")	Not completely. Sellers v. Powers, 426 S.W.2d 533, 536-537 (Tex. 1968) (citations omitted) (that the second presents "the principle of infectious invalidity or inseparability of the valid and invalid interests and the concomitant question" Is the invalid limitation so essential to the dispositive scheme of the testator . . . that it can be inferred that he would not wish the prior limitation to stand alone? "The balance of the disposition is not stricken out merely because the limitation is invalid unless additional language or circumstances are present which require an affirmative finding of this intent."). *See also* §5.043(c), providing that "a court shall enforce the provisions of the instrument that do not violate the rule and shall reform or construe under this section a provision that violates or might violate the rule."	No specific state case or statute. *See* Unif. Statutory Rule Against Perpetuities §1, 8B U.L.A. 256 (amended 1990) (explaining that "[t]he doctrine of infectious invalidity is superseded by this Act by Section 3, under which courts . . . are required to *reform* the disposition to approximate as closely as possible the transferor's . . . plan of distribution.")

Table 9
Rule Against Perpetuities

	TENNESSEE	TEXAS	UTAH
26. *Is there a rule against the suspension of the power of alienation? If so, how is it stated?*	Absolute prohibition. *See* Hankins v. Mathews, 425 S.W.2d 608, 610 (Tenn. 1968) (affirming the statement that "'The doctrine of most jurisdictions . . . is that where land is granted or devised in fee, a provision of any sort that the taker shall not alienate, or shall not have power to alienate, is void, whether amounting to a mere naked prohibition or direction, or expressed or construed to be a condition, or conjoined with a limitation over in the event of alienation or attempt to alienate.'")	Yes. Kelley v. Marlin, 714 S.W.2d 303, 309 (Tex. 1986) ("Probate law protects beneficiaries not only from being forced into unwanted relationships, but also against undue restrictions on their right to maintain and dispose of their property. The United States Supreme Court, as well as courts of this State, have consistently held that restraints on the power of alienation, when incorporated in a deed or will otherwise conveying a fee simple right to the property, are void.") *Cf.* Long v. RIM Operating, Inc., 345 S.W.3d 79, 91 (Tex. App. 2011) ("Texas courts have held that the rule against perpetuities is only a means of preventing unreasonable restraints on alienation and, therefore, does not bar enforcement of contractual rights to sell property that does not constitute an unreasonable restraint on alienation.").	Redd v. Western Sav. & Loan Co., 646 P.2d 761, 763-64 (Utah 1982) (affirming rule of free alienability, but permitting indirect restraints on alienation if reasonable).

Table 9
Rule Against Perpetuities

	TENNESSEE	TEXAS	UTAH
27. *Effective date.*	Effective for all nonvested interests and unexercised powers whenever created. (§ 66-1-206(a)) However, the law does not apply to interests and powers the validity of which was determined by a final judgment or settlement among interested parties prior to July 1, 1994. (§ 66-1-206(b))	Section 5.043, pertaining to reformation, applies to interests by instruments taking effect on or after September 1, 1969, and an appointment made on or after that date regardless of when the power was created. (§ 5.043(d))	December 31, 2003. *See also* #6.

---

[1] For questions #19 - 25, *see also* § 66-1-207 (noting that the state's USRAP supersedes the common law rule against perpetuities). The answers to questions #19 - 25 are not likely to apply in most cases because of the abolition of the rule with respect to the vast majority of many trusts.

Table 9
Rule Against Perpetuities

		VERMONT	VIRGINIA	WASHINGTON
1.	Which rule is in effect: the common law rule, the Uniform Statutory Rule Against Perpetuities (USRAP), other law, or none?	Variation on USRAP. (27 Vt. Stat. Ann. §§ 501-503)	USRAP. (Va. Code Ann. §§ 55-12.1 - 55-12.6)	Other. (Wash. Rev. Code Ann. § 11.98.130) Exception for provisions of instruments creating trusts and interests created due to a power of appointment under an instrument creating a trust.
2. a.	Is the common law rule relevant to any interests?	Yes, but only as a starting point of the analysis.	Yes, but only as a starting point of the analysis.	Common law rule. In re Estate of Lee, 299 P.2d 1066, 1068-69 (Wash. 1956) ("The rule against perpetuities prohibits the creation of future estates which, by possibility, may not become vested within a life or lives in being at the time of the testator's death and twenty-one years thereafter.")
b.	What is the relevant rule?	Under the orthodox rule against perpetuities no future interest in property is valid unless it must vest not later than 21 years (and the period of actual gestation) after some life in being at its creation. (Ransom v. Bebernitz, 782 A.2d 1155, 1160 n.3 (Vt. 2001)). But see questions #4 - 6 below (wait-and-see and reformation mean that this rule is not strictly applied)	A nonvested property interest is invalid unless: 1. When the interest is created, it is certain to vest or terminate no later than twenty-one years after the death of an individual then alive; or 2. The interest either vests or terminates within ninety years after its creation. (§ 55-12.1(A))	No provision of an instrument creating a trust, including the provisions of any further trust created, and no other disposition of property made pursuant to exercise of a power of appointment granted in or created through authority under such instrument is invalid under the rule against perpetuities, or any similar statute or common law, during the one hundred fifty years following the effective date of the instrument.

Table 9
Rule Against Perpetuities

	VERMONT	VIRGINIA	WASHINGTON
			Thereafter, unless the trust assets have previously become distributable or vested, the provision or other disposition of property is deemed to have been rendered invalid under the rule against perpetuities. (§ 11.98.130)
3. *Does the rule apply to other than private trusts?*	No. The rule does not apply to charitable trusts. (Ball v. Hall, 274 A.2d 1. 516, 523 (Vt. 1971))	Yes. The rule applies except to: A nonvested property interest or a power of appointment arising out of a nondonative transfer, except a nonvested property interest or a power of appointment arising out of (i) a premarital or postmarital agreement; (ii) a separation or divorce settlement; (iii) a spouse's election; (iv) a similar arrangement arising out of a prospective, existing, or previous marital relationship between the parties; (v) a contract to make or not to revoke a will or trust; (vi) a contract to exercise or not to exercise a power of appointment; (vii) a transfer in satisfaction of a duty of support; or (viii) a reciprocal transfer;	Unclear. *See* § 11.98.009 ("Except as provided in this section, this chapter applies to express trusts executed by the trustor after June 10, 1959, and does not apply to resulting trusts, constructive trusts, business trusts where certificates of beneficial interest are issued to the beneficiary, investment trusts, voting trusts, trusts in the nature of mortgages or pledges, trusts created by the judgment or decree of a court not sitting in probate, liquidation trusts, or trusts for the sole purpose of paying dividends, interest, interest coupons, salaries, wages, pensions or profits, trusts created in deposits in any financial institution pursuant to chapter 30.22 RCW, unless any such trust which is created in writing incorporates this chapter in whole or in part.")

Table 9
Rule Against Perpetuities

VERMONT	VIRGINIA	WASHINGTON
	2. A fiduciary's power relating to the administration or management of assets, including the power of a fiduciary to sell, lease, or mortgage property, and the power of a fiduciary to determine principal and income;	
	3. A power to appoint a fiduciary;	
	4. A discretionary power of trustee to distribute principal before termination of a trust to a beneficiary having an indefeasibly vested interest in the income and principal;	
	5. A nonvested property interest held by a charity, government, or governmental agency or subdivision, if the nonvested property interest is preceded by an interest held by another charity, government, or governmental agency or subdivision;	

Table 9
Rule Against Perpetuities

VERMONT	VIRGINIA	WASHINGTON
	6. A nonvested property interest in or a power of appointment with respect to a trust or other property arrangement forming part of a pension, profit-sharing, stock bonus, health, disability, death benefit, income deferral, or other current or deferred benefit plan for one or more employees, independent contractors, or their beneficiaries or spouses, to which contributions are made for the purpose of distributing to or for the benefit of the participants or their beneficiaries or spouses the property, income, or principal in the trust or other property arrangement, except a nonvested property interest or a power of appointment that is created by an election of a participant or a beneficiary or spouse; 7. A property interest, power of appointment, or arrangement that was not subject to the common law rule against perpetuities or is excluded by another statute of this Commonwealth; or	

Table 9
Rule Against Perpetuities

	VERMONT	VIRGINIA	WASHINGTON
		8. A nonvested interest in or power of appointment over personal propertyheld in trust, or a power of appointment over personal property granted under a trust, if the trust instrument, by its terms, provides that.§ 55-12.1 shall not apply B) The exception to the Uniform Statutory Rule Against Perpetuities under subdivision A does not extend to real property held in trust. For purposes of the subsection, real property does not include an interest in a corporation, limited liability company, partnership business trust, or other entity, even if such entity owns an interest in real property. (§ 55-12.4)	Wait-and-see for trust interests. Specifically, following 150 years after the effective date of the instrument, if the trust assets have not become distributable or vested, the provision or other disposition of property is deemed to have been rendered invalid under the rule against perpetuities. (§ 11.98.130) The common law rule applies for other interests. *See* Robroy Land Co. v. Prather, 622 P.2d 367, 373 (Wash. 1980).
4. *Does the rule invalidate the interest at its creation, or is the rule revised by a wait-and-see approach?*	Wait-and-see. Colby v. Colby, 596 A.2d 901, 903 (Vt. 1990) ("Vermont has, by passing 27 V.S.A. § 501 [see #6 below], aligned itself in a group of states adopting what is known as a 'wait and see' rule concerning perpetuities. This rule says that if, at the time of the event, the common law measure given as 'lives in being and twenty-one years' has not been violated, there is no violation of the rule.") .	Wait-and-see. (§ 55-12.1(A)(2))	

Table 9
Rule Against Perpetuities

	VERMONT	VIRGINIA	WASHINGTON
5. *Can the trust be reformed?*	Yes. (27 § 501)	Yes, but only if one of the following conditions is satisfied: 1. A nonvested property interest or a power of appointment becomes invalid under § 55-12.1 (see #2b); 2. A class gift is not but might become invalid under § 55-12.1 and the time has arrived when the share of any class member is to take effect in possession or enjoyment; or 3. A nonvested property interest that is not validated by subdivision A 1 of § 55-12.1, that is, the traditional common law rule, can vest but not within 90 years after its creation. (§ 55-12.3)	No specific state case or statute.
6. *If yes to 5., under what theory?*	Any interest in real or personal property which would violate the rule against perpetuities shall be reformed, within the limits of that rule, to approximate most closely the intention of the creator of the interest. In determining whether an interest would violate said rule and in reforming an interest the period of perpetuities shall be measured by actual rather than possible events. (27 § 501)	Upon the petition of an interested person, a court of equity in the county or city wherein the affected property or the greater part thereof is located shall reform a disposition in the manner that most closely approximates the transferor's manifested plan of distribution and is within the ninety years allowed by subdivision A 2, B 2 or C 2 of § 55-12.1. (§ 55-12.3)	See #5.

Table 9
Rule Against Perpetuities

	VERMONT	VIRGINIA	WASHINGTON
7. When is a general testamentary power of appointment invalid?	*See* Unif. Statutory Rule Against Perpetuities § 1, 8B U.L.A. 248 (amended 1990) ("Under the Common-law Rule . . . a *nongeneral power* (whether or not presently exercisable) or a *general testamentary power* is invalid as of the time of its creation if it *might* not terminate (by irrevocable exercise or otherwise) within a life in being plus 21 years.")	A general testamentary power of appointment is invalid unless one of the following conditions is satisfied: (1) When the power is created, it is certain to be irrevocably exercised or otherwise to terminate no later than 21 years after the death of an individual then alive. (2) The power is irrevocably exercised or otherwise terminates within 90 years after its creation. (§ 55-12.1(C))	*See* Unif. Statutory Rule Against Perpetuities § 1, 8B U.L.A. 248 (amended 1990) ("Under the Common-law Rule . . . a *nongeneral power* (whether or not presently exercisable) or a *general testamentary power* is invalid as of the time of its creation if it *might* not terminate (by irrevocable exercise or otherwise) within a life in being plus 21 years.")
8. *Same, but nongeneral testamentary power.*	*See* #7.	A nongeneral power of appointment . . . is invalid unless one of the following conditions is satisfied: (1) When the power is created, it is certain to be irrevocably exercised or otherwise to terminate no later than 21 years after the death of an individual then alive. (2) The power is irrevocably exercised or otherwise terminates within 90 years after its creation. (§ 55-12.1(C))	*See* #7.
9. *tamentary or inter vivos, not presently exercisable because of a condition precedent.*	*See* Unif. Statutory Rule Against Perpetuities § 1, 8B U.L.A. 248 (amended 1990) ("Under the Common-law Rule, a *general power not presently exercisable*	A general power of appointment not presently exercisable because of a condition precedent is invalid unless one of the following conditions is satisfied:	With respect to an inter vivos power, *see* Unif. Statutory Rule Against Perpetuities § 1, 8B U.L.A. 248 (amended 1990) ("Under the Common-law Rule, a

Table 9
Rule Against Perpetuities

	VERMONT	VIRGINIA	WASHINGTON
	because of a condition precedent is invalid as of the time of its creation if the condition *might* neither be satisfied nor become impossible to satisfy with a life in being plus 21 years."	(1) When the power is created, the condition precedent is certain to be satisfied or become impossible to satisfy no later than 21 years after the death of an individual then alive. (2) The condition precedent either is satisfied or becomes impossible to satisfy within 90 years after its creation. (§ 55-12.1(B))	*general power not presently exercisable because of a condition precedent* is invalid as of the time of its creation if the condition *might* neither be satisfied nor become impossible to satisfy with a life in being plus 21 years.") One hundred fifty years following the effective date of the instrument if created in a trust, otherwise common law rule. (See #2b.)
10. *Same, but nongeneral inter vivos power.*	See #7.	See #8.	See #9.
11. *Is a period of gestation added to the perpetuity period?*	Yes. (See #2a.)	No. The possibility that a child will be born to a person after that person's death is disregarded. (§ 55-12.1(D)) *See also* Unif. Statutory Rule Against Perpetuities § 1, 8B U.L.A. 243, 243 (amended 1990) ("[T]he possibility that a child will be born to [a testator] after his death must be disregarded; and the possibility that a child will be born to any of [the testator's] descendants after their deaths must also be disregarded. Note, however, that the rule of subsection (d) does *not* apply to the question of the entitlement of an after-born child to take a beneficial interest in the trust").	Yes. Kendall v. Kendall, 261 P.2d 422, 425 (Wash. 1953).

Table 9
Rule Against Perpetuities

	VERMONT	VIRGINIA	WASHINGTON
12. *What is the treatment of a "later of the traditional rule or 90 years" clause? See UPC 2-901(e).*	N/A	That language is inoperative to the extent it produces a period of time that exceeds twenty-one years after the death of the survivor of the specified lives. (§ 55-12.1(E))	N/A
13. *When is an interest created by the exercise of a general testamentary power deemed created?*	*See* comment to Unif. Probate Code § 2-902(a) ("general principles of property law determine that a nonvested property interest or power of appointment created by will is created at the decedent's death"); Unif. Statutory Rule Against Perpetuities § 2, 8B U.L.A. 268 (amended 1990) (stating the same).	Except as provided in subsections B and C and in § 55-12.5, the time of creation of a nonvested property interest or a power of appointment is determined under general principles of property law. (§ 55-12.2(A)) The first of the excepted provisions states that as long as a person with a general power to become the unqualified beneficial owner has that power, the nonvested interest is created when the power terminates. The second of the excepted provisions states that a nonvested property interest, which arises from a transfer to an existing trust, is created when the nonvested property interest in the trust was created. (§ 55-12.2(B)-(C)) *See generally* § 55-12.5 ("For the purposes of this section, a nonvested property interest or a power of appointment created by the exercise of a power of appointment is created when the power is irrevocably exercised or when a revocable exercise becomes irrevocable.")	*See* comment to Unif. Probate Code § 2-902(a) ("general principles of property law determine that a nonvested property interest or power of appointment created by will is created at the decedent's death"); Unif. Statutory Rule Against Perpetuities § 2, 8B U.L.A. 268 (amended 1990) (stating the same).

Table 9
Rule Against Perpetuities

	VERMONT	VIRGINIA	WASHINGTON
14. *Same, but nongeneral testamentary power.*	See #13.	See #13.	See #13.
15. *Same, but general inter vivos power.*	*See* comment to Unif. Probate Code § 2-902(a) ("With respect to an intervivos transfer, an interest or power is created on the date the transfer becomes effective for purposes of property law generally, normally the date of delivery of the deed or funding of the trust."); Unif. Statutory Rule Against Perpetuities § 2, 8B U.L.A. 268 (stating the same).	Except as provided in subsections B and C and in § 55-12.5, the time of creation of a nonvested property interest or a power of appointment is determined under general principles of property law. (§ 55-12.2(A)) The first of the excepted provisions states that as long as a person with a general power to become the unqualified beneficial owner has that power, the nonvested interest is created when the power terminates. The second of the excepted provisions states that a nonvested property interest, which arises from a transfer to an existing trust, is created when the nonvested property interest in the trust was created. (§ 55-12.2(B)-(C)) *See generally* § 55-12.5 ("For the purposes of this section, a nonvested property interest or a power of appointment created by the exercise of a power of appointment is created when the power is irrevocably exercised or when a revocable exercise becomes irrevocable.")	*See* comment to Unif. Probate Code § 2-902(a) ("With respect to an inter-vivos transfer, an interest or power is created on the date the transfer becomes effective for purposes of property law generally, normally the date of delivery of the deed or funding of the trust."); Unif. Statutory Rule Against Perpetuities § 2, 8B U.L.A. 268 (stating the same).
16. *Same, but nongeneral inter vivos power.*	See #15.	See #15.	See #15.

Table 9
Rule Against Perpetuities

	VERMONT	VIRGINIA	WASHINGTON
17. *When is an interest created if the grantor of a trust has a power to revoke?*	*See* comment to Unif. Probate Code § 2-902(b) (noting that "nonvested property interests and powers of appointment created in [a revocable inter-vivos trust] are created when the power to revoke expires, usually at the settlor's death"); Unif. Statutory Rule Against Perpetuities § 2, 8B U.L.A. 268 (amended 1990) (explaining that "any nonvested property interest subject to [a power to revoke] is not created … until the power terminates (by release, expiration at the death of the donee, or otherwise").	For the purposes of §§ 55-12.1 through 55-12.6, if there is a person who alone can exercise a power created by a governing instrument to become the unqualified beneficial owner of (i) a nonvested property interest or (ii) a property interest subject to a power of appointment described in subsection B or C in § 55-12.1, the nonvested property interest or power of appointment is created when the power to become the unqualified beneficial owner terminates. (§ 55.12.2(B)) *See also* comment to § 55-12.2 (explaining that "any nonvested property interest subject to [a power to revoke] is not created … until the power terminates (by release, expiration at the death of the donee, or otherwise"); Comment to Unif. Probate Code § 2-902(b) (noting that "nonvested property interest and powers of appointment created in [a revocable inter-vivos trust] are created when the power to revoke expires, usually at the settlor's death"). *See generally* § 55-12.5 ("For the purposes of this section, a nonvested property interest or a power of appointment created by the exercise of a power of appointment is created	Just as for a will, at the time of death. (§ 11.98.160) *See also* comment to Unif. Probate Code § 2-902(b) (noting that "nonvested property interests and powers of appointment created in [a revocable inter-vivos trust] are created when the power to revoke expires, usually at the settlor's death"); Unif. Statutory Rule Against Perpetuities § 2, 8B U.L.A. 268 (amended 1990) (explaining that "any nonvested property interest subject to [a power to revoke] is not created … until the power terminates (by release, expiration at the death of the donee, or otherwise").

9342

Table 9
Rule Against Perpetuities

	VERMONT	VIRGINIA	WASHINGTON
18. When does the period of the rule start re an interest contributed to an irrevocable trust? See UPC 2-902(c).	See comment to Unif. Probate Code 2-902(c). ("Arguably, at common law, each transfer [to an existing irrevocable inter-vivos trust] starts the period of the Rule running anew as to each transfer.")	A nonvested property interest or a power of appointment arising from a transfer of property to a previously funded trust or other existing property arrangement is created when the nonvested property interest or power of appointment in the original contribution was created. (§ 55-12.2(C))	For the purposes of RCW §§ 11.98.130 through 11.98.150, the effective date of an instrument purporting to create an irrevocable inter vivos trust is the date on which it is executed by the trustor. (§ 11.98.160) See also comment to Unif. Probate Code 2-902(c) ("Arguably, at common law, each transfer [to an existing irrevocable inter-vivos trust] starts the period of the Rule running anew as to each transfer.")
	when the power is irrevocably exercised or when a revocable exercise becomes irrevocable.")		

Table 9
Rule Against Perpetuities

	VERMONT	VIRGINIA	WASHINGTON
19. *Is there a conclusive presumption of fertility, that is, the "fertile octogenarian" rule?*	*See, e.g.,* Arkansas, question #19.	No specific state case or statute. *See* Unif. Statutory Rule Against Perpetuities §1, 813 U.L.A. 256 (amended 1990) (holding that "[t]his principle is not superseded by this Act, and in view of new advances in medical science . . . [this] is not unrealistic." *But see* C. P. Jhong, Annotation, *Modern Status of Presumption Against Possibility of Issue Being Extinct*, 98 A.L.R.2d 1285 (2003) (noting "a trend toward denying the conclusive or absolute nature of the presumption against the possibility of issue being extinct where there is competent evidence to the contrary has developed in the decisions, although some courts still adhere to the traditional view treating the presumption as conclusive or absolute").	Yes. Betchard v. Iverson, 212 P.2d 783, 787 (Wash. 1949) (noting that "the law conclusively presumes that [women] can bear additional children until the day of her death").

Table 9
Rule Against Perpetuities

	VERMONT	VIRGINIA	WASHINGTON
20. *What is the earliest age a child is deemed capable of bearing a child? What is the impact of illegitimacy?*	No specific case or statute. "Under the rule, courts must presume that living persons are capable of having or fathering children, no matter how young they are. *See* In re Graite's Will Trusts, [1949] 1 All E.R. 459, 460 (Ch.). Thus, the rule strikes down any interest whose vesting depends on the assertion that, for example, a toddler will not have children." (Keith L. Butler, Notes & Comments, *Long Live the Dead Hand: A Case for Repeal of the Rule Against Perpetuities in Washington,* 75 Wash. L. Rev. 1237, 1246 n.78 (2000)).	Not specifically addressed by USRAP, but the reasoning is the same as set forth in the comment to section 1 of USRAP, 2, Technical Violations of the Common Law Rule. Wait and see will typically result in no violation. Nevertheless, the common law rule ordinarily will be applied initially. "Under the rule, courts must presume that living persons are capable of having or fathering children, no matter how young they are. *See* In re Graite's Will Trusts, [1949] 1 All E.R. 459, 460 (Ch.). Thus, the rule strikes down any interest whose vesting depends on the assertion that, for example, a toddler will not have children." (Keith L. Butler, Notes & Comments, *Long Live the Dead Hand: A Case for Repeal of the Rule Against Perpetuities in Washington,* 75 Wash. L. Rev. 1237, 1246 n.78 (2000)).	No specific state case or statute. "Under the rule, courts must presume that living persons are capable of having or fathering children, no matter how young they are. See In re Graite's Will Trusts, [1949] 1 All E.R. 459, 460 (Ch.). Thus, the rule strikes down any interest whose vesting depends on the assertion that, for example, a toddler will not have children." (Keith L. Butler, Notes & Comments, *Long Live the Dead Hand: A Case for Repeal of the Rule Against Perpetuities in Washington,* 75 Wash. L. Rev. 1237, 1246 n.78 (2000)).

Table 9
Rule Against Perpetuities

	VERMONT	VIRGINIA	WASHINGTON
21. *Is the "unborn widow" rule observed?*	*See, e.g.,* Arkansas, question #21.	No specific state case or statute. *See* Unif. Statutory Rule Against Perpetuities §1, 8B U.L.A. 246 (amended 1990) (explaining that "[t]he chance that [an] interest will become invalid under the Statutory Rule is small" and so the unborn widow rule would rarely invalidate an interest); *see also* 61 Am. Jur. 2d *Perpetuities and Restraints on Alienation* §39 (2013) (noting the same).	*See, e.g.,* Arkansas, question #21.
22. *Does the "slothful executor" rule apply, i.e., an administrative contingency clause providing for a "distribution to, e.g., those issue living at the time of the satisfaction of the administrative condition precedent?"*	*See, e.g.,* California, question #22.	No specific state case or statute.	*See, e.g.,* California, question #22.
23. *Does the all-or-nothing rule apply to class gifts?*	*See, e.g.,* Alabama, question #23.	Yes. Rose v. Rose, 60 S.E.2d 45, 48 (Va. 1950) ("For if a contingent gift to a class is rendered void as to one or more members thereof by the rule against perpetuities, then the gift will fail as to all in that class."); Hagemann v. National Bank & Trust Co., 237 S.E.2d 388, 391 (Va. 1977) (noting the same).	Yes. Betchard v. Iverson, 212 P.2d 783, 786 (Wash. 1949) ("If a gift is to a class and it is void as to any member or members of the class, it is void as to all.")

Table 9
Rule Against Perpetuities

	VERMONT	VIRGINIA	WASHINGTON
24. *Is there an exception to the all-or-nothing rule in the case of subclasses or specific sums to each member of the class?*	No specific state case or statute. *See* Unif. Statutory Rule Against Perpetuities §2, 8B U.L.A. 257 ("The common law also recognizes a doctrine called the specific-sum doctrine which is derived from Storrs v. Benbow, 3 De G.M. & G. 390, 43 Eng. Rep 153 (Ch. 1853), and states: If a specified sum of money is to be paid to each member of a class, the interest of each class member is entitled to separate treatment and is valid or invalid under the Rule on its own. The common law also recognizes a doctrine called the sub-class doctrine, which is derived from Cattlin v. Brown, 11 Hare 372, 68 Eng. Rep. 1318 (Ch. 1853), and states: If the ultimate takers are not described as a single class but rather as a group of separate subclasses, and if the share to which each separate subclass is entitled will finally be determined within the period of the Rule, the gifts to the different subclasses are separate for the purpose of the Rule.").	No specific state case or statute. *See* Unif. Statutory Rule Against perpetuities §1, 8B U.L.A. 257 (amended 1990) ("The specific-sum and sub-class doctrines are not superseded by this Act.")	No specific state case or statute. *See* Unif. Statutory Rule Against Perpetuities §1, 8B U.L.A. 257 ("The common law also recognizes a doctrine called the specific-sum doctrine which is derived from Storrs v. Benbow, 3 De G.M. & G. 390, 43 Eng. Rep 153 (Ch. 1853), and states: If a specified sum of money is to be paid to each member of a class, the interest of each class member is entitled to separate treatment and is valid or invalid under the Rule on its own. The common law also recognizes a doctrine called the sub-class doctrine, which is derived from Cattlin v. Brown, 11 Hare 372, 68 Eng. Rep. 1318 (Ch. 1853), and states: If the ultimate takers are not described as a single class but rather as a group of separate subclasses, and if the share to which each separate subclass is entitled will finally be determined within the period of the Rule, the gifts to the different subclasses are separate for the purpose of the Rule.").

Table 9
Rule Against Perpetuities

	VERMONT	VIRGINIA	WASHINGTON
25. *Is the infectious invalidity rule followed outside class gifts?*	*See, e.g.,* Colorado, question #25.	Yes, but limits the rule. See Hagemann v. National Bank & Trust Co., 237 S.E.2d 388, 395 (Va. 1977) (citation omitted) (noting that "a remainder which is void because in violation of the rule against perpetuities does not necessarily render invalid the prior estate, but that the latter will be sustained notwithstanding the invalidity of the ulterior estate, where the two are not inseparable and dependent parts of a general testamentary scheme, and to uphold the one without the other would not defeat the primary or dominant purpose of the testator . . . ."). But see Unif. Statutory Rule Against Perpetuities § 1, 8B U.L.A. 256 (amended 1990) (explaining that "[t]he doctrine of infectious invalidity is superseded by this Act by Section 3, under which courts . . . are required to *reform* the disposition to approximate as closely as possible the transferor's . . . plan of distribution.").	*See, e.g.,* Colorado, question #25.

Table 9
Rule Against Perpetuities

	VERMONT	VIRGINIA	WASHINGTON
26. *Is there a rule against the suspension of the power of alienation? If so, how is it stated?*	No specific state statute. See Colby v. Colby, 596 A.2d 901, 902 (1991) ("restraints on alienation are not favored"). A "reasonableness" test is utilized, although the issue is analyzed by the court as if the matter involved the statutory wait-and-see version of the rule against perpetuities).	Reasonableness standard. See Lipps v. First Amer. Serv. Corp, 286 S.E.2d 215, 218 (Va. 1982) (discussing Virginia's law on restraints on alienation).	Reasonableness standard. See McCausland v. Bankers Life Ins. Co., 757 P.2d 941, 943-44 (Wash. 1988) (discussing whether due-on-sale clauses and prepayment provisions are unreasonable restraints on alienation).
27. *Effective date.*	When act "becomes operative," which was not defined. Act was approved, however, May 16, 1957. "This subchapter shall apply only to inter vivos instruments and wills taking effect after the subchapter becomes operative and to appointments made after the subchapter becomes operative including appointments by inter vivos instrument or will under powers created before the subchapter becomes effective." (27 § 502)	The law applies to a nonvested property interest or a power of appointment created on or after July 1, 2000. An interest or a power created by the exercise of a power of appointment is created when the power is irrevocably exercised or after a revocable exercise becomes irrevocable. (§ 55-12.5)	The act applies to any irrevocable trust with an effective date on or after January 1, 2002, as well as to a prior trust if the instrument so provides. (2001 ch. 60 § 4) It also does not apply to revocable and testamentary trusts if the settlor or testator was incapable since January 1, 2002, to revoke, amend or modify the instrument. (2001 ch. 60 § 4) Generally, an irrevocable trust is created when executed and a revocable trust or will is created at the time of the settlor's or testator's death. (§ 11.98.160)

Table 9
Rule Against Perpetuities

	WEST VIRGINIA	*WISCONSIN*	*WYOMING*
1. Which rule is in effect: the common law rule, the Uniform Statutory Rule Against Perpetuities (USRAP), other law, or none?	USRAP. (W. Va. Code §§ 36-1A-1 - 36-1A-8)	None (W.S.A. § 700.16(5) ("The common-law rule against perpetuities is not in force in this state."))	Common Law Rule, with exception for trusts created after July 1, 2003 that follow the requirements set forth in § 34-1-139. (Wyo. Stat. Ann. § 34-1-139)
2. a. Is the common law rule relevant to any interests?	Yes, but only as a starting point of the analysis. The provisions of the statute supersede the common law. (§ 36-1A-8)	N/A	Yes, with respect to certain interests.
b. What is the relevant rule?	A nonvested property interest is invalid unless: (1) When the interest is created, it is certain to vest or terminate no later than twenty-one years after the death of an individual then alive; or (2) The interest either vests or terminates within ninety years after its creation. (§ 36-1A-1(a))	N/A	No interest in real or personal property shall be good unless it must vest not later than twenty-one (21) years after some life in being at the creation of the interest and any period of gestation involved in the situation to which the limitation applies. (§ 34-1-139(a)) However, the common law rule does not apply to a trust created after July 1, 2003 if: (b) (i) The instrument creating the trust states that the rule against perpetuities as provided in subsection (a) of this section shall not apply to the trust; (ii) The instrument creating the trust states that the trust shall terminate no later than one thousand (1,000) years after the trust's creation; and

Table 9
Rule Against Perpetuities

	WEST VIRGINIA	WISCONSIN	WYOMING
			(iii) The trust is governed by the laws of this state and the trustee maintains a place of business, administers the trust in this state or is a resident of this state. (c) The election provided in (b) above is not available for real property owned and held in a trust otherwise making an election under subsection (b) of this section. The common law rule applies to such real property held in a trust making an election under (b), the election under (b) will apply to the remaining personal property assets of the trust. (§34-1-139) Note, however, that real property does not include a mineral interest or an interest in a corporation, limited liability company, partnership, business trust or other entity. (§34-1-139(d)) Thus, the continued application of the common law rule to real property held in trust can be easily avoided by reassigning the formal ownership of the real property.
3. *Does the rule apply to other than private trusts?*	Yes. The rule applies except to:	N/A	*See, e.g.,* Vermont, question #3.

Table 9
Rule Against Perpetuities

WEST VIRGINIA	WISCONSIN	WYOMING
(1) A nonvested property interest or a power of appointment arising out of a nondonative transfer, except a nonvested property interest or a power of appointment arising out of: (A) A premarital or postmarital agreement; (B) a separation or divorce settlement; (C) a spouse's election; (D) a similar arrangement arising out of a prospective, existing, or previous marital relationship between the parties; (E) a contract to make or not to revoke a will or trust; (F) a contract to exercise or not to exercise a power of appointment; (G) a transfer in satisfaction of a duty of support; or (H) a reciprocal transfer;		
(2) A fiduciary's power relating to the administration or management of assets, including the power of a fiduciary to sell, lease or mortgage property, and the power of a fiduciary to determine principal and income;		
(3) A power to appoint a fiduciary;		
(4) A discretionary power of a trustee to distribute principal before termination of a trust to a beneficiary having an indefeasibly vested interest in the income and principal;		

Table 9
Rule Against Perpetuities

WEST VIRGINIA	WISCONSIN	WYOMING

(5) A nonvested property interest held by a charity, government, or governmental agency or subdivision, if the nonvested property interest is preceded by an interest held by another charity, government, or governmental agency or subdivision;

(6) A nonvested property interest in or a power of appointment with respect to a trust or other property arrangement forming part of a pension, profit-sharing, stock bonus, health, disability, death benefit, income deferral, or other current or deferred benefit plan for one or more employees, independent contractors, or their beneficiaries or spouses, to which contributions are made for the purpose of distributing to or for the benefit of the participants or their beneficiaries or spouses the property, income, or principal in the trust or other property arrangement, except a nonvested property interest or a power of appointment that is created by an election of a participant or a beneficiary or spouse; or

Table 9
Rule Against Perpetuities

	WEST VIRGINIA	WISCONSIN	WYOMING
	(7) A property interest, power of appointment, or arrangement that was not subject to the common-law rule against perpetuities or is excluded by another provision of this code. (§ 36-1A-4)		
4. *Does the rule invalidate the interest at its creation, or is the rule revised by a wait-and-see approach?*	Wait-and-see. (§ 36-1A-1(a)(2))	N/A	At its creation. (See #2a)
5. *Can the trust be reformed?*	Yes, but only if one of the following conditions is satisfied: (1) A nonvested property interest or a power of appointment becomes invalid pursuant to the provisions of section one of this article (see #2b); (2) A class gift is not but might become invalid pursuant to the provisions of section one [§ 36-1A-1] of this article and the time has arrived when the share of any class member is to take effect in possession or enjoyment; or	N/A	N/A

Table 9
Rule Against Perpetuities

WEST VIRGINIA	WISCONSIN	WYOMING
(3) A nonvested property interest that is not validated by the provisions of subdivision (1), subsection (a), section one [§ 36-1A-1(a)(1)] of this article, that is, the traditional common law rule, can vest but not within ninety years after its creation. (§ 36-1A-3)		

Table 9
Rule Against Perpetuities

	WEST VIRGINIA	WISCONSIN	WYOMING
6. *If yes to 5., under what theory?*	Upon the petition of an interested person, a court shall reform a disposition in the manner that most closely approximates the transferor's manifested plan of distribution and is within the ninety years allowed by the provisions of subdivision (2), subsection (a), or subdivision (2), subsection (b), or subdivision (2), subsection (c), section one of this article. (§ 36-1A-3) *See also* § 36-1A-5(b) ("If a nonvested property interest or a power of appointment was created before the effective date of this article and is determined in a judicial proceeding, commenced on or after the effective date of this article, to violate this state's rule against perpetuities as that rule existed before the effective date of this article, a court upon the petition of an interested person may reform the disposition in the manner that most closely approximates the transferor's manifested plan of distribution and is within the limits of the rule against perpetuities applicable when the nonvested property interest or power of appointment was created.")	N/A	N/A
7. *When is a general testamentary power of appointment invalid?*	A general testamentary power of appointment is invalid unless one of the following conditions is satisfied:	N/A	*See* Unif. Statutory Rule Against Perpetuities § 1, 8B U.L.A. 248 (amended 1990) ("Under the Common-law Rule . . . a *nongeneral*

Table 9
Rule Against Perpetuities

	WEST VIRGINIA	WISCONSIN	WYOMING
			power (whether or not presently exercisable) or a *general testamentary power* is invalid as of the time of its creation if it *might* not terminate (by irrevocable exercise or otherwise) within a life in being plus 21 years.")
	(1) When the power is created, it is certain to be irrevocably exercised or otherwise to terminate no later than 21 years after the death of an individual then alive. (2) The power is irrevocably exercised or otherwise terminates within 90 years after its creation. (§36-1A-1(c))		
8. *Same, but nongeneral testamentary power.*	A nongeneral power of appointment . . . is invalid unless one of the following conditions is satisfied: (1) When the power is created, it is certain to be irrevocably exercised or otherwise to terminate no later than 21 years after the death of an individual then alive. (2) The power is irrevocably exercised or otherwise terminates within 90 years after its creation. (§36-1A-1(c))	N/A	See #7.
9. *Same, but general power, whether testamentary or inter vivos, not presently exercisable because of a condition precedent.*	A general power of appointment not presently exercisable because of a condition precedent is invalid unless one of the following conditions is satisfied:	N/A	*See* Unif. Statutory Rule Against Perpetuities §1, 8B U.L.A. 248 (amended 1990) ("Under the Common-law Rule, a *general*

Table 9
Rule Against Perpetuities

	WEST VIRGINIA	WISCONSIN	WYOMING
	(1) When the power is created, the condition precedent is certain to be satisfied or become impossible to satisfy no later than 21 years after the death of an individual then alive. (2) The condition precedent either is satisfied or becomes impossible to satisfy within 90 years after its creation. (§ 36-1A-1(b))		*power not presently exercisable because of a condition precedent* is invalid as of the time of its creation if the condition *might* neither be satisfied nor become impossible to satisfy with a life in being plus 21 years.")
10. *Same, but nongeneral inter vivos power.*	See #8.	N/A	See #7.
11. *Is a period of gestation added to the perpetuity period ?*	No. The possibility that a child will be born to a person after that person's death is disregarded. (§ 36-1A-1(d)) *See also* Unif. Statutory Rule Against Perpetuities § 1, 8B U.L.A. 242-43 (amended 1990) ("[T]he possibility that a child will be born to [a testator] after his death must be disregarded; and the possibility that a child will be born to any of [the testator's] descendants after their deaths must also be disregarded. Note, however, that the rule of subsection (d) does *not* apply to the question of the entitlement of an after-born child to take a beneficial interest in the trust").	N/A	Yes. (See #2a)

Table 9
Rule Against Perpetuities

	WEST VIRGINIA	WISCONSIN	WYOMING
12. *What is the treatment of a "later of the traditional rule or 90 years" clause? See UPC 2-901(e).*	West Virginia's USRAP does not specify how it will treat such clauses.	N/A	N/A
13. *When is an interest created by the exercise of a general testamentary power deemed created?*	Except as provided in subsections (b) and (c) of this section and in subsection (a), section five of this article, the time of creation of a nonvested property interest or a power of appointment is determined under general principles of property law. (§36-1A-2(a)) *See also* Unif. Statutory Rule Against Perpetuities §2, 8B U.L.A. 268 (amended 1990) (explaining that "general principles of property law determine that the time . . . [of creation] is at the decedent's death.") *See generally* §36-1A-5(a) ("a nonvested property interest or a power of appointment created by the exercise of a power of appointment is created when the power is irrevocably exercised or when a revocable exercise becomes irrevocable.")	N/A	*See* comment to Unif. Probate Code §2-902(a) ("general principles of property law determine that a nonvested property interest or power of appointment created by will is created at the decedent's death"); Unif. Statutory Rule Against Perpetuities §2, 8B U.L.A. 268 (amended 1990) (stating the same).
14. *Same, but nongeneral testamentary power.*	See #13.	N/A	See #13.

Table 9
Rule Against Perpetuities

WEST VIRGINIA	WISCONSIN	WYOMING
15. *Same, but general inter vivos power.*		
Except as provided in subsections (b) and (c) of this section and in subsection (a), section five of this article, the time of creation of a nonvested property interest or a power of appointment is determined under general principles of property law. (§ 36-1A-2(a)) The first of the excepted provisions states that as long as a person with a general power to become the unqualified beneficial owner has that power, the nonvested interest is created when the power terminates. The second of the excepted provisions states that a nonvested property interest, which arises from a transfer to an existing trust, is created when the nonvested property interest in the trust was created. *See also* Unif. Statutory Rule Against Perpetuities § 2, 8B U.L.A. 268 (amended 1990) (explaining that "the time when the interest or power is created is the date the transfer becomes effective for purposes of property law generally, normally the date of delivery of the deed"); Comment to Unif. Probate Code § 2-902(a) (stating same and adding "the funding of the trust" as "normally" the time when the interest is created). *See generally* § 36-1A-5(a) ("For the purposes of this section, a nonvested	N/A	*See* comment to Unif. Probate Code § 2-902(a) ("With respect to an intervivos transfer, an interest or power is created on the date the transfer becomes effective for purposes of property law generally, normally the date of delivery of the deed or funding of the trust."); Unif. Statutory Rule Against Perpetuities § 2, 8B U.L.A. 268 (stating the same).

9360

Table 9
Rule Against Perpetuities

	WEST VIRGINIA	WISCONSIN	WYOMING
	property interest or a power of appointment created by the exercise of a power of appointment is created when the power is irrevocably exercised or when a revocable exercise becomes irrevocable.")		
16. *Same, but nongeneral inter vivos power.*	See #15.	N/A	See #15.

Table 9
Rule Against Perpetuities

	WEST VIRGINIA	*WISCONSIN*	*WYOMING*
17. *When is an interest created if the grantor of a trust has a power to revoke?*	For purposes of this article, if there is a person who alone can exercise a power created by a governing instrument to become the unqualified beneficial owner of (1) a nonvested property interest or (2) a property interest subject to a power of appointment described in subsections (b) or (c), section one of this article, the nonvested property interest or power of appointment is created when the power to become the unqualified beneficial owner terminates. (§36-1A-2(b)) *See also* Unif. Statutory Rule Against Perpetuities §2, 8B U.L.A. 268 (amended 1990) (explaining that "any nonvested property interest subject to [a power to revoke] is not created . . . until the power terminates (by release, expiration at the death of the donee, or otherwise"); Comment to Unif. Probate Code §2-902(b) (noting that "nonvested property interest and powers of appointment created in [a revocable inter-vivos trust] are created when the power to revoke expires, usually at the settlor's death"). *See generally* §36-1A-5(a) ("A nonvested property interest or a power of appointment created by the exercise of a power of appointment is created	N/A	*See* comment to Unif. Probate Code §2-902(b) (noting that "nonvested property interests and powers of appointment created in [a revocable inter-vivos trust] are created when the power to revoke expires, usually at the settlor's death"); Unif. Statutory Rule Against Perpetuities §2, 8B U.L.A. 268 (amended 1990) (explaining that "any nonvested property interest subject to [a power to revoke] is not created . . . until the power terminates (by release, expiration at the death of the donee, or otherwise").

Table 9
Rule Against Perpetuities

	WEST VIRGINIA	WISCONSIN	WYOMING
	when the power is irrevocably exercised or when a revocable exercise becomes irrevocable.")		
18. *When does the period of the rule start re an interest contributed to an irrevocable trust? See UPC 2-902(c).*	A nonvested property interest or a power of appointment arising from a transfer of property to a previously funded trust or other existing property arrangement is created when the nonvested property interest or power of appointment in the original contribution was created. (§ 36-1A-2(c))	N/A	*See* comment to Unif. Probate Code 2-902(c) ("Arguably, at common law, each transfer [to an existing irrevocable inter-vivos trust] starts the period of the Rule running anew as to each transfer.")

Table 9
Rule Against Perpetuities

	WEST VIRGINIA	WISCONSIN	WYOMING
19. *Is there a conclusive presumption of fertility, that is, the "fertile octogenarian" rule?*	Yes. Carney v. Kain, 23 S.E. 650, 657 (W. Va. 1895) (noting that the "law considers that the possibility of issue continues so long as the person lives, no matter how improbable it may be.")[1] *See also* Unif. Statutory Rule Against Perpetuities § 1, 8B U.L.A. 256 (amended 1990) (holding that "[t]his principle is not superseded by this Act, and in view of new advances in medical science . . . [this] is not unrealistic."). *But see* C. P. Jhong, Annotation, *Modern Status of Presumption Against Possibility of Issue Being Extinct*, 98 A.L.R.2d 1285 (2003) (noting "a trend toward denying the conclusive or absolute nature of the presumption against the possibility of issue being extinct where there is competent evidence to the contrary has developed in the decisions, although some courts still adhere to the traditional view treating the presumption as conclusive or absolute").	N/A	*See, e.g.*, Arkansas, question #19.

Table 9
Rule Against Perpetuities

	WEST VIRGINIA	WISCONSIN	WYOMING
20. *What is the earliest age a child is deemed capable of bearing a child? What is the impact of illegitimacy?*	No specific state case or statute. "Under the rule, courts must presume that living persons are capable of having or fathering children, no matter how young they are. See In re Graite's Will Trusts, [1949] 1 All E.R. 459, 460 (Ch.). Thus, the rule strikes down any interest whose vesting depends on the assertion that, for example, a toddler will not have children." (Keith L. Butler, Notes & Comments, *Long Live the Dead Hand: A Case for Repeal of the Rule Against Perpetuities in Washington*, 75 Wash. L. Rev. 1237, 1246 n.78 (2000)).	N/A	"Under the rule, courts must presume that living persons are capable of having or fathering children, no matter how young they are. See In re Graite's Will Trusts, [1949] 1 All E.R. 459, 460 (Ch.). Thus, the rule strikes down any interest whose vesting depends on the assertion that, for example, a toddler will not have children." (Keith L. Butler, Notes & Comments, *Long Live the Dead Hand: A Case for Repeal of the Rule Against Perpetuities in Washington*, 75 Wash. L. Rev. 1237, 1246 n.78 (2000)).
21. *Is the "unborn widow" rule observed?*	Unclear. *See* Berry v. Union Nat'l Bank, 164 W. Va. 258, 266 (W. Va. 1980) (noting that "[o]ther jurisdictions have abolished the fertile octagenarian and unborn widow rules" while not deciding the issue); *see also* Unif. Statutory Rule Against Perpetuities § 1, 8B U.L.A. 246 (amended 1990) (explaining that "[t]he chance that [an] interest will become invalid under the Statutory Rule is small" and so the unborn widow rule would rarely invalidate an interest); 61 Am. Jur. 2d *Perpetuities and Restraints on Alienation* § 39 (2013) (noting the same).	N/A	*See, e.g.,* Arkansas, question #21.

Table 9
Rule Against Perpetuities

	WEST VIRGINIA	WISCONSIN	WYOMING
22. *Does the "slothful executor" rule apply, i.e., an administrative contingency clause providing for a "distribution to, e.g., those issue living at the time of satisfaction of the administrative condition precedent?"(cont'd)*	No specific state case or statute. *See* Unif. Statutory Rule Against Perpetuities §1, 8B U.L.A. 245 (amended 1990) (Under USRAP, an "interest becomes invalid only if it remains in existence and nonvested 90 years after [the testator's] death. Since it is almost certain that the final distribution of [an] estate will occur well within this 90-year period, the chance that [an] interest will be invalid is negligible.")	N/A	*See, e.g.,* California, question #22.
23. *Does the all-or-nothing rule apply to class gifts?*	No specific state case or statute. *See* Unif. Statutory Rule Against Perpetuities §1, 8B U.L.A. 257 (amended 1990) ("Although this Act does not supersede the basic idea of the much-maligned 'all-or-nothing' rule, the evils sometimes attributed to it are substantially if not entirely eliminated by the wait-and-see feature of the Statutory Rule and by the availability of reformation under Section 3.")	N/A	*See, e.g.,* Alabama, question #23.

Table 9
Rule Against Perpetuities

	WEST VIRGINIA	WISCONSIN	WYOMING
24. *Is there an exception to the all-or-nothing rule in the case of subclasses or specific sums to each member of the class?*	No specific state case or statute. *See* Unif. Statutory Rule Against Perpetuities §1, 8B U.L.A. 257 (amended 1990) ("The specific-sum and sub-class doctrines are not superseded by this Act.")	N/A	*See* Unif. Statutory Rule Against Perpetuities §1, 8B U.L.A. 257 ("The common law also recognizes a doctrine called the specific-sum doctrine which is derived from Storrs v. Benbow, 3 De G.M. & G. 390, 43 Eng. Rep. 153 (Ch. 1853), and states: If a specified sum of money is to be paid to each member of a class, the interest of each class member is entitled to separate treatment and is valid or invalid under the Rule on its own. The common law also recognizes a doctrine called the sub-class doctrine, which is derived from Cattlin v. Brown, 11 Hare 372, 68 Eng. Rep. 1318 (Ch. 1853), and states: If the ultimate takers are not described as a single class but rather as a group of separate subclasses, and if the share to which each separate subclass is entitled will finally be determined within the period of the Rule, the gifts to the different subclasses are separate for the purpose of the Rule.").

Table 9
Rule Against Perpetuities

	WEST VIRGINIA	WISCONSIN	WYOMING
25. *Is the infectious invalidity rule followed outside class gifts?*	Yes. Henderson v. Coombs, 453 S.E.2d 415, 418 (W. Va. 1994) (noting that "certain equitable rehabilitation methods, either reformation or the doctrine of infectious invalidity, could possibly be used in order to comport with the intentions of the grantor.") *But see* Unif. Statutory Rule Against Perpetuities §1, 8B U.L.A. 256 (amended 1990) (explaining that "[t]he doctrine of infectious invalidity is superseded by this Act by Section 3, under which courts . . . are required to *reform* the disposition to approximate as closely as possible the transferor's . . . plan of distribution.")	N/A	*See, e.g.,* Colorado, question #25.

Table 9
Rule Against Perpetuities

	WEST VIRGINIA	WISCONSIN	WYOMING
26. *Is there a rule against the suspension of the power of alienation? If so, how is it stated?*	Case law is limited. However, *see* Wallace v. St. Clair, 127 S.E.2d 742, 751 (W. Va. 1962) (noting that zoning regulations are not a restraint on regulation and will be upheld if reasonable.) A restraint is reasonable if "the beneficial enjoyment of the estate is not materially impaired, and the public good and interests are not violated, such restrictions are valid.").	A future interest or trust is void if it suspends the power of alienation for longer than the permissible period. The permissible period is a life or lives in being plus a period of 30 years. (W.S.A. §700.16(1)(A)) For more detailed rules on calculating the "permissible period," *see* W.S.A. §700.16(1)(b)-(c). For exceptions to the rule, *see* Wis. Stat. §700.16(4). Most importantly, there is no suspension of the power by a trustee or by equitable interests under a trust if the trustee has power to sell, either express or implied, or if there is an unlimited power to terminate in one or more persons then alive. (W.S.A. §700.16(3))	McGinnis v. McGinnis, 391 P.2d 927, 931 (Wyo. 1964) (holding that "there is no effective rule in Wyoming on restraints against alienation unless it be that which was derived from the common law" and not clearly deciding the common law rule, but finding oil royalties assigned in trust to a bank did not constitute a restraint on alienation.)
27. *Effective date.*	February 22, 1992. *See* W.V. Laws, 1992 Session, ch. 74 (1-1B. No. 2261). See also #6.	N/A	The special 1,000 year exemption applies in the case of certain trusts created after July 1, 2003. (§34-1-139 (b))

Note: Except for North Carolina, any comments from the UPC or USRAP have not been officially adopted by the state. Citations to them are for assistance in understanding the basic rules. Note also that much of the language within this Table is quoted directly from state statutes, although quotation marks are often not included.

[1] For questions #19 - 25, *see also* §36-1A-8 (noting that the state's USRAP supersedes the common law rule against perpetuities). The answers to questions #19 -25 are not likely to apply in most cases because of the abolition of the rule with respect to the vast majority of many trusts.

Table 10
Living Will
(current through 5/25/18)

Virtually every state has a living will statute. However, because of its controversial nature, states have developed quite diverse legislative responses to the topic. Certain states still have no comprehensive statute. In these states, a patient's right to terminate life is determined by a patchwork of statutory provisions and/or decisional law.

Increasingly, estate planners and elder law specialists are drafting living wills that address a host of issues not always considered in the more widely disseminated standard forms. This chapter considers in considerable depth these issues under the laws of the various states. It also considers in Table 10.06 the question of whether a living will executed in one state will be valid in another state. This question is not insubstantial, since it is common for a person to be hospitalized in a state other than the one in which he or she executed the living will.

The living will is not the only document likely to come into play. In situations in which the individual is not terminally ill, but is incapable of making health care decisions for herself, a health care directive is provided for in many jurisdictions. In some jurisdictions, a single document suffices, but in other jurisdictions, separate instruments are required. Table 10.01 indicates this for each state, as well as those states that simply do not provide for a health care directive.

As for the living will itself, many technical coverage issues arise. For example, there are difficult questions as to when a terminal condition exists and what sort of life support can legally be and not be withdrawn. These are addressed in Table 10.01. Table 10.02, on the other hand, is concerned with the formal requirements for executing a valid living will. For example, in some, but by no means the majority of states, a living will *must* be executed exactly like a testamentary instrument. A related question is the proper manner for revoking a living will. This matter is addressed on a state-by-state basis in Table 10.03. However, in numerous states, no clear consideration has been given to the question of the proper method to revoke a living will.

A major issue is the civil and criminal liability of medical personnel and hospitals if there is a failure to carry out the wishes expressed in the living will. These penalties serve as important leverage to compel observance of the living will. In this respect, the presence of a scienter requirement also has a considerable impact. In most cases, actual knowledge of the living will must have been present for liability to be imposed. These matters are explored in Table 10.04.

The presence of a living will can have an effect on the availability of insurance proceeds. First, with respect to health insurance, a person generally cannot be required to sign a living will in order to obtain health insurance. The state authority for this widespread position is set forth in Table 10.05. Second, state laws generally provide that the execution and giving effect to a living will is not suicide. Otherwise, life insurance proceeds could be denied under the terms of life insurance contracts.

Table 10.01, Part 1 Coverage of Living Will Statute

	Must There Be Separate Documents for Living Will and Health Care?	What Is the Specific Title of the Living Will Instrument?	Is a Terminal Condition Sufficient to Justify Withdrawing Support?	Is a Persistent Vegetative State or Permanent Unconsciousness Sufficient to Justify Withdrawing Support?	If a Different Standard Is Used, What Is it Exactly?	Has a "Terminal Condition," Persistent Vegetative State, or Permanent Unconsciousness or Other Standard Used Been Defined by Statute or Case Law?
Alabama	No. (§§ 22-8A-3(3), 22-8A-4(b))	Living Will. However, some provisions refer more generally to advance directive for health care which may also include a health care proxy. (§ 22-8A-3(3))	Yes. (§ 22-8A-4(d))	Yes. Permanent unconsciousness. (§ 22-8A-4(d))	An advance directive for health care becomes effective when a patient has a terminal illness or injury or a state of permanent unconsciousness. The declarant must also be unable to understand, appreciate, and direct his/her medical treatment. (§ 22-8A-4(d))	By statute "terminally ill or injured patient" (§ 22-8A-3(14)), and "permanent unconsciousness" have been defined. (§ 22-8A-3(10))

Table 10.01, Part 1 Coverage of Living Will Statute

	Must There Be Separate Documents for Living Will and Health Care?	What Is the Specific Title of the Living Will Instrument?	Is a Terminal Condition Sufficient to Justify Withdrawing Support?	Is a Persistent Vegetative State or Permanent Unconsciousness Sufficient to Justify Withdrawing Support?	If a Different Standard Is Used, What Is it Exactly?	Has a "Terminal Condition," Persistent Vegetative State, or Permanent Unconsciousness or Other Standard Used Been Defined by Statute or Case Law?
Alaska	Not specified, but probably no. However, an agent (appointed by a durable power of attorney for health care) can make any health care decision the principal could have made while having capacity. (§ 13.52.010(b))	Advance health care directive, which is defined as an individual instruction or a durable power of attorney for health care. (§§ 13.52.010; 13.52.390(1))	Yes. The existence of a "qualifying condition" is required to withdraw life-sustaining procedures. (§ 13.52.045) A qualifying condition under § 13.52.160 is determined by primary physician and one other. The term qualifying condition is defined as a terminal condition or permanent unconsciousness. (§ 13.52.390(32)) The optional statutory form in § 13.52.300 uses both terms, terminal condition and "condition of permanent unconsciousness," as being sufficient to withdraw support. Permanent unconsciousness shall be determined in consultation with a neurologist. (§ 13.52.160)	Yes. "Permanent unconsciousness." (§ 13.52.390(32))	N/A	Yes, "terminal condition" has been defined by statute as "an incurable or irreversible illness or injury." (§ 13.52.300 (Advanced Health Care Directive Optional Form: Pt. 2, Instructions for Health Care)) It is defined more extensively in § 13.52.390(37)(A)–(D). (§ 13.52.390(37)) "Permanent unconsciousness" is defined more extensively in § 13.52.390(27).

Table 10.01, Part 1 Coverage of Living Will Statute

	Must There Be Separate Documents for Living Will and Health Care?	What Is the Specific Title of the Living Will Instrument?	Is a Terminal Condition Sufficient to Justify Withdrawing Support?	Is a Persistent Vegetative State or Permanent Unconsciousness Sufficient to Justify Withdrawing Support?	If a Different Standard Is Used, What Is it Exactly?	Has a "Terminal Condition," Persistent Vegetative State, or Permanent Unconsciousness or Other Standard Used Been Defined by Statute or Case Law?
Arizona	No. A living will can be used as part of or instead of a health care power of attorney. (§ 36-3261) Also, any writing that complies with the living will requirements qualifies as a living will (§ 36-3262), presumably even if it addresses other health care matters. (§ 36-3262)	Living Will. (§ 36-3262)	Yes (as indicated in the statutory form). (§ 36-3262)	Yes (as indicated in the statutory form). (§ 36-3262)	N/A	No.
Arkansas	No. (§ 20-6-102(1)(e))	Living Will. (§ 20-6-102(13)(B))	Yes. (§ 20-17-202(b))	A "permanently unconscious" state will justify withdrawing support. (§ 20-17-202(c))	N/A	Yes. The statute defines "terminal condition" and "permanently unconscious." (§§ 20-17-201(11), 20-17-201(6))

Table 10.01, Part 1 Coverage of Living Will Statute

	Must There Be Separate Documents for Living Will and Health Care?	What Is the Specific Title of the Living Will Instrument?	Is a Terminal Condition Sufficient to Justify Withdrawing Support?	Is a Persistent Vegetative State or Permanent Unconsciousness Sufficient to Justify Withdrawing Support?	If a Different Standard Is Used, What Is it Exactly?	Has a "Terminal Condition," Persistent Vegetative State, or Permanent Unconsciousness or Other Standard Used Been Defined by Statute or Case Law?
California	No. (Prob. § 4671)	Individual health care instruction. (Prob. § 4670) A power of attorney for health care may be executed to give another person the authority to make health care decisions and may include individual health care instructions. (Prob. § 4671)	N/A	N/A	Either: (a) incurable and irreversible condition that will result in death within relatively short time; (b) unconsciousness, with reasonable degree of medical certainty that consciousness will not be regained; or (c) the likely risks of treatment will outweigh the expected benefits. (Prob. § 4701, statutory form (2.1))	Same as prior column.
Colorado	No. (§ 15-18-104(7))	Declaration as to Medical Treatment. (§ 15-18-104)	Yes. (§ 15-18-104(1))	Yes, "persistent vegetative state." (§ 15-18-104-1)	Terminal condition or in a persistent vegetative state and lacks decisional capacity to accept or reject medical or surgical treatment. (§ 15-18-104(1))	Yes. "Terminal condition," (§ 15-18-103(14) "persistent vegetative state," (§ 15-18-103(11) "decisional capacity" (§ 15-18-103(6))

Table 10.01, Part 1 Coverage of Living Will Statute

	Must There Be Separate Documents for Living Will and Health Care?	What Is the Specific Title of the Living Will Instrument?	Is a Terminal Condition Sufficient to Justify Withdrawing Support?	Is a Persistent Vegetative State or Permanent Unconsciousness Sufficient to Justify Withdrawing Support?	If a Different Standard Is Used, What Is it Exactly?	Has a "Terminal Condition," Persistent Vegetative State, or Permanent Unconsciousness or Other Standard Used Been Defined by Statute or Case Law?
Connecticut	No. An advance health care directive can be separate or part of a living will. There is also provision for a separate document ensuring the appointment of a health care representative, if not a part of the living will. (§§ 19a-570(1) & (8), 19a-575a)	Document concerning health care and withholding or withdrawal of life support systems. (§ 19a-575)	Yes, as indicated in the statutory form. (§ 19a-575, 19a-571(a)(2))	Yes, "permanently unconscious." (§§ 19a-575, 19a-571(a)(2))	N/A	Yes, by statute. Terminal condition: final stage of incurable/irreversible condition that will result in death within relatively short time without life support system. (§ 19a-570(11)) Permanently unconscious: permanent coma and persistent vegetative state or a condition that is irreversible, patient unaware of self/environment, and no behavioral response to environment. (§ 19a-570(10))
Delaware	No. An "advance health-care directive" can either mean an individual instruction or a power of attorney for health care, or both. (16 § 2501(a))	Advance health-care directive. (16 §§ 2503, 2501(a))	Yes. It is a "qualifying condition." (16 §§ 2505 (optional form), 2501(r)(2))	Yes. "Permanently unconscious." It is a "qualifying condition." (16 §§ 2505 (optional form), 2501(r)(1))	In addition to having a "qualifying condition," that is, either a terminal condition or the patient is "permanently unconscious," the patient must lack capacity for an advance health-care directive to become effective. (16 § 2503(c))	Yes. (16 § 2501(r)(1)&(2))

Table 10.01, Part 1 Coverage of Living Will Statute

	Must There Be Separate Documents for Living Will and Health Care?	What Is the Specific Title of the Living Will Instrument?	Is a Terminal Condition Sufficient to Justify Withdrawing Support?	Is a Persistent Vegetative State or Permanent Unconsciousness Sufficient to Justify Withdrawing Support?	If a Different Standard Is Used, What Is it Exactly?	Has a "Terminal Condition," Persistent Vegetative State, or Permanent Unconsciousness or Other Standard Used Been Defined by Statute or Case Law?
District of Columbia	No. (As indicated in statutory durable power of attorney for health care form) (§ 21-2207) Note that the attorney-in-fact is given very broad authority "to grant, refuse or withdraw consent to provision of any health care service, treatment, or procedure . . ." (§ 21-2206(a)(1))	Declaration. (§ 7-622)	Yes. (§ 7-622(a))	Not specified.	N/A	"Terminal condition" means an incurable condition which, regard less of the application of life-sustaining procedures, would produce death, and where the application of life-sustaining procedures would serve only to postpone the moment of death of the patient. (§ 7-621(6))

Table 10.01, Part 1 Coverage of Living Will Statute

	Must There Be Separate Documents for Living Will and Health Care?	What Is the Specific Title of the Living Will Instrument?	Is a Terminal Condition Sufficient to Justify Withdrawing Support?	Is a Persistent Vegetative State or Permanent Unconsciousness Sufficient to Justify Withdrawing Support?	If a Different Standard Is Used, What Is it Exactly?	Has a "Terminal Condition," Persistent Vegetative State, or Permanent Unconsciousness or Other Standard Used Been Defined by Statute or Case Law?
Florida	No. An "advance directive" can express the principal's desires concerning any aspect of health care, including designation of surrogate (§ 765.203), living will (§765.303), etc. (§765.101(1)) In addition, a health care surrogate may make decisions as to the withholding or withdrawing of life-prolonging procedures unless the designation of health care surrogate limits his authority to make such decisions. (§765.305(1))	Living will. (§765.303(1))	Yes. (§765.302)	Yes, persistent vegetative state. (§765.302)	"End stage condition" also qualifies. (§765.302)	Yes, statute. Terminal condition: injury disease or illness from which there is no reasonable probability of recovery and will cause death without treatment. (§765.101(17)) Persistent vegetative state: permanent/irreversible unconsciousness where there is no voluntary action/cognitive behavior and no ability to interact/communicate (§765.101(12)) End stage condition: irreversible condition that is caused by injury, disease, or illness which has resulted in progressively severe and permanent deterioration, and which, to a reasonable degree of medical probability, treatment of the condition would be ineffective. (§765.101(4))

Table 10.01, Part 1 Coverage of Living Will Statute

	Must There Be Separate Documents for Living Will and Health Care?	What Is the Specific Title of the Living Will Instrument?	Is a Terminal Condition Sufficient to Justify Withdrawing Support?	Is a Persistent Vegetative State or Permanent Unconsciousness Sufficient to Justify Withdrawing Support?	If a Different Standard Is Used, What Is it Exactly?	Has a "Terminal Condition," Persistent Vegetative State, or Permanent Unconsciousness or Other Standard Been Defined by Statute or Case Law?
Georgia	No. "Advance directive for health care" statutory form includes (1) health care agent, (2) treatment preferences, (3) guardianship. (§ 31-32-4)	"Advance Directive for Health Care" (§§ 31-32-2(1), 31-32-4)	Yes. (§ 31-32-5(a)(2))	Yes, "permanent unconsciousness." (§ 31-32-5(a)(2))	N/A	Yes. "Terminal condition" and "state of permanent unconsciousness" have been defined by statute. (§ 31-32-2(14) (terminal condition); § 31-32-2(13) (permanent unconsciousness)) "'Terminal condition' means an uncurable or irreversible condition which would result in the declarant's death in a relatively short period of time." As for "state of permanent unconsciousness," it "means an incurable or irreversible condition in which the declarant is not aware of himself or herself or his or her environment and in which the declarant is showing no behavioral response to his or her environment."

Table 10.01, Part 1 Coverage of Living Will Statute

	Must There Be Separate Documents for Living Will and Health Care?	What Is the Specific Title of the Living Will Instrument?	Is a Terminal Condition Sufficient to Justify Withdrawing Support?	Is a Persistent Vegetative State or Permanent Unconsciousness Sufficient to Justify Withdrawing Support?	If a Different Standard Is Used, What Is it Exactly?	Has a "Terminal Condition," Persistent Vegetative State, or Permanent Unconsciousness or Other Standard Used Been Defined by Statute or Case Law?
Hawaii	No. (§ 327E-3 (a) & (b))	Advance health-care directive (§ 327E-3), which may be in the form of an individual instruction or a power of attorney for health care, or both. (§ 327E-3(a) & (b))	N/A	N/A	Either: (a) incurable and irreversible condition that will result in death within relatively short time; (b) unconsciousness, with reasonable degree of medical certainty that consciousness will not be regained; or (c) the likely risks of treatment will outweigh the expected benefits. (§ 327E-16, statutory form Pt. 2 (6))	Same as prior column.

Table 10.01, Part 1 Coverage of Living Will Statute

	Must There Be Separate Documents for Living Will and Health Care?	What Is the Specific Title of the Living Will Instrument?	Is a Terminal Condition Sufficient to Justify Withdrawing Support?	Is a Persistent Vegetative State or Permanent Unconsciousness Sufficient to Justify Withdrawing Support?	If a Different Standard Is Used, What Is it Exactly?	Has a "Terminal Condition," Persistent Vegetative State, or Permanent Unconsciousness or Other Standard Used Been Defined by Statute or Case Law?
Idaho	No, as indicated in the statutory living will and durable power of attorney for health care form. (§39-4510)	Living will and Durable Power of Attorney for Health Care. (§39-4510)	Yes (as indicated in the statutory form, which states: "incurable or irreversible injury, disease, illness or condition, and a medical doctor who has examined me has certified: 1. That such injury, disease, illness or condition is terminal . . ."). (§39-4510)	Yes, persistent vegetative state (as indicated in the statutory form). (§39-4510)	N/A	Yes. Statutorily. "Terminal condition" is defined in §39-4502(17) (prior to July 1, 2012, §39-4502(14) as an incurable or irreversible condition which, without the administration of life-sustaining procedures, will, in the opinion of a physician, result in death if it runs its usual course. "Persistent Vegetative State" is defined in §39-4502(11) prior to July 1, 2012, §39-4502(10) as an irreversible state that has been medically confirmed by a neurological specialist in which the person has intact brain stem function but no higher cortical function and no awareness of self or environment.

Table 10.01, Part 1 Coverage of Living Will Statute

	Must There Be Separate Documents for Living Will and Health Care?	What Is the Specific Title of the Living Will Instrument?	Is a Terminal Condition Sufficient to Justify Withdrawing Support?	Is a Persistent Vegetative State or Permanent Unconsciousness Sufficient to Justify Withdrawing Support?	If a Different Standard Is Used, What Is it Exactly?	Has a "Terminal Condition," Persistent Vegetative State, or Permanent Unconsciousness or Other Standard Used Been Defined by Statute or Case Law?
Illinois	No, as indicated in the statutory durable power of attorney for health care form. (755 ILCS § 45/4-10(a))	Declaration. (755 ILCS §35/3(e))	Yes. (755 ILCS § 35/3(a))	Not specified.	Not specified.	Yes, statute. Terminal condition: "incurable/ and irreversible condition which is such that death is imminent and the application of death delaying procedures serves only to prolong the dying process." (755 ILCS §35/2(h))
Indiana	Not specified, although there is an implication that the documents can be the same, since the Living Will Declaration can contain "additional directions." (§16-36-4-9) See also §§ 16-36-1-14, 16-36-1-7 & 30-5-5-17) for requirements for appointing a representative to make health care decisions.	Living Will Declaration. (§16-36-4-10) Compare to the "Life Prolonging Procedures Declaration" in § 16-36-4-11.	Yes. (§16-36-4-13(a)(1))	Not specified.	N/A	A "terminal condition" means a condition caused by injury, disease or illness from which, to a reasonable degree of medical certainty: (a) there can be no recovery; and (b) death will occur within a short period of time without the provision of life-prolonging procedures. (§16-36-4-5)

Table 10.01, Part 1 Coverage of Living Will Statute

	Must There Be Separate Documents for Living Will and Health Care?	What Is the Specific Title of the Living Will Instrument?	Is a Terminal Condition Sufficient to Justify Withdrawing Support?	Is a Persistent Vegetative State or Permanent Unconsciousness Sufficient to Justify Withdrawing Support?	If a Different Standard Is Used, What Is it Exactly?	Has a "Terminal Condition," Persistent Vegetative State, or Permanent Unconsciousness or Other Standard Used Been Defined by Statute or Case Law?
Iowa	Not specified, but implied by § 144B, Durable Power of Attorney for Health Care. Note that sample form (§ 144B.5) does not mention any provisions relating to use of life-sustaining procedures, although it does allow the individual to include specific instructions including giving the agent the power to consent to the principal's physician not giving health care or stopping health care necessary to keep the principal alive.	Declaration (relating to use of life-sustaining procedures). (§ 144A.3)	Yes. (§ 144A.3(1))	Yes, (permanent unconsciousness) (as indicated in the statutory form). (§§ 144A.3(5) & 144A.2(13)) Actually, this term is subsumed within the statutory definition of "terminal condition."	N/A	Yes, "terminal condition" has been defined by statute. (§ 144A.2(13))
Kansas	Not specified.	Declaration (directing the withholding/with drawal of life sustaining procedures). (§ 65-28,103(a))	Yes. (§ 65-28,103(a))	Not specified.	Incurable injury, disease, or illness certified to be a terminal condition (as indicated in the statutory form). (§ 65-28,103(c))	Yes, "terminal condition" has been defined in the statutory form. (§ 65-28,103(c))

Table 10.01, Part 1 Coverage of Living Will Statute

	Must There Be Separate Documents for Living Will and Health Care?	What Is the Specific Title of the Living Will Instrument?	Is a Terminal Condition Sufficient to Justify Withdrawing Support?	Is a Persistent Vegetative State or Permanent Unconsciousness Sufficient to Justify Withdrawing Support?	If a Different Standard Is Used, What Is it Exactly?	Has a "Terminal Condition," Persistent Vegetative State, or Permanent Unconsciousness or Other Standard Used Been Defined by Statute or Case Law?
Kentucky	No, as indicated in the statutory living will directive form. (§311.625)	Living Will Directive. (§311.625)	Yes (as indicated in the statutory form). (§311.625(1))	Yes, "permanently unconscious" (as indicated in the statutory form). (§311.625(1))	N/A	"Terminal Condition" means a condition which, to a reasonable degree of medical probability, is incurable and irreversible and will result in death within a relatively short time, and where the application of life-prolonging treatment would serve only to artificially prolong the dying process. (§311.621(16)) "Permanently Unconscious" means a condition which, to a reasonable degree of medical probability, as determined by the patient's attending physician and one other physician on clinical examination, is characterized by an absence of cerebral cortical functions indicative of consciousness or behavioral interaction with the environment. (§311.621(12))

Table 10.01, Part 1 Coverage of Living Will Statute

	Must There Be Separate Documents for Living Will and Health Care?	What Is the Specific Title of the Living Will Instrument?	Is a Terminal Condition Sufficient to Justify Withdrawing Support?	Is a Persistent Vegetative State or Permanent Unconsciousness Sufficient to Justify Withdrawing Support?	If a Different Standard Is Used, What Is it Exactly?	Has a "Terminal Condition," "Persistent Vegetative State," or Permanent Unconsciousness or Other Standard Used Been Defined by Statute or Case Law?
Louisiana	No. The declaration may include designation of another to make treatment decisions. (§ 40:1151.2(C)(1))	Declaration. (§ 40:1151.2(C)(1))	Yes, "terminal and irreversible condition." (§ 40:1151.2(A)(1))	Yes, "profound comatose state" is used when defining "terminal condition." See prior column. (§§ 40:1151.2(C)(1) & 40:1151.2(15))	N/A	Yes, "terminal and irreversible condition" has been defined by statute. (§ 40:1157.2(14))
Maine	No (as indicated in the statutory form). (18-A § 5-804)	Advance Health-Care Directive. (18-A § 5-804)	Yes. Statutory form uses the phrase "incurable and irreversible condition" that will result in death within a relatively short time. (18-A § 5-804)	Yes. The statutory form also uses the phrase "unconsciousness that to a reasonable degree of a medical certainty will not end." (18-A § 5-804)	If the likely risks and burdens of treatment outweigh the expected benefits (as indicated in the statutory form). (18-A § 5-804)	Yes, both have been defined by statute. (18-A § 5-801(s) & (t))
Maryland	No (as indicated in the statutory form). (Health-Gen. § 5-603)	Advance Directive. (Health-Gen. § 5-603)	Yes (as indicated in the statutory form). (Health-Gen. §§ 5-603(II)(B), 5-606(b)(1))	Yes (as indicated in the statutory form). (Health-Gen. §§ 5-603(II)(C), 5-606(b)(2))	Also uses the term "end stage condition." (Health-Gen. § 5-606(b)(1))	Yes, "terminal condition," "persistent vegetative state," and "end-stage condition" have been defined by statute. (Health-Gen. § 5-601(u) ("terminal condition"), (q) ("persistent vegetative state") and (j) ("end-stage condition"))
Massachusetts[1]	No living will in Massachusetts.	Health care proxy. (201D § 2)	Not specified.	Not specified.	Not specified.	Not specified.
Michigan	No. (§ 700.5507(1))	Durable Power of Attorney and Patient Advocate Designation. (§700.5501)	Not specified.	Not specified.	Not specified.	N/A

Table 10.01, Part 1 Coverage of Living Will Statute

	Must There Be Separate Documents for Living Will and Health Care?	What Is the Specific Title of the Living Will Instrument?	Is a Terminal Condition Sufficient to Justify Withdrawing Support?	Is a Persistent Vegetative State or Permanent Unconsciousness Sufficient to Justify Withdrawing Support?	If a Different Standard Is Used, What Is it Exactly?	Has a "Terminal Condition," Persistent Vegetative State, or Permanent Unconsciousness or Other Standard Used Been Defined by Statute or Case Law?
Minnesota	No. (§ 145B.03)	Health Care Living Will. (§ 145B.04)	Yes (as indicated in the statutory form). (§ 145B.04(a))	Not specified. (§ 145B.04(a))	Not specified.	Yes, "terminal condition" has been defined by statute. (§ 145B.02 (Subd. 8))
Mississippi	No (as indicated in the statutory form. (§ 41-41-209))	Advanced health-care directive; if authority is given to an agent, that part is described as a power of attorney for health care. (§§ 41-41-205, 41-41-209, statutory form Pt. 1)	Yes, but statutory form uses the phrases "incurable and irreversible condition that will result in my death within a relatively short time." (§ 41-41-209, Pt. 2 (6)(a))	Implied by use of following language: "I become unconscious and, to a reasonable degree of medical uncertainty, I will not regain consciousness." (§ 41-41-209 statutory form, Pt. 2 (6)(a))	A third basis is that "the likely risks and burdens of treatment would outweigh the expected benefits." (§ 41-41-209, statutory form, Pt. 2 (6)(a)(iii))	No.
Missouri	Not specified, but the Declaration may contain other specific directions. (§ 459.015(3))	Declaration. (§ 459.015)	Yes (as indicated in the statutory form). (§ 459.015(3))	No. (§ 459.015(3))	Not specified. (§ 459.015(3))	Yes, "terminal condition" has been defined by statute. (§ 459.010(6))
Montana	Not specified, but the statutory forms deal with each separately. (§ 50-9-103(2) & (3))	Declaration. (§ 50-9-103(2))	Yes. (§§ 50-9-105(1)(b), 50-9-103(2))	Not specified.	N/A	"Terminal Condition" means an incurable or irreversible condition that, without the administration of life-sustaining treatment, will, in the opinion of the attending physician, result in death within a relatively short time. (§ 50-9-102(16))

Table 10.01, Part 1 Coverage of Living Will Statute

	Must There Be Separate Documents for Living Will and Health Care?	What Is the Specific Title of the Living Will Instrument?	Is a Terminal Condition Sufficient to Justify Withdrawing Support?	Is a Persistent Vegetative State or Permanent Unconsciousness Sufficient to Justify Withdrawing Support?	If a Different Standard Is Used, What Is it Exactly?	Has a "Terminal Condition," Persistent Vegetative State, or Permanent Unconsciousness or Other Standard Used Been Defined by Statute or Case Law?
Nebraska	No (as indicated in the health care power of attorney statutory form). (§ 30-3408)	Declaration. (§ 20-404)	Yes. (§ 20-405(2))	Yes, "persistent vegetative state." (§ 20-405(2))	Not specified.	Yes, statute. Terminal condition: incurable and irreversible condition that will result in death in a relatively short time without life-sustaining treatment. (§ 20-403(11)) Persistent vegetative state: to a reasonable degree of medical certainty in accordance with current medical standards is a total and irreversible loss of consciousness, no ability for cognitive interaction, and no reasonable hope for improvement. (§ 20-403(6)
Nevada	No (as indicated in the durable power of attorney for health care form). (§ 162A.860 Statement of Desires 3.)	Declaration. (§ 449.610)	Yes, assuming the declarant is determined by the attending physician to be no longer able to make decisions regarding administration of life-sustaining treatment. (§ 449.617)	Not specified.	Not specified.	"Terminal condition" means an incurable and irreversible condition that, without the administration of life-sustaining treatment, will, in the opinion of the attending physician, result in death within a relatively short time. (§ 162A.780)

Table 10.01, Part 1 Coverage of Living Will Statute

	Must There Be Separate Documents for Living Will and Health Care?	What Is the Specific Title of the Living Will Instrument?	Is a Terminal Condition Sufficient to Justify Withdrawing Support?	Is a Persistent Vegetative State or Permanent Unconsciousness Sufficient to Justify Withdrawing Support?	If a Different Standard Is Used, What Is it Exactly?	Has a "Terminal Condition," Persistent Vegetative State, or Permanent Unconsciousness or Other Standard Used Been Defined by Statute or Case Law?
New Hampshire	An advance directive can be a living will, a durable power of attorney for health care, a direction as to future medical care or designation of another person to make medical decisions. It can all be in one document or separate. (§§ 137-J:2(I); 137-J:20)	Living will or as part of an "Advance Directive." (§§ 137-J:2(I) & (XIV); 137-J:20)	Yes, "near death" (§ 137-J:2(XVI)) and as indicated in the statutory form. (§ 137-J:20(A)(2))	Yes, "permanently unconscious." (§ 137-J:2(XIV)) and as indicated in the statutory form (§ 137-J:20(A)(2))	Not specified.	Yes, "permanently unconscious" and "near death" have been defined by statute. (§§ 137-J:2(XVII) & (XVI))

Table 10.01, Part 1 Coverage of Living Will Statute

	Must There Be Separate Documents for Living Will and Health Care?	What Is the Specific Title of the Living Will Instrument?	Is a Terminal Condition Sufficient to Justify Withdrawing Support?	Is a Persistent Vegetative State or Permanent Unconsciousness Sufficient to Justify Withdrawing Support?	If a Different Standard Is Used, What Is it Exactly?	Has a "Terminal Condition," Persistent Vegetative State, or Permanent Unconsciousness or Other Standard Used Been Defined by Statute or Case Law?
New Jersey	No. (§ 26:2H-55)	Advance Directive for Health Care. (§ 26:2H-56)	Yes. (§§ 26:2H-67(3), 26:2H-55)	Yes, "permanently unconscious." (§§ 26:2H-67(2), 26:2H-55)	When patient is permanently unconscious or when life-sustaining treatment is experimental or is likely to be futile or ineffective, or is likely to merely prolong dying process; or when patient has a serious irreversible condition and likely risks of medical treatment outweigh likely benefits, or treatment of unwilling patient would be inhumane; but physician must consult with a reviewing body or get approval from a public agency set up for this purpose. (§ 26:2H-67(a)(1)-(2) & (4))	Permanently unconscious: a medical condition diagnosed in accord with currently accepted medical standards and with reasonable medical certainty as total and irreversible loss of consciousness, no capacity for interaction with environment which includes persistent vegetative state and irreversible comas (§ 26:2H-55); terminal condition: terminal stage of an irreversibly fatal illness, disease or condition (§ 26:2H-55). Specific life expectancy is not a requirement, but a prognosis of a life expectancy of six months or less will constitute a terminal condition. (Id.)

Table 10.01, Part 1 Coverage of Living Will Statute

	Must There Be Separate Documents for Living Will and Health Care?	What Is the Specific Title of the Living Will Instrument?	Is a Terminal Condition Sufficient to Justify Withdrawing Support?	Is a Persistent Vegetative State or Permanent Unconsciousness Sufficient to Justify Withdrawing Support?	If a Different Standard Is Used, What Is it Exactly?	Has a "Terminal Condition," Persistent Vegetative State, or Permanent Unconsciousness or Other Standard Used Been Defined by Statute or Case Law?
New Mexico	No. (§§ 24-7A-2(A), 24-7A-4))	Advance Health-Care Directive. (§ 24-7A-2)	Yes, but the term "incurable or irreversible condition" is used (as indicated in the statutory form). (§ 24-7A-4, Pt. 2)	Yes, but the term "become unconscious and to a reasonable degree of medical certainty I will not regain consciousness" is used (as indicated in the statutory form). (§ 24-7A-4, Pt. 2)	In addition to the standards in the prior two columns, support can be withdrawn if "the likely risks and burdens of treatment would outweigh the expected benefits." (§ 24-7A-4, Pt. 2)	Not defined, but described. (§ 24-7A-4, Pt. 2)
New York	No living will law in New York, but a health care proxy may include the principal's wishes or instructions as to health care and restrictions on the health care agent designated in the health care proxy. (Pub. Health § 2981(5)(b)) Specific instructions as to issues, such as artificial nutrition and hydrtion, may be provided to the agent, thereby limiting the agent's authority. (Pub. Health § 2981(5)(d) permissible form: Note)	Health care proxy. (Pub. Health §§ 2981(2), 2980(8)). Note that there is also provision for orders not to resuscitate. However, the provisions governing health care proxies and agents take precedence. (Pub. Health § 2962(5)(a)) Under certain circumstances, the patient, or if not capable, a surrogate or agent, can consent to an order not to resuscitate. See, e.g., Pub. Health § 2965(2). See generally Pub. Health § 2961 et seq.	Not specified.	Not specified.	Decision-making standard should be, after consultation with principal's physicians, (a) in accordance with the principal's wishes, including the principal's religious and moral beliefs, or (b) if the principal's wishes are not reasonably known and cannot with reasonable diligence be ascertained, in accordance with the principal's best interests. (Pub. Health § 2982(2))	Not specified.

Table 10.01, Part 1 Coverage of Living Will Statute

	Must There Be Separate Documents for Living Will and Health Care?	What Is the Specific Title of the Living Will Instrument?	Is a Terminal Condition Sufficient to Justify Withdrawing Support?	Is a Persistent Vegetative State or Permanent Unconsciousness Sufficient to Justify Withdrawing Support?	If a Different Standard Is Used, What Is it Exactly?	Has a "Terminal Condition," Persistent Vegetative State, or Permanent Unconsciousness or Other Standard Used Been Defined by Statute or Case Law?
North Carolina	No. (§ 90-321(j))	Advance Directive for a Natural Death ("Living Will"). (§ 90-321(d))	Yes (uses the term "incurable or irreversible" condition that will result in the declarant's death within a relatively short period of time). (§ 90-321(c)(1)(a))	Yes, uses the language "unconscious" with "high degree of medical certainty will never regain consciousness." (§ 90-321(c)(1)(b))	As a third ground, the statue provides for the situation in which the patient "suffers any condition resulting in the substantial loss of cognitive ability" which is not reversible. (§ 90-321(c)(1)(c))	No.
North Dakota	No (as indicated in the health care directive statutory form). (§ 23-06.5-17).	Health care directive. (§ 23-06.5-17; see also §§ 23-06.5-03(1), 23-06.5-02(5))	No. Not specified, but possibly. See optional statutory form, PART II(B) which allows declarant to state desires if he/she "were dying." (§ 23-06.5-17)	Not specified, but possibly. See optional statutory form, PART II, which allows declarant to state desires if he/she "were permanently unconscious." (§ 23-06.5-17).	N/A	Prior to its repeal by Laws 2005, ch. 232, § 19, § 23-06.4-02(7) provided, "terminal condition" means an incurable or irreversible condition that, without the administration of life-prolonging treatment, will result, in the opinion of the attending physician, in imminent death. The term did not include any form of senility, Alzheimer's disease, mental retardation, mental illness, or chronic mental or physical impairment, including comatose conditions that will not result in imminent death.

Table 10.01, Part 1 Coverage of Living Will Statute

	Must There Be Separate Documents for Living Will and Health Care?	What Is the Specific Title of the Living Will Instrument?	Is a Terminal Condition Sufficient to Justify Withdrawing Support?	Is a Persistent Vegetative State or Permanent Unconsciousness Sufficient to Justify Withdrawing Support?	If a Different Standard Is Used, What Is it Exactly?	Has a "Terminal Condition," Persistent Vegetative State, or Permanent Unconsciousness or Other Standard Used Been Defined by Statute or Case Law?
Ohio	No, in that the attorney in fact may also be authorized to make these decisions. However, if there are both a living will declaration and durable power of attorney for health care, the living will declaration supersedes a durable power of attorney declaration, even if the power of attorney was created after the declaration. (§§ 2133.03(B)(2); 1337.12 (D)(1)) However, the durable power of attorney supersedes a Do-Not-Resuscitate Order and Identification. (§ 1337.12(D)(1))	Declaration. (§ 2133.02(A)(1)) A person may also execute a declaration that authorizes the withholding or with drawal of CPR, known as a Do-Not-Resuscitate Order. (§ 2133.21(D))	Yes. (§ 2133.02(A)(2))	Yes, permanently unconscious state. (§ 2133.02(A)(2))	N/A	Yes, statute. Terminal condition: irreversible, incurable, untreatable condition caused by disease, illness, or injury from which there can be no recovery and death will occur in a relatively short time without life-sustaining treatment. (§ 2133.01(AA)) Permanently unconscious state: permanent unconsciousness where the declarant to a reasonable degree of medical certainty as determined in accordance with reasonable medical standards is irreversibly unaware of him self/ environment and there is a total loss of cerebral cortex functioning such that the declarant cannot experience pain or suffering. (§ 2133.01(U))

Table 10.01, Part 1 Coverage of Living Will Statute

	Must There Be Separate Documents for Living Will and Health Care?	What Is the Specific Title of the Living Will Instrument?	Is a Terminal Condition Sufficient to Justify Withdrawing Support?	Is a Persistent Vegetative State or Permanent Unconsciousness Sufficient to Justify Withdrawing Support?	If a Different Standard Is Used, What Is it Exactly?	Has a "Terminal Condition," Persistent Vegetative State, or Permanent Unconsciousness or Other Standard Used Been Defined by Statute or Case Law?
Oklahoma	No. (63 §3101.3(1))	Advance Directive for Health Care. (63 §3101.4(A))	Yes, if authorized (as indicated in the statutory form). (63 §3101.4(C)(I)(1)	Yes, "persistently unconscious" (as indicated in the statutory form). (63 §3101.4(C)(I)(2))	The form also allows for "end-stage condition" which results in complete physical dependency and is irreversible. (63 §3101.4(C)(1)(3))	Yes, "terminal condition," (63 §3101.3(12)) ("persistently unconscious," (63 §3101.3(7)) and "end-stage condition" are defined by statute. (63 §3101.3(4))

Table 10.01, Part 1 Coverage of Living Will Statute

	Must There Be Separate Documents for Living Will and Health Care?	What Is the Specific Title of the Living Will Instrument?	Is a Terminal Condition Sufficient to Justify Withdrawing Support?	Is a Persistent Vegetative State or Permanent Unconsciousness Sufficient to Justify Withdrawing Support?	If a Different Standard Is Used, What Is it Exactly?	Has a "Terminal Condition," Persistent Vegetative State, or Permanent Unconsciousness or Other Standard Used Been Defined by Statute or Case Law?
Oregon	No. (§ 127.531(2))	Advance Directive. (§ 127.531(2))	Yes. (§ 127.635(1)(a))	Yes, permanently unconscious. (§ 127.635(1)(b))	Statutory form indicates progressive illness, and extraordinary suffering. (§ 127.531(2), Pt. C; see also § 127.635(1)(c) & (d))	Yes, statute. Terminal condition: death is imminent irrespective of treatment and life-sustaining procedures or nutrition/hydration only postpone death. (§ 127.505(23)) Permanently unconscious: no awareness of self/environment, no reasonable possibility of returning to consciousness, and it has been confirmed by a neurological specialist. (§ 127.505(19)) Advanced progressive illness: fatal illness in its advanced stage where one cannot communicate, swallow food/water safely, care for oneself, recognize family, and unlikely condition will improve. (§ 127.531(2), Pt. C) Extraordinary suffering: life support does not help patient's condition and will only cause permanent and severe pain. (§ 127.531(2), Pt. C)

Table 10.01, Part 1 Coverage of Living Will Statute

	Must There Be Separate Documents for Living Will and Health Care?	What Is the Specific Title of the Living Will Instrument?	Is a Terminal Condition Sufficient to Justify Withdrawing Support?	Is a Persistent Vegetative State or Permanent Unconsciousness Sufficient to Justify Withdrawing Support?	If a Different Standard Is Used, What Is it Exactly?	Has a "Terminal Condition," Persistent Vegetative State, or Permanent Unconsciousness or Other Standard Used Been Defined by Statute or Case Law?
Pennsylvania	No. (20 § 5447)	Living Will. (20 § 5447) A proposed combined form is entitled "Durable Health Care Power of Attorney and Health Care Treatment Instructions (Living Will)." (20 § 5471)	Yes. Uses term "end-stage medical condition." (20 § 5443(a)(2) & 20 § 5443(g))	Yes, "permanently unconscious." (20 § 5443(a)(2) and 20 § 5443(g))	N/A	"End-stage medical condition" is "an incurable and irreversible medical condition in an advanced state caused by injury, disease or physical illness that will, in the opinion of the attending physician, to a reasonable degree of medical certainty, result in death, despite the introduction or continuation of medical treatment." (20 § 5422) "Permanent unconsciousness" is a condition diagnosed under current medical standards which with reasonable medical certainty is a total and irreversible loss of consciousness and capacity for interaction with the environment; includes irreversible vegetative state and irreversible coma. (20 § 5422)

Table 10.01, Part 1 Coverage of Living Will Statute

	Must There Be Separate Documents for Living Will and Health Care?	What Is the Specific Title of the Living Will Instrument?	Is a Terminal Condition Sufficient to Justify Withdrawing Support?	Is a Persistent Vegetative State or Permanent Unconsciousness Sufficient to Justify Withdrawing Support?	If a Different Standard Is Used, What Is it Exactly?	Has a "Terminal Condition," Persistent Vegetative State, or Permanent Unconsciousness or Other Standard Used Been Defined by Statute or Case Law?
Rhode Island	No (as indicated in the durable power of attorney for health care statutory form). (§ 23-4.10-2(4)(a))	Declaration. (§ 23-4.11-3(d))	Yes. (§ 23-4.11-3(c)(2))	Not specified.	N/A	Yes, statute. Terminal condition: incurable/irreversible condition that will cause death without life-sustaining procedures. (§ 23-4.11-2(13))
South Carolina	No. (§§ 44-77-40, 44-77-50)	Declaration of a Desire for a Natural Death. (§ 44-77-50)	Yes. (§ 44-77-40(1))	Yes, "permanently unconscious." (§ 44-77-40(1))	N/A	Yes, "terminal condition" and "permanent unconsciousness" are defined by statute. (§§ 44-77-20(4), 44-77-20(7))
South Dakota	A durable power of attorney may contain provisions as to medical procedures, intervention or treatment. (§ 59-7-2.1) If an individual has executed both a declaration and a durable power of attorney, the later executed document controls to the extent that the provisions conflict. (§ 34-12D-4)	Living Will Declaration. (§ 34-12D-3)	See last column. (§ 34-12D-5)	See next-to-last column for definition of "terminal condition."	"When the declarant is determined by the attending physician to be in a terminal condition, death is imminent, and the declarant is no longer able to communicate decisions about medical care." (§§ 34-12D-1(8), 34-12D-5)	Yes, statute. Terminal condition: incurable/irreversible condition that will result in death shortly or a coma/other permanently unconscious condition which will indefinitely last without improvement, person unable to communicate, no purposeful movement or motor activity, and cannot interact with environmental stimuli. (§ 34-12D-1(7))

Table 10.01, Part 1 Coverage of Living Will Statute

	Must There Be Separate Documents for Living Will and Health Care?	What Is the Specific Title of the Living Will Instrument?	Is a Terminal Condition Sufficient to Justify Withdrawing Support?	Is a Persistent Vegetative State or Permanent Unconsciousness Sufficient to Justify Withdrawing Support?	If a Different Standard Is Used, What Is it Exactly?	Has a "Terminal Condition," Persistent Vegetative State, or Permanent Unconsciousness or Other Standard Used Been Defined by Statute or Case Law?
Tennessee	No. (§ 34-6-204(a)(1) & (b)) (unless limited by the power, the attorney-in-fact can make the same decisions as the principal could. Presumably, then, living will provisions can be addressed in the durable power of attorney for health care)	Living Will. (§ 32-11-105)	Yes (as indicated in the statutory form). (§ 32-11-105)	Yes, "persistent vegetative state" is included in definition of terminal condition. (§ 32-11-103(9))	Loss of competency causes living will to become effective. (§ 32-11-104(a))	Yes, "terminal condition" has been defined by statute. (§ 32-11-103(9))
Texas	No. (Health & Safety §§ 166.033, 166.032(c))	Directive to Physicians and Family or Surrogates. (Health & Safety § 166.033)	Yes (as indicated in the statutory form). (Health & Safety § 166.033)	Not specified.	Incurable/ irreversible condition caused by injury, disease, or illness certified to be a terminal condition (as indicated in the statutory form). (Health & Safety § 166.033)	Yes, "terminal condition" and "irreversible condition" have been defined by statute. (Health & Safety § 166.002(13), (9))

Table 10.01, Part 1 Coverage of Living Will Statute

	Must There Be Separate Documents for Living Will and Health Care?	What Is the Specific Title of the Living Will Instrument?	Is a Terminal Condition Sufficient to Justify Withdrawing Support?	Is a Persistent Vegetative State or Permanent Unconsciousness Sufficient to Justify Withdrawing Support?	If a Different Standard Is Used, What Is it Exactly?	Has a "Terminal Condition," Persistent Vegetative State, or Permanent Unconsciousness or Other Standard Used Been Defined by Statute or Case Law?
Utah	No. They can be combined in an advance health care directive, per statutory form. (§75-2a-117 & §75-2a-107(1)(a))	Advance Health Care Directive. (§75-2a-117)	Statutory form uses the terms "progressive illness that will cause close to death," and "close to death and unlikely to recover" as two bases. (§75-2a-117, Pt. II(b))	Yes, persistent vegetative state (as indicated in the statutory form). (§75-2a-117, Pt. II(b))	Still other bases are the declarant "cannot communicate and my condition will unlikely improve," he or she does not "recognize my friends and family and it is unlikely my condition will improve." (§75-2a-117, Pt. II(b))	No.
Vermont	No. (18 §9702)	Advance Directive. (18 §9703)	Not relevant.	Not specified.	Not specified.	No.
Virginia	No. (§§54.1-2983, 54.1-2984)	Advance Medical Directive. (§54.1-2984)	Yes. (§54.1-2983) See also suggested form. (§54.1-2984, Option IV)	Yes, persistent vegetative state is included in definition of terminal condition. (§54.1-2982)	Not specified.	Yes, "terminal condition" and "persistent vegetative state" are defined by statute. (§54.1-2982)
Washington	Not specified.	Health Care Directive. (§70.122.030(1))	Yes. (§70.122.030(1))	Yes, "permanent unconscious condition" (§70.122.030(1)).	N/A	Yes, "terminal condition" and "permanent unconscious condition" are defined by statute. (§§70.122.020(9), 70.122.020(6))
West Virginia	No. (§16-30-4)	Living Will. (§16-30-4)	Yes (as indicated in the statutory form). (§16-30-4)	Yes, persistent vegetative state (as indicated in the statutory form). (§16-30-4)	N/A	Yes, "terminal condition" and "persistent vegetative state" have been defined by statute. (§§16-30-3(s), 16-30-3(aa))

Table 10.01, Part 1 Coverage of Living Will Statute

	Must There Be Separate Documents for Living Will and Health Care?	What Is the Specific Title of the Living Will Instrument?	Is a Terminal Condition Sufficient to Justify Withdrawing Support?	Is a Persistent Vegetative State or Permanent Unconsciousness Sufficient to Justify Withdrawing Support?	If a Different Standard Is Used, What Is it Exactly?	Has a "Terminal Condition," Persistent Vegetative State, or Permanent Unconsciousness or Other Standard Used Been Defined by Statute or Case Law?
Wisconsin	No (as indicated in the durable power of attorney statutory form). (§ 155.30)	Declaration to physicians; Wisconsin living will. (§ 154.03(2))	Yes. (§ 154.03(1))	Yes, persistent vegetative state. (§ 154.03(1))	May not be authorized when withholding or withdrawal of medication, life-sustaining procedure or feeding tube will cause pain that cannot be alleviated. (§ 154.03(1))	Yes, statute. Persistent vegetative state: complete/irreversible loss of all cerebral cortex functions causing complete, chronic, irreversible loss of all cognitive functioning and consciousness and no behavioral responses indicating cognitive functioning although autonomic functioning persists. (§ 154.01(5m)) Terminal condition: incurable condition caused by injury/illness, death is imminent, and life-sustaining procedures only postpone death. (§ 154.01(8))
Wyoming	There is a single document. (§ 35-22-403; see also § 35-22-402(a)(i))	Advance Health Care Directive. However, reference is also made to a power of attorney for health care. (§ 35-22-403)	No condition is required. An agent for a person who is incapacitated can simply refuse health care or artificial nutrition and hydration, just as an individual might for himself. (§ 35-22-402(a)(ix))	Condition not required. See prior column.	See third column.	See third column.

---

[1] Only deals with health care proxies.

Table 10.01, Part 2 Coverage of Living Will Statute

	Who Determines the Condition of the Patient?	What Sort of Medical Procedures Can Be Withheld or Withdrawn?	If "Life-Sustaining" Procedures or "Extraordinary Means," or Otherwise, Briefly What Does This Entail, If Defined?	Specifically, May Food and/or Hydration Be Withheld or Withdrawn?	Does the Statute Use "Artificially" or "Unnaturally" Prolonged in Describing When, e.g., Life-Sustaining Procedures or Extraordinary Means Can Be Withheld or Withdrawn?
Alabama	Attending physician and one other physician. (§ 22-8A-4(d))	Life-sustaining treatment and artificial nutrition and hydration. (§ 22-8A-4(a))	Life-sustaining treatment includes any medical treatment, procedure, or intervention that, in the judgment of the attending physician, when applied to the patient, would serve only to prolong the dying process where the patient has a terminal illness or injury, or would serve only to maintain the patient in a condition of permanent unconsciousness. These procedures shall include, but are not limited to, assisted ventilation, cardiopulmonary resuscitation, renal dialysis, surgical procedures, blood transfusions, and the administration of drugs and antibiotics. Life-sustaining treatment shall not include the administration of medication or the performance of any medical treatment where, in the opinion of the attending physician, the medication or	Yes, if specifically authorized in the living will. (§ 22-8A-4(a))	"Artificially" used to describe nutrition/hydration. (§ 22-8A-4)

Table 10.01, Part 2 Coverage of Living Will Statute

	Who Determines the Condition of the Patient?	What Sort of Medical Procedures Can Be Withheld or Withdrawn?	If "Life-Sustaining" Procedures or "Extraordinary Means," or Otherwise, Briefly What Does This Entail, If Defined?	Specifically, May Food and/or Hydration Be Withheld or Withdrawn?	Does the Statute Use "Artificially" or "Unnaturally" Prolonged in Describing When, e.g., Life-Sustaining Procedures or Extraordinary Means Can Be Withheld or Withdrawn?
			treatment is necessary to provide comfort or to alleviate pain. (§ 22-8A-3(8))		
Alaska	Primary physician and one other physician (when available). "Permanent unconsciousness" must be determined in consultation with a neurologist. (§ 13.52.160)	Life-sustaining procedures. (§ 13.52.045)	Life-sustaining procedure means any medical procedure or intervention that, in the judgment of the primary physician, when administered to a qualified patient, would serve only to prolong the dying process. (§ 13.52.390(23))	Yes, with respect to artificial nutrition and hydration. Artificial is used to describe nutirition/hydration. (§ 13.52.390(4)) As in statutory form (§ 13.52.300 (Explanation, Part I(c))	Neither term is used.
Arizona	Not specified. Likely the patient's doctors per the statutory form which indicates the patient has the option of providing for the continuation of all treatment until "my doctors reasonably conclude that my condition is terminal or is irreversible and incurable or I am in a persistent vegetative state". (§ 36-3262)	The patient can have the following treatment withheld: chest compressions, defibrillation, assisted ventilation, intubation, advanced life support medications, CPR, electric shock, artificial breathing, artificially administered food and drugs and all life-sustaining treatment generally. The patient can also add to this list of exclusions (as indicated in the statutory form). (§§ 36-3251, 36-3262)	Not defined.	Yes (as indicated in the statutory form). (§ 36-3262)	Artificially (as indicated in the statutory form). (§ 36-3262)

10,032

Table 10.01, Part 2 Coverage of Living Will Statute

	Who Determines the Condition of the Patient?	What Sort of Medical Procedures Can Be Withheld or Withdrawn?	If "Life-Sustaining" Procedures or "Extraordinary Means," or Otherwise, Briefly What Does This Entail, If Defined?	Specifically, May Food and/or Hydration Be Withheld or Withdrawn?	Does the Statute Use "Artificially" or "Unnaturally" Prolonged in Describing When, e.g., Life-Sustaining Procedures or Extraordinary Means Can Be Withheld or Withdrawn?
Arkansas	The attending physician and one other physician determine if a patient is in a "terminal condition" or "permanently unconscious state" and no longer able to make decisions regarding administration of life-sustaining treatment. (§ 20-17-203)	"Life-sustaining treatment." (§ 20-17-202(a))	"Life-sustaining treatment" is defined as any procedure or intervention that would only prolong death or maintain the person in a permanently unconscious state. (§ 20-17-201(5))	Maybe. The person may authorize the withdrawal of hydration and/or nutrition (as indicated in the statutory form). (§ 20-17-202) The attending physician has the responsibility to provide nutrition and/or hydration, however, for the patient's comfort or the alleviation of pain. (§ 20-17-206(b))	Not specified.
California	Primary physician. (Prob. § 4732)	Any care. (Prob. § 4701, Explanation (a))	N/A	Yes (as indicated in the statutory form); uses "artificial." (Prob. § 4701, Explanation (d))	Yes. Uses "artificial" to describe hydration/nutrition. (Prob. § 4701, Explanation (d))
Colorado	Attending physician and one other qualified physician. (§ 15-18-107)	Life-sustaining procedures and artificial nourishment. (§ 15-18-104(1)&(3)(a))	Life-sustaining procedure means any medical procedure or intervention that serves only to prolong the dying process. It does not include any procedure necessary to alleviate pain or provide nourishment. (§ 15-18-103(10))	Yes, but if such withholding causes the patient pain, a physician may order such nutrition/hydration as is necessary to alleviate pain. (§§ 15-18-104(4))	Not specified.

Table 10.01, Part 2 Coverage of Living Will Statute

	Who Determines the Condition of the Patient?	What Sort of Medical Procedures Can Be Withheld or Withdrawn?	If "Life-Sustaining" Procedures or "Extraordinary Means," or Otherwise, Briefly What Does This Entail, If Defined?	Specifically, May Food and/or Hydration Be Withheld or Withdrawn?	Does the Statute Use "Artificially" or "Unnaturally" Prolonged in Describing When, e.g., Life-Sustaining Procedures or Extraordinary Means Can Be Withheld or Withdrawn?
Connecticut	Incapacitation determined by attending physician. (§ 19a-579) Terminal condition determined by attending physician. (§ 19a-571(a)(2)) Permanently unconscious determined by attending physician and a physician qualified to make neurological diagnosis after examining the patient. (§ 19a-571(a)(2)	Life support systems. (§ 19a-575)	"Life support system" means any medical procedure/ intervention that would serve only to postpone death or maintain patient in state of permanent unconsciousness, including, but not limited to, mechanical or electronic devices, including artificial means of providing nutrition and hydration (§ 19a-570(7))	Yes. (§ 19a-570(1), (7) & (8))	Yes. The word "artificial" is used. (§ 19a-570(7))
Delaware	A determination that an individual lacks capacity or has recovered capacity must be made by the primary physician or other physician(s) as specified in the directive. Decisions to withdraw treatment from a patient must be made in consultation with a physician. (16 § 2503(e) & (f))	The patient can request that any medical procedures be withheld, including life-sustaining procedures and artificial nutrition and hydration (as indicated in the statutory form). (16 § 2505)	A "life-sustaining procedure" is any medical procedure that (a) utilizes mechanical or other artificial means to sustain, restore, or supplant a spontaneous vital function, or (b) does not afford the patient a reasonable chance of recovery from a terminal condition or permanent unconsciousness. (16§ 2501(1)) Includes artificial nutrition/ hydration as defined in 16 §2501(c).	Yes (as indicated in the statutory form). (16 §2505(e))	Yes. A life-sustaining procedure is one that "artificially sustains, restores, or supplants a spontaneous vital function." (16 §2501(l))

Table 10.01, Part 2 Coverage of Living Will Statute

	Who Determines the Condition of the Patient?	What Sort of Medical Procedures Can Be Withheld or Withdrawn?	If "Life-Sustaining" Procedures or "Extraordinary Means," or Otherwise, Briefly What Does This Entail, If Defined?	Specifically, May Food and/or Hydration Be Withheld or Withdrawn?	Does the Statute Use "Artificially" or "Unnaturally" Prolonged in Describing When, e.g., Life-Sustaining Procedures or Extraordinary Means Can Be Withheld or Withdrawn?
District of Columbia	A terminal condition must be certified by two physicians, one of whom shall be the attending physician (as indicated in the statutory form). (§§ 7-622(c), 7-621(3))	All life-sustaining procedures may be withheld. (§ 7-622(a))	The term "life-sustaining procedure" means any medical procedure that would serve only to artificially prolong the dying process. The term shall not include the administration of medication or the performance of medical procedures deemed necessary to provide comfort to the patient. (§ 7-621(3))	Not specified.	Yes. A life-sustaining procedure is one that would seem only to artificially prolong the dying process. (§ 7-621(3))
Florida	Attending/treating physician and one other physician after an examination. (§ 765.306)	Life-prolonging procedures. (§ 765.302(1))	Life-prolonging procedures: any medical procedure, treatment, intervention which uses mechanical/artificial means for vital function and only prolongs the dying process including artificially provided food and hydration. (§ 765.101(10))	Yes, since included in the definition of life-prolonging procedures. (§ 765.101(10)) Also, it is implied (as indicated in the statutory form which says that provision may be made only to receive medication or procedures to alleviate pain or provide comfort care). (§ 765.303(1))	Sample living will says "procedures would serve only to prolong artificially the process of dying." (§ 765.303(1)).

Table 10.01, Part 2 Coverage of Living Will Statute

	Who Determines the Condition of the Patient?	What Sort of Medical Procedures Can Be Withheld or Withdrawn?	If "Life-Sustaining" Procedures or "Extraordinary Means," or Otherwise, Briefly What Does This Entail, If Defined?	Specifically, May Food and/or Hydration Be Withheld or Withdrawn?	Does the Statute Use "Artificially" or "Unnaturally" Prolonged in Describing When, e.g., Life-Sustaining Procedures or Extraordinary Means Can Be Withheld or Withdrawn?
Georgia	Two physicians, one of whom must be the attending physician, make the determination after personally examining the declarant. (§31-32-9(b))	Life-sustaining procedures. (§31-32-5(a))	Life-sustaining procedures are defined as any medical procedures or interventions, which, when applied to a patient in a terminal condition or in a state of permanent unconsciousness which can keep the patient alive but cannot cure the patient and where death will occur without such procedures/interventions. This may include (at the declarant's option) the provision of nourishment and hydration, but does not include pain relief medications or procedures. (§31-32-2(9))	Yes, if authorized by the declarant. (§§31-32-2(9), 31-32-5(a))	Neither term is used. (§31-32-2)
Hawaii	Primary physician (unless otherwise specified in a written advance health-care directive) (§327E-3(f)) or supervising health care provider. (§327E-7(c))	Any healthcare, including the withholding or removal of artificially provided nutrition and hydration. (§§327E-3, 327E-16, Explanation (a))	N/A	Yes. (§327E-16, Explanation (d))	"Artificial" used in Optional Form to describe nutrition and hydration. (§327E-16, Pt.2(7))

Table 10.01, Part 2 Coverage of Living Will Statute

	Who Determines the Condition of the Patient?	What Sort of Medical Procedures Can Be Withheld or Withdrawn?	If "Life-Sustaining" Procedures or "Extraordinary Means," or Otherwise, Briefly What Does This Entail, If Defined?	Specifically, May Food and/or Hydration Be Withheld or Withdrawn?	Does the Statute Use "Artificially" or "Unnaturally" Prolonged in Describing When, e.g., Life-Sustaining Procedures or Extraordinary Means Can Be Withheld or Withdrawn?
Idaho	One examining phycician. (§ 39-4510 recommended form)	All medical treatment, including withdrawal of artificial nutrition and hydration. (§ 39-4510 recommended form)	"Artificial life-sustaining procedure" means any medical procedure or intervention that utilizes mechanical means to sustain or supplant a vital function which when applied to a qualified patient, would serve only to artificially prolong life. "Artificial life-sustaining procedure" does not include the administration of medication or the performance of any medical procedure deemed necessary to alleviate pain. (§ 39-4502(2))	Yes. (§ 39-4510 recommended form)	Artificially. (§ 39-4509) The statutory form mentions the term "artificial life-sustaining." (§ 39-4510 recommended form which uses other standards as well)
Illinois	Attending physician. (755 ILCS §§ 35/2(a), 35/6)	"Death delaying procedures." (755 ILCS § 35/3(a))	"Death delaying procedures": any medical procedure / intervention that only postpones death. Does not include treatments for care/ comfort. (755 ILCS § 35/2(d))	Yes, unless death would result solely from dehydration/ starvation. (755 ILCS § 35/2(d))	Artificially (as indicated in the statutory form). (755 ILCS § 35/3(e))

Table 10.01, Part 2 Coverage of Living Will Statute

	Who Determines the Condition of the Patient?	What Sort of Medical Procedures Can Be Withheld or Withdrawn?	If "Life-Sustaining" Procedures or "Extraordinary Means," or Otherwise, Briefly What Does This Entail, If Defined?	Specifically, May Food and/or Hydration Be Withheld or Withdrawn?	Does the Statute Use "Artificially" or "Unnaturally" Prolonged in Describing When, e.g., Life-Sustaining Procedures or Extraordinary Means Can Be Withheld or Withdrawn?
Indiana	The attending physician must determine the condition of the patient. (§§ 16-36-4-10, 16-36-4-13)	All life prolonging procedures can be withheld. (§16-36-4-10)	"Life prolonging procedure" means any medical procedure, treatment, or intervention that (1) uses mechanical or other artificial means to sustain, restore, or support a vital function, and (2) serves to prolong the dying process. (§ 16-36-4-1)	Yes. (§ 16-36-4-10)	Artificial. (§ 16-36-4-1)
Iowa	Attending physician and another physician. (§ 144A.5)	Life-sustaining procedures. (§ 144A.3(1))	Life-sustaining procedures means any medical procedure, treatment, or intervention which utilizes mechanical or artificial means to sustain, restore, or supplant a vital function which only serves to prolong dying. This does not include the provision of nutrition or hydration except when required to be provided parenterally or through intubation or pain relief medications or procedures. (§144A.2(8))	May only be withheld if provided parenterally or through intubation. (§ 144A.2(8) flush paragraph after (b))	Artificial. (§ 144A.2(8))

Table 10.01, Part 2 Coverage of Living Will Statute

	Who Determines the Condition of the Patient?	What Sort of Medical Procedures Can Be Withheld or Withdrawn?	If "Life-Sustaining" Procedures or "Extraordinary Means," or Otherwise, Briefly What Does This Entail, If Defined?	Specifically, May Food and/or Hydration Be Withheld or Withdrawn?	Does the Statute Use "Artificially" or "Unnaturally" Prolonged in Describing When, e.g., Life-Sustaining Procedures or Extraordinary Means Can Be Withheld or Withdrawn?
Kansas	Attending physician and one other physician (as indicated in the statutory form). (§ 65-28,103(c))	Life-sustaining procedures. (§ 65-28,103(a))	Life-sustaining procedure means any medical procedure or intervention that would serve only to prolong the dying process and where death would occur whether or not such procedures are used. This does not include pain relief medications or procedures. (§ 65-28,102(c))	Not specified.	Artificially (as indicated in the statutory form). (§ 65-28,103(c))
Kentucky	In the case of a patient who is permanently unconscious or in a terminal condition, it is determined by the patient's attending physician and one other physician. (§ 311.621(13) & (17))	All life-prolonging treatment and artificially provided nutrition/hydration can be withheld (as indicated in the statutory form). (§ 311.625(1), 311.623(1)(a)-(b))	"Life-prolonging treatment" means any medical procedure which: (a) utilizes mechanical or other artificial means to sustain, prolong, restore, or supplant a spontaneous vital function; and (b) when administered to a patient would serve only to prolong the dying process. This does not include treatment or medication for pain. (§ 311.621(11))	Yes. (§§ 311.625(1), 311.623(1)(b))	Artificial. (§ 311.621(11))

Table 10.01, Part 2 Coverage of Living Will Statute

	Who Determines the Condition of the Patient?	What Sort of Medical Procedures Can Be Withheld or Withdrawn?	If "Life-Sustaining" Procedures or "Extraordinary Means," or Otherwise, Briefly What Does This Entail, If Defined?	Specifically, May Food and/or Hydration Be Withheld or Withdrawn?	Does the Statute Use "Artificially" or "Unnaturally" Prolonged in Describing When, e.g., Life-Sustaining Procedures or Extraordinary Means Can Be Withheld or Withdrawn?
Louisiana	Attending physician and one other physician (as indicated in the statutory form). (§ 40:1151.2(C)(1))	Life-sustaining procedures. (§ 40:1151.2(A)(1))	Life-sustaining procedure means any medical procedure or intervention, such as the invasive administration of nutrition and hydration and administration of cardiopulmonary resuscitation which would serve only to prolong the dying process where the person has been diagnosed with a terminal and irreversible condition. This does not include pain relief medications or procedures. (§ 40:1151.2(8))	Yes (specifically the invasive administration of nutrition and hydration). (§§ 40:1151.2(A)(1), 40:1151.2(C)(1), 40:1151.2(8))	Artificially (as indicated in the statutory form). (§ 40:1151.2(C)(1))
Maine	Unless otherwise specified in a written advance health-care directive, a determination that a condition exists that affects the directive must be made by the primary physician or by a court of competent jurisdiction. (18-A § 5-802(d))	All forms of healthcare may be withheld (as indicated in the statutory form), including artificial nutrition and hydration. (18-A § 5-804)	"Life-sustaining treatment" means any medical procedure that will only serve to prolong the process of dying. It may include artificially administrated nutrition and hydration. (18-A § 5-801(r))	Yes (as indicated in the statutory form). (18-A § 5-804)	"Artificial" used to describe hydration/nutrition. (18A § 5-804)

Table 10.01, Part 2 Coverage of Living Will Statute

	Who Determines the Condition of the Patient?	What Sort of Medical Procedures Can Be Withheld or Withdrawn?	If "Life-Sustaining" Procedures or "Extraordinary Means," or Otherwise, Briefly What Does This Entail, If Defined?	Specifically, May Food and/or Hydration Be Withheld or Withdrawn?	Does the Statute Use "Artificially" or "Unnaturally" Prolonged in Describing When, e.g., Life-Sustaining Procedures or Extraordinary Means Can Be Withheld or Withdrawn?
Maryland	Attending physician and one other physician, certify patient is incapable of making health care decisions unless otherwise provided in document. If patient is unconscious, only one doctor's determination is needed. (Health-Gen. §§ 5-606(a)(1)-(2), 5-602(e))	Healthcare and/or life-sustaining procedures. (Health-Gen. § 5-602(a)&(d)(1))	Life-sustaining procedures means any medical procedure, treatment, or intervention which uses mechanical means to sustain or supplant a vital function which affords the patient no reasonable expectation of recovery. These procedures include artificially administered hydration and nutrition and cardiopulmonary resuscitation. (Health-Gen. § 5-601(n))	Yes, if authorized, artificially administered hydration and nutrition can be withheld/ withdrawn. (Health-Gen. §§ 5-601(n)(2); 5-602(a)&(d)(1))	"Artificially" is used to describe hydration and nutrition. (Health-Gen. §§ 5-601(n)(2))
Massachusetts	Attending physician decides the patient lacks capacity for health care decisions. (201D § 6)	Not specified. But proxy may make decisions regarding life-sustaining treatments, unless limited. (201D § 5)	Not specified.	Implies that artificial oral feeding can be withheld/ withdrawn. (201D § 13)	Not specified.
Michigan	The patient's attending physician and another physician or licensed psychologist shall determine, upon examination of the patient, the patient's ability to participate in medical treatment decisions. (§700.5508(1))	Treatment without which the patient would be allowed to die. (§ 700.5507)	Not specified.	Not specified.	Not specified.

Table 10.01, Part 2 Coverage of Living Will Statute

	Who Determines the Condition of the Patient?	What Sort of Medical Procedures Can Be Withheld or Withdrawn?	If "Life-Sustaining" Procedures or "Extraordinary Means," or Otherwise, Briefly What Does This Entail, If Defined?	Specifically, May Food and/or Hydration Be Withheld or Withdrawn?	Does the Statute Use "Artificially" or "Unnaturally" Prolonged in Describing When, e.g., Life-Sustaining Procedures or Extraordinary Means Can Be Withheld or Withdrawn?
Minnesota	Attending physician. (§ 145B.13)	Life-sustaining procedures and artificially administered sustenance (as indicated in the statutory form). (§ 145B.04(e)(5) & (6))	Not defined. (§ 145B.04(e)(6))	Yes, if specifically authorized. (§ 145B.03 (Subd. 2)(b)(1))	Not specified. "Artificial" used to describe nutrition/ hydration. (§ 145B.03 (Subd. 2(b)(1)))
Mississippi	The primary physician unless otherwise specified. (§ 41-41-205(6))	Treatment that would prolong life. (§ 41-41-209, statutory form Pt.2 (6))	Not specified.	Yes. (§ 41-41-209, statutory form (7), § 41-41-203(h)(iii))	"Artificial" is used to describe nutrition/ hydration. (§§ 41-41-203(h)(iii), 41-41-209, statutory form Pt. 2 (7))

Table 10.01, Part 2 Coverage of Living Will Statute

	Who Determines the Condition of the Patient?	What Sort of Medical Procedures Can Be Withheld or Withdrawn?	If "Life-Sustaining" Procedures or "Extraordinary Means," or Otherwise, Briefly What Does This Entail, If Defined?	Specifically, May Food and/or Hydration Be Withheld or Withdrawn?	Does the Statute Use "Artificially" or "Unnaturally" Prolonged in Describing When, e.g., Life-Sustaining Procedures or Extraordinary Means Can Be Withheld or Withdrawn?
Missouri	Attending physician. (§ 459.010(6))	Death-prolonging procedures (as indicated in the statutory form). (§ 459.015(3.))	Death-prolonging procedures include any medical procedure or intervention that only serves to artificially prolong the dying process when death will occur within a short time whether or not such procedures are used. These procedures do not include pain-alleviating medications or procedures or any procedures used to provide nutrition or hydration. (§ 459.010(3))	No. (§§ 459.010(3), 459.015(3.))	Artificially. (§ 459.010(3))
Montana	The attending physician or attending advanced practice registered nurse. (§ 50-9-105(1)(b))	All life-sustaining treatment can be withheld. (§ 50-9-103(1))	"Life-sustaining treatment" means any medical procedure or intervention that, when administered to a patient, serves only to prolong the dying process. (§ 50-9-102(9))	Not specified	Not specified.
Nebraska	Attending physician. (§ 20-405(2) & (3))	Life-sustaining treatment. (§ 20-404(1))	Life-sustaining treatment: any medical procedure/ intervention that would prolong the dying process or keep the patient in a persistent vegetative state. (§ 20-403(5))	Not if necessary for comfort care or alleviation of pain. (§ 20-408(2))	Not specified

Table 10.01, Part 2 Coverage of Living Will Statute

	Who Determines the Condition of the Patient?	What Sort of Medical Procedures Can Be Withheld or Withdrawn?	If "Life-Sustaining" Procedures or "Extraordinary Means," or Otherwise, Briefly What Does This Entail, If Defined?	Specifically, May Food and/or Hydration Be Withheld or Withdrawn?	Does the Statute Use "Artificially" or "Unnaturally" Prolonged in Describing When, e.g.; Life-Sustaining Procedures or Extraordinary Means Can Be Withheld or Withdrawn?
Nevada	The attending physician. (§ 449.617)	All life-sustaining treatment can be withheld. (§ 449.600(1))	"Life-sustaining treatment" means a medical procedure/intervention that serves only to prolong the process of dying. (§ 449.570)	Yes. (§ 449.624(3))	"Artificial" used to describe hydration/nutrition. (§ 449.624(3))
New Hampshire	Attending physician or APRN, or any other physician or APRN aware of the principal's execution of an advance directive. (§ 137-J:7(I)(c)) (§§ 137-J:20, 137-J:2, 137-J:5(I), 137-J:10(I)	Life-sustaining treatment. (§§ 137-J:2(XIV), 137-J:20)	"Life-sustaining treatment" means any medical procedure or intervention which uses mechanical or other medically administered means to sustain, restore, or supplant a vital function which when applied to a qualified patient would serve, in the written opinion of the attending physician or ARNP, only to artificially prolong the moment of death and where the person is near death or permanently unconscious. These procedures do not include medication, natural ingestion of food or fluids, or the performance of any medical procedure deemed necessary to provide comfort to the patient or to alleviate pain. (§ 137-J:2(XIII))	Yes, but only if there is a clear expression of intent in the directive, the principal objects, or it would actually hasten death. (§§ 137-J:7(III), 137-J:10(II))	Artificially. (§ 137-J:20)

Table 10.01, Part 2 Coverage of Living Will Statute

	Who Determines the Condition of the Patient?	What Sort of Medical Procedures Can Be Withheld or Withdrawn?	If "Life-Sustaining" Procedures or "Extraordinary Means," or Otherwise, Briefly What Does This Entail, If Defined?	Specifically, May Food and/or Hydration Be Withheld or Withdrawn?	Does the Statute Use "Artificially" or "Unnaturally" Prolonged in Describing When, e.g., Life-Sustaining Procedures or Extraordinary Means Can Be Withheld or Withdrawn?
New Jersey	Capacity determined by attending physician and confirmed by one or more physicians. (§ 26:2H-60) For permanently unconscious and terminal condition decided by attending physician and one other physician. (§ 26:2H-67(a)(2) & (3)) For irreversible illness/condition and decision is based on determination that risks outweigh possible benefits: attending physician in consultation with either a reviewing body or a public agency set up for that purpose. (§ 26:2H-67(a)(4))	Any form of health care including life-sustaining treatment. (§ 26:2H-58(b))	Life-sustaining treatment: any medical device or procedure, artificially provided fluids and nutrition, drugs, surgery or therapy which uses mechanical/artificial means to sustain, restore, or supplant a vital bodily function and thereby increase the expected lifespan of a patient. (§ 26:2H-55)	Yes, specifically artificial. (§§ 26:2H-55, 26:2H-58(b))	Yes, artificial means to sustain, restore or supplant vital bodily functions and artificially provided fluids and nutrition. (§ 26:2H-55)
New Mexico	Primary physician and one other qualified health-care professional. (§ 24-7A-11(C)) (See also § 24-7A-4, statutory form Pt. 2.)	Life-sustaining treatment and artificial nutrition and hydration and other forms of healthcare. (§§ 24-7A-4, 24-7A-1(G)(3)(4))	Life-sustaining treatment means any medical treatment or procedure without which the individual is likely to die within a relatively short time, as determined to a reasonable degree of medical certainty by the primary physician. (§ 24-7A-1(K))	Yes, artificially provided nutrition and hydration can be withdrawn, if authorized (as indicated in the statutory form). (§ 24-7A-4, Pt. 2 also § 24-7A-1(G)(4))	Artificial is used to describe nutrition and hydration. (§§ 24-7A-1(G)(4), 24-7A-4 Pt. 2)

Table 10.01, Part 2 Coverage of Living Will Statute

	Who Determines the Condition of the Patient?	What Sort of Medical Procedures Can Be Withheld or Withdrawn?	If "Life-Sustaining" Procedures or "Extraordinary Means," or Otherwise, Briefly What Does This Entail, If Defined?	Specifically, May Food and/or Hydration Be Withheld or Withdrawn?	Does the Statute Use "Artificially" or "Unnaturally" Prolonged in Describing When, e.g., Life-Sustaining Procedures or Extraordinary Means Can Be Withheld or Withdrawn?
New York	Attending physician and another physician for a decision to withdraw or withhold life-sustaining treatment. (Pub. Health § 2983(1))	Any treatment (Pub. Health § 2982(1)), including life-sustaining treatment (as indicated in Pub. Health § 2983(1)). But if the principal's wishes regarding the administration of artificial nutrition and hydration are not reasonably known and cannot with reasonable diligence be ascertained, the agent shall not have the authority to make decisions regarding these measures. (Pub. Health § 2982(2))	Not specified.	Yes, but if the principal's wishes regarding the administration of artificial nutrition and hydration are not reasonably known and cannot with reasonable diligence be ascertained, the agent shall not have the authority to make decisions regarding these measures. (Pub. Health § 2982(2))	Not specified.
North Carolina	Attending physician and one other physician. (§ 90-321(b)(1) & (2))	Life-prolonging measures. (§ 90-321(b))	Medical procedure or intervention that the attending physician determines would only serve to postpone death artificially by sustaining, restoring, or supplanting a vital function. Does not include care necessary to provide comfort or alleviate pain. (§§ 90-321(a)(2a), 32A-16(4))	Yes (if specifically authorized by declarant). (§§ 90-321(b), 32A-16(4))	Artificially. (§§ 90-321(a)(2a), 32A-16(4))

Table 10.01, Part 2 Coverage of Living Will Statute

	Who Determines the Condition of the Patient?	What Sort of Medical Procedures Can Be Withheld or Withdrawn?	If "Life-Sustaining" Procedures or "Extraordinary Means," or Otherwise, Briefly What Does This Entail, If Defined?	Specifically, May Food and/or Hydration Be Withheld or Withdrawn?	Does the Statute Use "Artificially" or "Unnaturally" Prolonged in Describing When, e.g., Life-Sustaining Procedures or Extraordinary Means Can Be Withheld or Withdrawn?
North Dakota	Principal's attending physician determines capacity to make healthcare decisions. (§ 23-06.5-03(3))	All treatment may be with held or withdrawn. (§ 23-06.5-02(4))	Not specified.	Yes. (§§ 23-06.5-02(4), 23-06.5-09(6))	Not specified.
Ohio	Attending physician and one other physician. In the case of permanent unconsciousness, the consulting physician must in some way be specifically qualified to make the assessment. (§ 2133.03(A)(1)-(2); also 2133.08(A)(1)(a) & (2))	Life-sustaining treatment. (§ 2133.02(A)(1))	Life-sustaining treatment: any medical procedure, treatment or intervention that will principally serve to prolong the dying process. (§ 2133.01(Q))	Yes, but only if the patient is in a permanently unconscious state. There are a number of requirements that the patient must meet in order to qualify which are too extensive and detailed to list, but which include obtaining an order from the county probate court. (§ 2133.09)	Not specified.
Oklahoma	Attending physician and one other physician (as indicated in the statutory form). (63 § 3101.4(C); also 63 §§ 3101.3(10) & (12), 3101.7))	Life-sustaining treatment (as indicated in the statutory form). (63 § 3101.4(C)(I)(1); also 63 § 3101.4(A))	Not defined.	Yes, artificially provided nutrition and hydration can be withdrawn, if specifically, clearly and separately authorized by the declarant. (63 § 3101.4(B)) The patient, however, will be provided with oral consumption of food and water. (63 § 3101.8)	Uses "Artificially" to describe nutrition and hydration (as indicated in the statutory form). (63 § 3101.4(B) & (C))

Table 10.01, Part 2 Coverage of Living Will Statute

	Who Determines the Condition of the Patient?	What Sort of Medical Procedures Can Be Withheld or Withdrawn?	If "Life-Sustaining" Procedures or "Extraordinary Means," or Otherwise, Briefly What Does This Entail, If Defined?	Specifically, May Food and/or Hydration Be Withheld or Withdrawn?	Does the Statute Use "Artificially" or "Unnaturally" Prolonged in Describing When, e.g., Life-Sustaining Procedures or Extraordinary Means Can Be Withheld or Withdrawn?
Oregon	Attending doctor and another knowledgeable doctor (as indicated in the statutory form). (§ 127.531(2) Pt.	Tube feeding and life support procedures (as indicated in the statutory form). (§ 127.531(2) Pt. C)	Tube feeding: artificially administered nutrition and hydration. (§ 127.505(24)) Life-sustaining procedures: any medical procedure, pharmaceutical, device, intervention that maintains life by sustaining, supporting, or supplanting a vital function; does not include care for cleanliness and comfort. (§ 127.505(17)) "Artificially administered nutrition and hydration" is also defined. (§ 127.505(4))	Yes, if artificial. (§§ 127.531(2) Pt. C, 127.505(23))	"Artificially" used to describe nutrition and hydration. (§§ 127.505(4), 127.580)
Pennsylvania	Attending physician. (20 § 5443)	Life-sustaining treatment. (20 § 5442(a))	Life-sustaining treatment: any medical procedure / intervention that prolongs death or maintains one in a state of permanent unconsciousness; this includes nutrition and hydration if artificial or invasive so long as the declaration specifically states this. (20 § 5422)	Yes, if specifically stated in the declaration and is artificial / invasive. (20 § 5422; also as in statutory form 20 § 5471)	"Artificially" is used to describe hydration and nutrition. (20 § 5422)

Table 10.01, Part 2 Coverage of Living Will Statute

	Who Determines the Condition of the Patient?	What Sort of Medical Procedures Can Be Withheld or Withdrawn?	If "Life-Sustaining" Procedures or "Extraordinary Means," or Otherwise, Briefly What Does This Entail, If Defined?	Specifically, May Food and/or Hydration Be Withheld or Withdrawn?	Does the Statute Use "Artificially" or "Unnaturally" Prolonged in Describing When, e.g., Life-Sustaining Procedures or Extraordinary Means Can Be Withheld or Withdrawn?
Rhode Island	Attending physician. (§ 23-4.11-3(c)(2))	Life-sustaining procedures. (§ 23-4.11-3(a))	Life-sustaining procedure: any medical procedure/ intervention that will only prolong the dying process but does not include anything that will provide comfort/care or alleviate pain. (§ 23-4.11-2(9))	Yes, if feeding is artificial (as indicated in the statutory form). (§ 23-4.11-3(d))	Artificially is used to describe feeding. (§ 23-4.11-3(d))
South Carolina	Attending physician and one other physician who have personally examined the patient. (§ 44-77-30)	Life-sustaining procedures. (§ 44-77-30)	Life-sustaining procedures means any medical procedure or intervention, including nutrition and hydration administered by tubes (if indicated by declarant), which would only serve to prolong dying. This does not include medications or treatments for pain relief nor the normal consumption of food and water. (§ 44-77-20(2))	Yes, artificially provided nutrition and hydration can be withdrawn, if specifically authorized. (§ 44-77-20(2))	Artificial is used. (§ 44-77-50)

Table 10.01, Part 2 Coverage of Living Will Statute

	Who Determines the Condition of the Patient?	What Sort of Medical Procedures Can Be Withheld or Withdrawn?	If "Life-Sustaining" Procedures or "Extraordinary Means," or Otherwise, Briefly What Does This Entail, If Defined?	Specifically, May Food and/or Hydration Be Withheld or Withdrawn?	Does the Statute Use "Artificially" or "Unnaturally" Prolonged in Describing When, e.g., Life-Sustaining Procedures or Extraordinary Means Can Be Withheld or Withdrawn?
South Dakota	Attending physician. (§ 34-12D-5)	"Life-sustaining treatment." (§ 34-12D-2)	Life-sustaining treatment: any medical procedure / intervention that will only postpone death or maintain patient's permanently unconscious state. Does not include: care for comfort, hygiene, human dignity, or orally administered food / water / medication / medical procedures that are necessary for pain. (§ 34-12D-1(4))	Yes, as long as the declarant specifically states in the living will that he desires artificial food / hydration to be withdrawn. (§ 34-12D-2)	Artificially, in context of food / hydration. (§ 34-12D-2)
Tennessee	Attending physician (as indicated in statutory form). (§ 32-11-105)	Artificially provided nourishment and fluids (if specifically indicated) and all medical care (not including pain relief medication or procedures). (§ 32-11-105 (in statutory form of declaration) (§ 32-11-103(5))	Medical care: any procedure or treatment rendered by a physician or health care provider designed to diagnose, assess, or treat a disease, illness, or injury. This does not include the withholding of nourishment and fluids unless the living will clearly so indicates. (§ 32-11-103(5))	Yes, if specifically and clearly indicated. (§ § 32-11-105; 32-11-103(5))	Not specified. "Artificially" describes only nourishment and fluids. (§ 32-11-105 (in form of declaration))

Table 10.01, Part 2 Coverage of Living Will Statute

	Who Determines the Condition of the Patient?	What Sort of Medical Procedures Can Be Withheld or Withdrawn?	If "Life-Sustaining" Procedures or "Extraordinary Means," or Otherwise, Briefly What Does This Entail, If Defined?	Specifically, May Food and/or Hydration Be Withheld or Withdrawn?	Does the Statute Use "Artificially" or "Unnaturally" Prolonged in Describing When, e.g., Life-Sustaining Procedures or Extraordinary Means Can Be Withheld or Withdrawn?
Texas	The attending physician (as indicated in the statutory form). (Health & Safety §§ 166.033, 166.040)	Life-sustaining treatment (as indicated in the statutory form). (Health & Safety § 166.033)	Life-sustaining treatment means treatment that, based on reasonable medical judgment, sustains the life of a patient and without which the patient will die. This does not include pain relief medications or procedures. (Health & Safety § 166.002(10))	Yes (as indicated in statutory form). (Health & Safety (§ 166.033)	Artificially. (Health & Safety § 166.002(10))
Utah	A physician who has personally examined the individual must assess the individual's healthcare decision making capacity and decide he lacks the capacity before the agent is empowered to make decisions. (§75-2a-104(2)	All health care decisions. (Statutory form—§75-2a-117(2)(Part I)(D))	Not relevant.	Yes. As in statutory form, §75-2a-117(2) (Part I)(D)	Not relevant.
Vermont	Principal's clinician determines principal's capacity. (18 §9706(1))	Life-sustaining treatments (as indicated in the statutory form). (18 §9702)	"Life-sustaining treatment" means any medical intervention, including nutrition and hydration administered by medical means and antibiotics, which is intended to extend life and without which the principal is likely to die. (18 §9701(19))	Yes. (18 §9702(a)(7))	Not specified.

Table 10.01, Part 2 Coverage of Living Will Statute

Who Determines the Condition of the Patient?	What Sort of Medical Procedures Can Be Withheld or Withdrawn?	If "Life-Sustaining" Procedures or "Extraordinary Means," or Otherwise, Briefly What Does This Entail, If Defined?	Specifically, May Food and/or Hydration Be Withheld or Withdrawn?	Does the Statute Use "Artificially" or "Unnaturally" Prolonged in Describing When, e.g., Life-Sustaining Procedures or Extraordinary Means Can Be Withheld or Withdrawn?
Virginia Attending physician and a capacity reviewer, if certification by a capacity reviewer is required. The certification is required unless the patient is unconscious or experiencing a profound impairment of consciousness due to trauma, stroke, or other acute physiological condition. (§ 54.1-2983.2(B))	Life-prolonging procedures. (§ 54.1-2983)	Life-prolonging procedures means any medical procedure, treatment, or intervention which uses mechanical means to sustain or supplant a vital function which affords the patient no reasonable expectation of recovery and would only serve to prolong the dying process. These procedures include artificially administered hydration and nutrition, but not pain-relieving medicines (even excessive dosages) or procedures done to provide physical comfort to the patient. (§ 54.1-2982)	Yes, artificially administered hydration and nutrition can be withheld/withdrawn. (§§ 54.1-2984, 54.1-2982)	Artificially (as indicated in the statutory form). (§ 54.1-2984)

Table 10.01, Part 2 Coverage of Living Will Statute

	Who Determines the Condition of the Patient?	What Sort of Medical Procedures Can Be Withheld or Withdrawn?	If "Life-Sustaining" Procedures or "Extraordinary Means," or Otherwise, Briefly What Does This Entail, If Defined?	Specifically, May Food and/or Hydration Be Withheld or Withdrawn?	Does the Statute Use "Artificially" or "Unnaturally" Prolonged in Describing When, e.g., Life-Sustaining Procedures or Extraordinary Means Can Be Withheld or Withdrawn?
Washington	Attending physician if terminal illness; two physicians if permanent unconscious state (as indicated in the statutory form). (§ 70.122.030(1))	Life-sustaining treatment. (§ 70.122.030(1))	Life-sustaining treatment means any medical or surgical intervention that uses mechanical or other artificial means, including artificially provided nutrition and hydration, to sustain, restore, or replace a vital function that only serves to prolong dying. This does not include pain relief medications or pain relief surgical intervention. (§ 70.122.020(5))	Artificially provided nutrition and hydration can be withdrawn. (§§ 70.122.030(1), 70.122.020(5))	Artificially (as indicated in the statutory form). (§ 70.122.030(1) and definition, § 70-122.020(5))
West Virginia	One physician (as indicated in the statutory form). (§ 16-30-4(d))	Life-prolonging medical intervention (as indicated in the statutory form). (§ 16-30-4)	Life-prolonging intervention means any medical procedure or intervention that would serve only to artificially prolong the dying process or maintain the person in a persistent vegetative state including nutrition and hydration through a feeding tube. This does not include pain relief medications or procedures. (§ 16-30-3(m))	Yes. (§§ 16-30-4, 16-30-3(m))	Artificially. (§ 16-30-3(m))

Table 10.01, Part 2 Coverage of Living Will Statute

	Who Determines the Condition of the Patient?	What Sort of Medical Procedures Can Be Withheld or Withdrawn?	If "Life-Sustaining" Procedures or "Extraordinary Means," or Otherwise, Briefly What Does This Entail, If Defined?	Specifically, May Food and/or Hydration Be Withheld or Withdrawn?	Does the Statute Use "Artificially" or "Unnaturally" Prolonged in Describing When, e.g., Life-Sustaining Procedures or Extraordinary Means Can Be Withheld or Withdrawn?
Wisconsin	Attending physician and one other physician after both have examined the patient (as indicated in the statutory form). (§ 154.03(2))	Life-sustaining procedures or feeding tubes. (§ 154.03(1))	Life-sustaining procedures: any medical procedure/intervention that only prolongs death, but will not avert death. Does not include: medication or procedures to alleviate pain or nutrition/hydration. (§ 154.01(5))	Yes, unless it will cause pain/discomfort or is administered through some means other than a feeding tube (unless it is determined medically contraindicated). (§ 154.03(1))	Artificially (as indicated in the statutory form) (§ 154.03(2))
Wyoming	If not otherwise specified, the primary physician unless unavailable. The treating primary health care provider may make the decision if the primary physician is unavailable. (§ 35-22-403(e)) The physician merely determines if the patient is capable. If not, the surrogate is allowed to make health care decisions.	Any treatments or procedures, including withholding of artificial nutrition and hydration. (§ 35-22-402(a)(ix))	"Artificial nutrition and hydration" defined in § 35-22-402(a)(iii).	Yes. (§ 35-22-402(a)(ix))	No, since the surrogate can make all health care decisions. (§§ 35-22-402(a)(ix), 35-22-406)

[1] Only deals with health care proxies.

Table 10.02, Part 1 Formal Requirements

What Formalities Satisfy the Requirements?

	Must the Living Will Be in Writing?	Just Like a Will?	Signed by the Person?	Signed By Someone (1) In His Presence and (2) At His Direction?	Signed Otherwise? Specify.
Alabama	Yes. (§ 22-8A-4(c)(1))	Shall be "substantially" in the form of living will provided in § 22-8A-4(h). [Note: no specific requirement that living will be in exact form of a will.] Not specified. (§ 22-8A-4)	Yes. (§ 22-8A-4(c)(2))	(1) Yes. (§ 22-8A-4(c)(2))(2)Yes. (§ 22-8A-4(c)(2))	Not specified. (§ 22-8A-4(c)(2))
Alaska	No. Can be oral or written. However, durable power of attorney for health care must be written. (§ 13.52.010(a), (b))	No specific form required. Sample "Advance Health Care Directive" provided. (§ 13.52.300)	Not required but does satisfy requirements. (§ 13.52.010(a))	Not specified.	The signatures of two witnesses or, alternatively the signature of a notary at a place in state is required for durable power of attorney. (§ 13.52.010(b))
Arizona	Yes. (§§ 36-3201(9), 36-3261, 36-3262)	No. "Any writing" may be used to create a living will. (§ 36-3262)	Yes. (§§ 36-3261, 36-3262)	Not specified, but probably not in light of alternate procedures provided in §§ 36-3221, 36-3221(B), 36-3261(B).	Sample form of living will calls for declarant to place initials next to his/her preferred health care options. (§ 36-3262) If unable to sign, a notary of each of two witnesses must verify that the declarant indicated that the document expressed his wishes and that he intended to adopt the document. (§§ 36-3221(B), 36-3261(B))

Table 10.02, Part 1 Formal Requirements

	Must the Living Will Be in Writing?	What Formalities Satisfy the Requirements?				
		Just Like a Will?	Writing?	Signed by the Person?	Signed By Someone (1) In His Presence and (2) At His Direction?	Signed Otherwise? Specify.
Arkansas	Yes. (§§ 20-17-202(a), 20-17-201(2))	Not specified. (Sample declarations provided.) (§ 20-17-202(b))	Yes. (§§ 20-17-201(2), 20-17-202(a))	Yes, or by someone at his or her direction. (§ 20-17-202(a))	Presence is not specified but it must be at the declarant's direction if the declarant himself is not signing it. (§ 20-17-202(a))	Not specified.
California	No, individual instructions may be oral or written. (Probate § 4670)	Not specified. (Sample directive provided.) (Probate § 4701, Pt. 2)	Yes. (Probate §§ 4673, 4670)	Yes, if written. (Probate § 4673(a)(2))	(1) Yes. (Probate § 4673(a)(2)) Yes. (Probate § 4673(a)(2))	Not specified.
Colorado	Yes. (§ 15-18-103(8))	Not specified. (§ 15-18-104) (Sample declaration provided.) (§ 15-18-104(3))	Yes. (§ 15-18-103(8))	Yes. (§§ 15-18-104(3), 15-18-106(1))	(1) Yes. (§§ 15-18-105(1)) (2) Yes. (§§ 15-18-105(1))	If declarant physically unable to sign, person signing for declarant cannot be a physician, employee of the health care facility, an attending physician, person with a claim against declarant's estate, or any person who believes he is an heir or beneficiary. (§ 15-18-105(1))
Connecticut	Yes. (§§ 19a-570(8), 19a-575)	Not specified. (Sample of living will provided.) (§ 19a-575)	Yes. (§ 19a-575)	Yes. (§ 19a-575)	Not specified.	Not specified.
Delaware	Yes. (16 § 2503(b)(1)(a))	Not specified. (Optional form of advance health-care directive provided.) (16 § 2505)	Yes. (16 § 2503(b)(1)(b))	Yes. (16 § 2503(b)(1)(b))	(1) Yes. (16 § 2503(b)(1)(b)) (2) Yes. (16 § 2503(b)(1)(b))	Not specified.

Table 10.02, Part 1 Formal Requirements

	Must the Living Will Be in Writing?	Just Like a Will?	*What Formalities Satisfy the Requirements?*			
			Writing?	Signed by the Person?	Signed By Someone (1) In His Presence and (2) At His Direction?	Signed Otherwise? Specify.
District of Columbia	Yes. (§7-622(a)(1))	Not specified. (Sample declaration provided.) (§7-622(c))	Yes. (§7-622(a)(1))	Yes. (§7-622(a)(2))	(1) Yes. (§7-622(a)(2)) (2) Yes. (§7-622(a)(2))	If patient is in intermediate or skilled care facility at time of declaration, one witness of the two must be a patient advocate or ombudsman. (§7-623)
Florida	No. (§765.101(1))	Not specified. (Sample form of living will provided.) (§765.303)	Yes, or a witnessed oral statement but nothing further is provided regarding the oral statement. (§765.101(11)(a) &(b))	Yes, if written. (§765.302(1))	(1) Yes, but must be one of the witnesses if declarant physically unable. (§765.302(1))(2) Yes, but must be one of the witnesses if declarant physically unable. (§765.302(1))	Not specified.
Georgia	Yes. (§31-32-5(a))	No. Any declaration expressing declarant's intent and complying substantially with the requirements of §31-32-4 (recommended form) shall be honored, regardless of form. (§31-32-5(b))	Yes. (§31-32-5(a))	Yes. (§31-32-5(a))	(1) Yes. (§31-32-5(a)) (2) Yes. (§31-32-5(a))	Not specified.
Hawaii	No. Instruction may be oral or written. (§327E-3(a)) [Note: Hawaii formal requirements specifically relate only to execution of power of attorney for health care.]	Not specified. (Sample directive provided.) (§327E-16)	Yes. (§§327E-3(a) & (b), 327E-16)	Yes (as indicated in the statutory form). (§§327E-16, 327E-3(b))	Not specified.	Not specified.

Table 10.02, Part 1 Formal Requirements

What Formalities Satisfy the Requirements?

	Must the Living Will Be in Writing?	Just Like a Will?	Writing?	Signed by the Person?	Signed By Someone (1) In His Presence and (2) At His Direction?	Signed Otherwise? Specify.
Idaho	Presumably, since living will is described as a "document" containing elements included in the statutory form. (§ 39-4510)	Substantially the same form as provided form. (§ 39-4510)	Yes. (§ 39-4510)	Yes (as indicated in the statutory form). (§ 39-4510)	Not specified. (§ 39-4510)	Not specified. (§ 39-4510)
Illinois	Yes. (755 ILCS § 35/2(b))	Not specified. (Sample declaration provided.) (755 ILCS § 35/3(e))	Yes. (755 ILCS §§ 35/2(b), 35/3(a))	Yes. (755 ILCS § 35/3(b))	(1) Not specified. (2) Yes. (755 ILCS § 35/3(b))	Not specified.
Indiana	Yes. (§ 16-36-4-8(b)(2))	Not specified. (Form of living will declaration provided.) (§ 16-36-4-10)	Yes. (§ 16-36-4-8(b)(2))	Yes. (§ 16-36-4-8(b)(3))	(1) Yes. (§ 16-36-4-8(b)(3)) (2) Yes. (§ 16-36-4-8(b)(3))	Not specified.
Iowa	Yes. (§§ 144A.2(3), 144A.3)	Not specified. (Sample declaration provided.) (§ 144A.3(5))	Yes. (§§ 144A.2(3), 144A.3)	Yes. (§ 144A.3(2))	(1) Not specified. (§ 144A.3(2)) (2) Yes. (§ 144A.3(2))	Not specified. (§ 144A.3(2))
Kansas	Yes. (§ 65-28,103 (a)(1))	Not specified. (Sample declaration provided.) (§ 65-28,103(c))	Yes. (§ 65-28,103(a)(1))	Yes. (§ 65-28,103(a)(2))	(1)(a) Yes. (§ 65-28,103(2)) (2) Yes. (§ 65-28,103(a)(2))	Not specified. (§ 65-28,103(a))
Kentucky	Yes. (§ 311.625(2))	Not specified. (Sample form of living will directive provided.) (§ 311.625(1))	Yes. (§ 311.625(2))	Yes. (§ 311.625(2))	(1) In grantor's presence. (2) Not specified. (§ 311.625(2))	Not specified.

Table 10.02, Part 1 Formal Requirements

	Must the Living Will Be in Writing?	What Formalities Satisfy the Requirements?				
		Just Like a Will?	Writing?	Signed by the Person?	Signed By Someone (1) In His Presence and (2) At His Direction?	Signed Otherwise? Specify.
Louisiana	No. Not if made subsequent to diagnosis of terminal condition when declarant cannot make written declaration. (§ 40:1299.58.3(A)(1) (3) & (B)(4)) An oral or nonverbal declaration can be made in the presence of two witnesses any time subsequent to the diagnosis of a terminal and irreversible condition. (§ 40:1299.58.3(A)(3))	Not specified. (Sample declaration provided.) (§ 40:1299.58.3(C)(1))	Yes. (§ 40:1299.58.3(A)(1))	Yes, required if written. (§ 40:1299.58.3(A)(2))	Not specified.	If patient cannot communicate, any person previously designated in a written instrument signed by the patient in the presence of at least two witnesses has authority to make a declaration for patient. (§ 40:1299.58.5(A)(2)(b))
Maine	No. The directive can be oral, but an oral directive is only valid if made to a health care provider or to a surrogate. (18-A § 5-802(a))	Not specified. (Sample directive provided.) (18-A § 5-804)	Yes. (18-A § 5-802(a))	Yes (as indicated in the statutory form). (18-A § 5-804)	Not specified.	Not specified.
Maryland	No, can be written or oral or electronic. (Health-Gen. § 5-602(a) & (d))	No. Different forms may be used. (Health-Gen. § 5-603) (Sample directive provided.) (Id.)	Yes. (Health-Gen. § 5-602(a))	Yes (if directive is written or electronic). (Health-Gen. § 5-602(c))	(1) Not specified. (2) Yes. (Health-Gen. § 5-602(c))	Documentation of oral directive shall be dated and signed by attending physician and a witness. (Health-Gen. § 5-602(d)(2))
Massachusetts[1]	Yes. (201D § 2)	Not specified. (Sample directive provided.) (Id.)	Yes. (201D § 2)	Yes. (201D § 2)	(1) Not specified. (2) Yes. (201D § 2)	In the presence of and signed by two adult witnesses. (§ 201D § 2)

Table 10.02, Part 1 Formal Requirements

What Formalities Satisfy the Requirements?

	Must the Living Will Be in Writing?	Just Like a Will?	Writing?	Signed by the Person?	Signed By Someone (1) In His Presence and (2) At His Direction?	Signed Otherwise? Specify.
Michigan	Yes. (§§ 700.5501, 700.5506(3))	Not specified. But see § 700.5507 for certain requirements of the Patient Advocate Designation. Note that a freestanding living will is not authorized by Michigan statute.	Yes. (§ 700.5506(3))	Yes. (§ 700.5506(3))	Not specified.	In the presence of and signed by 2 witnesses. (§ 700.5506(4))
Minnesota	Yes. (§§ 145B.03, 145B.02)	Not specified. (Sample living will provided.) (§ 145B.04)	Yes. (§§ 145B.03, 145B.02)	Yes. (§ 145B.03 (Subd. 2)(a))	(1) Not specified. (2) Yes, a witness can sign at the declarant's direction. (§ 145B.03 (Subd. 2)(c))	Must be signed by declarant and two witnesses or a notary public. (§ 145B.03 (Subd. 2)(a)) If declarant is physically unable to sign, one of the witnesses shall sign at declarant's direction. (§ 145B.03 (Subd. 2)(c))
Mississippi	No. May be oral or written. (§ 41-41-205(1))	No. Statutory form may be modified partially or in full. (§ 41-41-209)	Yes. (§§ 41-41-205(1), 41-41-205(2))	Yes. (§ 41-41-205(2))	Not specified; seemingly not, since all references are to the individual. (§§ 41-41-205, 41-41-209)	Not specified.
Missouri	Yes. (§ 459.015(1)(1))	Not specified. (Sample declaration provided.) (§ 459.015(3))	Yes. (§ 459.015(1)(1))	Yes. (§ 459.015(1)(2))	(1) Yes. (§ 459.015(1)(2)) (2) Yes. (§ 459.015(1)(2))	If not wholly in declarant's handwriting, must be signed in presence of two or more witnesses. (§ 459.015(1)(4))
Montana	Yes. (§ 50-9-103(1))	Not specified. (Sample declaration provided.) (§ 50-9-103(2))	Yes. (§ 50-9-103(1))	Yes. (§ 50-9-103(1))	(1) Not specified. (2) Yes. (§ 50-9-103(1))	Not specified.

Table 10.02, Part 1 Formal Requirements

	What Formalities Satisfy the Requirements?					
	Must the Living Will Be in Writing?	Just Like a Will?	Writing?	Signed by the Person?	Signed By Someone (1) In His Presence and (2) At His Direction?	Signed Otherwise? Specify.
Nebraska	Yes. (§§ 20-403(3), 20-404(1))	Not specified. (Sample declaration provided.) (§ 20-404(2))	Yes. (§§ 20-403(3), 20-404(1))	Yes. (§ 20-404(1))	(1) Not specified. (2) Yes. (§ 20-404(1))	Not specified.
Nevada	Yes. (§ 449.600(1))	Not specified. (Sample declaration provided.) (§ 449.610)	Yes. (§ 449.600(1))	Yes. (§ 449.600(1))	(1) Not specified. (2) Yes. (§ 449.600(1))	Not specified.
New Hampshire	Yes. (§§ 137-J:2(XIV), 137-J:14(I)(a))	Not specified. (Statutory form provided; § 137-J:20)	Yes. (§§ 137-J:14(I)(a))	Yes. (as indicated in the statutory form). (§ 137-J:14(I))	(1) Yes. (2) Yes. (§ 137-J:14(II))	Not specified.
New Jersey	May be supplemented by a video or audio tape recording. (§ 26:2H-56)	Not specified.	Yes. (§ 26:2H-55)	Yes. (§ 26:2H-56)	(1) Not specified. (2) Yes. (§ 26:2H-56)	Not specified.
New Mexico	No, it can be oral or written. If oral, directive must be made by personally informing a health care provider. (§ 24-7A-2(A))	No. Statutory form is optional and may be modified partially or in full. (§ 24-7A-4)	Yes. (§ 24-7A-2(A))	Yes (as indicated in statutory form). (§ 24-7A-4)	Not specified.	Not specified.
New York[2]	Yes. (Pub. Health § 2981(2))	Not specified. (Statutory form provided. See Pub. Health § 2981(5))	Yes. (Pub. Health § 2981(2))	Yes. (Pub. Health § 2981(2))	(1) Yes. (2) Yes. (Pub. Health § 2981(2))	Not specified.
North Carolina	Yes. (§ 90-321(a)(1a))	Not specified. (Sample declaration provided.) (§ 90-321(d))	Yes. (§ 90-321(a)(1a))	Yes. (§ 90-321(a)(1a))	Not specified.	Must also be "proved" before court clerk or notary who certified substantially as in form set forth in § 90-321(d1). See § 90-321(c)(4).

Table 10.02, Part 1 Formal Requirements

	Must the Living Will Be in Writing?	Just Like a Will?	What Formalities Satisfy the Requirements?			
			Writing?	Signed by the Person?	Signed By Someone (1) In His Presence and (2) At His Direction?	Signed Otherwise? Specify.
North Dakota	Yes. (§ 23-06.5-05(1)(a))	Not specified. (§ 23-06.5-05.1) (Sample declaration provided.) (§ 23.06.5-16)	Yes. (§ 23-06.5-05(1)(a))	Yes. (§ 23-06.5-05(1)(d))	(1) Yes. (§ 23-06.5-05(2)) (2) Yes. (§ 23-06.5-05(2))	Not specified.
Ohio	Yes. (§§ 2133.02(A)(1), 2133.01(F))	Not specified.	Yes. (§§ 2133.02(A)(1), 2133.01(F))	Yes. (§ 2133.02(A)(1))	(1) Not specified. (2) Yes. (§ 2133.02(A)(1))	Statute requires that declaration be signed "at the end." (§ 2133.02(A)(1))
Oklahoma	Yes. (63 §§ 3101.3(1), 3101.4(C))	Not specified. (Sample directive provided.) (63 § 3101.4(C))	Yes. (63 § 3101.4(C))	Yes. (63 § 3101.4(A))	Not specified.	Not specified.
Oregon	Yes. (§ 127.531)	No. Must be in statutory form. (§ 127.531(1))	Yes. (§ 127.531)	Yes. (§ 127.515(4))	Not specified.	Not specified.
Pennsylvania	Yes. (20 §§ 5442(a), 5447)	Not specified. (Sample declaration provided.) (20 § 5471)	Yes. (20 § 5447)	Yes. (20 § 5442(b)(1))	(1) Not specified. (2) Yes. (20 § 5442(b)(1))	Not specified.
Rhode Island	Yes. (§§ 23-4.11-2(4), 23-4.11-3(a))	Not specified. (Sample declaration provided.) (§ 23-4.11-3(d))	Yes. (§§ 23-4.11-2(4), 23-4.11-3(a))	Yes. (§ 23-4.11-3(a))	(1) Not specified. (2) Yes. (§ 23-4.11-3(a))	Not specified.
South Carolina	Yes. (§ 44-77-50)	Not specified. (Sample declaration provided.) (§ 44-77-50)	Yes. (§ 44-77-50)	Yes. (§ 44-77-40(2))	Not specified.	Must be signed in the presence of an officer authorized to administer oaths under the laws of the state where the signing occurs and in the presence of two witnesses. (§ 44-77-40(2))
South Dakota	Yes. (§§ 34-12D-2, 34-12D-1(2))	Not specified. (Sample living will provided.) (§ 34-12D-3)	Yes. (§§ 34-12D-1(2), 34-12D-2)	Yes. (§ 34-12D-2)	(1) Not specified. (2) Yes. (§ 34-12D-2)	Not specified.

Table 10.02, Part 1 Formal Requirements

What Formalities Satisfy the Requirements?

	Must the Living Will Be in Writing?	Just Like a Will?	Writing?	Signed by the Person?	Signed By Someone (1) In His Presence and (2) At His Direction?	Signed Otherwise? Specify.
Tennessee	Yes. (§§ 32-11-103(4), 32-11-105)	Not specified. (Sample living will provided.) (§ 32-11-105)	Yes. (§§ 32-11-103(4), 32-11-105)	Yes (can also be "a mark" by a declarant unable to fully sign). (§§ 32-11-104(a), 32-11-110(f), 1-3-105)	Not specified.	Not specified.
Texas	No, in addition to a written directive, the statute also allows a nonwritten directive to be made. (Health & Safety §§ 166.032(a), 166.034(a))	Not specified. (Sample written directive provided.) (Health & Safety § 166.033)	Yes. (Health & Safety § 166.032(a))	Yes (for written directives). (Health & Safety § 166.032(b))	Not specified.	The statute also allows for a nonwritten directive which must be issued in the presence of the attending physician and two witnesses. (Health & Safety § 166.034)
Utah	A health care directive may be oral or in writing. (§ 75-2a-107(1)(b))	Not specified. (§ 75-2a-107(1)(b)) Optional form provided. (§ 75-2a-117)	Not required. (§ 75-2a-107(1)(b))	Not specified. (§ 75-2a-107(1)(b)) But, implied by optional form. (§ 75-2a-117)	Not specified. But, implied in § 75-2a-107(1)(c)(i), which states that a witness may not be "the person who signed the directive on behalf of the declarant."	Regardless if oral or in writing, there must be one disinterested witness. (§ 75-2a-107(1)(c))
Vermont	Yes. (18 § 9703(b)).	Not specified.	Yes. (18 § 9703)	Yes. (18 § 9703(b))	(1) Yes. (18 § 9703(b)) (2) Yes. (18 § 9703(b))	Not specified.
Virginia	No, it can be written or oral. (§ 54.1-2983)	Not specified. (Sample directive provided.) (§ 54.1-2984)	Yes. (§ 54.1-2983)	Yes (if directive is written). (§ 54.1-2983)	Not specified.	If oral, it must be in front of the attending doctor and two witnesses. (§ 54.1-2983)
Washington	Yes. (§§ 70.122.020(3), 70.122.030(1))	Not specified. (Sample directive provided.) (§ 70.122.030(1))	Yes. (§ 70.122.030(1))	Yes. (§ 70.122.030(1))	Not specified.	Not specified.

Table 10.02, Part 1 Formal Requirements

	Must the Living Will Be in Writing?	What Formalities Satisfy the Requirements?				
		Just Like a Will?	Writing?	Signed by the Person?	Signed By Someone (1) In His Presence and (2) At His Direction?	Signed Otherwise? Specify.
West Virginia	Yes. (§ 16-30-4(a)(1))	Not specified. (Sample living will provided.) (§ 16-30-4(g))	Yes. (§ 16-30-4(a)(1))	Yes. (§ 16-30-4(a)(4))	(1) Yes. (§ 16-30-4(a)(2)) (2) Yes. (§ 16-30-4(a)(2))	Not specified.
Wisconsin	Yes. (§ § 154.02(1), 154.03(1))	Not specified. (Sample declaration provided.) (§ 154.03(2))	Yes. (§ § 154.02(1), 154.03(1))	Yes. (§ 154.03(1))	(1) Yes. (§ 154.03(1)) (2) Yes. (§ 154.03(1))	Declarant and witnesses must sign at the same time (as indicated in the statutory form). (§ 154.03(2))
Wyoming	An individual instruction may be oral or written (§ 35-22-403(a)). A power of attorney for health care must be written. (§ 35-22-403(b))	Not specified. (§ 35-22-403)	A power of attorney for health care must be in writing (§ 35-22-403(b)), but a writing is not required for an individual instruction by an adult or emancipated minor regarding a health care decision for the individual. (§ § 35-22-402(a)(xi), 35-22-403(a))	Yes, a power of attorney for health care must be signed by the principal. (§ 35-22-403(b))	(1) Yes. (§ 35-22-403(b)) (2) Yes. (§ 35-22-403(b))	Not specified.

[1] Only deals with health care proxies.
[2] Only deals with health care proxies.

Table 10.02, Part 2 Formal Requirements

What Formalities Satisfy the Requirements?

	Dated?	Number of Witnesses?	Age of Witnesses?	Other Witness Requirements? E.g., Is a Witness Statement Required?
Alabama	Yes. (§ 22-8A-4(c)(3))	At least two witnesses. (§ 22-8A-4(c)(4))	At least 19 years old. (§ 22-8A-4(c)(4))	Witnesses must attest (as indicated in the statement in the statutory form) to statement on the statutory form. (§ 22-8A-4(h))
Alaska	Yes, required for durable power for healthcare attorney. (§ 13.52.010(b))	For durable power of attorney, two qualified adult witnesses or a notary required. (Optional form, § § 13.52.300(15)(A) & 13.52.010(b)(1))	For durable power of attorney, adult. (optional form § 13.52.300)	Not specified. (§§ 13.52.300 & 13.52.010)
Arizona	Yes. (§§ 36-3261(B), 36-3221	One witness or notary. (§§ 36-3261(B), 36-3221)	Adult. (§§ 36-3221(A)(3), 36-3261(B))	Statement affirming witness was present at signing and that declarant was of sound mind and free from duress. (§ 36-3221(A)(3), 36-3261(B))
Arkansas	Yes (as indicated in the statutory form). (§ 20-17-202(b))	Two. (§ 20-17-202(a))	Not specified.	Statement that declarant voluntarily signed in the witness' presence (as indicated in the statutory form). (§ 20-17-202(b))
California	Yes. (Probate § 4673(a)(1))	Two, if not acknowledged before notary. (Probate § 4673(a)(3))	Adult. (Probate § 4674(a))	Witnesses declaration required. (Probate § 4674(d)) If declarant is a patient in a skilled nursing facility, a patient advocate or ombudsman must sign as a witness. (Probate § 4675(a))
Colorado	Not specified. (§ 15-18-104)	Two. (§ 15-18-106(1))	Not specified. (§ 15-18-106)	Not specified (§ 15-18-104(3))

Table 10.02, Part 2 Formal Requirements

What Formalities Satisfy the Requirements?

	Dated?	Number of Witnesses?	Age of Witnesses?	Other Witness Requirements? E.g., Is a Witness Statement Required?
Connecticut	Yes. (§ 19a-575)	Two. (§ 19a-575)	Not specified.	Declarant must sign in presence of witnesses. They must declare that declarant appeared to be of age, sound mind, able to understand the consequences, and under no improper influence (as indicated in the statutory form). (§ 19a-575)
Delaware	Yes. (16 § 2503(b)(1)(c))	Two. (16 § 2503(b)(1)(d))	Witnesses must be adults. (16 § 2503(b)(1)(d))	Witness statement is required. (16 § 2503(b)(2))
District of Columbia	Yes. (§ 7-622(a)(3))	Two. (§ 7-622(a)(4))	Witnesses must be 18 years of age. (§ 7-622(a)(4))	Witness statement included on statutory form. (§ 7-622(c))
Florida	Yes, if written, (as indicated in the statutory form). (§ 765.303(1))	Two. (§ 765.302(1))	Not specified.	At least one witness cannot be a spouse or blood relative of declarant. (§ 765.302(1))
Georgia	Yes (as indicated in the statutory form). (§ 31-32-4)	Two. (§ 31-32-5(c)(1))	18 or older. (§ 31-32-5(c)(1))	Witnesses must be competent, meaning of sound mind. (§§ 31-32-5(c)(1)) If the living will is executed by a patient in a hospital or skilled nursing facility, a qualified health care worker must also witness the signing. (§ 31-32-4) Witness statement required, as indicated on statutory form. (§ 31-32-4)
Hawaii	Yes (as indicated in the statutory form). (§ 327E-16)	Must be signed in the presence of two witnesses or acknowledged before notary (as indicated in the statutory form). (§ 327E-3(b)(1))	Witnesses must be adults (as indicated in the statutory form). (§ 327E-16)	Witness statement required (as indicated in the statutory form). (§ 327E-16)
Idaho	Yes (as indicated in the statutory form). (§ 39-4510)	Not specified. (§ 39-4510)	Not specified. (§ 39-4510)	Not specified. (§ 39-4510)

Table 10.02, Part 2 Formal Requirements

What Formalities Satisfy the Requirements?

	Dated?	Number of Witnesses?	Age of Witnesses?	Other Witness Requirements? E.g., Is a Witness Statement Required?
Illinois	Yes (as indicated in the statutory form). (755 ILCS §35/3(e))	Two. (755 ILCS §35/3(b))	18 or older. (755 ILCS §35/3(b))	Witness statement required (as indicated in statutory form). (755 ILCS §35/3(e))
Indiana	Yes. (§16-36-4-8(b)(4))	Two. (§16-36-4-8(b)(5))	18 or older. (§16-36-4-8(b)(5))	Witness statement required in the statutory form. (§16-36-4-10) Witness must be competent. (§16-36-4-8(b)(5))
Iowa	Yes. (§144A.3(2))	Two (if not acknowledged before notary). (§144A.3(2))	At least 18 years old. (§144A.3(2)(a)(3))	At least one cannot be a relative by blood, marriage, or adoption. (§144A.3 (2)(a))
Kansas	Yes. (§65-28,103(a)(3))	Two (if not acknowledged before notary). (§65-28,103(a)(4))	At least 18 years old. (§65-28,103(a)(4)(A))	Witness statement required (as indicated in statutory form). (§65-28,103(c))
Kentucky	Yes. (§311.625(2))	The directive must be signed before two witnesses or acknowledged before a notary public. (§311.625(2))	The witnesses must be 18 or over. (§§311.625(2), 311.621(1))	Not specified.
Louisiana	Yes (as indicated on the statutory form). (§40:1151.2(C)(1))	Two. (§40:1151.2(A)(2))	Adult. (§40:1151.2(16))	Not specified.
Maine	Yes (as indicated in the statutory form). (18-A §5-804)	Two witnesses required. (18-A §5-802(b), also see statutory form explanation part in 18-A §5-804)	Not specified.	Not specified.
Maryland	Yes (if directive is written). (Health-Gen. §5-602(c)) If oral, the recording of the declaration must be dated by the witness and physician. (§5-602(d)(2))	Two witnesses (if directive is written). (Health-Gen. §5-602(c)) If oral, the declaration must be witnessed by the attending physician and one witness. (§5-602(d)(2))	18 years of age. (Health-Gen. §§5-602(c)(2), 5-601(f))	Not specified.
Massachusetts[1]	Not specified.	Two. (201D §2)	Adult. (201D §2)	Witnesses must sign that they believe the declarant to be 18, of sound mind, and not under constraint or undue influence. (201D §2)

Table 10.02, Part 2 Formal Requirements

What Formalities Satisfy the Requirements?

	Dated?	Number of Witnesses?	Age of Witnesses?	Other Witness Requirements? E.g., Is a Witness Statement Required?
Michigan	Yes. (§ 700.5506(3))	Two. (§ 700.5506(4))	Not specified.	Must sign only if the patient appears to be of sound mind, signing voluntarily, and not under duress, fraud or undue influence. (§ 700.5506(4))
Minnesota	Yes (as indicated in the statutory form). (§ 145B.04)	Two witnesses (or a notary public). (§ 145B.03(Subd. 2)(a))	Adult (as indicated in the statutory form). (§ 145B.04)	Witness statement required. (§ 145B.03(Subd.2)(d))
Mississippi	Yes. (§ 41-41-205(2))	At least two witnesses (§ 41-41-205(2)(a)) or a notary. (§ 41-41-205(2)(b))	Adult (as indicated in the statutory form (13)). (§ 41-41-209)	Witnesses must declare under penalty of perjury the statement set forth in the statutory provisions. (§ 41-41-205(2)(a)
Missouri	Yes. (§ 459.015(1)(3))	At least two (only if the declaration is not wholly in the declarant's handwriting). (§ 459.015(1)(4))	At least 18 years old. (§ 459.015(1)(4))	Must sign statement (as indicated in statutory form). (§ 459.015(3))
Montana	Yes (as indicated in the statutory form). (§ 50-9-103(2))	A declaration must be signed before two witnesses. (§ 50-9-103(1))	Not specified.	Not specified.
Nebraska	Yes (as indicated in the statutory form). (§ 20-404(2))	Two or a notary. (§ 20-404(1))	Adult for witness and not specified for notary. (§ 20-404(1)) Adult defined as: 19 or older or a person who is/ has been married. (§ 20-403(1))	Witnesses sign under statement that "declarant signed voluntarily." (As in statutory form) (§ 20-404(2))
Nevada	Yes (as indicated in the statutory form). (§ 449.610)	Two witnesses must attest the declaration. (§ 449.600(1))	Not specified.	Not specified.
New Hampshire	Not specified. (§ 137-J:14(I)) However, the advance directive must be "in substantially" the form specified, which includes a date. (§ 137-J:20)	At least two witnesses. (§ 137-J:14(I)(a))	Witnesses must be 18 years or older. (§ 137-J:2(XXIII))	Witness must be competent. (§ 137-J:2(XIII))

Table 10.02, Part 2 Formal Requirements

What Formalities Satisfy the Requirements?

	Dated?	Number of Witnesses?	Age of Witnesses?	Other Witness Requirements? E.g., Is a Witness Statement Required?
New Jersey	Yes. (§ 26:2H-56)	Two or acknowledged by declarant before a notary, attorney, or another who can administer oaths. (§ 26:2H-56)	Adult, defined as 18 or older. (§§ 26:2H-55, 26:2H-56)	Must attest the declarant to be of sound mind and free of duress/ undue influence. (§ 26:2H-56)
New Mexico	Yes (as indicated in the statutory form). (§ 24-7A-4)	Not specified. Statutory form provides optional spot for two witnesses. (§ 24-7A-4)	Not specified.	Not specified.
New York	Yes. (Pub. Health § 2981(2))	Two. (Pub. Health § 2981(2))	Adult (18 years and older), or is the parent of a child, or has married. (Pub. Health §§ 2981(2), 2980(1))	Witness statement is required as to principal's state at signature/execution. (Pub. Health § 2981(2))
North Carolina	Yes. (§ 90-321(a)(1)(a))	Two. (§ 90-321(c)(3))	Not specified.	Witness statement required. (§ 90-321(c)(3))
North Dakota	Yes. (§ 23-06.5-05(1)(b))	A directive must be notarized or signed before two witnesses. (§ 23-06.5-17)	Adult (At least 18 years old). (§ 23-06.5-17)	Not specified.
Ohio	Yes. (§ 2133.02(A)(1))	Two, or acknowledged before a notary public. (§§ 2133.02(B)(1) & (2))	Adults defined as 18 or older. (§§ 2133.02(B)(1), 2133.01(A))	Requires witness statements that they believe the declarant to be of sound mind and not under duress, fraud, or undue influence. (§ 2133.02(B))
Oklahoma	Not specified (but implied by the statutory form). (63 § 3101.4(C))	Two witnesses. (63 § 3101.4(A))	At least 18 years old. (63 § 3101.4(A))	No statement required. (63 § 3101.4(A))

Table 10.02, Part 2 Formal Requirements

What Formalities Satisfy the Requirements?

	Dated?	Number of Witnesses?	Age of Witnesses?	Other Witness Requirements? E.g., Is a Witness Statement Required?
Oregon	Yes. (§ 127.515(4))	Two. (§ 127.515(4))	Adult, defined as an individual 18 or older, who has been adjudicated as an emancipated minor, or who is married. (§ § 127.515(4), 127.505(1))	Witness statement is required. (§ 127.515(4)(b)) Witness must declare that the declarant is personally known to them or shown proof of identification; signed or acknowledged the directive in their presence; appears to be of sound mind and is not under duress, fraud, or undue influences; that neither witness is appointed the declarant's health care representative; and that neither witness is the declarant's attending physician (as indicated in the statutory form). (§ 127.531(2)(Pt.D))
Pennsylvania	Yes (as indicated in the statutory form). (20 § 5442(b)(1))	Two. (20 § 5442(b)(2))	18 or older. (20 § 5442(b)(2))	Not specified.
Rhode Island	Yes (as indicated in the statutory form). (§ 23-4.11-3(d))	Two. (§ 23-4.11-3(a))	Not specified.	Witness must sign that they know the declarant and the declarant signed the declaration voluntarily in their presence (as indicated in the statutory form). (§ 23-4.11-3(d))

Table 10.02, Part 2 Formal Requirements

What Formalities Satisfy the Requirements?

	Dated?	Number of Witnesses?	Age of Witnesses?	Other Witness Requirements? E.g., Is a Witness Statement Required?
South Carolina	Yes. (§ 44-77-40(2))	Two witnesses (one of whom may be the required officer authorized to administer oaths). (§ 44-77-40(2))	Not specified.	Witnesses must subscribe to affidavit, which must be sworn to by at least one witness. (§ 44-77-40(2) & (4)) If declarant is patient in hospital or resident of nursing home, one of the two witnesses must be an ombudsman, with the same qualities required of witnesses. (§ 44-77-40(3))
South Dakota	Yes (as indicated in the statutory form). (§ 34-12D-3)	Two. (§ 34-12D-2)	Adult. (§ 34-12D-2)	Witnesses sign under statement that declarant voluntarily signed in their presence (as indicated in the statutory form). (§ 34-12D-3)
Tennessee	Yes (as indicated in the statutory form). (§ 32-11-105)	Two witnesses. (§ 32-11-104(a))	Adult. (§ 32-11-104(a))	Witness statement required. (§ 32-11-104(a)) Witness must be competent. (§§ 32-11-104(a), 32-11-105)
Texas	Yes (for written directives) (as indicated in the statutory form). (Health & Safety § 166.033)	Two witnesses (for both oral and written directives). (Health & Safety § 166.032(b))	Adult. (Health & Safety §§ 166.032(b), 166.003(1))	Not specified.
Utah	Not specified but implied on optional form. (§ 75-2a-117 Optional Form Pt. IV)	One. (§ 75-2a-117 Optional Form Pt. IV)	Not specified but optional form indicates 18 years or older. (§ 75-2a-117 Optional Form Pt. IV)	If oral declaration made, witness must "state the circumstances under which the directive was made." (§§ 75-2a-107(1)(d), 75-2a-117 Optional Form Pt. IV) Witness must be "disinterested." (§ 75-2a-107(1)(c))
Vermont	Yes (as indicated in the included statutory form). (18 § 9703(b))	Two or more witnesses. (18 § 9703(b))	At least 18 years old. (18 § 9703(b))	Witness statement required. (18 § 9703(b))

Table 10.02, Part 2 Formal Requirements

	What Formalities Satisfy the Requirements?			
	Dated?	*Number of Witnesses?*	*Age of Witnesses?*	*Other Witness Requirements? E.g., Is a Witness Statement Required?*
Virginia	Yes (as indicated in the statutory form if written directive). (§ 54.1-2984)	Two witnesses. (§ 54.1-2983)	Over the age of 18. (§ 54.1-2982)	Witness statement required (as indicated in statutory form). (§ 54.1-2984)
Washington	Yes (as indicated in the statutory form). (§ 70.122.030(1))	Two witnesses. (§ 70.122.030(1))	Not specified. (§ 70.122.030(1))	Witnesses must attest (as indicated in the statement in the statutory form) that the declarant is known to them and is capable of making health care decisions. (§ 70.122.030(1))
West Virginia	Yes. (§ 16-30-4(a)(3))	At least two witnesses. (§ 16-30-4(a)(4))	At least 18 years old. (§ 16-30-4(a)(4))	Witnesses must attest (as indicated in the statement in the statutory form) to statements on the statutory form. (§ 16-30-4(a)(5))
Wisconsin	Yes (as indicated in the statutory form). (§ 154.03(2))	Two. (§ 154.03(1))	Adult (as indicated in the statutory form). (§ 154.03(2))	Witness statement required (as indicated in the statutory form). (§ 154.03(2))
Wyoming	Not specified.	If a power of attorney for health care, notary or at least two witnesses. (§ 35-22-403(b))	Not specified.	No. (§ 35-22-403(b))

---

[1] Only deals with health care proxies.

Table 10.02, Part 3 Formal Requirements

What Formalities Satisfy the Requirements?

	What are Impermissible Conflicts of Witnesses Specified in the Statute?	Must Witnesses Affirm or Just Declare/Sign on the Basis of Knowledge and Belief?	Must Witnesses Sign the Document?	Must Attorney or Drafter Sign?	Capacity of Declarant: What Standard Is Used? E.g., Sound Mind, Sane?	Capacity of Declarant: Age Requirement?	Capacity of Declarant: Signed Before Notary?
Alabama	Witnesses cannot be related to the declarant by blood, adoption or marriage, entitled to any part of his/her estate, financially responsible for the declarant's medical care, the person who signed the advance directive, or appointed as the health care proxy therein. (§ 22-8A-4(c)(4))	Sign on knowledge/ belief (as indicated in the statutory form). (§ 22-8A-4(h))	Statutory form requires witness signatures. (§ 22-8A-4(c)(4) & (h))	Not specified.	Competent adult. (§§ 22-8A-4(a), 22-8A-3(5) [competent adult defined as alert, capable of understanding lay descriptions of medical procedures, and able to appreciate consequences of providing or withdrawing procedures] "Sound mind" used in statutory form. (§ 22-8A-4(h))	At least 19 years old. (§§ 22-8A-4(a), 22-8A-3(1))	Not specified. (§ 22-8A-4) "Sound mind" used in statutory form. (§ 22-8A-4(h))

Table 10.02, Part 3 Formal Requirements

What Formalities Satisfy the Requirements?

	What are Impermissible Conflicts of Witnesses Specified in the Statute?	Must Witnesses Sign the Document?	Must Witnesses Affirm or Just Declare/Sign on the Basis of Knowledge and Belief?	Must Attorney or Drafter Sign?	Capacity of Declarant: What Standard Is Used? E.g., Sound Mind, Sane?	Capacity of Declarant: Age Requirement?	Capacity of Declarant: Signed Before Notary?
Alaska	For durable power of attorney for health care the witness must not be a health care provider at the health care institution or health care facility where the principal is receiving health care; an employee there, the agent, and at least one witness should not be related to the principal by blood, marriage, or adoption, and should not be entitled to a portion of the estate of the principal upon the principal's death under a will or codicil of the principal existing at the time of execution of the durable power of attorney for health care or by operation of law then existing. (§ 13.52.010(d) & (e))	Yes. (§ 13.52.010(b))	No. The witnesses must sign and must personally know the principal. (§ 13.52.010(b)(1))	Not specified.	Not specified, but rebuttably presumed to have capacity to make health care decision. (§ 13.52.100) Statutory form provides "sound mind" and "under no duress, fraud, or undue influence." (§ 13.52.300)	Adult, aged 18, subject to certain exceptions. (§ 13.52.010(a))	Not specified. Required for durable power of attorney for health care if not signed by two witnesses. (§ 13.52.010(b)(2))

Table 10.02, Part 3 Formal Requirements

What Formalities Satisfy the Requirements?

	What are Impermissible Conflicts of Witnesses Specified in the Statute?	Must Witnesses Affirm or Just Declare/Sign on the Basis of Knowledge and Belief?	Must Witnesses Sign the Document?	Must Attorney or Drafter Sign?	Capacity of Declarant: What Standard Is Used? E.g., Sound Mind, Sane?	Capacity of Declarant: Age Requirement?	Capacity of Declarant: Signed Before Notary?
Arizona	Witness cannot be person designated to make decisions, or person directly involved in provision of health care; and if only one witness, the witness cannot be related to principal by blood, marriage or adoption and may not be entitled to any portion of principal's estate. (§§ 36-3261(C) & (D))	For living will, must notarize or affirm. (§§ 36-3261(B), 36-3221(A)(3))	Yes or notarize. (§§ 36-3261(B), 36-3221(A)(3))	Not specified.	The form requires a statement by the witness that "The patient then appeared to be of sound mind and free from duress." (§ 36-3261(B), 36-3221(A)(3))	Adult. (§ 36-3261(A))	Yes, or a witness. (§§ 36-3261(B), 36-3221(A)(3))
Arkansas	Not specified.	Attest it was voluntarily signed by declarant in the witness's presence (as indicated in the statutory form). (§ 20-17-202(b))	Yes (as indicated in the statutory form). (§ 20-17-202(b))	Not specified.	Sound mind. (§ 20-17-202(a))	18 or older. (§ 20-17-202(a))	Not specified.

Table 10.02, Part 3 Formal Requirements

What Formalities Satisfy the Requirements?

	What are Impermissible Conflicts of Witnesses Specified in the Statute?	Must Witnesses Affirm or Just Declare/Sign on the Basis of Knowledge and Belief?	Must Witnesses Sign the Document?	Must Attorney or Drafter Sign?	Capacity of Declarant: What Standard Is Used? E.g., Sound Mind, Sane?	Capacity of Declarant: Age Requirement? (Probate § 4670)	Capacity of Declarant: Signed Before Notary?
California	Witnesses cannot be health care provider or employee of provider; operator or employee of community care facility; or operator or employee of residential care facility for elderly. At least one witness cannot be related to declarant by blood, marriage, or adoption, or entitled to any part of declarant's estate. (Probate § 4674(c)–(f)) Witness requirements do not apply to notary. (Probate § 4674(g))	Witnesses affirmatively state, under penalty of perjury. (Probate §§ 4674, 4701 in optional form)	Yes, if not acknowledged by notary. (Probate § 4673(a)(3))	Not specified.	Capacity, meaning ability to understand nature, consequences, risks, benefits, and alternatives of health care decisions. (Probate §§ 4670, 4609) Sound mind and under no duress, fraud, or undue influence. (Probate § 4674(d))	Adult. (Probate § 4670)	Yes, if not signed by witnesses. (Probate § 4673(a)(3))
Colorado	Witnesses cannot include any physician, an employee of the physician or the health care facility, a person that knows or believes he is entitled to part of or has a claim against the declarant's estate (including heirs) or any other patient in the same health care facility. (§§ 15-18-105, 15-18-106(1)	Not Specified. (§ 15-18-104(5))	Not Specified. (§ 15-18-104(5))	Not specified. (§ 15-18-104)	With decisional capacity. (§ 15-18-104(1))	At least 18 years old. (§§ 15-18-104(2), 15-18-103(1) definition of adult)	Not specified. (§ 15-18-104)

Table 10.02, Part 3 Formal Requirements

What Formalities Satisfy the Requirements?

	What are Impermissible Conflicts of Witnesses Specified in the Statute?	Must Witnesses Affirm or Just Declare/Sign on the Basis of Knowledge and Belief?	Must Witnesses Sign the Document?	Must Attorney or Drafter Sign?	Capacity of Declarant: What Standard Is Used? E.g., Sound Mind, Sane?	Capacity of Declarant: Age Requirement?	Capacity of Declarant: Signed Before Notary?
Connecticut	Not specified.	Sign in declarant's presence on basis of appearance of declarant (as indicated in the statutory form). (§ 19a-575) Witnesses may also swear to an affidavit before a duly authorized officer. The affidavit shall be written on the living will, or attached thereto. (§ 19a-578(a))	Yes (as indicated in the statutory form). (§ 19a-575)	Not specified.	Sound mind and after careful reflection (as indicated in the statutory form). (§ 19a-575)	18 or older. (§ 19a-575)	Not specified.

Table 10.02, Part 3 Formal Requirements

What Formalities Satisfy the Requirements?

	What are Impermissible Conflicts of Witnesses Specified in the Statute?	Must Witnesses Affirm or Just Declare/Sign on the Basis of Knowledge and Belief?	Must Witnesses Sign the Document?	Must Attorney or Drafter Sign?	Capacity of Declarant: What Standard Is Used? E.g., Sound Mind, Sane?	Capacity of Declarant: Age Requirement?	Capacity of Declarant: Signed Before Notary?
Delaware	Witness must satisfy the following: The witness (a) is not related to the declarant; (b) is not entitled to any portion of the estate of the declarant under any will or trust; (c) does not have a claim against the declarant's estate; (d) does not have direct financial responsibility for the declarant's medical care; and (e) does not have a controlling interest in or is an operator of or an employee of a health care institution at which the declarant is a patient. (16 § 2503(b)(1)(d)(1)–(5)) An optional form lists these above the line for the witnesses' signatures as well as a statement that the witnesses are not under age 18. (16 § 2505)	Not specified.	Yes (as indicated in statutory form). (16 § 2505)	Not specified.	Mentally competent. (16 §§ 2503(a), 2505)	Adult. (16 § 2503(a))	Not specified.

Table 10.02, Part 3 Formal Requirements

What Formalities Satisfy the Requirements?

	What are Impermissible Conflicts of Witnesses Specified in the Statute?	Must Witnesses Affirm or Just Declare/Sign on the Basis of Knowledge and Belief?	Must Witnesses Sign the Document?	Must Attorney or Drafter Sign?	Capacity of Declarant: What Standard Is Used? E.g., Sound Mind, Sane?	Capacity of Declarant: Age Requirement?	Capacity of Declarant: Signed Before Notary?
District of Columbia	Witnesses cannot be: (a) the person who signed the declaration on behalf of and at the direction of the declarant; (b) related to the declarant by blood or marriage; (c) entitled to any portion of the estate of the declarant; (d) directly financially responsible for the declarant's medical care; or (e) an attending physician, employees of the attending physician, or employees of a health care facility where the declarant is a patient. (§7-622(a)(4)(A)–(E))	Sign on basis of belief that declarant is of sound mind. Witnesses must also declare they are of age and that there are no impermissible conflicts (as indicated in the statutory form). (§7-622(c))	Yes (as indicated in the statutory form). (§7-622(c))	Not specified.	Declarant must be of sound mind (as indicated in the statutory form). (§7-622(c))	18 years of age or older. (§7-622(a))	Not specified.
Florida	At least one witness cannot be a spouse or blood relative of declarant. (§765.302(1))	Not specified, but implied that witness must simply sign (as indicated in the statutory form). (§765.303(1))	Yes (as indicated in the statutory form). (§765.303(1))	Not specified.	Competent. (§765.302(1)) Willfully and voluntarily (as indicated in statutory form). (§765.303)	Adult. (§765.302(1))	Not specified.

Table 10.02, Part 3 Formal Requirements

What Formalities Satisfy the Requirements?

	What are Impermissible Conflicts of Witnesses Specified in the Statute?	*Must Witnesses Affirm or Just Declare/Sign on the Basis of Knowledge and Belief?*	*Must Witnesses Sign the Document?*	*Must Attorney or Drafter Sign?*	*Capacity of Declarant: What Standard Is Used? E.g., Sound Mind, Sane?*	*Capacity of Declarant: Age Requirement?*	*Capacity of Declarant: Signed Before Notary?*
Georgia	Neither witness can be: (a) individual selected to serve as declarant's health care agent; (b) one who will knowingly inherit anything from the declarant, or otherwise benefit financially from the declarant's death; (c) an individual directly involved in the declarant's health care. Only one witness may be an employee, agent or medical staff member of the facility where the declarant is receiving care. (§31-32-5(c)(2) & (3))	Not specified.	Yes (as indicated in the statutory form). (§31-32-4)	Not specified.	Sound mind. (§31-32-5(a))	18 or older. (§§31-32-5(a))	Not specified.

10,080

Table 10.02, Part 3 Formal Requirements

What Formalities Satisfy the Requirements?

	What are Impermissible Conflicts of Witnesses Specified in the Statute?	Must Witnesses Affirm or Just Declare/Sign on the Basis of Knowledge and Belief?	Must Witnesses Sign the Document?	Must Attorney or Drafter Sign?	Capacity of Declarant: What Standard Is Used? E.g., Sound Mind, Sane?	Capacity of Declarant: Age Requirement?	Capacity of Declarant: Signed Before Notary?
Hawaii	Witness must *not* be (a) a health care provider; (b) an employee of a health care provider or facility; or (c) the agent appointed in the document. At least *one* witness must not be (a) related to the principal by blood, marriage or adoption, or (b) entitled to any portion of the principal's estate. (§§ 327E-3(c) & (d), 327E-16)	Witnesses affirmatively declare under penalty of false swearing (as indicated in the statutory form). (§ 327E-16)	Yes (as indicated in the statutory form). (§ 327E-16)	Not specified.	Sound mind (as indicated in the statutory form). (§ 327E-16)	Adult or emancipated minor. (§ 327E-3)	Yes, if not signed before witnesses (as indicated in the statutory form). (§§ 327E-3(b), 327E-16)
Idaho	Not specified by the living will form. (§ 39-4510)	Not specified. (§ 39-4510)	Not specified. (§ 39-4510)	Not specified. (§ 39-4510)	"Competent person," that is, any emancipated minor or person eighteen or more years who is of sound mind. (§§ 39-4509(4); 39-4503)	Any person who comprehends the need for, nature of, and significant risks ordinarily inherent in a health care treatment or procedure. (§§ 39-4509(4), 39-4503)	Not specified.

Table 10.02, Part 3 Formal Requirements

What Formalities Satisfy the Requirements?

	What are Impermissible Conflicts of Witnesses Specified in the Statute?	Must Witnesses Affirm or Just Declare/Sign on the Basis of Knowledge and Belief?	Must Witnesses Sign the Document?	Must Attorney or Drafter Sign?	Capacity of Declarant: What Standard Is Used? E.g., Sound Mind, Sane?	Capacity of Declarant: Age Requirement?	Capacity of Declarant: Signed Before Notary?
Illinois	Witnesses must say they personally know declarant, believe him/her to be of sound mind, saw declarant sign, witness signed in the declarant's presence, did not sign it at the direction of the declarant, not entitled to anything through intestate and do not believe they are to receive anything under the will, and that they are not directly financially responsible for declarant's medical care (as indicated in statutory form). (755 ILCS §35/3(e))	Witnesses sign under affirmative statement (as indicated in statutory form). (755 ILCS §35/3(e))	Yes (as indicated in the statutory form). (755 ILCS §35/3(e))	Not specified.	Sound mind. (755 ILCS §35/3(a))	Age of majority or having obtained status of an "emancipated person." (755 ILCS §35/3(a))	Not specified.

Table 10.02, Part 3 Formal Requirements

What Formalities Satisfy the Requirements?

	What are Impermissible Conflicts of Witnesses Specified in the Statute?	Must Witnesses Affirm or Just Declare/Sign on the Basis of Knowledge and Belief?	Must Witnesses Sign the Document?	Must Attorney or Drafter Sign?	Capacity of Declarant: What Standard Is Used? E.g., Sound Mind, Sane?	Capacity of Declarant: Age Requirement?	Capacity of Declarant: Signed Before Notary?
Indiana	Witness cannot be: (a) the person who signed the declaration on behalf of and at the direction of the declarant; (b) the parent, spouse, or child of the decedent; (c) entitled to any portion of the estate of the decedent; or (d) directly financially responsible for the declarant's medical care. (§ 16-36-4-8(c)(1)(4))	Witnesses affirmatively state lack of listed conflicts (as indicated in the statutory form). (§ 16-36-4-10)	Yes (as indicated in the statutory form). (§ 16-36-4-10)	Not specified.	Declarant must be of sound mind. (§ 16-36-4-8(a))	Declarant must have reached 18 years of age. (§ 16-36-4-8(a))	Not specified.
Iowa	No statement required, but witnesses cannot be an attending health care provider, provider's employee, or a minor. Additionally, at least one witness cannot be related (by blood, marriage or adoption) to the declarant. (§ 144A.3(2)(a))	Presumably only have to sign on knowledge and belief. (§ 144A.3(2)(a))	Yes. (§ 144A.3(2)(a))	Not specified.	Competency. (§ 144A.3(1))	At least 18 years old. (§§ 144A.3(1), 144A.2(1))	Yes, if not signed before two witnesses. (§ 144A.3(2)(b))

Table 10.02, Part 3 Formal Requirements

What Formalities Satisfy the Requirements?

	What are Impermissible Conflicts of Witnesses Specified in the Statute?	Must Witnesses Affirm or Just Declare/Sign on the Basis of Knowledge and Belief?	Must Witnesses Sign the Document?	Must Attorney or Drafter Sign?	Capacity of Declarant: What Standard Is Used? E.g., Sound Mind, Sane?	Capacity of Declarant: Age Requirement?	Capacity of Declarant: Signed Before Notary?
Kansas	A witness cannot be the person signing on declarant's behalf, related by blood or marriage to the declarant, entitled to any portion of the declarant's estate (including under a will) or directly financially responsible for the declarant's medical care. (§65-28,103(a)(4)(A))	Witnesses affirmatively state lack of listed conflicts. (§65-28,103(c))	Yes (as indicated in the statutory form). (§65-28,103(c))	Not specified.	Sound mind (as indicated in the statutory form). (§65-28,103(c))	"Adult" (but not defined). (§65-28,103(a))	Yes, if not signed before two witnesses. (§65-28,103(a)(4)(B))
Kentucky	Witness cannot be (a) a blood relative of the grantor; (b) a beneficiary of the grantor via descent or distribution; (c) an employee of the health care facility where the grantor is a patient; (d) an attending physician of the grantor; or (e) any person directly financially responsible for the grantor's health care. (§311.625(2)(a)-(e))	Declare/sign on basis of belief (as indicated in statutory form). (§311.625(1))	Yes (as indicated in the statutory form). (§311.625(1))	Not specified.	Declarant must have emotional and mental decisional capacity. (§311.623(1))	Declarant must be at least 18 years old. (§§311.623(1), 311.621(1))	Notary can sign the document in lieu of two witnesses. (§311.625(2))

Table 10.02, Part 3 Formal Requirements

What Formalities Satisfy the Requirements?

	What are Impermissible Conflicts of Witnesses Specified in the Statute?	Must Witnesses Affirm or Just Declare/Sign on the Basis of Knowledge and Belief?	Must Witnesses Sign the Document?	Must Attorney or Drafter Sign?	Capacity of Declarant: What Standard Is Used? E.g., Sound Mind, Same?	Capacity of Declarant: Age Requirement?	Capacity of Declarant: Signed Before Notary?
Louisiana	Conflicts not listed in witness statement. (§ 40:1299.58.3(C)(1)) Must be a competent adult not related to the declarant by blood or marriage and who would not be entitled to any portion of the declarant's estate. (§ 40:1151.2(15))	Sign on knowledge/ belief. (§ 40:1151.2 (C)(1))	Yes (as indicated on the statutory form). (§ 40:1151.2(C)(1))	Not specified.	Sound mind (as indicated in the statutory form). (§ 40:1151.2(C)(1))	Adult. (§§ 40:1151.2(A)(1))	Not specified.
Maine	None listed.	Not specified. (18-A §§ 5-802(a), 5-804))	Two witnesses must sign. (18-A § 5-804, Part 4)	Not specified.	The patient must have capacity, meaning ability to understand condition, risks and benefits of health care, and consequences of health care decisions. (18-A §§ 5-802(b), 5-801(c))	The patient must be an adult or an emancipated minor. (18-A § 5-802(b))	Not specified.
Maryland	The witness cannot be a health care agent. At least one of the witnesses must be someone who will not knowingly inherit anything from the decedent or otherwise knowingly gain a financial benefit from the decedent's death. (Health-Gen. § 5-602)(c)(2)(ii)-(iii))	Witness must sign statement affirming that declarant signed or acknowledged signing the document in witness' presence (as in statutory form). (Health-Gen. § 5-603)	Yes. (Health-Gen. § 5-602(c)(1)) Witness must sign documentation of oral declaration. (Health-Gen. § 5-602(d)(2))	Not specified.	Competency. (Health-Gen. §§ 5-602(a), 5-601(f))	At least 18 years old. (Health-Gen. §§ 5-602(a), 5-601(f))	Not specified.

Table 10.02, Part 3 Formal Requirements

What Formalities Satisfy the Requirements?

	What are Impermissible Conflicts of Witnesses Specified in the Statute?	Must Witnesses Affirm or Just Declare/Sign on the Basis of Knowledge and Belief?	Must Witnesses Sign the Document?	Must Attorney or Drafter Sign?	Capacity of Declarant: What Standard Is Used? E.g., Sound Mind, Sane?	Capacity of Declarant: Age Requirement?	Capacity of Declarant: Signed Before Notary?
Massachusetts[1]	No witness can be the health care agent. (201D §2)	Belief. (201D §2)	Yes. (201D §2)	Not specified.	Competent. (201D §2)	18 years of age. (201D §2)	Not specified.
Michigan	Shall not be patient's spouse, parent, child, grandchild, sibling, presumptive heir, known devisee, physician, patient advocate or employee of life/health insurance provider for patient, health facility treating patient, home for the aged where patient resides, or community health services program or hospital providing mental health services to the patient. (§700.5506(4))	Must sign on the basis of knowledge and belief. (§700.5506(4))	Yes. (§700.5506(4))	Not specified.	Sound mind and not under duress, fraud or undue influence. (§700.5506(1))	18 years or older. (§700.5506(1))	Not specified.
Minnesota	A witness cannot be named as a proxy by the living will or be entitled to any part of the declarant's estate. (§145B.03(Subd. 2(d)))	Witnesses must certify to statement on statutory form. (§§145B.03 (Subd. 2)(d), 145B.04)	Yes, unless signed by notary. (§145B.03 (Subd. 2)(a))	Not specified.	Competency and sound mind. (§§145B.03 (Subd. 1), 145B.04)	States "adult," but does not define. (§145B.03 (Subd. 1)	Notary must sign, unless signed instead by two witnesses. (§145B.03 (Subd. 2)(a))

Table 10.02, Part 3 Formal Requirements

What Formalities Satisfy the Requirements?

	What are Impermissible Conflicts of Witnesses Specified in the Statute?	Must Witnesses Affirm or Just Declare/Sign on the Basis of Knowledge and Belief?	Must Witnesses Sign the Document?	Must Attorney or Drafter Sign?	Capacity of Declarant: What Standard Is Used? E.g., Sound Mind, Sane?	Capacity of Declarant: Age Requirement?	Capacity of Declarant: Signed Before Notary?
Mississippi	Witness must not be appointed as agent by the document; not be a health care provider; not be an employee of a health care provider or facility. At least one witness must not be related by blood, marriage, or adoption; and to the best of his or her knowledge, not be entitled to any part of the estate "under a will now existing or by operation of law." (§ 41-41-205(2)(a))	Acknowledge under penalties of perjury. (§ 41-41-205(2))	Yes or notary public. (§ 41-41-205(2))	Not specified.	Sound mind (in witness' required statements). (§ 41-41-205(2))	The declarant must be at least 18 years old or an emancipated minor. (§§ 41-41-205(1), 41-41-203(e) 41-41-211(2))	Yes, as an alternative to witnesses. (§ 41-41-205(2)(b))
Missouri	Witnesses cannot be the persons who signed declaration on declarant's behalf. (§ 459.015(1)(3))	Witnesses sign under affirmative statement (as indicated in statutory form). (§ 459.015(3))	Yes (as indicated in the statutory form). (§ 459.015(3))	Not specified. (§ 459.015(3))	Sound mind and competency. (§§ 459.015(1), 459.015(3))	At least 18 years old (as indicated in the statutory form). (§ 459.015(3))	Not specified.

Table 10.02, Part 3 Formal Requirements

What Formalities Satisfy the Requirements?

	What are Impermissible Conflicts of Witnesses Specified in the Statute?	Must Witnesses Affirm or Just Declare/Sign on the Basis of Knowledge and Belief?	Must Witnesses Sign the Document?	Must Attorney or Drafter Sign?	Capacity of Declarant: What Standard Is Used? E.g., Sound Mind, Sane?	Capacity of Declarant: Age Requirement?	Capacity of Declarant: Signed Before Notary?
Montana	Not specified.	Witnesses sign under statement that declarant signed voluntarily (as indicated in statutory form). (§ 50-9-103(2))	Yes (as indicated in the statutory form). (§ 50-9-103(2))	Not specified.	Patient must be of sound mind. (§ 50-9-103(1))	Patient must be at least 18 years of age. (§ 50-9-103(1))	Not specified.
Nebraska	No witness can be an employee of declarant's life/health insurance provider; only one witness can work for the health care provider treating the declarant. These restrictions do not apply to the notary. (§ 20-404(1))	Attest it was voluntarily signed in witnesses' presence (as indicated in the statutory form). (§ 20-404(2))	Yes (as indicated in the statutory form). (§ 20-404(2))	Not specified.	Sound mind. (§ 20-404(1))	Adult: 19 or older or a person who is/has been married. (§§ 20-403(1), 20-404(1))	Not required, but if signed before a notary then no other witnesses are necessary. (§ 20-404(1))
Nevada	Witnesses attest to statement that declarant signed voluntarily. (§ 449.610)	Attest. (§ 449.600(1))	Yes (as indicated in the statutory form). (§ 449.610)	Not specified.	Declarant must be of sound mind. (§ 449.600(1))	Declarant must beat least 18 years old. (§ 449.600(1))	Not specified.

Table 10.02, Part 3 Formal Requirements

What Formalities Satisfy the Requirements?

	What are Impermissible Conflicts of Witnesses Specified in the Statute?	Must Witnesses Affirm or Just Declare/Sign on the Basis of Knowledge and Belief?	Must Witnesses Sign the Document?	Must Attorney or Drafter Sign?	Capacity of Declarant: What Standard Is Used? E.g., Sound Mind, Sane?	Capacity of Declarant: Age Requirement?	Capacity of Declarant: Signed Before Notary?
New Hampshire	Witnesses cannot be declarant's spouse, heir, attending physician, ARNP, person under control of attending physician or ARNP, or any person employed by any part of principal's estate, trust, or deed. No more than one witness may be the principal's health or residential care provider or such provider's employee. (§ 137-J:14(I)(a)) Instead of witnesses, a notary or justice of the peace shall acknowledge the witness's signature. (§ 137-J:14(I)(b))	Affirm that principal appeared to be of sound mind and free from duress at the time the advance directive was signed and that the principal affirmed that he or she was aware of the nature of the document and signed it. (§ 137-J:14(I)(a))	Yes. (§ 137-J:14(I)(a))	Not specified.	Sound mind. (§ 137-J:14(I)(a))	At least 18 years old. (§ 137-J:2(XIX))	Instead of a witness. (§ 137-J:14(I)(b))
New Jersey	A designated health care representative cannot act as a witness. (§ 26:2H-56)	Must attest the declarant to be of sound mind, free of duress/undue influence and signed in witness' presence. (§ 26:2H-56)	Yes, "subscribing." (§ 26:2H-56)	No requirement, although attorney may sign in lieu of witnesses. (§ 26:2H-56)	Sound mind and free of duress/undue influence. (§ 26:2H-56)	Adult, 18 years of age or older. (§ 26:2H-55, definitions of "Declarant" and "Adult")	Yes, if not signed before witnesses. (§ 26:2H-56)

3

10,089

Table 10.02, Part 3 Formal Requirements

What Formalities Satisfy the Requirements?

	What are Impermissible Conflicts of Witnesses Specified in the Statute?	Must Witnesses Affirm or Just Declare/Sign on the Basis of Knowledge and Belief?	Must Witnesses Sign the Document?	Must Attorney or Drafter Sign?	Capacity of Declarant: What Standard Is Used? E.g., Sound Mind, Sane?	Capacity of Declarant: Age Requirement?	Capacity of Declarant: Signed Before Notary?
New Mexico	Not specified.	Not specified.	Statutory form indicates that witnesses' signatures are optional. (§ 24-7A-4)	Not specified.	Capacity. (§§ 24-7A-2(A), 24-7A-11)	Adult or emancipated minor. (§§ 24-7A-2(A), 24-7A-1(D))	Not specified.
New York	Witness shall *not* be the person appointed as agent in the proxy. (Pub. Health § 2981(2)(a))	Yes. (Pub. Health § 2981(2) & (5))	Yes. (Pub. Health § 2981(2) & (5))	Not specified.	Competent. (Pub.Health § 2981(2)) Language "sound mind and acting willingly and free from duress" is used in witness statement (Pub. Health § 2981(5))	Adult (18 years and older), or married, or the parent of a child. (Pub.Health §§ 2980(1), 2981(1))	Not specified.
North Carolina	A witness cannot be related to the declarant or the declarant's spouse within the third degree; cannot have a reasonable expectation of being entitled to or currently have a claim against any portion of the declarant's estate; and cannot be the attending physician or his or the health facility's/nursing home's employee. (§ 90-321(c)(3))	Affirm (as indicated in the statutory form). (§ 90-321(d1))	Yes (as indicated in the statutory form). (§ 90-321(d1))	Not specified.	Sound mind (as indicated in the statutory form). (§ 90-321(c)(3) & (d1))	Not specified.	Yes (or can instead be proved before a clerk or assistant clerk of a superior court). (§ 90-321(c)(4))

Table 10.02, Part 3 Formal Requirements

What Formalities Satisfy the Requirements?

	What are Impermissible Conflicts of Witnesses Specified in the Statute?	Must Witnesses Affirm or Just Declare/Sign on the Basis of Knowledge and Belief?	Must Witnesses Sign the Document?	Must Attorney or Drafter Sign?	Capacity of Declarant: What Standard Is Used? E.g., Sound Mind, Sane?	Capacity of Declarant: Age Requirement?	Capacity of Declarant: Signed Before Notary?
North Dakota	Witness cannot be: (a) the agent; (b) the spouse; (c) heir; (d) related to the declarant by blood or marriage or adoption; (e) entitled to any portion of the declarant's estate under a will or deed in existence or by operation of law; (f) claimants against any portion of the estate; (g) directly financially responsible for the declarant's medical care; or (h) the declarant's attending physician. In addition, at least one witness must not be a health care or long term care provider providing direct care to the principal on the date of execution. (§§ 23-06.5-05(2), 23-06.5-17)	Witnesses must "verify" the principal's signature. (§ 23-06.5-05(1))	Yes. (§ 23-06.5-05(2))	Not specified.	Principal must have ability to understand and appreciate nature and consequences of health care decisions including the significant benefits and harms of and reasonable alternatives to any proposed health care, and have ability to communicate a decision. (§ 23-06.5-02(3)) Principal is presumed to have capacity. (§ 23-06.5-13(3))	Declarant must be an adult at least 18 years of age. (§ 23-06.5-02(9)). Although not defined in Title 23, an adult is defined as age eighteen or older. (§14-10-02)	May be signed before notary in lieu of two witnesses. (§ 23-06.5-05 (1)(e)) Restrictions on witnesses are also applicable to notary, except that notary may be an employee of a health care or long term care provider providing care to the principal. (§ 23-06.5-05(2))

Table 10.02, Part 3 Formal Requirements

What Formalities Satisfy the Requirements?

	What are Impermissible Conflicts of Witnesses Specified in the Statute?	Must Witnesses Affirm or Just Declare/Sign on the Basis of Knowledge and Belief?	Must Witnesses Sign the Document?	Must Attorney or Drafter Sign?	Capacity of Declarant: What Standard Is Used? E.g., Sound Mind, Sane?	Capacity of Declarant: Age Requirement?	Capacity of Declarant: Signed Before Notary?
Ohio	Witness cannot be related to declarant by blood, marriage or adoption, cannot be an attending physician and cannot be an administrator of nursing home providing care to declarant. (§ 2133.02(B)(1))	Witnesses must attest to belief as to sound mind and not under duress, fraud, or undue influence. (§ 2133.02(B))	Yes, unless signed by notary. (§ 2133.02(B))	Not specified.	Sound mind. (§ 2133.02(A)(1))	Adult defined as 18 or older. (§§ 2133.02(A)(1), 2133.01(A))	May be signed by notary in lieu of two witnesses. (§ 2133.02(A)(1) & (B)(2))
Oklahoma	No statement required. Witnesses cannot be legatees, devisees or heirs of the declarant. (63 § 3101.4(A))	Sign only, attesting that declarant signed in their presence (as indicated in the statutory form). (63 § 3101.4(C))	Yes (as indicated in the statutory form). (63 § 3101.4(C))	Not specified.	Sound mind. (63 § 3101.4(A))	At least 18 years old. (63 § 3101.4(A))	Not specified.

Table 10.02, Part 3 Formal Requirements

What Formalities Satisfy the Requirements?

	What are Impermissible Conflicts of Witnesses Specified in the Statute?	Must Witnesses Affirm or Just Declare/Sign on the Basis of Knowledge and Belief?	Must Witnesses Sign the Document?	Must Attorney or Drafter Sign?	Capacity of Declarant: What Standard Is Used? E.g., Sound Mind, Sane?	Capacity of Declarant: Age Requirement?	Capacity of Declarant: Signed Before Notary?
Oregon	Witnesses shall not be (a) declarant's attorney-in-fact for health care or alternative attorney-in-fact; (b) declarant's attending physician. (§ 127.515(4)(d)) Additionally, at least one witness cannot be (a) related to the declarant by blood, marriage or adoption; (b) entitled to any portion of declarant's estate at time of signing or upon principal's death under will or operation of law; (c) owner, operator or employee of a health care facility where the declarant is a patient or resident. (§ 127.515(4)(c)(A)-(C))	Witnesses must affirm written declaration. (§ 127.531(2) Pt. D)	Yes (as indicated in the statutory form). (§ 127.531(2) Pt. D)	Not specified.	Sound mind (as indicated in the statutory form). (§ 127.531(2) Pt. A)	Capable adult, defined as 18 or older, person adjudicated as an emancipated minor, or who is married. (§§ 127.510(2), 127.505(1))	Not specified.

Table 10.02, Part 3 Formal Requirements

What Formalities Satisfy the Requirements?

	What are Impermissible Conflicts of Witnesses Specified in the Statute?	Must Witnesses Affirm or Just Declare/Sign on the Basis of Knowledge and Belief?	Must Witnesses Sign the Document?	Must Attorney or Drafter Sign?	Capacity of Declarant: What Standard Is Used? E.g., Sound Mind, Sane?	Capacity of Declarant: Age Requirement?	Capacity of Declarant: Signed Before Notary?
Pennsylvania	A witness cannot be the one who signs for the declarant, or the health care provider or an agent of the health care provider if the declarant's provider. (20 § 5442(c)(1)-(2))	Not specified.	Yes (as indicated in the statutory form). (20 § 5471)	Not specified.	Sound mind. (20 § 5442(a))	18 or older, high school graduate, or a person who has married or an emancipated minor. (20 § 5442(a)(1)-(4))	Not specified.
Rhode Island	Witnesses cannot be related by blood or marriage to the declarant. (§ 23-4.11-3(a))	Affirm that they personally know declarant and that the declarant voluntarily signed in the presence of the witness (as indicated in the statutory form). (§ 23-4.11-3(d))	Yes (as indicated in the statutory form). (§ 23-4.11-3(d))	Not specified.	Competent. (§ 23-4.11-3(a))	18 or older. (§ 23-4.11-3(a))	Not specified.

Table 10.02, Part 3 Formal Requirements

What Formalities Satisfy the Requirements?

	What are Impermissible Conflicts of Witnesses Specified in the Statute?	Must Witnesses Affirm or Just Declare/Sign on the Basis of Knowledge and Belief?	Must Witnesses Sign the Document?	Must Attorney or Drafter Sign?	Capacity of Declarant: What Standard Is Used? E.g., Sound Mind, Sane?	Capacity of Declarant: Age Requirement?	Capacity of Declarant: Signed Before Notary?
South Carolina	A witness cannot be: related to the declarant by blood, marriage, or adoption; entitled to any portion of the declarant's estate presently or under a will; financially responsible for the declarant's medical care; a beneficiary of the declarant's life insurance policy; the attending physician or his employee; or a person with a claim against any portion of declarant's estate. Not more than one of the witnesses can be employed by the health care facility in which the declarant is presently a patient. (§ 44-77-40(2))	Witnesses must affirm that they are qualified witnesses in required affidavit. Sign on "best information and belief" as to signing of declaration by a known, declarant of sound mind. (§ 44-77-50)	Yes. (§ 44-77-40(4))	Not specified.	Sound mind (as indicated in statutory form). (§ 44-77-50)	At least 18. (§ 44-77-30)	Yes. (§ 44-77-40(2))
South Dakota	Not specified.	Witnessing is all that is required. (§ 34-12D-2)	The statute simply states that the written declaration should be "witnessed." (§ 34-12D-2)	Not specified.	Competent. (§ 34-12D-2)	Adult. (§ 34-12D-2)	The signing may be in the presence of a notary public. (§ 34-12D-2)

Table 10.02, Part 3 Formal Requirements

What Formalities Satisfy the Requirements?

	What are Impermissible Conflicts of Witnesses Specified in the Statute?	Must Witnesses Affirm or Just Declare/Sign on the Basis of Knowledge and Belief?	Must Witnesses Sign the Document?	Must Attorney or Drafter Sign?	Capacity of Declarant: What Standard Is Used? E.g., Sound Mind, Sane?	Capacity of Declarant: Age Requirement?	Capacity of Declarant: Signed Before / attested to by Notary?
Tennessee	Witnesses must verify that they are not the declarant's appointed agent, not related to declarant by blood or marriage, that they are not entitled to and do not have a claim against any portion of declarant's estate, and that they are not an attending physician or an employee of the physician or health facility where declarant is a patient. (§ 32-11-104(a))	Witnesses affirmatively state lack of impermissible conflicts. (§ 32-11-105)	Yes (as indicated in the statutory form). (§§ 32-11-104(a), 32-11-105)	Not specified. (§ 32-11-105)	Sound mind and competency. (§§ 32-11-105, 32-11-104(a))	Only states "adult" (not defined). (§ 32-11-104(a))	Yes, if not signed before / attested to by two witnesses. (§ 31-11-104(a))

Table 10.02, Part 3 Formal Requirements

What Formalities Satisfy the Requirements?

	What are Impermissible Conflicts of Witnesses Specified in the Statute?	Must Witnesses Affirm or Just Declare/Sign on the Basis of Knowledge and Belief?	Must Witnesses Sign the Document?	Must Attorney or Drafter Sign?	Capacity of Declarant: What Standard Is Used? E.g., Sound Mind, Sane?	Capacity of Declarant: Age Requirement?	Capacity of Declarant: Signed Before Notary?
Texas	At least one witness may not be: (a) designated by declarant to make treatment decisions; (b) related to declarant by blood or marriage; (c) entitled to any part of declarant's estate after declarant's death; (d) declarant's attending physician; (e) an employee of the attending physician; (f) an employee of the health care facility where declarant is a patient if directly providing defendant's care or if an officer, director, partner or business office employee of the facility or its parent organization; or (g) a person with a claim against declarant's estate. (Health & Safety § 166.003)	Witnesses simply sign. (Health & Safety § 166.033)	Yes. (Health & Safety § 166.032(b))	Not specified.	Competent, meaning able to under stand the nature and consequences of treatment decisions. (Health & Safety §§ 166.032(a), 166.002(4))	Statute states "adult," but does not define. (Health & Safety § 166.032(a)) For a qualified patient under age of 18, the patient's spouse (if an adult), the patient's parents or the patient's guardian may execute a directive on the patient's behalf. (Health & Safety § 166.035)	Directive specifically does not have to be notarized. (Health & Safety § 166.036)

Table 10.02, Part 3 Formal Requirements

What Formalities Satisfy the Requirements?

	What are Impermissible Conflicts of Witnesses Specified in the Statute?	Must Witnesses Affirm or Just Declare/Sign on the Basis of Knowledge and Belief?	Must Witnesses Sign the Document?	Must Attorney or Drafter Sign?	Capacity of Declarant: What Standard Is Used? E.g., Sound Mind, Sane?	Capacity of Declarant: Age Requirement?	Capacity of Declarant: Signed Before Notary?
Utah	A witness cannot be related to the declarant by blood or marriage; the person who signed on the behalf of the declarant; entitled to any portion of the declarant's estate presently or under a will; directly financially responsible for the declarant's medical care; a health care provider to the declarant; or an administrator of the health care facility in which the declarant is receiving care; or the appointed agent. (§75-2a-107(1)(c)(i)-(vi))	No provision, except if oral directive then witness must state the circumstances under which the directive was made. (§75-2a-107(1)(d))	Implied by optional form. (§75-2a-117)	Not specified.	The declarant is presumed to have the capacity to complete a health care directive. (§75-2a-105)	At least 18 years old, unless the declarant is an emancipated minor as defined in §78A-6-803. (§75-2a-103(1))	Not specified.
Vermont	Witnesses cannot be the declarant's agent, spouse, reciprocal beneficiary, parent, adult sibling, adult child, or adult grandchild. (18 §9703(c))	Witnesses affirm. (18 §9703(b))	Yes. (18 §9703(b))	Not specified.	"Capacity" means an individual's ability to make and communicate a decision regarding the issue that needs to be decided. (18 §9701(4))	Adult. (18 §§9702(a), 9703(a))	Not specified.

Table 10.02, Part 3 Formal Requirements

What Formalities Satisfy the Requirements?

	What are Impermissible Conflicts of Witnesses Specified in the Statute?	Must Witnesses Affirm or Just Declare/Sign on the Basis of Knowledge and Belief?	Must Witnesses Sign the Document?	Must Attorney or Drafter Sign?	Capacity of Declarant: What Standard Is Used? E.g., Sound Mind, Sane?	Capacity of Declarant: Age Requirement?	Capacity of Declarant: Signed Before Notary?
Virginia	None listed. (§ 54.1-2982)	Witnesses affirmatively state that declarant signed in their presence. (§ 54.1-2984)	Yes. (as indicated in the statutory form). (§ 54.1-2984)	Not specified.	"Capable of making an informed decision." (§ 54.1-2983)	Only states "adult." (§ 54.1-2983)	Not specified.
Washington	Affirmative statement not required, but a witness cannot be: an attending physician or his/her or the health facility's employee; related by blood or marriage to the declarant; or entitled to or have a claim against the declarant's estate. (§ 70.122.030(1))	Sign on knowledge/belief (as indicated in the statutory form). (§ 70.122.030(1))	Yes (as indicated in the statutory form). (§ 70.122.030(1))	Not specified.	"Capacity to make health care decisions" (as indicated in the statutory form). (§ 70.122.030(1))	Must be an "adult person." (§ 70.122.030(1)) 18 years. (§ § 26.28.010, 26.28.015)	Not specified.

Table 10.02, Part 3 Formal Requirements

What Formalities Satisfy the Requirements?

	What are Impermissible Conflicts of Witnesses Specified in the Statute?	Must Witnesses Affirm or Just Declare/Sign on the Basis of Knowledge and Belief?	Must Witnesses Sign the Document?	Must Attorney or Drafter Sign?	Capacity of Declarant: What Standard Is Used? E.g., Sound Mind, Sane?	Capacity of Declarant: Age Requirement?	Capacity of Declarant: Signed Before Notary?
West Virginia	A witness cannot be: an attending physician; related by blood or marriage to the declarant; entitled to any portion of the declarant's estate; directly financially responsible for the declarant's medical care; the person who signed the living will for the declarant on the behalf and direction of the declarant; or declarant's medical power of attorney representative. (§ 16-30-4(b))	Witnesses affirm lack of impermissible conflicts. (§ 16-30-4(a)(5))	Yes. (§ 16-30-4(a)(5))	Not specified.	Competency. (§ 16-30-4(a))	Adult, meaning a person 18 or older, an emancipated minor, or a mature minor. (§§ 16-30-4(a), 16-30-3(b))	Yes. (§ 16-30-4(a)(5))

Table 10.02, Part 3 Formal Requirements

What Formalities Satisfy the Requirements?

	What are Impermissible Conflicts of Witnesses Specified in the Statute?	*Must Witnesses Affirm or Just Declare/Sign on the Basis of Knowledge and Belief?*	*Must Witnesses Sign the Document?*	*Must Attorney or Drafter Sign?*	*Capacity of Declarant: What Standard Is Used? E.g., Sound Mind, Sane?*	*Capacity of Declarant: Age Requirement?*	*Capacity of Declarant: Signed Before Notary?*
Wisconsin	Cannot be related by blood, marriage or adoption; cannot have knowledge they are entitled to, or have a claim against any part of the estate; cannot be directly responsible for the declarant's health care; and cannot be a health care provider, employee of the health care provider, or an employee of an inpatient health care facility serving the declarant (chaplains and social workers are allowed). (§ 154.03(1)(a)–(d))	Sign on belief as to declarant's sound mind. Witnesses affirmatively state that they are free of impermissible conflicts. (§ 154.03(2))	Yes. (§ 154.03(1))	Not specified.	Sound mind. (§ 154.03(1))	18 or older. (§ 154.03(1))	Not specified.

Table 10.02, Part 3 Formal Requirements

What Formalities Satisfy the Requirements?

	What are Impermissible Conflicts of Witnesses Specified in the Statute?	Must Witnesses Affirm or Just Declare/Sign on the Basis of Knowledge and Belief?	Must Witnesses Sign the Document?	Must Attorney or Drafter Sign?	Capacity of Declarant: What Standard Is Used? E.g., Sound Mind, Sane?	Capacity of Declarant: Age Requirement?	Capacity of Declarant: Signed Before Notary?
Wyoming	A witness cannot be: a treating health care provider or an employee thereof; the attorney-in-fact nominated in the writing; the operator of a community care facility or employee thereof; the operator of a residential care facility or employee thereof. (§ 35-22-403(c))	Sign on penalty of perjury that the person signing is the principal, that the principal signed in his presence. (§ 35-22-403(c)).	Yes, or sworn before a notary public. (§ 35-22-403(b))	Not specified.	Not specified. (§§ 35-22-403(a) & (b))	Statute states "adult," but does not define, as well as emancipated minor. (§ 35-22-403(b))	If not signed before two witnesses. (§ 35-22-403(b))

[1] Only deals with health care proxies.

Table 10.02, Part 4 Formal Requirements

	Effect of Pregnancy?	Must Pregnancy Test Be Administered?	Is There a Requirement That a Notified Attending Physician Make the Declaration Part of the Medical Record?	Is There Automatic Severability of Defective Clauses or Does Entire Living Will Fail (Or No Provision)?	Must There Be a Registration of the Living Will?	Must You Follow the Living Will Form in the Statute or Is Something "Substantially Equivalent a Satisfactory Alternative?
Alabama	If pregnancy is known by the physician, the living will has no effect during the course of the pregnancy. (§ 22-8A-4(e))	Not specified. (§ 22-8A-4(e))	Yes. (§ 22-8A-4(f))	Automatic severability. (§ 22-8A-4(h))	Not specified.	Language provides: "shall be substantially in the following form, but in addition may include other specific directions." (§ 22-8A-4(h))

Table 10.02, Part 4 Formal Requirements

Effect of Pregnancy?	Must Pregnancy Test Be Administered?	Is There a Requirement That a Notified Attending Physician Make the Declaration Part of the Medical Record?	Is There Automatic Severability of Defective Clauses or Does Entire Living Will Fail (Or No Provision)?	Must There Be a Registration of the Living Will?	Must You Follow the Living Will Form in the Statute or Is Something "Substantially" Equivalent a Satisfactory Alternative?
Alaska	The supervising health care provider must determine if a woman of child-bearing age is pregnant before implementing a health-care decision involving her. (§ 13.52.055(a)). The health-care directive may not be given effect if the patient is pregnant and lacks capacity; the directive or decision is to withhold or withdraw life-sustaining procedures; the withholding or withdrawal of the life-sustaining procedures would, in reasonable medical judgment, be likely to result in the death of the patient; and it is probable that the fetus could develop to the point of live birth if the life-sustaining procedures were provided. However, the foregoing does not apply to emergency services in the field. (§ 13.52.055(b))	Yes, if a woman of childbearing age, the supervising health care provider is required to take reasonable steps to determine whether the woman is pregnant. (§ 13.52.055(a))	Yes. (§ 13.52.060(b))	Yes. (§ 13.52.290)	Not specified.	No. May be, but "need not be" in the statutory form or substantially similar. (§ 13.52.300)

Table 10.02, Part 4 Formal Requirements

	Effect of Pregnancy?	Must Pregnancy Test Be Administered?	Is There a Requirement That a Notified Attending Physician Make the Declaration Part of the Medical Record?	Is There Automatic Severability of Defective Clauses or Does Entire Living Will Fail (Or No Provision)?	Must There Be a Registration of the Living Will?	Must You Follow the Living Will Form in the Statute or Is Something "Substantially" Equivalent a Satisfactory Alternative?
Arizona	The patient can request that life-sustaining treatment not be removed, notwithstanding any directive to the contrary, if she is known to be pregnant (as indicated in the statutory form). (§ 36-3262)	Not specified.	Not specified.	Not specified.	Not specified.	A living will can be in any form that complies with the requirements of § 36-3261.
Arkansas	If the physician knows the declarant is pregnant the declaration will not be given effect if there is a possibility "the fetus could develop to the point of live birth" by continuing to give the declarant life-sustaining treatment. (§ 20-17-206(c))	Not specified.	Yes. (§§ 20-17-202(d), 20-17-205)	Severability. (§ 20-17-216)	Not specified.	Declaration "may, but need not" be in the statutory form. (§ 20-17-202(b))
California	Not specified, but statute does not authorize consent to abortion. (Probate § 4652(e))	Not specified.	Yes. (Probate § 4731(a))	Severability. (Probate § 11)	Registration is optional. (Probate §§ 4800, 4803)	Directive, may, but need not, follow statutory form, which may be modified partially or in full. (Probate §§ 4700, 4701)
Colorado	If the attending physician knows that the declarant is pregnant, a medical evaluation must be conducted to determine if the fetus is viable. If so, the declaration has no effect. (§ 15-18-104(2))	Not specified. (§ 15-18-104(2))	Yes. (§ 15-18-104(1))	Not specified.	Not specified.	Declaration "may, but need not" be in the statutory form. (§ 15-18-104(3))

Table 10.02, Part 4 Formal Requirements

	Effect of Pregnancy?	Must Pregnancy Test Be Administered?	Is There a Requirement That a Notified Attending Physician Make the Declaration Part of the Medical Record?	Is There Automatic Severability of Defective Clauses or Does Entire Living Will Fail (Or No Provision)?	Must There Be a Registration of the Living Will?	Must You Follow the Living Will Form in the Statute or Is Something "Substantially" Equivalent a Satisfactory Alternative?
Connecticut	Living will without effect if pregnant. (§ 19a-574)	Not specified.	Yes, as well as any oral communication made by the patient to the physician, other health care person or agent, legal guardian, conservator, or next of kin concerning health care. (§ 19a-578(b))	Not specified.	Not specified. The living will or appointment of health care representative becomes operative when furnished to the attending physician and the declarant is determined to be incapacitated. (§ 19a-579)	Living will may be "substantially" in statutory form. (§ 19a-575)
Delaware	A life-sustaining procedure may not be withheld from a patient known to be pregnant so long as it is probable that the fetus will develop to be viable outside of the uterus. (16 § 2503(j))	Not specified.	Yes. (16 § 2508(b))	Not specified.	Not specified.	Statutory form "may, but need not" be used to create an advance health-care directive. Individuals may complete or modify all or any part of the following form. (16 § 2505)
District of Columbia	Not specified.	N/A	Yes. (§7-622(b))	Severability of additional specific directions found to be invalid. (§7-622(c))	Not specified.	A declaration must be substantially in the form set forth in §7-622, but may include other specific directions of the declarant. (§7-622(c))

Table 10.02, Part 4 Formal Requirements

	Effect of Pregnancy?	Must Pregnancy Test Be Administered?	Is There a Requirement That a Notified Attending Physician Make the Declaration Part of the Medical Record?	Is There Automatic Severability of Defective Clauses or Does Entire Living Will Fail (Or No Provision)?	Must There Be a Registration of the Living Will?	Must You Follow the Living Will Form in the Statute or Is Something "Substantially" Equivalent a Satisfactory Alternative?
Florida	Surrogate/proxy cannot consent to the withdrawal of life-prolonging procedures prior to viability unless principal expressly delegated such authority in writing. (§765.113)	Not specified.	Yes. (§765.302(2))	Not specified.	Not specified.	May be in same form, but need not to be valid. (§765.303(1))
Georgia	If the attending physician determines that the declarant is pregnant, physician must determine that fetus is not viable and that living will specifically indicates that living will is to be carried out. Otherwise, the living will cannot be in effect. (§31-32-9(a)(1)	Not specified, but states that physician, to the best of his knowledge, shall determine if declarant is pregnant and if fetus is viable. (§31-32-9(a)(1))	Yes. (§31-32-8(1))	Not specified.	Not specified.	"Any declaration" expressing declarant's intent shall be honored, regardless of form. Declarations "similar to" statutory form or "substantially" in form specified under prior law shall be presumed valid. (§§31-32-5(b), 31-32-3)
Hawaii	Not specified.	Not specified.	Yes. (§327E-7(b))	Not specified.	Not specified.	Statutory form is optional and may be modified in any way, or a different form that contains the substance of the optional form may be used. (§§327E-16, 327E-3(j))
Idaho	If diagnosed as pregnant, living will has no force during course of pregnancy. (§39-4510)	Not specified. (§39-4510)	Not specified. (§39-4510)	Not specified.	No. (§§39-4514(9); 39-4510(2))	Living will shall be "substantially" in statutory form or another form that contains the same elements. (§39-4510(1))

Table 10.02, Part 4 Formal Requirements

	Effect of Pregnancy?	Must Pregnancy Test Be Administered?	Is There a Requirement That a Notified Attending Physician Make the Declaration Part of the Medical Record?	Is There Automatic Severability of Defective Clauses or Does Entire Living Will Fail (Or No Provision)?	Must There Be a Registration of the Living Will?	Must You Follow the Living Will Form in the Statute or Is Something "Substantially" Equivalent a Satisfactory Alternative?
Illinois	Void if attending physician believes the fetus could develop to live birth. (755 ILCS §35/3(c))	Not specified.	Yes. (755 ILCS §35/3(d))	Severability. (755 ILCS §35/3(e))	Not specified.	Declaration "may, but need not" be in the statutory form, and may include other specific directions. (755 ILCS §35/3(e))
Indiana	A living will declaration of a person diagnosed as pregnant by the attending physician has no effect during the person's pregnancy. (§16-36-4-8(d))	Not specified.	Yes. (§16-36-4-8(e))	The invalidity of any additional specific directions does not affect the validity of the declaration. (§16-36-4-9)	Not specified.	A living will declaration must substantially follow the form set forth in §16-36-4-10, but may also include additional specific directions of the declarant. (§16-36-4-9)
Iowa	If the attending physician knows patient is pregnant, the living will cannot be in effect as long as fetus could develop to live birth. (§144A.6(2))	Not specified. (§144A.6(2))	Not specified, but implied, since revocation of the directive *must* be made part of the declarant's medical record. (§144A.4(2))	Not specified.	Not specified.	Declaration may be, but "need not be" in the statutory form. (§144A.3(5))
Kansas	If the attending physician has diagnosed declarant as pregnant, the declaration is ineffective during the course of pregnancy. (§65-28,103(a))	Not specified. (§65-28,103(a))	Yes. (§65-28,103(b))	Automatic severability. (§65-28,103(c))	Not specified.	Must be in substantially the same form but may include other specific directions. (§65-28,103(c))

Table 10.02, Part 4 Formal Requirements

	Effect of Pregnancy?	Must Pregnancy Test Be Administered?	Is There a Requirement That a Notified Attending Physician Make the Declaration Part of the Medical Record?	Is There Automatic Severability of Defective Clauses or Does Entire Living Will Fail (Or No Provision)?	Must There Be a Registration of the Living Will?	Must You Follow the Living Will Form in the Statute or Is Something "Substantially" Equivalent a Satisfactory Alternative?
Kentucky	If the patient is diagnosed as pregnant the directive shall have no force during the course of the pregnancy unless the life-prolonging procedures will not allow for the continuing development and live birth of the unborn child, or will be physically harmful to the woman, or will prolong severe pain. (§ 311.629(4))	Not specified.	Yes. (§ 311.633(1))	If any additional specific directions are held to be invalid, that invalidity shall not affect the directive. (§ 311.625(1))	Not specified.	§ 311.625(1) states that a living will directive shall be substantially in the form set forth in that section and may include additional specific directions. However, § 311.637(6) states that persons can make advance directives outside the provisions of § 311.625.
Louisiana	Not specified.	Not specified.	Yes (or a copy of the declaration). (§ 40:1151.2(B)(3) & (4))	Automatic severability. (§ 40:1151.2(C)(2))	Declarant or attorney "may" register. (§ 40:1151.2 (D)(1))	Declaration may be, but "need not be" in the statutory form and can include other specific directions. (§ 40:1151.2(C)(1))
Maine	Not specified.	N/A	Yes. (18-A § 5-807(b))	Not specified.	Not specified.	The advance healthcare directive form set forth in 18-A § 5-804 is optional and may be modified partially or in its entirety. (18-A § 5-804)
Maryland	Declarant can give specific instructions to be followed if she is pregnant as stated in the statutory form. (Health-Gen. § 5-603(II)(F))	Not specified. (Health-Gen. § 5-603)	Yes. (Health-Gen. § 5-602(f)(2))	Not specified.	Not specified.	Form is only suggested as a guide. Forms may be partially completed, and different forms may be used. (Health-Gen. § 5-603)

Table 10.02, Part 4 Formal Requirements

	Effect of Pregnancy?	Must Pregnancy Test Be Administered?	Is There a Requirement That a Notified Attending Physician Make the Declaration Part of the Medical Record?	Is There Automatic Severability of Defective Clauses or Does Entire Living Will Fail (Or No Provision)?	Must There Be a Registration of the Living Will?	Must You Follow the Living Will Form in the Statute or Is Something "Substantially" Equivalent a Satisfactory Alternative?
Massachusetts[1]	Not specified.	Not specified.	Yes. (201D § 5)	Not specified.	Not specified.	No form provided, only specified what is provided in Table 10.02, Parts 1–3.
Michigan	Patient advocate cannot make medical treatment decision to withhold or withdraw treatment from a pregnant patient that would result in the patient's death. (§§ 700.5512(1), 700.5509(1)(d))	Not specified.	Yes. (§ 700.5506(3))	Not specified.	Not specified.	No form provided.
Minnesota	If the attending physician knows that the declarant is pregnant, the living will cannot be in effect as long as the fetus can develop to the point of live birth if life-sustaining treatment is continued. (§ 145B.13(3))	Not specified.	Yes. (§ 145B.06 (Subd. 1)(a))	Not specified.	Not specified.	Must be substantially in the statutory form. (§ 145B.04) Must state all information required in § 145B.03(subd. 2)(b)(1)-(2).
Mississippi	Not specified, except to extent the advanced health-care directive does not override the abortion laws. (§ 41-41-227(7))	Not specified.	Yes. (§ 41-41-215(2))	Not specified.	No specified.	Yes. Although the form "may" be used, "any other writing" may also suffice. (§ 41-41-209)
Missouri	The declaration is not in effect during the declarant's pregnancy if the attending physician diagnosed the declarant as being pregnant. (§ 459.025)	Not specified. (§ 459.025)	Yes. (§ 459.015(2))	Automatic severability. (§ 459.015(3))	Not specified.	The declaration may be in the statutory form, but it is not necessary to use the sample form. In addition, the declaration may include other specific directions. (§ 459.015(3))

Table 10.02, Part 4 Formal Requirements

	Effect of Pregnancy?	Must Pregnancy Test Be Administered?	Is There a Requirement That a Notified Attending Physician Make the Declaration Part of the Medical Record?	Is There Automatic Severability of Defective Clauses or Does Entire Living Will Fail (Or No Provision)?	Must There Be a Registration of the Living Will?	Must You Follow the Living Will Form in the Statute or Is Something "Substantially" Equivalent a Satisfactory Alternative?
Montana	Life-sustaining treatment cannot be withheld from a person known to the attending physician to be pregnant so long as it is probable that the fetus will develop to the point of live birth with the continued application of life-sustaining treatment. (§§ 50-9-106(7), 50-9-202(3))	Not specified.	Yes. (§ 50-9-103(5))	Not specified.	Failure to file the declaration with the attorney general does NOT affect the validity of the registration. (§ 50-9-502(3)(a))	The declaration may, but need not, be in the statutory form. (§ 50-9-103(2))
Nebraska	If physician knows of pregnancy and it is probable that the fetus can develop to live birth if life-sustaining treatment is administered, then the declaration will not be given effect. (§ 20-408(3))	Not specified.	Yes. (§ 20-404(3))	No provision.	Not specified.	Need not be in the statutory form. (§ 20-404(2))
Nevada	Life-sustaining treatment may not be withheld from a patient known to the attending physician to be pregnant so long as it is probable that the fetus will develop to the point of live birth with the continued application of life-sustaining treatment. (§§ 449.624(4), 449.626(6))	Not specified.	Yes. (§ 449.600(2))	Not specified.	Not specified.	Declaration may, but need not, be in statutory form. (§ 449.610)

Table 10.02, Part 4 Formal Requirements

	Effect of Pregnancy?	Must Pregnancy Test Be Administered?	Is There a Requirement That a Notified Attending Physician Make the Declaration Part of the Medical Record?	Is There Automatic Severability of Defective Clauses or Does Entire Living Will Fail (Or No Provision)?	Must There Be a Registration of the Living Will?	Must You Follow the Living Will Form in the Statute or Is Something "Substantially" Equivalent a Satisfactory Alternative?
New Hampshire	Agent does not have authority to consent to a withdrawal of life-sustaining treatment, unless treatment will not permit continuing development and live birth of fetus or will be physically harmful to principal or prolong severe pain which cannot be alleviated by medication. (§§ 137-J:5(V)(c); 137-J:10(IV)(a))	Not specified.	Yes. (§§ 137-J:5(II), 137-J:7(I)(a))	Severability. (§ 137-J:4)	Not specified.	Advance directive must be in substantially similar form). (§ 137-J:20)
New Jersey	Female declarants may include instructions to be followed in the event of pregnancy. (§ 26:2H-56)	Not specified.	Yes. (§ 26:2H-62(a))	Not specified.	Not specified.	Statutory form not provided.
New Mexico	Not specified.	Not specified.	Yes. (§ 24-7A-7(B))	Automatic severability. (§ 24-7A-18)	Not specified.	Directive may, but need not, follow statutory form. Form can be modified partially or in full. (§ 24-7A-4)
New York	Not specified.	Not specified.	Yes. (Pub. Health § 2984(1))	Not specified.	Not specified.	No, a health care proxy may, but need not, be in the statutory form. (Pub. Health § 2981(5)(d))
North Carolina	Not specified.	Not specified.	Not specified.	Not specified.	No, optional. (§ 130A-467)	No (§ 90-321(a)(1a) & (c)), but sample form is "specifically determined to meet the requirements" of the statute. (§ 90-321(d1))

Table 10.02, Part 4 Formal Requirements

	Effect of Pregnancy?	Must Pregnancy Test Be Administered?	Is There a Requirement That a Notified Attending Physician Make the Declaration Part of the Medical Record?	Is There Automatic Severability of Defective Clauses or Does Entire Living Will Fail (Or No Provision)?	Must There Be a Registration of the Living Will?	Must You Follow the Living Will Form in the Statute or Is Something "Substantially" Equivalent a Satisfactory Alternative?
North Dakota	Medical treatment must be provided to a pregnant patient with a terminal condition unless, to a reasonable degree of medical certainty, such medical treatment will not maintain the patient in such a way as to permit the continuing development and live birth of the unborn child or will prolong severe pain. (§ 23-06.5-09(5))	Not specified.	Yes, by implication in § 23-06.5-07(2).	Not specified.	Not specified.	No. The statutory form is an optional, but not a required, form. (§§ 23-06.5-16, 23-06.5-17)
Ohio	Declaration is ineffective if removing the treatments would terminate pregnancy, unless the fetus would not be born alive. (§§ 2133.06(B), 2133.08(G))	Not specified.	Yes. (§ 2133.02(C))	Not specified.	Not specified.	No statutory form is provided. Must follow requirements for execution in § 2133.02. Section 2133.07(B) states that a printed form of a declaration may be sold or distributed for use by adults not advised by an attorney.
Oklahoma	If declarant has been diagnosed as pregnant and the attending physician knows it, the directive has no effect during the course of the pregnancy, unless patient has specifically authorized, "in her own words," that the directive has effect during the course of the pregnancy. (63 § 3101.8(C))	Yes (implied), where appropriate considering age and other factors. (63 § 3101.8(C))	Yes. (63 § 3101.4(D))	Not specified, but implied, since the directive may be revoked "in whole or part." (63 § 3101.6(A))	Not specified.	Advance directive shall be "substantially" in the statutory form. (63 § 3101.4(C))

Table 10.02, Part 4 Formal Requirements

	Effect of Pregnancy?	Must Pregnancy Test Be Administered?	Is There a Requirement That a Notified Attending Physician Make the Declaration Part of the Medical Record?	Is There Automatic Severability of Defective Clauses or Does Entire Living Will Fail (Or No Provision)?	Must There Be a Registration of the Living Will?	Must You Follow the Living Will Form in the Statute or Is Something "Substantially" Equivalent a Satisfactory Alternative?
Oregon	Not specified, but a health care representative may not make any health decision with respect to abortion on behalf of the principal. (§ 127.540(4))	Not specified.	Yes. (§ 127.510(5))	If not in compliance with statutory form or formal requirements, the directive is not valid, but will constitute evidence of the patient's desires. (§ 127.535(6))	Not specified.	Must be in the statutory form, although declarant may cross out or add words to express wishes better. (§ 127.531(1))
Pennsylvania	Life-sustaining treatment, nutrition and hydration must be provided unless, to a reasonable degree of medical certainty, they will not maintain the pregnant woman in a way as to permit continuing development and live birth of the unborn child, will be physically harmful to the pregnant woman, or will cause pain to the pregnant woman that cannot be alleviated by medication. (20 §5429)	No, unless the physician has reason to believe the woman may be pregnant. (20 §5429(c))	Yes. (20 §§ 5443(d), 5462(d))	Severability. (20 §5443(c))	Not specified.	Declaration may, but need not, be in the statutory form, and may include other specific directions. (20 §§5447 (living will); 5465 (health care power of attorney); 5471 (combined form)) (20 §5433
Rhode Island	Declaration is void as long as it is probable that the fetus could develop to live birth. (§23-4.11-6(c))	Not specified.	Yes. (§ 23-4.11-3(b))	Severability. (§ 23-4.11-15)	Not specified.	Declaration may, but need not, be in the statutory form. (§ 23-4.11-3(d))
South Carolina	If declarant has been diagnosed as pregnant, the declaration is not effective during the course of the pregnancy. (§ 44-77-70)	Not specified. (§ 44-77-70)	Not specified.	Not specified.	Not specified.	Declaration must be substantially in statutory form, with revocation provisions appearing in upper case or boldface. (§ 44-77-50)

Table 10.02, Part 4 Formal Requirements

	Effect of Pregnancy?	Must Pregnancy Test Be Administered?	Is There a Requirement That a Notified Attending Physician Make the Declaration Part of the Medical Record?	Is There Automatic Severability of Defective Clauses or Does Entire Living Will Fail (Or No Provision)?	Must There Be a Registration of the Living Will?	Must You Follow the Living Will Form in the Statute or Is Something "Substantially" Equivalent a Satisfactory Alternative?
South Dakota	Pregnant woman will be given life-sustaining treatment and food/hydration unless these procedures will not result in live birth or will be harmful/painful to the female as decided by attending physician and one other physician. (§34-12D-10)	Not specified.	Yes. (§34-12D-7)	No provision.	Not specified.	May, but need not, be in the statutory form. (§34-12D-3)
Tennessee	Not specified.	Not specified.	Yes. (§32-11-104(b))	Automatic severability. (§32-11-110(g))	Not specified.	Declaration shall be "substantially" in the statutory form provided for in §32-11-105. (§32-11-104(a)) This is not to the exclusion of other written and clear expressions of intent to accept, refuse, or withdraw medical care. (§32-11-105)
Texas	A person may not withdraw/withhold life-sustaining procedures from a pregnant patient. (Health & Safety §166.049)	Not specified. (Health & Safety §166.049)	Yes. (Health & Safety §§166.032(d) & 166.034(c) (for unwritten directive))	Not specified.	Not specified.	Only states that directive "may be" written in the statutory form, not specified otherwise. (Health & Safety §166.033)
Utah	A directive has no force during a declarant's pregnancy. (§75-2a-123)	Not specified. (§75-2a-123)	Yes. (§75-2a-115(2)(b)(1))	Not specified.	Not specified.	A health care directive is presumed valid if in the optional form of the statute or a substantially similar form. (§75-2a-117(1))

Table 10.02, Part 4 Formal Requirements

	Effect of Pregnancy?	Must Pregnancy Test Be Administered?	Is There a Requirement That a Notified Attending Physician Make the Declaration Part of the Medical Record?	Is There Automatic Severability of Defective Clauses or Does Entire Living Will Fail (Or No Provision)?	Must There Be a Registration of the Living Will?	Must You Follow the Living Will Form in the Statute or Is Something "Substantially" Equivalent a Satisfactory Alternative?
Vermont	Can direct which life sustaining procedures the principal would or would not desire if pregnant. (18 §9702(8)(a))	Not specified.	Yes, every health care provider must develop a system to ensure directive is available when services are rendered. (18 §9709)	Severability. (18 §9720)	Individuals may submit directive to registry. (18 §9701(28))	No statutory form.
Virginia	Not specified.	Not specified.	Yes. (§54.1-2983)	Not specified. (§54.1-2984)	Not specified.	Directive may, but need not, be in statutory form. (§54.1-2984)
Washington	If declarant has been diagnosed as pregnant and the physician knows it, the health-care directive has no effect during the pregnancy (as indicated in the statutory form). (§70.122.030(1)(d))	Not specified. (§70.122.030(1)(d))	Yes. (§70.122.030(1))	Automatic severability. (§§70.122.905, 70.122.920)	No, but it may be registered. (§§70.122.040(1)(d), 70.122.130(2)(b) & (d))	Directive may be in statutory form, but it may include other specific directions. (§70.122.030(1))
West Virginia	Not specified, but the statute expressly states that the common law doctrine of medical necessity is not abrogated. (§16-30-17)	Not specified.	Yes. (§16-30-4(d))	Automatic severability. (§16-30-4(g))	Not specified.	May but "need not be" in the statutory form and can include other specific directions. (§16-30-4(g))
Wisconsin	Declaration has no effect during pregnancy. (§154.07(2))	Not specified.	Yes. (§§154.03(1), 154.11(8))	No provision.	No, registration for a fee is optional. (§154.13(1))	No, not limited to the statutory form but declarations prepared and provided by department of health and family services shall be in statutory form. (§§154.02(1), 154.03(2))
Wyoming	Not specified. (§35-22-403)	Not specified. (§35-22-403)	Yes. (§35-22-408(c))	Not specified.	Not specified.	No form provided.

[1] Only deals with health care proxies.

Table 10.03, Part 1 Revocation

	What Physical Acts Accomplish This?	If a Writing, Is It Sufficient If:				
		By a Writing?	Signed by Declarant?	Signed by a Person (1) In His Presence and (2) At His Direction?	Dated?	Witnessed?
Alabama	Burning, obliteration, tearing, destroying, or defacing in a manner showing intention to revoke. (§ 22-8A-5(a)(1))	Yes. (§ 22-8A-5(a)(2))	Yes. (§ 22-8A-5(a)(2))	(1) Not specified. (2) Yes. (§ 22-8A-5(a)(2))	Yes. (§ 22-8A-5(a)(2))	No. (§ 22-8A-5(a)(2))
Alaska	States any manner that communicates an intent to revoke advance health care directives. (§ 13.52.020(b)) However, to revoke appointment of agent must be by writing or personal notification to health care provider. (§ 13.52.020(a)	Yes (implied, since any manner qualifies). (§ 13.52.020(b)) Required to revoke appointment of agent. (§ 13.52.020(a))	Not specified for advance health care directive. (§ 13.52.020(b)) Yes, for revocation of agent. (§ 13.52.020(a))	Not specified. (§ 13.52.020(a) &(b))	Not specified. (§ 13.52.020(a) & (b))	Not specified. (§ 13.52.020(b))
Arizona	Making a new health-care directive or any act that demonstrates a specific intent to revoke a directive. (§ 36-3202(3) & (4))	Yes. (§ 36-3202(1))	Not specified.	Not specified.	Not specified.	Not specified.
Arkansas	"Communication [in any manner] to the attending physician or other health care provider by the declarant or a witness to the revocation." (§ 20-17-204(a))	Yes, but presumably not required, since "communication" is used. (§ 20-17-204(a)	Not specified.	Not specified.	Not specified.	Not specified. But revocation can be "communicated" by a witness. (§ 20-17-204(a))

Table 10.03, Part 1 Revocation

| | What Physical Acts Accomplish This? | If a Writing, Is It Sufficient If: | | | | |
		By a Writing?	Signed by Declarant?	Signed by a Person (1) In His Presence and (2) At His Direction?	Dated?	Witnessed?
California	Patient having capacity can revoke advance health care directive at any time and in any manner that communicates an intent to revoke. (Probate § 4695(b))	Yes, presumably. (Probate § 4695(b)) A writing (or oral notification) is required for revocation of designation of an agent. (§ 4695(a))	Not specified. Yes, for revocation of agent designation. (Probate § 4695(a))	Not specified.	Not specified.	Not specified.
Colorado	Burning, tearing, canceling, obliterating, or destroying. (§ 15-18-109)	Yes, but oral declaration is allowed as well. (§ 15-18-109)	Not specified. (§ 15-18-109)	Not specified. (§ 15-18-109)	Not specified. (§ 15-18-109)	Not specified. (§ 15-18-109)
Connecticut	Can be done in any manner by the declarant. (§ 19a-579a(a))	Yes (but not specifically required). (§ 19a-579a(a))	Not specified.	Not specified.	Not specified.	Not specified.
Delaware	A health-care directive may be revoked in any manner that communicates an intent to revoke. It must be done in the presence of two competent persons, one of whom is a health care provider. (16 § 2504(a)(2))	Yes. (16 § 2504(a)(1))	Written revocation must be signed by the declarant. (16 § 2504(a)(1))	Not specified.	Not specified.	A revocation must be witnessed only if it is not done by a signed writing. (16 § 2504(a)(2))

Table 10.03, Part 1 Revocation

	What Physical Acts Accomplish This?	If a Writing, Is It Sufficient If:				
		By a Writing?	Signed by Declarant?	Signed by a Person (1) In His Presence and (2) At His Direction?	Dated?	Witnessed?
District of Columbia	A declaration may be revoked by being obliterated, burned, torn, or otherwise destroyed by the declarant or by some person in the declarant's presence and at the declarant's direction. (§7-624(a)(1))	Yes. (§7-624(a)(2))	Yes. (§7-624(a)(2))	(1) Not specified. (2) Yes. (§7-624(a)(2))	Yes. (§7-624(a)(2))	Not specified.
Florida	Physical cancellation/ destruction by principal or by another in the principal's presence/direction. (§765.104(1)(b))	Yes. (§765.104(1)(a))	Yes. (§765.104(1)(a))	Not specified.	Yes. (§765.104(1)(a))	Not specified.
Georgia	Being defaced, obliterated, burned, canceled, torn, or destroyed by the declarant (or person in his presence at his direction). (§31-32-6(a)(2))	Yes. (§31-32-6(a)(3))	Yes. (§31-32-6(a)(3))	(1) Not specified. (§31-32-6(a)(3)) (2) Yes. (§31-32-6(a)(3))	Yes. (§31-32-6(a)(3))	Not specified. (§31-32-6(a)(3))

Table 10.03, Part 1 Revocation

	What Physical Acts Accomplish This?	By a Writing?	Signed by Declarant?	If a Writing, Is It Sufficient If: Signed by a Person (1) In His Presence and (2) At His Direction?	Dated?	Witnessed?
Hawaii	Advanced health care directive can be revoked at any time and in any manner that communicates an intent to revoke. (§327E-4(b)) Designation of agent may be revoked only in writing or in direct communication to health care provider. (§372E-4(a))	Yes, presumed for advance health care directive. (§327E-4(b)) Required for revocation of agent designation. (§327E-4(a))	Yes, for revocation of agent designation. (§327E-4(a))	Not allowed for revocation of agent designation. (§327E-4(a))	Not specified.	Not specified.
Idaho	Intentionally defacing, cancelling, burning, tearing, obliteration, or destroying by the declarant or another person at the declarant's direction. (§39-4511A(1)(a))	Yes. (§39-4511A(1)(b))	Yes. (§39-4511A(1)(b))	Can be revoked by destruction by some person in declarant's presence and by his direction. But, not specified for writing. (§39-4511A(1)(a))	Not specified. (§39-4511A)	Not specified. (§39-4511A)
Illinois	Obliterating, burning, tearing, or otherwise destroying or defacing the declaration in a manner indicating an intent to cancel. (755 ILCS §35/5(a)(1))	Yes. (755 ILCS §35/5(a)(2))	Yes. (755 ILCS §35/5(a)(2))	(1) Not specified. (2) Yes. (755 ILCS §35/5(a)(2))	Yes. (755 ILCS §35/5(a)(2))	Not specified.

Table 10.03, Part 1 Revocation

	What Physical Acts Accomplish This?	If a Writing, Is It Sufficient If:		Signed by a Person (1) In His Presence and (2) At His Direction?	Dated?	Witnessed?
		By a Writing?	Signed by Declarant?			
Indiana	A living will declaration can be revoked by physical cancellation or destruction of the declaration by the declarant or another person in the declarant's presence and at the declarant's direction. (§16-36-4-12(a)(2))	Yes. (§16-36-4-12(a)(1))	Yes. (§16-36-4-12(a)(1))	Not specified.	Yes. (§16-36-4-12(a)(1))	Not specified.
Iowa	Any manner by which the declarant is able to communicate his intent to revoke causes revocation. (§144A.4(1))	Yes (implied since any manner with intent satisfies). (§144A.4(1))	Not specified.	Not specified.	Not specified.	Not specified.
Kansas	Being obliterated, burned, torn, or destroyed or defaced in a manner indicating intention to cancel. (§65-28,104(a)(1))	Yes. (§65-28,104(a)(2))	Yes. (§65-28,104(a)(2))	(1) Not specified. (§65-28,104(a)(2)) (2) Yes. (§65-28,104(a)(2))	Yes. (§65-28,104(a)(2))	Not specified. (§65-28,104(a)(2))
Kentucky	A directive may be revoked by destruction of the document by the grantor, or by some person in the grantor's presence and at the grantor's direction. (§311.627(1)(c))	Yes. (§311.627(1)(a))	Yes. (§311.627(1)(a))	Not specified.	Yes. (§311.627(1)(a))	Not specified.

Table 10.03, Part 1 Revocation

| | What Physical Acts Accomplish This? | If a Writing, Is It Sufficient If: | | | |
		By a Writing?	Signed by Declarant?	Signed by a Person (1) In His Presence and (2) At His Direction?	Dated?	Witnessed?
Louisiana	Being defaced, canceled, obliterated, burned, torn, or destroyed by the declarant or someone in his presence and at his direction. (§ 40:1151.3(A)(1))	Yes. (§ 40:1151.3(A)(2))	Yes. (§ 40:1151.3(A)(2))	Not specified. (§ 40:1151.3(A)(2))	Yes. (§ 40:1151.3(A)(2))	Not specified. (§ 40:1151.3(A)(2))
Maine	An individual with capacity may revoke all or part of an advance health-care directive at any time and in any manner that communicates an intent to revoke. (18-A § 5-803(b)) Revocation of agent designation must be in writing or by personally informing the supervising health care provider. (18-A § 5-803(a))	Yes (presumed, since "any manner" is sufficient). (18-A § 5-803(b)) Required for revocation of agent designation. (18-A § 5-803(a))	Not specified. Required for revocation of agent designation. (18-A § 5-803(a))	Not specified.	Not specified.	Not specified.
Maryland	"Physical cancellation" or destruction. (Health-Gen. § 5-604(a))	Yes. (Health-Gen. § 5-604(a))	Yes. (Health-Gen. § 5-604(a))	Not specified. (Health-Gen. § 5-604)	Yes. (Health-Gen. § 5-604(a))	Not specified. (Health-Gen. § 5-604)
Massachusetts[1]	Any act evidencing an intent to revoke. (201D §7)	Yes. (201D §7)	Not specified.	Not specified.	Not specified.	Not specified.

Table 10.03, Part 1 Revocation

	What Physical Acts Accomplish This?	If a Writing, Is It Sufficient If:				
		By a Writing?	Signed by Declarant?	Signed by a Person (1) In His Presence and (2) At His Direction?	Dated?	Witnessed?
Michigan	Any manner by which the patient is able to communicate his intent to revoke causes revocation. (§ 700.5510(d))	Yes. (§ 700.5510(d))	Not specified. (§ 700.5510(d))	Not specified. (§ 700.5510(d))	Not specified. (§ 700.5510(d))	Not specified. (§ 700.5510(d))
Minnesota	Declaration can be revoked in any manner by the declarant. (§ 145B.09(Subd. 1))	Yes (implied since can be revoked in any manner). (§ 145B.09 (Subd.1))	Not specified.	Not specified.	Not specified.	Not specified.
Mississippi	Advance health care directive may be revoked "at any time and in any manner that communicates an intent to revoke." (§ 41-41-207(2)) Designation of agent must be revoked in writing or by personally informing health care providers. (§ 41-41-207(1))	Yes (implied) since can be revoked in any manner. (§ 41-41-207(2)) Required for agent designation revocation. (§ 41-41-207(2))	No specified.	Not specified.	Not specified.	Not specified.
Missouri	Any manner by which the declarant is able to communicate his intent to revoke causes revocation. (§ 459.020(1))	Yes. (§§ 459.015(3, 459.020(1))	Yes (as indicated in the statutory form). (§ 459.015(3))	Not specified. (§ 459.015(3))	Yes (as indicated in the statutory form). (§ 459.015(3))	No (not required in the statutory form). (§ 459.015(3))

Table 10.03, Part 1 Revocation

	What Physical Acts Accomplish This?	If a Writing, Is It Sufficient If:				Witnessed?
		By a Writing?	Signed by Declarant?	Signed by a Person (1) In His Presence and (2) At His Direction?	Dated?	
Montana	A declarant may revoke a declaration at any time and in any manner, without regard to mental or physical condition. Such declaration must be communicated to the attending physician. (§ 50-9-104(1))	Presumably, since any manner is sufficient. (§ 50-9-104(1))	Not specified.	Not specified.	Not specified.	Presumably yes. If not directly witnessed by or communicated by declarant to attending physician, attending advance practice registered nurse, emergency medical care personnel or health care provider is not valid unless attending physician is informed of revocation (by witness—presumably) before patient needs life-sustaining treatment. (§ 50-9-104(1))
Nebraska	Declaration may be revoked "at any time" and in "any manner." (§ 20-406(1))	Yes, presumably, since "any manner" is sufficient. (§ 20-406(1))	Not specified.	Not specified.	Not specified.	Not specified.
Nevada	A declarant may revoke a declaration at any time and in any manner, without regard to mental or physical condition. Such declaration must be communicated to the attending physician or other health-care provider. (§ 449.620(1))	Yes, presumably, since "any manner" is sufficient. (§ 449.620(1))	Not specified.	Not specified.	Not specified.	Not specified.

Table 10.03, Part 1 Revocation

| | What Physical Acts Accomplish This? | If a Writing, Is It Sufficient If: | | | |
		By a Writing?	Signed by Declarant?	Signed by a Person (1) In His Presence and (2) At His Direction?	Dated?	Witnessed?
New Hampshire	Burning, tearing, obliterating, or other act evidencing a specific intent to revoke or causing the same to be done by another person at the principal's direction and in the principal's presence. (§ 137-J:15(I)(a))	Yes. (§ 137-J:15(I)(a)-(b))	Yes. (§ 137-J:15(I)(a)-(b))	Not specified.	Yes, with respect to a written revocation but not necessarily by a subsequent executed advance directive. (§ 137-J:15(I)(a)-(b))	No, if written revocation. Yes, if by a subsequent executed advance directive, except if a notary is used. (§ 137-J:15(I)(a)-(b))
New Jersey	Oral or written notification to health care representative, physician, nurse/ other health care person, or a reliable witness, execution of another advance directive, or any other act showing an intent to revoke. (§ 26:2H-57(b)(1) & (2))	Yes. (§ 26:2H-57(b)(1))	Not specified.	Not specified.	Not specified.	Not specified.

Table 10.03, Part 1 Revocation

	What Physical Acts Accomplish This?	If a Writing, Is It Sufficient If:				
		By a Writing?	Signed by Declarant?	Signed by a Person (1) In His Presence and (2) At His Direction?	Dated?	Witnessed?
New Mexico	States any manner that communicates an intent to revoke. (§24-7A-3(B)) The statutory form allows for "personally informing the supervising healthcare provider." (§24-7A-4) Revocation of agent designation must be by signed writing or personally informing health care provider. (§24-7A-3(A))	Yes (implied, since any manner qualifies). (§24-7A-3(B)) Required for revocation of agent designation. (§24-7A-3(A))	Not specified for revocation of advance health care directive. (§24-7A-3(B)) Revocation of agent designation must be signed by the patient. (§24-7A-3(A))	Not specified for revocation of advance health care directive. (§24-7A-3(B)) For revocation of agent designation—two individuals. (§24-7A-3(A))	Not specified. (§24-7A-3(B))	Not specified. (§24-7A-3(B)) Yes, if written revocation of agent designated by patient who does not have ability to sign for self.
New York	Any act evidencing a specific intent to revoke the proxy. (Pub. Health §2985(1)(a))	Yes. (Pub. Health §2985(1)(a))	Yes, presumably if in writing. (Pub. Health §2985(1)(a))	Not specified.	Not specified.	Not specified.
North Carolina	Any manner by which the declarant is able to communicate his intent to revoke. (§90-321(e))	Yes. (§§90-321(e), 90-321(d1)—statutory form)	Yes. (§§90-321(e), 90-321(d1)—statutory form)	Not specified. (§90-321(e))	Not specified. (§90-321(e))	Not specified. (§90-321(e))

Table 10.03, Part 1 Revocation

	What Physical Acts Accomplish This?	By a Writing?	*If a Writing, Is It Sufficient If:*			
			Signed by Declarant?	Signed by a Person (1) In His Presence and (2) At His Direction?	Dated?	Witnessed?
North Dakota	A health care directive is revoked by notification by the principal to the agent or a health care or long-term care services provider orally, or in writing, or by any other act evidencing a specific intent to revoke the directive; or by execution by the principal of a subsequent health care directive. (§ 23-06.5-07(1)(a) & (b))	Yes. (§ 23-06.5-07(1)(a)))	Not specified. (§ 23-06.5-07)	Not specified. (§ 23-06.5-07)	Not specified. (§ 23-06.5-07)	Not specified.
Ohio	Revocation can occur at any time and in any manner. (§ 2133.04(A))	Presumably yes since revocation can be done "in any manner." (§ 2133.04(A))	Not specified.	Not specified.	Not specified.	Not specified.
Oklahoma	Directive may be revoked in whole or in part at any time and in any manner by the declarant. (63 § 3101.6(A))	Yes (implied), since it can be revoked in any manner by the declarant. (63 § 3101.6(A))	Not specified.	Not specified. (63 § 3101.6(A))	Not specified. (63 § 3101.6(A))	Not specified. (63 § 3101.6(A))
Oregon	Revocation may occur at any time and in any manner that communicates the intent to revoke. (§ 127.545(1))	Presumably yes since "any manner." (§ 127.545(1))	Not specified but can be revoked at any time and in any manner by a capable principal. (§ 127.545(1)(b))	Not specified.	Not specified.	Not specified.

Table 10.03, Part 1 Revocation

	What Physical Acts Accomplish This?	If a Writing, Is It Sufficient If:				
		By a Writing?	Signed by Declarant?	Signed by a Person (1) In His Presence and (2) At His Direction?	Dated?	Witnessed?
Pennsylvania	Revocation may occur at any time and in any manner. (20 § 5444(a))	Presumably yes since "any manner" is sufficient. (20 § 5444(a))	Not specified.	Not specified.	Not specified.	Not specified.
Rhode Island	Any manner which communicates an intent to revoke. (§ 23-4.11-4(a)(1))	Presumably yes since "any manner." (§ 23-4.11-4(a)(1))	Not specified.	Not specified.	Not specified.	Not specified.
South Carolina	Being defaced, obliterated, torn, or otherwise destroyed in any manner indicating an intention to revoke. (§ 44-77-80(1))	Yes. (§ 44-77-80(2))	Yes. (§ 44-77-80(2))	Not specified, but can be revoked in writing by the declarant's designee. (§ 44-77-80(1) & (4))	Yes. (§ 44-77-80(2))	Not specified. (§ 44-77-80(2))
South Dakota	Declaration can be revoked at any time and in any manner. (§ 34-12D-8)	Presumably yes. (§ 34-12D-8)	Not specified.	Not specified.	Not specified.	Not specified.
Tennessee	Statute only refers to written or oral revocation. (§ 32-11-106)	Yes. (§ 32-11-106(1))	Yes. (§ 32-11-106(1))	Not specified. (§ 32-11-106(1))	Yes. (§ 32-11-106(1))	Not specified. (§ 32-11-106(1))
Texas	Being defaced, canceled, obliterated, burned, torn, or otherwise destroyed by the declarant or someone at his direction/presence. (Health & Safety § 166.042(a)(1))	Yes. (Health & Safety § 166.042(a)(2))	Yes. (Health & Safety § 166.042(a)(2))	Not specified.	Yes. (Health & Safety § 166.042(a)(2))	Not specified.

Table 10.03, Part 1 Revocation

	What Physical Acts Accomplish This?	If a Writing, Is It Sufficient If:				
		By a Writing?	Signed by Declarant?	Signed by a Person (1) In His Presence and (2) At His Direction?	Dated?	Witnessed?
Utah	Being obliterated, burned, torn, or otherwise destroyed or defaced in any manner indicating an intention to revoke, including writing "void" across it or instructing another to do such acts. (§75-2a-114)	Yes. (§75-2a-114(1)(d))	Yes. (§75-2a-114(1)(d))	Presence not specified. The person must be at the direction of the declarant. (§75-2a-114(1)(d)(ii))	Yes. (§75-2a-114(1)(d))	Not specified.
Vermont	Burning, tearing, or obliterating by declarant or another in declarant's presence and at his direction. (18 §9704(b)(1)(C))	Yes. (18 §9704(b)(1)(A))	Not specified.	Not specified.	Not specified	Not specified.
Virginia	"Physical cancellation" or destruction. (§54.1-2985(ii))	Yes. (§54.1-2985(i))	Yes. (§54.1-2985(i))	Not specified. (§54.1-2985)	Yes. (§54.1-2985(i))	Not specified. (§54.1-2985)
Washington	Being defaced, canceled, obliterated, burned, torn, or otherwise destroyed by declarant or at his direction in his presence. (§70.122.040(1)(a))	Yes. (§70.122.040(1)(b))	Yes. (§70.122.040(1)(b))	Not specified. (§70.122.040(1)(b))	Yes. (§70.122.040(1)(b))	Not specified. (§70.122.040(1)(b))
West Virginia	By being destroyed by the declarant or someone at his direction and in his presence. (§16-30-18(a)(1))	Yes. (§16-30-18(a)(2))	Yes. (§16-30-18(a)(2))	(1) Not specified. (2) Yes. (§16-30-18(a)(2))	Yes. (§16-30-18(a)(2))	Not specified.

Table 10.03, Part 1 Revocation

	What Physical Acts Accomplish This?	If a Writing, Is It Sufficient If:				
		By a Writing?	Signed by Declarant?	Signed by a Person (1) In His Presence and (2) At His Direction?	Dated?	Witnessed?
Wisconsin	By being cancelled, defaced, obliterated, burned, torn, or otherwise destroyed by declarant or another at declarant's direction and in declarant's presence. (§ 154.05(1)(a))	Yes. (§ 154.05(1)(b))	Yes. (§ 154.05(1)(b))	Not specified.	Yes. (§ 154.05(1)(b))	Not specified.
Wyoming	An individual with capacity may revoke all or part of an advance health care directive, other than the designation of an agent at any time and in any manner that communicates an intent to revoke. (§ 35-22-404(b)) Revoking the designation of an agent must be in a signed writing. (§ 35-22-404(a))	Yes. (§ 35-22-404(b)) Any oral revocation shall, as soon as possible, be documented in a writing signed and dated by the individual or a witness to the revocation. (§ 35-22-404(b))	Yes. (§ 35-22-404(b))	(1) Not specified. (§ 35-22-404) (2) Not specified. (§ 35-22-404)	Yes. (§ 35-22-404(b))	Not specified. (§ 35-22-404)

[1] Only deals with health care proxies.

Table 10.03, Part 2 Revocation

	Witnesses	Capacity of Witnesses	Subsequent Confirmatory Writing by Witness Required	Requirement of Doctor Recording Notice of Revocation in Medical Record	Verbally — Sufficient If Physician Sees Actual Confirmatory Writing Revoking Living Will?	Is Another Form of Notification Satisfactory?	If So, from Whom?
Alabama	One witness is required for oral statement. (§ 22-8A-5(a)(3))	At least 19 years old. (§ 22-8A-5(a)(3))	Yes. (§ 22-8A-5(a)(3))	Yes. (§ 22-8A-5(a)(3))	Yes. A health care provider or attending physician must receive the writing. (§ 22-8A-5(a)(3))	Not specified. A health care provider or attending physician must receive the writing. (§ 22-8A-5(a)(3))	Not specified. (§ 22-8A-5(a)(3))

Table 10.03, Part 2 Revocation

	Witnesses	Capacity of Witnesses	Subsequent Confirmatory Writing by Witness Required	Verbally — Requirement of Doctor Recording Notice of Revocation in Medical Record	Sufficient If Physician Sees Actual Confirmatory Writing Revoking Living Will?	Is Another Form of Notification Satisfactory?	If So, from Whom?
Alaska	Not specified, but implied that oral revocation satisfies since any manner qualifies. (§ 13.52.020(b)) However, in the case of revocation of agent, verbal revocation must be made personally to the health care provider. (§ 13.52.020(a)) Special rules apply to a principal suffering from mental illness (§ 13.52.020(c)). Communication of revocation given to a health care provider, agent, guardian, or surrogate, must be communicated immediately to the supervising health care provider and any health care institution at which the patient is receiving care. (§ 13.52.020(d))	Not specified. See Col. 1.	Not specified. (§ 13.52.020(b))	Yes. (§ 13.52.020(c))	Not specified. (§ 13.52.020(c))	Yes. (§ 13.52.020(b))	Not specified. (§ 13.52.020)

Table 10.03, Part 2 Revocation

	Witnesses	Capacity of Witnesses	Subsequent Confirmatory Writing by Witnesses Required	Requirement of Doctor Recording Notice of Revocation in Medical Record (Verbally)	Sufficient If Physician Sees Actual Confirmatory Writing Revoking Living Will?	Is Another Form of Notification Satisfactory?	If So, from Whom?
Arizona	Oral notification must be made to surrogate or health care provider. (§36-3202(2))	Not specified.	Not specified.	Not specified.	Not specified.	Not specified.	Not specified.
Arkansas[1]	Not specified.	Not specified.	Not specified.	Yes. (§20-17-204(b))	Not specified, but implied. (§20-17-204(a))	Yes, any communication from the declarant or a witness to the revocation. (§20-17-204(a))	Yes, any communication from the declarant or a witness to the revocation. (§20-17-204(a))
California	Not specified, but implied that oral revocation satisfies since any manner qualifies. (Probate §4695(b)) However, in case of revocation of agent, verbal revocation must be made personally to the health care provider. (Probate §4695(a))	Not specified.	Not specified.	Yes. (Probate §4731(a))	Not specified.	Not specified.	Not specified, but provider, agent, conservator, or surrogate who is informed of revocation is obligated to notify provider. (Probate §4696)
Colorado	Oral revocation is permitted, but no witness requirement is specified. (§15-18-109)	Not specified. (§15-18-109)	Not specified. (§15-18-109)	Not specified. (§15-18-109)	Not specified.	Not specified. (§15-18-109)	Not specified. (§15-18-109)

Table 10.03, Part 2 Revocation

					Verbally		
	Witnesses	Capacity of Witnesses	Subsequent Confirmatory Writing by Witness Required	Requirement of Doctor Recording Notice of Revocation in Medical Record	Sufficient If Physician Sees Actual Confirmatory Writing Revoking Living Will?	Is Another Form of Notification Satisfactory?	If So, from Whom?
Connecticut	Not specified, but statute refers to revocation "by the declarant." (§19a-579a(a))	Not specified.	Not specified.	Yes. (§19a-579a(b))	Not specified.	Revocation "at any time and in any manner" is satisfactory. (§19a-579a(a))	Not specified.
Delaware	A verbal revocation must be done in the presence of two competent persons, one of whom is a health care provider. (16 §2504(a)(2))	Competent. (16 §2504(a)(2))	Yes. Witnesses must memorialize the revocation in writing. It must be signed and dated by both witnesses. (16 §2504(b))	Yes. (16 §2508(b))	Not specified, but presumed. (16 §2504(b) & (c))	Any manner that communicates an intent to revoke is sufficient if done in the presence of two competent witnesses, one of whom is a health care provider. (16 §2504(a)(2))	Not specified.
District of Columbia	Declarant must verbally revoke in the presence of a witness. (§7-624(a)(3))	Witness must be 18 years or older. (§7-624(a)(3))	Yes. (§7-624(a)(3))	Yes. (§7-624(a)(3))	Yes. (§7-624(a)(3))	Revocation effective upon "communication" to physician. (§7-624(a)(3))	Communication from declarant or person acting on his/her behalf. (§7-624(a)(3))
Florida[2]	Not specified.	Not specified.	Not specified.	Not specified, but implied in requirement that "advance directives shall travel with the patient as part of the patient's medical record." (§765.110(2))	Not specified.	Yes, effective when "communicated" to surrogate, health care provider or facility. (§765.104(3))	Yes, effective when "communicated" to surrogate, health care provider or facility. No specific party mentioned. (§765.104(3))

Table 10.03, Part 2 Revocation

	Witnesses	Capacity of Witnesses	Subsequent Confirmatory Writing by Witness Required	Requirement of Doctor Recording Notice of Revocation in Medical Record	Sufficient If Physician Sees Actual Confirmatory Writing Revoking Living Will?	Is Another Form of Notification Satisfactory?	If So, from Whom?
	Verbally						
Georgia	Oral expression of intent to revoke must be made in the presence of one witness. (§31-32-6(a)(4))	Witness must be 18 years or older. (§31-32-6(a)(4))	Yes, within 30 days. (§31-32-6(a)(4))	Yes. (§31-32-6(a)(3)-(4))	Presumably. Sufficient if revocation is communicated to physician, by declarant or at declarant's direction. (§31-32-6(a)(3)-(4))	Yes. Revocation is effective upon "communication." (§31-32-6(a)(3)-(4))	A person acting at the direction of the declarant can notify the physician. (§31-32-5(a)(3))
Hawaii	Not specified. May be used for agent revocation only if needed, directly to health care provider. (§327E-4(a)) Presumably for advance health care directive which can be made in "any manner." Oral revocation possible but with witness requirements. (§327E-4(b))	Not specified.	Not specified.	Yes. (§327E-7(b))	Not specified.	Revocation shall be "communicated" to provider. (§327E-4(c))	Can be communicated by provider, agent, guardian, or surrogate who is informed of revocation. (§327E-4(c))
Idaho	Oral revocation allowed but nothing specified about witnesses. (§39-4511A(1)(C))	Not specified. (§39-4511A)	Not specified. (§39-4511A)	Not specified. (§39-4511A)	Not specified. (§39-4511A)	Maker of revoked living will and durable power of attorney is responsible for notifying physician of revocation. (§39-4511A(2))	Declarant. (§39-4511A(2))

Table 10.03, Part 2 Revocation

	Witnesses	Capacity of Witnesses	Subsequent Confirmatory Writing by Witness Required	Requirement of Doctor Recording Notice of Revocation in Medical Record	Sufficient If Physician Sees Actual Confirmatory Writing Revoking Living Will?	Is Another Form of Notification Satisfactory?	If So, from Whom?
					Verbally		
Illinois[3]	One. (755 ILCS §35/5(a)(3))	Not specified, but must be 18 or older. (755 ILCS §35/5(a)(3))	Yes. (755 ILCS §35/5(a)(3))	Yes. (755 ILCS §35/5(b))	Yes. (755 ILCS §35/5(b))	Revocation effective upon "communication" to physician, by declarant or witness. (755 ILCS §35/5(b))	By a witness to the revocation or declarant. (755 ILCS §35/5(b))
Indiana[4]	Not specified.	Not specified.	Not specified.	Not specified.	Revocation effective when "communicated" to physician. (§16-36-4-12(b))	Not specified.	Not specified.
Iowa	Not specified. (§144A.4(1))	Not specified. (§144A.4(1))	Not specified. (§144A.4(1))	Yes. (§144A.4(2))	Revocation effective only upon "communication" to attending physician. (§144A.4(1))	Revocation effective upon any communication. (§144A.4(1))	By declarant or by another to whom the revocation was communicated. (§144A.4(1))
Kansas	One witness. (§65-28,104(a)(3))	At least 18 years old. (§65-28,104(a)(3))	Yes. (§65-28,104(a)(3))	Yes. (§65-28,104(a)(3))	Yes. (§65-28,104(a)(3))	Not specified. (§65-28,104(a))	Not specified. (§65-28,104(a))
Kentucky	Must be revoked in the presence of two adults, one of whom shall be a health care provider. (§311.627(1)(b))	18 or older, and of sound mind. (§§311.627(1)(b), 311.621(1))	Not specified.	Yes. (§311.627(3))	Not specified.	Not specified.	Not specified.
Louisiana	Not specified, but can revoke verbally. (§40:1151.3(A)(3)(a))	Not specified. (§40:1151.3(A)(3)(a))	Not specified. (§40:1151.3(A)(3)(a))	Yes. (§40:1151.3(A)(3)(c))	Not specified. (§40:1151.3(A)(3)(a))	Yes. Oral or nonverbal revocation effective upon "communication" to physician. (§40:1151.3(A)(3)(b))	Not specified.

Table 10.03, Part 2 Revocation

	Witnesses	Capacity of Witnesses	Subsequent Confirmatory Writing by Witness Required	Requirement of Doctor Recording Notice of Revocation in Medical Record	Verbally — Sufficient If Physician Sees Actual Confirmatory Writing Revoking Living Will?	Is Another Form of Notification Satisfactory?	If So, from Whom?
Maine[5]	Not specified for revocation of advance health care directive. For revocation of agent designation, communication must be made personally to health care agent. (§5-803(c))	Not specified for revocation of advance health care directive. For revocation of agent designation, communication must be made personally to health care agent. (18-A §5-803(c))	Not specified.	Yes. (18-A §5-807(b))	Not specified.	Any communication to physician or facility is presumably sufficient. (18-A §5-803(c))	Revocation can be communicated by declarant, provider, agent, guardian, or surrogate. (18-A §5-803(c))
Maryland	A health care practitioner and another witness are required to witness an oral revocation. (Health-Gen. §5-604(b))	One witness must be a health care practitioner. (Health-Gen. §5-604(a))	Yes. (Health-Gen. §5-604(b))	Yes. (Health-Gen. §5-604(b))	Not specified. (Health-Gen. §5-604)	Not specified. (Health-Gen. §5-604)	Not specified. (Health-Gen. §5-604)
Massachusetts[6]	Not specified.	Not specified.	Not specified.	Yes. (201D §7)	Presumably yes, since any act is used. (201D §7)	Yes, by the principal informing the agent or nursing staff who then will tell the attending physician. (201D §7)	By the principal informing the agent or nursing staff who then will tell the attending physician. (201D §7)
Michigan	If revocation is *not* written, witness is required. (§700.5510(d))	Not specified. (§700.5510(d))	Yes. (§700.5510(d))	Yes. (§700.5510(d))	Presumably, yes. (§700.5510(d))	Not specified. (§700.5510(d))	Not specified. (§700.5510(d))

Table 10.03, Part 2 Revocation

	Verbally						
	Witnesses	Capacity of Witnesses	Subsequent Confirmatory Writing by Witness Required	Requirement of Doctor Recording Notice of Revocation in Medical Record	Sufficient If Physician Sees Actual Confirmatory Writing Revoking Living Will?	Is Another Form of Notification Satisfactory?	If So, from Whom?
Minnesota	Not specified. (§ 145B.09 (Subd.1))	Not specified.	Not specified.	Yes. (§ 145B.09 (Subd. 1))	Presumably, yes. (§ 145B.09 (Subd.1))	Yes, effective when declarant "communicates" revocation to physician. (§ 145B.09 (Subd.1))	None other than declarant specified. (§ 145B.09 (Subd.1))
Mississippi	Not specified, only states that the advance health-care directive may be revoked "at any time and in any manner that communicates an intent to revoke." (§ 41-41-207(2)) Oral revocation of agent designation, however, must be witnessed by health care provider. (§ 41-41-207(1))	Not specified.	Merely requires that health care provider, agent, guardian, or surrogate "promptly communicate the fact of the revocation to the supervising health care provider and to any health care institution at which the patient is receiving care." (§ 41-41-207(3))	Yes, with respect to a supervising health care provider. (§ 41-41-215(2))	Not specified.	Not specified.	Not specified.
Missouri	Not specified, but any manner by which the declarant is able to communicate his intent to revoke causes revocation. Statute does not specify number of witnesses, if any, needed. (§ 459.020(1))	Not specified. (§ 459.020(1))	Not specified. (§ 459.020(1))	Yes. (§ 459.020(2))	Not specified. (§ 459.020(2))	Not specified. (§ 459.020(2))	Not specified. (§ 459.020(2))

Table 10.03, Part 2 Revocation

				Verbally		
	Witnesses	Capacity of Witnesses	Subsequent Confirmatory Writing by Witness Required	Requirement of Doctor Recording Notice of Revocation in Medical Record	Sufficient If Physician Sees Actual Confirmatory Writing Revoking Living Will?	Is Another Form of Notification Satisfactory?	If So, from Whom?
Montana[7]	Presumably, yes. If not directly witnessed or communicated by declarant to attending physician, attending advanced practice registered nurse, emergency medical personnel or health care provider is not valid unless attending physician is informed of revocation by witness presumably before patient needs life-sustaining treatment. (§ 50.9.104(1))	Not specified.	Not specified.	Yes. (§ 50-9-104(2))	Yes, presumably. (§ 50-9-104(1))	Revocation is effective upon "communication" to physician or provider by declarant or witness. (§ 50-9-104(1))	Presumably, anyone can serve as a witness to a revocation as long as it is communicated to the physician. (§ 50-9-104(1))
Nebraska	Not specified, but communication to physician by a witness is sufficient. (§ 20-406(1))	Not specified.	Not specified.	Yes. (§ 20-406(2))	Yes, presumably. (§ 20-406(1))	Any communication from a witness to the revocation or the declarant to the attending physician health care provider. (§ 20-406(1))	Any witness to the revocation or the declarant. (§ 20-406(1))

Table 10.03, Part 2 Revocation

	Witnesses	Capacity of Witnesses	Subsequent Confirmatory Writing by Witness Required	*Verbally* Requirement of Doctor Recording Notice of Revocation in Medical Record	Sufficient If Physician Sees Actual Confirmatory Writing Revoking Living Will?	Is Another Form of Notification Satisfactory?	If So, from Whom?
Nevada[8]	Not specified, but communication to physician by a witness is sufficient. (§ 449.620(1))	Not specified.	Not specified.	Yes, if unformed. (§ 449.620(2))	Yes, presumably. (§ 449.620(1))	Yes, any "communication" to physician. (§ 449.620(1))	By declarant or a witness. (§ 449.620(1))
New Hampshire	Yes, at least two witnesses. (§ 137-J:15(I)(a))	No witness can be the principal's spouse or heir at law. (§ 137-J:15(I)(a))	Not specified.	Yes. (§ 137-J:15(II))	Yes, presumably, although statute only refers to duty of person to make physician or ARNP aware of revocation. (§ 137-J:7(I)(b))	Presumably any communication. (§ 137-J:15(II))	Declarant or agent. (§ 137-J:15(II))
New Jersey[9]	Written or oral notification of revocation to a witness is sufficient. (§ 26:2H-57(b)(1))	Notification of revocation can be made to health care representative, physician, nurse, or other reliable witness. (§ 26:2H-57(b)(1))	Not specified.	Yes. (§ 26:2H-62(a))	Yes, presumably. (§ 26:2H-57(e))	Revocation effective upon "communication" to any person capable of transmitting the information. (§ 26:2H-57(e))	Presumably, anyone who communicates the revocation. (§ 26:2H-57(e))

Table 10.03, Part 2 Revocation

	Witnesses	Capacity of Witnesses	Subsequent Confirmatory Writing by Witness Required	Requirement of Doctor Recording Notice of Revocation in Medical Record	Verbally Sufficient If Physician Sees Actual Confirmatory Writing Revoking Living Will?	Is Another Form of Notification Satisfactory?	If So, from Whom?
New Mexico	Not specified for revocation of advance health care directive. (§24-7A-3(B)) Must be witnessed by health care provider for revocation of agent designation. (§24-7A-3(A))	Not specified. (§24-7A-3(B))	Not specified. (§24-7A-3(B))	Yes. (§24-7A-7(B))	Not specified. (§24-7A-3(B))	Communication of revocation is required. (§24-7A-3(C))	Communication to physician can be by health care provider, agent, guardian, or surrogate. (§24-7A-3(C))
New York	Not specified.	Not specified.	Not specified, except that a physician informed of or provided with a revocation must record it. (Pub. Health §2985(2)(a)(i))	Yes, presumably. (Pub. Health §2985(2)(a))	Yes. (Pub. Health §2985(2)(a)(i))	It is satisfactory by notifying the agent or a health care provider orally or in writing or by any other act evidencing a specific intent to revoke the proxy. (Pub. Health §2985(1)(a))	Health care agent. (Pub. Health §2985(1)(a))
North Carolina	Not specified, but revocation is effective only upon communication to the attending physician by declarant or an individual acting on his behalf. (§90-321(e))	Not specified. (§90-321(e))	Not specified. (§90-321(e))	Not specified. (§90-321(e))	Yes, presumed. (§90-321(e))	Revocation effective upon "communication" to physician. (§90-321(e))	By declarant or an individual acting on his behalf. (§90-321(e))

Table 10.03, Part 2 Revocation

	Witnesses	Capacity of Witnesses	Subsequent Confirmatory Writing by Witness Required	Requirement of Doctor Recording Notice of Revocation in Medical Record	Sufficient If Physician Sees Actual Confirmatory Writing Revoking Living Will?	Verbally — Is Another Form of Notification Satisfactory?	If So, from Whom?
North Dakota[10]	Not specified. (§ 23–06.5-07)	Not specified. (§ 23–06.5-07)	Not specified. (§ 23–06.5-07)	Yes. (§ 23–06.5-07(2))	Yes, presumed. (§ 23–06.5-07(1)(a))	Revocation effective upon "notification" to physician. (§ 23–06.5-07(1)(a))	Only principal is specified. (§ 23–06.5-07(1)(a))
Ohio	Not specified.	Not specified.	Not specified.	Yes. (§ 2133.04(B))	Yes, presumed. (§ 2133.04(A))	Revocation effective upon its "communication" to attending physician. (§ 2133.04(A))	Communication can be from declarant, a witness to the revocation, or other health care personnel to whom witness communicates the revocation. (§ 2133.04(A))
Oklahoma	Not specified.	Not specified. (63 § 3101.6(A))	Not specified. (63 § 3101.6(A))	Yes. (63 § 3101.6(B))	Yes, presumed. (63 § 3101.6(A))	Revocation is effective upon "communication" to attending physician. (63 § 3101.6(A))	Communication can be by declarant or a witness to the revocation. (63 § 3101.6(A))
Oregon[11]	Not specified.	Not specified.	Not specified.	Yes. (§ 127.545(3))	Presumably yes. (§ 127.545(2))	Revocation is effective upon "communication" by principal to attending physician, provider, or health care representative. If made to representative, the representative must inform physician or provider. (§ 127.545(2))	The declarant or health care representative who then notifies the attending or health care provider. (§ 127.545(2))

Table 10.03, Part 2 Revocation

	Witnesses	Capacity of Witnesses	Subsequent Confirmatory Writing by Witness Required	Requirement of Doctor Recording Notice of Revocation in Medical Record	Verbally — Sufficient If Physician Sees Actual Confirmatory Writing Revoking Living Will?	Is Another Form of Notification Satisfactory?	If So, from Whom?
Pennsylvania[12]	Not specified.	Not specified.	Not specified.	Yes. (20 §5444(c))	Presumably yes since "communication" used. (20 §5444(b))	Revocation effective upon "communication" to physician or provider. (20 §5444(b))	Communication can be by declarant or a witness to the revocation. (20 §5444(b))
Rhode Island[13]	Not specified.	Not specified.	Not specified.	Yes. (§23-4.11-4(a)(2))	Presumably yes since "any communication" is effective. (§23-4.11-4(a)(1))	Revocation effective as to physician or provider upon "communication" to that physician or provider. (§23-4.11-4(a)(1))	Communication can be by declarant or another who witnessed the revocation. (§23-4.11-4(a)(1))
South Carolina	Not specified, but oral revocation is effective if communicated to physician by a witness. (§44-77-80(3))	Not specified.	No (revocation must only be "communicated" to physician within a reasonable time). (§44-77-80(3)) However, physician must be able to confirm revocation by conversation with principal. (§44-77-80(3)(c))	Yes. (§44-77-80(1)-(4))	Presumably yes. (§44-77-80(3))	Revocation effective upon "communication" to physician. (§44-77-80(3))	Communication can be directly from declarant to the attending physician or from another witness if declarant is not capable of communicating. (§44-77-80(3))
South Dakota[14]	Not specified.	Not specified.	Not specified.	Yes. (§34-12D-8)	Presumably yes since communication used. (§34-12D-8)	Revocation effective upon "communication" to physician or provider. (§34-12D-8)	Not specified.

Table 10.03, Part 2 Revocation

	Verbally						
	Witnesses	Capacity of Witnesses	Subsequent Confirmatory Writing Required by Witnesses	Requirement of Doctor Recording Notice of Revocation in Medical Record	Sufficient If Physician Sees Actual Confirmatory Writing Revoking Living Will?	Is Another Form of Notification Satisfactory?	If So, from Whom?
Tennessee	Oral revocation must be made "to the attending physician." (§ 32-11-106(2))	Not specified (only attending physician can witness). (§ 32-11-106(2))	N/A	Yes. (§ 32-11-106(2))	States only that oral statement or revocation is to be made "by the declarant to the attending physician." (§ 32-11-106(2))	Not specified. (§ 32-11-106(2))	Not specified. (§ 32-11-106(2))
Texas	Oral revocation is permitted, but unspecified if any witnesses needed. (Health & Safety § 166.042(a)(3))	Not specified.	Not specified.	Yes. Physician must also enter the word "void" on each page of the directive in the record. (Health & Safety § 166.042(c))	Yes, presumed, since any "notification" is sufficient. (Health & Safety § 166.042(c))	Revocation effective upon any "notification" of physician. (Health & Safety § 166.042(c))	Notification to the physician can be by the declarant or a person acting on his/her behalf. (Health & Safety § 166.042(c))

Table 10.03, Part 2 Revocation

	Witnesses	Capacity of Witnesses	Verbally				
			Subsequent Confirmatory Writing by Witness Required	Requirement of Doctor Recording Notice of Revocation in Medical Record	Sufficient If Physician Sees Actual Confirmatory Writing Revoking Living Will?	Is Another Form of Notification Satisfactory?	If So, from Whom?
Utah	One witness in the case of an oral directive. (§75-2a-114(1)(e))	At least 18 years old. (§75-2a-114(1)(e)) Must not be related to declarant by marriage or blood, entitled to any portion of the declarant's estate, directly financially responsible for the declarant's medical care; health care provider providing care to declarant; an administrator of health care facility in which declarant is receiving care, or designated to become agent or surrogate upon the revocation. (§75-2a-114(e))	Not specified.	Yes. (§75-2a-115 (2)(b)(1))	The health care provider must be notified of the existence of the revocation. (§75-2a-115(1))	No specific type of notifications specified. (§75-2a-115(1))	Declarant or surrogate. (§75-2a-115(1)).

Table 10.03, Part 2 Revocation

	Witnesses	Capacity of Witnesses	Subsequent Confirmatory Writing by Witness Required	Requirement of Doctor Recording Notice of Revocation in Medical Record	Verbally Sufficient If Physician Sees Actual Confirmatory Writing Revoking Living Will?	Is Another Form of Notification Satisfactory?	If So, from Whom?
Vermont	Not specified. (18 §9704) To revoke appointment of an agent, the oral revocation must be made directly to principal clinician. (18 §9704(b)(1)(B))	Not specified. (18 §9704)	Not specified. (18 §9704)	Yes. (18 §9704((c)(1)(C))	Yes, presumably. (18 §9704(c)(1)(A))	Yes, presumably. (18 §9704(c)(1)(A))	Not specified. (§9704)
Virginia	Not specified, only mentions oral expression of intent to revoke. (§54.1-2985(iii))	Not specified. (§54.1-2985)	Not specified. (§54.1-2985)	Not specified. (§54.1-2985)	Not specified. (§54.1-2985)	Revocation effective when "communicated" to physician. (§54.1-2985)	Implied that any person can communicate the revoca tion to the attending physician. (§54.1-2985)
Washington	Not specified, but oral communication to the attending physician by the declarant or by a person acting on the behalf of the declarant is required. (§70.122.040(1)(c))	Not specified. (§70.122.040(1)(c))	Not specified. (§70.122.040(1)(c))	Yes. (§70.122.040(1) (b) & (c))	Yes, presumed. (§70.122.040(1)(c))	Revocation effective upon "communication" to physician. (§70.122.040(1)(c))	Communication can be by declarant or someone acting on his / her behalf. (§70.122.040(1)(c))
West Virginia	One witness. (§16-30-18(a)(3))	At least 18 years old. (§16-30-18(a)(3))	Yes. (§16-30-18(a)(3))	Yes. (§16-30-18(a)(2) & (3))	Yes, presumed. (§16-30-18(a)(3))	Revocation is effective only upon communication to physician. (§16-30-18(a)(3))	Communication to the physician can be by the declarant or a person acting on his behalf. (§16-30-18(a)(3))

Table 10.03, Part 2 Revocation

	Witnesses	Capacity of Witnesses	Subsequent Confirmatory Writing by Witness Required	Requirement of Doctor Recording Notice of Revocation in Medical Record	Verbally	Is Another Form of Notification Satisfactory?	If So, from Whom?
					Sufficient If Physician Sees Actual Confirmatory Writing Revoking Living Will?		
Wisconsin	Not specified.	Not specified.	Not specified.	Yes. (§ 154.05(2))	Not specified, but presumed. (§ 154.05(1)(c))	Revocation effective only if physician is "notified." (§ 154.05(1)(c))	Notification can be by declarant or person acting on declarant's behalf. (§ 154.05(1)(c))
Wyoming	Witness to oral revocation can sign subsequent written document memorializing revocation in lieu of the individual. (§ 35-22-404(b))	Not specified.	Possibly. If individual does not sign subsequent written document memorializing revocation, witness must. (§ 35-22-404(b))	No, but must communicate the fact of the revocation to the primary health care provider and to any heath care institution at which the patient is receiving care. (§ 35-22-404(c))	Yes, presumed. (§ 35-22-404)	Revocation effective when health care provider is "informed" of it. (§ 35-22-404(c)).	Not specified. (§ 35-22-404)

---

[1] Generally any communication, so revocation can be verbal. (§ 20-17-204(a))

[2] Can do it verbally. (§ 765.104(1)(c))

[3] Oral revocation is authorized. (755 ILCS § 35/5(a)(3))

[4] A living will declaration can be revoked by an oral expression of intent to revoke. (§ 16-36-4-12(a)(3))

[5] An individual with capacity may revoke all or part of an advance health-care directive at any time and in any manner that communicates an intent to revoke. (18-A § 5-803(b))

[6] Only deals with health care proxies. Revocation is automatic when a new health care proxy is executed or there is a divorce and the former spouse was the agent. (Id. 201D § 7)

[7] A declarant may revoke a declaration at any time and in any manner, without regard to mental or physical condition. Such declaration must be communicated to the attending physician. (§ 50-9-104(1))

[8] A declarant may revoke a declaration at any time and in any manner, without regard to mental or physical condition. Such declaration must be communicated to the attending physician or other health care provider. (§ 449.620(1))

[9] Oral revocation is authorized. (§ 26:2H-57(b)(1))

[10] A declaration may be revoked by an oral expression of intent to revoke. (§ 23-06.5-07(1)(a))

[11] Presumably, verbal revocation is effective, since "any manner" is used. (§ 127.545(1))

[12] Presumably, verbal revocation is effective, since "any manner" is used. (20 § 5444(a))

[13] Presumably, verbal revocation is effective, since "any manner" is used. (§ 23-4.11-4(a)(1))

[14] Presumably, verbal revocation is effective, since "any manner" is used. (§ 34-12D-8)

Table 10.04 Civil or Criminal Liability for Failure to Act

	Is There Any Civil or Criminal Liability for Failing to Act Without Actual Knowledge?	Is There Any Civil or Criminal Liability for Failing to Act With Actual Knowledge?	Is a Physician's Confirmation of a Terminal Condition in Writing Required Before the Living Will Can Be Given Effect?	Is the Physician Liable If There Is Mistaken Withholding or Withdrawing of Life Support?	Is There Criminal Liability for Destroying a Living Will?	Is There Criminal Liability for Forging a Living Will?
Alabama	No, not if the health care provider is acting in good faith. (§ 22-8A-5(b), 22-8A-7(c))	Yes. (§§ 22-8A-5(b), 22-8A-7(c))	Yes, it must be "documented" in the medical record by two physicians. (§ 22-8A-4(d))	Physician not liable if acted in good faith, pursuant to reasonable medical standards and without actual knowledge of revocation. (§ 22-8A-7(c))	Yes, if destroyed without declarant's consent. (§ 22-8A-8(c))	Yes. (§ 22-8A-8(d))
Alaska	No, not if the health care provider is acting in good faith. (§ 13.52.080(a)) Equitable relief may also be available. (§ 13.52.140)	Yes, there must be intent to violate the law. (§ 13.52.090(a)) Equitable relief may also be available. (§ 13.52.140(a))	No, but physician is required to make confirmation part of declarant's medical record. (§ 13.52.160)	No. (§ 13.52.080) The health care provider must act in good faith and in "accordance with generally accepted health care standards applicable to health care provider."	Not specified.	Not specified.

Table 10.04 Civil or Criminal Liability for Failure to Act

	Is There Any Civil or Criminal Liability for Failing to Act Without Actual Knowledge?	Is There Any Civil or Criminal Liability for Failing to Act With Actual Knowledge?	Is a Physician's Confirmation of a Terminal Condition in Writing Required Before the Living Will Can Be Given Effect?	Is the Physician Liable If There Is Mistaken Withholding or Withdrawing of Life Support?	Is There Criminal Liability for Destroying a Living Will?	Is There Criminal Liability for Forging a Living Will?
Arizona	Surrogates, guardians for health care and health care providers are not subject to civil or criminal liability if they act in good faith. (§§ 36-3203(D), 36-3205(A), 36-3261(c)) A surrogate acts in good faith if the surrogate "acts [or refuses] to act based on [the] surrogate's reasonable belief of [the] patient's desires . . ." (§ 36-3203(D)) A health care provider acts in good faith if the provider acts or refuses to act in reliance on the provisions of a health-care directive or directions of a surrogate. (§ 36-3205(B)) A health care provider is not subject to civil or criminal liability if the provider fails to comply with a direction that violates the	Surrogates, guardians for health care and health care providers are not subject to civil or criminal liability if they act in good faith. (§§ 36-3203(D), 36-3205(A)) A surrogate acts in good faith if the surrogate "acts [or refuses] to act based on [the] surrogate's reasonable belief of [the] patient's desires . . ." (§ 36-3203(D)) A health care provider acts in good faith if the provider acts or refuses to act in reliance on the provisions of a health-care directive or directions of a surrogate. (§ 36-3205(B)) A health care provider is not subject to civil or criminal liability if the provider fails to comply with a direction that violates the provider's conscience, provided that the provider transfer the patient to a health care provider who will comply with the patient's or guardian's directions. (§ 36-3205(C))	Not specified.	Health care providers are not released from civil or criminal liability for the negligent treatment of a patient if the negligence is unrelated to the provider's reliance on a health care directive or directions from a surrogate. (§ 36-3205(D))	Not specified.	Not specified.

10,149

Table 10.04 Civil or Criminal Liability for Failure to Act

	Is There Any Civil or Criminal Liability for Failing to Act Without Actual Knowledge?	Is There Any Civil or Criminal Liability for Failing to Act With Actual Knowledge?	Is a Physician's Confirmation of a Terminal Condition in Writing Required Before the Living Will Can Be Given Effect?	Is the Physician Liable If There Is Mistaken Withholding or Withdrawing of Life Support?	Is There Criminal Liability for Destroying a Living Will?	Is There Criminal Liability for Forging a Living Will?
	provider's conscience, provided that the provider transfer the patient to a health care provider who will comply with the patient's or guardian's directions. (§ 36-3205(C))					
Arkansas	No. (§ 20-17-208(a))	If the physician will not comply, then that person must transfer the patient to another physician. (§ 20-17-207) If the person fails to transfer the patient then that person is guilty of a Class A misdemeanor. (§ 20-17-209(a)) Any person who withholds personal knowledge of a revocation is guilty of a Class D felony. (§ 20-17-209(d))	Declaration becomes effective when (i) communicated to physician and (ii) attending physician and another physician in consultation determines that declarant is in terminal condition, unable to make medical decisions, or permanently unconscious. Although this determination must be entered in the declarant's medical record, a writing is not specifically required for effectiveness. (§ 20-17-203)	No, so long as the physician's actions comport with "reasonable medical standards." (§ 20-17-208(b))	Yes, if without the declarant's consent. (§ 20-17-209(c))	Yes. (§ 20-17-209(d))

Table 10.04 Civil or Criminal Liability for Failure to Act

	Is There Any Civil or Criminal Liability for Failing to Act Without Actual Knowledge?	Is There Any Civil or Criminal Liability for Failing to Act With Actual Knowledge?	Is a Physician's Confirmation of a Terminal Condition in Writing Required Before the Living Will Can Be Given Effect?	Is the Physician Liable If There Is Mistaken Withholding or Withdrawing of Life Support?	Is There Criminal Liability for Destroying a Living Will?	Is There Criminal Liability for Forging a Living Will?
California	No, so long as in good faith. (Probate §§ 4740, 4741)	Civil liability for any intentional violation. (Probate § 4742(a))	Not specified.	No. (Probate § 4740(c))	Yes. Only civil damages specified. (Probate § 4742(b))	Yes. (Probate § 4743)
Colorado	No. (§ 15-18-110)	Only states that it is unprofessional conduct, if physician also refuses to transfer care. (§ 15-18-113(5))	Yes. (§ 15-18-107)	No, with respect to an apparently valid declaration and in the absence of actual knowledge of revocation, fraud, or improper execution. (§ 15-18-110(1))	Yes, if destroyed without the declarant's knowledge and consent. (§ 15-18-113(1))	Yes. (§ 15-18-113 (2) &(3))

Table 10.04 Civil or Criminal Liability for Failure to Act

	Is There Any Civil or Criminal Liability for Failing to Act Without Actual Knowledge?	Is There Any Civil or Criminal Liability for Failing to Act With Actual Knowledge?	Is a Physician's Confirmation of a Terminal Condition in Writing Required Before the Living Will Can Be Given Effect?	Is the Physician Liable If There Is Mistaken Withholding or Withdrawing of Life Support?	Is There Criminal Liability for Destroying a Living Will?	Is There Criminal Liability for Forging a Living Will?
Connecticut	Not specified.	Affirmative duty to transfer patient but no mention of liability. (§ 19a-580a)	"If attending physician does not deem an incapacitated person to be in a terminal condition or permanently unconscious, beneficial medical treatment, including nutrition and hydration must be provided." Does not mention writing. (§ 19a-571(a)) Living will becomes operative when (1) furnished to physician and (2) physician determines declarant to be incapacitated. Writing not specifically required. (§ 19a-579) However, within a reasonable time prior to withholding or causing the removal of any life support system, the attending physician must make reasonable efforts to notify the declarant's health care representative, next-of-kin, guardian, conservator, or other person designated for decision-making under § 1-56r. (§ 19a-580).	No. (§ 19a-579a(c))	Not specified.	Probably under Penal Code. (§ 53a-139)

Table 10.04 Civil or Criminal Liability for Failure to Act

	Is There Any Civil or Criminal Liability for Failing to Act Without Actual Knowledge?	Is a Physician's Confirmation of a Terminal Condition in Writing Required Before the Living Will Can Be Given Effect?	Is the Physician Liable If There Is Mistaken Withholding or Withdrawing of Life Support?	Is There Criminal Liability for Destroying a Living Will?	Is There Criminal Liability for Forging a Living Will?
Delaware	No liability for providing treatment in an emergency if existence of health-care directive is unknown. (16 § 2510(a)(4)) No liability for declining to comply with advance health-care directive because the instruction is contrary to conscious or good faith medical judgment of the provider, or the written policies of the institution or based on a good faith belief that the patient lacked authority. (16 § 2510(a)(2) & (5)) See also 16 § 2508(e)-(g), which allows declining to comply if it is for reasons of conscience (e), or medically ineffective treatment or health care(f), although the patient must be promptly informed and the health care provider must provide continuing care, including continuing life sustaining care, to the patient until a transfer can be effected; and not impede the transfer of the patient to another health care provider or institution identified by the patient, the patient's agent or the patient's surrogate (g).	Advance health-care directive becomes effective after "determination" that declarant lacks capacity. Physician's written confirmation is required before withdrawing food/hydration. (16 §§ 2503(c), 2501(r)) Writing not specifically required. (16 §2503(c))	No liability if, in good faith and according to generally accepted standards, advance health-care directive is complied with and lack of revocation or termination is assumed. (16 § 2510(a)(3)	Yes. (16 § 2513(b))	Yes. (16 § 2513(b))

Table 10.04 Civil or Criminal Liability for Failure to Act

	Is There Any Civil or Criminal Liability for Failing to Act Without Actual Knowledge?	Is There Any Civil or Criminal Liability for Failing to Act With Actual Knowledge?	Is a Physician's Confirmation of a Terminal Condition in Writing Required Before the Living Will Can Be Given Effect?	Is the Physician Liable If There Is Mistaken Withholding or Withdrawing of Life Support?	Is There Criminal Liability for Destroying a Living Will?	Is There Criminal Liability for Forging a Living Will?
District of Columbia	Not specified. (§7-627(a))	Physicians who cannot comply with declaration must effect a transfer of the patient. Failure to transfer shall constitute unprofessional conduct. Civil or criminal liability not specified. (§7-627(b))	Yes. (§7-625)	There is no civil or criminal liability for failure to act on a declaration unless such person has actual knowledge of the revocation. (§7-624(b))	Yes, if without the declarant's consent. (§7-627(c))	Yes, if contrary to wishes of declarant and if it results in hastening of death. (§7-627(d))
Florida	No, with respect to an amendment or revocation. (§765.104(3))	Must transfer if refusal to comply based on moral or ethical beliefs, but no mention of liability. (§765.1105)	Yes, in the medical record. (§765.306)	No. (§765.104(3))	Yes, if without principal's consent. (§765.1115(1))	Yes. (§765.1115(2))
Georgia	Not specified, but probably no civil liability. (§31-32-10(b))	No civil liability for failing to comply with living will in good faith. Physician refusing to comply shall notify next of kin and either transfer patient or allow next of kin to obtain another physician. (§§31-32-10(a)(1) & (b), 31-32-9(d)) But withdrawal of life-sustaining care based on directive, when there is actual knowledge of the revocation of such directive will eliminate immunity. (§31-32-10(e))	Yes. (§31-32-9(a)(2))	No, as long as acted in good faith. (§31-32-10(c))	Yes. (§31-32-13(1))	Yes. (§31-32-13(1) & (2))
Hawaii	No. (§327E-9(a)(3))	Not if based on good faith belief that person lacked authority. (§327E-9(a)(2))	Yes. (§327E-7(c))	No. (§327E-9(a)(3))	Only civil damages specified. (§327E-10)	Only civil damages specified. (§327E-10)

Table 10.04 Civil or Criminal Liability for Failure to Act

	Is There Any Civil or Criminal Liability for Failing to Act Without Actual Knowledge?	Is There Any Civil or Criminal Liability for Failing to Act With Actual Knowledge?	Is a Physician's Confirmation of a Terminal Condition in Writing Required Before the Living Will Can Be Given Effect?	Is the Physician Liable If There Is Mistaken Withholding or Withdrawing of Life Support?	Is There Criminal Liability for Destroying a Living Will?	Is There Criminal Liability for Forging a Living Will?
Idaho	No criminal or civil liability for acts in good faith. (§ 39-4513(1))	Physician who cannot comply for ethical or professional reasons may withdraw without incurring liability provided he/she makes a good faith effort to assist in obtaining another physician. (§ 39-4513(2))	Not specified. (§ 39-4510)	No. (§ 39-4513)	Not specified.	Not specified.
Illinois	No (implied). (755 ILCS § 35/8(c))	Yes, if physician fails to notify patient of unwillingness to comply. (755 ILCS § 35/8(c)&(d))	Yes. (755 ILCS § 35/6)	No. (755 ILCS §§ 35/5(c), 35/7)	No, civil liability only. (755 ILCS § 35/8(a))	Yes, if contrary to wishes of patient thereby hastening death. (755 ILCS § 35/8(b))
Indiana	Not specified.	Not specified, but physicians violating transfer provisions of § 16-36-4-13(e) are subject to disciplinary sanctions. (§ 16-36-4-21)	Yes. (§ 16-36-4-13)	There is no civil or criminal liability for failing to act upon a revocation unless the person had actual knowledge of the revocation. (§§ 16-36-4-12(c), 16-36-4-13(d))	Yes, if without the declarant's consent. (§ 16-36-4-15(1))	Yes. (§§ 16-36-4-16, 16-36-4-15(2))
Iowa	Not specified, but no liability for actions in accord with reasonable medical standards. (§ 144A.9(2))	Not specified, but no liability for actions in accord with reasonable medical standards. (§ 144A.9(2)) Compliance with statute is absolute defense. (§ 144A.9(3)) If physician or provider cannot comply, transfer shall be effected. (§ 144A.8)	The physician is required to record determination of terminal condition in the declarant's record. It is unclear whether it is required before the living will can be given effect. (§ 144A.5)	No. (§ 144A.9(1)(a))	Yes, if destroyed without the declarant's consent. (§ 144A.10(1))	Yes. (§ 144A.10(2))

Table 10.04 Civil or Criminal Liability for Failure to Act

	Is There Any Civil or Criminal Liability for Failing to Act Without Actual Knowledge?	Is There Any Civil or Criminal Liability for Failing to Act With Actual Knowledge?	Is a Physician's Confirmation of a Terminal Condition in Writing Required Before the Living Will Can Be Given Effect?	Is the Physician Liable If There Is Mistaken Withholding or Withdrawing of Life Support?	Is There Criminal Liability for Destroying a Living Will?	Is There Criminal Liability for Forging a Living Will?
Kansas	Not specified.	Only constitutes unprofessional conduct if physician does not comply with declaration and fails to transfer patient to another physician. (§ 65-28,107(a))	Yes. (§ 65-28,105)	No. (§ 65-28,104(b))	Yes, if destroyed without the declarant's consent. (§ 65-28,107(b))	Yes, if directly intends and causes life-sustaining procedures to be withdrawn/withheld contrary to the wishes of the declarant and, consequently, death is hastened (§ 65-28,107(c)) or, if without declarant's consent. (§ 65-28,107(b))
Kentucky	Not specified.	Not specified, but physicians and facilities refusing to comply with living will directive shall notify patient (or responsible party) of refusal and seek a transfer. (§ 311.633(2)) If notification and transfer not carried out, physician or facility may be liable. (§ 311.635)	Not specified.	No health care provider shall be subject to any liability for acting in good faith upon the knowledge, or lack thereof, of the existence of a revocation of a living will directive. (§ 311.627(3))	Not specified. The destruction of a living will does result in civil liability. (§ 311.641(1))	Yes. (§ 311.641(2))

Table 10.04 Civil or Criminal Liability for Failure to Act

	Is There Any Civil or Criminal Liability for Failing to Act Without Actual Knowledge?	Is There Any Civil or Criminal Liability for Failing to Act With Actual Knowledge?	Is a Physician's Confirmation of a Terminal Condition in Writing Required Before the Living Will Can Be Given Effect?	Is the Physician Liable If There Is Mistaken Withholding or Withdrawing of Life Support?	Is There Criminal Liability for Destroying a Living Will?	Is There Criminal Liability for Forging a Living Will?
Louisiana	Not specified.	Not specified, but only states that if physician cannot comply, he shall transfer patient to another physician. (§ 40:1151.6(B))	Yes. (§ 40:1151.6(A))	No, not if acting in good faith. (§ 40:1151.7(B)) States that health care worker can assume that the declaration is valid until notified of revocation. (§ 40:1151.3(B))	Not specified. Destruction without consent does result in civil liability. (§ 40:1151.8(A))	Yes, if directly causes life-sustaining procedures to be withdrawn/withheld contrary to the wishes of the declarant and, consequently, death is hastened. (§ 40:1151.8(B))
Maine	Not specified.	No liability for declining to comply if based on belief that person lacked capacity or that decision did not comply with statute. (18-A § 5-809(a)(2)) Otherwise, a provider or institution intentionally violating the statute is liable for, including the notification and transfer requirements of 18-A § 5-807(g), damages. (18-A § 5-810)	Physician is required to note condition in the patient's record. It is unclear whether it is required before the living will can be given effect. (18-A § 5-807(c))	A health care provider acting in good faith and in accordance with generally accepted health care standards is not subject to civil or criminal liability for complying with a health-care directive and assuming that the directive is valid and has not been revoked or terminated. (18-A § 5-809(a)(3))	No. Person is subject to civil liability. (18-A § 5-810(b))	No. Person is subject to civil liability. (18-A § 5-810(b))

Table 10.04 Civil or Criminal Liability for Failure to Act

	Is There Any Civil or Criminal Liability for Failing to Act Without Actual Knowledge?	Is There Any Civil or Criminal Liability for Failing to Act With Actual Knowledge?	Is a Physician's Confirmation of a Terminal Condition in Writing Required Before the Living Will Can Be Given Effect?	Is the Physician Liable If There Is Mistaken Withholding or Withdrawing of Life Support?	Is There Criminal Liability for Destroying a Living Will?	Is There Criminal Liability for Forging a Living Will?
Maryland	Not specified.	Not specified, but the health care provider should make every reasonable effort to transfer the patient. Also, the statute does not authorize the provider to provide health care over the objection of competent individuals. (Health-Gen. §5-613)	Yes. (Health-Gen. §5-606(b)(1))	Not specified, but generally, not if the physician acted in good faith. (Health-Gen. §5-609(c))	Yes, if without the declarant's consent and thereby contravenes the intent of the patient. (Health-Gen. §5-610(a))	Yes, if contravenes the intent of the patient and death is hastened. (Health-Gen. §5-610(b))
Massachusetts[1]	Not specified.	Must transfer patient but no mention of liability. (201D §14)	Not specified.	No (implied) if it is done in good faith. (201D §8)	Not specified.	Not specified.
Michigan	Not specified.	Not specified.	Not specified.	No. (§700.5511(2))	Not specified.	Not specified.
Minnesota	Not specified.	Not specified, but states that if cannot comply, the declarant can be transferred. (§145B.06(subd. 1))	Not specified.	Not specified, only states physician's actions after diagnosis must be based on reasonable medical practice. (§145B.13)	Yes, if it is done wilfully without the declarant's consent. (§145B.105(subd.1)(1)	Yes. (§145B.105(subd.1)(3))
Mississippi	No. (§§ 41-41-219, 41-41-221)	No, if decision is made in good faith. (§41-41-219(2)) A physician may refuse to comply if he believes the declarant lacked authority. (§41-41-219(1)) Physician may also refuse to comply for reasons of conscience, but must then transfer the patient. (§41-41-215)	Not specified.	No, if made in good faith or based on the belief that person lacked authority. (§41-41-219 (1)(b) &(2))	There is civil liability. (§41-41-221)	Not specified. There is civil liability. (§41-41-221)

Table 10.04 Civil or Criminal Liability for Failure to Act

	Is There Any Civil or Criminal Liability for Failing to Act Without Actual Knowledge?	Is There Any Civil or Criminal Liability for Failing to Act With Actual Knowledge?	Is a Physician's Confirmation of a Terminal Condition in Writing Required Before the Living Will Can Be Given Effect?	Is the Physician Liable If There Is Mistaken Withholding or Withdrawing of Life Support?	Is There Criminal Liability for Destroying a Living Will?	Is There Criminal Liability for Forging a Living Will?
Missouri	Not specified.	Only states that it constitutes unprofessional conduct if a physician acts contrary to desires in a declaration of which he has actual knowledge without serious reason. (§ 459.045(1)) Any person so failing to act, without serious reason, shall lose rights of inheritance under patient's will. (§ 459.045(2)) A physician who is unwilling to comply with a declaration must transfer the declarant. (§ 459.030(1))	Yes. (§ 459.025)	No (unless revocation is in medical record or person has actual knowledge of revocation). (§ 459.020(3))	Yes, if destroyed without the declarant's consent. (§ 459.045(3))	Yes. (§ 459.045(3) & (4))

Table 10.04 Civil or Criminal Liability for Failure to Act

	Is There Any Civil or Criminal Liability for Failing to Act Without Actual Knowledge?	Is There Any Civil or Criminal Liability for Failing to Act With Actual Knowledge?	Is a Physician's Confirmation of a Terminal Condition in Writing Required Before the Living Will Can Be Given Effect?	Is the Physician Liable If There Is Mistaken Withholding or Withdrawing of Life Support?	Is There Criminal Liability for Destroying a Living Will?	Is There Criminal Liability for Forging a Living Will?
Montana	Not specified although no liability for withdrawal or withholding of life-sustaining treatment if the doctor or advanced practice registered nurse acted consistent with the requirements of the law, especially the exercise of "reasonable medical judgment," per "reasonable medical standards," or "actions undertaken in good faith." (§ 50-9-204(1)-(4))	Yes, if physician willfully fails to comply with transfer provisions of § 50-9-203. (§ 50-9-206(1)) However, if physician fails to comply because good faith belief that declaration is *not* valid, he is not liable. (§ 50-9-204(3))	Physician is required to record the patient's terminal condition in the medical record. It is unclear whether this is necessary before the living will can be given effect. (§ 50-9-201)	No, unless there was actual notice of a revocation. (§ 50-9-204(1))	Yes, if without consent. (§ 50-9-206(3))	Yes. (§ 50-9-206(3) & (4))
Nebraska	Not specified, but not if within "reasonable medical standards." (§ 20-410(2))	Yes, if physician will fully fails to comply with transfer provisions. (§ 20-411(1))	Yes. (§§ 20-405(2), 20-407)	No. (§ 20-410(1))	Yes, if without consent. (§ 20-411(3))	Yes. (§ 20-411(3) & (4))
Nevada	Not specified.	Yes, if physician willfully fails to comply with transfer provisions. (§ 449.660(1)) No, if physician refuses to comply because good faith belief that consent is not valid. (§ 449.630(3))	Physician is required to note the terminal condition in the patient's medical record. It is unclear whether this is required before the living will can be given effect. (§§ 449.617, 449.622)	No, in the absence of knowledge of revocation. (§ 449.630(1))	Yes, if without consent. (§ 449.660(3))	Yes, if contrary to declarant's wishes and death is hastened. (§ 449.660(3) &(4))

Table 10.04 Civil or Criminal Liability for Failure to Act

	Is There Any Civil or Criminal Liability for Failing to Act Without Actual Knowledge?	Is There Any Civil or Criminal Liability for Failing to Act With Actual Knowledge?	Is a Physician's Confirmation of a Terminal Condition in Writing Required Before the Living Will Can Be Given Effect?	Is the Physician Liable If There Is Mistaken Withholding or Withdrawing of Life Support?	Is There Criminal Liability for Destroying a Living Will?	Is There Criminal Liability for Forging a Living Will?
New Hampshire	No (implied). (§ 137-J:10(II)(a))	There is immunity if there is a good-faith belief that a directive of an agent is in conflict with or exceeds the scope of the authority of the agent or the advance directive. (§ 137-J:12(II)(b)) There is also provision for transfer of a qualified patient of the physician or ARNP, who because of personal beliefs or conscience cannot comply with the advance directive. (§ 137-J:7(II))	Yes. (§ § 137-J:7(I)(c); 137-J:10(I)(a)-(b))	There is liability for a failure to exercise due care. (§ 137-J:12(III)) Presumably, however, there is no liability if the physician did not have knowledge of a revocation. (§ § 137-J:15, 137-J:12)	Yes, if done knowingly and falsely. (§ 137-J:23)	Yes, if done knowingly and falsely. (§ 137-J:23)
New Jersey	The physician has an affirmative duty to inquire if there is an advance directive. (§ 26:2H-62(a)) No liability for any action if in good faith and in accord with the statute. (§ 26:2H-73)	Yes, if in the absence of timely notification of unwillingness to act and arrange a transfer (§ 26:2H-62(b)), professional misconduct and civil liability. (§ 26:2H-78(a) & (b))	Physician must confirm, but does not mention writing. (§ 26:2H-67)	No liability for any action if in good faith and in accord with the statute. (§ 26:2H-73)	Yes, if without consent. (§ 26:2H-78(c)(1))	Yes. (§ 26:2H-78(c)(2))

Table 10.04 Civil or Criminal Liability for Failure to Act

	Is There Any Civil or Criminal Liability for Failing to Act Without Actual Knowledge?	Is There Any Civil or Criminal Liability for Failing to Act With Actual Knowledge?	Is a Physician's Confirmation of a Terminal Condition in Writing Required Before the Living Will Can Be Given Effect?	Is the Physician Liable If There Is Mistaken Withholding or Withdrawing of Life Support?	Is There Criminal Liability for Destroying a Living Will?	Is There Criminal Liability for Forging a Living Will?
New Mexico	Not specified.	Civil damages or fine of $5,000 (whichever is greater) if done intentionally and caused a violation. (§ 24-7A-10(A)) However, a physician can refuse to comply as long as he transfers the patient. (§ 24-7A-7(G)) A physician may also refuse to comply if he has good faith belief that person lacked authority. (§ 24-7A-9(A))	Yes. (§ 24-7A-7(C))	No, if based on a good faith assumption that directive was valid and there has been no revocation. (§ 24-7A-9(A)(3))	Not specified criminally (but alludes to the possibility), only specifies a fine/civil damages if done without the declarant's consent. (§ 24-7A-10(B) & (C))	Not specified criminally (but alludes to the possibility), only specifies a fine/civil damages if done without the declarant's consent. (§ 24-7A-10(B) & (C))
New York	No, so long as in good faith. (Pub. Health § 2986(1))	Not specified, but transfer is required if unwilling to act. (Pub. Health § 2984(4))	Not specified.	No, so long as in good faith. (Pub. Health § 2986(1))	Not specified.	Not specified.
North Carolina	Not specified.	Not specified.	Not specified. Confirmation is required, but a writing is not specified. (§ 90-321(b)(2))	No, in the absence of knowledge of a revocation. (§ 90-321(b))	Not specified.	Not specified.
North Dakota	No, so long as in good faith and ordinary care. (§ 23-06.5-12(2))	No, but notification and transfer required if unwilling to act. (§ 23-06.5-12(3))	Not specified.	No, in the absence of a knowledge of a revocation. (§ 23-06.5-12)	Yes. (§ 23-06.5-18(1) & (2))	Yes. (§ 23-06.5-18(1) & (2))

Table 10.04 Civil or Criminal Liability for Failure to Act

	Is There Any Civil or Criminal Liability for Failing to Act Without Actual Knowledge?	Is There Any Civil or Criminal Liability for Failing to Act With Actual Knowledge?	Is a Physician's Confirmation of a Terminal Condition in Writing Required Before the Living Will Can Be Given Effect?	Is the Physician Liable If There Is Mistaken Withholding or Withdrawing of Life Support?	Is There Criminal Liability for Destroying a Living Will?	Is There Criminal Liability for Forging a Living Will?
Ohio	Not if actions are in good faith, using reasonable medical standards, and the person not acting outside the scope of authority. (§ 2133.11(A) & (D)).	Not if in good faith, person does not prevent or attempt to prevent or delay or attempt to delay the transfer of the patient and the person is not acting out side their authority. (§ 2133.11(A)(4) & (D))	Yes. (§§ 2133.03(A)(1), 2133.05(A))	No, if declaration is carried out in good faith and without actual knowledge of a revocation or defect. (§ 2133.11(A)(1))	Not specified.	Not specified.
Oklahoma	Not specified.	Civil or criminal liability is not specified, but physician is guilty of unprofessional conduct if willfully fails to act without arranging for transfer to another physician/health care worker. (63 §§ 3101.9, 3101.11(A))	Not required to give effect, but physician is required to make confirmation part of declarant's medical record. (63 § 3101.7)	No, in absence of knowledge of revocation. (63 § 3101.10(A))	Yes, if destroyed without the declarant's consent. (63 § 3101.11(C))	Yes. (63 § 3101.11(D))

Table 10.04 Civil or Criminal Liability for Failure to Act

	Is There Any Civil or Criminal Liability for Failing to Act Without Actual Knowledge?	Is There Any Civil or Criminal Liability for Failing to Act With Actual Knowledge?	Is a Physician's Confirmation of a Terminal Condition in Writing Required Before the Living Will Can Be Given Effect?	Is the Physician Liable If There Is Mistaken Withholding or Withdrawing of Life Support?	Is There Criminal Liability for Destroying a Living Will?	Is There Criminal Liability for Forging a Living Will?
Oregon	Not specified.	Yes, unless compliance with notification and transfer provisions. (§§ 127.625, 127.654)	Confirmation required, but writing not mentioned. (§ 127.640)	No, there is liability only if the provider relied on a directive that he/she knew to be revoked, suspended, superseded, or subject to other legal infirmity (§ 127.555(3)(d)(A)), a court challenge is pending (§ 127.555(3)(d)(B)), or the health care representative has withdrawn or has been disqualified. (§ 127.555(3)(d)(C))	Yes. (§ 127.995)	Yes. (§ 127.995)
Pennsylvania	No. (20 § 5431)	Not if attending physician or other health care provider cannot do so in good conscience. However, the attending physician or health care provider must make every reasonable effort to assist the transfer to a physician or other health care provider who will comply. (20 § 5424(a) & (b))	Yes. (20 § 5443)	No, so long as following, in good faith, declarant's previous wishes as outlined in the declaration. (20 § 5431(a))	Yes, if without consent. (20 § 5432(b)(1))	Yes. (20 § 5432(b)(3))

Table 10.04 Civil or Criminal Liability for Failure to Act

	Is There Any Civil or Criminal Liability for Failing to Act Without Actual Knowledge?	Is There Any Civil or Criminal Liability for Failing to Act With Actual Knowledge?	Is a Physician's Confirmation of a Terminal Condition in Writing Required Before the Living Will Can Be Given Effect?	Is the Physician Liable If There Is Mistaken Withholding or Withdrawing of Life Support?	Is There Criminal Liability for Destroying a Living Will?	Is There Criminal Liability for Forging a Living Will?
Rhode Island	No specific provision but generally no liability if actions are within reasonable medical standards. (§ 23-4.11-8(b))	Failure to transfer is unprofessional conduct and may result in civil liability. (§ 23-4.11-9(a) & (e))	Yes. (§§ 23-4.11-3(c)(2), 23-4.11-5)	No. (§ 23-4.11-8(a)(1))	Yes. (§ 23-4.11-9(c))	Yes. (§ 23-4.11-9(d))
South Carolina	Not specified.	Civil or criminal liability is not specified, but physician is guilty of unprofessional conduct if willfully fails to act without transferring patient to another physician/facility. (§ 44-77-100)	Not specified, only states that condition must be "certified." (§ 44-77-30)	No, if relying on an apparently valid declaration without actual notice of revocation. (§ 44-77-90)	No, only civil liability for damages. (§ 44-77-160(C))	Yes, if declarant dies as a result. (§ 44-77-160(A))
South Dakota	Not specified.	No, but physician must transfer patient. (§ 34-12D-11)	Yes. (§§ 34-12D-5, 34-12D-7)	No, absent actual knowledge of revocation. (§ 34-12D-13)	Not specified.	Not specified.
Tennessee	No. (§ 32-11-108(b))	Yes. Civil liability and professional disciplinary actions for failing to comply with notification and transfer provisions. (§ 32-11-108(a))	Not specified.	No, presumably, if action taken without notice of revocation. (§ 32-11-108(b)) Statute also states no liability if physician complies with reasonable medical standards. (§ 32-11-110(i))	Yes, if destroyed without the declarant's consent. (§ 32-11-109)	Yes. (§ 32-11-109)

Table 10.04 Civil or Criminal Liability for Failure to Act

	Is There Any Civil or Criminal Liability for Failing to Act Without Actual Knowledge?	Is There Any Civil or Criminal Liability for Failing to Act With Actual Knowledge?	Is a Physician's Confirmation of a Terminal Condition in Writing Required Before the Living Will Can Be Given Effect?	Is the Physician Liable If There Is Mistaken Withholding or Withdrawing of Life Support?	Is There Criminal Liability for Destroying a Living Will?	Is There Criminal Liability for Forging a Living Will?
Texas	No. (Health & Safety § 166.045(a))	Not specified, but physician refusing to comply is subject to review and disciplinary action by licensing board. (Health & Safety § 166.045(b)) No liability if physician complies with provisions of § 166.046. (Health & Safety § 166.045(d))	Yes. (Health & Safety §§ 166.040(a), 166.031(2))	No, as long as physician exercises reasonable care in applying directive. (Health & Safety § 166.044) Generally no liability for failure to act on revocation without actual knowledge. (Health & Safety § 166.042(d))	Yes, if without the declarant's consent. (Health & Safety § 166.048(a))	Yes if contrary to patient's desires and death is hastened. (Health & Safety § 166.048(b))
Utah	No. (§ 75-2a-115(2)(a))	Not if based on the belief that a surrogate ordering withholding or withdrawing of care had no decision-making authority (§ 75-2a-115(3)(b) & (4)(b)(i)) or the instructions are inconsistent with the patient's wishes (§ 75-2a-115(4)(b)(i)(c) & (4)(e) or on account of reasons of conscience. (§§ 75-2a-115(4)(b)(ii), 75-2a-115(4)(b) & (c)) If refusing to comply, the physician must follow transfer procedures. (§ 75-2a-115(4)(d))	Not specified.	Yes. (§ 75-2a-115(1)(a)) Not for failing to act on an unknown revocation or disqualification of a surrogate. (§§ 75-2a-115(2)(a), 75-2a-115(3)(e))	Yes. (§ 75-2a-118(1)(a)	Yes. (§ 75-2a-118(1)(b) & (2))

Table 10.04 Civil or Criminal Liability for Failure to Act

	Is There Any Civil or Criminal Liability for Failing to Act Without Actual Knowledge?	Is There Any Civil or Criminal Liability for Failure to Act With Actual Knowledge?	Is a Physician's Confirmation of a Terminal Condition in Writing Required Before the Living Will Can Be Given Effect?	Is the Physician Liable If There Is Mistaken Withholding or Withdrawing of Life Support?	Is There Criminal Liability for Destroying a Living Will?	Is There Criminal Liability for Forging a Living Will?
Vermont	No, so long as acts in good faith. (18 §9713(b))	No, so long as the provider informs the principal, assists the principal in the transfer of care to a provider who is willing to honor the instruction, provides care until a new provider has been found, and documents the conflict, the steps taken to resolve it, and its resolution in the principal's medical record. (18 §§9707(b)(3), 9714(a))	Not specified.	No, as long as "relying in good faith on a suspended or revoked directive." (18 §9713(b)(1)(B))	Not specified.	Not specified.
Virginia	Not specified.	Civil or criminal liability is not specified, but attending physician can transfer the patient to another physician if unwilling to comply. (§54.1-2987)	This is specified in the statutory form, but the form is optional. (§54.1-2984)	No, unless actual knowledge of a revocation. (§§54.1-2985, 54.1-2988)	Yes, if caused life-prolonging procedures to be used in contravention of the declarant's intent. (§54.1-2989)	Yes, if contrary to declarant's wishes and death is hastened. (§54.1-2989)
Washington	No, as long as acting "in good faith" and "without negligence." (§70.122.051(4))	No, if acting in good faith and in accordance with provisions for a written plan to control in cases of inability to act. (§70.122.060(3))	Yes. (§70.122.030(2))	No. Requires action in "good faith." (§70.122.051(2) & (4))	Yes, if destroyed without the declarant's consent. (§70.122.090(1))	Yes, if contrary to declarant's wishes and death is hastened. (§70.122.090(2))

Table 10.04 Civil or Criminal Liability for Failure to Act

	Is There Any Civil or Criminal Liability for Failing to Act Without Actual Knowledge?	Is There Any Civil or Criminal Liability for Failing to Act With Actual Knowledge?	Is a Physician's Confirmation of a Terminal Condition in Writing Required Before the Living Will Can Be Given Effect?	Is the Physician Liable If There Is Mistaken Withholding or Withdrawing of Life Support?	Is There Criminal Liability for Destroying a Living Will?	Is There Criminal Liability for Forging a Living Will?
West Virginia	No. (§ 16-30-22(a))	Liability not specified, but subject to review and disciplinary action by licensing board for failure to comply. (§ 16-30-22(b)) There is transfer provision for conscience objectors. (§ 16-30-12)	Yes. (§§ 16-30-7(a) & (b), 16-30-19(a))	No, unless actual knowledge of a revocation. (§ 16-30-18(b))	Not specified.	Not specified.
Wisconsin	Not specified.	No, only that it is unprofessional conduct if a physician fails to make good faith attempt to transfer. (§ 154.07(1)(a)(3))	Yes. (§ 154.02(3))	No, if no actual knowledge of revocation. (§ 154.07(1)(a)(2))	Yes, if without consent. (§ 154.15(1))	Yes. (§ 154.15(2))
Wyoming	Not specified.	Not if acting in good faith (§ 35-22-410) or in good conscience (§ 35-22-408(e)). If acting on the basis of conscience, must inform and transfer patient to provider willing to comply with the instruction and provide life-sustaining care until such a transfer can be effected. (§ 35-22-408(g))	Not specified.	No, so long as acting in good faith and in accordance with generally accepted health care standard. (§ 35-22-410(a)(iii))	Civil liability, if destroyed without the declarant's consent. (§ 35-22-411(b)). Criminal liability not specified.	Yes, civil liability. (§ 35-22-411(b)) Criminal liability not specified.

[1] Only deals with health care proxies.

Table 10.05 Effect Regarding Insurance

	Are Persons Protected from Being Required to Sign a Living Will in Order to Be Given Health Insurance or Health Care?	Is the Execution and Giving Effect to the Living Will Expressly Considered Not to Be Suicide for Life Insurance Contracts?
Alabama	Yes. (§22-8A-9(c))	Yes (states not suicide for any purpose). (§22-8A-9(a))
Alaska	Yes. (§§13.52.060(h), 13.52.130)	Yes (states not suicide for any purpose). (§13.52.120(b))
Arizona	Yes. (§36-3207(A) relating to all health-care directives)	Yes. (§36-3207(C)) (relating to all health-care directives)
Arkansas	Yes. (§§20-17-210(c), 20-17-209(e))	Yes. (§§20-17-210(a) & (b))
California	Yes. (Probate §4677)	Yes. (Probate §4656)
Colorado	Yes. (§15-18-111)	Yes (states not suicide for any purpose). (§15-18-111)
Connecticut	Yes. (§19a-580b)	Not specified.
Delaware	Yes. (16 §2512(c))	Yes. (16 §2512(a))
District of Columbia	Yes. (§7-628(c))	Yes. (§7-628(a))
Florida	Yes. (§§765.108, 765.110(2))	Yes. (§§765.309(2), 765.108)
Georgia	Yes. (§31-32-12(a))	Yes (states not suicide for any purpose). (§31-32-11(a))
Hawaii	Yes (for health care services). (§327E-7(h)) Does not address insurance plans.	Yes. (§327E-13(b))
Idaho	Yes. (§39-4514(8)(b))	Not specified, but states that no life insurance policy can be impaired or invalidated by withholding or withdrawal of artificial life-sustaining procedures. (§39-4514(8)(a))
Illinois	Yes. (755 ILCS §§35/8(e), 35/9(c))	Yes. (§755 ILCS §35/9(a) & (b))
Indiana	Yes. (§16-36-4-17(d))	Yes. (§16-36-4-17(a) & (c))
Iowa	Yes. (§144A.11(3))	Yes (states not suicide for any purpose). (§§144A.11(1), 144A.11(2))
Kansas	Yes. (§65-28,108(c))	Yes. States not for any purpose, suicide. (§65-28,108(a)) States that no life insurance policy can be impaired or invalidated by withholding or withdrawal of artificial life-sustaining procedures. (§65-28,108(b))
Kentucky	Yes. (§311.637(2))	Yes. (§311.637(1))
Louisiana	Yes. (§40:1151.9(B)(4))	Yes (states not suicide for any purpose). (§40:1151.9(B)(1))
Maine	Yes, as to health care. (18-A §5-807(h))	Yes. (18-A §5-813(b))
Maryland	Yes. (Health-Gen. §5-614(c))	Yes (states not suicide for any purpose). (Health-Gen. §5-614(a))
Massachusetts[1]	Yes. (201D §10)	"Nothing in this chapter shall be construed to constitute . . . suicide." (201D §12)

Table 10.05 Effect Regarding Insurance

	Are Persons Protected from Being Required to Sign a Living Will in Order to Be Given Health Insurance or Health Care?	Is the Execution and Giving Effect to the Living Will Expressly Considered Not to Be Suicide for Life Insurance Contracts?
Michigan	Yes. (§§ 333.5659, 700.5512(2) & (3))	Yes. (§§ 333.5659(e), 700.5512(3)(e) & (4))
Minnesota	Yes. Requiring patient to sign is a misdemeanor. (§ 145B.105(subd.1)(5))	Not specified, but states that no life insurance policy can be affected, impaired, or modified by the effectuation of a living will. (§ 145B.11)
Mississippi	Yes, as to health care. (§ 41-41-215(8))	Yes (states not suicide for any purpose). (§ 41-41-227(2))
Missouri	Yes. (§ 459.050(2))	Not specified, but no life insurance policy can be impaired or invalidated by the withholding or withdrawal of death-prolonging procedures. (§ 459.050(1))
Montana	Yes. (§ 50-9-205(3))	Yes. (§ 50-9-205(1))
Nebraska	Yes. (§§ 20-411(5), 20-412(3))	Yes. (§ 20-412(1))
Nevada	Yes. (§ 449.650(3))	Yes. (§ 449.650(1) & (2))
New Hampshire	Yes. (§ 137-J:3(I))	Yes, not suicide. (§§ 137-J:10(III); 137-J:3(II))
New Jersey	Yes. (§§ 26:2H-75, 26:2H-78(c)(4))	Yes. (§§ 26:2H-75, 26:2H-77(a))
New Mexico	Yes. (§§ 24-7A-2.1(A) & (B), 24-7A-7(H))	Yes (states not suicide for any purpose). (§ 24-7A-13(B))
New York	Yes. (Pub. Health § 2988)	An order to not resuscitate shall not affect, in any manner, life insurance. (Pub. Health § 2975)
North Carolina	Yes. (§ 90-321(g))	Yes (states not suicide for any purpose). (§ 90-321(f))
North Dakota	Yes. (§ 23-06.5-13(11))	Yes. (§ 23-06.5-13(9)) (states not suicide for any purpose) (§ 23-06.5-13(10))
Ohio	Yes. (§ 2133.12(B)(4))	Yes. (§§ 2133.12(A), 2133.12(B)(1) & (2))
Oklahoma	Yes. (63 § 3101.12(C))	Yes (states not suicide for any purpose). (63 § 3101.12(A) & (B))
Oregon	Yes. (§ 127.565(2))	Yes. (§§ 127.570(2), 127.565(3))
Pennsylvania	Yes. (20 § 5428(1))	Yes. (20 §§ 5426, 5427)
Rhode Island	Yes. (§ 23-4.11-10(b) & (c))	Yes. (§ 23-4.11-10(a) & (b))
South Carolina	Yes. (§ 44-77-120)	Yes (states not suicide for any purpose). (§ 44-77-110)
South Dakota	Yes. (§ 34-12D-16)	Yes. (§§ 34-12D-14, 34-12D-15)
Tennessee	Yes. (§ 32-11-110(c))	Yes. (§ 32-11-110(a) & (b))
Texas	Yes. (Health & Safety § 166.007)	No life insurance policy can be impaired or invalidated by withholding or withdrawal of artificial life-sustaining procedures. (Health & Safety § 166.006(b))
Utah	Yes. (§ 75-2a-119(3)(a))	Yes. (§ 75-2a-119(2)(b))
Vermont	Yes. (18 § 9709(e))	Yes (states shall not be construed as suicide). (18 § 9715(a))

Table 10.05 Effect Regarding Insurance

	Are Persons Protected from Being Required to Sign a Living Will in Order to Be Given Health Insurance or Health Care?	Is the Execution and Giving Effect to the Living Will Expressly Considered Not to Be Suicide for Life Insurance Contracts?
Virginia	Yes. (§ 54.1-2991)	Yes (states not suicide for any purpose). (§ 54.1-2991)
Washington	Yes. (§ 70.122.070(3))	Yes (states not suicide for any purpose). (§ 70.122.070(1) & (2))
West Virginia	Yes. (§ 16-30-14(d))	Yes (states not suicide for any purpose). (§ 16-30-14(b))
Wisconsin	Yes. (§ 154.11(3))	Yes. (§ 154.11(1) & (2))
Wyoming	Yes, as to health care. (§ 35-22-408(h))	Yes (states not suicide). (§ 35-22-414(b))

[1] Only deals with health care proxies.

Table 10.06 Governing Law

Will a Foreign-Executed Living Will Be Given Effect? (Note If Says "State" and Does Not Include Foreign Country)

State	
Alabama	Yes, but it does not authorize the administration, withholding/withdrawal of health care that is prohibited under Alabama law. Uses term "another state." (§22-8A-12) Does not include foreign countries.
Alaska	Declarations issued and authorized in compliance with laws of another state are effective in Alaska to the extent that it complies with Alaska law. (§13.52.010)(k) Does not include foreign countries.
Arizona	A health-care directive in another "state, district or territory of the U.S." is valid in Arizona if it was valid in the place where and at the time when it was adopted and only to the extent that it does not conflict with Arizona's criminal laws. (§36-3208) Does not include foreign countries.
Arkansas	A declaration executed in another "state" in compliance with the law of that state or of Arkansas is validly executed. (§20-17-212) Does not include foreign countries.
California	Any instrument executed in another "state" or "jurisdiction" in compliance with the law of that state or jurisdiction or of California is valid in and enforceable in California to the same extent as a written advance directive validly executed in California. (Probate §4676(a)
Colorado	Any declaration executed in compliance with the laws of the state where it was executed shall be considered effective for use in Colorado to the extent it does not violate any Colorado laws. The law uses the term "state." It does not apply to foreign countries. (§15-18-108(6), effective Aug. 11, 2010)
Connecticut	Yes, if not violative of Connecticut public policy. A health care provider can rely on health care instructions or appointment of a health care proxy from outside Connecticut if there is an order from a court of competent jurisdiction, there is a notarized statement from the patient or holder of the proxy that is valid where executed, not against Connecticut public policy, or based on the health care provider's own good faith analysis. (§19a-580g)
Delaware	Yes, a living will executed in another state in compliance with the laws of that state or of Delaware is valid. Does not include foreign countries. (16 §2517)
District of Columbia	Not specified.
Florida	If executed in compliance with law of another state or of Florida, the directive is considered validly executed in Florida. (§765.112) Does not include foreign countries.
Georgia	Yes, a declaration executed in another "state" and valid under the law of the state where executed shall be recognized. Does not include foreign countries. (§31-32-5(b))
Hawaii	Yes, a document executed in another state will be considered valid if the document complies with Hawaii law or with laws of the state where enacted. (§327E-3(j)) Does not include foreign countries.
Idaho	Yes, health care directives executed in another state that substantially comply with the Idaho statute will be recognized. (§39-4514(7))
Illinois	A declaration executed in another "state" in compliance with the law of that state or Illinois is validly executed. (755 ILCS §35/9(h)) Does not include foreign countries.
Indiana	Not specified.

Table 10.06 Governing Law

Will a Foreign-Executed Living Will Be Given Effect? (Note If Says "State" and Does Not Include Foreign Country)

State	Will a Foreign-Executed Living Will Be Given Effect?
Iowa	A document executed in another "state" or "jurisdiction" shall be deemed valid and enforceable in Iowa, to the extent the document is consistent with the laws of Iowa. (§ 144A.3(4))
Kansas	Not specified.
Kentucky	Not specified.
Louisiana	A declaration properly executed in another state is valid. (§ 40:1151.9(D)) Does not include foreign countries.
Maine	Yes, as long as it complies with Maine law, or if valid where executed. (18-A § 5-802(h))
Maryland	Yes, if in compliance with the laws of Maryland or the state in which it was executed. Uses the term "another state." (Health-Gen. § 5-617) Does not include foreign countries.
Massachusetts	A health care proxy executed in another state or jurisdiction is enforceable if it is in compliance with the laws of the other state or jurisdiction. (201D § 11) Will not be enforced if enforcement would violate 201D § § 14 & 15.
Michigan	Not specified.
Minnesota	Yes, if it "substantially" complies with the Minnesota chapter on living wills. Uses the term "another state." (§ 145B.16) Does not include foreign countries.
Mississippi	Yes, if it complies with the local law. (§ 41-41-205(10))
Missouri	Not specified.
Montana	Yes, as long as it meets the laws of the state where executed and substantially complies with Montana laws. (§ 50-9-111) Does not include foreign countries.
Nebraska	Yes, a declaration executed in another state in compliance with the law of that state or of Nebraska is valid. (§ 20-414) Does not include foreign countries.
Nevada	Yes, as long as it is in compliance with the laws of that state or with Nevada laws. (§ 449.690(1)) An instrument executed anywhere before July 1, 1977 is effective if it clearly expresses the declarant's voluntary intent to withhold treatment. (§ 449.690(2)) An instrument executed anywhere before October 1, 1991 is effective if in substantial compliance with current Nevada law and not revoked. (§ 449.690(2)) Does not include foreign countries. (§ 449.690(3)
New Hampshire	Yes, but "any exercise of power" under a foreign living will must comply with the laws of New Hampshire. Uses the term "another state or jurisdiction." (§ 137-J:17)
New Jersey	Yes, if valid in that state, country, or New Jersey and if not contrary to New Jersey public policy. A living will valid under the law of another state or country is valid even if executed there, if not contrary to New Jersey public policy. (§ 26:2H-76)
New Mexico	Yes, directive from another state or jurisdiction is valid if it complies with the laws of the state where it was made. (§ 24-7A-16(C)) Enforceable to the same extent as a directive made in New Mexico. (Id.)
New York	A health care proxy or similar instrument executed in another state or jurisdiction in compliance with the law of that state or jurisdiction shall be considered validly executed. (Pub. Health § 2990)
North Carolina	Declaration of similar document executed in a jurisdiction other than North Carolina shall be valid in North Carolina if it appears to have been executed in accordance with the requirements of that jurisdiction or of North Carolina. (§ 90-321(l))

Table 10.06 Governing Law

Will a Foreign-Executed Living Will Be Given Effect? (Note If Says "State" and Does Not Include Foreign Country)

State	
North Dakota	Yes, directive or similar instrument from another state or jurisdiction is valid if it was executed in compliance with the laws of the other state or jurisdiction. (§ 23-06.5-11)
Ohio	Yes, as long as the declaration is in compliance with the laws of that state or in substantial compliance with Ohio law. (§ 2133.14) Does not include foreign countries.
Oklahoma	Yes, if complies with Oklahoma state law or another state's law that does not exceed authorizations permitted under Oklahoma state law. Uses the term "another state." (63 § 3101.14) Does not include foreign countries.
Oregon	An advance directive executed by an adult who at the time of execution resided in another state, in compliance with the laws of that state, the laws of the state where the person was located at the time, or Oregon laws, is validly executed. (§ 127.515(5)) Does not include foreign countries.
Pennsylvania	Living will or document appointing health care agent executed in another "state" or "jurisdiction" and in conformity with the laws of that state or jurisdiction shall be valid in Pennsylvania, except to the extent that those documents allow a principal to direct procedures inconsistent with the laws of Pennsylvania. (20 § 5446(b))
Rhode Island	A declaration executed in another state in compliance with the law of that state is valid. (§ 23-4.11-12) Does not include foreign countries.
South Carolina	Yes, if the law of the state of the declarant's domicile when the declaration was made expresses a substantially similar intent to applicable South Carolina law. Uses the term "state." (§ 44-77-30)
South Dakota	Statute states that declaration which meets the execution requirements of the jurisdiction where executed, where declarant was a resident, or of South Dakota is valid. (§ 34-12D-22)
Tennessee	Yes, if in compliance with either the laws of Tennessee or of the state of the declarant's residence. (§ 32-11-111) Does not include foreign countries.
Texas	Directive or similar instrument validly executed in "another state or jurisdiction" shall be effective as long as it does not violate Texas law. (Health & Safety § 166.005)
Utah	Directive executed in another state shall be presumed to comply with Utah law, unless otherwise provided in the directive and, in good faith, may be relied upon by health care provider or health care facility. (§ 75-2a-121) Does not include foreign countries.
Vermont	A declaration executed in another state in compliance with the law of that state is valid. (18 § 9716)
Virginia	Yes, if it complies with Virginia state law or the law of the state where the directive was made. Uses the term "another state." (§ 54.1-2993) Does not include foreign countries.
Washington	Yes, to the extent permitted by Washington state law and federal constitutional law. Uses the term "another political jurisdiction." (§ 70.122.030(3))

Table 10.06 Governing Law

Will a Foreign-Executed Living Will Be Given Effect? (Note If Says "State" and Does Not Include Foreign Country)

West Virginia	A declaration executed in another state is valid if it is in compliance with West Virginia law or the state law in which it was executed. Uses the term "another state." (§16-30-21) Does not include foreign countries.
Wisconsin	A valid document executed in another state or jurisdiction in compliance with the laws of that state or jurisdiction is valid in Wisconsin to the extent that the document is consistent with Wisconsin laws. (§154.11(9))
Wyoming	Not specified, although states "This act shall be applied and construed to effectuate its general purpose to make uniform the law with respect to the subject matter of this act among states enacting it." (§35-22-416)

Table 11
Status of Children Conceived By Assisted Reproduction Techniques
(current through 5/1/18)

With the increasing use of assisted reproduction techniques, many legal questions bearing on the status of the individuals produced have taken center stage. States have been slow to address by statute the numerous permutations that the varied techniques give rise to and their legal consequences in terms of the parent-child relationship and rights under the inheritance law as well as wills and trusts. This Table 11 seeks to detail the current state of the law, recognizing that this is a developing area of the law, with many issues still not adequately addressed in a large number of states. Of course, an awareness that an issue is not yet addressed can itself be quite important information.

The Table is organized into three major categories. First, a series of questions address the status and rights of posthumously conceived children generally. Second, the question of who is the mother is addressed in the context of gestational surrogacy and other arrangements in which a woman does not contribute both the egg and womb but contracts for one or the other or even both. The third category considers assisted reproduction techniques from the standpoint of the man, apart from the first category involving posthumous conception.

As for the first category, the Table considers initially whether the state law recognizes as the parent of a child the contributor of genetic material, even though the child is conceived by assisted reproduction techniques after the contributor of the genetic material is deceased. In a number of states, there is provision made for this situation, but only in the spousal setting. Moreover, the provision that is made does not necessarily address inheritance rights or membership in a class of "children" for purposes of will and trust distributions. Finally, the matter under consideration here is a child conceived posthumously. This is to be distinguished from the standard posthumous child statute, that principally addresses the birth of a child conceived before the decedent's death, but born thereafter.

The first category then considers whether the rules addressing spouses also applies to the unmarried contributor of procreative material. The Table proceeds to consider whether and what sort of consent is required to have been given by the decedent prior to the decedent's death and precisely for what consent must be given. Finally, the Table explores whether the state law addresses inheritance rights and right under a will or trust with respect to the posthumously conceived child. In many states, these rights have not been addressed. There are a few cases that have sought to delineate the rights of the child, but these do not typically give much guidance and may not have much influence outside the particular jurisdiction.

The second category addresses parentage when a situation is involved in which the woman claims to be the mother, but has not contributed both egg and womb. First, consideration is given to whether there is a distinction in treatment depending on the marital status of the woman. This is followed by the issue of who is the mother if one woman contributed the egg, but uses the womb of another woman, the standard gestational surrogacy case. The next question considers the outcome when the woman contracts for an egg, but provides the womb. Finally, consideration is given to the situation in which a woman contracts for both an egg and a womb. Can she still be deemed the mother under these circumstances? If not, who is the mother?

The third category deals with the interested men. First, the situation is considered in which a man consents to another man's sperm fertilizing his wife's egg, with his wife carrying the embryo in her womb. Consideration is also given to authorities that have addressed the matter when the parties are not married, but are partners, such as in the same-sex scenario. For example, can a lesbian partner of the woman who gives birth to the child also be presumed the parent, much as the husband in the typical situation? The next question investigates the status of the contributor of sperm and how he can assure that he is not deemed the father. Most typically, donation of sperm anonymously through a licensed physician is the safest route, but even this path is not always an assured method for avoiding paternity.

Alabama
Status of Children Conceived by Assisted Reproduction Techniques

A. Posthumously Conceived Individuals

1.	Can an individual have legal status as a child even though conceived and born after the parent's death?	Yes, if the parents are married at the deceased parent's death. (§ 26-17-707)
2.	What if the deceased contributor of procreative material was not married?	No authority.
3.	Is the consent of the deceased contributor of procreative material required and, if so, what kind of consent, and consent to what?	If the spouse dies before placement of eggs, sperm, or embryos, the decedent is not the parent unless the decedent consented in a record kept by a licensed physician that if assisted reproduction occurred after death the decedent would be the parent. (§ 26-17-707)
4.	Is there specific authority addressing the posthumous child's right of inheritance?	No.
5.	Is there specific authority addressing the posthumous child's status under a will or a trust?	No.

B. Mother does not provide both womb and egg

6.	Is there a distinction drawn between a married and unmarried woman?	No. (§ 26-17-202)
7.	Who is the mother if a woman contributes the egg but the child is carried in a surrogate's womb?	Apparently, the woman giving birth to the child would be the mother. (§ 26-17-201(a)(1)) See also § 26-17-702 (Uniform Comment).
8.	Who is the mother if a woman contracts for the egg but carries the child in her womb?	Apparently, the woman carrying the child. (§ 26-17-201(a)(1))
9.	Who is the mother if a woman contracts for both the egg and the womb?	Apparently, the woman giving birth to the child would be the mother. (§ 26-17-201(a)(1)) See also § 26-17-702 (Uniform Comment).

C. When the man is not the biological father or is not married to the mother

10.	If a husband does not contribute sperm but consents to his wife providing the womb with the intention of being the mother, is he the father?	Yes, if consent by wife is in a record signed by wife and her husband and maintained by the assisting licensed physician. (§§ 26-17-704(a), 26-17-201(b)(5)) See also § 26-17-703 ("If a husband . . . consents to assisted reproduction by his wife as provided in Section 26-17-704, he is the father of the resulting child.").

11. *If a man contributes sperm how can he avoid being father?*

As long as the donor provided the semen to a licensed physician for use in artificial insemination of a married woman other than the donor's wife, the donor is not the father. (§ 26-17-702) The outcome is not clear if the sperm was not provided to a licensed physician, the husband does not give consent, or the recipient is not married. A comment accompanying the statute indicates that the donor would be the father in these situations, since this "eliminates the potential created in the Uniform Parentage Act [the source of the Alabama law] of having a child intentionally created who would have no legal father."

Alaska
Status of Children Conceived by Assisted Reproduction Techniques

A. Posthumously Conceived Individuals

1.	Can an individual have legal status as a child even though conceived and born after the parent's death?	No authority.
2.	What if the deceased contributor of procreative material was not married?	No authority.
3.	Is the consent of the deceased contributor of procreative material required and, if so, what kind of consent, and consent to what?	No authority.
4.	Is there specific authority addressing the posthumous child's right of inheritance?	No authority.
5.	Is there specific authority addressing the posthumous child's status under a will or a trust?	No authority.

B. Mother does not provide both womb and egg

6.	Is there a distinction drawn between a married and unmarried woman?	No authority in the case of an unmarried woman using another woman's egg or womb.
7.	Who is the mother if a woman contributes the egg but the child is carried in a surrogate's womb?	No authority.
8.	Who is the mother if a woman contracts for the egg but carries the child in her womb?	If the woman is married and she and her husband consent in writing to the procedure, the woman is the mother. (§ 25.20.045)
9.	Who is the mother if a woman contracts for both the egg and the womb?	No authority.

C. When the man is not the biological father or is not married to the mother

10.	If a husband does not contribute sperm but consents to his wife providing the womb with the intention of being the mother, is he the father?	Yes, if consent by both spouses is given in writing and the insemination is performed by a licensed physician. (§ 25.20.045)
11.	If a man contributes sperm how can he avoid being father?	If the woman is married and both she and her husband consent in writing to the procedure, the sperm donor is not the father. (§ 25.20.045) No authority if woman is unmarried. Donor might not be able to avoid being father if genetic test shows him to be the father within 95% probability. (§ 25.20.050(d)) However, this provision has never been applied to sperm donors.

Arizona
Status of Children Conceived by Assisted Reproduction Techniques

A. Posthumously Conceived Individuals

1.	Can an individual have legal status as a child even though conceived and born after the parent's death?	The only relevant provision is that if, within 10 months of death a child is born and a man was married to the mother during the ten-month period, he is presumed the father, regardless of whether child was conceived through artificial reproduction. (§ 25-814(A)(1)) The presumption can be overcome by clear and convincing evidence. (§ 25-814(C)) See also Gillett-Netting v. Barnhart, 371 F.3d 593, 599 (9th Cir. 2004) ("Although Arizona law does not deal specifically with posthumously-conceived children, every child in Arizona . . . is the legitimate child of her or his natural parents.").
2.	What if the deceased contributor of procreative material was not married?	Unclear. See Gillett-Netting v. Barnhart, 371 F.3d 593, 599 n.7 (9th Cir. 2004). The critical question is who is a "natural parent?" For example, an unmarried sperm donor would not be.
3.	Is the consent of the deceased contributor of procreative material required and, if so, what kind of consent, and consent to what?	No authority.
4.	Is there specific authority addressing the posthumous child's right of inheritance?	No authority.
5.	Is there specific authority addressing the posthumous child's status under a will or a trust?	No authority.

B. Mother does not provide both womb and egg

6.	Is there a distinction drawn between a married and unmarried woman?	No authority.
7.	Who is the mother if a woman contributes the egg but the child is carried in a surrogate's womb?	Uncertain. The surrogate is the legal mother under the relevant statute. (§ 25-218(B)) However, the statute has been held violative of the equal protection clause. The reasoning offered is that the biological father is permitted to establish parentage, but the biological mother contributing genetic material is not. (Soos v. Superior Ct., 897 P.2d 1356 (Ct. App. 1994))
8.	Who is the mother if a woman contracts for the egg but carries the child in her womb?	The woman carrying the child in her womb is the legal mother under the relevant statute. (§ 25-218(B)) However, the statute has been held violative of the equal protection clause. The reasoning offered is that the biological father is permitted to establish parentage, but the biological mother contributing genetic material is not. (Soos v. Superior Ct., 897 P.2d 1356 (Ct. App. 1994))

9.	*Who is the mother if a woman contracts for both the egg and the womb?*	The woman carrying the child in her womb is the legal mother under the relevant statute. (§ 25-218(B)) However, the statute has been held violative of the equal protection clause. The reasoning offered is that the biological father is permitted to establish parentage, but the biological mother contributing genetic material is not. (Soos v. Superior Ct., 897 P.2d 1356 (Ct. App. 1994)) In the situation presented, the woman has no biological connection and will have the weakest case.

C. When the man is not the biological father or is not married to the mother

10.	*If a husband does not contribute sperm but consents to his wife providing the womb with the intention of being the mother, is he the father?*	Yes, although the presumption is rebuttable. (§ 25-218(C))
11.	*If a man contributes sperm how can he avoid being father?*	A sperm donor could avoid being the legal father if (i) the woman recipient of the sperm is married at any time in the ten months immediately preceding the birth of the child or the child is born within ten months of the termination of the marriage by death, annulment, declaration of invalidity or dissolution or after the court enters a decree of legal separation, or (ii) both parents sign a notarized or witnessed statement acknowledging paternity. (§ 25-814(A)(1)&(4)) Such written statement must be accompanied by written consent from the presumed father, the sperm donor. (§ 25-814(B)) Another presumption, however, provides that a person is the father if genetic testing affirms at least a 95% probability of paternity. (§ 25-814(A)(2)) If presumptions clash, then the one "based on weightier considerations of policy and logic will control. A court decree establishing paternity of the child by another man rebuts the presumption." (§ 25-814(C)) However, in Gillett-Netting v. Barnhart, 371 F.3d 593 (9th Cir. 2004), the court states that if the sperm donor had not been married to the mother, Arizona would not treat him as the child's natural parent, and he likely would have no obligation to support the child if he were alive. Id. at 599 n.7. The applicability of the decision to inheritance is uncertain. Id. at 599 n.8.

Arkansas
Status of Children Conceived by Assisted Reproduction Techniques

A. Posthumously Conceived Individuals

1.	Can an individual have legal status as a child even though conceived and born after the parent's death?	No authority.
2.	What if the deceased contributor of procreative material was not married?	No authority.
3.	Is the consent of the deceased contributor of procreative material required and, if so, what kind of consent, and consent to what?	No authority.
4.	Is there specific authority addressing the posthumous child's right of inheritance?	Posthumously conceived children have no rights to inherit under intestate succession. A child created as an embryo during parents' marriage but implanted in mother's womb after death of father has no right to inherit as a surviving child under Arkansas intestacy law. Finley v. Astrue, 270 S.W.3d 849 (Ark. 2008). See also Finley v. Astrue, 601 F. Supp. 2d 1092 (E.D. Ark. 2009).
5.	Is there specific authority addressing the posthumous child's status under a will or a trust?	No authority.

B. Mother does not provide both womb and egg

6.	Is there a distinction drawn between a married and unmarried woman?	No distinction. (§ 9-10-201(b) & (c))
7.	Who is the mother if a woman contributes the egg but the child is carried in a surrogate's womb?	If the "woman intended to be the mother" is the wife of the biological father, the woman is the legal mother. (§ 9-10-201(b)(1), (c)(1)(A)) If the sperm was provided by an anonymous donor, the "woman intended to be the mother" is the legal mother. (§ 9-10-201(b)(3), (c)(1)(C)) This is true even if the woman is unmarried. (Id.) For birth registration purposes, in cases of surrogate mothers, the woman giving birth shall be presumed to be the natural mother and shall be listed as such on the certificate of birth, but a substituted certificate of birth may be issued upon orders of a court of competent jurisdiction. (§ 9-10-201(c)(2))
8.	Who is the mother if a woman contracts for the egg but carries the child in her womb?	The woman, assuming "artificial insemination," an undefined term in the statute, includes implantation of another woman's egg. (§ 9-10-201(b))

9.	*Who is the mother if a woman contracts for both the egg and the womb?*	If the "woman intended to be the mother" is the wife of the biological father, she is the legal mother. (§ 9-10-201(b)(1), (c)(1)(A)) If the sperm was provided by an anonymous donor, the "woman intended to be the mother" is the legal mother. (§ 9-10-201(b)(3), (c)(1)(C)) This is true even if the woman is unmarried. (Id.) For birth registration purposes, in cases of surrogate mothers, the woman giving birth shall be presumed to be the natural mother and shall be listed as such on the certificate of birth, but a substituted certificate of birth may be issued upon orders of a court of competent jurisdiction. (§ 9-10-201(c)(2))

C. When the man is not the biological father or is not married to the mother

10.	*If a husband does not contribute sperm but consents to his wife providing the womb with the intention of being the mother, is he the father?*	Yes, if the consent is in writing. (§ 9-10-201(a)) This does not apply to surrogate mother cases. In those cases, the biological father is the father, along with his wife if she is intended to be the mother. (§ 9-10-201(b)(1)) However, if there was an anonymous sperm donor, then the woman intended to be the mother is the mother. (§ 9-10-201(b)(3)) In this case, the husband appears not to be deemed the natural father and would, presumably, have to adopt the child. (§ 9-10-201(b)(3))
11.	*If a man contributes sperm how can he avoid being father?*	A sperm donor is presumed not to be the father if the "woman intended to be the mother" is married and her husband consents in writing to the artificial insemination (§ 9-10-201(a), (c)), or if the woman is unmarried (unless there is a surrogate mother and the sperm donor is not anonymous). (§ 9-10-201(c)(1)(c))

California
Status of Children Conceived by Assisted Reproduction Techniques

A. Posthumously Conceived Individuals

1.	Can an individual have legal status as a child even though conceived and born after the parent's death?	The child must be in utero within two years of the issuance of a certificate of the decedent's death or entry of a judgment determining the fact of the decedent's death, whichever occurs first. (Prob. § 249.5(c)) The child is treated as born during the decedent's lifetime. A child who is the product of human cloning is not covered by this section. (Id.)
2.	What if the deceased contributor of procreative material was not married?	The statute makes no distinction based on marital status. (Prob. § 249.5)
3.	Is the consent of the deceased contributor of procreative material required and, if so, what kind of consent, and consent to what?	Yes. The child or his representative must prove by clear and convincing evidence that the decedent, in writing, specified that his or her genetic material shall be used for the posthumous conception of a child of the decedent. (Prob. § 249.5(a)) The specification must be signed and dated by the decedent. (Prob. § 249.5(a)(1)) A person is designated by the decedent to control the use of the genetic material. (Prob. § 249.5(a)(3)) The person designated by the decedent to control the use of the genetic material shall give written notice by certified mail, return receipt requested, that the decedent's genetic material was available for the purpose of posthumous conception. The notice shall be given to a person who has the power to control the distribution of either the decedent's property or death benefits payable by reason of the decedent's death, within four months of the date of issuance of a certificate of the decedent's death or entry of a judgment determining the fact of the decedent's death, whichever event occurs first. (Prob. § 249.5(b)) See also Vernoff v. Astrue, 568 F.3d 1102, 1110-11 (9th Cir. 2009) (no right to intestate succession by posthumously conceived child under § 249.5 if there is no consent).
4.	Is there specific authority addressing the posthumous child's right of inheritance?	Yes. The child will be deemed born during the decedent's life if certain conditions are satisfied. (Prob. § 249.5) See #3 above.
5.	Is there specific authority addressing the posthumous child's status under a will or a trust?	Yes. The child will be deemed born during the decedent's life if certain conditions are satisfied. (Prob. § 249.5) See #3 above.

B. Mother does not provide both womb and egg

6.	Is there a distinction drawn between a married and unmarried woman?	Certain distinctions are drawn. See, e.g., #8 below.

7.	*Who is the mother if a woman contributes the egg but the child is carried in a surrogate's womb?*	No direct authority. "[T]he UPA states that provisions applicable to determining a father and child relationship shall be used to determine a mother and child relationship 'insofar as practicable' . . . " '[G]enetic consanguinity' could be the basis for a finding of maternity just as it is for paternity.' K.M. v. E.G., 37 Cal. 4th 130, 138 (2005) On the other hand, the provision protecting the unmarried sperm donor from paternity, see #11 below, will not bar the assertion of maternity by an egg donor in an unmarried, lesbian relationship situation. Johnson v. Calvert, 851 P.2d 776 (Cal. 1993) suggests that the intent of the parties would control when parentage could be determined differently by genetic donor or by birth mother. Thus, the woman supplying the egg could be the mother if it was not "donated" for the benefit of the surrogate. Even if there is donation, if it is for the purpose of the surrogate bearing a child to be raised by the lesbian donor and her partner/surrogate, the donor is a parent as well. K.M., 37 Cal. 4th at 138. Note also that if spouses divorce after entering into the surrogacy contract, the child born to the surrogate will have to act promptly if one of the spouses dies in order to assert entitlement under the contract, even assuming the child can do so. The one-year statute of limitations for claims against a decedent's estate will apply. See Farb v. Superior Court, 174 Cal. App. 4th 678, 683 (2009).
8.	*Who is the mother if a woman contracts for the egg but carries the child in her womb?*	The child of a wife cohabitating with her husband, if he is not impotent or sterile, is conclusively presumed to be a child of the marriage. (Fam. §§ 7540, 7541) In the case of an unmarried woman, the outcome depends on the case law. Johnson v. Calvert, 851 P.2d 776 (Cal. 1993) suggests that the intent of the parties would control when parentage would be determined differently by genetic material than by birth. See also K.M. v. E.G., 37 Cal. 4th 130 (Cal. 2005) (woman who gave birth was a parent; lesbian partner who donated eggs was also a parent, since she did not just donate, but designed the donation so that the child who was born could be raised in their joint home).

9.	*Who is the mother if a woman contracts for both the egg and the womb?*	Just as a husband is deemed to be the lawful father of a child unrelated to him when his wife gives birth after artificial insemination, so should a husband *and* wife be deemed the lawful parents of a child after a surrogate bears a biologically unrelated child on their behalf. In re Marriage of Buzzanca, 61 Cal. App. 4th 1410, 1413 (Cal. Ct. App. 1998).

C. When the man is not the biological father or is not married to the mother

10.	*If a husband does not contribute sperm but consents to his wife providing the womb with the intention of being the mother, is he the father?*	Yes, if the husband consents in writing in a document signed by both husband and wife and certified by the attending physician and surgeon. (Fam. § 7613(a)) In the same sex situation, the partner is a parent if she receives the child into her home and openly holds out the child as her natural child, and she actively participated in causing the child to be conceived with the understanding that she would raise the child with the birth mother and assuming there are no competing claims to being a second parent. (Elisa B. v. Superior Court, 117 P.3d 660 (Cal. 2005))
11.	*If a man contributes sperm how can he avoid being father?*	The donor of semen provided to a licensed physician and surgeon for use in artificial insemination of a woman other than the donor's wife is treated in law as if he were not the natural father of a child thereby conceived. (Fam. § 7613(b))

Colorado
Status of Children Conceived by Assisted Reproduction Techniques

A. Posthumously Conceived Individuals[1]

1.	Can an individual have legal status as a child even though conceived and born after the parent's death?	U.P.A. — Yes. (§ 19-4-106(8)) U.P.C. — Yes. (§ § 15-11-120(11), 15-11-121(8)) The child must be in utero not later than 36 months after the decedent's death or born not later than 45 months after the decedent's death. (§ 15-11-121(8))
2.	What if the deceased contributor of procreative material was not married?	U.P.A. — The statute only addresses a "spouse." U.P.C. — A parent-child relationship exists between a child of assisted reproduction and an individual other than the birth mother who consented to assisted reproduction by the birth mother with intent to be treated as the other parent of the child. Intent to be treated as a parent of a posthumously conceived child must be established by clear and convincing evidence. (§ 15-11-120(6)(III))
3.	Is the consent of the deceased contributor of procreative material required and, if so, what kind of consent, and consent to what?	U.P.A. — If a spouse dies before placement of eggs, sperm, or embryos, the deceased spouse is not a parent of the resulting child unless the deceased spouse consented in a record that if assisted reproduction were to occur after death, the deceased spouse would be a parent of the child. (§ 19-4-106(8)) U.P.C. — If married, consent is presumed. (§ 15-11-120(8)(b)) If not married, there either needs to be written consent, or else functioning as a parent or intending to function as a parent but prevented from doing so. (§ 15-11-120(6))
4.	Is there specific authority addressing the posthumous child's right of inheritance?	U.P.A. — No. U.P.C. — Yes. (§ § 15-11-120(11), 15-11-121(8))
5.	Is there specific authority addressing the posthumous child's status under a will or a trust?	No. The U.P.C. provisions only apply to intestacy. (§ 15-11-116) However, the intestacy provisions might be incorporated by reference, depending on how the instrument is written. Also, it would apply to a class gift. (§ 15-11-705(7)(b) & (c))

B. Mother does not provide both womb and egg

6.	Is there a distinction drawn between a married and unmarried woman?	U.P.A. — Yes. The statute only addresses a woman who is married. (§ 19-4-106) U.P.C. — No. (§ § 15-11-117, 15-11-121(1)(d))

7.	Who is the mother if a woman contributes the egg but the child is carried in a surrogate's womb?	U.P.A. — Generally, a donor of an egg is not the parent. (§ 19-4-106(2)) This situation of the intended mother donating the egg does not appear to have been considered by the drafters, who addressed the wife as recipient and not as donor of an egg. U.P.C. — The intended parent is the mother, here, typically the contributor of the egg. (§ 15-11-121(1)(d) & (4))
8.	Who is the mother if a woman contracts for the egg but carries the child in her womb?	U.P.A. — If, under the supervision of a licensed physician and with the consent of her husband, a wife consents to assisted reproduction with an egg donated by another woman, to conceive a child for herself, not as a surrogate, the wife is treated in law as if she were the natural mother of a child thereby conceived. (§ 19-4-106(1)) There is no consideration of the situation of a recipient who is unmarried or if the consents are not given. However, generally a donor is not a parent. (§ 19-4-106(2)) U.P.C. — The woman who carries the child in her womb. (§ 15-11-120(2)-(3))
9.	Who is the mother if a woman contracts for both the egg and the womb?	U.P.A. — No authority. See #7 above. U.P.C. — The intended parent. (§ 15-11-121(1)(d) & (4))

C. When the man is not the biological father or is not married to the mother

10.	If a husband does not contribute sperm but consents to his wife providing the womb with the intention of being the mother, is he the father?	U.P.A. — Yes, per § 19-4-106(3), as long as both husband and wife consent in writing, pursuant to § 19-4-106(1). Even if the husband does not sign a consent, this does not preclude finding him to be the father. (§ 19-4-106(5)) U.P.C. — Yes. (§ 15-11-120(6)&(8)(a))
11.	If a man contributes sperm how can he avoid being father?	U.P.A. — A donor is not a parent of a child conceived by means of assisted reproduction, unless he is married to the mother. (§ 19-4-106(2)) U.P.C. — A parent-child relationship does not exist with a third-party donor. (§ 15-11-120(2))

[1] Colorado has enacted both U.P.C. §§ 2-120 and 2-121, as well as the Uniform Parentage Act. The U.P.C. and U.P.A. are not necessarily consistent, and the manner in which conflicts are to be resolved is not specified. Presumably, the enacted U.P.C. provisions apply exclusively to intestacy and class gifts, but this is not certain. The only provision addressing the matter is § 15-11-121(9), which states that the provision concerning gestational agreements "does not affect laws of this state other than this [probate] code regarding the enforceability or validity of a gestational agreement."

Connecticut
Status of Children Conceived by Assisted Reproduction Techniques

A. Posthumously Conceived Individuals

1.	*Can an individual have legal status as a child even though conceived and born after the parent's death?*	Yes. (§ 45a-774)
2.	*What if the deceased contributor of procreative material was not married?*	The statute is written in terms of "spouse." (§ 45a-774)
3.	*Is the consent of the deceased contributor of procreative material required and, if so, what kind of consent, and consent to what?*	Yes. (§ 45a-785(a)(1)) Consent must be in writing, (Id.) and must provide for custody of the deceased's procreative material. Further, the child must be in utero within one year of death of the contributor. (§ 45a-785-(a)(2))
4.	*Is there specific authority addressing the posthumous child's right of inheritance?*	Yes. The law requires that the decedent executed a written document that (A) specifically set forth that his sperm or her eggs may be used for the posthumous conception of a child, (B) specifically provided his or her spouse with authority to exercise custody, control, and use of the sperm or eggs in the event of his or her death, and (C) was signed and dated by the decedent and the surviving spouse. In addition, the child was in utero not later than one year after the date of death of the decedent spouse. (§ 45a-785(a)(1)-(2))
5.	*Is there specific authority addressing the posthumous child's status under a will or a trust?*	Yes. (§§ 45a-778(b), 45a-785)

B. Mother does not provide both womb and egg

6.	*Is there a distinction drawn between a married and unmarried woman?*	Yes, since the statute only addresses married women. (§ 45a-774; Raftopol v. Ramey, 12 A.3d 783 (Conn. 2011))
7.	*Who is the mother if a woman contributes the egg but the child is carried in a surrogate's womb?*	No direct authority if there is no gestational agreement. Doe v. Doe, 710 A.2d 1297, 1314 (Conn. 1998) *may* still be relevant when there is not a gestational agreement and the parties are married. It holds that a child of the marriage is limited to a child conceived by both parties, a child adopted by both parties, a child born to the wife and adopted by the husband, a child conceived by the husband adopted by the wife, and a child born to the wife and conceived through artificial insemination by a donor pursuant to §§ 45a-771-45a-779. If there is a gestational agreement, see 9.
8.	*Who is the mother if a woman contracts for the egg but carries the child in her womb?*	Any child or children born as a result of A.I.D. shall be deemed to acquire, in all respects, the status of a naturally conceived legitimate child of the husband and wife who consented to and requested the use of A.I.D. [artificial insemination with donor sperm or eggs]. (§§ 45a-771a(2), 45a-774)

| 9. | Who is the mother if a woman contracts for both the egg and the womb? | If there is a valid gestational agreement, the intended parents under the agreement are the parents. (Raftopol v. Ramey, 12 A.3d 783 (Conn. 2011) (involving same-sex male companion of biological father)). Previously, in a case of two unmarried homosexual men who entered into a gestational agreement with a woman, the men were deemed the parents. (Griffiths v. Taylor, 2008 WL 2745130, at *7 (Super. Ct. June 13, 2008) (parentage based on intention and not biology)) In these cases, the birth certificate initially indicates that the birth mother is the mother, but then a replacement certificate is issued. (§ 7-48a) |

C. When the man is not the biological father or is not married to the mother

| 10. | If a husband does not contribute sperm but consents to his wife providing the womb with the intention of being the mother, is he the father? | Any child or children born as a result of A.I.D. shall be deemed to acquire, in all respects, the status of a naturally conceived legitimate child of the husband and wife who consented to and requested the use of A.I.D. (§ 45a-774) |
| 11. | If a man contributes sperm how can he avoid being father? | An identified or anonymous donor of sperm or eggs used in A.I.D., or any person claiming by or through such donor, shall not have any right or interest in any child born as a result of A.I.D. (§ 45a-775) The child cannot inherit from the natural father, and the natural father cannot inherit from the child. (§ 45a-777) |

Delaware
Status of Children Conceived by Assisted Reproduction Techniques

A. Posthumously Conceived Individuals

1.	Can an individual have legal status as a child even though conceived and born after the parent's death?	If the parent died before placement of egg, sperm, and embryos, he is "not a parent of the resulting child unless the deceased individual consented in a record that if assisted reproduction were to occur after death, the deceased individual would be a parent of the child." (13 § 8-707)
2.	What if the deceased contributor of procreative material was not married?	As the statute does not address marital status, any contributor who offers valid consent presumably is the legal parent. (13 § 8-707; See also 13 § 8-202)
3.	Is the consent of the deceased contributor of procreative material required and, if so, what kind of consent, and consent to what?	Yes. (13 § 8-707) Consent for all assisted reproduction must be given under 13 § 8-704(a). Consent must be in writing by both a woman and an intended parent. (Id.) However, even without consent, there still may be a finding of paternity if the woman and man, during the first two years of the child's life, resided together in the same household with the child and openly held out the child as their own. (13 § 8-704(b) (referencing 13 § 8-201)) Obviously, this would not apply to a posthumously conceived child.
4.	Is there specific authority addressing the posthumous child's right of inheritance?	No.
5.	Is there specific authority addressing the posthumous child's status under a will or a trust?	No.

B. Mother does not provide both womb and egg

6.	Is there a distinction drawn between a married and unmarried woman?	No. (13 §§ 8-201, 8-202)
7.	Who is the mother if a woman contributes the egg but the child is carried in a surrogate's womb?	Provisions of this chapter of the Delaware Code relating to determinations of paternity apply to determinations of maternity. (13 § 8-106) In this respect, a man who provides sperm for, or consents to, assisted reproduction by a woman as provided in § 8-704 with intent to be the parent of her child, is a parent of the resulting child. (13 § 8-703) A woman who provides an egg to a surrogate with the intent to be the parent of the resulting child would be the mother. (13 § 8-704(a) if there is a record signed by the gestational carrier and the intended parent; (13 § 8-704(a); 13 § 8-703(b))
8.	Who is the mother if a woman contracts for the egg but carries the child in her womb?	The intended parent if a gestational carrier agreement. (13 § 8-703(b))
9.	Who is the mother if a woman contracts for both the egg and the womb?	See ##7-8 above.

C. When the man is not the biological father or is not married to the mother

10.	*If a husband does not contribute sperm but consents to his wife providing the womb with the intention of being the mother, is he the father?*	Yes, although he may challenge his paternity within 2 years of the child's birth if he did not consent to the assisted reproduction before or after the birth of the child. (13 § 8-705(a)) However, a husband may challenge paternity at any time if, in addition to not having consented to the assisted reproduction before or after the birth of the child, the husband did not provide the sperm, the husband and mother did not co-habitate together since the probable time of conception, and the husband never openly held out child as his own. (13 § 8-705(b))
11.	*If a man contributes sperm how can he avoid being father?*	A donor is not a parent of a child conceived by means of assisted reproduction. (13 § 8-702) A donor is defined, *inter alia*, as a producer of the eggs or sperm, other than a husband or wife of the woman recipient. (13 § 8-102(8)) On the other hand, a man who provides sperm for, or consents to, assisted reproduction by a woman as provided in § 8-704 with intent to be the parent of her child, is a parent of the resulting child. (13 § 8-703)

District of Columbia
Status of Children Conceived by Assisted Reproduction Techniques

A. Posthumously Conceived Individuals

1.	Can an individual have legal status as a child even though conceived and born after the parent's death?	On its face, § 19-314, addressing posthumous children in the case of intestacy, does not explicitly bar posthumously *conceived* children from inheriting by intestacy, but it also does not directly address the issue. It states that "a child or descendant of the intestate born after the death of the intestate has the same right of inheritance as if born before death."
2.	What if the deceased contributor of procreative material was not married?	No authority.
3.	Is the consent of the deceased contributor of procreative material required and, if so, what kind of consent, and consent to what?	No authority.
4.	Is there specific authority addressing the posthumous child's right of inheritance?	Unclear. See #1 above.
5.	Is there specific authority addressing the posthumous child's status under a will or a trust?	On its face, § 42-704 addressing posthumous children in the case of a future estate where the future estate is limited to heirs, issue, or children, includes "posthumous children." However, the term "posthumous children" is not defined.

B. Mother does not provide both womb and egg

6.	Is there a distinction drawn between a married and unmarried woman?	No. (§ 16-401(16))
7.	Who is the mother if a woman contributes the egg but the child is carried in a surrogate's womb?	The intended parent, in this case, the contributor of the egg. (§ 16-407(a)(1))
8.	Who is the mother if a woman contracts for the egg but carries the child in her womb?	The woman carrying the child, since she is the intended parent. (§§ 16-407(a)(4); 16-407(b)(1))
9.	Who is the mother if a woman contracts for both the egg and the womb?	No authority.

C. When the man is not the biological father or is not married to the mother

10.	If a husband does not contribute sperm but consents to his wife providing the womb with the intention of being the mother, is he the father?	Yes. (§ 16-407(a)(1))
11.	If a man contributes sperm how can he avoid being father?	He is not the parent if not the intended parent. (§ 16-407(a)(4))

Florida
Status of Children Conceived by Assisted Reproduction Techniques

A. Posthumously Conceived Individuals

1.	Can an individual have legal status as a child even though conceived and born after the parent's death?	No. See 4. below.
2.	What if the deceased contributor of procreative material was not married?	At least with regard to inheritance, the statute is not limited to spouses. (§ 742.17(4))
3.	Is the consent of the deceased contributor of procreative material required and, if so, what kind of consent, and consent to what?	For inheritance purposes, see 4. below.
4.	Is there specific authority addressing the posthumous child's right of inheritance?	A child conceived from eggs or sperm of a person or persons who died before the transfer of the eggs, sperm or preembryos to a woman's body shall not be eligible for a claim against the decedent's estate, unless the child has been provided for by the decedent's will. (§ 742.17(4))
5.	Is there specific authority addressing the posthumous child's status under a will or a trust?	A child conceived from the eggs or sperm of a person or persons who died before the transfer of their eggs, sperm, or preembryos to a woman's body shall not be eligible for a claim against the decedent's estate unless the child has been provided for by the decedent's will. (§ 742.17(4)) In the event of the death of one member of a commissioning couple (that is, the intended father and mother, one of whom has contributed the egg or sperm (§ 742.13(2)), "[a]bsent a written agreement" the surviving member is entitled to maintain control over all eggs, sperm, and preembryos. (§ 742.17(3))

B. Mother does not provide both womb and egg

6.	Is there a distinction drawn between a married and unmarried woman?	Yes. For a married couple, see § 742.16(7). See also 7. below. In the case of an unmarried couple, see T.M.H. v. D.M.T., 79 So. 3d 787 (Dist. Ct. App. 2011) which held that, the lesbian partner who contributed the egg was a parent despite § 742.14, which provides that a donor "shall relinquish maternal or paternal rights and obligations with respect to the donation or the resulting children." The lesbian partner was not a "donor," because her intent was not simply to give her ova, but to give her ova in order to be a parent. According to the majority, an interpretation that barred her from parentage would be a violation of equal protection rights. However, the dissent maintained that the constitutional right to procreate has not been extended to include a right to procreate outside one's body.

7.	*Who is the mother if a woman contributes the egg but the child is carried in a surrogate's womb?*	When at least one member of the commissioning couple is the genetic parent of the child, the commissioning couple* shall be presumed to be the natural parents of the child. (§ 742.16(7)) The couple must be married and both at least 18 years old. (§ 742.15(1))
8.	*Who is the mother if a woman contracts for the egg but carries the child in her womb?*	The woman who carries the child in her womb. The donor of the egg or preembryo "shall relinquish all maternal . . . rights and obligations with respect to the donation or the resulting children" (§ 742.14) But see 7. above. If the egg is fertilized by the male member of the commissioning couple*, they are presumed to be the natural parents. (§ 742.16(7)) "[E]xcept in the case of gestational surrogacy, any child born within wedlock" from donated egg or preembryos "shall be irrebuttably presumed to be the child of the recipient gestating woman and her husband provided that both parties have consented in writing to the use of donated eggs or preembryos." (§ 742.11(2)) There is no provision regarding an unmarried woman.
9.	*Who is the mother if a woman contracts for both the egg and the womb?*	A surrogate assumes parental rights and responsibilities if the child born to her is not genetically related to either commissioning* parent. (§ 742.15(3)(e))

C. When the man is not the biological father or is not married to the mother

10.	*If a husband does not contribute sperm but consents to his wife providing the womb with the intention of being the mother, is he the father?*	Yes. If both mother and father, within wedlock, have provided consent in writing, the presumption is irrebuttable. (§ 742.11(2))
11.	*If a man contributes sperm how can he avoid being father?*	Case law holds that he is not the father. See Lamaritata v. Lucas, 823 So. 2d 316, 319 (Dist. Ct. App. 2002); Brown v. Gadson, 654 S.E.2d 179, 180 (Ga. Ct. App. 2007) (interpreting the Florida law). See also § 742.14 compelling the donor to relinquish all paternal rights. Note, however, that § 742.14 has been held unconstitutional as applied in T.M.H. v. D.M.T., 79 So. 3d 787 (Dist. Ct. App. 2011). Note also that the statute does not apply if there is a "commissioning couple* or a father who has executed a preplanned adoption agreement . . . " Still, a typical donor, who is seeking to avoid paternity should not be affected.

* "Commissioning couple" means "the intended mother and father." (§ 742.13(2)) Thus, the provision would not protect parental rights in the case of a same-sex couple, as they could not be a "commissioning couple." This has been held unconstitutional as applied by one district court of appeals in T.M.H. v. D.M.T., 79 So. 3d 787 (Dist. Ct. App. 2011) (involving biological mother who donated egg to birth mother when they were in a lesbian relationship).

Georgia
Status of Children Conceived by Assisted Reproduction Techniques

A. Posthumously Conceived Individuals

1.	Can an individual have legal status as a child even though conceived and born after the parent's death?	No specific authority. However, a child born within wedlock or "within the usual period of gestation thereafter ... by means of artificial insemination" is presumed legitimate. (§ 19-7-21) Thus, a child immediately conceived by ART after death of father might well be presumed his child. This would, apparently, only be the case if the mother was married to the decedent or the child was born within the usual period after wedlock ended.
2.	What if the deceased contributor of procreative material was not married?	No authority.
3.	Is the consent of the deceased contributor of procreative material required and, if so, what kind of consent, and consent to what?	Yes, as to use and administration of artificial insemination. (§ 19-7-21)
4.	Is there specific authority addressing the posthumous child's right of inheritance?	No specific authority.
5.	Is there specific authority addressing the posthumous child's status under a will or a trust?	No specific authority.

B. Mother does not provide both womb and egg

6.	Is there a distinction drawn between a married and unmarried woman?	Yes.
7.	Who is the mother if a woman contributes the egg but the child is carried in a surrogate's womb?	No authority.
8.	Who is the mother if a woman contracts for the egg but carries the child in her womb?	If the woman is married, the child is presumed to be the legitimate child of the woman and her husband, assuming there was consent. See #3 above. (§ 19-7-21) No authority currently exists as to the status of an unmarried woman who has a child through artificial reproduction or the situation in which a husband has not consented.
9.	Who is the mother if a woman contracts for both the egg and the womb?	No authority.

C. When the man is not the biological father or is not married to the mother

10.	If a husband does not contribute sperm but consents to his wife providing the womb with the intention of being the mother, is he the father?	Yes. (§ 19-7-21)

| 11. | If a man contributes sperm how can he avoid being father? | If the recipient is married and both she and her husband consent in writing to the procedure, they are irrebuttably presumed the parents. (§ 19-7-21)
On the other hand, "Georgia's statutes neither provide for nor contemplate . . . circumstances . . . where a man and woman who are not married to each other, have employed artificial insemination under an agreement releasing the donor father from the duties and responsibilities of parenthood." Brown v. Gadson, 654 S.E.2d 179, 180 n.2 (Ga. Ct. App. 2007) (holding Florida law not violative of Georgia public policy, so that Florida statute governing unmarried donor and recipient could be applied in Georgia court, thereby relieving donor of liability based on their agreement). |

Hawaii
Status of Children Conceived by Assisted Reproduction Techniques

A. Posthumously Conceived Individuals

1.	Can an individual have legal status as a child even though conceived and born after the parent's death?	No authority.
2.	What if the deceased contributor of procreative material was not married?	No authority.
3.	Is the consent of the deceased contributor of procreative material required and, if so, what kind of consent, and consent to what?	No authority.
4.	Is there specific authority addressing the posthumous child's right of inheritance?	"Posthumous children" are allowed to inherit. (§ 532-9) However, the term is not defined.
5.	Is there specific authority addressing the posthumous child's status under a will or a trust?	See #10 below.

B. Mother does not provide both womb and egg

6.	Is there a distinction drawn between a married and unmarried woman?	No. (§ 584-2)
7.	Who is the mother if a woman contributes the egg but the child is carried in a surrogate's womb?	No authority.
8.	Who is the mother if a woman contracts for the egg but carries the child in her womb?	No authority.
9.	Who is the mother if a woman contracts for both the egg and the womb?	No authority.

C. When the man is not the biological father or is not married to the mother

10.	If a husband does not contribute sperm but consents to his wife providing the womb with the intention of being the mother, is he the father?	Although the statute does not reference assisted reproduction, a man is presumed to be the father of a child born to his wife during the marriage or within 300 days of its termination. (§ 584-4(a)(1)) Furthermore, the period for establishing the parent-child relationship does not extend the time within which a right of inheritance or right to succession may be asserted beyond the time provided by law relating to distribution and closing of decedent's estates or to the determination of heirship, or otherwise. (§ 584-6(a)(3))
11.	If a man contributes sperm how can he avoid being father?	No authority.

Idaho
Status of Children Conceived by Assisted Reproduction Techniques

A. Posthumously Conceived Individuals

1.	Can an individual have legal status as a child even though conceived and born after the parent's death?	No authority.
2.	What if the deceased contributor of procreative material was not married?	No authority.
3.	Is the consent of the deceased contributor of procreative material required and, if so, what kind of consent, and consent to what?	No authority.
4.	Is there specific authority addressing the posthumous child's right of inheritance?	§ 15-2-108 appears to limit their right of inheritance to children conceived prior to death of the parent.
5.	Is there specific authority addressing the posthumous child's status under a will or a trust?	No authority.

B. Mother does not provide both womb and egg

6.	Is there a distinction drawn between a married and unmarried woman?	No authority.
7.	Who is the mother if a woman contributes the egg but the child is carried in a surrogate's womb?	No authority.
8.	Who is the mother if a woman contracts for the egg but carries the child in her womb?	No authority. Title 39, Chapter 54, generally assumes that a woman giving birth to a child is the mother, but it does not envision the situation of egg donation and no case has dealt with the subject.
9.	Who is the mother if a woman contracts for both the egg and the womb?	No authority.

C. When the man is not the biological father or is not married to the mother

10.	If a husband does not contribute sperm but consents to his wife providing the womb with the intention of being the mother, is he the father?	The husband of a woman who has a child through artificial insemination is the child's legal father if he consented to the procedure. (§ 39-5405(3))
11.	If a man contributes sperm how can he avoid being father?	The donor (a man who is not the husband of the woman upon whom the artificial insemination is performed) (§ 39-5401) has no rights, obligations or interests as to the child (§ 39-5405(1)), nor does the child with respect to the donor (§ 39-5405(2)).

Illinois
Status of Children Conceived by Assisted Reproduction Techniques

A. Posthumously Conceived Individuals

1.	Can an individual have legal status as a child even though conceived and born after the parent's death?	No. (750 ILCS § 46/706; 755 ILCS § 5/1-1)
2.	What if the deceased contributor of procreative material was not married?	No legal status as a child. (Id.)
3.	Is the consent of the deceased contributor of procreative material required and, if so, what kind of consent, and consent to what?	Irrelevant. No legal status as a child. (Id.)
4.	Is there specific authority addressing the posthumous child's right of inheritance?	No authority.
5.	Is there specific authority addressing the posthumous child's status under a will or a trust?	No authority.

B. Mother does not provide both womb and egg

6.	Is there a distinction drawn between a married and unmarried woman?	No.
7.	Who is the mother if a woman contributes the egg but the child is carried in a surrogate's womb?	The woman who contributes the egg is the mother upon birth of the child if all of the requirements in § 750 ILCS § 47/15(d) are met. These include surrogate and intended parent requirements (outlined in section 20), and a gestational surrogacy contract requirement (outlined in Section 25).
8.	Who is the mother if a woman contracts for the egg but carries the child in her womb?	The woman who carries the child in her womb is the mother unless the requisite steps are taken to identify another woman as the intended mother. (§ 750 ILCS 47/15(a))
9.	Who is the mother if a woman contracts for both the egg and the womb?	The intended mother is the mother upon birth of the child if she complies with 750 ILCS § 47/15. Importantly, however, in order for a gestational surrogacy contract to have a valid intended parent, as a required by 750 ILCS § 47/25, at least one gamete must be contributed by an intended parent. (750 ILCS § 47/20(b)(1))

C. When the man is not the biological father or is not married to the mother

10.	If a husband does not contribute sperm but consents to his wife providing the womb with the intention of being the mother, is he the father?	Yes, if an "intended parent." (750 ILCS § 46/703(a)) An "intended parent" is a person "who entered into an assisted reproduction technology arrangement . . . under which he or she will be the legal parent of the resulting child." (750 ILCS § 46/103(m-3)) It is not clear how one "enters into" an assisted reproduction technology arrangement. In any event, such arrangement would not cover reproduction by actual sexual intercourse. (750 ILCS § 46/103(d))

11. *If a man contributes sperm how can he avoid being father?*	By being a "donor," which entails relinquishing all legal rights in a writing. (750 ILCS §46/703 (a)-(b))

Indiana
Status of Children Conceived by Assisted Reproduction Techniques

A. Posthumously Conceived Individuals

1.	Can an individual have legal status as a child even though conceived and born after the parent's death?	No authority.
2.	What if the deceased contributor of procreative material was not married?	No authority.
3.	Is the consent of the deceased contributor of procreative material required and, if so, what kind of consent, and consent to what?	No authority.
4.	Is there specific authority addressing the posthumous child's right of inheritance?	No authority.
5.	Is there specific authority addressing the posthumous child's status under a will or a trust?	No authority.

B. Mother does not provide both womb and egg

6.	Is there a distinction drawn between a married and unmarried woman?	No authority.
7.	Who is the mother if a woman contributes the egg but the child is carried in a surrogate's womb?	The birth mother, unless the other woman can establish by clear and convincing evidence that she is the biological mother. (In re Paternity and Maternity of Infant R., 922 N.E.2d 59 (Ct. App. 2010)) **Note**: Surrogacy contracts are prohibited in Indiana. (§§ 31-20-1-1; 31-20-1-2) However, the court in the above case did not consider these statutory provisions. In a later decision, In re Paternity of Infant T., 991 N.E.2d 596 (Ct. App. 2013), the court held that if the birth mother does not present clear and convincing evidence that another woman is the biological mother then she cannot disestablish her maternity.
8.	Who is the mother if a woman contracts for the egg but carries the child in her womb?	No direct authority.
9.	Who is the mother if a woman contracts for both the egg and the womb?	No authority.

C. When the man is not the biological father or is not married to the mother

10.	If a husband does not contribute sperm but consents to his wife providing the womb with the intention of being the mother, is he the father?	Yes, at least for purposes of providing support after divorce. Where the husband and wife knowingly and voluntarily consent to artificial insemination, the resulting child is a child of the marriage within the meaning of the Dissolution of Marriage Act. (Engelking v. Engelking, 982 N.E.2d 326 (Ct. App. 2013))

11. *If a man contributes sperm how can he avoid being father?*	Provide the sperm to a licensed physician and have a donor contract between the parties that reflects a "careful consideration of the implications and a thorough understanding of the agreement's meaning and import." (In re Paternity of M.F., 938 N.E.2d 1256, 1262 (Ind. Ct. App. 2010))

Iowa
Status of Children Conceived by Assisted Reproduction Techniques

A. Posthumously Conceived Individuals

1.	Can an individual have legal status as a child even though conceived and born after the parent's death?	Yes. §633.220A provides that, for rules relating to intestate succession, a child conceived and born after the intestate's death is deemed a child of the intestate if: (a) a genetic parent-child relationship between the child and intestate is established, (b) the intestate, in a signed writing, authorized the surviving spouse to use the decedent's genetic material to initiate the posthumous procedure that resulted in the child's birth, and (c) the child is born within 2 years of the death of the intestate.
2.	What if the deceased contributor of procreative material was not married?	See above. As element (b) requires that authorization is granted to a spouse to use the descendants' genetic material, an unmarried contributor falls outside the scope of §633.220A.
3.	Is the consent of the deceased contributor of procreative material required and, if so, what kind of consent, and consent to what?	Yes. See above.
4.	Is there specific authority addressing the posthumous child's right of inheritance?	See 1, above.
5.	Is there specific authority addressing the posthumous child's status under a will or a trust?	Yes, with regard to a will. (§633.267(1)) The child conceived after the testator's death, if satisfying the criteria of 1. above, is treated as a child (§633.267(2)) and, thus, entitled to an intestate share, unless it appears from the will that the omission was intentional. (§633.267(1))

B. Mother does not provide both womb and egg

6.	Is there a distinction drawn between a married and unmarried woman?	No authority.
7.	Who is the mother if a woman contributes the egg but the child is carried in a surrogate's womb?	No authority. "Iowa courts have never decided a surrogacy case, and the state legislature has not regulated surrogacy practice." 51 Drake L. Rev. 605, 607 (2003).
8.	Who is the mother if a woman contracts for the egg but carries the child in her womb?	No authority.
9.	Who is the mother if a woman contracts for both the egg and the womb?	No authority.

C. When the man is not the biological father or is not married to the mother

10.	If a husband does not contribute sperm but consents to his wife providing the womb with the intention of being the mother, is he the father?	No authority.
11.	If a man contributes sperm how can he avoid being father?	No authority.

Kansas
Status of Children Conceived by Assisted Reproduction Techniques

A. Posthumously Conceived Individuals

1.	Can an individual have legal status as a child even though conceived and born after the parent's death?	No authority.
2.	What if the deceased contributor of procreative material was not married?	No authority.
3.	Is the consent of the deceased contributor of procreative material required and, if so, what kind of consent, and consent to what?	No authority.
4.	Is there specific authority addressing the posthumous child's right of inheritance?	No authority.
5.	Is there specific authority addressing the posthumous child's status under a will or a trust?	No authority.

B. Mother does not provide both womb and egg

6.	Is there a distinction drawn between a married and unmarried woman?	No. (§ 23-2206)
7.	Who is the mother if a woman contributes the egg but the child is carried in a surrogate's womb?	With respect to the mother-child relationship, § 23-2220 provides: "Insofar as practicable, the provisions of this act applicable to the father and child relationship apply." § 23-2208 indicates that a man is presumed to be the father of the child if test results indicate a probability of 97% or greater that the man is the father of the child. If this provision were applied to a woman who's fertilized egg was carried in a surrogate's womb, the woman could be declared the mother of the child.
8.	Who is the mother if a woman contracts for the egg but carries the child in her womb?	"The mother may be established by proof of her having given birth to the child or under this act." (§ 23-2207(a))
9.	Who is the mother if a woman contracts for both the egg and the womb?	See 7, above.

C. When the man is not the biological father or is not married to the mother

10.	If a husband does not contribute sperm but consents to his wife providing the womb with the intention of being the mother, is he the father?	No definite authority. Of possible relevance may be § 23-2208 and the presumptions regarding paternity.
11.	If a man contributes sperm how can he avoid being father?	The donor of semen provided to a licensed physician for use in artificial insemination of a woman other than the donor's wife is treated in law as if he were not the birth father of a child thereby conceived, unless agreed to in writing by the donor and the woman. (§ 23-2208(f))

Kentucky
Status of Children Conceived by Assisted Reproduction Techniques

A. Posthumously Conceived Individuals

1.	Can an individual have legal status as a child even though conceived and born after the parent's death?	No authority.
2.	What if the deceased contributor of procreative material was not married?	No authority.
3.	Is the consent of the deceased contributor of procreative material required and, if so, what kind of consent, and consent to what?	No authority.
4.	Is there specific authority addressing the posthumous child's right of inheritance?	No authority.
5.	Is there specific authority addressing the posthumous child's status under a will or a trust?	No authority.

B. Mother does not provide both womb and egg

6.	Is there a distinction drawn between a married and unmarried woman?	Yes.
7.	Who is the mother if a woman contributes the egg but the child is carried in a surrogate's womb?	No authority. Surrogate mother contracts for consideration are void under § 199.590(4). A married couple cannot legally contract with a surrogate mother that for a stated consideration she will agree to be artificially inseminated with the natural father's sperm, carry the fetus to delivery and consent to the wife's adoption of the child since under subsection (5) [of § 199.500] the surrogate mother cannot give legally binding consent for the adoption of a child until five days after the birth of the child, and even a contract providing for future consent by the surrogate mother would be illegal since it would be against public policy to contract as a means of avoiding the language of this section. (Opin. Attorney Gen. 81-18)
8.	Who is the mother if a woman contracts for the egg but carries the child in her womb?	Depending on timing and marital status, the woman can be the mother. "A child born during lawful wedlock, or within ten (10) months thereafter, is presumed to be the child of the husband and wife." (§ 406.011)
9.	Who is the mother if a woman contracts for both the egg and the womb?	No direct authority. Surrogate mother contracts are void under § 199.590(4).

C. When the man is not the biological father or is not married to the mother

10.	If a husband does not contribute sperm but consents to his wife providing the womb with the intention of being the mother, is he the father?	Presumably the husband is the father. "A child born during lawful wedlock, or within ten (10) months thereafter, is presumed to be the child of the husband and wife." (§ 406.011)

11.	*If a man contributes sperm how can he avoid being father?*	No authority. Generally, the birth certificate of a child born as a result of artificial insemination is completed in accordance with the provisions of § 213.046, which does not set forth specific rules addressing this situation. There is no general provision relieving the donor of paternity.

Louisiana
Status of Children Conceived by Assisted Reproduction Techniques

A. Posthumously Conceived Individuals

1.	Can an individual have legal status as a child even though conceived and born after the parent's death?	Yes. Child must be born within 3 years of the death of the decedent. (R.S. 9:391.1(A)) An heir or legatee has one year thereafter to challenge paternity. (R.S. 9:391.1(B)) See also R.S. 9:133, which provides that an in vitro fertilized ovum must develop into an unborn child that is born alive in order to have inheritance rights.
2.	What if the deceased contributor of procreative material was not married?	The statute only addresses spouses.
3.	Is the consent of the deceased contributor of procreative material required and, if so, what kind of consent, and consent to what?	The decedent must have specifically authorized in writing his surviving spouse to use his gametes. (R.S. 9:391.1(A))
4.	Is there specific authority addressing the posthumous child's right of inheritance?	Yes. (R.S. 9:391.1(A))
5.	Is there specific authority addressing the posthumous child's status under a will or a trust?	Yes, entitled to "all rights" as a child of the decedent. (R.S. 9:391.1(A))

B. Mother does not provide both womb and egg

6.	Is there a distinction drawn between a married and unmarried woman?	The "mother" is the woman who gives birth to the child, that is, who provides the womb. There is an exception if a surrogate who provides the womb is a relative of a married husband or wife. (C.C. Art. 184)
7.	Who is the mother if a woman contributes the egg but the child is carried in a surrogate's womb?	A husband and wife are the "biological parents" of a child if they provide the sperm and egg for in vitro fertilization performed by a licensed physician, and the resulting fetus is carried by a surrogate who is related by blood or affinity to either the husband or wife. (R.S. 40:32)
8.	Who is the mother if a woman contracts for the egg but carries the child in her womb?	Maternity may be established by a preponderance of the evidence that the child was born of a particular woman. (C.C. Art. 184) Revision Comments state: "This Article clarifies present law by explicitly establishing that the mother of a child is the woman who gives birth to the child, and that maternity may be proved by any evidence at any time." For an exception to this rule, see #7, above.
9.	Who is the mother if a woman contracts for both the egg and the womb?	No authority.

C. When the man is not the biological father or is not married to the mother

10.	If a husband does not contribute sperm but consents to his wife providing the womb with the intention of being the mother, is he the father?	Yes, if he consented to the assisted conception. (C.C. Art. 188)

11. *If a man contributes sperm how can he avoid being father?*

No specific authority. R.S. 9:133 provides that a child born as a result of in vitro fertilization and in vitro fertilized ovum donation to another couple does not retain its inheritance rights from the in vitro fertilization patients. R.S. 9:126 implies that an anonymous sperm donor may avoid being a father, but no case has dealt with the subject. See also R.S. 9:130, which defines a fertilized human ovum as a juridical person. The married fertilization patients may renounce by notarial acts their parental rights for implantation in favor of another married couple.

Maine
Status of Children Conceived by Assisted Reproduction Techniques

A. Posthumously Conceived Individuals

1.	Can an individual have legal status as a child even though conceived and born after the parent's death?	No authority.
2.	What if the deceased contributor of procreative material was not married?	No authority.
3.	Is the consent of the deceased contributor of procreative material required and, if so, what kind of consent, and consent to what?	No authority.
4.	Is there specific authority addressing the posthumous child's right of inheritance?	No authority.
5.	Is there specific authority addressing the posthumous child's status under a will or a trust?	No authority.

B. Mother does not provide both womb and egg

6.	Is there a distinction drawn between a married and unmarried woman?	No authority.
7.	Who is the mother if a woman contributes the egg but the child is carried in a surrogate's womb?	The woman contributing the egg, at least in an undisputed case where the genetic parents seek a judgment declaring their legal parentage and the gestational carrier and her husband have assented that they do not wish to be recognized as the child's parents. (Nolan v. LaBree, 52 A.3d 923, 925 (Me. 2012))
8.	Who is the mother if a woman contracts for the egg but carries the child in her womb?	No authority.
9.	Who is the mother if a woman contracts for both the egg and the womb?	No authority.

C. When the man is not the biological father or is not married to the mother

10.	If a husband does not contribute sperm but consents to his wife providing the womb with the intention of being the mother, is he the father?	There is no specific provision. However, the husband is presumed to be the father under M.R. Evid. 302, unless evidence "beyond a reasonable doubt" is presented in support of illegitimacy. The wife may also acknowledge that the father is not the husband. (Denbow v. Harris, 583 A.2d 205, 207 (Me. 1990))
11.	If a man contributes sperm how can he avoid being father?	For inheritance purposes, he is not the father. (In re I.H., 834 A.2d 922, 925-26 (Me. 2003) (citing 18-A §5-207(a), 18-A §1-201(28), and 18-A §2-109)) There is no explicit statute. The dicta in the case regarding interstate succession is based on interpretation of the cited sections of Maine's version of the U.P.C.

Maryland
Status of Children Conceived by Assisted Reproduction Techniques

A. Posthumously Conceived Individuals

1.	Can an individual have legal status as a child even though conceived and born after the parent's death?	Yes, if the decedent gave consent in a written record and the child is born within 2 years after the decedent's death. (Est. & Tr. § 3-107(b))
2.	What if the deceased contributor of procreative material was not married?	Statute does not distinguish. (Est. & Tr. § 3-107(b))
3.	Is the consent of the deceased contributor of procreative material required and, if so, what kind of consent, and consent to what?	Decedent must have consented in a written record to (1) use of decedent's genetic material for posthumous conception in accordance with the requirements of § 20-111 of the Health-General Article, and (2) be the parent of a child posthumously conceived using the person's genetic material. (Est. & Tr. § 3-107(b))
4.	Is there specific authority addressing the posthumous child's right of inheritance?	Yes. If the conditions of Est. & Tr. § 3-107 are met then the child is entitled to a distribution. (Est. & Tr. § 3-107(a) & (b))
5.	Is there specific authority addressing the posthumous child's status under a will or a trust?	Yes, specifically with respect to a trust, a "child" includes a posthumously conceived child conceived from the genetic material of the grantor. (Est. & Tr. § 1-205(a)(2))

B. Mother does not provide both womb and egg

6.	Is there a distinction drawn between a married and unmarried woman?	No authority.
7.	Who is the mother if a woman contributes the egg but the child is carried in a surrogate's womb?	No authority.
8.	Who is the mother if a woman contracts for the egg but carries the child in her womb?	No authority.
9.	Who is the mother if a woman contracts for both the egg and the womb?	No authority.

C. When the man is not the biological father or is not married to the mother

10.	If a husband does not contribute sperm but consents to his wife providing the womb with the intention of being the mother, is he the father?	Yes. (Est. & Tr. § 1-206(b)) Consent of husband is presumed. (Id.)
11.	If a man contributes sperm how can he avoid being father?	For an unmarried man, he is not the father unless he has taken certain steps or there is a judicial determination. (Est. & Tr. § 1-208(b))

Massachusetts
Status of Children Conceived by Assisted Reproduction Techniques

A. Posthumously Conceived Individuals

1.	Can an individual have legal status as a child even though conceived and born after the parent's death?	Likely yes under Woodward v. Comm'r, 760 N.E.2d 257 (Mass. 2002) (construing a since-repealed statute "in a manner that advanced the purposes of the intestacy law." (See research references on Westlaw under § 2-108)) Not clear whether one-year requirement for commencing paternity claims mandated by intestacy statute, 3-803, applies. The court did not decide in *Woodward*, although it did express doubt whether the period imposed significant burdens on the parents and consequently on the child.
2.	What if the deceased contributor of procreative material was not married?	No specific authority.
3.	Is the consent of the deceased contributor of procreative material required and, if so, what kind of consent, and consent to what?	Yes, with respect to posthumous conception. Woodward v. Comm'r, 760 N.E.2d 257 (Mass. 2002). In addition, there must be consent to the support of any resulting child. (Id.) *Woodward* did not discuss particulars of consent, and subsequent cases have not clarified the issue, for example, whether it must be in writing. The evidentiary standards under Massachusetts law are explored further in Hanson v. Astrue, 733 F. Supp. 2d 214 (D. Mass. 2010).
4.	Is there specific authority addressing the posthumous child's right of inheritance?	No definite authority. *Woodward* involved a social security claim interpreting the intestacy statute and did recognize a right to inherit if the consents discussed in #3 above were given.
5.	Is there specific authority addressing the posthumous child's status under a will or a trust?	No authority.

B. Mother does not provide both womb and egg

6.	Is there a distinction drawn between a married and unmarried woman?	Yes.
7.	Who is the mother if a woman contributes the egg but the child is carried in a surrogate's womb?	Unclear. If the woman and the woman's spouse are the sole genetic sources for the child, and the surrogate does not contest, the woman may be the mother. See Culliton v. Beth Isr. Deaconess Med. Ctr., 435 Mass. 285, 291-92 (2001). R.R. v. M.H., 689 N.E.2d 790, cites to Johnson v. Calvert, 851 P.2d 776 (1993), as authority that the egg donor is the mother. (689 N.E.2d at 795 n.10)
8.	Who is the mother if a woman contracts for the egg but carries the child in her womb?	The woman is the mother. (46 § 4B) See also R.R. v. M.H., 689 N.E.2d 790, 795 (Mass. 1998).
9.	Who is the mother if a woman contracts for both the egg and the womb?	No authority.

C. When the man is not the biological father or is not married to the mother

10.	If a husband does not contribute sperm but consents to his wife providing the womb with the intention of being the mother, is he the father?	Yes, the husband is the father if he consents to the insemination. (46, § 4B) See also R.R. v. M.H., 689 N.E.2d 790 (Mass. 1998). Note that the nonmarital situation is not addressed.
11.	If a man contributes sperm how can he avoid being father?	No direct authority. Woodward v. Comm'r, 760 N.E.2d 257, 270 n.23, suggests that the relinquishment of all rights and responsibilities under contract with a sperm bank by the donor relieves him of legal parentage.

Michigan
Status of Children Conceived by Assisted Reproduction Techniques

A. Posthumously Conceived Individuals

1.	Can an individual have legal status as a child even though conceived and born after the parent's death?	No. See #4.
2.	What if the deceased contributor of procreative material was not married?	No authority.
3.	Is the consent of the deceased contributor of procreative material required and, if so, what kind of consent, and consent to what?	For intestacy purposes. See #4.
4.	Is there specific authority addressing the posthumous child's right of inheritance?	Posthumous children conceived after parent's death have no right of inheritance. (In re Certified Question from U.S. Dist. Court for Western Michigan, 825 N.W.2d 566, 570 (Mich. 2012)) "Because plaintiff's twins were not in gestation at [the decedent's]death, no inheritance right vested in them . . . pursuant to MCL 700.2108. Moreover, because the twins were not living at the time of his death, they had no inheritance rights as heirs pursuant to MCL 700.2104." (Id.)
5.	Is there specific authority addressing the posthumous child's status under a will or a trust?	No authority. But note that the law favors construction of a will most nearly in accordance with statutes of descent and distribution. (Gardner v. City Nat. Bank & Trust Co., 267 Mich. 270, 279 (1934))

B. Mother does not provide both womb and egg

6.	Is there a distinction drawn between a married and unmarried woman?	No authority.
7.	Who is the mother if a woman contributes the egg but the child is carried in a surrogate's womb?	No authority. Note: surrogate contracts are void in Michigan. (§722.855; Doe v. Kelley, 307 N.W.2d 438, 441 (Ct. App. 1981))
8.	Who is the mother if a woman contracts for the egg but carries the child in her womb?	Unsure. In disputed cases of surrogate carriers, the party having physical custody of the child maintains it until the dispute is settled. But legal custody is ultimately determined by the best interests of the child. (§722.861) Relationship for purposes of inheritance is not addressed.
9.	Who is the mother if a woman contracts for both the egg and the womb?	No authority.

C. When the man is not the biological father or is not married to the mother

10.	If a husband does not contribute sperm but consents to his wife providing the womb with the intention of being the mother, is he the father?	Yes. A child conceived by a married woman with the consent of her husband following utilization of assisted reproductive technology is considered as their child for purposes of intestate succession. Consent is presumed unless the contrary is shown by clear and convincing evidence. (§ 700.2114(1)(a))
11.	If a man contributes sperm how can he avoid being father?	No authority.

Minnesota
Status of Children Conceived by Assisted Reproduction Techniques

A. Posthumously Conceived Individuals[2]

1.	Can an individual have legal status as a child even though conceived and born after the parent's death?	No. (§ 524.2-120 subd. 10)
2.	What if the deceased contributor of procreative material was not married?	See #1 above.
3.	Is the consent of the deceased contributor of procreative material required and, if so, what kind of consent, and consent to what?	See #1 above.
4.	Is there specific authority addressing the posthumous child's right of inheritance?	See #1 above.
5.	Is there specific authority addressing the posthumous child's status under a will or a trust?	Not specifically, but #1 relates to the parent-child relationship for intestacy purposes and would likely affect the construction of a will or trust, the posthumous child being a child born out of wedlock. In this case, § 524.2-705 applies to class gifts the terms of relationship in accordance with the rules for intestate succession.

B. Mother does not provide both womb and egg

6.	Is there a distinction drawn between a married and unmarried woman?	No authority. Generally, a parent-child relationship can exist regardless of marital status of the parents. (§ 524.2-117)

7.	*Who is the mother if a woman contributes the egg but the child is carried in a surrogate's womb?*	Unclear. Effective Aug. 1, 2010, for inheritance purposes, a parent-child relationship exists with the "birth mother." (§ 524.2-120 Subd. 2) While this would appear to point to the surrogate, § 524.1-201(7) makes clear that a "child of assisted reproduction" does not include a child conceived pursuant to a gestational agreement. Furthermore, the term "'birth mother' does not include a woman who gives birth pursuant to a gestational agreement." (§ 524.1-201(5)) While the statute also defines "intended parents" for purposes of a gestational agreement, there is no statutory provision specifically dealing with the parent-child relationship under a gestational agreement. Earlier, one Minnesota case, involving property rights, In re Paternity and Custody of Baby Boy A., 2007 Westlaw 4304448 (Ct. App. Dec. 11, 2007), held that a gestational surrogate was not the mother. The decision recognizes that the mother-child relationship is not determined necessarily by the biological or genetic relationship. The court held that gestational surrogacy agreements are not void as a matter of Minnesota public policy. However, the court applied the governing Illinois law, rather than Minnesota law, to determine the parent-child relationship. See also § 524.2-121, indicating that the chapters on intestate succession, including § 524.2-120, dealing with assisted reproduction, do not change state law on gestational agreements.
8.	*Who is the mother if a woman contracts for the egg but carries the child in her womb?*	Uncertain result. In A.L.S. ex rel J.P. v. E.A.G., 2010 Westlaw 4181449 (Ct. App. Oct. 26, 2010), discussed in 9. below, the court noted in dicta that § 257.62, relating to blood and genetic tests, should not be read as allowing egg donors to become the parent of the resulting child. (See A.L.S. at *3)
9.	*Who is the mother if a woman contracts for both the egg and the womb?*	No direct authority. Most recently, in A.L.S. ex rel. J.P. v. E.A.G., 2010 Westlaw 4181449 (Ct. App. Oct. 26, 2010), the court addressed the situation where two men contracted with a surrogate, who had her egg fertilized intrauterine by the sperm of one of the men. The surrogate was deemed the mother. The male partner not contributing any procreative material was held not a parent. For inheritance purposes, it appears that the surrogate birth mother is the mother. (§ 524.2-120 Subd. 2)

C. When the man is not the biological father or is not married to the mother

10.	*If a husband does not contribute sperm but consents to his wife providing the womb with the intention of being the mother, is he the father?*	U.P.A. — Yes, if, under the supervision of a licensed physician, the husband consented in a writing signed by both him and his wife. The consent must be retained by the physician for at least 4 years after confirmation of pregnancy from artificial insemination. (§ 257.56 Subd. 1) U.P.C. — Yes. (§ 524.2-120 Subds. 5 & 7)
11.	*If a man contributes sperm how can he avoid being father?*	U.P.A. — If the woman is married to a person other than the donor, the donor is not the father. (§ 257.56 Subd. 2) No authority in the case of an unmarried woman. U.P.C. — A parent-child relationship does not exist between a child of assisted reproduction and a third party donor. (§ 524.2-120 Subd. 1)

[2] Minnesota has enacted U.P.C. § 2-120 and parts of U.P.C. § 2-121, as well as the Uniform Parentage Act. These statutes are not necessarily consistent, but the manner in which conflicts are to be resolved is not specified. Presumably, the enacted U.P.C. provisions apply exclusively to intestacy and class gifts, but this is not certain. In particular, § 524.2-121 makes clear that none of the provisions of the Uniform Probate Code affect the law of the state relating to gestational agreements.

Mississippi
Status of Children Conceived by Assisted Reproduction Techniques

A. Posthumously Conceived Individuals

1.	Can an individual have legal status as a child even though conceived and born after the parent's death?	No authority.
2.	What if the deceased contributor of procreative material was not married?	No authority.
3.	Is the consent of the deceased contributor of procreative material required and, if so, what kind of consent, and consent to what?	No authority.
4.	Is there specific authority addressing the posthumous child's right of inheritance?	No authority.
5.	Is there specific authority addressing the posthumous child's status under a will or a trust?	No authority.

B. Mother does not provide both womb and egg

6.	Is there a distinction drawn between a married and unmarried woman?	No authority.
7.	Who is the mother if a woman contributes the egg but the child is carried in a surrogate's womb?	No authority.
8.	Who is the mother if a woman contracts for the egg but carries the child in her womb?	No authority.
9.	Who is the mother if a woman contracts for both the egg and the womb?	No authority.

C. When the man is not the biological father or is not married to the mother

10.	If a husband does not contribute sperm but consents to his wife providing the womb with the intention of being the mother, is he the father?	Apparently yes. (Wells v. Wells, 35 So. 3d 1250 (Miss. Ct. App. 2010))
11.	If a man contributes sperm how can he avoid being father?	No authority.

Missouri
Status of Children Conceived by Assisted Reproduction Techniques

A. Posthumously Conceived Individuals

1.	Can an individual have legal status as a child even though conceived and born after the parent's death?	No authority.
2.	What if the deceased contributor of procreative material was not married?	No authority.
3.	Is the consent of the deceased contributor of procreative material required and, if so, what kind of consent, and consent to what?	No authority.
4.	Is there specific authority addressing the posthumous child's right of inheritance?	No authority.
5.	Is there specific authority addressing the posthumous child's status under a will or a trust?	No authority.

B. Mother does not provide both womb and egg

6.	Is there a distinction drawn between a married and unmarried woman?	No authority.
7.	Who is the mother if a woman contributes the egg but the child is carried in a surrogate's womb?	No authority.
8.	Who is the mother if a woman contracts for the egg but carries the child in her womb?	No authority.
9.	Who is the mother if a woman contracts for both the egg and the womb?	No authority.

C. When the man is not the biological father or is not married to the mother

10.	If a husband does not contribute sperm but consents to his wife providing the womb with the intention of being the mother, is he the father?	Yes, if the husband consented in a writing signed by both him and his wife, certified by a supervising licensed physician. (§ 210.824(1))
11.	If a man contributes sperm how can he avoid being father?	If the woman is married to a person other than the donor, he is not the father. (§ 210.824(2)) If the woman is unmarried, no authority.

Montana
Status of Children Conceived by Assisted Reproduction Techniques

A. Posthumously Conceived Individuals

1.	Can an individual have legal status as a child even though conceived and born after the parent's death?	No authority.
2.	What if the deceased contributor of procreative material was not married?	No authority.
3.	Is the consent of the deceased contributor of procreative material required and, if so, what kind of consent, and consent to what?	No authority.
4.	Is there specific authority addressing the posthumous child's right of inheritance?	No authority.
5.	Is there specific authority addressing the posthumous child's status under a will or a trust?	No authority.

B. Mother does not provide both womb and egg

6.	Is there a distinction drawn between a married and unmarried woman?	No authority.
7.	Who is the mother if a woman contributes the egg but the child is carried in a surrogate's womb?	No authority.
8.	Who is the mother if a woman contracts for the egg but carries the child in her womb?	No authority.
9.	Who is the mother if a woman contracts for both the egg and the womb?	No authority.

C. When the man is not the biological father or is not married to the mother

10.	If a husband does not contribute sperm but consents to his wife providing the womb with the intention of being the mother, is he the father?	Yes, if the husband consented in a writing signed by both him and his wife, certified by a supervising licensed physician. (§ 40-6-106(1))
11.	If a man contributes sperm how can he avoid being father?	If the woman is married to a person other than the donor, the donor is not the father. (§ 40-6-106(2)) No authority if the woman is not married.

Nebraska
Status of Children Conceived by Assisted Reproduction Techniques

A. Posthumously Conceived Individuals

1.	Can an individual have legal status as a child even though conceived and born after the parent's death?	No. See 4, below.
2.	What if the deceased contributor of procreative material was not married?	No authority.
3.	Is the consent of the deceased contributor of procreative material required and, if so, what kind of consent, and consent to what?	No authority. See 4, below.
4.	Is there specific authority addressing the posthumous child's right of inheritance?	Yes. "A child conceived after her biological father's death through intrauterine insemination using his sperm . . . cannot inherit from her father as his surviving issue under current Nebraska intestacy law. A child conceived after her biological father's death does not 'survive' her father as required under 30-2304 . . . [and is] excluded from inheriting under 30-2308 because she was not conceived prior to her father's death." (Amen v. Astrue, 822 N.W.2d 419, 422 (Neb. 2012))
5.	Is there specific authority addressing the posthumous child's status under a will or a trust?	No authority.

B. Mother does not provide both womb and egg

6.	Is there a distinction drawn between a married and unmarried woman?	No authority.
7.	Who is the mother if a woman contributes the egg but the child is carried in a surrogate's womb?	No authority.
8.	Who is the mother if a woman contracts for the egg but carries the child in her womb?	No authority.
9.	Who is the mother if a woman contracts for both the egg and the womb?	No authority.

C. When the man is not the biological father or is not married to the mother

10.	If a husband does not contribute sperm but consents to his wife providing the womb with the intention of being the mother, is he the father?	Likely, yes; however, this may be subject to the equities of the case. (See Deterding v. Deterding, 18 Neb. App. 922, 926 (Ct. App. 2011) (interpreting § 43-1412.01 as to prevent a formerly married man from renouncing his status as a father to a child conceived via artificial insemination when the consented to the use of another's sperm for artificial insemination))
11.	If a man contributes sperm how can he avoid being father?	No authority.

Nevada
Status of Children Conceived by Assisted Reproduction Techniques

A. Posthumously Conceived Individuals

1.	Can an individual have legal status as a child even though conceived and born after the parent's death?	No authority.
2.	What if the deceased contributor of procreative material was not married?	No authority.
3.	Is the consent of the deceased contributor of procreative material required and, if so, what kind of consent, and consent to what?	No authority.
4.	Is there specific authority addressing the posthumous child's right of inheritance?	No authority.
5.	Is there specific authority addressing the posthumous child's status under a will or a trust?	No authority.

B. Mother does not provide both womb and egg

6.	Is there a distinction drawn between a married and unmarried woman?	No. See the definition of intended parent. (§ 126.590)
7.	Who is the mother if a woman contributes the egg but the child is carried in a surrogate's womb?	Assuming a valid gestational agreement, with all parties having legal counsel, the intended parent would be the mother. (§ 126.720)
8.	Who is the mother if a woman contracts for the egg but carries the child in her womb?	In St. Mary v. Damon, 309 P.3d 1027 (Nev. 2013), the court held that a woman who contributed the womb could be a mother along with the woman who contributed the egg and that the Uniform Parentage Act did not foreclose this. The best interests of the child are key. Since the decision, Nevada has enacted provisions regarding "gestational agreements." Under § 126.720, the intended parent or parents would be the parents. The result might be the same in St. Mary under the law if it was established that both donors intended to be parents and had been represented by legal counsel. If not, § 126.720 would appear to make the birth mother the sole mother.
9.	Who is the mother if a woman contracts for both the egg and the womb?	The intended parent. See 7. and 8. above.

C. When the man is not the biological father or is not married to the mother

10.	If a husband does not contribute sperm but consents to his wife providing the womb with the intention of being the mother, is he the father?	Yes, as a husband is presumed to be the father. (§ 126.051(1)(a)). More generally, a "person who provides gametes for, or consents to, assisted reproduction by a woman . . . , with the intent to be a parent of her child is a parent of the resulting child." (§ 126.670)
11.	If a man contributes sperm how can he avoid being father?	A donor is generally not a parent. (§ § 126.660, 126.510)

New Hampshire
Status of Children Conceived by Assisted Reproduction Techniques

A. Posthumously Conceived Individuals

1.	Can an individual have legal status as a child even though conceived and born after the parent's death?	Yes. (§ 168-B:2(II) & (IV))
2.	What if the deceased contributor of procreative material was not married?	No authority.
3.	Is the consent of the deceased contributor of procreative material required and, if so, what kind of consent, and consent to what?	Consent in writing prior to death that if assisted reproduction were to occur after death, the deceased individual would be a parent of the child. (§ 168-B:2(IV))
4.	Is there specific authority addressing the posthumous child's right of inheritance?	See #1 above.
5.	Is there specific authority addressing the posthumous child's status under a will or a trust?	No authority.

B. Mother does not provide both womb and egg

6.	Is there a distinction drawn between a married and unmarried woman?	No. (§ 168-B:7)
7.	Who is the mother if a woman contributes the egg but the child is carried in a surrogate's womb?	The intended parent is the mother, assuming there is a valid gestational carrier agreement. (§ 168-B:7)
8.	Who is the mother if a woman contracts for the egg but carries the child in her womb?	No authority.
9.	Who is the mother if a woman contracts for both the egg and the womb?	§ 5-C:29 indicates that the wife of the natural father is the mother, if it is intended that she adopt the child. However, under another statutory provision, the intended mother would be deemed the child's mother from birth provided that the woman used a gestational carrier agreement under § 168-B:11. Importantly, however, a gestational carrier, as defined in § 168-B:1, excludes surrogates with a genetic relation to the child. (§ 168-B:1(IX)). Presumably, in order to satisfy the statute, an intended parent would have to contract for an egg from a party unrelated to the surrogate. (§ 168-B:7)

C. When the man is not the biological father or is not married to the mother

10.	If a husband does not contribute sperm but consents to his wife providing the womb with the intention of being the mother, is he the father?	Yes. (§§ 5-C:30(I)(a)) Note also that, notwithstanding any other provision of law, there is a presumption of a parent-child relationship between the husband and the child born to his spouse. (§ 168-B:2(v)(a))

11. *If a man contributes sperm how can he avoid being father?*

If the woman is married to a person other than the donor, he is not the father. (§ 5-C:30(I)(a)) Rather, the husband is. If the woman is unmarried, the sperm donor may still avoid being the father if he is unwilling to be identified on the birth record, assuming he can even be identified. (§ 5-C:30(I)(b)) More generally, a donor is not a parent of a child conceived through assisted reproduction. (§ 168-B:2(III)) A donor is only an individual with no claim or claims to present or future parental rights and obligations to any resulting child. (§ 168-B:1(v)) The meaning of "claim" is uncertain.

New Jersey
Status of Children Conceived by Assisted Reproduction Techniques

A. Posthumously Conceived Individuals

1.	Can an individual have legal status as a child even though conceived and born after the parent's death?	No statutory authority. In the principal New Jersey decision, In re Estate of Kolacy, 753 A.2d 1257 (Ch. Div. 2000), twin children were born more than 18 months after their father's death and they were found to be his legal heirs. [Note, however, that the opinion was only an advisory opinion].
2.	What if the deceased contributor of procreative material was not married?	No distinction is drawn based on marital status.
3.	Is the consent of the deceased contributor of procreative material required and, if so, what kind of consent, and consent to what?	Implied consent was given in the principal New Jersey case to deal with posthumous conception in that the man, about to undergo chemotherapy, allowed his sperm to be harvested. (In re Estate of Kolacy, 753 A.2d 1257, 1263 (Ch. Div. 2000)) There was no direct evidence any express consent was actually given, though the court stated that it "accept(s) Mariantonia Kolacy's statement that her husband unequivocally expressed his desire that she use his stored sperm after his death to bear his children." (Id.)
4.	Is there specific authority addressing the posthumous child's right of inheritance?	The children in In re Estate of Kolacy, 753 A.2d 1257 (Ch. Div. 2000), were deemed the decedent's legal heirs (Id. at 1263-64). [Note, however, that the opinion was an advisory opinion.] The precise parameters of the law after Kolacy are unclear. The court does suggest a system where distributions to others prior to the "advent of after born children could be treated as vested and left undisturbed, while distributions made following the birth of after born children could be made to both categories of children." (Id. at 1262)
5.	Is there specific authority addressing the posthumous child's status under a will or a trust?	No authority, although the reasoning of In re Kolacy would presumably apply. See #4 above.

B. Mother does not provide both womb and egg

6.	Is there a distinction drawn between a married and unmarried woman?	No.
7.	Who is the mother if a woman contributes the egg but the child is carried in a surrogate's womb?	In A.H.W. v. G.H.B., 772 A.2d 948 (Super. Ch. 2000), the court held that the surrogate could choose to surrender the child within the 72 hours after birth, citing § 9:3-41(e). If so, the biological mother would be thereafter listed on the birth certificate as the mother. If the surrogate did not voluntarily surrender the child during the 72-hour period, her status as parent would have to be litigated. Thus, the court did not decide the question of maternity.

8.	*Who is the mother if a woman contracts for the egg but carries the child in her womb?*	No authority.
9.	*Who is the mother if a woman contracts for both the egg and the womb?*	The contracting woman is not the mother and is required to adopt the child. (In re T.J.S., 16 A.3d 386 (Super. A.D. 2011, *aff'd per curiam*, by an equally divided court, 54 A.3d 263 (N.J. 2012))

C. When the man is not the biological father or is not married to the mother

10.	*If a husband does not contribute sperm but consents to his wife providing the womb with the intention of being the mother, is he the father?*	Yes, if he consents in a writing signed by both husband and wife and certified by the supervising physician. (§ 9:17-44(a)) In In re Parentage of Robinson, 890 A.2d 1036 (Super. Ch. 2005), the court held that a woman who was not the biological parent, but was the same-sex partner of the birth mother, could claim parentage. The Artificial Insemination Act was construed as not requiring the person seeking to be a parent to establish a genetic link. Rather, the person has to "show indicia of commitment to be a spouse and to be a parent to the child." Id. at 1042. The Artificial Insemination statute only refers to situations involving a "husband and wife." Nevertheless, the court explained that the partners had married in Canada and were recognized as domestic partners in New York. Thus, while New Jersey, at the time did not recognize same-sex marriage, it was in the child's best interest and did not violate any state public policy to recognize parentage of a partner who was clearly in a committed relationship.
11.	*If a man contributes sperm how can he avoid being father?*	The donor who gives the sperm to a licensed physician is not the father unless the woman receiving the sperm is his wife. (§ 9:17-44(b))

New Mexico
Status of Children Conceived by Assisted Reproduction Techniques

A. Posthumously Conceived Individuals[3]

1.	Can an individual have legal status as a child even though conceived and born after the parent's death?	U.P.A. — Yes, if the decedent was married and consented in a signed record stating that if assisted reproduction were to occur after death, the deceased person would be a parent. (§ 40-11A-707) No specific time requirement for the conception or birth is set forth. U.P.C. — Yes. (§ § 45-2-120(K), 45-2-121(H)) The child must be in utero not later than 36 months after the decedent's death or born not later than 45 months after the decedent's death.
2.	What if the deceased contributor of procreative material was not married?	Sections 45-2-120(K) and 45-2-121(H) do not indicate that the decedent must have been married.
3.	Is the consent of the deceased contributor of procreative material required and, if so, what kind of consent, and consent to what?	U.P.A. —The decedent is not a parent unless the decedent was a spouse and consented in a signed record that if the assisted reproduction occurred after death, the decedent would be a parent of the child. (§ 40-11A-707) U.P.C. — If married, consent is presumed. (§ 45-2-120(H)(2)) If not married, there either needs to be written consent, or else functioning as a parent or intending to function as a parent but prevented from doing so. (§ 45-2-120(F))
4.	Is there specific authority addressing the posthumous child's right of inheritance?	U.P.A. — No. U.P.C. — Yes. (§ § 45-2-116, 45-2-120(F)(2)(c))
5.	Is there specific authority addressing the posthumous child's status under a will or a trust?	U.P.A. — No. U.P.C.—The U.P.C. provisions only apply to intestacy. (§ 45-2-116) However, the intestacy provisions might be incorporated, depending on how the instrument is written. In addition, the parent-child relationship for intestacy would apply to a class gift. (§ 45-2-705(B))

B. Mother does not provide both womb and egg

6.	Is there a distinction drawn between a married and unmarried woman?	U.P.A. — No. (§ 40-11A-703 (at least with respect to donors who are intended parents)) U.P.C. — No. (§ § 45-2-120(C) (non-gestational assisted reproduction), 45-2-121(A)(4) (gestational agreement))

7.	*Who is the mother if a woman contributes the egg but the child is carried in a surrogate's womb?*	U.P.A. — The woman who contributes the egg appears to be the mother under § 40-11A-703. However, the New Mexico Uniform Parentage Act explicitly does not authorize or prohibit agreements. (§ 40-11A-801(A)) If the agreement is unenforceable under other New Mexico laws, the parent-child relationship is determined under § 40-11A-201, which would consider the woman giving birth to be the mother. (§§ 40-11A-201(A)(1), 40-11A-801(B)) U.P.C. — The woman contributing the egg with the intention to be the mother is the mother. (§ 45-2-121(A)(4))
8.	*Who is the mother if a woman contracts for the egg but carries the child in her womb?*	U.P.A. — The woman carrying the child. (§ 40-11A-702) U.P.C. — The birth mother is the mother (§ 45-2-120(C)), unless some other woman was the intended mother. (§ 45-2-120(F)) That would not be the case here, so the woman who carries the child is the mother.
9.	*Who is the mother if a woman contracts for both the egg and the womb?*	U.P.A. — See #7 above. U.P.C. — The woman. (§ 45-2-121(A)(4))

C. When the man is not the biological father or is not married to the mother

10.	*If a husband does not contribute sperm but consents to his wife providing the womb with the intention of being the mother, is he the father?*	U.P.A. — Yes, if he is the intended parent and consents with the other intended parent in a record signed by them before placement of the egg, sperm, or embryos. (§§ 40-11A-703, 40-11A-704(A)) Even if consent is not given, the person can still be the parent if, during the first two years of the child's life, the parent lived in the same household and openly held out the child as his own. (§§ 40-11A-704(B), 40-11A-201(B)(5)) U.P.C. — Even without consent, the husband is the father, if there is not clear and convincing evidence to the contrary. (§ 45-2-120(F)) If he gave actual consent, his status is reinforced, but can be overcome by clear and convincing evidence to the contrary presented typically within two years of birth.

| 11. | If a man contributes sperm how can he avoid being father? | U.P.A. — "Donors of eggs, sperm or embryos are not the parents of a child conceived by means of assisted reproduction." (§ 40-11A-702) However, a person who provides eggs, sperm or embryos, with intent to be the parent is the parent. (§ 40-11A-703) U.P.C. — A third-party donor is not a parent. (§ § 45-2-120(B), 45-2-120(A)(3)) |

[3] New Mexico has enacted both U.P.C. § § 2-120 and 2-121, as well as the Uniform Parentage Act. These statutes are not necessarily consistent, but the manner in which conflicts are to be resolved is not specified. Presumably, the enacted U.P.C. provisions apply exclusively to intestacy and class gifts, but this is not certain. Section 40-11A-203 specifies that the U.P.A. governs, "except determinations of parental rights pursuant to the Children's Code or as otherwise provided by other law of New Mexico." The U.P.C. provisions should fit within the meaning of "otherwise."

Note also that gestational agreements are neither authorized nor prohibited. (§ 40-11A-801) If a birth results from an agreement, which is unenforceable under other laws of the state, then parentage is determined pursuant to Article 2 of the New Mexico Parentage Act. Presumably, the determination would be governed by § 40-11A-201. However, this is not an especially helpful provision, since it provides for determination of maternity based on either giving birth or adjudication. Adjudication, unlike giving birth, would likely lead to a determination of maternity based on genetic relationship. (§ § 40-11A-106; 40-11A-505)

New York
Status of Children Conceived by Assisted Reproduction Techniques

A. Posthumously Conceived Individuals

1.	*Can an individual have legal status as a child even though conceived and born after the parent's death?*	Yes, (EPTL §4-1.3) if the genetic parent gave consent in writing to use genetic material to conceive no more than seven years prior to death.
2.	*What if the deceased contributor of procreative material was not married?*	Does not alter the result. (EPTL §4-1.3(b))
3.	*Is the consent of the deceased contributor of procreative material required and, if so, what kind of consent, and consent to what?*	Consent to conceive posthumously in writing. (EPTL §4-1.3(b)(1)(a))
4.	*Is there specific authority addressing the posthumous child's right of inheritance?*	Yes. (EPTL §4-1.3(b))
5.	*Is there specific authority addressing the posthumous child's status under a will or a trust?*	Yes. (EPTL §4-1.3(b))

B. Mother does not provide both womb and egg

6.	*Is there a distinction drawn between a married and unmarried woman?*	No authority.
7.	*Who is the mother if a woman contributes the egg but the child is carried in a surrogate's womb?*	**Note**: Surrogate parenting contracts are void and unenforceable in New York. (Dom. Rel., Law §122) However, this does not negate the court's need to determine the child's parent, which is determined on the basis of "intent," at least in the case of maternity. See In re Doe, 793 N.Y.S.2d 878, 881-82 (Sur. Ct. 2005). The same power of the court, recognized more broadly under the state law, which was not addressed in *Doe*, is granted under New York City regulatory provisions. (See T.V. v. New York Dept. of Health, 929 N.Y.S.2d 139 (App. Div. 2011)) *T.V.* appears to recognize the right to have the genetic contributor treated as the mother, where she and the gestational contributor do not dispute motherhood, but the Department of Health is resisting. In this situation, the issue of the invalidity of the surrogacy agreement is not being raised, at least by the interested individuals.
8.	*Who is the mother if a woman contracts for the egg but carries the child in her womb?*	The woman carrying the child. (McDonald v. McDonald, 608 N.Y.S.2d 477 (App. Div. 1998))

9. *Who is the mother if a woman contracts for both the egg and the womb?*	At least one case has held that the woman that contracts for the egg and womb is the mother. (In re Doe, 793 N.Y.S.2d 878 (Sur. Ct. 2005)) The court so holding gave full faith and credit to California law, where the surrogacy contract extended, and concluded that the children were *not* adoptees and, thus, were eligible under a trust established for the benefit of the issue of the settlor's children. Under the trust instrument, children by adoption were not to be regarded as "issue" or descendants." (Id.)

C. When the man is not the biological father or is not married to the mother

10. *If a husband does not contribute sperm but consents to his wife providing the womb with the intention of being the mother, is he the father?*	Yes, if both husband and wife consent in writing and a duly authorized physician certifies that he had rendered the service. (Dom. Rel. Law § 73) However, the amendments to Fam. Ct. Act §§ 418 and 532 imply that the written consent requirement of Dom. Rel. Law § 73 does not apply in paternity and support proceedings where there is a presumption of legitimacy, e.g., due to marriage or an equitable estoppel. Thus, strict compliance with the procedure set forth in § 73 is not required, and consent by the husband of a married woman to artificial insemination may be proved by other clear and convincing evidence. (Laura G. v Peter G., 830 N.Y.S.2d 496, 499-500 (Sup. Ct. 2007))
11. *If a man contributes sperm how can he avoid being father?*	No clear authority. Currently, there is no statute and no recorded decision has touched upon the rights of a surrogate child to inherit from the donor of the sperm in the event the child is not adopted by him. (11-191 Warren's Heaton on Surrogate's Court Practice § 191.05(k)); see also Practice Commentary to Dom. Rel. § 73: "Where the statute has been followed . . . implicitly, any claim to natural fatherhood by the donor of the sperm used for the insemination is extinguished.") On the other hand, if he gave consent to the artificial insemination, the children will be his for inheritance purposes. In re Martin B., 841 N.Y.S.2d 207, 211-12 (Sur. Ct. 2007), holds that child born with consent of father to use of his semen makes the child his child.

North Carolina
Status of Children Conceived by Assisted Reproduction Techniques

A. Posthumously Conceived Individuals

1.	Can an individual have legal status as a child even though conceived and born after the parent's death?	No authority. "As to the legal status of conceived-after-death children, that question has not yet been resolved." (Official Comment, § 41-15)
2.	What if the deceased contributor of procreative material was not married?	No authority.
3.	Is the consent of the deceased contributor of procreative material required and, if so, what kind of consent, and consent to what?	No authority.
4.	Is there specific authority addressing the posthumous child's right of inheritance?	No authority.
5.	Is there specific authority addressing the posthumous child's status under a will or a trust?	No authority.

B. Mother does not provide both womb and egg

6.	Is there a distinction drawn between a married and unmarried woman?	No authority.
7.	Who is the mother if a woman contributes the egg but the child is carried in a surrogate's womb?	No authority.
8.	Who is the mother if a woman contracts for the egg but carries the child in her womb?	No authority.
9.	Who is the mother if a woman contracts for both the egg and the womb?	No authority.

C. When the man is not the biological father or is not married to the mother

10.	If a husband does not contribute sperm but consents to his wife providing the womb with the intention of being the mother, is he the father?	Yes, if he and his wife have requested and consented to the procedure in writing. (§ 49A-1)
11.	If a man contributes sperm how can he avoid being father?	If the mother is married to a person other than the donor and her husband consents in writing to the procedure, the sperm donor is not the father. (§ 49A-1) No authority if the mother is not married.

North Dakota
Status of Children Conceived by Assisted Reproduction Techniques

A. Posthumously Conceived Individuals[4]

1.	Can an individual have legal status as a child even though conceived and born after the parent's death?	U.P.A. —Yes, if the decedent was married and consented in a signed record stating that if assisted reproduction were to occur after death, the deceased person would be a parent. (§ 14-20-65) No specific time requirement for the conception or birth is set forth. U.P.C. — Yes. (§ § 30.1-04-19(11), 30.1-04-20(8)) The child must be in utero not later than 36 months after the decedent's death or born not later than 45 months after the individual's death. (Id.)
2.	What if the deceased contributor of procreative material was not married?	U.P.A. — No. Reference is to a "deceased spouse." (§ 14-20-65) U.P.C. — Yes. (§ 30.1-04-16) ("parent-child relationship exists between a child and the child's *genetic* parents, regardless of their marital status.") An intended parent in the case of a gestational agreement or assisted reproduction also does not have to be married. (§ § 30.1-04-19, 30.1-04-20(1)(d))
3.	Is the consent of the deceased contributor of procreative material required and, if so, what kind of consent, and consent to what?	U.P.A. — Yes. The deceased spouse is not a parent unless he "consented in a record that if assisted reproduction were to occur after death, the deceased individual would be a parent of the child." (§ 14-20-65) U.P.C. — If married, consent is presumed. (§ 30.1-04-19(8)) If not married, there either needs to be written consent, or else functioning as a parent no later than two years after the child's birth or intending to function as a parent no later than two years after the child's birth, but prevented from doing so. (§ 30.1-04-19(6))
4.	Is there specific authority addressing the posthumous child's right of inheritance?	U.P.A. — No. U.P.C. — Yes. (§ § 30.1-04-15, 30.1-04-19(11), 30.1-04-20(8))
5.	Is there specific authority addressing the posthumous child's status under a will or a trust?	U.P.A. — No. U.P.C. — The U.P.C. provisions only apply to intestacy. (§ 30.1-04-15) However, the intestacy provisions might be incorporated, depending on how the instrument is written. In addition, the meaning of the parent-child relationship for intestacy would apply to a class gift. (§ 30.1-09.1-05(2))

B. Mother does not provide both womb and egg

6.	Is there a distinction drawn between a married and unmarried woman?	U.P.A. — No authority. There are certain presumptions as to paternity of a husband that may also apply to a wife. (§ § 14-20-06, 14-20-10) U.P.C. — No. (§ § 30.1-04-16, 30.1-04-20(1)(d))

7.	Who is the mother if a woman contributes the egg but the child is carried in a surrogate's womb?	U.P.A. — No authority. There is a conflict in the statute as maternity can be established by giving birth (§ 14-20-07(1)) or by an adjudication establishing genetic link (§§ 14-20-29, 14-20-06)). U.P.C. — The intended parent is the mother; here, typically the contributor of the egg. (§ 30.1-04-20(1)(d) & (4))
8.	Who is the mother if a woman contracts for the egg but carries the child in her womb?	U.P.A. — No authority. But see #7 above. U.P.C. — The woman who carries the child in her womb. (§ 30.1-04-19(2)-(3))
9.	Who is the mother if a woman contracts for both the egg and the womb?	U.P.A. — No authority, especially no statutory basis for the contracting woman to be regarded as the mother. U.P.C. — The intended parent. (§ 30.1-04-20(1)(d)&(4))

C. When the man is not the biological father or is not married to the mother

10.	If a husband does not contribute sperm but consents to his wife providing the womb with the intention of being the mother, is he the father?	U.P.A. — Yes. (§ 14-20-61) U.P.C. – Yes. (§ 30.1-04-19(6)&(8))
11.	If a man contributes sperm how can he avoid being father?	U.P.A. — "A donor [of sperm]is not a parent of a child conceived by means of assisted reproduction." (§ 14-20-60) U.P.C. — A parent-child relationship does not exist with a third-party donor. (§ 30.1-04-19(2))

---

[4] North Dakota has enacted both U.P.C. §§ 2-120 and 2-121, as well as the Uniform Parentage Act. These statutes are not necessarily consistent, but the manner in which conflicts are to be resolved is not specified. Presumably, the enacted U.P.C. provisions apply exclusively to intestacy and class gifts, but this is not certain. (§ 30.1-04-20(9) (stating that the gestational agreement provision does not affect other law of the state regarding enforceability or validity of a gestational agreement)) In addition, § 14-20-03(3) states that: "This chapter does not create, enlarge, or diminish, parental rights or duties under other laws of this state." This provision would not appear to bear on the inheritance rights of children. To the extent it affects parental rights, the provision suggests that the Probate Code would be given priority.

Ohio
Status of Children Conceived by Assisted Reproduction Techniques

A. Posthumously Conceived Individuals

1.	Can an individual have legal status as a child even though conceived and born after the parent's death?	No authority.
2.	What if the deceased contributor of procreative material was not married?	No authority.
3.	Is the consent of the deceased contributor of procreative material required and, if so, what kind of consent, and consent to what?	No authority.
4.	Is there specific authority addressing the posthumous child's right of inheritance?	No authority.
5.	Is there specific authority addressing the posthumous child's status under a will or a trust?	No authority.

B. Mother does not provide both womb and egg

6.	Is there a distinction drawn between a married and unmarried woman?	No distinction.
7.	Who is the mother if a woman contributes the egg but the child is carried in a surrogate's womb?	The woman is the mother if she is identified as the genetic parent of the child and she has not relinquished her parental rights. Belsito v. Clark, 644 N.E.2d 760, 767 (Com. Pl. 1994).
8.	Who is the mother if a woman contracts for the egg but carries the child in her womb?	The woman, at least in the case of the implantation of an embryo. (§ 3111.97(A))
9.	Who is the mother if a woman contracts for both the egg and the womb?	In S.N. v. M.B., 935 N.E.2d 463 (Ct. App. 2010), the court held that the surrogate of a valid agreement is not the mother if she agreed not to be. The intended mother is the mother.

C. When the man is not the biological father or is not married to the mother

10.	If a husband does not contribute sperm but consents to his wife providing the womb with the intention of being the mother, is he the father?	Yes. (§ 3111.95(A)) See also Brooks v. Fair, 532 N.E.2d 208 (Ct. App. 1988).
11.	If a man contributes sperm how can he avoid being father?	The donor is not the father if it is a non-spousal artificial insemination. (§ 3111.95(B))

Oklahoma
Status of Children Conceived by Assisted Reproduction Techniques

A. Posthumously Conceived Individuals

1.	Can an individual have legal status as a child even though conceived and born after the parent's death?	No authority.
2.	What if the deceased contributor of procreative material was not married?	No authority.
3.	Is the consent of the deceased contributor of procreative material required and, if so, what kind of consent, and consent to what?	No authority.
4.	Is there specific authority addressing the posthumous child's right of inheritance?	No authority.
5.	Is there specific authority addressing the posthumous child's status under a will or a trust?	No authority.

B. Mother does not provide both womb and egg

6.	Is there a distinction drawn between a married and unmarried woman?	Yes. Authorization and consent may only be given by husband and wife. (10 §§ 551, 553)
7.	Who is the mother if a woman contributes the egg but the child is carried in a surrogate's womb?	No authority.
8.	Who is the mother if a woman contracts for the egg but carries the child in her womb?	The woman is the mother. (10 § 554)
9.	Who is the mother if a woman contracts for both the egg and the womb?	No authority.

C. When the man is not the biological father or is not married to the mother

10.	If a husband does not contribute sperm but consents to his wife providing the womb with the intention of being the mother, is he the father?	"Any child or children born as a result of a heterologous oocyte [egg] donation shall be considered for all legal intents and purposes, the same as a naturally conceived legitimate child of the husband and wife which consent to and receive an oocyte pursuant to the use of the technique of heterologous oocyte donation." (10 § 554; see also 10 § 551) In the case of a human embryo transfer from one married couple to another receiving married couple, if there are appropriate consents of the parties obtained by a licensed physician, the receiving couple are the parents of the child (10 § 556(B)(1)), and the child has no right, obligation or interest with respect to the spouses who donated the embryo. (10 § 556(D))
11.	If a man contributes sperm how can he avoid being father?	If the woman is married to a person other than the donor, the donor is not the father. (10 § 552) If the woman is unmarried, no authority.

Oregon
Status of Children Conceived by Assisted Reproduction Techniques

A. Posthumously Conceived Individuals

1.	Can an individual have legal status as a child even though conceived and born after the parent's death?	No authority.
2.	What if the deceased contributor of procreative material was not married?	No authority.
3.	Is the consent of the deceased contributor of procreative material required and, if so, what kind of consent, and consent to what?	No authority.
4.	Is there specific authority addressing the posthumous child's right of inheritance?	No authority.
5.	Is there specific authority addressing the posthumous child's status under a will or a trust?	No authority.

B. Mother does not provide both womb and egg

6.	Is there a distinction drawn between a married and unmarried woman?	No distinction.
7.	Who is the mother if a woman contributes the egg but the child is carried in a surrogate's womb?	46 Op. Atty Gen. 221 (Apr. 19, 1989) indicates that the surrogate would be the mother, not the woman. Consent to adoption before birth would be invalid. An adoption would be necessary after birth and would only be approved by a court if it "is fit and proper."
8.	Who is the mother if a woman contracts for the egg but carries the child in her womb?	No authority.
9.	Who is the mother if a woman contracts for both the egg and the womb?	No authority.

C. When the man is not the biological father or is not married to the mother

10.	If a husband does not contribute sperm but consents to his wife providing the womb with the intention of being the mother, is he the father?	Yes. (§ 109.243) In Shineovich v. Shineovich, 214 P.3d 29 (Ct. App. 2009), the contention was made by a former lesbian companion who had consented to artificial insemination that not presuming her to be the other parent was unconstitutional on equal protection grounds under the state constitution because it favored men who were married. The court held that the provision was unconstitutional, despite a constitutional amendment in force recognizing only heterosexual marriage. The court held that the state legislature had expressed a strong interest in protecting children from being denied support and that recognizing the parentage in the case of mothers in same-sex relationships would further that interest, especially in light of the recognition in the state of same-sex civil unions and adoptions.

11. *If a man contributes sperm how can he avoid being father?*

If the donor is not the husband of the mother, the donor would not be the father. (§ 109.239(2))

Pennsylvania
Status of Children Conceived by Assisted Reproduction Techniques

A. Posthumously Conceived Individuals

1.	Can an individual have legal status as a child even though conceived and born after the parent's death?	No. (Seaman v. Colvin, 145 F. Supp. 3d 421, 432 (E.D. Pa. On August 31, 2015))
2.	What if the deceased contributor of procreative material was not married?	No authority.
3.	Is the consent of the deceased contributor of procreative material required and, if so, what kind of consent, and consent to what?	No authority.
4.	Is there specific authority addressing the posthumous child's right of inheritance?	No authority.
5.	Is there specific authority addressing the posthumous child's status under a will or a trust?	No authority.

B. Mother does not provide both womb and egg

6.	Is there a distinction drawn between a married and unmarried woman?	No distinction.
7.	Who is the mother if a woman contributes the egg but the child is carried in a surrogate's womb?	Unclear. In J.F. v. D.B., 897 A.2d 1261, 1279 (Super. Ct. 2006), the court held that the gestational "mother" did not have standing to seek custody. It overturned the lower court ruling that the surrogacy contract was void, thereby giving the surrogate standing because she was "the legal mother." The court, however, declined to address directly who was the "legal mother."
8.	Who is the mother if a woman contracts for the egg but carries the child in her womb?	See #7 above.
9.	Who is the mother if a woman contracts for both the egg and the womb?	See #7 above.

C. When the man is not the biological father or is not married to the mother

10.	If a husband does not contribute sperm but consents to his wife providing the womb with the intention of being the mother, is he the father?	No authority.
11.	If a man contributes sperm how can he avoid being father?	No settled authority. In one case involving a private sperm donation, the court enforced an agreement where the donor provided sperm and the mother agreed not to seek child support from the donor. (Ferguson v. McKiernan, 940 A.2d 1236 (Penn. 2007))

Rhode Island
Status of Children Conceived by Assisted Reproduction Techniques

A. Posthumously Conceived Individuals

1.	Can an individual have legal status as a child even though conceived and born after the parent's death?	No authority.
2.	What if the deceased contributor of procreative material was not married?	No authority.
3.	Is the consent of the deceased contributor of procreative material required and, if so, what kind of consent, and consent to what?	No authority.
4.	Is there specific authority addressing the posthumous child's right of inheritance?	No authority.
5.	Is there specific authority addressing the posthumous child's status under a will or a trust?	No authority.

B. Mother does not provide both womb and egg

6.	Is there a distinction drawn between a married and unmarried woman?	No authority.
7.	Who is the mother if a woman contributes the egg but the child is carried in a surrogate's womb?	No authority.
8.	Who is the mother if a woman contracts for the egg but carries the child in her womb?	No authority.
9.	Who is the mother if a woman contracts for both the egg and the womb?	No authority.

C. When the man is not the biological father or is not married to the mother

10.	If a husband does not contribute sperm but consents to his wife providing the womb with the intention of being the mother, is he the father?	No authority.
11.	If a man contributes sperm how can he avoid being father?	No authority.

South Carolina
Status of Children Conceived by Assisted Reproduction Techniques

A. Posthumously Conceived Individuals

1.	Can an individual have legal status as a child even though conceived and born after the parent's death?	No authority.
2.	What if the deceased contributor of procreative material was not married?	No authority.
3.	Is the consent of the deceased contributor of procreative material required and, if so, what kind of consent, and consent to what?	No authority.
4.	Is there specific authority addressing the posthumous child's right of inheritance?	No authority.
5.	Is there specific authority addressing the posthumous child's status under a will or a trust?	No authority.

B. Mother does not provide both womb and egg

6.	Is there a distinction drawn between a married and unmarried woman?	No authority.
7.	Who is the mother if a woman contributes the egg but the child is carried in a surrogate's womb?	No authority.
8.	Who is the mother if a woman contracts for the egg but carries the child in her womb?	No authority.
9.	Who is the mother if a woman contracts for both the egg and the womb?	No authority.

C. When the man is not the biological father or is not married to the mother

10.	If a husband does not contribute sperm but consents to his wife providing the womb with the intention of being the mother, is he the father?	Apparently, yes. In one case, a court declared the ex-husband to be the father where he knew of, and thus impliedly consented to, his ex-wife undergoing artificial insemination while they were married. (In re Baby Doe, 353 S.E.2d 877, 878-89 (S.C. 1987))
11.	If a man contributes sperm how can he avoid being father?	No authority.

South Dakota
Status of Children Conceived by Assisted Reproduction Techniques

A. Posthumously Conceived Individuals

1.	Can an individual have legal status as a child even though conceived and born after the parent's death?	No authority.
2.	What if the deceased contributor of procreative material was not married?	No authority.
3.	Is the consent of the deceased contributor of procreative material required and, if so, what kind of consent, and consent to what?	No authority.
4.	Is there specific authority addressing the posthumous child's right of inheritance?	No authority.
5.	Is there specific authority addressing the posthumous child's status under a will or a trust?	No authority.

B. Mother does not provide both womb and egg

6.	Is there a distinction drawn between a married and unmarried woman?	No authority.
7.	Who is the mother if a woman contributes the egg but the child is carried in a surrogate's womb?	No authority.
8.	Who is the mother if a woman contracts for the egg but carries the child in her womb?	No authority.
9.	Who is the mother if a woman contracts for both the egg and the womb?	No authority.

C. When the man is not the biological father or is not married to the mother

10.	If a husband does not contribute sperm but consents to his wife providing the womb with the intention of being the mother, is he the father?	No authority.
11.	If a man contributes sperm how can he avoid being father?	No direct authority. At least one case has distinguished between an anonymous sperm donor contributing sperm for artificial insemination for use by a woman to whom he is not married, in which case he should not be the father, and the case where a man has natural intercourse, but the man and woman agreed, he would have no support obligation. In this latter case, the man is the father. (Estes v. Albers, 504 N.W.2d 607 (S.D. 1993))

Tennessee
Status of Children Conceived by Assisted Reproduction Techniques

A. Posthumously Conceived Individuals

1.	Can an individual have legal status as a child even though conceived and born after the parent's death?	No authority.
2.	What if the deceased contributor of procreative material was not married?	No authority.
3.	Is the consent of the deceased contributor of procreative material required and, if so, what kind of consent, and consent to what?	No authority.
4.	Is there specific authority addressing the posthumous child's right of inheritance?	No authority.
5.	Is there specific authority addressing the posthumous child's status under a will or a trust?	No authority.

B. Mother does not provide both womb and egg

6.	Is there a distinction drawn between a married and unmarried woman?	Yes.
7.	Who is the mother if a woman contributes the egg but the child is carried in a surrogate's womb?	The woman, if there has been a union of her egg and her husband's sperm. (§ 36-1-102(48)(A)(i)) No surrender or adoption required. (§ 36-1-102(48)(B)) Nonmarital situations are not addressed.
8.	Who is the mother if a woman contracts for the egg but carries the child in her womb?	In re C.K.G., 173 S.W.3d 714 (Tenn. 2005), relying in part on Tenn. Code Ann. § 68-3-306, suggests that the woman would be the mother.
9.	Who is the mother if a woman contracts for both the egg and the womb?	The woman, if the contract states the parties' "intent that the woman who carries the fetus shall relinquish the child to the biological father and the biological father's wife to parent." (§ 36-1-102(48)(A)(ii)) Nonmarital situations are not addressed, nor are situations addressed in which the husband does not contribute the sperm. However, see In re Baby, 447 S.W.3d 807 (Tenn. 2014), where the Tennessee Supreme Court held that a surrogacy contract did not transfer rights from a "traditional surrogate" (where surrogate was the biological mother) to unmarried intended parents (one of which was the sperm donor) because "the statutory procedures for terminating the parental rights of a traditional surrogate are limited to involuntary termination, parental consent to adoption, and surrender." (Id. at 836, discussing § 36-1-102 (48))

C. When the man is not the biological father or is not married to the mother

10.	If a husband does not contribute sperm but consents to his wife providing the womb with the intention of being the mother, is he the father?	Yes. (§ 68-3-306)
11.	If a man contributes sperm how can he avoid being father?	No authority.

Texas
Status of Children Conceived by Assisted Reproduction Techniques

A. Posthumously Conceived Individuals

1.	Can an individual have legal status as a child even though conceived and born after the parent's death?	Yes. (Fam. § 160.707)
2.	What if the deceased contributor of procreative material was not married?	The statute only references the death of a "spouse." (§ 160.707)
3.	Is the consent of the deceased contributor of procreative material required and, if so, what kind of consent, and consent to what?	If the spouse dies before placement of eggs, sperm, or embryos, the decedent is not the parent unless the decedent consented in a record kept by a licensed physician that if assisted reproduction occurred after death the decedent would be the parent. (Fam. Code § 160.707)
4.	Is there specific authority addressing the posthumous child's right of inheritance?	No direct authority.
5.	Is there specific authority addressing the posthumous child's status under a will or a trust?	No direct authority.

B. Mother does not provide both womb and egg

6.	Is there a distinction drawn between a married and unmarried woman?	No. (Fam. § 160.202) However, there are certain presumptions as to paternity of a husband that may also apply to a wife. (Fam. §§ 160.106, 160.201(a))
7.	Who is the mother if a woman contributes the egg but the child is carried in a surrogate's womb?	The woman, assuming an adjudication pursuant to a valid gestational agreement. (Fam. § 160.760(a)-(b)) If the agreement is invalid, the determination of parentage is less certain. (Fam. § 160.762(b)) There is a conflict in the statute, as maternity can be established by giving birth (§ 160.201(a)(1)) or by an adjudication establishing a genetic link (Fam. §§ 160.505, 160.106)
8.	Who is the mother if a woman contracts for the egg but carries the child in her womb?	No authority.
9.	Who is the mother if a woman contracts for both the egg and the womb?	The woman who was the intended parent. (Fam. § 160.760(a)-(b)) One case held that when a surrogate bore an unrelated child, the intended parent was not married, and there was no written surrogacy agreement, then the woman who gave birth was the mother. Her lack of a genetic connection did not alter this result. See In re M.M.M., 428 S.W.3d 389 (Ct. App. 2014) (the case involved a man seeking to be the sole parent based on an alleged understanding with a female friend and gestational carrier, who then claimed parentage and sought custody and support)

C. When the man is not the biological father or is not married to the mother

10.	If a husband does not contribute sperm but consents to his wife providing the womb with the intention of being the mother, is he the father?	Yes. (Fam. § 160.703) Technically, both spouses must give consent kept by a licensed physician. If the husband did not give the consent, he is the father of a child "born to his wife if the wife and husband openly treated the child as their own." (Fam. § 160.704(a)-(b))
11.	If a man contributes sperm how can he avoid being father?	In the case of an unmarried man, by not having the intent to be the father. (Fam. Code § 160.7031(a)) Consent to be the father must be in a record signed by the man and the unmarried woman and kept by a licensed physician. (Fam. § 160.7031(b)) Also, a "donor" is not a parent of a child conceived by means of assisted reproduction. (Fam. Code § 160.702) A man does not qualify as a donor, however, if he is a husband or an unmarried man who contributes sperm with the intent to be the father. (Fam. Code § 160.102 (6)(A), (C)) In this last case, however, he will likely not be able to exclude the person who serves as birth mother from parentage status. (In re M.M.M., 428 S.W.3d 389 (Ct. App. 2014))

Utah
Status of Children Conceived by Assisted Reproduction Techniques

A. Posthumously Conceived Individuals

1.	Can an individual have legal status as a child even though conceived and born after the parent's death?	Yes, but apparently only if a spouse. (§ 78B-15-707)
2.	What if the deceased contributor of procreative material was not married?	The statute only addresses a "spouse." (§ 78B-15-707)
3.	Is the consent of the deceased contributor of procreative material required and, if so, what kind of consent, and consent to what?	If the spouse dies before placement of eggs, sperm, or embryos, the decedent is not the parent unless the decedent consented in a record that if assisted reproduction occurred after death the decedent would be the parent. (§ 78B-15-707)
4.	Is there specific authority addressing the posthumous child's right of inheritance?	No direct authority.
5.	Is there specific authority addressing the posthumous child's status under a will or a trust?	No direct authority.

B. Mother does not provide both womb and egg

6.	Is there a distinction drawn between a married and unmarried woman?	Yes, at least with respect to a gestational agreement. (§ 78B-15-801(3))
7.	Who is the mother if a woman contributes the egg but the child is carried in a surrogate's womb?	The woman is the mother if the gestational agreement was validated by a tribunal. (§§ 78B-15-803, 78B-15-807) If the agreement is invalid, the determination of parentage is less certain. (§ 78B-15-809)
8.	Who is the mother if a woman contracts for the egg but carries the child in her womb?	The woman carrying the child as an egg donor is not a parent of a child conceived via assisted reproduction. (§ 78B-15-702; see § 78B-15-102 (defining artificial insemination and donor))
9.	Who is the mother if a woman contracts for both the egg and the womb?	See #7 above. Also noted that "The gestational mother's eggs may not be used in the assisted reproduction procedure." (§ 78B-15-801(7))

C. When the man is not the biological father or is not married to the mother

10.	If a husband does not contribute sperm but consents to his wife providing the womb with the intention of being the mother, is he the father?	Yes. (§ 78B-15-703) Technically, both spouses must give consent kept by a licensed physician. If the husband did not give the consent, he is the father of a child "born to his wife if the wife and husband openly treated the child as their own." (§ 78B-15-704)
11.	If a man contributes sperm how can he avoid being father?	A donor is not a parent. (§ 78B-15-702) A donor is a person other than a husband who provides the sperm or a parent determined otherwise under the law. (§ 78B-15-102(10))

Vermont
Status of Children Conceived by Assisted Reproduction Techniques

A. Posthumously Conceived Individuals

1.	Can an individual have legal status as a child even though conceived and born after the parent's death?	No authority.
2.	What if the deceased contributor of procreative material was not married?	No authority.
3.	Is the consent of the deceased contributor of procreative material required and, if so, what kind of consent, and consent to what?	No authority.
4.	Is there specific authority addressing the posthumous child's right of inheritance?	No authority.
5.	Is there specific authority addressing the posthumous child's status under a will or a trust?	No authority.

B. Mother does not provide both womb and egg

6.	Is there a distinction drawn between a married and unmarried woman?	No authority.
7.	Who is the mother if a woman contributes the egg but the child is carried in a surrogate's womb?	No authority.
8.	Who is the mother if a woman contracts for the egg but carries the child in her womb?	No authority.
9.	Who is the mother if a woman contracts for both the egg and the womb?	No authority.

C. When the man is not the biological father or is not married to the mother

10.	If a husband does not contribute sperm but consents to his wife providing the womb with the intention of being the mother, is he the father?	Probably yes. Miller-Jenkins v. Miller-Jenkins, 912 A.2d 951, 970 (Vt. 2006), (relying on People v. Sorensen, 437 P.2d 495 (Cal. 1968), and cases from other jurisdictions). The decision actually relies on this authority to recognize the parental status of a same-sex partner previously in a Vermont civil union at the time of procreation, birth, and early upbringing. The couple's civil union was equated to the husband-wife situation present in the cases cited. Also heavily emphasized was the intent of the parties that the non-child-bearing partner also be a parent. The court also noted that otherwise the child would only have one parent. The court refused to give full faith and credit to a Virginia decision that the partner was not a parent.
11.	If a man contributes sperm how can he avoid being father?	No direct authority. If the sperm donor does not intend to father the child, he is likely not the father. (See Miller-Jenkins discussion above) On the other hand, the sperm donor may have a right to make a claim. (Id.)

Virginia
Status of Children Conceived by Assisted Reproduction Techniques

A. Posthumously Conceived Individuals

1.	Can an individual have legal status as a child even though conceived and born after the parent's death?	Generally no. (Schafer v. Astrue, 641 F.3d 49, 53 (4th Cir. 2011) (dicta)) § 20-164 only applies to a child born not later than 10 months after a parent's death. Technically, this could apply to a child conceived after the death of a parent, if conceived shortly thereafter. It appears as well that there would need to be written consent "to be a parent . . . " Furthermore, the parents must have been married. (§ 20-158(B))
2.	What if the deceased contributor of procreative material was not married?	No authority.
3.	Is the consent of the deceased contributor of procreative material required and, if so, what kind of consent, and consent to what?	Written consent is required, unless implantation occurs before the notice of death can be reasonably communicated to the physician performing the procedure. (§ 20-158(B))
4.	Is there specific authority addressing the posthumous child's right of inheritance?	No authority.
5.	Is there specific authority addressing the posthumous child's status under a will or a trust?	No authority.

B. Mother does not provide both womb and egg

6.	Is there a distinction drawn between a married and unmarried woman?	In part. See #8 below.
7.	Who is the mother if a woman contributes the egg but the child is carried in a surrogate's womb?	If a court has approved a valid surrogacy contract that so stipulates, the woman is the mother. (§ 20-160(D)) Without an approved surrogacy contract, the surrogate is the mother, unless the intended mother is a genetic parent. (§§ 20-158(A)(1), 20-158(E)(1))
8.	Who is the mother if a woman contracts for the egg but carries the child in her womb?	The intended parents are the parents if the surrogacy contract is valid and approved by the court. (§ 20-158(D)) If the surrogacy contract is not approved, the result is uncertain. If the woman is married, her husband contributed genetic material, her husband consented to the agreement, and she retains custody pursuant to § 20-162, then she is the mother. (§ 20-158(E)(2)) § 20-158(A)(3) suggests that the woman would be the mother.

9. *Who is the mother if a woman contracts for both the egg and the womb?*	Generally, one of the intended parents must be a genetic parent. (§ 20-160(B)(9)) If a court has approved a valid surrogacy contract that so stipulates, the woman is the mother. (§ 20-160) If neither of the intended parents is a genetic parent, then the surrogate mother is the legal mother and, if married, her husband is the father. (§ 20-160(D)) In this situation, the intended parents may obtain parental status through adoption. (Id.) Note that in the case of a woman who served as a gestational mother and was artificially inseminated with the sperm of two same-sex male partners, one court, Prashad v. Copeland, 685 S.E.2d 199 (Ct. App. 2009), honored a North Carolina custody order, awarding custody to the non-genetic male partner rather than the gestational and genetic surrogate mother. The court made a point of emphasizing that the recognition of the North Carolina order was due to its being based on the relationship between the man and the child, the non-genetically related male partner having been a full-time parent to the child, and not on the marital status of the same-sex partners. It also did not address parentage.

C. When the man is not the biological father or is not married to the mother

10. *If a husband does not contribute sperm but consents to his wife providing the womb with the intention of being the mother, is he the father?*	Yes, unless he can show that he did not consent to the procedure and commences an action within 2 years after he discovers or, in the exercise of due diligence, reasonably should have discovered the child's birth and in which action it is determined that he did not consent to the performance of assisted conception. (§ 20-158(A)(2))
11. *If a man contributes sperm how can he avoid being father?*	The donor is not the father unless he is married to the mother. (§ 20-158(A)(3)) On the other hand, if the donor, who may be cohabiting with the mother, donates sperm to facilitate assisted conception and acknowledges the child when born, he is not foreclosed from being the father. (See L.F. v. Breit, 736 S.E.2d 711 (Va. 2013)) The policy that each child have a mother and a father trumps the assisted conception statute that states that a donor of procreative material is not a parent. In *Breit*, the court held that the statute was intended to apply only to a married couple using a third party donor. In the nonmarital context, paternity may be established by genetic tests or a voluntary acknowledgement of paternity by father and mother. (Id.; § 20-49.1) Importantly, the man in Breit wanted to be declared the father. (736 S.E.2d at 715-16)

Washington
Status of Children Conceived by Assisted Reproduction Techniques—2018

A. Posthumously Conceived Individuals

1.	Can an individual have legal status as a child even though conceived and born after the parent's death?	Yes. (§ 26.26.730)
2.	What if the deceased contributor of procreative material was not married?	When read in tandem, § 26.26.106 and § 26.26.730 would grant the same legal status to the child regardless of contributor's marital status.
3.	Is the consent of the deceased contributor of procreative material required and, if so, what kind of consent, and consent to what?	If the contributor dies before placement of eggs, sperm, or embryos, the decedent is not the parent unless the decedent consented in a signed record that if assisted reproduction occurred after death the decedent would be the parent of the child. (§ 26.26.730)
4.	Is there specific authority addressing the posthumous child's right of inheritance?	No authority.
5.	Is there specific authority addressing the posthumous child's status under a will or a trust?	No authority.

B. Mother does not provide both womb and egg

6.	Is there a distinction drawn between a married and unmarried woman?	No. (§ 26.26.106)
7.	Who is the mother if a woman contributes the egg but the child is carried in a surrogate's womb?	The woman is the mother if she is the intended mother under a valid surrogate contract. (§§ 26.26.210–26.26.260 et seq.) If there is no valid surrogate contract, the surrogate is the mother. (§ 26.26.101(1)) See also § 26.26.735. Without an agreement a donor is not a parent. (§ 26.26.705)
8.	Who is the mother if a woman contracts for the egg but carries the child in her womb?	The woman is the mother, if certified by physician to whom the ovum is given. (§ 26.26.735) The couple, including the woman, must consent to being parents, or must reside in the same household with the child after the child's birth and hold the child out as their own. (§ 26.26.715(1)) The parties can agree in a signed writing otherwise as to who is the parent. (§ 26.26.735)
9.	Who is the mother if a woman contracts for both the egg and the womb?	The woman is the mother if she is the intended mother under a valid surrogate contract. (§§ 26.26.210–26.26.260). If there is no valid surrogate contract, the surrogate is the mother. (§ 26.26.101(1)) See also § 26.26.735. Without an agreement, a donor is not a parent. (§ 26.26.705) A donor is a person other than a husband who provides the sperm or a parent determined otherwise under the law. (§ 26.26.011(9))

C. When the man is not the biological father or is not married to the mother

10.	If a husband does not contribute sperm but consents to his wife providing the womb with the intention of being the mother, is he the father?	Yes. (§§ 26.26.710, 26.26.715) Note that spousal presumptions of parentage have extended to domestic partners. (§§ 26.26.116, 26.26.720, 26.26.903)
11.	If a man contributes sperm how can he avoid being father?	If he has not signed a consent, he is generally not the father. However, failure by a person to sign a consent does not preclude a finding that the person is a parent if the person resided in the same household with the child and "openly held out the child as their own." (§ 26.26.715(2)) The situation in which the intended parties are not married or not domestic partners is not addressed. Generally, a donor is not a parent unless otherwise agreed in a signed record by the donor and the person or persons intending to be parents. (§ 26.26.705)

Washington
Status of Children Conceived by Assisted Reproduction Techniques—
2019

A. Posthumously Conceived Individuals

1.	*Can an individual have legal status as a child even though conceived and born after the parent's death?*	Yes. (§ 26.26.608)
2.	*What if the deceased contributor of procreative material was not married?*	When read in tandem, § 26.26.202 and § 26.26.608 would grant the same legal status to the child regardless of contributor's marital status.
3.	*Is the consent of the deceased contributor of procreative material required and, if so, what kind consent, and consent to what?*	If the contributor dies before transfer of a gamete or embryo, the decedent is not the parent unless the decedent consented in a signed record that if assisted reproduction occurred after death the decedent would be the parent of the child or the individual's intent to be a parent of the child is (i) established by clear and convincing evidence and (ii) the embryo is in utero not later than 36 months after the contributor's death or the child is born not later than 45 months after the contributor's death. (§ 26.26.608)
4.	*Is there specific authority addressing the posthumous child's right of inheritance?*	No authority.
5.	*Is there specific authority addressing the posthumous child's status under a will or trust?*	No authority.

B. Mother does not provide both womb and egg

6.	*Is there a distinction drawn between a married and Unmarried woman?*	No. (§ 26.26.202)
7.	*Who is the mother if a woman contributes the egg but the child is carried in a surrogate's womb?*	The woman is the mother if she is the intended mother under a valid surrogate contract. (§ 26.26.709). If there is no valid surrogate contract, the surrogate is the mother. (§ 26.26.101(1); see also § 26.26.602) Without an agreement, a donor is not a parent. (§ 26.26.602)
8.	*Who is the mother if a woman contracts for the egg, but carries the child in her womb?*	The woman is the mother, not the genetic surrogate. (§ 26.26.709(b)&(d)) The couple, including the woman, must consent to being parents, or must reside in the same household with the child after the child's birth, generally for 4 years, and hold the child out as their own. (§ 26.26.604)

| 9. | Who is the mother if a woman contracts for both the egg and the womb? | The woman is the mother if she is the intended mother under a valid surrogate contract. (§§ 26.26.704; 26.26.709) if there is no valid or validated surrogate contract, the surrogate is the mother if she withdraws her consent before 48 hours before the birth of the child. (§ 26.26.716(3)). If consent is withdrawn later, a court decides parentage in the "best interest of the child." (§ 26.26.716(4)) A surrogate can withdraw consent even if the agreement is otherwise valid, if done within 48 hours of birth (26.26.714(b)). Without an agreement, a donor is not a parent. (§ 26.26.602) A donor is a person who contributes gametes but is not a woman who gave birth other than pursuant to a surrogate agreement or a parent or intended parent pursuant to sections 601-608 or 701-718. (§ 26.26.102(9)) |

C. When the man is not the biological father or is not married to the mother

| 10. | If a husband does not contribute sperm but consents to his wife providing the womb with the intention of being the mother, is he the father? | Yes. (§ 26.26.603) The provision extends to any individual and not just a husband with respect to a husband who is deemed the parent unless he did not provide consent, in which case procedures are set forth for challenging his parentage. (§ 26.26.605) |
| 11. | If a man contributes sperm, how can he avoid being the father? | If he has not signed a consent, he is generally not the father. However, failure by a person to sign a consent does not preclude a finding that the person is a parent if the person resided in the same household with the child generally for 4 years after birth and "openly held out the child as their own." (§ 26.26.604(2)(b)) Generally, a donor is not a parent unless otherwise agreed in a signed record by the donor and the person or persons intending to be parents. (§ 26.26.602) |

West Virginia
Status of Children Conceived by Assisted Reproduction Techniques

A. Posthumously Conceived Individuals

1.	Can an individual have legal status as a child even though conceived and born after the parent's death?	No authority.
2.	What if the deceased contributor of procreative material was not married?	No authority.
3.	Is the consent of the deceased contributor of procreative material required and, if so, what kind of consent, and consent to what?	No authority.
4.	Is there specific authority addressing the posthumous child's right of inheritance?	No authority.
5.	Is there specific authority addressing the posthumous child's status under a will or a trust?	No authority.

B. Mother does not provide both womb and egg

6.	Is there a distinction drawn between a married and unmarried woman?	No authority.
7.	Who is the mother if a woman contributes the egg but the child is carried in a surrogate's womb?	No authority.
8.	Who is the mother if a woman contracts for the egg but carries the child in her womb?	No authority.
9.	Who is the mother if a woman contracts for both the egg and the womb?	No authority.

C. When the man is not the biological father or is not married to the mother

10.	If a husband does not contribute sperm but consents to his wife providing the womb with the intention of being the mother, is he the father?	§§ 48-22-110(1) and (2) suggest that the husband would be the father, but the statute was not designed to address this situation.
11.	If a man contributes sperm how can he avoid being father?	No authority.

Wisconsin
Status of Children Conceived by Assisted Reproduction Techniques

A. Posthumously Conceived Individuals

1.	Can an individual have legal status as a child even though conceived and born after the parent's death?	No authority.
2.	What if the deceased contributor of procreative material was not married?	No authority.
3.	Is the consent of the deceased contributor of procreative material required and, if so, what kind of consent, and consent to what?	No authority.
4.	Is there specific authority addressing the posthumous child's right of inheritance?	No authority.
5.	Is there specific authority addressing the posthumous child's status under a will or a trust?	No authority.

B. Mother does not provide both womb and egg

6.	Is there a distinction drawn between a married and unmarried woman?	No authority.
7.	Who is the mother if a woman contributes the egg but the child is carried in a surrogate's womb?	The surrogate is initially the mother until a court determines parental rights. (§ 69.14(1)(h))
8.	Who is the mother if a woman contracts for the egg but carries the child in her womb?	No authority.
9.	Who is the mother if a woman contracts for both the egg and the womb?	The surrogate is initially the mother until a court determines parental rights. (§ 69.14(1)(h)) While the surrogate cannot be denied her parental rights, a surrogacy agreement that addresses custody, if in the best interests of the child, may be given effect and any void provisions regarding termination of parental rights can be severed without invalidating the entire agreement. (In re Paternity of F.T.R., 833 N.W.2d 634 (Wis. 2013))

C. When the man is not the biological father or is not married to the mother

10.	If a husband does not contribute sperm but consents to his wife providing the womb with the intention of being the mother, is he the father?	Yes, if consent is given by a husband in writing and signed by him and his wife. The artificial insemination must take place under the supervision of a licensed physician, who shall certify their signatures and the date of the insemination and file the husband's consent with the department of health services. Failure to file by the physician does not affect the legal status of the child. (§ 891.40(1)) However, if the requirements in § 891.40 are not complied with, the father's information is omitted from the birth certificate. (§ 69.14(1)(g)) A court determination would be required. For example, § 891.40(1) would not apply if the couple is not married. (See also § 767.87(9))
11.	If a man contributes sperm how can he avoid being father?	The donor, if not married to the woman, is not the father. (§ 891.40(2))

Wyoming
Status of Children Conceived by Assisted Reproduction Techniques

A. Posthumously Conceived Individuals

1.	Can an individual have legal status as a child even though conceived and born after the parent's death?	Yes. (§ 14-2-907)
2.	What if the deceased contributor of procreative material was not married?	No distinction based on marital status.
3.	Is the consent of the deceased contributor of procreative material required and, if so, what kind of consent, and consent to what?	If an individual consented in a record to be a parent by assisted reproduction dies before placement of eggs, sperm, or embryos, the decedent is not the parent, unless the decedent consented in a record that if assisted reproduction were to occur after death, the decedent would be a parent. (§ 14-2-907)
4.	Is there specific authority addressing the posthumous child's right of inheritance?	No authority.
5.	Is there specific authority addressing the posthumous child's status under a will or a trust?	No authority.

B. Mother does not provide both womb and egg

6.	Is there a distinction drawn between a married and unmarried woman?	No. (§ 14-2-502)
7.	Who is the mother if a woman contributes the egg but the child is carried in a surrogate's womb?	Although there is no statute directly on point, the surrogate probably is the mother. (§ 14-2-501(a)(i))
8.	Who is the mother if a woman contracts for the egg but carries the child in her womb?	The woman giving birth would probably be the mother. (§ 14-2-501(a)(i))
9.	Who is the mother if a woman contracts for both the egg and the womb?	Although there is no statute directly on point, the surrogate probably is the mother. (§ 14-2-501(a)(i))

C. When the man is not the biological father or is not married to the mother

10.	If a husband does not contribute sperm but consents to his wife providing the womb with the intention of being the mother, is he the father?	The husband is required to give consent in a record signed by him and his wife. (§ 14-2-904) In fact, the man and woman do not have to be married. Failure to sign does not preclude the man intended to be the father from being the father if, during the first 2 years of the child's life, he and the woman resided in the same household with the child and openly held out the child as their own. (Id.)
11.	If a man contributes sperm how can he avoid being father?	The donor is not the father. (§ 14-2-902) However, a man who provides sperm for, or consents to assisted reproduction as in #10 above, with the intent to be the parent, is the parent of the resulting child. (§ 14-2-903) A donor is a person other than (i) a husband who provides the sperm or (ii) a parent determined otherwise under the law. (§ 14-2-402(a)(viii))

Table 12
Contacts Resulting in State Taxation of An Estate's Income
(current through 5/1/17)

A state must have some contact with an estate before it can tax the estate's entire income. The typical contact relied upon is the decedent's domicile in the state at the time of death. On this basis, the state claims the appropriate nexus to justify the taxation of the income of the estate following the decedent's death until the estate is closed. The residence of the personal representative, the situs of estate administration, the sources of income, the situs of the underlying assets, and the residence or domicile of the beneficiaries are not given consideration.

Not all states, however, apply the domicile at death contact. Several states, instead, apply the residence at death standard. The concept of "residence" for this purpose ordinarily includes domicile but goes beyond it. Commonly, the standard also incorporates physical presence in the state for at least more than one-half of the taxable year and/or the maintenance of a permanent place of abode. In the case of a decedent, this standard may well not be satisfied if the decedent dies during the first half of the taxable year. In this case, the domicile branch of the residence standard will often provide the appropriate nexus permitting taxation of the estate's income.

The remaining states employ somewhat more unique standards, such as a multifactor contacts test. Exposure of the estate to state income tax will be determined by an imprecise weighing of these factors. On the other hand, the state may look simply to the situs of estate administration. Generally, if situs of estate administration is a factor in a multifactor test, or the factor, the law likely will refer to domiciliary administration. In effect, this is an adoption of the domicile at death test for estate income taxation. However, a state may make reference to "administration" without distinguishing between domiciliary and ancillary administration, thus, leaving unsettled whether a rather tangential connection with the state may suffice.

When the required nexus exists, the estate is deemed to be a resident estate and the estate's entire net income, whether derived from within or without the state, is subject to taxation. While this is commonly the case, certain states impose no income tax on estates at all, regardless of the nexus with the state. Other states may only tax certain types of income. Tennessee, for example, taxes just dividends on stocks and interest on bonds. Although not addressed by this Table, states also have exemptions, with only amounts over the exemption subject to taxation or even to reporting.

When an estate is not a resident estate, it is not taxed by the state on its entire net income. Rather, it is likely to be taxed exclusively on its locally-sourced income. The present Table does not specify these contacts, the purpose being to identify those contacts that justify the state in taxing the entire income of the estate, whether derived from sources within or without the state.

State	Jurisdictional Basis for Taxation
Alabama	Residence of the decedent at the time of death (§ 40-18-1(32)) A person is presumed to be "residing" in Alabama if (1) domiciled in Alabama, (2) maintains a permanent place of abode in Alabama, or (3) spends in the aggregate more than 7 months of the income year in Alabama. (§ 40-18-2(b)) *See also* § 40-18-25, providing for the taxation of the income of a resident estate.
Alaska	No income tax.
Arizona	Residence of the decedent at the time of death (§ 43-1301(4)) "Resident" includes every individual who (1) is in the state for other than a temporary or transitory purpose, (2) is domiciled in the state and who is outside the state for a temporary or transitory purpose, or (3) spends in the aggregate more than 9 months of the taxable year in the state. This last basis is only a presumption and can be overcome by evidence that the individual is in the state for a temporary or transitory purpose. (§ 43-104(19)(a)-(c)) *See also* § 43-1301(1)-(2), providing for the taxation of the income of a resident estate.
Arkansas	No tax of estate created by a "nonresident" donor, trustor, or settlor or by a "nonresident testator." (§ 26-51-201(b)) Thus, an estate created by a "resident" is subject to tax. (§ 26-51-201(a)) "Resident" includes any individual (1) domiciled in the state or (2) who maintains a permanent place of abode within the state and spends in the aggregate more than 6 months in the taxable year within the state. (§ 26-51-102(14)) Note that the statute does not refer to those who leave an estate and die intestate. (§ 26-51-201(b)) This is not explained in regulations nor in instructions to AR 1002, the Fiduciary Return.
California	Residence of the decedent (Rev. & Tax § 17742(a)) Residence includes every individual who is (1) in the state for other than a temporary or transitory purpose or (2) domiciled in the state and who is outside the state for a temporary or transitory purpose. A person is not domiciled in the state if absent from the state for at least 546 consecutive days under an employment-related contract, and even if returning for no more than 45 days in a taxable year. However, in order for this exception to "domicile" to apply, the income from intangible property cannot exceed $200,000 for the taxable year. Moreover, no exception applies if the "principal purpose" of absence from the state is avoidance of tax. (Rev. & Tax § 17014) Rev. & Tax § 17742(a) provides for the taxation of the income of a resident estate.
Colorado	The estate is being administered in the state, other than in an ancillary proceeding. (§ 39-22-103(7)) *See, e.g.,* In re McLaughlin's Will, 128 Colo. 581, 585-86, 265 P.2d 691, 693 (1954). *See also* §§ 39-22-104(1.7) & 39-22-401, providing for the taxation of the income of a resident estate.
Connecticut	The decedent was a "resident of this state" at the time of death. (§ 12-701(a)(4)(A)). A "resident of this state" means:
	(1) a domiciliary, unless the domiciliary (a) maintains no permanent place of abode in the state, does maintain a permanent place of abode elsewhere, and spends no more than 30 days in the aggregate in the state during the taxable year or (b) in the course of 548 consecutive days spends 450 days in a foreign country or countries, spends no more than 90 days in the state, does not maintain a permanent place of abode at which a spouse or minor children spend more than 90 days, and during the nonresident portion of any taxable year ending in the 548 day period, the number of days spent in the state does not exceed the ratio that 90 bears to 548 days;
	(2) a nondomiciliary, who maintains a permanent place of abode in the state and "is in this state" in the aggregate for more than 183 days during the taxable year unless in active military service. (§ 12-701(a)(1))
	See also § 12-700(a)(9)(E), providing for the taxation of the income of a resident estate.

State	Jurisdictional Basis for Taxation
Delaware	The term "resident estate" means the estate of a decedent who was domiciled in Delaware at death. (30 § 1601(7)) *See also* 30 § § 1632, 1635 providing for the taxation of the income of a resident estate. Under 30 § 1636(a), a deduction is allowed for taxable income, set aside under the terms of the governing instrument, for future distribution to nonresident beneficiaries.
District of Columbia	The term "resident estate" means the estate of a decedent who was domiciled in the District of Columbia at death. (§ 47-1809.01) *See also* § 47-1809.03, providing for the taxation of the income of a resident estate.
Florida	No income tax.
Georgia	The tax is imposed on fiduciaries (1) receiving income from business done in Georgia; (2) managing funds or property located in the state; or (3) managing funds or property for the benefit of a resident of the state. (§ 48-7-22(a)) A "resident" beneficiary under (3) would be one who (1) is a legal resident on income tax day, (2) resides within the state on "a more or less regular or permanent basis and not on the temporary or transitory basis of a visitor or sojourner and who resides in the state on income tax day"; and (3) on income tax day has been residing in the state for at least 183 days or part-days in the aggregate of the immediately preceding 365 days. Once a person is a resident, that person has the burden of showing to the satisfaction of the commissioner that he has become a legal resident or domiciliary of another state and that he does not fit within (3) immediately above. (§ 48-7-1(10)(A)-(B)) "Income tax day" is generally December 31 or the end of the fiscal year if the fiscal year for tax reporting has already been established. (§ 48-7-1(5))
Hawaii	Three criteria must be satisfied: (1) The decedent was a resident, (2) the fiduciary of the estate was appointed by an Hawaiian court, and (3) estate administration is carried out in the state. (§ 235-1) A "resident" is an individual who is (1) domiciled in the state or (2) resides in the state. A person resides in the state if in the state for other than a temporary or transitory purpose. There is a presumption of residence if the person is in the state more than 200 days during the taxable year. The presumption can be overcome by showing the maintenance of a permanent place of abode elsewhere and a presence in Hawaii for a temporary or transitory purpose. Presence due to military or naval orders of the U.S., while engaged in aviation or navigation, or while a student, does not count toward residence. (Id.) *See also* § 235-4(e)(1), providing for the taxation of the income of a resident estate.
Idaho	A resident estate is subject to tax on income from all sources. (§ § 63-3026, 63-3030(a)(5)) "Resident estate" is not defined by statute. A resident estate is the estate of a person domiciled in Idaho on the date of his death. (§ 63-3015(i)) A decedent was a resident if he was domiciled in the estate for the entire taxable year or maintained a place of abode for the entire taxable year and spent more than 270 days of the taxable year in the state. (§ 63-3013(1)(a)-(b))
Illinois	The term "resident" includes the estate of a decedent who was domiciled in Illinois at death. (35 § 5/1501(20)(B)) *See also* 35 § 5/201(a), providing for the taxation of the income of an estate receiving income in or as a resident of Illinois.
Indiana	Residence. (§ 6-3-1-12(c)) A deceased person was resident if he was (1) domiciled in the state during the taxable year or (2) maintained a permanent place of residence in the state and spent more than 183 days of the taxable year in the state. (§ 6-3-1-12(a)-(b)) *Quaere* whether the decedent had to be domiciled in the state on the date of death. *See also* § 6-3-2-1(a), providing for the taxation of the income of a resident person and § 6-3-1-14 defining an estate as a "person."

State	Jurisdictional Basis for Taxation
Iowa	There is no clear statement of the relevant contact making an estate a resident estate. The Iowa Admin. Code requires reporting of income from all sources of "[e]states of Iowa resident decedents." (Adm. Code § 701-89.8(3)) *See also* § 422.8(3), which states that a resident estate's income is allocated like that of a resident individual. A resident individual is one who is (1) domiciled in the state or (2) maintains a permanent place of abode in the state. (Ia. Code Ann. § 422.4(15))
Kansas	Section 79-32,134 provides for taxation of the income of a "resident estate." "Resident estate" means the estate of a deceased person whose domicile was in Kansas at the time of such person's death. (§ 79-32,109(c))
Kentucky	An estate is taxed like an individual under § 141.020. (§ 141.030) A person is a resident if the person is domiciled in the state or maintains a place of abode in the state and spends in the aggregate more than 183 days of the taxable year in the state. (§ 141.010(17)) However, there is no clear statement of when an estate is a resident, so as to be taxed like a resident individual. Neither the regulations nor Form 741 clarify this.
Louisiana	Domicile at death. (Rev. Stat. § 47:300.10(2))
Maine	The term "resident estate" means the estate of a decedent who was domiciled in Maine at death. (36 § 5102(4)(A)) *See also* 36 §§ 5160, 5111, providing for the taxation of the income of a resident estate.
Maryland	"Resident" means a personal representative of an estate if the decedent was domiciled in Maryland on the date of the decedent's death. (Tax-Gen. § 10-101(k)(1)(ii)) The tax is imposed on individuals (Tax-Gen. § 10-102), which term includes within its meaning fiduciaries. (Tax-Gen. § 10-101(g) & (f)(1)) Unlike a nonresident, a resident, that is, domiciliary estate, is generally taxed on the resident's income, whatever its source. (Tax-Gen. §§ 10-203, 10-206, 10-210)
Massachusetts	Residence at death. (62 § 9) A resident is an individual (1) domiciled in the commonwealth or (2) who maintains a permanent place of abode in the commonwealth and spends more than 183 days during the taxable year there, including partial days. However, days spent in the commonwealth while on active duty in the armed forces do not count. (62 § 1(f))
Michigan	The term "resident" means estate of a decedent who was domiciled in Michigan at death. (§ 206.18(1)(b)) "Domicile" means the place of true, fixed, and permanent home and principle establishment to where one intends to return until establishing another. It also includes living in the state at least 183 days in the tax year (§ 206.18(1)(a)) *See also* § 206.110(1), providing for the taxation of the income of a resident estate.
Minnesota	The term "resident estate" means any one of the following: (1) the decedent was domiciled in Minnesota at death, (2) the personal representative was appointed by a Minnesota court in a proceeding other than an ancillary proceeding, or (3) the administration of the estate is carried out in Minnesota in a proceeding other than an ancillary proceeding. (§ 290.01(7a.)) *See also* § 290.22, providing for the taxation of the income of an estate and § 290.17 subd. (1)(a), which specifies that only Minnesota-source income and losses are taken into account. If an estate is resident, income from intangibles is deemed to have a Minnesota source.
Mississippi	The entire net income of every "resident estate" is subject to tax. (§ 27-7-5(1)) "Resident estate" is not defined. The taxing authorities take the position that a resident estate "is the estate of a person who was a Mississippi resident at the time of death." See Instructions for Completing Form 81-110, Fiduciary Income Tax Return for Estates and Trusts (2012).

State	Jurisdictional Basis for Taxation
Missouri	The term "resident estate" means the estate of a decedent who was domiciled in Missouri at death. (§ 143.331(1)) *See also* § 143.341, providing for the taxation of the income of a resident estate.
Montana	Although not set forth in the statute, the instructions for Form FID-3 (p. 15, FAQ 2 (2012)) state that "[a]n estate is a resident estate if the decedent was a Montana resident on the date of his or her death." The Adm. Rules of Montana 42.15.301(3)(a) refers to "the estate of a decedent who was a resident," but there is no amplification as to its application.
Nebraska	The term "resident estate" means the estate of a decedent who was domiciled in Nebraska at death. (§ 77-2714.01(6)(a)) *See also* § 77-2717, providing for the taxation of the income of a resident estate.
Nevada	No income tax.
New Hampshire	"[L]ast dwelt in this state" (§ 77:9) In Stark v. Parker, 56 N.H. 481 (1876), this terminology was interpreted to mean domiciled in the state, rather than resident in the state.
New Jersey	The term "resident estate" means the estate of a decedent who was domiciled in New Jersey at death. (§ 54A:1-2(o)(1)) *See also* § 54A:2-1, providing for the taxation of the income of a resident estate.
New Mexico	The Instructions for Form FID-1 (p. 1 (2013)) are quite ambiguous. On the one hand, they require the filing of a return if "the estate is of a decedent who was a resident of New Mexico." However, in bold letters thereafter they state "An estate is DOMICILED IN NEW MEXICO if the decedent was domiciled in New Mexico." The significance of this latter statement is not clear. A resident estate is not defined by statute. However, the term "individual" includes an estate. (§ 7-2-2(I)) A broad definition is given to the term "resident" so that it includes a person (1) domiciled in the state or (2) physically present for at least 185 days in the taxable year. (§ 7-2-2(S))
New York	The term "resident estate" means the estate of a decedent who was domiciled in New York at death. (Tax § 605(b)(3)(A)) *See also* § 618, providing for the taxation of the income of a resident estate.
North Carolina	Any estate that (1) derives income from North Carolina sources and such income is attributable to ownership of an interest in real or tangible personal property in the state or the income is derived from a business, trade, profession, or occupation carried on in the state, or (2) derives income which is for the benefit of a North Carolina resident. (§ 105-160.2) *See also* Instructions for Estates and Trusts Income Tax Return. With respect to a beneficiary, a "resident" of the state includes a domiciliary or a person residing in the state other than on a temporary or transitory basis. A person residing in the state more than 183 days during the taxable year is presumed a resident, but, the fact that a person is absent from the state for more than 183 days does not give rise to a presumption against residence. If a person leaves the state, residence is not deemed abandoned until a "domicile" elsewhere is adopted. (§ 105-153.3(15))

State	Jurisdictional Basis for Taxation
North Dakota	An estate is resident if it has a relationship to the state sufficient to "create nexus." This includes, but is not limited to, the following contacts: (1) a beneficiary of the estate is a domiciliary or resident of the state, (2) the executor is a domiciliary or resident of the state, (3) assets making up part of the estate have a situs in the state, (4) any or all of the administration or income production of the estate takes place in the state, and (5) the laws of the state are specifically made applicable to the estate or to the opposite parties with respect to their fiduciary relationship. (N.D. Adm. Code § 81-03-02.1-04) A resident is (1) a domiciliary or (2) a person who maintains a permanent place of abode and who spends more than 7 months in the state during the taxable year, but an active duty military member and that person's spouse are not residents simply because they voted in the state. (N.D. Cent. Code § 57-38-01(11)) *See also* N.D. Cent. Code § 57-38-30.3(1)(e), providing for the taxation of the income of an estate generally. N.D. Cent. Code § 57-38-30.3(1)(f) then provides for taxation of a nonresident estate based on a formula that is equal to the portion of the federal adjusted gross income allocable and apportionable to North Dakota.
Ohio	The term "resident estate" means the estate of a decedent who was domiciled in Ohio at death. (§ 5747.01(I)(2)) *See also* § 5747.02(A), providing for the taxation of the income of a resident estate. Note that the domicile test of § 5747.24 is not controlling. Thus, case law and administrative decisions are controlling.
Oklahoma	The term "resident estate" means the estate of a decedent who was domiciled in Oklahoma at death. (68 § 2353(5)) *See also* 68 § 2355(G), providing for the taxation of the income of fiduciaries.
Oregon	If the fiduciary is appointed by an Oregon court or the administration of the estate is carried on in Oregon. (§§ 316.282(1)(b), 316.282(2)) *Quaere* whether the foregoing includes appointment of an ancillary fiduciary. *Quaere* whether an estate is resident if there is only partial administration in Oregon.
Pennsylvania	The term "resident estate" means the estate of a decedent who was a resident of the state at the time of death. (72 § 7301(r)) "Resident Individual" is defined as an individual domiciled in Pennsylvania, unless he maintains no permanent place of abode there, maintains a permanent place of abode elsewhere, and spends not more than 30 days in the taxable year in Pennsylvania. If not domiciled, an individual is a resident if the individual has a permanent place of abode in Pennsylvania and spends in the aggregate more than 183 days of the taxable year in Pennsylvania. (72 § 7301(p)) *See also* 72 § 7302(a), providing for the taxation of the income of a resident estate.
Rhode Island	The term "resident estate" means the estate of a resident of the state at death. (§ 44-30-5(c)(1)) "Resident" means an individual either (1) domiciled in the state or (2) who maintains a permanent place of abode in the state and is in the state more than 183 days during the taxable year, unless the individual is in the armed forces of the U.S. (§ 44-30-5(a)(1)-(2)) In determining domicile, the geographic location of professional advisors, including medical, financial, legal, insurance, fiduciary, or investment services, as well as charitable contributions to Rhode Island organizations, is not taken into account. (§ 44-30-5(a)(1)) *See also* §§ 44-30-1(a) & 44-30-16 providing for the taxation of the income of a resident estate.
South Carolina	The term "resident estate" means the estate of a decedent who was domiciled in South Carolina at death. (§ 12-6-30(4)) *See also* § 12-6-610, providing for the taxation of the income of a resident estate.
South Dakota	No income tax.

State	Jurisdictional Basis for Taxation
Tennessee	The tax is just on dividends and interest from stocks and bonds. Executors and administrators receiving income taxable from stocks or bonds that were the property of a decedent who, at the time of death, resided in Tennessee, pay tax on the income until the stocks or bonds have been distributed or transferred to distributees or legatees of the decedent. (§ 67-2-110(b)) Although not free of ambiguity, a resident would appear to be any individual who maintains a legal domicile in the state or who maintains a place of residence in Tennessee for more than 6 months in the tax year. (§ 67-2-101(5))
Texas	No income tax.
Utah	Domicile at death. (§ 75-7-103(1)(i)(i)) *See also* § § 59-10-201, 59-10-201.1, providing for the taxation of the income of a resident estate.
Vermont	Domicile at death. (32 § 5811(12)) *See also* 32 § 5822, providing for the taxation of the income of a resident estate.
Virginia	Domicile at death. (§ 58.1-302) *See also* § 58.1-361(A), providing for the taxation of the income of a resident estate.
Washington	No income tax.
West Virginia	Domicile at death. (§ 11-21-7(c)(1)) *See also* § 11-21-18, providing for the taxation of the income of a resident estate.
Wisconsin	Tax is imposed on the personal representative of an estate of an individual residing in the state in case of death. (§ 71.02(1)) The estate of a decedent is considered resident at the domicile of the decedent at the time of his or her death. (§ 71.14(1))
Wyoming	No income tax.

Table 13
Income Tax Rates for Trusts and Estates
(current through 5/1/18)

This table indicates the actual rates of taxation imposed on trusts and estates. The table should be considered along with Table 2 which details the circumstances under which a state will exercise its jurisdiction to tax an estate's income.

As is apparent from the state-by-state analysis, there is a considerable range of rates from state to state. Thus, even if a trust or estate does have the necessary contacts for a particular state to tax the income, the rates are still important in terms of just how onerous the anticipated or actual tax will be. However, this table is only intended to provide a snapshot of the tax imposed, since no consideration is given to the exclusions, deductions, and credits that may affect taxable income and the ultimate tax payable to the state. The table also does not set forth the principles under the particular state's law for determining how much income is to be allocated to the trust or estate and how much to the grantor or the beneficiaries. Finally, rates of *individual* taxation are not provided, even though this could prove helpful in deciding whether accumulation of income or distribution to beneficiaries in the case of a discretionary trust would be most tax-advantageous.

The reader should also be aware of the deduction allowed at the federal level for state income taxes paid. The value of this deduction will increase, and, thus, the burden of the state tax will decline, as the taxpayer moves into a higher federal tax bracket. On the other hand, the deduction will come into play in determining alternative minimum tax, thus potentially limiting the deduction's benefit. Indeed, federal tax law will drive many decisions relating to the income taxation of trusts and estates. Still, this table will afford an important indication of the maximum exposure to income tax at the state level.

Note should be taken that an attempt has been made to provide the most current rate tables. A large number of states make annual adjustments based on cost-of-living index increases or increases in state revenues. Unfortunately, these adjustments may not be determined until later in the calendar year, after the effective date of this table.

Table 13
Income Tax Rates for Trusts and Estates
Chart

	Comments	
Alabama	The tax rate imposed on trusts and estates is the same tax rate as individuals who are single persons. (§§ 40-18-25(a)–(c), 40-18-5(1); AL ADC 810-3-25-.04(1)) However, a resident estate or trust that has gross income taxable in Alabama and another state will be allowed a credit for net income taxes paid to the other state on such income as provided in § 40-18-21. (AL ADC 810-3-25-.04(2)) If the amount paid another state is actually greater than what would have been due with Alabama's income tax rate, then only the excess is entitled to a credit. (§ 40-18-25(c)(2))	a. Two percent of taxable income not in excess of five hundred dollars ($500). b. Four percent of taxable income in excess of five hundred dollars ($500) and not in excess of three thousand dollars ($3,000). c. Five percent of taxable income in excess of three thousand dollars ($3,000). (§ 40-18-5(1))
Alaska	No Income Tax on Trusts and Estates	

Table 13
Income Tax Rates for Trusts and Estates

Comments	Chart
Arizona	
The tax rate imposed on trusts and estates is the same tax rate as "individuals," except for trusts that are taxable as partnerships or corporations under the Internal Revenue Code. However, individual is not defined. Arizona Administrative Code R15-5-2215(3)(d) defines an individual taxpayer filing as a "single" person as including trusts and estates. (§43-1311) The income dollar amounts for each bracket will be adjusted for tax years beginning in 2015. (§43-1011(C))	*If taxable income is:* *The tax is:* $0–$10,000 2.59% of taxable income $10,001–$25,000 $259, plus 2.88% of the excess over $10,000 $25,001–$50,000 $691, plus 3.36% of the excess over $25,000 $50,001–$150,000 $1,531, plus 4.24% of the excess over $50,000 $150,001 and over $5,771, plus 4.54% of the excess over $150,000 (§43-1011(A)(5)(a))
Arkansas	
Trusts and estates are taxed like individuals. (§26-51-201(a)) The tax tables are adjusted for inflation. (§26-51-201(a)(11)) There is a capital gains exemption. It is 45% from February 1, 2015 through June 30, 2016. Thereafter, it increases to 50%. (§26-51-8158(b)(2)(A)–(C)) There is an exemption of net capital gains in excess of $10 million. (§26-51-815(b)(3))	For tax years beginning in or after 2015, if net income is less than $21,000:

For tax years beginning in or after 2015, if net income is less than $21,000:

From	Less Than or Equal To	Rate
$0	$4,299	0.9%
$4,300	$8,399	2.4%
$8,400	$12,599	3.4%
$12,600	$20,999	4.4%

(§26-51-201(a)(8))

For tax years beginning on or after 2016, if net income is equal to or greater than $21,000, but not greater than $75,000:

From	Less Than or Equal To	Rate
$0	$4,299	0.9%
$4,300	$8,399	2.5%
$8,400	$12,599	3.5%
$12,600	$20,999	4.5%
$21,000	$35,099	5.0%
$35,100	$75,000	6.0%

(§26-51-201(a)(7))

Table 13
Income Tax Rates for Trusts and Estates
Chart

Comments	

For tax years beginning in or after 2016, if net income is more than $75,000:

From	*Less Than or Equal To*	*Rate*
$0	$4,299	0.9%
$4,300	$8,399	2.5%
$8,400	$12,599	3.5%
$12,600	$20,999	4.5%
$21,000	$35,099	6.0%
$35,100 and above		6.9%

(§ 26-51-201(a)(9))

For tax years beginning in or after 2016, if net income is more than $75,000 but not more than $80,000, a deduction for a bracket adjustment is allowed in amount in accordance with the table set forth below:

From	*Equal To*	*Bracket Adjustment Amount*
$75,001	$76,000	$440
$76,001	$77,000	$340
$77,001	$78,000	$240
$78,001	$79,000	$140
$79,001	$80,000	$40
$80,001 and above		$0

(§ 26-51-201(a)(10))

California

The tax is imposed on federal taxable income, as modified and at rates for an individual. (Rev. & Tax §§ 17041(a)(1) & (e), 17731) There is also a 7% alternative minimum tax on alternative minimum taxable income determined under the IRC. (Rev. & Tax § 17062(b)(3)(A)(iv)). Finally, and not to be overlooked, there is a 1% "millionaire's tax" on taxable income in excess of $1,000,000. (Rev. & Tax § 17043) The rates shown are adjusted annually (Rev. & Tax § 17041(h))

If taxable income is over:	*The tax is:*
$0 but not over $8,015	$80.15 + 2% of excess over $8,015
$8,015 but not over $19,011	$299.87 + 4% of excess over $19,011
$19,011 but not over $29,989	$739.39 + 6% of excess over $29,989
$29,989 but not over $41,629	$1,437.79 + 8% of excess over $41,629
$41,629 but not over $52,612	$2,316.43 + 9.30% of excess over $52,612
$52,612 but not over $268,750	$22,417.26 + 10.30% of excess over $268,750
$268,750 but not over $322,499	$29,953.41 + 11.30% of excess over $322,499
$322,499 but not over $537,498	$52,248.30 + 12.30% of excess over $537,498
$537,498 and over	

Table 13
Income Tax Rates for Trusts and Estates
Chart

Comments	
	Rates shown are for 2015. (See Form 541 Booklet 2015; see also Proposition 30, increasing rates over $250,000)
Colorado	4.63% of federal taxable income, with certain modifications. (§ 39-22-104(1.7))
Connecticut	For resident trusts or estates, the rate of tax is 6.99% of their Connecticut taxable income for taxable years commencing on or after January 1, 2015. (§ 12-700(a)(9)(E); For nonresident trusts, the rate is the same but is based on a fraction, the numerator of which is the Connecticut taxable income derived from within the state and the denominator of which is all Connecticut taxable income (§ 12-700(b)), which is basically federal taxable income with certain adjustments. (§ 12-701(a)(9))

Delaware: The trust or estate is taxed like an individual. (30 §§ 1631, 1632).
However, the following trusts are not subject to tax: trusts taxable as corporations, tax-exempt trusts, and real estate investment trusts. (30 § 1633). There is also a separate tax on the ordinary income portion of a lump-sum distribution received by every resident estate or trust. (30 § 1102(b))

IMPORTANT BENEFIT: 30 § 1636(a) permits a deduction to be taken by a resident estate or trust to the extent its federal taxable income is "set aside for future distribution to nonresident beneficiaries."

If taxable income is:	*The tax is:*
Not in excess of $2,000	0%
In excess of $2,000 but not in excess of $5,000	2.2%
In excess of $5,000, but not in excess of $10,000	3.9%
In excess of $10,000, but not in excess of $20,000	4.8%
In excess of $20,000, but not in excess of $25,000	5.2%
In excess of $25,000, but not in excess of $60,000	5.55%
In excess of $60,000	6.6%

(30 § 1102(a)(14))

District of Columbia: The tax rate imposed on trusts and estates is the same tax rate as for individuals. (§§ 47-1809.03, 47-1806.03(a)(8)(A))

For taxable years beginning after December 31, 2014

Table 13
Income Tax Rates for Trusts and Estates

Chart

Comments	
	If taxable income is: *The tax is:*
	Not over $10,000 4%% of the taxable income
	Over $10,000 but not over $40,000 6% of the excess over $10,000, plus $400
	Over $40,000 but not over $60,000 7% of the excess over $40,000, plus $2,200
	Over $60,000 but not over $350,000 8.5% of the excess over $60,000, plus $3,600
	Over $350,000 8.95% of the excess over $350,000, plus $28,250

*Note that for taxable years beginning after December 31, 2015, the same schedule below shall apply (§ 47-1806.03(a)(10)(C)), except if superseded by any funded provision of § 47-181, and until § 47-1806.03(a)(10)(B) is fully applicable, which depends on available funding.

If taxable income is:	*The tax is:*
Not over $10,000	4% of the taxable income
Over $10,000 but not over $40,000	$400 + 6% of the excess over $10,000
Over $40,000 but not over $60,000	$2,200 + 6.5% of the excess over $40,000
Over $60,000 but not over $350,000	$3,500 + 8.5% of the excess over $60,000
Over $350,000 but not over $1,000,000	$28,150 + 8.75% of the excess over $350,000
Over $1,000,000	$85,025 + 8.95% of the excess over $1,000,000

Florida	*No income tax on trusts and estates.* (§ 220.02)

Georgia	The tax rate imposed on trusts and estates is the same tax rate as individuals. (§§ 48-7-22(b), 48-7-20(d))

If Georgia taxable income is:	*The tax is:*
Not over $750.00	1%
Over $750.00 but not over $2,250.00	$7.50 plus 2% of amount over $750.00
Over $2,250.00 but not over $3,750.00	$37.50 plus 3% of amount over $2,250.00
Over $3,750.00 but not over $5,250.00	$82.50 plus 4% of amount over $3,750.00
Over $5,250.00 but not over $7,000.00	$142.50 plus 5% of amount over $5,250.00
Over $7,000.00	$230.00 plus 6% of the amount over $7,000

(§§ 48-7-22(b), 48-7-20(b)(1))

Table 13
Income Tax Rates for Trusts and Estates

Chart

	Comments	Chart
Hawaii	Regarding net capital gain, the maximum tax cannot be greater than (1) the tax on the greater of taxable income without net capital gain or the tax on taxable income taxed at a rate below 7.25%, plus 7.25% of taxable income in excess of the amount under (1). (§ 235-51(f))	For taxable years beginning after December 31, 2001: *If the taxable income is:* Not over $2,000 ... 1.40% of taxable income Over $2,000 but not over $4,000 ... $28.00 plus 3.20% of excess over $2,000 Over $4,000 but not over $8,000 ... $92.00 plus 5.50% of excess over $4,000 Over $8,000 but not over $12,000 ... $312.00 plus 6.40% of excess over $8,000 Over $12,000 but not over $16,000 ... $568.00 plus 6.80% of excess over $12,000 Over $16,000 but not over $20,000 ... $840.00 plus 7.20% of excess over $16,000 Over $20,000 but not over $30,000 ... $1,128.00 plus 7.60% of excess over $20,000 Over $30,000 but not over $40,000 ... $1,888.00 plus 7.90% of excess over $30,000 Over $40,000 ... $2,678.00 plus 8.25% of excess over $40,000 (§ 235-51(d))
Idaho	Each year the brackets are adjusted for inflation. (§ 63-3024(a))	*When Idaho taxable income for taxable year 2018 is:* Less than $1,454 ... 1.25% $1,000 but less than $2,000 ... $23.26, plus 3.6% of the amount over $1,454 $2,000 but less than $4,362 ... $75.60, plus 4.1% of the amount over $2,908 $4,362 but less than $5,816 ... $135.21, plus 5.1% of the amount over $4,362 $5,816 but less than $7,270 ... $209.36, plus 6.1% of the amount over $5,816 $7,270 but less than $10,905 ... $298.05, plus 7.1% of the amount over $7,270 Over $10,905 ... $556.14, plus 7.4% of the amount over $10,905 (§ 63-3024(a))

Taxable Income Over	But Not Over	Rate*
$0	$1,472	1.6% [1.25%]
$1,472	$2,945	3.60% [3.125%]
$2,945	$4,417	4.10% [3.625%]
$4,417	$5,890	5.10% [4.624%]
$5,890	$7,362	6.10% [5.625%]
$7,362	$11,043	7.10% [6.625%]
$11,043		7.40% [6.625%]

*Bracketed rates are the reduced rates beginning with 2018. However, the brackets for 2018 have not yet been adjusted for inflation as of 5-23-18.

Table 13
Income Tax Rates for Trusts and Estates
Chart

	Comments
Illinois	In the case of a trust or estate, for taxable years beginning in 2018, the tax is a flat rate of 4.95%. (35 ILCS 5/201(b)(5.4) In addition, trusts, but not estates, are subject to a Personal Property Tax Replacement Income Tax of 1.5% imposed on net income of resident trusts for the taxable year reduced by any investment credits. (35 ILCS 5/201(c)-(d), (e) (investment tax credit)
Indiana	The tax rate imposed on trusts and estates is the same tax rate as individuals, defined resident. (§6-3-1-12) The tax rate is 3.3% of adjusted gross income (as defined in §6-3-1-3.5) of every resident, and on the adjusted gross income derived from sources within Indiana of every nonresident. For tax years beginning after December 31, 2016, the tax rate is 3.23% of adjusted gross income of every resident, and on the adjusted gross income derived from sources within Indiana of every non-resident. (§6-3-2-1(a)(3))

Iowa

The tax rate imposed on individuals applies as well to trusts and estates. (§422.6) The rate is adjusted annually for inflation. (§422.5(6)) An alternative minimum tax may be imposed. (§422.5(2)).

Adjusted Rates for 2017

Taxable Income Over	But Not Over	The Tax is:
$0	$1,598	0.36%
$1,598	$3,196	0.72%
$3,196	$6,392	2.43%
$6,392	$14,382	4.50%
$14,382	$23,970	6.12%
$23,970	$31,960	6.48%
$31,960	$47,940	6.80%
$47,940	$71,910	7.92%
$71,910		8.98%

There is imposed upon every resident and nonresident of Iowa, including estates and trusts, the greater of the tax determined above or the state alternative minimum tax equal to seventy-five percent of the maximum state individual income tax rate for the tax year, rounded to the nearest one-tenth of one percent, of the state alternative minimum taxable income of the taxpayer (§422.5(2)(a)), which also sets forth the computation of the alternative minimum tax. (§422.5(1)(a)-(i)) (See Form 1A 1041 for any year to see the new rates for that year)

Kansas

The tax rate imposed on the Kansas taxable income of trusts and estates is the same as rates as imposed on unmarried resident individuals. (§§79-32,110(d), 79-32,110(a)(2)(D)-(E))

For the tax year 2018, and all tax years thereafter:

If the taxable income is:	But not over:	The tax is:
Over $3,500	$15,000	3.10%
$15,000	$30,000	5.25%
$30,000	----	5.70%

(§79-32,110 (d)&(a)(2)(F))

Table 13
Income Tax Rates for Trusts and Estates

Chart

Comments	
Kentucky	The tax rate imposed on trusts and estates is the same tax rate as imposed on individuals. (§§ 141.030(1), 141.020))	For taxable years beginning after December 31, 2004: (1) Two percent (2%) of the amount of net income not exceeding three thousand dollars ($3,000); (2) Three percent (3%) of the amount of net income in excess of three thousand dollars ($3,000) but not in excess of four thousand dollars ($4,000); (3) Four percent (4%) of the amount of net income in excess of four thousand dollars ($4,000) but not in excess of five thousand dollars ($5,000); (4) Five percent (5%) of the amount of net income in excess of five thousand dollars ($5,000) but not in excess of eight thousand dollars ($8,000); (5) Five and eight-tenths percent (5.8%) of the amount of net income in excess of eight thousand dollars ($8,000) but not in excess of seventy-five thousand dollars ($75,000); (6) Six percent (6%) of the amount of net income in excess of seventy-five thousand dollars ($75,000). (§ 141.020(2)(b))
Louisiana	An income tax is imposed for each taxable year upon the Louisiana taxable income of every estate or trust, whether resident or nonresident. (Rev. Stat. § 47:300.1)	The tax to be assessed, levied, collected, and paid upon the Louisiana taxable income of an estate or trust is computed at the following rates: (1) Two percent on the first ten thousand dollars of Louisiana taxable income. (2) Four percent on the next forty thousand dollars of Louisiana taxable income. (3) Six percent on Louisiana taxable income in excess of fifty thousand dollars. (Rev. Stat. § 47:300.1)
Maine	The rates are imposed as for resident individuals. (36 §§ 5160, 5111)	For tax years beginning on or after 1-1-17: *Maine Taxable Income:* *The tax is:* Less than $21,050 5.8% At least $21.050 but less than $50,000 $1,221 plus 6.75% of excess over $21,050 $50,000 or more $3,175 plus 7.15% of excess over $50,000 (36 § 5111(1-F))

Table 13
Income Tax Rates for Trusts and Estates

Chart

Comments	
Maryland	The tax rate imposed on trusts and estates is the same tax rate as individuals (Tax-Gen. §§ 10-101(g), 10-105(a)) in that the term "individual" is defined to include a fiduciary.	(i) 2% of Maryland taxable income of $1 through $1,000; (ii) 3% of Maryland taxable income of $1,001 through $2,000; (iii) 4% of Maryland taxable income of $2,001 through $3,000; (iv) 4.75% of Maryland taxable income of $3,001 through $100,000; (v) 5% of Maryland taxable income of $100,001 through $125,000; (vi) 5.25% of Maryland taxable income of $125,001 through $150,000; (vii) 5.5% of Maryland taxable income of $150,001 through $250,000; and (viii) 5.75% of Maryland taxable income in excess of $250,000. (§ 10-105(a)(1))

Table 13
Income Tax Rates for Trusts and Estates

Comments	Chart	
Massachusetts	Trusts and estates are taxed at the same rates as individuals. (62 § 10(a)&(c)) Massachusetts gross income is divided into three parts. Part A gross income consists of certain interest that is not exempted, such as non-Massachusetts bank account interest, (62 § 2(b)(1)(A)) dividends, and short-term capital gains. (62 § 2(b)(1)(C)) Dividends and interest, however, are taxed at the same rate as Part B income. (62 § 2(a)(2)) Part B gross income is the rest of Massachusetts gross income that is not Part A or Part C. (62 § 2(b)(2)) Part C gross income is capital gain income of capital assets held for more than one year. (62 § 2(b)(3)) The tax rates for Part B are adjusted based on an annual report of the Commission, but Part B income cannot be taxed at a rate lower than 5%. (62 § 4(b)) There is also an additional tax measured by an interest charge on deferred tax on installment sales with a sales price over $150,000 and aggregate outstanding face amount of such obligations at the end of the year exceeding $5,000,000. (62C § 32A(a))	*Part* A, e.g., short-term capital gains and long-term gains from collectibles (after 50% deduction) A, e.g., interest and dividends B, such as business, income and rents C, long-term capital gain** ** Long-term gains from the sale of qualified small business stock as defined in Ch. 62 sec. 4(c) are taxed at 3%.	*Rate* 12.0% (62 § 4(a)(1)) 5.1% (62 § 4(a)(2)) 5.25%* (62 § 4(b)) 5.1% (62 § 4(c)) *If $24,000 or less, lower rates of tax tables apply. (62 § 4) (See also www.mass.gov/dor/all-taxes/tax-rate-table.html) (Tax rates as of Jan. 1, 2016)

Table 13

Income Tax Rates for Trusts and Estates

Chart

Comments	
Michigan	For tax years that begin on or after October 1, 2012, the rate is 4.25%. The tax rate imposed on trusts and estates is the tax rate "levied and imposed upon the taxable income of every person other than a corporation." (§§ 206.51(9)(c)(i)-(iii), 206.51(1))
Minnesota	Estates and trusts must compute their income tax by applying the rates imposed upon married individuals filing joint returns and surviving spouses to their taxable income, **except that the income brackets will be one half of the amounts listed on the accompanying chart** (§ 290.06 Subd. 2c(a)) There is also an adjustment for inflation. (§ 290.06 Subd. 2d)) 2017 adjusted rates: http://www.revenue.state.mn.us/individuals/individ_income/Pages/Minnesota_Income_Tax_Rates_and_Brackets.aspx (1) On the first $25,890, 5.35 percent; (2) On all over $25,890, but not over $85,060, 7.050 percent; (3) On all over $85,060, but not over $160,020, 7.850 percent; (4) On all over $160,020, 9.850 percent. (§ 290.06 Subd. 2c(a) & 2d)
Mississippi	*Taxable Income Over:* / *But Not Over:* / *Rate* 0 / $5,000 / 3% $5,000 / $10,000 / $150 plus 4% of excess over $5,000 $10,000 / / $350 plus 5% of excess over $10,000 (§ 27-7-5(1)) For 2018, there is no tax on the first $1,000 of taxable income and for 2019, this exemption is increased to $2,000. (§ 27-7-5(1)(a)(1)(ii)-(iii))

Table 13
Income Tax Rates for Trusts and Estates

Chart

Comments		

Missouri

The tax rate imposed on trusts and estates is the same as is imposed on resident individuals, with some modifications. Rate tables are actually provided for "resident individuals."
(§§ 143.311, 143.061, 143.011)

2017 adjusted rates:

If the Missouri taxable income is:	The tax is:
Not over $100	$0
At least $101 but not over $1,008	1.5% of the Missouri taxable income
Over $1,008 but not over $2,016	$15 plus 2% of excess over $1,008
Over $2,016 but not over $3,024	$35 plus 2.5% of excess over $2,016
Over $3,024 but not over $4,032	$60 plus 3% of excess over $3,024
Over $4,032 but not over $5,040	$90 plus 3.5% of excess over $4,032
Over $5,040 but not over $6,048	$125 plus 4% of excess over $5,040
Over $6,048 but not over $7,056	$165 plus 4.5% of excess over $6,048
Over $7,056 but not over $8,064	$210 plus 5% of excess over $7,056
Over $8,064 but not over $9,072	$260 plus 5.5% of excess over $8,064
Over $9,072	$315 plus 5.9% of excess over $9,072

(§ 143.011)

Montana

The determination of taxable income is set forth in § 15-30-2150. By November 1 of each year, the department shall multiply the bracket amount contained in subsection (1) of the inflation factor for that tax year and round the cumulative brackets to the nearest $100.
(§ 15-30-2103(2))

2017 Adjusted Rates:

Taxable Income Over	But Not Over	Rate	Minus
$0	$3,000	1%	$0
$3,000	$5,200	2%	$29
$5,200	$8,000	3%	$81
$8,000	$10,800	4%	$160
$10,800	$13,900	5%	$206
$13,900	$17,900	6%	$402
More than $17,900		6.9%	$560

13,014

Table 13
Income Tax Rates for Trusts and Estates

Comments		Chart

Nebraska

In the case of taxable years beginning on or after January 1, 2014, resident trusts are taxed at the rates shown (§77-2715.03(2)) with adjustments for inflation beginning in 2015. (§77-2715.03(3)) See also §77-2717(1)(a)(ii). No estimated tax payments are required to be made. (Form 1041N Instructions)

2015 Adjusted Rates

Taxable Income Over	But Not Over	Rate
0	$510	2.46%
$510	$4,830	3.51%
$4,830	$15,580	5.01%
$15,580		6.84%

(§77-2715.03(2))

Nevada

No income tax on trusts and estates.

New Hampshire

For taxable periods ending on or after December 31, 2013, a trust is no longer taxable (§77:3) or required to file an income tax return. Furthermore, trusts are exempted from interest and dividends tax. Beneficiaries are taxable on distributed interest and dividends reported on a federal K-1. (§77:10) There is no tax on accumulated income in an employee benefit plan. (§77:11) There is also a separate business profits tax of 8.5% imposed on taxable business profits. (§77-A:2) (§§77:1, 77:3(c), 77:4, 77:9, 77:10) Executors appointed by a court of the state are liable for tax on interest and dividends. (77:3.I(c)). The rate of tax is 5%. (§77:1)

New Jersey

A tax is imposed for each taxable year on the New Jersey gross income of every estate or trust (other than a charitable trust or a trust forming part of a pension or profit-sharing plan). (§54A:2-1)

If the taxable income is:

Not over $20,000

Over $20,000 but not over $35,000

Over $35,000 but not over $40,000

Over $40,000 but not over $75,000

Over $75,000 but not over $500,000

Over $500,000

(§54A:2-1(b)(5))

The tax is:

1.400% of taxable income

$280.00 plus 1.750% of the excess over $20,000

$542.50 plus 3.500% of the excess over $35,000

$717.50 plus 5.525% of the excess over $40,000

$2,651.25 plus 6.370% of the excess over $75,000

$29,723.75 plus 8.970% of the excess over $500,000

Table 13
Income Tax Rates for Trusts and Estates

Comments		Chart
	New Mexico	The tax rate imposed on estates and trusts is the same tax rate imposed on single individuals. (§7-2-2(I)) No adjustment for inflation.	2016 Form 2016 FID-1: *If the taxable income is:* Not over $5,500 *The tax shall be:* 1.7% of taxable income Over $5,500 but not over $11,000 $93.50 plus 3.2% of excess over $5,500 Over $11,000 but not over $16,000 $269.50 plus 4.7% of excess over $11,000 Over $16,000 $504.50 plus 4.9% of excess over $16,000 (§7-2-7)
	New York	For taxable years beginning in 2017, as adjusted for the cost-of-living (Tax Law § 601-1(a)): *If the New York taxable income is:* *The tax is:* Not over $8,500 4% of the New York taxable income Over $8,500 but not over $11,700 $340 plus 4.5% of excess over $8,500 Over $11,700 but not over $13,900 $484 plus 5.25% of excess over $11,700 Over $13,900 but not over $21,400 $600 plus 5.9% of excess over $13,900 Over $21,400 but not over $80,650 $1,042 plus 6.45% of excess over $21,400 Over $80,650 but not over $215,400 $4,864 plus 6.65% of excess over $80,650 Over $215,400 but not over $1,077,550 $13,825 plus 6.85% of excess over $215,400 Over $1,077,550 $72,882 plus 8.82% of excess over $1,070,350 (Tax Law § 601(c)(1)(A)) The tax rate for taxable income over $21,400 and under $80,650, is reduced to 6.33% and for taxable income over $80,650 and under $215,400 is reduced to 6.57%. The other percentage brackets remain the same.
	New York City	In addition to the regular city income tax, there is a special tax on the ordinary income portion of lump sum distributions pursuant to an election made by the taxpayer under IRC § 402(e). (Tax Law § 1301-B Admin. Code § 11-1724(a)).	For taxable years beginning after 2017: *If the city taxable income is:* *The tax is:* Not over $12,000 3.078% of the city taxable income Over $12,000 but not over $25,000 $369 plus 3.762% of excess over $12,000 Over $25,000 but not over $50,000 $858 plus 3.819% of excess over $25,000 Over $50,000 but not over $500,000 $1,813 plus 3.876% of excess over $50,000 Over $500,000 (Tax Law §§ 1304(a)(3) & 1304B(a)(1)(ii))

Table 13
Income Tax Rates for Trusts and Estates
Chart

Comments	
Yonkers, New York	Yonkers imposes a tax which is 16.75% of the net New York state tax. (Tax § 1321; 20 NYCRR 250.1; art IX of the Code and Ordinances of the City of Yonkers § 15-111.) The tax is imposed on an estate of a decedent who died domiciled in Yonkers, a testamentary trust of such decedent, or on an inter vivos irrevocable trust otherwise subject to New York state tax where a resident of Yonkers made a transfer to an irrevocable trust at the time of the creation of the trust or was resident when it became irrevocable, or was a resident when transferring to a revocable trust and the trust is still resident.
North Carolina	The rate of tax for tax years beginning in 2017 is 5.499%. (§ 105-153.7(a))
North Dakota	The tax rate imposed on trusts and estates is the same tax rate as imposed on individuals. (§§ 57-38-07) The rates are revised for cost-of-living adjustment each taxable year in accordance with IRC § 1(f). (§ 57-38-30.3(1)(g)) 2017 rates Taxable Income

2017 rates Taxable Income

Over	Up to	Rate
$0	$2,550	1.10%
$2,550	$6,000	2.04% of the excess over $2,550
$6,000	$9,150	2.27% of the excess over $6,000
$9,150	$12,500	2.64% of the excess over $9,150
$12,500		2.90% of the excess over $12,500

(§ 57-38-30.3(e))

Table 13
Income Tax Rates for Trusts and Estates
Chart

Comments		For taxable year 2015:

Ohio

The tax rate imposed on the modified taxable income of trusts and the taxable income of estates is the same as is imposed on the adjusted gross income of individuals, less exemptions. (§ 5747.02) After 2015, the rates will be adjusted annually. (§ 5747.02 (flush paragraph after (A)(4))) Reductions in tax are to be made as well if the director of budget and management certifies there is surplus revenue. (§ 5747.02(B))

Taxable Income (Estates) or Modified Ohio Taxable Income (Trusts)	*Tax*
$10,630 or less	$0
More than $10,651 but not more than $16,000	$1.980%
More than $16,000 but not more than $21,350	2.476%
More than $21,350 but not more than $42,650	2.969%
More than $42,650 but not more than $85,300	3.465%
More than $85,300 but not more than $106,650	3.960%
More than $106,650 but not more than $213,350	4.597%
More than $213,350	4.997%

(§ 5747.02(A)(3))

Oklahoma

The tax rate imposed on trusts and estates is the same tax rate as single individuals, (68 § 2355(G)) There is a special rate for nonresident aliens of 8% instead of the 30% of the Internal Revenue Code. (68 § 2355(D))

For taxable year 2016:
(a) 0.5% tax on first $1,000.00 or part thereof,
(b) 1% tax on next $1,500.00 or part thereof,
(c) 2% tax on next $1,250.00 or part thereof,
(d) 3% tax on next $1,150.00 or part thereof,
(e) 4% tax on next $2,300.00 or part thereof,
(f) if the State Board of Equalization makes a determination pursuant to Section 4 of the Act, or 4.85% tax on the remainder if the State Board of Equalization makes a determination pursuant to Section 5 of the Act.
(68 § 2355(C.1.))

Table 13
Income Tax Rates for Trusts and Estates
Chart

Comments		
Oregon	The tax rate imposed on trusts and estates is the same tax rate as individuals. (§§316.267, 316.272). The dollar amounts for each rate bracket are increased for a cost-of-living adjustment for each tax year by the Department of Revenue. (§316.037(1)(b)(A)) No estimated tax needs to be filed.	*2017 Adjusted Rates*

2017 Adjusted Rates

Taxable Income	Rates
Not over $3,450	5% of taxable income
Over $3,450 but not over $8,700	7%
Over $8,700 but not over $125,000	9%
Over $125,000	9.9%

(§316.037(1)(a)); Form 41. p.3

Pennsylvania — Tax rate is 3.07%, including as to capital gains. (72 §§7302(a), 7303) The tax is imposed on income or gains not required to be distributed to a beneficiary and, in fact, not paid or credited to a beneficiary. (72 §7305) A credit is allowed against the tax of another state. (72 §7314)

Rhode Island

Taxable Income for 2018

Taxable Income	Rate
Not over $2,500	3.75%
Over $2,500 but not over $7,950	4.75%
Over $7,950	5.99%

(§44-30-2.6(C)(3)(A)(11)) These rates are adjusted for inflation. (§44-30-2.6(3)(E))

South Carolina — Brackets are indexed. (§12-6-510(A))

Taxable Income for 2018

Taxable Income	Rate
Not over $2,970	0% of taxable income
Over $2,970 but not over $5,940	3%
Over $5,940 but not over $8,910	4%
Over $8,910 but not over $11,880	5%
Over $11,880 but not over $14,360	6%
Over $14,360	7%

South Dakota — *No income tax on trusts or estates.*

Tennessee — Tax rate is 3% on dividends and interest in 2018; 2% in 2019. (§§67-2-102(2)&(3), 67-2-101(5))

Texas — *No income tax on trusts or estates.*

Table 13
Income Tax Rates for Trusts and Estates
Chart

Comments	
Utah	The tax rate imposed on trusts and estates is the same tax rate as is imposed on individuals filing separately. (§§ 59-10-201(1), 59-10-201.1, 59-10-104(2)) It is 5% of state taxable income. (§ 59-10-104(2)) A resident estate or trust is allowed the credit provided in § 59-10-1003, relating to an income tax imposed by another state, or D.C., or a possession of the U.S.
Vermont	A special tax rate is imposed on the taxable income of estates and trusts. (32 § 5822(a)(5)) Further adjustments are presented. (32 § 5822(c)). In particular, the amount of tax is increased by 24% of the federal tax liability for (1) additional taxes on qualified retirement plans, (2) recapture of federal investment tax credit, (3) tax on qualified lump-sum distributions of pension income not included in federal taxable income, and decreased by 24% of the reduction in tax liability due to farm income averaging. (32 § 5822(c))	Form FIT-161 *For 2017: If taxable income is:* $2,550 or less Over $2,550 but not over $5,950 Over $5,950 but not over $9,150 Over $9,150 but not over $12,450 Over $12,450 (32 § 5822(a)(5)) *The tax is:* 3.55% of taxable income $91 plus 6.80% of taxable income over $2,550 $322 plus 7.80% of taxable income over $5,950 $571 plus 8.80% of taxable income over $9,150 $862 plus 8.95% of taxable income over $12,450
Virginia	The tax rate imposed on trusts and estates is the same tax rate as individuals. (§§ 58.1-360, 58.1-320)	Two percent on income not in excess of $3,000. Three percent on income in excess of $3,000 but not in excess of $5,000. Five percent on income in excess of $5,000 but not in excess of $17,000. Five and three-quarters percent on income in excess of $17,000 for taxable years beginning on and after January 1, 1990. (§ 58.1-320)

Table 13
Income Tax Rates for Trusts and Estates
Chart

Comments		
Washington	No income tax on trusts or estates. However, they may be subject to the Business and Occupation Tax at rates applied to gross proceeds of sales or gross income of the business that vary with the business activity. (§ § 82.04.220 et seq.) To the extent profits are in the form of return on investments, they are not subject to the tax. See John H. Sellen Const. Co. v. State Dep't Rev., 558 P.2d 1342 (1976).	
West Virginia	*If the West Virginia taxable income is:* Not over $10,000 Over $10,000 but not over $25,000 Over $25,000 but not over $40,000 Over $40,000 but not over $60,000 Over $60,000 (§ 11-21-4e(a)	*The tax is:* 3% of the taxable income $300.00 plus 4% of excess over $10,000 $900.00 plus 4.5% of excess over $25,000 $1,575.00 plus 6% of excess over $40,000 $2,775.00 plus 6.5% of excess over $60,000
Wisconsin	The tax rate imposed on trusts and estates is the same tax rate as individuals. (§71.125(1)) There is an adjustment for inflation. (§71.06(2e))	*For taxable years beginning in 2016:* *Base Taxable Income* Not over $11,120 Over $11,120 but not over $22,230 Over $22,230 but not over $244,750 Over $244,750 (§71.06(1q); *see also* www.revenue.wi.gov/ pages/FAQS/pcs-taxrates.aspx)	*Rates* 4.0% of taxable income $444.80 plus 5.84% of the excess over $11,120 $1,093.62 plus 6.27% of the excess over $22,230 $15,045.63 plus 7.65% of the excess over $244,750
Wyoming	*No income tax on trusts or estates.*	

Table 14
State Inheritance, Estate, Generation-Skipping Transfer, and Gift Taxes
(current through 5/1/18)

Under Section 2011 of the Internal Revenue Code, the federal government was prepared to avoid the collection of double death taxes at both the federal and state level by allowing the state to keep a specified amount. This was accomplished by a credit for state taxes. See Table 14.08. In view of the availability of this credit, state legislation was drafted in every state so as to soak up the maximum amount of the credit but in most states not to impose a tax liability in excess of the federal credit. Nevertheless, there might still have been actual tax liability in excess of the maximum credit amount if more than one state sought to claim in death taxes the maximum amount of the federal credit. Moreover, not every state limited itself to a death tax based on the federal credit. In a number of states an independent inheritance or succession tax was imposed on the beneficiaries or an independent estate or succession tax was imposed on the estate of the decedent. A separate tax geared to the credit was generally imposed in these states when the independent tax yielded an amount that was less than the available federal credit amount.

While the independent taxes remain unaffected, the "soak-up" tax has been affected by the total elimination of the credit in 2005. The effect is to repeal the state soak-up tax. A number of states have enacted legislation to deem the IRC § 2011 credit still in force as of a particular date prior to its repeal. Note also that the sharing of revenues between states will likely be altered with more going to states that have frozen the credit in place if the other state has not done so. Table 14.08 is a State-by-State Summary of the Current State Estate Inheritance Tax Situation.

Table 14.01 reviews, for each state, whether a tax not dependent on the federal § 2011 credit is imposed. Although often imposed on the beneficiaries in the nature of an inheritance tax, with different levels of taxation often based on relationship to the decedent, the question still remains what property is subject to tax. The table indicates fair uniformity among states in taxing all sorts of interests in property, as well as allowing for exemptions, such as for transfers to a spouse or a charity. In terms of a key concern of this work, Table 14.01 reviews precisely what property is subject to tax, depending on whether the decedent was a domiciliary or nondomiciliary. The taxation of nondomiciliaries is often considerably less expansive in its scope. But while nondomiciliary status is obviously preferable, it does not mean there is no tax. The attorney must be aware that states other than the domiciliary state may also be taxing certain interests in property. There are also substantial traps, since a state like New York may impose tax based on the maximum credit amount prior to reduction or repeal of IRC § 2011. It may then reduce this amount only by the lesser of the tax imposed by the residence state or the proportion of the total gross estate value represented by the local property of the nonresident. If the residence state no longer has a tax or defers to another state so as to pick up only whatever is left of the former credit, e.g., Florida, there may be a disproportionate tax paid to the nonresidence state. As can be seen, reference simply to the tax law of the domicile is insufficient for obtaining a true picture of the potential tax burden during the estate planning process or in determining to which states tax must be paid once the individual has died.

Table 14.02 continues the analysis with regard to the estate tax. The estate tax, which is imposed on the estate rather than the beneficiaries, typically was capped in an amount equal to the maximum federal credit. This table indicates whether the state imposes an estate tax, when payment is to be made, and whether the tax is linked to the federal credit, and as of what date if relevant. The table explains for each state which property is subject to tax in the case of a domiciliary and a nondomiciliary, as is done in Table 14.01 with regard to any tax not dependent on the federal credit for state death taxes.

In addition, the table indicates how each state addresses the problem of other states also claiming the federal credit amount. As was previously indicated, certain states, like New York, have a problematic formula. In many cases, but not all, a state will claim only a pro rata portion of the credit amount, based on the fraction of the total gross estate that the property being taxed by the particular state represents.

Furthermore, in some cases, the estate tax will be imposed, as noted, only if the independent inheritance, succession, or estate tax is less than the federal credit amount.

Of course, caution must be exercised. With the repeal of the federal credit for state death taxes, there may not be an actual estate tax imposed, even though the statutory framework is still on the books and is analyzed in Table 14.02.

Limitations on tax may also come in the form of an applicable exclusion amount/unified credit. A state may only impose an inheritance tax or an estate tax to the extent a calculation based on (1) the federal gross estate, (2) the federal taxable estate, or (3) the combined federal taxable estate and adjusted gross estate exceeds the applicable exclusion amount/unified credit in effect under federal law at a certain point in time, such as 2009. Some states opt in this regard for the Internal Revenue Code as in force in 2000, which Code also provided for a phase-in of the applicable exclusion amount reaching $1,000,000 in 2006. See I.R.C. § 2010(c). The determination of tax liability based on the federal tax credit for state death taxes does not come into play unless the estate, as measured under (1), (2), or (3) above exceeds the applicable exclusion/unified credit amount.

A state may provide for a Q-TIP marital deduction election that is independent of the federal election. While this imposes a distinct election requirement that must be carefully observed, it also permits the claiming of the deduction for state tax purposes, even though no federal estate tax return is required, a situation that could arise if the federal applicable exclusion/unified credit is greater than that provided by the state.

In addition, because the taxable base typically is determined under a modified version of federal law, the question arises as to how to deal with the I.R.C. § 2058 deduction for state death taxes. If the deduction is allowed in computing the taxable base, it will be necessary to utilize an interrelated calculation to determine the deduction. This is because the deduction cannot be determined until the state tax is determined, but the state tax cannot be determined until the tax deduction is determined. To avoid the issue, a number of states have provided that the deduction is not to be taken into account in determining the state tax base, even though the federal law is generally relied upon for this purpose.

As the foregoing discussion reveals, a state death tax law computation can be rather complex. Generally state law may adopt the current Internal Revenue Code for determining the taxable base. However, it may then deviate by enacting an applicable exclusion amount/unified credit that was in force under an earlier version of the Internal Revenue Code or has been independently arrived at under state law. The tax itself may be based on the state death credit, which is no longer in force under federal law. This will mean the incorporation into state law of a provision from the Internal Revenue Code again from an earlier date. Thus, several different versions of federal law might be involved and incorporated as part of a freestanding state law that is now decoupled from the current federal law and which will be unaffected by future changes in the status of the applicable exclusion/unified credit, the state death tax credit, the marital deduction, or the deduction for state death taxes.

Table 14.03 proceeds with an analysis with respect to state generation-skipping transfer taxes. Many, but by no means all, states impose this tax. Those that do so, however, rely exclusively on the federal credit for state generation-skipping transfer taxes set forth in IRC § 2604. The federal credit, which is pegged at a maximum 5 percent of the federal generation-skipping transfer tax, is available for generation-skipping transfers other than direct skips. However, some states do not explicitly exclude direct skips from their tax, thus raising the prospect of both federal and state taxation.

The § 2604 credit is repealed effective January 1, 2005. Unlike the case of the § 2011 state death tax credit, few states have enacted legislation to deem this credit still in effect. Consequently, the repeal of the federal credit has had the effect of repealing almost all state generation-skipping transfer taxes.

As with the estate tax, a major issue is which property is subject to tax by a particular state. This is an especially difficult topic because links that existed when a trust was created may no longer exist when the generation-skipping transfer occurs. Moreover, the property itself may no longer be located in the state. Depending on domiciliary or nondomiciliary status at a particular point in time specified in the statute, the taxing state is likely to seek a prorated portion of tax based on the maximum federal credit, at least when another state is also claiming some or all of the maximum credit amount with respect to the same property.

Table 14.04 addresses the imposition of gift tax by the states. Only one state, Connecticut, presently imposes this tax. With regard to this, the date for payment of the tax is set forth. In addition, the property subject to taxation in the cases of a domiciliary and nondomiciliary is also addressed. Note that a state, see, e.g., Minnesota, may take certain gifts into account for estate tax purposes, even though there is not a separate gift tax.

Table 14.05 explores the matter of waivers, that is, the state requirement for a formal release by the government, often based on payment of taxes, before assets can be transferred after the death of the decedent. This information should be especially helpful when there is a tax liability in another state as well as at the domicile. The table indicates the appropriate person from whom waivers must be obtained for each state imposing the requirement. It also indicates those states that do not require waivers. In some states, waivers are not required, but the fiduciary is not permitted to make any transfer or distribution until all taxes are paid. A liability for taxes may be imposed by statute on a fiduciary who makes a prior transfer or distribution.

Table 14.06 addresses how states resolve conflicts over death taxation. In particular, many states have adopted the Uniform Act on Interstate Compromise of Death Taxes and/or the Uniform Act on Arbitration of Inheritance Taxes. These acts set forth a procedure whereby states can resolve disputes over the domicile of the decedent. Domicile is critical, since it affords a constitutionally sound basis for taxing all of the decedent's assets. Moreover, the Supreme Court has held that as long as there is a reasonable basis, more than one state can claim to be the domicile. Thus, state resolution of the conflict is vital to avoid multiple taxation of the same property. The attorney must, therefore, be aware of these relief procedures.

Table 14.07 sets forth the actual rates of transfer taxes imposed.

Table 14.08 summarizes the status of each state's transfer taxes in light of the repeal of the federal tax credit for state death taxes.

Table 14.09 sets forth the schedule of IRC § 2011(b) before its repeal.

Likewise, the attorney must be aware of the reciprocal exemption provisions of many state statutes. These statutes often provide that a state will not tax a nondomiciliary with regard to certain property, usually intangible personal property, if the nondomiciliary's state of domicile affords a reciprocal exemption to the taxing state's domiciliaries. Thus, a careful analysis of these provisions can result in an avoidance of multiple state tax exposure with respect to substantial assets. The earlier tables detailing tax liability need to be considered in light of Table 14.06, which may eliminate the liability that those tables indicate would otherwise be imposed.

The foregoing tables should prove helpful for estate planning as well as postmortem tax compliance. The estate planner will be able to evaluate the jurisdictional bases of different states to tax and the likely tax to be imposed. If necessary, links of the client or the property with certain states can be terminated. After death, the attorney can use the tables to determine readily the exposure to tax in the various states, the need for waivers, and the availability of conflict resolution and reciprocal exemption provisions to reduce the tax burden.

To facilitate the determination of the actual tax exposure, Table 14.07 sets forth the rate schedules of state inheritance, succession, estate, generation-skipping transfer, and gift taxes for those states with such independent rate schedules. The rate schedules are organized on a state-by-state basis. Brief consideration is given to the availability of key deductions/exemptions and various credits and exclusions which is also addressed in Table 14.01. Since many states rely on the federal credit for state death taxes in determining the state tax, the relevant portions of IRC § 2011 are set forth for quick reference in Table 14.09.

One final note on terminology is in order. Many states utilize the terms "resident" and "nonresident." In the transfer tax area, these terms, for federal constitutional reasons, ordinarily mean "domiciliary" and "nondomiciliary." This definitional approach should be contrasted with the income taxation of trusts and estates, see Table 12 where "residence" means actual residence and not domicile. Of course, as those tables demonstrate, states may well have different concepts of when a trust or estate is an actual "resident" of the state.

Table 14.01

Freestanding Inheritance, Estate and Succession Tax

	Is There an Inheritance, Estate, or Succession Tax Not Based on the §2011 Federal Credit?	When Must Payment Be Made?	Are Interests Other Than Outright Ownership Subject to Tax?	Are Broad Deductions for Charitable and Marital Transfers, as Well as Administrative Expenses, Allowed?	With Regard to a Domiciliary,* What Property Is Subject to Tax?	With Respect to a Nondomiciliary,* What Property Is Subject to Tax?
Alabama	No.	N/A	N/A	N/A	N/A	N/A
Alaska	No.	N/A	N/A	N/A	N/A	N/A
Arizona	No.	N/A	N/A	N/A	N/A	N/A
Arkansas	No.	N/A	N/A	N/A	N/A	N/A
California	No. (Rev. & Tax. §13301)	N/A	N/A	N/A	N/A	N/A
Colorado	No.	N/A	N/A	N/A	N/A	N/A
Connecticut	Yes. For the rate, see Table 14.07.	The estate tax is due 6 months after the date of death. (§12-392)	Yes. (§12-391(f)(2))	Yes. (§12-391)	The property includes real property in this state, tangible personal property having an actual situs in this state, and all intangible property. (§12-391(d)(3))	The property includes real property situated in this state and tangible personal property having an actual situs in this state. (§12-391(e)(2)
Delaware	No.	N/A	N/A	N/A	N/A	N/A

Table 14.01
Freestanding Inheritance, Estate and Succession Tax

	Is There an Inheritance, Estate, or Succession Tax Not Based on the § 2011 Federal Credit?	When Must Payment Be Made?	Are Interests Other Than Outright Ownership Subject to Tax?	Are Broad Deductions for Charitable and Marital Transfers, as Well as Administrative Expenses, Allowed?	With Regard to a Domiciliary,* What Property Is Subject to Tax?	With Respect to a Nondomiciliary,* What Property Is Subject to Tax?
District of Columbia	Yes. For the rate, see Table 14.07.	The estate tax is due 10 months after the date of death (§ 47-3705(a)-(c))	Yes, same as under federal tax law. (§ 47-3701(5))	Yes, same as under federal tax law (§ 47-3701(12)(c))	Essentially the federal taxable estate, but the tax is reduced by the proportionate value of the gross estate represented by non-D.C.-situs property (§ 47-3702(a-1)(2))	The portion of the gross estate represented by property having a taxable situs in D.C. This includes real property, tangible personal property, and intangible property used in a trade or business in D.C. Other intangible property is situated where the decedent died domiciled. (§ 47-3703(b-1) & 47-3701(12A))
Florida	No.	N/A	N/A	N/A	N/A	N/A
Georgia	No. (Ga. Code Ann. § 48-12-1)	N/A	N/A	N/A	N/A	N/A

Table 14.01
Freestanding Inheritance, Estate and Succession Tax

	Is There an Inheritance, Estate, or Succession Tax Not Based on the § 2011 Federal Credit?	When Must Payment Be Made?	Are Interests Other Than Outright Ownership Subject to Tax?	Are Broad Deductions for Charitable and Marital Transfers, as Well as Administrative Expenses, Allowed?	With Regard to a Domiciliary,* What Property Is Subject to Tax?	With Respect to a Nondomiciliary,* What Property Is Subject to Tax?
Hawaii	Yes. For the rate, see Table 14.07.	The estate tax is due at the time the federal estate tax return or applicable generation-skipping transfer tax return must be filed. (§ 236E-9(b))	N/A	Yes. (§ 236E-4)	The Hawaii taxable estate, which is essentially computed the same as the federal taxable estate. (§ 236E-7(1))	However, inclusions are limited to real and tangible personal property located in Hawaii. (§ 236E-8(a)(2)) But in § 236E-7, reference is made to the federal gross estate and, in the case of non-resident aliens, to IRC § 2106. (§ 236E-7(2)-(3))
Idaho	No.	N/A	N/A	N/A	N/A	N/A
Illinois	No.	N/A (405/6)	N/A	N/A	N/A	N/A
Indiana	No. Repealed effective Jan. 1, 2013, P.L. § 205-2013, § 105.	N/A	N/A	N/A	N/A	N/A
Iowa	Yes. (§ 450.2) For the rate, See Table 14.07. There is also an additional qualified use inheritance tax if a qualified heir disposes of qualified use property for which an election has been made. (§ 450B.3)	The inheritance tax is due nine months after the decedent's death. (§ 450.6)	Yes. (§ 450.3)	Yes. (§§ 450.9, 450.12)	(1) real estate and tangible personal property located in this state regardless of whether the decedent was a resident of Iowa at death, (2) intangible personal property owned by a decedent domiciled in this state. (§ 450.2)	Real estate and tangible personal property located in Iowa. (§ 450.2)

Table 14.01
Freestanding Inheritance, Estate and Succession Tax

	Is There an Inheritance, Estate, or Succession Tax Not Based on the §2011 Federal Credit?	When Must Payment Be Made?	Are Interests Other Than Outright Ownership Subject to Tax?	Are Broad Deductions for Charitable and Marital Transfers, as Well as Administrative Expenses, Allowed?	With Regard to a Domiciliary,* What Property Is Subject to Tax?	With Respect to a Nondomiciliary,* What Property Is Subject to Tax?
Kansas	No.	N/A	N/A	N/A	N/A	N/A
Kentucky	Yes. (§ 140.010) For the rate, see Table 14.07.	The inheritance tax is due at death and is delinquent if not paid within 18 months. If paid within 18 months, there is no interest charge. There is, on the other hand, a discount of 5% if the taxes are paid within nine months. (§ 140.210(1)) If the tax liability on a beneficiary's net distributive share exceeds $5,000, payments may be paid in 10 annual installments, with interest beginning 18 months after the date of death. (§ 140.222)	Yes. (§ 140.010) For the rate of taxation, See Table 14.07.	In part, with respect to exemption of transfers to educational, religious, and charitable institutions, and to cities and public institutions (§ 140.060) and with respect to certain payments under employee's trusts (§ 140.063). The marital deduction, including qualified terminable interest property, is exempt if an election is made. The marital deduction is independent of whether the federal estate tax marital deduction is elected. (§ 140.080)	The property includes any interest of an "inhabitant" in real or personal property in the state, all tangible personal property "wherever situated" if it has "not acquired a situs for tax purposes of taxation outside of this state," and all intangibles belonging to a Kentucky domiciliary, except partnership property located in another state and subject to an inheritance or estate tax there. (§ 140.010)	Intangible property with a "business situs" in the state, all real property in the state and interest therein, and all tangible personal property with a situs in this state if "not taxable elsewhere." (§ 140.010)
Louisiana	No. § 47:2401 repealed by Acts 2008, No. 822, effective Jan. 1, 2010.	N/A	N/A	N/A	N/A	N/A

Table 14.01

Freestanding Inheritance, Estate and Succession Tax

	Is There an Inheritance, Estate, or Succession Tax Not Based on the §2011 Federal Credit?	When Must Payment Be Made?	Are Interests Other Than Outright Ownership Subject to Tax?	Are Broad Deductions for Charitable and Marital Transfers, as Well as Administrative Expenses, Allowed?	With Regard to a Domiciliary,* What Property Is Subject to Tax?	With Respect to a Nondomiciliary,* What Property Is Subject to Tax?
Maine	Yes. For the rate, see Table 14.07.	9 months after the date of death. (36 § 4107)	Yes. (36 §§ 4102(7), 4103(1)) Note also that taxable gifts within one year of death increase the Maine taxable estate. (36 § 4102(7)(c)) potential clasification for 1 year preceding death.	Yes, as per federal law. However, Maine allows a separate Q-TIP election at the state level in an amount that is no greater than the amount by which the federal applicable exclusion amount exceeds the Maine exclusion amount. The federal applicable exclusion amount does not include the deceased spousal unused exclusion amount under IRC § 2810. (36 § 4102(6)(B))	See Table 14.02.	See Table 14.02.

Table 14.01
Freestanding Inheritance, Estate and Succession Tax

	Is There an Inheritance, Estate, or Succession Tax Not Based on the §2011 Federal Credit?	When Must Payment Be Made?	Are Interests Other Than Outright Ownership Subject to Tax?	Are Broad Deductions for Charitable and Marital Transfers, as Well as Administrative Expenses, Allowed?	With Regard to a Domiciliary,* What Property Is Subject to Tax?	With Respect to a Nondomiciliary,* What Property Is Subject to Tax?
Maryland	Yes. (Tax-Gen. §7-202) For the rate, see Table 14.07.	The inheritance tax is due at the time of accounting for the distribution. (Tax-Gen. §7-217(a)) An information report, however, is due within three months of the appointment of a personal representative. (Tax-Gen. §7-224)	Yes. (Tax-Gen. §7-202)	Yes. (Tax-Gen. §7-203)	Property with a "taxable situs" in the state is subject to the tax. (Tax-Gen. §7-202)	Same as for a domiciliary (Tax-Gen. §7-203), with the exception of no tax on the receipt of personal property from a nonresident decedent if the state or country of decedent's residence at death does not impose death tax on such property or affords a reciprocal exemption similar to Maryland's provision. (Tax-Gen. §7-203(f))
Massachusetts	No. (65A §1)	N/A	N/A	N/A	N/A	N/A
Michigan	No.	N/A	N/A	N/A	N/A	N/A
Minnesota	No.	N/A	N/A	N/A	N/A	N/A
Mississippi	No.	N/A	N/A	N/A	N/A	N/A
Missouri	No.	N/A	N/A	N/A	N/A	N/A
Montana	No.	N/A	N/A	N/A	N/A	N/A

Table 14.01
Freestanding Inheritance, Estate and Succession Tax

	Is There an Inheritance, Estate, or Succession Tax Not Based on the §2011 Federal Credit?	When Must Payment Be Made?	Are Interests Other Than Outright Ownership Subject to Tax?	Are Broad Deductions for Charitable and Marital Transfers, as Well as Administrative Expenses, Allowed?	With Regard to a Domiciliary,* What Property Is Subject to Tax?	With Respect to a Nondomiciliary,* What Property Is Subject to Tax?
Nebraska	Yes. (§77-2004) For the rate, see Table 14.07. The tax is payable to the county of residence except for (i) real property situated in another county or (ii) personal property listed and assessed in another county. (§77-2014(2)(a)) If a nonresident decedent is involved, then the tax is based on situs as in (i) and (ii) above. (§77-2014(2)(b)) The tax assessed against the estate is apportioned among counties based on the foregoing rules using values of the respective properties. (§77-2014(3))	The inheritance tax is due 12 months after the decedent's death. (§77-2010) Interest is charged from date the tax became payable if the tax is not paid within 12 months of death. There is also a monthly penalty of 5% of taxes due, up to a maximum of 25%. (*Id.*)	Yes. (§77-2002)	The inheritance tax does not apply to transfers to the surviving spouse if property is valued at less than $40,000. (§77-2004) Property transferred to the United States or to any state, or any political subdivision of either, is exempt from the inheritance tax. (§77-2007.03) The inheritance tax does not apply to transfers for religious, charitable or educational purposes provided that the recipient is located in Nebraska or in a state with a reciprocal exemption. (§77-2007.04)	All property in the probate estate, as well as retained interests, such as revocable trusts, and joint interests are subject to tax. Transfers in contemplation of death, within 3 years of death, and for which a federal gift tax return was filed, are subject to tax. (§77-2002) (§77-2001)	Same as for a domiciliary, but only with respect to property "within the state." (§77-2001)
Nevada	No.	N/A	N/A	N/A	N/A	N/A
New Hampshire	The tax, Chapter 86, was repealed, effective January 1, 2003.	N/A	N/A	N/A	N/A	N/A

Table 14.01

Freestanding Inheritance, Estate and Succession Tax

	Is There an Inheritance, Estate, or Succession Tax Not Based on the §2011 Federal Credit?	When Must Payment Be Made?	Are Interests Other Than Outright Ownership Subject to Tax?	Are Broad Deductions for Charitable and Marital Transfers, as Well as Administrative Expenses, Allowed?	With Regard to a Domiciliary,* What Property Is Subject to Tax?	With Respect to a Nondomiciliary,* What Property Is Subject to Tax?
New Jersey	Yes, an inheritance tax. (§54:34-1) For the rate, see Table 14.07.	Inheritance taxes are due at the death of the decedent. (§54:35-1) All taxes not paid within eight months thereafter accrue interest at 10% per annum. If the delay is for necessary litigation or other unavoidable cause of delay, 6% per annum. (§54:35-3)	Yes. (§54:34-1)	Yes. (§54:34-4)	The property on which the tax is imposed is real or tangible personal property of the value in the aggregate of $500 or over, whether in trust or not within the state, and all intangible personal property. (§54:34-1)	All real and tangible personal property "within" the state exceeding in the aggregate $500 (§54:34-1), and not specifically exempted by §54:34-4, is taxed according to the beneficiary's relation to the decedent and the value of the property.
New Mexico	No.	N/A	N/A	N/A	N/A	N/A
New York	Yes. (Tax Law §952) There was also an estate tax. Beginning in 2018, there is no estate tax. (§54:38-1(a)(4))	Due on or before date fixed for filing return which is 9 months of death. (Tax Law §§974, 972)	Yes. (Tax Law §955)	Yes. (Tax Law §955(b))	All property except real or tangible personal property sitused outside N.Y. (Tax Law §955)	Real and tangible personal property with situs in N.Y. (Tax Law §960)
North Carolina	No.	N/A	N/A	N/A	N/A	N/A
North Dakota	No.	N/A	N/A	N/A	N/A	N/A

Table 14.01

Freestanding Inheritance, Estate and Succession Tax

	Is There an Inheritance, Estate, or Succession Tax Not Based on the § 2011 Federal Credit?	When Must Payment Be Made?	Are Interests Other Than Outright Ownership Subject to Tax?	Are Broad Deductions for Charitable and Marital Transfers, as Well as Administrative Expenses, Allowed?	With Regard to a Domiciliary,* What Property Is Subject to Tax?	With Respect to a Nondomiciliary,* What Property Is Subject to Tax?
Ohio	Tax repealed for those dying on or after Jan. 1, 2013, part of the Budget Bill, H.B. 153.	N/A	N/A	N/A	N/A	The tax is computed by calculating the tax as if the decedent were a domiciliary of Ohio with all his property located in the state and then multiplying the tax by a fraction the numerator of which is the property taxable by Ohio in the case of a nondomiciliary and the denominator of which is the worldwide gross estate. (§ 5731.19)
Oklahoma	No. Repealed by Laws 2006, 2d Ex. Sess., Ch. 42, § 6, effective Jan. 1, 2010.	N/A	N/A	N/A	N/A	N/A

Table 14.01
Freestanding Inheritance, Estate and Succession Tax

	Is There an Inheritance, Estate, or Succession Tax Not Based on the §2011 Federal Credit?	When Must Payment Be Made?	Are Interests Other Than Outright Ownership Subject to Tax?	Are Broad Deductions for Charitable and Marital Transfers, as Well as Administrative Expenses, Allowed?	With Regard to a Domiciliary,* What Property Is Subject to Tax?	With Respect to a Nondomiciliary,* What Property Is Subject to Tax?
Oregon	Yes. (§118.010) For the rate, see Table 14.07.	Accrues upon death. Payable when federal and estate tax is due, or if no federal estate tax return, then 9 months after death. (§118.100)	Yes, the starting point is the federal taxable estate. (§118.010(3))	Yes. Oregon also provides a deduction for special marital property (§118.010(3)(b)(A)), which is in a trust or other property interest whereby the surviving spouse alone is entitled to a distribution or to have accumulated for his or her benefit, principal or income. No power can be exercised during the surviving spouse's lifetime for the benefit of any other person. The executor must elect this deduction. (§§118.013, 118.016) The deduction is independent of a federal estate tax marital deduction.	Federal taxable estate with changes. (§118.010(3))	Yes, any interest in real property and tangible personal property in Oregon. (§118.010(6))

Table 14.01

Freestanding Inheritance, Estate and Succession Tax

	Is There an Inheritance, Estate, or Succession Tax Not Based on the §2011 Federal Credit?	When Must Payment Be Made?	Are Interests Other Than Outright Ownership Subject to Tax?	Are Broad Deductions for Charitable and Marital Transfers, as Well as Administrative Expenses, Allowed?	With Regard to a Domiciliary,* What Property Is Subject to Tax?	With Respect to a Nondomiciliary,* What Property Is Subject to Tax?
Pennsylvania	Yes. (72 §9116) For the rate, see Table 14.07.	The inheritance tax is due at the date of the decedent's death and is delinquent if not paid after nine months. There is a 5% discount if paid within three months of the death. (72 §9142)	Yes. (72 §9107)	Yes. (72 §9111 et seq.)	All real and tangible personal property with a situs in Pennsylvania, as well as intangible personal property. All real and tangible personal property with a situs outside Pennsylvania is taxed if the decedent had contracted to sell it and the state of situs of the property does not subject it to death tax. (72 §9102, definition of "Property" or "Estate")	The tax is computed upon the value of real property and tangible personal property located in Pennsylvania, in excess of unpaid property taxes assessed on the property and any indebtedness for which it is liened, mortgaged, or pledged. (72 §§9116(b)(2); 9102)
Rhode Island	No.	N/A	N/A	N/A	N/A	N/A
South Carolina	No.	N/A	N/A	N/A	N/A	N/A

Table 14.01

Freestanding Inheritance, Estate and Succession Tax

	Is There an Inheritance, Estate, or Succession Tax Not Based on the § 2011 Federal Credit?	When Must Payment Be Made?	Are Interests Other Than Outright Ownership Subject to Tax?	Are Broad Deductions for Charitable and Marital Transfers, as Well as Administrative Expenses, Allowed?	With Regard to a Domiciliary,* What Property Is Subject to Tax?	With Respect to a Nondomiciliary,* What Property Is Subject to Tax?
South Dakota	No. Art. XI, § 15 of the South Dakota Constitution provides that "No tax may be levied on any inheritance, and the legislature may not enact any law imposing such a tax. The effective date of this Section is July 1, 2001." The former Inheritance Tax was abolished by Amendment C, voted on by the public November 7, 2000. There was also an estate tax on the books. However, it was based on the federal credit for state death taxes, which was abolished. Therefore, there was also no estate tax imposed. Both the inheritance and estate taxes were officially repealed by Ch. 59 (H.B. 1057),	N/A	N/A	N/A	N/A	N/A

Table 14.01

Freestanding Inheritance, Estate and Succession Tax

	Is There an Inheritance, Estate, or Succession Tax Not Based on the § 2011 Federal Credit?	When Must Payment Be Made?	Are Interests Other Than Outright Ownership Subject to Tax?	Are Broad Deductions for Charitable and Marital Transfers, as Well as Administrative Expenses, Allowed?	With Regard to a Domiciliary,* What Property Is Subject to Tax?	With Respect to a Nondomiciliary,* What Property Is Subject to Tax?
	approved February 2, 2014.					
Tennessee	No. Repealed eff. 2016. (§ 67-8-314(b))	N/A	N/A	N/A	N/A	N/A
Texas	No. (Repealed effective September, 1 2015 by S.B. 752 Ch. 161, § 1).	N/A	N/A	N/A	N/A	N/A
Utah	No.	N/A	N/A	N/A	N/A	N/A
Vermont	No.	N/A	N/A	N/A	N/A	N/A
Virginia	No. However, there is a minor tax on the probate of wills and grant of administration. See Table 14.07 and § 58.1-1712.	N/A	N/A	N/A	N/A	N/A

Table 14.01

Freestanding Inheritance, Estate and Succession Tax

	Is There an Inheritance, Estate, or Succession Tax Not Based on the §2011 Federal Credit?	When Must Payment Be Made?	Are Interests Other Than Outright Ownership Subject to Tax?	Are Broad Deductions for Charitable and Marital Transfers, as Well as Administrative Expenses, Allowed?	With Regard to a Domiciliary,* What Property Is Subject to Tax?	With Respect to a Nondomiciliary,* What Property Is Subject to Tax?
Washington	Yes, with respect to decedents dying on or after May 17, 2005. (§83.100.040) For the rate, see Table 14.07.	On or before the date Washington return is required. (§§83.100.050, 83.100.060)	Yes, just as under federal tax law determination of the gross estate. (§83.100.020(5))	Yes, closely resembles the federal taxable estate. Instead of a unified credit, there is a deduction of $2,000,000 in 2014, adjusted for inflation thereafter. In 2018, the exemption is $2,193,000. (Washington Department of Revenue Estate Tax Tables) (§83.100.020(1)(a)(iii)) In addition, the deduction for state death taxes under IRC §2058 is not taken into account. (§83.100.020(16)) The election of the marital deduction for qualified terminable interest property is partially independent from the federal election. The Department of Revenue may provide for a separate election if the election is made	Every transfer of property located in Washington is subject to tax. This includes any intangible property of a resident, wherever located. (§83.100.040(1))	Property located in Washington is subject to tax. (§83.100.040)

Table 14.01

Freestanding Inheritance, Estate and Succession Tax

on the federal return or if no return is required to be filed. (§83.100.047(1)) In fact, the Department of Revenue has so provided on the instructions to the state return. The situation in which an election on a federal return is not made is not specifically mentioned. (§83.100.020(14))

	Is There an Inheritance, Estate, or Succession Tax Not Based on the §2011 Federal Credit?	When Must Payment Be Made?	Are Interests Other Than Outright Ownership Subject to Tax?	Are Broad Deductions for Charitable and Marital Transfers, as Well as Administrative Expenses, Allowed?	With Regard to a Domiciliary,* What Property Is Subject to Tax?	With Respect to a Nondomiciliary,* What Property Is Subject to Tax?
West Virginia	No.	N/A	N/A	N/A	N/A	N/A
Wisconsin	No.	N/A	N/A	N/A	N/A	N/A
Wyoming	No.	N/A	N/A	N/A	N/A	N/A

* The terms domiciliary and nondomiciliary are used herein. Many statutes use the terms "resident" or "nonresident." However, the case law makes clear "domiciliary" and "nondomiciliary" are intended. Still, caution is advised.

Table 14.02
Estate Tax

	Is There an Estate Tax?	When Must Payment of Tax Be Made?	In the Case of an Estate Tax, How Is It Computed for a Domiciliary?	In the Case of an Estate Tax, How Is It Computed for a Nondomiciliary, U.S. Resident?
Alabama	Yes. (§ 40-15-2)	Estate tax must be paid on or before nine months after the decedent's death (§§ 40-15-4, 40-15-7(g)) (same for nondomiciliaries).	The tax equals the full amount of state tax permissible as a credit or deduction in computing the federal estate tax. (§ 40-15-2) The tax is the proportion that the value of the estate within or subject to the jurisdiction of Alabama bears to the value of the gross estate. (§ 40-15-17) With the repeal of the federal credit, no tax is currently imposed.	The tax is imposed on real property or tangible personal property "located" in Alabama and other items "lawfully subject to the imposition of an estate tax by the state of Alabama." (§ 40-15-7(a)) It is also imposed on real property and tangible personal property in Alabama or such property transferred in contemplation of death or, e.g., held in trust and intended to pass in possession or enjoyment at or after the death are taxed. (§ 40-15-7(h)) Moneys, credits, securities, and other intangible personal property in Alabama, but not employed by the owner in carrying on a business in the state are deemed located at the domicile of the owner. If held in trust, they shall not be deemed to be located in Alabama simply because the owner was domiciled in the state, except if no other state subjects this property to death taxation. (§ 40-15-8) The tax due is the proportion of the federal estate tax available as a credit or deduction as would be leviable upon an estate of similar taxable net value, less the proportion of any exemption to which the estate is entitled, which the actual value

Table 14.02
Estate Tax

Is There an Estate Tax?	When Must Payment of Tax Be Made?	In the Case of an Estate Tax, How Is It Computed for a Domiciliary?	In the Case of an Estate Tax, How Is It Computed for a Nondomiciliary, U.S. Resident?
			of the real estate and tangible personal property located in Alabama bears to the actual value of the gross estate wherever situated. (§40-15-7(b)) With the repeal of the federal credit, no tax is currently imposed.

Table 14.02
Estate Tax

	Is There an Estate Tax?	When Must Payment of Tax Be Made?	In the Case of an Estate Tax, How Is It Computed for a Domiciliary?	In the Case of an Estate Tax, How Is It Computed for a Nondomiciliary, U.S. Resident?
Alaska	Yes. (§ 43.31.011)	The tax is payable 15 months after decedent's death. (§ 43.31.141)	The tax is the amount of the federal estate tax credit for state death taxes actually paid to states reduced by the smaller of (1) the amount of the credit allocable to those "constitutional" estate, inheritance, legacy and succession taxes actually paid to other states; or (2) with respect to the property located in another state that is owned by the decedent or subject to tax, the portion of the credit allocated to that state based on the proportion that the value of the property taxed by the state bears to the value of the total gross estate. (§ 43.31.011) With the repeal of the federal credit, no tax is currently imposed.	The tax is the amount of the credit allowable under the federal estate tax laws for state death taxes actually paid to the states, as the value of Alaska real and tangible personal property, intangible personal property with a business situs in Alaska, and the securities and obligations of corporations organized under Alaska's laws in Alaska bears to the entire gross estate wherever situated. (§ 43.31.021) In the case of a nonresident *alien*, the property included is real, tangible personal, and "intangible personal property physically present" in Alaska. (§ 43.31.031(a)) Stock of an Alaska corporation is deemed physically present in Alaska, but life insurance proceeds and money on deposit with a bank with respect to a nonresident alien are not deemed physically present in Alaska. (§ 43.31.031(b)) The tax equals the proportion of the state death tax credit "actually paid to the several states" as the value of the aforesaid property taxable in Alaska bears to the value of the estate taxable by the U.S. wherever situated. (§ 43.31.031(a)) With the repeal of

Table 14.02
Estate Tax

	Is There an Estate Tax?	When Must Payment of Tax Be Made?	In the Case of an Estate Tax, How Is It Computed for a Domiciliary?	In the Case of an Estate Tax, How Is It Computed for a Nondomiciliary, U.S. Resident?
				the federal credit, no tax is currently imposed.
Arizona	No. Repealed by Laws 2006, ch. 262, §3, eff. Sept. 21, 2006.	N/A	N/A	N/A
Arkansas	No. (§26-59-103)	N/A	N/A	N/A
California	Yes. (Rev. & Tax. §13302) However, the tax paid to California and at the federal level cannot exceed the death tax liability to the U.S. if this section were not in effect. (*Id.*)	The tax is due at the date of the decedent's death and is delinquent if not paid within nine months of the death. (Rev. & Tax. §§13531–13532)	The tax is the maximum allowable amount of the federal tax credit for state death taxes allocable to California situs property. This is determined by multiplying the credit by the percentage that the gross value of the property located in California bears to the gross value of the entire estate subject to the federal estate tax. (Rev. & Tax. §§13302–13304) With the repeal of the federal credit, no tax is currently imposed.	Same as for a domiciliary. (Rev. & Tax. §§13302–13304) With the repeal of the federal credit for state death taxes, no tax is currently imposed.

Table 14.02
Estate Tax

	Is There an Estate Tax?	When Must Payment of Tax Be Made?	In the Case of an Estate Tax, How Is It Computed for a Domiciliary?	In the Case of an Estate Tax, How Is It Computed for a Nondomiciliary, U.S. Resident?
Colorado	Yes. (§ 39-23.5-103)	The estate tax must be paid at the time for filing the federal estate tax return. (§§ 39-23.5-108(1), 39-23.5-107(1)	The tax is the amount of the federal credit for state death taxes. (§ 39-23.5-103(1)) The Colorado estate tax is reduced by the lesser of (1) the amount of the death tax paid to the other state which is allowed as a credit against the federal estate tax or (2) the amount which is determined by multiplying the federal credit by a fraction with the numerator equal to the value of the gross estate less the value of the property located in Colorado and with the denominator equal to the value of the gross estate. (§ 39-23.5-103(2)) Property of a domiciliary includes real property held in trust or otherwise that is not situated in another state; tangible personal property with an actual situs in Colorado; and all intangible personal property where physically located or wherever the banks or debtors are located or domiciled; except that real property in a personal trust shall not be taxed if it has a situs in another state. (§ 39-23.5-103(3)) With the repeal of the federal credit, no tax is currently imposed.	The tax is the amount determined by multiplying the federal credit for state death taxes by a fraction, with the numerator equal to the value of the property located in Colorado which is included in the gross estate and with the denominator equal to the value of the gross estate for purposes of the federal estate tax. (§ 39-23.5-104(2)) Property of a nondomiciliary that is located in Colorado includes real property situated in Colorado held in trust, and tangible property in the state, but intangibles that have acquired an actual or business situs in this state are not taxable. (§ 39-23.5-104(3)) With the repeal of the federal credit, no tax is currently imposed.

Table 14.02
Estate Tax

	Is There an Estate Tax?	When Must Payment of Tax Be Made?	In the Case of an Estate Tax, How Is It Computed for a Domiciliary?	In the Case of an Estate Tax, How Is It Computed for a Nondomiciliary, U.S. Resident?
Connecticut	Yes. (§ 12-391)	The tax becomes due at the date of the decedent's death and is delinquent if not paid within six months of death. (§ 12-392(a)(1))	The tax is imposed on the Connecticut taxable estate determined as under the federal estate tax with this amount taxed under the rates set forth in § 12-391(g). The exemption for 2018 is $2,600,000 (§ 12-391(g)(4)), for 2019 it is $3,600,000 (§ 12-391(g)(5)), and thereafter is equal to the federal exemption amount. (§ 12-391(g)(6)) The Connecticut taxable estate includes taxable gifts since 2005. A credit is allowed for taxes paid on these gifts to the state. (§ § 12-391(c)(1), (d)(1)) See Table 14.07 and § 12-391(g) for the actual rates of tax. Taxable gifts are the same as for federal purposes, but not including transfers of real property and tangible personal property situated outside of the state. (§ 12-643(c)) The amount of tax paid should not exceed $20 million reduced by gift taxes paid by the decedent and spouse with respect to gifts made on or after January 1, 2016 and includable in the decedent's gross estate. (§ 12-391(d)(1)(D))	Property subject to the tax includes real property in the state and tangible personal property having an actual situs in the state. (§ 12-391(e)(2)) The amount of the tax is computed by multiplying the tax determined under the rate schedule in § 12-391(g) by a fraction, the numerator of which is the value of the gross estate over which the state has jurisdiction, and the denominator of which is the value of the gross estate. A credit is allowed for gift tax paid to the state beginning in 2005. (§ 12-391(e)(1)) Taxable gifts are the same as for federal purposes, but only pertain to transfers of real property and tangible personal property situated in the state. (§ 12-643(c)) As for the actual rate of tax, see Table 14.07 and § 12-391(g)) The same taxable rate applies as for domiciliaries. Thus, the exemptions discussed in the prior column also apply. The $20 million cap is reduced to $15 million for 2019 and thereafter. (§ 12-391(d)(1)(E)) However, note that there are probate fees capped at $40,000 for estates as to Connecticut situs property forming part of the gross estate, not just the

Table 14.02
Estate Tax

	Is There an Estate Tax?	When Must Payment of Tax Be Made?	In the Case of an Estate Tax, How Is It Computed for a Domiciliary?	In the Case of an Estate Tax, How Is It Computed for a Nondomiciliary, U.S. Resident?
				probate estate, at $5,615 plus 0.5% over $2,000,000.
Delaware	The tax is repealed effective July 2, 2017 for estates beginning January 1, 2018 (81 Laws 2017, Ch. 52, §1)	N/A	N/A	N/A
District of Columbia	Yes. (§§ 47-3702, 47-3703)	Payment within 10 months of death. (§ 47-3705(a)-(c))	The tax is calculated the same as for federal tax purposes, except there is no deduction as under IRC § 2058. (§ 47-3701(12)(C)) (§ 47-3701(14)) The exemption for 2018 is equal to the basic exclusion amount of IRC § 2010(c)(3)(A) and any cost of living adjustment. The tax is reduced by the proportionate value of the gross estate represented by assets situated outside D.C. (§ 47-702(a-1(2)) There is no provision for portability.	First, the tax is computed the same as for a resident. The tax is then multiplied by the fraction, the numerator of which is the value of the gross estate represented by D.C.-situs property and the denominator of which is the total value of the gross estate. (§ 47-3703(b-1))

Table 14.02
Estate Tax

	Is There an Estate Tax?	When Must Payment of Tax Be Made?	In the Case of an Estate Tax, How Is It Computed for a Domiciliary?	In the Case of an Estate Tax, How Is It Computed for a Nondomiciliary, U.S. Resident?
Florida	Yes. (§ 198.02)	Payment of the estate tax must be made at the time for filing the federal estate tax return. (§ 198.15) A filing is required even if there is no Florida tax liability whenever a federal estate tax return is required to be filed. Tax Information and Publication, No. 06C03-01, Fla. Dep't Rev., Feb. 15, 2006. There is a 10% penalty for any unpaid tax if the failure is for not more than 30 days, or 20% if for more than 30 days. (§ 198.15(2))	The tax is the amount of the federal credit. (§ 198.02) The tax is the amount by which the federal credit exceeds the aggregate amount of all constitutionally valid death taxes actually paid to other states in connection with the decedent's estate. (§ 198.02) With the repeal of the federal credit, no tax is currently imposed.	The tax is imposed on "every person who at the time of death was not a resident of this state but was a resident of the United States. . . ." The tax is the sum equal to the proportion of the amount of the federal credit, as the value of the real and tangible personal property with a situs in Florida, the intangible personal property having a business situs in the state, and the securities and obligations of corporations organized under Florida law bears to the value of the gross estate. (§ 198.03) In the case of a nonresident alien, the denominator of the fraction is the estate taxable by the U.S. wherever situated. Life insurance on a nonresident alien, and deposits in a bank not engaged in a business in the U.S. are not deemed physically situated in Florida. (§ 198.04) With the repeal of the federal credit, no tax is currently imposed.
Georgia	No. (§ 48-12.1.1) Repealed by Laws 2005, Act 31, § 26, effective April 12, 2005 for estates of decedents who died after January 1, 2005. All estate taxes were abolished on or after July 1, 2014. (§ 48-12-1)	N/A	N/A	N/A

Table 14.02
Estate Tax

	Is There an Estate Tax?	When Must Payment of Tax Be Made?	In the Case of an Estate Tax, How Is It Computed for a Domiciliary?	In the Case of an Estate Tax, How Is It Computed for a Nondomiciliary, U.S. Resident?
Hawaii	Yes. (§ 236E-8)	The payment of the estate tax is due at the time that the federal estate tax return or applicable generation-skipping transfer tax return must be filed. Extensions of time for filing either will be followed by Hawaii. (§§ 236D-6 and 236E-9(b))	The federal taxable estate under IRC § 2051 but without regard for the deduction for state death taxes paid under IRC § 2058. (§ 236E-7(1)) There is also an exclusion of 100% of the federal exclusion amount. (§ 236E-6(a)(1)) The tax is imposed on the Hawaii taxable estate taxed under the rates set forth in Table 14.07. (§ 236E-8(b)) If any property of a resident is subject to a death tax imposed by another state, and there is no reciprocal provision by the other state allowing property to be taxed in Hawaii, the amount of tax due will be credited with the lessor of (1) the amount of death tax paid to the other state or (2) an amount equal to multiplying the Hawaii estate tax by a fraction, the numerator equal to the value of the property subject to the death tax imposed by the other state and the denominator equal to the decedent's gross estate. (§ 236E-8(c)) The tax applies to decedents dying after January 25, 2012.	The federal taxable estate under IRC § 2051 but without regard for the deduction for state death taxes paid under § 2058, multiplied by a fraction, the numerator equal to the value of the property in the state and the denominator equal to the federal gross estate. (§ 236E-7(2)) The tax is multiplied by the rates in Table 14.07. (§ 236E-8(b)) There is also an exclusion for an amount equal to the applicable federal exclusion amount multiplied by a fraction the numerator equal to value of property in Hawaii subject to tax, and the denominator equal to the federal gross estate. (§ 236E-6(a)(2)) The tax applies to decedents dying after January 25, 2012.

Table 14.02
Estate Tax

	Is There an Estate Tax?	When Must Payment of Tax Be Made?	In the Case of an Estate Tax, How Is It Computed for a Domiciliary?	In the Case of an Estate Tax, How Is It Computed for a Nondomiciliary, U.S. Resident?
Idaho	Yes. (§ 14-403)	Payment is due on or before the federal estate tax return filing deadline. (§ 14-406(1))	The starting point is the "property of a resident," which includes Idaho real property, tangible personal property with a situs in Idaho, and all intangible personal property owned by the resident, regardless of where it is located. (§ 14-403(3)) The tax is the amount of the federal credit. (§ 14-403(1)) The tax is reduced by the lesser of: (a) the amount of tax paid to the other state or (b) the amount computed by multiplying the federal credit by a fraction with a numerator equal to the value of the property subject to the death tax paid to the other state and with a denominator equal to the value of the gross estate. (§ 14-403(2)) With the repeal of the federal credit, no tax is currently imposed.	The tax is computed by multiplying the federal credit by a fraction with the numerator equal to the value of the property "located in Idaho" and with the denominator equal to the value of the gross estate. (§ 14-404(2)) Property is exempt from tax to the extent that the same types of property of a resident are exempt from taxation under the nondomiciliary's state. (§ 14-404(3)) With the repeal of the federal credit, no tax is currently imposed.

Table 14.02
Estate Tax

	Is There an Estate Tax?	When Must Payment of Tax Be Made?	In the Case of an Estate Tax, How Is It Computed for a Domiciliary?	In the Case of an Estate Tax, How Is It Computed for a Nondomiciliary, U.S. Resident?
Illinois	Yes. See Col. 3.	The payment of the estate tax is due at the same time as the dead line for paying the federal estate tax. (35 ILCS § 405/6(a))	For decedents dying on or after December 31, 2010 the tax is the amount of the federal credit as of December 31, 2001. However, there is an initial $4 million exemption. (35 ILCS § 405/2(b)) The tax is reduced by multiplying the state tax credit with respect to the taxable transfer by the percentage which the gross value of the transferred property not having a tax situs in Illinois bears the gross value of the total transferred property. (35 ILCS § 405/3(c)) Note that there is a marital deduction for qualified terminable interest property independent of any election of the federal deduction under IRC § 2056(b)(7). (35 ILCS § 405/2(b-1))	Same as for a domiciliary. (35 ILCS § 405/3(c)) However, the property subject to tax is Illinois-situs real property and tangible personal property, including such property held in trust. (35 ICLS § 405/5 (a))
Indiana	Repealed, eff. January 1, 2013, by P.L. 205-2013, Sec. 115.			
Iowa	Repealed, eff. July 1, 2014, by Acts 2014 (85 G.A.) Ch. 1076, H.F. 2435, § 25.			
Kansas	The estate tax was repealed by Laws 2006, ch. 199, § 54.	N/A	N/A	N/A

Table 14.02
Estate Tax

	Is There an Estate Tax?	When Must Payment of Tax Be Made?	In the Case of an Estate Tax, How Is It Computed for a Domiciliary?	In the Case of an Estate Tax, How Is It Computed for a Nondomiciliary, U.S. Resident?
Kentucky	Yes. (§ 140.130)	The estate tax is due at death and is delinquent if not paid within 18 months. There is a discount of 5% if the taxes are paid within nine months. (§ 140.210(1))	The tax is computed by multiplying the federal credit for state death taxes by the ratio that the portion of the net estate over which Kentucky has jurisdiction bears to the total net estate. The total amount of inheritance taxes paid, less any discount taken, is credited against the estate tax. (§ 140.130) With the repeal of the federal credit, no tax is currently imposed.	Same as for a domiciliary. (§ 140.130(2)) With the repeal of the federal credit, no tax is currently imposed.
Louisiana	Yes. (§ 47:2431)	Estate taxes must be paid prior to the filing of the federal estate tax return or nine months after the death of the decedent, whichever comes first. (§ 47:2432(B))	Louisiana does not provide for the accommodation of other states. The maximum amount of the credit for the state death taxes must be paid to the state. (§ 47:2432) The tax is not explicitly limited as to individuals or property and is, thus, apparently, limited only by federal constitutional constraints. With the repeal of the federal credit, no tax is currently imposed.	Same as for domiciliary to the extent Louisiana has jurisdiction over some of estate property. (§ 47:2432(A)) With the repeal of the federal credit, no tax is currently imposed.

Table 14.02
Estate Tax

	Is There an Estate Tax?	When Must Payment of Tax Be Made?	In the Case of an Estate Tax, How Is It Computed for a Domiciliary?	In the Case of an Estate Tax, How Is It Computed for a Nondomiciliary, U.S. Resident?
Maine	Yes. (36 §§ 4101 and 4103)	9 months after date of death. (36 § 4107)	The tax is imposed on "Maine taxable estate," (36 § 4103(1)) which is essentially the federal taxable estate, decreased by Maine QTIP, increased by Maine elective property, and increased by all taxable gifts within one year of death. (36 § 4102(7)) The Main exclusion amount is equal to the federal basic exclusion for the year pursuant to IRC § 2010(c)(3). (36 § 4102(5)) To the extent that there is a tax, the amount is multiplied by a fraction, the numerator of which is the value of that portion of the adjusted federal gross estate that consists of real and tangible property in Maine and all intangible personal property and the denominator of which is the value of the adjusted federal gross estate. (36 § 4103(1)) The adjusted federal gross estate is the federal gross estate modified by Maine QTIP, Maine elective property (basically the surviving spouse's qualified income interest under a QTIP trust), and taxable gifts made within one year before death. (36 § 4103(2) provides a credit for taxes actually paid to another jurisdiction that is a state, D.C., a U.S. possession or	The amount of tax computed under 36 § 4103 (resident) on the Maine taxable estate is multiplied by the ratio of the value of the portion of the adjusted federal gross estate consisting of real and tangible personal property located in Maine to the value of the adjusted federal gross estate as defined in 36 § 4102(1). (36 § 4104) See prior column for the computation of the tax.

Table 14.02
Estate Tax

Is There an Estate Tax?	When Must Payment of Tax Be Made?	In the Case of an Estate Tax, How Is It Computed for a Domiciliary?	In the Case of an Estate Tax, How Is It Computed for a Nondomiciliary, U.S. Resident?
		territory or any political subdivision of a foreign country analogous to a U.S. state. The credit is determined by multiplying the tax due by a fraction, the numerator of which is property in the foreign jurisdiction subject to the credit on which tax was actually paid and the denominator of which is the adjusted federal gross estate.	

Table 14.02
Estate Tax

	Is There an Estate Tax?	When Must Payment of Tax Be Made?	In the Case of an Estate Tax, How Is It Computed for a Domiciliary?	In the Case of an Estate Tax, How Is It Computed for a Nondomiciliary, U.S. Resident?
Maryland	Yes. (Tax-Gen. §7-302)	Generally, the payment must be made nine months after the decedent's death. (Tax-Gen. §§ 7-305, 7-306)	The tax is the difference between the inheritance tax and any greater amount of the federal credit allocable to Maryland, which is the amount of the federal state death tax credit reduced by the proportion that the amount of the estate not included in the Maryland estate bears to the amount of the entire estate. (Tax-Gen. §7-304) Notwithstanding a reduction upon repeal of the federal credit, the Maryland estate tax will remain in force without reduction as if there had been no reduction or repeal in the federal credit. (Tax-Gen. §7-309(a)) The federal credit should be determined as in effect on December 31, 2001. (Tax-Gen. §7-309(b)) The federal credit used to determine the Maryland estate tax may not exceed 16% of the amount by which the decedent's taxable estate, as defined under IRC §2051, exceeds, $3,000,000 in 2017, $4,000,000 in 2018, the federal applicable exclusion amount in 2019 and thereafter, but capped at $5,000,000. (Tax-Gen. §7-309(b)(3)(i)(6)) The federal deduction for state death taxes, IRC §2058, is ignored in calculating Maryland estate tax. (Tax-Gen.	Same as for a domiciliary. (Tax-Gen. §7-304) The tax is imposed on the transfer of the Maryland estate of each decedent who was a nonresident whose estate includes any interest in real or tangible personal property located in Maryland. (Tax-Gen. §7-302(2)) A provision indicates that Maryland will tax the out-of-state tangible personal property of a nonresident otherwise being taxed, if its state does not accord a reciprocal benefit to Maryland residents. The provision is meaningless, since there is a federal constitutional prohibition against taxing the out-of-state tangible personal property of a nonresident decedent. (Tax-Gen. §7-303(a))

Table 14.02
Estate Tax

	Is There an Estate Tax?	When Must Payment of Tax Be Made?	In the Case of an Estate Tax, How Is It Computed for a Domiciliary?	In the Case of an Estate Tax, How Is It Computed for a Nondomiciliary, U.S. Resident?
			§7-309(b)(5)(ii)) The Maryland marital deduction election for qualified terminable interest property is independent of the federal election. (Tax-Gen. §7-309(b)(5)) The law provides for portability beginning in 2019. (Tax-Gen. 7-309(b)(i)(6)&(9))	
Massachusetts	Yes. (65C § 2A)	The estate tax is due and payable 9 months from the date of death.	The tax is the amount by which the federal state death tax credit (as in effect on December 31, 2000) exceeds the lesser of (a) the aggregate amount of constitutionally valid estate, inheritance, legacy and succession taxes actually paid to the several states other than Massachusetts or (b) an amount equal to such proportion of such allowable credit as the value of properties taxable by other states bears to the value of the entire federal gross estate wherever situated. (65C § 2A(a)) An independent state election for a marital deduction for qualified terminable interest property can be made. (65C § 3A; Mass. Dep't Rev. Directive 03-2 Issue 1) There is an exemption amount of $1,000,000. (65C§§ 2A, 3)	A tax is imposed on real and tangible personal property located in Massachusetts. The amount of the tax is the sum equal to the proportion of the federal state death credit (as on effect on December 31, 2000) which the value of Massachusetts real and tangible personal property taxed in Massachusetts which qualifies for such credit bears to the value of the decedent's total federal gross estate. (65C § 2A(b)) 65C § 4;

Table 14.02
Estate Tax

	Is There an Estate Tax?	When Must Payment of Tax Be Made?	In the Case of an Estate Tax, How Is It Computed for a Domiciliary?	In the Case of an Estate Tax, How Is It Computed for a Nondomiciliary, U.S. Resident?
Michigan	Yes. (§ 205.232) Because a taxpayer can choose the maximum allowable federal credit now in effect, zero, the tax has been effectively repealed.	Taxes are due and payable on or before the last day prescribed by law for paying the corresponding federal transfer taxes, pursuant to the federal return, excluding extensions. The department shall extend the time for payment of the tax if the time for paying the federal transfer tax is extended. (§ 205.236)	Tax is equal to the maximum allowable federal credit for state death taxes, IRC § 2011, in effect on January 1, 1998 or, at the option of the personal representative, in effect on the date of the decedent's death. (§ 205.256(g)) The personal representative has the option of choosing the federal credit in effect on January 1, 1998 or at the date of the decedent's death. (§ 205.256(g)) The tax is reduced by the amount of all estate, inheritance, legacy and succession taxes paid to states other than Michigan, which amount is not to exceed an amount equal to the proportionate share of that maximum allowable federal credit that the gross value of all real and tangible personal property located in states other than Michigan bears to the gross value of all property included in the decedent's gross estate wherever located. (§ 205.232(1)) With the repeal of the federal credit, no tax is currently imposed.	Tax is an amount equal to the proportionate share of the maximum allowable federal state death tax credit that the gross value of all real and tangible personal property located in Michigan bears to the gross value of all property included in the decedent's gross estate wherever located. (§ 205.232(2)) The allowable federal credit means the federal credit for state death taxes, IRC § 2011, in effect on January 1, 1998 or, at the option of the personal representative, in effect on the date of the decedent's death. (§ 205.256(g)) With the repeal of the federal credit, no tax is currently imposed.

Table 14.02
Estate Tax

	Is There an Estate Tax?	When Must Payment of Tax Be Made?	In the Case of an Estate Tax, How Is It Computed for a Domiciliary?	In the Case of an Estate Tax, How Is It Computed for a Nondomiciliary, U.S. Resident?
Minnesota	Yes. (§ 291.01)	The tax is due nine months after the decedent's death. (§ 289A.20(Subd.3))	The tax is the proportion of the maximum federal credit, as amended through December 31, 2000, for state death taxes that the "Minnesota gross estate" bears to the value of the federal gross estate. Also, the Minnesota adjusted taxable estate, rather than the federal adjusted taxable estate, is used in determining the maximum credit for state death taxes. (§ 291.03(1)) The Minnesota gross estate is equal to the federal gross estate, but does not include any property with a situs outside Minnesota. (§ 291.005(4)) The Minnesota taxable estate equals the federal taxable estate increased by the deduction for state death taxes under IRC § 2058, the deduction for foreign death taxes allowed under IRC § 2053(d) and the aggregate of taxable gifts as defined in IRC § 2503 made by the decedent within three years of death. (§ 291.016 subd. 2) The taxable estate is also reduced by the exclusion amount, which is $2,400,000 for 2018, $2,700,000 for 2019, and $3,000,000 thereafter and the lesser of (1) the value of qualified small business property under § 291.03 (subd. 9) and qualified farm property under	The tax is the proportion of the federal credit for state death taxes that the "Minnesota gross estate" bears to the value of the federal gross estate. (§ 291.03(1))

Table 14.02
Estate Tax

	Is There an Estate Tax?	When Must Payment of Tax Be Made?	In the Case of an Estate Tax, How Is It Computed for a Domiciliary?	In the Case of an Estate Tax, How Is It Computed for a Nondomiciliary, U.S. Resident?
			§ 291.03 (subd. 10) *or* (2) the result of $5,000,000 less the exclusion amount referenced above. (§ 291.016 subd. (3)) There is an option for a state Q-TIP election independent of the federal election. (§ 291.03 subd. 1d(a))	
Mississippi	Yes. (§ 27-9-5)	Taxes are due nine months after the decedent's death. (§ 27-9-27)	The tax is the maximum amount of state death tax credit or deduction. The tax imposed shall not exceed the aggregate amounts which may be credited against or deducted for federal estate tax. The tax imposed shall be in the proportion that the Mississippi estate bears to the entire estate wherever located. (§ 27-9-5) With the repeal of the federal credit, no tax is currently imposed.	Same as for domiciliary. (§ 27-9-5) With the repeal of the federal credit, no tax is currently imposed.

Table 14.02
Estate Tax

	Is There an Estate Tax?	When Must Payment of Tax Be Made?	In the Case of an Estate Tax, How Is It Computed for a Domiciliary?	In the Case of an Estate Tax, How Is It Computed for a Nondomiciliary, U.S. Resident?
Missouri	Yes. (§145.011)	The estate tax must be paid when the return is filed (i.e., within nine months of the death). (§145.511)	The tax is the amount of the federal state death tax credit, reduced by an amount computed by multiplying the tax by a fraction with the numerator equal to the gross estate excluding all property having a "tax situs" outside of Missouri and with the denominator equal to the value of the gross estate for federal tax purposes. (§§145.011, 145.041) With the repeal of the federal credit, no tax is currently imposed.	Same as for a domiciliary. (§§145.011, 145.041) With the repeal of the federal state death tax credit, no tax is currently imposed.
Montana	Yes. (§72-16-904)	Estate taxes are due 18 months from the death of the decedent. (§72-16-909)	The tax is equal to the maximum federal state death tax credit allowable against the federal estate tax imposed with respect to the portion of the decedent's estate having a taxable situs in Montana. If only a portion of the estate has a tax situs in Montana, the credit is determined by multiplying the federal state death tax credit by the percentage that the value of the estate property having a tax situs in Montana bears to the value of the entire estate. (§72-16-905) With the repeal of the federal credit, no tax is currently imposed.	Same as for domiciliary. (§72-16-905) With the repeal of the federal state death tax credit, no tax is currently imposed.
Nebraska	No. (§77-2101.01)	N/A	N/A	N/A

Table 14.02
Estate Tax

	Is There an Estate Tax?	When Must Payment of Tax Be Made?	In the Case of an Estate Tax, How Is It Computed for a Domiciliary?	In the Case of an Estate Tax, How Is It Computed for a Nondomiciliary, U.S. Resident?
Nevada	Yes. (§375A.100)	The estate tax payment is due at the date of death and is delinquent if not paid within nine months. (§375A.200(3))	The tax is imposed on interests in real and tangible personal property with a situs in Nevada, as well as interests in all intangible personal property. (§375A.100(1)) The tax is the amount of the federal credit allocable to Nevada property. (§375A.100(1)) The allocable portion of the credit is determined by multiplying the federal credit by the percentage that the gross value of the property taxable by Nevada bears to the gross value of the total estate subject to federal estate tax. (§375A.105) With the repeal of the federal credit, no tax is currently imposed.	Same as for domiciliaries, except that the tax is imposed only on interests in Nevada situs real property, tangible personal property, and, in the case of a nonresident of the U.S., interests in intangible personal property in Nevada, including stock of a corporation recognized or having its principal place of business in Nevada or doing a "major part of its business in Nevada" or a federal corporation or national bank with its principal place of its business or a major part of business in Nevada. However, savings accounts in S&Ls, and bank deposits not used in connection with a business conducted or operating in Nevada are excluded. (§375A.100(2)) With the repeal of the federal credit, no tax is currently imposed.

Table 14.02
Estate Tax

	Is There an Estate Tax?	When Must Payment of Tax Be Made?	In the Case of an Estate Tax, How Is It Computed for a Domiciliary?	In the Case of an Estate Tax, How Is It Computed for a Nondomiciliary, U.S. Resident?
New Hampshire	Yes. (§ 87:1)	The estate tax is due at the same time the federal estate tax is payable. (§ 87:2)	Tax equals the maximum federal credit allowable with respect to property subject to New Hampshire state tax. The tax is imposed in every case in which the credit for state death taxes paid is available as a credit on the decedent's federal estate tax return. (§ 87:1) With the repeal of the federal credit, no tax is currently imposed.	Same as for domiciliary. (§ 87:1) With the repeal of the federal credit, no tax is currently imposed.
New Jersey	No.	N/A	N/A	N/A
New Mexico	Yes. (§ 7-7-3(A))	The tax must be paid at the time that the federal return is filed. (§ 7-7-6)	The tax is the amount of the federal credit. (§ 7-7-3(A)) The tax is credited with the lesser of the amount of the death tax paid to another state and credited against the federal estate tax or of the amount determined by multiplying the federal credit by a fraction with the numerator equal to the value of the property subject to the death tax of another state and with the denominator equal to the value of the gross estate for federal tax purposes. (§ 7-7-3(B)) With the repeal of the federal credit, no tax is currently imposed.	The tax is determined by multiplying the federal state death tax credit by the fraction with the numerator equal to the value of the property located in New Mexico and with the denominator equal to the value of the gross estate for federal tax purposes. (§ 7-7-4(B)) With the repeal of the federal credit, no tax is currently imposed.

Table 14.02
Estate Tax

	Is There an Estate Tax?	When Must Payment of Tax Be Made?	In the Case of an Estate Tax, How Is It Computed for a Domiciliary?	In the Case of an Estate Tax, How Is It Computed for a Nondomiciliary, U.S. Resident?
New York	Yes. (Tax § 952)	Estate taxes are due within nine months after the date of death. (Tax §§ 972 & 974)	The tax is calculated on the basis of a rate table derived from the IRC § 2011 Table. (Tax § 952(b); See Table 14.07) The tax is only imposed if the New York taxable estate exceeds the "basic exclusion amount." For 2018, the basic exclusion amount is $5,250,000. Thereafter, the basic exclusion amount is equal to $5 million times 1 plus cost of living adjustment (% by which consumer price index in prior year exceeds 2010 consumer price index). (Tax § 952(c)(2)(A)–(C)) Thus, for 2019, the exclusion will be the pre-2018 amount of $5,490,000, indexed for inflation. The New York taxable estate is arrived at by starting with the federal gross estate, subject to certain adjustments. Thus, the New York gross estate is the federal gross estate reduced by the value of real or tangible personal property with "an actual situs outside New York state." (Tax § 954) The New York gross estate includes gifts made within 3 years of death with some exceptions, such as if the decedent was not a New York resident when the gift was made (Tax § 954(a)(3)). In arriving at the New York taxable estate, federal estate tax deductions	Nonresidents are taxed on the transfer of real and tangible personal property that is located in the state and that would be includible in the decedent's federal estate or New York gross estate if the decedent were a resident of the state. The tax otherwise is generally computed the same as for domiciliaries. However, the "New York gross estate" in the numerator does not include intangible personal property. (Tax § 960) This can lead to a major New York liability as the state death tax credit is phased out since it allows New York to keep taxes equal to the former allowable state death tax credit and determined under the harsher federal tax law as in effect in 1998.

Table 14.02
Estate Tax

Is There an Estate Tax?	When Must Payment of Tax Be Made?	In the Case of an Estate Tax, How Is It Computed for a Domiciliary?	In the Case of an Estate Tax, How Is It Computed for a Nondomiciliary, U.S. Resident?
		are generally allowed, with certain adjustments. With regard to the marital deduction, the election of the Q-TIP marital deduction is only allowed if taken on the federal return. (Tax § 955(c)) However, if no federal return is filed, then a New York return election suffices. (Id.) **The basic exclusion amount is completely lost when the taxable estate exceeds 105% of the basic exclusion amount. (Tax § 952(c)(1)) This is known as the "cliff phase-out."** There is also inclusion in the amount subject to tax any gift made within 3 years of death beginning April 1, 2014, but only if the gift was made when the person was a N.Y. resident. (Tax § 954(a)(3)) A marital deduction is available through June 30, 2019, regarding a noncitizen surviving spouse without the need to use a Qualified Domestic Trust. This only applies, however, if a federal estate tax return is not required for federal estate tax purposes. (Tax § 951(b))	
North Carolina	No. Repealed by S.L. 2013-316 (H.B. 998) § 7(a), effective Jan. 1, 2013	N/A	N/A	N/A

Table 14.02
Estate Tax

	Is There an Estate Tax?	When Must Payment of Tax Be Made?	In the Case of an Estate Tax, How Is It Computed for a Domiciliary?	In the Case of an Estate Tax, How Is It Computed for a Nondomiciliary, U.S. Resident?
North Dakota	Yes. (§57-37.1-02)	The tax is due at the death of the decedent and is late if not paid within 15 months. (§57-37.1-07)	The tax is the amount of the federal credit that is allocable for the portion of the estate having a "taxable situs" in North Dakota, which is determined by multiplying the credit by the percentage that the value of the estate having a "taxable situs" in North Dakota bears to the entire federal gross estate. (§57-37.1-04(1)) Situs rules are set forth in §57-37.1-01(6). In the case of tangible personal property, its situs is where "it was normally kept or located at the time of the decedent's death." For intangible property, it is the state of residence at the time of death. With the repeal of the federal credit, no tax is currently imposed.	Same as for a domiciliary. (§57-37.1-04) With the repeal of the federal credit, no tax is currently imposed.
Ohio	No. Repealed for persons dying on or after Jan. 1, 2013, as part of the Budget Bill, H.B. 153.	N/A	N/A	N/A
Oklahoma	No. Repealed by Laws 2006 2d Ex. Sess., Ch. 42, §6, effective Jan. 1, 2010.	N/A	N/A	N/A

Table 14.02
Estate Tax

	Is There an Estate Tax?	When Must Payment of Tax Be Made?	In the Case of an Estate Tax, How Is It Computed for a Domiciliary?	In the Case of an Estate Tax, How Is It Computed for a Nondomiciliary, U.S. Resident?
Oregon	Yes. (§ 118.010) Although the legislation is described as an act relating to "inheritance tax," it is actually an estate tax. (H.B. 2541, approved June 28, 2011) The law is effective for decedents dying on or after January 1, 2012. (Id. § 30) See Table 14.01.	Tax is due at same time the federal estate tax is payable, or if no federal estate tax return is required, no later than 9 months after death. (§ 118.100(1))	The tax is determined by multiplying the Oregon taxable estate by rates in § 118.010(4). See Table 14.07. The Oregon taxable estate is the federal taxable estate *increased* by (i) the deduction for state death taxes under IRC § 2058 and (ii) if decedent is the surviving spouse, unless included in the federal taxable estate, property for which a deduction for Oregon special marital property was previously allowed (typically a QTIP trust of which the decedent was the beneficiary surviving spouse) or property for which a separate Oregon election under IRC § 2056 or § 2056A was previously allowed, and *decreased* by Oregon special marital property (typically a QTIP trust for benefit of surviving spouse) on the date of the decedent's death and any other applicable exclusions or deductions. (§ 118.010(3)) In the case of a resident, the tax otherwise determined is reduced by multiplying the tax by a ratio, the numerator being real property in Oregon, tangible personal property in Oregon, and all intangible personal property (not subject to death tax by another state or	The tax is determined for a nonresident the same as for a resident. However, the tax imposed is determined by multiplying the initial tax by a ratio, the numerator of which is the sum of real property and tangible personal property in Oregon. The denominator is the total value of the decedent's gross estate. (§ 118.010(6))

Table 14.02
Estate Tax

Is There an Estate Tax?	When Must Payment of Tax Be Made?	In the Case of an Estate Tax, How Is It Computed for a Domiciliary?	In the Case of an Estate Tax, How Is It Computed for a Nondomiciliary, U.S. Resident?
		country). The denominator is the total value of decedent's gross estate, as defined by IRC §2031 (§§ 118.010(5), 118.005(6)) There is a $1,000,000 exemption. (118,010(4))	
Pennsylvania Yes. (72 §9117)	The tax is due nine months after the decedent's death. (72 §9145(c))	If the inheritance tax paid is less than the federal state death tax credit, then an estate tax for the difference is imposed. (72 §9117) The tax is reduced by the greater of: (a) the amount of death taxes actually paid to other states except for any death tax expressly imposed to receive the benefit of the federal credit; or (b) the amount determined by multiplying the federal credit by a fraction with the numerator equal to the value of the real property and tangible personal property located in another state and with the denominator equal to the value of the decedent's gross estate for federal estate tax purposes. (72 §9117(a)) With the repeal of the federal credit, no tax is currently imposed.	The tax is computed by multiplying the maximum federal credit for state death taxes by a fraction with the numerator equal to the value of the real or tangible personal property having a situs in Pennsylvania and with the denominator equal to the value of the gross estate for purposes of the federal estate tax. The tax is reduced by the amount of any inheritance tax paid. (72 §9117(b)) With the repeal of the federal credit, no tax is currently imposed.

Table 14.02
Estate Tax

	Is There an Estate Tax? (§ 44-22-1.1)	When Must Payment of Tax Be Made?	In the Case of an Estate Tax, How Is It Computed for a Domiciliary?	In the Case of an Estate Tax, How Is It Computed for a Nondomiciliary, U.S. Resident?
Rhode Island	Yes. (§ 44-22-1.1)	Taxes due nine months from the death of the decedent. (§ 44-23-16)	The tax is equal to the maximum federal credit for state death taxes allowed by § 2011 as in effect on January 1, 2001. (§ 44-22-1.1(a)(3)). However, the tax only applies if the net taxable estate exceeds $1,500,000 on or after Jan. 1, 2015. The $1,500,000 is reached by a standard $60,000 exemption plus a $64,000 credit, which is the equivalent of a $1,440,000 exemption. (§ 44-22-1.1(a)(4)) Beginning in 2016, the Rhode Island credits are adjusted by changes in the CPI-index for all Urban Consumers (CPI-U). (Id.) Thus, for 2018, the exemption is $1,537,656. (R.I. Department of Revenue, Division of Tax and Advisory for Tax Professionals, dated November 15, 2017) A marital deduction election for qualified terminable interest property is allowed independent of a federal election. (R.I. Div. of Taxation, Rul. Request No. 2003-03) State tax is reduced to an amount determined by multiplying the tax by a fraction whose numerator is the gross estate excluding all property not having a "tax situs" in the state and whose denominator is the gross estate. (§ 44-22-1.1(b))	The provision is the same as for residents, except that nonresidents are not subject to estate tax for intangible personal property. (§ 44-22-1.1)

Table 14.02
Estate Tax

Is There an Estate Tax?	When Must Payment of Tax Be Made?	In the Case of an Estate Tax, How Is It Computed for a Domiciliary?	In the Case of an Estate Tax, How Is It Computed for a Nondomiciliary, U.S. Resident?
		Property has a tax situs in Rhode Island if it is real or tangible personal property with an actual situs in the state or any intangible personal property of a decedent who was a resident. (§ 44-22-1.1(e))	

Table 14.02
Estate Tax

	Is There an Estate Tax?	When Must Payment of Tax Be Made?	In the Case of an Estate Tax, How Is It Computed for a Domiciliary?	In the Case of an Estate Tax, How Is It Computed for a Nondomiciliary, U.S. Resident?
South Carolina	Yes. (§ 12-16-510)	The estate tax is due nine months after the death. (§ 12-16-1110)	The tax is the amount of the federal state death tax credit based on the Internal Revenue Code on December 31, 2015. Since on that same date the Code did not provide for a federal credit for state death taxes, there is no actual tax imposed by South Carolina. (§§ 12-16-510(A); 12-16-20(5); 12-6-40(A)) Assuming there was a tax credit, then if real or tangible property is located out of state, the tax due is credited with the lesser of: (a) the amount of the death tax paid to another state that is credited against the federal tax; or (b) the amount computed by multiplying the credit by a fraction with the numerator equal to the value of the gross estate over which another state has jurisdiction but only to the same extent South Carolina would exert jurisdiction to tax a resident of the other state(s) and with the denominator equal to the value of the gross estate. (§ 12-16-510(B))	The federal state death tax credit is multiplied by a fraction with the numerator equal to the portion of the gross estate over which South Carolina has jurisdiction for estate tax purposes and with the denominator equal to the value of the gross estate. Intangible personal property is not included. (§ 12-16-520)
South Dakota	No. See Table 14.01.	N/A	N/A	N/A

Table 14.02
Estate Tax

	Is There an Estate Tax?	When Must Payment of Tax Be Made?	In the Case of an Estate Tax, How Is It Computed for a Domiciliary?	In the Case of an Estate Tax, How Is It Computed for a Nondomiciliary, U.S. Resident?
Tennessee	Yes. (§ 67-8-204)	Estate taxes are payable at the same time at which the federal estate tax is payable. (§ 67-8-207)	The tax is equal to the amount of the excess of the federal state death tax credit over the aggregate of Tennessee inheritance and other state taxes payable out of the "Tennessee estate." (§ 67-8-204) The Tennessee estate is the property the transfer of which Tennessee has the power to tax. (§ 67-8-202(8)) The estate tax is a pick-up tax and does not yield additional tax because of the repeal of the federal credit. With the repeal of the federal credit, no tax is currently imposed.	Same as for domiciliaries if owned real property situated within the state or tangible personal property having an actual situs in the state. (§§ 67-8-202(2), 67-8-204)
Texas	No. Repealed by S.B. 752, Ch 1161, §1 effective September 1, 2015.	N/A	N/A	N/A

Table 14.02
Estate Tax

	Is There an Estate Tax?	When Must Payment of Tax Be Made?	In the Case of an Estate Tax, How Is It Computed for a Domiciliary?	In the Case of an Estate Tax, How Is It Computed for a Nondomiciliary, U.S. Resident?
Utah	Yes. (§ 59-11-103)	Payment is due on or before the date that the federal return is due, including extensions. (§§ 59-11-106(1), 59-11-105(1))	The tax is imposed on the taxable estate in an amount equal to the federal state death tax credit. If another state is taxing "property of a resident," then the Utah tax is reduced by the lesser of the amount of the death tax paid to another state and credited against federal estate tax or of the amount computed by multiplying the federal credit by a fraction with the numerator equal to the value of the property subject to the death tax of another state and with the denominator equal to the value of the gross estate. (§ 59-11-103) The "property of a resident" includes real property located in the state, tangible personal property having an "actual situs" in the state, and all intangible personal property owned by the resident. (§ 59-11-103(3)) With the repeal of the federal credit, no tax is currently imposed.	The tax is equal to an amount computed by multiplying the federal credit for state death taxes by a fraction, the numerator of which is the value of "property located in this state," and the denominator of which is the value of the gross estate. The "property located in this state" includes (a) real property and interests such as mineral interests, royalties, production payments, leasehold interests, or working interests in minerals; (b)tangible personal property with an actual situs in Utah, including money; (c) intangible personal property having a trade or business situs in Utah; and (d) the securities of a corporation organized in Utah. (§ 59-11-104(3)) With the repeal of the federal credit, no tax is currently imposed.

Table 14.02
Estate Tax

	Is There an Estate Tax?	When Must Payment of Tax Be Made?	In the Case of an Estate Tax, How Is It Computed for a Domiciliary?	In the Case of an Estate Tax, How Is It Computed for a Nondomiciliary, U.S. Resident?
Vermont	Yes. (32 §7442a)	The tax is payable within 9 months of the death of the decedent. (32 §§7447 & 7446)	Initially, the tax is based on the "Vermont estate," which term is not defined by statute. However, the return relies on the federal tentative taxable estate from federal Form 706, p. 1, and 3a. Thus, if a federal Q-TIP deduction is claimed there will also be one at the state level. Probably, a state level deduction can be claimed even though no federal return is actually required to be filed. The tax is the amount of the federal state death tax credit as in effect on January 1, 2001, Table 14.09, that exceeds the lesser of (a) the amount of all constitutionally valid state death taxes actually paid to other states, or (b) a sum equal to the proportion of the federal state death tax credit which the value of the property taxed by other states bears to the value of the decedent's gross estate for federal estate tax purposes. (32 §7442a) The Vermont estate tax, however, cannot exceed the tax that would be imposed under the federal estate tax if the applicable exclusion amount were $2,750,000 and there was no deduction under IRC § 2058 (the modified federal estate tax). (32 §7442a(c)) As a result, until a Vermont taxable estate amounts to	The tax is the amount equal to the proportion of the federal credit for state death taxes that the value of the Vermont real and tangible personal property taxed in Vermont bears to the value of the total gross estate for federal estate tax purposes. (32 §7442a(b))

Table 14.02
Estate Tax

Is There an Estate Tax?	When Must Payment of Tax Be Made?	In the Case of an Estate Tax, How Is It Computed for a Domiciliary?	In the Case of an Estate Tax, How Is It Computed for a Nondomiciliary, U.S. Resident?
		slightly less than $3,400,000, the modified federal estate tax will be the lower applicable amount. Thereafter, the Vermont tax on the estate will apply. Estates above $2,750,000 are taxed at 16% on the excess. (32 §7442a(b)) See Ron R. Morgan, Planning for the Vermont Estate Tax (posted online July 3, 2012).	

Table 14.02
Estate Tax

	Is There an Estate Tax?	When Must Payment of Tax Be Made?	In the Case of an Estate Tax, How Is It Computed for a Domiciliary?	In the Case of an Estate Tax, How Is It Computed for a Nondomiciliary, U.S. Resident?
Virginia	Yes. (§58.1-902) However, there is no tax for estates of decedents dying on or after July 1, 2007, because the tax is based on the repealed IRC §2011 credit for state death taxes. (§58.1-901) See ch. 4, H.B. No. 5019, §§1, 6. (Aug. 28, 2006)	The estate tax is due at the time the federal estate tax return must be filed. (§58.1-905)	The tax is imposed on the taxable estate, which is determined as per IRC §2051. (§58.1-901) However, the "property of a resident" subject to tax is limited to real property in Virginia, tangible personal property with an "actual situs" there, and all intangible property regardless of where it is located. The tax is equal to the amount of the federal state death tax credit. (§58.1-902) If the Virginia resident had real and tangible personal property located outside the state and subject to a death tax for which the IRC §2011 federal credit for state death taxes is allowed, then the tax due will be credited with an amount equal to the lesser of (a) the amount of the death tax paid to another state and credited against the federal credit or (b) the amount computed by multiplying the federal credit by a fraction the numerator of which is equal to the value of the property over which another state has jurisdiction to the same extent to which Virginia would exert jurisdiction on other states' residents and the denominator of which is equal to the value of the gross estate. (§58.1-902(B)) With the	The tax is the amount determined by multiplying the federal credit for state death taxes by a fraction with the numerator equal to the value of the gross estate over which Virginia has jurisdiction and with the denominator equal to the value of the gross estate for federal estate tax purposes. (§58.1-903) The tax does not apply to intangible personal property. (§58.1-903(B))

14,055

Table 14.02
Estate Tax

	Is There an Estate Tax?	When Must Payment of Tax Be Made?	In the Case of an Estate Tax, How Is It Computed for a Domiciliary?	In the Case of an Estate Tax, How Is It Computed for a Nondomiciliary, U.S. Resident?
Washington	Yes. (§ 83.100.040) This is the independent tax identified in Table 14.01 and the rates for which are set forth in Table 14.07.	The payment of the estate tax coincides with the filing requirements for the federal tax return including any extensions for filing, generally within 9 months of decedent's date of death. (§ 83.100.050)	Every transfer of property located in Washington is subject to tax. This includes any intangible property of a resident, wherever located. (§ 83.100.040(1); see also Table 14.01) The taxable estate is determined much like the federal taxable estate. (§ 83.100.020(7)&(15)) The applicable exclusion amount equals $2,000,000, adjusted by increases in the CPI since October 2012. For 2018, it is $2,193,000. (Dep't of Rev. Estate Tax Tables, Filing Thresholds and Exclusion Amounts)	Property located in Washington is subject to tax. (§ 83.100.040(2)(b)) The tax is calculated on the basis of the property located in Washington, which is the numerator of the fraction and the gross estate of the decedent is the denominator of the fraction. (Id.) The fraction is multiplied by the value of the Washington taxable estate, which is the same as the value of the federal taxable estate. (§ 83.100.040(2)(a)) Also, intangibles are presumably not Washington property of a nondomiciliary of Washington. (§ 83.100.040(1))

repeal of the federal credit, no tax is currently imposed.

Table 14.02
Estate Tax

	Is There an Estate Tax?	When Must Payment of Tax Be Made?	In the Case of an Estate Tax, How Is It Computed for a Domiciliary?	In the Case of an Estate Tax, How Is It Computed for a Nondomiciliary, U.S. Resident?
West Virginia	Yes. (§ 11-11-3)	The tax is due on the date of the decedent's death and is delinquent if the tax is unpaid nine months after the payment due date. (§ 11-11-13)	The tax is imposed on the net taxable estate, (§ 11-11-4(a)) which is determined as per IRC § 2051. (§ 11-11-2(10)) However, the "property of a resident" subject to tax is limited to real property in West Virginia, tangible personal property with an "actual situs" there, and all intangible property. (§ 11-11-4(c)) The tax is the amount of the federal credit for state death taxes. (§ 11-11-4(a)) The tax is reduced by the lesser of (a) the amount of the death tax paid to another state and credited against the federal estate tax and the federal generation-skipping tax, and (b) the amount computed by multiplying the federal credit by a fraction the numerator of which is equal to the value of the property over which the other state has jurisdiction "to the same extent to which West Virginia would exert jurisdiction . . . with respect to residents of such other state (or states)," and the denominator of which is equal to the value of the gross estate for federal tax purposes. (§ 11-11-4(b)) With the repeal of the federal credit, no tax is currently imposed.	The tax is computed by multiplying the federal state death tax credit by a fraction with the numerator equal to the value of the property over which West Virginia exerts jurisdiction for purposes of the estate tax and with the denominator equal to the value of the gross estate for purposes of the federal estate tax. The estate tax of a nondomiciliary applies to real and tangible personal property located in West Virginia, but it does not apply to intangible personal property. (§ 11-11-5) With the repeal of the federal credit, no tax is currently imposed.

Table 14.02
Estate Tax

	Is There an Estate Tax?	When Must Payment of Tax Be Made?	In the Case of an Estate Tax, How Is It Computed for a Domiciliary?	In the Case of an Estate Tax, How Is It Computed for a Nondomiciliary, U.S. Resident?
Wisconsin	Yes. (§72.02)	The payment is due nine months after the death. (§72.22)	The tax is equal to the amount of the federal credit. (§72.02) "Federal credit" means, for deaths occurring after December 31, 2007, the federal estate tax credit allowed for state death taxes as computed under the federal estate tax law in effect on the day of the decedent's death. (§72.01(11m)) The tax is imposed on all transfers by the decedent of any property with a "taxable situs" in the state (§72.02), although another provision refers to taxing "any transfer of property" (§72.11(1)(a)). Transfer is simply defined as "the passing of property." (§72.01(21)) If only a portion of the decedent's property is located in Wisconsin, the tax is determined by multiplying the credit by a fraction the numerator of which equals the value of the property with a taxable situs in Wisconsin and the denominator of which equals the value of the estate that qualifies for the federal credit. (§72.02) For persons dying in 2008 and thereafter the reference is to the current federal credit for state death taxes, which has been repealed, so there is no estate tax liability.	Same as for a domiciliary. Property having a "taxable situs" in the case of a nonresident would, presumably, not include intangible personal property. Even if it does, it is not taxed by Wisconsin, if the decedent's state, territory, or district of residence affords a reciprocal exemption to residents of Wisconsin or does not impose a tax on the transfer at death at the time of the death of the decedent. (§72.11(2))

Table 14.02
Estate Tax

	Is There an Estate Tax?	When Must Payment of Tax Be Made?	In the Case of an Estate Tax, How Is It Computed for a Domiciliary?	In the Case of an Estate Tax, How Is It Computed for a Nondomiciliary, U.S. Resident?
Wyoming	Yes. (§39-19-103)	The payment of the tax must be made whenever the federal tax return is due. (§39-19-107(b))	The tax is imposed on the transfer of the "Wyoming gross estate" and equals the maximum federal state death tax credit. The tax is the greater of an amount equal to the credit multiplied by a fraction, the numerator of which is the value of the Wyoming gross estate, and the denominator of which is the federal gross estate, or the actual credit allowable to the Wyoming gross estate. (§39-19-103(b)) The Wyoming gross estate is the value of the federal gross estate, except for real or tangible personal property having an "actual situs" outside Wyoming. (§39-19-101(a)(v)) With the repeal of the federal credit, no tax is currently imposed.	Same as domiciliary, but the Wyoming estate does not include intangible personal property. (§§39-19-101(a)(v), 39-19-103(c)) With the repeal of the federal state death tax credit, no tax is currently imposed.

Table 14.03
Generation-Skipping Transfer Tax

	Is There a Generation-Skipping Transfer Tax?	Is the Generation-Skipping Transfer Tax Limited to the § 2604 Credit?*	When Must Payment of Tax Be Made?	In the Case of a Generation-Skipping Transfer Tax, How Is It Computed for a Domiciliary?*	In the Case of a Generation-Skipping Transfer Tax, How Is It Computed for a Nondomiciliary,*U.S. Resident?
Alabama	Yes. (§ 40-15A-2)	Yes. (§ 40-15A-2)	This tax is due and payable at the same time as the federal tax on generation-skipping transfers. (§ 40-15A-5(b))	It applies to intangible property of a person domiciled in the state as of the date of transfer or death, if the transfer occurs after death, as well as real and tangible personal property in Alabama at the time of the generation-skipping transfer. (§ 40-15A-3) The tax equals the full amount of state tax permissible as a credit in computing any federal generation-skipping transfer tax. (§ 40-15A-2)	Same as for a domiciliary, but limited to real and tangible personal property in the state at the time of the generation-skipping transfer. (§§ 40-15A-3, 40-15A-2)
Alaska	No.	N/A	N/A	N/A	N/A
Arizona	No. (Repealed Laws 2006, ch. 262 § 3, beginning with 2006)	N/A	N/A	N/A	N/A
Arkansas	No.	N/A	N/A	N/A	N/A

Table 14.03

Generation-Skipping Transfer Tax

	Is There a Generation-Skipping Transfer Tax?	Is the Generation-Skipping Transfer Tax Limited to the § 2604 Credit?*	When Must Payment of Tax Be Made?	In the Case of a Generation-Skipping Transfer Tax, How Is It Computed for a Domiciliary?*	In the Case of a Generation-Skipping Transfer Tax, How Is It Computed for a Nondomiciliary,*U.S. Resident?
California	Yes. (Rev. & Tax. § 16710)	Yes. (Rev. & Tax. § 16710)	On or before the same date as the last date for filing the federal generation-skipping transfer return. (Rev. & Tax. § 16752)	The tax is the amount of the federal credit for state generation-skipping transfer taxes. If transferred property is real property located out side of California or personal property having a "business situs" out of the state and is taxable by another state, the tax is reduced by an amount that bears the same ratio to the total federal credit as the value of the property taxable in another state bears to the value of the gross generation-skipping transfer for federal tax purposes. (Rev. & Tax. § 16710)	The tax applies to "generation-skipping transfers." This term is defined as under federal law, but only applies if the original transferor was a resident of California at the date of the original transfer or the property transferred is real or personal property in California. (Rev. & Tax. § 16702)

Table 14.03
Generation-Skipping Transfer Tax

	Is There a Generation-Skipping Transfer Tax?	Is the Generation-Skipping Transfer Tax Limited to the § 2604 Credit?*	When Must Payment of Tax Be Made?	In the Case of a Generation-Skipping Transfer Tax, How Is It Computed for a Domiciliary?*	In the Case of a Generation-Skipping Transfer Tax, How Is It Computed for a Nondomiciliary,*U.S. Resident?
Colorado	Yes. (§ 39-23.5-106)	Yes. (§ 39-23.5-106)	Generation-skipping transfer taxes must be paid at the time for filing the federal generation-skipping transfer return. (§§ 39-23.5-108(1), 39-23.5-107(1))	The tax is the amount of the federal credit multiplied by a fraction with the numerator equal to the value of the property located in Colorado which is included in the generation-skipping transfer and with the denominator equal to the value of the entire generation- skipping transfer for purposes of the federal tax. (§ 39-23.5-106(2)) Property located in Colorado includes real property held in trust or otherwise, tangible personal property in the state, and intangible personal property owned by a trust with its principal place of administration in the state at the time of the generation-skipping transfer. (§ 39-23.5-106(3))	Same as for a domiciliary. (§ 39-23.5-106)

Table 14.03
Generation-Skipping Transfer Tax

	Is There a Generation-Skipping Transfer Tax?	Is the Generation-Skipping Transfer Tax Limited to the § 2604 Credit?*	When Must Payment of Tax Be Made?	In the Case of a Generation-Skipping Transfer Tax, How Is It Computed for a Domiciliary?*	In the Case of a Generation-Skipping Transfer Tax, How Is It Computed for a Nondomiciliary,* U.S. Resident?
Connecticut	Yes. (§ 12-390b)	Yes. (§ 12-390b)	Upon a taxable distribution or termination on the day for filing a return (§ 12-390c(a)(1)), which is due at the time for filing the federal return. (§ 12-390c(b)(1))	The tax equals the federal credit except if real or tangible personal property located out of the state is subject to the tax by another state. In that case, the tax is reduced by the lesser of (a) the taxes paid the other state(s) (allowed as a credit against federal generation-skipping transfer tax), or (b) an amount computed by multiplying the credit by a fraction, the numerator of which is the value of transferred real and tangible personal property over which the other state(s) has jurisdiction to the same extent Connecticut would exert jurisdiction and the denominator of which is the value of all transferred property subject to the generation-skipping transfer tax wherever located. A transferor is a resident if one at the time of the original transfer. (§ 12-390b(a))	A tax is imposed if real or tangible personal property located in the state is the subject of the generation-skipping transfer. To determine the tax, the credit is multiplied by a fraction, the numerator of which is the property located in Connecticut subject to the tax and over which Connecticut has taxing jurisdiction and the denominator of which is the value of all transferred property "subject to generation-skipping transfer taxes, wherever located." (§ 12-390b(b))
Delaware	No.	N/A	N/A	N/A	N/A
District of Columbia	No.	N/A	N/A	N/A	N/A

Table 14.03
Generation-Skipping Transfer Tax

	Is There a Generation-Skipping Transfer Tax?	Is the Generation-Skipping Transfer Tax Limited to the § 2604 Credit?*	When Must Payment of Tax Be Made?	In the Case of a Generation-Skipping Transfer Tax, How Is It Computed for a Domiciliary?*	In the Case of a Generation-Skipping Transfer Tax, How Is It Computed for a Nondomiciliary,*U.S. Resident?
Florida	Yes. (§ 198.021)	Yes. (§ 198.021)	The generation-skipping transfer tax must be paid at the time for filing the federal generation-skipping transfer tax return. (§ 198.155(2) & (3))	The tax is the amount of the federal credit, to the extent that the credit exceeds the aggregate amount of all "constitutionally valid" taxes on the same transfer actually paid to other states. The tax only applies if the original transferor was a resident at the date of the original transfer. (§ 198.021)	The tax applies to real or personal property in the state. The tax is the amount allowable as a federal credit reduced by the amount which bears the same ratio to the federal credit as the value of the generation-skipping transfer property taxable by other states bears to the gross generation-skipping transfer property. (§ 198.031)
Georgia	No.	N/A	N/A	N/A	N/A

Table 14.03

Generation-Skipping Transfer Tax

	Is There a Generation-Skipping Transfer Tax?	Is the Generation-Skipping Transfer Tax Limited to the §2604 Credit?*	When Must Payment of Tax Be Made?	In the Case of a Generation-Skipping Transfer Tax, How Is It Computed for a Domiciliary?*	In the Case of a Generation-Skipping Transfer Tax, How Is It Computed for a Nondomiciliary,*U.S. Resident?
Hawaii	Yes. (§ 236E-17)	No. (§ 236E-17(b))	The generation-skipping transfer tax is due at the time that the federal generation-skipping transfer tax return must be filed, including an extension to file the federal return. (§§ 236E-17(c), 236E-9(c)(1))	The tax applies if the transfer is of "[p]roperty located in [Hawaii]" or of "[p]roperty from a resident trust." (§ 236E-17(a)) The tax is the applicable generation-skipping transfer tax rate multiplied by the taxable amount under IRC Chapter 13 multiplied by a fraction, where the numerator equals the taxable transfer as calculated from § 236E-17(a), and the denominator equals the total amount of taxable transfers subject to the federal generation-skipping tax. (§ 236E-17(b)) If another state taxes the transfer under a state law that does have a reciprocal provision allowing the property to be taxed in Hawaii, the tax is reduced by the leeser of the amount of tax paid to the other state or the amount computed by multiplying the Hawaii generation-skipping transfer tax by a fraction with a numerator equal to the value of the property subject to the tax paid to the other state and with a denominator equal to the value of all property subject to the federal generation-skipping tax. (§ 236E-17(e)) For purposes of the tax, a resident trust is a trust of which is carried on in Hawaii or, if	Same as for a domiciliary. (§ 236E-17)

Table 14.03
Generation-Skipping Transfer Tax

Is There a Generation-Skipping Transfer Tax?	Is the Generation-Skipping Transfer Tax Limited to the § 2604 Credit?*	When Must Payment of Tax Be Made?	In the Case of a Generation-Skipping Transfer Tax, How Is It Computed for a Domiciliary?*	In the Case of a Generation-Skipping Transfer Tax, How Is It Computed for a Nondomiciliary,*U.S. Resident?
			carried on partly outside the state, a trust of which one-half or more of the fiduciaries reside in Hawaii. (§ 236E-2)	
Idaho Yes. (§§ 14-403, 14-404)	Yes. (§§ 14-402-14-404)	The generation-skipping transfer tax is due on or before the date the federal return is due. (§§ 14-406, 14-405)	Although the term "federal credit" is defined as referring to the generation-skipping transfer tax credit allowed under IRC § 2604 (§ 14-402(3)) no provision actually addresses the calculation of the tax, e.g., which property is taken into account when more than one state is imposing the tax. (§ 14-403) As the credit has been repealed, there is no tax actually imposed.	See prior col. (§ 14-404)

Table 14.03
Generation-Skipping Transfer Tax

	Is There a Generation-Skipping Transfer Tax?	Is the Generation-Skipping Transfer Tax Limited to the § 2604 Credit?*	When Must Payment of Tax Be Made?	In the Case of a Generation-Skipping Transfer Tax, How Is It Computed for a Domiciliary?*	In the Case of a Generation-Skipping Transfer Tax, How Is It Computed for a Nondomiciliary,*U.S. Resident?
Illinois	Yes. (35 ILCS § 405/4)	Yes. (35 ILCS § 405/4(b)) For decedents dying on or after January 1, 2011, the tax is the amount of credit as of December 31, 2001. However, the exclusion amount is only $4,000,000 (405/2)	The payment of the generation-skipping transfer tax is due at the same time as the deadline for filing the federal generation-skipping transfer tax return. (35 ILCS §§ 405/6(a), 405/2)	The tax is imposed on every generation-skipping transfer involving "transferred property" having a "tax situs" in Illinois. (35 ILCS § 405/4(a)) The time when the tax situs must exist and whether the original or later generation-skipping "transfer" is being referred to are unclear. The tax is the amount of the federal credit reduced by the lesser of the amount of the federal credit paid to any other state and the amount computed by multiplying the federal credit by the fraction with the numerator equal to the gross value of the transferred property located in another state and with the denominator equal to the gross value of all the transferred property. (35 ILCS § 405/4(b))	Same as for a domiciliary. (35 ILCS § 405/4(b))
Indiana	No. Repealed eff. Jan. 1, 2013 by P.L. 205-2013, sec. 122.				
Iowa	No. Repealed eff. July 1, 2014 by Acts 2014 (85 G.A.) Ch. 1076, H.F. 2435, § 25.				
Kansas	No.	N/A	N/A	N/A	N/A
Kentucky	No.	N/A	N/A	N/A	N/A
Louisiana	No	N/A	N/A	N/A	N/A
Maine	No.	N/A	N/A	N/A	N/A

Table 14.03
Generation-Skipping Transfer Tax

	Is There a Generation-Skipping Transfer Tax?	Is the Generation-Skipping Transfer Tax Limited to the §2604 Credit?*	When Must Payment of Tax Be Made?	In the Case of a Generation-Skipping Transfer Tax, How Is It Computed for a Domiciliary?*	In the Case of a Generation-Skipping Transfer Tax, How Is It Computed for a Nondomiciliary,*U.S. Resident?
Maryland	Yes. (Tax-Gen. §7-402)	Yes. (Tax-Gen. §7-403)	The payment must be made no later than the date for filing the return (Tax-Gen. §7-406), which is the same date as required for filing the federal return. (Tax-Gen. §7-405)	The tax is only imposed on a generation-skipping transfer due to death. The original transferor must have been a resident on the date of the original transfer. If not, the generation-skipping transfer must involve Maryland-situs property. The tax does not apply to a direct skip. (Tax-Gen. §7-402) The tax is the amount of the federal credit. (Tax-Gen. §7-403)	Same as for a domiciliary. (Tax-Gen. §7-403)
Massachusetts	Yes. (65C §4A)	Yes. (65C §4A)	The federal law requirements for payment in the case of a taxable termination or distribution apply. (65C §4A(e))	The tax applies to every generation-skipping transfer if the original transferor was a resident at the time of the original transfer or the property "transferred" is "in" the state. (§65C §4A(a)(1) The tax is the amount allowable as a federal credit for state death taxes under IRC §2604. (65C §4A(b)) Note that the Massachusetts statute mistakenly refers to IRC §2602. Importantly, the tax is currently preserved due to the reference to the credit as in effect on December 31, 1981. (65C §4A(c))	The tax is only applied to transferred real or personal property that is located in the state. The tax is the amount allowable as a federal credit. (65C §4A(2)(c))

Table 14.03
Generation-Skipping Transfer Tax

	Is There a Generation-Skipping Transfer Tax?	Is the Generation-Skipping Transfer Tax Limited to the § 2604 Credit?*	When Must Payment of Tax Be Made?	In the Case of a Generation-Skipping Transfer Tax, How Is It Computed for a Domiciliary?*	In the Case of a Generation-Skipping Transfer Tax, How Is It Computed for a Nondomiciliary,* U.S. Resident?
Michigan	Yes. (§ 205.233)	Yes. (§ 205.233)	Tax is due and payable on or before the last day prescribed by law for paying the corresponding federal transfer tax, pursuant to the federal return, excluding extensions. The department shall extend the time for payment of the tax if the time for paying the federal transfer tax is extended. (§ 205.236)	The tax is equal to the maximum allowable federal credit reduced by the amount of all generation-skipping transfer taxes paid to other states, which amount is not to exceed an amount equal to the proportional share of the maximum allowable federal credit that the gross value of all real and tangible personal property located outside Michigan bears to the gross value of all transferred property wherever located. (§ 205.233(1)) The allowable federal credit means the federal credit for state generation-skipping transfer tax, I.R.C. § 2604, in effect on January 1, 1998, or, at the option of the personal representative, in effect on the date of the decedent's death. (§ 205.256(g)) Note that this optimal date appears to have been addressing the estate tax rather than the generation-skipping transfer tax.	The tax is an amount equal to the proportional share of the maximum allowable federal credit that the gross value of all transferred real and tangible personal property located in Michigan bears to the gross value of all transferred property subject to generation-skipping transfer taxes wherever located. (§ 205.233(2)) The allowable federal credit means the federal credit for state generation-skipping transfer tax, IRC § 2604, in effect on January 1, 1998, or, at the option of the personal representative, in effect on the date of the decedent's death. (§ 205.256(g)) Note that this optimal date appears to have been addressing the estate tax rather than the generation-skipping transfer tax.
Minnesota	No.	N/A	N/A	N/A	N/A
Mississippi	No.	N/A	N/A	N/A	N/A

Table 14.03

Generation-Skipping Transfer Tax

	Is There a Generation-Skipping Transfer Tax?	Is the Generation-Skipping Transfer Tax Limited to the §2604 Credit?*	When Must Payment of Tax Be Made?	In the Case of a Generation-Skipping Transfer Tax, How Is It Computed for a Domiciliary?*	In the Case of a Generation-Skipping Transfer Tax, How Is It Computed for a Nondomiciliary,*U.S. Resident?
Missouri	Yes. (§ 145.995)	Yes. (§ 145.995)	The generation-skipping transfer tax must be paid when the return is filed, which is within 9 months after the death of the decedent, and as provided by the director of revenue. (§§ 145.511, 145.995)	The tax is the amount of the IRC § 2604 credit, reduced by the amount computed by multiplying the tax by a fraction with the numerator equal to the property included in the generation-skipping transfer, excluding all property not having a "tax situs" in Missouri, and with the denominator equal to the value of the property included in the generation-skipping transfer for federal tax purposes. (§§ 145.995, 145.041 & 145.011) In determining the fraction, no deductions shall be considered and the gross estate shall not be reduced by a mortgage or other indebtedness for which the decedent's estate is not liable.	Same as for a domiciliary. (§§ 145.995 & 145.011)
Montana	Yes. (§ 72-16-1002)	Yes. (§ 72-16-1002(1))	The generation-skipping transfer tax must be paid on or before the deadline for filing the federal generation-skipping transfer tax return. (§ 72-16-1003(2))	Tax is imposed on all generation-skipping transfers, other than direct skips, occurring as a result of the decedent's death, in an amount equal to the maximum federal credit. If any of the property transferred is located in another state, the tax is reduced by an amount that bears the same ratio to the federal credit as the value of the property taxed in the other state bears to the value of the gross transfer. (§ 72-16-1002)	Same as for domiciliary. (§ 72-16-1002)

Table 14.03
Generation-Skipping Transfer Tax

	Is There a Generation-Skipping Transfer Tax?	Is the Generation-Skipping Transfer Tax Limited to the § 2604 Credit?*	When Must Payment of Tax Be Made?	In the Case of a Generation-Skipping Transfer Tax, How Is It Computed for a Domiciliary?*	In the Case of a Generation-Skipping Transfer Tax, How Is It Computed for a Nondomiciliary,*U.S. Resident?
Nebraska	No.	N/A	N/A	N/A	N/A
Nevada	Yes. (§ 375B.100)	Yes. (§ 375B.100(1))	The tax is due on or before the date the federal generation-skipping transfer tax is due. (§ 375B.240)	The tax is limited to generation-skipping transfers due to a death other than a direct skip. (§ 375B.100) The tax is the amount determined by multiplying the federal credit by the percentage which the gross value of the transferred property located in Nevada bears to the gross value of the entire property transferred for purposes of the federal generation-skipping tax. (§ 375B.110(2))	Same as for a domiciliary. (§ 375B.110)
New Hampshire	No.	N/A	N/A	N/A	N/A
New Jersey	No.	N/A	N/A	N/A	N/A
New Mexico	No.	N/A	N/A	N/A	N/A
New York	No. Repealed L. 2014, ch.59, pt. 4, § 8, eff. April 1, 2014.	N/A	N/A	N/A	N/A
North Carolina	No. Repealed S.L. 2013-316, § 7(a), eff. Jan. 1, 2013.	N/A	N/A	N/A	N/A
North Dakota	No.	N/A	N/A	N/A	N/A

Table 14.03
Generation-Skipping Transfer Tax

	Is There a Generation-Skipping Transfer Tax?	Is the Generation-Skipping Transfer Tax Limited to the § 2604 Credit?*	When Must Payment of Tax Be Made?	In the Case of a Generation-Skipping Transfer Tax, How Is It Computed for a Domiciliary?*	In the Case of a Generation-Skipping Transfer Tax, How Is It Computed for a Nondomiciliary,*U.S. Resident?
Ohio	Yes. (§ 5731.181)	Yes. (§ 5731.181(B))	The taxes must be paid when the return is due, which is the same time as for federal tax law. (§ 5731.181(C) & (D))	The tax is imposed on property with a situs in Ohio and involving a transfer as a result of the death of an individual. (§ 5731.181(B)) Such property includes real and tangible personal property in the state, intangible personal property employed in carrying on a business in the state, intangible personal property owned by a trust where the trustee resides or has its principal place of business in the state, or if more than one trustee, then the trust's principal place of administration is in Ohio. (*Id.*) The tax is the amount of the federal credit. (*Id.*) If another state imposes a generation-skipping transfer tax, the tax commissioner may enter into a compromise. (§ 5731.181(E))	Same as for a domiciliary. (§ 5731.181)
Oklahoma	No.	N/A	N/A	N/A	N/A
Oregon	No.	N/A	N/A	N/A	N/A
Pennsylvania	No.	N/A	N/A	N/A	N/A

Table 14.03
Generation-Skipping Transfer Tax

	Is There a Generation-Skipping Transfer Tax?	Is the Generation-Skipping Transfer Tax Limited to the § 2604 Credit?*	When Must Payment of Tax Be Made?	In the Case of a Generation-Skipping Transfer Tax, How Is It Computed for a Domiciliary?*	In the Case of a Generation-Skipping Transfer Tax, How Is It Computed for a Nondomiciliary,*U.S. Resident?
Rhode Island	Yes. (§ 44-40-3)	Yes. (§ 44-40-3)	The payment is due at the same time as under the federal tax law. (§ 44-40-13) Provision is only made for a payment of tax in the case of a taxable distribution or termination, although the tax would appear to apply to direct skips as well.	The tax is imposed with regard to "every" generation-skipping transfer. (§ 44-40-3(a)) A generation-skipping transfer is the same as for federal tax purposes, but only if the original transferor was a resident of Rhode Island at the time of the original transfer, "the deemed transferor is a resident at the time of his death," and the property transferred is real or personal property "in" Rhode Island. (§ 44-40-2(4)) However, if another state is taxing real property or personal property in another state, then the Rhode Island tax is reduced by an amount which is determined by multiplying the federal credit by a fraction, the numerator of which is the value of the property taxable in the other state and the denominator of which is the gross generation-skipping transfer. (§ 44-40-3(b))	Based on the definition of "generation-skipping transfer," there would be no tax. See prior column.

Table 14.03
Generation-Skipping Transfer Tax

	Is There a Generation-Skipping Transfer Tax?	Is the Generation-Skipping Transfer Tax Limited to the § 2604 Credit?*	When Must Payment of Tax Be Made?	In the Case of a Generation-Skipping Transfer Tax, How Is It Computed for a Domiciliary?*	In the Case of a Generation-Skipping Transfer Tax, How Is It Computed for a Nondomiciliary,*U.S. Resident?
South Carolina	Yes. (§ 12-16-720)	Yes. (§ 12-16-720)	The tax is due as determined pursuant to federal tax law on a taxable distribution or termination. (§ 12-16-730)	The tax is imposed where the original transferor was a resident of South Carolina at the time of the original transfer or, if not then resident, the tax is imposed with respect to transfers of real and personal property with a situs in South Carolina. In the first case, the tax is the amount that the federal credit exceeds the aggregate amount of all taxes paid to other states on the same transfer. In the second case, the tax is the amount equal to the amount of the federal credit reduced by the amount which bears the same ratio to the federal credit as the value of the transferred property taxable by other states bears to the value of the gross transfer for federal generation-skipping transfer tax purposes. (§ 12-16-720)	The tax is the maximum federal credit for state generation-skipping taxes reduced by the amount which bears the same ratio to the federal credit as the value of the transferred property taxable by other states bears to the value of the gross generation-skipping transfer for purposes of the federal generation-skipping tax. Intangible personal property is not included. (§ 12-16-720)
South Dakota	No. (§ 10-41-65 repealed by 2014 S.D. Laws, Ch. 59 (HB 1057))	N/A	N/A	N/A	N/A

Table 14.03
Generation-Skipping Transfer Tax

	Is There a Generation-Skipping Transfer Tax?	Is the Generation-Skipping Transfer Tax Limited to the § 2604 Credit?*	When Must Payment of Tax Be Made?	In the Case of a Generation-Skipping Transfer Tax, How Is It Computed for a Domiciliary?*	In the Case of a Generation-Skipping Transfer Tax, How Is It Computed for a Nondomiciliary,*U.S. Resident?
Tennessee	Yes. (§ 67-8-603)	Yes. (§ 67-8-603)	The tax must be paid at the time required under the federal law. (§ 67-8-604(a))	Tax is imposed on every generation-skipping transfer in an amount equal to the amount allowable as a credit for state taxes under I.R.C. § 2604. If any of the property transferred is real property located in another state or tangible personal property located in another state which requires the payment of a tax for which credit is received against the federal generation-skipping transfer tax, any tax otherwise due shall be reduced by an amount which bears the same ratio to the total state tax credit allowable for federal generation-skipping transfer tax purposes as the value of such property taxable in such other states bears to the value of the gross generation-skipping transfer for generation-skipping transfer tax purposes. (§ 67-8-603)	Same as for a domiciliary.
Texas	No. Repealed by S.B. 752, Ch 1161, §1 effective September 1, 2015.	N/A	N/A	N/A	N/A
Utah	No.	N/A	N/A	N/A	N/A

Table 14.03

Generation-Skipping Transfer Tax

	Is There a Generation-Skipping Transfer Tax?	Is the Generation-Skipping Transfer Tax Limited to the § 2604 Credit?*	When Must Payment of Tax Be Made?	In the Case of a Generation-Skipping Transfer Tax, How Is It Computed for a Domiciliary?*	In the Case of a Generation-Skipping Transfer Tax, How Is It Computed for a Nondomiciliary,*U.S. Resident?
Vermont	Yes. (32 §7460)	Yes as it was in effect on January 1, 2001. (32 §7460(b))	On or before the last day prescribed for filing the federal return. (32 §7460(d))	The tax is imposed on all transfers subject to the federal generation-skipping transfer tax if the original transferor was a resident at the time of the original transfer. The amount is equal to the amount allowable as a credit for state death taxes under IRC §2604. (32 §7460(b)) The tax is currently preserved due to reference to the credit in effect on January 1, 2001. (32 §7460(b))	Same as in the case of domiciliary, except only to the extent of real or tangible personal property in Vermont. (32 §7460(c))

Table 14.03
Generation-Skipping Transfer Tax

	Is There a Generation-Skipping Transfer Tax?	Is the Generation-Skipping Transfer Tax Limited to the § 2604 Credit?*	When Must Payment of Tax Be Made?	In the Case of a Generation-Skipping Transfer Tax, How Is It Computed for a Domiciliary?*	In the Case of a Generation-Skipping Transfer Tax, How Is It Computed for a Nondomiciliary,* U.S. Resident?
Virginia	Yes. (§ 58.1-936)	Yes. (§ 58.1-936)	The payment of the tax is due when a federal tax would be due for a taxable distribution or taxable termination. (§ 58.1-937(B))	The tax is imposed on all property where the original transferor was a resident of Virginia at the time of the original transfer or, if not, then on the generation-skipping transfer of real or personal property having a situs in Virginia. (§ 58.1-936) In the first case, the tax is the amount that the federal credit exceeds the aggregate amount of all taxes paid to other states on the same transfer. (§ 58.1-936) In the second situation, the tax is the amount equal to the amount of the federal credit reduced by the amount which bears the same ratio to the federal credit as the value of the transferred property taxable by other states bears to the value of the gross transfer for federal generation-skipping transfer tax purposes. (§ 58.1-936)	Same as in the case of domiciliary.
Washington	No. Repealed. (§ 83.100.045), L. 2005, ch. 516, § 17, effective April 22, 2005.	N/A	N/A	N/A	N/A

Table 14.03
Generation-Skipping Transfer Tax

	Is There a Generation-Skipping Transfer Tax?	Is the Generation-Skipping Transfer Tax Limited to the §2604 Credit?*	When Must Payment of Tax Be Made?	In the Case of a Generation-Skipping Transfer Tax, How Is It Computed for a Domiciliary?*	In the Case of a Generation-Skipping Transfer Tax, How Is It Computed for a Nondomiciliary,*U.S. Resident?
West Virginia	No.	N/A	N/A	N/A	N/A
Wisconsin	No.	N/A	N/A	N/A	N/A
Wyoming	No.	N/A	N/A	N/A	N/A

* The federal credit for state generation-skipping transfer taxes terminated at the end of 2004. (Pub.L. No. 107-16, §532(d) (June 7, 2001)) As a result, if a state tax is based on the credit and the state law does not grandfather in the credit, the state generation-skipping transfer tax will no longer be in effect. Unless expressly indicated in this Table, the credit has not been grandfathered.

1. Under §77-2101(2), a generation-skipping transfer tax is imposed on taxable transfers that give rise to federal tax liability. Federal tax law, however, does not have separate categories for transfers or distributions.

2. Note that there is no reference to distributions, as in the case of domiciliaries.

Table 14.04
Gift Tax

	Is There a Gift Tax?	If So, When Is Payment Due?	In the Case of a Gift Tax, How Is It Computed for a Domiciliary?	In the Case of a Gift Tax, How Is It Computed for a Non-domiciliary, U.S. Resident?
Connecticut	Yes. (§ 12-640) For the rate, see Table 15.07.	The tax is payable by April 15 following the close of the calendar year in which the gift was made. (§ 12-647(a))	The tax is imposed on the transfers by gift which are included as taxable gifts for federal gift tax purposes. (§ 12-643(a)) The first $2,000,000 of taxable gifts since Jan. 1, 2005 is not subject to tax. (§ 12-642(a)(5)) The deductions allowed under IRC §§ 2522 to 2524 are available in computing taxable gifts. (§ 12-643(a)) "Connecticut taxable gifts" does not apply to the transfer of real property and tangible personal property having a situs outside the state. (§ 12-641) No reference is made to intangible property in the statute. But see Dept. Rev. Services, Conn. Informational Publication, IP 2004(24) (Sept. 13, 2004), 2004 WL 2294152 at *3, 2004 Conn. Tax LEXIS 43, stating that gifts of intangible property are subject to tax.	Same as for domiciliary. (§ 12-643(a)) However, the "Connecticut taxable gifts" in the case of a non-domiciliary only includes the transfer of real property and tangible personal property situated in the state. (§ 12-643(c)) (see also Dept. Rev. Services, Conn. Informational Publication, IP 2004(24), (Sept. 13, 2004), 2004 WL 2294152, 2004 Conn. Tax LEXIS 43)

Table 14.05

Waivers

	Are Waivers Required for Transfer of Assets or Payment Required Before Transfer?	From Whom Are Waivers Obtained?
Alabama	Only with respect to nonresident decedents. With respect to delivery of property to a foreign legal representative, the tax must first be paid or security posted. (§ 40-15-7(d))	The Department of Revenue. (§ 40-15-7(d))
Alaska	No. However, executor is liable for tax if property is distributed to heirs, next of kin, distributees, legatees, or devisees without having paid or secured the tax due to the state, or obtained the release of the property from the lien of the tax. (§ 43.31.221)	N/A
Arizona	N/A	N/A
Arkansas	No. However, executor is liable for tax if property is distributed to heirs, next of kin, distributees, legatees, or devisees without having paid or secured the tax due to the state, or obtained the release of the property from the lien of the tax. (§ 26-59-117)	N/A
California	No. However, see Rev. & Tax § 13530.	N/A
Colorado	No. (§ 39-23.5-107(5))	N/A
Connecticut	No. However, "[n]o executor, administrator or other person acting in a fiduciary capacity shall be required to transfer, pay over or distribute any property . . . until the amount of such tax or taxes due . . . is paid or, if the apportionment of tax has not been determined, until adequate security is furnished by the transferee for such payment." (§ 12-403)	N/A
Delaware		N/A
District of Columbia	No. However, "[t]he personal representative of every decedent subject to the tax imposed by this chapter *shall*, before distribution of the estate, pay to the mayor any taxes, penalties, and interest due under this chapter." (emphasis added) (§ 47-3713). The personal representative is liable if the estate is distributed before payment. (§ 47-3712) A certificate of payment may be obtained from the Mayor. (§ 47-3710)	The Mayor will certify payment. (§ 47-3710)

Table 14.05
Waivers

	Are Waivers Required for Transfer of Assets or Payment Required Before Transfer?	From Whom Are Waivers Obtained?
Florida	No. However, "[i]f any personal representative shall make distribution either in whole or part of any of the property of an estate to the heirs, next of kin, distributes, legatees, or devisees without having paid or secured the tax due . . . he or she shall become personally liable for the tax so due the state . . ." (§ 198.23)	N/A
Georgia	No.	N/A
Hawaii	A release gives the personal representative the authority to transfer all property composing the decedent's estate. (§ 236E-12) Although this language appears mandatory, the Department of Revenue simply makes a release available as the only way to be certain of no tax liability before distribution of the estate. The personal representative is liable for tax on property distributed before payment. (§ 236E-16(a))	The Department of Taxation. (§ 236E-12)
Idaho	No. However, "[a]ny personal representative who distributes any portion of the property without first paying the tax imposed . . . is personally liable for the tax." (§ 14-410(2)) Also, a receipt, a certificate of transfer, and any other appropriate instrument is issued upon payment of amounts due. (§ 14-409(2))	Tax Commission. (§ 14-409(2))
Illinois	No.	N/A
Indiana	No transfer is permissible until the tax has been paid. (§ 6-4.1-8-2(a)) For the transfer of personal property in possession of another, the Department of State Revenue or the county assessor must give written consent. (§ 6-4.1-8-4(a)) Notice must also be given when money is transferred or life insurance paid, or other types of assets transferred primarily in the case of a resident decedent, without obtaining consent. (§ 6-4.1-8-4) If a person violates the consent or notice requirements of § 6-4.1-8-4, that person is liable for the taxes and is subject to an additional penalty not to exceed $1,000. (§§ 6-4.1-8-7)	Department of State Revenue or in certain instances the county assessor for the county in which the decedent was domiciled may give written consent to the transfer of personal property. (§ 6-4.1-8-4)

Table 14.05
Waivers

	Are Waivers Required for Transfer of Assets or Payment Required Before Transfer?	From Whom Are Waivers Obtained?
Iowa	A foreign personal representative cannot transfer Iowa stock before the tax is paid to the Department of Revenue and Finance. Otherwise, the corporation permitting its stock to be transferred is liable to pay the tax, interest, and costs. (§450.87)	N/A
Kansas	No.	N/A
Kentucky	No.	N/A
Louisiana	Repealed by Acts 2008, No. 822, effective Jan. 1, 2010.	N/A
Maine	No.	N/A
Maryland	Tax must be paid before property is distributed. (Tax-Gen. §7-216(a)(1)) The person distributing the property is liable for the tax until the tax is paid. (Tax-Gen. §7-216(a)(2))	N/A
Massachusetts	No. However, the executor is liable for the tax. (65C §6)	N/A
Michigan	No. The personal representative must obtain a release from the tax lien or pay the tax before distribution to avoid personal liability. (§205.244)	N/A
Minnesota	No. No personal representative shall be required to transfer property unless all taxes are paid. (§291.12 subd. 3)	N/A
Mississippi	No. However, every executor or administrator who pays any debts due by the estate before he satisfies and pays the tax due is personally liable. (§27-9-37)	N/A
Missouri	No.	N/A
Montana	No. However, administrators, executors, trustees, and grantees are liable for the tax with interest until it has been paid. (§72-16-908)	N/A

Table 14.05
Waivers

	Are Waivers Required for Transfer of Assets or Payment Required Before Transfer?	*From Whom Are Waivers Obtained?*
Nebraska	An administrator, executor, or trustee may not deliver or be compelled to deliver any specific legacy or property subject to tax until he has collected the tax thereon. (§77-2011)	N/A
Nevada	No. However, the estate tax must be paid by the personal representative to the extent of assets subject to his or her control. Liability for payment of the tax continues until the tax is paid. (§375A.200(1))	N/A
New Hampshire	No.	N/A
New Jersey	No property owned by the decedent as of the date of death may be transferred without the written consent of the director of the Division of Taxation in the Department of the Treasury. (§54:38-6) No corporation of the state can transfer any of its stock belonging to a resident decedent unless notice of the time of the intended transfer is served upon the State Tax Commissioner at least 10 days prior to the transfer, nor until the Commissioner consents thereto in writing. (§54:35-21) No executor or trustee shall turn over any property until payment of tax. To do so, incurs personal liability. (§54:36-7) A fiduciary is not required to transfer funds or property until tax is paid. (§3B:24-7)	The State Tax Commissioner must consent. (§54:35-21) The State Tax Commissioner shall issue a statement of payment or exemption upon determination of such. (§54:35-9)
New Mexico	The tax must be paid before property is transferred or the transferor becomes liable for the tax. (§7-7-12(A))	N/A
New York	An executor who distributes any asset of the estate prior to payment in full of the tax shall be personally liable. (Tax §975(b))	N/A
North Carolina	No.	N/A
North Dakota	No.	N/A

Table 14.05
Waivers

	Are Waivers Required for Transfer of Assets or Payment Required Before Transfer?	From Whom Are Waivers Obtained?
Ohio	No waivers are required for asset transfers with respect to resident decedents dying on or after Jan. 1, 2013. (§ 5731.39) No waiver is necessary in the case of a nonresident decedent for the transfer of intangible personal property. (§ 5731.40) An administrator, executor, or trustee may not deliver or be compelled to deliver any property, the transfer of which is subject to taxes until the taxes have been collected. If the property is transferred before payment of the tax, the executor will be personally liable. (§ 5731.37(B))	Tax Commissioner. (§ 5731.39(G)(1))
Oklahoma	Title 63, art. 8 was repealed by Laws 2006, 2d Ex. Sess., ch. 42, § 6, effective Jan. 1, 2010.	N/A
Oregon	If a foreign executor, administrator or trustee assigns or transfers any stock in the state standing in the name of the decedent liable for any such tax, the tax shall be paid to the Department of Revenue on or before the transfer thereof. No such transfer is valid until the tax is paid. (§ 118.310)	Oregon Tax Court. (§ 118.410)
Pennsylvania	No. However, no personal representative may be compelled to pay or deliver property to the transferee except upon payment of the tax due. If the property is delivered before payment of the tax, the personal representative will be personally liable. (72 § 9146)	N/A
Rhode Island	No person having possession of property forming a part of the estate of a resident decedent may deliver or transfer the property unless the transferor furnishes the tax administrator with a statement under oath describing the property and the person to whom the property is being delivered. If a statement is not provided, the transferor is liable for the tax. (§ 44-23-35) A permit is required for the transfer of securities of a corporation incorporated in the state or doing business in the state. (§ 44-23-34) With respect to other property, the executor is personally liable until tax is paid. (§ 44-23-9)	Waivers must be obtained from the Tax Administrator for transfers of securities. A statement under oath is required to be submitted for other property. (§ 44-23-35)

Table 14.05
Waivers

	Are Waivers Required for Transfer of Assets or Payment Required Before Transfer?	*From Whom Are Waivers Obtained?*
South Carolina	Upon payment of tax a certificate releasing all property from a tax lien is issued. (§12-16-1510(D)) The tax on transfers of in-state stocks or obligations must be paid "on transfer" by foreign executors, administrators, or trustees. (§12-16-1210) If a personal representative distributes property without having paid the tax, he is personally liable. (§12-16-1150)	Department of Revenue. (§12-16-1510(D))
South Dakota	No. §10-41-65 repealed by 2014 S.D. Laws Ch. 59 (H.B. 1057).	Repealed. See prior col.
Tennessee	Yes, in the case of stocks, bonds, and real estate. (§67-8-417(a)(2)) Property subject to taxation shall not be transferred unless the Commissioner consents in writing. (§67-8-417(e)(1)) The law provides that no part of the property should be distributed until the tax thereon is paid. (§67-8-417(a)(1))	Commissioner of Revenue. (§67-8-417(a)(2) & (e)(1))
Texas	Repealed by S.B. 752, Ch 1161, §3, effective September 1, 2015.	N/A
Utah	No. However, the personal representative is liable for tax on property transferred before payment. (§59-11-111(2))	N/A
Vermont	No. However, the transferor is liable for tax on property transferred before payment. (32 §7452)	N/A
Virginia	No. However, if a personal representative distributes any property without paying or securing payment of the tax thereon, he is personally liable for the tax due. (§58.1-909)	N/A

Table 14.05
Waivers

	Are Waivers Required for Transfer of Assets or Payment Required Before Transfer?	*From Whom Are Waivers Obtained?*
Washington	No. However, a personal representative who distributes any property without first paying, securing another's payment of, or furnishing security for payment of taxes is personally liable for taxes to extent of value of property that comes into personal representative's possession. (§ 83.100.120(1)) Furthermore, any person who has control, custody, or possession of property and delivers any property to the personal representative or legal representative of the decedent outside Washington without first paying, securing another's payment of, or furnishing security for payment of the taxes due is liable for the taxes to the extent of the value delivered. (§ 83.100.120(2)) However, such person is not liable if a release certificate or a release of nonliability certificate is first obtained from the Department of Revenue. (§ 83.100.120(4))	N/A
West Virginia	No. However, any person exercising control who transfers property before payment is liable for the tax. (§ 11-11-20(b))	N/A
Wisconsin	No.	N/A
Wyoming	No. However, the court shall not issue a decree of final distribution until tax is paid. (§ 39-19-107(c)(ii)(B))	N/A

Table 14.06
Conflicts Between States

	Are There Compromise or Arbitration Provisions for Disputes over the Decedent's Domicile?	Is There a Provision for the Reciprocal Exemption of Taxes?
Alabama	No provision.	There is a reciprocal exemption for the intangible personal property of a nonresident if the property is not employed in carrying on business within Alabama and if the property is subject to a death tax in another state. (§ 40-15-8) This is true even if the trustee is domiciled in this state. (*Id.*) These provisions apply only if the decedent's state of residence has similar reciprocal provisions. (§ 40-15-9)
Alaska	There is a general provision for compromise of the tax if the liability of the taxpayer is in doubt. (§ 43.05.070) The Department of Revenue may compromise the tax if there is doubt as to the liability of the tax payer for the collectibility of the tax. (*Id.*) To facilitate estate settlement and distribution, the Department and executor may agree to a compromise amount of tax in full satisfaction of the tax due. (§ 43.31.260).	Personal property of a nonresident, other than tangible personal property located in Alaska, is not taxed if the state of residence of the decedent allowed a reciprocal exemption as to all personal property, except tangible personal property having an actual situs therein and allowed a similar exemption to residents of the state of residence of the decedent. (§ 43.31.410(2))
Arizona	There is a general provision that allows the Department of Revenue to enter into a closing agreement to satisfy a taxpayer's tax liability. (§ 42-1113)	No.
Arkansas	The Director of the Department of Finance and Administration may compromise any controversy relating to a state tax. (§ 26-18-705)	With respect to property of a nonresident located in Arkansas, Arkansas will not tax if the other state has a reciprocal provision regarding Arkansas residents. (§ 26-59-107(c))
California	California has adopted both the Uniform Act on Interstate Compromise of Death Taxes and the Uniform Act on Interstate Arbitration of Death Taxes. (Rev. & Tax. §§ 13801, 13820)	No.
Colorado	Colorado has adopted both the Uniform Act on Interstate Compromise of Death Taxes and the Uniform Act on Interstate and Arbitration of Inheritance Taxes. (§ 39-24-101)	No.

Table 14.06
Conflicts Between States

	Are There Compromise or Arbitration Provisions for Disputes over the Decedent's Domicile?	Is There a Provision for the Reciprocal Exemption of Taxes?
Connecticut	The Commissioner of Revenue Services has the authority to make a written agreement with other taxing authorities to compromise the controversy or submit the controversy to arbitration. (§§ 12-372, 12-395a)	No.
Delaware	Delaware has adopted both the Uniform Act on Interstate Compromise of Death Taxes and the Uniform Act on Interstate Arbitration of Death Taxes. (30 §§ 1703, 1704)	No.
District of Columbia	Yes. The Mayor has the authority to compromise. (§ 47-3704)	No.
Florida	No. Presumption of domiciliary status. Determined solely under Ch. 198 proceeding. (§ 198.015)	There is an exemption from all transfer taxes if the nonresident was a resident of a state that did not tax Floridians, except on tangible personal property in the state, or if there is a reciprocal exemption provision regarding death taxes on personal property, other than tangible personal property with an actual situs in the state and permitted a similar exemption to residents of the state. (§ 198.44)
Georgia	There is a provision allowing for a compromise agreement when a dispute over the collection of taxes exists. (§ 48-2-18.1)	No.
Hawaii	Yes. The department of taxation may enter into an agreement with other taxing authorities that a certain sum be accepted as full payment of the tax, but only to the extent of property with a situs in Hawaii. (§ 236E-24)	No.
Idaho	No provision.	The estate tax exempts the property of a resident taxed by another state if that state has a reciprocal provision allowing the property to be taxed in the state of domicile. (§ 14-403(2)) The estate tax exempts the property of a nonresident to the extent that the decedent's state of residence exempts the same types of property of a resident of Idaho. (§ 14-404(3))

Table 14.06
Conflicts Between States

	Are There Compromise or Arbitration Provisions for Disputes over the Decedent's Domicile?	Is There a Provision for the Reciprocal Exemption of Taxes?
Illinois	The Attorney General may enter into a written compromise agreement with the taxing authorities of another state or states. The person required to file the Illinois state tax return or pay the Illinois tax also has full power and authority to enter into the written compromise agreement with the taxing authorities of another state or states. (35 ILCS §405/17)	No.
Indiana	The Department of State Revenue may, with the approval of the attorney general, enter into a compromise agreement concerning the amount of the inheritance tax. (§6–4.1-12-5(a)) The department may enter into a compromise agreement if there is substantial doubt as to whether the decedent was a resident of Indiana. (§6–4.1-12-5(b)(6))	No.
Iowa	No provision.	
Kansas	No provision.	No. The Kansas reciprocal exemption of death taxes has been repealed effective July 1, 1998.
Kentucky	The Commissioner of the Department of Revenue may enter into a written compromise agreement. (§ 140.285(1))	The intangible personal property of a nonresident decedent held in trust by a Kentucky trustee is exempt from taxation if the decedent's state of residence has a reciprocal provision and if the personal representative presents evidence the tax has been or will be paid in the other state. (§ 140.275(1))
Louisiana	No provision.	The tax was repealed by Acts 2008, No. 822, effective Jan. 1, 2010.
Maine	Maine has adopted both the Uniform Interstate Arbitration of Death Taxes Act and the Uniform Interstate Compromise of Death Taxes Act. (36 §§ 3911, 3981)	Yes. A reciprocal exemption will apply to any state where Maine is given reasonable assurance of the collection of death taxes when a Maine domiciliary's estate is administered in that other state. The statute should be construed to ensure that the state of domicile receives all death taxes due it. (36 §4045)

Table 14.06
Conflicts Between States

	Are There Compromise or Arbitration Provisions for Disputes over the Decedent's Domicile?	*Is There a Provision for the Reciprocal Exemption of Taxes?*
Maryland	Maryland has adopted both the Uniform Act on Interstate Compromise of Death Taxes and the Uniform Act on Interstate Arbitration of Death Taxes. (Tax-Gen. §§ 7-118, 7-115)	The inheritance and estate taxes do not apply to the personal property of a nonresident, except for tangible personal property located in Maryland, if the decedent's state or country of residence does not tax "the receipt of similar personal property of a resident of this State" or has a reciprocal exemption provision "similar to" the Maryland provision. (Tax-Gen. §§ 7-203(f), 7-303)
Massachusetts	Massachusetts has adopted both the Uniform Act on Interstate Arbitration of Death Taxes and the Uniform Interstate Compromise of Death Taxes Act. (65B §§ 1-7)	No.
Michigan	Michigan has adopted both the Uniform Act on Interstate Compromise of Death Taxes and the Uniform Act on Interstate Arbitration of Death Taxes. (§ 205.601, *et seq.*)	There is an exemption from all transfer taxes if the nonresident was a resident of a state that did not tax residents of Michigan, except on tangible personal property in the state, or if there is a reciprocal exemption provision regarding death taxes on personal property, other than tangible personal property with an actual situs in the state and permitted a similar exemption to residents of the state. (§ 205.201(2)(b))
Minnesota	Repealed by Laws 2014, c. 150, art. 3, § 8, par. (c), eff. Mar. 22, 2014.	
Mississippi	The commissioner, with the approval of the attorney general may agree upon the amount of taxes at any time due or to become due. (§ 27-9-41)	There is an exemption from all transfer taxes if the nonresident was a resident of a state that did not tax residents of Mississippi, except on tangible personal property in the state, or if there is a reciprocal exemption provision regarding death taxes on personal property, other than tangible personal property with an actual situs in the state and permitted a similar exemption to residents of the state. (§ 27-9-13)
Missouri	The Director of Revenue may make a written agreement of Compromise with the taxing authorities of another state. (§ 145.201)	No.
Montana	No provision.	No.

Table 14.06
Conflicts Between States

	Are There Compromise or Arbitration Provisions for Disputes over the Decedent's Domicile?	Is There a Provision for the Reciprocal Exemption of Taxes?
Nebraska	Nebraska has adopted both the Uniform Act on Interstate Compromise of Death Taxes and the Uniform Act on Interstate Arbitration of Death Taxes. (§77-3301)	There is an exemption from all transfer taxes if the nonresident was a resident of a state that did not tax residents of Nebraska, except on tangible personal property in the state, or if there is a reciprocal exemption provision regarding death taxes on personal property, other than tangible personal property with an actual situs in the state and permitted a similar exemption to residents of the state. (§77-2007.01)
Nevada	Nevada has adopted both the Uniform Act on Interstate Compromise of Death Taxes and the Uniform Act on Interstate Arbitration of Death Taxes. (§§ 375A.410, 375A.460, see also § 375A.640 for general authority to settle tax disputes)	No.
New Hampshire	The Department of Revenue Administration has the power to enter into written agreements with taxing authorities of other states if there is a conflict over the decedent's domicile. If an agreement cannot be reached, the Department of Revenue Administration can enter arbitration. (§ 90:3)	No.
New Jersey	New Jersey has adopted the Uniform Interstate Compromise of Death Taxes Act. The Director of the Division of Taxation has the power to compromise and enter into agreements with other states claiming the domicile of the decedent. (§ 54:38A-1)	No.
New Mexico	No provision.	The transfer of the personal property of a nonresident is exempt to the extent that the decedent's state of residence exempts the property of New Mexico residents from death taxes. (§7-7-4(D))
New York	New York has adopted the Uniform Interstate Compromise of Death Taxes Act. The Commissioner of Taxation and Finance has the power to enter into written agreements with taxing authorities of other states if there is a conflict over the decedent's domicile. (Tax § 978(a))	Taxes imposed by the state on personal property (except tangible personal property located in the state) are not payable if the transferor is a resident of a state or territory of the United States, the laws of which contain a reciprocal provision under which nonresidents are exempted from death and transfer taxes on all personal property other than tangible personal property located in the state. (Tax § 960-a)

Table 14.06
Conflicts Between States

	Are There Compromise or Arbitration Provisions for Disputes over the Decedent's Domicile?	Is There a Provision for the Reciprocal Exemption of Taxes?
North Carolina	The Secretary of Revenue, with the approval of the Attorney General, has authority to make agreements with the taxing officials of other states or with taxpayers in cases of disputes as to the domicile of the decedent. (§ 105-240.1)	No.
North Dakota	No provision.	No.
Ohio	Yes. The Tax Commissioner, with the permission of the probate court, may enter into a compromise with the taxing authorities of another state claiming that the decedent was domiciled in that state. (§ 5731.35)	Intangible personal property of a nonresident is not taxed if the state of residence of the decedent allowed a reciprocal exemption as to all personal property, except tangible personal property having an actual situs therein and allowed a similar exemption to residents of the state. (§ 5731.34)
Oklahoma	No provision.	Repealed by Laws 2006, 2d Ex. Sess., ch. 42, § 6, effective Jan. 1, 2010.
Oregon	No provision. Prior provision repealed by Laws 2011, c. 526, 529, eff. Sept. 29, 2011.	Intangible personal property of a nonresident is not included in the numerator of the ratio for determining tax liability. (§ 118.010(6))
Pennsylvania	Yes, Pennsylvania has adopted both the Uniform Act on Interstate Compromise of Death Taxes and the Uniform Act on Interstate Arbitration of Death Taxes. (72 §§ 9157, 9158)	No. However intangibles of non-residents are specifically exempt from inheritance tax. (72 § 9111)
Rhode Island	The State Tax Administrator can enter into agreements with other taxing officials claiming the domicile of the decedent. (§ 44-23-29) If an agreement cannot be reached, the taxing administrator can enter into arbitration. (§ 44-23-30)	No.
South Carolina	South Carolina has adopted both the Uniform Act on Interstate Compromise of Death Taxes and the Uniform Act on Interstate Arbitration of Death Taxes. (§§ 12-16-210 through 12-16-320)	No.
South Dakota	No provision.	Repealed by 2014 S.D. Laws Ch. 59 (H.B. 1057)

Table 14.06
Conflicts Between States

	Are There Compromise or Arbitration Provisions for Disputes over the Decedent's Domicile?	Is There a Provision for the Reciprocal Exemption of Taxes?
Tennessee	The Commissioner of Revenue may enter into written agreements with other taxing officials if there is a dispute as to the decedent's domicile. (§ 67-8-503) If no agreement can be reached, the Commissioner of Revenue can appoint a person to a board of arbitration to resolve the dispute. (§ 67-8-504)	No.
Texas	Repealed by S.B. 752, Ch 1161, § 3, effective September 1, 2015.	No.
Utah	No provision.	Transfers of intangible personal property having a situs in the state and of securities of any corporation or entity organized under the laws of the state are exempt from taxation, to the extent that the same types of property of a Utah resident are exempt in the nonresident's state. (§ 59-11-104(4))
Vermont	Vermont has adopted both the Uniform Act on Interstate Compromise of Death Taxes and the Uniform Act on Interstate Arbitration of Death Taxes. (32 §§ 7202, 7102)	No.
Virginia	Virginia has adopted both the Uniform Act on Interstate Compromise of Death Taxes and the Uniform Act on Interstate Arbitration of Death Taxes. (§§ 58.1-922, 58.1-923)	No.
Washington	The department may enter into an agreement in writing with any person relating to the liability of such person in respect of any tax imposed by any of the preceding chapters of this title for any taxable period or periods. (§ 82.32.350)	No. Repealed L. 2005, Ch. 516, § 17 (§ 83.100.040(3)). Effective 5/17/2005.
West Virginia	West Virginia has adopted both the Uniform Act on Interstate Compromise of Death Taxes and the Uniform Act on Interstate Arbitration of Death Taxes. (§§ 11-11A-1, 11-11B-1)	No.
Wisconsin	The Department of Revenue may enter into a written agreement with the taxing authority of another state to settle the dispute before a panel of arbitrators. (§ 72.35(1))	The estate tax does not apply to the intangible personal property of a nonresident if the decedent's state of residence has a reciprocal provision. (§ 72.11(2))
Wyoming	No provision.	No.

Table 14.07
Inheritance, Estate, Succession, Transfer, and Gift Tax Rates
Connecticut

Estate Tax (§ 12-391(g)(3))

Amount of Taxable Estate	Tax Rate
Not over $2,000,000	None
Over $2,000,000 but not over $3,600,000	7.2% of the excess over $2,000,000
Over $3,600,000 but not over $4,100,000	$115,200 plus 7.8% of the excess over $3,600,000
Over $4,100,000 but not over $5,100,000	$154,200 plus 8.4% of the excess over $4,100,000
Over $5,100,000 but not over $6,100,000	$238,200 plus 9.0% of the excess over $5,100,000
Over $6,100,000 but not over $7,100,000	$328,200 plus 9.6% of the excess over $6,100,000
Over $7,100,000 but not over $8,100,000	$424,200 plus 10.2% of the excess over $7,100,000
Over $8,100,000 but not over $9,100,000	$526,200 plus 10.8% of the excess over $8,100,000
Over $9,100,000 but not over $10,100,000	$634,200 plus 11.4% of the excess over $9,100,000
Over $10,100,000	$748,200 plus 12% of the excess over $10,100,000

Table 14.07
Inheritance, Estate, Succession, Transfer, and Gift Tax Rates
Connecticut

Gift Tax (§ 12-642(a)(5))

*Amount of Taxable Gifts**	*Tax Rate*
Not over $2,000,000	None
Over $2,000,000 but not over $3,600,000	7.2% of the excess over $2,000,000
Over $3,600,000 but not over $4,100,000	$115,200 plus 7.8% of the excess over $3,600,000
Over $4,100,000 but not over $5,100,000	$154,200 plus 8.4% of the excess over $4,100,000
Over $5,100,000 but not over $6,100,000	$238,200 plus 9.0% of the excess over $5,100,000
Over $6,100,000 but not over $7,100,000	$328,200 plus 9.6% of the excess over $6,100,000
Over $7,100,000 but not over $8,100,000	$424,200 plus 10.2% of the excess over $7,100,000
Over $8,100,000 but not over $9,100,000	$526,200 plus 10.8% of the excess over $8,100,000
Over $9,100,000 but not over $10,100,000	$634,200 plus 11.4% of the excess over $9,100,000
Over $10,100,000	$748,200 plus 12% of the excess over $10,100,000

* The Connecticut taxable estate includes "the aggregate amount of all Connecticut taxable gifts made by the donor during all calendar years on or after January 1, 2005." A credit is then allowed to the extent of tax previously paid but not in excess of the tax. (§ 12-642(a)(5))

Table 14.07
Inheritance, Estate, Succession, Transfer, and Gift Tax Rates
District of Columbia

Amount of Taxable Estate	Tax Rate
Not over $1,000,000	None
Over $1,000,000 but not over $1,500,000	6.4%
Over $1,500,000 but not over $2,000,000	7.2%
Over $2,000,000 but not over $2,500,000	8% Over $2,500,000 but not over $3,000,000
8.8% Over $3,000,000 but not over $3,500,000	9.6% Over $3,500,000 but not over $4,000,000
10.4% Over $4,000,000 but not over $5,000,000	11.2% Over $5,000,000 but not over $6,000,000
12% Over $6,000,000 but not over $7,000,000	12.8%
Over $7,000,000 but not over $8,000,000	13.6%
Over $8,000,000, but not over $9,000,000	14.4%
Over $9,000,000, but not over $10,000,000	15.2%
Over $10,000,000	16%

Table 14.07
Inheritance, Estate, Succession, Transfer, and Gift Tax Rates
Hawaii

Estate Tax (§ 236E-8)

If the Hawaii net taxable estate is:	The tax shall be:
$1,000,000 or less	10% of Hawaii net taxable estate
Over $1,000,000 but not over $2,000,000	$100,000 plus 11% of amount exceeding $1,000,000
Over $2,000,000 but not over $3,000,000	$210,000 plus 12% of amount exceeding $2,000,000
Over $3,000,000 but not over $4,000,000	$330,000 plus 13% of amount exceeding $3,000,000
Over $4,000,000 but not over $5,000,000	$460,000 plus 14% of amount exceeding $4,000,000
Over $5,000,000	$600,000 plus 15.7% of amount exceeding $5,000,000

Table 14.07
Inheritance, Estate, Succession, Transfer, and Gift Tax Rates
Iowa

Inheritance Tax (§ 450.10)

(1) For transfers to the brother or sister, son-in-law, or daughter-in-law, the tax rate is:

Taxable Property	Tax Rate
$0–12,500	5%
$12,501–25,000	6%
$25,001–75,000	7%
$75,001–100,000	8%
$100,001–150,000	9%
Over $150,000	10%

(2) For transfers to persons not included in subsections 1 and 6, the tax rate is:

Taxable	Tax Rate
$0–50,000	10%
$50,001–100,000	12%
Over $100,000	15%

(3) For transfers to societies, institutions or associations incorporated or organized under the laws of another state, territory, province or country for charitable, educational or religious purposes or to cemetery associations not organized under Iowa laws or to resident trustees for uses outside of Iowa, the tax rate is 10% on the entire amount so transferred. (§ 450.10(3))

(4) For transfers to any firm, corporation or society organized for profit, or fraternal or social organizations which do not qualify for exemption under Sections 170(c) and 2055 of the Internal Revenue Code, the tax rate is 15% on the entire amount so transferred. (§ 450.10(4))

(5) For transfers to persons included under subsection (1), there is a credit applied to the tax imposed on the individual share in an amount equal to the tax imposed by Iowa on the decedent on any property or the proportionate share on property passing to the person taxed, which is identifiable as having been received by the decedent as a share in the estate of another decedent who died within two years prior to the death of the decedent or which is identifiable as having been acquired by the decedent in exchange for property so received. (§ 450.10(5))

(6) For transfers to the surviving spouse, and parents, grandparents, great-grandparents, and other lineal ascendants, children, stepchildren, grandchildren, great-grandchildren, and other lineal descendants (including legally adopted children), there is no tax. (§ § 450.9; 450.10(6))

Table 14.07
Inheritance, Estate, Succession, Transfer, and Gift Tax Rates
Kentucky

Inheritance tax (§ 140.070)

Transfer to Class A Beneficiary	Tax Rate
$0–20,000	2%
$20,001–30,000	3%
$30,001–45,000	4%
$45,001–60,000	5%
$60,001–100,000	6%
$100,001–200,000	7%
$200,001–500,000	8%
Over $500,000	10%

Note: Class A beneficiaries are exempt from tax. (§ 140.080(1)(c)(4))

Class A beneficiary includes decedent's parent, surviving spouse, child by blood, stepchild, child adopted during infancy, child adopted during adulthood who was reared by the decedent during infancy or a grandchild who is the issue of a child by blood, the issue of a stepchild, the issue of a child adopted during adulthood who was reared by the decedent during infancy, the issue of a child adopted during infancy, brother, sister, or brother or sister of the half blood. (§ 140.070(1))

Table 14.07
Inheritance, Estate, Succession, Transfer, and Gift Tax Rates
Kentucky

Transfer to Class B Beneficiary	Tax Rate
$0–10,000	4%
$10,001–20,000	5%
$20,001–30,000	6%
$30,001–45,000	8%
$45,001–60,000	10%
$60,001–100,000	12%
$100,001–200,000	14%
Over $200,000	16%

Class B beneficiary consists of decedent's nephew, niece, or a nephew or niece of the half-blood, daughter-in-law, son-in-law, aunt or uncle, or a great-grandchild who is the grandchild of a child by blood, of a stepchild or of a child adopted during infancy. (§ 140.070(2))

Transfer to Class C Beneficiary	Tax Rate
$0–10,000	6%
$10,001–20,000	8%
$20,001–30,000	10%
$30,001–45,000	12%
$45,001–60,000	14%
Over $60,000	16%

Class C beneficiary includes any educational, religious, or other institutions, societies, or associations, or any cities, towns, or public institutions not exempted by § 140.060, or to any person not included in either Class A or Class B. (§ 140.070(3))

Exemptions: Exemptions are dependent on the class, as follows:

Class A – 100% (§ 140.080(1)(c)(4))

Class B – $1,000 (§ 140.080(1)(d))

Class C – $500 (§ 140.080(1)(e))

Table 14.07
Inheritance, Estate, Succession, Transfer, and Gift Tax Rates
Maine

Taxable Estate (36 § 4103)		
More than	Less than	Tax
$0	Maine Exclusion Amount (MEA)	0
MEA	MEA + $3,000,000	8% on excess over $2,000,000
MEA + $3,000,000	MEA + $6,000,000	$240,000 plus 10% on excess over MEA + $3,000,000
MEA + $6,000,000	—	$540,000 plus 12% on excess over MEA + $6,000,000

Table 14.07
Inheritance, Estate, Succession, Transfer, and Gift Tax Rates
Maryland

Inheritance Tax Rate (Tax-Gen. § 7-204)

Collateral tax rate: The inheritance tax rate is 10% of the "clear value" of the property that passes from a decedent. (Tax-Gen. § 7-204(b)) "Clear value" is fair market value minus expenses (Tax-Gen. § 7-204(a)). A family allowance bars application of the inheritance tax to ancestors of the decedent up to the grandparent generational level, lineal descendants, the spouse of the decedent, or spouse of a child of the decedent, a spouse of a lineal descendant, or a spouse of a lineal descendant of a child of the decedent, a sibling, a parent or child, or a corporation, partnership, or limited liability company, if all the stockholders, partners, or members, consist of the above persons. (Tax-Gen. § 7-203(b)(2)) There is also a $1,000 per person exemption with regard to receipt of property by persons other than those referenced above. (Tax-Gen. § 7-203(g))

Table 14.07
Inheritance, Estate, Succession, Transfer, and Gift Tax Rates
Nebraska

Inheritance Tax (§§ 77-2001–77-2006)

For transfers to any parent, lineal descendant, grandparent, sibling, child or adopted child, lineal descendant legally adopted, person to whom the decedent stood for not less than 10 years prior to death in the acknowledged relation of a parent, or the spouse or surviving spouse of any such persons, married to the decedent at the time of the decendant's death, and persons having any of these relationships to a spouse who is married to the decedent at the time of his death, the tax is 1% of the value of the property received in excess of $40,000. (§§ 77-2004, 77-2005.01)

For transfers to any aunt, uncle, niece or nephew related by blood or adoption, or other lineal descendant of the same, or the spouse or surviving spouse of any such persons, or the same relatives of a former spouse who was married to the decedent at the time of the former spouse's prior death, and persons having any of these relations to a spouse who is married to the decedent at the time of the decedent's death, the tax is 13% of the value of the property received by each person in excess of $15,000. (§§ 77-2005, 77-2005.01)

For all other transfers, the tax is 18% of the clear market value of the beneficial interest in excess of $10,000. (§ 77-2006)

Table 14.07
Inheritance, Estate, Succession, Transfer, and Gift Tax Rates
New Jersey

Inheritance Tax (§ 54:34-2)

No tax is imposed on transfers to spouses after January 1, 1985 or domestic partners (as defined in Section 3 of Pub. L. No. 2003, C. 246, (§ 26:8A-3) effective 180 days after its enactment on January 12, 2004), or transfers to parents, grandparents, children, or grandchildren after July 1, 1988. (§ 54:34-2(a)(1) & (a)(2))

Transfers made after July 1, 1988 to brother, sister, wife, or widow of son of decedent, or husband or widower of a daughter of decedent:

Amount of Transfer	Tax Rate
$0–25,000	0%
$25,001–1,100,000	11%
$1,100,001–1,400,000	13%
$1,400,001–1,700,000	14%
Over $1,700,000	16%

(§ 54:34-2(c)(2))

Transfers to all transferees not listed above:

Amount of Transfer	Tax Rate
$0–700,000	15%
Over $700,000	16%

(§ 54:34-2(d))

Table 14.07
Inheritance, Estate, Succession, Transfer, and Gift Tax Rates
New York

Estate Tax Rates (Tax § 952) (On or after 4-1-14)

If the New York taxable estate is:	The Tax Is:
Not over $500,000	3.06% of taxable estate
Over $500,000 but not over $1,000,000	$15,300 plus 5.0% of excess over $500,000
Over $1,000,000 but not over $1,500,000	$40,300 plus 5.5% of excess over $1,000,000
Over $1,500,000 but not over $2,100,000	$67,800 plus 6.5% of excess over $1,500,000
Over $2,100,000 but not over $2,600,000	$106,800 plus 8.0% of excess over $2,100,000
Over $2,600,000 but not over $3,100,000	$146,800 plus 8.8% of excess over $2,600,000
Over $3,100,000 but not over $3,600,000	$190,800 plus 9.6% of excess over $3,100,000
Over $3,600,000 but not over $4,100,000	$238,800 plus 10.4% of excess over $3,600,000
Over $4,100,000 but not over $5,100,000	$290,800 plus 11.2% of excess over $4,100,000
Over $5,100,000 but not over $6,100,000	$402,800 plus 12.0% of excess over $5,100,000
Over $6,100,000 but not over $7,100,000	$522,800 plus 12.8% of excess over $6,100,000
Over $7,100,000 but not over $8,100,000	$650,800 plus 13.6% of excess over $7,100,000
Over $8,100,000 but not over $9,100,000	$786,800 plus 14.4% of excess over $8,100,000
Over $9,100,000 but not over $10,100,000	$930,800 plus 15.2% of excess over $9,100,000
Over $10,100,000	$1,082,800 plus 16.0% of excess over $10,100,000

Table 14.07
Inheritance, Estate, Succession, Transfer, and Gift Tax Rates
Oregon

Estate Tax Rates (§ 118.010(4))

(1) Taxable Estate At Least	(2) But Not More Than	(3) Tax	(4) Excess Over (1) Multiplied by:
$1,000,000	$1,500,000	$0	10%
$1,500,000	$2,500,000	$50,000	10.25%
$2,500,000	$3,500,000	$152,500	10.5%
$3,500,000	$4,500,000	$257,500	11.0%
$4,500,000	$5,500,000	$367,500	11.5%
$5,500,000	$6,500,000	$482,500	12.0%
$6,500,000	$7,500,000	$602,500	13.0%
$7,500,000	$8,500,000	$732,500	14.0%
$8,500,000	$9,500,000	$872,500	15.0%
$9,500,000		$1,022,500	16.0%

Table 14.07
Inheritance, Estate, Succession, Transfer, and Gift Tax Rates
Pennsylvania

Inheritance Tax Rate (72 § 9116)

---

(1)   The inheritance tax rate is 4.5% for transfers of property to the (a) grandfather, grandmother, father, mother and lineal descendants of decedent or (b) wife or widow and husband or widower of a child; subject to (1.2) below.

(1.1)   The inheritance tax rate for transfers to the surviving spouse is 0% for decedents dying on or after January 1, 1995.

(1.2)   The inheritance tax upon the transfer of property from a child 21 years of age or younger to or for the use of a natural or adoptive parent, or stepparent, is taxed at a rate of 0%.

(1.3)   The inheritance tax upon the transfer of property passing to or for the use of a sibling is taxed at a rate of 12%.

---

(2)   The inheritance tax rate for transfers for all persons other than those designated in subclauses (1), (1.1), (1.2), or (1.3) is 15%.

---

(3)   When property passes to or for the use of a husband and wife with right of survivorship, one of whom is taxable at a rate lower than the other, the lower rate of tax shall be applied to the entire interest.

Table 14.07
Inheritance, Estate, Succession, Transfer, and Gift Tax Rates
Virginia

Tax on the probate of wills: A tax equal to 10 cents for every $100 of value, or fraction of $100, is imposed on estates with a value over $15,000. (§ 58.1-1712)

Table 14.07
Inheritance, Estate, Succession, Transfer, and Gift Tax Rates
Washington

Estate Tax Rates (§ 83.100.040(2)(a))				
If Washington Taxable Estate is at least	But Less Than	The amount of Tax Equals	Plus Tax Rate %	Of Washington Taxable Rate
		Initial Tax Amount		Value Greater Than
$0	$1,000,000	$0	10.00%	$0
$1,000,000	$2,000,000	$100,000	14.00%	$1,000,000
$2,000,000	$3,000,000	$240,000	15.00%	$2,000,000
$3,000,000	$4,000,000	$390,000	16.00%	$3,000,000
$4,000,000	$6,000,000	$550,000	18.00%	$4,000,000
$6,000,000	$7,000,000	$910,000	19.00%	$6,000,000
$7,000,000	$9,000,000	$1,100,000	19.50%	$7,000,000
Above $9,000,000		$1,490,000	20.00%	Above $9,000,000

Table 14.08
State-by-State Summary of Current State Inheritance and Estate Tax Situation

State	Alt. #1: State Estate Tax is the Federal Credit Frozen at a Certain Date	Alt. #2: State Tax Independent of Federal Credit	Alt. #3: No State Estate Tax Due to Repeal of Federal Credit in 2005 or Otherwise
Alabama	N/A	N/A	§ 40-15-2
Alaska	N/A	N/A	§ 43.31.011
Arizona	N/A	N/A	§ 42-4051[a]
Arkansas	N/A	N/A	§ 26-59-103
California	N/A	N/A	Rev. & Tax § § 13301 & 13302
Colorado	N/A	N/A	§ § 39-23.5-103
Connecticut	N/A	§ 12-391(d), with exception of $2,600,000 exemption in 2018, $3,600,000 in 2019, and then the federal exemption amount. Maximum tax is $20,000,000 in 2018 and $15,000,000 thereafter	N/A
Delaware	N/A	N/A	N/A
District of Columbia	N/A	§ 47-3702(a-1) with federal exemption amount	N/A
Florida	N/A	N/A	§ § 198.02 & 198.41
Georgia	N/A	N/A	§ 48-12-1[b]
Hawaii	N/A	N/A § 236E-8 (for decedents dying after Jan. 25, 2012), with an exemption equal to the federal applicable exclusion.	N/A
Idaho	N/A	N/A	§ 14-403
Illinois	35 ILCS § § 405/2 & 405/3 December 31, 2001, but also a $4,000,000 applicable exclusion amount	N/A	N/A
Indiana	N/A	N/A	N/A
Iowa	N/A	§ 450.10	N/A

Table 14.08
State-by-State Summary of Current State Inheritance and Estate Tax Situation

State	Alt. #1: State Estate Tax is the Federal Credit Frozen at a Certain Date	Alt. #2: State Tax Independent of Federal Credit	Alt. #3: No State Estate Tax Due to Repeal of Federal Credit in 2005 or Otherwise
Kansas	N/A	N/A	N/A
Kentucky	N/A	§ 140.070	§ 140.130
Louisiana	N/A	N/A	§ 47:2432
Maine	N/A	However, there is an exemption amount equal to the federal applicable exclusion amount, 36 § § 4101 and 4103	N/A
Maryland	Tax-Gen. § 7-304 December 31, 2001, with a $4,000,000 exemption in 2018 and $5,000,000 in 2019.	Tax-Gen. § 7-202	N/A
Massachusetts	65C § 2A December 31, 2000ᶜ, with a $1,000,000 exemption	N/A	N/A
Michigan	§ 205.256(g) The credit as in effect on January 1, 1998 or, at the option of the personal representative, at time of death of decedent. This means that the state's estate tax is effectively repealed.	N/A	§ 205.256(g) The credit as in effect on January 1, 1998 or, at the option of the personal representative, at the time of death of decedent. This means that the state's estate tax is effectively repealed.
Minnesota	§ 291.03 December 31, 2000, with a $2,400,000 exemption for 2018, a $2,700,000 exemption for 2019, and a $3,000,000 exemption thereafter.	N/A	N/A
Mississippi	N/A	N/A	§ 27-9-5
Missouri	N/A	N/A	§ 145.011 & § 145.1000
Montana	N/A	N/A	§ 72-16-905
Nebraska	N/A	§ 77-2001 (county inheritance tax)	N/A
Nevada	N/A	N/A	§ 375A.100
New Hampshire	N/A	N/A	§ § 87:1 & 87:9

Table 14.08
State-by-State Summary of Current State Inheritance and Estate Tax Situation

State	Alt. #1: State Estate Tax is the Federal Credit Frozen at a Certain Date	Alt. #2: State Tax Independent of Federal Credit	Alt. #3: No State Estate Tax Due to Repeal of Federal Credit in 2005 or Otherwise
New Jersey	N/A	Yes. (§ 54:34-1) (inheritance tax)	N/A
New Mexico	N/A	N/A	§ 7-7-3
New York	Tax § 951 July 22, 1998[e], with a $5,250,000 exemption through 2018.	N/A	N/A
North Carolina	N/A	N/A	N/A
North Dakota	N/A	N/A	§ 57-37.1-04
Ohio	N/A	N/A	N/A
Oklahoma	N/A	N/A	68 § 804
Oregon	N/A	§ 118.010(2)	N/A
Pennsylvania	N/A	72 § 9116 (Inheritance tax)	72 § 9117
Rhode Island	§ 44-22-1.1 January 1, 2001, with 2018 exemption of $1,537,656	N/A	N/A
South Carolina	N/A	N/A	§§ 12-16-20(5) & 12-6-40(A)
South Dakota	N/A	N/A	N/A
Tennessee	N/A	—	§ 67-8-204
Texas	N/A	N/A	N/A
Utah	N/A	N/A	§ 59-11-103
Vermont	32 §§ 7442a, 7475 January 1, 2001[d], with $2,750,000 exemption	N/A	N/A
Virginia	N/A	N/A	§ 58.1-901, eff. July 1, 2007
Washington	N/A	§ 83.100.040	N/A
West Virginia	N/A	N/A	§ 11-11-4

Table 14.08
State-by-State Summary of Current State Inheritance and Estate Tax Situation

State	Alt. #1: State Estate Tax is the Federal Credit Frozen at a Certain Date	Alt. #2: State Tax Independent of Federal Credit	Alt. #3: No State Estate Tax Due to Repeal of Federal Credit in 2005 or Otherwise
Wisconsin	N/A	N/A	§§ 72.02 & 72.01 (11m)
Wyoming	N/A	N/A	§§ 39-19-103 & 39-19-104

[a] The tax was repealed independent of the federal credit by Laws 2006, Ch. 262, § 3, eff. September 21, 2006.

[b] All estate taxes were abolished on or after July 1, 2014, even if the federal credit comes back into force. (§ 48-12-1)

[c] The generation skipping transfer tax is also preserved by reference to the IRC § 2602 credit in effect on December 31, 1981. (65C § 4A(c))

[d] The generation skipping transfer tax is also preserved by reference to the IRC § 2604 credit in effect on January 1, 2001 (32 § 7460(b))

Table 14.09
Internal Revenue Code Section 2011(b): State Death Tax Credit Before Repeal

(b) Amount of credit.

(1) In general. Except as provided in paragraph (2), the credit allowed by this section shall not exceed the appropriate amount stated in the following table:

If the adjusted taxable estate is:	The maximum tax credit shall be:
Not over $90,000	8/10ths of 1% of the amount by which the adjusted taxable estate exceeds $40,000
Over $90,000 but not over $140,000	$400 plus 1.6% of the excess over $90,000
Over $140,000 but not over $240,000	$1,200 plus 2.4% of the excess over $140,000
Over $240,000 but not over $440,000	$3,600 plus 3.2% of the excess over $240,000
Over $440,000 but not over $640,000	$10,000 plus 4% of the excess over $440,000
Over $640,000 but not over $840,000	$18,000 plus 4.8% of the excess over $640,000
Over $840,000 but not over $1,040,000	$27,600 plus 5.6% of the excess over $840,000
Over $1,040,000 but not over $1,540,000	$38,800 plus 6.4% of the excess over $1,040,000
Over $1,540,000 but not over $2,040,000	$70,800 plus 7.2% of the excess over $1,540,000
Over $2,040,000 but not over $2,540,000	$106,800 plus 8% of the excess over $2,040,000
Over $2,540,000 but not over $3,040,000	$146,800 plus 8.8% of the excess over $2,540,000
Over $3,040,000 but not over $3,540,000	$190,800 plus 9.6% of the excess over $3,040,000
Over $3,540,000 but not over $4,040,000	$238,800 plus 10.4% of the excess over $3,540,000
Over $4,040,000 but not over $5,040,000	$290,800 plus 11.2% of the excess over $4,040,000
Over $5,040,000 but not over $6,040,000	$402,800 plus 12% of the excess over $5,040,000
Over $6,040,000 but not over $7,040,000	$522,800 plus 12.8% of the excess over $6,040,000
Over $7,040,000 but not over $8,040,000	$650,800 plus 13.6% of the excess over $7,040,000
Over $8,040,000 but not over $9,040,000	$786,800 plus 14.4% of the excess over $8,040,000
Over $9,040,000 but not over $10,040,000	$930,800 plus 15.2% of the excess over $9,040,000
Over $10,040,000	$1,082,800 plus 16% of the excess over $10,040,000

(2) Reduction of maximum credit.

(A) In general. In the case of estates of decedents dying after December 31, 2001, the credit allowed by this section shall not exceed the applicable percentage of the credit otherwise determined under paragraph (1).

(B) Applicable percentage.

In the case of estates of decedents dying during:	The applicable percentage is:
2002	75 percent
2003	50 percent
2004	25 percent

(3) Adjusted taxable estate. For purposes of this section, the term "adjusted taxable estate" means the taxable estate reduced by $ 60,000.

IRC § 2604 Federal Credit for State Generation-Skipping Transfer Taxes

The credit terminates for transfers made after December 31, 2004 (Pub. L. No. 107-16, § 532(c)(10), June 7, 2001)